THE GREAT HOLLYWOOD MUSICAL PICTURES

by
James Robert Parish
and
Michael R. Pitts

The Scarecrow Press, Inc.
Metuchen, N.J., & London
1992

Other *GREAT* books by James Robert Parish and Michael R. Pitts:

The Great Detective Pictures
The Great Gangster Pictures
The Great Gangster Pictures II
The Great Science Fiction Pictures
The Great Science Fiction Pictures II
The Great Spy Pictures
The Great Spy Pictures II
The Great Western Pictures
The Great Western Pictures II
Hollywood on Hollywood

Also available by James Robert Parish:

The Great Combat Pictures
The Great Cop Pictures

British Library Cataloguing-in-Publication data available

Library of Congress Cataloging-in-Publication Data

Parish, James Robert.
The great Hollywood musical pictures / by James Robert Parish and Michael R. Pitts.
p. cm.
ISBN 0-8108-2529-5 (alk. paper)
1. Musical films—United States—History and criticism. I. Pitts, Michael R. II. Title.
PN1995.9.M86P37 1992
791.43'6—dc20 92-7483

Manufactured in the United States of America

Printed on acid-free paper

For Miss Alice Faye

CONTENTS

ACKNOWLEDGMENTS

John Cocchi
Howard Davis
Film Favorites (Karen Martin, Paula Phillips)
Sharon R. Fox
Alex Gildzen
Kent State University Library
Doug McClelland
Jim Meyer
Peter Miglierini
Barry Rivadue
Margie Schultz
Vincent Terrace

Editorial Consultant: Allan Taylor

INTRODUCTION

Having covered such movie genres as the spy, gangster, western, science fiction and detective films in our THE GREAT . . . PICTURES series, we now focus on musicals. Since the inception of the sound era, song-and-dance films have been a popular part of movie fare. However, unlike the other genres we have already covered, the musical remains almost solely in the realm of the feature film, with few TV movie musicals. In this volume we have also chosen only to cover Hollywood product and not foreign productions. As we have noted in our other volumes in this series, the word "Great" refers to the genre covered and not to all of its product.

Ever since Al Jolson first announced "You ain't heard nothin' yet!" in THE JAZZ SINGER (1927), movie musicals have been a part of our lives. In the early sound period, a rash of "All-Talking, All-Singing, All-Dancing" motion pictures flooded the market. By 1930 the onslaught of so many films (and so many of them inferior) caused this special art form to fade in popularity. It was revived in 1932 by Warner Bros.' 42ND STREET and, later, through the teamings of Fred Astaire and Ginger Rogers as well as Jeanette MacDonald and Nelson Eddy. Since then, movie musicals have had their ups and downs in the public's esteem. However, the genre itself has retained its strength, whether the films' plots and music were borrowed from stage shows or were conceived especially for celluloid. As fads in music have changed, so have the complexity of movie musicals.

The continuing interest in movie musicals can be gauged by the fact that a number of genre productions are among the biggest money making movies of all time, including GREASE, MARY POPPINS, SATURDAY NIGHT FEVER and THE SOUND OF MUSIC. While our other volumes have endeavored to include a wide variety of titles, including the product of poverty row, this book basically looks at the output of the major studios because minor outfits—wanting to avoid the prohibitive costs involved—rarely made musicals. Unlike other types of films, musicals are more expensive to produce because the music either must be purchased for the film or composed for it. In addition, production number settings also require more financial investment than motion pictures that can get by using already standing sets.

In this volume we examine nearly 350 musical movies from Hollywood, with the coverage running the gamut from the best to some of the least enticing genre productions; from the beginning of the sound era to the present. Not every musical movie could be included in the book and if your favorite is missing, let us know (in care of the publisher) and we will try to include it in a follow-up edition. Also, we would appreciate any additions or corrections the reader might have, or any comments.

As with other types of movies, the videocassette/laser disc boom has made available many titles from the past for viewing and evaluation and we hope this book will not only bring back memories but also whet the reader's appetite to see the films included here, either in theatre or on television, or via video or laser disc. The movie musicals have kept us humming for more than six decades and we hope this book will complement the genre and the joys it has brought the viewing public.

James Robert Parish

Michael R. Pitts

GREAT HOLLYWOOD MUSICAL PICTURES

AFTER THE DANCE (Columbia, 1935) 60 minutes.

Director, Leo Bulgakov; story, Harrison Jacobs; screenplay, Harold Shumate; additional dialogue, Bruce Manning; costumes, Murray Mayer; choreographer, Albertina Rasch; sound, George Cooper; camera, Joseph August; editor, Otto Meyer.

Songs: "Without You, I'm Just Drifting," "Tomorrow Night" (Harry Akst); "I Heard a Blind Man Singing in the Street" (Clarence Muse).

Nancy Carroll (Anne Taylor); George Murphy (Jerry Davis); Thelma Todd (Mabel Kane); Jack LaRue (Mitch); Arthur Hohl (Louis); Wyrley Birch (Warden); Victor Kilian (Kennedy); George McKay (Danny); and: Harry Barris, Thurston Hall, Robert Middlemass, Virginia Sale.

Night club singer Jerry Davis (George Murphy) is framed for manslaughter by his partner Mabel Kane (Thelma Todd) and is sent to prison. After he proves himself there, the warden (Wyrley Birch) makes him a trustee and assigns him, with cellmate Danny (George McKay), to outside duty as a truck driver. Corrupt convict Mitch (Jack LaRue) and his cohorts use the truck to escape and in a shootout a guard is killed. Fearing he will be blamed for the jailbreak, Jerry runs away. For several weeks he tries to elude the law and when he attempts to steal food and milk from the doorstep of Anne Taylor (Nancy Carroll), the young woman befriends him. She is a night club singer and when she hears Jerry sing, he is hired as her partner. Feigning stage fright he wears a mask and bills himself as the "Knave of Hearts." The singer proves to be very successful but trouble develops when Mabel joins the show as a hoofer and tries to disrupt Jerry's love affair with Anne by attempting to blackmail him. Jerry plans to leave after telling Anne the truth, but the warden arrives to tell him he has been cleared in the jailbreak by Danny's testimony and his record will be clean if he serves his remaining two years in prison. Jerry leaves with the warden after Anne promises to marry him when he is free.

The career of dancing-singing star Nancy Carroll had been waning since she left Paramount in 1933. This minor Columbia musical was her third and final co-starring role with George Murphy, who was on the way up. The film proved to be Carroll's final starring musical feature. *Variety* noted, "Apparently intended for the big time, but the story fails to come through. . . ." The *New York American* pointed out, ". . . Neither Mr. Murphy's song 'n dance, nor Miss Carroll's pulchritude are sufficient to rescue it. . . ."

To be noted is that the tune "I Heard a Blind Man Singing in the Street" was written by black character actor Clarence Muse.

ALEXANDER'S RAGTIME BAND (20th Century-Fox, 1938) 105 minutes.

Producer, Darryl F. Zanuck; associate producer, Harry Joe Brown; director, Henry King; screenplay, Kathryn Scola, Lamar Trotti; art directors, Bernard Herzbrun, Boris Leven; set decorator, Thomas Little; costumes, Gwen Wakeling; music director, Alfred Newman; choreographer, Seymour Felix; sound, Arthur Von Kirbach, Roger Heman; camera, Peverell Marley; editor, Barbara McLean.

Songs: "Alexander's Rag-Time Band," "Rag-Time Violin," "The International Rag," "Everybody's Doing It Now," "This Is the Life," "When the Midnight Choo-Choo Leaves for Alabam," "For Your Country and My Country," "I Can Always Find a Little Sunshine at the YMCA," "Oh! How I Hate to Get Up in the Morning," "We're on Our Way to France," "Say It with Music," "A Pretty Girl Is Like a Melody," "Blue Skies," "Pack Up Your Sins and Go to the Devil," "What'll I Do?" "Remember," "Everybody Step," "All Alone," "Gypsy in Me," "Easter Parade," "Heat Wave," "Cheek to Cheek," "Lazy," "Marie," "Some Sunny Day," "The Song Is Ended," "When I Lost You," "Now It Can Be Told," "I'm Marching Along with Time," "My Walking Stick" (Irving Berlin).

Tyrone Power (Roger Grant); Alice Faye (Stella Kirby); Don Ameche (Charlie Dwyer); Ethel Merman (Jerry Allen); Jack Haley (Davey Lane); Jean Hersholt (Professor Heinrich); Helen Westley (Aunt Sophie Heinrich); John Carradine (Taxi Driver); Paul Hurst (Bill); Wally Vernon (Himself); Ruth Terry (Ruby); Douglas Fowley (Snapper); Eddie Collins (Corporal Collins); Joseph Crehan (Stage Manager); Robert Gleckler (Eddie); Dixie Dunbar (Specialty); Joe King (Charles Dillingham); Charles Coleman (Head Waiter); Stanley Andrews (Colonel); Charles Williams (Agent); Jane Jones, Otto Fries, Mel Kalish (Trio); Grady Sutton (Babe); Selmer Jackson (Manager of Radio Station); Tyler Brooks (Assistant Stage Manager); Donald Douglas (Singer); James Flavin, Jack Pennick (Sergeant); Harold Goodwin (M.P.); Edward Keane (Major); Ralph Dunn (Captain); Charles Tannen (Secretary);

Alice Faye in ALEXANDER'S RAGTIME BAND (1938).

Robert Lowery (Reporter); Eleanor Wesselhoeft (Martha); Sam Ash, Lynne Barkley, Pop Byron, Kay Griffith, Kings Men Quartet, Arthur Rankin, Cully Richard, Edwin Stanley, Cecil Weston.

One of the brightest and most popular movie musicals of the 1930s, ALEXANDER'S RAGTIME BAND boasted a $2 million budget and thirty songs, all by Irving Berlin, whose name appeared on the opening credits before the stars. The well-mounted film was in production for two years and was nominated for a half-dozen Academy Awards, including Best Picture. It won for Alfred Newman's Music Scoring.* This movie established Alice Faye as one of the screen's most popular female stars and solidified her screen teaming with both Tyrone Power and Don Ameche. (The trio had just scored a big success with IN OLD CHICAGO [1938].) W. Franklyn Moshier wrote of this production in *The Films of Alice Faye* (1972), ". . . The musical film gained new status; it was

*The other Oscar nominations for ALEXANDER'S RAGTIME BAND were Best Original Story, Interior Decoration, Best Song ("Now It Can Be Told"), and Editing.

lifted from the ranks of trite backstage stories to a respectable place of honor and prestige. It was the coming of age for musical films both in America and abroad."

Before the First World War, Nob Hill's Professor Heinrich (Jean Hersholt) and his wife Sophie (Helen Westley) are disappointed when their nephew Roger Grant (Tyrone Power) forsakes his classical music training to play a new style music called ragtime in a Barbary Coast honky tonk. There he meets singer Stella Kirby (Alice Faye) who joins his act. Soon Roger's "Alexander and His Ragtime Band" are the sensation of San Francisco and Stella falls in love with the bandleader. The band gets a long-lasting job at the ritzy Cliff House and a New York theatrical producer (Joe King) offers Stella a high-paying job, but rejects Roger and his band. Bandsman-composer Charlie Dwyer (Don Ameche) urges her to take the job and as a result she and Grant break up. Stella goes to New York while Grant joins the army. While he is overseas fighting in World War I, Stella marries Dwyer. He is now a successful Broadway songwriter and she has developed as a big attraction on the Great White Way. When Roger returns he hires Jerry Allen (Ethel Merman) as his vocalist and they begin a romance. Meanwhile, Stella and Dwyer agree to divorce. Grant and Jerry realize they do not love each other, and Stella drifts back to honky tonks. When Roger, once again a big success, is about to perform at Carnegie Hall, a taxi driver (John Carradine), who recognizes Stella, takes her there. Roger notices her in the wings and urges her to come on stage to sing "Alexander's Ragtime Band." They are now reunited romantically.

Not only did ALEXANDER'S RAGTIME BAND deftly present the music of the ragtime era—from before the First World War to the eve of the Second—but it also interpolated beautifully the rhythms of the period, so many of which were contributed by Irving Berlin. In addition, Berlin composed a trio of tunes ("Now It Can Be Told," "I'm Marching Along with Time" and "My Walking Stick") which debuted in the feature, the first song becoming associated with Alice Faye. Although Merman was subordinated to Faye, she had a wide range of songs to perform, from the gentle "A Pretty Girl Is Like a Melody" to the more boisterous "Hand Me Down My Walking Stick" and "Pack Up Your Sins and Go to the Devil." Roy Hemming (*The Melody Lingers On,* 1986) observed, "Most of the numbers are staged in a straightforward way, as they would be on a stage in the era in which they're supposedly taking place within the story. There are no Busby Berkeley-style overhead angles or complex dance patterns—just an unadorned emphasis on the songs and on the singers. . . . Perhaps more than any other major musical of the '30s, ALEXANDER'S RAGTIME BAND reaffirms music as the great bringer-together, the common bond that can help anybody overcome any problem. . . ."

Alice Faye recreated the part of Stella with Robert Preston on NBC's "Lux Radio Theatre." In the mid-1940s Tyrone Power redid his part from the movie for radio's "Showtime," teamed with Al Jolson, Dinah Shore, Dick Haymes and Margaret Whiting.

ALL THAT JAZZ (Columbia/20th Century-Fox, 1979) Color 123 minutes.

Executive producer, Daniel Melnick; producer, Robert Alan Aurthur; associate producers, Kenneth Utt, Wolfgang Gattes; director, Bob Fosse; screenplay, Aurthur, Fosse; production designer, Philip Rosenberg; costumes, Albert Wolksky; makeup, Fern Buchner; music director/arranger, Ralph Burns; music supervisor, Stanley Lebowsky; dance music arranger, Arnold Gross; choreographer, Fosse; assistant directors, Gattes, Joseph Ray; technical advisers, Nancy Bird, Dr. John E. Hutchinson, II; sound, Chris Newman, Peter Ilardi, Glenn Berger; sound re-recording, Dick Vorisek; supervising sound editor, Maurice Schell; camera, Giuseppe Rotunno; editor, Alan Heim.

Songs: "On Broadway" (Barry Mann, Cynthia Weil, Jerry Leiber, Mike Stoller); "A Perfect Day" (Harry Nilsson); "Take Off with Us" (Fred Tobias, Stanley Lebowsky); "Everything Old Is New Again" (Peter Allen, Carole Bayer Sager); "There's No Business Like Show Business" (Irving Berlin); "After You've Gone" (Henry Creamer, Turner Layton); "There'll Be Some Changes Made" (W. Benton Overstreet, Billy Higgins, Herbert Edwards); "Who's Sorry Now" (Ted Snyder, Bert Kalmar, Harry Ruby); "Some of These Days" (Shelton Brooks); "Pack Up Your Troubles in Your Old Kit Bag" (Felix Powell, George H. Powell); "Bye, Bye Love (Life)" (B. Bryant, F. Bryant).

Roy Scheider (Joe Gideon); Jessica Lange (Angelique); Ann Reinking (Kate Jagger); Leland Palmer (Audrey Paris); Cliff Gorman (David Newman); Ben Vereen (O'Connor Flood); Erzebet Foldi (Michelle); Michael Tolan (Dr. Ballinger); Max Wright (Joshua Benn); William La Messena (Jonesy Hecht); Chris Chase (Leslie Perry); Deborah Geffner (Victoria); Kathryn Doby (Kathryn); Anthony Holland (Paul Dann); Robert Hitt (Ted Christopher); David Margulies (Larry Goldie); Sue Paul (Stacy); Keith Gordon (Young Joe); Frankie Man (Comic); Alan Heim (Eddie); John Lithgow (Lucas Sergeant); Sloane Shelton (Mother); Ben Masters (Dr. Garry); Robert Levine (Dr. Hyman); Phil Friedman (Murray Nathan); Stephen Strimpell (Alvin Rackmil);

Leonard Drum (Insurance Man); Eugene Troobnick (Insurance Doctor); Jules Fisher (Himself); Catherine Shirriff (Nurse Briggs); Joanna Merlin (Nurse Pierce); Leah Ayres (Nurse Capobianco); Nancy Beth Bird (Nurse Bates); Harry Agress (Resident MD); C. C. H. Pounder (Nurse Gibbons); Tito Goya (Attendant); Tiger Haynes (Porter); Otta Palfi-Andor (Old Woman); K. C. Townsend, Melanie Hunter, Rita Bennett (Strippers); Gary Bayer (Intern); Wayne Carson (Assistant Stage Manager); Kerry Casserly, Judi Paseltiner (Dancers Backstage); Steve Elmore, I. M. Hobson, Mary McCarty, Theresa Merritt, Sammy Smith (Cast of *NY/LA*); Nichole Fosse (Dancer); Vicki Frederick, P. J. Mann (Menage Partners); Minnie Gaster (Script Supervisor); Michael Green, Bruce MacCallum (Clapper Boys); Joyce Ellen Hill (Nurse Collins); Edith Kramer (Manager, Rehearsal Studio); Barbara McKinley (Diane); Gavin Moses (Apprentice Editor); Mary Mon Toy (Dietician); Wallace Shawn (Assistant Insurance Man); Jacqueline Solotar (Autograph Seeker); Arnold Gross (Pianist); Sandahl Bergman, Eileen Casey, Bruce Davis, Gary Flannery, Jennifer Nairn-Smith, Denny Ruvolo, Leland Schwantes, John Sowinski, Candace Tovar, Rima Vetter (Principal Dancers); Trudy Carson, Mary Sue Finnerty, Lesley Kingley, P. J. Mann, Cathy Rice, Sonja Stuart, Terri Treas (Fan Dancers); Ralph E. Berntsen, Jan Flato, John Paul Fetta, Andy Schwartz (Rock Band).

Bob Fosse's semi-autobiographical and very personal musical statement, ALL THAT JAZZ proved to be one of the more popular musicals of the 1970s, grossing $20,030,000 in distributors' domestic film rentals at the box-office. It netted Fosse an Oscar nomination as Best Director, along with his script co-authored with Robert Alan Aurthur. Roy Scheider (who replaced Richard Dreyfuss in the role) was nominated for Best Actor, and the picture itself received a nomination. The somber fantasy received Academy Awards for Best Scoring, Art Direction-Set Decoration, Costumes, and Editing. Giuseppe Rotunno's cinematography received an Oscar nomination and he won the British Academy Award, as did Alan Heim for editing. The soundtrack album was on *Billboard* magazine's hits chart for three weeks, rising to position #36.

Multi-talented Joe Gideon (Roy Scheider) is busy preparing a new musical, which stars his ex-wife (Jessica Lange), and at the same time is editing a major motion picture he has just directed. All of these activities, plus trying to carry on a relationship with his live-in lover (Ann Reinking), prove to be too much for Joe's constitution and he suffers a major heart attack. While in the hospital and hovering near death, the man visualizes many of the creative aspects of his life as a master of ceremonies (Ben Vereen) appears and sings

"Bye Bye Life." After a series of dances featuring anatomy model girls and death-mask-wearing guitarists, Joe finally succumbs. However, his death is not a sad affair, but a celebration of his life.

In *The Best, Worst and Most Unusual: Hollywood Musicals* (1983), the editors of *Consumer Guide* and Phillip J. Kaplan commented, "Few show business people have bared their souls as much as Bob Fosse does in ALL THAT JAZZ. He presents an unflattering portrait of himself, one acknowledging not only his talent, but also his excesses. The film, like Fosse, walks a tightrope between talent and excess. . . . The problem with the film is that there is no discipline to Fosse's revelations about himself and thus, while he shows everything, he reveals nothing. Even with Fosse's lapses in judgment, ALL THAT JAZZ is one of the more interesting and flashy musicals of the 1970s." Richard Combs (British *Monthly Film Bulletin*) analyzed, "In ALL THAT JAZZ, the backstage musical dies as surely as its choreographer-hero. . . . Underneath its triumphant razzmatazz, ALL THAT JAZZ is as dull and uninformative as the plainest Hollywood-on-Hollywood or art-in-the-making subject. . . . Only in the last half-hour, when Gideon begins dying in earnest, does the pretentious triviality of the theme intersect with the show-biz vulgarity in transcendently black-comic camp. . . ."

For all its downsides, ALL THAT JAZZ remains an offbeat example of creative risk-taking. It is an intriguing movie that improves with re-viewings.

AN AMERICAN IN PARIS (Metro-Goldwyn-Mayer, 1951) Color 113 minutes.

Producer, Arthur Freed; director, Vincente Minnelli; story/screenplay, Alan Jay Lerner; art directors, Cedric Gibbons, Preston Ames, (uncredited): Jack Martin Smith, Irene Sharaff; set decorators, Edwin B. Willis, Keogh Gleason; costumes, Orry-Kelly; Beaux Arts Ball costumes, Walter Plunkett; ballet costumes, Sharaff; makeup, William Tuttle; music directors, John Green, Saul Chaplin; choreographer, Gene Kelly; choreographer assistant, Carol Haney; assistant director, Al Raboch; color consultants, Henri Jaffa, James Gooch; technical adviser, Alan Antik; special effects, Warren Newcombe, Irving Reis; sound supervisor, Douglas Shearer; camera, Alfred Gilks; ballet camera, John Alton; editor, Adrienne Fazan.

Songs: "How Long Has This Been Going On?", "Nice Work If You Can Get It," "Fascinating Rhythm," "By Strauss," "I Got Rhythm," "But Not for Me," "Do Do Do," "Bidin' My Time," "Love Is Here to Stay," "Someone to Watch Over Me," "Tra-La-

La," "I Don't Think I'll Fall in Love Today," " 'S Wonderful," "Liza," "An American in Paris," "Embraceable You," "Strike Up the Band," "Oh Lady Be Good," "That Certain Feeling," "Clap Yo Hands," "Love Walked In" (George Gershwin, Ira Gershwin); "I'll Build a Stairway to Paradise" (George Gershwin, Ira Gershwin, Buddy G. DeSylva); "Concerto in F" [Third Movement] (George Gershwin).

Gene Kelly (Jerry Mulligan); Leslie Caron (Lise Bouvier); Oscar Levant (Adam Cook); Georges Guetary (Henri Baurel); Nina Foch (Milo Roberts); Eugene Borden (George Mattieu); Martha Barnattre (Mathilde Mattieu); Mary Jones (Old Lady Dancer); Ann Codee (Therese); George Davis (Francois); Hayden Rorke (Tommy Baldwin); Paul Maxey (John McDowd); Dick Wessel (Ben Macrow); Adele Coray, Don Quinn (Honeymoon Couple); Lucian Planzoles, Christian Pasques, Antony Mazola (Boys with Bubble Gum); Jeanne Lafayette, Louise Laureau (Nuns); Alfred Paix (Postman); Noel Neill (American Girl); Nan Boardman (Maid); John Eldredge (Jack Jansen); Anna Q. Nilsson (Kay Jansen); Madge Blake (Customer); Dudley Field (Winston Churchill); Andre Charisse (Dancing Partner); Jean Romaine, Mary Jane French, Pat Dean Smith, Joan Barton, Ann Robin, Mary Ellen Gleason, Judy Landon, Beverly Thompson, Beverly Baldy, Angela Wilson, Sue Casey, Ann Brendon, Marietta Elliott, Lorraine Crawford, Lola Kenricks, Meredith Leeds, Marilyn Rogers, Pat Hall, Madge Journery, Marlene Todd ("Stairway" Girls); *An American in Paris Ballet Company:* Mary Menzies, Svetlana McLee, Florence Brundage, Dee Turnell (Furies); Harriet Scott, Janet Lavis, Sheila Meyers, Lila Zali, Betty Scott, Eileen Locklin, Pat Sims, Linda Scott, Shirley Lopez, Shirley Glickman, Phyllis Sutter (Place de la Concorde Ensemble); Dick Lenner, Don Hulbert, John Stanley, Ray Weamer, Harvey Karels, Bert Madrid, Dick Landry, Rudy Silva, Rodney Bieber, Manuel Petroff, Robert Ames, Betty Hannon, Linda Heller, David Kasday, Marion Horosko, Pamela Wells, Dorothy Tuttle, Tommy Ladd, Albert Ruiz, Alex Goudovitch, Eric Freeman, Dick Humphries, Alan Cooke, John Gardner, Ricky Gonzales, Bill Chatham, Ernie Flatt, Ricky Riccardi (Firemen); Ernie Flatt, Alex Romero, Bill Chatham (Servicemen in Rousseau Place); Betty Scott, Shirley Lopez, Pat Sims, Dee Turnell, Sheila Meyuers, Janet Lavis (Can-can Dancers); Dick Lenner (Toulouse-Lautrec); Gino Corrado (Oscar Wilde); Alba No Valero (Aristide Briand).

Voted the Best Picture of 1951 by the Academy of Motion Picture Arts and Sciences, AN AMERICAN IN PARIS also netted a half-dozen other Oscars, including photography, art direction, sets and scoring for a musical, plus star Gene Kelly was given a special Academy Award for "his brilliant achievements in the art of choreography on film." The picture's best moments came in a seventeen-minute fantasy ballet sequence which cost a mammoth (at the time) $450,000 to produce and was added to the film after the production was finished. Clive Hirschhorn in *The Hollywood Musical* (1981) reported, "Like the Impressionist and post-Impressionist canvases from which it drew its inspiration, the superb ballet . . . was full of light and movement. Nothing of its kind from Hollywood had quite possessed its class, sense of style, and chic."

Following World War II, American soldier Jerry Mulligan (Gene Kelly) remains in Paris where he lives in a cramped one-room garret and paints. However, he is not successful. His two best friends, dour pianist Adam Cook (Oscar Levant) and cabaret singer Henri Baurel (Georges Guetary), both encourage him to try different career avenues. Cook advises him he has no talent and suggests he give up the arts, while Baurel tells him to stick with his painting. Rich widow Milo Roberts (Nina Foch), who has romantic designs on Jerry, becomes his patron. She prods her wealthy friends

Gene Kelly and Leslie Caron in AN AMERICAN IN PARIS (1951).

to buy his works and suddenly he finds himself a success. Celebrating one night he meets pretty young Lise Bouvier (Leslie Caron). The two fall in love, but they decide not to see each other again when Mulligan discovers she is engaged to Baurel. Because Jerry refuses to romance his patron she drops him and things look bad for him again. However, Baurel, realizing that Jerry and Lise are in love, gives up the girl and the two lovers are reunited.

Besides the acclaimed ballet sequence (which in retrospect seems more pretentiously stylized than creative), the musical highlights of AN AMERICAN IN PARIS include the revival of several George Gershwin favorites like " 'S Wonderful," "Embraceable You" and "Nice Work If You Can Get It," plus Oscar Levant's effective piano solo of Gershwin's "Concerto in F." Georges Guetary also does a fine vocal on "I'll Build a Stairway to Paradise" (the film's sole "production" number) while Kelly and Levant perform a duet on "Tra-La-La" and "By Strauss." AN AMERICAN IN PARIS was the screen debut of Leslie Caron and reflected the typical sophisticated visual style of director Vincente Minnelli, who did his best to disguise the squeaky clean plot structure.

In analyzing the virtues of this film, Ted Sennett (*Hollywood Musicals,* 1981) decided, "Most of its musical numbers contain moments of shimmering beauty and striking originality, and surprisingly, considering the thinness and triteness of the story, many of the songs flow smoothly from the events and the characters, in the best musical fashion."

Made at a cost of $2,723,903, AN AMERICAN IN PARIS grossed over $8,005,000 in its initial release.

ANCHORS AWEIGH (Metro-Goldwyn-Mayer, 1945) Color 143 minutes.

Producer, Joe Pasternak; director, George Sidney; based on the novel *You Can't Fool a Marine* by Natalie Marcin; screenplay, Isobel Lennart; art directors, Cedric Gibbons, Randall Duell; set decorators, Edwin B. Willis, Richard Pefferle; costumes, Irene, Kay Dean; music director, George Stoll; vocal arranger, Earl Brent; orchestrator, Alex Stordahl; choreographer, Gene Kelly; cartoon sequence director, Fred Quimby; assistant director, George Rheim; sound supervisor, Douglas Shearer; camera, Robert Planck, Charles Boyle; editor, Adrienne Fazan.

Songs: "The Charm of You," "We Hate to Leave," "I Fall in Love Too Easily," "What Makes the Sunset?", "I Begged Her," "We Hate to Leave" (Jule Styne, Sammy Cahn); "Jealousy" (Vera Bloom, Jacob Gade); "Donkey Serenade" (Bob Wright, Chet

Frank Marlowe, Frank Sinatra, Gene Kelly and Douglas Cowan in ANCHORS AWEIGH (1945).

Forrest, Rudolf Friml); "(All of a Sudden) My Heart Sings" (Harold Rome, Henri Jamblan Herpin); "If You Knew Susie" (Joseph Meyer, Buddy G. DeSylva); "La Cumparsita" (G. H. Matos Rodriguez); "The Worry Song" (Ralph Freed, Sammy Fain); "Piano Concerto No. 1 in B-Flat Minor (Opus 23)" "Waltz from Serenade in C Major for String Orchestra (Opus 48)" (Peter Ilyich Tchaikovsky); "Second Hungarian Rhapsody" (Franz Liszt); "Cradle Song (Wiegenlied, Opus 49, No. 4)" (Johannes Brahms); "Largo Al Factotum," from the opera *The Barber of Seville* (Gioacchino Rossini, Cesare Sterbin; adapted); "Anchors Aweigh" (Alfred H. Miles, Royal Lovell, Charles A. Zimmerman).

Frank Sinatra (Clarence Doolittle); Gene Kelly (Joseph Brady); Kathryn Grayson (Susan Abbott); Jose Iturbi (Himself); Dean Stockwell (Donald Martin); Carlos Ramirez (Carlos); Henry O'Neill (Admiral Hammond); Leon Ames (Commander); Rags Ragland (Police Sergeant); Edgar Kennedy (Police Captain); Pamela Britton (Girl from Brooklyn); Henry Armetta (Hamburger Man); Billy Gilbert (Cafe Manager); Sharon McManus (Little Girl Beggar); James Burke (Studio Cop); James Flavin (Radio Cop); Chester Clute (Iturbi's Assistant); Grady Sutton (Bertram Kramer);

Peggy Maley (Lana Turner Double); Sondra Rodgers (Iturbi's Secretary); Gary Owen, Steve Brodie (Soldiers); Charles Coleman (Butler); Milton Parsons (Bearded Man); Renie Riano (Waitress); Alex Callam (Commander); Harry Barris, John James, Wally Cassell, Douglas Cowan, Henry Daniels, Jr., William "Bill" Phillips, Tom Trout (Sailors); Esther Michelson (Hamburger Woman); William Forrest (Movie Director); Ray Teal (Assistant Movie Director); Milton Kibbee (Bartender); and Frank Marlowe.

Sailors Joseph Brady (Gene Kelly) and Clarence Doolittle (Frank Sinatra) are on shore leave in Hollywood; slick Brady is telling naive Doolittle he will get him a date with a glamorous movie star. Meeting film bit player Susan Abbott (Kathryn Grayson), who has aspirations of being a singing star, Joe advises her he can gain her an audition with acclaimed pianist Jose Iturbi (himself). When he fails to do so, he attempts to persuade shy Clarence to become romantically involved with the young lady. By now, Clarence, however, has fallen in love with a pretty girl (Pamela Britton) from Brooklyn whom he met at the Hollywood Canteen. Much to Joe's surprise, Susan wins an audition with Iturbi and even earns a movie contract. Joe now realizes he is in love with Susan, and he and Clarence end their brief shore leave, each having met the woman of his dreams. And Susan's little orphaned nephew (Dean Stockwell) has found a new role model: Brady.

ANCHORS AWEIGH was one of the 1940s films which helped to solidify Gene Kelly's popularity with movie audiences. A miscast Frank Sinatra (as a girl-shy [!] gob) was experiencing a decline in popularity. It was the first of their three MGM musicals together. The picture provided Kelly with two well-staged dance numbers: one was a charming fantasy sequence in which he danced with cartoon characters Tom and Jerry, while the second had him doing a sparkling Mexican hat dance with a little girl (Sharon McManus). Kelly and Sinatra sang together on "I Begged Her" and Sinatra crooned "The Charm of You," "We Hate to Leave" and the Oscar-nominated "I Fall in Love Too Easily." It was Kathryn Grayson, however, who had the movie's best numbers as she vibrantly sang "Jealousy" and "(All of a Sudden) My Heart Sings."

ANCHORS AWEIGH is noted for its on-location lensing of such Los Angeles landmarks as the Hollywood Bowl and Olvera Street. To date, the film has grossed $4,778,679 in distributors' domestic film rentals.

ANNIE (Columbia, 1982) Color 130 minutes.

Executive producer, Joe Layton; producer, Ray Stark; associate producer, Carol Sobieski; director, John Huston; based on the musical play by Thomas Meehan, Charles Strouse & Martin Charnin, and the comic strip, "Little Orphan Annie"; screenplay, Sobieski; production designer, Dale Hennesy; art directors, Robert Guerra, Diane Wager; set decorator, Marvin March; costumes, Theoni V. Aldredge; makeup, Ben Lane, Dan Striepeke, Jeff Hamilton; music director/arranger, Ralph Burns; vocal/dance arranger, Peter Howard; music editors, Shinichi Yamazaki, Jeff Carson, La Da Productions; music research, David Kurtz; musical sequences created by Layton; choreographer, Arlene Phillips; second unit director, James Arnett; assistant directors, Jerry Ziesmer, Chris Soldo, Phil Morini; stunt coordinators, James Arnett, Gerald E. Brutsche; sound, Gene Cantamessa, Dan Wallin; sound re-recording, Michael J. Kohut, Jay M. Harding, Carlos de Larios, Gregory H. Watkins; sound effects, Pat Somerset, Jeffrey Bushelman, Burbank Editorial Services; sound editors, Steve Bushelman, Ian McGregor Scott, Robert Gutknecht; special effects coordinator, Phil Cory; special camera effects, Howard A. Anderson Co.; camera, Richard Moore; second unit camera, Rex Metz; supervising editor, Margaret Booth; editor, Michael A. Stevenson.

Songs: "Tomorrow," "Sandy," "It's the Hard-Knock Life,"

Aileen Quinn and Sandy in ANNIE (1982).

"Maybe," "Dumb Dog," "I Think I'm Gonna Like It Here," "Little Girls," "We Got Annie," "Let's Go to the Movies," "Sign," "You're Never Fully Dressed Without a Smile," "Easy Street," "Tomorrow (White House Version)," "Finale: I Don't Need Anything But You/We Got Annie/Tomorrow" (Charles Strouse, Martin Charnin).

Albert Finney (Daddy Warbucks); Carol Burnett (Miss Hannigan); Bernadette Peters (Lily); Ann Reinking (Grace Farrell); Tim Curry (Rooster); Aileen Quinn (Annie); Geoffrey Holder (Punjab); Roger Minami (Asp); Toni Ann Gisondi (Molly); Rosanne Sorrentino (Pepper); Lara Berk (Tessie); April Lerman (Kate); Lucie Stewart (Duffy); Robin Ignico (July); Edward Herrmann (Franklin D. Roosevelt); Lois DeBanzie (Eleanor Roosevelt); Peter Marshall (Bert Healy); Lori Ackerman, Murphy Cross, Nancy Sinclair (Boylan Sisters); I. M. Hobson (Drake); Lu Leonard (Mrs. Pugh); Mavis Ray (Mrs. Greer); Pam Blair (Annette); Colleen Zenk (Celette); Victor Griffin (Saunders); Jerome Collamore (Frick); John Richards (Frack); Wayne Cilento (Photographer); Ken Swofford (Weasel); Larry Hankin (Pound Man); Irving Metzman (Bundles); Angela Martin (Mrs. McKracky); Kurtis Epper Sanders (Spike); and: Karei Baca, The Big Apple Circus, Jophery Brown, Gerald E. Brutsche, Tina Maria Caspary, Jamie Flowers, Sonja Haney, Victoria Hartman, Janet Marie Jones, Lisa Keldrup, Angela Lee, Liz Marsh, Cherie Michan, Danielle Miller, Jan Mackie, Mandy Peterson, Bob M. Porter, Linda Saputo, Shawnee Smith, Julie Whitman.

Costing an estimated $40–50 million, ANNIE was based on the long-running Broadway musical (2,377 performances) which was taken from the long-time popular comic strip which, in turn, derived from the perennially popular James Whitcomb Riley poem. Sadly, the film ranks as one of Hollywood's biggest box-office fiascos. Directed by an unlikely John Huston (it was his first and last musical), with dance numbers helmed by Joe Layton and uninspired choreography by Arlene Phillips, ANNIE emerged as a major bore. It failed to gain a wide audience among either adults or their offspring, grossing $37,316,783 in distributors' domestic film rentals. The soundtrack album remained on *Billboard* magazine's hits chart for only six weeks, rising to position #35.

During the Depression, cute young Annie (Aileen Quinn) is housed in an orphanage run by cruel Miss Hannigan (Carol Burnett), who especially despises the child because of her bubbly optimistic outlook on life. When Grace Farrell (Ann Reinking) comes to the institution looking for a child to spend a few days with her rich employer, Daddy Warbucks (Albert Finney), Miss Hannigan tries to hide Annie. However, it is to no avail as Grace spots the child and immediately takes her home to meet Warbucks. The billionaire is completely captivated by the moppet's charms and takes her on a tour of Broadway, introduces her to President Franklin D. Roosevelt (Edward Herrmann) and offers a hefty reward for finding Annie's parents. Miss Hannigan, her corrupt brother Rooster (Tim Curry) and his girlfriend Lily (Bernadette Peters) then attempt to get this money for themselves. When that fails, they kidnap the child. Annie manages to escape. Both her captors and Warbucks give chase, and Miss Hannigan and her crew are captured and arrested. Little Annie goes to live with Warbucks and Grace on a permanent basis.

While ANNIE does include the beautiful song "Tomorrow" and a comedy dance routine around "Easy Street," for the most part the music is sluggish going and the performances too oversized. Regarding this screen failure the editors of *Consumer Guide* and Phillip J. Kaplan wrote in *The Best, Worst and Most Unusual: Hollywood Musicals* (1983) that it ". . . Squandered so much talent and money with such poor results that it joins the ranks of great musical disasters. The only thing the movie had going for it was hype." *Variety* observed, "In an effort to be more 'realistic,' ANNIE winds up exposing just how weak a story it had to start with, not helped here by the music. . . . Four new tunes penned for the film aren't any better."

In 1990, a musical sequel, ANNIE II, failed to open on Broadway, after out-of-town tryouts.

ANNIE GET YOUR GUN (Metro-Goldwyn-Mayer, 1950) Color 107 minutes.

Producer, Arthur Freed; director, George Sidney; based on the musical play by Herbert and Dorothy Fields, Irving Berlin; screenplay, Sidney Sheldon; art directors, Cedric Gibbons, Paul Groesse; set decorators, Edwin B. Willis, Richard A. Pefferle; women's costumes, Helen Rose; men's costumes, Walter Plunkett; makeup, Jack Dawn; music director, Adolph Deutsch; music adaptor, Roger Edens; choreographer, Robert Alton; color consultants, Henri Jaffa, James Gooch; assistant director, George Rheim; sound, Douglas Shearer, Norman Fenton; special effects, A. Arnold Gillespie, Warren Newcombe; montage, Peter Ballbusch; camera, Charles Rosher; editor, James E. Newman.

Songs: "Colonel Buffalo Bill," "Doin' What Comes Natur'lly," "The Girl That I Marry," "You Can't Get a Man with a Gun," "There's No Business Like Show Business," "They Say It's Wonderful," "My Defenses Are Down," "I'm an Indian Too," "Anything You Can Do," "I'm a Bad Bad Man" (Irving Berlin).

Betty Hutton (Annie Oakley); Howard Keel (Frank Butler); Louis Calhern (Buffalo Bill); J. Carrol Naish (Chief Sitting Bull); Edward Arnold (Pawnee Bill); Keenan Wynn (Charlie Davenport); Benay Venuta (Dolly Tate); Clinton Sundberg (Foster Wilson); James H. Harrison (Mac); Bradley Mora (Little Jake); Susan Odin (Jessie); Diane Dick (Nellie); Chief Yowlachie (Little Horse); Eleanor Brown (Minnie); Evelyn Beresford (Queen Victoria): Andre Charlot (President Loubet of France); John Mylong (Kaiser Wilhelm II); Nino Pipitone (King Victor Emanuel of Italy); Carl Sepulveda, Carol Henry, Fred Gilman (Cowboys); John Hamilton (Ship Captain); William Bill Hall (Tall Man); Edward Earle (Footman); Marjorie Wood (Constance); Elizabeth Flournoy (Helen); Mae Clarke Langdon (Mrs. Adam); Frank Wilcox (Mr. Clay).

Irving Berlin's classic stage musical, *Annie Get Your Gun,* debuted on Broadway on May 16, 1946, with Ethel Merman and Ray Middleton starring in the vigorous production which ran for 1,147 performances and became one of the great songfests of the American stage. Metro-Goldwyn-Mayer purchased the movie rights to the musical for $650,000. After deciding that Ethel Merman was too old (at age forty) and not box-office enough, the studio set about miscasting its own Judy Garland (after turning down Betty Hutton, Judy Canova, Doris Day and Betty Garrett for the part), with disastrous results. After completing the soundtrack numbers and a few scenes under Busby Berkeley's direction, Garland's emotional instability led to her replacement in the production by Paramount's "Blonde Bombshell," Betty Hutton.* This ball-of-fire actress gave the performance of her life in bringing the title character alive on screen. She was ably abetted by co-star Howard Keel as the self-centered Frank Butler.

Homely sharpshooter Annie Oakley (Betty Hutton) is hired to perform in Buffalo Bill Cody's (Louis Calhern) wild west show. Immediately she is attracted to the show's star, Frank Butler (Howard Keel), but he does not reciprocate the feeling. Also in the show is Chief Sitting Bull (J. Carrol Naish), who befriends Annie and tries to advise her on the best method to win Butler's affections. Meanwhile, showman rival Pawnee Bill (Edward Arnold) tries to lure Annie away from Cody, but eventually Butler falls in love with the markswoman and they marry.

---

*After Garland was removed from ANNIE GET YOUR GUN, director Busby Berkeley was replaced, first by Charles Walters and then by George Sidney. During the transition, actor Frank Morgan died and his part as Buffalo Bill was assumed by Louis Calhern.

Betty Hutton (top center), Louis Calhern, J. Carrol Naish, Benay Venuta, Howard Keel, Edward Arnold and Keenan Wynn in ANNIE GET YOUR GUN (1950).

"A whale of a musical picture, if minus the throb and tingle from Broadway," The *New York Times* opined, adding, "With diligence, fidelity and gobs of bright color, this movie makes handsome use of Irving Berlin's dandy score, the lavish riggings of an expensive production and a pip of a singing hero. . . . What matters is that great gusto and that ribald regard for 'show business' are still rampant."

Costing $3.8 million and grossing $4.65 million in its initial release, ANNIE GET YOUR GUN retained most of the fabulous Irving Berlin score* and these numbers were beautifully staged. Among the highlights were Howard Keel's plaintive "My Defenses

---

*"Let's Go West Again" had been cut from the Broadway version, but was reinstated for the movie. It was prerecorded by Garland and later by Hutton, but still not used in the film. Other songs from the stage score, including "Who Do You Love, I Hope" and "Moonshine Lullaby," were not considered for the film edition.

Are Down," Betty Hutton's rowdy "Doin' What Comes Naturally" and the big boisterous finale around "There's No Business Like Show Business."

Both Ethel Merman and Ray Middleton continued to be associated with *Annie Get Your Gun* on stage and in 1966 Miss Merman headlined Lincoln Center's (New York) revival of the production for which Irving Berlin contributed a new song, "An Old Fashioned Wedding." In the spring of 1967 Merman did the role on an NBC-TV special and in the 1970s she would record the score for London Records. The year Ethel Merman reprised her Annie Oakley role on TV, a sad footnote occurred regarding the stars of the 1950 film. Producer A.C. Lyles hoped to revive some of the box-office magic of ANNIE GET YOUR GUN by casting Betty Hutton and Howard Keel in the lead roles of his economy Western RED TOMAHAWK. However, after a few days of shooting Miss Hutton, who had trouble with the fast paced production schedule, was replaced by Joan Caulfield, repeating what happened to Judy Garland seventeen years prior.

It should be noted that the film ANNIE GET YOUR GUN won an Oscar for Adolph Deutsch and Roger Edens' music scoring, but overall the bright musical was bypassed in a year that also produced ALL ABOUT EVE, CYRANO DE BERGERAC, HARVEY and SUNSET BOULEVARD.

ANYTHING GOES *see* CALL ME MADAM (essay).

APPLAUSE (Paramount, 1929) 87 minutes. (Silent version: 6,896′)

Producers, Jesse L. Lasky, Walter Wanger; associate producer, Monta Bell; director, Rouben Mamoulian; based on the novel by Betty Brown; screenplay, Garrett Fort; sound, Ernest F. Zatorsky; camera, George Folsey; editor, John Bassler.

Songs: "What Wouldn't I Do for That Man" (E. Y. Harburg, Jay Gorney); "Yaaka Hula Hickey Dula" (E. Ray Goetz, Joe Young, Pete Wendling); "Give Your Little Baby Lots of Lovin' " (Dolly Morse, Joe Burke); "I've Got a Feelin' I'm Fallin' " (Billy Rose, Harry Link, "Fats" Waller).

Helen Morgan (Kitty Darling); Joan Peers (April Darling); Fuller Mellish, Jr. (Hitch Nelson); Henry Wadsworth (Tony); Jack Cameron (Joe King); Dorothy Cumming (Mother Superior); Jack Singer (Producer); Paul Barrett (Slim Lamont).

Kitty Darling (Helen Morgan), a not-too-bright but optimistic burlesque star whose husband died in prison, wants a better life for her little daughter and sends her to a convent school. When she is grown, the girl, April (Joan Peers), comes to the big city. Kitty's lover, a drunk named Hitch (Fuller Mellish, Jr.), who is a comedian in the show in which Kitty works, wants to use the girl to bring some youth into the tawdry stage effort. When Kitty finds her daughter does not approve of her relationship with Hitch, Kitty marries the man, even though he has told her she is old and ugly. He also tries to make advances to April, but she rejects him. Meanwhile, April falls in love with sailor Tony (Henry Wadsworth) and they become engaged. However, when she overhears Hitch tell Kitty she is a has-been, the girl rejects Tony and joins the chorus of the burlesque show. Thinking her daughter is now married, the distraught and emotionally defeated Kitty poisons herself. April agrees to take her mother's place in the show, and she and Tony are reconciled.

"Remarkable enough even today, the film must have seemed . . . a real eye-opener in those days of talk, talk and more talk, . . . The very opening sequence indicates that [director Rouben] Mamoulian was thinking in terms of movement rather than sound, and in terms of cinema rather than theatre." (Tom Milne, *Mamoulian,* 1969). Lee Edward Stein (*The Movie Musical,* 1974) championed the film: ". . . An unusually realistic and cynical look at backstage life. Fighting advice from his Paramount bosses, Mamoulian insisted on showing the world of burlesque as grim, seamy and ultimately heartbreaking." The production, Mamoulian's first film, was made at Paramount's Astoria (Long Island, New York) studio and displayed an amazing camera fluidity and non-static soundtrack. Unfortunately APPLAUSE failed to recoup its costs, although over the years it has grown into one of the screen's early musical movie classics.

Renowned torch singer Helen Morgan was near-brilliant as the disillusioned, aging performer Kitty and provided memorable renditions of "What Wouldn't I Do for That Man" and "I've Gotta Feelin' I'm Fallin'."

APRIL SHOWERS (Warner Bros., 1948) 93 minutes.

Producer, William Jacobs; director, James V. Kern; based on the story "Barbary Host" by Joe Laurie, Jr.; screenplay, Peter Milne; art director, Hugh Reticker; set decorator, Ben Bone; costumes, Travilla; makeup, Perc Westmore; music, Ray Heindorf; music director, Leo F. Forbstein; choreographer, LeRoy Prinz; sound, Stanley Jones; montages, James Leicester; special effects, William McGann, Wesley Anderson; camera, Carl Guthrie; editor, Thomas Reilly.

Songs: "Little Trouper" (Kim Gannon, Walter Kent); "The

World's Most Beautiful Girl" (Kim Gannon, Ted Fetter); "It's Tulip Time in Holland" (Dave Radford, Richard A. Whiting); "April Showers" (Buddy G. DeSylva, Louis Silvers); "Carolina in the Morning" (Gus Kahn, Walter Donaldson); "Mr. Lovejoy and Mr. Jay" (Jack Scholl, Ray Heindorf).

Jack Carson (Joe Tyme); Ann Sothern (June Tyme); Robert Alda (Billy Shay); S. Z. Sakall (Mr. Curly); Robert Ellis (Buster); Richard Rober (Al Wilson); Joseph Crehan (Mr. Barnes); Ray Walker (Mr. Barclay); John Gallaudet (Mr. Gordon); Phillip van Zandt (Mr. Swift); Billy Curtis (Vanderhouten).

One of the most underrated and unjustly forgotten musicals of the late 1940s was Warner Bros.' APRIL SHOWERS. It had the misfortune to come along in the post-war years when light fluff such as this was eschewed in favor of stark and realistic "message" pictures. Morever, it was shot in economical black-and-white. "Even with expert presentation, this would be an insufferable tale," the *New York Times* criticized. However, seen today, this movie, despite its maudlin plotline, is quite entertaining, not only for its well staged production numbers but also for its very fine period detail.

At the turn of the century, third-rate vaudevillians Joe (Jack Carson) and June Tyme (Ann Sothern) struggle with their dancing act, but they begin to have some success when their small son Buster (Robert Ellis) joins the act. The family trio has a major success in California and this leads to Broadway, where they score big at the vaudeville mecca, The Palace Theatre. Just as they are enjoying their new-found success, the Gerry Society, which monitors the activities of performers under the age of sixteen, steps in and tries to control Buster's activities. Joe, whose inflated ego makes him think he is the big star of the act, begins drinking heavily and he and June fight. She and Buster sign with agent Billy Shay (Robert Alda), who has designs on June, and mother and son take the act back to the West Coast, leaving a sullen Joe behind. Returning to his senses, Joe heads westward, has a showdown with Shay and is reconciled with June and Buster. The family continues its act.

Based on Joe Laurie Jr.'s story, "Barbary Host," APRIL SHOWERS nicely interpolates old and new numbers in its score, among the latter being "The World's Most Beautiful Girl" and "Little Trouper," while stalwarts like the title tune and "Carolina in the Morning" were also highlighted. One of the nicest features of the film was the opportunity to see MGM's "Maisie" series star, Ann Sothern, starring in a musical, a format in which she shone but had too little opportunity to perform in at her home lot.

AT LONG LAST LOVE (20th Century-Fox, 1975) Color 118 minutes.

Producer, Peter Bogdanovich; associate producer, Frank Marshall; director/screenplay, Bogdanovich; art director, John Lloyd; set decorator, Jerry Wonderlich; costumes, Bobbie Mannix; music directors, Artie Butler, Lionel Newman; orchestrators, Gus Levene, Harry Betts; choreographers, Albert Lantieri, Rita Abrams; assistant directors, Mickey McArdle, Jerry Balew; sound, Victor Goode, Eugene O'Brien; sound re-recording, Barry Thomas, Theodore Soderberg; sound editor, Don Hall; special effects, Charlie Spurgeon; camera, Laszlo Kovacs; editor, Douglas Robertson.

Songs: "Which," "Tired of Living Alone," "You're the Top," "Find Me a Primitive Man," "Friendship," "But in the Morning, No!" "At Long Last Love," "Well Did You Evah?" "From Alpha to Omega," "Let's Misbehave," "It's De-Lovely," "Just One of Those Things," "I Get a Kick Out of You," "Most Gentlemen Don't Like Love," "I Love Him (But He Didn't Love Me)," "A Picture of Me Without You" (Cole Porter).

Burt Reynolds (Michael Oliver Pritchard III); Cybill Shepherd (Brooke Carter); Madeline Kahn (Kitty O'Kelly); Duilio Del Prete (Johnny Spanish [Giovani Spagnoli]); Eileen Brennan (Elizabeth); John Hillerman (Rodney James); Mildred Natwick (Mabel Pritchard); Quinn Redeker (Phillip); J. Edward McKinley (Billings); John Stephenson (Abbott); Peter Dane (Williams); William Paterson (Murray); Lester Dorr (Doorman); Liam Dunn (Harry); Elvin Moon (Elevator Boy); M. Emmet Walsh (Harold the Doorman); Burton Gilliam (Man at Racetrack); Albert Lantieri (Bookmaker); Len Lookabaugh (Workman); Anna Bogdanovich (1st Salesgirl); Alexandra Bogdanovich, Antonia Bogdanovich (Children at Lord & Taylor); Rita Loewen (2nd Salesgirl); Maurice Prince (Power Room Attendant); Christa Lang (Pregnant Lady); William Shepherd (Tall Young Man at 400 Dance); Manny Harmon (Bandleader); Tanis Van Kirk (Usherette); Ned Wertimer (1st Man at Nightclub); Arthur Peterson (George); Barbara Ann Walters (Mildred); Violet Cane (Vi); Roger Price (Alfred, Mabel's Chauffeur); Loutz Gage (Captain Craig); Diana Wyatt, Clive Morgan (1st Couple at Racquet Club); Patricia O'Neal, Nelson Welch (2nd Couple at Racquet Club); Morgan Farley (3rd Man at Racquet Club); Robert Terry (4th Man at Racquet Club); Artie Butler (Cab Driver); Gene Lebelle (Boxer); Basil Hoffman (Movie Theatre Manager); Donald Journeaux (Man in Lobby); Jeffrey Byron, Lloyd Catlett (Bellboys); Kevin O'Neal (Telegram Bellboy); and: Rita Abrams, Tony

Barberio, William Bartlett, Ian Bruce, Maria Cokkinos, Sheila Condit, Bill Couch, Ross Divito, Elizabeth Edwards, Roy Goldman, Roberta Lynn Haines, Stephanie Haines, John Houy, Merlena Joyh, Sam Kwasman, Fran Lee, Bert May, Jim Mohlman, Jack Onzal, David Panaieff, Mary K. Peters, Tucker Smith, Bill Taliaferro, Nelson Welch, Roy Wilson, Diana Wyatt, Joan Zajac.

Legend has it that Cole Porter was awaiting medical help for a broken leg when he composed the song "At Long Last Love" to take his mind off the pain of his injury. Legend also has it the song never brought him luck and was one of his lesser efforts, having first been used in the Broadway show, *You Never Know* (1938). Attempting to revive the moribund movie musical, iconoclastic producer-director Peter Bogdanovich chose the song as the title tune for this sad screen outing, which also attempted to bring back the screwball comedy genre. The mixture of the two, plus the focus on the limited talents of uncharismatic Cybill Shepherd, sank the film from the start. Not even the inclusion of fifteen additional Porter tunes, some of them his best, could buoy this embarrassing farrago.

Although it runs almost two hours, AT LONG LAST LOVE has a frail storyline. Society girl Brooke Carter (Cybill Shepherd) is sought after by bored playboy Michael Oliver Pritchard III (Burt Reynolds) and Venetian gambler Johnny Spanish, né Giovani Spagnoli (Duilio Del Prete). Also involved in the love triangle are showgirl Kitty O'Kelly (Madeline Kahn) and Brooke's love-starved maid, Elizabeth (Eileen Brennan), who has her romantic ambitions set on Rodney (John Hillerman), Pritchard's dour butler. Observing the shenanigans with a level-headed sarcasm is Pritchard's mother (Mildred Natwick; the one saving grace of the picture). Eventually Brooke and Pritchard are united, as are Kitty and Johnny Spanish as well as the maid and butler.

Variety pointed out, "The principals sang their numbers while being filmed, with orchestrations dubbed in later, in an attempt to eliminate the lifelessness of post-sync when it is done poorly. On the basis of this experiment, pre-recording can rest its case." When AT LONG LAST LOVE was sold to TV, Bogdanovich re-edited the film, but the end result was still one of the most dismally bad movie musicals.

This film can be recommended only for the strong at heart. Above and beyond the wretched singing by most of the cast, watching Eileen Brennan, Cybill Shepherd and Madeline Kahn kick up their heels is not a harmonious sight.

BABES IN ARMS (Metro-Goldwyn-Mayer, 1939) 93 minutes.

Producer, Arthur Freed; director, Busby Berkeley; based on

the musical play by Richard Rodgers, Lorenz Hart; screenplay, Jack McGowan, Kay Van Riper, (uncredited): Florence Ryerson, Edgar Allan Woolf, Joe Laurie, John Meehan, Walter DeLeon, Irving Brecher, Ben Freedman, Anita Loos; art directors, Cedric Gibbons, Merrill Pye; costumes, Dolly Tree; music director, George Stoll; orchestrator, Conrad Salinger, (uncredited) Leo Araud; music adaptor, Roger Edens; camera, Ray June; editor, Frank Sullivan.

Songs: "Babes in Arms," "Where or When," "The Lady Is a Tramp" (Richard Rodgers, Lorenz Hart); "Ja-Da" (Bob Carlton); "Rock-a-Bye Baby" (Effie T. Crockett); "Silent Night" (Franz Gruber; arranger, Roger Edens); "Good Morning," "Broadway Rhythm," "You Are My Lucky Star," "I Cried for You," "Broadway Melody," "Singin' in the Rain" (Nacio Herb Brown, Arthur Freed); "Darktown Strutters Ball" (Shelton Brooks); "Opera vs. Jazz" (arranger, Edens); sextette from the opera *Lucia di Lammermoor* (Gaetano Donizetti); "Bob White" (Bernard D. Hanighen, Johnny Mercer); "Indignation March," "Nursery March" (Edens); "My Daddy Was a Minstrel Man" (Edens); "Oh! Susanna" (Stephen Foster); "Ida, Sweet As Apple Cider" (Eddie Leonard, Eddie Munson); "On Moonlight Bay" (Edward Madden, Percy Wenrich); "I'm Just Wild about Harry" (Noble Sissle, Eubie Blake); "The Stars and Stripes Forever" (John Philip Sousa); "God's Country" (Harold Arlen, E. Y. Harburg); "Give My Regards to Broadway" (George M. Cohan); "Toot Toot Tootsie" (Gus Kahn, Ernie Erdman, Dan Russo).

Mickey Rooney (Mickey Moran); Judy Garland (Patsy Barton); Charles Winninger (Joe Moran); Guy Kibbee (Judge Black); June Preisser (Rosalie Essex); Grace Hayes (Florrie Moran); Betty Jaynes (Molly Moran); Douglas McPhail (Don Brice); Rand Brooks (Jeff Steele); Leni Lynn (Doby Martini); John Sheffield (Bobs); Henry Hull (Maddox); Barnett Parker (William); Ann Shoemaker (Mrs. Barton); Margaret Hamilton (Martha Steele); Joseph Crehan (Mr. Essex); George McKay (Brice); Henry Roquemore (Shaw); Lelah Taylor (Mrs. Brice); Lon McCallister (Boy); and: Charles Brown, Rube Demarest, Kay Deslys, Irene Franklin, Sidney Miller, Patsy Moran.

"The film is fresh, amiable, spirited and is perhaps best summed up by [director Busby] Berkeley's staging of the title song. Mickey, Judy, and all the other show-biz kids march through the streets lustily singing about who they are and what they are going to do. . . . Just to watch them is to know there is no stopping them" (Tony Thomas, Jim Terry, *The Busby Berkeley Book,* 1973).

Veteran vaudevillians Joe (Charles Winninger) and Florrie Moran (Grace Hayes) put together a touring show which uses many

Judy Garland and Mickey Rooney in BABES IN ARMS (1939).

of their comrades of yore. However, troubles ensue when their offspring want a part in the production and are refused. The enterprising youngsters, led by Mickey Moran (Mickey Rooney) and Patsy Barton (Judy Garland), decide to stage their own show with Mickey doing the writing and co-starring with Patsy. The youngsters have a month to prove their worth or they will be sent to a state trade school as a local busybody (Margaret Hamilton) insists. Money for the youthful production is forthcoming from former child star Rosalie Essex (June Preisser) who, in return, is given the lead in the show, with Patsy now reduced to being her understudy. Problems develop with both Rosalie and the weather (it is an outdoor show). Eventually, all turns out well when the skies clear and Rosalie cannot go on. Patsy takes her place, and the production is a big success. Broadway producer Maddox (Henry Hull), a pal of Joe Moran, attends the revue, and decides to take it to Broadway, where Mickey, Patsy and company are sure to be a big success.

BABES IN ARMS was the third of ten MGM movies to co-star Mickey Rooney and Judy Garland. It was the first of four Busby Berkeley musicals to star the popular young pair and was produced by Arthur Freed's new production unit at MGM, which the same year starred Garland in THE WIZARD OF OZ. BABES IN ARMS was based on Richard Rodgers' and Lorenz Hart's Broadway show which had enjoyed a 289-performance run in 1937. The plot was revamped to build up Mickey Rooney's role and to display the youthful exuberance and vitality of its leads. Only the title tune, "Where or When," and bits of "The Lady Is a Tramp" were used from the original stage score, and Freed utilized several of his own compositions to bolster the proceedings. This was *the* film in which the cliché of the kids deciding "Gee let's put on a show!" became a Hollywood reality and began a snowballing Hollywood trend.

In contrast to Busby Berkeley's prior musical extravaganzas at Warner Bros., which typically featured Dick Powell, Ruby Keeler and a bevy of bleached blonde chorines in adult tales of gold diggers, BABES IN ARMS was tailored to the more intimate talents of Rooney and Garland and the more family-oriented tenets of Metro-Goldwyn-Mayer screen product. Nevertheless, Berkeley included three mammoth production numbers: the title tune, which is a call to arms led by baritone Douglas McPhail, the minstrel show interlude, and the grand finale, "God's Country."

When BABES IN ARMS opened in October 1939 the *New York Daily News* proclaimed, "As an entertainment, it has lost some of its original sophistication and the elastic snap with which it went over on the stage. But it has gained in comic interludes and serves to introduce several new screen personalities." Made at a cost of $748,000, the musical grossed $3,335,000 in its initial release. Rooney was Oscar-nominated for his role (which included imitations of Lionel Barrymore and Clark Gable, dancing, singing and playing musical instruments) and soon rose to number one at the box-office. Roger Edens and George E. Stoll were nominated for their scoring of the film.

So successful was BABES IN ARMS that it resulted in a sequel two years later called BABES ON BROADWAY, again with Busby Berkeley helming and Rooney and Garland starring. Here the youngsters, although using different character names, try for success on the Great White Way; a highlight was Mickey Rooney's outrageous impersonation of Carmen Miranda.

BABES IN TOYLAND (Metro-Goldwyn-Mayer, 1934) 77 minutes.

Producer, Hal Roach; directors, Gus Meins, Charles Rogers; based on the operetta by Victor Herbert, Glen MacDonough; screenplay, Nick Grinde, Frank Butler; music director, Henry Jackson; camera, Art Lloyd, Francis Corby; editors, William Terhune, Bert Jordan.

Songs: "Toyland," "Don't Cry Bo-Peep," "A Castle in Spain," "I Can't Do That Sum," "Go to Sleep, Slumber Deep" (Victor Herbert, Glen MacDonough); "Who's Afraid of the Big Bad Wolf" (Ann Ronnell, Frank Church); "March of the Toys" (Herbert).

Stan Laurel (Stanley Dum); Oliver Hardy (Oliver Dee); Charlotte Henry (Bo-Peep); Felix Knight (Tom-Tom); Henry Kleinbach [Brandon] (Barnaby); Florence Roberts (Widow Peep); Ferdinand Munier (Santa Claus); William Burress (Toymaker); Virginia Karns (Mother Goose); Johnny Downs (Little Boy Blue); Jean Darling (Curly Locks); Frank Austin (Justice of the Peace); Gus Leonard (Candle Snuffer); Alice Dahl (Little Miss Muffett); Peter Gordon (Cat and the Fiddle); Sumner Getchell (Tom Thumb); Kewpie Morgan (Old King Cole); John George (Barnaby's Minion); Billy Bletcher (Chief of Police); Alice Cook (Mother Hubbard); Alice Moore (Queen of Hearts).

Reissue titles: MARCH OF THE TOYS; MARCH OF THE WOODEN SOLDIERS; REVENGE IS SWEET. TV title: MARCH OF THE WOODEN SOLDIERS.

See: BABES IN TOYLAND (1961) (essay).

BABES IN TOYLAND (Buena Vista, 1961) Color 106 minutes.

Producer, Walt Disney; director, Jack Donahue; based on the

operetta by Victor Herbert, Glen MacDonough; screenplay, Ward Kimball, Joe Rinaldi, Lowell S. Hawley; Donough; added material, Mel Leven; art directors, Carroll Clark, Marvin Aubrey Davis; set decorators, Emile Kuri, Hal Gausman; costumes, Bill Thomas; makeup, Pat McNalley; choreographer, Tommy Mahoney; music adaptor/conductor, George Bruns; orchestrator, Franklyn Marks; choral arranger, Jud Conlon; assistant director, Austen Jewell; sound supervisor, Robert O. Cook; sound, Dean Thomas; animated effects, Joshua Meader; special effects, Eustace Lycett, Robert A. Mattey; camera, Edward Colman; editor, Robert Stafford.

Songs: "Castle in Spain," "I Can't Do the Sum," "Just a Toy," "Floretta," "We Won't Be Happy Till We Get It," "Lemonade," "Just a Whisper Away," "March of the Toys," "Toyland" (Victor Herbert, Glen MacDonough); "Slowly He Sank into the Sea," "The Workshop Song," "The Forest of No Return" (George Bruns, Mel Leven).

Ray Bolger (Barnaby); Tommy Sands (Tom Piper); Annette Funicello (Mary Contrary); Ed Wynn (Toymaker); Tommy Kirk (Grumio); Kevin Corcoran (Boy Blue); Henry Calvin (Gonzorgo); Gene Sheldon (Roderigo); Mary McCarty (Mother Goose); Ann Jillian (Bo Peep); Brian Corcoran (Willie Winkie); Marilee and Melanie Arnold (Twins); Jerry Glen (Simple Simon); John Perri (Jack-Be-Nimble); David Pinson (Bobby Shaftoe); Bryan Russell (The Little Boy); James Martin (Jack); Ilana Dowding (Jill).

Victor Herbert's operetta, *Babes in Toyland,* with book and lyrics by Glen MacDonough, has delighted audiences since it debuted in 1903. Two screen versions of the children's fantasy have appeared, the 1934 version by Hal Roach being far more satisfying than the 1961 Walt Disney remake.

BABES IN TOYLAND takes place in a fairy tale world called Toyland where pretty Bo-Peep (Charlotte Henry, who had starred in the title role of Paramount's ALICE IN WONDERLAND the year before) is in love with Tom-Tom (Felix Knight), but she is lusted after by the evil Silas Barnaby (Henry Kleinbach [Henry Brandon]). Also in Toyland are the Toymaker (William Burress) and his two bumbling assistants, Stannie Dum (Stan Laurel) and Ollie Dee (Oliver Hardy), who board with Bo-Beep's mother, Widow Peep (Florence Roberts). The evil Barnaby has Tom-Tom abducted to the underworld of Bogeyland so he can marry Bo-Peep. However, Stannie and Ollie come to her rescue by operating an army of giant wooden soldiers who route Barnaby and his sinister minions. Happiness is restored to Toyland.

Containing an appealing variety of fairy tale characters, the Hal Roach production of BABES IN TOYLAND was a delight for audiences young and old and for the most part it faithfully retained most of Victor Herbert's score (only four songs were deleted). Felix Knight was especially impressive singing "Toyland." Of course, the main interest of the production was the comedy antics of Laurel and Hardy as the toymaker's inept assistants. Their screen personalities in no way hampered the operetta; indeed, they enhanced it. Judging the results, the *New York Times* enthused, "The film is an authentic children's entertainment and quite the merriest of its kind that Hollywood has turned loose on the nation's screen in a long time. . . . Since the comic team of Laurel and Hardy has wandered into it, the elders, as well as their young charges, are advised to check their dignity at the door." Over the years the 1934 edition became a holiday favorite and was reissued theatrically several times.

Disney's 1961 Technicolor version of BABES IN TOYLAND, for a time, halted showings of the Hal Roach feature, but in no way can it compare to the 1934 original. Overlong, the musical utilized basically the original Victory Herbert operetta plot and employed most of the songs, but its casting was very weak except for Ray Bolger as Barnaby. Tommy Sands and Annette Funicello were not particularly appealing in the undemanding roles of the young lovers. Ed Wynn's exaggerated bumbling Toymaker was especially irritating. Perhaps Leonard Maltin best summed up the film's problems in *The Disney Films* (1973), "BABES IN TOYLAND is filled to the brim with gimmicks, ranging from minor (animated stars bursting out of Tom's head when he is bopped with a sledge-hammer by the two henchmen) to major (talking/singing/dancing trees in the Forest of No Return), an endless procession of songs, staged in a variety of fashions to avoid repetition from one to the next, and a large cast performing in the most colorful settings ever devised for a live-action Disney film. Unfortunately, all these elements combined cannot overcome some basic and serious flaws that hamper the picture."

BABES ON BROADWAY *see* BABES IN ARMS (essay).

BACK TO THE BEACH *see* BEACH PARTY (essay).

BAJA OKLAHOMA (HBO-Cable TV, 1988) Color 99 minutes.

Executive producer, Hunt Lowry; producer, Mary-Kay Powell; associate producer, Fred Baron; director, Bobby Roth; based on the novel by Dan Jenkins; screenplay, Roth, Jenkins; production designer, Al Brenner; art director, David M. Haber; costumes, Ruth Myers; makeup, Annie D'Angelo; music, Stanley Myers; music supervisor, Dick Rudolph; choreographer, Jerry Evans;

assistant directors, Josh McLaglen, Tom Archuleta; camera, Michael Ballhaus; editors, John Carnochan, Gail Yasunaga.

Songs: "I Think You've Got Me" (Billy Vera, Larry Brown); "Three Minute Thing" (Chip Taylor, Paul Gayten); "Faded Love" (Bob Wills, John Wills); "In My Dreams" (Paul Kennerly); "No Place to Have a Heart" (Dick Rudolph, Michael Sembello); "I'll Be Your San Antone Rose" (Susanna Clark); "It's Just Living (Slick's Song)" (Karla Bonoff); "Baja Oklahoma" (Willie Nelson, Dan Jenkins).

Lesley Ann Warren (Juanita Hutchins); Peter Coyote (Slick Henderson); Swoosie Kurtz (Doris Steadman); Billy Vera (Lonnie Slocum); Anthony Zerbe (Ol' Jeemy Williams); William Forsythe (Tommy Earl Browner); John M. Jackson (Lee Steadman); Bruce Abbott (Dove Christian); Julia Roberts (Candy Hutchins); Carmen Argenziano (Roy Simmons); Paul Bartel (Minister); Jordan Charney (Beecher Perry); Carole Davis (Tina Busher); Alice Krige (Patsy Cline); Bob Wills, Jr. (Bob Wills); Willie Nelson, Emmylou Harris (Themselves).

Few musicals have been made for television in recent years; except Barry Manilow's glittery gangster yarn, COPACABANA (1985). Thus BAJA OKLAHOMA was a welcome arrival with its breezy story of a good time girl who yearns to be a successful country music composer. The production garnered solid reviews and, in addition to its cable TV debut, received some theatrical distribution.

Texas barmaid Juanita Hutchins (Lesley Ann Warren) has become somewhat jaded thanks to an endless succession of disappointments, lovers and two broken marriages. Still she has optimism and tries to escape from her humdrum existence by writing country songs. Slick Henderson (Peter Coyote), an ex-boyfriend of two decades before, returns suddenly to her life, wanting to renew their romance, while Juanita has constant trouble with her teenage daughter Candy (Julia Roberts). She fears the latter will repeat her romantic mistakes, especially since she has taken up with a dope peddler (Bruce Abbott). Eventually Juanita composes a song she likes but she has difficulty in getting an entertainer friend, Lonnie Slocum (Billy Vera), to listen to it. Finally a local promoter (Anthony Zerbe) provides her with an opportunity and the song is introduced by Willie Nelson (himself), which gives Juanita hope for future success.

An interesting aspect of BAJA OKLAHOMA has Willie Nelson making a brief appearance singing the title song which he wrote with Dan Jenkins. Also appearing are Emmylou Harris, Bob Wills Jr. playing his famous fiddler father, and Alice Krige as Patsy

Cline. The critics mostly liked this homey feature, the *San Francisco Chronicle* calling it "a bull's eye for HBO." The *New York Daily News* opined, "BAJA is in a class by itself. . . . It may well be 'the sleeper' of the season." The *Chicago Sun-Times* judged it ". . . A rich and raunchy romp." More demanding was *Variety,* which labeled the outing ". . . An amiable little country-western fairy tale none too high on plausibility but pleasant enough. . . . Along with its easy-going predictability, film has no strong urgency about it. . . ."

BALALAIKA (Metro-Goldwyn-Mayer, 1939) 102 minutes.

Producer, Lawrence Weingarten; director, Reinhold Schunzel; based on the operetta by Eric Maschwitz, George Ponford, Bernard Gruen; screenplay, Leon Gordon, Charles Bennett, Jacques Deval; music, Herbert Stothart; sound supervisor, Douglas Shearer; camera, Joseph Ruttenberg, Karl Freund.

Songs: "At the Balalaika" (George Posford, Eric Maschwitz; with new lyrics by Bob Wright, Chet Forrest); "After Service" (arranger, Herbert Stothart); "A Life for the Czar" (from the opera by Mikhail Glinka, Georgy Rosen; as adapted); "Ride Cossack, Ride," "Tanya," "Wishing Episode (Mirror Mirror)" (Stothart, Wright, Forrest); "Gorko" (traditional; adaptor, Stothart); "Polonaise in A Flat Major, Opus 53" (Frederick Chopin); "Song of the Volga Boatman" (traditional; arrangers, Feodor Chaliapin, T.H. Koeneman); "Chanson Bohème," "Chanson du Toréador," "Si Tu M'Aime" (all from the opera *Carmen* [Georges Bizet]); "Shadows on the Sand" (based on themes from the symphonic suite "Scheherezade" for orchestra by Nikolai Rimsky-Korsakov, arranged by Wright, Forrest); "God Save the Czar" (Alexei Kvov, Vasili Zhukovsky); "Stille Nacht [Silent Night]" (Franz Gruber, Joseph Mohr); "Otchichornia" (traditional); "Flow, Flow, White Wine" (Stothart, Gus Kahn); "The Magic of Your Love" (Franz Lehar; new lyrics: Kahn, Clifford Grey).

Nelson Eddy (Prince Peter Karagin); Ilona Massey (Lydia Pavlovna Marakov); Charles Ruggles (Nicki Popoff); Frank Morgan (Danchenoff); Lionel Atwill (Professor Marakov); C. Aubrey Smith (General Karagin); Joyce Compton (Masha); Dalies Frantz (Dimitri Marakov); Walter Woolf King (Sibirski); Phillip Terry (Lieutenant Smimoff); Frederick Worlock (Ramensky); Abner Biberman (Leo); Arthur W. Cernitz (Captain Pavloff); Roland Varno (Lieutenant Nikitin); George Tobias (Slaski); Paul Sutton (Anton); Willy Costello (Captain Testoff); Paul Irving (Prince Morodin); Mildred Shay (Jeanette Sibirsky); Alma Kruger (Mrs. Danchenoff); Zeffie Tilbury (Princess); Charles Judels (Cafe Proprietor).

Balalaika debuted on the London stage late in 1936 and this operetta by Eric Maschwitz, George Ponford and Bernard Gruen had a run of 446 performances starring Muriel Angelus and Roger Treville. MGM obtained the screen rights to the production and transformed it into a lavish movie starring Nelson Eddy and Ilona Massey. Its many musical interludes varied from new material by Herbert Stothart, Bob Wright and Chet Forrest to traditional Russian folk ballads. Douglas Shearer earned an Academy Award nomination for Best Sound Recording for the production.

Although the picture sumptuously deals with the ambiance of the Russian Revolution of the 1910s, one learns very little about the historical events. (Since Russia was then an ally of the U.S. in the emerging World War II, MGM was fearful of taking sides regarding the Revolution.) As Eleanor Knowles noted in *The Films of Jeanette MacDonald and Nelson Eddy* (1975), "BALALAIKA, as a musical, refrains from commenting on the struggle between the nobility and the revolutionaries while making it the center of the action. And although the irony and nostalgia of royal expatriates working as waiters and tailors is beautifully handled, the conflict of the drama is never realized. . . . This is not to say that the film is dull. It is richly mounted, excitingly photographed, and full of tender and funny moments. Eddy is in especially good voice and delivers some outstanding numbers."

Prince Peter Karagin (Nelson Eddy) rides with his Cossack troops into a small Russian village near St. Petersburg in 1914, on their way to a cafe called Maxim's where beautiful Lydia Pavlovna Marakov (Ilona Massey) sings while her brother Dimitri (Dalies Frantz) plays the piano and their father, Professor Marakov (Lionel Atwill), is the conductor. Karagin is attracted to the girl and sends his orderly, Nicki Popoff (Charlie Ruggles), to arrange a meeting with her, but Popoff mistakes her maid Masha (Joyce Compton) for the singer. When the matter is straightened out, it is Popoff who is in love with the maid. Meanwhile, the cafe proprietor (Charles Judels) tells Lydia to sing for the Cossacks. She does so against her will, and thwarts the advances of an officer named Sibirski (Walter Woolf King). Wanting to be near Lydia, Peter poses as a student and the two form a romantic attraction. His father, General Karagin (C. Aubrey Smith), is opposed to the rising revolutionary tide in Russia, while Peter is unaware that Lydia and her family are supporters of the cause. The prince uses his influence to gain Lydia a post at the Imperial Opera run by Danchenoff (Frank Morgan), and continues to romance her in the guise of a student. Later Peter leads his Cossacks against a group of revolutionaries and in the fracas Lydia's brother is killed. Finding out the truth of Peter's identity, Lydia agrees to lead him and his father into a trap, but when Peter resigns from the army to marry her, she thwarts the plot, although General Karagin is injured. Just then World War I breaks out and Peter is assigned to lead troops in the conflict. Lydia is arrested for her role in the assassination attempts. During the war, the two lovers are separated. After the conflict ends, the Russian nobility goes in exile to Paris where Nicki and his wife Masha run the Cafe Balalaika, a Russian restaurant, with Peter as a singing waiter and his father as the wine steward. On New Year's Eve all of the former nobility have a party and Lydia arrives. She and Peter renew their romance.

The opulent BALALAIKA uses several plot situations familiar to moviegoers from Warner Bros.' TOVARICH (1937) and from MGM's own NINOTCHKA (1939), with the defrocked Russian nobility surviving and cavorting in Paris. As the *New York Times* reminded, ". . . the picture is long on formula and short on originality and . . . nine out of ten sequences have been blue-printed before." It was made in the year that MGM sought to merchandise its screen operetta team of Jeanette MacDonald and Nelson Eddy in *separate* movie vehicles, thus paving the way for beautiful Ilona Massey to take the co-lead in BALALAIKA. (She had had a supporting part in the Nelson Eddy-Eleanor Powell musical, ROSALIE [1937] *q.v.*) The exotic Massey proved to be a fetching soprano with her rendition of "Tanya" and in "Magic of Your Love" with Eddy. However, she lacked tne warmth of personality or the showmanship of MacDonald; more importantly there was no great chemistry between the Hungarian actress and Eddy. Eddy had a best-selling record for Columbia with "At the Balalaika" and also recorded five other songs from the film, including "Silent Night," "Song of the Volga Boatman," and "The Toreador Song."

THE BAND WAGON (Metro-Goldwyn-Mayer, 1953) Color 111 minutes.

Producer, Arthur Freed; associate producer, Roger Edens; director, Vincente Minnelli; screenplay, Betty Comden, Adolph Green; art directors, Cedric Gibbons, Preston Ames; set decorators, Edwin B. Willis, Keogh Gleason; costumes, Mary Ann Nyberg; makeup, William Tuttle; music director, Adolph Deutsch; orchestrators, Conrad Salinger, Skip Martin, Alexander Courage; choreographers, Michael Kidd, Oliver Smith; assistant director, Jerry Thorpe; color consultants, Henri Jaffa, Robert Brower; special effects, Warren Newcombe; camera, Harry Jackson, (uncredited) George Folsey; editor, Albert Akst.

Songs: "By Myself," "Dancing in the Dark," "I Love Louisa," "Shine on Your Shoes," "That's Entertainment!" "New Sun in the

Sky," "Louisiana Hayride," "Beggar's Waltz," "You and the Night and the Music," "High and Low," "Something to Remember You By," "Right at the Start of It," "Is It All a Dream?" "Sweet Music" (Arthur Schwartz, Howard Dietz); "Girl Hunt Ballet" (Schwartz; narration by Alan Jay Lerner); "The Egg" (Conrad Salinger); "Carriage in the Park" (Roger Edens, Salinger); "Off-Scene Noodles" (Adolph Deutsch); "Oedipus Rex Bridge" (Edens, Alexander Courage).

Fred Astaire (Tony Hunter); Cyd Charisse (Gaby Bernard); Oscar Levant (Lester Marton); Nanette Fabray (Lily Marton); Jack Buchanan (Jeffrey Cordova); James Mitchell (Paul Byrd); Robert Gist (Hal Benton); Thurston Hall (Colonel Tripp); Ava Gardner (The Movie Star); LeRoy Daniels (Shoeshine Boy); Jack Tesler (Ivan); Dee Turnell, Elynne Ray, Peggy Murray, Judy Landon (Girls in Troupe); Jimmie Thompson, Bert May (Boys in Troupe); John Lupton (Jack the Promoter); Owen McGivney (Prop Man); Sam Hearn (Agent); Herb Vigran, Emory Parnell (Men on Train); Ernest Anderson (Porter); Frank Scannon, Stu Wilson, Roy Engel (Reporters); Al Hill (Shooting Gallery Operator); Paul Bradley (Dancer in Park/Waiter); Bobby Watson (Bobby the Dresser);

Fred Astaire, Nanette Fabray, Jack Buchanan and Oscar Levant in THE BAND WAGON (1953).

Lotte Stein (Chambermaid); Smoki Whitfield (Chauffeur); Dick Alexander, Al Ferguson (Stagehands); Betty Farrington (Fitter); Bess Flowers (Lady on Train); Matt Mattox (Specialty Dancer); Sue Casey (Tall Woman in Penny Arcade); Eden Hartford, Julie Newmar (Girls in "Private Eye" Number); Steve Forrest (Man); Madge Blake (Gushy Woman); India Adams (Singing Voice of Gaby Bernard).

The *New York Times* called THE BAND WAGON "A brilliantly sophisticated, warm and wonderful musical film, one of the best ever made, that takes the old putting-on-a-Broadway-show theme and sets it delightfully spinning, with a fine cast taking their cues from Fred Astaire. . . . Add, emphatically, a bright, witty script . . . the splendidly knowing direction of Vincente Minnelli and a grand flow of tunes. . . ." On the other hand, Lee Edward Stern (*The Movie Musical,* 1974) cautioned, "THE BAND WAGON, with its many delights, is not perfect. Nanette Fabray's number, 'Louisiana Hayride,' is embarrassingly coy and arch; and the final ballet, a spoof of the then-popular Mickey Spillane tough-guy novels, is so convinced of its own cleverness that its effect is jarring rather than amusing." Julia Johnson (*Magill's American Film Guide,* 1983) summarized, "Underlying the visual style and elegance of the film is the pensive theme of loneliness and the passage of time. It is, in fact, the image of Fred Astaire striding jauntily down the train platform singing 'By Myself' that sets the mood of the film and remains in the mind's eye." Johnson also noted ". . . The brilliant performance of British musical star Jack Buchanan as Cordova. . . . With its sharp, witty dialogue, his role is a well-drawn, fully realized characterization which gains added resonance from the fact that it has certain resemblances to director Vincente Minnelli."

Once famous movie star-dancer Tony Hunter (Fred Astaire), whose career needs revitalization, arrives in New York City to star in a musical written for him by his friends Lester (Oscar Levant) and Lily Marton (Nanette Fabray). To enhance the plotline of the vehicle, its director, Jeffrey Cordova (Jack Buchanan), turns it into a Faust allegory. Trouble ensues when leading lady-ballerina Gaby Bernard (Cyd Charisse) and Tony take an immediate dislike to each other; she thinks he is too old and he fears she is too tall to be his dance partner. Matters are not helped when Tony begins to fall in love with Gaby; she is the girlfriend of show choreographer Paul Byrd (James Mitchell). When the musical opens on the road in New Haven it is a dud and all concerned agree to pull together and do the best they can. As a result the show blossoms as a Broadway hit.

The genesis of THE BAND WAGON dates back to a 1931 Broadway revue with book and lyrics by George S. Kaufman and

Howard Dietz and music by Arthur Schwartz. The stars were Fred and Adele Astaire and Clifton Webb. For the film, MGM producer Arthur Freed revamped the old show (which had been loosely filmed by 20th Century-Fox in 1949 as DANCING IN THE DARK, with William Powell and Betsy Drake), using only three of the original production's songs ("I Love Louisa", "New Sun in the Sky," and "Dancing in the Dark"), and adding two new numbers: "That's Entertainment" and "Girl Hunt Ballet." With a shooting schedule running from October 1952 to January 1953 (with retakes in early February 1953), THE BAND WAGON reached completion at a cost of $2,169,120. It debuted at Radio City Music Hall in July 1953 and grossed $5,655,505 in initial release, turning it into one of Hollywood's more profitable musicals.

There were some numbers moviegoers never saw in the release print: Astaire and Charisse dancing to "You Have Everything," Astaire and Fabray in "Gotta Bran' New Suit," Levant and Fabray performing "Sweet Music to Worry the Wolf Away," and, among others, India Adams' singing of "Two-Faced Woman," which would be used instead for the studio's TORCH SONG (1953), with Joan Crawford lip-synching the Schwartz-Dietz tune.

Off-camera during THE BAND WAGON there was a great reserve between Cyd Charisse and Fred Astaire. While she termed him "the most perfect gentleman I have ever known" and a "perfectionist," he would recall that of all his dance partners she was the heaviest, and that he dreaded their dance lifts together. (It was during this period that his wife Phyllis—mother of his children, Ava and Fred—was terminally ill, thus adding to Astaire's misery during this production.) Nevertheless, on-camera Charisse proved to be one, if not the best, of Astaire's many screen partners. As Clive Hirshhorn (*The Hollywood Musical,* 1981) noted, "She seemed to bring out an erotic quality in his dancing, especially in the exquisite 'Dancing in the Dark,' with its Central Park setting which recalled some of the more lyrical of the Astaire-Rogers dances in the thirties." Astaire and Charisse would be reteamed in SILK STOCKINGS (1957), *q.v.*

When MGM filmed its nostalgia tribute, THAT'S ENTERTAINMENT! (1974), co-narrator-host Fred Astaire returned to the studio and was photographed visiting the old train set on the Culver City lot. As Astaire would recall, "The set was a mess. All the windows on the train were broken. Nobody had tried to sweep or clean up. It was just a wreck. The Twentieth Century Limited looked so black and dreary. As I walked along, I noticed that the carpeting was torn and the seats of the train were missing. But I suppose nothing should last forever."

THE BARKLEYS OF BROADWAY (Metro-Goldwyn-Mayer, 1949) Color 109 minutes.

Producer, Arthur Freed; associate producer, Roger Edens; director, Charles Walters; screenplay, Betty Comden, Adolph Green, (uncredited) Sidney Sheldon; art directors, Cedric Gibbons, Edward Cafagno; set decorators, Edwin B. Willis, Arthur Krams; Miss Rogers' costumes, Irene; men's costumes, Valles; makeup, Jack Dawn; music director, Lennie Hayton; orchestrator, Conrad Salinger; vocal arranger, Robert Tucker; music numbers stager/director, Robert Alton; "Shoes with Wings On" director, Hermes Pan; assistant director, Wallace Worsley; color consultants, Natalie Kalmus, Henri Jaffa; sound, Douglas Shearer, Charles E. Wallace; dancing shoes effects, Irving Ries; special effects, Warren Newcombe; camera, Harry Stradling; editor, Albert Akst.

Songs: "You'd Be Hard to Replace," "Manhattan Downbeat," "A Weekend in the Country," "Swing Trot," "Bouncin' the Blues," "My One and Only Highland Fling," "Shoes with Wings On" (Harry Warren, Ira Gershwin); "They Can't Take that Away from Me" (George Gershwin, Ira Gershwin); "Piano Concerto No. 1" (Peter Ilich Tchaikovsky); "Sabre Dance" (Aram Khatchaturian); "Angel," "This Heart of Mine" (Warren, Freed); "Ginger Comes Home" (Lennie Hayton).

Fred Astaire (Josh Barkley); Ginger Rogers (Dinah Barkley); Oscar Levant (Ezra Miller); Billie Burke (Mrs. Livingston Belney); Gale Robbins (Shirlene May); Jacques Francois (Jacques Pierre Barredout); George Zucco (The Judge); Clinton Sundberg (Bert Fisher); Inez Cooper (Pamela Driscoll); Carol Brewster (Gloria Amboy); Wilson Wood (Larry); Jean Andren (First Woman); Laura Treadwell (Second Woman); Margaret Bert (Mary the Maid); Hans Conreid (Ladislaus Ladi); Frank Ferguson (Mr. Perkins); Dee Turnell (Blonde); Joyce Mathews (Genevieve); Roger Moore (First Man); Lois Austin, Betty Blythe, Bill Tannen, Bess Flowers (Guests in Theatre Lobby); Allen Wood (Taxi Driver); Alphonse Martell, Howard Mitchell, Marcel de la Brosse, Wilbur Mack (Ad Lib Judges); Larry Steers, Lillian West (Ad Lib Guests); Pat Miller, Betty O'Kelly, Bobbie Brooks, Charles Van, Richard Winters, Mickey Martin, Dick Barron (Bobby-Soxers); Lorraine Crawford (Cleo Fernby); Mahlon Hamilton (Apartment Doorman); Reginald Simpson (Husband); Sherry Hall (Chauffeur); Frank Ferguson (Mr. Perkins); George Boyce, John Albright, Butch Terrell (*Look* Magazine Photographers); Edward Kilroy (Standee); Nolan Leary (Stage Doorman); Joe Grandby (Duke de Morny); Esther Somers (Sarah's Mother); Helen Eby-Rock (Sarah's Aunt); Bob Purcell

Ginger Rogers and Fred Astaire in THE BARKLEYS OF BROADWAY (1949).

(Voice); Max Willenz (Clerk); Jack Rice (Ticket Man); Robert Jackson (Clementine); Wheaton Chambers (Man).

Following RKO's THE STORY OF VERNON AND IRENE CASTLE (1939), their ninth picture together, co-stars Fred Astaire and Ginger Rogers went their separate screen ways. A decade later, they were reunited on-camera in MGM's Technicolor production of THE BARKLEYS OF BROADWAY; Judy Garland left the production due to emotional illness and was replaced by Rogers. While the film lacked sufficient plot and production numbers, Ginger and Fred retained the old magic, as noted by *Time* magazine. "Their dance numbers, though more sedate than ever before, are enchanting examples of the breezy, sophisticated style which they themselves brought to perfection."

The musical comedy team of Josh (Fred Astaire) and Dinah Barkley (Ginger Rogers) have enjoyed stage success for years, but Dinah wants to become a dramatic actress and prove she can hold her own as a solo performer. (With Rogers in the role it was a case of art imitating life.) As a result the bickering team splits, much to the consternation of their producer-playwright-friend, Ezra Miller (Oscar Levant). She succumbs to the blandishments of Jacques Pierre Barredout (Jacques Francois) to appear in his newest dramatic play. Josh, who has continued to appear in the musical, now teamed with Dinah's understudy, secretly watches her rehearsals and phones her one night with suggestions on how to improve her performance. Because he adopts a French accent for these phone calls, she thinks the help is coming from Jacques. Dinah eventually realizes that Josh is the Frenchman-in-disguise and, after teasing him into believing that she intends to wed the playwright, the two reunite. Together again romantically, they plan to star in a new musical comedy, continuing onward as the dancing toasts of Broadway.

With Garland no longer part of the proceedings, the musical numbers had to be altered to fit Rogers' more sophisticated personality. Thus several Harry Warren-Ira Gershwin's selections were deleted: the hillbilly "Courtship of Elmer and Ella," the comic ballet "Poetry in Motion," and "Natchez on the Mississip'." Roger Edens suggested that one of the replacement numbers should be a reprise of George and Ira Gershwin's "They Can't Take That Away from Me," which Astaire and Rogers had used so memorably in the ferryboat scene of SHALL WE DANCE (1937). It was thought that this would make a wonderfully nostalgic bridge between the Astaire-Rogers outings of the 1930s and this celluloid rematch.

The movie offers a sterling range of singing and dancing. In the opening scene, Astaire and Rogers dance to "Swing Trot." The trio of Astaire, Rogers and acerbic Oscar Levant scamper about the countryside to "A Weekend in the Country." Then there is the "You'd Be Hard to Replace" number, set in the team's New York apartment, which finds Astaire wooing Rogers, with both partners clad in bathrobes. The comical "My One and Only Highland Fling" has the star duo performing in kilts and brogues, while the instrumental "Bouncin' the Blues" provides a background for the team's dancing. Garbed in formal attire, the two dance to "They Can't Take That Away from Me," and at the elegant finale, "Manhattan Heartbeat," they swirl about a replica of the Plaza Hotel fountain surrounded by several dozen pairs of dancers.

The *New York Times* reported, "Next to the patching of relations between Russia and the United States, there is probably no rapprochement that has been more universally desired than the bringing back together of Ginger Rogers and Fred Astaire. . . . Metro has joined the two again . . . and the health of the world should improve. . . . Age cannot wither the enchantment of Ginger and Fred." Shot at a cost of $2,325,420, THE BARKLEYS OF BROADWAY grossed $5,421,000 in its initial release. Astaire received a special Oscar statuette ". . . For his unique artistry and his contributions to the technique of musical pictures."

THE BARKLEYS OF BROADWAY was the final screen teaming of Astaire and Rogers.

BEACH PARTY (American International Pictures, 1963) Color 101 minutes.

Executive producer, Samuel Z. Arkoff; producers, James H. Nicholson, Lou Rusoff; associate producer, Robert Dillon; director, William Asher; screenplay, Rusoff; production designer/art director, Daniel Haller; set decorator, Harry Reif; costume supervisors, Marjorie Corso, Tom Welsh; makeup, Carlie Taylor; music, Les Baxter; music coordinator, Al Simms; music editor, Eve Newman; sound, Don Rush, Roger White; sound editor, Al Bird; assistant directors, Clark Paylow, Lew Borzage; special effects, Butler-Glouner, Inc.; camera, Kay Norton; editor, Homer Powell.

Songs: "Beach Party," "Swingin' and a-Surfin'," "Secret Surfin' Spot" (Gary Usher, Roger Christian); "Promise Me Anything (Give Me More)," "Treat Him Nicely" (Guy Hemric, Jerry Styner); "Don't Stop Now" (Bob Marcucci, Russ Faith).

Bob Cummings (Professor Sutwell); Dorothy Malone (Marianne); Frankie Avalon (Frankie); Annette Funicello (Dolores); Harvey Lembeck (Eric Von Zipper); Jody McCrea (Deadhead); Morey Amsterdam (Cappy); John Ashley (Ken); Eva Six (Ava); Dick Dale and the Del Tones (Musicians); David Landfield (Ed); Dolores Wells (Sue); Valora Noland (Rhonda); Bobby Payne (Tom); Duane Ament (Big Boy); Andy Romano, John Macchia, Jerry Brutsche, Bob Harvey (Motorcycle Rats); Linda Rogers, Alberta Nelson (Motorcycle Mice); Candy Johnson (Perpetual Motion Dancer); Roger Bacon (Tour Guide); Yvette Vickers, Sharon Garrett (Yogi Girls); Mickey Dora, John Fain, Pam Colbert,

Donna Russell, Mike Nader, Ed Garner, Laura Lynn, Susan Yardley, Brian Wilson (Surfers); Lorie Summers, Meredith MacRae, Luree Nicholson, Paulette Rapp, Marlo Baers (Beach Girls); John Beach, Bill Slosky, Brent Battin, Roger Christian, Gary Usher, Bill Parker (Beach Boys); Vincent Price (Big Daddy).

In retrospect, it seemed the most logical thing to do: team rock 'n' roll heartthrob Frankie Avalon with Walt Disney contractee (and TV Mouseketeer alumnus) Annette Funicello in a series of harmless romance-and-sand romps filled with forgettable pop tunes and peppered with guest cameos from once-famous screen stars. But in reality it was a fluke of coincidence that brought together fading teen star Avalon with fast maturing Funicello in BEACH PARTY. The film was produced on the cheap by American International Pictures, best known for its low-budget science fiction and horror entries. To give the production marquee appeal, the studio featured mature performers Bob Cummings and Dorothy Malone as the production's "stars." One of the film's songs, "Don't Stop Now," was co-authored by Bob Marcucci, the discoverer of both Frankie Avalon and his rival Fabian.

Anthropology professor Sutwell (Bob Cummings) and his faithful secretary Marianne (Dorothy Malone) are undertaking research on the sex habits of teenagers at a southern California beach. In their investigation, they observe the antics of Frankie (Frankie Avalon) and his girlfriend Dolores (Annette Funicello) and their pals, who are having a holiday after high school graduation. Frankie wants his sexual way with Dolores but she demands marriage and commitment. To make her jealous and more accommodating he flirts with shapely waitress Ava (Eva Six). Meanwhile, biker Eric Von Zipper (Harvey Lembeck) and his gang abduct Dolores, but Sutwell saves her. They strike up a friendship that makes Frankie jealous. When the beach gang discovers what the professor's research is really about and that they have been his guinea pigs, they confront him in the local beer hall. A pie fight ensues. When the melee is over, Frankie and Dolores are reunited, and Sutwell finally proposes to Marianne.

Variety enthused of the lightweight entertainment, "It moves quickly and easily and has been dressed with handsome production values." On the other hand, *Time* magazine carped, "It makes Gidget's Roman Misadventures look like a scene from Tosca." Filled with comedy, chaste sexual flirting, light rock music, comely bikini-clad teenagers and attractive location shooting in Balboa, Laguna, Malibu and Newport, California, BEACH PARTY proved a box-office boom for AIP. The series was continued with MUSCLE BEACH PARTY (1964), BIKINI BEACH (1964),

BEACH BLANKET BINGO (1965), HOW TO STUFF A WILD BIKINI (1965), and the science fiction-tinged PAJAMA PARTY (1964) (*q.v.*).

Years later, when everyone thought it was safe to go back into the water, Frankie Avalon and Annette Funicello reteamed for Paramount's BACK TO THE BEACH (1987), a send-up of their surf-and-sand outings of the 1960s. The *Hollywood Reporter* alerted, "It's a good-humored nostalgia trip. . . . Both Frankie and Annette are once again delights: he's snazzy and casually electric, while she's, as ever, the all-American proper heartthrob. . . ." *Daily Variety* noted, "BACK TO THE BEACH is a wonderfully campy trip down pop culture's trash-filled memory lane."

BELLS ARE RINGING (Metro-Goldwyn-Mayer, 1958) Color 126 minutes.

Producer, Arthur Freed; director, Vincente Minnelli; based on the musical play by Betty Comden, Adolph Green, Jule Styne; screenplay, Comden, Green; art directors, George W. Davis, Preston Ames; set decorators, Henry Grace, Keogh Gleason; costumes, Walter Plunkett; makeup, William Tuttle; music adaptor/conductor, Andre Previn; orchestrators, Alexander Courage, Pete King; choreographer, Charles O'Curran; assistant director, William McGarry; sound supervisor, Franklin Milton; special effects, A. Arnold Gillespie, Lee Leblanc; camera, Milton Krasner; editor, Adrienne Fazan.

Songs: "Bells Are Ringing," "The Party's Over," "Just in Time," "Long Before I Knew You," "It's a Perfect Relationship," "Do It Yourself," "It's a Simple Little System," "Better Than a Dream," "Hello, Hello There!" "I Met a Girl," "I Love Your Sunny Teeth," "Oh How It Hurts," "Hot and Cold," "The Midas Touch," "Mississippi Steamboat," "Mu Cha Cha," "Drop that Name," "Is It a Crime?" "I'm Going Back" (Jule Styne, Betty Comden, Adolph Green).

Judy Holliday (Ella Peterson); Dean Martin (Jeffrey Moss); Fred Clark (Larry Hastings); Eddie Foy, Jr. (Otto Prantz); Jean Stapleton (Sue); Ruth Storey (Gwynne); Dort Clark (Inspector Barnes); Frank Gorshin (Blake Barton); Ralph Roberts (Francis); Valerie Allen (Olga); Bernie West (Dr. Joe Kitchell); Steven Peck (First Gangster); Gerry Mulligan (Ella's Blind Date); Hal Linden (Master of Ceremonies); Madge Blake (Woman); Olan Soule (Nervous Man); and: Nancy Walters.

Judy Holliday scored a huge success on Broadway in 1956 with *Bells Are Ringing,* which ran for 926 performances. Four years later she appeared in the screen version of the Betty Comden-Adolph

Green-Jule Styne musical, with the music adapted and conducted by Andre Previn. Five numbers (including "Saltzburg" and "On My Own") from the stage version were dropped and two new numbers were added: "Do It Yourself" and "Better Than a Dream." Holliday's "Is It a Crime?", a showstopper on stage, was filmed for the movie but deleted from the release print, as was Dean Martin's rendition of "My Guiding Star" (a newly created number). The *New York Times* judged, "Lifted almost bodily from the stage, this extremely thin musical comedy, as before, pushes the blonde Judy out front and more or less leaves her there, with little help from Dean Martin, slouching around as her leading man. . . . The Jule Styne score, still, has two good numbers ['Just in Time,' 'The Party's Over']. And the gags are still there, glibly lined out for Miss Holliday, who, of course, is darling."

In New York City, Ella Peterson (Judy Holliday) is employed as a telephone answering service operator by Susanswerphone. A romantic and a passionate busybody, she becomes personally involved with her customers and soon finds herself attracted to playboy-playwright Jeffrey Moss (Dean Martin). The two eventually meet and begin a romance, but the down-to-earth Ella finds it difficult socializing with Jeffrey's sophisticated friends. The duo become involved with a number of zesty characters, including: J. Otto Prantz (Eddie Foy, Jr.), a bookmaker who runs a record company as a front for his syndicate; beatnik Blake Barton (Frank Gorshin), who wants to become a dramatic actor; a dentist (Bernie West) who has ambitions to write pop tunes; and Ella's zany friend Sue (Jean Stapleton). Eventually, though, Ella and Jeffrey overcome their cultural differences.

On stage *Bells Are Ringing* was wonderfully alive and fresh, showcasing admirably the talents of Judy Holliday and, to a lesser extent, her onstage vis-à-vis, Sydney Chaplin. In the translation to the screen in CinemaScope and color, the spontaneity was emasculated and there was little chemistry between Holliday (overly refined and glamorized in the MGM tradition) and too laid-back Dean Martin. The film emerged as overly talky and under-choreographed. It lacked director Minnelli's usual sophisticated visual style and was too often a pedestrian celluloid copy of the stage original.

Costing $2,203,123, BELLS ARE RINGING grossed $3,985,950. This was Judy Holliday's final film before she died in 1965 of cancer. Gerry Mulligan, who played Holliday's blind date in the picture, was married to her at the time she died; he is a famous jazz saxophonist.

THE BENNY GOODMAN STORY *see* THE GLENN MILLER STORY (essay).

THE BEST LITTLE WHOREHOUSE IN TEXAS (Universal, 1982) Color 114 minutes.

Producers, Thomas Miller, Edward Milkis, Robert Boyett; assistant producer, Dow Griffith; director, Colin Higgins; based on the musical play by Larry L. King, Peter Masterson, Carol Hall; screenplay, King, Masterson, Higgins; production designer, Robert F. Boyle; art directors, Norman Newberry, Frank Richwood; set decorator, Arthur J. Parker; costumes, Theodora Van Runkle; makeup, Marvin Westmore, Peter Altobelli, Brad Wilder, Tom Ellingwood; choreographer, Tony Stevens; music, Pat Williams; music consultant, Richard Baskin; music supervisors, Dolly Parton, Gregg Perry; music producer/arranger, Perry; additional music arrangers, Bob Alcivar, Shorty Rogers; underscore orchestrator, Herb Spencer; music editors, George Brand, Michael Fowler, Don Woods; assistant directors, Jack Frost Sanders, Jim Van Wyck, Emmitt-Leon O'Neil; stunt coordinator, Eddie Hice; sound, William B. Kaplan; sound re-recording, John J. Stephens, Stanley H. Polinsky, Dan Wallin; supervising sound editor, John Stacy; sound editors, Bruce Stambler, Glenn Hoskinson, Walter Jenevein, Kyle Wright, Gil Hudson; special effects, Fred Gebler; special visual effects, Albert Whitlock; camera, William A. Fraker; additional camera, Bobby Byrne, Steven Poster; matte camera, Bill Taylor; editors, Pembroke J. Herring, David Bretherton, Jack Hofstra, Nicholas Elipoulous, Walter Hanneman.

Songs: "Twenty Fans," "Aggie Song," "A Lil' Ole Bitty Pissant Country Place," "Sidestep," "Watch Dog Theme," "Texas Has a Whorehouse in It," "Hard Candy Christmas" (Carol Hall); "Sneakin' Around," "I Will Always Love You" (Dolly Parton).

Burt Reynolds (Sheriff Ed Earl Dodd); Dolly Parton (Mona Strangely); Dom DeLuise (Melvin P. Thorpe); Charles Durning (Governor); Jim Nabors (Deputy Fred); Robert Mandan (Senator Wingwood); Lois Nettleton (Dulcie Mae); Theresa Merritt (Jewel); Noah Beery (Edsel); Raleigh Bond (Mayor Rufus); Barry Corbin (C.J.); Ken Magee (Mansel); Mary Jo Catlett (Rita); Mary Louise Wilson (Rita); Howard K. Smith (Himself); Paula Shaw (Wulla Jean); Lee Ritchey (Governor's Aide); Alice Drummond (Governor's Secretary); Karyn Harrison (Chicken Girl); Randy Bennett (Privates Boy); Gail Benedict, Valerie Leigh Bixler, Leslie Cook, Carol Culver, Lorraine Fields, Trish Garland, Sandi Johnson, Lee Lund, Paula Lynn, Lily Mariye, Andrea Pike, Terrie M. Robinson,

Dolly Parton in THE BEST LITTLE WHOREHOUSE IN TEXAS (1982).

Jennifer Nairn-Smith, Terrie Treas, Melanie Winter (Chicken Ranch Girls); Stephen Bray, Brian Bullard, Jeffrey Calhoun, Gary Chapman, John Dolf, David Engel, Ed Forsyth, Mark Fotopoulos, Michael Fullington, David Warren Gibson, Joe Hart, Jeffrey Hornaday, Patrick Maguire, Ted Marriot, Jerry Mitchell, Steven Moore, Douglas Robb, Kevin Ryan, Tim Topper, Marvin Tunney, Randy Van Cupp, Robert Warners (Aggies); Robin Lynn Funk, Larry Kenton, Edie Lehmann, Mark McGee, Karen McLain, Benjamin Taylor, Arnette Walker, Ty Whitney (Dogettes); Robert Briscoe, John Walter Davis, Gregory Itzin, Timothy Stack, Larry B. Williams (Melvin's Crew); Robert Ginnaven, John Edson, Sharon Ammann, Claudette Gardner, Suzi McLaughlin (Reporters); and: Cadence Cloggers of Austin, Texas; Southwest Texas State University Marching Band.

Based on a true story, this musical comedy was a stage success which debuted off Broadway in October 1977 and moved to Broadway in June 1978 for a 1,584-performance run. When it was translated into a motion picture in 1982 the production received much publicity due to the teaming of then top box-office star Burt Reynolds with buxomy country music-turned-pop singer Dolly Parton, and the inclusion of such regular Reynolds cronies as Dom DeLuise and Jim Nabors. However, the resultant film was minor entertainment at best. While Charles Durning was nominated for a Best Supporting Actor Oscar for his flavorful work as a crooked politician (he sings/dances a wonderful "Sidestep") and Parton did okay by her Mae West imitation, the overall film dragged badly. It lacked any of the zest associated with the stage original.

In the arid Texas town of Gilbert, Mona Strangely (Dolly Parton) operates the Chicken Ranch brothel with Dulcie Mae (Lois Nettleton). Miss Mona is carrying on an affair with local lawman Ed Earl Dodd (Burt Reynolds), who has a financial interest in the Chicken Ranch. He, along with his deputy (Jim Nabors), gives Miss Mona a free rein to run her long-established business. Meanwhile, Melvin P. Thorpe (Dom De Luise), a self-centered TV newsman, plans to make himself famous by exposing the illegal activities at the Chicken Ranch, and putting Miss Mona and her lover behind bars. Getting involved in his exploitive scheme are the governor (Charles Durning) and local bigwigs (Noah Beery, Raleigh Bond). Eventually, it is Melvin who is exposed as being corrupt. Ed Earl decides on a career in politics himself and proposes to Miss Mona, who accepts his offer.

Costing $26 million, THE BEST LITTLE WHOREHOUSE IN TEXAS failed to recoup its expenses at the box-office. Analyzing the bloated production, Tom Milne (British *Monthly*

Film Bulletin) pondered, "Difficult to image how this tiresomely winsome musical—boasting a set of songs which drone indistinguishably on like country and western muzak and a book which is as coy about brothels as any Naughty Nineties farce—ever became a big Broadway hit. . . . There is nothing much they [Parton and Reynolds] can do about the spiritless choreography, the fortune-cookie dialogue . . . or the endless wastes devoted to . . . a disastrously miscalculated performance from Dom Deluise. . . ."

The two songs ("Sneakin' Around" and "I Will Always Love You") composed by Dolly Parton for the film became best-selling records for her on RCA. It is interesting to note that Parton's younger (and more petite) sister, Stella, toured in the play after Dolly made the movie.

THE BIG BROADCAST (Paramount, 1932) 80 minutes.

Director, Frank Tuttle; based on the play *Wild Waves* by William Ford Manley; screenplay, George Marion, Jr.; camera, George Folsey.

Songs: "Where the Blue of the Night Meets the Gold of the Day" (Roy Turk, Bing Crosby, Fred Ahlert); "When the Moon Comes over the Mountain" (Kate Smith, Harry Woods, Howard Johnson); "Shout, Sister, Shout" (Clarence Williams); "Minnie the Moocher" (Cab Calloway, Irving Mills, Clarence Gatskill); "Goodbye Blues" (Arnold Johnson, Jimmy McHugh); "Marta" (L. Wolfe Gilbert, Moises Simons); "Nola" (James F. Burns, Felix Arndt); "Hot Today" (Benny Carter); "Dinah" (Sam M. Lewis, Joe Young, Harry Akst); "Please," "Here Lies Love" (Ralph Rainger, Leo Robin); "Tiger Rag" (B. J. La Rocca and the Original Dixieland Jazz Band); "Trees" (Joyce Kilmer, Oscar Rasbach); "Crazy People" (Edgar Leslie, James V. Monaco); "It Was So Beautiful" (Arthur Freed, Harry Barris); "Kicking the Gong Around" (Ted Koehler, Harold Arlen).

Bing Crosby (Bing Hornsby); Stuart Erwin (Leslie McWhinney); Leila Hyams (Anita Rogers); Sharon Lynn (Mona); George Burns (George); Gracie Allen (Gracie); George Barbier (Clapsaddle); Ralph Robertson (Announcer); Alex Melish (Bird and Animal Man); Spec O'Donnell (Office Boy); Anna Chandler (Mrs. Cohen); Tom Carrigan (Officer); Dewey Robinson (Basso); The Boswell Sisters, Cab Calloway and His Orchestra, Vincent Lopez and His Orchestra, The Mills Brothers, Donald Novis, Kate Smith, Arthur Tracy (Themselves); Don Ball, William Brenton, Norman Brokenshire, James Wallington (Announcers).

Although it took a few years, Hollywood finally came to grips with the rival medium of radio. In THE BIG BROADCAST

Paramount joined forces with the new medium not only to make a film about radio but to make one featuring a number of its most popular stars. The result was not only sensational box-office, but the movie launched Bing Crosby's starring film career.

Wealthy Leslie McWhinney (Stuart Erwin) purchases a financially unstable radio station and soon realizes he is in trouble, especially after meeting the station's fast-talking manager (George Burns) and his bird-brained secretary (Gracie Allen). In order to save his investment, Leslie asks his friend, crooner Bing Hornsby (Bing Crosby), to perform on a big all-star show. Bing agrees, but at the station the singer meets another employee, Anita Rogers (Leila Hyams), and he and McWhinney quickly become rivals for her affections. The big show goes on with talent like Kate Smith, The Mills Brothers, The Boswell Sisters, Arthur "The Street Singer" Tracy, Donald Novis, Vincent Lopez and Cab Calloway (themselves). Fearing he will lose McWhinney's friendship because of his interest in Anita, Hornsby fails to show up. Finally he is located in a local speakeasy, the conflict with McWhinney is settled, and Hornsby arrives in time to close the talent show. The radio station is saved.

The *New York American* reported, "It's a sort of combination film-play musical, and well done shorts, features personalities of show business, and it's worth anyone's time and money." *Variety* was more discerning about this property, based on a short-lived Broadway play which Paramount had financed. "BIG BROADCAST is neither the expose on the crooners that the play set out to be, and never achieved . . . nor is it an inside on radio or any of its manifestations, as may have been the intent for celluloid purposes." Among the musical highlights of this potpourri production are: Bing Crosby's crooning "Please" (which became a big hit for him), "Here Lies Love" and "Where the Blue of the Night Meets the Gold of the Day" (his trademark song); Kate Smith's spectacular rendition of "It Was So Beautiful" (which was written especially for her to perform in the feature); The Mills Brothers' fast version of "The Tiger Rag"; Arthur Tracy performing his theme, "Marta"; and Donald Novis singing "Trees." For comedy relief Burns and Allen performed two skits: "Take a Letter" and "Moneymaking Brother."

After THE BIG BROADCAST other studios jumped on the bandwagon and employed radio stars and motifs in their films. Paramount later turned out three more entries in their series, THE BIG BROADCAST OF 1936, 1937 and 1938 (*qq.v.*). The same studio also produced INTERNATIONAL HOUSE (1933), a similarly structured cavalcade of (radio) performers, including W. C. Fields, George Burns and Gracie Allen, Cab Calloway and Rudy Vallee.

THE BIG BROADCAST OF 1936 (Paramount, 1935) 97 minutes.

Producer, Benjamin Glazer; director, Norman Taurog; story/ adaptors, Walter DeLeon, Francis Martin, Ralph Spence; choreographer, LeRoy Prinz; camera, Leo Tover; editor, Ellsworth Hoagland.

Songs: "I Wished on the Moon" (Dorothy Parker, Ralph Rainger); "It's the Animal in Me" (Mack Gordon, Harry Revel); "Aramgura," "Through the Doorway of Dreams I Saw You" (Richard A. Whiting, Leo Robin); "Double Trouble," "Miss Brown to You," "Why Dream?" (Whiting, Robin, Rainger); "Crooner's Lullaby" (Arthur Johnston, Sam Coslow); "Why Stars Come Out at Night" (Ray Noble); "Goodnight Sweetheart" (Noble, James Campbell, Reg Connelly).

Jack Oakie (Speed); George Burns (George); Gracie Allen (Gracie); Lyda Roberti (Countess Ysobel de Naigila); Wendy Barrie (Sue); Henry Wadsworth (Smiley); C. Henry Gordon (Gordonio); Benny Baker (Herman); Bing Crosby, Ethel Merman, Richard Tauber, Ray Noble and His Band, Ina Ray Hutton and Her Band (Themselves); Amos 'n Andy (Grocery Clerks); Mary Boland (Mrs. Sealingsworth); Charles Ruggles (Mr. Sealingsworth); David Holt (Brother); Virginia Weidler (Sister); Sir Guy Standing (Doctor); Gail Patrick (Nurse); Bill Robinson (Dancer); Harold and Fayard Nicholas (Dot and Dash); Vienna Choir Boys (Choir); Akim Tamiroff (Boris); Samuel S. Hinds (Captain); Willy West and McGinty (Builders).

See: THE BIG BROADCAST OF 1938 (essay).

THE BIG BROADCAST OF 1937 (Paramount, 1936) 100 minutes.

Producer, Lewis E. Gensler; director, Mitchell Leisen; story, Barry Trivers, Arthur Kober, Erwin Gelsey; screenplay, Walter DeLeon, Francis Martin; art directors, Hans Dreier, Robert Usher; music director, Boris Morros; camera, Theodore Sparkuhl; editor, Stuart Heisler.

Songs: "Hi-Ho the Radio," "La Bomba," "You Came to My Rescue," "There's Love in Your Eyes," "I'm Talking Through My Heart," "Vote for Mr. Rhythm" (Ralph Rainger, Leo Robin); "Here Comes the Bride" (traditional); "Fugue in G Minor" (Johann S. Bach).

Jack Benny (Jack Carson); George Burns (Mr. Platt); Gracie Allen (Mrs. Platt); Bob Burns (Bob Black); Benny Fields (Himself); Frank Forest (Frank Rossman); Ray Milland (Bob Miller); Shirley Ross (Gwen Holmes); Martha Raye (Patsy); Benny Goodman and His Orchestra, Leopold Stokowski and His Symphony Orchestra (Themselves); Louis Da Pron, Eleanore Whitney, Larry Adler

Gracie Allen, George Burns and Martha Raye in THE BIG BROADCAST OF 1937 (1936).

(Specialties); Sam Hearn (Schlepperman); Stan Kavanaugh (Kavvy); Virginia Weidler (Flower Girl); David Holt, Billy Lee (Train Bearers); Irving Bacon (Property Man); Ernest Cossart (The Uncle); Billie Bellport (Mrs. Peters); Billy Bletcher (Property Man); Harry Depp (Assistant Stage Manager); Pat West (Stage Manager); Cupid Ainsworth (Penelope); Don Hulbert (Page Boy); Frank Hagney (Cowboy); Frank Jenks (Trombone Player); Avril Cameron (Woman Singer); Hal Greene (Elevator Boy); Nora Cecil (Home Economics Woman); Harrison Greene (Violinsky); Leonid Kinskey (Russian); John Marlowe (Anemic Character); Gino Corrado (Violinist); Rosemary Glosz (Fat Lady); Henry Arthur (Tap Dancer); Ann Evers (Information Clerk); Alex Schonberg (Scientist); Maurice Cass (Announcer); Edward J. LeSaint (Minister); Gail Sheridan, Irene Bennett, Priscilla Lawson (Bridesmaids); Jack Mulhall (Clerk); Ted Thompson (Hotel Clerk); Ellen Drew (Telephone Girl/Member of Bridal Party); Florence Dudley (Telephone Operator); Murray Alper (Taxi Driver); Paddy O'Flynn (Attendant); Billy Arnold (Jones); Robert Cochrane (Newsboy); Bob Littlefield (Starter); Eddie Dunn (Clerk); Nell Craig, Jeanne Hart, Peggy Leon, John Tyrrell, Louis Natheaux, Matt McHugh,

Art Rowlands (Bits); Paul Gustin (Headwaiter); Jeanne Perkins, Nick Luckats, William Hopper, Marten Lamont, John Morley (Members of Bridal Party); Mitchell Leisen (Bit).

See: THE BIG BROADCAST OF 1938 (essay).

THE BIG BROADCAST OF 1938 (Paramount, 1937) 94 minutes.

Producer, Harlan Thompson; director, Mitchell Leisen; story, Frederick Hazlitt Brennan; adaptors, Howard Lindsay, Russel Crouse; screenplay, Walter DeLeon, Francis Martin, Ken Englund; art directors, Hans Dreier, Ernst Fegte; costumes, Edith Head; choreographer, LeRoy Prinz; music director, Boris Morros; animator, Leon Schlesinger; special effects, Gordon Jennings; camera, Harry Fischbeck; editors, Eda Warren, Chandler House.

Songs: "Thanks for the Memory," "Mama, That Moon Is Here Again," "You Took the Words Right Out of My Heart," "Don't Tell a Secret to a Rose," "This Little Ripple Had Rhythm," "The Waltz Lives On" (Ralph Rainger, Leo Robin); "Zuni Zuni" (Tito Guizar); "Sawing a Woman in Half" (Jack Rock); "Ho-Jo-To-Ho" from the opera *Die Walküre* (Richard Wagner).

W. C. Fields (T. Frothingill Bellows/S. B. Bellows); Martha Raye (Martha Bellows); Dorothy Lamour (Dorothy Wyndham); Shirley Ross (Cleo Fielding); Russell Hicks (Captain Stafford); Dorothy Howe (Joan Fielding); Lionel Pape (Lord Droopy); Patricia Wilder (Honey Chile); Rufe Davis (Turnkey); Grace Bradley (Grace Fielding); Lynne Overman (Scoop McPhail); Bob Hope (Buzz Fielding); Ben Blue (Mike); Leif Erickson (Bob Hayes); Tito Guizar (Himself); Virginia Vale (Joan Fielding); Leonid Kinskey (Ivan); Shep Field and His Rippling Rhythm Orchestra, Kirsten Flagstad, Wilfred Pelletier (Themselves); Archie Twitchel, James Craig (Stewards); Richard Denning, Michael Brooke, Jack Hubbard, Bill Roberts, Clive Morgan, John Huettner, Bruce Wyndham, Kenneth Swartz (Officers); Rex Moore, Bernard Punsley, Don Marton (Caddies); James Conlin (Reporter); Irving Bacon (Prisoner-Harmonica Player); Wally Maher (Court Clerk); Muriel Barr (Showgirl); Mary MacLaren, Florence Wix, Carol Holloway, Gertrude Astor, Nell Craig, Ethel Clayton, Gloria Williams (Women); Ray Hanford (Pilot); Jerry Fletcher, Robert Allen (Gas Station Attendants); Bud Geary (Helmsman).

Paramount had a big success with THE BIG BROADCAST (*q.v.*) in 1932 and used the loose format again in the mid-1930s for a trio of big-budget, all-star efforts which had public appeal more because of their casts than the silly plots concocted to hold the threads of these productions together. Still, the three movies, which like the original featured songs by the team of Ralph Rainger and Leo Robin, offer a wide range of entertainers, from the comedy antics of W.C. Fields, Burns and Allen and Jack Benny to highbrow classical artists like Leopold Stokowski and Kirsten Flagstad. Despite their variety, however, none of these follow-ups—or all of them combined for that matter—were as good as the studio's first genre effort.

Of the three, THE BIG BROADCAST OF 1936 (1935) has the easiest plot to follow. Jack Oakie starred as Speed, the manager of a poorly financed radio station who also dubs the singing voice of a mysterious radio crooner called "The Great Lover." George (George Burns) and Gracie (Gracie Allen), who own the rights to a television device invented by her uncle, work for the radio station. The man-hungry Countess Ysobel de Naigila (Lyda Roberti) abducts Speed when she finds out he is the crooner, and eventually her money is used to finance the TV invention. Interpolated into this merry, madcap adventure are a series of musical and comedy blackouts, including Bing Crosby crooning "I Wished on the Moon" (which was soon ranked on radio's new show "Your Hit Parade"), the Ethel Merman number cut from WE'RE NOT DRESSING (1934), called "It's the Animal in Me," Ray Noble and His Orchestra performing "Why the Stars Come Out at Night," and vaudeville turns by the likes of Bill "Bojangles" Robinson, The Nicholas Brothers and Amos 'n Andy. One particularly amusing sequence had Benny Baker as a young man trying to concoct a meal from the many directions given by Gracie Allen on her cooking show. Despite all the talent involved, THE BIG BROADCAST OF 1936 was not financially successful due to its ever-ballooning talent budget.

Jack Benny *and* Burns and Allen headlined THE BIG BROADCAST OF 1937 (1936) and again a slim radio industry backdrop was used to parade a variety of diverse special turns. Here Jack Benny played Jack Carson, the manager of a small town radio station who has difficulties with Mrs. Platt (Gracie Allen), who with her husband (George Burns) manufactures golf balls and sponsors the biggest show on the station. Working for Carson as his secretary is Patsy (Martha Raye), while announcer Gwen Holmes (Shirley Ross) falls in love with press agent Bob Miller (Ray Milland). Sandwiched into the plot were Benny Goodman and His Orchestra performing "Here's Love in Your Eye," Martha Raye belting out, in her best bombastic swing style, "Here Comes the Bride," and a Bach fugue conducted by highbrow Leopold Stokowski. Shirley Ross, a much ignored vocalist in some 1930s movies, richly sang "I'm Talking Through My Heart." Frank S. Nugent (*New York*

Times) pointed out, ". . . It is a picture worthy of seeing for its unusual photographic effects. The staging is modern, almost impressionistic, and Mr. Leisen and his cameramen have created a number of interesting studies in black and white." To be noted in a brief bit featuring Bob Burns is director Mitchell Leisen.

The final series entry was THE BIG BROADCAST OF 1938 (1937), directed with élan by Mitchell Leisen, who had handled the previous edition.* Here the plot was nearly non-existent. It centered on a trans-Atlantic boat race between two luxury ships, one of which is owned by W.C. Fields who stages various entertainment acts from his vessel's showroom which are broadcast on radio. Thus the movie had an excuse to present Bob Hope (in his feature film debut) and Shirley Ross dueting on their famous song, "Thanks for the Memory" (which won an Academy Award); Tito Guizar performing "Zuni Zuni"; the Wagnerian soprano Kirsten Flagstad performing Brünnhilde's War Cry from Richard Wagner's opera *Die Walküre;* Martha Raye enthusiastically delivering "Mama, That Moon Is Here again," and Dorothy Lamour singing "You Took the Words Right Out of My Heart." *Variety* enthused, "It abounds with the kind of tunes that fit every radio receiving set. It's pictorially original and alluring, upholding the showmanship tradition of Paramount's annual parade of radio and screen talent."**

BILLY ROSE'S JUMBO (Metro-Goldwyn-Mayer, 1962) Color 123 minutes.

Producers, Joe Pasternak, Martin Melcher; associate producer, Roger Edens; director, Charles Walters; second unit director,

*In *Hollywood Director* (1973), David Chierichetti noted, "The scene of Kirsten Flagstad singing . . . was shot by an unknown director in Paramount's Astoria [Long Island] studio, and the Rippling Rhythm cartoon that accompanied Shep Fields' Orchestra was the work of Leon Schlesinger. The film's one big production number, 'The Waltz Goes On,' was stylishly staged by LeRoy Prinz, although Leisen created the visual concept, all glossy blacks and glaring whites. Leisen handled the slapstick interludes between the number competently but could do little more."

**For THE BIG BROADCAST OF 1938, director Mitchell Leisen was insistent on creating a better means than simple dialogue to show that the characters played by Bob Hope and Shirley Ross (who were once married and who meet again accidentally aboard ship) are still in love. He asked songwriters Ralph Rainger and Leo Robin to handle the situation with music and lyrics and they came up with "Thanks for the Memory." Not only did the song rise to number one on radio's "Your Hit Parade" but it won an Academy Award, beating out the competition: Irving Berlin's "Now It Can Be Told" from ALEXANDER'S RAGTIME BAND, Berlin's "Change Partners" from CAREFREE, Jimmy McHugh and Harold Adamson's "My Own" from THAT CERTAIN AGE, and Harry Warren and Johnny Mercer's "Jeepers Creepers" from GOING PLACES.

Busby Berkeley; based on the play by Ben Hecht, Charles MacArthur, Richard Rodgers, Lorenz Hart; screenplay, Sidney Sheldon; art directors, George W. Davis, Preston Ames; set decorators, Henry Grace, Hugh Hunt; costumes, Morton Haack; makeup, William Tuttle, Jack Wilson; music supervisor/conductor, George Stoll; orchestrators, Conrad Salinger, Leo Arnaud, Robert Van Epp; vocal arranger, Robert Tucker; assistant directors, William Shanks, Carl Roup; color consultant, Charles K. Hagedon; circus acts coordinator, Al Dobritch; sound supervisor, Franklin Milton; special visual effects, Arnold Gillespie, J. McMillan Johnsson, Robert R. Hoag; camera, William H. Daniels; editor, Richard Farrell; assistant editor, Alex Beaton.

Songs: "The Circus Is on Parade," "Little Girl Blue," "Over and Over Again," "Why Can't I?" "This Can't Be Love," "My Romance," "The Most Beautiful Girl in the World," "What Is a Circus?" "Sawdust, Spangles and Dreams" (Richard Rodgers, Lorenz Hart; adapted by Roger Edens).

Doris Day (Kitty Wonder); Stephen Boyd (Sam Rawlins); Jimmy Durante (Pop Wonder); Martha Raye (Lulu); Dean Jagger (John Noble); Joseph Waring (Harry); Lynn Wood (Tina); Charles Watts (Ellis); James Chandler (Parsons); Robert Burton (Madison); Wilson Wood (Hank); Norman Leavitt (Eddie); Grady Sutton (Driver); Sydney the Elephant (Jumbo); John Hart (Marshal); Roy Engel, Jack Boyle (Reporters); Robert Williams (Deputy); Sue Casey (Dottie); Fred Cob (Andy); William Hines (Roustabout); Michael Kostrick (Michaels); Ralph Lee (Perry); Paul Wexler (Sharpie); Otto Reichow (Hans); Billy Barty (Joey); Chuck Haren (Lennie); J. Lewis Smith (Dick); Ron Henon, The Carlisles, The Pedrolas, The Wazzans, The Hannefords, Billy Barton, Corky Cristians, Victor Julian, Richard Berg, Joe Monahan, Miss Lani, Adolph Dubsky, Pat Anthony, Janos Prohaska, The Barbettes (Circus Performers).

In 1910 the Wonder Circus sets up in a small Midwestern town with its main attraction, the talented elephant, Jumbo. The circus is owned by aerialist Kitty (Doris Day) and her dad, Pop Wonder (Jimmy Durante). Pop has long been engaged to a performer in the circus, Madame Lulu (Martha Raye), but she has never been able to get him to set a wedding date. As the performance is about to begin, Kitty's high-wire aerialist partner quits for a higher paying job and they are in a quandary until stranger Sam Rawlins (Stephen Boyd) suddenly shows up, takes over and saves the show. Later he helps Kitty to recover the box-office receipts that Pop lost in a crap game. Unknown to Kitty and Pop, Sam is really the son of their rival, John Noble (Dean Jagger), who intends to buy up the notes on the show

Doris Day and Martha Raye in BILLY ROSE'S JUMBO (1962).

and take it over because he wants Jumbo for his own bigtop. Sam and Kitty fall in love but Sam has second thoughts about his father's scheme and decides to avoid Kitty. However, one night he saves her life during an aerial accident. As the two announce their feelings for each other, Pop and Lulu finally set their wedding date. When Kitty learns about Noble's scheme, she leaves Sam, but he follows her and convinces her that he now wants no part of his father's scheme. Together they rebuild the Wonder Circus and defeat their rival.

BILLY ROSE'S JUMBO was based on the 1935 Hippodrome

Theatre production (233 performances) of *Jumbo* which was produced by Billy Rose and starred Jimmy Durante, Donald Novis and Gloria Grafton. In addition to its circus sequences the motion picture was highlighted by several fine Richard Rodgers and Lorenz Hart songs, some of which were "borrowed" from other of the composers' Broadway shows: "This Can't Be Love" (sung by Doris Day) came from *The Boys from Syracuse* (1938) and "Why Can't I?" (sung by Day and Martha Raye) derived from *Spring Is Here* (1929). One of the nicest moments in the production was the finale, "Sawdust, Spangles and Dreams" (arranged by Roger Edens from various Rodgers and Hart melodies), performed by all four leads. The soundtrack album remained on *Billboard* magazine's hits chart for six weeks, rising to position #33.

There were several reasons why this expensive film failed to catch on with the public. The *New York Times* noted that there were "Two mistakes here, both fatal. This is the kind of old-fashioned circus musical that was routinely stylish back in the 'thirties' with nice tunes, sweethearts and the invariable comic support roles that in this case save it. For all the festive color production, the format is being offered as a contemporary package, minus the necessary style and imagination of today." Other problems were that only a few years before at Paramount, Cecil B. DeMille had produced a real circus extravaganza, THE GREATEST SHOW ON EARTH (1952), which caused JUMBO to pale in contrast.* Then too, Doris Day, at age thirty-eight, was too mature to play the ingenue. Her strident performance in this musical cost her the leads in THE UNSINKABLE MOLLY BROWN (1964), *q.v.,* and THE SOUND OF MUSIC (1965), *q.v.,* which were given to Debbie Reynolds and Julie Andrews respectively. Moreover, Stephen Boyd, while physically virile as Day's vis-à-vis, was too leaden in his characterization and too hesitant in his few singing spots. Lastly, the sawdust plot creaks.

For the record, this was Busby Berkeley's final screen work; here he handled the second unit direction, in particular guiding the picture through the opening scene of the circus arriving in town and the production number, "Over and Over Again," featuring Day and several agile trapeze artists performing under the dazzling Big Top. Orchestrator Conrad Salinger, after completing the scoring for the

*There had been several other circus movies in the 1950s, including: THREE RING CIRCUS (1954) with Dean Martin and Jerry Lewis; TRAPEZE (1956) with Burt Lancaster, Gina Lollabrigida and Tony Curtis; MERRY ANDREW (1958) with Danny Kaye and Pier Angeli; and THE BIG CIRCUS (1959) with Victor Mature and Red Buttons.

number "Little Girl Blue," committed suicide. During production, a despondent Martha Raye attempted suicide. Little wonder that the resultant film is too often so joyless.

A.k.a.: JUMBO.

BITTER SWEET (Metro-Goldwyn-Mayer, 1940) Color 92 minutes.

Producer, Victor Saville; director, W. S. Van Dyke, II; based on the musical play *Bittersweet* by Noel Coward; screenplay, Lester Samuels; art directors, Cedric Gibbons, John S. Dieterle; set decorator, Edwin B. Willis; gowns, Adrian; men's costumes, Gile Steele; makeup, Jack Dawn; music director, Herbert Stothart; vocal/orchestrators, Murray Cutter, Ken Darby; choreographer, Ernst Matray; sound supervisor, Douglas Shearer; camera, Oliver T. Marsh, Allan Davey; editor, Harold F. Kress.

Songs: "I'll See You Again," "If You Could Only Come with Me," "What Is Love?" "Tokay," "Dear Little Cafe," "Kiss Me," "Ladies of the Town," "Zigeuner (finale)," "Love in Any Language" (Noel Coward, with new lyrics by Gus Kahn); "Una Voce Poco Fa," from the opera *The Barber of Seville* (Gioacchino Rossini).

Jeanette MacDonald (Sari [Sarah] Millick); Nelson Eddy (Carl Linden); George Sanders (Baron Von Tranisch); Ian Hunter (Lord Shayne); Felix Bressart (Max); Edward Ashley (Harry Daventry); Lynne Carver (Dolly); Diana Lewis (Jane); Curt Bois (Ernst); Fay Holden (Mrs. Millick); Sig Rumann (Herr Schlick); Janet Beecher (Lady Daventry); Charles Judels (Herr Wyler); Veda Ann Borg (Manon); Herman Bing (Market Keeper); Greta Meyer (Mama Luden); Philip Winter (Edgar); Armand Kaliz (Headwaiter); Alexander Pollard (Butler); Colin Campbell (Sir Arthur Fenchurch); Art Berry, Sr. (Cabbie); Sam Savitsky (Bearded Man); Howard Lang (Pawnbroker); Lester Sharpe, Hans Joby, Jeff Corey (Boarders); Paul E. Burns (Lathered Man); Hans Conreid (Rudolph); John Hendrick (Fritz); Ruth Tobey (Market Keeper's Child); Warren Rock (Wyler's Secretary); William Tannen (Secretary of Employment Agency); Davison Clark (Attendant); Jean De Briac (Croupier); Ernest Verebes (Orderly); Pamela Randall (Hansi); Muriel Goodspeed (Freda); Earl Wallace (Wine Waiter); Louis Natheaux (Officer); Margaret Bert (Woman on Stairs); Julius Tannen (Schlick's Companion); Armand Cortes (Croupier); Irene Colman, June Wilkins (Girls in Casino); Jack Chefe, Gino Corrado (Waiters); Eugene Beday (Civilian); Max Barwyn (Bartender); Major Sam Harris (Officer Seen Dining); Kay Williams (Entertainer).

Noel Coward's 1929 operetta *Bittersweet* served as the basis for the seventh and penultimate screen teaming of Jeanette Mac-

Donald and Nelson Eddy. The famed playwright was so distraught with the final product that he vowed never again to let one of his works be filmed in Hollywood. The original London production had starred Evelyn Laye and Gerald Nodin, and when it arrived on Broadway, also in 1929, *Bittersweet* headlined Peggy Wood and George Metaxa. In 1933 Herbert Wilcox directed his wife Anna Neagle in the first screen version of BITTERSWEET, a British film co-starring Fernand Gravet. While the 1940 MGM edition was a lush production—Oliver T. Marsh and Allen Davey received Oscar nominations for their color cinematography—the film retains too little of the charm of the original stage work. On the other hand, it did provide MacDonald and Eddy with one of their more popular duets, "I'll See You Again," which they later recorded for RCA Victor.

In Victorian England Viennese voice teacher Carl Linden (Nelson Eddy) is about to bid farewell to his beautiful student, Sarah Millick (Jeanette MacDonald), and return home. Sarah is engaged to snobbish Harry Daventry (Edward Ashley) but she has fallen in love with Linden and that night, after her engagement party, the two elope. They travel to Vienna where they are greeted by Linden's friends Ernst (Curt Bois) and Max (Felix Bressart). Now calling herself Sari, the new bride tries to encourage her husband in the composition of his new opera and, by chance, gives him the note he needs to complete the work called "Zigeuner." Time passes and the two make a sparse living by singing for the wealthy, including arrogant Captain Von Tranisch (George Sanders) and gaming enthusiast Lord Shayne (Ian Hunter). Von Tranisch lusts for Sari and arranges for her to sing and Linden to accompany her on the piano at a posh cafe where, one night, he makes a pass at Sari. Linden comes to her defense and Von Tranisch challenges him to a duel and kills him in the ensuing fight. Linden's opera is produced by Herr Wyler (Charles Judels) with Sari performing the lead, and it is a great success. In her mind's eye, Sari is reunited with her husband.

BITTER SWEET did little to allay the slipping screen popularity of Jeanette MacDonald and Nelson Eddy (both of whom were noticeably too old for their youthful roles) or to uphold waning audience interest in the movie operetta genre. The *New York Times* called the offering "battered," saying it was ". . . patched together out of Mr. Coward's fragile and tender work." The *New York Daily News* was a bit kinder, insisting the film "drips with Technicolor and sentimentality." Perhaps the picture's greatest disappointment was not in its schmaltzy plot but in its lack of substantial music. Outside of the team's duet on "I'll See You

Again" and Jeanette's solo of "Zigeuner," the two stars did not have a great deal to work with musically, although Eddy managed to make something out of "If You Could Only Come with Me." Cut from the release print of BITTER SWEET was MacDonald and Eddy's duet to "The Call of Life."

On January 31, 1949 Jeanette MacDonald recreated the role of Sari when "Bitter Sweet" was presented on NBC radio's "The Railroad Hour" with series star Gordon MacRae as Carl.

BLACK GOLD *see* HIGH, WIDE AND HANDSOME

BLUE HAWAII (Paramount, 1961) Color 101 minutes.

Producer, Hal B. Wallis; associate producer, Paul Nathan; director, Norman Taurog; story, Allan Weiss; screenplay, Hal Kanter; art directors, Hal Pereira, Walter Tyler; set decorators, Sam Comer, Frank McKelvy; costumes, Edith Head; makeup supervisor, Wally Westmore; choreographer, Charles O'Curran; music arranger/conductor, Joseph J. Lilley; assistant director, D. Michael Moore; sound, Philip Mitchell, Charles Grenzbach; special camera effects, John P. Fulton; process camera, Farciot Edouart; camera, Charles Lang, Jr.; second unit camera, W. Wallace Kelley; supervising editor, Warren Low; editor, Terry O. Morse.

Songs: "Blue Hawaii" (Ralph Rainger, Leo Robin); "Almost Always True" (Fred Wise, Ben Weisman); "Aloha Oe" (Ludia Kamekeha Liliuodalani; arranged/adapted by Elvis Presley); "No More" (Don Robertson, Hal Blair); "I Can't Help Falling in Love," "Ku-U-I-Po" (Hugo Peretti, Luigi Creatore, George David Weiss); "Rock-a-Hula Baby (Wise, Weisman, Dolores Fuller); "Moonlight Swim" (Sylvia Dee, Weisman); "Ito Eats," "Slicin' Sand," "Hawaiian Sunset," "Beach Boy Blues," "Island of Love" (Sid Tepper, Roy C. Bennett); "Hawaiian Wedding Song" (Charles E. King, Al Hoffman, Dick Manning).

Elvis Presley (Chad Gates); Joan Blackman (Maile Duval); Nancy Walters (Abigail Prentace); Roland Winters (Fred Gates); Angela Lansbury (Sarah Lee Gates); John Archer (Jack Kelman); Howard McNear (Mr. Chapman); Flora Hayes (Mrs. Manaka); Gregory Gay (Mr. Duval); Steve Brodie (Tucker Garvey); Iris Adrian (Enid Garvey); Darlene Tompkins (Patsy); Pamela Akert (Sandy); Christian Kay (Beverly); Jenny Maxwell (Ellie); Frank Atienza (Ito O'Hara); Lani Kai (Carl); Jose De Vega (Ernie); Ralph Hanalie (Wes); Michael Ross (Lieutenant Grey); Richard Reeves (Harmonica-Playing Convict); Tiki Hanalie (Bit); Hilo Hattie (Waihila); The Jordanaires (Accompanists).

Returning to Hawaii from the service, Chad Gates (Elvis

Presley) goes against the wishes of his domineering mother Sarah (Angela Lansbury), and instead of working for his father's (Roland Winters) pineapple processing business, takes a job as a tour guide so he can work with Maile Duval (Joan Blackman), his girlfriend. He is assigned to guide Abigail Prentace (Nancy Walters), a school teacher with four teenage girl charges, and at a luau when a drunk makes a play for one of the girls Chad comes to her defense, and lands in jail as a result. Mrs. Gates informs Chad that Maile is a bad influence on him, while Maile fears that Abigail is too interested in her boyfriend. She is unaware that the teacher is actually in love with his uncle, Jack Kelman (John Archer). Eventually all is resolved happily and Maile and Chad plan to marry. Mrs. Gates is content to be planning the Hawaiian wedding and the newlyweds are given the convention account from his dad's company.

"Elvis fans, rejoice. Here is Presley at his peak," wrote Jay Robert Nash and Stanley Ralph Ross in *The Motion Picture Guide* (1985). "Lots of tunes, romance, a good job of acting by Lansbury as Elvis' mother. . . . Basically slim premise but plenty of clever lines from Hal Kanter, dean of Hollywood's after-dinner wits." At the time of its issuance, the *New York Times* reported, "Balmy is the word for this Elvis Presley showcase, amiable, light and blandly uneventful movie, with its sunkist backgrounds and lush foliage encircling a slender plot like a blossom lei and providing the prettiest color poster ever for Honolulu and pineapples—in about that order." The film grossed $4.7 million in distributors' domestic film rentals. The soundtrack album stayed on *Billboard* magazine's hits chart for fifty-three weeks, rising to position #1.

Besides the gorgeous Hawaiian locales and a serviceable plot, BLUE HAWAII was a delight for Elvis fans in that the star performed over a dozen songs, including one of his most famous, "Can't Help Falling in Love" and the title tune sung decades before by Bing Crosby in WAIKIKI WEDDING (1937). Five years later, Presley made another, similarly-structured musical, PARADISE—HAWAII STYLE, which was far less effective.

BLUE SKIES (Paramount, 1946) Color 104 minutes.

Producer, Sol C. Siegel; director, Stuart Heisler; screen idea, Irving Berlin; adaptor, Allan Scott; screenplay, Arthur Sheekman; art directors, Hans Dreier, Hal Pereira; set decorators, Sam Comer, Maurice Goodman; music director, Robert Emmett Dolan; vocal arrangers, Joseph J. Lilley, Troy Sanders; choreographer, Hermes Pan; color consultants, Natalie Kalmus, Robert Brower; assistant director, C. C. Coleman, Jr.; sound, Hugo Grenzbach, John Cope; special camera effects, Gordon Jennings, Paul K. Lepal; process camera, Farciot Edouart; camera, Charles Lang, Jr., William Snyder; editor, LeRoy Stone.

Songs: "Puttin' on the Ritz," "A Pretty Girl Is Like a Melody," "I've Got My Captain Working for Me Now," "You'd Be Surprised," "Serenade to an Old-Fashioned Girl," "I'll See You in C-U-B-A," "A Couple of Song and Dance Men," "Always," "You Keep Coming Back Like a Song," "The Little Things in Life," "Not for All the Rice in China," "Everybody Step," "How Deep Is the Ocean?" "Heat Wave," "Any Bonds Today?" "This Is the Army, Mr. Jones," "White Christmas," "Nobody Knows," "Tell Me, Little Gypsy," "Some Sunny Day," "Mandy," "When You Walked Out," "Because I Love You," "How Many Times," "The Song Is Ended," "Lady" (Irving Berlin).

Bing Crosby (Johnny Adams); Fred Astaire (Jed Potter); Joan Caulfield (Mary O'Hara); Billy De Wolfe (Tony); Olga San Juan (Nita Nova); Robert Benchley (Business Man); Frank Faylen (Mack); Victoria Horne (Martha the Nurse); Karolyn Grimes (Mary Elizabeth); Roy Gordon (Charles Dillingham); Jack Norton (Drunk); Jimmy Conlin (Valet); Len Hendry (Electrician); John M. Sullivan (Sugar Daddy); Charles La Torre (Mr. Rakopolis); Joan Woodbury (Flo); John Kelly (Tough Guy); Roberta Jonay (Hat Check Girl); Frances Morris (Nurse); John "Skins" Miller (Ed); Roxanne Collins, Paula Rauy, Larry Steers, Major Sam Harris (Guests); John Gallaudet (Stage Manager); Reverend Neal Dodd (Minister); Peggy McIntyre (Mary Elizabeth); Michael Brandon (Charlie the Stage Manager); Will Wright (Dan, the Stage Manager); Albert Ruiz, Joel Friend (Specialty Dance); Vicki Jasmund, Norman Grieger, Joanne Lybrook, Louise Saraydar (Girls in Quartette); Barbara Slater (Myrtle); Carol Andrews (Dolly).

Having teamed relaxed Bing Crosby and perfectionist Fred Astaire so lucratively in HOLIDAY INN (1942), *q.v.,* Paramount united the stars again in BLUE SKIES.* Irving Berlin concocted the story idea for this delightful escapade, but it is his more than twenty songs which make this Technicolor film so enduringly entertaining. Among the highlights are Bing Crosby crooning "White Christmas" (Berlin's most popular number ever) and "You Keep Coming Back Like a Song," and his performance of "A Couple of Song and Dance Men" with Fred Astaire. Astaire does fine vocalizing and dancing (the latter choreographed by Hermes Pan) in "Puttin' on the Ritz," which featured a mirrored chorus of miniaturized Astaires, while in

*Dancer Paul Draper had been assigned to star in BLUE SKIES with Bing Crosby; but when director Mark Sandrich died, producer Sol C. Siegel and new director Stuart Heisler chose to replace Draper with Fred Astaire.

novelty routines Billy De Wolfe scores with his drag performance of "Mrs. Murgatroyd" and Olga San Juan belts out "You'd Be Surprised." Stuart Heisler directed this musical, taking over for producer-director Mark Sandrich, who fell ill after beginning the picture (he died soon after). Paramount spent $3 million on the package and it grossed nearly $10 million worldwide. As in their last joint screen outing, it is Bing Crosby who is top-billed and who wins the film's heroine. Astaire was to have co-starred with Bing Crosby in WHITE CHRISTMAS (1954), *q.v.,* but he became ill and was replaced first by Donald O'Connor and then by Danny Kaye.

Radio star Jed Potter (Fred Astaire), once a famous dancer, recounts how years before, in 1919, he and singer Johnny Adams (Bing Crosby) both loved the same girl, Mary O'Hara (Joan Caulfield). Mary and Johnny are married but he can not make a go of his business and after their daughter Mary Elizabeth (Karolyn Grimes) is born, they separate and divorce. Jed and Mary then begin a romance, but when Johnny comes back into the picture Mary leaves Jed for Johnny. The dancer becomes a drunk and while performing a number, falls off the stage, injuring himself, and he can no longer dance. At the radio station where Jed is recounting the story to his audience as he is about to introduce Johnny, who will sing, Mary arrives and the three are happily reunited.

In *The Films of Bing Crosby* (1977), Robert Bookbinder termed the film ". . . An expertly produced and touching allegory about human relationships that uses a simple and entertaining premise to relate a message about life and love."

BLUE SKIES grossed $5,700,000 in distributors' domestic film rentals.

BODY ROCK (New World, 1984) Color 93 minutes.

Executive producers, Jon Feltheimer, Phil Ramone, Charles J. Weber; producer, Jeffrey Schechtman; associate producer, Chuck Russell; director, Marcelo Epstein; story, Desmond Nakano, Kimberly Lynn White; screenplay, Nakano; production designer, Guy Comtois; art director, Craig Stearns; set designer, Charles R. Moore; set decorator, Cricket Rowland; costumes, Marlene Stewart; makeup, Richard Arlington, Pamela L. Peitzman, Tim D'Arcy; choreographer, Susan Scanlan; music, Sylvester Levay; music supervisor, Gaylon Horton; music editors, Jim Hendrikson, Mike Tronick; sound track supervisor, Ramone; production coordinator, Rebecca Greeley; technical consultant, Kimberly Lynn White; stunt coordinator, Chuck Gaylord; assistant directors, Leon Dudevoir, Gerald Fleck; sound, Lee Alexander, Jean DeFeaver, Tony

Gonzalez; sound re-recording, David Dockendorf, Kevin F. Cleary, Hoppy Mehterian; supervising sound editor, William Stevenson; sound editors, Carl Mahakian, John Post; special effects, Bill Harrison, Special Effects Unlimited; camera, Robby Muller; additional camera, Ed Lachman, Burleigh Wartes; editor, Richard Halsey.

Songs: "Body Rock" (Sylvester Levay, John Bettis); "Spray It On" (Ralph MacDonald, William Salter, William Eaton, Anthony MacDonald); "Let Your Body Rock (Don't Stop)" (Ralph MacDonald, Salter, Eaton); "Everybody's Breakin'," "Drastic Measures" (Morris "Butch" Stewart, Phillip Lane Stewart); "Teamwork" (Bruce Roberts, Andy Goldmark); "One Thing Leads to Another" (Goldmark, Phil Galdston); "Vanishing Point" (Baxter Robertson); "Sharpshooter" (Marc Blatte, Larry Gottlieb); "In the Neighborhood" (Julian Lennon, Galdston); "Fools Like Me" (Sylvester Levay, Goldmark, Galdston); "Smooth Talker" (Mark Hudson, Michael Sembello, Danny Sembello); "Why You Wanna Break My Heart?" (Dwight Twilley); "The Jungle," "Closest to Love," "Do You Know Who I Am?" (Nickolas Ashford, Valerie Simpson); "Deliver" (Martin Briley, Galdston).

Lorenzo Lamas (Chilly D); Vicki Frederick (Claire); Cameron Dye (E-Z); Michelle Nicastro (Darlene); Ray Sharkey (Terrence); Grace Zabriskie (Chilly's Mother); Carole Ita White (Carolyn); Joseph Whipp (Donald); Oz Rock (Ricky); LaRon A. Smith (Magick); Rene Elizondo (Snake); Seth Kaufman (Jama); Russell Clark (Jay); Robin Menken (Jodie); Tony Ganios (Big Mac); Shashawnee Hall (Theo); Barbara Beaman (Cashier); Mimi Kinkade (Little Freak); Ellen Gerstein (Secretary); Mark Sellers (D.J.); Ken Powell (Fred); Dark Hoffman, James Greene (Chilly's Friends); Robert Kessler (Doctor); Shawn Patrick Whittington (Dwayne); Gino Garcia (First Kid); Alison Suzanne (Girl in Rhythm Nation); Kim "Popsicle" Delfin, Ted "Rock" Devoux, T. C. Diamond, James "Jazzy" Everett, Jimmy "Bic" Greene, Charlie "Heckle" Histake, Stephan "Skeeter" Nicholas, Dane "Robot" Parker, Anthony "Bam Bam" Thomas, Tangerine Valentine, Wayne C. Ward, Shawn "Little Cagney" Whittington, Pete "Deadrock" Gonzalez, "Decky" Solomon, "Rockin" Rob Stafford, Steward Foy Wilson (Rhythm Nation and Skeleton Dancers); Don Bernstein, Christopher Boatwright, Kirk Hansen, Eddie Jr., Greg Ramos, Daniel Lorenzo, Scott Grossman, Robert Brady, Randy Digrazio, Joseph Taylor (Ghetto Blaster Dancers); Lalanya Fair, Margit Haut, Page Leongng, Nanette Tarpey (Smoothtalker Dancers); Donald Devoux, Richard "Skate" Diaz, Ann Williams, Sabrina

Garcia, Camille Garcia, Che Garcia, Trish Lashmett, Kevin Foster, Tescia "Miss T" Harris (Additional Finale Dancers).

The break-dancing craze took the nation by storm in the mid-1980s and it was predictable that Hollywood would capitalize on such a popular, if short-lived, fad. One of the better exponents of celluloid break-dancing was New World Pictures' BODY ROCK, starring Lorenzo Lamas, the TV matinee idol son of Fernando Lamas and Arlene Dahl. Unfortunately, Lamas was miscast in the lead role, *TV Movie and Video Guide* (1989) noting unkindly, "Watching L.L. clomp to the beat is like watching Victor Mature do the boogaloo."

Chilly D (Lorenzo Lamas) is the head of a tough New York City street gang but he loves to dance. When he meets hoofer Magick (LaRon A. Smith) the latter becomes the young man's mentor, teaching him how to hone his break-dancing speciality. Chilly and his friends put together an act which is seen by promoter Terrence (Ray Sharkey). He is so impressed with Chilly that he hires him to be the emcee and star attraction at his new-wave nightclub. This new-found success quickly goes to the young man's head. He moves out of his mother's apartment, drops his friends and neglects girlfriend Darlene (Michelle Nicastro) while beginning a love affair with his new roommate, Claire (Vicki Frederick). Eventually Chilly has a career comedown and finally realizes the true worth of Darlene and his pals.

A number of well-known recording artists and dancers contributed the music and break-dance sequences to BODY ROCK, and when they are present the movie has some interest. The musical sequences are coordinated by FLASHDANCE (1983) supervisor, Phil Ramone. Unfortunately the PG-13 feature is on the dull side dramatically, with little of the sex or dramatic action its targeted audience had come to expect of such a melodrama.

Variety complained that the picture ". . . would be in better shape if it lived up to its energetic soundtrack, but wobbly breakdance picture offers too little. . . ."

BOLERO (Paramount, 1934) 85 minutes.

Associate producer, Benjamin Glazer; directors, Wesley Ruggles, (uncredited) Mitchell Leisen; story, Carey Wilson, Kubec Glasmon, Ruth Ridenour; screenplay, Horace Jackson; composition "Bolero" by Maurice Ravel; new music, Ralph Rainger; choreographer, LeRoy Prinz; sound, Earl Hayman; camera, Leo Tover; editor, Hugh Bennett.

George Raft (Raoul DeBaere); Carole Lombard (Helen Hathaway); Sally Rand (Annette); Frances Drake (Leona); William Frawley (Mike DeBaere); Raymond Milland (Lord Robert Coray); Gloria Shea (Lucy); Gertrude Michael (Lady Claire D'Argon); Del Henderson (Theatre Manager); Frank G. Dunn (Hotel Manager); Martha Bamattre (Belgian Landlady); Paul Panzer (Bailiff); Adolph Millar (German Beer Garden Manager); Anne Shaw (Young Matron); Phillips Smalley (Leona's Angel); John Irwin (Porter); Gregory Golubeff (Orchestra Leader); Ralph Rainger (Pianist in "Raftero" Tango Dance Scene).

BOLERO was a different kind of musical in that it featured no popular songs and no lavishly staged production numbers. Instead, the film was centered around a sensuous dance to the music of Maurice Ravel's "Bolero."* While the critics were not overly enthused about the feature, the public went to see it in droves, making it one of Paramount's more successful releases of the year. Highlighting George Raft's dancing abilities,** the movie also has historic importance in that it presents Sally Rand doing a version of her famous fan dance. The finale number was restaged by uncredited director Mitchell Leisen.

In the years before World War I, coal miner Raoul DeBaere (George Raft) is financed by his brother Mike (William Frawley) and goes to Paris to become a dancer and to make his fortune. First he makes a living dancing for pay at tea dances, but eventually he works up a routine with Leona (Frances Drake) and they become headliners at the Cabaret Montmartre, although Raoul rejects her romantic overtures. Mike arrives in Paris to manage his brother's career and Raoul is sponsored by rich Lady Claire D'Argon (Gertrude Michael) and co-stars with fan-dancer Annette (Sally Rand). Finally he takes American Helen Hathaway (Carole Lombard) as his new partner and the two dance the "Bolero" and become a sensation. Raoul falls in love with Helen but she rejects him for the attention of wealthy Lord Robert Coray (Ray Milland). When World I erupts, Raoul enlists in the service for the publicity value and this deception turns Helen against him. During the hostilities, Raoul is gassed and this leaves him with a weak heart. After the war ends he returns to Paris and opens his own club. On opening night his partner cannot perform and Helen substitutes.

---

*BOLERO used an abridged version of Maurice Ravel's 1928 concert piece, "Bolero." For this motion picture, Ralph Rainger composed a special new tango, "The Raftero," as music to which star George Raft could dance. Rainger can be seen playing the piano with the orchestra in the background of this tango scene.

**Despite George Raft's dancing prowess, doubles were used for him and Carole Lombard in some long shots of the "Bolero" dance number.

Again they cause a sensation with the "Bolero," but after the exhibition the weakened Raoul dies in his dressing room.

Thanks to the success of BOLERO, Paramount reteamed Raft and Lombard for a less successful follow-up, RUMBA, the next year. For that picture Ralph Rainger composed an eleven-minute orchestral number entitled "The Rhythm of the Rhumba" for stars Raft and Lombard to dance to.

BORN TO DANCE (Metro-Goldwyn-Mayer, 1936) 108 minutes.

Associate producer, Jack Cummings; director, Roy Del Ruth; story, Jack McGowan, Sid Silvers, B. G. De Sylva; screenplay, McGowan, Silvers; music director, Alfred Newman; music arranger, Roger Edens; choreographer, Dave Gould; camera, Ray June; editor, Blanche Sewell.

Songs: "Rolling Home," "I've Got You Under My Skin," "Rap-Rap-Tap on Wood," "Love Me, Love My Pekinese," "Hey Babe, Hey," "Entrance of Lucy James," "Easy to Love," "Swingin' the Jinx Away" (Cole Porter); "Dance of the Hours" from the opera *La Gioconda* (Amilcare Ponchielli).

Eleanor Powell (Nora Paige); James Stewart (Ted Barker); Virginia Bruce (Lucy James); Una Merkel (Jenny Saks); Sid Silvers (Gunny Saks); Frances Langford (Peppy Turner); Raymond Walburn (Captain Percival Dingby); Alan Dinehart (James McKay); Buddy Ebsen (Mush Tracy); Juanita Quigley (Sally Saks); George & Jalna (Themselves); Reginald Gardiner (Policeman); Barnett Parker (Floorwalker); J. Marshall Smith, L. Dwight Snyder, Jay Johnson, Del Porter (The Foursome); Charles Trowbridge (Store Demonstrator); Helen Troy (Telephone Operator); William & Joe Mandel (Acrobats); Anita Brown (Anita, the Maid); Wally Maher, Johnny Tyrrell, Franklin Parker (Reporters); Harry Strang (Sailor); Dennis O'Keefe (Man with Girl on Couch); Geraldine Robertson, Mary Dees, Jacqueline Dax, Ginger Wyatt, Gay DeLys, Jean Joyce (Girls); John Kelly (Recruiting Officer); Fuzzy Knight (Pianist); George King (Assistant Stage Manager); Jonathan Hale (Hector, the Columnist); Bobby Watson (Costumes/Assistant Stage Manager); Charles Coleman (Waiter); James Flavin (Ship's Officer).

Eleanor Powell, considered by many to be the screen's premiere dancer, had her first starring role in movies in BORN TO DANCE, and Cole Porter, who provided the songs for the expansive vehicle, personally selected James Stewart to be her crooner leading man. While gangling Stewart did fairly well vocalizing Porter's "Easy to Love" in the proceedings, the picture proved Stewart was far more at home in non-musical product, a fact he readily admitted in his hosting segment of THAT'S ENTER-

Eleanor Powell in BORN TO DANCE (1936).

TAINMENT! (1974), *q.v.* On the other hand, BORN TO DANCE also proved that MGM star Eleanor Powell could carry a film with her outstanding dancing abilities and spritely personality.

Nora Paige (Eleanor Powell) works at the Lonely Hearts Club in New York City where she meets gob Ted Barker (James Stewart). Despite his shyness they fall in love. Meanwhile, Broadway show star Lucy James (Virginia Bruce) visits Ted's ship for publicity purposes and meets Barker when he rescues her dog after it has fallen overboard. Lucy's press agent (Alan Dinehart) builds a romance between Lucy and Ted, which causes Nora to break off with him. He nevertheless arranges for Nora to be given a spot in Lucy's show as her understudy. Later, the sailor deliberately breaks a story about himself and Lucy to the press which causes the musical comedy star to walk out on the show on opening night. Nora takes her place and is a sensation. She and Ted are joyfully reunited and plan to wed.

"What counted in BORN TO DANCE wasn't its thimbleful of plot . . . but the splendour of Cole Porter's tip-top score and the razz-a-matazz of its staging (by Dave Gould)" (Clive Hirshhorn, *The Hollywood Musical,* 1981). Among the delights of the film are

Powell's rapid-fire tapping to "Rap-Rap-Tap on Wood," Virginia Bruce's singing of 'I've Got You Under My Skin" and the remarkably lavish finale number, "Swingin' the Jinx Away," sung by Frances Langford, tap-danced, front-and-center, by Powell, and featuring an amazing art deco battleship set. Rounding out the film were the comic presence of Una Merkel (as Powell's sassy friend/mentor), Sid Silvers (as Merkel's spouse and Stewart's buddy), Buddy Ebsen (as a singing/dancing gob), and Reginald Gardiner (as the cop in Central Park who mock conducts a non-existent orchestra to Ponchielli's "Dance of the Hours").

With such a cornucopia of entertainment, it was little wonder that *Variety* endorsed "BORN TO DANCE [as] corking entertainment, more nearly approaching the revue type than most musical films, despite the presence of a 'book'. . . . Dance direction by Dave Gould is big time. . . . The budget provided for plenty of girls and scenery without overdoing it."

BOTH ENDS OF THE CANDLE *see* THE HELEN MORGAN STORY.

THE BOYS FROM SYRACUSE (Universal, 1940) 72 minutes.

Producer, Jules Levey; director, Edward Sutherland; based on the musical play by George Abbott, Richard Rodgers, Lorenz Hart, as adapted from the play *A Comedy of Errors* by William Shakespeare; screenplay, Leonard Spigelgass, Charles Grayson; music director, Charles Previn; choreographer, Dave Gould; camera, Joe Valentine; editor, Milton Carruth.

Songs: "Sing for Your Supper," "Falling in Love with Love," "He and She," "This Can't Be Love," "Who Are You?" "The Greeks Have No Word for It" (Richard Rodgers, Lorenz Hart).

Allan Jones (Antipholus of Ephesus/Antipholus of Syracuse); Martha Raye (Luce); Joe Penner (Dromio of Ephesus/Dromio of Syracuse); Rosemary Lane (Phyllis); Charles Butterworth (Duke of Ephesus); Irene Hervey (Adriana); Alan Mowbray (Angelo); Eric Blore (Pinch); Samuel S. Hinds (Aegeon); Tom Dugan (Octavius); Spencer Charters (Turnkey); Doris Lloyd (Woman); Larry Blake (Announcer); Eddie Acuff (Taxi Cab Driver); Matt McHugh (Bartender); David Oliver (Messenger); June Wilkins (Secretary); Bess Flower (Woman); Cyril Ring (Guard); Julie Carter (Girl).

George Abbott based this comedy on Shakespeare's play *A Comedy of Errors,* and with songs by Richard Rodgers and Lorenz Hart it opened on Broadway late in 1938. With a cast which included Teddy Hart (Lorenz Hart's brother), Jimmy Savo, Eddie Albert, Wynn Murray, Muriel Angelus and Burl Ives, the show had a 235-performance run. Universal acquired the rights to the work and Jules Levey, in his debut as a producer, brought it to the screen. In typical Hollywood fashion, the screen version tampered mightily with the original. Several songs were dropped (including "The Shortest Day of the Year," "What Can You Do with a Man?"), others were truncated in the release print, while Rodgers and Hart contributed two middling new numbers ("The Greeks Have No Word for It" and "Who Are You?"). What had been satire on stage became low farce on screen. As *Variety* politely put it, "Sophisticated audiences will find the gags too unsubtle and the action too obvious, but the greater part of the film audience will relish the out-and-out screwiness of the whole idea." On the plus side, film techniques allowed for the two male leads (Allan Jones, Joe Penner) each to play twins, whereas on Broadway it had required four performers.

In ancient Greece, twin brothers Antipholus of Ephesus (Allan Jones) and Antipholus of Syracuse (Allan Jones) are parted as infants, as are their respective slaves, Dromio of Ephesus (Joe

Irene Hervey, Allan Jones, Joe Penner, Alan Mowbray, Martha Raye, Eric Blore in THE BOYS FROM SYRACUSE (1940).

Penner) and Dromio of Syracuse (Joe Penner). The aristocratic brothers grow up to become rulers, one controlling Ephesus and the other conquering Syracuse. Since the two cities are rivals and the rulers do not know they are siblings, trouble erupts when their father Aegeon (Samuel S. Hinds) comes to Ephesus looking for his son, the ruler of Syracuse, and ends up being sentenced to death by his other, unknown, offspring. Meanwhile, slave girl Luce (Martha Raye) is in love with Dromio of Ephesus and becomes romantically confused when she sees his identical twin, the invading sibling from Syracuse, who has come in search of his father. After many identity mix-ups, the problem is settled, the two brothers are joyfully reunited and peace reigns between the two cities.

The cast starred players on the decline: ex-MGM star Allan Jones and ex-Paramount comedy star Martha Raye were trying to re-establish their film careers, while both Rosemary Lane (best known for working in concert with her sisters Priscilla and Lola at Warner Bros.) and Joe "Want a Duck?" Penner (a nasal comedian of stage/radio fame) were treading water with this box-office misfire.

Among the musical "highlights" of the film are Jones's rendering of "Falling in Love with Love" and "Who Are You?", which he recorded successfully for Victor Records, Martha Raye's vocals on "Sing for Your Supper" (pleasantly lively, not done too broadly), "The Greeks Had No Word for It" (a would-be witty ditty) and her lyrics-laundered duet with Joe Penner on "He and She"; and Rosemary Lane performing "This Can't Be Love."

BRIGADOON (Metro-Goldwyn-Mayer, 1954) Color 108 minutes.

Producer, Arthur Freed; associate producer, Roger Edens; director, Vincente Minnelli; based on the musical play by Alan Jay Lerner, Frederick Loewe; screenplay, Lerner, Loewe; art directors, Cedric Gibbons, Preston Ames; set decorators, Edwin B. Willis, Keogh Gleason; costumes, Irene Sharaff; makeup, William Tuttle; music director, John Green; choral arranger, Robert Tucker; choreographer, Gene Kelly; assistant director, Frank Baur; technical adviser, Commander T. A. Murray; color consultant, Alvord Eiseman; sound supervisor, Wesley C. Miller; special effects, Warren Newcombe; camera, Joseph Ruttenberg; editor, Albert Akst.

Songs: "Prologue," "Entrance of the Clans," "Waitin' for My Dearie," "Once in the Highlands," "Down on MacConnachy Square," "The Heather on the Hill," "Almost Like Being in Love," "I'll Go Home with Bonnie Jean," "Vendor's Calls," "Wedding

Dance," "The Chase," "Brigadoon" (Alan Jay Lerner, Frederick Loewe).

Gene Kelly (Tommy Albright); Van Johnson (Jeff Douglas); Cyd Charisse (Fiona Campbell); Elaine Stewart (Jane Ashton); Barry Jones (Mr. Lundie); Hugh Laing (Harry Beaton); Albert Sharpe (Andrew Campbell); Virginia Bosler (Jean Campbell); Jimmy Thompson (Charlie Chisholm Dalrymple); Tudor Owen (Archie Beaton); Owen McGiveney (Angus); Dee Turnell (Ann); Dody Heath (Meg Brocie); Eddie Quillan (Sandy); Madge Blake (Mrs. McIntosh); Stuart Whitman (Man at Bar); George Chakiris (Specialty Dancer); Pat O'Malley (Townsman); Carole Richards (Singing Voice of Fiona Campbell).

"Strangely, sadly, the very one of all the post-war Broadway musicals with the most ready-made potential for the camera falls as flat as a pancake," the *New York Times* determined. "On the screen, the charming little Scottish village, Brigadoon, rising from the misty past and enveloping two modern American hunters in its local romances and intrigues, generally seems—for all the expensive trimmings and the apt casting—like a lifeless, overstuffed, Christmas goose."

Alan Jay Lerner and Frederick Loewe's musical fantasy *Brigadoon* debuted on Broadway in March 1947, and had a run of 581 performances, starring Marion Bell, David Brooks, George Keane and Pamela Britton. It introduced such memorable songs as "Heather on the Hill," "Come to Me, Bend to Me," and "Almost Like Being in Love." When MGM translated the production to film in 1954, it was decided at the last minute that the studio could save money by filming BRIGADOON on soundstages rather than on location. The result was a lumbering, not often entertaining picture, shot in garish Ansco Color and widescreen CinemaScope. Although no new numbers were added for the picture version, several numbers were cut: "Come to Me, Bend to Me," "There But for You Go I" (both of which were recorded but dropped from the movie, yet are included in the soundtrack album), "The Love of My Life," "My Mother's Wedding Day" and "The Sword Dance."

Bored Gotham businessmen Tommy Albright (Gene Kelly) and Jeff Douglas (Van Johnson) take a holiday in Scotland and one day, while they are grouse shooting, they become lost. They stumble onto the mystical village of Brigadoon, which becomes visible only once every century. A wedding is about to take place in the tradition-clad glen and there is much merriment. Tommy and Jeff join in, Tommy meets beautiful Fiona Campbell (Cyd Charisse) and the two fall in love, forcing him to decide whether to stay forever in the mystical town or return with Jeff to his routine life in

New York City. Finally, he succumbs to his pal's urgings and they fly home. However, Tommy finds life boring and unbearable and he returns to Scotland. His love for Fiona is so great that the village of Brigadoon reappears. He and his lady love are reunited forever.

"The pity of MGM's version of *Brigadoon* is that it was made in 1954, at a time when the public interest in musicals had passed its peak. . . . Few Hollywood directors have ever favored CinemaScope and in viewing this picture it is apparent that [director Vincent] Minnelli was uncomfortable in his first encounter with the long rectangular frame. It would have been difficult to fill the frame with dancers and singers on location, but even harder in the confines of a studio"—Tony Thomas (*The Films of Gene Kelly,* 1974). On the other hand, the virtues of the picture are its color costumes, the musical scoring/arrangements and the vivid sets of Preston Ames. As the choreographer for the film Kelly is at his best in handling the Scottish (traditional) dances and the ballet-like steps assembled for his courting of Cyd Charisse. (The latter, ever graceful in motion, was wooden in her characterization; and, as was the custom, her vocals were dubbed, this time by Carole Richards.)

Gene Kelly and Van Johnson, both MGM stars of the 1940s and early 1950s, had appeared together on Broadway in *Pal Joey* (1940).

BRIGADOON, made at a cost of $2,352,625, grossed $3,385,000 in its initial release.

THE BROADWAY MELODY (Metro-Goldwyn-Mayer, 1929) 102 minutes. (Silent version: 5,943′)

Director, Harry Beaumont; story, Edmund Goulding; screenplay, Sarah Y. Mason; dialogue, Norman Houston, James Gleason; titles, Earl Baldwin; art director, Cedric Gibbons; wardrobe, David Cox; sound supervisor, Douglas Shearer; sound, Wesley Miller, Louis Kolb, O. O. Ceccarini, G. A. Burns; camera, John Arnold; editor (sound version), Sam S. Zimbalist; editor (silent version), William Le Vanway.

Songs: "The Broadway Melody," "You Were Meant for Me," "Harmony Babies," "The Wedding of the Painted Doll," "The Boy Friend," "Love Boat" (Arthur Freed, Nacio Herb Brown); "Truthful Parson Brown" (Willard Robinson); "Give My Regards to Broadway" (George M. Cohan).

Anita Page (Queenie Mahoney); Bessie Love ("Hank" Mahoney); Charles King (Eddie Kearns); Jed Prouty (Uncle Bernie); Kenneth Thomson (Jock Warriner); Edward Dillon (Dillon, the Stage Manager); Mary Doran (Flo, the Blonde); Eddie Kane (Francis Zanfield); J. Emmett Beck (Babe Hatrick); Marshall Ruth

(Stew); Drew Demarest (Turpe); James Burrows (Singer); James Gleason (Jimmy Gleason, the Music Publisher); Ray Cooke (Bellhop); Nacio Herb Brown (Pianist at Gleason's).

If any one motion picture can be credited with starting the popularity of the backstage movie musical in the early sound era it is MGM's THE BROADWAY MELODY. This was the film which MGM promoted as "ALL TALKING! ALL SINGING! ALL DANCING!"* It was the first movie to have a (largely) original score composed for it. *Photoplay* magazine dubbed it a "Brilliant all-talkie of backstage life, with Bessie Love astonishing." *Motion Picture News* extolled, "Metro-Goldwyn-Mayer have stolen a march on all their competitors in the talkie production field by being the first on the market with a combination drama and musical revue that will knock the audiences for a goal. Others have had revues and musical comedies in work but MGM is the first to hit the screen with theirs and to them will have to go the glory for all time of being the pioneers." In retrospect, Edward Lee Stern wrote in *The Movie Musical* (1974), "Its success was phenomenal. It was the first sound film as well as the first musical to win an Academy Award as best picture of the year. It won an Oscar nomination for Bessie Love. And, more important in terms of its influence, it was a tremendous box-office draw. In a year when the average price of admission was about 35 cents, it grossed more than $4,000,000. [THE BROADWAY MELODY was made at a cost of $280,000.]"

None too successful vaudeville performer Eddie Kearns (Charles King) writes a successful song and is hired by producer Frances Zanfield (Eddie Kane) to sing it in his Broadway revue. Eddie is in love with "Hank" Mahoney (Bessie Love), who has a vaudeville act with her sister Queenie (Anita Page). Due to his success he is able to persuade the sisters to quit the road and come to Manhattan. Later, Eddie finds himself attracted to Queenie, although she becomes the mistress of one of the financial backers of the show so that Hank and Eddie can stay together. When Hank finds out about her sister's love affair with Eddie, she persuades him to take Queenie away from the backer. When this happens, Hank gets another partner for her sister act and returns to the road.

With its fast-paced action and good use of early sound equipment (although music, songs and dialogue were recorded directly on the sound track), THE BROADWAY MELODY also

*MGM had originally planned to shoot THE BROADWAY MELODY as only a part-talkie, but studio producer Irving Thalberg was so impressed with the initial rushes that he revised the budget to have the film be all-talking. Nevertheless, for those theatres not yet equipped for sound, a silent film version was distributed.

Bessie Love and Anita Page in THE BROADWAY MELODY (1929).

had an outstanding music score. It not only included such standards as "Give My Regards to Broadway" and "You Were Meant for Me," but also the popular title song (which Charles King recorded for Victor Records) and "The Wedding of the Painted Doll" sequence which was filmed in Technicolor.

Seen today, BROADWAY MELODY is a quaint curio filled with crude staging, hefty, lumbering chorines, and hackneyed situations. But in its day, it was considered fresh, daring and exciting.* It led *Variety* to ponder, "The possibilities are what jolt the imagination. . . . If the talker studios can top the production efforts of the stage and get the camera close enough to make the [dance] ensemble seem to be in the same theatre, what's going to happen in Boston between a musical comedy stage at $4.40 and screen at 75 cents."

Bessie Love and Charles King were reunited by MGM for CHASING RAINBOWS (1930), another backstage romance musical, but by then the novelty of the format had worn thin. THE BROADWAY MELODY was remade by MGM as TWO GIRLS ON BROADWAY (1940), starring Lana Turner, George Murphy, Joan Blondell and Kent Taylor. It emerged a near programmer. *Variety* chronicled, "This being a remake, the basic pattern is once more reprised to make it decidedly dated in dramatic elements. Script revisions brush up the dialog considerably and reblocking processing, for modernization, has a night club background instead of the vaudeville stage of the original." Meanwhile, MGM had filmed three musicals under the umbrella title of BROADWAY MELODY OF 1936 (1935), BROADWAY MELODY OF 1938 (1937) and BROADWAY MELODY OF 1940 (1940), *qq.v.*

BROADWAY MELODY OF 1936 (Metro-Goldwyn-Mayer, 1935) 103 minutes.

Producer, John W. Considine, Jr.; director, Roy Del Ruth; story, Moss Hart; screenplay, Jack McGowan, Sid Silvers; additional dialogue, Harry Cohn; art director, Cedric Gibbons; costumes, Adrian; music director, Alfred Newman; dance choreographer, Dave Gould; ballet choreographer, Albertina Rasch; assistant director, Bill Scully; sound supervisor, Douglas Shearer; camera, Charles Rosher; editor, Blanche Sewell.

Songs: "I've Got a Feeling You're Fooling," "Sing Before

---

*Ethan Mordden (*The Hollywood Musical,* 1981) noted, "THE BROADWAY MELODY established the rule in backstagers that The Show be a revue rather than a story musical. That way, no one has to work around a plot, set characters, or context songs; in a revue, anything—from solo specialty to big number—goes."

Breakfast," "You Are My Lucky Star," "Broadway Rhythm," "On a Sunday Afternoon" (Nacio Herb Brown, Arthur Freed).

Jack Benny (Bert Keeler); Eleanor Powell (Irene Foster); Robert Taylor (Bob Gordon); Una Merkel (Kitty Corbett); Sid Silvers (Snoop); Buddy Ebsen (Ted); June Knight (Lillian Brent); Vilma Ebsen (Sally); Nick Long, Jr. (Basil); Robert Wildhack (Snorer); Paul Harvey (Managing Editor); Frances Langford, Harry Stockwell (Themselves); Irene Coleman, Beatrice Coleman, Georgina Gray, Mary Jane Halsey, Lucille Lund, Ada Ford (Show Girls); Theresa Harris (Maid); Max Barwyn (Headwaiter); Bernadene Hayes, Treva Lawler (Waitresses); Bud Williams (Pullman Porter); Lee Phelps (Conductor); Andre Cheron (Hotel Manager); Rolfe Sedan (Assistant Hotel Manager); Eddie Tamblyn (Bellhop); Bert Moorhouse (Hotel Clerk); Neely Edwards (Character Man); Bobby Gordon (Copy Boy); Anya Teranda, Luana Walters, Patricia Gregory (Chorus Girls); Marjorie Lane (Singing Voice of Irene Foster).

See: BROADWAY MELODY OF 1940 (essay).

BROADWAY MELODY OF 1938 (Metro-Goldwyn-Mayer, 1937) 115 minutes.

Producer, Jack Cummings; director, Roy Del Ruth; story, Jack McGowan, Sid Silvers; screenplay, McGowan; music director, George Stoll; choreographer, Dave Gould; camera, William Daniels; editor, Blanche Sewell.

Songs: "Dear Mr. Gable" (James V. Monaco, Joseph McCarthy; special adaptation, Roger Edens); "I'm Feeling Like a Million," "Yours and Mine," "Everybody Sing," "Your Broadway and My Broadway," "Broadway Rhythm," "Sun Showers" (Nacio Herb Brown, Arthur Freed); "Some of These Days" (Shelton Brooks).

Robert Taylor (Steve Raleigh); Eleanor Powell (Sally Lee); George Murphy (Sonny Ledford); Binnie Barnes (Caroline Whipple); Buddy Ebsen (Peter Trot); Sophie Tucker (Alice Clayton); Judy Garland (Betty Clayton); Charles Igor Gorin (Nicki Papaloopas); Raymond Walburn (Herman Whipple); Robert Benchley (Duffy); Willie Howard (The Waiter); Charley Grapewin (James K. Blakeley); Robert Wildhack (The Sneezer); Billy Gilbert (George Papaloopas); Barnett Parker (Jerry Jason); Helen Troy (Emma Snipe); Marjorie Lane (Singing Voice of Sally Lee).

See: BROADWAY MELODY OF 1940 (essay).

BROADWAY MELODY OF 1940 (Metro-Goldwyn-Mayer, 1940) 102 minutes.

Producer, Jack Cummings; director, Norman Taurog; story, Jack McGowan, Dore Schary; screenplay, Leon Gordon, George

Oppenheimer; music director, Alfred Newman; choreographers, Bobby Connolly, Luigi Arditi; camera, Oliver T. Marsh, Joseph Ruttenberg; editor, Blanche Sewell.

Songs: "Begin the Beguine," "Please Don't Monkey with Broadway," "Between You and Me," "I Concentrate on You," "Juke Box Dance" (Cole Porter); "Il Bacio" (Luigi Arditi).

Fred Astaire (Johnny Brett); Eleanor Powell (Clara Bennett); George Murphy (King Shaw); Frank Morgan (Bob Casey); Ian Hunter (Bert C. Matthews); Florence Rice (Amy Blake); Lynne Carver (Emmy Lou Lee); Ann Morriss (Pearl); Trixie Firschke (Juggler); Douglas McPhail (Masker Singer); Charlotte Arren (Singer).

MGM produced the original THE BROADWAY MELODY (*q.v.*) in 1929 and several years later made three more entries with that title, competing with THE GOLDDIGGERS series at Warner Bros. and THE BIG BROADCAST pictures at Paramount. The first two BROADWAY MELODY follow-ups used traditional on-with-the-show themes as the springboard for a variety of song and dance routines, while the 1940 edition of the group was a showcase for the hoofing of Fred Astaire, Eleanor Powell and George Murphy. Snappy, expert tap-dancing Powell was, in fact, in all three of these MGM series films. The first, by far, was the best of the lot.

BROADWAY MELODY OF 1936 (1935) featured Jack Benny as scheming Gotham gossip columnist Bert Keeler, who is at odds with handsome young Broadway producer Bob Gordon (Robert Taylor). Tart-mouthed Keeler learns that no-talent, acid-tongued singer Lillian Brent (June Knight) is backing Gordon's new musical, *Broadway Rhythm,* so she can have the lead in the production, and Keeler prints the tantalizing facts, whereupon Gordon socks him in the jaw. Meanwhile, Irene Foster (Eleanor Powell), Bob's hometown sweetheart, comes to New York City, hoping to audition for the lead in his show. However, he is too preoccupied to give her any attention. In order to get the audition, she assumes the guise of masked French performer, Mlle. Arlette. She wins not only the key part, but also Bob's affection. Keeler becomes aware of Irene's deception and plans to run the exclusive story. However, she unmasks herself first. The show goes on and she and it are both tremendous hits.

"BROADWAY MELODY OF 1936 . . . was in no way a sequel to the epoch-making THE BROADWAY MELODY. . . . And, apart from its similarity of title and milieu, the only other points it had in common with the earlier were a marvellous Arthur Freed-Nacio Herb Brown score, its overwhelming entertainment value, and its enormous potency at the box office"—Clive Hirschhorn (*The Hollywood Musical,* 1981). Among the dance numbers, highlights were Eleanor Powell and the Ebsens (Buddy and his sister Vilma) dancing on a rooftop to "Sing Before Breakfast," and Powell spotlighted in the elaborately staged "I've Got a Feeling You're Fooling." Robert Taylor, better known for his looks than for his acting or singing prowess, proved amateurish but adequate in tandem vocalizing of "I've Got a Feeling You're Fooling" with June Knight. Talented Frances Langford, whose popularity as a radio/record artist was never matched on screen, efficiently sang "You Are My Lucky Star" and "Broadway Rhythm," both of which numbers showcased Powell's dancing. (Cut from the release print was Langford's singing of "Something's Gotta Happen Soon.")

When BROADWAY MELODY OF 1936 opened in New York on September 15, 1936 (the same day that Paramount's THE BIG BROADCAST OF 1936, *q.v.,* debuted down the street on Broadway), the *New York Times* alerted, "If THE BROADWAY MELODY OF 1936 sounds dangerously modern, there is no cause for alarm. . . . The faces are new, and so are the songs and the dances and some of the jests, but the work is in the familiar back-stage tradition of the original BROADWAY MELODY. . . ."

For BROADWAY MELODY OF 1938 (1937), Robert Taylor and Eleanor Powell (with Marjorie Lane again dubbing her vocals) were back as a Broadway producer and his star hoofer in this tale of Steve Raleigh (Robert Taylor) needing funds to keep his show afloat. The money is raised from star Sally Lee's (Powell) race horse's win at the Saratoga Track. Naturally, both the star and the musical are a resounding success and the producer and Sally become involved romantically. Unlike the 1936 edition, this outing underplayed the plot in deference to a series of opulent production numbers, with basically ho-hum results. Today the picture is best remembered for Judy Garland's heart-felt rendition of "You Made Me Love You," sung to Clark Gable's photograph. Another highlight is Sophie Tucker—cast as Garland's mother!—belting out "Your Broadway and My Broadway" and her trademark, "Some of These Days." The tune "Broadway Rhythm" was also reprised from the 1936 outing. Not to be overlooked was angular Buddy Ebsen, a strong tap dancer in his own right who had appeared in BROADWAY MELODY OF 1936 (1935) and BORN TO DANCE (1936), *qq.v.* "Buddy Ebsen, who has come to be regarded as Eleanor Powell's shadow because he always plays with and up to her, handles some first class comedy bits on his own in addition to his eccentric dancing." (*Variety*).

The final series entry, BROADWAY MELODY OF 1940, promised to be the best of the lot with its trio of dancing stars—Fred Astaire, Eleanor Powell and George Murphy—and its songs by Cole Porter. But, a too maudlin plot premise got in the way of the music, resulting in a frequently mediocre production. "The staples, notably Eleanor Powell and a sumptuous Metro-Goldwyn-Mayer production, are still there and so is the customary hypocritical plot, comfortably designed with large gaps into which carefully prefabricated 'production numbers' may duly be fitted." (*New York Times*)

When the dance team of Johnny Brett (Fred Astaire) and King Shaw (George Murphy) can find no other show business work, they accept jobs as hosts at Manhattan's Dawnland Ballroom. When they perform one night for the customers at the Ballroom, they are spotted by addled producer Bob Casey (Frank Morgan), who decides he wants to hire Johnny for his upcoming musical, *Broadway Melody.* By error, King is asked to audition for the show, opposite the queen of Broadway musicals, Clara Bennett (Eleanor Powell). Johnny coaches King for his role although King does not have the talent to carry it off properly. King is cast in the show and quickly becomes egocentric and a heavy drinker. On opening night, King is too drunk to go on, so Johnny dons a mask and does the part for him, to critical acclaim. King thus basks in the glory and success that rightfully belongs to his ex-partner. One night King, now wanting to set matters right, pretends to be drunk so that Johnny will take his place. While he and Clara are performing, King comes on stage and reveals the truth as the three dance together.

Many felt Eleanor Powell would be an ideal partner for Fred Astaire following Ginger Rogers' departure for dramatic roles. In fact Metro-Goldwyn-Mayer promoted BROADWAY MELODY OF 1940 with: "It took mighty MGM to bring the world's two greatest dancers together. And what a show of shows they're in! You've never seen its like . . . for song, for spectacle, for thrilling romance!" But the film revealed Powell outdistancing Astaire in the hoofing department, thus terminating that hoped-for arrangement. As *Variety* weighed the picture, it ". . . Lacks ingredients to carry it into the smash hit class."

On the plus side was a sophisticated Cole Porter score, far more cosmopolitan than the tunes turned out by Arthur Freed and Nacio Herb Brown for earlier editions of the studio's musical revue. (One has only to compare Porter's "Please Don't Monkey with Broadway" with the more mundane, obvious work by Freed-Brown: "Broadway Melody" [THE BROADWAY MELODY], "Broadway Rhythm" [BROADWAY MELODY OF 1936] or "Your Broadway and My Broadway" [BROADWAY MELODY OF 1938]. In the 1940 film the song-and-dance numbers are much more integrated into the plotline. Among the interludes there is Powell tapping, singing and being tossed about by the chorus of sailors in "I Am the Captain"; "Between You and Me," which is Murphy's audition for Powell's show; "I've Got My Eyes on You," Astaire dancing elegantly on an empty stage; "Juke Box Dance," with Powell-Astaire dancing to a boogie woogie beat; "Begin the Beguine," a nine-minute multi-part production number with Powell-Astaire dancing on an elaborate mirrored set; and the finale, a reprise of "I've Got My Eyes on You" featuring Powell, Astaire and Murphy.*

Originally, BROADWAY MELODY OF 1940 was to have been filmed in color, but the advent of World War II had closed down many European release markets. Thus MGM decided to cut back on production expenditures for this and other studio product. Two songs ("I Happen to Be in Love" and "I'm So in Love with You") were discarded from the release print. A projected BROADWAY MELODY OF 1943, to star Eleanor Powell and Gene Kelly, was abandoned in pre-production.

BROADWAY MELODY OF 1943 *see* BROADWAY MELODY OF 1940 (essay).

THE BUDDY HOLLY STORY (Columbia, 1978) Color 114 minutes.

Executive producer, Edward H. Cohen; co-executive producer, Fred T. Kuehnert; producer, Fred Bauer; associate producer, Frances Avrut-Bauer; director, Steve Rash; based on the book *Buddy Holly: His Life and Music* by John Colrosen; story, Rash, Bauer; screenplay, Robert Gittler; production designer, Joel Schiller; set decorator, Tom Roysden; costumes, Michael Butler, Thalia Phillips, William Flores; makeup, Marvin Westmore, Doris Alexander; music/music director, Joe Renzetti; choreographer, Maggie Rush; assistant directors, Carol Himes, Bob Smally; sound, Willie Burton; sound re-recording, Tex Rudloff, Joel Fein, Curly Rhirlwell, Walter Gest; special audio, Joel Fein; sound editor, Jerry

*In analyzing the "Begin the Beguine" dance sequence in *The Melody Lingers On,* 1986, Roy Hemming noted, about the finale portion of the number, ". . . Astaire and Powell reappear in casual, all-white, modern dress. As the soundtrack shifts into a swing version of 'Begin the Beguine' dominated by a clarinet solo . . . Astaire and Powell begin the sharpest, fast-stepping, show-stopping tap dance any duo has ever put on film."

Stanford; special effects, Robbie Knott; camera, Steven Lamer; editor, David Blewitt.

Songs: "Rock Around with Ollie Vee" (Sonny Curtis); "That'll Be the Day," "Peggy Sue" (Jerry Allison, Buddy Holly, Norman Petty); "Rave On," "Oh Boy" (Sonny West, Bill Tilghman, Petty); "It's So Easy," "Maybe Baby," "True Love Ways" (Holly, Petty); "Words of Love" (Holly); "Listen to Me" (Charles Hardin, Petty); "Every Day I Have the Blues" (Peter Chatman); "Well, All Right" (Frances Faye, Don Raye, Dan Howell); "Chantilly Lace" (J.P. Richardson); "Whole Lotta Shakin' Goin' On" (Dave Williams, Sunny David); "You Send Me" (L. C. Cooke).

Gary Busey (Buddy Holly); Don Stroud (Jesse); Charles Martin Smith (Ray Bob); Bill Jordan (Riley Randolph); Maria Richwine (Maria Elena Santiago); Conrad Janis (Ross Turner); Albert Popwell (Eddie Foster); Amy Johnston (Jenny Lou); Jim Beach (Mr. Wilson); John F. Goff (T. J.); Fred Travalena (Madman Mancuso); Dick O'Neil (Sol Zuckerman); Stymie Beard (Luther); M. G. Kelly (M.C.); Paul Mooney (Sam Cooke); Bill Phillips Murray (Desk Clerk); Freeman King (Tyrone); Steve Camp (Cook); Jody Berry (Engineer Sam); Bob Christopher (Cadillac Salesman); Arch Johnson (Mr. Holly); Neva Patterson (Mrs. Holly); Gloria Irricari (Mrs. Santiago); Rajah Bergman, Joe Renzetti (Violinists); Gilbert Melgar (Richie); Gailaird Sartain (Big Bopper); George Simonelli (Dion); Steve Doubet (Roger); Jack Dembo (Cabbie); Richard Kennedy (Reverend Hargiss); Anthony Johnson (Singer on Bus); Rod Grier (Singer on Show); Peter Griffin (Director); Maxine Green, Mary Hyland, Susan Morse (Group Singers); Buster Jones (Soloist); Jerry Zaremba (Eddie); Paul Carmello (Parker); Bill Lytle (Delbert); Raymond Schockey (Sheriff); Loutz Gage (Producer); John Waldron, Alan Peterson (Little Boys); Jack Jozefson (Stage Manager); Craig White (King Curtis); John B. Jarvis (Pianist, Cochran Band); Richie Hayward (Drummer, Cochran Band); David Miner (Bass Player, Cochran Band).

Buddy Holly (1936–59) was one of the premier stars of 1950s rock 'n' roll, with resounding hits like "Peggy Sue," "That'll Be the Day," "Words of Love" and "Rave On" on the Coral label. His death in a plane crash in 1959 (which also took the lives of Ritchie Valens and the Big Bopper [Jape Richardson]) made him a legend and his music popularity has continued to this day. This 1978 biopic is a straightforward, vibrant account of Holly's life. However, despite critical praise, it failed to generate much business (only $5.9 million in distributors' domestic film rentals) in contrast to the 1987 film about Ritchie Valens, LA BAMBA (*q.v.*), which became one of the big moneymakers of its year.

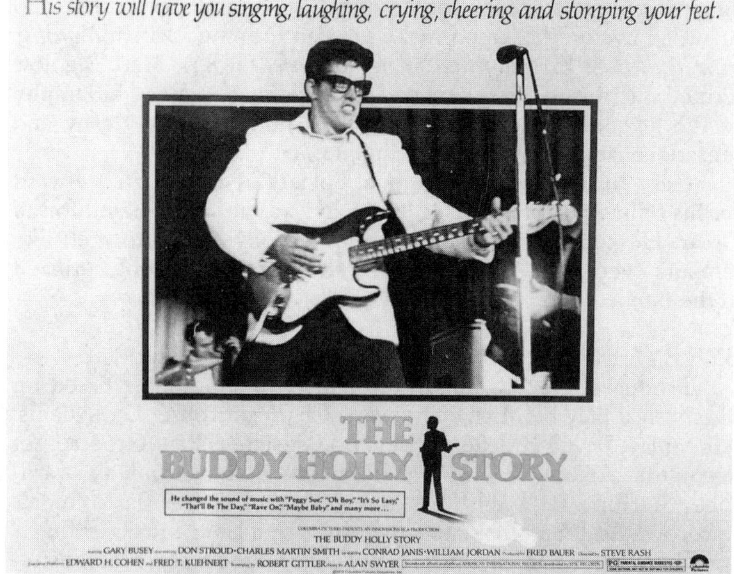

Advertisement for THE BUDDY HOLLY STORY (1978).

Growing up in Lubbock, Texas, teenager Buddy Holly (Gary Busey) becomes an ardent fan of rock 'n' roll, much to the chagrin of his parents (Arch Johnson, Neva Patterson). He begins writing and performing this type of music and forms a band called "The Crickets." He soon becomes an industry success. Having given up his hometown girlfriend, Jenny Lou (Amy Johnston), he falls in love with and marries Coral Records' secretary, Maria Elena Santiago (Maria Richwine), despite the initial objections of her aunt (Gloria Irricari). Buddy enjoys the success music brings him, although he hates being away so much from his bride as a result of his heavy performing schedule on the road. On February 3, 1959, while on tour from Clear Lake, Iowa to his next one-night stand in Minnesota, he is killed in a plane crash in a snowstorm.

"That the ending of THE BUDDY HOLLY STORY leaves a more-than-average size lump in the throat is a tribute to the throb of loyal emotion which pulses throughout the film. Certainly, there is as little meretricious sensationalising of the star's tragically premature death at the age of twenty-two as there is of his earlier, rapid steps up the ladder of fame. . . . That the film-makers maintain their emphasis on the music . . . is a particularly brave risk in the light of their determination to have the music performed and recorded live on the soundtrack . . ." (Jan Dawson, British *Monthly Film Bulletin*). In *The Films of the Seventies* (1984), Marc Sigoloff termed the film an "Excellent and surprisingly restrained biography of the legendary rock singer, which is not the usual trashy and sensationalized Hollywood film biography."

Gary Busey won the National Society of Film Critics Award for his telling performance as Holly and was also nominated for an Oscar. He not only looked like Buddy Holly but performed like him and even did his own vocals on the many Holly songs utilized in the movie.

BYE BYE BIRDIE (Columbia, 1963) Color 112 minutes.

Producer, Fred Kohlmar; director, George Sidney; based on the musical play by Michael Stewart, Charles Strouse, Lee Adams; screenplay, Irving Brecher; production designer, Paul Groesse; set decorator, Arthur Krams; wardrobe coordinator/women's wardrobe, Marjorie B. Wahl; Miss Leigh's costumes, Pat Barto; men's wardrobe, Ed Ware; makeup supervisor, Ben Lane; music arranger/conductor, John Green; music coordinator, Fred Karger; orchestrators, Green, Al Woodbury; choreographers, Onna White, Tom Panko; sound director, Charles Rice; special effects, Geza Gaspar; camera, Joseph Biroc; editor, Charles Nelson.

Songs: "How Lovely to Be a Woman," "Put on a Happy Face," "The Telephone Hour," "Bye Bye Birdie," "Honestly Sincere," "One Boy," "Kids," "A Lot of Livin' to Do," "One Last Kiss," "We Love You, Conrad," "Hymn for a Sunday Evening," "Sultan's Ballet" (Charles Strouse, Lee Adams).

Janet Leigh (Rosie DeLeon); Dick Van Dyke (Albert Peterson); Ann-Margret (Kim McAfee); Maureen Stapleton (Mama Peterson); Bobby Rydell (Hugo Peabody); Jesse Pearson (Conrad Birdie); Ed Sullivan (Himself); Paul Lynde (Mr. McAfee); Mary LaRoche (Mrs. McAfee); Michael Evans (Claude Paisley); Robert Paige (Bob Precht); Gregory Morton (Borov); Byran Russell (Randolph McAfee); Milton Frome (Mr. Maude); Ben Astar (Ballet Manager); Trudi Ames (Ursula); Cyril Delevanti (Mr. Nebbitt); Frank Albertson (Mayor); Beverly Yates (Mayor's Wife); Frank Sully (Bartender); Bo Peep Karlin (Ursula's Mother); Melinda Marx (Teenager); Mell Turner, Gil Lamb (Shriners); Lee Aaker (Leader); Karel Shimoff (Prima Ballerina); Donald Lawton (Russian Consul); Yvonne White (Telephone Operator); Debbie Stern (Debbie); Sheila Denner (Sheila); Pete Menefee (Harvey); George

Janet Leigh in BYE BYE BIRDIE (1963).

Spicer (Tommy); Dick Winslow (Leader of Firemen's Band); Hazel Shermet (Marge, Birdie's Secretary); John Daly (Himself).

A satire on Elvis Presley and rock 'n' roll music, *Bye Bye Birdie* opened on Broadway in 1960 starring Dick Van Dyke, Chita Rivera, Kay Medford, Paul Lynde, Dick Gautier, Michael J. Pollard and Susan Watson. It enjoyed a 607-performance run. Three years later—in the midst of a renewed vogue in filming Broadway musicals*—the property was translated to the screen with Van Dyke and Lynde recreating their stage roles. The satire had a healthy gross of $6.2 million in distributors' domestic film rentals. The *New York Times* wrote, "Best by far when musically spoofing the vigor of young people and their adulation of a hip-swiveling, rubber-lipped jive crooner . . . [with] plenty of musical punch and sparkle." The soundtrack album to BYE BYE BIRDIE remained on *Billboard* magazine's hits chart for forty-one weeks, rising to position #2.

---

*In 1962 Hollywood had translated GYPSY, THE MUSIC MAN and BILLY ROSE'S JUMBO (*qq.v.*) to the screen.

Singing idol Conrad Birdie (Jesse Pearson) is about to be inducted into the army. This upsets the nation's teenagers as well as broke composer Albert Peterson (Dick Van Dyke), who has written the title tune for Conrad's next movie, which now has to be shelved. Albert wants to marry his beautiful secretary Rosie DeLeon (Janet Leigh) but his domineering Mama (Maureen Stapleton) does not approve of her. Rosie has Albert write a farewell ditty for Conrad to sing on Ed Sullivan's (himself) TV show, and a typical teenage girl is selected to give him a farewell kiss. The young miss turns out to be Kim McAfee (Ann-Margret), from Sweet Apple, Ohio, where Sullivan will originate his TV variety show. Albert goes to Sweet Apple, pursued by his vigilant mother. There he finds out that Kim's father (Paul Lynde) will not permit Conrad to stay in his home. Teenagers nearly riot when the singer arrives in the small town and then it is learned that his TV spot has been cut to thirty seconds to accommodate the visiting Russian ballet. When the show goes on, Rosie and Albert spike the Russian conductor's milk and his ballet becomes a shambles. On the air Conrad sings to Kim, but her boyfriend Hugo (Bobby Rydell) hits him. Kim now realizes that she really loves Hugo, not Conrad. Albert and Rosie decide to wed. His overpossessive Mama is planning to remain in Ohio, because she has found a boyfriend.

In its adaptation to the screen, several numbers from the Broadway original vanished ("What Did I Ever See in Him?" "Normal American Boy," "Spanish Rose"). The leading lady's role of Rose was not only homogenized to accommodate the personality and talent differences between Chita Rivera and Janet Leigh, but the focus on Rose was diminished so that the part of Kim (played sirenishly by rising sex kitten Ann-Margret) could be expanded. *Time* magazine observed, "Broadway musicals, like rural beauty-contest winners, rarely survive a round trip to Hollywood without a loss of innocence. This one . . . had an apple-cheekiness about it on the stage that seems slightly worm-eaten on film, and the result is more goof than spoof."

BYE BYE BIRDIE received Oscar nominations for Best Sound and Best Scoring of Music (Adaptation or Treatment). *Bring Back Birdie,* a sequel to *Bye Bye Birdie,* opened on Broadway early in March 1981, starring Donald O'Connor, but the musical comedy lasted for only four performances.

CABARET (Allied Artists, 1972) Color 124 minutes.

Producer, Cy Feuer; associate producer, Harold Nebenzal; director, Bob Fosse; based on the musical play *Cabaret* by Joe Masteroff, John Kander and Fred Ebb, the stage play *I Am A*

Camera by John Van Druten, and "Goodbye to Berlin" by Christopher Isherwood; screenplay, Jay Presson; art directors, Jurgen Kiebach, Rolf Zehetbauer; set decorator, Herbert Strabel; costumes, Charlotte Flemming; music director, Ralph Burns; choreographer, Fosse; assistant directors, Douglas Green, Wolfgang Glattes; sound, Robert Knudson, Avid Hildyard; camera, Geoffrey Unsworth; editor, David Bretherton.

Songs: "Wilkommen," "Mein Herr," "Two Ladies," "Maybe This Time," "If You Could See Her," "Money, Money," "Sitting Pretty," "Tiller Girls," "Heinraten," "Tomorrow Belongs to Me," "Cabaret" (John Kander, Fred Ebb).

Liza Minnelli (Sally Bowles); Michael York (Brian Roberts); Helmut Griem (Maximilian von Heune); Joel Grey (Master of Ceremonies); Fritz Wepper (Fritz Wendel); Marisa Berenson (Natalia Landauer); Elisabeth Neumann-Viertel (Fraulein Schneider); Sigrid Von Richthhofen (Fraulein Maur); Helen Vita (Fraulein Kost); Gerd Vespermann (Bobby); Ralf Wolter (Herr Ludwig); Georg Hartmann (Willi); Ricky Renee (Elke); Estrongo Nachama (Cantor); Kathryn Doby, Inge Jaeger, Angelika Koch, Helen Velkovorska, Gitta Schmidt, Louise Quick (Kit Kat Dancers); Greta Keller (Voice on Phonograph); Oliver Collignon (Young Nazi); Mark Lambert (Singing Voice of the Young Nazi).

Although it lost the Oscar to THE GODFATHER as the Best Picture of 1972, CABARET garnered nine Academy Awards including Liza Minnelli as Best Actress and Joel Grey as Best Supporting Actor. Other Oscars won by the musical included Bob Fosse as Best Director, the cinematography of Geoffrey Unsworth, art direction by Rolf Zehetbauer and Jurgen Kiebach and set decorator Herbert Strabel, editing by David Bretherton, Ralph Burns' music adaptation and Robert Knudson and Avid Hildyard for sound. Grossing $20,250,000 in distributors' domestic film rentals, CABARET had a long creative history. It originated in the Christopher Isherwood story, "Goodbye to Berlin," which was published in Isherwood's compilation, *Berlin Stories* (1954), two years after it served as the basis for the 1952 play *I Am a Camera* by John Van Druten. That property was filmed in England in 1955 as I AM A CAMERA starring Julie Harris, Laurence Harvey, Shelley Winters and Ron Randell. In 1967 Joe Masteroff adapted the Van Druten work to the Broadway stage as a musical called *Cabaret.* Starring Joel Grey, Jill Haworth, Bert Convy, Jack Gifford and Lotte Lenya, it lasted for 1,166 performances. The music and lyrics for the production were composed by John Kander and Fred Ebb, who would later do the original songs for the Barbra Streisand movie musical, FUNNY LADY (*q.v.*), in 1975.

The sophisticated CABARET compares the decadence of post-World War I Germany and the rise of the Nazis to power. The focal point of the drama is set in a third-rate nightclub whose chief attraction is hedonistic American Sally Bowles (Liza Minnelli). The Master of Ceremonies (Joel Grey) of the sleazy Kit Kat cabaret is an evil, dwarfish man who delights in the degeneracy and near perversion of the acts presented, such as a song ("If You Could See Her") about his girlfriend who turns out to be a gorilla. Coming to the garish cabaret is handsome Brian Roberts (Michael York), an aimless young Britisher who is involved with Baron Maximilian von Heune (Helmut Griem), a rich nobleman who has also paid Sally for her sexual services. Roberts and Sally meet and fall in love and carry on a romance while gigolo Fritz Wendel (Fritz Wepper) romances Natalia Landauer (Marisa Berenson), with Fritz hiding his Jewish origins from her in order to gain upward social mobility. While these characters and the people who come to the cabaret to forget their trouble continue their idle existence, the Nazi party rises to power and takes revenge on them for their political complacency.

Several songs from the Broadway original disappeared in the picture version, including: "So What?" "Don't Tell Mama," "Perfectly Marvelous," "It Couldn't Please Me More (Pineapple)," "Why Should I Wake Up?" and "What Would You Do?" They were replaced by several Kander and Ebb tunes, including "Maybe This Time," and two numbers written by them especially for the movie: "Mein Herr" and "Money, Money." While the ABC Records soundtrack album of CABARET remained on the charts for more than a year, the title song provided Herb Alpert and the Tijuana Brass with a tepid single chart record on the A&M label in the spring of 1968. The title song, as performed on-camera by Liza Minnelli, is the best remembered number from the film, and became *de rigueur* in her subsequent club act. Also impressive is Joel Grey's singing of "Wilkommen" and the grimly patriotic Hitler Youths' ballad, "Tomorrow Belongs to Me," the latter being the film's only musical sequence not lensed in the cabaret setting. CABARET's soundtrack album remained on *Billboard* magazine's hits chart for nine weeks, rising to position #25.

Originally Gene Kelly was to have directed the screen musical, but due to his wife's ailing health he did not want to go on location to Germany. Bob Fosse, a former stage-film dancer turned choreographer-director, who had helmed SWEET CHARITY (1969), *q.v.* and would reach his apogee in ALL THAT JAZZ (1979), *q.v.*, was substituted. He imposed a dark, brooding intensity on the project, refusing to "open it up" as was traditional with stage musicals converted into motion pictures. He employed a series of quick cutting scenes to create an energy and pace that scarcely slackens in the film. To accommodate its new stars, the play's British heroine became American and the stage hero was transformed from American to English. The bisexual character of the German aristocrat von Heune was added especially for the movie. Clive Hirschhorn (*The Hollywood Musical,* 1981) observed. "It was part of a radical re-assessment of the . . . stage show . . . and, like everything else in the movie, was a distinct improvement on its Broadway counterpart. All the songs . . . commented on the action as opposed to being integrated into it. . . ." In *The Best, Worst and Most Unusual: Hollywood Musicals* (1983), the editors of *Consumer Guide* and Phillip J. Kaplan wrote, "By concentrating on the inhabitants of a decadent night club, the film shows the manner in which many people ignore turbulent social events by desperately searching for fun. CABARET shows both the fun and the pain, with unwavering honesty. Using the backstage musical for serious purposes, CABARET performs a daring feat—it creates a frightening real world and uses music to convey the horror."

CABARET appeared in a year which saw the release of two other major Hollywood musicals: 1776 and LADY SINGS THE BLUES, *qq.v.*

CABIN IN THE SKY (Metro-Goldwyn-Mayer, 1942) Sepia 99 minutes.

Producer, Arthur Freed; associate producer, Albert Lewis, (uncredited) Roger Edens; directors, Vincente Minnelli, (uncredited) Busby Berkeley; based on the musical play by Lynn Root, John LaTouche, Vernon Duke; screenplay, Joseph Schrank, (uncredited) Eustace Cocrell, Marc Connelly; art directors, Cedric Gibbons, Leonid Vasian; set decorators, Edwin B. Willis, Hugh Hunt; costume supervisor, Irene; costume associate, Howard Shoup; men's costumes, Gile Steele; music adaptor, Edens; music director, George Stoll; orchestrators, George Bassman, Conrad Salinger; choral arranger, Hall Johnson; sound supervisor, Douglas Shearer; camera, Sidney Wagner; editor, Harold F. Kress.

Songs: "Cabin in the Sky," "Honey in the Honeycomb," "Love Me Tomorrow," "In My Old Virginia Home" (Vernon Duke, John LaTouche); "Taking a Chance on Love" (Duke, LaTouche, Ted Fetter); "Happiness Is Just a Thing Called Joe," "Li'l Black Sheep," "That Ole Debbil Consequence," "Some Folk Work," "Ain't It the Truth" (Harold Arlen, E. Y. Harburg); "Going Up" (Duke Ellington); "Forward," "The Prayer," "Dusky Jezebel," "Sweet Petunia," "But the Flesh Is Weak," "Revelations," "Jezebel Jones"

(Roger Edens); "Old Ship of Zion" (arranger, Hall Johnson); "Shine" (Lew Brown, Ford Dabney, Cecil Mack); "Things Ain't What They Used to Be" (Mercer Ellington).

Ethel Waters (Petunia Jackson); Eddie "Rochester" Anderson (Little Joe Jackson); Lena Horne (Georgia Brown); Louis Armstrong (The Trumpeter); Rex Ingram (Lucius/Lucifer, Jr.); Kenneth Spencer (Reverend Green/The General); John Bubbles [John W. Sublett] (Domino Johnson); Oscar Polk (The Deacon/Fleetfoot); Mantan Moreland (First Idea Man); Willie Best (Second Idea Man); Fletcher Rivers (Moke, the Third Idea Man); Leon James (Poke, the Fourth Idea Man); Bill Bailey (Bill); Buck [Ford L. Washington] (Messenger Boy); Butterfly McQueen (Lily); Ruby Dandridge (Mrs. Kelso); Nicodemus (Dude); Ernest Whitman (Jim Henry); Duke Ellington and His Orchestra, The Hall Johnson Choir (Themselves).

"Broadway's big, fun-jammed musical is on the screen at last! Crowded with stars—and songs—and spectacle—in the famed MGM manner." Such was the ad campaign for CABIN IN THE SKY, Hollywood's first major all-black film since MGM's HALLELUJAH (1929), *q.v.**

Cabin in the Sky, under the guidance of director/choreographer George Balanchine, had bowed on Broadway in October 1940, starring Ethel Waters, Todd Duncan, Dooley Wilson, Rex Ingram and Katherine Dunham and Her Dancers. With a book by Lynn Root and lyrics and music by John LaTouche and Vernon Duke, the musical boasted a score including "Taking a Chance on Love" and "Cabin in the Sky." Because ethnic-oriented productions in that period had limited audience appeal, the show closed after 156 performances, at a loss of $25,000. At that juncture, MGM producer Arthur Freed, unable to acquire the screen rights to *Porgy and Bess,* "settled" for obtaining film rights to *Cabin in the Sky* at a cost of $40,000.

MGM hired Ethel Waters and Rex Ingram to repeat their Broadway roles and a rising black singer named Lena Horne was put under studio contract to handle the part of sultry Georgia Brown, the temptress. For marquee allure, Eddie "Rochester" Anderson (famous for his role on Jack Benny's radio program), Butterfly McQueen (of GONE WITH THE WIND), Louis Armstrong, Duke Ellington and His Band and the Hall Johnson Choir were

---

*In 1943, 20th Century-Fox distributed the all-black musical, STORMY WEATHER, *q.v.,* a fictionalized account of the life of Bill "Bojangles" Robinson, starring Robinson, Cab Calloway and His Band, Lena Horne, Fats Waller and Katherine Dunham.

added to the talent lineup. There was immediate and persistent friction between Waters and Horne, the former agitated with Hollywood in general, over the way MGM was treating religion in the picture, and with Horne in particular (because the latter was young, thin and had a major assignment which diverted from Waters' spotlight). The cast took sides in the on-going feud. Director Vincente Minnelli, too engulfed in coping with his first feature film and in dealing with studio politics, was unable to halt the feud. Despite the friction, CABIN IN THE SKY was completed in two months of shooting at a cost of $662,141.

In the black community of a small southern town, the loyal Petunia (Ethel Waters) must contend with her womanizing husband, Little Joe Jackson (Eddie "Rochester" Anderson), a shiftless man driven to drink and gamble. Jackson is wounded in a crap game and wavers between life and death. In his delirium, he dreams that the devil, Lucifer, Jr. (Rex Ingram) has claimed his soul. Meanwhile, because his staunch wife Petunia has prayed for his deliverance, the Lawd's General (Kenneth Spencer) grants Jackson a six-month reprieve to make amends. In the struggle for Jackson's soul, Lucifer, Jr. utilizes the seductive Georgia Brown (Lena Horne) to lead Jackson astray. Between Georgia's wiles and Jackson suddenly winning a sweepstakes ticket, the victim falls back into his old dissolute ways. Petunia goes to Jim Henry's (Ernest Whitman) cafe to woo her husband back. A melee develops and both Petunia and Little Joe are wounded. As the faithful Petunia and her errant Joe head to heaven, The General destroys the cafe with a fierce tornado. The noise of the annihilation awakens Jackson from his dream. He now insists he will one day share a "cabin in the sky" with his patient, beloved Petunia.

The musical highlights of CABIN IN THE SKY, which was filmed entirely in sepia, are Ethel Waters' rendition of the title song, "Taking a Chance on Love" and "Happiness Is Just a Thing Called Joe," the latter two written especially for the movie. Sultry Lena Horne sparkles with her rendition of "Honey in the Honeycomb" and in a fantasy sequence Louis Armstrong appears as the Angel Gabriel playing his trumpet to "Shine." Also appearing are Duke Ellington and His Orchestra performing "Going Up" and "Things Ain't What They Used to Be." Two songs by Arlen-Harburg, "Ain't It the Truth" (sung by Lena Horne; later used in the Broadway show, *Jamaica,* 1957, starring Horne) and "I Got a Song" (sung by John Bubbles; later used in the Broadway show, *Bloomer Girl*, 1944) were cut. (The song "Cabin in the Sky" was nominated for an Oscar but lost to "You'll Never Know" from the Alice Faye musical, HELLO, FRISCO, HELLO [1943], *q.v.*)

At the time of its release the *New York Times* referred to the film as "an inspiring expression of a simple people's faith in the hereafter," and *Variety* weighed, "CABIN is a worthwhile picture for Metro to have made, if only as a step toward recognition of the place of the colored man in American life." However, today the movie is considered more of a whimsical fable. Herb Sterne, in *Rob Wagner's Script* magazine, complained, "Much of the zing of the original has been lost between the boards and the Culver City stages . . . some of the loss must be attached to the studio's over-elaboration, and fondness for the theatrical geegaws of cliché." Sterne also blamed director Minnelli for ". . . The complete camera mismanagement. . . . Minnelli has photographed the film with a preponderance of close-ups. . . ." In *The Best, Worst and Most Unusual: Hollywood Musicals* (1983), the editors of *Consumer Guide* and Phillip J. Kaplan decided, "Unfortunately it was an all-black musical written and directed by whites. While the intentions of those making it were good, some strange stereotypes still crept in." Roy Hemming (*The Melody Lingers On,* 1986) judged, "For all its once-overpraised folkloristic whimsy, CABIN IN THE SKY today seems more simplistic than simple, more whimpering than whimsical. But it does give us one of the great [Harold] Arlen songs, 'Happiness Is Just a Thing Called Joe.' "

For the record, some of the special effects sequences for the tornado in CABIN IN THE SKY were borrowed from footage of the studio's THE WIZARD OF OZ (1939), *q.v.*

CALAMITY JANE (Warner Bros., 1953) Color 101 minutes.

Producer, William Jacobs; director, David Butler; screenplay, James O'Hanlon; art director, John Beckman; set decorator, G. W. Bertsen; costumes, Howard Shoup; music director, Ray Heindorf; choreographer, Jack Donahue; sound, Stanley Jones, David Forrest; camera, Wilfrid M. Cline; editor, Irene Morra.

Songs: "Secret Love," "The Deadwood Stage," "Higher Than a Hawk," " 'Tis Harry I'm Plannin' to Marry," "I Can Do Without You," "I've Got a Hive Full of Honey," "Keep It Under Your Hat," "Just Blew in from the Windy City," "A Woman's Touch," "The Black Hills of Dakota" (Sammy Fain, Paul Francis Webster).

Doris Day (Calamity Jane); Howard Keel (Wild Bill Hickok); Allyn McLerie (Katie Brown); Philip Carey (Lieutenant Gilmartin); Dick Wesson (Francis Fryer); Paul Harvey (Henry Miller); Chubby Johnson (Rattlesnake); Gale Robbins (Adelaide Adams); Lee Shumway (Bartender); Rex Lease (Buck); Francis McDonald (Hank); Monte Montague (Pete); Emmett Lynn (Artist); Forrest Taylor (MacPherson); Lane Chandler, Glenn Strange, Zon Murray,

Budd Buster, Terry Frost, Tom London, Billy Bletcher (Prospectors); and: Stanley Blystone, Kenne Duncan, Bill Hale, Reed Howes, Tom Monroe, Lee Morgan, Buddy Roosevelt.

When MGM acquired the screen rights to ANNIE GET YOUR GUN (1950), *q.v.*, Doris Day was one of the hopefuls who wanted mightily to play Annie Oakley. Three years after losing that coveted role to Judy Garland (who was replaced midstream by Paramount's Betty Hutton), Day was given the opportunity by her home lot to portray a similar brusque cowgirl in CALAMITY JANE. The new musical also used MGM's Howard Keel (the co-lead of ANNIE GET YOUR GUN) as her leading man, Wild Bill Hickok. Enacting the rough and tumble Calamity Jane* was a decided departure from the fluffy (and often empty) musicals she had been churning out at Warner Bros. The film itself produced the Academy Award-winning song, "Secret Love." In addition there were ten other tunes by Paul Francis Webster and Sammy Fain. These melodies carried the movie, which was saddled with a thin, frequently bland, plotline. Thanks to the bouncy music, and the (over) enthusiastic work of Doris Day and Howard Keel, CALAMITY JANE emerged as one of the more exuberant musicals of the year.

Calamity Jane (Doris Day) is a frontier gal who can do anything most men can do, and often better. To help dancehall owner Henry Miller (Paul Harvey), she goes to Chicago to bring back a big theatrical performer to save Miller's operation from bankruptcy. By error, she escorts the great lady's maid, Katie Brown (Allyn McLerie), back to Deadwood. With Jane's support, Katie carries off her ruse and succeeds as a dancehall entertainer. In the process, Katie attracts the attention of both Wild Bill Hickok (Howard Keel) and Lieutenant Gilmartin (Philip Carey), the two men in Jane's life. It is the bemused Hickok who intervenes when Jane becomes jealous of the growing romance between Katie and Gilmartin. Before long, Wild Bill comes to realize he loves the buckskin-wearing sharpshooter. When Jane leaves town in embarrassment, he follows her and brings her back. Both couples plan to wed.

---

*Among the other actresses who have played Calamity Jane on screen are: Ethel Grey Terry (WILD BILL HICKOK, 1923), Louise Dresser (CAUGHT, 1931), Jean Arthur (THE PLAINSMAN, 1937), Sally Payne (YOUNG BILL HICKOK, 1940), Frances Farmer (BADLANDS OF DAKOTA, 1941), Jane Russell (THE PALEFACE, 1948), Yvonne De Carlo (CALAMITY JANE AND SAM BASS, 1949), Evelyn Ankers (THE TEXAN MEETS CALAMITY JANE, 1950), Judi Meredith (THE RAIDERS, 1964), Gloria Milland (SEVEN HOURS OF GUNFIRE, 1964), Abby Dalton (THE PLAINSMAN, 1966), Kim Darby (THAT WAS THE WEST THAT WAS, TV-1974), Jane Alexander (CALAMITY JANE, TV-1984).

"Miss Day stomps and hollers her way around the town of Deadwood like Betty Hutton in a holiday moon," insisted the *New York Herald Tribune.* The *New York Times* judged, "As for Miss Day's performance, it is tempestuous to the point of becoming just a bit frightening—a bit terrifying—at times. The scenery is fat and highly flavored. In Technicolor, it looks good enough to eat. But the voracity with which Miss Day has at it and wolfs it down is unnerving to see."

CALAMITY JANE also received Oscar nominations for Scoring of a Musical Picture and Sound Recording.

CALL ME MADAM (20th Century-Fox, 1953) Color 117 minutes.

Producer, Sol C. Siegel; director, Walter Lang; based on the musical play by Howard Lindsay, Russel Crouse and Irving Berlin; screenplay, Arthur Sheekman; art directors, Lyle Wheeler, John De Cuir; music directors, Alfred Newman, Ken Darby; choreographer, Robert Alton; color consultant, Leonard Doss; camera, Leon Shamroy; editor, Robert Simpson.

Songs: "Welcome to Lichtenberg," "Mrs. Sally Adams," "The Ocarina," "What Chance Have I with Love?" "Something to Dance About," "The Best Thing for You," "The Hostess with the Mostes'," "That International Rag," "Can You Use Any Money Today?" "Marry for Love," "It's a Lovely Day Today" (Irving Berlin).

Ethel Merman (Mrs. Sally Adams); Donald O'Connor (Kenneth Gibson); Vera-Ellen (Princess Maria); George Sanders (Cosmo Constantine); Billy De Wolfe (Pemberton Maxwell); Helmut Dantine (Prince Hugo); Walter Slezak (Tantinnin); Steven Geray (Sebastian); Ludwig Stossel (Grand Duke); Lilia Skala (Grand Duchess); Charles Dingle (Senator Brockway); Emory Parnell (Senator Gallagher); Percy Helton (Senator Wilkins); Leon Belasco (Leader); Oscar Beregi (Chamberlain); Nestor Paiva (Miccoli); Sidney Marion (Proprietor); Richard Garrick (Supreme Court Justice); Walter Woolf King (Secretary of State); Olan Soule (Clerk); John Wengraf (Ronchin); Fritz Feld (Hat Clerk); Erno Verebes (Music Clerk); Hannelore Axman (Switchboard Operator); Lal Chand Mehra (Minister from Magrador); Charles Conrad, Don Dillaway, Frank Gerstle, Rennie McEvoy (Reporters); Allen Wood, Johnny Downs (Cameramen); Gene Roth (Equerry); Carole Richards (Singing Voice of Princess Maria).

Ethel Merman was perhaps the most distinctive and vivacious personality of the twentieth-century American musical theatre. For several decades she was the boisterous belter from the Bronx whose vocal dynamics were only exceeded by her high-voltage

Ethel Merman and George Sanders in CALL ME MADAM (1953).

personality. She made several stabs at the movies, but her oversized personality was never suited to the big screen (she was too much for movie audiences to absorb). One of her best and biggest screen assignments was CALL ME MADAM, only the second* of her many stage roles that she recreated on screen. Howard Lindsay and Russel Crouse had concocted the stage script for *Call Me Madam* expressly for Merman, basing it loosely on the lively Washington socialite hostess, Perle Mesta, and treading amusingly on the mores of the nation's capital. Irving Berlin wrote the show score for Merman and co-star Paul Lukas. The musical opened on Broadway on October 12, 1950 for a 644-performance run.

Because of her influence in Washington D.C. as a result of her years as a society hostess, salty Sally Adams (Ethel Merman) is appointed by the President to the post of ambassador to the small European country of Lichtenstein. Making the trip with Sally is her press attaché Kenneth Gibson (Donald O'Connor). Once they are settled there, he immediately falls in love with Princess Maria (Vera-Ellen), the daughter of Prince Hugo (Helmut Dantine), the country's ruler. Earthy Sally also finds romance with the country's foreign minister, Cosmo Constantine (George Sanders), but must cope with the machinations of the corrupt finance minister, Tantinnen (Walter Slezak).

It was Merman who socked across "International Rag" (added to the film from Berlin's repertoire), "Can You Use Any Money Today?" and "The Hostess with the Mostes'," and outshone Donald O'Connor in the duet, "You're Just in Love." George Sanders, in his only screen musical and using a jarring "foreign" accent, was more than adequate as a baritone delivering "Marrying for Love," while Donald O'Connor and Vera-Ellen (dubbed by Carole Richards) sang/danced to "It's a Lovely Day Today" and the lesser "What Chance Have I With Love?"—the latter added to the film's score from Berlin's 1940 stage musical, *Louisiana Purchase.* The efficient choreography was by Robert Alton, formerly of MGM. Dropped from the original Broadway score were "They Like Ike" (about Dwight D. Eisenhower running for the presidency) and "Once Upon a Time Today" (sung by the press attaché).

"The one and only Ethel, strutting her stuff in top form and resounding vocal brass. . . . It makes a fine, assembly-line cornucopia of entertainment. . . . It moves bouncily, with director Walter Lang in control—but with nobody, obviously, controlling Miss Merman, who, gowned to the teeth, belting out Berlin and

*In Paramount's ANYTHING GOES (1936), Ethel Merman repeated her stage role (1934) in the musical film co-starring Bing Crosby, Ida Lupino and Charlie Ruggles.

squelching the one fly in the ointment (Billy De Wolfe), makes it her ointment and almost makes it seem original" (*New York Times*). In retrospect, Roy Hemming (*The Melody Lingers On,* 1986) judged, "The movie version of CALL ME MADAM is as much a '50s period piece as TOP HAT [1935, *q.v.*] is a '30s one. Its dialogue is filled with fast-flying jabs at everything from contemporary fads and politics to Margaret Truman's singing. Berlin's songs spur much of the spoofing spirit along. . . ."

CAMELOT (Warner Bros.-Seven Arts, 1967) Color 179 minutes.

Producer, Jack L. Warner; director, Joshua Logan; based on the musical play by Alan Jay Lerner & Frederick Loewe and the book *The Once and Future King* by T. H. White; screenplay, Lerner; production scenery/costumes, John Truscott; art director, Edward Carrere; set decorator, John W. Brown; makeup supervisor, Gordon Bau; music supervisor/conductor, Alfred Newman; associate music supervisor, Ken Darby; orchestrators, Leo Shuken, Jack Hayes, Pete King, Gus Levene; music staging associate, Buddy Schwab; music liaison, Trude Rittman; assistant directors, Arthur Jacobson, Jack Aldworth; directors of action sequences, Tap Canutt, Joe Canutt; sound, M. A. Merrick, Dan Wallin; camera, Richard H. Kline; editor, Folmar Blangsted.

Songs: "Camelot," "If Ever I Would Leave You," "Then You May Take Me to the Fair," "C'est Moi," "How to Handle a Woman," "The Lusty Month of May," "Guinevere," "What Do the Simple Folk Do?", "I Wonder What the King Is Doing Tonight," "Follow Me," "I Loved You Once in Silence," "Wedding Ceremony," "The Simple Joys of Maidenhood" (Alan Jay Lerner, Frederick Loewe).

Richard Harris (King Arthur); Vanessa Redgrave (Queen Guinevere); Franco Nero (Lancelot Du Lac); David Hemmings (Mordred); Lionel Jeffries (King Pellinore); Laurence Naismith (Merlyn); Pierre Olaf (Dap); Estelle Winwood (Lady Clarinda); Gary Marshall (Sir Lionel); Anthony Rogers (Sir Dinaden); Peter Bromilow (Sir Sagramore); Sue Casey (Lady Sybil); Garry Marshal (Tom of Warwick); Nicholas Beauvy (King Arthur as a Boy); Gene Merlino (Singing Voice of Lancelot Du Lac).

With the tremendous success of Broadway's *My Fair Lady* (1956) and Hollywood's GIGI (1958), the musical comedy team of Alan Jay Lerner and Frederick Loewe next ventured into translating T. H. White's book *The Once and Future King* (1960) into a stage musical. With Julie Andrews (*My Fair Lady*) as the Queen, Richard Burton as the King and rising singer Robert Goulet as Sir Lancelot, the production was pronounced to be sure-fire. However, such was

Franco Nero, Richard Harris and Vanessa Redgrave in CAMELOT (1967).

not the case with *Camelot,* which struggled to Broadway on December 3, 1960, having coped with the illness of its director (Moss Hart), multiple mammoth production problems, and staggering costs for the elaborate sets, costumes, and expensive performing talent. Despite the presence of such numbers as "The Lusty Month of May," "How to Handle a Woman" and "If Ever I Would Leave You," most critical plaudits went to the sumptuous staging. This led one pundit to decree, "You come out humming the sets." Nevertheless, the pre-sold musical package lasted for 873 performances. Warner Bros., which had filmed several stage musicals recently: GYPSY (1962), THE MUSIC MAN (1962) and MY FAIR LADY (1964), *qq.v.,* outbid everyone for the movie rights.

CAMELOT proved to be the last personal production at Warner Bros.-Seven Arts by studio head Jack L. Warner, costing $15 million. The picture was a great disappointment. Granted, there was visual grandeur of epic proportions on the screen, but that could not disguise the miscasting of the three lead roles, nor Joshua Logan's ponderous direction.

In the Dark Ages, King Arthur (Richard Harris) meets beautiful Guinevere (Vanessa Redgrave) in an enchanted forest near his castle, Camelot. They are soon wed. Arthur then forms his Knights of the Round Table and calls for members who will defend chivalry and the oppressed. One of those answering the call is Lancelot Du Lac (Franco Nero), who becomes Arthur's best friend and most trusted Knight. At first Guinevere is jealous of Lancelot because he has the King's ear, but soon she grows to admire him. Eventually they fall in love and mate. Arthur at first refuses to believe the vile rumors about his wife and Lancelot. However, when Arthur's illegitimate son Mordred (David Hemmings) arrives and is refused acceptance by the King, Mordred schemes with other knights to expose the trysting of Lancelot and Guinevere. When the two are found together, Lancelot escapes but the Queen is captured and Arthur orders her to be burned at the stake. Lancelot, however, arrives at the execution site and rescues the queen. She retreats to a convent, Lancelot and King Arthur prepare to battle to the finish, and the wondrous, idealistic days of Camelot are finished.

"If ever there was a Broadway musical that cried for simple clarification and opening up of its story—a drenching in cinema magic to remove all the dull and pretentious patches of realism and romantic cliché that kept it from sparkling in the theatre—it's this stunningly-opulent but cumbersome and pretentious color movie. . . ." (*New York Times*). "What the well-disposed considered 'a wisp of glory' on the stage sloshes across the screen as a gaudy, mawkish, pretentious, disorganized bore. . . . Whatever meaning Lerner's book once had is defeated by one of the worst examples of screen direction in recent years and is crushed beneath gargantuan, tasteless production" (Robert Downing, *Films in Review* magazine, December 1967).

CAMELOT was not helped by having Vanessa Redgrave (who unfortunately did her own singing) and Franco Nero (whose voice was dubbed by Gene Merlino) in such pivotal vocal assignments. At least Richard Harris, who gave a too exaggerated interpretation to the role of King Arthur, had a musical background and had enjoyed some success as a modern troubadour (especially with his hit pop song, "MacArthur Park"). Songs dropped from the original Broadway score were: "The Parade," "The Jousts," "Before I Gaze At

You Again," "The Seven Deadly Virtues," "The Persuasion" and "Fie on Goodness." Because of its pre-sold qualities, the soundtrack album did last for twenty-three weeks on *Billboard* magazine's hits chart, rising to position #11.

CAMELOT was a relative box-office failure, only grossing $14,000,000 in distributors' domestic film rentals. It won Academy Awards for Best Art Direction-Set Decoration (John Truscott, Edward Carrere; John W. Brown); Best Scoring of Music—Adaptation or Treatment (Alfred Newman, Ken Darby); Best Costume Design (John Truscott); and Oscar nominations for its Cinematography and Sound.

CAN-CAN (20th Century-Fox, 1960) Color 131 minutes.

Producer, Jack Cummings; associate producer, Saul Chaplin; director, Walter Lang; based on the musical play by Abe Burrows, Cole Porter; screenplay, Dorothy Kingsley, Charles Lederer; art directors, Lyle Wheeler, Jack Martin Smith; music arranger/conductor, Nelson Riddle; choreographer, Hermes Pan; camera, William H. Daniels; editor, Robert Simpson.

Songs: "Maidens Typical of France," "It's All Right with Me," "Come Along with Me," "Live and Let Live," "Adam and Eve Ballet," "Montmartre," "Snake Dance," "Apache Dance," "C'est Magnifique," "I Love Paris," "Let's Do It," "Just One of Those Things," "You Do Something to Me" (Cole Porter).

Frank Sinatra (François Durnais); Shirley MacLaine (Simone Pistache); Maurice Chevalier (Paul Barrière); Louis Jourdan (Philippe Forrestier); Juliet Prowse (Claudine); Marcel Dalio (Andre, the Headwaiter); Leon Belasco (Arturo, the Orchestra Leader); Nestor Paiva (Bailiff); John A. Neris (Photographer); Jean Del Val (Judge Merceaux); Ann Codee (League President); Eugene Borden (Chevrolet); Jonathan Kidd (Recorder); Marc Wilder (Adam); Peter Coe (Policeman Dupont); Marcel de la Broesse (Plainclothesman); Rene Godfrey, Lili Valenty (Dowagers); Charles Carman (Knife Thrower); Carole Bryan (Gigi); Barbara Carter (Camille); Jane Earl (Renée); Ruth Earl (Ruth); Laura Fraser (Germine); Vera Lee (Gabrielle); Lisa Mitchell (Fifi); Wanda Shannon (Maxine); Darlene Tittle (Gisele); Wilda Taylor (Lili); Ambrogio Malerba (Apache Dancer); Alphonse Martell (Butler); Geneviève Aumont (Secretary); Edward Le Veque (Judge); Maurice Marsac (Bailiff).

In 1890s Paris, Judge Philippe Forrestier (Louis Jourdan), newly appointed to the bench, declares he will bring to court cafe owners who allow the illegal dance, the risqué can-can, to be performed in their establishments. One such cafe proprietor is Simone Pistache (Shirley MacLaine) who has been protected to date by her lawyer, François Durnais (Frank Sinatra) and by an accommodating older judge, Paul Barrière (Maurice Chevalier). When Simone meets Forrestier her worries are over because he quickly falls in love with her. Forrestier asks Simone to marry him and she, who really loves Durnais, hopes the proposal will bring her lawyer around to the subject of matrimony. Trying to thwart Forrestier's attempts to marry Simone, Durnais insults the judge in front of his society friends. However, the scheme fails to work. Thus he is forced to propose to Simone, who readily accepts his invitation to marriage.

The original 1953 Broadway musical, *Can-Can,* starring Lilo, Hans Conreid, Gwen Verdon and Erik Rhodes, had run for 893 performances, buoyed by its lively Cole Porter score, saucy dance numbers and a serviceable script by Abe Burrows. 20th Century-Fox acquired the screen rights and cast Frank Sinatra (who owed the studio a film after walking out on *Carousel,* 1956, *q.v.*). and fellow rat-packer Shirley MacLaine as the leads. For additional audience allure, two Gallic alumnae from GIGI (1958), *q.v.*—Maurice Chevalier and Louis Jourdan—were hired as top support. But somehow, veteran Walter Lang, who had directed many Betty Grable song-and-dance entries as well as two recent Ethel Merman musicals (CALL ME MADAM, 1953, THERE'S NO BUSINESS LIKE SHOW BUSINESS, 1954., *qq.v*), could not come to grips with the fluff. What emerged was 134 minutes of unengaging fluff, more ponderous and crass than sparkling. Each of the stars had his or her song moments: "It's All Right with Me" (Sinatra), "Come Along with Me" (MacLaine), "Live and Let Live" (Chevalier, Jourdan), but their vocal interpretations were more perfunctory than inspired. There was plenty of heel-kicking dancing by MacLaine et al., especially in the scandalous "Can-Can" number, but the terpsichorean highlight was definitely Juliet Prowse's "Snake Dance." Many Porter numbers (including "I Am Love," "If You Loved Me Truly," "Every Man Is a Stupid Man") were dropped from the film, while several Porter tunes ("Just One of Those Things," "You Do Something to Me" and "Let's Do It") were added from the composer's song trunk.

Pinpointing the film's flaws, *Variety* decided, "It's Las Vegas, 1960; not Montmartre, 1896. . . . [The picture] somehow conveys the feeling that Clan members Sinatra and Miss MacLaine would soon be joined by other members of the group for another 'summit' meeting. . . . Even if you accept CAN-CAN as a tongue-in-cheek offering, the basic premise is still hard to swallow." Nevertheless, due its name cast the film grossed $4.2 million in distributors' domestic film rentals. Revenues were helped by the tremendous publicity garnered when Nikita Krushchev, then premier of the Soviet Union, visited the 20th Century-Fox studios and later denounced the title dance as immoral.

CAN-CAN received Oscar nominations for Best Scoring of a Musical Picture and Best Costume Design (Color). The soundtrack album was on *Billboard* magazine's hits chart for twenty weeks, reaching third position.

CAN'T STOP THE MUSIC (Associated Film Distribution, 1980) Color 118 minutes.

Producers, Allan Carr, Jacques Morali, Henri Belolo; associate producer, Neil A. Machlis; director, Nancy Walker; screenplay, Bronte Woodward, Carr; production designer, Steve Hendrickson; art director, Harold Michelson; set decorator, Richard McKenzie, Eric Orburn; costumes, Jane Greenwood, Theoni V. Aldredge; makeup, Dan Stripeke, Jim McCoy; music, Morali; music arranger/director, Horace Ott; choreographer, Arlene Phillips; second unit director, Charles Braverman; assistant directors, Bill Beasley, Paul Moen, Candace Suerstedt; stunts, Bill Anagnos, Arthur Edwards; sound, Barry Thomas; sound re-recording, Michael J. Kohut, Aaron Rochin, Jay M. Harding, Carlos F. deLarios; sound effects editor, Don S. Walden; electronic visual effects, Roy Hays; special effects, Michael Sullivan; camera, Bill Butler; second unit camera, Richard Kratina; editor, John F. Burnett.

Songs: "Can't Stop the Music," "Liberation," "I Love You to Death" (Jacques Morali, Henri Belolo, Phil Hurtt, Beauris Whitehead); "YMCA," "Magic Night," "Milk Shake" (Morali, Belolo, Victor Willis); "Give Me a Break" (Morali, Belolo, The Ritchie Family [Vera Brown, Jacqui Smith-Lee, Dodie Draher]); "Samantha," "The Sound of the City," "Sophistication," "I'm a Singing Juggler" (Morali, Belolo, Hurtt).

Village People: Ray Simpson (Policeman), David Hodo (Construction Worker), Felipe Rose (Indian), Randy Jones (Cowboy), Glenn Hughes (Leatherman), Alex Briley (G.I.); Valerie Perrine (Samantha Simpson); Bruce Jenner (Ron White); Steve Guttenberg (Jack Morell); Paul Sand (Steve Waits); Tammy Grimes (Sydney Channing); June Havoc (Helen Morell); Barbara Rush (Norma White); Altovise Davis (Alicia Edwards); Marilyn Sokol (Lulu Brecht); Russell Nype (Richard Montgomery); Jack Weston (Benny Murray); Leigh Taylor-Young (Claudia Walters); Dick Patterson (Record Store Manager); Bobo Lewis (Bread Woman); Paula Trueman (Stickup Lady); Portia Nelson (Law Office Receptionist); Selma Archerd (Mrs. Williams); Muriel Slatkin (Mrs. Slatkin); Aaron Gold (TV Reporter); Vera Brown, Jacqui Smith-

Lee, Dodie Draher (The Ritchie Family); Greg Zadikov (Singing Vendor); Danone Camden (Stewardess in Record Store); Rasa Allen, Gabriel Barre (Mimes); Donald Blanton (Relief D.J.); Roger LeClaire (Disco Photographer); Cindy Roberts (Jean Harlow); Maggie Brendler (Marilyn Monroe); Bradley Bliss (Betty Grable); Bill Bartman (Wino); Victor Davis (Buster Sirwinski); William L. Arndt (Commercial Director); Jerry Layne (Ventriloquist); Terry Dunne (James the Flame); Maria Roosakos (Steve Waits's Secretary); Mike Kulik (Milk Commercial Director); Richard Bruce Friedman (Recording Technician); Deborah Louise Ash, Seamus Brennan, Wade Collings, Jane Margaret Colthorpe, Edyie Fleming,

Valerie Perrine and The Village People in CAN'T STOP THE MUSIC (1980).

Roy Hamilyn Gayle, Virginia Francis Hartley, Alison Jane Herlihy, Richard King, Kim Elizabeth Leeson, Perri Lister, Sarah Miles, Gene Montoya, Floyd Anthony Pearce, Blane Savage, Peter Tramm, Robert Warners, Christine Anne Wickman (Dancers).

One of the 1980s' first attempts to make a tongue-in-cheek big screen musical was CAN'T STOP THE MUSIC, which immodestly proclaimed it was "The Musical Event of the '80s." Producer Allan Carr hoped to recapture the glories of the old Judy Garland-Mickey Rooney "let's put on a show" musicals, updated to a modern idiom. Costing some $20 million and helmed by comedienne-director

Nancy Walker (an alumnus of 1940s MGM), the film vexed audiences with its extremely peculiar casting. Among the diverse personalities signed for the project were the singing group The Village People, Valerie Perrine (replacing Olivia Newton-John), ex-comic Steve Guttenberg, Olympic decathlon champ Bruce Jenner, and dancer Altovise Davis (the wife of Sammy Davis, Jr.), as well as such veterans as June Havoc, Barbara Rush, Tammy Grimes and Jack Weston. The less said about the emoting of The Village People and Bruce Jenner the better, but it was refreshing to have Gypsy Rose Lee's sister, June Havoc, back on screen.

Model Samantha Simpson (Valerie Perrine) has retired while still in demand. She decides to aid her platonic friend, Jack Morell (Steve Guttenburg), a disco disc jockey who wants to be a composer, by making a demonstration tape of one of his songs for Steve Waits (Paul Sands), the head of Marrakesh Records and one of Samantha's former intimates. She puts together a group called The Village People (themselves) to do the song, and it and the singers are a big success. Meanwhile, Samantha is attracted to conservative lawyer Ron White (Bruce Jenner) and is encouraged to continue her relationship with him both by his mother (Barbara Rush) and by Jack's mother (June Havoc). White proposes to Samantha.

With its many in-house tributes to old Hollywood genre classics and the staging of production numbers like "Y.M.C.A.," an aquatic ensemble reminiscent of the Esther Williams' routines of yore, CAN'T STOP THE MUSIC had appeal to nostalgia buffs. But on the other hand, it catered to the now-audience with near nudity, risqué dialogue and exploitation of the then currently voguish The Village People (a gay-oriented group which had brief popularity with mainstream youths). Tom Milne (British *Monthly Film Bulletin*) labeled the movie an "uneasy amalgam of Broadway show and disco musical." In cataloging the picture's vices, he noted, "Nor are matters helped by the way in which Nancy Walker . . . encourages them [the cast] to mouth their lines with stultifying over-emphasis, meanwhile hurling themselves about in a non-stop frenzy. . . . It would all be absolutely unbearable but for some admirable sets. . . . The choreography executed in front of these sets, unfortunately, is nothing to create a song-and-dance about."

Most of the film's songs were written by Jacques Morali, who created/managed The Village People.

CAREFREE (RKO, 1938) 83 minutes.

Producer, Pandro S. Berman; director, Mark Sandrich; story, Marian Ainslee, Guy Endore; adaptors, Dudley Nichols, Hagar

Wilde; screenplay, Ernest Pagano, Allan Scott; art directors, Van Nest Polglase, Carroll Clark; set decorator, Darrell Silvera; gowns for Miss Rogers, Howard Greer; costumes, Edward Stevenson; music director, Victor Baravalle; choreographers, Hermes Pan, Fred Astaire; sound, Hugh McDowell; special effects, Vernon L. Walker; camera, Robert de Grasse; editor, William Hamilton.

Songs: "I Used to Be Color Blind," "Since They Turned Loch Lomond into Swing," "The Yam," "Change Partners" (Irving Berlin).

Fred Astaire (Dr. Tony Flagg); Ginger Rogers (Amanda Cooper); Ralph Bellamy (Stephen Arden); Luella Gear (Aunt Cora); Jack Carson (Connors); Clarence Kolb (Judy Travers); Franklin Pangborn (Roland Hunter); Walter Kingsford (Dr. Powers); Kay Sutton (Miss Adams); Tom Tully (Policeman); Hattie McDaniel (Maid); Robert B. Mitchell, St. Brendan's Boys Choir (Themselves).

Fred Astaire and Ginger Rogers were paired on-camera for the eighth time in CAREFREE. Since their two previous musicals, SWING TIME (1936) and SHALL WE DANCE? (1937), *qq.v.* had not been big money makers, RKO decided to tamper with the plot formula by having *less* music and *more* comedy in this outing. *Variety* forecast, "The result may inspire some to wonder if the psyching shouldn't have started in the studio. It's a disappointing story. . . ." CAREFREE, the team's first box-office flop, did not break even at the turnstiles.

Wealthy Stephen Arden (Ralph Bellamy) wants to know why his fiancée, Amanda Cooper (Ginger Rogers), has broken off their engagement three times. He sends her to psychiatrist Tony Flagg (Fred Astaire), a follower of Sigmund Freud's theories. Amanda agrees to undergo psychoanalysis with Dr. Flagg, but during their sessions together she finds herself falling in love with the bachelor. To counteract this, the doctor places her under hypnosis and attempts to impress on her subsconscious that she is meant for Arden, not himself. Dr. Flagg, however, slowly realizes that he loves Amanda and sets out to undo the subliminal ideas he has given her. Eventually the two realize they love one another.

Irving Berlin composed eight songs for CAREFREE but RKO cut half of them. Of the surviving numbers, "Change Partners," which was nominated for an Oscar, was the biggest success. Dapper Fred Astaire was not too believable as the psychiatrist but he was at his dancing best in "Since They Turned Loch Lomond Into Swing" (a golfing number he choreographed with Hermes Pan). Ginger Rogers had the lion's share of screen attention and shone in "The Yam," another of those concocted dance crazes that were integral to the Astaire-Rogers outings. Initially the "I Used to Be Color

Blind" number was intended to be filmed in color, but financially plagued RKO was cutting costs in all areas and it was instead shot in black-and-white. Nevertheless, the dance/song duet with its slow motion photography captured all the finesse of the screen team's best attributes.

CAREFREE earned Oscar nominations for Interior [Art] Direction (Van Nest Polglase) and for its musical score (Victor Baravalle). This movie was the fifth and final Astaire-Rogers entry directed by Mark Sandrich, who soon thereafter left RKO in a dispute and signed on with Paramount.

CARMEN JONES (20th Century-Fox, 1954) Color 105 minutes.

Producer/director, Otto Preminger; based on the musical play by Oscar Hammerstein, II, with music by Georges Bizet; screenplay, Harry Kleiner; art director, Edward L. Ilou; music, Georges Bizet; music director, Herschel Burke Gilbert; music conductor, Dimitri Tiomkin; choreographer, Herbert Ross, Gilbert; camera, Sam Leavitt; editor, Louis R. Loeffler.

Songs: "Dat's Love (Habanera)," "You Talk Just Like My Maw," "Dere's a Cafe on De Corner," "Dis Flower (Flower Song)," "Beat Out Dat Rhythm on a Drum," "Stand Up and Fight (Toreador Song)," "Card Song," "My Joe," "Whizzin' Away Along De Tracks," "Duet," "Finale" (Oscar Hammerstein, II, with music by Georges Bizet).

Dorothy Dandridge (Carmen Jones); Harry Belafonte (Joe); Olga James (Cindy Lou); Pearl Bailey (Frankie); Diahann Carroll (Myrt); Roy Glenn (Rum); Nick Stewart (Dink); Joe Adams (Husky Miller); Brock Peters (Sergeant Brown); Sandy Lewis (T-Bone); Mauri Lynn (Sally); DeForest Covan (Trainer); Marilyn Horne (Singing voice of Carmen Jones); LeVern Hutcherson (Singing voice of Joe); Marvin Hayes (Singing voice of Husk Millery); Bernice Peterson (Singing Voice of Myrt); and: Max Roach, Carmen de Lavallade; Brock Peters (Singing Voice of Rum).

Oscar Hammerstein II adapted the opera *Carmen* by Georges Bizet and Prosper Merimée to the Broadway stage late in 1943 with an all-black cast, setting his *Carmen Jones* in the contemporary South. The successful musical ran for 502 performances with the three strenuous leading roles being played alternately by two different casts: Muriel Smith and Muriel Rohn in the title role, Luther Saxon and Napoleon Reed as Joe, and Carlotta Franzell and Elton J. Warren as Cindy Lou. A half-dozen years after the Broadway musical debuted, Roland Petit created a ballet version of the production. After that, producer-director Otto Preminger began making plans to bring *Carmen Jones* to screen.

Twentieth Century-Fox issued CARMEN JONES in DeLuxe Color and CinemaScope but despite good critical reaction, the feature was not overly successful. Sticking close to the Bizet opera (set originally in Spain), the film had the morally loose Carmen Jones (Dorothy Dandridge) working at a parachute factory in Jacksonville, Florida. She is loved by the good-hearted but bland Joe (Harry Belafonte). Boxer Husky Miller (Joe Adams) arrives on the scene and Carmen takes up with the virile man, leaving the loyal Joe. Joe, a GI who has deserted the Army and become a factory guard for the love of Carmen, vows to takes revenge on Miller and to regain Carmen's affections. He realizes eventually how no good she is and strangles her.

While the film retained Oscar Hammerstein II's music score, it was weakened by an over-abundance of dubbing for the leading players' singing. Marilyn Horne sang for Dorothy Dandridge, LeVern Hutcherson for Harry Belafonte, Marvin Hayes for Joe Adams, and Bernice Peterson for Diahann Carroll. Brock Peters, who played Sergeant Brown in the feature, dubbed in the singing for the character of Rum. Providing her own singing voice was Pearl Bailey as Frankie, doing the delightful "Beat Out Dat Rhythm on a Drum."*

Films in Review magazine (December 1954) wrote, "The best thing about CARMEN JONES is that it provides an opportunity for talented Negro actors and actresses to appear in a film of their own." Regarding the combination of Bizet's plot and music to contemporary blacks, the reviewer opined, "The resulting cultural confusion is occasionally bewildering." The *New York Times* reported, ". . . The picture seems primarily a sex melodrama, whose ghost-sung operatic music fits neither the words nor the characters. And for all the fine, splashy color photography and the handsomeness of the two leads, they and the others convey none of the power of the original opera drama."

CARNIVAL ROCK (Howco, 1957) 75 minutes.

Producer/director, Roger Corman; screenplay, Leo Lieberman; set designer, Robert Kinoshita; music, Walter Greene, Buck Ram; camera, Floyd Crosby; editor, Charles Gross, Jr.

Songs: "Ou-Shoo-Blad-d," "The Creep" (Walter Greene, Buck Ram).

---

*Regarding Pearl Bailey's solo, Donald Bogle in *Blacks in American Film and Television* (1988) noted, "When Bailey belts 'Beat Out That Rhythm on a Drum,' she does for her sequence what Paul Robeson did for his when he sang 'Ol' Man River' in *Show Boat:* she takes the whole high-falutin' nonsense to another level, in this instance one of transcendent fun and high spirits."

Susan Cabot (Natalie); Brian Hutton (Stanley); David J. Stewart (Christy); Dick Miller (Ben); Iris Adrian (Celia); Jonathan Haze (Max); Ed Nelson (Cannon); Chris Alcaide (Slug); Horace Logan (Master of Ceremonies); Yvonne Peattie (Mother); Gary Huntley (Boy); Frankie Ray (Billy); Dorothy Neman (Clara); Clara Andressa, Terry Blake (Cleaning Ladies); and: The Platters, David Houston, Bob Luman, The Shadows, The Blockbusters (Themselves).

Purportedly a very loose remake of DER BLAUE ENGEL (The Blue Angel) (1930), CARNIVAL ROCK was one of two features producer-director Roger Corman made from financing supplied by theatre owners in the South. The other picture was TEENAGE THUNDER and both were issued on a double bill by Howco-International, a small outfit trying to break into the lucrative juvenile drive-in trade.

"The pent-up fury of today's rock 'n' rollers—hungry for kicks!" and "I'll have your heart before the sun comes up" read the catchlines for this quickie. The story deals with the owner (David J. Stewart) of a small-time nightclub who lusts for his lead singer (Susan Cabot). A roving gambler (Brian Hutton) arrives on the scene and wins not only the club from its owner, but also the girl's affections. Because the gambler and the singer plan to wed, the former owner seeks revenge and sets fire to the club on the night of the wedding.

CARNIVAL ROCK was laced with performances from a variety of guest artists, including Bob Luman, The Platters, David Houston, The Blockbusters and The Shadows. Leading lady Susan Cabot sang "Ou-Shoo-Blad-d," while most of the music was handled by Luman, a twenty-year-old rocker who was especially popular in the South. Both he and David Houston (Gene Austin's godson) later became staples in country music. Houston also sang "Teen Ages Kisses" in TEENAGE THUNDER.

Having previously made ROCK ALL NIGHT (1956) with The Platters, Roger Corman was able to knock out CARNIVAL ROCK quickly for nice returns from its intended market. By now, major studios like Warner Bros. were turning out "big-budget" rock movies like JAMBOREE (1957), which featured some seventeen name recording artists. These more elaborate outings were fast squeezing out the economy-level rock movies.

CAROUSEL (20th Century-Fox, 1956) Color 128 minutes.

Producer, Henry Ephron; director, Henry King; based on the musical play by Richard Rodgers & Oscar Hammerstein II, and the play *Liliom* by Ferenc Molnar as adapted by Benjamin F. Glazer;

screenplay, Phoebe Ephron, Henry Ephron; costumes, Mary Wills; music director, Alfred Newman; choreographer, Rod Alexander; Louise's ballet choreographed by Agnes De Mille; camera, Charles G. Clarke; editor, William Reynolds.

Songs: "Carousel Waltz," "When I Marry Mister Snow," "If I Loved You," "When the Children Are Asleep," "Soliloquy," "June Is Bustin' Out All Over," "Stonecutters Cut It on Stone," "What's the Use of Wondrin'," "A Real Nice Clambake," "You'll Never Walk Alone," "Carousel Ballet" (Richard Rodgers, Oscar Hammerstein II).

Gordon MacRae (Billy Bigelow); Shirley Jones (Julie Jordan); Cameron Mitchell (Jigger); Barbara Ruick (Carrie); Claramae Turner (Cousin Nettie); Robert Rounseville (Mr. Snow); Gene Lockhart (The Starkeeper); Audrey Christie (Mrs. Mullin); Susan Luckey (Louise); William Le Massena (Heavenly Friend); John Dehner (Mr. Bascombs); Jacques D'Amboise (Louise's Dancing Partner); Frank Tweddel (Captain Watson); Richard Deacon (Policeman); Dee Pollock (Enoch Snow, Jr.); and: Marion Dempsey, Harry "Duke" Johnson, Tor Johnson, Ed Mundy, Mary Orozco, Sylvia Stanton, Angelo Rossitto.

"The movie CAROUSEL has an abundance of riches, from the opening 'Carousel Waltz,' which sweeps the audience up with the irresistible lilt of its music, to the sentimental but touching climax

Audrey Christie, Gordon MacRae, Shirley Jones and Barbara Ruick in CAROUSEL (1956).

in which the dead Billy returns to earth to make a mystical contact with his wife and daughter. The hectic activity of a 'real nice' Maine clambake, the unfettered joy of a bright June day are beautifully realized in the settings, the costumes, and the entrancing Rodgers melodies. Also, Shirley Jones makes a fetching and poignant heroine and sings with charm and grace." (Ted Sennett, *Hollywood Musicals,* 1981).

Based on Ferenc Molnar's fantasy stage production, *Liliom* (1909), Richard Rodgers and Oscar Hammerstein II's musical *Carousel* opened on Broadway on April 19, 1945, starring Jan Clayton and John Raitt.* It was the composers' first stage collaboration since their enormously successful *Oklahoma!* (1943). *Carousel* ran for 890 performances. The production was considered another milestone in the modern American musical theatre, for not only did the songs help to establish the mood and settings, but they served to develop characterization (e.g., the show-stopping seven-minute "Soliloquy"). More than a decade after the musical bowed on Broadway it reached the screen, a year after OKLAHOMA!, *q.v.,* became a movie. Initially Frank Sinatra was to star in CAROUSEL, but he walked off the film, allegedly because he refused to shoot each scene twice (once for the CinemaScope 55 version, once for the "flat" version). The role was offered to Gene Kelly and he rejected it (when they wanted to dub his voice with a more full-timbre singer). Instead, Gordon MacRae was signed, thus reuniting the ex-Warner Bros. star with his OKLAHOMA! co-lead, Shirley Jones. Both—she in particular—gave the finest performances of their movie careers, although Jones later went on to win a Best Supporting Actress Oscar for ELMER GANTRY (1960).

In a small town in Maine in 1873, carefree carousel barker Billy Bigelow (Gordon MacRae) falls in love with cotton mill factory worker Julie Jordan (Shirley Jones). The two go off together and lose their jobs, and when they return they are married, but the town's inhabitants are now hostile toward them. Billy cannot/will not get work and Julie becomes pregnant. By June, when the town is preparing for its annual clambake, a desperate and bitter Billy joins forces with his dishonest pal, Jigger (Cameron Mitchell), and they agree to undertake a robbery. During the crime, however, everything goes wrong and Billy dies as he tries to escape and falls on his own knife. Fifteen years pass and as Billy looks down from heaven he sees that his timid teenage daughter (Susan Luckey) is

*The dramatic play *Liliom* has been filmed in 1930 by Fox Films starring Charles Farrell and Rose Hobart. In 1934, director Fritz Lang had filmed the story in France as *Liliom,* starring Charles Boyer and Madeleine Ozeray.

unhappy and rejected. He is given a chance to return to Earth for a single day and he "gives" his daughter a star. With his advice she becomes very happy. Satisfied that he has helped his only child, Billy returns to heaven.

Some critics carped that the storyline was too syrupy and old-fashioned, that Gordon MacRae's Billy Bigelow missed out on the complexity of the braggart's character, that Shirley Jones was too wholesome and innocent and that the mixture of fantasy and reality scene sets (the latter filmed on location in Boothbay Harbor, Maine and Zuma Beach, California) created a confused ambiance in the picture. But the *New York Times* concluded, "Under Henry King's direction, the grand score soars on. . . . And Rod Alexander's dances have lusty vitality." Moreover, by this period filmmakers had worked out the glitches in using a widescreen process and it was no longer an artistic deficit; in fact, during the "June Is Bustin' Out All Over" number the dancers sprint across the elongated screen with great abandon.

While CAROUSEL was quite faithful to the Broadway original, some songs were deleted: "You're a Queer One, Julie Jordan," "June Dance," "Blow High, Blow Low," "Hornpipe Dance," "Geraniums in the Winder" and "The Highest Judge of All." CAROUSEL sadly received no Oscar nominations, losing out in many categories to 20th Century-Fox's other Rodgers-Hammerstein II adaptation that year, THE KING AND I, *q.v.* CAROUSEL was not a moneymaker for 20th Century-Fox. The soundtrack album to CAROUSEL remained on *Billboard* magazine's hit charts for fifty-six weeks, rising briefly to position #2.

CENTENNIAL SUMMER (20th Century-Fox, 1946) Color 104 minutes.

Producer/director, Otto Preminger; based on the novel by Albert E. Idell; screenplay, Michael Kanin; art directors, Lyle Wheeler, Lee Fuller; set decorator, Thomas Little; music, Jerome Kern; music director, Alfred Newman; orchestrators, Maurice de Packh, Herbert Spencer, Conrad Salinger; vocal arranger, Charles Henderson; choreographer, Dorothy Fox; assistant director, Arthur Jacobson; color consultants, Natalie Kalmus, Richard Mueller; sound, W. D. Flick, Roger Heman; special effects, Fred Sersen; camera, Ernest Palmer; editor, Harry Reynolds.

Songs: "All Through the Day" (Jerome Kern, Oscar Hammerstein II); "In Love in Vain," "The Right Romance," "Centennial," "Up with the Lark," "Railroad Song" (Kern, Leo Robin); "Cinderella Sue" (Kern, E. Y. Harburg).

Jeanne Crain (Julia Rogers); Cornel Wilde (Philippe Lascalles);

Linda Darnell (Edith Rogers); William Eythe (Benjamin Franklin Phelps); Walter Brennan (Jesse Rogers); Constance Bennett (Zenia Lascalles); Dorothy Gish (Harriet Rogers); Barbara Whiting (Susanna Rogers); Larry Stevens (Richard Lewis, Esq.); Kathleen Howard (Deborah); Buddy Swan (Dudley Rogers); Charles Dingle (Snodgrass); Avon Long (Specialty); Gavin Gordon (Trowbridge); Eddie Dunn (Mr. Phelps); Lois Austin (Mrs. Phelps); Harry Strang (Mr. Dorgan); Frances Morris (Mrs. Dorgan); Reginald Sheffield (President Ulysses S. Grant); William Frambes (Messenger Boy); Paul Everton (Senator); James Metcalfe (Bartender); John Farrell (Drunk); Billy Wayne (Attendant); Robert Malcolm (Kelly); Edna Holland (Nurse); Ferris Taylor (Governor); Winifred Harris (Governor's Wife); Rodney Bell (Master of Ceremonies); Glancy Cooper (Carpenter); Florida Sanders (Dance Specialty); Sam McDaniel, Fred "Snowflake" Toones, Napoleon Whiting, Nicodemus Stewart (Red Caps); Hans Moebus (Subject in Still Life); Joe Whitehead (Railroad Clerk); Louanne Hogan (Singing Voice of Julia Rogers).

In hope of garnering some of the box-office receipts which MGM enjoyed with its warm-hearted, nostalgic MEET ME IN ST. LOUIS (*q.v.*) two years before, 20th Century-Fox produced a lavish musical entitled CENTENNIAL SUMMER, centered around the 1876 Philadelphia Exposition. Today this mixture of romance, music, patriotism and colorful scenery is best remembered for being Jerome Kern's final film. (He died on November 11, 1945 of a cerebral hemorrhage, while CENTENNIAL SUMMER was still in production.) The story is very routine and the abundance of nonsinger leads creates liabilities that are almost unsurmountable.

It is 1876 and Philadelphia is honoring the one-hundredth anniversary of the founding of the United States by having a mammoth Exposition. Among those preparing for the celebration are the Rogers family, composed of parents Jesse (Walter Brennan) and Harriet (Dorothy Gish), just grown daughters Julia (Jeanne Crain) and Edith (Linda Darnell), younger sister Susanna (Barbara Whiting) and little brother Dudley (Buddy Swan). Arriving in the city to help with the French Pavilion at the Exposition is Frenchman Philippe Lascalles (Cornel Wilde), who is introduced to the Rogers family by their mutual relative, the glamorous, flirtatious Paris-based Zenia Lascalles (Constance Bennett). Both Julia and Edith are attracted to Philippe, who has trouble with the English language, and are also courted by handsome American Benjamin Franklin Phelps (William Eythe). After a number of romantic complications, each of the two young women eventually pairs off with the man of her choice: Julia with Lascalles and Edith with Phelps.

Linda Darnell and Jeanne Crain in CENTENNIAL SUMMER (1946).

While very fetching Jeanne Crain and Linda Darnell mouthed the songs in the film, both of them were dubbed. Jerome Kern's "Up with the Lark" was also sung by various cast members and Avon Long performed an eye-catching specialty dance to "Cinderella Sue." The movie's two most memorable ballads, "In Love in Vain" and "All Through the Night" were popularized on Capitol Records by Margaret Whiting, whose sister Barbara played little sister Susanna in the movie.

In retrospect, John Kobal would write in *Gotta Sing, Gotta Dance* (1971), ". . . Though the film is not without pleasure, the final result suffers from coyness, ornate self-indulgence and a sluggish pace, lacking that most vital ingredient, imagination." He blamed the movie's failings on director Otto Preminger, ". . . whose feelings for music and eye for decor were woefully inadequate." The director himself would admit to Gerald Pratley in *The Cinema of Otto Preminger* (1971), "Today, I would not be capable of spending three or four months on CENTENNIAL SUMMER—neither the story nor the characters would interest me. That is really a film I wouldn't do today. It was successful and it worked, and at that time it probably served some purpose in my life, and in my career. It's hard to say why, I can't tell you why I did it." Despite his misadventures with CENTENNIAL SUMMER, Preminger directed three additional musicals: THAT LADY IN ERMINE (1948), CARMEN JONES (1954), *q.v.,* and PORGY AND BESS (1959), *q.v.,* none of them notable successes.

CENTENNIAL SUMMER was nominated for two Academy Awards: Best Song ("All Through the Day") and Best Scoring of a Musical Picture (Alfred Newman), but lost, respectively, to: "I Can't Begin to Tell You" from 20th Century-Fox's THE DOLLY SISTERS, and Columbia's THE JOLSON STORY.

CHITTY CHITTY BANG BANG (United Artists, 1969) Color 145 minutes.

Producer, Albert R. Broccoli; associate producer, Stanley Sopel; director, Richard Taylor; based on the book *Chitty Chitty Bang Bang, the Magical Car* by Ian Fleming; screenplay, Roald Dahl, Ken Hughes; additional dialogue, Richard Maibaum; production designer, Ken Adam; art director, Harry Pottle; costumes, Elizabeth Haffenden, Joan Bridge; music supervisor/conductor, Irwin Kostal; choreographers, Marc Breaux, Dee Dee Wood; assistant director, Gus Agosti; sound, John Mitchell, Fred Hynes; special effects, John Stears; Potts' inventions created by Rowland Emmett; camera, Christopher Challis; second unit camera, Skeets Kelly; aerial camera, John Jordan; editor, John Shirley.

Songs: "You Two," "Toot Sweets," "Hushabye Mountain," "New O'Bam-Boo," "Truly Scrumptious," "Chitty Chitty Bang Bang," "Lovely Lonely Man," "Posh!" "The Roses of Success," "Chu-Chi Face," "Doll on a Music Box" (Richard M. Sherman, Robert B. Sherman).

Dick Van Dyke (Caractacus Potts); Sally Ann Howes (Truly Scrumptious); Lionel Jeffries (Grandpa Potts); Gert Frobe (Baron Bomburst); Anna Quayle (Baroness Bomburst); Benny Hill (Toymaker); James Robertson Justice (Lord Scrumptious); Robert Helpmann (Child Catcher); Heather Ripley (Jemima Potts); Adrian Hall (Jeremy Potts); Barbara Windsor (Blonde); Davy Kaye (Admiral); Alexander Dore, Bernard Spear (Spies); Stanley Unwin (Chancellor); Peter Arne (Captain of Guard); Desmond Llewelyn (Coggins); Victor Maddern (Junkman); Arthur Mullard (Big Man); Ross Parker (Chef); Gerald Campion, Felix Felton, Monti De Lyle (Ministers); Totti Truman-Taylor (Duchess); Larry Taylor (Lieutenant); Max Bacon (Orchestra Leader); Max Wall, John Heawood, Michael Darbyshire, Kenneth Maller, Gerald Taylor, Eddie Davis (Inventors); John Raddock (Minister of Finance); Richard Wattis (Secretary at Sweets Factory); Colin Rix (Chauffeur); John Bascomb (Castle Chef); Janette Rowsell, Miranda Hampton (Scullery Maids); Jessie Robins (Pastry Cook); John Crocker (Under Chef); Theo Agar (Fourth Minister); Gabrielle Daye (Lady in Waiting); Grace Newcombe (Second Duchess); Kay Hamilton (Third Duchess); Dickie Owen (Major Domo); and: Teddy Kiss.

With the tremendous popularity of the children's fantasy musical, MARY POPPINS (1964), *q.v.,* everyone wanted to duplicate its success. United Artists offered the very expensively ($10 million) mounted CHITTY CHITTY BANG BANG which boasted not only a score by the composers of MARY POPPINS and dances created by MARY POPPINS' choreographers but that film's leading man, Dick Van Dyke. Taken from Ian Fleming's popular children's story,* CHITTY CHITTY BANG BANG was a highly touted family musical in the late 1960s, but it only grossed $7,120,217 in distributors' domestic film rentals.

In Edwardian England unsuccessful inventor Caractacus Potts (Dick Van Dyke) resides with his children, Jemima (Heather Ripley) and Jeremy (Adrian Hall), and their Grandpa (Lionel Jeffries). Since the children need funds to acquire a worn out racing

---

*CHITTY CHITTY BANG BANG was supervised by Albert R. Broccoli, who had translated Ian Fleming's James Bond novels into a successful film series. Scriptwriters Roald Dahl and Richard Maibaum, production designer Ken Adam, and villain Gert Frobe had all been involved in entries in the James Bond series.

car, Caractacus attempts to parlay his newest invention—whistling sweets—to candy manufacturer Lord Scrumptious (James Robertson Justice). However, his demonstration of the product is a flop. Caractacus then gets the money by dancing at a county fair with a folk dancing troupe, and is soon able to make the wreck of a car into a handsome new auto he dubs "Chitty Chitty Bang Bang." He then takes his children to the seaside, along with Truly Scrumptious (Sally Ann Howes), the daughter of the candy maker. Later, Caractacus recites a fable about the wicked Baron Bomburst (Gert Frobe) who covets the car because it can travel over water and mistakenly kidnaps Grandpa Potts. Caractacus, Truly and the youngsters pursue the Baron to his kingdom of Vulgaria in their flying auto. Eventually they help liberate the imprisoned youth of the country—the Baron's wife (Anna Quayle) has forbidden children in her kingdom—and Vulgaria is now freed of the Baron's control. Back in England and into the reality of everyday life, Lord Scrumptious decides to purchase Potts' candy invention, while Caractacus and Truly plan to wed. As they leave with the children none of them is aware that Chitty Chitty Bang Bang—their "fine four-fendered friend"—is flying through the air.

There were several structural problems plaguing CHITTY CHITTY BANG BANG. Not only was the picture overly long, but it suffered from an uneasy mixture of reality and fantasy. In contrast to his vital, whimsical performance in MARY POPPINS, Dick Van Dyke seemed to walk through his Cockney role herein. Matters were not helped by Sally Ann Howes' bland appearance as the heroine; she was colorless in contrast to Julie Andrews of MARY POPPINS. Pinpointing the marketing problem with CHITTY CHITTY BANG BANG, *Variety* noted, ". . . . The mistake seems to have been made again that a 'children's film' is synonymous with a 'family film.' If SOUND OF MUSIC was certainly the latter, then MARY POPPINS remains the only example of the former which succeeded in drawing adults to theatres sans their progeny." Analyzing the musical in perspective, Ronald Bergen (*The United Artists Story,* 1981) offered, "Some of the sets and machines were amusing but . . . the movie was 145 minutes of badly-acted, sugar-coated whimsy, punctuated by dreadful songs and shoddy special effects."

In a year when FUNNY GIRL and OLIVER!, *qq.v.,* were *the* screen's major musicals, CHITTY CHITTY BANG BANG received only one Oscar nomination: Best Song ("Chitty Chitty Bang Bang") but lost to "The Windmills of Your Mind," the theme song from THE THOMAS CROWN AFFAIR.

THE CHOCOLATE SOLDIER (Metro-Goldwyn-Mayer, 1941) 102 minutes.

Producer, Victor Saville; director, Roy Del Ruth; based on the play *The Guardsman* by Ferenc Molnar; screenplay, Keith Winter, Leonard Lee, Ernest Vajda, Claudine West; art director, Cedric Gibbons; set decorator, Edwin B. Willis; costumes, Adrian; music, Oscar Straus; music director, Merrill Pye; music adaptors, Herbert Stothart, Bronislau Kaper; choreographer, Ernst Matray; sound supervisor, Douglas Shearer; camera, Karl Freund; editor, James E. Newcom.

Songs: "My Hero," "Sympathy," "The Flower Presentation," "Thank the Lord the War Is Over," "Ti-ra-la-la," "Seek the Spy" (Oscar Straus, Stanislaus Strange); "While My Lady Sleeps" (Bronislau Kaper, Gus Kahn); "Mephistopheles' Song of the Flea" (Modest Moussorgsky); "Mon Coeur S'Ouvre à Ta Voix" from the opera *Samson and Delilah* (Camille Saint-Saens).

Nelson Eddy (Karl Lang/Vasili Vasilovitch Vronofsky); Rise Stevens (Maria Lanyl); Nigel Bruce (Bernard Fischer); Florence Bates (Pugsy [Mme. Helene]); Dorothy Gilmore (Magda); Nydia Westman (Liesel, the Maid); Max Barwyn (Anton); Charles Judels (Klementor); Jack Lipson (Captain Masakroff); Leon Belasco (Waiter); Sig Arno (Emile); Dave Willock (Messenger Boy).

THE CHOCOLATE SOLDIER has a most intriguing history. It was based on the 1903 play, *Arms and the Man* by George Bernard Shaw, which was made into an opera by Oscar Straus, Rudolph Bernaurer and Leopold Jacobson in 1909 called *Der Tapfere Soldat* (The Chocolate Soldier). MGM acquired the rights to the music (but not to Shaw's play) and blended it into a remake of THE GUARDSMAN (1931), which had starred Alfred Lunt and Lynn Fontanne, who had first played in the stage production of the work in 1924. Despite the fact that it was only a medium-budget production, THE CHOCOLATE SOLDIER was nominated for three Academy Awards: Karl Freund's cinematography, Best Sound Recording by Douglas Shearer, and Herbert Stothart and Bronislau Kaper's music score.

Although they have been married for only six months, opera stars Karl Lang (Nelson Eddy) and Maria Lanyl (Rise Stevens) are constantly fighting, mainly because Karl believes Maria is having affairs and she thinks the same of him. Maria's friend Pugsy (Florence Bates) enjoys the scraps and does nothing to avert them, while their mutual friend, newspaper critic Bernard Fischer (Nigel Bruce), attempts to patch up their marital problems. After a performance one evening, the trio go to a restaurant. Karl has to leave suddenly and the jealous Maria insists it must be for a romantic rendezvous. Soon thereafter she meets noted Russian singer, Vasili Vasilovitch Vronofsky (Nelson Eddy), to whom she is attracted. Later Karl finds out about Vasili and he and Maria quarrel, but she continues to see the Russian. When Karl is away, Vasili spends the night with Maria. However, the next evening, during the new opera in which Maria and Karl co-star, he reveals that he was Vasili. When he accuses his wife of intentional infidelity, she tells him she knew of his ruse all along and that his kisses had given him away. The two then realize they are very much in love.

Nelson Eddy and Rise Stevens, who made her screen debut in the movie, recorded most of the score from THE CHOCOLATE SOLDIER for Columbia Records and it provided them with duets on the title song, "Forgive," "My Hero" and "Sympathy," while Nelson Eddy did outstanding solos on "While My Lady Sleeps," "Evening Star" and "Song of the Flea," and Stevens sang "Ti-ra-la-la."

In *The Films of Jeanette MacDonald and Nelson Eddy* (1975), Eleanor Knowles wrote, "THE CHOCOLATE SOLDIER is an agreeable little film that one wishes fervently had had better production numbers and that Eddy's 'Karl' scenes had not been misdirected. We also might have liked Miss Stevens a little more if she had been permitted to smile a little less." While viewers and critics did not take well to Nelson Eddy's work as the jealous Karl, most thoroughly enjoyed his hamming as the lusty Cossack. THE CHOCOLATE SOLDIER was sandwiched between NEW MOON (1940) and I MARRIED AN ANGEL (1942), *qq.v.,* the last two features starring Jeanette MacDonald and Nelson Eddy. THE CHOCOLATE SOLDIER was yet another effort to find a new leading lady for Eddy in the waning operetta film genre.

CITY IN FLAMES *see* IN OLD CHICAGO (essay).

CLOSE HARMONY (Paramount, 1929) 66 minutes.

Directors, John Cromwell, Edward Sutherland; story, Elsie Janis, Gene Markey; adaptor, Percy Heath; dialogue, John V. A. Weaver, Heath; sound, Franklin Hansen; camera, J. Roy Hunt; editor, Tay Malarkey.

Songs: "She's So I Dunno," "I Want to Go Places and Do Things," "I'm All A-Twitter, I'm All A-Twirl" (Richard A. Whiting, Leo Robin); "Twelfth Street Rag" (Euday L. Bowman, Spencer Williams).

Charles "Buddy" Rogers (Al West); Nancy Carroll (Marjorie Merwin); Harry Green (Max Mindel); Jack Oakie (Ben Barney); Richard "Skeets" Gallagher (Johnny Bey); Matty Roubert (Bert);

Ricca Allen (Mrs. Prosser); Wade Boteler (Kelly the Cop); Baby Mack (Sybil the Maid); Oscar Smith (George Washington Brown); Greta Grandstedt (Eva Larue); Gus Partos (Gustav); Jesse Stafford and His Orchestra (Themselves).

Singer-dancer Marjorie Merwin (Nancy Carroll), who headlines the posh Babylon Theatre for its manager, Max Mindel (Harry Green), takes a fancy to young bandleader Al West (Charles "Buddy" Rogers) and gets him an audition with Max. The band is a sensation and is signed for the season. However, Max is jealous over Marjorie's affection for Al and to make him look bad he hires the singing duo of Ben Barney (Jackie Oakie) and Johnny Bey (Richard "Skeets" Gallagher) to steal away the band's thunder. Marjorie sees through this ruse and causes a rift between the two singers by romancing each of them. Eventually, however, Al makes her tell the two men the truth. During a performance, Al plays all the band's instruments and is such a hit with the audience that Max offers him a lucrative contract. Marjorie and Al are reconciled.

Charles "Buddy" Rogers, known as "America's Boy Friend," had first teamed with pert, talented Nancy Carroll in the silent feature, ABIE'S IRISH ROSE (1928), and in the sound era they would follow CLOSE HARMONY with ILLUSION (1929) and FOLLOW THROUGH (1930). CLOSE HARMONY contained Leo Robin and Richard Whiting's "I Want to Go Places and Do Things" and "I'm All A-Twitter, I'm All A-Twirl" plus Euday L. Bowman's classic "Twelfth Street Rag." Perhaps the highlight of the film is the sequence where versatile musician-star Charles "Buddy" Rogers performs on *all* the band's instruments. This was actually a part of his own stage act and he allegedly also played a variety of instruments on his 1930 Columbia recording of "Sweepin' the Clouds Away," from PARAMOUNT ON PARADE (1930), *q.v.*, in which he also appeared, as did Nancy Carroll.

Reporting on this entry in a year crammed full with all-talking song-and-dance pictures, the *New York Times* judged it "An entertaining musical film," and added, "The plot is trivial and contains one of those situations that could have been explained away in few words . . . . The lines are delivered in a series of wise-cracking epigrams that caused those in the Rialto audience much amusement yesterday."

COAL MINER'S DAUGHTER (Universal, 1980) Color 125 minutes.

Executive producer, Bob Larson; producer, Bernard Schwartz; associate producer, Zelda Barron; director, Michael Apted; based on the autobiography by Loretta Lynn with George Vescey;

screenplay, Tom Richman; production designer, John Corso; art director, Lou Mann; set decorator, John M. Dwyer; costumes, Joe L. Tompkins; makeup, Mark Reedall; music supervisor, Owen Bradley; assistant directors, Dan Kolsrud, Katy Emde; technical adviser, David Skepner; sound, Jim Alexander; sound re-recording, Richard Portman, Roger Heman; supervising sound editor, Gordon Ecker, Jr.; special effects, Floyd Van Wey, Tom Delgenio; camera, Ralf D. Bode; second unit camera, William Birch; editor, Arthur Schmidt.

Songs: "I'm a Honky Tonk Girl," "You Ain't Woman Enough to Take My Man," "You're Lookin' at Country," "Coal Miner's Daughter" (Loretta Lynn); "The Great Titanic" (traditional); "There He Goes" (Eddie Miller, Derwood Haddock); "I Fall to Pieces" (Hank Cochran, Harlan Howard); "One's on the Way" (Shel Silverstein); "Back in My Baby's Arms" (Bob Montgomery); "Sweet Dreams" (Don Gibson); "Walking after Midnight" (Don Hecht, Alan Block); "Crazy" (Willie Nelson); "Walking the Floor Over You" (Ernest Tubb); "Blue Moon of Kentucky" (Bill Monroe); "It Wasn't God Who Made Honky Tonk Angels" (J. D. Miller); "Satisfied Mind" (Red Hayes, Jack Rhodes); "Amazing Grace" (traditional).

Sissy Spacek (Loretta Webb Lynn); Tommy Lee Jones (Doolittle "Mooney" Lynn); Levon Helm (Ted Webb); Phyllis Boyers (Clara Webb); Bill Anderson, Jr., Foister Dickerson, Malla McCown, Pamela McCown, Kevin Salvilla (Webb Children); William Sanderson (Junior Webb at Age Sixteen); Sissy Lucas, Pat Paterson, Brian Warf, Elizabeth Watson, (Loretta and Mooney's Children); Beverly D'Angelo (Patsy Cline); Robert Elkins (Bobby Day); Bob Hannah (Charlie Dick); Ernest Tubb (Himself); Jennifer Beasley (Patsy Lynn); Jessica Easley (Peggy Lynn); Michael Baisch (Storekeeper); Susan Kingsley (Girl at Fairgrounds); David Gray (Doc Turner); Royce Clark (Hugh Cherry); Gary Parker (Radio Station Manager); Billy Strange (Speedy West); Bruce Newman (Opry Stage Manager); Grant Turner (Opry Announcer); Frank Mitchell (Washington Neighbor); Merle Kilgore (Cowboy at Tootsie's); Rhonda Rhoton (Lizzie); Vernon Oxford (Preacher); Ron Hensley (John Nenn); Doug Bledsoe (Cowboy at Grange Hall); Aubrey Wells (Red Lynn); Russell Varner (Bidder at Pie Auction); Tommie O'Donnell, Lou Headley, Ruby Caudrill (Teachers at Pie Auction); Charles Kahlenberg (Business Manager); Alice McGeachy (Woman with Doll); Ken Riley (Road Manager); Jim Webb (Bus Driver); Dave Thornhill, Don Ballinger, Zeke Dawson, Gene Dunlap, Durwood Edwards, Chuck Flynn, Lonnie Godfrey, Bob Hempker (Coal Miner's Band); Danny Faircloth, Charles

Gore, Doug Hauseman, Mike Noble, Daniel Sarenana, Billy West (Patsy Cline's Band); Roy Acuff, Minnie Pearl (Themselves).

Country singer Loretta Lynn's best-selling 1976 autobiography, *Coal Miner's Daughter* (the title of her 1970 Decca hit record), was brought to the screen in 1980. The Universal release not only grossed $38.5 million in distributors' domestic film rentals, but it also earned star Sissy Spacek an Academy Award as Best Actress. For her well-rounded performance as Loretta Lynn, which ranged from early teen years to Lynn's years of stardom. Spacek provided her own vocals on such Loretta Lynn standards as the title song (which also became a chart single for Spacek on MCA Records in 1980), "One's on the Way," "You Ain't Woman Enough to Take My Man," "Back in My Baby's Arms," "There He Goes" and "You're Lookin' at Country." The soundtrack album to COAL

Sissy Spacek in COAL MINER'S DAUGHTER (1980).

MINER'S DAUGHTER was on *Billboard* magazine's hits chart for one week at position #40.

In the post-World War II period, teenager Loretta Lynn (Sissy Spacek) lives in Butcher Holler, Kentucky, an impoverished coal mining area, with her parents (Levon Helm, Phyllis Boyers) and several siblings. At fourteen she meets ex-G.I. Doolittle "Mooney" Lynn (Tommy Lee Jones) at a church social and the two fall in love. They marry and later move to Washington state where they have four children while Loretta continues to compose songs and hopes to become a country singer. With Mooney's urging, she begins to perform in local bars and she composes a tune called "Honky Tonk Girl" which she records for Zero Records. It becomes a best-selling single. Relocating to Nashville with Mooney, Loretta is befriended by country music great Ernest Tubb (himself) and later becomes a close friend with singing star Patsy Cline (Beverly D'Angelo), both of whom help Loretta in her career climb. Within a few years Loretta is a top country singer. After taking time out to give birth to twin girls she begins the long grind of constant touring, which takes its toll on her health. She suffers a nervous breakdown, then, after recovering, continues her successful career.

Variety termed the movie ". . . A thoughtful, endearing film . . . [which] mostly avoids the sudsy atmosphere common to many showbiz tales and emerges as both a wonderful love story and convincing portrayal of one woman's life." While the two-hour-plus feature moved quickly, it did bog down at the finale, and suffered from a weak ending. Tom Milne (British *Monthly Film Bulletin*) observed, ". . . The last third of the film is something of a comedown after a lengthy stretch in which he [director Michael Apted] not only builds up a credibly complex relationship with equal injections of tenderness and humour, but brings the fresh, unprejudiced eye of a foreigner to backwoods America."

In addition to Sissy Spacek's topnotch emoting as Loretta Lynn, Beverly D'Angelo was most convincing as country-western legend Patsy Cline. She matched Spacek's vocal prowess by performing her own singing on such noted Cline hits as "Walking After Midnight," "Crazy" and "Sweet Dreams." Not only did COAL MINER'S DAUGHTER revitalize interest in Loretta Lynn, it also brought about a revival in the late Patsy Cline's popularity. In 1985 Jessica Lange starred as the singer in SWEET DREAMS, which used Patsy Cline's original recordings for its soundtrack.

COLLEGE HUMOR (Paramount, 1933) 68 minutes.

Director, Wesley Ruggles; story, Dean Fales; screenplay, Claude Binyon, Frank Butler; camera, Leo Tover.

Songs: "Down the Old Ox Road," "Learn to Croon," "Moonstruck," "Play Ball," "Alma Mater," "Colleen of Killarney," "I'm a Bachelor of the Art of Ha-Cha-Cha" (Arthur Johnston, Sam Coslow).

Bing Crosby (Professor Frederick Danvers); Jack Oakie (Barney Shirrel); Richard Arlen (Mondrake); Mary Carlisle (Barbara Shirrel); Mary Korman (Amber); George Burns (Himself); Gracie Allen (Herself); Joseph Sauers [Sawyer] (Tex Roust); Lona Andre (Ginger); and: James Burke, Jimmy Conlin, James Donlin, Lumsden Hare, Howard Jones, Jack Kennedy, Eddie Nugent, Robert Quirk, Churchill Ross, Grady Sutton.

Following his success in THE BIG BROADCAST (*q.v.*) the previous year, Bing Crosby received top billing for the first time in a breezy Paramount feature which combined music by Arthur Johnston and Sam Coslow with the studio's penchant for making college comedies. In the course of its brief running time (68 minutes), Bing Crosby crooned a quartet of songs: "Play Ball," "Moonstruck," "Down the Old Ox Road" and "Learn to Croon," the latter two becoming big hits for him on Brunswick Records. While Crosby handled the role of the music professor-crooner quite well and rambunctious Jack Oakie was in his element as his wise-cracking sidekick, it was Richard Arlen who stole the acting honors as the dumb football hero. As was traditional in such campus melees, the movie contained the *de rigueur* last reel football match.

Professor Frederick Danvers (Bing Crosby) begins teaching at a midwestern college where he attracts the attention of co-ed Barbara Shirrel (Mary Carlisle), thus making the school's football hero, Mondrake (Richard Arlen), jealous. Danver's pal, Barney Shirrel (Jack Oakie), also a gridiron star, tries to keep Mondrake away from him. Also mixed up in the mess are zany George (George Burns) and Grace (Gracie Allen) who operate a bizarre catering service on campus. While Mondrake and Barney help win the big football game for their alma mater, Danvers wins Barbara's love.

COLLEGIATE (Paramount, 1936) 80 minutes.

Producer, Louis D. Lighton; director, Ralph Murphy; based on the story "The Charm School" by Alice Duer Miller; screenplay, Walter DeLeon, Francis Martin; music director, George Stoll; camera, William Mellor; editor, Doane Harrison.

Songs: "I Feel Like a Feather in the Breeze," "You Hit the Spot," "Rhythmatic," "My Grandfather's Clock in the Hallway," "Who Am I?" "Guess Again," "Will I Ever Know," "Learn to Be Lovely" (Mack Gordon, Harry Revel).

Joe Penner (Joe); Jack Oakie (Jerry Craig); Ned Sparks

("Scoop" Oakland); Frances Langford (Miss Hay); Betty Grable (Dorothy); Lynne Overman (Sour Puss); Betty Jane Cooper (Dance Instructress); Mack Gordon, Harry Revel (Themselves); Henry Kolker (Mr. MacGregor); Donald Gallagher (Thomas J. Bloodgood); Albert Conti (Headwaiter); Julius Tannen (Detective Browning); Helen Brown (Dance Teacher); Johnny Wrey, Ted Shea, Bob Goodstein, Ruby Shaeffer, Jimmy Dime, Jack and Bob Crosby (Chorus Boys); Dorothy Jarvis, Katherine Hankin, Nancy Emery, Irene Bennett, Martha O'Driscoll (Chorus Girls); Edgar Dearing (State Trooper); Guy Usher (Lawyer); Marjorie Reynolds (Girl).

Paramount continued its 1930s infatuation with campus hi-jinks with COLLEGIATE, a remake of CHARM SCHOOL (1921, with Wallace Reid); SOMEONE TO LOVE (1928, with Charles "Buddy" Rogers) and SWEETIE (1929, with Nancy Carroll), *q.v.* It was an average musical comedy which boasted a number of listenable tunes by Mack Gordon and Harry Revel, both of whom appear as themselves as a part of the school's musical faculty. The two best songs in the feature are "You Hit the Spot" and "I Feel Like a Feather in the Breeze," both of which are sung by Frances Langford. Joe Penner, who romances Betty Grable on-camera, does the novelty tune, "Who Am I?" Betty Jane Cooper, appearing as herself, plays the dance instructor and does two tap-dance sequences, "Rhythmatic" being done in tandem with Jack Oakie.

Brash burlesque comic Jerry Craig (Jack Oakie) inherits a girls' charm school and attempts to get out of the deal. However, when he finds out that amnesiac Joe (Joe Penner) will provide all the money he needs to keep the school operating, Jerry decides to stay with it, especially after he meets one of the instructors, Miss Hay (Frances Langford). Also involved in the happenings are newspaperman "Scoop" Oakland (Ned Sparks) and his pal, Sour Puss (Lynne Overman), pretty co-ed Dorothy (Betty Grable) and Detective Browning (Julius Tannen), who eventually proves that Joe is really comedian Joe Penner!

While the snappy COLLEGIATE proved to be an amiable vehicle for the nonsense comedy of Joe Penner (who was far more popular on radio than in film), the programmer miscast double-take comedian Jack Oakie as the male lead. By now, at age thirty-three, he had become heavy set (to say the least) and hardly looked the romantic leading man the part required for its plot premise. The assignment might have better gone to studio contractees Fred MacMurray or Kent Taylor.

British release title: THE CHARM SCHOOL.

COVER GIRL (Columbia, 1944) Color 107 minutes.

Producer, Arthur Schwartz; director, Charles Vidor; based on the script by Erwin Gelsey; adaptors, Marion Parsonnet, Paul Gangelin; screenplay, Virginia Van Upp; art directors, Lionel Banks, Cary Odell; set decorator, Fay Babcock; music director, Morris W. Stoloff; music arranger/orchestrator, Carmen Dragon; choreographers, Val Raset, Seymour Felix, Gene Kelly, Stanley Donen; assistant directors, Jack Voglin, Bud Boetticher; sound, Lambert Day; camera, Rudolph Mate, Allen M. Davey; editor, Viola Lawrence.

Songs: "Make Way for Tomorrow" (Jerome Kern, E. Y. Harburg); "Long Ago and Far Away," "Put Me to the Test," "Sure Thing," "That's the Best of All," "The Show Must Go On," "Who's Complaining?", "Alter Ego" (Kern, Ira Gershwin); "Poor John" (Fred W. Leigh, Harry E. Pether).

Rita Hayworth (Rusty Parker/Maribelle Hicks); Gene Kelly (Danny McGuire); Lee Bowman (Noel Wheaton); Phil Silvers (Genius); Jinx Falkenburg (Jinx); Leslie Brooks (Maurine Martin); Eve Arden (Cornelia Jackson); Otto Kruger (John Coudair); Jess Barker (John Coudair as a Young Man); Anita Colby (Anita); Curt Bois (Chem); Edward Brophy (Joe); Thurston Hall (Tony Pastor); Jean Colleran, Francine Counihan, Helen Mueller, Cecilia Meagher, Betty Jane Hess, Dusty Anderson, Eileen McClory, Cornelia B. von Hessert, Karen X. Gaylord, Cheryl Archibald, Peggy Lloyd, Betty Jane Graham, Martha Outlaw, Susann Shaw, Rose May Robson (Cover Girls); Jack North (Harry the Drunk); Robert Homans (Pop, the Doorman); Eddie Dunn (Mac, the Cop); Sam Flint (Butler); Shelley Winters (Girl); Kathleen O'Malley (Cigarette Girl); William Kline (Chauffeur); Victor Travers (Bartender); Robert F. Hill (Headwaiter); John Tyrrell (Electrician); Frank O'Connor (Cook); Eugene Anderson, Jr. (Busboy); Sam Ash (Assistant Cook); Vin Moore (Waiter); Ralph Sanford, Ralph Peters (Truckmen); Barbara Pepper, Grace Leonard (Chorus Girls); Gwen Seager, Sally Cairns, Eloise Hart, Diane Griffith, Wesley Brent, Lucille Allen, Virginia Gardner, Helene Garron, Muriel Morris, Patti Sacks, Marion Graham (Cover Girl Contestants); Frances Morris (Coudair's Secretary); Billy Benedict (Florist Boy); William Sloan (Naval Officer); Grace Hayle, Fern Emmett (Women Columnists); Rudy Wissler, Glenn Charles, Jackie Brown (Boys); Ilene [Betty] Brewer (Autograph Hound); Warren Ashe (Rusty's Interviewer); John Dislon (Rusty's Photographer); Jack Rice (Reporter); Sam Flint (Coudair's Butler); Ed Allen (Best Man); George Lessey (Minister); Miriam Lavelle, Miriam Franklin, Ronald Wyckoff (Specialty Dancers); Grace Gillern, Eddie Cutler,

Randolph Hughes, Jack Bennett, George Dobbs, Al Norman, Larry Rio, Jack Boyle, Virginia Wilson, Betty Brodel (Dancers); Johnny Mitchell (Pianist, Maribelle's Love); Patti Sheldon (Girl); Martha Mears (Singing Voice of Rusty Parker).

"In 1944, the same year in which MEET ME IN ST. LOUIS [*q.v.*] was released by MGM, another musical turned up to alter the direction of the genre . . . . It was perhaps the quintessential musical film of the forties, a movie perched squarely between past and future. COVER GIRL looks backward in its foolish backstage plot and in some of its conventional musical numbers. Yet it also looks forward to the late forties and beyond in the emergence of Gene Kelly as an important film dancer and in the unforced exuberance and innovative style of other of its musical numbers." (Ted Sennett, *Hollywood Musicals,* 1981).

COVER GIRL was one of redheaded pin-up queen Rita Hayworth's most popular World War II starring vehicles. More-

Rita Hayworth and Gene Kelly in COVER GIRL (1944).

over, this stylish motion picture did a great deal to boost the film stock of dancer Gene Kelly. Hayworth, Kelly and Phil Silvers (who delivered a funny comedy performance as their pal) delightfully danced to the exuberant "Make Way for Tomorrow" (on roller skates!), while the film's romantic ballad, "Long Ago and Far Away," was nominated for an Oscar, as was the picture's color cinematography and its interior color decorations. On her vocals Rita Hayworth was dubbed by Martha Mears. A subplot in the picture had Rita's character playing her own grandmother in turn-of-the-century flashbacks, with both women almost making the same romantic error, since the grandmother had once loved, and given up, the magazine editor played by Otto Kruger. To parade a rash of beauties before the camera, the movie incorporated a sequence featuring contemporary cover girl models.

Wise-cracking magazine editor Cornelia "Stonewall" Jackson (Eve Arden) is ordered by her suave boss John Coudair (Otto Kruger) to locate the perfect cover girl for his magazine. Following a nationwide contest, the prize goes to Brooklyn nightclub chorine Rusty Parker (Rita Hayworth), who loves her dance partner, Danny McGuire (Gene Kelly). The publicity surrounding her appearance on the publication's cover makes Rusty a well known personality, and Broadway producer Noel Wheaton (Lee Bowman) offers to star her in his stage production. She and Danny argue over her new-found fame and Rusty begins a romance with Wheaton, agreeing not only to star in his show but also to marry him. At the altar, Rusty has a change of heart and returns to Danny.

". . . COVER GIRL was important in that it marked [Gene] Kelly's transition from hoofer to dancer, his famous 'alter ego' sequence being remarkably advanced for its time. . . . The rest of the numbers . . . were far less innovative. . . . COVER GIRL was important to Gene Kelly's career in that it contained several elements which he would later refine, rework and enlarge in some of his musicals at MGM" (Clive Hirschhorn, *The Hollywood Musical,* 1981). COVER GIRL was the continuation of the working relationship between Gene Kelly and choreographer (later director) Stanley Donen; they had worked together in the Broadway production of *Pal Joey* (1940).

To be noted: COVER GIRL was the first producing assignment for songwriter Arthur Schwartz; the first musical film for Hungarian-born director Charles Vidor, and *the* motion picture which elevated borrowed MGM performer Gene Kelly to major screen stardom. This was Rita Hayworth's third 1940s musical at her home studio; she had already co-starred in Columbia's YOU'LL NEVER GET RICH (1941) and YOU WERE NEVER LOVELIER

(1942), *q.v.*, teamed in both with Fred Astaire. After the triumph of COVER GIRL, Columbia Pictures' head Harry Cohn purchased the screen rights to *Pal Joey* to reteam Hayworth and Kelly. But by then, MGM would not reloan Kelly and the project was shelved until 1957 (*q.v.*) when Frank Sinatra starred with Kim Novak in the musical. In the resultant film Rita Hayworth was relegated to playing the sophisticated older woman.

CURLY TOP (Fox, 1935) 75 minutes.

Producer, Winfield Sheehan; director, Irving Cummings; based on the novel *Daddy Long Legs* by Jean Webster; screenplay, Patterson McNutt, Arthur Beckhard; music, Ray Henderson; music director, Oscar Bradley; choreographer, Jack Donohue; camera, John Seitz.

Songs: "Curly Top" (Ted Koehler, Ray Henderson); "The Simple Things in Life," "When I Grow Up" (Edward Heyman, Henderson); "Animal Crackers," "It's All So New to Me" (Koehler, Irving Caesar, Henderson).

Shirley Temple (Elizabeth Blair); John Boles (Edward Morgan); Rochelle Hudson (Mary Blair); Jane Darwell (Mrs. Denham);

John Boles, Shirley Temple and Rochelle Hudson in CURLY TOP (1935).

Rafaela Ottiano (Mrs. Higgins); Esther Dale (Aunt Genevieve Graham); Etienne Girardot (Mr. Wyckoff); Maurice Murphy (Jimmie Rogers); Arthur Treacher (Butler).

Shirley Temple had become Fox's top box-office draw and one of the most popular of film stars following her big splash in STAND UP AND CHEER (*q.v.*) for the studio in 1934. Thanks to the Fox features, BABY TAKE A BOW, BRIGHT EYES (both 1934), THE LITTLE COLONEL and OUR LITTLE GIRL (both 1935), Shirley was keeping the lot afloat financially during the bleak years of the Depression. While CURLY TOP was in production, Fox merged with 20th Century Pictures to become 20th Century-Fox, with Darryl F. Zanuck becoming studio chief. Until the end of the decade, Shirley Temple would remain a potent box-office draw for the new company.

Little Elizabeth Blair (Shirley Temple) and older sister Mary (Rochelle Hudson) are orphaned following the death of their parents. Playboy Edward Morgan (John Boles) takes a shine to Elizabeth and wants to adopt her. However, in order to do, he must also become Mary's guardian. Two society bluenoses (Jane Darwell, Rafaela Ottiano) attempt to block Edward's actions, while his Aunt Genevieve Graham (Esther Dale) and Elizabeth try to promote a romance between Edward and Mary. Eventually their ploy is successful; Edwin and Mary plan to wed and to legally keep Elizabeth.

An endearing remake of DADDY LONG LEGS, which had been filmed with Mary Pickford in 1919 and again by Fox in 1931 with Janet Gaynor and Warner Baxter, CURLY TOP was a loose reworking of the old chestnut which would be filmed yet again under its original title by 20th Century-Fox in 1955 (*q.v.*) with Fred Astaire and Leslie Caron. CURLY TOP provided a showcase for Shirley Temple to be adorable and precocious, to ooze optimism, dance (including a hula) and be musically versatile. The picture contains two of her best remembered songs, "Animal Crackers" and "When I Grow Up." John Boles crooned the title song (while Shirley danced on a piano top) and "It's All So New to Me." Also memorable were Esther Dale as the wise old aunt and Arthur Treacher as the stuffy butler, constantly intoning "my word" and succumbing to Shirley's charms.

DADDY LONG LEGS (20th Century-Fox, 1955) Color 126 minutes.

Producer, Samuel G. Engel; director, Jean Negulesco; based on the novel and the play by Jean Webster; screenplay, Phoebe Ephron, Henry Ephron; art directors, Lyle Wheeler, John De Cuir; set decorators, Walter M. Scott, Paul S. Fox; music, Johnny Mercer,

Alex North; music director, Alfred Newman; choreographers, Roland Petit, David Robel, Fred Astaire; camera, Leon Shamroy; editor, William Reynolds.

Songs: "Something's Gotta Give," "The Slue-Foot," "The Daydream Sequence," "Dancing through Life," "History of the Beat," "C-A-T Spells Cat," "Daddy Long Legs," "Welcome Egghead," "Dream" (Johnny Mercer).

Fred Astaire (Jarvis Pendleton); Leslie Caron (Julie); Terry Moore (Linda); Thelma Ritter (Miss Pritchard); Fred Clark (Griggs); Charlotte Austin (Sally); Larry Keating (Alexander Williamson); Kathryn Givney (Gertrude); Kelly Brown (Jimmy McBride); Sara Shane (Pat); Numa Lapeyre (Jean); Ann Codee (Madame Sevanne); Steven Geray (Emile); Percival Vivian (Professor); Helen Van Tuyl (College Dean); Damian O'Flynn (Larry Hamilton); Ralph Dumke (Mr. Bronson); Ray Anthony and His Orchestra (Themselves); Joseph Kearns (Guide); Larry Kent (Butler); Charles Anthony Hughes (Hotel Manager); Kathryn Card (Miss Carrington); Harry Seymour (Cab Driver); J. Anthony Hughes (Deliveryman); George Dunn (Chauffeur); Janice Carroll (Athletic Girl Dancer); Gertrude Astor (Woman); David Hoffman, Paul Bradley (Jewelers); Guy Des Rochers (French Lieutenant); Carleton Young, Paul Power (Commission Members); William Hines (Army Sergeant); Frank Kreig (French Farmer); Bob Adler (Deliveryman); Diane Jergens, Marjorie Hellen [Leslie Parrish] (College Girls).

Veteran dancing star Fred Astaire had been with MGM since 1945, except for loanouts to Paramount for BLUE SKIES (1946) and LET'S DANCE (1950), *qq.v.*, and he had success in a number of screen musicals. But by the mid-1950s the popularity of such movie fare was fading. In 1955 Astaire went to 20th Century-Fox for DADDY LONG LEGS, one of his lesser musical efforts. In fact, he was to make only two more 1950s musicals, FUNNY FACE (1957) and SILK STOCKINGS (1957), *qq.v.*, before turning to character parts. Although DADDY LONG LEGS was slickly made, there was no real on-camera chemistry between fifty-five-year-old Astaire and twenty-four-year-old Caron. The latter was far more at home partnered with Gene Kelly in AN AMERICAN IN PARIS (1951), *q.v.* DADDY LONG LEGS' main appeal came in its music score by Johnny Mercer, chiefly in the catchy song, "Something's Gotta Give."

As a small homeless girl in France, Julie (Leslie Caron) was cared for by an unknown sponsor she dubbed "Daddy Long Legs," and as the years went by she attempted unsuccessfully to learn his identity. Entering an American college, Julie continues her efforts. Meanwhile, the benefactor's personal secretary, Miss Pritchard

Fred Astaire and Leslie Caron in DADDY LONG LEGS (1955).

(Thelma Ritter), finally convinces her employer, Jarvis Pendleton (Fred Astaire), a wealthy businessman, to reveal himself. Reluctantly Jarvis goes to the college and there meets Julie, but only belatedly admits that he has been her sponsor. The two become attracted to one another and, after considerable discussion about their age difference, they plan to marry, as does Miss Pritchard, who is romantically involved with Griggs (Fred Clark), Jarvis' business manager.

To fill out the musical portion of DADDY LONG LEGS there was "The Slue-Foot," danced by Astaire, Caron and a room full of students (including Terry Moore) to the sounds of Ray Anthony and His Orchestra. The number was conceived in the hopes of repeating the success of those invented dance crazes that appeared in several of the 1930s Astaire-Ginger Rogers movies. The weakest talent link in DADDY LONG LEGS was choreographer Roland Petit, whose chief "contributions" were two extended dream ballets ("The Daydream" and "Dancing through Life") designed for Astaire, Caron and company. Shot in widescreen and gaudy color, these fantasy sequences were obvious and uninspired. Much better was Astaire's Drum Dance.

The *New York Times* wrote, "Fred Astaire's durable, incomparable footwork and the grace of the lovely Leslie Caron as his newest partner highlight an otherwise okay but rather frail and worn story structure. . . . It's a picture whose heart—along with the feet of the two stars—is in the right place, no question about it."

DADDY LONG LEGS was nominated for an Oscar for Best Song ("Something's Gotta Give") as well as for Best Scoring of a Musical Picture and for Best Art Direction—Color. Based on the 1912 novel by Jean Webster, DADDY LONG LEGS was first made as a silent movie in 1919 starring Mary Pickford, and in 1931 a talkie version starred Janet Gaynor at Fox. The same studio reworked the old chestnut into a Shirley Temple musical in 1935 called CURLY TOP (*q.v.*).

DAMES (Warner Bros., 1934) 90 minutes.

Producer, Darryl F. Zanuck; director, Ray Enright; story, Robert Lord, Delmer Daves; screenplay, Daves; art directors, Robert Haas, Willy Pogany; costumes, Orry-Kelly; music director, Leo F. Forbstein; choreographer, Busby Berkeley; camera, Sid Hickox, George Barnes; editor, Harold McLernon.

Songs: "Dames," "The Girl at the Ironing Board," "I Only Have Eyes for You" (Al Dubin, Harry Warren); "When You Were a Smile on Your Mother's Lips" (Irving Kahal, Sammy Fain); "Try to See It My Way" (Mort Dixon, Allie Wrubel).

Joan Blondell (Mabel Anderson); Dick Powell (Jimmy Higgens); Ruby Keeler (Barbara Hemingway); ZaSu Pitts (Mathilda Hemingway); Hugh Herbert (Ezra Ounce); Guy Kibbee (Horace); Arthur Vinton (Bulger); Sammy Fain (Buttercup Baumer); Phil Regan (Johnny Harris); Arthur Aylesworth (Conductor); Leila Bennett (Laura, the Maid); Berton Churchill (H. Elsworthy Todd); Patricia Harper, Ruth Eddings, De Don Blunier, Gloria Faythe, Diana Douglas (Chorus Girls); Lester Dorr (Elevator Starter); Eddy Chandler (Guard); Harry Holman (Spanish War Veteran); Fred "Snowflake" Toones (Porter); Frank Darien (Druggist); Eddie Kane (Harry, the Stage Manager); Charlie Williams (Dance Director); Phil Tead (Reporter); Johnny Arthur (Billings, the Secretary).

By this point the Busby Berkeley-directed Warner Bros. musicals were more showcases for his elaborate musical numbers than anything else. They were becoming threadbare in terms of plot. Thus, despite fine casts drawn from the studio's stock company, these outings were beginning to wear thin. "DAMES differed so little from the previous Berkeley musicals that only an expert can separate it from the others. . . . The title song—[co-composer Harry] Warren claims that he and [co-composer Al]

Dubin tried to come up with a song in every picture that more or less summed up the whole thing—serves a good purpose for Berkeley to launch into another of his complicated, fanciful routines involving geometrically displayed girls" (Tony Thomas, *The Hollywood Musical,* 1975).

Rich reformer Ezra Ounce (Hugh Herbert) promises his cousin Horace P. Hemingway (Guy Kibbee) ten million dollars because he is a moral man. However, the gift will be made only on condition that Hemingway head the Ounce Society for the Elevation of American Morals and that he keeps out their young relative, Jimmy Higgens (Dick Powell), who is involved in theatrics. Taking a train home, Horace finds himself stranded in a sleeping compartment with chorus girl Mabel Anderson (Joan Blondell) and he gives her money on condition that she keep the matter quiet. When she reaches New York City, Mabel tries to get into Jimmy's new Broadway show but he informs her he does not

Joan Blondell, Dick Powell and Ruby Keeler in DAMES (1934).

have the money to produce it. She acquires the funds by blackmailing Horace about the train incident. Meanwhile, Jimmy's girlfriend, Barbara (Ruby Keeler), Horace's daughter, becomes jealous of his involvement with Mabel and breaks off their engagement. When the show is cast, Barbara wins a dancing role. Later, Ezra plans to close the show by hiring hooligans to break up the musical production. Taking medicine which is laced with liquor, Ezra and Horace go to the theatre to witness the show being closed. When the fracas orchestrated by Ezra's hirelings commences, the police arrive and everyone is carted off to jail. Behind bars, Ezra decides he prefers the company of chorus girls to reforming, while Horace must explain the situation to his strait-laced wife Mathilda (ZaSu Pitts), as Jimmy and Barbara become re-engaged.

This was the fourth of seven Warner Bros. musicals to team Ruby Keeler and Dick Powell and the fourth of them to be directed by Busby Berkeley.* As in all these mind-boggling collaborations, the plot formula had boy meeting and winning the girl in a backstage setting, with several musical segments filled with chorines dancing to precision Berkeley choreography. The three song-and-dance highlights of DAMES were the snappy "Dames," the love ballad "I Only Have Eyes for You," and the surrealistic "The Girl at the Ironing Board," all created by songwriters Warren and Dubin. "Dames" featured a bevy of blonde chorus girls weaving to and fro in intricate patterns bolstered by trick photography while Powell crooned the lyrics about the joys of gorgeous womanhood. Set in a Gay Nineties' atmosphere, "The Girl at the Ironing Board" focused on Joan Blondell (who knew how to sock across a number in talk-song fashion) as a young laundress reciting her tale of lovelorn woe to the collection of men's long underwear and pajamas she is ironing. As the number proceeds, the laundry begins dancing about on its own. "By far the most memorable item . . . is 'I Only Have Eyes for You.' One of the best songs ever written for a film, it is sung by Powell and beautifully staged by Berkeley. Dick and Ruby meet in front of a movie theatre, then take a long subway ride during which they fall asleep. As Powell dreams—hordes of girls appear, all wearing Benda masks of Ruby so that an army of Keelers assaults the eye. Each girl, with a board on her back, bends over, and fitting the boards together, a gigantic jigsaw picture of

---

*The seven Dick Powell-Ruby Keeler musicals at Warner Bros. were: 42nd STREET (1933), THE GOLDDIGGERS OF 1933 (1933), FOOTLIGHT PARADE (1933), DAMES (1934), *qqv.*, and FLIRTATION WALK (1934), SHIPMATES FOREVER (1935), COLLEEN (1936).

Ruby's face appears." (Tony Thomas, Jim Terry, *The Busby Berkeley Book,* 1973).

The *New York Herald Tribune* noted, "The plot is trite, the jokes are rather stale, and the coherence of the story is often far from clear. The songs, however, are gay and lilting." The *New York Times* decided, "Does not quite attain the standard set by FORTY-SECOND STREET, even though it is amply eye-filling."

DAMN YANKEES (Warner Bros., 1958) Color 110 minutes.

Producers/directors, George Abbott, Stanley Donen; based on the musical play by Abbott, Douglas Wallop, Richard Adler, Jerry Ross, and the novel *The Year the Yankees Lost the Pennant* by Wallop; screenplay, Abbott; production designers/costumes, William Eckart, Jean Eckart; art director, Stanley Fleischer; choreographers, Bob Fosse, Pat Ferrier; camera, Harold Lipstein; editor, Frank Bracht.

Songs: "Heart," "Whatever Lola Wants," "Shoeless Jo from Hannibal Mo," "There's Something about an Empty Chair," "Two Lost Souls," "A Little Brains, a Little Talent," "Those Were the Good Old Days," "Goodbye, Old Girl," "Six Months out of Every Year," "The Game," "Who's Got the Pain" (Adler, Ross).

Tab Hunter (Joe Hardy); Gwen Verdon (Lola); Ray Walston (Applegate); Russ Brown (Van Buren); Shannon Bolin (Meg); Nathaniel Frey (Smokey); Jimmie Komack (Rocky); Rae Allen (Gloria); Robert Shafer (Joe Boyd); Jean Stapleton (Sister); Albert Linville (Vernon); Bob Fosse (Mambo Dancer); Elizabeth Howell (Doris); Pat Ferrer (Dancer).

George Abbott and Douglas Wallop based their two-act musical comedy *Damn Yankees* on Wallop's unpublished novel *The Year the Yankees Lost the Pennant,* which finally saw print in 1957. With music and lyrics by Richard Adler and Jerry Ross, the show debuted on Broadway on May 5, 1955, starring Gwen Verdon and Ray Walston, and ran for 1,019 performances. In 1958, Warner Bros., which had filmed Broadway's PAJAMA GAME the year before, brought the production to the screen with Gwen Verdon, Ray Walston and Jean Stapleton repeating their stage parts.* As with PAJAMA GAME there was a concerted effort to mold the property into the demands of the motion picture medium without losing the qualities that had made the musical work on stage.

*DAMN YANKEES, like THE PAJAMA GAME on the Broadway stage, had employed the talents of songwriters Richard Adler and Jerry Ross, director George Abbott and choreographer Bob Fosse. PAJAMA GAME, on screen, starred Doris Day and John Raitt, and was co-directed by Abbott and Stanley Donen.

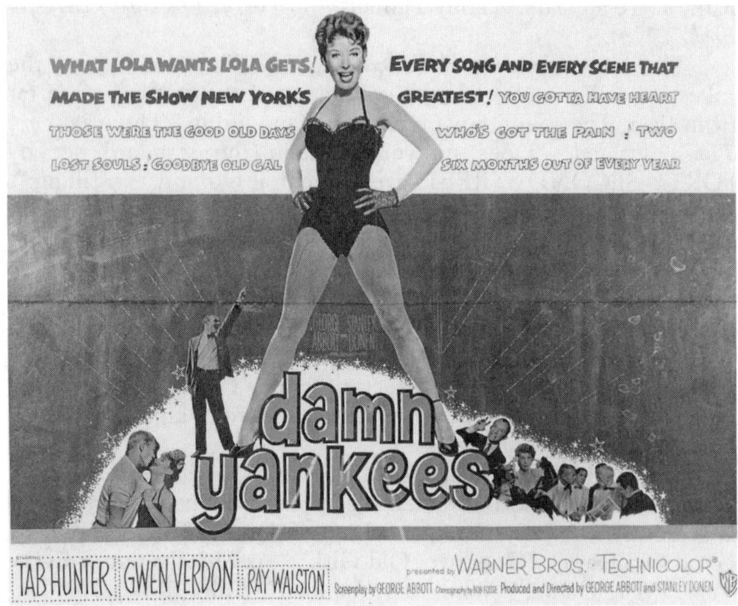

Advertisement for DAMN YANKEES (1958).

Wanting to be the greatest baseball player in history, aging Joe Boyd (Robert Shafer) readily sells his soul to the Devil, known as Mr. Applegate (Ray Walston). As a result he becomes young Joe Hardy (Tab Hunter) and soon is turned into the sensation of the Washington Senators baseball team. He leads his teammates to winning the national pennant over the New York Yankees and then, using an escape clause in his contract with Satan, returns to his wife Meg (Shannon Bolin). Wanting Joe's soul, Applegate enlists the aid of sexy Lola (Gwen Verdon) to bring Joe to Hell. However, Joe resists the seductive Lola and remains with his wife, thus thwarting the devil's machinations.

While the songs in DAMN YANKEES fit well into the musical's plot, the best remembered number was Gwen Verdon's energetic solo, "Whatever Lola Wants." She also performed a fine modern ballet to "Two Lost Souls." The *New York Times* noted, "Gwen Verdon's screen debut as a star . . . puts real zing and fire into this reasonable screening of the stage musical comedy. . . . The idea of a baseball musical now comes across, amid actual game sequences, as a little too earthbound. The stage suggestion was more intriguing. And there are some arid, conversational patches now. But Miss Verdon is wonderful, lifting the movie bodily as the torrid, wiggling vamp. . . ." As for Tab Hunter in the lead male role, what he lacked in dramatic ability or singing talent was made up for (according to studio logic) by his appeal to young moviegoers. The soundtrack album popped onto *Billboard* magazine's hits chart for one week at position #20.

British release title: WHAT LOLA WANTS.

A DAMSEL IN DISTRESS (RKO, 1937) 100 minutes.

Producer, Pandro S. Berman; director, George Stevens; based on the play by P. G. Wodehouse, Ian Hay and the novel by Wodehouse; screenplay, Wodehouse, S. K. Lauren, Ernest Pagano; art directors, Van Nest Polglase, Carroll Clark; music director, Victor Baravelle; orchestrator, Robert Russell Bennett; additional arrangements, Ray Noble, George Bassman; choreographer, Hermes Pan, (uncredited) Fred Astaire; assistant director, Argyle Nelson; special effects, Vernon L. Walker; camera, Joseph H. August; editor, Henry Berman.

Songs: "A Foggy Day," "Nice Work If You Can Get It," "The Jolly Tar and Milkmaid," "Stiff Upper Lip," "I Can't Be Bothered Now," "Put Me to the Test," "Sing of Spring," "Things Are Looking Up" (George Gershwin, Ira Gershwin); "Ah Che A Voi Perdoni Iddio" from the opera *Martha* (Friedrich von Flotow).

Fred Astaire (Jerry Halliday); George Burns (Himself); Gracie Allen (Herself); Joan Fontaine (Lady Alyce Marshmorton); Reginald Gardiner (Keggs); Ray Noble (Reggie); Constance Collier (Lady Caroline Marshmorton); Montagu Love (Lord John Marshmorton); Harry Watson (Albert); Jan Duggan (Miss Ruggles); Pearl Amatore, Betty Rone, Mary Dean, Jac George (Madrigal Singers); Joe Niemeyer (Halliday Impersonator); Bill O'Brien (Chauffeur); Mary Gordon (Cook); Ralph Brooks, Fred Kelsey (Sightseers); Major Sam Harris (Dance Extra); Mario Berini (Singing Voice of Keggs).

Wanting to make a feature without Ginger Rogers, dapper Fred Astaire starred in A DAMSEL IN DISTRESS. RKO contractee Joan Fontaine was cast as his leading lady when British musical comedy star Jessie Matthews turned down the part. Besides the elegant dancing and pleasing vocals of Fred Astaire, the well-appointed movie contained a pleasing George and Ira Gershwin music score, the comedy (and dancing) antics of George Burns and Grace Allen, plus a fine supporting cast. Nevertheless, it did *not* catch on with the public and was a box-office disappointment (the first such for Astaire). It caused RKO to quickly reteam the charming Astaire with spunky Ginger Rogers in CAREFREE (1937), *q.v.*

DAMSEL IN DISTRESS cast Fred Astaire as footloose American dancing star Jerry Halliday, who arrives in London with zany cohorts George Burns and Gracie Allen. The elegant dancer quickly falls in love with upper crust British heiress Lady Alyce Marshmorton (Joan Fontaine), who is kept a near prisoner at the family estate at Totleigh Castle. He must combat the prejudice of her snobbish relatives to win her affections.

DAMSEL IN DISTRESS was ably directed by George Stevens, who took great pains to hide Joan Fontaine's lack of dancing ability by using various camera angles in near long shots. In fact, the Astaire-Fontaine dance to "Things Are Looking Up," as staged by Hermes Pan, is one of the lesser moments in the production. Among the movie's better moments are the Gershwins' songs, "A Foggy Day" (sung by Astaire in a dense atmosphere near the Marshmorton estate) and "Nice Work If You Can Get It" (during which he enthusiastically plays an assortment of percussion instruments), and to a lesser extent, "Put Me to the Test" (danced by Astaire, Burns and Allen). Perhaps the surprise highlight of the feature was Astaire and Burns and Allen dancing/cavorting to "Stiff Upper Lip" as they go through a funhouse. The sequence earned Hermes Pan an Oscar.

In analyzing the film, *Variety* weighed, "Libretto is bright and the dialog funny. Some of it is more Burns and Allen than P. G. Wodehouse, but what price screen-credit?. . . . Astaire is Astaire all the way. . . . Joan Fontaine is passively fair as the ingenue, nicely looking the role but otherwise undistinguished."

A DAMSEL IN DISTRESS was a remake of a 1920 silent film starring June Caprice, issued by Pathé. The 1937 edition was Oscar-nominated for Best Interior Decoration.

DANCE OF LIFE (Paramount, 1929) Color Sequences 115 minutes. (Also silent version: 7,488′).

Associate producer, David O. Selznick; directors, John Cromwell, A. Edward Sutherland; based on the play *Burlesque* by George Manker Watters, Arthur Hopkins; screenplay, Benjamin Glazer, Watters; titles, Julian Johnson; choreographer, Earl Lindsay; sound, Harry D. Mills; camera, J. Roy Hunt; editor, George Nichols, Jr.

Songs: "True Blue Lou," "King of Jazzmania," "Cuddlesome Baby," "Flippity Flop," "Ladies of the Dance" (Sam Coslow, Richard A. Whiting, Leo Robin).

Nancy Carroll (Bonny Lee King/Bonny Kane); Hal Skelly

(Ralph "Skid" Johnson); Ralph Theodore (Harvey Howell); Charles D. Brown (Lefty); Dorothy Revier (Sylvia Marco); Al St. John (Bozo the Clown); May Boley (Gussie); Oscar Levant (Jerry); Gladys Du Bois (Miss Sherman); James T. Quinn (Jimmy); James Farley (Champ Melvin); George Irving (Minister); Thelma McNeal ("Lady of India"); Gordona Bennett, Miss La Reno, Cora Beach Shumway, Charlotte Ogden, Kay Deslys, Magda Blom (Amazon Chorus Girls); John Cromwell (Doorkeeper); A. Edward Sutherland (Theatre Attendant).

Hal Skelly came to Hollywood in 1929 to recreate his stage role in the successful theatrical production of *Burlesque* which he originated on Broadway in 1927 opposite Barbara Stanwyck; he also headlined the 1928–29 road company of the drama, which included Oscar Levant in the cast. Skelly proved to be a marvel in the film version, THE DANCE OF LIFE, and he made a half-dozen more features before his untimely death in 1934 at the age of forty-three.

Third-rate comic Skid Johnson (Hal Skelly) is fired from his burlesque job and ends up teaming with specialty dancer reject, Bonny Kane (Nancy Carroll). The duo form a successful act and soon marry. When Bonny becomes ill, Skid has a flirtation with dancer Sylvia Marco (Dorothy Revier), but he soon returns to Bonny. When she recovers, their act is resumed. Later Skid is signed for a Broadway show. He and Bonny are forced to separate as she goes on the road with a burlesque review. Skid is a hit on Broadway and again takes up with Sylvia, the star of the show. Meanwhile, Bonny meets rancher Harvey Howell (Ralph Theodore) and they fall in love. Skid, however, muffs his chance and loses his stage job. When he returns to the burlesque circuit he becomes a heavy drinker and frequently fails to appear for work. The stage manager (Charles D. Brown) asks Bonny to find him, and she does so. Her faith in him gets Skid through the opening night and the duo renew their love for each other.

Offering such Richard Whiting, Leo Robin and Sam Coslow songs as "True Blue Lou," "King of Jazzmania" and "Cuddlesome Baby," DANCE OF LIFE was one of the most successful of Hollywood's early talkies. It was bolstered by having one of the Ziegfeld-like stage production numbers lensed in two-color Technicolor. "It is the 'actingest' talkie seen so far, and at the same time, the most convincing," wrote *Motion Picture* magazine. Mordaunt Hall commented in the *New York Times,* "While the edges are taken off the story for those who witnessed the stage production, Mr. Skelly's portrayal of Skid Johnson is so excellent that it complements for patches of forced dialogue and unskilled acting by others in the cast of the picture."

DANCE OF LIFE was turned out by the directorial duo of John Cromwell (who plays a doorman) and Edward Sutherland (portraying the theatre attendant in the film), who had previously directed co-star Nancy Carroll in CLOSE HARMONY (*q.v.*) the same year. The support cast featured Oscar Levant and Charles D. Brown repeating their stage roles, while the part of Bozo the Clown went to silent film comedy star Al St. John.

The 1927 George Manker Watters and Arthur Hopkins play *Burlesque* has become a show business perennial. In addition to its many stage adaptations, it was filmed twice more: Paramount's SWING HIGH, SWING LOW (1937, with Carole Lombard and Fred MacMurray) and 20th Century-Fox's WHEN MY BABY SMILES AT ME (1948, with Betty Grable and Dan Dailey). In addition, there have been several television versions of *Burlesque,* with Bert Lahr headlining "NBC Dramatic Theatre" in 1949 and "Prudential Playhouse" in 1951. Buddy Ebsen was Skid Johnson in 1952 on "Broadway Television Theatre," Art Carney played the part on "Kraft Theatre" in 1954, and Dan Dailey, who starred as Skid in WHEN MY BABY SMILES AT ME, repeated the role on CBS-TV's "Shower of Stars" in 1955, with Marilyn Maxwell as Bonny and a supporting cast which included Joan Blondell, Jack Oakie (also from the 1948 film), Dick Foran, James Burke, Helen Stanley and Jack Benny in a cameo as himself.

DANCING LADY (Metro-Goldwyn-Mayer, 1933) 90 minutes.

Executive producer, David O. Selznick; associate producer, John W. Considine, Jr.; director, Robert Z. Leonard; based on the novel by James Warner Bellah; screenplay, Allen Rivkin, P. J. Wolfson; art directors/set decorators, Cedric Gibbons, Harry Oliver; costumes, Adrian; music/music director, Lou Silvers; choreographers, Sammy Lee, Edward Prinz; special effects, Slavko Vorkapich; camera, Oliver T. Marsh; editor, Margaret Booth.

Songs: "Heigh Ho, The Gang's All Here," "Let's Go Bavarian," "Everything I Have Is Yours" (Burton Lane, Harold Adamson); "That's the Rhythm of the Day" (Richard Rodgers, Lorenz Hart); "Hold Your Man" (Arthur Freed, Nacio Herb Brown); "Hey Young Fella," "Close Your Old Umbrella," "My Dancing Lady" (Dorothy Fields, Jimmy McHugh).

Joan Crawford (Janie Barlow); Clark Gable (Patch Gallagher); Franchot Tone (Tod Newton); Fred Astaire (Himself); Nelson Eddy (Himself); May Robson (Dolly Todhunter); Winnie Lightner (Rosette Henrietta La Rue); Robert Benchley (Ward King); Ted Healy (Steve); Moe Howard, Jerry Howard, Larry Fine (The Three Stooges); Gloria Foy (Vivian Warner); Maynard Holmes (Jasper

Bradley, Jr.); Sterling Holloway (Pinky, the Author); Florine McKinney (Grace Newton); Bonita Barker, Dale Dean, Shirley Aranson, Katharine Barnes, Lynn Bari (Chorus Girls); Jack Baxley (Barker); Frank Hagney (Cop); Pat Somerset (Tod's Friend); Charles Williams (Man Arrested in Burlesque House); Ferdinand Gottschalk (Judge); Eve Arden (Marcia, the "Southern" Actress); Matt McHugh (Marcia's Agent); Charlie Sullivan (Dabby); Harry Bradley, John Sheehan (Author's Pals); Stanley Blystone (Traffic Cop); Charles C. Wilson (Club Manager); Gordon [Bill] Elliott (Cafe Extra); Larry Steers, C. Montague Shaw (First Nighters); Art Jarrett (Art); Grant Mitchell (Bradley, Sr.)

After the overabundance of all-talking, all-singing, all-dancing movie musicals in the 1929–1930 period, the public was sated with such fare and Hollywood went out of its way to avoid the genre. Then Darryl F. Zanuck produced 42nd STREET (1933), *q.v.,* at Warner Bros. and it was such an enormous hit that not only did that studio produce a rash of similar ventures, but MGM wanted to join the celluloid hit parade. Meticulous producer David O. Selznick concocted the musical package known as DANCING LADY, a sumptuously mounted (in the great Metro tradition) backstage story which showcased the popular screen love team of Joan Crawford and Clark Gable.* (Ironically, off-camera it was Franchot Tone who was Crawford's then romantic interest and who became her husband from 1935 to 1939.) DANCING LADY proved to be a box-office bonanza.

Burlesque dancer Janie Barlow (Joan Crawford) wants to be a big musical comedy dancing star on Broadway. She uses her experience as a hoofer to land a job on the Great White Way but she wants to remain a moral young woman. Wealthy playboy Tod Newton (Franchot Tone) is attracted to Janie but she rejects his advances, so he proposes. He also offers her a job in the chorus of a new Broadway musical in which he has a financial interest. Janie accepts the dancing job and advises Tod she will marry him *only* if the show is a failure. So he sets out to sabotage the venture. Meanwhile, Janie begins rehearsals with the show's tough dance director, Patch Gallagher (Clark Gable). The latter dislikes Janie because he believes she used her influence through Newton to win the role. Patch makes fun of Janie in front of the cast, but she takes

*Joan Crawford and Clark Gable starred in several MGM features together: DANCE, FOOLS, DANCE (1931), LAUGHING SINNERS (1931), POSSESSED (1931), DANCING LADY (1933), CHAINED (1934), FORSAKING ALL OTHERS (1934), LOVE ON THE RUN (1936) and STRANGE CARGO. Of this group, only DANCING LADY was a musical.

it and soon proves herself to be a hard-working and talented performer. When it later appears that the show, through Tod's manipulations, will not open, the cast rallies behind Patch. They bring up the curtain on what turns out to be a big hit, with Janie becoming the show's major attraction. Tod relinquishes his claim to Janie, leaving her free to romance Patch.

While dynamic Joan Crawford was better suited to dramatic parts than to musicals, she acquits herself quite admirably in the title role of DANCING LADY. In the course of this gilt-edged musical drama, she tap-dances, sings, grimaces, swallows hard, cajoles and makes glittering lights shine from her ever so expressive eyes. On the other hand, Clark Gable's harassed and harassing dance director appears to be just an offshoot of Warner Baxter's trend-setting work on 42nd STREET. Both Fred Astaire and Nelson Eddy make their feature film debuts in the picture. The former danced with Crawford in the lavish "Let's Go Bavarian" number, while Eddy was the focal singer/tour guide in the "That's the Rhythm of the Day" routine which chronicled a historical montage of dances through the ages. The top song in the feature is "Everything I Have Is Yours," which was crooned by Art Jarrett and became a standard.* For comedy relief, the film boasted Robert Benchley as well as Ted Healy and The Three Stooges. The choreography by Sammy Lee and Edward Prinz owed a great deal to the influence of Busby Berkeley.

In evaluating DANCING LADY, Mordaunt Hall (*New York Times*) offered, "It is for the most part quite a lively affair. . . . The closing interludes are given over to a lavishly staged spectacle which by some stroke of magic the leading male character is supposed to put on in an ordinary sized theatre. It looks as though it might be better suited to the Yale Bowl or Chicago's Soldier Field."

Made at a cost of $923,000 during sixty-five days of production, the film grossed $1,667,000.

A DATE WITH JUDY (Metro-Goldwyn-Mayer, 1948) Color 113 minutes.

Producer, Joe Pasternak; director, Richard Thorpe; based on characters created by Aleen Leslie; screenplay, Dorothy Cooper, Dorothy Kingsley; art directors, Cedric Gibbons, Paul Groesse; set decorators, Edwin B. Willis, Richard A. Pefferie; costumes, Helen

*Originally Joan Crawford was to have sung "Everything I Have Is Yours," but it was decided her vocal range was too narrow. However, so that promotion could claim that she sings this number, during Art Jarrett's renditions she passes by the camera and hums a few bars of the melody.

Rose; music director, George Stoll; orchestrators, Leo Arnaud, Albert Sendrey, Robert Franklyn; choreographer, Stanley Donen; color consultants, Natalie Kalmus, Henri Jaffa; assistant director, Jerome Bergman; sound, Douglas Shearer, Norwood A. Fenton; special effects, Warren Newcombe; camera, Robert Surtees; editor, Harold F. Kress.

Songs: "Strictly on the Corny Side" (Stella Unger, Alec Templeton); "It's a Most Unusual Day" (Harold Adamson, Jimmy McHugh); "Judaline" (Don Raye, Gene De Paul); "I've Got a Date with Judy," "I'm Gonna Meet My Mary" (Bill Katz, Calvin Jackson); "Temptation" (Arthur Freed, Nacio Herb Brown); "Cuanto Le Gusta" (Ray Gilbert, Gabriel Ruiz); "Mulligatawny."

Wallace Beery (Melvin R. Foster); Jane Powell (Judy Foster); Elizabeth Taylor (Carol Pringle); Carmen Miranda (Rosita Conchellas); Xavier Cugat (Cugat); Robert Stack (Stephen Andrews); Selena Royle (Mrs. Foster); Scotty Beckett (Ogden "Oogie" Pringle); Leon Ames (Mr. Lucien T. Pringle); George Cleveland (Gramps); Lloyd Corrigan (Pop Scully); Clinton Sundberg (Jameson); Jean McLaren (Mitzie); Jerry Hunter (Randolph Foster); Buddy Howard (Jo-Jo Hoffenpepper); Lillian Yarbo (Nightingale); Eula Guy (Miss Clarke); Francis Pierlot (Professor Green); Rena Lenart (Olga); Sheila Stein (Little Girl in Drugstore); Alice Kelley (Girl); Polly Bailey (Elderly Woman); Fern Eggen (Miss Sampson); Paul Bradley (Headwaiter).

Based on the popular NBC radio series, "A Date with Judy" by Aleen Leslie, which ran from 1943–49, with Louise Erickson in the title role, this musical boasted a variety of tunes, most of which were performed by fast maturing teenager Jane Powell, the best being "Love Is Where You Find It" and "It's a Most Unusual Day." She also sang "Through the Years," "Judaline" and did a duet with Scotty Beckett on "I'm Strictly on the Corny Side" (with choreographed action by Stanley Donen). Carmen Miranda, in a comeback of sorts from earlier 1940s' stardom in 20th Century-Fox musicals, displayed her fiery style, backed by Xavier Cugat and His Band on "Cuanto Le Gusta" and "Cooking with Gas."

Judy Foster (Jane Powell) is a Santa Barbara, California teenager who has been dating Oogie Pringle (Scotty Beckett), but she meets and falls in love with older Stephen Andrews (Robert Stack). More problems arise for Judy when she mistakenly thinks her father Melvin (Wallace Beery) is romancing Rosita Conchellas (Carmen Miranda), south-of-the-border singer who works for bandleader Xavier Cugat (himself). To complicate problems even further, Judy discovers she has a rival for Stephen in beautiful Carol Pringle (Elizabeth Taylor), Oogie's sister. Eventually all works out well when Judy understands that she really cares for Oogie and that her dad is not romancing Rosita but is taking rumba dance lessons from her in order to surprise her mother (Selena Royle).

Running nearly two hours, the modestly-budgeted A DATE WITH JUDY ". . . is loaded with youthful zest, making for gay, light entertainment" (*Variety*). The same trade paper added, "Joe Pasternak's production guidance is showmanly, backing the story with lusty, but not ostentatious, trappings that provided top-notch setting for music and fan. Casting is particularly apt. . . ."

A sitcom version of A DATE WITH JUDY came to television in 1951–52 on ABC-TV with Patricia Crowley as Judy Foster, while a summer 1952 and 1953 ABC-TV edition featured a new cast with Mary Linn Beller as Judy.

THE DAUGHTER OF ROSIE O'GRADY (Warner Bros., 1950) Color 104 minutes.

Producer, William Jacobs; director, David Butler; story, Jack Rose, Melville Shavelson; screenplay, Rose, Shavelson, Peter Milne; art director, Douglas Bacon; set decorator, Ben Bone; music, David Bullolph; orchestrator, Frank Perkins; music director, Ray Heindorf; choreographer, LeRoy Prinz; assistant director, Phil Quinn; color consultant, Michael Kovaleski; sound, Dolph Thomas; special effects, William McGann, H. F. Koenekamp; camera, Wilfrid M. Cline; editor, Irene Morris.

Songs: "My Own True Love and I" (M. K. Jerome, Jack Scholl); "As We Are Today" (Ernesto Lecuona, Charles Tobias); "Ma Blushin' Rosie" (Edgar Smith, John Stromberg); "The Rose of Tralee" (Charles Glover); "A Farm Off Old Broadway," "A Picture Turned to the Wall," "Winter, Winter" (A. Bryan-Gumble); "Winter Serenade," "The Daughter of Rosie O'Grady" (Monty C. Brice, Walter Donaldson).

June Haver (Patricia O'Grady); Gordon MacRae (Tony Pastor); James Barton (Dennis O'Grady); Debbie Reynolds (Maureen O'Grady); S. Z. "Cuddles" Sakall (Miklos Teretzky); Gene Nelson (Doug Martin); Sean McClory (James Moore); Marsha [Marcia Mae] Jones (Katie O'Grady); Jane Darwell (Mrs. Murphy); Irene Seidner (Mama Teretzky); Oscar O'Shea (Mr. Flannigan); Jack Lomas (Sergeant); Kendall Kapps (Actor); and Virginia Lee.

As the 1950s dawned in the age of the Cold War, Hollywood still continued to churn out fluffy period musicals. All this, despite the fact that audiences were quickly tiring of this type of fare, which had reached its crest during the World War II years. By now June Haver was enjoying a brief vogue as a top musical comedy star, and was still considered the likely replacement at her home lot (20th

Century-Fox) for fading Betty Grable. In 1949 Warner Bros. had borrowed Haver to star in LOOK FOR THE SILVER LINING, *q.v.* As part of the same deal Haver made THE DAUGHTER OF ROSIE O'GRADY for Warner Bros.* This color outing featured several vintage songs, but it also boasted two nice new melodies: "As We Are Today," sung by Gordon MacRae, and "My Own True Love and I," performed by June Haver and James Barton.

In post-Spanish-American War New York City, Patricia O'Grady (June Haver) is the daughter of widower Dennis O'Grady (James Barton), a drunken ex-vaudevillian who has learned to hate show business since the death of his performer wife. Dennis makes a living as a horse cab driver to support Patricia and her two sisters, older Katie (Marsha [Marcia Mae] Jones), who is secretly wed to a policeman, and younger sibling Maureen (Debbie Reynolds). Much to her father's chagrin, Patricia wants to become a musical star like her late mother and is encouraged by family friend Miklos Teretzky (S. Z. "Cuddles" Sakall). After meeting show business impresario Tony Pastor (Gordon MacRae), Patricia breaks with her father and sets out to establish herself as a singing star. En route, she has romances with both Pastor and dancer Doug Martin (Gene Nelson) before finding success and reconciling with her dad.

Variety termed the picture ". . . Another of those familiarly patterned musicals with a backstage plot. It has charm, some wit, nice music and good pace. . . . Some of the dance numbers are expressive of the old school of vaude, in keeping with the story's period, and there are several good tunes ably delivered by MacRae and Miss Haver." While the picture was overburdened by stale genre formulas, a too bland performance by Haver and uninspired choreography by LeRoy Prinz, it did benefit from the presence of a very young, bubbling Debbie Reynolds.

THE DAUGHTER OF ROSIE O'GRADY would be June Haver's last loanout to Warner Bros., which by then was developing its own new musical comedy star, Doris Day.

DEEP IN MY HEART (Metro-Goldwyn-Mayer, 1954) Color 130 minutes.

Producer, Roger Edens; director, Stanley Donen; based on the book by Elliott Arnold; screenplay, Leonard Spigelgass; art directors Cedric Gibbons, Edward Caragno; music, Sigmund Romberg; music director, Adolph Deutsch; choral arranger, Robert Tucker;

---

*Betty Grable had starred in SWEET ROSIE O'GRADY (1943) at 20th Century-Fox, teamed with Robert Young and Reginald Gardiner.

choreographer, Eugene Loring; special effects, Warren Newcombe; camera, George Folsey; editor, Adrienne Fazan.

Songs: "The Leg of Mutton Rag," "One Kiss," "Deep in My Heart," "Riff Song," "The Desert Song," "Jazz Jazza, Doo, Do," "Miss U.S.A." (Sigmund Romberg); "It," "One Alone" (Romberg, Otto Harbach, Oscar Hammerstein); "I Love to Go Swimmin' with Wimmen" (Romberg, Ballard MacDonald); "Mr. and Mrs." (Romberg, Cyrus Wood); "The Road to Paradise," "Will You Remember?" (Romberg, Rida Johnson Young); "Serenade," "Your Land and My Land," (Romberg, Dorothy Donnelly); "Lover Come Back to Me," "You Will Remember Vienna," "Softly As in a Morning Sunrise," "When I Grow Too Old to Dream," "Stout-Hearted Men" (Romberg, Oscar Hammerstein II); "Auf Wiedersehn" (Romberg, Herbert Reynolds).

Jose Ferrer (Sigmund Romberg); Merle Oberon (Dorothy Donnelly); Helen Traubel (Anna Mueller); Doe Avedon (Lillian Romberg); Walter Pidgeon (J. J. Shubert); Paul Henreid (Florenz Ziegfeld); Tamara Toumanova (Gaby Delys); Paul Stewart (Bert Townsend); Isobel Elsom (Mrs. Harris); David Burns (Lazar Berrison, Sr.); Jim Backus (Ben Judson); Douglas Fowley (Harold Butterfield); Russ Tamblyn (Berrison, Jr.); Rosemary Clooney, Gene Kelly, Fred Kelly, Jane Powell, Vic Damone, Ann Miller, William Olvis, Cyd Charisse, James Mitchell, Howard Keel, Tony Martin, Joan Weldon (Guest Stars); Robert Easton (Cumberly); Suzanne Luckey (Arabella Bell); Ludwig Stossel (Mr. Novak); Else Neft (Mrs. Novak); Norbert Schiller, Torben Meyer (Card Players); Reuben Wendorff, Franz Roehn (Men); Laiola Wendorff (Woman); Henri Letondal (Francois); Lane Nakano (Japanese Butler); John Alvin (Mr. Mulvaney); Jean Vander Pyl (Miss Zimmerman); Mary Alan Hokanson (Miss Cranbrook); Maudie Prickett (Lady); Henry Sylvester (Judge); Bob Carson (Orchestra Leader); Robert Watson (Florist); Marjorie Liszt (Waitress); Gail Bonney, Jean Dante (Women Guests); Dulce Daye, Margaret Bacon, Gloria Moore, Lullumae Bohrman, Tailor Bosell, Richard Beavers (Bits); Gordon Wynne (Treasurer); Mitchell Kowall (Oscar Hammerstein); Joe Roach (Groom); Dee Turnell (Bride); Barrie Chase (Dancer in "I Love to Go Swimmin' with Wimmen" number).

Hollywood's penchant for biopics of famous composers was coming to a close when MGM filmed Sigmund Romberg's life (1887–1951) as DEEP IN MY HEART. Running well over two hours, the expensively mounted production followed the usual path for such affairs, complete with a sugar-coated look at its subject, surrounded by many guest stars (here a cornucopia!) performing the composer's works. More than a dozen Romberg tunes were featured in the proceedings, ranging from his best known works to lesser but still pleasing melodies culled from his more than fifty Broadway operettas and musicals.

The film opens with a special dedication: "To all those who love the music of Sigmund Romberg." Hungarian engineer-turned-composer Sigmund Romberg (Jose Ferrer) arrives in America in the pre-World War I era, makes a living as a musician and begins composing dance music. He soon has a cafe orchestra and eventually he is hired to compose songs for Broadway producer J. J. Shubert (Walter Pidgeon). For a time he writes popular shows, then, finally, he gets to do what he wants: create operettas. His first major success is *Maytime* in 1917. He has worked for cafe owner Anna Mueller (Helen Traubel), the woman becomes Romberg's mentor, and now begins teaming with elegant Dorothy Donnelly (Merle Oberon), who becomes his lyricist. Eventually illness takes Dorothy's life, but Romberg's success continues. He meets beautiful Lillian (Doe Avedon) and the two fall in love and marry.

"Unless the sweet, sentimental melodies of Sigmund Romberg lie deep in your heart and you don't mind clichés, you'd better have a strong digestive system for this Hollywoodized bilge, stringing out a harmless vaudeville cavalcade of his numbers of the years and threading them with an asinine little drama purporting to represent the composer's life." (*New York Times*).

In terms of songs DEEP IN MY HEART has its rewards, particularly in Helen Traubel's film debut, in which she sings "Auf Wiedersehn, "Softly As in a Morning Sunrise" and "Stout Hearted Men." There was Tony Martin's robust rendition of "Lover Come Back to Me" and Gene and Fred Kelly dancing to the comical "I Love to Go Swimmin' with Wimmen." On the other hand, there was Jane Powell and Vic Damone's embarrassing duet of "Will You Remember?" which only made audiences recall more fondly Jeanette MacDonald and Nelson Eddy singing this famous tune in MAYTIME (1937), *q.v.* The soundtrack album to DEEP IN MY HEART stayed on *Billboard* magazine's hits chart for sixteen weeks, rising to position #4.

Originally, in 1950, Arthur Freed was to have produced THE ROMBERG STORY (as it was then called), Kurt Kasznar was to have starred, with Lana Turner making a special guest appearance as continental-style performer Gaby Delys. Romberg himself was to have appeared in a special prologue. By the time the production became an actuality, Freed's long-time associate Roger Edens was given his first solo production assignment and Jose Ferrer (a very strange casting choice that proved fortuitous) was hired to play

Romberg. Ballerina Tamara Toumanova was cast as Gaby Delys, while Romberg did not make the special prologue, having died in 1951. An equally surprising bit of casting was the hiring of Metropolitan Opera star Helen Traubel to make her screen bow. Despite her age, height and girth, she proved a delightful presence. Cut from the final release print was Traubel singing "Dance My Darlings," Jane Powell's rendition of "One Kiss," and Esther Williams performing as an American Beauty Rose in an aqua pageant, for which George Murphy was the master of ceremonies and dancer.

Several months before the December 1954 premiere of DEEP IN MY HEART (Radio City Music Hall in New York; the Egyptian and Loew's State Theatres in Los Angeles), Romberg's final musical, *The Girl in Pink Tights,* opened posthumously on Broadway, running for 115 performances.

THE DESERT SONG (Warner Bros., 1929) Color Sequences 125 minutes.

Director, Roy Del Ruth; based on the operetta by Laurence Schwab, Otto Harbach, Frank Mandel, Oscar Hammerstein II, Sigmund Romberg; screenplay, Harvey Gates; costumes, Earl Luick; music, Romberg; sound, George R. Groves; camera, Bernard McGill; editor, Ralph Dawson.

Songs: "The Riff Song," "French Marching Song," "Then You Will Know," "The Desert Song," "Song of the Brass Key," "Sabre Song," "Romance," "One Alone," "One Flower Grows Alone in Your Garden," "My Little Catagnette" (Sigmund Romberg, Oscar Hammerstein II, Otto Harbach).

John Boles (The Red Shadow/Pierre Birbeau); Carlotta King (Margot); Louise Fazenda (Susan); Johnny Arthur (Bennie Kid, a Reporter); Edward Martindel (General Birbeau); Jack Pratt (Pasha); Otto Hoffman (Hasse); Robert E. Guzman (Sid El Kar); Marie Wells (Clementina); John Miljan (Captain Fontaine); Del Elliott (Rebel); Myrna Loy (Azuri).

See: THE DESERT SONG (1953) (essay).

THE DESERT SONG (Warner Bros., 1943) Color 90 minutes.

Producer, Robert Buckner; director, Robert Florey; based on the operetta by Laurence Schwab, Otto Harbach, Frank Mandel, Oscar Hammerstein II, Sigmund Romberg; screenplay, Buckner; art director, Charles Novi; music, Romberg, Heinz Roemheld; choreographer, LeRoy Prinz; camera, Bert Glennon; editor, Frank Magee.

Songs: "The Riff Song," "The Desert Song," "One Alone,"

"Romance," "French Military Marching Song," "One Flower Grows Alone in Your Garden" (Otto Harbach, Oscar Hammerstein II, Sigmund Romberg); "Fifi's Song" (Jack Scholl, Romberg); "Gay Parisienne" (Scholl, Serge Walters); "Long Live the Night" (Scholl, Mario Silva, Romberg).

Dennis Morgan (Paul Hudson); Irene Manning (Margot); Bruce Cabot (Captain Fontaine); Victor Francen (Caid Yousseff); Lynne Overman (Johnny Walsh); Gene Lockhart (Pere FanFan); Faye Emerson (Hajy); Marcel Dalio (Tarbouch); Felix Basch (Heinzelman); Gerald Mohr (Haasan); Noble Johnson (Abdel Rahman); Curt Bois (Francois); Albert Morin (Muhammad); Jack LaRue (Lieutenant Bertin); William Edmunds (Suliman); Wallis Clark (Pajot); Sylvia Opert (Dancer); and: Egon Brecher, Fritz Leiber, Nestor Paiva, Duncan Renaldo, George Renevent.

See: THE DESERT SONG (1953) (essay).

THE DESERT SONG (Warner Bros., 1953) Color 110 minutes.

Producer, Rudi Fehr; director, Bruce Humberstone; based on the operetta by Laurence Schwab, Otto Harbach, Frank Mandel, Oscar Hammerstein II, Sigmund Romberg; screenplay, Roland Kibbee; art director, Stanley Fleischer; music, Romberg, Max Steiner; music director, Ray Heindorf; choreographer, LeRoy Prinz; camera, Robert Burks; editor, William Ziegler.

Songs: "The Riff Song," "The Desert Song," "Long Live the Night," "Romance," "One Alone," "One Flower Grows Alone in Your Garden" (Otto Harbach, Oscar Hammerstein II, Sigmund Romberg); "Gay Parisienne" (Jack Scholl, Serge Walters, Romberg).

Kathryn Grayson (Margot); Gordon MacRae (Paul Bonnard/El Khobar); Steve Cochran (Captain Fontaine); Raymond Massey (Yousseff); Dick Wesson (Benjy Kidd); Allyn McLerie (Azuri); Ray Collins (General Birabeau); Paul Picerni (Hassan); Frank DeKova (Mindar); William Conrad (Lachmed); Trevor Bardette (Meri); Mark Dana (Lieutenant Duvalle).

Since its Broadway debut in 1926, *The Desert Song,* with songs by Sigmund Romberg, Oscar Hammerstein II, and Otto Harbach, has been one of the perennially favorite operettas of the stage with its romantic plot and resplendent songs (including "One Alone," "The Riff Song," "One Flower Grows Alone in Your Garden" and the title tune). The property first appeared on the Great White Way and ran for 471 performances with Robert Halliday and Vivienne Segal in the leading roles. Since that time there have been scores of major stagings of the operetta, both in the U.S. and abroad, and on three occasions it has been transferred to the big screen.

THE DESERT SONG was first made by Warner Bros. in 1929

and, like the other screen renditions, it adhered closely to the stage plot concocted by Laurence Schwab, Otto Harbach, Frank Mandel and Oscar Hammerstein II. The narrative is set in North Africa with the mysterious Red Shadow as the leader of a band of daring horsemen known as The Riffs. The Red Shadow is actually Pierre Birbeau (John Boles), the son of the French general (Edward Martindel) who commands his country's forces in the desert. Pierre pretends to be both weak-willed and light-minded to disguise his Riff activities. However, when his father favors a marriage between the girl, Margot (Carlotta King), he loves and Captain Pierre Fontaine (John Miljan), who is secretly in league with local sheiks, Pierre takes on the guise of The Red Shadow and carries Margot to the desert palace of an ally (Jack Pratt). The commandant arrives at the palace and challenges The Red Shadow to a duel. Rather than fight his own father he refuses, and loses the respect of his men. He then disappears into the desert. Meanwhile, General Birbeau is told by Margot about his son's identity. After Fontaine's nefarious activities are exposed, Pierre is welcomed home as a hero and wins Margot's love.

Issued in the spring of 1929, THE DESERT SONG was the first sound film operetta with Technicolor sequences. *Photoplay* magazine said it was "a bit old fashioned and stagey" (which was being kind), but noted "Some good singing by John Boles." The highlight of the picture was its use of the fine music score plus the effective work of John Boles as the elusive The Red Shadow and Myrna Loy as an evil but alluring native dancer. Released as musical films were nearing their apex in popularity at the beginning of the sound era, THE DESERT SONG was a big box-office hit, despite its primitive sound (the industry was then making vast technical leaps almost weekly) and the very wooden performance of Carlotta King.

Warner Bros. remade the vehicle during World War II to accommodate the public's demand for light, non-depressing fare. The resulting production, with its updated storyline to encompass the Allies versus Axis struggle, again captured the flavor of the operetta with Dennis Morgan as Paul Hudson, The Red Shadow, Irene Manning as Margot and Bruce Cabot as the evil Captain Fontaine. The *New York Times* reported, "This brash and gaudy picture is relaxing entertainment and spirited fun." This edition excised some of the original songs and added other operetta standards like "Gay Parisienne" and "Long Live the Night."

A decade after the remake, the studio filmed the project for the third time, in Technicolor like the second outing. Gordon

Kathryn Grayson and Gordon MacRae in THE DESERT SONG (1953).

MacRae was Paul Bonnard, now alias El Khobar, Kathryn Grayson (of MGM) was Margot, Steve Cochran played Captain Fontaine and Raymond Massey was an evil sheik. The production harkened back to the original score, but the operetta's creaking plot showed through, as the *New York Times* noted: "Rudi Fehr's new production, alas, batters the old war horse with such a wealth of dull, slipshod absurdities that, songs notwithstanding, the wonders now is how it ever got by in the first place. . . . At this point, THE DESERT SONG may be considered dying of thirst."

By now the evergreen operetta was looking far better on stage than on screen. On July 7, 1955 producer Max Liebman presented a ninety-minute production of "The Desert Song" on NBC-TV with Nelson Eddy as The Red Shadow, Gale Sherwood as Margot and John Conte as Fontaine. On TV the old warhorse proved to be fine entertainment, especially when Nelson Eddy (then fifty-four years old) and Gale Sherwood sang the beautiful Romberg-Hammerstein II melodies. In this same period, Nelson Eddy and Doretta Morrow recorded the venerable score for Columbia Records.

DIRTY DANCING (Vestron, 1987) Color 100 minutes.

Executive producers, Mitchell Cannold, Steven Reuther; producer, Linda Gottlieb; co-producer, Eleanor Bergstein; associate producer, Doro Bachrach; director, Emile Ardolino; screenplay, Bergstein; production designer, David Chapman; art directors, Mark Haack, Stephen Lineweaver; set decorator, Clay Duffy; costumes, Hilary Rosenfeld; makeup, Gilbert La Chapelle, David Forrest; music, John Morris; music supervisors, Danny Goldberg, Michael Lloyd; period music consultant, "Cousin Brucie" Morrow; music editor, Joseph S. DeBeasi; choreographer, Kenny Ortega; sound, John Pritchett, George Baetz, Doug Axtell, Roger Rhodes; sound re-recording, Rick Dior; supervising sound editor, Dan Sable; ADR editor, Anne Stein; camera, Jeff Jur; editor, Peter C. Frank; associate editor, Farrel Levy.

Songs: "Be My Baby" (Jeff Barry, Ellie Greenwich, Phil Spector); "Big Girls Don't Cry" (B. Gaudio, B. Crewe); "Merengue," "Johnny's Mambo" (Erich Bulling, John D'Andrea, Michael Lloyd); "Fox Trot," "Waltz" (Michael Lloyd, D'Andrea); "Where Are You Tonight?" (Mark Scola); "Do You Love Me?" (Berry Gordy); "Love Man," "These Arms of Mine" (Otis Redding); "Stay" (Maurice Williams); "Wipe Out" (The Surfaris); "Hungry Eyes" (Frank Previte, John DeNicola); "Overload" (Alfie Zappacosta,

Cynthia Rhodes, Jennifer Grey and Patrick Swayze in DIRTY DANCING (1987).

Marko Luciani); "Hey Baby" (Bruce Channel, M. Cobb); "De Todo un Poco" (Lou Perez); "Some Kind of Wonderful," "Will You Love Me Tomorrow?" (C. King, G. Goffin); "Cry to Me" (B. Russell); "Love Is Strange" (E. Smith, M. Baker, S. Robinson); "You Don't Own Me" (D. White, J. Madara); "Yes" (Terry Fryer, Neal Cavaugh, Tom Graf); "In the Still of the Night" (F. Parris); "She's Like the Wind" (Patrick Swayze, Stacy Widelitz); "(I've Had) The Time of My Life" (Previte, Donald Markowtiz, DeNicola).

Jennifer Grey (Frances "Baby" Houseman); Patrick Swayze (Johnny Castle); Jerry Orbach (Jake Houseman); Cynthia Rhodes (Penny Johnson); Jack Weston (Max Kellerman); Jane Bruckner (Lisa Houseman); Kelly Bishop (Marjorie Houseman); Lonny Price (Neil Kellerman); Max Cantor (Robbie Gould); Charles Honi Coles (Tito Suarez); Neal Jones (Billy Kostecki); "Cousin Brucie" Morrow (Magician); Wayne Knight (Stan); Paula Trueman (Mrs. Schumacher); Alvin Myerovich (Mr. Schumacher); Miranda Garrison (Vivian Pressman); Garry Goodrow (Moe Pressman); Antone Pagan (Staff Kid); Tom Cannold (Busboy); M. R. Fletcher, Jesus Fuentes, Heather Lee Gerdes, Karen Getz, Andrew Charles Koch, D. A. Pauley, Dorian Sanchez, Jennifer Stahl (Dirty Dancers); Jonathan Barnes, Dwyght Bryan, Tom Drake, John Gotz, Dwayne Malphus, Dr. Clifford Watkins (Tito's Band).

The highest grossing independent film of 1987, DIRTY DANCING, with an intake of $2,009,305 in distributors' domestic film rentals, was one of the surprise hits of the year's movie season. The feature was highlighted by Kenny Ortega's choreography and several songs, including the Oscar-winning "Time of My Life" and "She's Like the Wind" and "Hungry Eyes." "The title refers to the last touch-dancing craze to hit the country, a concatenation of undulating hips and rippling chests that bore white working class kids on a wave of soulful black music." (*Los Angeles Reader*). As a result of DIRTY DANCING (the title alone sold theatre tickets!), Patrick Swayze became a major movie star and the musical film genre continued to enjoy a minor rebirth begun by FAME (1980), *q.v.*, FLASHDANCE (1983) and FOOTLOOSE (1984).

In 1963 top-grade high school graduate Frances "Baby" Houseman (Jennifer Grey) vacations at Kellerman's Mountain House in the Catskills with her family: her doting physician father (Jerry Orbach), her loving mother (Kelly Bishop) and her bubble-headed sister (Jane Bruckner). After this annual summer vacation, Baby is scheduled to go to college in the fall, with eventual hopes of joining the Peace Corps. At Kellerman's Baby meets dancer Penny Johnson (Cynthia Rhodes), who is pregnant and wants to get an abortion. Befriending Penny, Baby is able to get the money for the operation from her father and at the same time she finds herself attracted to handsome Johnny Castle (Patrick Swayze). He is Penny's dance partner and also moonlights as a gigolo for the bored and rich housewives who frequent the upstate New York resort operated by Max Kellerman (Jack Weston). When Penny becomes ill after her bungled abortion—and is then medically treated by Dr. Houseman—Johnny teaches Baby the various dance steps he does with Penny and Baby takes over as his partner. She is also willingly seduced by the dancer. As the summer progresses, Baby finds herself growing up emotionally as she and Johnny perfect the dances which will get him and Penny work in the fall.

Variety reported, "Good production values, some nice dance sequences and a likeable performance by [Jennifer] Grey make the film more than watchable, especially for those acquainted with the Jewish tribal mating rituals that go on in the Catskill Mountain resorts." C. M. Firillo in *Films in Review* magazine (December 1987) judged, "Director Emile Ardolino, best known for his 1984 Academy Award-winning documentary feature, HE MAKES ME FEEL LIKE DANCIN', has put on film several terrific dance/seduction scenes and a spectacular grand finale reminiscent of music videos featuring ensemble dancers and marred only by a silly, melodramatic speech at the beginning."

The soundtrack album from the film (which incorporated many hit tunes from the Sixties with their original artists) sold more than eight million copies, while a follow-up disc, MORE DIRTY DANCING, passed the million mark in sales. The movie engendered a 1988 nation-wide concert tour of *The Dirty Dancing Show* (a portion of which was syndicated as a television special in 1989) as well as a rightfully short-lived 1988 CBS TV series, "Dirty Dancing," starring Patrick Cassidy as Johnny Castle and Melora Hardin as Baby. There is still occasional talk of producing a sequel, DIRTY DANCING II, to co-star Patrick Swayze and Jennifer Grey.

DISC JOCKEY (Allied Artists, 1951) 77 minutes.

Producer, Maurice Duke; director, Will Jason; story/screenplay, Clark E. Reynolds; art director, David Milton; set decorator, Otto Siegel; wardrobe, Courtney Haslam, Esther Krebs; makeup, Lou Filippi; music/music director, Russ Morgan; assistant director, Edward Morey, Jr.; sound, Tom Lambert; camera, Harry Neumann; editor, Otho Lovering.

Songs: "Let's Meander Through the Meadow," "Show Me You Love Me" (S. Steuben, Roz Gordon); "Nobody Wants Me," "After

Advertisement for DISC JOCKEY (1951).

Hours" (Gordon); "Disc Jockey," "In My Heart" (Herb Jeffries, Dick Hazard); "Peaceful Country," "Riders of the Purple Sage" (Foy Willing); "Brain Wave" (George Shearing); "Oh Look at Me Now" (John De Vries, Joe Bushkin); "The Roving Kind" (Jessie Cavanaugh, Arnold Stanton).

Ginny Simms (Vickie Peters); Tom Drake (Johnny); Jane Nigh (Marion); Michael O'Shea (Mike Richards); Lenny Kent (Happy); Jerome Cowan (Marley); Tommy Dorsey, George Shearing, Sarah Vaughan, Herb Jeffries, Nick Lucas, The Weavers, Jack Fina, Vito Musso, Red Nichols, Red Norvo, Ben Pollack, Joe Block (Themselves); Joe Adams, Joe Allison, Bill Anson, Doug Arthur, Don Bell, Paul Brenner, Bob Clayton, Paul Dixon, Ed Gallaher, Dick Gilbert, Bill Gordon, Maurice Hart, Bruce Hayes, Eddie Hubbard, Bea Kalmus, Les Malloy, Paul Masterson, Ed McKenzie, Tom Mercein, Gill Newsome, Gene Norman, Art Pallans, Bob Poole, Norman Prescott, Fred Robbins, Ernie Simon, Larry Wilson (Disc Jockeys).

Disc jockey-radio promoter Mike Richards (Michael O'Shea) is told by his main sponsor, Marley (Jerome Cowan), that disc jockeys are passé. He refuses to sign a new contract unless his advertising rates are greatly reduced. Marley also challenges Richards to develop a radio and recording star from an unknown by using disc jockeys to prove they are still effective. Meanwhile, Richards' secretary, Marion (Jane Nigh), is jealous because her boyfriend, Johnny (Tom Drake), has brought in a new singer, Vickie Peters (Ginny Simms) for Richards to audition, and Marion fears they are involved romantically. Richards likes Vickie's singing voice and decides to promote her as his new star. However, he does not have time to listen to Happy's (Lenny Kent) new discovery, vocalist H. J. Ball (Herb Jeffries). Enlisting the aid of a number of recording artists (Russ Morgan, Tommy Dorsey, Sarah Vaughan, Nick Lucas, George Shearing, The Weavers, Foy Willing and the Riders of the Purple Sage) and two dozen leading national disc jockeys, Richards transforms Vickie into a huge star in just a few weeks. When Vickie also becomes a disc jockey, jealous Marion deliberately mixes up the script of her on-the-air sales pitch for Marley's candy product. However, the ploy backfires and his sales skyrocket. As a result, Vickie is more popular than ever. Marion and Johnny reconcile and Marley signs a new contract with Richards as well as having romantic designs on Vickie.

By the early 1950s, disc jockeys virtually controlled the record market and which platters were played on the airwaves. This low-budget but pleasant musical featured a number of popular DJs from around the country, including Chicago's Eddie Hubbard and Ernie Simon, Paul Dixon from Cincinnati, Nashville's Joe Allison, Paul Brenner from Newark, and Los Angeles' Paul Masterson, Bill Anson, Gene Norman, Joey Adams and Maurice Hart. The movie was also loaded with musical numbers, the best being Nick Lucas crooning "Let's Meander Through the Meadow," George Shearing's "Brain Wave," "Peaceful Country" by Foy Willing and the Riders of the Purple Sage, The Weavers doing "The Roving Kind" and Herb Jeffries performing the title song and "In My Heart."

DIVINE MADNESS (Warner Bros., 1980) Color 94 minutes.

Executive producer, Howard Jeffrey; producer/director, Michael Ritchie; screenplay, Jerry Blatt, Bette Midler, Bruce Vilanch; production designer, Albert Brenner; costumes, choreographer, Toni Basil; music arrangers/supervisors, Tony Berg, Randy Kerber; Robert DeMora; assistant directors, Jack Roe, John Kretchmer; camera, William A. Fraker; editor, Glenn Farr.

Songs: "Big Noise from Winnetka" (Gil Rodin, Bob Crosby, Bob Haggart, Ray Bauduc); "Paradise" (Harry Nilsson, Gil Garfield, Perry Botkin, Jr.); "Shiver Me Timbers" (Tom Waits); "The Rose" (Amanda McBroom); "Fire Down Below" (Bob Seger);

"Stay with Me" (Jerry Ragovoy, George Weiss); "Chapel of Love" (Jeff Barry, Ellie Greenwich, Phil Spector); "Boogie Woogie Bugle Boy" (Don Raye, Hughie Prince); "E Street Shuffle" (Bruce Springsteen); "Summer (The First Time)" (Bobby Goldsboro); "Leader of the Pack" (George Morton, Barry, Greenwich); "I'm Ready to Begin Again" (Jerry Leiber, Mike Stoller); "Do You Wanna Dance?" (Bobby Freeman), "You Can't Always Get What You Want" (Mick Jagger, Keith Richards); "I Shall Be Released" (Bob Dylan).

Bette Midler (The Divine Miss M); Jocelyn Brown, Ula Hedwig, Diva Gray (The Harlettes); Irving Sudrow (Head Usher); Tony Berg, Jon Bonine, Joey Carbone, Randy Kerber (Band Vocals).

Wonderfully iconoclastic Bette Midler had long had a strong cult following for her outrageous stage persona when she won dramatic accolades for her performance in THE ROSE (*q.v.*) in 1979. No doubt due to its success, her then current stage show was brought to the screen the next year by Warner Bros., produced and directed by Michael Ritchie. On screen the "Divine Miss M" is backed by the Harlettes (Jocelyn Brown, Ula Hedwig, Diva Gray—replacing earlier Harlettes with whom she was feuding) and band vocalists Tony Berg, Jon Bonine, Joey Carbone and Randy Kerber. Increasingly, the concert film—especially of contemporary rock stars performing—was becoming the focus of film producers who wanted to turn out a musical entertainment, but did not want to chance creating a new score and/or book.

The film opens with some comedy by a character called Head Usher (Irving Sudrow), warning his subordinates how to act with the customers in the upcoming Bette Midler (herself) concert. The concert then begins and for the next one-and-one-half hours Midler sings, tells raunchy jokes and ingratiates herself with those in attendance. Her vocals range from such standard (and oldie) tunes as "The Rose," her version of the Andrews Sisters' "Boogie Woogie Bugle Boy," Bob Crosby's "Big Noise from Winnetka" and "Chapel of Love," to "Leader of the Pack" and "The E Street Shuffle." Along the way the star sports assorted outrageous costumes, pokes fun at Princess Margaret of England, imitates Bruce Springsteen, and recites her repertoire of Sophie Tucker jokes.

Janet Maslin wrote in the *New York Times*, "Miss Midler sings songs that don't necessarily suit her, trots about in outfits no one else could get away with and tells bawdy jokes so sweetly she makes the bawdiness almost beside the point. She gets away with most of this, and more. . . . Mr. Ritchie's style is generally unobtrusive; the direction calls attention to itself only when he abandons a close shot of Miss Midler to show a glimpse of her audience, or to view her from a distance. For all its elaborate staging—and the sets and costumes are often spectacular—Miss Midler's act is an intimate one, and it doesn't need to be interrupted in this way." Kevin Thomas (Los Angeles Times) enthused, ". . . For those of us who think Miss M really is divine, DIVINE MADNESS is pure, exhilarating joy, a definitive concert film culled from more than 90 hours of footage shot during three shows. . . . DIVINE MADNESS is definitely not for prudes."

Bette! Divine Madness had played on Broadway in December 1979 for forty performances. The movie version (94 minutes compared to the 2½-hour stage original) was shot at the Pasadena Civic Auditorium in March 1980 over a three-week period using ten cameras. Because she was ill during much of the filming, she re-recorded several of the numbers back at the studio. Midler called the movie "the time-capsule version of my act." The movie was a commercial disappointment and the Atlantic album of the movie (which contains "My Mother's Eye" by Tom Waits—cut from the film) was not a major seller. Regarding the film's lack of success, Midler would later admit, "It was all my fault. I made all the mistakes. The concert picture is a scary form. I felt it should have been peddled as a spectacle rather than as a concert, because there I was, making a spectacle of myself. In France, it was sold that way and did very, very well."

Perhaps the most creative aspect of DIVINE MADNESS (the film) was the promotional art work, which featured a shot of Mount Rushmore with Midler's profile sandwiched in between the carved stone faces of George Washington and Theodore Roosevelt, replacing that of Abraham Lincoln. The soundtrack album appeared briefly (three weeks) on *Billboard* magazine's hits chart, rising to #3 position.

THE DOLLY SISTERS (20th Century-Fox, 1945) Color 114 minutes.

Producer, George Jessel; director, Irving Cummings; based on the story by John Kenyon Nicholson; screenplay, John Larkin, Marian Spitzer; art directors, Lyle Wheeler, Leland Fuller; set decorators, Thomas Little, Walter M. Scott; music settings designer, Joseph C. Wright; costumes, Orry-Kelly; music directors, Alfred Newman, Charles Henderson; orchestrator, Gene Rose; choreographer, Seymour Felix; color consultants, Natalie Kalmus, Richard Mueller; assistant director, Henry Weinberg; sound, Arthur Kurbach; camera, Ernest Palmer; editor, Barbara McLean.

Songs: "I Can't Begin to Tell You" (Mack Gordon, James V. Monaco); "I'm Always Chasing Rainbows" (Joseph McCarthy, Harry Carroll); "Powder, Lipstick and Rouge" (Gordon, Harry Revel); "Give Me the Moonlight" (Lew Brown, Albert von Tilzer); "On the Mississippi" (Ballard MacDonald, Arthur Fields, Harry Carroll); "We Have Been Around" (Gordon, Charles Henderson); "Carolina in the Morning" (Gus Kahn, Walter Donaldson); "Arrah Go On, I'm Gonna Go Back to Oregon" (Joe Young, Sam Lewis, Bert Grant); "Darktown Strutters' Ball" (Shelton Brooks); "The Vamp" (Byron Gay); "Hungarian Dance No. 5 in F Sharp Minor" (Johannes Brahms); "Smiles" (Will Callahan, Lee S. Roberts); "Oh Frenchie" (Sam Ehrlich, Con Conrad); "Pack Up Your Troubles" (Felix Powell, George Asaf); "Mademoiselle from Armentières" (traditional); "The Sidewalks of New York" (James Blake, Charles B. Lawlor).

Betty Grable (Jenny Dolly); John Payne (Harry Fox); June Haver (Rosie Dolly); S. Z. Sakall (Uncle Latsie); Reginald Gardiner (Duke); Frank Latimore (Irving Netcher); Gene Sheldon (Professor Winnup); Sig Rumann (Tsimmis); Trudy Marshall (Lenore); Colette Lyons (Flo Daly); Evon Thomas (Jenny as a Child); Donna Jo Gribble (Rosie as a Child); Robert Middlemass (Oscar Hammerstein); Paul Hurst (Dowling); Lester Allen (Morrie Keno); Frank Orth (Stage Manager); Sam Garrett (Will Rogers); J. C. Fowler (Al Smith); Betty Farrington (Mrs. Al Smith); Virginia Brissac (Nun); Charles Evans (Man); George O'Hara (Frank Tinny); Ricki Van Dusen (Madame Polaire); J. Farrell MacDonald (Doorman); Herbert Ashley (Fields); William Nye (Bartender); Julius Tannen (Man); Walter Soderling (Train Conductor); Harry Seymour (Pianist); George Davis (French Juggler); Trudy Berliner (German Actress); Igor Lolgoruki (Russian Actress); Nino Bellni (French Actor); Theresa Harris (Ellabelle); Mary Currier (Hammerstein's Secretary); Andre Charlot (Phillipe); Edward Kano (Harris); Mae Marsh (Flower Lady); Else Janssen (Kathi).

Twentieth Century-Fox mogul Darryl F. Zanuck wanted to bring Alice Faye back to the screen in 1945 to appear with Betty Grable in THE DOLLY SISTERS. When she refused the part, it went to producer George Jessel's protégé, June Haver, who became a star thanks to the picture and a studio rival to Grable. The Dolly Sisters (Jenny and Rosie) were popular performers, primarily dancers, in pre-World War I musicals and they had success abroad in the early 1920s. This screen offering was only very loosely based on their lives, even to the point of having two blonde stars doing the leads, when the real Dolly Sisters were brunettes.

In 1912 two eighteen-year-old Hungarian girls, Jenny (Betty

Grable) and Rosie (June Haver), who have been in the United States since 1904, begin singing in beer gardens with their doting Uncle Latsie (S. Z. "Cuddles" Sakall) as their manager. They become headliners at Hammerstein's (Robert Middlemass) music hall in New York City and this leads to their becoming the singing and dancing stars of Broadway. Jenny, meanwhile, has met and fallen in love with song-and-dance man-composer Harry Fox (John Payne). She and Fox marry and Harry continues growing in stature as a songwriter-performer. When World War I breaks out, Harry enlists and is shipped to France. Jenny, who has been downplaying her career in favor of domesticity, agrees to go to Paris to perform with her sister at the Folies Bergère. They are a huge hit. With the war over, Harry begs Jenny to return to the States but she refuses to abandon her sister in the midst of their show business success. Fox tells her to get a divorce and he returns to New York to pursue his career, while the Dolly Sisters become the toast of Continent. Romantically, Jenny is pursued by a British nobleman (Reginald Gardiner), with whom she is riding the night his car crashes. While Jenny recuperates, she urges her sister to wed wealthy young

Betty Grable and June Haver in THE DOLLY SISTERS (1945).

American Irving Netcher (Frank Latimore). Rosie and Irving return to America. In 1921 Jenny comes to New York, having recovered from her injuries but now financially strapped. At an all-star benefit performance, she and Harry are joyfully reunited.

With two gorgeous stars, lavish sets and costumes, Technicolor, and a catalog of old and new songs, THE DOLLY SISTERS could not help but be a financial success. As the trade paper *Harrison's Reports* noted, "The production values are up to the customary lavish stand set by this company for musicals of this type, and the staging of the different musical sequences, particularly the 'Darktown Strutter's Ball' number, is novel and ingenious." *Variety* endorsed, "As with many another yesteryear showbiz figure . . . historical, chronological and biographical accuracy takes to the Hollywoods when the main intent is to entertain. . . . Regardless of biographical authenticity, this film resurrects a a golden era of the theatre and the international set of the early 1900s." The *New York Times* was less appreciative, "It is a tired and long-drawn stencil of so many old musical film plots that even the legs of Betty Grable and June Haver fail as adequate support. . . . [It is] the purely mechanical agitation of a couple of modern pinup girls." In retrospect, Clive Hirschhorn (*The Hollywood Musical,* 1981) observed, "The musical numbers were staged by Seymour Felix with such kitschy vulgarity (especially a gaudy item glorifying a woman's make-up kit called 'Powder, Lipstick and Rouge' . . .) that viewed today, they cannot be considered as anything other than monuments to bad taste. At the same time, what cannot be denied is just how compulsively enjoyable they are."

THE DOLLY SISTERS revived many popular turn-of-the-century tunes like "Carolina in the Morning," "Dear Old Pal of Mine" and "Frenchy," and introduced a hauntingly appealing new song entitled "I Can't Begin to Tell You," along with "Don't Be Too Old-Fashioned." The film's main theme, however, was "I'm Always Chasing Rainbows." In the picture its composition is accredited to Harry Fox, but in reality it was written by Harry Carroll and Joseph McCarthy.

John Payne was one of the better but more overlooked cinema leading men in musical comedies. This dependable performer came to 20th Century-Fox in 1940 and appeared in several musicals with Betty Grable, including FOOTLIGHT SERENADE (1942) and SPRINGTIME IN THE ROCKIES. He had co-starred with Alice Faye in TIN PAN ALLEY (1940), *q.v.*, THE GREAT AMERICAN BROADCAST (1941) WEEKEND IN HAVANA (1941) and HELLO, FRISCO, HELLO (1943), *q.v.* Payne's only other picture with June Haver was the moody fantasy, WAKE UP AND

DREAM (1946). Two other staples of Hollywood's musical comedies found in THE DOLLY SISTERS were S. Z. "Cuddles" Sakall,* the bespectacled, bulky Hungarian actor known for his nervous mannerism (and his shaking wattles), and British Reginald Gardiner,** noted for portraying snobbish butlers or charming noblemen.

DOWN ARGENTINE WAY (20th Century-Fox, 1940) Color 92 minutes.

Producer, Darryl F. Zanuck; associate producer, Harry Joe Brown; director, Irving Cummings; story, Rian James, Ralph Spencer; screenplay, Darrell Ware, Karl Tunberg; art directors, Richard Day, Joseph C. Wright; music director, Emil Newman; choreographers, Nick Castle, Geneva Sawyer; camera, Leon Shamroy, Ray Rennahan; editor, Barbara McLean.

Songs: "South American Way" (Al Dubin, Jimmy McHugh); "Down Argentine Way," "Sing to Your Senorita," "Two Dreams Met," "Nenita" (Mack Gordon, Harry Warren); "Mama Yo Quiero" (Al Stillman, Jaraca Paiva, Vincente Paiva); "Doin' the Conga" (Gene Rose); "Bambu" (Patricia Teixeira, Donga).

Don Ameche (Ricardo Quintana); Betty Grable (Glenda Crawford); Carmen Miranda (Herself); Charlotte Greenwood (Binnie Crawford); J. Carrol Naish (Casiano); Henry Stephenson (Don Diego Quintana); Katharine Aldridge (Helen Carson); Leonid Kinskey (Tito Acuna); Chris-Pin Martin (Esteban); Robert Conway (Jimmy Blake); Gregory Gaye (Sebastian); Bobby Stone (Panchito); Charles Judels (Ambassador); Nicholas Brothers, Thomas and Catherine Dowling (Dance Specialties); Six Hits and a Miss, Flores Brothers, Banda Da Lua (Themselves); Edward Fielding (Willis Crawford); Edward Conrad (Anastasio); Fortunio Bonanova, Armand Kaliz (Hotel Managers); Frank Puglia (Montero); Carlos Albert (Spanish Singing Voice of Ricardo Quintana).

Ricardo Quintana (Don Ameche) brings a group of horses to the United States from his ranch in the Argentine Pampas where his father, Don Diego Quintana (Henry Stephenson), raises the thoroughbreds. Ricardo is supposed to sell the animals to wealthy New Yorker Glenda Crawford (Betty Grable) and her mother

---

*S. Z. Sakall would be reteamed with June Haver in three additional features: OH YOU BEAUTIFUL DOLL (1949), LOOK FOR THE SILVER LINING (1949), *q.v.*, and THE DAUGHTER OF ROSIE O'GRADY (1950), *q.v.*

**Reginald Gardiner additionally played with Betty Grable in SWEET ROSIE O'GRADY (1943), THAT LADY IN ERMINE (1948), and WABASH AVENUE (1950). He was with June Haver in I WONDER WHO'S KISSING HER NOW (1947) and I'LL GET BY (1951).

Binnie (Charlotte Greenwood). However, when he arrives in the United States he discovers that the two families have a feud of long standing. Although stymied in his plan to sell his prize-winning jumpers to Glenda, he and Glenda begin a romance. Later he has to return to South America. Glenda and Binnie soon travel to Argentina and there they meet entertainer Carmen Miranda (herself). Glenda and Ricardo resume their romance. They try to convince his proud, stubborn father to end the feud and to recognize that his best, a prize-winning jumper, is actually a championship racing horse. Eventually all is cleared up and the two lovers are free to wed.

By signing Brazilian bombshell Carmen Miranda (then performing on Broadway in *Streets of Paris;* her scenes were shot in New York City) and featuring her in this Technicolor musical, 20th Century-Fox smartly played up the then voguish interest in South America. The studio's recurring interest in Latin themes in the early 1940s would be a wise decision. When World War II shut off many European and Asian film markets, 20th Century-Fox could still count on good grosses south-of-the-border. Here Carmen Miranda is well showcased in numbers like "South [Souse] American Way" (which she was singing on Broadway), "Mama Yo Quiero" and "Bambu," while Don Ameche and Betty Grable do well by the title song* and "Two Dreams Met," among others. The film, lensed in the old gorgeous, gaudy Technicolor, also highlighted Grable's simple but effective dancing, acrobatic tap numbers by the Nicholas Brothers, and some wisecracks and high kicks by veteran Charlotte Greenwood in her "Sing to Your Senorita" duet with Leonid Kinskey.

Originally, Alice Faye was to have starred in DOWN ARGENTINE WAY, but dropped out due to illness. Betty Grable, who had been performing in Hollywood films since the age of fourteen in 1930, was hired for the lead. (At the time she was on Broadway playing second fiddle to Ethel Merman and Bert Lahr in Cole Porter's *DuBarry Was a Lady.*) DOWN ARGENTINE WAY did a great deal to consolidate Grable's position in Hollywood and was her first major step up the ladder and to replacing Alice Faye as the studio's queen of musical comedies. Betty was noted for her shapely legs and peaches-and-cream complexion.

The success of DOWN ARGENTINE WAY proved studio head Darryl F. Zanuck's point that movie musicals could still be

---

*To be noted was that Carlos Albert sang the Spanish lyrics for Don Ameche in the song "Down Argentine Way."

successful *if* they had exotic locales, luscious Technicolor, shapely leading ladies and, of course, a solid score.

EASTER PARADE (Metro-Goldwyn-Mayer, 1948) Color 103 minutes.

Producer, Arthur Freed; associate producer, Roger Edens; director, Charles Walters; story, Frances Goodrich, Albert Hackett; screenplay, Sidney Sheldon, Goodrich, Hackett, (uncredited) Guy Bolton; art directors, Cedric Gibbons, Jack Martin Smith; set decorators, Edwin B. Willis, Arthur Krams; women's costumes, Irene; men's costumes, Valles; makeup, Jack Dawn; music director, Johnny Green; orchestrators, Conrad Salinger, Mason Van Cleave, Leo Arnaud; vocal arranger, Robert Tucker; choreographer, Robert Alton; color consultants, Natalie Kalmus, Henri Jaffa; assistant director, Wallace Worsley; sound supervisor, Douglas Shearer; camera, Harry Stradling; editor, Albert Akst.

Songs: "Happy Easter," "Drum Crazy," "It Only Happens When I Dance with You," "Everybody's Doin' It Now," "I Want to Go Back to Michigan," "Beautiful Faces," "A Fella with an Umbrella," "I Love a Piano," "Snookey Ookums," "Ragtime Violin," "When the Midnight Choo-Choo Leaves for Alabam'," "Shaking the Blues Away," "Steppin' Out with My Baby," "A Couple of Swells," "The Girl on the Magazine Cover," "Better Luck Next Time," "Easter Parade," "When I Lost You," "At the Devil's Ball," "This Is the Life," "Along Came Ruth," "Call Me Up Some Rainy Afternoon," "That International Rag." (Irving Berlin).

Judy Garland (Hannah Brown); Fred Astaire (Don Hewes); Peter Lawford (Jonathan Harrow, III); Ann Miller (Nadine Gale); Clinton Sundberg (Mike, the Bartender); Jules Munshin (François, the Headwaiter); Jeni Legon (Essie); Richard Beavers (Singer); Dick Simmons (Al, the Stage Manager for Ziegfeld); Jimmy Bates (Boy in "Drum Crazy"); Jimmy Dodd (Cabby); Robert Emmett O'Connor (Cop Who Gives Jonathan Harrow a Ticket); Patricia Jackson, Bobbie Priest, Dee Turnell (Specialty Dancers); Lola Albright, Joi Lansing (Hat Models); Lynn Romer, Jean Romer ("Delineator" Twins); Helen Heigh (Modiste); Wilson Wood (Marty); Hector [Carmi Tryon] and His Pals (Dog Act); Peter Chong (Sam, the Valet); Nolan Leary (Drug Clerk); Doris Kemper (Mary); Frank Mayo (Headwaiter); Benay Venuta (Bar Patron).

In a catalog of sparkling MGM musicals, EASTER PARADE certainly fits near the top, an expert blend of superior talent on both sides of the cameras. It represents the finest that the Arthur Freed musical unit at MGM could develop. The *New York Daily News* praised the motion picture as, ". . . Gay, witty, tuneful and filled with the magic rhythm of Fred Astaire's and Ann Miller's dancing and with Judy Garland's warbling of [Irving] Berlin's enticing tunes. . . ." Songwriter Irving Berlin reportedly was paid $500,000 plus a percentage of the film's profit; a unique contractual deal for that period.

Originally, in 1947 when MGM announced EASTER PARADE as an upcoming vehicle, its star cast was to include Judy Garland, Gene Kelly, Kathryn Grayson, Frank Sinatra and Red Skelton. As the project was refined, the players changed to Garland, Kelly, Ann Miller (replacing Cyd Charisse who had suffered an accident), Peter Lawford and Jules Munshin (as François, the headwaiter). During rehearsals in mid-September 1947 for Kelly's "Drum Crazy" routine, Kelly broke his ankle (playing football in his backyard). With Kelly's approval, Fred Astaire was coaxed out of a thirteen-month retirement to take over the lead role. Initially Vincente Minnelli was set to direct his wife (Judy Garland) in EASTER PARADE, as he had in the still-completing THE PIRATE (1948), *q.v.* However, the emotional stress level between director and star was already great, so he was replaced after five days by Charles Walters. The latter had come to MGM in 1942 as a sometimes on-screen dancer and choreographer. His first directorial venture at the studio had been GOOD NEWS (1947), *q.v.* It was Walters who requested that the screenplay by the husband-and-wife team of Albert Hackett and Frances Goodrich be amended to avoid its being too much of a PYGMALION-like story. Sidney Sheldon and Guy Bolton contributed the rewrites.

It was Roger Edens, long a staple at MGM and of the Arthur Freed unit in particular, who had the task of selecting which of the vast array of songs from Irving Berlin's catalog should be used in EASTER PARADE, and of those picked, having new arrangements provided. For the movie, Berlin composed such new melodies as "Drum Crazy," "It Only Happens When I Dance with You," "I Love You—You Love Him," "A Fella with an Umbrella," "Steppin' Out with My Baby" and "Mister Monotony." When Freed did not care for the newly written novelty number "Let's Take an Old-Fashioned Walk," Berlin readily agreed to create a new number and supposedly turned out "A Couple of Swells" in an hour. Before its release, the song "Mister Monotony" (sung by Judy Garland) was cut from the release print, as were "I Love You—You Love Him" and "A Pretty Girl Is Like a Melody."

In 1912 New York, Nadine Gale (Ann Miller) advises dance partner Don Hewes (Fred Astaire) that she has contracted for a Broadway show and that, from now on, she intends to be a solo performer. Despite this disappointment, Don still loves the egocentric Nadine, although she prefer Hewes' wealthy young friend, Jonathan Harrow (Peter Lawford). A dejected Hewes boasts that he can make any chorus girl into a new star/partner. He selects novice cafe performer Hannah Brown (Judy Garland) and attempts to mold the neophyte into a new edition of Nadine. Later he realizes his error. Hannah is an individual and her special talents must be highlighted. By now Hannah is in love with Don, despite his loyalty to Nadine and the fact that Jonathan is interested in Hannah. Eventually Don and Hannah star in their own Broadway show, *Walking Up the Avenue* and, in particular, their number "A Couple of Swells." They are now bona fide stars. This leads the opportunistic Nadine to attempt to steal back her ex-partner. However, at the Easter Parade—the first anniversary of their meeting—it is with Hannah that Don parades down the fashionable avenue.

In a program full of extremely appealing numbers there are two major highlights. Vivacious Ann Miller shines in her snappy solo, "Shaking the Blues Away," gyrating at her sexy best with proficient dance steps. What makes this number unique is that she is not surrounded by a squad of chorus boys but performs on a bare stage supported only by a chorus of unseen voices. The other standout interlude is "A Couple of Swells," which features Garland and Astaire in hobo garb deciding to stroll up ritzy Fifth Avenue. That is not to say that the other songs are not well done. There is the dance duet ("It Only Happens When I Dance with You") between Miller and Astaire, with her matching her partner step for step. Astaire has his solo spot with "Steppin' Out with My Baby" (a slow motion dance) and he and Garland duet/dance to the "When the Midnight Choo-Choo Leaves for Alabam' " (among other joint ragtime routines). It is Garland who sings the plaintive "Better Luck Next Time" and Peter Lawford who handles "A Fella with an Umbrella." Cut from the release print was Garland's number "Mr. Monotony," in which she wore the identical outfit she would wear in the "Get Happy" number of SUMMER STOCK (1950), *q.v.*

Technically, one of the most impressive moments in EASTER PARADE is the finale showing midtown Fifth Avenue. Because it was the time before location shooting became common, art director Jack Martin Smith took advantage of a backlot section to construct two city blocks containing, among other Fifth Avenue landmarks, St. Patrick's Church (bottom portion only). To fill out the structure and to fill in for the non-built other side of the street, process camera work was used. When seven hundred extras, cars, buggies and other conveyances were put into motion on the set, the finished results were breathtaking.

The ads for EASTER PARADE proclaimed, "Judy pours out her heart in glorious love songs . . . and inspires debonair Astaire to his greatest triumph. . . . in a musical romance as gay and tender as Irving Berlin's melodies." *Newsweek* magazine reported of the musical, "The important thing is that Fred Astaire is back again with Irving Berlin calling the tunes." *Cue* magazine endorsed, "Splendiferously Technicolored, fancily decorated, it is probably the most elaborate package of musical entertainment since MGM's ZIEGFELD FOLLIES [*q.v.*]. The plot is familiar but funny, the lines and lyrics are comic, and the direction light and quick."

Made at a cost of $2,503,654, EASTER PARADE grossed $6,803,000 in its initial release. Johnny Green and Roger Edens won an Academy Award for Best Score of a Musical Film.

As a result of EASTER PARADE, Judy Garland and Fred Astaire were to be reunited in THE BARKLEYS OF BROADWAY (1949), *q.v.*, but because of Garland's continuing erratic behavior and recurrent ailments, she was replaced in the musical by Ginger Rogers.

EASY TO LOVE (Metro-Goldwyn-Mayer, 1953) Color 96 minutes.

Producer, Joe Pasternak; director, Charles Walters; story, Laslo Vadnay; screenplay, Vadnay, Williams Roberts; art directors, Cedric Gibbons, Jack Martin Smith; music directors, Lennie Hayton, George Stoll; choreographer, Busby Berkeley; camera, Ray June; editor, Gene Ruggiero.

Songs: "Easy to Love" (Cole Porter); "Coquette" (Carmen Lombardo, Johnny Green, Gus Kahn); "Beautiful Spring" (Paul Lincke); "That's What a Rainy Day Is For," "Look Out! I'm Romantic," "Didja Ever" (Vic Mizzy, Mann Curtis).

Esther Williams (Julie Hallerton); Van Johnson (Ray Lloyd); Tony Martin (Barry Gordon); John Bromfield (Hank); Edna Skinner (Nancy Parnell); King Donovan (Ben); Paul Bryar (Mr. Barnes); Carroll Baker (Clarice); Eddie Oliver (Band Leader); Benny Rubin (Oscar Levenson); Edward Clark (Gardener); June Whitley (Costumes); Emory Parnell (Mr. Huffnagel); David Newell (Makeup Man); Sondra Gould (Ben's Wife); Lillian Culver (Flora); Fenton Hamilton (Fat Man); Harriett Brest, Helen Dickson, Ann Luther, Maude Erickson, Peggy Remington, Violet Seton, Dorothy Vernon (Women Guests in Lobby); Richard Downing Pope, Bud Gaines (Tourists); Byron Kane, Reginald Simpson (Photographers); Joe Mell (Sleepy Waiter); Hal Berns (Melvin, the Pianist); Margaret Bert (Mrs. Huffnagel); Cyd Charisse (Walk-On).

Beautiful Julie Hallerton (Esther Williams) is the swimming

star of the aqua show at the Cypress Gardens, Florida resort owned by Ray Lloyd (Van Johnson). (She also works for him as a secretary, all for $75 a week!) Julie loves Ray but he does not realize it because all he thinks about is business. Thus she is forced to date swimming instructor Hank (John Bromfield). When Ray takes Julie with him on a business trip to New York City she meets nightclub singer Barry Gordon (Tony Martin), who immediately falls in love with her. He follows her back to Florida where he proceeds to romance the star swimmer. Finally Ray realizes what is happening and that he too loves Julie. She plays her suitors off against each other until she finally settles down with Ray.

Musically, it is Tony Martin who supports EASY TO LOVE. He sings "Didja Ever" and "Look Out! I'm Romantic" in the New York nightclub setting; for "That's What a Rainy Day Is For" he has a chorus of sixteen elderly ladies. He also vocalizes on Cole Porter's old tune, "Easy to Love," and performs Carmen Lombardo and Johnny Green's number, "Coquette." Visually it was choreographer Busby Berkeley who took best advantage of the on-location filming at Cypress Gardens, Florida. One aquatic scene has the beautiful Williams dressed in clown attire, romping about a swimming pool with an oversized chimpanzee, as delighted children look on. In another, Williams and one (John Bromfield) of her suitors swim and court in a moon-drenched cove with a mass of floating white gardenias as backdrop. Most impressive was the finale. Berkeley would recall of this spectacular sequence shot (largely from a hovering helicopter) at Lake Eloise, Florida, "This was the kind of thing I loved. I had Esther and eighty boy and girl skiers whizzing along on skis carrying big flags. I mapped out an intricate pattern of movements for them through the cypress trees and around huge geysers that shot sixty-foot sprays into the air. I had twelve boy skiers going over twelve-foot-high jumps simultaneously. In one part of the routine I used a hundred girls in a huge swimming pool that I had had built in the shape of the state of Florida. I used a helicopter in another part of this sequence, with Esther standing on a trapeze while hanging from the plane, then diving from a height of eighty feet into a V-shaped formation of skiers traveling at thirty-five miles per hour across the lake. She then comes up on skis for a furious ride that takes her looping over several ramps, finally hurtling over the heads of the bandsmen, who are merrily playing away, and comes right up to the camera." Of this latter sequence, the *New York Journal-American* would assess, "I'd say this was Busby Berkeley's crowning achievement. . . . [It] is showier than the recent Coronation and paced faster than a Keystone Cops comedy."

The *New York Times* judged of EASY TO LOVE, "Esther Williams, never yummier or wetter, in one of her better watercade musicals, one that works in every department. . . . Charles Walters has directed the picture exactly for what it is, a bright rainbow-hued entertainment."

ELVIS (ABC-TV, 2/11/79) Color 150 minutes.

Executive producer, Dick Clark; producer, Anthony Lawrence; supervising producer, Tony Bishop; associate producer, James Ritz; director, John Carpenter; teleplay, Lawrence; art directors, Tracy Bousman, James Newport; set decorator, Bill Harp; costume supervisors, Tony Faso, Suzanne Grace, Richard Mahoney; makeup, Marv Westmore; music/music director, Joe Renzetti; music coordinator, Frank Capp; assistant directors, Larry Franco, Craig Beaudine, Glen Sanford; technical advisors, Charlie Hodge, Larry Geller, Becky Yancy, Cliff Linedecker; stunt coordinator, Aaron Norris; sound, Willie Burton; camera, Donald M. Morgan; supervising editor, Tom Walls; editor, Ron Moler.

Songs: "Mystery Train" (Sam C. Phillips, Herman Parker, Jr.); "The Wonder of You" (Baker Knight); "That's Alright Mama" (Arthur "Big Boy" Crudup); "Blue Moon of Kentucky" (Bill Munroe); "My Happiness" (Barney Bergantine, Betty Peterson); "Old Shep" (Red Foley, E. M. Jones); "Heartbreak Hotel" (Mae Boren Axton, Tommy Durden, Elvis Presley); "Rip It Up" (Robert A. Blackwell, John Marascalco); "Are You Lonesome Tonight?" (Roy Turk, Lou Handman); "Love Me Tender" (Elvis Presley, Vera Matson); "Crying in the Chapel" (Artie Glenn); "Until It's Time for You to Go" (Buffy Sainte-Marie); "Pledging My Love" (Ferdinand Washington, Don Robey); "Separate Ways" (Mainegra, West); "Suspicious Minds" (Fred Zambon); "Burning Love" (Dennis Linde); "Blue Suede Shoes" (Carl Perkins); "Lawdy Miss Clawdy" (Lloyd Price); "Shake, Rattle and Roll" (Charles Calhoun); "Long Tall Sally" (R. Penniman, Robert A. Blackwell, E. Johnson); "Fool Such as I" (B. Trader); "Battle Hymn of the Republic" (Julia Ward Howe, music attributed to William Steffe).

Kurt Russell (Elvis Presley); Shelley Winters (Gladys Presley); Bing Russell (Vernon Presley); Robert Gray (Red West); Pat Hingle (Colonel Tom Parker); Season Hubley (Priscilla Presley); Melody Anderson (Bonnie); Ed Begley, Jr. (D. C. Fontana); James Canning (Scotty); Charles Cyphers (Sam Phillips); Peter Hobbs (Jim Denny); Les Lannom (Sonny West); Elliott Street (Bill Black); Will Jordan (Ed Sullivan); Joe Mantegna (Joe Esposito); Galen Thompson (Hank Snow); Ellen Travolta (Marion); Abi Young (Natalie Wood); Felicia Fenske (Lisa Marie Presley); Randy Gray

(Elvis as a Boy); Meg Wyllie (Grandma); Charlie Hodge (Himself); Nora Boland (Teacher); Larry Geller (Himself); Jim Greenleaf (Second Reporter); Ronnie McDowell (Singing Voice of Elvis Presley); and: Christian Berrigan, Mark Dennis, Bill Erwin, Mario Gallo, Del Hinkley, Ted Lehman, Jack McCulloch, Larry Pennell, Ed Ruffalo, Ken Smolka, David Stafford, Dennis Stewart, Dick Young.

Following his sudden death in the summer of 1978, Elvis Presley became the subject of tremendous renewed publicity, including various types of merchandizing. Early in 1979 Dick Clark Productions made a biopic of the singer's life called ELVIS and this handsome TV movie was helmed by John Carpenter, who had just scored with the shock-gore entry, HALLOWEEN (1978). Kurt Russell won an Emmy Award nomination for his adept performance in the title role (his singing was dubbed by Elvis soundalike, Ronnie McDowell, who had a successful single with his co-penned Elvis tribute, "The King Is Gone," on Scorpion Records). Also nominated for Emmy Awards were Donald M. Morgan for his cinematography and Marv Westmore for makeup. The scenario at best was superficial drama on which to recreate events in Presley's life and peg the trademark song numbers.

ELVIS covers the turbulent life of the rock legend from his early childhood in Tennessee through his return to the limelight in the late 1960s. It does not touch on his last, lonely tragic years when he battled prescription drugs and weight problems. The narrative shows Elvis (Randy Gray) as a boy who is very close to his dowdy, overprotective mother (Shelley Winters) while his father (Bing Russell) ekes out a living. The youngster becomes interested in music, and when he becomes an adult (Kurt Russell) he emerges as a fine guitarist and singer. When he cuts a record for his mother at Sam Phillips' (Charles Cyphers) Memphis Sun Records studio, he comes to the attention of the enterprising record producer. His records do well enough for him to go on tour with country star Hank Snow (Galen Thompson). Snow and his manager Colonel Tom Parker (Pat Hingle) are impressed with the young man and take him to RCA Records, while Parker becomes his manager. Following an appearance on Ed Sullivan's (Will Jordan) TV show, Elvis becomes a national sensation and the number-one rocker in the U.S. Despite the death of his mother, Elvis continues to be a success. While serving a stint in the Army in West Germany he meets teenager Priscilla (Season Hubley) and they are later married and have a daughter, Lisa Marie (Felicia Fenske). As the years go by, Elvis' career begins to decline. However, in 1968 he returns in a highly-rated TV special and then begins working with great success in the showrooms of Las Vegas.

ELVIS was a big ratings success when it was first telecast. *TV Movies and Video Guide* (1989) weighed, "The Presley saga affectionately and believably retold. . . . Russell surprisingly effective as Elvis. . . ." Naturally the TV movie employed many of Elvis' landmark hit songs, all nicely dubbed by Ronnie McDowell. Dick Clark Records issued the soundtrack album with McDowell backed by The Jordanaires, the group which often sang with Elvis on his recording sessions.

In 1981 NBC-TV telecast the small screen movie, ELVIS AND THE BEAUTY QUEEN, which told of the singer's (Don Johnson) romance with Linda Thompson (Stephanie Zimbalist), and in 1988 the telefeature ELVIS AND ME, in which Priscilla Presley's (Susan Walters) years with Elvis (Dale Midkiff) are detailed, debuted. (Priscilla Presley served as executive producer on the production.) As in ELVIS, the singer's vocals were dubbed by Ronnie McDowell. In the theatrical feature HEARTBREAK HOTEL (1988), set in 1972, David Keith played Elvis in a badly-executed, whimsical story about the great performer suddenly popping into the lives of a small town Ohio family.

ELVIS AND ME *see* ELVIS (essay).

ELVIS AND THE BEAUTY QUEEN *see* ELVIS (essay).

THE EMPEROR WALTZ (Paramount, 1948) Color 106 minutes.

Producer, Charles Brackett; director, Billy Wilder; screenplay, Brackett, Wilder; art directors, Hans Dreier, Franz Bachelin; set decorators, Sam Comer, Paul Huldschinsky; costumes, Edith Head, Gile Steele; makeup, Wally Westmore; music, Victor Young; vocal arranger, Joseph J. Lilley; choreographer, Billy Daniels; color consultants, Natalie Kalmus, Robert Brower; assistant director, C. C. Coleman, Jr.; sound, Stanley Cooley, John Cope; process camera, Farciot Edouart; special effects, Gordon Jennings; camera, George Barnes; editor, Doane Harrison.

Songs: "Get Yourself a Phonograph," (Johnny Burke, Jimmy Van Heusen); "I Kiss Your Hand, Madame" (Ralph Erwin, Sam M. Lewis, Joe Young; German lyrics, Fritz Rotter); "The Kiss in Your Eyes" (adapted by Burke from "Im Chambre Separee" by Richard Heuberger); "Friendly Mountains" (adapted by Burke from traditional Swiss songs); "The Emperor Waltz" (adapted by Burke from a waltz by Johann Strauss II).

Bing Crosby (Virgil Smith); Joan Fontaine (Johanna Augusta

Joan Fontaine and Bing Crosby in THE EMPEROR WALTZ (1948).

Franziska); Roland Culver (Baron Holenia); Lucile Watson (Princess Bitotska); Richard Haydn (Emperor Franz Joseph); Harold Vermilyea (Chamberlain); Sig Rumann (Dr. Zwieback); Julia Dean (Archduchess Stephanie); Bert Prival (Chauffeur); Alma Macrorie (Proprietress of the Inn); Roberta Jonay (Chambermaid); John Goldsworthy (Obersthofmeister); James Vincent (Abbe); Harry Allen (Gamekeeper); Eleanor Tennant (Tennis Player); Vesey O'Davoren (Butler); Norbert Schiller (Assistant to Dr. Zwieback); Frank Elliott (Von Usedom); Paul de Corday (Hungarian Officer); Jack Gargan (Master of Ceremonies); Doris Dowling, Renee Randall, Jean Marshall, Kathy Young (Tyrolean Girls); Len Hendry (Palace Guard); Cyril Delevanti (Diplomat); Frank Mayo (Parliamentary Politician); Hans Moebus, Albert Petit, Albert Pollet, Count Stefenelli (Elderly Aristocrats); Franco Corsaro (Spanish Marques); Jerry James, William Meader (King's Guards); Gene Ashley, John "Skins" Miller, Jac Fisher, Leo Lynn (Tyrolean Men); Bob Stephenson, James Logan (Beaters).

"The film exudes a distinctive 'story book' enchantment that is saved from being juvenile by the complete conviction with which it is presented. THE EMPEROR WALTZ is a kind of adult fairy story, admittedly overflowing with romantic idealism but still managing to depict the 'perfect love' in such a way as to make it almost believable." (Robert Bookbinder, *The Films of Bing Crosby,* 1977).

Fast-talking American phonograph salesman Virgil Smith (Bing Crosby) comes to Austria during the reign of Emperor Franz Joseph (Richard Haydn) to convince the royal family of the popularity of recordings. He is given an impromptu audience with the monarch at his palace in the Tyrolean Alps but when he attempts to demonstrate his product, he is thrown out because guards believe he has a bomb. Undaunted, Virgil next approaches the emperor's favorite niece, Countess Franziska von Stultzenberg (Joan Fontaine), hoping to get into her good graces and thus win another audience with her uncle. The countess, however, is snobbish and refuses to have anything to do with Smith. Meanwhile, complications arise when Virgil's mongrel dog Buttons becomes attracted to the countess's pet poodle. Eventually the countess decides the two dogs should be friends. As a result, she becomes acquainted with Virgil and they fall in love.

"Billy Wilder directing a Viennese operetta sounds like pouring vinegar over a chocolate sundae. However there was not a trace of his acidulated cynicism in THE EMPEROR WALTZ, a sugary confection for Bing Crosby . . ." (John Douglas Eames, *The Paramount Story,* 1985). Shot on an 89-day production schedule, THE EMPEROR WALTZ grossed $4 million in distributors' domestic film rentals. It proved to be a solid showcase for both Bing Crosby and Joan Fontaine. Crosby had several pleasing numbers in the production, including the title song which Johnny Burke based on the music of Johann Strauss II, "The Kiss in Your Eyes," "Friendly Mountains" and an old popular songs from the 1920s, "I Kiss Your Hand, Madame."

THE EMPEROR WALTZ was nominated for Oscars for Best Scoring of a Musical Picture and Best Costume Design—Color.

EVERY NIGHT AT EIGHT (Paramount, 1935) 80 minutes.

Producer, Walter Wanger; director, Raoul Walsh; based on the story "Three on a Mike" by Stanley Garvey; screenplay, Gene Towne, Graham Baker; additional dialogue, Bert Hanlon; art director, Alexander Tobuloff; costumes, Helen Taylor; assistant director, Eric Stacey; sound, Hugo Grenzbach; camera, James Van Trees; editor, W. Donn Hayes.

Songs: "I'm in the Mood for Love" (Dorothy Fields, Jimmy McHugh); "I Feel a Song Comin' On," "Take It Easy," "Speaking

Confidentially," "Every Night at Eight" (Fields, George Oppenheimer); "Then You've Never Been Blue" (Ted Fio Rito, Joe Young, Sam Lewis, Frances Langford); "Il Bacio" (Luigi Arditi).

George Raft ("Tops" Cardona); Alice Faye (Dixie Dean); Patsy Kelly (Daphne O'Connor); Frances Langford (Susan Moore); Jimmie Hollywood, Henry Taylor, Eddie Bartel (Three Radio Rogues); Harry Barris (Snorky); Walter Catlett (Master of Ceremonies); Dillon Ober (Trick Drummer); Florence Gill (Henrietta, the Chicken Lady); Eddy Conrad (Italian Singer); Charles Forsyth (Sound Effects Man); Herman Bing (Joe Schmidt); Boothe Howard (Martin); John H. Dilson (Huxley); Louise Larabee, Louise McNamee (New Employees); Herb Ashley (Piano Mover); Louise Carver (Mrs. Snyder); Richard Powell (Fresh Sailor); Lynton Brent (Mail Sorter); Phyllis Crane, Gertie Green (Telephone Operators); Nina Gilbert (Chief Operator); Eddie Fetherston (Photo Layout Man, Gold Strike Cigarettes); Harry Holman (Jacksonville Colonel); Claud Allister (Rich Bore); Stephen Chase ("Barrymore"); Bud Flanagan [Dennis O'Keefe] (Extra).

By the mid-1930s the motion picture industry was no longer able to snub the medium of radio and was beginning to interpolate

Frances Langford, Alice Faye, Patsy Kelly and George Raft in EVERY NIGHT AT EIGHT (1935).

radio themes into movie plots for added box-office strength. One such effort was Paramount's EVERY NIGHT AT EIGHT, which starred George Raft as a Ben Bernie-type bandleader and featured Alice Faye, Frances Langford and Patsy Kelly as a singing trio obviously patterned after the very popular Boswell Sisters. *Photoplay* magazine even observed, ". . . It's a photographed radio program, but there's plenty to entertain you. . . ." The *New York Times* found the proceedings "simple, light-hearted and unpretentious." Among the musical highlights of ths undemanding, very entertaining picture are the title tune, "I'm in the Mood for Love" (a very popular song which was on radio's "Your Hit Parade" for twelve weeks) and Alice Faye's rendition of "I Feel a Song Coming On." Sadly, sultry Faye (on loan from Fox Films) was subordinated to round-faced Frances Langford (under Paramount contract), as the radio star was making her big screen debut in this musical. As for George Raft, an acquired taste, he was particularly charming and relaxed in this offering. It was an amusing change of pace to see brash comedienne Patsy Kelly, usually looking the worst for wear, so well coiffed and garbed.

Three attractive young women, Dixie Dean (Alice Faye), Daphne O'Connor (Patsy Kelly) and Susan Moore (Frances Langford), work for Huxley's Mint Julep Company and cause a sensation when they sing as a trio at the organization's variety program. They make a recording on the company dictaphone and lose their jobs. Without funds, they are soon evicted from their rented room. They enter an amateur radio contest but lose when Susan faints from hunger and the prize goes to Tops Cardona and His Band. Tops, however, is impressed with the girls and hires them to perform with the group. Ironically, the band is signed to appear on radio, sponsored by the Huxley company, and Tops and the girls become a big success. Meanwhile, Susan and Tops fall in love. Still, the overworked girls are tired of radio work and accept a yachting party invitation. They find their hosts are snobs and so return to the radio show, and Tops and Susan renew their romance.

Alice Faye, here still in her Jean Harlow look-alike period, would star in three additional radio-themed musicals back at her home lot, 20th Century-Fox: SING, BABY, SING (1936), *q.v.*, WAKE UP AND LIVE (1937), *q.v.*, and THE GREAT AMERICAN BROADCAST (1941).

FAME (Metro-Goldwyn-Mayer, 1980) Color 134 minutes.

Producer, David de Silva, Alan Marshall; director, Alan Parker; screenplay, Christopher Gore; production designer, Geoffrey Kirkland; art director, Ed Wittstein; set decorator,

George DeTitta, costumes, Kristi Zea; makeup, Joseph Cuervo; choreographer, Louis Falco; music, Michael Gore; sound, Chris Newman, Arthur Bloom, Chuck Irwin; assistant directors, Robert F. Colesberry, Raymond L. Greenfield; sound re-recording, Michael J. Kohut, Aaron Rochin, Jay M. Harding; sound editors, Les Wiggins, Rusty Coppleman; camera, Michael Seresin; editor, Gerry Hambling; additional editor, Yoshio Kishi.

Songs: "Fame" (Michael Gore, Dean Pitchford; arranger, Leon L. Pendarvis); "Out Here with My Own" (Michael Gore, Lesley Gore); "Hot Lunch Jam" (Michael Gore, Lesley Gore, Robert F. Colesberry); "Dogs in the Yard" (Dominic Bugatti, Frank Musker; arranger, Steve Margoshes); "Red Lights" (Michael Gore, Dean Pitchford; arranger, Gil Askey); "Is It Okay If I Call You Mine?" (Paul McCrane); "Never Alone" (Anthony Evans); "I Sing the Body Electric" (Michael Gore, Dean Pitchford; arranger, Margoshes);

Irene Cara (Coco Hernandez); Lee Curreri (Bruno Martelli); Laura Dean (Lisa Monroe); Antonio Franceschi (Hilary Van Doren); Paul McCrane (Montgomery MacNeil); Barry Miller (Ralph Garcy [Raoul Garcia]); Gene Anthony Ray (Leroy Johnson); Maureen Teefy (Doris Finsecker); Eddie Barth (Angelo); Boyd Gaines (Michael); Albert Hague (Professor Shorofsky); Tresa Hughes (Naomi Finsecker); Steve Inwood (Francois Lafete); Anne Meara (Mrs. Sherwood); Joanna Merlin (Miss Berg); Jim Moody (Farrell); Debbie Allen (Lydia Grant); Richard Belzer (Richard, the Master of Ceremonies at Catch a Rising Star Club); Frank Bongiorno (Truck Driver); Bill Britten (Mr. England); Eric Brockington (Plump Eric); Nicholas Bunin (Bunsky); Cindy Canuelas (Cindy); Nora Cotrone (Topless Student); Mbewe Escobar (Phenicia); Gennady Filimonov (Violinist); Victor Fischbarg (Harvey Finsecker); Penny Frank (Dance Teacher); Willie Henry, Jr. (Bathroom Student); Sang Kim (Oriental Violinist); Darrell Kirkman (Richard III); Judith L'Heureux (Nurse); Nancy Lee (Oriental Student); Sarah Malament (Dance Accompanist); James Manis (Bruno's Uncle); Carol Massenburg (Shirley, Leroy's Partner); Isaac Mizrahi (Touchstone); Raquel Mondin (Ralph's Sister); Alba Oms (Ralph's Mother); Frank Oteri (Schlepstein); Traci Parnell (Hawaiian Dancer); Sal Piro (Master of Ceremonies at ROCKY HORROR SHOW Screening); Leslie Quickley ("Towering Inferno" Student); Ray Ramirez (Father Morales); Ilse Sass (Mrs. Tossoff); Dawn Steinberg (Monitor on Stairs); Jonathan Strasser (Orchestra Conductor); Yvette Torres (Ralph's Little Sister); Frank X. Vitolo (Frankie); Stefanie Zimmerman (Dance Teacher); Tracy Burnett, Greg De Jean, Laura Delano, Michael DeLorenzo, Aaron Dugger, Neisha Folkes, Karen Ford, Robin Gray, Hazel Green, Eva

Grubler, Patrick King, Cynthia Lochard, Julian Montenaire, Holly Reeve, Kate Snyder, Meg Tilly, Louis Venosta, Philip Wright, Ranko Yokoyana (Principal Dancers); Adam Abeshouse, Yvette D. Carrington, Fima Ephron, Anthony Evans, Crystal Garner, Lisa Herman, Thais Hockaday, Karen Hoppe, Frankie Laino, April Lang, Richard Latimer, Lisa Lowell, Ann Marie McDermott, Kerry McDermott, Maureen McDermott, Josh Melville, Peter Rafelson, Anne Roboff, Boris Slutsky, Alan Vetter, Eva Weinstein (Principal Musicians and Vocalists).

The intertwining lives of a group of students at the High School of Performing Arts in New York City made up the complex plotline for FAME, which enjoyed distributors' domestic film rentals of $7,798,235 and spawned a very popular teleseries (NBC, 1982–83; syndicated 1983–87) which featured several members from the original motion picture. Although overlong and dramatically involved without ever really bringing much delineation to its diverse characters (frequently ethnic stereotypes), FAME struck a chord with the young moviegoing audience. It became one of the more favorably received musicals of the early 1980s. *Variety* reported, "What director Alan Parker has come up with is exposure for some of the most talented youngsters seen on screen in years. There isn't a bad performance in the lot and the handful of older actors are hard put not to be overwhelmed by the outpouring of sheer energy of the colorful admixture of boys, girls, whites, blacks, Puerto Ricans and the cross-sections that make up New York teenagers."

Several teenagers are attending the Performing Arts School (the actual institution refused to participate in the making of the film): Leroy Johnson (Gene Anthony Ray), a black youth who is a fine dancer but who has spurned the educational system to the point that he will fail to graduate because he cannot read, has a cultural battle with white English teacher, Mrs. Sherwood (Anne Meara), who wants to assist him; Montgomery MacNeil (Paul McCrane), the homosexual son of a famous, and absent, movie star; Doris Finsecker (Maureen Teefy), who is unwillingly being pushed into a singing career by her ambitious mother (Tresa Hughes); Lisa Monroe (Laura Dean) who is also controlled by her manipulative mother; would-be comic Ralph Garcy (Barry Miller), the son of an ex-convict, whose real name is Raoul Garcia and who has a fixation with the late comedian Freddie Prinz; Italian student Angelo (Eddie Barth); music student Bruno Martelli (Lee Curreri), who wants his own electronic music compositions to be a part of the school's curriculum, and his friend, the overly ambitious Coco Hernandez (Irene Cara), who is intent on becoming a singing star.

Judging the results, John Pym (British *Monthly Film Bulletin*) decided, "The fragments of these youngsters' stories are cut together with a breathless immediacy that many will find irresistible; and the punctuating sequences of non-stop entertainment . . . communicate a genuine if limited sense of the world occupied by starry-eyed, over-energised student performers, as opposed to the grittily or woefully determined old pros in the chorus lines of show business." Pym added that the film's faults derive from the fact that director Alan Parker "does not appear interested in why people become performers" and ". . . The fantasy is so relentlessly overplayed that what might have been . . . endearingly charming, for the most part ends up ludicrously overblown."

FAME won an Academy Award for Best Song ("Fame"). It was nominated for Best Original Score, Best Sound and Best Film Editing. The soundtrack album to FAME was on *Billboard* magazine's hits chart for sixteen weeks and rose to position #7.

FANTASIA (RKO, 1940) Color 120 minutes.

Producer, Walt Disney.

Toccata and Fugue in D Minor by Johann Sebastian Bach; director, Samuel Armstrong; story development, Lee Blair, Elmer Plummer, Phil Dike; art director, Robert Cormack; animators, Cy Young, Art Palmer, Daniel MacManus, George Rowley, Edwin Aardal, Joshua Meador, Cornett Wood; background paintings, Joe Stanley, John Hench, Nino Carbe.

The Nutcracker Suite by Peter Ilich Tchaikovsky; director, Samuel Armstrong; story development, Sylvia Moberly-Holland, Norman Wright, Albert Heth, Bianca Majolie, Graham Heid; character designers, John Walbridge, Elmer Plummer, Ethel Kulsar; art directors, Robert Cormack, Al Zinnen, Curtiss D. Perkins, Arthur Byram, Bruce Bushman; animators, Arthur Babbitt, Les Clark, Don Lusk, Young, Robert Stokes; background paintings, John Hench, Ethel Kulsar, Nino Carbe.

The Sorcerer's Apprentice by Paul Dukas; director, James Algar; story development, Perce Pearce, Carl Fallberg; art directors, Tom Codrick, Charles Philippi, Zack Schwartz; animation supervisor, Fred Moore, Vladimir Tytla; animators, Lee Clark, Riley Thompson, Marvin Woodward, Preston Blair, Edward Love, Ugo D'Orsi, George Rowley, Cornett Wood; background paintings, Claude Coats, Stan Spohn, Albert Dempster, Eric Hansen.

The Rite of Spring by Igor Stravinsky; directors, Bill Roberts, Paul Satterfield; story development/research, William Martin, Leo Thiele, Robert Sterner, John Fraser McLeish; art directors, MacLaren Stewart, Dick Kelsey, John Hubley; animation supervisors, Wolfgang Reitherman, Joshua Meador; animators, Philip Duncan, John McManus, Paul Busch, Art Palmer, Don Tobin, Edwin Aardal, Paul B. Kossoff; background paintings, Ed Starr, Brice Mack, Edward Levitt; special camera effects, Gail Papineau, Leonard Pickley.

Pastoral Symphony by Ludwig van Beethoven; directors, Hamilton Luske, Jim Handley, Ford Beebe; story development, Otto Englander, Webb Smith, Erdman Penner, Joseph Sabo, Bill Peet, George Stallings; character design, James Bodrero, John P. Miller, Lorna S. Soderstrom; art directors, Hugh Hennessy, Kenneth Anderson, J. Gordon Legg, Herbert Ryman, Yale Gracey, Lance Nolley; animation supervisors, Fred Moore, Ward Kimball, Eric Larson, Arthur Babbitt, Oliver M. Johnston, Jr., Don Towsley; animators, Berny Wolf, Jack Campbell, John Bradbury, James Moore, Milt Neil, Bill Justice, John Elliotte, Walt Kelly, Don Lusk, Lynn Karp, Murray McLennan, Robert W. Youngquist, Harry Hamsel; background paintings, Claude Coats, Ray Huffine, W. Richard Anthony, Arthur Riley, Gerald Nevius, Roy Forkum.

Dance of the Hours by Amilcare Ponchielli; directors, T. Hee, Norman Ferguson; character design, Martin Provensen, James Bodrero, Duke Russell, Earl Hurd; art directors, Kendall O'Connor, Harold Doughty, Ernest Nordli; animation supervisor, Norman Ferguson; animators, John Lounsbery, Howard Swift, Preston Blair, Hugh Fraser, Harvey Toombs, Norman Tate, Hicks Lokey, Art Elliott, Grant Simmons, Ray Patterson, Franklin Grundeen; background paintings, Albert Dempster, Charles Conner.

Night on Bald Mountain by Modest Mussorgsky and *Ave Maria* by Franz Schubert; director, Wilfred Jackson; story development, Campbell Grant, Arthur Heinemann, Phil Dike; art directors, Kay Nielsen, Terrell Stapp, Charles Payzant, Thor Putnam; animation supervisor, Vladimir Tytla; animators, John McManus, William N. Shull, Robert W. Carlson, Jr., Lester Novros, Don Paterson; background paintings, Merle Cox, Ray Lockrem, Robert Storms, W. Richard Anthony; special animation effects, Joshua Meador, Miles E. Pike, John F. Reed, Daniel MacManus; special camera effects, Gail Papineau, Leonard Pickley; special lyrics for "Ave Maria" by Rachel Field; "Ave Maria" chorus director, Charles Henderson.

Deems Taylor (Himself); Leopold Stokowski and the Philadelphia Symphony Orchestra (Themselves); Julietta Novis ("Ave Maria" Soloist).

After producing the extremely successful animated features, SNOW WHITE AND THE SEVEN DWARFS (1937) and PINOCCHIO (1940), Walt Disney took a huge risk by turning out

FANTASIA, a combination of classical music and animation. It received mixed critical reaction and only polite audience acceptance. For the initial engagements of the first release in special selected houses, FANTASIA was shown with Fantasound, an advanced (for its time) technology stereo sound system. Thereafter, for the rest of the first release engagement it was distributed with standard sound, so theatres would not have to be re-equipped for the engagements. Thanks to several reissues (which restored the stereo sound and even added a widescreen effect), FANTASIA (which cost $2.5 million) took on new life. To date it has grossed $28,660,000 in distributors' domestic film rentals. During the 1970s it gathered a cult following among young people who used it as a background stimulus for drug use, much to the chagrin of the Disney organization with its wholesome family image. In any event, FANTASIA today is considered a cinematic masterpiece.

Originally Walt Disney had envisioned using Paul Dukas' "The Sorcerer's Apprentice" for a Mickey Mouse cartoon, and Leopold Stokowski agreed to conduct the background music for the short. Stokowski, however, urged Disney to expand the concept into a feature employing other classical pieces. Musicologist Deems Taylor was enlisted to narrate the production, and he and Stokowski both make appearances in FANTASIA.

Johann Sebastian Bach's "Toccata and Fugue in D Minor" opens the film, followed by firefly ballerinas, which becomes Peter Ilich Tchaikovsky's "The Dance of the Sugar Plum Fairies." Next, Oriental-appearing mushrooms do the "Chinese Dance" while falling petals perform "The Dance of the Reed Flutes." "Arabian Dance" is executed underwater as bubbles enact the "Russian Dance," followed by "The Waltz of the Flowers." Next comes the originally conceived "The Sorcerer's Apprentice" in which Mickey Mouse uses his master's power to make a broom do all his chores, with near catastrophic results. Igor Stravinsky's "The Rite of Spring" is the springboard to show the world's creation. Characters in Greek mythology are used to animate the "Pastoral Symphony" by Beethoven, while various animals perform Amilcare Ponchielli's "Dance of the Hours." The feature concludes with a duel between good and evil in a combination of Modest Mussorgsky's "Night on Bald Mountain" and Franz Schubert's "Ave Maria."

Perhaps the best remembered sequences in FANTASIA are Mickey Mouse in "The Sorcerer's Apprentice" and the "Night on Bald Mountain" segment. The latter includes the particularly frightening Tchernobog, the Black God, whose animation was modeled from live action by Bela Lugosi, who posed in the part for the studio animators.

In 1941 the Academy of Motion Picture Arts and Sciences gave a Special Award to Leopold Stokowski and his associates for their "unique achievement in the creation of a new form of visualized music" in FANTASIA.

FIDDLER ON THE ROOF (United Artists, 1971) Color 180 minutes.

Producer, Norman Jewison; associate producer, Patrick Palmer; director, Jewison; based on the musical play by Joseph Stein, Jerry Bock, Sheldon Harnick; adapted from the play *Tevye and His Daughters* by Sholom Aleichem [Solomon Rabinowitz]; screenplay, Stein; production designer, Robert Boyle; art director, Michael Stringer; set decorator, Peter Lamont; costumes, Elizabeth Haffenden, Joan Bridge; music, Bock; music director, John Williams; choreographer, Tom Abbott (based on Jerome Robbins' stage choreography); assistant directors, Terry Nelson, Paul Ibbetson, Terry Churcher; sound, David Hilyard; sound re-recording, Gordon K. McCallum; sound editor, Les Wiggins; special effects, John Stears; camera, Oswald Morris; editors, Antony Gibbs, Robert Lawrence.

Songs: "Tradition," "Matchmaker, Matchmaker," "If I Were a Rich Man," "Sabbath Prayer," "To Life," "Miracle of Miracles," "Tevye's Dream," "Sunrise, Sunset," "Bottle Dance," "Do You Love Me?" "Far from the Home I Love," "Anatevka" (Jerry Bock, Sheldon Harnick).

Topol (Tevye); Norma Crane (Golde); Leonard Frey (Motel); Molly Picon (Yente); Paul Mann (Lazar Wolf); Rosalind Harris (Tzeitel); Michele Marsh (Hodel); Neva Small (Chava); [Paul] Michael Glaser (Perchik); Raymond Lovelock (Fyedka); Elaine Edwards (Shprintze); Candy Bonstein (Bielke); Shimen Ruskin (Mordcha); Zvee Scooler (Rabbi); Louis Zorich (Constable); Alfie Scopp (Avram); Howard Goorney (Nachum); Barry Dennen (Mendel); Vernon Dobtcheff (Russian Official); Ruth Madoc (Fruma Sarah); Patience Collier (Grandma Tzeitel); Tutte Lemkow (Fiddler); Larry Bianco (Igor); Stella Courney (Shandel); Jacob Kalich (Yankel); Brian Coburn (Berl); George Little (Hone); Stanley Fleet (Farcel); Arnold Diamond (Moishe); Marika Rivera (Rifka); Mark Malicz (Ezekial); Aharon Ipale (Sheftel); Otto Diamant (Yussel); Judith Harte (Gnessi); Harry Ditson (Leibesh); Michael Lewis (Joshua); Hazel Wright (Rebecca); Carl Jaffe (Isaac); Miki Iveria (Bess); Hilda Kriseman (Zelda); Sarah Cohen (Bashe); Susan Sloman (Nechama); Roger Lloyd Pack (Sexton); Vladimir Medar (Priest); Walter Cartier, Peter Johnston, Guy Lutman, Donald MacLennan, Rene Sartoris, Sammy Bayes (Russian Dancers); Ivan Baptie, Jody Hall, Michael Ingleton, Barry Lines, Ken Robson, Adam Scott, Bob Stevenson, Lou Zamprogna, Roy Durbin, Albin Pahernik (Jewish Male Dancers); Ina Claire, Tanya Bayona, Karen Trent, Petra Siniawski (Jewish Female Dancers); Cyril Bass (Drummer); A. Haverstock (Violinist); Leo Wright (Trumpeter); C. C. Bilham (Bassist); M. Winter (Clarinettist); H. Krein (Accordionist); Isaac Stern (Solo Violin).

Fiddler on the Roof, from the 1964 season, was the fifth-longest-running Broadway musical, with 3,242 performances, and additionally was an international hit. Garnering $38,255,196 in distributors' domestic film rentals, the film was Oscar-nominated for Best Picture (losing to THE FRENCH CONNECTION) and star Topol was nominated for Best Actor (losing to Gene Hackman in THE FRENCH CONNECTION). FIDDLER ON THE ROOF did win Academy Awards for John Williams' Music, Oswald Morris' Cinematography, and Sound by Gordon K. McCallum and David Hilyard.

Based on the stories of Sholom Aleichem [Solomon Rabinowitz], FIDDLER ON THE ROOF is set in 1905 in the village of Anatevka in Czarist Russia. In the Jewish community there, middle-aged milkman Tevye (Topol) and his patient wife Golde (Norma Crane) are hoping to marry off their five daughters. They use the services of village matchmaker Yente (Molly Picon) to accomplish this "overwhelming" task. Tevye's efforts go awry as Tzeitel (Rosalind Harris) weds Motel (Leonard Frey), a poor tailor who is not her intended groom; Hodel (Michele Marsh) weds Perchik ([Paul] Michael Glaser) without her father's consent, the young man/tutor being in league with anti-government guerrillas (which eventually results in the couple to be sent to Siberia); and daughter Chava (Neva Small) chooses Lazar Wolf (Paul Mann), a gentile, as her groom, leading Tevye to tell his family to forget she exists. Meanwhile, as the result of yet another pogrom against the Jewish citizens, Tevye and his remaining brood must flee and begin their exodus to new homes in other countries. Behind the fleeing villagers follows the lonely fiddler (a symbolic figure from traditional Jewish life in Russia).

United Artists went to great expense to recreate the Ukrainian village of Anatevka (created and shot on location near Zagreb, Yugoslavia). However, many were incensed that Zero Mostel, the creator of the role of impatient Tevye, who frequently talks with God, was not used for the screen version instead of the more genteel, younger Israeli actor, Topol, who had also played the role on stage. Ingredients found lacking in the screen adaptation were: ". . . The vitality of Jerome Robbins' choreography (ruined here by insensitive

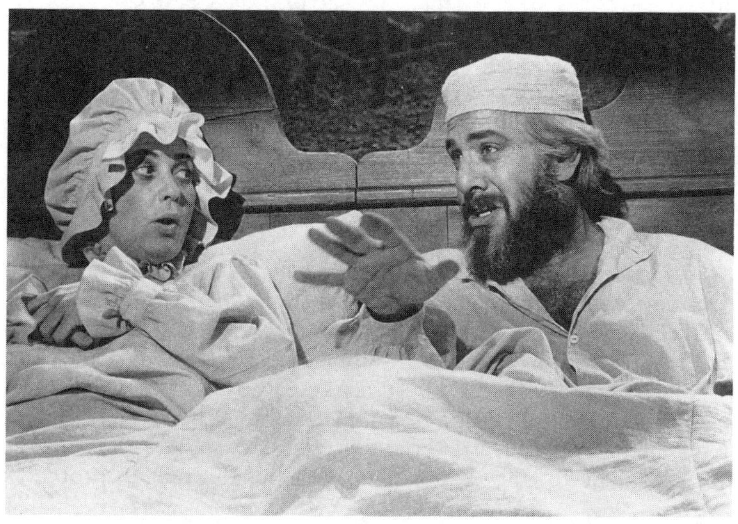

Norma Crane and Topol in FIDDLER ON THE ROOF (1971).

cutting), and the splendid Chagall-inspired setting. The opening out into real locations . . . also reduced its impact, and the . . . photography by Oswald Morris was inappropriately glossy for the subject, distancing the film even further from the original short story . . ." (Ronald Bergan, *The United Artists Story,* 1986). Other symptomatic problems were noted by Colin Ford (British *Monthly Film Bulletin*): "In the New York and London theatres, Zero Mostel and Topol made ['If I Were a Rich Man'] a virtuoso show-stopper night after night; in the cinema, it is almost thrown away, a hiatus in the development of the plot. A vehicle for voice and personality has become a production number for singer, cameraman and editor; even Topol cannot be expected to pull off in so many short takes what cries out for a sustained build-up. This apparent insensitivity to the needs of performers in a musical extends to the dance routines, where the camera rarely shows the dancers' feet."

Three songs from the Broadway score were cut from the movie: "Wedding Dance," "Now I Have Everything" and "I Just Heard." When FIDDLER ON THE ROOF was re-released in 1979, the film's running time was cut by thirty-eight minutes and Dolby Stereo sound was brought into play. The soundtrack album to FIDDLER ON THE ROOF was on *Billboard* magazine's hits charts for four weeks, rising to position #30.

FINE AND DANDY *see* THE WEST POINT STORY.

THE FIREFLY (Metro-Goldwyn-Mayer, 1937) Sepia 138 minutes.

Producer, Hunt Stromberg; director, Robert Z. Leonard; based on the operetta by Otto A. Harbach and Rudolf Friml; adaptor, Ogden Nash; screenplay, Frances Goodrich, Albert Hackett; art directors, Cedric Gibbons; music director, Herbert Stothart; choreographer, Albertina Rasch; camera, Oliver Marsh; editor, Robert J. Kern.

Songs: "Giannina Mia" (Otto A. Harbach, Rudolf Friml); "The Donkey Serenade" (arranged by Herbert Stothart from "Chanson" by Friml; new lyrics, Bob Wright, Chet Forrest); "Love Is Like a Firefly," "English March," "A Woman's Kiss" (Friml; new lyrics, Wright, Forrest); "He Who Loves and Runs Away" (Friml, Gus Kahn); "Sympathy" (Friml, Kahn, Harbach); "When a Maid Comes Knocking at Your Heart" (Friml; lyrics, Harbach, Wright, Forrest); "Danse Jeanette" (Stothart); "Para La Salud" (arranger, Stothart);

Jeanette MacDonald and Ralph Byrd in THE FIREFLY (1937).

"Ojos Rojos" (Argentine folk song; arranger, Manuel Alvarez Maciste).

Jeanette MacDonald (Nina Maria Azara); Allan Jones (Don Diego Manrique de Lara [Captain Francois DeCourcourt]); Warren William (Colonel De Rougemont); Billy Gilbert (Innkeeper); Henry Daniell (General Savary); Douglass Dumbrille (Marquis De Melito); Leonard Penn (Etienne); Tom Rutherford (King Ferdinand); Belle Mitchell (Lola); George Zucco (St. Clair, Chief of French Secret Service); Matthew Boulton (Corbett Morris, the Duke of Wellington); Robert Spindola (Juan); Ian Wolfe (Izquierdo, the Minister); Manuel Alvarez Maciste (Pedro); Frank Puglia (Pablo); John Picorri (Cafe Proprietor); James B. Carson (Smiling Waiter); Jason Robards (Spanish Patriot); Alan Curtis (French Soldier); Ralph Byrd (French Lieutenant); Bud Flanagan [Dennis O'Keefe] (French Soldier-Admirer); Maurice Cass (Strawberry Vendor); Sam Appel (Fruit Vendor); Maurice Black (Pigeon Vendor); Rolfe Sedan (Hat Vendor); Inez Palange (Flower Woman); Harry Worth (Adjutant); John Merton, Hooper Atchley (French Officers); Stanley Price (Joseph Bonaparte); Brandon Hurst (English General); Pedro de Cordoba (Spanish General); Theodore von Eltz (Captain Pierlot); Lane Chandler (Captain of the Guard); Edward Keane (Colonel, the Chief of Staff); Sidney Bracy (Secretary); Eddie Phillips (Captain); Russ Powell (Stablehand); Agostino Borgato (Peasant); Robert Z. Leonard, Albertina Rasch (Cafe Extras).

The title of this operetta comes from the title character, singer Nina Maria Azara, who is known as "Mosca del Fuego" or "The Firefly." Rudolf Friml and Otto A. Harbach composed the production for Italian singer Emma Trentini, who first performed it on Broadway late in 1912. For the screen version, Jeanette MacDonald, after being in motion pictures for eight years, received solo star billing for the first time. Her leading man was fellow MGM contractee Allan Jones, who had sung with MacDonald the year prior in the operatic sequences of ROSE MARIE (*q.v.*). In THE FIREFLY Allan Jones performed "The Donkey Serenade," which Rudolf Friml composed specifically for the film (it was based on his 1920 piano piece, "Chanson"). Jones' RCA Victor recording of the melody sold in excess of a million copies and for years was the company's third best selling platter.

In Spain, at the time of its conquest by Napoleon Bonaparte, beautiful cafe singer Nina Maria Azara (Jeanette MacDonald) is romancing the Marquis De Melito (Douglass Dumbrille), but she is really a spy for the Spanish loyalists. When a French officer (Leonard Penn) wants to court her, Nina Maria distracts him by claiming to love a stranger, Don Diego (Allan Jones), who promptly returns her affections. Don Diego pursues the singer and eventually she finds herself attracted to him, although she has now been assigned to focus on Colonel De Rougemont (Warren William). Nevertheless, Don Diego remains persistent. With a message intended for the Colonel in her possession, Nina Maria is cornered and asks Don Diego for help. However, St. Clair (George Zucco), the chief of the French Secret Police, forces him to get a confession out of the young woman. When he succeeds it is revealed that he is really Captain Francois Decourcourt, who works for St. Clair. Nina Maria is ordered out of the country, just as Spain and France go to war. Later, she is imprisoned on the orders of De Rougemont. Francois comes to see her but is later reported missing in action. The tide turns in favor of the Spanish and Nina Maria is released from prison. She is cheered by an awaiting crowd. She searches out the injured Francois and the two are happily reunited.

Despite a number of good songs ably performed—Jones's "The Donkey Serenade," "Giannina Mia" and "A Woman's Kiss," Jeanette's "Love Is Like a Firefly," "He Who Loves and Runs Away" and her reprise of "Giannina Mia," and their duet of "Sympathy"—the film was overlong. In spite of plush production trappings, THE FIREFLY emerged too frequently boring. The *New York World-Telegram* explained, "Done in the manner of old-fashioned operettas, it throws right out the window all the crusading work done by directors such as W.S. Van Dyke, Rouben Mamoulian and others in trying to convert the screen operetta into a realistic pungent, believable medium."

THE FIRST NUDIE MUSICAL (Paramount, 1976) Color 97 minutes.

Executive producers, Stuart W. Phelps, Peter S. Brown; producer, Jack Reeves; directors, Mark Haggard, Bruce Kimmel; screenplay, Kimmel; art director, Tom Rassmussen; set decorator, Timothy J. Block; costumes, Rassmussen; music, Kimmel; choreographer, Lloyd Gordon; camera, Douglas H. Knapp; editor, Allen Leuso.

Songs: "The First Nudie Musical," "The Lights and the Smiles," "Orgasm," "Lesbian Butch Dyke," "Dancing Dildos," "Perversion," "Honey, What Ya Doin' Tonight?" "Let 'Em Eat Cake," "I Don't Have to Hide Anymore," "Where Is a Man?" (Kimmel).

Stephen Nathan (Harry Schecter); Cindy Williams (Rosie); Bruce Kimmel (John Smithee); Leslie Ackerman (Susie); Alan Abelew (George Brenner); Diana Canova (Juanita); Alexandra Morgan (Mary La Rue); Frank Doubleday (Arvin); Kathleen

Hietala (Eunice); Art Marino (Eddie); Hy Pyke (Benny); Greg Finley (Jimmy); Herb Graham (Frankie); Rene Hall (Dick Davis); Susan Stewart (Joy Full); Artie Shafer (Actor); Jerry Hoffman (Schlong); Wade Crookham (Mr. "Orgasm"); Nancy Chadwick (Lesbian); John Kirby (Bad Actor); Vern Joyce (Assistant Director); Jan Praise (Cameraman); Eileen Ramsey (Brenda); Jane Ralston (Buck & Wing Girl); Claude Spence (Old Man Schecter); Chris Corso (Pervert); Alison Cohen (Jane); Susan Gelb (Tapper); Kathryn Kimmel (The Hand); Nancy Bleier, Susan Underwood, Cindy Ashley, Jane Ralston, Jeff Greenberg, Susan Buckner, Diana Vance, Lauren Lucas, Lloyd Gordon, Kathy Wigglet, Chris Malott, Alana Reed, Joe Blum, Rick Nickerson (Dancers).

Hollywood executive Harry Schecter (Stephen Nathan), the head of once famous Schecter Studios, has to make pornographic movies in order to keep from going bankrupt. However, when several of his films fail to recoup their cost at the box-office he cannot obtain backing to do another movie. His secretary-lover, Rosie Brady (Cindy Williams), suggests to Harry that he produce a musical with naked performers, and he easily gets backing for this project. He is forced to hire the naive nephew (Bruce Kimmel) of one of the money men to direct the venture. When scores of applicants answer the casting call for the project, the new director proves to be entirely inept. Harry takes over the production reins, but he keeps running into roadblocks and ends up with only two weeks left to make the film or lose his financing. When the picture's leading lady (Diana Canova) tries to seduce Harry, Rosie maneuvers her out of the way. With no one left to play the star roles, Rosie and Harry take over the parts and get the film into the can. At its preview, the new movie is a hit. Harry now has the opportunity to make only "good" films, while he and Rosie plan to wed.

Shot in eighteen days at a cost of approximately $150,000, THE FIRST NUDIE MUSICAL was picked up by Paramount and dropped after initial test showings demonstrated that there was little box-office interest in it. (Some sources claim the studio scratched the film because they were fearful it might hurt the image of star Cindy Williams, by then popular on TV in "Laverne and Shirley," being shot at Paramount.) Writing in *Cult Movies 2* (1983), Danny Peary noted, "Ironically, when I first saw THE FIRST NUDIE MUSICAL, I realized that the title perfectly reflects the innocence of the filmmakers—and it is this innocence when dealing with the supposedly perverse adult material that gives the picture its charm. . . . Probably the most remarkable thing about this movie, considering its subject matter, is that it is totally inoffensive, which leads one to believe it might have done better if it had not been."

THE FLOWER DRUM SONG (Universal, 1961) Color 133 minutes.

Producer, Ross Hunter in association with Joseph Fields; director, Henry Koster; based on the novel by C.Y. Lee and the musical play by Fields, Richard Rodgers, Oscar Hammerstein, II; screenplay, Fields; art directors, Alexander Golitzen, Joseph Wright; set decorator, Howard Bristol; costumes, Irene Sharaff; makeup, Bud Westmore; music supervisor/director, Alfred Newman; choreographer, Hermes Pan; assistant director, Phil Bowles; technical advisors, H. K. Wong, Albert Lim; sound, Waldon O. Watson, Joe Lapis; camera, Russell Metty; editor, Milton Carruth.

Songs: "Fan Tan Fanny," "Grant Avenue," "You Are Beautiful," "I Am Going to Like it Here," "The Other Generation," "Chop Suey," "Love Look Away," "I Enjoy Being a Girl," "Gliding through My Memoree," "Sunday," "Don't Marry Me" (Richard Rodgers, Oscar Hammerstein, II).

Nancy Kwan (Linda Low); James Shigeta (Wang Ta); Juanita Hall (Auntie [Madame Liang]); Jack Soo (Sammy Fong); Miyoshi Umeki (Mei Li); Benson Fong (Wang Chi-Yang); Reiko Sato (Helen Chao); Patrick Adiarte (Wang San); Kam Tong (Dr. Li); Victor Sen Yung (Frankie Wing); Soo Young (Madame Fong); Ching Wah Lee (Professor); James Hong (Headwaiter); Spencer Chan (Dr. Chon); Arthur Song (Dr. Fong); Weaver Levy (Policeman); Herman Rudin (Holdup Man); Cherylene Lee, Virginia Lee (San's Girlfriends); Virginia Grey (TV Heroine); Paul Sorensen (TV Sheriff); Ward Ramsey (Great White Hunter); Laurette Luez (Mexican Girl); Robert Kino (Bank Manager); Beal Wong (Tailor); Jon Fong (Square Dance Caller); Willard Lee, Frank Kumagai (Tradesmen); B. J. Baker (Singing Voice of Linda Low); John Dodson (Singing Voice of Dr. Li); Marilyn Horne (Singing Voice of Helen Chao).

Having dealt successfully with the Polynesian in *South Pacific* (1948), and with the Siamese in *The King and I* (1952), Richard Rodgers and Oscar Hammerstein turned to the Chinese in San Francisco for the musical *Flower Drum Song,* which opened on Broadway on December 1, 1958 for a 600-performance run. Gene Kelly directed the hit production, which starred Pat Suzuki, Miyoshi Umeki, Larry Blyden, Juanita Hall, Keye Luke and Jack Soo. Producer Ross Hunter, most associated with glossy cinema soap operas such as IMITATION OF LIFE (1959), purchased the screen rights and cast Miyoshi Umeki, Juanita Hall and Jack Soo from the Broadway version. Not content with using San Francisco's real Chinatown, he constructed his own Grant Avenue on the Universal backlot. ". . . The scale and gloss of the enterprise did little to disguise its overly 'cutesy-cutesy' tone that succeeded in being uncomfortably condescending to the Chinese community of San Francisco . . ." (Clive Hirschhorn, *The Universal Story,* 1983). Critics also noted that the cast was not particularly Chinese (the leads were part-English, Japanese and mulatto) and that the Rodgers and Hammerstein score was more Broadway than Oriental.

San Francisco Chinatown nightclub proprietor Sammy Fong (Jack Soo) has Hong Kong girl Mei Li (Miyoshi Umeki) chosen as his "picture" bride-to-be, although he really wants to marry sensual Linda Low (Nancy Kwan), a singer in his club. This modern man, who rebels against old-world marriage traditions, attempts to persuade the Wang family to have their son Wang Ta (James Shigeta) marry Mei Li, who has just arrived in the United States, but Wang Ta has been dating Linda, who is eager to become related to his family's wealth. A party is given to celebrate both Wang Ta's college graduation and his aunt's (Juanita Hall) graduation from citizen school. There Ta's impending marriage to Linda is announced. Sammy, however, is intent on winning Linda. He invites the Wang family to his club and when they see Linda perform a striptease they call off the wedding. By now Ta realizes he loves Mei Li, but he is still aching over his desire for Linda. Mei Li demands that Sammy live up to the marriage contract. However, in the midst of the ceremony confesses she entered the country illegally, which makes the marriage agreement invalid. Ta, nevertheless, wants to marry her and so a double wedding takes place, with Sammy also marrying Linda.

The best ingredients of this colorful but compromised production were Juanita Hall's singing of "Chop Suey" and Hermes Pan's choreography of the "Love Look Away" ballet sequence. Other pleasing moments were the duet, "A Hundred Million Miracles," sung by Miyoshi Umeki and Kam Tong (dubbed), and curvaceous Nancy Kwan (dubbed) performing "I Enjoy Being a Girl," a brassy paean to the joys of pre-emancipated womanhood. The *New York Times* assessed, "Colorfulness and pleasant music were the strong points of this Rodgers-and-Hammerstein package on Broadway. Likewise the richly-technicolored movie, with the same plot, behavior and attitudes as so much slick razzle-dazzle of San Francisco's Chinatown. But the melodies, the sumptuous settings and a few personalities surmount the near-caricatures of the characters." Despite its flaws, FLOWER DRUM SONG received five Oscar nominations: Scoring—Musical Picture, Costume Design—Color, Art Direction-Set Decoration—Color, Sound, and Cinematography—Color. The movie grossed $4,833,077 in distributors' domestic film rentals. The soundtrack album appeared on *Billboard* magazine's hits chart for twenty-four weeks, rising to position #15.

Having survived FLOWER DRUM SONG, Ross Hunter returned to the musical film genre again, this time with the disastrous LOST HORIZONS (1974), *q.v.*

FLYING DOWN TO RIO (RKO, 1933) 89 minutes.

Executive producer, Merian C. Cooper; associate producer, Lou Brock; director, Thornton Freeland; based on the play by Anne Caldwell, from an original story by Brock; screenplay, Cyril Hume, H. W. Hanemann, Erwin Gelsey; art directors, Van Nest Polglase, Carroll Clark; costumes, Walter Plunkett; music, Vincent Youmans; music director, Max Steiner; choreographers, Dave Gould, (uncredited) Hermes Pan; sound, P. J. Faulkner; camera effects, Vernon Walker; camera, J. Roy Hunt; editor, Jack Kitchin.

Songs: "Music Makes Me," "The Carioca," "Orchids in the Moonlight," "Flying Down to Rio" (Vincent Youmans, Edward Eliscu, Gus Kahn).

Dolores Del Rio (Belinha de Rezende); Gene Raymond (Roger Bond); Raul Roulien (Julio Ruberio); Ginger Rogers (Honey Hale); Fred Astaire (Fred Ayres); Blanche Frederici (Dona Elena); Walter Walker (Senor de Rezende); Etta Moten (Black Singer); Roy D'Arcy, Maurice Black, Armand Kaliz (The Three Greeks); Paul Porcasi (Mayor); Reginald Barlow (Banker); Eric Blore (Butterbass, the Head Waiter); Franklin Pangborn (Hammersmith, the Hotel Manager); Luis Alberni (Carioca Casino Manager); Jack Goode, Jack Rice, Eddie Borden (Yankee Clipper Musicians); Alice Gentle (Concert Singer); Martha La Venture (Dancer); Ray Cooke (Banjoist); Harry Bowen (Airport Mechanic); Lucile Browne, Mary Kornman (Belinha's Friends); Sidney Bracy (Rodriguez, the Chauffeur); Clarence Muse (Caddy in "Haiti"); Movita Castaneda (Singer); Harry Semels (Sign Poster); Manuel Paris (Extra at Aviators' Club); Gino Corrado (Messenger); Adrian Rosley (Club Manager); Wallace MacDonald (Corrado, the Pilot [Messenger]); Adrian Rosley (Club Manager); The American Clippers Band, The Brazilian Turunas (Themselves); Howard Wilson, Betty Furness, Francisco Maran, Helen Collins, Carol Tevis, Eddie Tamblyn, Alice Ardell, Rafael Alivir, Barbara Sheldon, Douglas Williams, Alma Traver, Juan Duval, Eddie Boland, Julian Rivero, Pedro Regas (Bits).

"FLYING DOWN TO RIO was a watershed film in RKO history. It introduced one of the famous teams in the chronicle of Hollywood musical filmmaking—Fred Astaire and Ginger Rogers—and it inaugurated a series of pictures that would make the studio a leader in the production of musicals throughout the rest of the decade" (Richard B. Jewell, Vernon Harbin, *The RKO Story,* 1982). In actuality, Dorothy Jordan had been contracted to play the role of Honey Hale in FLYING DOWN TO RIO, but when she chose instead to marry studio executive producer Merian C. Cooper, Ginger Rogers was substituted. Rogers' on-screen dance/love interest partner was thirty-four-year-old Fred Astaire, who had recently made his screen debut in MGM's DANCING LADY (1933), *q.v.*, supporting Joan Crawford in a song-and-dance number. The actual leads of this trend-setting film were Dolores Del Rio and Gene Raymond (who replaced Joel McCrea).

Orchestra leader-aviator Roger Bond (Gene Raymond) and his performers, including the dance team of Fred Ayres (Fred Astaire) and Honey Hale (Ginger Rogers), earn a big break by being hired to perform at a posh resort hotel in Rio de Janeiro. They fly down to Rio for the engagement. Once there, Roger falls in love with sultry Brazilian entertainer Belinha de Rezende (Dolores Del Rio), who is engaged to wealthy Julio Ruberio (Raul Roulien). The band scores a major success in Rio, especially Fred and Honey when they dance "The Carioca." Eventually Julio realizes that his relationship with Belinha is hopeless and he relinquishes his rights to her, so she can have happiness with Roger.

Within the deliciously conceived film the song numbers are divided evenly among the cast: "Music Makes Me" (Ginger Rogers), "Orchids in the Moonlight" (Raul Roulien, Fred Astaire, Dolores Del Rio), "Flying Down to Rio" (Astaire and the chorus) and "The Carioca" (Etta Moten). The film accidentally established several ingredients that would become standard in future Astaire-Rogers outings: glorious art deco sets by Van Nest Polglase (filmed in black-and-white), choreography by Hermes Pan (in this production he was the uncredited assistant dance director), a fabricated dance craze (herein "The Carioca"), and a simplistic plot thread of elegant Astaire feuding, courting and winning feisty but graceful Rogers.

Two particular numbers stand out in FLYING DOWN TO RIO: the title tune, sung as a line of chorus girls strapped to the wings of airplanes dance and throw off clothing high above Rio, abetted by apache dancers and trapeze artists. The other is the infectious "The Carioca" number, whose title refers to a native of Rio de Janeiro. The dance is presented at the Carioca Casino, first by the Brazilian Turunas (themselves), followed with a terpsichorean demonstration by casino guests. Astaire and Rogers are fascinated by this avant-garde dance (a variation of the samba) which demands partners dance with foreheads touching. They try out the intricate steps and soon have the dance floor to themselves. Thereafter, three vocalists (including black songstress Etta Moten) sing the lyrics as first twenty-five couples and then sixteen Brazilians perform the dance. The scene climaxes with Astaire and Rogers dancing atop seven white grand pianos which have been arranged to form a circular dance floor. It is inspired moviemaking at its grandest.

The *New York American* termed the production "a glorious Hollywood holiday" and it paved the way for the successful starring screen teamings of Fred Astaire and Ginger Rogers at RKO. It also demonstrated that, with the assistance of special effects, a musical need not be bound to the soundstage and could also succeed without a backstage setting.

FOLIES BERGERE (United Artists, 1935) 83 minutes.

Executive producer, Darryl F. Zanuck; associate producers, William Goetz, Raymond Griffith; director, Roy Del Ruth; based on the play *The Red Cat* by Rudolph Lothar, Hans Adler; screenplay, Bess Meredyth, Hal Long; art director, William Darling; costumes, Albert M. Levy, Omar Kiam; music arranger/conductor, Alfred Newman; choreographer, Dave Gould; sound, E. H. Hansen; camera, Barney McGill, Peverell Marley; editors, Allen McNeil, Sherman Todd.

Songs: "Singing a Happy Song," "I Was Lucky," "Au Revoir l'Amour," "Rhythm of the Rain" (Jack Meskill, Jack Stern); "You Took the Words Right Out of My Mouth" (Harold Adamson, Burton Lane); "I Don't Stand a Ghost of a Chance with You" (Victor Young, Ned Washington, Bing Crosby); "Valentine" (Henri Christine; English lyrics, Herbert Reynolds; French lyrics, Albert Willemetz).

Maurice Chevalier (Eugene Charlier/Fernand, the Baron Cassini); Merle Oberon (Baroness Genevieve Cassini); Ann Sothern (Mimi); Walter Byron (Rene); Lumsden Hare (Gustave); Robert Grief (Henri); Eric Blore (Francois); Halliwell Hobbes (Paulet); Philip Dare (Victor); Frank McGlynn, Sr. (Joseph); Ferdinand Munier (Morizet); Ferdinand Gottschalk (Ferdinand); Barbara Leonard (Josephine); Georges Renavent (Premier); Olin Howland (Stage Manager); Sailor Vincent (Rubber Bit); Robert Graves, Paul Kruger (Doormen); Olga Borget, Irene Bentley, Vivian Martin, Jenny Gray, Doris Morton (Usherettes); Joseph E. Bernard (Butler); Albert Pollet (Secretary); Perry Ivins (Airport Official); Mario Dominici (Doctor); Paul Toien (Page Boy); Lew Hicks, Leon Baron (Attendants); Nam Dibot (Ticket Man); Harry

Holman (Cafe Waiter); Leonard Walker (Assistant Stage Manager); Albert Pollet, Max Barwyn (Waiters in Box); Ed Reinach, Joe Mack, Pop Garso, Bruce Covington, Charles Hagen, Adolph Faylauer, Harry Milton, Conrad Seidermann, Austin Browne (Bearded Men); Marbeth Wright, Lucille Lund, Jeanne Hart, Joan Woodbury, Bernadene Hayes, Marie Wells, Fay Worth, Maryan Dowling (Girls in Bar); Pauline Rosebrook, Shirley Hughes, Dixie McKinley, Libby Marks, Rosa Milano, Zandra Dvorak (Girl Models); Roy Seagus, Eugene Beday, Harry Semek, Hans Schumm, Alex Chevron, Luis Hanore, Rene Mimieux, Dick Allen, Henri Runique (Bartenders); Bob Von Dobeneck, Al Mazzola, Bill O'Brien, Al Constance, Jack Raymond (Waiters); Audrey Hall, Pokey Champion, Rita Dunn, Claudia Fargo, Myra Jones, Billie Lee, Mary Jane Hodge (Girls in Shell); Helen Mann, Joan Sheldon, Jill Evans, Barbara Roberts, Angela Blue, Nell Rhoades, June Gale, Mae Madison (Girls in Secretary Number); Jenny Gray, Thaya Foster, Ruth Day, Barbara Beall, Gail Goodson, Virginia Dabney (Girls in Hat Store); Wedgwood Nowell, Barlowe Borland, Anders Van Haden, John Ince, Wilson Millar, Yorke Sherwood, Cyril Thornton, Vesey O'Davoren, Robert Cody (Principals in Montage).

After coming to Hollywood in 1929 and becoming one of the top stars of musical films (at Paramount and briefly at MGM), Frenchman Maurice Chevalier concluded his first U.S. tenure in 1935 with FOLIES BERGERE in which he sang "I Was Lucky," "Rhythm of the Rain," "I Don't Stand a Ghost of a Chance with You" and "Valentine," among others. The lavish production proved to be a solid vehicle for him, as noted by the *Los Angeles Examiner:* "FOLIES BERGERE is a natural so far as that attractive debonair Frenchman, Maurice Chevalier, is concerned. He fairly radiates that expressive personality of his, singing, dancing, making love and proving himself so magnetic the ladies should flock in large numbers to where it is being shown."

A financial crisis prevents Baron Cassini (Maurice Chevalier) from being in two places at once. He decides he must attend a clandestine business meeting and, because he is also required at a ball, his associates do not know what to do. They decide to engage Folies Bergere entertainer Eugene Charlier (Maurice Chevalier) to impersonate their employer at the society event, although no one informs Baroness Cassini (Merle Oberon), who has recently been estranged from her husband. At the ball Charlier finds himself attracted to the Baroness but she shuns him, learning that her spouse has been wooing Charlier's stage partner, Mimi (Ann Sothern). The next day the Baron does not return and Charlier again impersonates him. In so doing he convinces Mimi to give up Cassini and she, in turn, realizes she really loves Charlier. Successful in his business venture, the Baron returns home to find his wife loves him again. When he learns of the identity ruse, he is left wondering how far Charlier went in restoring his wife's affections.

Although Maurice Chevalier sparkled in FOLIES BERGERE and for many was the saving grace of this movie, otherwise burdened with an obvious and over-extended plotline, he was not the original choice for the lead. Darryl F. Zanuck, having left Warner Bros. where he was responsible for 42ND STREET (1933), *q.v.,* wanted to produce a lavish musical at 20th Century Pictures, where he had been hired as executive producer. Once he had selected FOLIES BERGERE as his ambitious musical project, he wanted Charles Boyer for the lead assignment. When Boyer refused the part, he suggested his countryman and friend Chevalier. Not to be overlooked in this entertainment potpourri is Ann Sothern, who had shone in the Eddie Cantor musical, KID MILLIONS (1934). Sothern provides solid counterpoint to Chevalier in their two song numbers together: "Singing a Happy Song" and "Rhythm in the Rain."

A French-language version of FOLIES BERGERE, called L'HOMME DES FOLIES BERGERE, was shot simultaneously with the American edition, also starring Maurice Chevalier. The more risque French version— which included topless Folies girls—had Natalie Paley as the Baroness and Sim Viva as Mimi. The plotline from FOLIES BERGERE would be reworked twice by 20th Century-Fox: THAT NIGHT IN RIO (1941, with Don Ameche, Alice Faye, Carmen Miranda) and ON THE RIVIERA (1951, with Danny Kaye, Gene Tierney, Corinne Calvet).

British release title: THE MAN FROM THE FOLIES BERGERE.

FOLLOW THE BOYS (Metro-Goldwyn-Mayer, 1963) Color 96 minutes.

Producer, Lawrence P. Bachmann; director, Richard Thorpe; story, Bachmann; screenplay, David T. Chantler, David Osborn; art director, Bill Andrews; music, Ron Goodwin, Alexander Courage; music conductor, Goodwin; song arranger/conductor, Geoff Love; production supervisor, Basil Somner; assistant director, Jack Causey; sound, Rusty Coppleman; camera, Ted Scaife; editor, John Victor Smith.

Songs: "Follow the Boys," "Tonight's My Night," "Intrigue," "Waiting for Billy," "Sleepyland" (Benny Davis, Ted Murry, Dramato Palumbo); "Italian Lullabye" (Connie Francis).

Connie Francis (Bonnie Pulaski); Paula Prentiss (Toni Denham); Dany Robin (Michele); Russ Tamblyn (Lieutenant Smith); Richard Long (Lieutenant Peter Langley); Ron Randell (Commander Ben Bradville); Roger Perry (Radarman Bill Pulaski); Janis Paige (Liz Bradville); Robert Nicholas (Hulldown); Paul Maxwell (C.M.A.A.); Eric Pohlmann (Italian Farmer); David Sumner (Vittorio); Sean Kelly (Duty Officer); John McClaren (Commentator); Roger Snowdon (Italian Barman).

Pop singer Connie Francis made a good impression when she co-starred in Metro-Goldwyn-Mayer's WHERE THE BOYS ARE (1960); she also had a hit record of the title song on the MGM label. Three years later she headlined MGM's modestly-budgeted FOLLOW THE BOYS, but her next two outings for the studio, LOOKING FOR LOVE (1964) and WHERE THE BOYS MEET THE GIRLS (1966), doomed her screen career. FOLLOW THE BOYS not only had the buoyant Connie performing her self-penned "Italian Lullabye" but she also sang the title song (which was very derivative of "Where the Boys Are"), "Tonight's My Night," "Sleepyland," "Intrigue" and "Waiting for Billy." The highlight of the feature was its French Riviera and Cannes locations, shot in Metrocolor and widescreen. Unfortunately, the *New York Times* was correct when it labeled the feature ". . . A flat, frazzled stencil of WHERE THE BOYS ARE. . . . This is a jerky account of four women and their variously fickle men, all of whom seem to have in common excessively meager brains."

In Europe Bonnie Pulaski (Connie Francis) has to give up her new husband Billy (Roger Perry), who has been recalled to duty on the *U.S.S. Independence,* after only two hours of marriage. In order to get to her man, Bonnie joins forces with older Liz Bradville (Janis Paige), who wants her commander husband (Ron Randell) to take a non-sea position so they can have children. Then there are Toni Denham (Paula Prentiss) and local girl Michele (Dany Robin), both of whom have their ambition set on winning Lieutenant Peter Langley (Richard Long). Toni is out to marry Peter so that he will go into business with her father, while Michele is really a bill collector. The four women, known as "seagulls," purchase a run-down car and pursue their men from Cannes to Santa Margharita in Italy, where Billy becomes angry at Bonnie for hounding him, while Peter abandons Toni for Michele. At the annual festival for the crushing of grapes, Toni becomes smitten with Lieutenant Smith (Russ Tamblyn), Commander Bradville agrees to abandon the sea, and Bonnie and Billy are reunited.

Not only was Richard Thorpe's direction flat and the scenario predictable, but FOLLOW THE BOYS failed to allow Francis to shine at that self-deprecating comedy which had made her so engaging in WHERE THE BOYS ARE.

FOLLOW THE FLEET (RKO, 1936) 110 minutes.

Producer, Pandro S. Berman; director, Mark Sandrich; based on the play *Shore Leave* by Herbert Osborne; screenplay, Dwight Taylor, Allan Scott; art directors, Van Nest Polglase, Carroll Clark; set decorator, Darrell Silvera; gowns, Bernard Newman; music director, Max Steiner; choreographers, Hermes Pan, Fred Astaire; technical advisor, Lieutenant Commander Harvey Haislip; special effects, Vernon Walker; camera, David Abel; editor, Henry Berman.

Songs: "We Saw the Sea," "I'd Rather Lead a Band," "Let Yourself Go," "I'm Putting All My Eggs in One Basket," "Get Thee Behind Me, Satan," "But Where Are You?" "Let's Face the Music and Dance" (Irving Berlin).

Fred Astaire (Bake Baker); Ginger Rogers (Sherry Martin); Randolph Scott (Bilge Smith); Harriet [Nelson] Hilliard (Connie Martin); Astrid Allwyn (Iris Manning); Harry Beresford (Captain Ezra Hickey); Russell Hicks (Jim Nolan); Brooks Benedict (Sullivan); Ray Mayer (Dopey); Lucille Ball (Kitty Collins); Addison [Jack] Randall (Lieutenant Williams); Maxine Jennings (Hostess); Jane Hamilton (Waitress); Kay Sutton (Telephone Operator); Doris Lloyd (Mrs. Courtney); Huntley Gordon (Touring Officer); James Pierce (Bouncer); Herbert Rawlinson (Webber); Gertrude Short (Cashier at Dance Joint); George Magrill (Quartermaster); Betty Grable, Joy Hodges, Jeanne Gray (Trio); Thelma Leeds, Lita Chevret (Girls); Tony Martin, Edward Burns, Frank Mills, Frank Jenks (Sailors); Dorothy Fleiesman, Bob Cromer (Contest Dancers).

For the fifth screen teaming of Fred Astaire and Ginger Rogers, RKO dusted off the 1922 Herbert Osborne play *Shore Leave,* which had been filmed as a silent in 1925 by First National with Richard Barthelmess and Dorothy Mackaill, again at the beginning of the sound era in 1930 as HIT THE DECK (*q.v.*) and remade under that title by MGM in 1955. As in TOP HAT (1935), *q.v.,* Irving Berlin supplied the score and Mark Sandrich directed. However, except for "Let's Face the Music and Dance" it was not on par with Berlin's music for their previous film. In comparing FOLLOW THE FLEET to TOP HAT, Roy Hemming (*The Melody Lingers On,* 1986) noted, "It's different not only in locale and style, but also in the way Berlin's songs are used. Instead of being plot motivated, most of the songs seem more arbitrarily inserted and are sometimes even out of joint with the script. . . . Instead of the Continental elegance and sophistication of TOP HAT, FOLLOW THE FLEET is a more homespun romp about a couple of sailors. . . ."

Getting shore leave in San Francisco, sailor pals Bake Baker (Fred Astaire) and Bilge Smith (Randolph Scott) find themselves romantically linked with two dancehall girl sisters, Sherry (Ginger Rogers) and Connie Martin (Harriet [Nelson] Hilliard). Bake and Sherry had once been a vaudeville team together and they meet again at the Paradise Ballroom. The two couples have all kinds of romantic problems, often fighting and then making up. Eventually they team up to fix up an old ship and turn it into a posh showboat. There they stage a big musical revue that is well received.

Tony Martin can be glimpsed briefly in FOLLOW THE FLEET as a sailor. Originally he was given "Let's Face the Music and Dance" to croon, but star Fred Astaire usurped the number for himself and it provided his finest showcase in the feature. (It also allowed him to don his trademark white tie and tails, which were in sharp contrast to the flavor of the earlier portions of the movie.) Astaire's best work with Ginger Rogers in this production was on the gag dance, "I'm Putting All My Eggs in One Basket," while Harriet Hilliard sang "Here Am I, But Where Are You?" and "Get Thee Behind Me, Satan," the latter melody composed originally for TOP HAT. To be noted in small roles are Lucille Ball and Betty Grable, the latter as part of a singing trio.

Liberty magazine assessed: "FOLLOW THE FLEET, the latest Astaire-Rogers music-fest, supplies just what audiences have come to expect from these nimble stars. The picture is well dressed, spirited, and imbued with a lighthearted gaiety. . . . [It] is close to flawless during its lyric moments." On the other hand, handsome Randolph Scott, who had been the second male lead in Irene Dunne-Astaire-Rogers's ROBERTA (1935), *q.v.,* was again awkward and far from nimble, a very ill-equipped participant. Then too, there were several variations from the by now standard Astaire-Rogers formula. As Stanley Green (*Encyclopaedia of the Musical Film,* 1987) pointed out, "Except for a divorcee's palatial estate, the film's chief locales—a battleship, a dancehall, and a steam schooner—made it the least opulent of any that starred Astaire and Rogers. . . . But the image-change was most noticeable in the casting of Astaire as a gum-chewing gob, which not only lowered his social standing but severely limited his wardrobe."

After FOLLOW THE FLEET, Astaire and Rogers returned to more traditional, more elegant doings in SWING TIME (1936), *q.v.* FOLLOW THE FLEET appeared in the same year as MGM's BORN TO DANCE, *q.v.,* a more satisfying study of gobs intermingling in the world of show business. The latter feature boasted a zippy Cole Porter score and starred Eleanor Powell, James Stewart, Virginia Bruce and Buddy Ebsen.

FOOTLIGHT PARADE (Warner Bros., 1933) 104 minutes.

Director, Lloyd Bacon; screenplay, Manuel Self, James Seymour; art directors, Anton Grot, Jack Okey; costumes, Milo Anderson; makeup, Perc Westmore; music director, Leo F. Forbstein; dance numbers creator/stager, Busby Berkeley; dialogue director, William Keighley; camera, George Barnes; editor, George Amy.

Songs: "Honeymoon Hotel," "Shanghai Lil" (Al Dubin, Harry Warren); "By a Waterfall," "Ah, the Moon Is Here," "Sitting on a Backyard Fence" (Irving Kahal, Sammy Fain);

James Cagney (Chester Kent); Joan Blondell (Nan Prescott); Ruby Keeler (Bea Thorn); Dick Powell (Scotty Blair); Guy Kibbee (Silas Gould); Ruth Donnelly (Harriet Bowers Gould); Claire Dodd (Vivian Rich); Hugh Herbert (Charlie Bowers); Frank McHugh (Francis); Arthur Hohl (Al Frazer); Gordon Westcott (Harry Thompson); Renee Whitney (Cynthia Kent); Philip Faversham (Joe Farrington); Juliet Ware (Miss Smythe); Herman Bing (Fralick, the Music Director); Paul Porcasi (George Appolinaris); William Granger (Doorman); Charles C. Wilson (Cop); Barbara Rogers (Gracie); Billy Taft (Specialty Dancer); Marjean Rogers, Pat Wing, Donna Mae Roberts, Donna La Barr, Marlow Dwyer (Chorus Girls); Dave O'Brien (Chorus Boy); George Chandler (Drugstore Attendant); Hobart Cavanaugh (Title Thinker-Upper); William V. Mong (Auditor); Lee Moran (Mac, the Dance Director); Billy Barty (Mouse in "Sittin' on a Backyard Fence" Number); Harry Seymour (Desk Clerk in "Honeymoon Hotel" Number); Sam McDaniel (Porter); Fred Kelsey (House Detective); Jimmy Conlin (Uncle); Roger Gray (Sailor in "Shanghai Lil" Number); John Garfield (Sailor Behind Table); Duke York (Sailor on Table); Harry Seymour (Joe, the Assistant Dance Director).

Producer Darryl F. Zanuck reteamed director Lloyd Bacon and dance director Busby Berkeley from 42ND STREET (1933), *q.v.*, for this expansive musical affair which also included several cast members and technical talent from that movie and its Berkeley follow-up, GOLD DIGGERS OF 1933 (*q.v.*). All three of these films utilized a backstage storyline. The big surprise of FOOTLIGHT PARADE was Jimmy Cagney as the energetic director-hoofer, breaking his tough gangster image and paving the way for his Oscar-winning role in YANKEE DOODLE DANDY (*q.v.*) eight years later. FOOTLIGHT PARADE also contains some of Berkeley's best remembered symmetrical production numbers, all

Ruby Keeler, James Cagney, Joan Blondell, Frank McHugh and Dick Powell in FOOTLIGHT PARADE (1933).

presented in the final portion of the picture: "Honeymoon Hotel" with Dick Powell and Ruby Keeler as newlyweds; the two in a woodsy love song "By a Waterfall" (which focused extensively on chorus girl bathing beauties parading by, plunging into and cavorting above and beneath the water); and the finale, "Shanghai Lil," involving Cagney and Ruby Keeler in a saucy story within a story, which had both of them (and the multitudinous chorus) singing, tap dancing and involved in military precision steps. Lesser numbers in the picture included "Ah, the Moon Is Here" and "Sittin' on a Backyard Fence."

While staging abbreviated revues ("prologues") for New York City movie theatre owners Silas Gould (Guy Kibbee) and Al Frazer (Arthur Hohl), hot-tempered Chester Kent (James Cagney) has all his best ideas stolen by spies for rival operators. When chorus line director Francis (Frank McHugh) becomes overworked, a substitute is brought in by Gould's sister Harriet (Ruth Donnelly)—young crooner Scotty Blair (Dick Powell). The latter is soon attracted to secretary Bea Thorn (Ruby Keeler), who proves to be an excellent tap dancer. Scotty romances Bea during rehearsals while brassy actress Nan Prescott (Joan Blondell), who is interested in Chester, is frustrated to see him being vamped by wealthy Vivian Rich (Claire Dodd). To stop the theft of his latest production numbers, Chester orders the theatre locked and all the players and dancers are kept there in a dormitory-like setting until opening night. When the tryout is ready, lead performer Joe Farrington (Philip Faversham) becomes drunk and Chester must take his place. He and Nan work well together. As a result he dumps Vivian for ever patient Nan.

While FOOTLIGHT PARADE was one of Warner Bros.' most costly Busby Berkeley musicals, it met with mixed critical reception from the jaded press. (There should only be such bountiful entertainment in a contemporary musical film!) The *New York Times* complained that it was "a dull and turgid musical film" while *Time* magazine noted, "Most of the mass-maneuvers in FOOTLIGHT PARADE only remotely resemble dances but they are sufficiently bizarre—in many cases, pretty—to be worth watching." On the other hand, the *New York Herald Tribune* enthused, "FOOTLIGHT PARADE is elaborate, fantastically extravagant in its chorus numbers, slightly less tuneful and considerably more disrobed than its predecessors, well acted and pretty certain to be a smashing economic success." "Those who weren't lost in the image of a silly plot were suffocated by the sheer vulgar lavishness of the piece," decided the *New York Evening Post,* while the *Los Angeles Times* reported, "This Warner Brothers feature is just about the biggest song, dance and story picture to date and I would hesitate to name any in its class for spectacular numbers. It's easy to figure this as a sensational hit."

Originally, when FOOTLIGHT PARADE went into production, Dick Powell was suffering from a throat problem and Stanley Smith was brought in to replace him, but Powell "recovered" in time to join the cast, thus allowing for the third screen teaming of Powell and Ruby Keeler. The latter was not initially intended to "sing" in the "Shanghai Lil" number; it had been planned for Renee Whitney (seen in the film as Cynthia Kent), but at the last minute it was decided to have Keeler perform in the interlude. (For the record, kinetic Jimmy Cagney outdances, outsings, and outshines Keeler throughout this number, which features her as a Oriental whore.) The reason that usual songwriters Al Dubin and Harry Warren did not compose the "By the Waterfall" number (Sammy Fain and Irving Kahal did) was that they were on holiday when Berkeley conceived the notion for the aquacade production routine and required a splashy new song to accompany the hundreds of water nymphs frolicking in the gallons of water.

FOR ME AND MY GAL (Metro-Goldwyn-Mayer, 1942) 104 minutes.

Producer, Arthur Freed; director, Busby Berkeley; based on the original story "The Big Time" by Howard Emmett Rogers; screenplay, Richard Sherman, Fred Finklehoffe, Sid Silvers, (uncredited): Jack McGowan, Irving Brecher; art directors, Cedric Gibbons, Gabriel Scognamillo; set decorators, Edwin B. Willis, Keogh Gleason; costumes, Gile Steele; makeup, Jack Dawn; music director, George Stoll; vocals/orchestrators, Conrad Salinger, George Bassman, Leo Arnaud, (uncredited) Roger Edens; music adaptor, Edens; choreographers Bobby Connolly, (uncredited) Gene Kelly; (uncredited) technical advisor, Elsie Janis; sound supervisor, Douglas Shearer; montage, Peter Ballbusch; camera, William Daniels; editor, Ben Lewis.

Songs: "For Me and My Gal" (Edgar Leslie, F. Ray Goetz, George W. Meyer); "The Doll Shop," "The Confession," "Vaudeville Montage," "Love Song," "The Small Time" (Roger Edens); "Oh Johnny, Oh" (Ed Rose, Abe Olman); "They Go Wild, Simply Wild Over Me" (Joseph McCarthy, Fred Fisher); "Oh You Beautiful Doll" (A. Seymour Brown, Nat D. Ayer); "Don't Leave Me Daddy" (Joe Verges); "Sailors' Hornpipe" (traditional); "By the Beautiful Sea" (Harold Atteridge, Harry Carroll); "When You Wore a Tulip" (Jack Mahoney, Percy Wenrich); "Do I Love You?" (E. Ray Goetz, Henri Christine); "After You've Gone" (Henry Creamer, Turner Layton); "Tell Me" (Max Kortlander, J. Will Callahan); "Till We Meet Again" (Ray Egan, Richard A. Whiting); "We Don't Want the Bacon" (Howard Carr, Harry Russell, Jimmie Havens); "Ballin' the Jack" (Jim Burris, Chris Smith); "What Are You Going to Do to Help the Boys?" (Gus Kahn, Egbert Van Alstyne); "Mademoiselle from Armentieres" (unknown); "How Ya Gonna Keep 'Em Down on the Farm?" (Sam M. Lewis, Joe Young, Walter Donaldson); "Where Do We Go from Here" (Howard Johnson, Percy Wenrich); "It's a Long Way to Tipperary" (Jack Judge, Harry Williams); "Goodbye Broadway, Hello France" (C. Francis Riesner, Benny Davis, Billy Baskette); "Smiles" (J. Will Callahan, Lee M. Roberts); "Oh Frenchy" (Sam Ehrlich, Con Conrad); "Pack Up Your Troubles" (George Asaf, Felix Powell); "When Johnny Comes Marching Home" (Louis Lambert; adaptor, Edens)

Judy Garland (Jo Hayden); George Murphy (Jimmy K. Metcalf); Gene Kelly (Harry Palmer); Martha Eggerth (Eve Minard); Ben Blue (Sid Simms); Richard Quine (Danny Hayden); Keenan Wynn (Eddie Milton); Horace [Stephen] McNally (Mr. Waring); Lucille Norman (Lily Duncan); Betty Welles, Anne Rooney (Members of Jimmy's Company).

"They love! It's a swift-paced romance of vaudeville's golden days! He was a fresh guy but he stole his way into her heart. . . . Step out with Judy and a screenful of entertainers in her grandest hit! . . . A love story that brings tears! It's got everything . . . for you and your gal." So proclaimed the ads FOR ME AND MY GAL, which was Judy Garland's first solo starring feature as an adult in a musical picture. It was also Gene Kelly's screen debut and the first of his several starring roles at MGM with Garland.

In the pre-World War I era, entertainers Jo Hayden (Judy Garland), Red Metcalf (George Murphy), Lily Duncan (Lucille Norman) and Sid Simms (Ben Blue) play the vaudeville circuit. Jo endures the rigors of touring to finance her younger brother's (Richard Quine) medical school education and so that, one day, she can realize her dream—playing the Palace Theatre in New York City. When Jo meets handsome, glib Harry Palmer (Gene Kelly) he convinces her to abandon the act and to become his partner. Ironically it is Red's and Sid's careers that advance, while Jo and Harry continue playing the small time. During these years, Jo has fallen in love with Harry. Meantime, Harry takes up with internationally popular singing star Eve Minard (Martha Eggerth) in order to advance his career. Finally, he realizes his love for Jo and gives up Eve. Just as the duo win a booking at the Palace Theatre, Harry gets his draft notice. To avoid being mobilized into the service, he smashes his hand in a wardrobe trunk "accident." When Jo learns what he has done, she leaves him, still grieving over her brother who died fighting in France. A remorseful Harry attempts to make amends. Because of his maimed hand he cannot join the Army. However, he and Sid sign up with a YMCA entertainment unit heading for the front lines. While entertaining troops he performs a heroic act. Thereafter, he is reunited with Jo who has come to France to sing for the troops. After the Armistice the couple resume their stage partnership and finally get to play the Palace Theatre in New York City.

FOR ME AND MY GAL was conceived as MGM's answer to 20th Century-Fox's ALEXANDER'S RAGTIME BAND (1938), *q.v.*, a rousing hosannah to vaudeville. Moreover, its strong patriotic theme was appropriate for the rising tide of nationalism as the United States was drawn into World War II. Initially George Murphy was assigned the role of Harry Palmer, but producer Arthur Freed had second thoughts once he realized how similar that part was to the role of the heel Kelly had played on Broadway in *Pal Joey* (1940). Freed made a deal with producer David O. Selznick to share Kelly's contract, and thus Kelly made his screen debut at Metro-Goldwyn-Mayer. Murphy was relegated to the tertiary role, although he retained second billing. During production there were strained relations between Murphy and Kelly, as well as between Kelly and director Busby Berkeley, who had favored Murphy for the assignment. After FOR ME AND MY GAL was previewed, it was realized that audience sympathy was with Murphy, not Kelly, winning Garland's affections at the film's finale. Thus there were twenty-one days of retakes, including two major scenes to show the heel-becoming-a-hero and becoming more humane. The finale was restaged, this time removing Murphy from the spotlight.

Looking rather wan in the picture (she was absent on sick leave for a total of four weeks during filming), Judy Garland had a bevy of songs to perform, including "Don't Leave Me Daddy," "After You've Gone," "How Ya Gonna Keep Them Down on the Farm?" (with quartet), "Where Do We Go from Here" (with quartet), "Smiles" and "It's a Long Way to Tipperary" (with chorus). She and Kelly danced and sang to "Ballin' the Jack" and the title tune; Kelly and Ben Blue performed "Frenchie, Frenchie"; Kelly hoofed solo to such numbers as "Oh, Johnny, Oh" and "They Go Wild, Simply Wild Over Me"; Martha Eggerth performed "Do I Love You?" "Tell Me" and "Till We Meet Again"; and the not-to-be-overlooked George Murphy dueted on "Oh You Beautiful Doll" with Lucille Norman and harmonized with Garland on "By the Beautiful Sea" and the film's first presentation of "For Me and My Gal." To be noted, Bobby Connolly, *not* director/choreographer Busby Berkeley, staged the dances for this film.

Bosley Crowther noted of the movie in the *New York Times,* "The songs are good, the story maudlin—that is the long and short of it. But maybe that was vaudeville." Nevertheless, FOR ME AND MY GAL was a crowd pleaser. Judy Garland and Gene Kelly would reteam for THE PIRATE (1948), *q.v.*, and SUMMER STOCK (1950), *q.v.*, and appear in separate sequences in MGM's all-star salutes: THOUSANDS CHEER (1943) and ZIEGFELD FOLLIES (1946), *q.v.*

Made at a cost of $802,980, FOR ME AND MY GAL grossed $4,371,000 in distributors' domestic film rentals.

42ND STREET (Warner Bros., 1933) 98 minutes.

Producer, Darryl F. Zanuck; director, Lloyd Bacon; based on the novel by Bradford Ropes; screenplay, James Seymour, Rian James; art director, Jack Okey; costumes, Orry-Kelly; choreographer, Busby Berkeley; assistant director, Gordon Hollingshead; camera, Sol Polito; editor, Thomas Pratt.

Songs: "It Must Be June," "You're Getting to Be a Habit with

Me," "Young and Healthy," "Shuffle Off to Buffalo" (Al Dubin, Harry Warren).

Warner Baxter (Julian Marsh); Bebe Daniels (Dorothy Brock); George Brent (Pat Denning); Una Merkel (Lorraine Fleming); Ruby Keeler (Peggy Sawyer); Guy Kibbee (Abner Dillon); Dick Powell (Billy Lawler); Ginger Rogers (Anytime Annie [Ann Lowell]); George E. Stone (Andy Lee); Robert McWade (Al Jones); Ned Sparks (Thomas Barry); Eddie Nugent (Terry Neil); Allen Jenkins (MacElory); Harry Akst (Jerry); Clarence Nordstrom (Groom in "Shuffle Off to Buffalo" Number); Henry B. Walthall (The Actor); Al Dubin, Harry Warren (Songwriters); Toby Wing ("Young and Healthy" Number Girl); Tom Kennedy (Slim Murphy); Wallis Clark (Dr. Chadwick); Jack La Rue (A Mug); Louise Beavers (Pansy); Dave O'Brien (Chorus Boy); Patricia Ellis (Secretary); George Irving (House Doctor); Charles Lane (An Author); Milton Kibbee (News Spreader); Rolfe Sedan (Stage Aide); Lyle Talbot (Geoffrey Waring); Harry Seymour (Aide);

Bebe Daniels, George Brent, Ruby Keeler, Warner Baxter and Wallis Clark in 42ND STREET (1933).

Gertrude Keeler, Helen Keeler, Pat Wing, Geraine Grear [Joan Barclay], Ann Hovey, Renee Whitney, Dorothy Coonan, Barbara Rogers, June Glory, Jayne Shadduck, Adele Lacy, Loretta Andrews, Margaret La Marr, Mary Jane Halsey, Ruth Eddings, Edna Callaghan, Patsy Farnum, Maxine Cantway, Lynn Browning, Donna Mae Roberts, Lorena Layson, Alice Jans (Chorus Girls); Kermit Maynard (Dancer Who Catches Girl).

Credited with revitalizing the popularity of the movie musical, 42ND STREET is one of the best musicals in the history of the genre. With its adult, fast-paced plot, a quartet of sparkling songs by Al Dubin and Harry Warren, and an appealing cast, 42ND STREET remains a viewing delight no matter how many times it is watched (even in its new computerized color version).

Ace Broadway producer Julian Marsh (Warner Baxter), in failing health, is set to put on his greatest musical (*Pretty Lady*), a lavish affair starring veteran actress Dorothy Brock (Bebe Daniels). Marsh, in addition to all his other problems in piecing together the show, has to deal with the temperamental star, her "backer," Abner Dillon (Guy Kibbee), and her new boyfriend, Pat Denning (George Brent). Marsh also has troubles trying to coach the show's ingenue, Peggy Sawyer (Ruby Keeler), who is falling in love with leading man Billy Lawler (Dick Powell), while a member of the chorus, Ann "Anytime Annie" Lowell (Ginger Rogers), keeps pushing for a bigger part in the proceedings. When Dorothy sprains her ankle on the night of dress rehearsal in Philadelphia and cannot go on, Anytime Annie is given the lead, but she realizes she cannot pull it off. The part goes to Peggy, who after much coaching from Marsh, goes forth to perform, with the director commanding her, "You're going out a youngster, but you've got to come back a star." Peggy does just that and helps to make the show a hit. She and Billy rejoice together. Despite his success, it is a hollow victory for Julian, who is a worn-out man.

Busby Berkeley directed the large-scale production numbers for 42ND STREET. This film established his reputation as an innovative craftsman, especially in his intriguing placement of cameras and his cutting techniques to highlight the kaleidoscopic effects of his dance troupe's movements. This is especially evident in the "Shuffle Off to Buffalo" number as well as in his handling of "Young and Healthy," which is crooned by Dick Powell. Additionally, there was Berkeley's staging of the big "42nd Street" production number, which tells a sharp, sophisticated story-within-a story, a panorama of seamy life on the gaudy thoroughfare. It is a marvel of showmanship! Director Lloyd Bacon matches Berkeley in helming the rest of the film and brings about some snappy performances, especially Warner Baxter as the harried producer who makes the part the epitome of all such characters in many films to come. Also worthy of note is Ginger Rogers' flashy work as Anytime Annie, the quick-tongued, monocle-wearing chorine who is nicely featured with Ruby Keeler and Una Merkel in the "Shuffle Off to Buffalo" segment.

The film launched Dick Powell as one of filmdom's most popular singers. It was also the beginning of Ruby Keeler's movie hoofing career, which included nine musicals at the studio. (Ironically her singing voice was squeaky at best and her tap dancing was thumpish; but, somehow, few people at the time minded, focusing instead on her winning enthusiasm and the fact that she was then the wife of Al Jolson.) As the fading star, Bebe Daniels comes off extremely well, not only in the dramatics but in her off-handed rendering of the torch song, "You're Getting to Be a Habit with Me."

Audiences flocked to 42ND STREET and critics, for the most part, were enthusiastic about the trend-setting feature. "The singing cinema comes into its own once again . . . we're offered a comprehensive study of theatrical life, replete with the vernacular of the stage world; the customers, the cues, the lingo, the laughs, the songs, the sorrows; action every minute, packed into a full picture at a breath-taking pace" (*New York Daily News*). 42ND STREET grossed over $2.25 million and generated a new cycle of movie musicals which quickly got stuck in a formula. 42ND STREET received Oscar nominations for Best Picture and Sound.

For the record, the Helen and Gertrude Keeler in the film's chorus line were Ruby's real life siblings. Composers Harry Warren and Al Dubin were seen briefly playing songwriters. On August 25, 1980 a Broadway musical version of *42nd Street* debuted, starring Tammy Grimes, Jerry Orbach, Wanda Richert and Carole Cook. The long-running show (3,486 performances) was directed and choreographed by Gower Champion, who died on the day of the opening.

THE FOX MOVIETONE FOLLIES (Fox, 1929) Color Sequences 80 minutes.

Presenter, William Fox; director, David Butler; revue director, Marcel Silver; screenplay, Butler; costumes, Sophie Wachner, Alice O'Neill; music conductor, Arthur Kay; ensemble directors, Archie Gottler, Fanchon & Marco; sound, Joseph E. Aiken; camera, Charles Van Enger; editor, Ralph Dietrich.

Songs: "Walking with Susie," "Why Can't I Be Like You?" "Legs," "The Breakaway," "That's Your Baby," "Look What You've

Sharon Lynn and John Breeden in THE FOX MOVIETONE FOLLIES (1929).

Done to Me," "Big City Blues," "Pearl of Old Japan" (Con Conrad, Sidney Mitchell, Archie Gottler).

John Breeden (George Shelby); Lola Lane (Lila Beaumont); De Witt Jennings (Jay Darrell); Sharon Lynn (Ann Foster); Arthur Stone (Al Leaton); Stepin Fetchit (Swifty); Warren Hymer (Martin); Archie Gottler (Stage Manager); Arthur Kay (Orchestra Leader); Mario Dominici (Le Maire); Vina Gale, Arthur Springer, Helen Hunt, Charles Huff, Harriet Griffith, John Griffith (Adagio Dancers); Sue Carol, Dixie Lee, Melva Cornell, Paul Langlen, Carolynne Snowden, Jeanette Dancey, David Percy, David Rollins, Bob Burns, Frank Richardson, Henry M. Mollandin, Frank La Mont (Song and Dance Numbers).

Issued in the summer of 1929, THE FOX MOVIETONE FOLLIES was the studio's contribution to the major companies' parade of all-star, all-talking, all-singing, all-dancing motion pictures. The ads boasted "Now through the Magic of FOX MOVIETONE . . . [comes] this gorgeous extravaganza with a conviction that you will await it each year with expectancy. No theatre anywhere can duplicate this unrivaled revue with a brilliant cast of

200. . . ." In actuality, although this entry had a wisp of a plot, it lacked big star names and was not the most popular of the lot by any means. "By now the singing-talkie revue has lost its novelty," decided *Photoplay* magazine, which added that this outing had "comedy, fair songs, and a bit of a love story."

George Shelby (John Breeden) comes to New York City from his southern home to persuade his girlfriend, Lila Beaumont (Lola Lane), to abandon her dreams of a stage career. When she wins a part in a musical revue, George buys the controlling interest in the show from its producer, Jay Darrell (De Witt Jennings), so that he can dismiss Lila from the cast. When the show bows, however, the temperamental star (Sharon Lynn) refuses to go on. Lila takes her place and is a terrific success. Because the revue is a hit, George sells his interest back to Darrell. He and Lila plan to wed.

THE FOX MOVIETONE FOLLIES was loaded with song-and-dance numbers, but few of the Con Conrad, Sidney Mitchell and Archie Gottler songs were memorable. Perhaps the best was "The Breakaway," which was sung by Sue Carol. Making her movie debut in this revue was Dixie Lee. She and Sue Carol became good friends and later both were more famous as the wives of noted movie stars; Sue Carol (who became an agent) married Alan Ladd, while Dixie Lee wed Bing Crosby. It should be noted that pert Sue Carol, while only a mediocre performer, was quite popular in the early sound era. She is associated with several standard tunes from the period such as "The Kiss Waltz," "Sweet Sue" and "Three Little Words."

The next year Fox released MOVIETONE FOLLIES OF 1930 starring El Brendel, William Collier, Jr., Marjorie White, Miriam Seegar and Noel Francis, with fourteen-year-old Betty Grable in the chorus. This time the publicity for the picture insisted, "The most thrilling musical entertainment ever put on the screen! Better than the record-breaking Fox Follies of 1929!" But, by then, the musical film craze was fast fading and there were no more annual entries in this movie revue series.

British release title: MOVIETONE FOLLIES OF 1929.

FUNNY FACE (Paramount, 1957) Color 103 minutes.

Producer, Roger Edens; director, Stanley Donen; based on an unproduced musical libretto to *Wedding Day* by Leonard Gershe; screenplay, Gershe; art directors, George W. Davis, Hal Pereira; set decorators, Sam Comer, Ray Moyer; costumes, Edith Head, Hubert de Givenchy; makeup, Wally Westmore; music director, Adolph Deutsch; orchestrators, Conrad Salinger, Van Cleave, Alexander Courage, Skip Martin; choreographers, Fred Astaire,

Eugene Loring; special camera effects, John P. Fulton; process camera, Farciot Edouart; camera, Ray June; editor, Frank Bracht.

Songs: "Funny Face," "How Long Has This Been Going On?" "Clap Yo' Hands," "Basal Metabolism" (instrumental), "Let's Kiss and Make Up," "He Loves and She Loves," " 'S Wonderful" (George Gershwin, Ira Gershwin); "Think Pink!" "Bonjour, Paris!" "On How to Be Lovely" (Leonard Gershe, Roger Edens); "Marche Funèbre" (Edens).

Audrey Hepburn (Jo Stockton); Fred Astaire (Dick Avery); Kay Thompson (Maggie Prescott); Michel Auclair (Professor Emile Flostre); Robert Flemyng (Paul Duval); Dovima (Marion); Virginia Gibson (Babs); Suzy Parker, Sunny Harnett, Don Powell, Carole Astman (Specialty Dancers); Sue England (Laura); Ruta Lee (Lettie); Alex Gerry (Dovitch); Iphigenie Castiglioni (Armande); Jean Del Val (Hairdresser); Albert D'Arno (Beautician); Nina Borget (Assistant Hairdresser); Marilyn White, Dorothy Colbert (Receptionists); Louise Glenn, Heather Hopper, Cecile Rogers (Junior Editors); Nancy Kilgas (Melissa); Emilie Stevens (Assistant Dance Director); Paul Smith (Steve); Diane Du Bois (Mimi); Karen Scott (Gigi); Gabriel Curtiz (Man Next to Hand Stand); Peter Camlin (Man Buyer); Elizabeth Slifer (Mme. La Farge); Donald Lawton (Airport Clerk); Karine Nordman (French Girl); Genevieve Aumont (French Actress); Nesdon Booth (Southern Man); George Dee, Marcel de la Brosse, Albert Godderis (Seedy Men); Jerry Lucas (Bruiser); Jack Chefe (Frenchman); Jan Bradley (Crying Girl); Jerry Chiat (Man on Head); Elsa Peterson (Woman Buyer); Fern Barry (Southern Wife).

Fred Astaire and his sister Adele first starred with Victor Moore in *Funny Face* on Broadway in the fall of 1927, for a 244-performance run. The musical by George and Ira Gershwin introduced such song standards as the title melody, " 'S Wonderful," "My One and Only" and "He Loves and She Loves." Jump ahead three decades. MGM producer Roger Edens purchased Leonard Gershe's story, "Wedding Day," as a potential musical. It was Edens' concept to blend the score of *Funny Face* with Gershe's story and to have Fred Astaire and Audrey Hepburn co-star in a *Pygmalion*-like tale. However, the Gershwins' score was owned by Warner Bros., Astaire and Hepburn had picture commitments to Paramount, while Edens, Gershe and the selected director (Stanley Donen) were based at MGM. Finally, after much negotiations, all rights and services were sold to Paramount, including the use of such other MGM-Arthur Freed unit staples as cinematographer Ray June, music arrangers Adolph Deutsch and Conrad Salinger and choreographer Eugene Loring. Filming began in April 1956;

concluding that June on the Eiffel Tower with Astaire, Hepburn and Kay Thompson singing "Bonjour Paris."

Fashion magazine editor Maggie Prescott (Kay Thompson) develops an idea of doing a layout called "Clothes for Women Who Aren't Interested in Clothes." She assigns ace fashion photographer Richard Avery (Fred Astaire) not only to do the layout but to find a suitable model for the project. He stumbles onto a studious Greenwich Village girl who works at an avant garde book shop, Jo Stockton (Audrey Hepburn), and he signs her for the magazine spread. The two, accompanied by Maggie, go to Paris. There Avery has Jo learn the modeling trade. During the process the two fall in love, while Jo is transformed into the perfect model.

Moira Walsh wrote in *America* magazine, "The film offers two agreeable, though not uncommon, added attractions: a color and Vista Vision tour of Paris, and, for the ladies, a mouth-watering fashion show. It also offers for the delectation of more critical audiences two strikingly original features; some unique camera trickery involving color effects (supervised by fashion photographer Richard Avedon); and an intelligent script which pokes pointed fun at both the world of high fashion and the world of Left Bank philosophers." The *New York Times* reported, "A scrumptiously delicious and filling musical with real gleam from all sides . . . a truly lovely and beguiling color production that makes the scenic most of some Paris backgrounds." In retrospect, John Douglas Eames (*The Paramount Story,* 1985) judged, "FUNNY FACE was pure joy from start to finish. Ravishing to the eye . . . the ear was beguiled by a succession of superb songs. . . . Astaire and Hepburn shimmered with charm and talent, but the revelation was Thompson, with a presence so magnetic that she even stole a song and dance ["Clap Yo' Hands"] from Astaire." The fact that Fred Astaire, at fifty-seven, was nearly twice Audrey Hepburn's age seemed magically unimportant in the course of their lyrical FUNNY FACE courtship.

Most of the Gershwins' original score (except "My One and Only") was retained for the Paramount production. These included Fred Astaire singing and dancing to the title song, he and Kay Thompson singing and dancing to the electric "Clap Yo' Hands" (borrowed from the Gershwins' *Oh, Kay!,* 1926), Astaire vocalizing "He Loves and She Loves," which he and Audrey Hepburn dance to, Astaire singing "Let's Kiss and Make Up" before doing his bullfight dance, and " 'S Wonderful," sung and danced to by Astaire and Hepburn. Also Hepburn (making her movie musical debut) sings "How Long Has This Been Going On?" (written for *Funny*

Face but used in the Gershwins' *Rosalie,* 1928) and in a Left Bank Cafe dances to "Basal Metabolism." Roger Edens and Leonard Gershe also composed a trio of new tunes for the film, including Kay Thompson's solo on "Think Pink!" Thompson, Astaire and Hepburn do the split-screen trio, "Bonjour, Paris!" and the two ladies harmonize and dance to "On How to Be Lovely."

The chic and joyful FUNNY FACE was nominated for four Academy Awards: Best Story and Screenplay—Written for the Screen, Cinematography, Costume Design, and Art Direction.

FUNNY GIRL (Columbia, 1968) Color 151 minutes.

Producer, Ray Stark; director, William Wyler; based on the musical play by Jule Styne, Bob Merrill, Isobel Lennart; screenplay, Lennart; production designer, Gene Callahan; art director, Robert Luthardt; set decorator, William Kiernan; Miss Streisand's costumes, Irene Sharaff; makeup supervisor, Ben Lane; music supervisor/ conductor, Walter Scharf; orchestrators, Jack Hayes, Scharf, Leo Shuken, Herbert Spencer; vocal/dance arranger, Betty Walberg; music editor, Ted Sebern; musical numbers directed by Herbert Ross; sound supervisor, Charles J. Rice; sound, Arthur Piantadosi, Jack Solomon; sound effects editor, Joe Henrie; camera, Harry Stradling; supervising editor, Robert Swink; editors, Maury Winetrobe, William Sands.

Songs: "If a Girl Isn't Pretty," "The Swan," "Roller Skate Rag," "People," "Sadie, Sadie," "His Love Makes Me Beautiful," "Don't Rain on My Parade," "I'm the Greatest Star," "You Are Woman, I Am Man," "Funny Girl" (Jule Styne, Bob Merrill); "I'd Rather Be Blue Over You (Than Happy with Somebody Else)" (Fred Fisher, Billy Rose); "Second Hand Rose" (James F. Hanley, Grant Clark); "My Man" (Maurice Yvain, A. Willemetz, Jacques Charles; English adaptor, Channing Pollock).

Barbra Streisand (Fanny Brice); Omar Sharif (Nick Arnstein); Kay Medford (Rose Brice); Anne Francis (Georgia James); Walter Pidgeon (Florenz Ziegfeld); Lee Allen (Eddie Ryan); Mae Questel (Mrs. Strakosh); Gerald Mohr (Branca); Frank Faylen (Keeney); Mittie Lawrence (Emma); Gertrude Flynn (Mrs. O'Malley); Penny Santon (Mrs. Mecker); John Harmon (Company Manager); Thordis Brandt, Bettina Brenna, Virginia Ann Ford, Alena Johnston, Karen Lee, Mary Jane Mangler, Inga Neilsen, Sharon Vaughn (Ziegfeld Girls).

Unique talent Barbra Streisand shot to Broadway stardom in 1964 portraying show business legend Fanny Brice (1891–1951) in the musical *Funny Girl,* which ran for 1,348 performances on

Broadway. Four years later she recreated the role in the William Wyler-Ray Stark Columbia Pictures production.* She garnered an Academy Award for her performance, tying with Katharine Hepburn who starred in THE LION IN WINTER. The musical was also nominated for an Oscar as Best Picture, but lost to another musical, OLIVER (*q.v.*).** FUNNY GIRL grossed $26,325,000 in distributors' domestic film rentals and resulted in a sequel, the far less satisfying FUNNY LADY (1975), *q.v.*

In 1910s New York City, Fanny Brice (Barbra Streisand), although not a glamour girl, longs to become a Broadway star. When she loses her job in a chorus she wangles her way into a roller skating number and through her innate comedy abilities becomes a hit. She impresses handsome gambler Nick Arnstein (Omar Sharif), who helps her get a raise. Soon she is hired by Broadway producer Florenz Ziegfeld (Walter Pidgeon) to appear in his famous *Follies.* She quickly raises the producer's ire when she makes a comedy out of the lavish wedding finale sequence by appearing as a very pregnant bride. However, the routine is such a sensation with the audience that the showman permits her to choose her own skits thereafter. Fanny briefly renews her relationship with Nick but then does not see him again for a year. While she is on tour, they rekindle their budding romance. Later, Fanny leaves the annual *Follies* to marry Arnstein. They have a daughter and live lavishly. Fanny returns to the stage and learns that her husband has lost all his money gambling and they are forced to sell their home. Jealous of Fanny's success, Nick leaves her and falls more heavily into debt. He is sent to prison for his participation in a bogus bond operation. A year later he is released and comes to his wife's backstage dressing room. He bids her a final farewell.

FUNNY GIRL represented several firsts. It was Barbra Streisand's screen debut, it was the first musical comedy for Egyptian actor Omar Sharif (who joins in a few strains of the duet, "I Am Woman, You Are Man"), and it was the first and only movie musical for veteran director William Wyler, a three-time Oscar winner. In actuality, choreographer Herbert Ross directed all the musical scenes (about 50% of the picture) and many insist that most of Streisand's scenes were controlled by the star herself. In translating the play into a film, several songs were excised,

---

*Producer Ray Stark was Fanny Brice's son-in-law. He had conceived of the musical story initially as a film, but finally first produced it as a stage show and then in its screen adaptation.

**Other Oscar nominations for FUNNY GIRL were: Best Supporting Actress (Kay Medford), Best Song ("Funny Girl"), Best Score of a Musical Picture—Original or Treatment, Cinematography, Sound, and Editing.

including "Cornet Man," "Who Taught Her Everything?" "I Want to Be Seen with You Tonight," "Henry Street," "Find Yourself a Man," "Rat-Tat-Tat-Tat," "Who Are You Now?" and "The Music that Makes Me Dance." Added for the movie were three new Jule Styne-Bob Merrill numbers ("Roller Skate Rag," "The Swan" and "Funny Girl") and three old standards associated with Fanny Brice ("Second Hand Rose," "I'd Rather Be Blue Over You" and "My Man"). Shot, but cut from the release print, was the Styne-Merrill number, "Locked in a Pink Velvet Jail." Among special highlights of the picture is Streisand's rendition of "Don't Rain on My Parade," which was opened up to follow her from a railway station, to a train ride, to driving a car, and then to standing on the bridge of a tugboat as she pursues Nick Arnstein who is sailing away on an ocean vessel. Then there is the touching torch song finale, "My Man," accomplished in close up as Fanny sings of her lost love. The soundtrack album to FUNNY GIRL was on *Billboard* magazine's hits chart for thirty-one weeks, rising to position #12.

When the film FUNNY GIRL debuted, *Variety* endorsed, "The charismatic ingredients of the smash musical, the star's inspired song styling . . . casting of Omar Sharif . . . combine into one of the more important roadshow filmusicals. . . . The face-value unreality of the suave confidence man falling for the ungainly comedienne is overcome by their personal performances. . . . It is to the credit of all concerned that the romance remains thoroughly believable." In retrospect, Ethan Mordden (*The Hollywood Musical,* 1981) noted, "The blockbuster [movie musical] syndrome might have collapsed by the late 1960s if some of the big musicals hadn't done so well. OLIVER! and FUNNY GIRL in 1968 proved that there were more SOUNDS OF MUSIC [1965, *q.v.*] to be heard after all, and FUNNY GIRL promised fresh gala for the form in the successful launching of Barbra Streisand in cinema."

It should be noted that ROSE OF WASHINGTON SQUARE (1939), *q.v.,* starring Alice Faye, Tyrone Power and Al Jolson, was an unofficial retelling of the Fanny Brice-Nick Arnstein story. Brice sued 20th Century-Fox and settled out of court.

FUNNY LADY (Columbia, 1975) Color 136 minutes.

Producer, Ray Stark; director, Herbert Ross; story, Arnold Schulman; screenplay, Schulman, Jay Presson Allen; production designer, George Jenkins; set decorator, Audrey Blasdel; costumes, Ray Aghayan, Bob Mackie, Shirley Strahm; music director, Peter Matz; choreographer, Betty Walberg; special effects, Albert Whitlock; camera, James Wong Howe; editor, Marion Rothman.

Songs: "Blind Date," "So Long, Honey Lamb," "Let's Hear It

for Me," "I Like Him/I Like Her," "Isn't This Better?" "How Lucky Can You Get?" (John Kander, Fred Ebb); "(It's Gonna Be a) Great Day," "More Than You Know" (Vincent Youmans, Edward Eliscu, Billy Rose); "It's Only a Paper Moon" (Harold Arlen, E. Y. Harburg, Rose); "I Found a Million Dollar Baby in a Five and Ten Cent Store" (Harry Warren, Mort Dixon, Rose); "Beautiful Face," "Have a Heart" (James V. Monaco, Fred Fisher, Rose); "If You Want the Rainbow, You Must Have the Rain" (Oscar Levant, Dixon, Rose); "I Got a Code in My Dose" (Arthur Fields, Fred Hall, Rose); "Am I Blue?" (Harry Akst, Grant Clarke, Rose); "Clap Hands, Here Comes Charley" (Joseph Meyer, Ballard MacDonald, Rose); "Me and My Shadow" (Al Jolson, Dave Dreyer, Rose); "If I Love Again" (Jack Murray, Ben Oakland).

Barbra Streisand (Fanny Brice); James Caan (Billy Rose); Omar Sharif (Nick Arnstein); Roddy McDowall (Bobby); Ben Vereen (Bert Robbins); Carole Wells (Norma Butler); Larry Gates (Bernard Baruch); Heidi O'Rourke (Eleanor Holm); Samantha Huffaker (Fran); Matt Emery (Buck Bolton); Joshua Shelley (Painter); Corey Fischer (Conductor); Garrett Lewis (Production Singer); Don Torres (Man at Wedding); Raymond Guth (Buffalo Handler); Gene Troobnick (Ned); Royce Wallace (Adele); and: Paul Bryar, Cliff Norton.

Having starred in additional Broadway hits-into-screen musicals (HELLO, DOLLY!, 1969, ON A CLEAR DAY YOU CAN SEE FOREVER, 1970, *qq.v.*) since her screen debut in FUNNY GIRL, *q.v.,* Barbra Streisand returned to the role of entertainer Fanny Brice in FUNNY LADY. The sequel picks up where FUNNY GIRL left off in detailing the life and career of legendary Fanny Brice, covering not only her reinvolvement with gangster Nick Arnstein but also her relationship with feisty showman Billy Rose. Again the film was a stylish production by Ray Stark, with FUNNY GIRL choreographer Herbert Ross now in charge as director. In this super showcase for Streisand—no one else really had an opportunity to shine—she performed many Fanny Brice song favorites. However, the results proved to be contrived, with Streisand more stylized and far less spontaneous than in the past. Although it was not as successful as the first film, FUNNY LADY grossed $19,313,000 in distributors' domestic film rentals.

In 1930 Fanny Brice (Barbra Streisand) is a successful star of the *Ziegfeld Follies* and has a young daughter, Fran (Samantha Huffaker). Although she is divorced from crook Nick Arnstein (Omar Sharif) she still loves the man. Meanwhile, it is the Depression and famed showman Florenz Ziegfeld has difficulty financing his newest show. At this juncture, Fanny meets brash,

Barbra Streisand in FUNNY LADY (1975).

young songwriter-club owner Billy Rose (James Caan). Although they are opposites, the two are attracted. The uncouth, ambitious Rose wants to star Fanny in his spectacular shows. Eventually the two fall in love, but Nick re-enters Fanny's life. For a time they renew their romance but Arnstein realizes he is bad for Fanny and leaves her again. She returns to Billy Rose, who stars her in a Broadway show, *Crazy Quilt.* Although she is not in love with him, Fanny marries Rose and for a time they are content. However, on a surprise trip from Hollywood (where she is starring on radio in "The Baby Snooks Show") to Cleveland, she discovers Billy is having an affair with his aquacade swimming star, Eleanor Holm (Heidi O'Rourke). Fanny and Rose divorce. Fanny realizes that while she may bring happiness to others through her singing and comedy (on stage, radio and films), she will never find marital bliss. Years pass, and Fanny encounters an older, wealthier Billy Rose who hopes to star Fanny on Broadway. While she says no, there is a hint that she may yet change her mind.

Among the many songs in FUNNY LADY are several co-written by Billy Rose, including "It's Only a Paper Moon," "Me and My Shadow" and "Great Day." Also included in the score was a Fanny Brice favorite, "Am I Blue?" John Kander and Fred Ebb, who had composed the songs for the stage and film version of CABARET (1972), *q.v.,* created a quartet of new songs for this project, with Streisand having her best moments with "How Lucky Can You Get?"* Far less felicitous was the production mounting for Kander-Ebb's "Let's Hear It for Me," which was stridently sung as Brice flies to meet Billy Rose. It emerged as an imitative parallel to "Don't Rain on My Parade" (of FUNNY GIRL) and brought unintentional laughter from filmgoers. The soundtrack album to FUNNY LADY appeared on *Billboard* magazine's hits chart for nine weeks, rising to position #6.

One of the creative highlights of FUNNY LADY was James Wong Howe's cinematography, which was Oscar-nominated. FUNNY LADY received four other Academy Award nominations: Best Song ("How Lucky Can You Get"), Scoring, Costume Design and Sound.

When FUNNY LADY bowed, Pauline Kael decreed in *The New Yorker* magazine, "The moviemakers weren't just going to make a sequel to FUNNY GIRL—they were going to kill us. . . . The picture is overproduced and badly edited, with a '40s-movie-heartbreak plot. A great deal of talent has been badly used."

---

*Fred Ebb and John Kander also wrote the bridging "I Like Him/I Like Her" interlude which was tagged onto the "It's Only a Paper Moon" number.

A FUNNY THING HAPPENED ON THE WAY TO THE FORUM (United Artists, 1966) Color 99 minutes.

Producer, Melvin Frank; associate producer, Bob McNaught; director, Richard Lester; based on the musical comedy by Burt Shevelove, Larry Gelbart, Stephen Sondheim; screenplay, Frank, Michael Pertwee; production designer/costumes, Tony Walton; art director, Syd Cain; makeup, Trevor Crole-Rees; incidental music/music director, Ken Thorne; music conductor, Irwin Kostal; choreographers, Ethel Martin, George Martin; second unit director, Bob Simmons; assistant director, Jose Lopez Rodero; sound, Gerry Humphreys; special effects, Cliff Richardson; camera, Nicholas Roeg; editor, John Victor Smith.

Songs: "Comedy Tonight," "Free," "Lovely," "Everybody Ought to Have a Maid," "Bring Me My Bride," "The Dirge" (Stephen Sondheim).

Zero Mostel (Pseudolus); Phil Silvers (Lycus); Buster Keaton (Erronius); Jack Gilford (Hysterium); Michael Crawford (Hero); Annette Andre (Philia); Patricia Jessel (Domina); Michael Hordern (Senex); Leon Greene (Miles Gloriosus); Pamela Brown (High Priestess); Inga Neilsen (Gymnasia); Myrna White (Vibrata); Lucienne Bridou (Panacea); Helen Funai (Tintinabula); Jennifer Baker, Susan Baker (Geminac); Janet Webb (Fertilla); Beatrix Lehmann (Domina's Mother); Alfie Bass (Gatekeeper); Roy Kinnear (Instructor); and: Frank Elliott, Bill Kerr, Jack May, Frank Thornton.

Zany, outrageous Zero Mostel created the role of the wily, lying and cheating Roman slave Pseudolus on Broadway in 1964 in the very funny, bawdy musical comedy, *A Funny Thing Happened on the Way to the Forum,* which delighted audiences for 964 performances. Two years later he repeated his part in the United Artists film version. Given lush production trimming, the picture benefitted from an excellent supporting cast which included a diverse range of comedians: Phil Silvers, Jack Gilford and Buster Keaton (in his final American film role). Although the movie recaptured some of the hilarity of the original stage work, the film was not overly successful at the box-office. As Ronald Bergan (*The United Artists Story,* 1986) explained, "Jump cuts, rapid editing, speeded up and slow motion, fine for the Beatles movies, was fatal to the enjoyable old-fashioned burlesque musical. . . . Yet, so strong were the personalities of the cast that they managed to break through the style."

In ancient Rome Pseudolus (Zero Mostel) is the slave of Senex (Michael Hordern). Despite Pseudolus being lazy and a liar and always trying to become emancipated, his master is tolerant of him.

When Pseudolus discovers that his master's son Hero (Michael Crawford), who is none too bright, is in love with Philia (Annette Andre), a slave girl employed in a brothel controlled by Lycus (Phil Silvers), Pseudolus promises to aid Hero in "rescuing the girl" in return for his freedom. Finding out that Philia has already been sold to soldier Miles Gloriosus (Leon Greene), Pseudolus blackmails another slave, Hysterium (Jack Gilford), into putting on Philia's clothes and pretending to be her corpse, with Pseudolus insisting she has died of the plague. Meanwhile, Philia thinks Senex is her new owner, and he believes she is his newest slave. Pseudolus attempts to keep Senex and Philia separated, but when Miles Gloriosus arrives to claim her, Philia despairs of ever having Hero and goes to the temple to sacrifice herself. In stopping her rash action, Pseudolus involves everyone in a wild chariot race which results in a meeting with a wealthy old man, Erronius (Buster Keaton), who has spent years searching for his lost children and now finds them in Philia and Miles Gloriosus. Thus Philia is unencumbered to wed Hero and Pseudolus is set free by Senex. He now takes up with a beautiful young woman (Inga Neilsen).

As with most musicals, the score of A FUNNY THING HAPPENED ON THE WAY TO THE FORUM fits best in the play's framework and no hit songs resulted from it, although the opening "Comedy Tonight" is amusing, as is the delightfully risque "Everybody Ought to Have a Maid." To open up the film and to focus more on daffy, slapstick comedy (a specialty of director Richard Lester), several songs from the stage original were dropped, including: "Love I Hear," "Pretty Little Picture," "I'm Calm," "That Dirty Old Man" and "That'll Show Him." The *New York Times* weighed, "A few tricks with the camera and a slight toning down of the original madcap spirit haven't spoiled the fun from Broadway and Old Rome, still a cockeyed arena of nubile, busty girls, lusty warriors and lecherous slaves and connivers, all racing around in mad, naughty confusion." Lily N. L. Smith noted in *Films in Review* magazine (November 1966), "Director Richard Lester has given us much more than just a stage musical filmed with lavish sets and gorgeous girls. A good part of the credit for this should go to the camera, since much of the humor comes from sight-gags, which require close-ups on the actors. Slapstick, at its funniest, also requires quick takes (to keep the audience from reflecting). Some of the film's best laughs come from dream sequences repeated several times with different characters and photographed in slow tempo. A song, 'Lovely,' is sung through these passages."

A FUNNY THING HAPPENED ON THE WAY TO THE

Jack Gilford, Michael Hordern, Zero Mostel and Phil Silvers in A FUNNY THING HAPPENED ON THE WAY TO THE FORUM (1966).

FORUM won an Academy Award for Best Scoring of Music—Adaptation or Treatment (Ken Thorne).

On March 30, 1972 a revival of *A Funny Thing Happened on the Way to the Forum* opened on Broadway, starring Phil Silvers (as Pseudolus) and a cast that included Mort Marshall, Larry Blyden and Reginald Owen. The show lasted 156 performances but closed due to Silvers' sudden illness. A 1980 American tour of the stage comedy featured Arte Johnson, Aubrey Schreiber, John Carradine (who was in the original Broadway production), Hans Conreid and Benny Baker.

THE GANG'S ALL HERE (20th Century-Fox, 1943) Color 103 minutes.

Producer, William LeBaron; director, Busby Berkeley; story, Nancy Wintner, George Root, Jr., Tom Bridges; screenplay, Walter Bullock; art directors, James Basevi, Joseph C. Wright; set decorators, Thomas Little, Yvonne Wood; music directors, Alfred Newman, Charles Henderson; choreographer, Berkeley; color consultant, Natalie Kalmus; assistant director, Tom Dudley; sound,

George Leverett, Roger Heman; special camera effects, Fred Sersen; camera, Edward Cronjager; editor, Ray Curtiss.

Songs: "No Love, No Nothing," "A Journey to a Star," "The Lady in the Tutti-Frutti Hat," "The Polka-Dot Polka," "You Discover You're in New York," "Paducah," "Minnie's in the Money" (Leo Robin, Harry Warren); "Brazil" (Ary Barroso, S. K. Russell); "Soft Winds" (Benny Goodman); "Polka-Dot Polka" (David Raksin).

Alice Faye (Eadie Allen); Carmen Miranda (Dorita); Phil Baker (Himself); Benny Goodman and His Orchestra (Themselves); Eugene Pallette (Mr. Mason, Sr.); Charlotte Greenwood (Mrs. Peyton Potter); Edward Everett Horton (Peyton Potter); Tony DeMarco (Himself); James Ellison (Andy Mason); Sheila Ryan (Vivian); Dave Willock (Sergeant Casey); June Haver (Maybelle); Miriam Lavelle (Specialty Dancer); Charles Saggau, Dedre Gale (Jitterbug Dancers); George Dobbs (Benson); Leon Belasco (Waiter); Frank Faylen (Marine); Russell Hoyt (Sailor); Virginia Sale (Secretary); Leyland Hodgson (Butler); Lee Bennett (Man); Jeanne Crain (Girl by the Pool); Lillian Yarbo (Maid); Frank Darien (Doorman); Al Murphy (Stage Manager); Hallene Hill (Old Lady); Gabriel Canzona (Organ Grinder); Fred Walburn (Newsboy); Virginia Wilson (Dancing Partner).

"The STARS Are All Here! The GALS Are All Here! The TUNES Are All Here! The LAUGHS Are All Here!" So read the ads for THE GANG'S ALL HERE. As handled by ace genre director Busby Berkeley, the movie was a lavish confection reteaming two of the most popular film music stars of the 1940s (Alice Faye, Carmen Miranda), highlighting the big band sound of Benny Goodman and his group, and showcasing the comedy relief of Charlotte Greenwood and Edward Everett Horton. That the storyline was so insipid was almost incidental.

Pretty Eadie Allen (Alice Faye) works in the chorus of the Club New York, where the star attractions are Brazilian dancer-singer Dorita (Carmen Miranda) and crooner Phil Baker (himself). One night Sergeant Andy Mason (James Ellison) drops into the club to talk to pal Baker. He spots his wealthy father (Eugene Pallette) there with their neighbor, Peyton Potter (Edward Everett Horton). Andy sees Eadie and after he dances with her at a military canteen, the two fall in love. (To gain her interest and sympathy, Andy has pretended to be "Sergeant Casey," a lonely soldier with no one to see him off to military action.) But the next day he ships out for army duty in the Pacific. Several months go by and Eadie becomes the top singing attraction at the club. When Andy returns home a war hero, his father arranges to stage the Club New York show at

Alice Faye, Phil Baker and Carmen Miranda in THE GANG'S ALL HERE (1943).

his rose garden, much to the chagrin of Mrs. Potter (Charlotte Greenwood), who has known Baker in the past. Dorita then finds out that Andy is engaged to the Potters' daughter, Vivian (Sheila Ryan). Learning this, Eadie informs Andy that she actually loves his pal (Dave Willock). The elaborate show is staged, with Benny Goodman (himself) and His Orchestra. It is a big success for the War Bond cause, but by now Vivian, who has replaced one of the dancers in the production as Tony DeMarco's (himself) partner, prefers show business to Andy. The way is paved for Eadie and Andy's reconciliation.

THE GANG'S ALL HERE was a very expensively mounted affair, in production for over six months. It was Busby Berkeley's first color feature and his first and only teaming with Alice Faye. While its story was hampered by genre conventions, its wilder, creative moments make the movie a fascinating viewing experience.

In the film's quieter musical moments, Faye warbles "No Love, No Nothing" (a tribute to romantic sacrifices on the homefront) and "A Journey to a Star" (a warm ballad), both of which became big hits for her. Then there was Carmen Miranda singing "Paducah" to the harmonies of Benny Goodman and His Orchestra, while Charlotte Greenwood and Charles Saggau danced to a Goodman rhythm number. The orchestra leader himself sang "Minnie's in the Money." Far more typical of Berkeley's extravagant touch were the two massive production numbers. "The Lady in the Tutti-Frutti Hat" has become a classic of its species, with its lush depiction of the South American star entering the tropical isle scene in an oxen-drawn gold cart and wearing one of her massive piled-high fruit headdresses. Sixty chorus ladies carrying giant bananas soon are positioning themselves in assorted geometrical patterns. (The obvious phallic symbolism of the number was so offensive to Brazilian officials that the movie was banned in that country.) The other visual attraction is the finale, "The Polka-Dot Polka," which finds Faye and company on a revolving platform backed by two huge neon-lit mirrors which reflect the intricate steps of the dance troupe.

Photoplay magazine pronounced the film, ". . . Overlavish, plush-cushioned production, so beautiful to look at, so lovely to listen to, but so fragile in story it floats like a feather." But moviegoers were agog at the abundance of lavishness; certainly the apex of wartime musicals. Ironically, it proved to be Alice Faye's last starring musical at 20th Century-Fox; shortly after, she abandoned moviemaking to raise a family.

In 1971 THE GANG'S ALL HERE, with a freshly struck color

print, received several art house release engagements in the United States, amazing a new generation of moviegoers with the plushness of entertainment values that once was the special domain of Hollywood musicals.

British release title: THE GIRLS HE LEFT BEHIND

THE GAY DIVORCEE (RKO, 1934) 107 minutes.

Producer, Pandro S. Berman; director, Mark Sandrich; based on the musical play *The Gay Divorce* by Dwight Taylor and Cole Porter, and the novel *The Gay Divorce* by Taylor; screenplay, George Marion, Jr., Dorothy Yost, Edward Kaufman; art directors, Van Nest Polglase, Carroll Clark; costumes, Walter Plunkett; music director, Max Steiner; music adaptors, Kenneth Webb, Samuel Hoffenstein; choreographers, Dave Gould, (uncredited) Fred Astaire, Hermes Pan; special effects, Vernon Walker; camera, David Abel; editor, William Hamilton.

Songs: "Needle in a Haystack" (Con Conrad, Herb Magidson); "Don't Let It Bother You," "Let's K-nock K-nees" (Mack Gordon, Harry Revel); "The Continental" (Con Conrad, Herb Magidson); "Night and Day" (Cole Porter).

Fred Astaire (Guy Holden); Ginger Rogers (Mimi Glossop); Alice Brady (Hortense Ditherwell); Edward Everett Horton (Egbert Fitzgerald); Erik Rhodes (Rodolfo Tonetti); Eric Blore (Waiter); Lillian Miles, Betty Grable (Hotel Guests); Charles Coleman (Valet); William Austin (Cyril Glossop); Paul Porcasi (Nightclub Proprietor); E. E. Clive (Customs Inspector); George Davis, Alphonse Martell (French Waiters); Charles Hall (Call Boy at Dock); and: Art Jarrett.

Following their successful teaming in FLYING DOWN TO RIO (*q.v.*) the previous year, Fred Astaire and Ginger Rogers were given their first starring vehicle as a team in THE GAY DIVORCEE. This was the black-and-white screen version of the musical comedy, *The Gay Divorce,* in which Astaire had starred on both the New York and London stages.* With a marvelous twenty-two-minute production number of Astaire and Rogers dancing "The Continental" and songs like "Night and Day" (a song-and-dance courtship duet for the leads, set in a ballroom), "A Needle in a Haystack" (an Astaire song/dance solo), "Don't Let It Bother You" (performed by Astaire) and "Let's K-nock K-nees" (performed by Betty Grable and Edward Everett Horton), THE GAY DIVOR-

**The Gay Divorce* opened on Broadway on November 29, 1932 and ran for 248 performances. Only Porter's "Night and Day" was retained for the film from the New York stage production.

CEE solidified the popularity of the Astaire and Rogers' teaming. It launched their magical series of 1930s moneymakers at RKO.

Pretty Mimi Glossop (Ginger Rogers) wants to get a divorce and her busybody Aunt Hortense (Alice Brady) and none-too-smart lawyer Egbert Fitzgerald (Edward Everett Horton) send her to a British resort. There she is to meet a hired co-respondent, Rodolfo Tonetti (Erik Rhodes), who will give the impression that they are lovers, thus providing Mimi with a legal basis for obtaining a divorce. On the docks of London, Mimi meets assured American dancer Guy Holden (Fred Astaire) and he is immediately smitten with her. His pursuit of the attractive young lady leads him to the Brighton resort hotel where she thinks he is the co-respondent and she thus takes a great dislike to him. When Rodolfo arrives on the scene, Guy believes he is Mimi's lover. All kinds of misunderstandings occur before all is settled and Guy and Mimi begin a romance.

Andre Sennwald reported in the *New York Times,* "Last season it was the Carioca which persuaded the foolhardy to bash their heads together. Now the athletic RKO Radio strategists have created the Continental, an equally strenuous routine in which you confide your secret dreams to your partner under the protective camouflage of the music. . . . Both as a romantic comedian and as a lyric dancer Mr. Astaire is an urbane delight, and Miss Rogers keeps pace with him even in his rhythmic flights over the furniture." In retrospect, Ted Sennett (*Hollywood Musicals,* 1981) appraised, "Although THE GAY DIVORCEE triumphed . . . it retained one heavy burden from the stage version: its dated, rather empty-headed book. A throwback to the old Princess Theater musicals of the twenties, the plot was gossamer nonsense. . . . Luckily, the music numbers are outstanding." Roy Hemming (*The Melody Lingers On,* 1986) pointed out, "More than any previous dance number in a movie, 'Night and Day' showed how a song and dance could be more than a plot interruption or aside, how it could instead advance the action and express important aspects of character. . . . 'Night and Day' can be called the number by which Fred Astaire and Ginger Rogers, together, really seduced the moviegoing public with the magic of their dancing and established the screen persona that was to remain basic to their partnership for the rest of the decade."

This was the first of five Astaire-Rogers pictures to be directed by Mark Sandrich, and the first of seven RKO musicals to be produced by Pandro S. Berman. The play's title was altered to appease the Hays (censorship) Office, which insisted that a divorce could never be happy, but a divorcee might be. Only "Night and Day" survived from the original Broadway score, while Con Conrad and Herb Magidson wrote four new songs for the movie. THE GAY DIVORCEE won an Academy Award for Best Song ("The Continental"). The movie received Oscar nominations for Best Picture, Score, Interior Decoration and Sound.

THE GAY IMPOSTERS *see* GOLD DIGGERS IN PARIS.

GENTLEMEN MARRY BRUNETTES (United Artists, 1955) Color 97 minutes.

Executive producer, Robert Bassler; producers, Richard Sale, Robert Waterfield; associate producer, Mary Loos; director, Sale; based on the book *But Gentlemen Marry Brunettes* by Anita Loos; screenplay, Mary Loos, Sale; costumes, Travilla; gowns, Christian Dior; music/music director, Frobert Farnon; choreographer, Jack Cole; assistant directors, Basil Keys, Robert Genore; camera, Desmond Dickinson; editor, G. Turney-Smith.

Songs: "Gentlemen Marry Brunettes" (Herbert Spencer, Earle Hagen); "You're Driving Me Crazy" (Walter Donaldson); "Miss Annabelle Lee" (Sidney Clare, Lew Pollack); "Have You Met Miss Jones?" "My Funny Valentine" (Richard Rodgers, Lorenz Hart); "I Wanna Be Loved By You" (Bert Kalmar, Harry Ruby); "Ain't Misbehavin' " (Andy Razaf, Fats Waller).

Jane Russell (Bonnie Jones/Mimi Jones); Jeanne Crain (Connie Jones/Mitzi Jones); Alan Young (Charlie Biddle, Mrs. Biddle, Mr. Biddle, Sr.); Scott Brady (David Action); Rudy Vallee (Himself); Guy Middleton (Earl of Wickenware); Erich Pohlmann (Monsieur Ballard); Ferdy Mayne (Monsieur Dufond); Leonard Sachs (Monsieur Dufy); Guido Lorraine (Monsieur Marcel); Derek Sydney (Stage Manager); Body Caheen (Pilot); Robert Favart (Hotel Manager); Duncan Elliot (Couturier); Edward Tracy (Chauffeur); Michael Balfour (Stage Doorman); Penny Dane (Wardrobe Woman); Anita Ellis (Singing Voice of Connie Jones).

Following the triumph of GENTLEMEN PREFER BLONDES (*q.v.*) two years before, Jane Russell, now teamed with Jeanne Crain, starred in a humdrum sequel of sorts, GENTLEMEN MARRY BRUNETTES. Despite Paris settings and an attractive cast, the film was a very pale follow-up to the original and failed to generate any of its financial or artistic success.

Bonnie (Jane Russell) and Connie Jones (Jeanne Crain) have a singing sisters act but they run into difficulties when Bonnie agrees to marry half a dozen different men at the same time. To escape the furor, they head to Paris where their agent, David Action (Scott Brady), negotiates for them an engagement at the Folies Club. On arrival they meet Rudy Vallee (himself) who once romanced their mothers, Mimi (Jane Russell) and Mitzi (Jeanne Crain), some two decades before when they were the toasts of the city. While in Paris the girls also encounter wealthy Charlie Biddle (Alan Young) who becomes smitten with Connie. Bonnie meanwhile becomes romantically involved with Action.

Bosley Crowther (*New York Times*) decided, "Despite such rich ingredients as music, CinemaScope and Technicolor, the comedy . . . is an aimless, uninspired charade that is saved from being a complete dud by a clutch of sturdy tunes and a quick Cook's Tour of Paris and the Riviera." Most of the singing in the film was done by Jeanne Crain (who was dubbed by Anita Ellis), the best number being "My Funny Valentine," sung at the Rodin Museum. Rudy Vallee, kidding his image as a singing idol, contributed much of the movie's comedy and also sang "Have You Met Miss Jones?" with Crain and Alan Young and "I Wanna Be Loved by You" with Jane Russell and Crain.

GENTLEMEN PREFER BLONDES (20th Century-Fox, 1953) Color 91 minutes.

Producer, Sol C. Siegel; director, Howard Hawks; based on the play by Anita Loos, Joseph Fields; screenplay, Charles Lederer; art directors, Lyle Wheeler, Joseph C. Wright; set decorator, Claude Carpenter; costumes, Travilla; music director, Lionel Newman; choreographer, Jack Cole; special effects, Ray Kellog; camera, Harry J. Wild; editor, Hugh S. Fowler.

Songs: "A (Two) Little Girl(s) from Little Rock," "Bye Bye Love," "Diamonds Are a Girl's Best Friend" (Jule Styne, Leo Robin); "Ain't There Anyone Here for Love," "When Love Goes Wrong" (Hoagy Carmichael, Harold Adamson).

Jane Russell (Dorothy); Marilyn Monroe (Lorelei Lee); Charles Coburn (Sir Francis Beekman); Elliott Reid (Malone); Tommy Noonan (Gus Esmond); George "Foghorn" Winslow (Henry Spofford III); Marcel Dalio (Magistrate); Taylor Holmes (Esmond, Sr.); Norma Varden (Lady Beekman); Howard Wendell (Watson); Henri Letondal (Grotier); Steven Geray (Hotel Manager); Alex Frazer (Pritchard); Robert Fuller (Man); George Chakiris (Dancer); Leo Mostovoy (Phillipe); George Davis (Cab Driver); Alphonse Martell (Headwaiter); Jimmie Moultrie, Freddie Moultrie (Boy Dancers); Jean De Briac, Peter Camlin, George Dee (Gendarmes); Harry Carey, Jr. (Winslow); Jean Del Val (Ship's Captain); Ray Montgomery (Peters); Alvy Moore (Anderson); Robert Nichols (Eans); Charles Tannen (Ed); Jimmy Young (Stevens); Charles De Ravanne (Purser); John Close (Coach); William Cabanne (Sims); Philip Sylvestre

Marilyn Monroe and Jane Russell in GENTLEMEN PREFER BLONDES (1953).

(Steward); Jack Chefe (Proprietor); John Hedloe (Athlete); Max Willenz (Court Clerk); Rolfe Sedan (Waiter); Robert Foulk, Ralph Peters (Passport Officials); Harris Brown, A. Cameron Grant (Men); Harry Seymour (Captain of Waiters); Donald Moray (Airport Porter); Deena Dikkers (Hotel Clerk); Richard La Marr (Man); Fred Stevens (Stagehand).

Unique Carol Channing caused a sensation on Broadway late in 1949 when she starred in Anita Loos' *Gentlemen Prefer Blondes,* singing the golddiggers' anthem, "Diamonds Are a Girl's Best Friend." The show ran for 740 performances and 20th Century-Fox purchased the screen rights to the musical for $150,000, planning it as a vehicle for Betty Grable in 1951. Two years later the company made the movie version starring sex symbols Marilyn Monroe and Jane Russell, altering the plotline to suit the two stars and deleting most of the stage song numbers. The resulting feature garnered $5,100,000 in distributors' domestic film rentals and greatly boosted the careers of its two curvaceous stars.

Show girls Dorothy (Jane Russell) and Lorelei Lee (Marilyn Monroe) are sailing for Paris on the *Ile de France,* the trip financed by a letter of credit from Gus Esmond (Tommy Noonan), Lorelei's fiancé. On the trip Dorothy becomes involved with sailor Malone (Elliott Reid) who is really a detective hired by Gus's father (Taylor Holmes) to gain incriminating evidence on Lorelei. Wanting her friend to marry a rich man, Lorelei tries to get her fixed up with mysterious Henry Spofford III (George "Foghorn" Winslow), who turns out to be a small boy with a deep voice. Meanwhile, Lorelei romances a wealthy merchant, the elderly Sir Francis Beekman (Charles Coburn), who gives her a diamond tiara belonging to his wife (Norma Varden). In Paris the young women gain employment in a nightclub, but when Gus learns about the tiara he leaves Lorelei. When she is later accused of stealing the jewelry, they end up in a court battle where they prove that Beekman willingly gave Lorelei the diamonds. As a result, in a double ceremony, Lorelei marries Gus and Dorothy weds Malone.

Much of director Howard Hawks' famous style (robust naughtiness combined with screwball comedy) spilled over in GENTLEMEN PREFER BLONDES. This musical comedy showcased both Marilyn Monroe and Jane Russell extremely effectively; the former as the not-so-dumb blonde, the latter as the smart but vulnerable brunette. Monroe sang "Diamonds Are a Girl's Best Friend" while Russell had an engaging production number (set in the ship's gym) with "Ain't There Anyone Here for Love." They each sang "Bye Bye Love" and dueted on "When Love Goes Wrong" and "Two Little Girls from Little Rock."

A sequel, GENTLMEN MARRY BRUNETTES (*q.v.*), emerged two years later.

GEORGE WHITE'S 1935 SCANDALS (Fox, 1935) 83 minutes.

In charge of production, Winfield R. Sheehan; producer/director/screen idea, George White; screenplay, Jack Yellen, Patterson McNutt; art director, Gordon Wiles; costumes, Charles Le Maire; music director, Louis De Francesco; camera, George Schneiderman.

Songs: "You Belong to Me" (Jack Yellen, Cliff Friend); "It's an Old Southern Custom," "I Was Born Too Late" (Yellen, Joseph Meyer); "Oh, I Didn't Know," "According to the Moonlight" (Yellen, Herb Magidson, Meyer); "I Got Shoes, You Got Shoesies," "Hunkadola" (Yellen, Friend, Meyer); "It's Time to Say Goodnight" (Friend, Meyer).

Alice Faye (Honey Walters); James Dunn (Eddie Taylor); Ned Sparks (Elmer White); Lyda Roberti (Manya); Cliff Edwards (Dude Holloway); Arline Judge (Midgie Malone); Eleanor Powell (Marilyn Collins); Emma Dunn (Aunt Jane); Benny Rubin (Louis); Charles Richman (Harriman); Roger Imhof (Officer Riley); Donald Kerr (Grady); Walter Johnson (Daniels); Fred Santley (Master of Ceremonies); Jack Mulhall (Ticket Seller); Sam McDaniel (Porter); George White (Himself); Lois Eckhart (Mme. DuBarry); Fuzzy Knight (Sam Fagel); Jed Prouty (Al Lee); Lynn Bari, Anne Nagel (Chorus Girls); Tamara Shayne (Russian Girl); and: Esther Brodelet, Florine Dickson, Harry Dunkinson, Madelyn Earle, Kay Hughes, Thomas Jackson, Edna Mae Jones, Mildred Morris, Iris Shunn, Aloha Wray, Marbeth Wright.

Alice Faye attained screen stardom in her film debut in GEORGE WHITE'S SCANDALS (*q.v.*) in 1934 and the next year she received top billing for the first time on film in its sequel, GEORGE WHITE'S 1935 SCANDALS. This feature introduced tap dancing great Eleanor Powell to the cinema and included a number of well mounted production numbers. James Dunn took over the lead from Rudy Vallee, who had toplined the first film. The sequel was pale compared to the original and no more offshoots based on the George White reviews ensued until the very standard 1945 RKO revue, GEORGE WHITE'S SCANDALS (*q.v.*), with Jack Haley and Joan Davis.

When his *Scandals* concludes its Broadway run, producer George White (himself) and star Manya (Lyda Roberti) head to Florida for a vacation. Along the way they stop in a small Georgia town where they witness a hick rendition of their New York show. White is impressed with singer Honey Walters (Alice Faye) and signs her for his next production. Thanks to Honey's fast-talking Aunt Jane (Emma Dunn), he also agrees to take along performers Eddie Taylor (James Dunn), Elmer (Ned Sparks), Midge (Arline Judge) and Dude (Cliff Edwards). When the new *Scandals* debuts in New York City it is a big success, but Eddie begins romancing dancer Marilyn Collins (Eleanor Powell). This upsets Honey and eventually White fires both of them. When Aunt Jane arrives in Gotham and comes to view the show, White enlists the aid of a booking agent (Benny Rubin) to bring back Honey and Eddie. He succeeds and the two young lovers are reconciled.

"According to the Moonlight," dueted by Alice Faye and James Dunn, was the most memorable song in the film. Other good numbers included "I Was Born Too Late," "Oh, I Didn't Know" (which featured rows of chorines in vocal support), "You Belong to Me" and "It's an Old Southern Custom" (repeated too frequently throughout the picture)—all performed by Faye. Lyda Roberti and Cliff Edwards shared a duet of "Hunkadola," which relied on acrobatic dancing for its novelty.

Howard Barnes (*New York Times*) wrote, "Alice Faye is the premiere chanteuse of the musical and is exceedingly resourceful in putting over its most infectious songs . . . but neither the tunes nor pageantry are potent enough to charm away . . . [the picture's] frequent laggard stretches."

GEORGE WHITE'S SCANDALS (Fox, 1934) 83 minutes.

In charge of production, Winfield R. Sheehan; producer, George White; directors, White, Thornton Freeland, Harry Lackman; story, White; screenplay, Jack Yellen; costumes, Charles LeMaire; music director, Louis De Francesco; choreographer, Chester Hale; camera, Lee Garmes, George Schneiderman; editor, Paul Weatherwax.

Songs: "Oh, You Nasty Man," "So Nice," "My Dog Loves Your Dog," "Sweet and Simple," "Six Women," "Following in Mother's Footsteps," "Every Day Is Father's Day with Baby," "Hold My Hand" (Ray Henderson, Jack Yellen, Irving Caesar); "Picking Cotton" (Buddy G. DeSylva, Lew Brown, Henderson); "The Man on the Flying Trapeze" (adaptor, Walter O'Keefe).

Rudy Vallee (Jimmy Martin); Jimmy Durante (Happy McGillicuddy); Alice Faye (Kitty Donnelly); Adrienne Ames (Barbara Loraine); Gregory Ratoff (Nicholas Mitwoch); Cliff Edwards (Steve Hart); Dixie Dunbar (Patsy Dey); Gertrude Michael (Miss Lee); Richard Carle (Minister); Warren Hymer (Pete Pandos); George White (Himself); Thomas Jackson (Al Burke); Armand Kaliz (Count Dekker); Roger Grey (Sailor Brown); William Bailey

(Harold Bestry); George Irving (John R. Loraine); Edward Le Saint (Judge O'Neill); Edna May Jones (Eleanor Sawyer); Irving Bacon (Hick); Dewey Robinson (Garbage King); Creighton Hale (Theatre Treasurer); Alma Mott, Lee Lawrence, Ethlyn Howard (Sally, Irene and Mary); Dick Alexander (Iceman); Frances Raymond (Landlady); Howard Hickman (Doctor).

Between 1919 and 1939 George White produced his popular *Scandals* revue on Broadway as well as other shows. He was one of New York's most successful and influential producers. In 1934 he sold the idea of having a motion picture based on his *Scandals* and Fox produced the concept starring Rudy Vallee, who sandwiched it between starring in the 1931 and 1936 editions of *George White's Scandals* on Broadway. The movie also introduced Alice Faye to the screen. She had impressed Rudy Vallee as a chorus girl in the 1931 show and he had featured her on his radio show. He had negotiated a small spot for her in the movie. However, when leading lady Lillian Harvey withdrew from the project because she felt her role was too inconsequential, Alice was promoted to the part. Writing in *The Films of Alice Faye* (1972), W. Franklyn Moshier stated, "Despite the weakest of story threads on which to hang almost a dozen musical numbers, SCANDALS holds up remarkably well today due to impressive work on the part of a capable cast, some excellent music, cleverly staged musical numbers. . . ." The musical highlights were Rudy Vallee's crooning "Hold My Hand" and "Sweet and Simple" to Alice Faye, and her rousing rendition of "You Nasty Man." Jimmy Durante, whose screen career was fading since he had left MGM, had a blackface number. As with so many movie musicals of this period, the choreography (here by Chester Hale) was derivative of Busby Berkeley's kaleidoscopic screen effects, but without the creative inspiration that earmarked Berkeley's efforts.

Newspaper reporter Miss Lee (Gertrude Michael) goes backstage at George White's (himself) *Scandals* and finds that singer Kitty Donnelly (Alice Faye) is smitten with star Jimmy Martin (Rudy Vallee) who, in turn, is romancing socialite Barbara Loraine (Adrienne Ames). When the two girls quarrel over Martin, he sides with Barbara. Kitty leaves the production, as does Happy (Jimmy Durante), who has had a falling out with his partner, Patsy (Dixie Dunbar). When the *Scandals* cast performs some of the show's songs on radio, Barbara arrives with a boxer (Warren Hymer) and Jimmy realizes that she does not love him. White then works it so Jimmy and Kitty sign a marriage license, each believing it is a contract for the next season. At the finale of the night's show a minister (Richard Carle) marries the lovebirds.

GEORGE WHITE'S SCANDALS (RKO, 1945) 95 minutes.

Executive producers, Jack J. Gross, Nat Holt; producer, George White; director, Felix E. Feist; story, Hugh Wedlock, Howard Snyder; screenplay, Wedlock, Snyder, Parke Levy, Howard Green; art directors, Albert S. D'Agostino, Ralph Berger; set decorators, Darrell Silvera, Harley Miller; musical settings, Carroll Clark; music director, Constantin Bakaleinikoff; musical associate, Norman Bennett; choreographer, Ernest Matray; assistant directors, Fred A. Fleck, Clem Beauchamp; sound, Jean L. Speak, James G. Stewart; special effects, Vernon L. Walker; camera, Robert de Grasse; editor, Joseph Noriega.

Songs: "I Wake Up in the Morning," "I Want to Be a Drummer," "Who Killed Vaudeville?" (Jack Yellen, Sammy Fain); "Bolero in the Jungle" (Tommy Peterson); "Wishing" (Buddy G. DeSylva); "Life Is Just a Bowl of Cherries" (Lew Brown, Ray Henderson); "Liza" (George Gershwin, Ira Gershwin).

Joan Davis (Joan Mason); Jack Haley (Jack Williams); Philip Terry (Tom McGrath); Martha Holliday (Jill Martin); Ethel Smith (Swing Organist); Margaret Hamilton (Clarabelle); Glenn Tryon (George White); Bettejane [Jane] Greer (Billie Randall); Audrey Young (Maxine Manners); Rose Murphy (Hilda); Fritz Feld (Montescu); Beverly Wills (Joan, as a Child); Gene Krupa and His Band (Themselves); Rufe Davis (Impersonations); Wesley Brent, Grace Young, Lorraine Clark, Diane Mumby, Linda Claire, Susanne Rossder, Marilyn Buford, Marie McCardle, Vivian Mason, Vivian McCoy, Virginia Belmont, Rusty Farrell, Nan Leslie, Chili Williams, June Frazer, Virgina Cruzon, Annelle Hayes, John Barlow, Barbara Thorson, Ruth Hall, Ethelreda Leopold, Alice Eyland, Linda Ennis, Lucy Cochrane, Zas Varka (Showgirls); Frank Mitchell, Lyle Latell (Ladder Gag); Effie Laird, Hope Landin (Scrubwomen); Shelby Hamilton, Walter Stone (Dancers); Carmel Myers (Leslie); Ed O'Neil (John the Baptist); Neely Edwards (Lord Quimby); Dorothy Christy (Lady Asbury); Holmes Herbert (Lord Asbury); Harry Monty, Buster Brodie (Box Gag); Betty Farrington (Buxom Woman); Harold Minjur (Hotel Clerk); Rosalie Ray (Chorus Dame); Tom Noonan (Joe); Edmund Glover (Production Man); Nino Tempo (Drummer); Sammy Blum (Cafe Proprietor); Larry Wheat (Pop).

George White's popular Broadway *Scandals* revues were a part of history when RKO tossed together this low-budgeted musical comedy with White as co-producer. This picture was nowhere in the same class with his two earlier film efforts, GEORGE WHITE'S SCANDALS (1934) and GEORGE WHITE'S 1935 SCANDALS (1935), *qq.v.,* in both of which he had made on-screen appearances.

With its all too apparent slapdash qualities, this offering was unworthy of knockabout comedienne Joan Davis.

Each year members of George White's (Glenn Tryon) *Scandals* put on a show, and hoofer Joan Mason (Joan Davis) arrives hoping to get the lead. She finds the star part has gone to Jill Martin (Martha Holliday), whose dancer sister married British royalty. Meanwhile, Joan is in love with the show's co-star, Jack Williams (Jack Haley), but his prissy sister Clarabelle (Margaret Hamilton) opposes the match. Also romantically involved is Jill, who is entranced with the stage manager, Tom McGrath (Philip Terry). However, due to a silly misunderstanding they have a spat. Jill walks out on opening night and Joan has to take over the lead. She saves the show.

The wispy plot was the least asset of GEORGE WHITE'S SCANDALS. The film was produced largely as a showcase for a variety of musical numbers ranging from a quintet of jazz tunes by Gene Krupa and His Band to organ playing by Ethel Smith and torch songs performed by Rose Murphy. Joan Davis and Jack Haley did rowdy versions of "Life Is Just a Bowl of Cherries" (introduced by Ethel Merman in the 1931 Broadway *Scandals*) and "Who Killed Vaudeville?" In a flashback sequence, Joan Davis's daughter, Beverly Wills, played her character at age twelve. To pad the proceedings there were also clips from several other studio films, including John Wayne and Ella Raines in TALL IN THE SADDLE (1944).

This was producer George White's last film. He was later imprisoned for killing a young bride and groom in a hit-and-run car accident.

G.I. BLUES (Paramount, 1960) Color 115 minutes.

Producer, Hal Wallis; associate producer, Paul Nathan; director, Norman Taurog; (uncredited) based on the play *Sailor Beware* by Kenyon Nicholson, Charles Robinson; screenplay, Edmund Beloin, Henry Garson; art directors, Hal Pereira, Walter Tyler; set decorators, Sam Comer, Ray Mayer; costumes, Edith Head; choreographer, Charles O'Curran; music director, Joseph J. Lilley; assistant director, D. Michael Moore; technical advisor, Colonel Tom Parker; special effects, John P. Fulton; camera, Loyal Griggs; editor, Warren Low.

Songs: "Wooden Heart" (Fred Wise, Ben Weisman, Kay Twomey, Bert Kaempfert); "G.I. Blues" (Sid Tepper, Roy C. Bennett); "Shoppin' Around" (Tepper, Bennett, Aaron Schroder); "Tonight Is So Right for Love," "What's She Really Like?" (Sid Wayne, Abner Silver); "Frankfurt Special," "Didya Ever," "Big

Elvis Presley in G.I. BLUES (1960).

Boots" (Wayne, Sherman Edwards); "Pocketful of Rainbows" (Wise, Weisman); "Doin' the Best I Can" (Pornus, Schumann); "Blue Suede Shoes" (Carl Perkins).

Elvis Presley (Tulsa McCauley); James Douglas (Rick); Robert Ivers (Cooky); Juliet Prowse (Lili); Leticia Roman (Tina); Sigrid Maier (Marla); Arch Johnson (Sergeant McGraw); Mickey Knox (Jeeter); John Hudson (Captain Hobart); Ken Becker (Mac); Jeremy Slate (Turk); Beach Dickerson (Warren); Trent Dolan (Mickey); Carl Crow (Walter); Fred Essler (Papa Mueller); Ronald Starr (Harvey); Erika Peters (Trudy); Ludwig Stossel (Owner of Puppet Show); Robert Boon (Guitarist/Leader); Edit Angold (Mrs. Hagermann); Dick Winslow (Orchestra Leader); Edward Coch (Band Leader); Ed Faulkner (Red); Fred Kruger (Herr Klugmann); Torben Meyer (Headwaiter); Gene Roth, Roy C. Wright (Businessmen); Harper Carter, Tip McClure (M.P.s); Walter Conrad (Chaplain); Edward Stroll (Dynamite); William Kaufmann (Kaffeehouse Manager); Hannerl Melcher (Strolling Girl Singer); Elisha Matthew [Bitsy] Mott, Jr. (Sergeant); Judith Rawlins (Fritzie); Marianne Gaba (Bargirl); and: The Jordanaires.

Following his highly publicized two-year stint in the Army in Europe, Elvis Presley returned to civilian life and movies in 1960 with G.I. BLUES. It effectively (with $4.3 million in distributors' domestic film rentals) exploited his military sojourn. In this musical outing Elvis sang ten tunes but, for the first time in his six movies to date, the picture failed to provide him with a single hit record, although his RCA soundtrack album for the picture remained on the record charts for a year. Not to be overlooked was the dynamic presence of Juliet Prowse, who performed some sensational dancing.

Stationed in West Germany as a tank gunner, Tulsa McCauley (Elvis Presley) plans to open a nightclub with his G.I. pals Cooky (Robert Ivers) and Rick (James Douglas), but they need funds to start the establishment. On a lark, Tulsa makes a bet he can spend the night with shapely dancer Lili (Juliet Prowse); if he wins he will get enough money to open the night spot. Tulsa sets out to romance Lili in such settings as a Rhine River steamboat, a cable car and a park. He finally realizes that he truly loves the young woman. Lili, on the other hand, learns of the bet and drops Tulsa. He then attempts to win her back, and eventually does.

Variety reported, "G.I. BLUES restores Elvis Presley to the screen in a picture that seems to have been left over from the frivolous filmusicals of World War II. . . . About the creakiest 'book' in musicomedy annals has been revived . . . as a framework within which Presley warbles 10 wobbly songs and costar Julie

Prowse steps out in a pair of flashy dances." The *New York Times* noted, "Elvis Presley's first post-Army stint vehicle finds him changed into a subdued, forthright, mannerly young gent, minus the rolling eyes and swivel hips of yore, in this scrubbed little color yarn. . . . Our boy, formerly movement personified, has become a fine young man, but there are limits to everything."

G.I. BLUES was an uncredited remake of the 1933 play, *Sailor Beware,* which had already been adapted several times by Paramount Pictures: LADY BE CAREFUL (1936, with Lew Ayres); THE FLEET'S IN (1942, with William Holden), and SAILOR BEWARE (1951, with Dean Martin). This was the first of nine Elvis Presley screen vehicles to be directed by Norman Taurog.

G.I. BLUES remained on *Billboard* magazine's hits chart for forty-nine weeks and was in number #1 position for ten weeks.

GIGI (Metro-Goldwyn-Mayer, 1958) Color 116 minutes.

Producer, Arthur Freed; directors, Vincente Minnelli, (uncredited) Charles Walters; based on the novel by Colette; screenplay, Alan Jay Lerner; production designer/scenery/costumes, Cecil Beaton; art directors, William A. Horning, Preston Ames; set decorators, Henry Grace, Keogh Gleason; set decorator for French location, Maurice Petri; makeup, William Tuttle, Charles Parker; music supervisor/conductor, Andre Previn; orchestrator, Conrad Salinger; color consultant, Charles K. Hagedon; assistant directors, William McGarry, William Shanks, Michel Wyn; sound supervisor, Dr. Wesley C. Miller; camera, Joseph Ruttenberg, (uncredited) Ray June; second unit camera, George Barsky; editor, Adrienne Fazan.

Songs: "Thank Heaven for Little Girls," "It's a Bore!" "The Parisians," "Gossip," "She's Not Thinking of Me (Waltz at Maxim's)," "The Night They Invented Champagne," "A Toujours," "Ah Yes, I Remember It Well," "Gaston's Soliloquy," "Gigi," "I'm Glad I'm Not Young Anymore," "Say A Prayer for Me Tonight" (Alan Jay Lerner, Frederick Loewe).

Leslie Caron (Gigi); Maurice Chevalier (Honoré Lachaille); Louis Jourdan (Gaston Lachaille); Hermione Gingold (Madame Alvarez); Eva Gabor (Liane d'Exelmans); Jacques Bergerac (Sandomir); Isabel Jeans (Aunt Alicia); John Abbott (Manuel); Monique Van Vooren (Showgirl); Mauja Ploss (Mannequin); Edwin Jerome (Charles, the Butler); Marilyn Sims (Redhead); Richard Bean (Harlequin); Pat Sheahan (Blonde); Dorothy Neuman (Designer); Leroy Overacker (Lifeguard at Deauville); Betty Wand (Singing Voice of Gigi).

A "sheer delight" is how the *Motion Picture Herald* trade journal described the dazzling GIGI, a major attraction in the era that saw the decline of the movie musical. This charming collaboration by Alan Jay Lerner (who provided the screenplay, based on Colette's novel, along with the lyrics) and Frederick Loewe won nine Academy Awards. GIGI's Oscars included: Best Picture, Vincente Minnelli as Best Director, Lerner for Best Screenplay, and "Gigi" as Best Song. Star Maurice Chevalier, who injected such insouciance into the lyrical proceedings, was given a Special Oscar for his contributions to entertainment.*

In 1948 there had been a French film of GIGI, based on Colette's novel and starring Danielle Delmore (Gigi), Frank Villard (Gaston) and Yvonne De Bray (Mme. Alvarez). In 1951 Audrey Hepburn starred in a Broadway adaptation of Colette's work and became a major name. When Arthur Freed decided to picturize GIGI as a musical, he hired Alan Jay Lerner and Frederick Loewe who had just had tremendous success on Broadway with *My Fair Lady* (1956).** Not only did the Freed unit have to overcome tremendous censorship problems (the basic story contains a very controversial sexual theme and had to be considerably toned down), but the casting created continued controversy. Lerner had hoped Audrey Hepburn would be given the lead, while some at Metro wanted Pier Angeli for the part. However, it was Freed who decreed that French actress Leslie Caron, who had scored so effectively in MGM's AN AMERICAN IN PARIS (1951) and LILI (1953), *qq.v.,* should have the choice assignment. (Her singing would be dubbed by Betty Wand.) There was little discussion about the appropriateness of casting boulevardier Maurice Chevalier (he had been a friend of the late Colette) as the roué Honoré. But there was some conflict over the part of Gaston. Lerner thought Britisher Dirk Bogarde would be right, but when he was unavailable, Frenchman Louis Jourdan was signed (although he doubted his own abilities to carry the tunes). When Eva Gabor was hired to play Gaston's disloyal mistress, she insisted that Jacques Bergerac (the ex-husband of Ginger Rogers) be hired to play the licentious skating instructor, Sandomir. George Cukor suggested Isabel Jeans for the role of Gigi's worldly grandmama, but veteran Hermione

---

*GIGI also won Oscars for Scoring, Cinematography—Color, Art and Set Direction, Costume Design and Editing.

**The story parallels between GIGI and *My Fair Lady* were so great, that when GIGI (the movie) opened, Bosley Crowther (*New York Times*) wrote, "There won't be much point in anybody trying to produce a film of MY FAIR LADY for a while, because Arthur Freed has virtually done it with GIGI . . . a musical film that bears such a basic resemblance to MY FAIR LADY that the authors may want to sue themselves." The song "Say a Prayer for Me Tonight," sung by Leslie Caron in GIGI, had been created originally for the stage version of *My Fair Lady.*

Gingold had come to Freed's attention because of her many appearances on Jack Paar's late-night TV talk show.

GIGI involved twenty-four days of location shooting in France. When the project went $500,000 over budget, the crew was forced to return to the MGM home lot in Culver City for thirty-five additional days of filming. During production director Vincente Minnelli became very ill as the result of being bitten by a swan in the Jardin de Bagatelle (France); uncredited Charles Walters directed some of the retakes/new sequences; and there was a period when Louis Jourdan walked off the set temporarily when he felt Freed had insulted him (stating that his singing sounded just like that of Rex Harrison). After the film's initial previews, Freed demanded eleven days of retakes and lensing of additional scenes. The final cost of GIGI was $3,319,335.

In fin-de-siècle Paris, dapper Gaston Lachaille (Louis Jourdan), a bored bon vivant, finds distraction from the tedium of his elegant life and beautiful women in the companionship of his playboy

Maurice Chevalier in GIGI (1958).

uncle, Honoré Lachaille (Maurice Chevalier). Gaston also is entertained by the innocence of a gawky, illegitimate young girl named Gigi (Leslie Caron) who lives with her grandmother, Madame Alvarez (Hermione Gingold) and her struggling show business mother (never seen in the narrative). Growing into womanhood and becoming very beautiful, Gigi is being trained by her grandmother—who once was a romantic interlude for Honoré—and her Aunt Alicia (Isabel Jeans) to become a courtesan. When Gaston is thrown over by his fickle mistress (Eva Gabor), who takes up with her opportunistic skating instructor (Jacques Bergerac), the dejected Gaston takes Gigi and her grandmother on a vacation to Trouville. Once there, Gaston finds himself attracted to the maturing young lady whom he has previously regarded as a child. Upon their return to Paris, Gaston starts escorting Gigi about the city and intends to make her his mistress. However, Gigi is too naive to fit into Gaston's social swirl as a kept woman. By now Gaston has fallen in love with Gigi and proposes marriage. Gigi accepts.

Arthur Knight (*Saturday Review* magazine) enthused, "Visually, GIGI is one of the most elegant and tasteful musicals that MGM has ever turned out. Nor does it lag too far behind musically. . . ." *Variety* endorsed, "Replete with taste from its sartorial investiture to the ultimate histrionic performances." Stanley Kauffman (*The New Republic*) pointed out, "GIGI is consistently pleasant, but is extraordinary in only one way. Do not be deceived by the advertising; the real star is Cecil Beaton, who designed the costumes and scenery. When the story ambles and the songs don't quite soar, the clothes and settings continue to enchant."

Actually GIGI harbors many romantic and witty musical treats, from Louis Jourdan's very special rendition of the title song to Leslie Caron's plaintive "Say a Prayer for Me Tonight," to the rollicking "The Night They Invented Champagne" and "The Parisians." However, charming Maurice Chevalier, of the broad smile, winking eyes and gesturing walking stick, steals the show singing "Thank Heaven for Little Girls," "I'm Glad I'm Not Young Anymore" and his touching duet with Hermione Gingold, "I Remember It Well."

GIGI placed third in *Film Daily* trade newspaper's Ten Best Pictures poll and tenth in the National Board of Review's Top Ten Pictures, and won the *Photoplay*'s Gold Medal. GIGI grossed $7,263,000 in distributors' domestic film rentals. The soundtrack album to GIGI won the first Grammy Award given for "best original cast motion picture sound track." The soundtrack album was on *Billboard* magazine's hits chart for forty-three weeks and in #1 position for ten weeks.

In May 1973 the Los Angeles-San Francisco Civic Light Opera produced an expensive stage version of the Lerner and Loewe film classic. It premiered on Broadway on November 16, 1973. The cast included Alfred Drake (Honoré), Daniel Massey (Gaston), Agnes Moorehead (Aunt Alicia), Maria Karnilova (Grandmama) and Karen Wolfe (Gigi). The unspectacular show won a Tony Award for Best Musical Score but closed on February 10, 1974.

GIRL CRAZY (RKO, 1932) 75 minutes.

Producer, Wiliam Le Baron; director, William A. Seiter; based on the musical play by John McGowan, Guy Bolton, George Gershwin, Ira Gershwin; screenplay, Tim Whelan, Herman J. Mankiewicz, Edward Welch, Walter DeLeon; art director, Max Ree; camera, Roy Hunt; editor, Artie Roberts.

Songs: "Could You Use Me?" "But Not for Me," "Embraceable You," "Sam and Delilah," "I Got Rhythm," "You've Got What Gets Me" (George Gershwin, Ira Gershwin).

Bert Wheeler (Jimmy Deegan); Robert Woolsey (Slick Foster); Eddie Quillan (Danny Churchill); Dorothy Lee (Patsy Deegan); Mitzi Green (Tessie Deegan); Kitty Kelly (Kate Foster); Arline Judge (Molly Gray); Stanley Fields (Lank Sanders); Lita Chevret (Mary); Chris-Pin Martin (Pete); and: Brooks Benedict, Lon Chaney, Jr., Monte Collins.

See: GIRL CRAZY (1943) (essay).

GIRL CRAZY (Metro-Goldwyn-Mayer, 1943) 99 minutes.

Producer, Arthur Freed; directors, Norman Taurog, (uncredited) Busby Berkeley; based on the musical play by Guy Bolton, John McGowan, George Gershwin, Ira Gershwin; screenplay, Fred F. Finklehoffe, (uncredited): William Ludwig, Dorothy Kingsley, Sid Silvers; art director, Cedric Gibbons; set decorators, Edwin B. Willis, Mac Alper; costume supervisor, Irene; costumes, Irene Sharaff; music director, George Stoll; music adaptor, Roger Edens; orchestrators, Conrad Salinger, Axel Sordahl, Sy Oliver; vocal arrangers, Hugh Martin, Ralph Blaine; music arranger, Roger Edens; choreographer, Charles Walters; "I Got Rhythm" staged by Berkeley; assistant director, Joseph Boyle; sound supervisor, Douglas Shearer; camera, William Daniels, Robert Planck; editor, Albert Akst.

Songs: "Treat Me Rough," "Bidin' My Time," "But Not for Me," "Could You Use Me?" "Fascinatin' Rhythm," "Cactus Time in Arizona," "I Got Rhythm" (George Gershwin, Ira Gershwin); "Happy Birthday, Ginger" (Roger Edens).

Mickey Rooney (Danny Churchill, Jr.); Judy Garland (Ginger

Gray); Gil Stratton (Bud Livermore); Robert E. Strickland (Henry Lathrop); Rags Ragland (Rags); June Allyson (Specialty); Nancy Walker (Polly Williams); Guy Kibbee (Dean Phineas Armour); Tommy Dorsey and His Band (Themselves); Frances Rafferty (Marjorie Tait); Howard Freeman (Governor Tait); Henry O'Neill (Mr. Churchill, Sr.); Sidney Miller (Ed); Eve Whitney (Brunette); Carol Gallagher, Kay Williams (Blondes); Jess Lee Brooks (Buckets); Roger Moore (Cameraman); Charles Coleman (Maitre d'Hotel); Harry Depp (Nervous Man); Richard Kipling (Dignified Man); Henry Roquemore (Fat Man); Alponse Martel (Waiter); Frances MacInerney, Sally Cairns (Checkroom Girls); Barbara Bedford (Churchill's Secretary); Victor Potel (Stationmaster); Joseph Geil, Jr., Ken Stewart (Students); William Beaudine, Jr. (Tom); Irving Bacon (Reception Clerk); George Offerman, Jr. (Messenger); Mary Elliott (Southern Girl); Katharine Booth (Girl); Georgia Carroll, Aileen Haley, Noreen Nash, Natalie Draper, Hazel Brooks, Mary Jane French, Inez Cooper, Linda Deane (Showgirls); Don Taylor, Jimmy Butler, Peter Lawford, John Estes, Bob Lowell (Boys); Sarah Edwards (Governor's Secretary); William Bishop, James Warren, Fred Beckner, Jr. (Radio Men); Blanche Rose, Helen Dickson, Melissa Ten Eyck, Vangie Beilby, Julia Griffith, Lillian West, Sandra Morgan, Peggy Leon, Bess Flowers (Committee Women); Harry C. Bradley (Governor's Crony); Bill Hazlett (Indian Chief); Rose Higgins (Indian Squaw); Spec O'Donnell (Fiddle Player).

Girl Crazy, with music by George Gershwin and lyrics by brother Ira, had a 272-performance run on Broadway following its opening in the middle of October 1930. Its cast included Willie Howard, Ethel Merman, Ginger Rogers and Red Nichols and His Orchestra. Among the standards which originated in this lively musical comedy were "I Got Rhythm," "Bidin' My Time," "Embraceable You" and "But Not for Me." By the time RKO brought the work to the screen two years later, the public had tired of movie musicals. Thus the emphasis of the film was switched to the zany comedy antics of the studios' in-house top comedy team, Bert Wheeler and Robert Woolsey.

The convoluted plot of the 1932 version of GIRL CRAZY has Jimmy Deegan (Bert Wheeler) and his wife Patsy (Dorothy Lee) being driven to the rugged Arizona town of Custerville by cab driver Slick Foster (Robert Woolsey). Upon arrival (with the broken down cab being drawn by two horses!) the trio finds the area is controlled by tough Lank Sanders (Stanley Fields). The locals draft city slicker Jimmy to run for sheriff—the previous holders of the office have all met with violent ends. Complicating Jimmy's life is the arrival of little sister Tessie (Mitzi Green), who constantly performs imitations. While the *New York Times* lauded the film as "Fun of the boisterous kind," the movie was only a pale offshoot of the zippy stage production. To its credit, it did retain most of the Gershwins' original score, with the brother songwriters composing "You've Got What Gets Me" especially for the picture. The costly film was not a moneymaker.

RKO's 1932 version of GIRL CRAZY is little seen today because of the 1943 MGM remake of the project which became one of Mickey Rooney and Judy Garland's most popular joint vehicles. While the plot was no nearer the 1930 stage show than the first film outing, the MGM edition better captured the spirit of the Gershwins' work and made better use of the score.

In 1943's GIRL CRAZY, when self-centered New York City playboy Danny Churchill (Mickey Rooney) gets into another publicity-generating misadventure, his father (Henry O'Neill) dispatches him to Cody College, an all-male institution in the wilds of Arizona. Arriving at Cody, Danny meets the Dean (Guy Kibbee) and his granddaughter Ginger Gray (Judy Garland), who also operates the local post office. Danny is soon at odds with most everyone because he rebels at the rigors of the school. His only friend is Rags (Rags Ragland), the school's custodian. Later, spunky Ginger persuades Danny to remain at Cody and soon the two are in love. When a state legislative decision threatens to close Cody College (because of an enrollment decline), Danny and Ginger visit Governor Tait (Howard Freeman). The Governor agrees to postpone signing the bill for a few months while Danny and Ginger organize a western rodeo geared to attract publicity and win more applicants for the school. Enterprising Danny woos all of the local debutantes to Cody's rodeo, promising each she will be chosen rodeo queen. At the big event, the finalists are Ginger and Marjorie (Frances Rafferty), the governor's daughter. Marjorie is chosen and a disappointed Ginger feigns enthusiasm. Later Danny explains his reasoning to Ginger, and her spirits are buoyed by the rash of new applications to Cody.

The ads for 1943's GIRL CRAZY read: "Judy and Mickey! Joy and Music! They're Together Again and When They're Together It's a Grand, Happy Show! It's Got Rhythm! It's Got Comedy! It's Got G-A-L-S!" This was the ninth joint appearance of Garland and Rooney in an MGM production. But it had a difficult time coming to be. Originally MGM had planned to remake GIRL CRAZY in 1939 as a project for Eddie Cantor. A few years later the property was revamped to suit the talents of Garland and Rooney. Busby Berkeley was initially set to direct the picture, but after filming of the "I Got Rhythm" number (which was to be the finale), there was severe disagreement between Roger Edens (music adaptor for the

Arthur Freed musical film unit at MGM) and Berkeley over how the number should be staged: Edens wanted it simple, while Berkeley had filled the segment with hundreds of chorus girls in western garb, shooting cannons, and his usual wild camera shots. Garland, who abhorred having to rehearse and execute the precision steps demanded by Berkeley's choreography, sided with Edens. After the expensive "I Got Rhythm" was completed, Berkeley was discharged from the film and was loaned (shipped) to 20th Century-Fox, where he directed Alice Faye in THE GANG'S ALL HERE, *q.v.* The much more congenial Norman Taurog was substituted. Meanwhile, there were more production delays as Rooney, recently divorced from Ava Gardner and acting rambunctious, demanded that the crew relocate shooting to Palm Springs for ten days where he was vacationing. Garland would appear/disappear from the set according to her moods and the course of her latest extracurricular romance (she was then stuck in an unhappy marriage to composer David Rose). Finally, by mid-May 1943, the film was completed at a cost of $1,410,850.85, some $323,000 over its estimated budget.

GIRL CRAZY (1943) employed the bulk of the original Broadway score, most as vocal numbers, but a few ("Boy, What Love Has Done to Me!" and "When It's Cactus Time in Arizona") as background music. "Fascinatin' Rhythm" was borrowed from the Gershwins' *Lady, Be Good*! (1924), while Roger Edens contributed the interlude music, "Happy Birthday, Ginger." A boisterous number, "Bronco Busters" (also from the original score)—featuring Rooney, Garland and Nancy Walker—was recorded, but deleted from the release print.

There are many treats in the 1943 GIRL CRAZY. Garland's touching renditions of "But Not for Me," "Bidin' My Time" and "Embraceable You," and Rooney's duet with Garland on "Could You Use Me?" Not to be overlooked was June Allyson's specialty number in which she cavorts with Rooney in a nightclub setting ("Treat Me Rough"), the self-deprecating humor of sharp-tongued comedienne Nancy Walker and the touching drama of the dumb but sensitive handyman, played by Rags Ragland. Among the newcomers in the cast were Peter Lawford and Don Taylor, cast as Cody College students. During the "Embraceable You" segment Garland is seen dancing with Charles Walters, who had choreographed much of the film.

The *New York Herald Tribune* endorsed, "Chalk up another musical comedy triumph for the Rooney-Garland team." *Time* magazine decided that Rooney was "a natural dancer and comedian" and, of his co-star, Judy Garland: ". . . [Her] presence is open, cheerful and warming. If she were not so profitably good at her own game, she could obviously be a dramatic cinema actress with profits to all."

GIRL CRAZY (1943) grossed $3,771,000 in its initial release.

In 1965 MGM redid GIRL CRAZY in the color production, WHEN THE BOYS MEET THE GIRLS, starring Connie Francis and Harve Presnell. By now the storyline was no more than a thin thread for guest shots by the likes of Liberace, Louis Armstrong and Herman's Hermits. The setting was changed from a dude ranch to a hotel in Nevada for divorcees. The *New York Times* branded the proceedings, "A miserable and parched dredging-up of the old Garland-Rooney musical. . . ."

THE GIRL OF THE GOLDEN WEST (Metro-Goldwyn-Mayer, 1938) Sepiatone 120 minutes.

Producer, William Anthony McGuire; director, Robert Z. Leonard; based on the play by David Belasco; screenplay, Isabel Dawn, Boyce DeGaw; art director, Cedric Gibbons; costumes, Adrian; music director, Herbert Stothart; choreographer, Albertina Rasch; special effects, Slavko Vorkapich; camera, Oliver T. Marsh; editor, W. Donn Hayes.

Songs: "Sun-Up to Sun-Down," "Shadows on the Moon," "Soldiers of Fortune," "The Wind in the Trees," "Senorita," "The West Ain't Wild Anymore," "Who Are We to Say," "Mariachie" (Sigmund Romberg, Gus Kahn); "Ave Maria" (Johann Bach; Charles Gounod); "Liebestraum" (Franz Liszt; lyrics by Gus Kahn).

Jeanette MacDonald (Mary Robbins); Nelson Eddy (Lieutenant Johnson [Ramerez]); Walter Pidgeon (Jack Rance); Leo Carrillo (Mosquito); Buddy Ebsen (Alabama); Leonard Penn (Pedro); Priscilla Lawson (Nina Martinez); Bob Murphy (Sonora Slim); Olin Howland (Trinidad Joe); Cliff Edwards (Minstrel Joe); Billy Bevan (Nick); Brandon Trynan (The Professor); H. B. Warner (Father Sienna); Monty Woolley (Governor); Charley Grapewin (Uncle Davy); Noah Beery, Sr. (General Ramerez); Billy Cody, Jr. (Gringo); Jeanne Ellis (Mary as a Girl); Ynez Seabury (Wowkle); Victor Potel (Stage Driver); Nick Thomason (Billy Jack Rabbit); Tom Mahoney (Handsome Charlie); Phillip Armenta (Long Face); Chief Big Tree (Indian Chief); Russell Simpson (Pioneer); Armand "Curley" Wright, Pedro Regas (Renegades); Gene Coogan (Manuel); Sergei Arabeloff (Jose); Alberto Morin (Juan); Joe Dominguez (Felipe); Frank McGlynn (Pete, a Gambler); Cy Kendall (Hank, a Gambler); E. Alyn Warren, Francis Ford (Miners); Hank Bell (Deputy); Walter Bonn (Lieutenant Johnson); Richard Tucker (Colonel); Virginia Howell (Governor's Wife).

For the fourth screen vehicle for Jeanette MacDonald and Nelson Eddy as a team, MGM chose the old chestnut, *The Girl of the Golden West* by David Belasco, which had first been produced as a drama in 1905 starring Blanche Bates, Robert Hilliard and Frank Keenan. Giacomo Puccini transformed the property into an opera which premiered late in 1910 with Emmy Destinn, Enrico Caruso and Pasquale Amato. The drama was also filmed twice in the silent period, first by director Cecil B. DeMille in 1914, starring Mabel Van Buren, and again in 1923 by First National with Sylvia Breamer, J. Warren Kerrigan and Russell Simpson (who would have a bit in the 1938 picture). The first sound version of the Belasco play came in 1930 when First National-Warner Bros. produced it with Ann Harding and James Rennie starring. For the 1938 edition, Sigmund Romberg and Gus Kahn composed several songs, none of them memorable. The final production proved to be too long, resulting in Ray Bolger and Carol Tevis being cut from the film and Cliff "Ukulele Ike" Edwards being left with only a bit part. The *New York Times* judged that the plot was ". . . dated as a tin bathtub, but redeemed by the singing of its stars."

As a child, Mary Robbins (Jeanne Ellis) is kidnapped from her wagon heading West by bandit Ramerez (Noah Beery, Sr.) and his boy pal Gringo (Bill Cody, Jr.). Soon she and Gringo are swearing undying love. Ramerez is killed by the settlers and, years later, Gringo, grown to adulthood, has adopted his late friend's name, and this Ramerez (Nelson Eddy) is also a bandit, teamed with his pal Mosquito (Leo Carrillo). Meanwhile, the grown Mary (Jeanette MacDonald), who owns the Polka Saloon in the town of Cloudy Mountain, plans to go to Monterey accompanied by Alabama (Buddy Ebsen). Before she leaves she talks with the local sheriff, Jack Rance (Walter Pidgeon), who wants to marry her. Along the way Ramerez tries to rob Mary but instead falls in love with her. Later he takes on the guise of Lieutenant Dick Johnson to continue the courtship. Soon the two are in love. Ramerez follows Mary back to Cloudy Mountain and there encounters Rance. Mary soon learns that her new suitor is really a bandit. Later, when she finds him hiding in her cabin, she orders him out into a snow storm. However, when he is shot she protects him. Rance quickly realizes that Ramerez is in Mary's cabin. He and Mary play cards to determine the man's fate, and Mary wins by cheating. When the sheriff confronts her about being cheated, Mary offers herself in exchange for the bandit's release. On the day she is to marry the sheriff, he overhears the two lovers talking and accepts the fact that the two are in love. He permits them to leave, and the lovers wed, planning to start life anew elsewhere.

The premise of THE GIRL OF THE GOLDEN WEST was far from ideal for the two leads. It was a near impossible feat for Jeanette MacDonald to pose as a swaggering cowgirl, full of slangy talk and displaying a knack for playing poker. It was no easier for Nelson Eddy to play the rugged dark-haired Mexican bandit or to pose as the dashing Lieutenant Johnson, the latter part demanding the likes of an Errol Flynn.

Nelson Eddy recorded "Senorita," "Solders of Fortune," "Sun-up to Sundown" and "Who Are We to Say?" for RCA Victor from the film, while in the movie Jeanette sang "The Wind in the Trees," "Liebestraum" and Bach's "Ave Maria." She and Eddy dueted on "Shadows on the Moon," "Mariachie" and, in the finale, "Senorita."

After the leaden THE GIRL OF THE GOLDEN WEST, it was two years before MacDonald and Eddy reteamed, this time for NEW MOON, *q.v.*

THE GIRLS HE LEFT BEHIND *see* THE GANG'S ALL HERE.

THE GLENN MILLER STORY (Universal, 1954) Color 115 minutes.

Producer, Aaron Rosenberg; director, Anthony Mann; screenplay, Valentine Davies, Oscar Brodney; art directors, Bernard Herzbrun, Alexander Golitzen; music director, Joseph Gershenson; music adaptor, Henry Mancini; choreographer, Kenny Williams; technical advisor, Chummy MacGregor; sound, Leslie I. Carey; camera, William Daniels; editor, Russell Schoengarth.

Songs: "Basin Street Blues" (Spencer Williams); "Moonlight Serenade" (Mitchell Parish, Glenn Miller); "In the Mood" (Andy Razaf, Joe Garland); "Tuxedo Junction" (Buddy Feyne, Erskine Hawkins, William Johnson, William Dash); "Little Brown Jug" (J. E. Winner); "Adios" (Eddie Woods, Enric Madriguera); "String of Pearls" (Eddie DeLange, Jerry Gray); "Pennsylvania 6–5000" (Gray, Carl Sigman); "Stairway to the Stars" (Parish, Matt Malneck, Frank Signorelli); "American Patrol" (E. H. Meacham); "I Know Why," "Chattanooga Choo Choo" (Mack Gordon, Harry Warren); "Bidin' My Time" (George Gershwin, Ira Gershwin); "I Dreamed I Dwelt in Marble Halls" (Alfred Bunn, Michael Balfe); "St. Louis Blues March" ("St. Louis Blues" by W. C. Handy; arrangers, Ray McKinley, Perry Burgett, Gray, Miller).

James Stewart (Glenn Miller); June Allyson (Helen Burger Miller); Charles Drake (Don Haynes); George Tobias (Si Schribman); Henry [Harry] Morgan (Chummy MacGregory); Marion Ross (Polly Haynes); Irving Bacon (Mr. Miller); Kathleen

Lockhart (Mrs. Miller); Barton MacLane (General Arnold); Sig Rumann (Mr. Krantz); Phil Garris (Joe Becker); James Bell (Mr. Burger); Katherine Warren (Mrs. Burger); Frances Langford, Louis Armstrong, Gene Krupa, Cozy Cole, Ben Pollack, Archie Savage Dancers, The Modernaires with Paula Kelly (Themselves); Dayton Lummis (Colonel Spaulding); Deborah Sydes (Jonnie Dee); Anthony Sydes (Herbert); Ruth Hampton (Girl Singer); Damien O'Flynn (Colonel Baker); Carleton Young (Adjutant General); William Challee (Sergeant); Steve Pendleton (Lieutenant Colonel Baessell); Harry Harvey, Sr. (Doctor); Leo Mostovoy (Schillinger); Dick Ryan (Garage Man); Hal K. Dawson (Doctor); Lisa Gaye (Bobby-Soxer); Nino Tempo (Wilbur Schwartz); Babe Russin (Himself); Carl Vernell (Music Cutter); Bonnie Eddy (Irene); Robert A. Davis (Boy); The Mello Men, the Rolling Robinsons (Specialties); Roland Jones (Waiter); Kevin Cochran (Boy); Cicily Carter (Bobby Soxer); Joe Yukl (Trombone Playing for Glenn Miller).

The swing music of Glenn Miller (1904–1944) has endured for many decades, making him the most remembered and popular figure of the big band era. Over the years nearly all of Miller's myriad recordings, radio broadcasts and live appearances have been reissued and there continues to be a major demand for his distinctive music. In 1954 Universal brought Glenn Miller's story to the screen in a polished biopic which was highlighted by its recreation of many trademark Miller songs such as "Moonlight Serenade" (Miller's theme song), "In the Mood," "Chattanooga Choo Choo," "String of Pearls," "Elmer's Tune" and many more.

All of his life Glenn Miller (James Stewart) had a consuming ambition to play trombone and to write musical arrangements according to his standards. At the University of Colorado he meets Helen Burger (June Allyson) and they begin a romance which culminates in marriage, after Glenn works with bandleader Ben Pollack (himself) and as a bandsman on Broadway productions. On their wedding night, however, Miller becomes involved in a Harlem jazz session with Louis Armstrong, Gene Krupa, Cozy Cole (themselves) and other musicians. Always studying music, Glenn takes lessons in music theory and is befriended by Si Schribman (George Tobias), a Boston dancehall operator. After years of playing in other musicians' bands, Glenn finally forms his own orchestra. Within a few years, he is the most popular of the big band leaders, famous for his distinctive sound. When World War II breaks out, Miller joins the service and is placed in charge of the Army band. While appearing in England late in 1944 he embarks on a plane for a Paris concert for Allied troops. The flight is lost in the fog and no trace is ever found of the craft or its passengers. For Helen and the thousands of Miller fans, there is only the memory of his work.

In addition to the fine recreation of the music of the Glenn Miller Orchestra, there was the bonus appearances of many notable musicians, including big band vocalists Frances Langford, Paula Kelly and the Modernaires. This production benefitted greatly from James Stewart's apt portrayal of the bespectacled title character. As the *New York Herald Tribune* noted, "James Stewart plays the role of the scholarly looking band leader with discretion and clarity and the shy good humor which clings to most of his roles." Joe Yukl provided the trombone playing for Jimmy Stewart.

This was the second of three films teaming Jimmy Stewart and June Allyson. THE GLENN MILLER STORY grossed $7,590,994 in distributors' domestic film rentals. The movie won an Academy Award for Best Sound Recording and received Oscar nominations for Best Story/Screenplay and Scoring of a Musical Picture. Its success led the studio to produce another screen biography of a bandleader, THE BENNY GOODMAN STORY (1956), starring Steve Allen and Donna Reed. It was conceived by the same talent which brought THE GLENN MILLER STORY to the screen. For the new biopic, Aaron Rosenberg again produced, while Valentine Davies both prepared the screenplay and served as director. The prefabricated THE BENNY GOODMAN STORY failed to live up to the quality and entertainment values of its predecessor.

GOING HOLLYWOOD (Metro-Goldwyn-Mayer, 1933) 80 minutes.

Producer, Walter Wanger; director, Raoul Walsh; story, Frances Marion; screenplay, Donald Ogden Stewart; music director, Lennie Hayton; camera, George Folsey; editor, Frank Sullivan.

Songs: "We'll Make Hay While the Sun Shines," "Our Big Love Scene," "Going Hollywood," "Cinderella's Fella," "After Sundown," "Beautiful Girl," "Temptation" (Arthur Freed, Nacio Herb Brown); "Just an Echo in the Valley" (Reginald Connelly, Jimmy Campbell, Harry Woods).

Bing Crosby (Bill Williams); Marion Davies (Sylvia Bruce); Fifi D'Orsay (Lili Yvonne); Stuart Erwin (Ernest P. Baker); Patsy Kelly (Jill); Bobby Watson (Jack Thompson); Ned Sparks (Bert); and: Lennie Hayton, The Three Radio Rogues.

Publishing magnate William Randolph Hearst provided the funds for this Walter Wanger production which starred Hearst's mistress, Marion Davies, in one of her better sound vehicles.

Actually, the film belongs to Bing Crosby who was borrowed from Paramount for this assignment, which director Raoul Walsh filmed over a very leisurely half-year period. *Variety,* however, was not impressed and labeled it a "Pretentious musical. . . . It has names, girls and good music, but its story is weak from hunger. . . ." *Harrison's Reports* complained, "Just a fair musical, with some comedy . . . the outcome obvious. . . . There is only one lavish set—that of a dance number, which is used in the filming of a motion picture in which Marion Davies stars."

Sylvia Bruce (Marion Davies), a teacher at a girls school, is bored with academics and wants to explore the world. Moreover, she idolizes radio crooner Bill Williams (Bing Crosby). Deciding she cannot live without him, she abandons her job and goes in pursuit. He is heading to Hollywood to make a motion picture and she follows. Once there, he becomes infatuated with his leading lady, Lili Yvonne (Fifi D'Orsay), who is a bad influence on the screen newcomer. Sylvia gains an extra's job on the film and manages always to get in Bill's way. When the temperamental Lili throws a tantrum, the producer (Stuart Erwin) replaces her with Sylvia, who proves successful in the assignment. Jealous over Sylvia's enthusiasm for Bill, Lili convinces him to abandon the picture and go on a spree with her to Mexico. Sylvia follows them and talks Bill into completing his film. Sylvia and Bill admit their love for one another.

Musically, the best ingredient of GOING HOLLYWOOD is Bing Crosby's rendition of Arthur Freed and Nacio Herb Brown's classic song, "Temptation," which was penned for the production. Also impressive was Marion Davies' work on the big number, "We'll Make Hay While the Sun Shines." Highlighting the movie was a fine (if overexaggerated) comic performance by Fifi D'Orsay as the hot-tempered movie star.

GOING MY WAY (Paramount, 1944) 130 minutes.

Producer/director/story, Leo McCarey; screenplay, Frank Butler, Frank Cavett; art directors, Hans Dreier, William Flannery; set decorator, Gene Merritt; costumes, Edith Head; music director, Robert Emmett Dolan; assistant director, Alvin Ganzer; sound, Gene Merritt; special effects, Gordon Jennings; camera, Lionel Lindon; editor, Leroy Stone.

Songs: "The Day After Forever," "Going My Way," "Swingin' on a Star" (Johnny Burke, Jimmy Van Heusen); "Silent Night" (Franz Gruber); "Habañera" from the opera *Carmen* by Georges Bizet; "Ave Maria" (Franz Schubert); "Too-ra-loo-ra-loo-ra" (J. R. Shannon).

Bing Crosby (Father Chuck O'Malley); Rise Stevens (Genevieve Linden); Barry Fitzgerald (Father Fitzgibbon); Frank McHugh (Father Timothy O'Dowd); Gene Lockhart (Ted Haines, Sr.); William Frawley (Max Dolan); James Brown (Ted Haines, Jr.); Jean Heather (Carol James); Porter Hall (Mr. Belknap); Fortunio Bonaova (Tomasso Bozzani); Eily Malyon (Mrs. Carmody); George Nokes (Pee Wee); Tom Dillon (Officer McCarthy); Stanley Clements (Tony Scaponi); Carl "Alfalfa" Switzer (Herman Langerhanke); Hugh Maguire (Pitch Pie); Sybyl Lewis (Maid at Metropolitan Opera House); George McKay (Mr. Van Heusen); Jack Norton (Mr. Lilley); Anita Bolster (Mrs. Quimp); Jimmie Dundee (Fireman); Adeline de Walt Reynolds (Mother Fitzgibbon); Gibson Gowland (Churchgoer); Julia Gibson (Taxi Driver); Bill Henry (Intern); Robert Tafur (Don Jose); Marti Garralaga (Zuniga); and the Robert Mitchell Boy Choir.

Father Fitzgibbon (Barry Fitzgerald) has been the curate of St. Dominick's Church in New York City for nearly a half-century. Set in his ways and not open to new ideas, he has permitted the church to come under the shadow of mortgages and unhappy parishioners. Church officials dispatch younger priest Father Chuck O'Malley (Bing Crosby) to help the church in its day-to-day operation, but he is opposed in his actions by Father Fitzgibbon. Father O'Malley, an amateur songwriter, sells one of his tunes to music publisher Max Dolan (William Frawley). It becomes a big hit and he uses the royalties to relieve the church of its debts. This causes stern Father Fitzgibbon to soften in his attitude toward Father O'Malley. However, tragedy strikes when St. Dominick's is burned to the ground. To raise funds to construct a new church, Father O'Malley signs the church choir to go on a singing tour with famous opera singer Genevieve Linden (Rise Stevens). They make enough money not only to build a new edifice but also to bring Father Fitzgibbon's aged mother (Adeline Reynolds) from Ireland to live with her son whom she has not seen in forty-five years. Knowing his mission is completed, Father O'Malley leaves for another assignment.

Shot over a six-month period and filled with improvisational scenes, GOING MY WAY grossed $6.5 million in distributors' domestic film rentals. This heartwarming but unsaccharine picture proved to be one of the most popular films of the 1940s. It was named the Best Picture of 1944 by the Academy of Motion Picture Arts and Sciences and also netted Oscars for Bing Crosby as Best Actor, Barry Fitzgerald as Best Supporting Actor, Leo McCarey for both Best Director and Best Original Story, Frank Butler and Frank Cavett for Best Screenplay, and Johnny Burke and James Van

Heusen for Best Song ("Swinging on a Star").* The two songwriters also composed the title song and "Day After Forever" for the movie, which also included J.R. Shannon's "Too-ra-loo-ra-loo-ra," all three sung successfully by Bing Crosby. The film's leading lady, Metropolitan Opera star Rise Stevens, had made her screen bow in MGM's THE CHOCOLATE SOLDIER (1941), *q.v.,* opposite Nelson Eddy.

James Agee (*Time* magazine) endorsed, "[GOING MY WAY] . . . presents Bing Crosby as a Catholic priest, and gets away with it so gracefully that Crosby, the priesthood and the audience are equal gainers." Agee termed the movie "often a beautiful piece of entertainment." He reasoned that "Leo McCarey's leisured, limpid direction and . . . [the] splendid sets are partly responsible for this. . . . But the best reasons are the loving attention to character, and some magnificent acting."

Bing Crosby repeated the role of Father O'Malley the next year in RKO's THE BELLS OF ST. MARY'S, which co-starred Ingrid Bergman.** In it he crooned the title song, "Aren't You Glad You're You?" and "In the Land of Beginning Again." On October 16, 1947, the two stars recreated their roles when "The Bells of St. Mary's" was presented as an episode of CBS radio's "Screen Guild Players." Crosby would play a priest one final time on screen, in 20th Century-Fox's SAY ONE FOR ME (1959), co-starring Debbie Reynolds and Robert Wagner.

GOLD DIGGERS IN PARIS (Warner Bros., 1938) 100 minutes.

Producer, Sam Bischoff; director, Ray Enright; story, Jerry Wald, Richard Macaulay, Maurice Leo, Jerry Horwin, James Seymour; screenplay, Earl Baldwin, Warren Duff; art director, Robert Haas; music director, Leo F. Forbstein; choreographer, Busby Berkeley; camera, Sol Polito, George Barnes; editor, George Amy.

Songs: "The Latin Quarter," "I Wanna Go Back to Bali," "Put That Down in Writing," "A Stranger in Paree" (Al Dubin, Harry Warren); "Day Dreaming All Night Long," "Waltz of the Flowers," "My Adventure" (Warren, Johnny Mercer); "Tiger Rag," "Mr. Corn."

Rudy Vallee (Terry Moore); Rosemary Lane (Kay Morrow); Hugh Herbert (Maurice Giraud); Allen Jenkins (Duke Dennis);

---

* GOING MY WAY was also Oscar-nominated for Best Cinematography—Black and White and for Best Editing. In a most unusual situation, Barry Fitzgerald was nominated for both Best Actor and Best Supporting Actor for his role of Father Fitzgibbon in GOING MY WAY, winning in the latter category.

**Father Eugene O'Malley, age eighty-four, the Roman Catholic priest who inspired the character played by Bing Crosby in GOING MY WAY died in Chicago on August 14, 1989.

Gloria Dickson (Mona); Melville Cooper (Pierre LeBrec); Mabel Todd (Leticia); Fritz Feld (Luis Leoni); Ed Brophy (Mike Coogan); Curt Bois (Padrinsky); Victor Kilian, George Renevant (Gendarmes); Armand Kaliz (Stage Manager); Maurice Cass (Vail); Eddie "Rochester" Anderson (Doorman); and: The Schnickelfritz Band.

Warner Bros.' "The Gold Diggers" series was showing noticeable wear and experiencing audience antipathy towards such musicals at this time. Thus the studio moved the format abroad to take advantage of the Paris Exposition and modeled the chorine line dancers after the popular New York City Music Hall Rockettes. The tame result was a "moderately successful but unmemorable [movie]" (Ted Sennett, *Warner Brothers Presents,* 1971) which proved to be the finale to the once profitable series.

A group of Gotham showgirls heads to Paris under the leadership of crooner Terry Moore (Rudy Vallee). With them is a comedy team (Allen Jenkins, Mabel Todd) and good-humored gangster Mike Coogan (Edward Brophy) who is financing the trip in the hope that the girls will make it big at the Paris Exposition. En route, Terry carries on a romance with dancer Kay Morrow (Rosemary Lane), although another girl in the troupe, Mona (Gloria Dickson), has set her sights on Terry and tries to break up their activities. In Paris the dancers are mistaken for an American ballet company, much to the chagrin of its high-strung leader, Padrinsky (Curt Bois). Eventually, though, the mix-up is straightened out and Terry and the dancers enjoy a success. The crooner and Kay find happiness together.

"Rudy Vallee successfully carries off the stellar burden of GOLD DIGGERS IN PARIS, which is a tough assignment basically," decreed *Variety.* Although the tightly-budgeted feature has a nice gloss about it, with steady direction by Ray Enright and well-staged dance numbers by Busby Berkeley, the music is mediocre and the tone very unsophisticated (in contrast to the earlier entries). Vallee is provided no outstanding material to deliver, although he does pleasantly with "Stranger in Paree" and "Day Dreaming" and also scores with his outstanding Maurice Chevalier imitation. For novelty the movie features Freddie Fisher's Schnickelfritz Band which offers comedy variations of "Tiger Rag" and "Mr. Corn."

British release title: GAY IMPOSTERS.

GOLD DIGGERS OF BROADWAY (Warner Bros., 1929) Color 105 minutes. (Also silent version).

Director, Roy Del Ruth; based on the play *The Gold Diggers* by Avery Hopwood; screenplay, Robert Lord; titles, De Leon Anthony; costumes, Earl Luick; music conductor, Louis Silvers; choreographer, Larry Ceballos; assistant director, Ross Lederman; sound, George R. Groves; camera, Barney McGill, Ray Rennahan; editor, William Holmes.

Songs: "Tiptoe Through the Tulips," "Painting the Clouds with Sunshine," "In a Kitchenette," "Go to Bed," "And They Still Fall in Love," "What Will I Do Without You?" "Mechanical Man," "Song of the Gold Diggers" (Al Dubin, Joe Burke).

Nancy Welford (Jerry); Conway Tearle (Stephen Lee); Winnie Lightner (Mabel); Ann Pennington (Ann Collins); Lilyan Tashman (Eleanor); William Bakewell (Wally); Nick Lucas (Nick); Helen Foster (Violet); Albert Gran (Blake); Gertrude Short (Topsy); Neely Edwards (Stage Manager); Julia Swayne Gordon (Cissy Gray); Lee Moran (Dance Director); Armand Kaliz (Barney Barnett).

"Picture a profuse procession of revue spectacle scenes in amazing settings . . . superbly staged chorus dancing numbers . . . the flashing wit of Winnie Lightner . . . the charm of Nancy Welford

Conway Tearle, Lilyan Tashman (standing), Nancy Welford (standing), Nick Lucas, Winnie Lightner and Ann Pennington in GOLD DIGGERS OF BROADWAY (1929).

. . . the astounding dancing of Ann Pennington. . . . The crooning of Nick Lucas. . . . Love scenes as only Conway Tearle can play them. . . . A story that had New York gasping and giggling for one solid year . . . You have only begun to imagine the treat that is in store for you." So proclaimed the ads for GOLD DIGGERS OF BROADWAY.

One of the brightest and most successful of the early sound film's all-talking, all-singing, all-dancing features was GOLD DIGGERS OF BROADWAY. It was based on Avery Hopwood's play *The Gold Diggers,* which was first staged in 1919 and filmed under that title by Warner Bros. as a silent in 1923 with Hope Hampton, Louise Fazenda and Gertrude Short. This sound version, however, was replete with numerous songs by Al Dubin and Joe Burke plus Larry Ceballos' well-staged dance numbers. *Variety* reviewed, "Lots of color—Technicolor—lots of comedy, girls, songs, music, dancing, production and Winnie Lightner, with Nick Lucas the main warbler. . . . That's what's going to send the picture into the money class for the Warners. . . ."

The plot of the remake stayed close to that of the 1923 film version in that wealthy Stephen Lee (Conway Tearle) does not approve of his nephew Wally's (William Bakewell) engagement to showgirl Violet (Helen Foster) because he insists that all actresses are gold diggers. Violet's pal Jerry (Nancy Welford) comes to her friend's defense, setting up a scheme by which she will vamp Stephen to prove to him what an honest girl Violet really is, all so that Violet can marry Wally. At a swank party, Jerry carries out her ploy while showgirl Mabel (Winnie Lightner) sets her cap for older lawyer Blake (Albert Gran) as Ann (Ann Pennington) and Eleanor (Lilyan Tashman) dance and guitar-playing crooner Nick (Nick Lucas) serenades the group. Stephen sees through the romantic hoax, but also realizes that he adores Jerry, and the two plan to wed. He approves of the upcoming nuptials between Wally and Violet.

In addition to its splashy Technicolor (called Natural Color in the film's advertising), the highlights of GOLD DIGGERS OF BROADWAY are its music and production numbers, Nick Lucas' crooning and Winnie Lightner's smart-mouthed comedy antics. The movie's two biggest songs were "Tiptoe Through the Tulips" and "Painting the Clouds with Sunshine," which Nick Lucas sang against the backdrop of elaborate production ensembles. Lucas' recordings of the songs for Brunswick Records resulted in one of the biggest selling discs of 1929, with sales well over the one-million mark. The sheet music for the two melodies became the best-selling in the nation late in 1929 and early in 1930. Broadway's Winnie Lightner remained in Hollywood where her earthy comedy highlighted several early sound films before her retirement in the mid-1930s. Among her films was an appearance in THE SHOW OF SHOWS (1929), the same year Nick Lucas rejected a seven-year Warner Bros. contract in favor of returning to the more lucrative field of vaudeville and, later, radio.

Like many early sound features, GOLD DIGGERS OF BROADWAY apparently no longer exists, although its soundtrack survives thanks to the fact it was recorded on Vitaphone Discs. Also existing only in this form is the special trailer for the movie that the studio issued to exploit the musical. Although the film was in re-release as late as 1939, it sadly disappeared after that date. However, its format was rehashed in the 1930s by Warner Bros. for its popular series of "Gold Diggers" features. It also provided the basis for Warner Bros.' PAINTING THE CLOUDS WITH SUNSHINE (1951), a musical remake starring Virginia Mayo, Dennis Morgan and Gene Nelson.

GOLD DIGGERS OF 1933 (Warner Bros, 1933) 94 minutes.

Producer, Robert Lord; director, Mervyn LeRoy; based on the play *The Gold Diggers* by Avery Hopwood; screenplay, Erwin Gelsey, James Seymour, David Boehm, Ben Markson; art director, Anton Grot; costumes, Orry-Kelly; music director, Leo F. Forbstein; choreographer, Busby Berkeley; sound, Nathan Levinson; camera, Sol Polito; editor, George Amy.

Songs: "We're in the Money," "I've Got to Sing a Torch Song," "Pettin' in the Park," "The Shadow Waltz," "Remember My Forgotten Man" (Al Dubin, Harry Warren).

Warren William (J. Lawrence Bradford); Joan Blondell (Carol King); Aline MacMahon (Trixie Lorraine); Ruby Keeler (Polly Parker); Dick Powell (Brad Roberts [Robert Treat Bradford]); Guy Kibbee (Faneuil H. Peabody); Ned Sparks (Barney Hopkins); Ginger Rogers (Fay Fortune); Clarence Nordstrom (Gordon); Robert Agnew (Dance Director); Sterling Holloway (Messenger Boy); Tammany Young (Gigolo Eddie); Ferdinand Gottschalk (Clubman); Lynn Browning (Gold Digger Girl); Charles C. Wilson (Deputy); Billy Barty ("Pettin' in the Park" Baby); Fred "Snowflake" Toones, Theresa Harris (Black Couple); Joan Barclay (Chorus Girl); Wallace MacDonald (Stage Manager); Charles Lane, Wilbur Mack, Grace Hayle (Society Reporters); Hobart Cavanaugh (Dog Salesman); Gordon [Bill] Elliott (Dance Extra); Bud Flanagan [Dennis O'Keefe] (Extra During Intermission); Busby Berkeley (Call Boy); Fred Kelsey (Detective Jones); Frank Mills (1st Forgotten Man); Etta Moten ("Forgotten Man" Singer); Billy West (Medal of Honor Winner); Eddie Foster (Zipky's Kentucky Hill

Billies, 2nd Man); Loretta Andrews, Adrien Brier, Lynn Carthew, Kitty Cunningham, Gloria Faythe, Muriel Gordon, June Glory, Ebba Hally, Amo Ingraham, Lorena Layson, Alice Jans, Jayne Shadduck, Bee Stevens, Anita Thompson, Pat Wing, Renee Whitney, Ann Hovey, Dorothy Coonan (Gold Diggers).

See: GOLD DIGGERS OF 1937 (essay).

GOLD DIGGERS OF 1935 (Warner Bros., 1935) 95 minutes.

Director, Busby Berkeley; story, Peter Milne, Robert Lord; screenplay, Manuel Seff, Milne; art director, Anton Grot; choreographer, Berkeley; camera, George Barnes; editor George Amy.

Songs: "I'm Going Shopping with You," "Lullaby of Broadway," "The Words Are in My Heart" (Al Dubin, Harry Warren).

Wini Shaw and Dick Powell in GOLD DIGGERS OF 1935 (1935).

Dick Powell (Dick Curtis); Gloria Stuart (Amy Prentiss); Adolphe Menjou (Nicoleff); Glenda Farrell (Betty Hawes); Grant Mitchell (Louis Larnson); Dorothy Dare (Arline Davis); Alice Brady (Mrs. Mathilda Prentiss); Frank McHugh (Humboldt Prentiss); Hugh Herbert (T. Mosely Thorpe); Winifred Shaw (Winny); Joseph Cawthorn (August Schultz); Ramon & Rosita (Dancers); Matty King (Tap Dancer); Thomas Jackson (Haggarty); Virginia Grey (Singer in "The Words Are in My Heart" Number); Emily LaRue (Girl); Phil Tead (Head Bellhop); Eddie Kane (Maitre d'Hotel); Arthur Aylesworth (Head Barman); Gordon [Bill] Elliott (Martin the Clerk); John Quillan, Ray Cooke (Bellhops); Don Brodie (Photographer); Eddie Fetherstone, Billy Newell, George

Riley, Harry Seymour (Reporters); Franklyn Farnum (Bellhop); Charles Coleman (Manders the Doorman); E. E. Clive (Westbrook the Chauffeur); Leo White (Perfume Clerk).

See: GOLD DIGGERS OF 1937 (essay).

GOLD DIGGERS OF 1937 (First National, 1936) 101 minutes.

Producer, Hal B. Wallis; associate producer, Earl Baldwin; director, Lloyd Bacon; based on the play *Sweet Mystery of Life* by Richard Maibaum, Michael Wallace, George Haight; screenplay, Warren Duff; music director, Leo F. Forbstein; choreographer, Busby Berkelely; camera, Arthur Edeson; editor, Thomas Richards.

Songs: "Let's Put Our Heads Together," "Speaking of the Weather," "Life Insurance Song," "Hush Ma Mouth" (E. Y. Harburg, Harold Arlen); "All's Fair in Love and War," "With Plenty of Money and You" (Al Dubin, Harry Warren).

Dick Powell (Rosmer Peek); Joan Blondell (Norma Parry); Glenda Farrell (Genevieve Larkin); Victor Moore (J. J. Hobart); Lee Dixon (Boop Oglethorpe); Osgood Perkins (Mory Wethered); Charles D. Brown (John Huge); Rosalind Marquis (Sally); Irene Ware (Irene); William Davidson (Andy Callahan); Joseph Crehan (Chairman of Insurance Convention); Susan Fleming (Lucille Bailey); Charles Halton (Dr. Warshoff); Olin Howland (Dr. McDuffy); Paul Irving (Dr. Henry); Harry Bradley (Dr. Bell); Fred "Snowflake" Toones (Snowflake); Pat West (Drunken Salesman); Iris Adrian (Verna); Cliff Saum (Conductor); Jane Wyman, Irene Coleman, Shirley Lloyd, Betty Mauk, Naomi Judge, Betty McIvor, Sheila Bromley, Lois Lindsay, Marjorie Weaver, Lucille Keeling, Virginia Dabney, Jane Marshall (Girls); Wedgwood Nowell (Penfield); Tom Ricketts (Reginald); Bobby Jarvis (Stage Manager); Myrtle Stedman, Jacqueline Saunders (Nurses); Gordon Hart (White).

Following the triumph of 42ND STREET (1933), *q.v.,* Warner Bros. was eager to capitalize on the resurgence of the musical movie genre. It reworked one of its greatest successes of the early sound era, GOLD DIGGERS OF BROADWAY (1929), *q.v.,* and tagged the remake GOLD DIGGERS OF 1933. Directed by Mervyn LeRoy in forty-five days on a budget of $300,000, the film brought back many of the craftsmen (dance director Busby Berkeley, cameraman Sol Polito, composers Al Dubin and Harry Warren) and some of the cast from 42ND STREET to create a movie that was even more of a success. (Considering the dispatch with which GOLD DIGGERS OF 1933 was pushed through production, it was something of a miracle.) In the perspective of cinema history,

GOLD DIGGERS OF 1933 confirmed that ". . . The musical had indeed dispensed with its stagebound, muscle bound ways and was becoming a new and different art form" (Ted Sennett, *Warner Brothers Presents,* 1971).

Composer Brad Roberts (Dick Powell) uses his family's fortune to back a Broadway show for producer Barney Hopkins (Ned Sparks) and the production gives work to needy showgirls Carol King (Joan Blondell), Trixie Lorraine (Aline MacMahon), Polly Parker (Ruby Keeler) and Fay Fortune (Ginger Rogers). The girls are all focused on snaring millionaire husbands and when Brad's conservative blueblood brother, J. Lawrence Bradford (Warren William), learns of his brother's folly he and his equally wealthy friend, Faneuil H. Peabody (Guy Kibbee), rush to New York City to save the youth from his folly. Stuffy Lawrence encounters Carol and is convinced she is out to vamp Brad, who really is in love with Polly. Meanwhile blustering but vulnerable Peabody becomes the object of the grasping attentions of both Trixie and Fay. Eventually, Lawrence comes to accept that the show girls are not really gold diggers at heart, and, meanwhile, the musical show meets with a favorable reception. Brad and Polly plan to wed while Lawrence admits he loves no-nonsense Carol.

Thanks to the strong comedy playing of versatile Joan Blondell, the straight work of debonair Warren William, the bumbling characterization by Guy Kibbee and the smart-aleck wisecracking by Aline MacMahon and Ginger Rogers, the plotline of GOLD DIGGERS OF 1933 holds up quite well—even today. But it is the quintet of songs by Al Dubin and Harry Warren and Busby Berkeley's staging of the expansive production numbers which make the film such a sustained treat.* The movie opens on a strong note with Ginger Rogers singing "The Gold Diggers' Song (We're in the Money)," some of it in Pig Latin. Dick Powell does well crooning "I've Got to Sing a Torch Song" and he and Ruby Keeler are nicely spotlighted in the entertainingly staged story number, "Pettin' in the Park" (which was considered risqué in its day). Berkeley also prepared imaginatively the elaborate and haunting "Shadow Waltz," with Powell vocalizing the love song, and there are a seemingly endless number of dancing girls playing white, illuminated violins. Joan Blondell (in a talk song fashion)

---

*In *The Hollywood Musical* (1981), Ethan Mordden notes, "Just as the numbers in 42ND STREET progressively grew beyond the boundaries of a theatre stage, in GOLD DIGGERS OF 1933 Berkeley disbands an attempt to formulate a theatre style for more than a few minutes at the beginnings and ends of numbers. . . . Berkeley and his disciples do not pretend to be filming theatre: they give us the cinematic equivalent of what theatre does."

closes the proceedings with the poignant "Remember My Forgotten Man" number, an elongated ode to World War I veterans caught in the turmoil of the Depression once they were back home.* While it may be a dated paean today, in its time the segment was considered highly emotional, especially the scene where returning soldiers are transformed into beggars in a breadline.

The *New York Times* wrote, "Imaginatively staged, breezy show with a story of no greater consequence than is to be found in this type of picture. . . . More than once the audience applauded the excellent camera work and the artistry of the scenic effects." *Photoplay* magazine enthused, "If you thought 42ND STREET was good, you have a date with any theatre showing this one. It's another Ruby Keeler show that has everything 42ND STREET did! . . . it's rich, we promise you, and at that it's only the foundation upon which director Mervyn LeRoy and dance impresario Busby Berkeley have built music, ensemble numbers, and acting that are splendid."

GOLD DIGGERS OF 1933 was Oscar-nominated for Best Sound Recording, and this thrilling movie persuaded the studio to continue "The Gold Diggers" series.

Busby Berkeley was riding the crest of his fame and took over the entire direction of GOLD DIGGERS OF 1935, which featured Dick Powell but was minus such pivotal players as spirited Joan Blondell and enthusiastic Ruby Keeler. Overall, the results were pedestrian, except for the extraordinary "Lullaby of Broadway" production number sung by Wini Shaw in an elaborate exposé of life on the tough side on Broadway. However, it must be admitted, Berkeley was saddled with a stale script and two other mediocre Al Dubin-Harry Warren tunes, "The Words Are in My Heart" (a production number waltz with the chorines playing white pianos that "move" around the stage) and "I'm Going Shopping with You."

Rich Mathilda Prentiss (Alice Brady) takes her pretty daughter Amy (Gloria Stuart) to New Hampshire to the Wentworth Plaza, a luxury hotel. By going there, she hopes that she can help her offspring land addled millionaire and snuffbox expert Mosely Thorpe (Hugh Herbert), who has been carrying on with a hard-line, gold-digging stenographer (Glenda Farrell) named Betty Hawes. Amy, however, spoils the plans by becoming attracted to Dick

*In the "Remember My Forgotten Man" number of GOLD DIGGERS OF 1933 it is Joan Blondell who talks the opening verse and chorus of the song. Later a repeat chorus of the lyrics is sung by Etta Moten, and for the finale of the rousing routine it is Blondell who mouths the words to the song while Moten provides the voice. Etta Moten's strong voice had been featured in "The Carioca" number of FLYING DOWN TO RIO (1933), *q.v.*

Curtis (Dick Powell), a financially strapped medical student who has been working at the hotel as a desk clerk. Mrs. Prentiss finally permits Curtis to escort Amy around town on one final fling before the young woman marries Thorpe. Also involved is Mathilda's none-too-bright son, Humboldt (Frank McHugh), who is always chasing girls. Then there is down-and-out Russian movie director Nikolai Nicoleff (Adolphe Menjou), who decides to bilk gullible Mrs. Prentiss of her money. Matters become complicated when Betty files a breach of promise suit against Thorpe. Fortunately all ends happily for the two young lovers.

Admitting the weak points of the film, the *New York Times* acknowledged, "Busby Berkeley, the master of scenic prestidigitation, continues to dazzle the eye and stun the imagination in the latest of the Warner Brothers musical comedies." The movie received Oscar nominations for Best Song ("Lullaby of Broadway") and Best Dance Direction.

Lloyd Bacon took over as director of GOLD DIGGERS OF 1937 (1936) while Busby Berkeley remained as dance director. Dick Powell and his off-screen wife, Joan Blondell, as well as Glenda Farrell were back on hand, but with the addition of stage comic Victor Moore, band singer Rosalind Marquis and dancer Lee Dixon. There was also the infusion of new songwriters (Harold Arlen and E. Y. Harburg) to provide four tunes in addition to two from the series' old standby tunesmiths (Harry Warren and Al Dubin). The resulting movie was worse in terms of plot. However, it was better musically, thanks to two tunes ("With Plenty of Money and You" and "All's Fair in Love and War") by Al Dubin and Harry Warren and a trio ("Speaking of the Weather," "Let's Put Our Heads Together" and "The Life Insurance Song") by E. Y. Harburg and Harold Arlen.

Meek insurance agent Ross Peek (Dick Powell), at the urging of the company secretary (Joan Blondell), is able to land a big policy on bumbling millionaire J. J. Hobart (Victor Moore). He then must protect his investment when Hobart's partners decide to collect on the policy. Hobart gets involved with a gold digger (Glenda Farrell) and also backs a musical show starring Peek and his girlfriend. The musical is a hit and all ends happily.

Although the music in GOLD DIGGERS OF 1937 is better, Berkeley's staging is less inventive than before. The exceptions are "With Plenty of Money and You," "Let's Put Our Heads Together" (which features fifty couples in huge rocking chairs singing) and "All's Fair in Love and War" (which, despite its merits, was a wan reminder of the similar military number from GOLD DIGGERS OF 1933). Overall, this movie musical has a tired look about it, and is not helped by the Production Code of 1934, which forced filmmakers to be far more decorous in presenting the seamier realities of life, even on the Great White Way. Seen today, GOLD DIGGERS OF 1937 reminds one that the insurance industry still employs the same worn sales techniques it used a half century ago. After this entry, Warner Bros. issued the break-the-mold GOLD DIGGERS IN PARIS (1937), *q.v.,* and then dropped the once innovative series.

GOLD DIGGERS OF 1937 earned an Academy Award nomination for Best Dance Direction (Busby Berkeley for the "All's Fair in Love and War" number).

GOOD NEWS (Metro-Goldwyn-Mayer, 1930) 78 minutes.

Directors, Nick Grinde, Edgar J. McGregor; based on the musical play by Laurence Schwab, Frank Mandel, Buddy G. DeSylva, Lew Brown, Ray Henderson; screenplay, Frances Marion; dialogue, Joe Farnman; art director, Cedric Gibbons; wardrobe, David Cox; choreographer, Sammy Lee; sound, Russell Franks, Douglas Shearer; camera, Percy Hilburn; editor, William Levanway.

Songs: "He's a Lady's Man," "Good News," "Tait Song," "Students Are We," "Varsity Drag," "The Best Things in Life Are Free" (Buddy G. DeSylva, Lew Brown, Ray Henderson); "If You're Not Kissing Me," "Football" (Arthur Freed, Nacio Herb Brown); "I Feel Pessimistic" (J. Russell Robinson, George Waggner); "I'd Like to Make You Happy" (Reggie Montgomery).

Mary Lawlor (Connie); Stanley Smith (Tom); Bessie Love (Babe); Cliff Edwards (Kearney); Gus Shy (Bobby); Lola Lane (Patricia); Thomas Jackson (Coach); Delmer Daves (Beef); Billy Taft (Freshman); Frank McGlynn (Professor Kenyon); Dorothy McNulty [Penny Singleton] (Flo); Vera Marsh, Helen Virgil (Girls); Abe Lyman and His Band (Themselves).

See: GOOD NEWS (1947) (essay).

GOOD NEWS (Metro-Goldwyn-Mayer, 1947) Color 92 minutes.

Producer, Arthur Freed; associate producer, Roger Edens; director, Charles Walters; based on the musical play by Laurence Schwab, Frank Mandel, Buddy G. DeSylva, Lew Brown, Ray Henderson; screenplay, Betty Comden, Adolph Green; art directors, Cedric Gibbons, Edward Carfagno; set decorators, Edwin B. Willis, Paul G. Chamberlain; women's costumes, Helen Rose; men's costumes, Valles; makeup, Jack Dawn; music director, Lennie Hayton; vocal arranger, Kay Thompson; choreographers, Walters, Robert Alton; assistant director, Al Jennings; color consultants, Natalie Kalmus, Henri Jaffa; sound supervisor, Douglas Shearer; camera, Charles Schoenbaum; editor, Albert Akst.

Songs: "Good News," "Varsity Drag," "Just Imagine," "Lucky in Love," "He's a Lady's Man," "The Best Things in Life Are Free" (Buddy G. DeSylva, Lew Brown, Ray Henderson; additional lyrics for "Tait Song" "He's a Lady's Man," "Varsity Drag" and "Good News" by Roger Edens, Kay Thompson); "Pass that Peace Pipe" (Edens, Ralph Blane, Hugh Martin); "The French Lesson" (Edens, Betty Comden, Adolph Green); "My Blue Heaven" (Walter Donaldson); "Wedding of the Painted Doll" (Nacio Herb Brown, Arthur Freed).

June Allyson (Connie Lane); Peter Lawford (Tommy Marlowe); Patricia Marshall (Pat McClellan); Joan McCracken (Babe Doolittle); Ray McDonald (Bobby Turner); Mel Torme (Danny); Robert Strickland (Peter Van Dyne, III); Donald MacBride (Coach Johnson); Tom Dugan (Pooch); Clinton Sundberg (Professor Burton Kennyone); Loren Tindall (Beef); Connie Gilchrist (Cora, the Cook); Morris Ankrum (Dean Griswold); Georgia Lee (Flo); Jane Green (Mrs. Drexel); Andy Williams (Off-screen Vocalist for "He's a Lady's Man" number); and: Richard Tripper, Bill Harbach.

College hijinks used to be a popular subject for musicals, providing an idealized atmosphere for youthful exuberance and the wonders of new love. Such a show was *Good News,* which debuted in the fall of 1927 and ran for 551 performances starring Mary Lawlor, John Price Jones, Zelma O'Neal, Inez Courtney and George Olsen and His Orchestra. Buddy G. DeSylva, Lew Brown and Ray Henderson penned a number of popular songs for this musical, including "Good News," "The Best Things in Life Are Free," "The Varsity Drag," "Lucky in Love" and "Just Imagine." When MGM filmed the musical comedy in 1930 it retained only a few items from the original score but did cast Mary Lawlor to repeat her stage role and utilized the director (Edgar J. McGregor) of the stage production to work with director Nick Grinde on supervising the movie adaptation.

At Tait College, football hero Tom Marlowe (Stanley Smith) has done so little studying that he is about to be expelled from school, to the detriment of his teammates who need him to win the big game. Marlowe is loved by pretty co-ed Connie (Mary Lawlor), but he is attracted to exotic Pat (Lola Lane). His pal Bobby (Gus Shy) is after school vamp Babe (Bessie Love). With the help of Professor Kenyon (Frank McGlynn), Tom manages to remain in school and has the opportunity to win the season's final football game. He also realizes he loves Connie, while Bobby wins Babe.

In transferring GOOD NEWS to the screen, MGM deleted several of the numbers from the stage version, including "Just Imagine," "Flaming Youth," "Football Drill," "Baby! What?" "The Girl of the Pi Beta Phi" and "In the Meantime." For the movie, Nacio Herb Brown and Arthur Freed contributed "Football" and "If You're Not Kissing Me," while Reggie Montgomery provided "I'd Like to Make You Happy" and George Waggner and J. Russell Robinson wrote "I Feel Pessimistic."

When GOOD NEWS was released in the early fall of 1930, MGM's promotional copy boasted: "AT LAST THE GREAT BROADWAY HIT COMES TO THE TALKING SCREEN. . . . A greater, more complete, more realistic production of this sensational musical comedy than was possible on the stage. GOOD NEWS brings you the soul of college life—its swift rhythm, its pulsing youth, its songs, its pep, its loves, its laughter—crowded into one never-to-be-forgotten picture. A cocktail of hilarious, riotous entertainment!"

There were two major problems with GOOD NEWS by the time it was issued. The first was that the overabundance of Hollywood musicals in 1929–30 had surfeited audience tastes, and the genre was becoming anathema at the box-office. A worried MGM therefore belatedly deleted several already filmed musical interludes from GOOD NEWS (thus its relatively short running time). Among the tunes excised were: "That's How You Know We're Co-eds" (sung by Lola Lane) and the duet reprises of "The Best Things in Life Are Free" and "Lucky in Love." The other problem was aptly described by *Photoplay* magazine: "GOOD NEWS has been stolen so many times that now it's no longer news. But it is done in a sprightly manner and if you haven't seen the Varsity Drag so often that you're bored, you'll love it. It is college run rampant. . . ."

In 1941, following the success of MGM's BABES ON BROADWAY starring Mickey Rooney and Judy Garland, the studio planned to star this popular screen team in a remake of GOOD NEWS. However, for various scheduling reasons, the project was postponed. By the time it went into production in March 1947, June Allyson and Peter Lawford (he replacing such earlier choices as Van Johnson and Mickey Rooney) were the stars, with Patricia Marshall substituting for Gloria De Haven (who went on suspension) as the college vamp. MGM choreographer and sometimes performer Charles Walters was given his first directorial assignment with GOOD NEWS. Six of the original songs from the Broadway production were retained for the new movie. Roger Edens, Betty Comden and Adolph Green wrote two new numbers for GOOD NEWS (1947): "An Easier Way" and "The French Lesson." "Pass that Peace Pipe" (by Edens, Hugh Martin and Ralph Blane) had been prepared for ZIEGFELD FOLLIES (1946), *q.v.,* for Judy Garland, Gene Kelly and Nancy Walker, but after it was cut from that musical, it was eventually decided to use it in GOOD NEWS.

In advertising its remake, MGM exclaimed, "A tonic in Technicolor! Oh how the audiences are loving it. The fun and the hit songs, the beautiful girls and the wild and wonderful dancing, the mad and merry cast of youthful stars and the sheer pace of it!" This colorful remake remained close to the plot of the original with its Tait College setting in the Roaring Twenties. Here June Allyson is co-ed Connie, also the campus librarian, in love with football hero Tommy Marlowe (Peter Lawford); he is infatuated with French student Pat McClellan (Patricia Marshall). June Allyson sang "Just Imagine," Joan McCracken and Ray McDonald sang and danced energetically to the drugstore production number, "Pass That Peace Pipe," Patricia Marshall performed "Lucky in Love" (which was reprised by all the principals), Peter Lawford did "He's a Lady's Man" and a French version of "The Best Things in Life Are Free," and Mel Torme did the latter song much better in English. Allyson and Lawford dueted on "The French Lesson" (ironically, in real life he spoke perfect French) and joined together for the high-stepping finale, "Varsity Drag." Cut from the film were such numbers as "An Easier Way," sung by Allyson and Marshall.

A rather jaded *New York Times* complained of the new GOOD NEWS, "It is just another college musical . . . recalling the verve of the original, it seems rather woodenly done, until one remembers all the duplicates—and some pretty good ones—that have come between." Moviegoers, on the other hand, responded favorably to this ebullient musical. Made at a cost of $1,662,718, it grossed $2,956,000 at the box-office in its initial release.

GOOD NEWS made a star out of Britisher Peter Lawford, who had been so reluctant to try his hand as a song-and-dance man. He and June Allyson would co-star again in the family drama, LITTLE WOMEN (1949), and a bizarre murder mystery, THEY ONLY KILL THEIR MASTERS (1972). In the compilation feature, THAT'S ENTERTAINMENT! (1974), *q.v.,* co-host Lawford would reminisce about the making of GOOD NEWS and walk through, on-camera, the surviving remains of the Tait College set. The songwriting team of Comden and Green would do such other MGM musicals as ON THE TOWN (1949), SINGIN' IN THE RAIN (1952) and THE BAND WAGON (1953), *qq.v.*

In 1973 *Good News,* much revamped, was revived for a

successful national tour starring Alice Faye and John Payne (replaced for the brief Broadway run in 1974 by Gene Nelson).

THE GRACE MOORE STORY *see* SO THIS IS LOVE.

GREASE (Paramount, 1978) Color 110 minutes.

Producers, Robert Stigwood, Allan Carr; associate producer, Neil A. Machlis; director, Randal Kleiser; based on the musical play by Jim Jacobs, Warren Casey; adaptor, Carr; screenplay, Bronte Woodard; production designer, Phil Jefferies; set decorator, James Bekey; makeup, Dan Striepeke, Eddie Allen; music supervisor, Bill Oakes; special music consultant, Louis St. Louis; choreographer, Patricia Birch; dance consultant, Tommy Smith; assistant directors, Jerry Grandley, Lynn Morgan and Paula Marcus; stunt coordinator, Wallace Dwight Taylor; sound, Jerry Jost; sound re-recording, Bill Varney; sound effects editor, Charles Moran; electronic visual effects, Rony Hays; camera, Bill Butler; editor, John F. Burnett.

Songs: "Summer Nights," "Hopelessly Devoted to You," "Beauty School Dropout," "Look at Me, I'm Sandra Dee,"

Annette Charles, John Travolta and Eve Arden in GREASE (1978).

"Greased Lightnin'," "It's Raining on Prom Night," "Alone at a Drive-in-Movie," "Blue Moon," "Those Magic Changes," "Hound Dog," "Born to Hand-Jive," "Mooning," "Freddy My Love," "Rock 'n' Roll Party Queen," "There Are Worse Things I Could Do," "We Go Together," (Jim Jacobs, Warren Casey); "Love Is a Many Splendored Thing" (Sammy Fain, Paul Francis Webster); "Grease" (Barry Gibb); "You're the One that I Want" (John Farrar); "Sandy" (Louis St. Louis, Scott Simon); "Rock 'n' Roll Is Here to Stay" (D. White); "Blue Moon" (Richard Rodgers, Lorenz Hart); "Tears on My Pillow" (S. Bradford, A. Lewis).

John Travolta (Danny Zucco); Olivia Newton-John (Sandy Olsson); Stockard Channing (Betty Rizzo); Jeff Conaway (Kenickie); Barry Pearl (Doody); Michael Tucci (Rizzo); Kelly Ward (Putzie); Didi Conn (Frenchie); Jamie Donnelly (Jan); Dinah Manoff (Marty); Eve Arden (Principal McGee); Frankie Avalon (Teen Angel); Joan Blondell (Vi, the Waitress); Edd Byrnes (Vince Fontaine); Sid Caesar (Coach Calhoun); Alice Ghostley (Mrs. Murdoch); Dody Goodman (Blanche); Sha-Na-Na (Johnny Casino and the Gamblers); Susan Buckner (Patty Simcox); Lorenzo Lamas (Tom Chisum); Fannie Flagg (Nurse Wilkins); Dick Patterson (Mr. Rudie); Eddie Deezen (Eugene); Darrell Zwerling (Mr. Lynch); Ellen Travolta (Waitress); Annette Charles (Cha Cha); Dennis C. Stewart (Leo).

See: GREASE 2 (essay).

GREASE 2 (Paramount, 1982) Color 114 minutes.

Executive producer, Bill Oakes; producers, Robert Stigwood, Allan Carr; associate producer, Neil A. Machlis; director, Patricia Birch; based on characters created by Jim Jacobs, Warren Casey; screenplay, Ken Finkleman; production designer, Gene Callahan; set decorator, Lee Poll; costumes, Robert De Mora; music/music arranger, Louis St. Louis; music director/arranger, Artie Butler; horn arranger, Andy Muson; additional orchestrator, Michael Gibson; music editor, June Edgerton; choreographer, Birch; assistant directors, Gar Daigler, David Arntzen, Venita Ozols; stunt coordinator, James Arnett; sound, Lawrence O. Jost, Murray McFadden, Gary Luchs; sound re-recording, James R. Cook, Don Cahn, Robert L. Harman; sound effects editor, Robert C. Gutknecht; camera, Frank Stanley; editor, John F. Burnett.

Songs: "Back to School Again," "Who's That Guy?", "(Love Will) Turn Back the Hands of Time" (Louis St. Louis, Howard Greenfield); "Charades" (St. Louis, Michael Gibson); "Girl for All Seasons," "Rock-a-Hula Luau (Summer Is Coming)" (Dominic Bugatti, Frank Musker); "Score Tonight" (Bugatti, Musker, St.

Louis); "Prowlin' " (Bugatti, Musker, Christopher Cerf); "Brad" (Cerf); "Reproduction," "Cool Rider" (Dennis Linde); "We'll Be Together" (Bob Morrison, Johnny MacRae); "Do It for Our Country" (Rob Hegel); "Our Day Will Come" (Bob Hilliard, Mort Garson); "Rebel Walk" (Duane Eddy, Lee Hazelwood); "Cry."

Maxwell Caulfield (Michael Carrington); Michelle Pfeiffer (Stephanie Zinone); Adrian Zmed (Johnny Nogerilli); Christopher McDonald (Goose); Peter Frechette (Lou DiMucci); Leif Green (Davey); Lorna Luft (Paulette Rebchuck); Maureen Teefy (Sharon Cooper); Alison Price (Rhonda Ritter); Pamela Segall (Dolores); Didi Conn (Frenchie); Eve Arden (Principal McGee); Sid Caesar (Coach Calhoun); Dody Goodman (Blanche); Tab Hunter (Mr. Stuart); Connie Stevens (Miss Mason); Dick Patterson (Mr. Spears); Eddie Deezen (Eugene); Matt Lattanzi (Brad); Jean Sagal, Liz Sagal (Sorority Girls); Dennis C. Stewart (Balmudo); Brad Jeffries, Henry Dickey, Vernon Scott (Preptones); Steve M. Davison, Richard Epper, Pat Green, Freddie Hice, Steve Holladay, Gary Hymes, Mike Runyard, Scott Wilder (Cycle Lords); Helena Andreyko, Ivy Austin, Lucinda Dickey, Sandra Grauy, Vicki Hunter, Donna King, Evelyn Tosi, Dallace Winkler (Girl Greasers); Dennis Daniels, John Robert Garrett, Bernardo Hiller, Roy Luthringer, Charles McGowan, Aurelio Padron, Andy Tennant, Tom Villard (Boy Greasers).

When *Grease* bowed on Broadway in 1972 it was billed as "A New 50's Rock 'n' Roll Musical" and its cast included Adrienne Barbeau, Walter Bobbie and Barry Bostwick. The show, with music by Jim Jacobs and Warren Casey, had a run of 3,388 performances. In 1978 the acclaimed musical was brought to the big screen starring John Travolta, who had just scored extremely well in SATURDAY NIGHT FEVER (1977), *q.v.* He was teamed with English-Australian recording star Olivia Newton-John. The results were explosive: the movie grossed $96,300,000 in distributors' domestic film rentals, making it the biggest money-making movie musical of all time. It made strutting (some insisted Simian-like) Travolta and peaches-and-cream Olivia Newton-John the musical superstars of the cinema, at least for the moment.

In the late 1950s at Rydell High School in California, self-centered biker Danny Zucco (John Travolta), a senior, succumbs romantically to a new student, beautiful Sandy Olsson (Olivia Newton-John), whom he had met that past summer on the beach. Danny tries to impress his "tough" pals with how easily he will be able to seduce the innocent Sandy. At the same time, he—and every other boy in school—is pursued by the sexually loose Betty Rizzo (Stockard Channing). The latter eventually settles on Danny's pal, Kenickie (Jeff Conaway), as her man. Romancing Sandy, Danny fails to get to fourth base with her; hoping to impress the moral young lady, he goes out for sports. However, the school's coach (Sid Caesar) can do nothing to make him look like an athletic hero. Finally, it is Sandy who sheds her too-good-to-be-true image. By the time of the school carnival she has transformed herself into a groovy chick. She and Danny confirm their love for one another, while Betty and Kenickie decide to marry.

Highlighted by Patricia Birch's energetic choreography and the exuberance of its mostly youthful cast, GREASE is a pulsating parody of 1950s rock movie musicals. The producers wisely populated the picture with acting veterans who carry the film's dramatic load. In particular, Eve Arden is outstanding as the school's principal. (One of the screen's priceless moments is her double-take after urging the students over the public address system to back the local team by becoming athletic supporters.) Then there is Dody Goodman as the principal's air-head secretary who, in one joyful sequence, fights a losing battle with a typewriter ribbon. The two leads, particularly Newton-John when she is the wholesome Sandy, fill the bill most satisfactorily. The picture is loaded with both old and new songs, the best remembered being Newton-John's rendering of "Hopelessly Devoted to You" which was a best-selling single for her on RSO Records, the label also having big sales with the film's original soundtrack. Frankie Valli performs the title theme while Frankie Avalon (a refugee from 1960s beach party screen musicals) makes a welcome appearance in a dream sequence, singing the satirical "Beauty School Drop-Out." Travolta and Olivia Newton-John duet on "Summer Nights," "You're the One that I Want" and "We Go Together." Travolta solos on "Sandy" (performed imaginatively at a drive-in movie theatre) and feisty Stockard Channing does "Look at Me, I'm Sandra Dee" and "There Are Worse Things I Could Do." Most of the movie's soundtrack oldies ("Blue Moon," "Hound Dog," "Tears on My Pillow") are sung by the group Sha-Na-Na. The soundtrack album to GREASE lingered on *Billboard* magazine's hits chart for thirty-nine weeks and was in #1 position for twelve weeks.

While it is difficult to argue with such huge financial affirmation, the editors of *Consumer Guide* and Philip J. Kaplan (*The Best, The Worst and The Most Unusual: Hollywood Musicals,* 1983), pointed out, "For a musical set in the 1950s, the score is surprisingly contemporary, and that is one of the film's problems." The authors did admit, "Although GREASE does not succeed as a

1950s parody or a 1950s celebration, it is often amusing and entertaining."

Four years later, producers Robert Stigwood and Allan Carr turned out GREASE 2, also for Paramount. Patricia Birch, who had provided the choreography for the first film, served in the dual capacity of director and choreographer for the new edition. John Travolta and Olivia Newton-John declined to appear in this follow-up,* and the leads went to relative newcomers, Maxwell Caulfield and Michelle Pfeiffer. Eve Arden, Dody Goodman and Sid Caesar were retained from the original film (although given little to do), as was Didi Conn. Additionally, there were cameos by such nostalgia purveyors as Connie Stevens and Tab Hunter. Judy Garland's daughter, Lorna Luft, was cast as a ranking member of Rydell High's Pink Ladies sorority.

British student Michael Carrington (Maxwell Caulfield) decides to join his cousin Frenchie (Didi Conn) at California's Rydell High School to complete his senior year. He is soon attracted to student Stephanie Zinone (Michelle Pfeiffer), the leader of the Pink Ladies sorority (who date only bikers and Thunderbird car owners). Although she is bored with Johnny Nogerilli (Adrian Zmed), head of the T-Bird motorcycle gang at school, she is slow to react to Michael's advances. To win his lady love, Michael takes on the disguise of a super hero and manages to save Stephanie from the Cycle Lords, the rivals to the T-Birds. At the school talent show, Stephanie admits her feelings for the mysterious biker. Because of his daring against the Cycle Lords, Michael is admitted to the T-Birds and he and Stephanie declare their love for one another.

GREASE 2 simply lacked the zest of the 1978 movie; its two leads did not match the charisma of John Travolta and Olivia Newton-John. *Variety* pinpointed one of the movie's major weaknesses: "Rarely has a Hollywood film offered a slimmer plotline than in the case here—even Sam Katzman's rock 'n' roll cheapies of the period boasted the phoney tension stemming from the kids wanting to swing to the evil beat in face of parental and official disapproval." The same reviewer did admit, "Choreographer and director Patricia Birch has come up with some unusual settings (a bowling alley, a bomb shelter) for some of the scenes, and employs some sharp montage to give most of the songs and dances a fair amount of punch."

GREASE 2 grossed a relatively weak $6,500,000 in distributors' domestic film rentals.

---

*John Travolta and Olivia Newton-John would team up again for the fantasy comedy, TWO OF A KIND (1983), which proved to be a box-office dud.

THE GREAT CARUSO (Metro-Goldwyn-Mayer, 1951) Color 109 minutes.

Producer, Joe Pasternak; director, Richard Thorpe; story, Dorothy Caruso; screenplay, Sonia Levien, William Ludwig; art directors, Cedric Gibbons, Gabriel Scognamillo; set decorators, Edwin B. Willis, Jack D. Moore; costumes, Gile Steele, Helen Rose; makeup, William J. Tuttle; music/music director, Johnny Green; assistant director, Sid Sidman; color consultants, Henri Jaffa, James Gooch; sound supervisor, Douglas Shearer; special effects, Warren Newcombe; montage, Peter Ballbusch; camera, Joseph Ruttenberg; editor, Gene Ruggiero.

Songs: "Vesti La Giubba" from the opera *I Pagliacci* by Ruggiero Leoncavallo; "M'Appari" from the opera *Martha* by Friedrich von Flotow; "Celeste Aida," "Numi, Pieta," "La Fatal Pietra" from the opera *Aida* by Guiseppe Verdi; "Sextet" from the opera *Lucia di Lammermoor* by Gaetano Donizetti; "La Donne e Mobile" from the opera *Rigoletto* by Verdi; "Che Gelida Manina" from the opera *La Boheme* by Giacomo Puccini; "E Lucevan Le Stelle" from the opera *Tosca* by Puccini; "Because" (Edward Teschemacher, Guy d'Hardelot); "Sweethearts" (Victor Herbert, Robert B. Smith); "The Loveliest Night of the Year" (from "Over the Waves" by Juventino Rosas; adaptor, Irving Aaronson; new lyrics, Paul Francis Webster); "The Last Rose of Summer" (Thomas Moore, Richard Alfred Milliken); "Ave Maria" (Charles Gounod; adapted from a Prelude by Johann Sebastian Bach).

Mario Lanza (Enrico Caruso); Ann Blyth (Dorothy Benjamin); Dorothy Kirsten (Louise Heggar); Jarmila Novotna (Maria Selka); Richard Hageman (Carlo Santi); Carl Benton Reid (Park Benjamin); Eduard Franz (Giulio Gatti-Casazza); Ludwig Donath (Alfredo Brazzi); Alan Napier (Jean de Reszke); Paul Javor (Antonio Scotti); Carl Milletaire (Gino); Shepard Menken (Fucito); Vincent Renno (Tullio); Nestor Paiva (Egisto Barretto); Peter Edward Price (Caruso as a Boy); Mario Siletti (Papa Caruso); Angela Clarke (Mama Caruso); Ian Wolfe (Hutchins); Yvette Duguay (Musetta); Argentina Brunetti (Mrs. Barretto); Edit Angold (Hilda); Peter Brocco (Father Bronzetti); David Bond (Father Angelico); Matt Moore (Max); Anthony Mazola (Fucito at Age Eight); Mae Clarke (Woman); Blanche Thebom, Teresa Celli, Nicola Moscona, Giuseppe Valengo, Lucina Amara, Marina Koshetz, Robert E. Bright, Gilbert Russell (Opera Singers); Mario DeLaval (Ottello Carmini); Sherry Jackson (Musetta as a Child); Maurice Samuels (Papa Gino).

Mario Lanza scored his greatest cinema triumph in the title role of THE GREAT CARUSO, the biopic of his idol, famed Italian opera singer Enrico Caruso (1873–1921). Although the movie bore little resemblance to Caruso's actual life and took many liberties, it was brimming over with songs and arias associated with the famed tenor. Star Mario Lanza performed these many musical interludes beautifully, even introducing a new number, "The Loveliest Night of the Year," which became a best seller for him on RCA Victor Records. He shares a few of the musical numbers with such noted classical singers as Dorothy Kirsten, Blanche Thebom and Lucina Amara.

Beginning with his birth in Naples, Italy to poor parents and the sudden death of his mother (Angela Clarke), the narrative jumps to Enrico Caruso (Mario Lanza) as a youth with a talent for singing in the church choir. As an adult he becomes a cafe singer. Next come his years studying and performing opera in Italy and other European countries, and his later success in London. Now well-to-do he returns to Italy, planning to marry the girl he loved, but he finds that she has already married. Next, Caruso travels to America where he eventually becomes a major attraction at the New York Metropolitan Opera. There he meets beautiful Dorothy Benjamin (Ann Blyth). The two fall in love but their romance is opposed by her wealthy father (Carl Benton Reid), a patron of the arts whom Caruso once accidentally offended. The two lovers are befriended by another opera star, Louise Heggar (Dorothy Kirsten). Eventually Enrico and Dorothy marry and have a child. Caruso rises to the heights as the most famous singer of his time, before his sudden death from pleurisy at the age of forty-seven.

The *New York Times* judged THE GREAT CARUSO "A fine, thumping earful of operatic and semi-classical songs, piercingly rendered by Mario Lanza. . . . Also, as handsomely dressed and color-wrapped a production as anyone could expect of a film on the life and career of the great Italian tenor. . . . As drama, filling in between the musical interludes, [it] is the silliest, sappiest and soggiest beading-together of clichés imaginable."

THE GREAT CARUSO won an Academy Award for Best Sound. It received Oscar nominations for Best Scoring and Costume Design—Color. The movie grossed $4,531,000 in distributors' domestic film rentals. The success of this motion picture led to such other biopics of opera stars as SO THIS IS LOVE (1953, with Kathryn Grayson as Grace Moore), *q.v.;* MELBA (1953, with Patrice Munsel as Nellie Melba); and INTERRUPTED MELODY (1955, with Eleanor Parker as Marjorie Lawrence).

THE GREAT VICTOR HERBERT (Paramount, 1939) 96 minutes.

Producer/director, Andrew L. Stone; story, Robert Lively, Stone; screenplay, Russel Crouse, Lively; art directors, Hans Dreier, Ernst Fegte; music, Victor Herbert; music director, Phil Boutelje; choreographer, LeRoy Prinz; sound, Loren Ryder; camera, Victor Milner; editor, James Smith.

Songs: "Someday" (Victor Herbert, William LeBaron); "Al Fresco," "Thine Alone," "Puncinello," "Kiss Me Again," "All for You," "Neapolitan Love Song" (Herbert, Henry Blossom); "Absinthe Frappe," "Rose of the World," "March of the Toys" (Herbert, Glen Macdonough); "There Once Was an Owl," "To the Land of Romance" (Herbert, Harry B. Smith); "Ah, Sweet Mystery of Life," "I'm Falling in Love with Someone" (Herbert, Rida Johnson Young); "Sweethearts" (Herbert, Robert B. Smith).

Allan Jones (John Ramsey); Mary Martin (Louise Hall); Walter Connolly (Victor Herbert); Lee Bowman (Dr. Richard Moore); Susanna Foster (Peggy Ramsey); Judith Barrett (Marie Clark); Jerome Cowan (Barney Harris); John Garrick (Warner Bryant); Pierre Watkin (Albert Martin); Richard Tucker (Michael Brown); Hal K. Dawson (George Faller); Emmett Vogan (Forbes); Mary Currier (Mrs. Victor Herbert); James Finlayson (Lamp Lighter).

Victor Herbert (1859–1924) was one of the most popular composers of the late nineteenth and early twentieth centuries, composing such shows as *Cyrano De Bergerac* (1899), *Babes in Toyland* (1903), *Naughty Marietta* (1910), *Sweethearts* (1913), *Eileen* (1917), *Angel Face* (1920) and the 1921 and 1923 editions of *The Ziegfeld Follies.* In 1939 Paramount turned out a biopic of the maestro. While Walter Connolly was well cast in the part, the picture actually had little to do with Herbert's life, other than gloriously featuring sixteen of his songs. It is best remembered today for having cast both Mary Martin and Susanna Foster in their screen debuts.

Temperamental tenor John Ramsey (Allan Jones), who has made a great success of appearing in Victor Herbert (Walter Connolly) operettas, meets Louise Hall (Mary Martin), a small-town girl with ambitions to become a stage actress. Ramsey falls in love with her and convinces Herbert to hire Louise for his new production. She is sensational in her debut. Thereafter, both because she is fearful of professionally overshadowing her husband and because she is going to have a baby, she retires. Ramsey's career wanes and marital problems increase between him and his wife. Louise and their child go to Switzerland. Later she returns to

America where she is reconciled with him. His career is now at a nadir. To help make expenses meet, she gives singing lessons. When their daughter Peggy (Susanna Foster) is fourteen, Louise agrees to star in a revival of one of Herbert's operettas. On opening night Ramsey, who does not want to stand in his wife's career path, announces he is going to Australia. A distraught Louise is unable to perform and Peggy goes on in her place. Peggy is extremely nervous and does not come across to the audience, until her father puts on a costume and joins the chorus on stage. Now filled with confidence, Peggy is well received. The Ramseys celebrate their reconciliation.

Despite its anemic plot, THE GREAT VICTOR HERBERT is an entertaining package, due mainly to the handsome staging it offers of the many Herbert compositions presented. Allan Jones gives fine renderings of "Sweethearts," "Some Day," "Thine Alone" and "I'm Falling in Love with Someone," all of which he recorded for Victor Records. Susanna Foster was quite impressive in her screen bow as a teenage coloratura performing "Kiss Me Again." Ironically, while much hype was given to Broadway's Mary Martin in her first major screen role, her voice seemed ineffective singing the Herbert songs.

Variety termed the results "elaborately produced, visually effective," and added, "With the advantage of Victor Herbert's superlative score, the film should please the musically inclined." In *The Paramount Story* (1985), John Douglas Eames rated the film, ". . . An enjoyable musical with a less idiotic script than most composer biopics inflicted on their audiences."

THE GREAT VICTOR HERBERT was Oscar-nominated for Best Score, Cinematography, and Sound.

THE GREAT ZIEGFELD (Metro-Goldwyn-Mayer, 1936) 170 minutes.

Producer, Hunt Stromberg; director, Robert Z. Leonard; screenplay, William Anthony McGuire; art director, Cedric Gibbons; costumes, Adrian; music director, Arthur Lange; orchestrator, Frank Skinner; choreographer, Seymour Felix; technical advisor, Billie Burke; sound, Douglas Shearer; camera, Oliver T. Marsh, Ray June, George Folsey, Merritt B. Gerstad; editor, William S. Gray.

Songs: "Yiddle on Your Fiddle," "A Pretty Girl Is Like a Melody" (Irving Berlin); Interpolated music within "A Pretty Girl Is Like a Melody" number: "Humoresque No. 7 in G flat" (Antonin Dvorak), "One Fine Day" from the opera *Madame Butterfly*

(Giacomo Puccini), "Liebestraum" (Franz Liszt), "The Blue Danube Waltz" (Johann Strauss II), "On with the Motley" from the opera *Pagliacci* (Ruggiero Leoncavallo), and "Rhapsody in Blue" (George Gershwin); "You Gotta Pull Strings," "She's a Ziegfeld Follies Girl," "You," "You Never Looked So Beautiful" (Walter Donaldson, Harold Adamson); "A Circus Must Be Different in a Ziegfeld Show" (Con Conrad, Herb Magidson); "My Man" (Maurice Yvain; English lyrics, Channing Pollock); "Won't You Come and Play with Me" (adapted from the German by Anna Held); "It's Delightful to Be Married" (adapted by Held, Vincent Scotto from "La Petite Tonkinoise" by Scotto, Henri Christine); "If You Knew Susie" (Buddy G. DeSylva, Joseph Meyer).

William Powell (Florenz Ziegfeld); Luise Rainer (Anna Held); Myrna Loy (Billie Burke); Frank Morgan (Billings); Reginald Owen (Sampston); Nat Pendleton (Sandow the Great); Virginia Bruce (Audrey Lane); Ernest Cossart (Sidney); Robert Greig (Joe); Raymond Walburn (Sage); Fanny Brice (Herself); Jean Chatburn (Mary Lou); Ann Pennington (Herself); Ray Bolger (Himself); Harriet Hoctor (Herself); Gilda Gray (Herself); Charles Trowbridge (Julian Mitchell); A. A. Trimble (Will Rogers); Joan Holland (Patricia Ziegfeld); Buddy Doyle (Eddie Cantor); Charles Judels (Pierre); Leon Errol (Himself); Marcelle Corday (Marie); Esther Muir (Prima Donna); Herman Bing (Customer); Paul Irving (Erlanger); William Demarest (Gene Buck); Stanley Morner [Dennis Morgan] (Vocalist in "Pretty Girl" Number); Allan Jones (Voice Dubber in "Pretty Girl" Number); Alfred P. James (Stage Doorman); Sarah Edwards (Wardrobe Woman); Suzanne Kaaren (Miss Blair); Mickey Daniels (Telegraph Boy); Alice Keating (Alice); Charles Coleman (Carriage Starter); Mary Howard (Miss Carlisle); Evelyn Dockson (Fat Woman); Susan Fleming (Girl with Sage); Charles Fallon (French Ambassador); Adrienne d'Ambricourt (Wife of French Ambassador); Edwin Maxwell (Charles Frohman); Ruth Gillette (Lillian Russell); John Hyams (Dave Stamper); Wallis Clark (Broker); Ray Brown (Inspector Doyle); Rosina Lawrence (Marilyn Miller); Pat Nixon (Extra).

Enterprising Florenz Ziegfeld (William Powell) begins his show business career as a sideshow barker at the Chicago Fair, exploiting Sandow the Strong Man (Nat Pendleton). With the money derived from this venture, Florenz sails for Europe, where he nearly goes broke gambling at Monte Carlo. However, there he also discovers actress Anna Held (Luise Rainer) and he outwits friendly rival Billings (Frank Morgan) in signing the star to a personal contract. During their professional relationship back in the States, the flamboyant Ziegfeld and Anna Held fall in love and

The "A Pretty Girl Is Like a Melody" production number from THE GREAT ZIEGFELD (1936). Virginia Bruce is seated at the top of the column.

they wed, but they have troubles due to her temperament and jealousy and his extravagant ways. Anna finally divorces Florenz because of his philandering but he continues to become the top producer on Broadway. He meets and marries actress Billie Burke (Myrna Loy). Their marriage is a relatively happy one, with Billie somewhat restraining her husband financially. They are further united following the birth of their daughter Patricia (Joan Holland). When Ziegfeld has financial reverses, Billie sells her jewelry to back his new shows and Ziegfeld again finds great success. The stock market crash of 1929, however, wipes out the Ziegfeld fortune and, not long after, he dies, a broken man.

Initially it was Universal Pictures that planned to present a pictorial glorification to the great showman, Florenz Ziegfeld (1869–1932). But that studio suffered financial reverses and MGM acquired the screen rights to the project, including the screenplay by William Anthony McGuire (longtime friend of Ziegfeld) for $250,000. To topline this $1,500,000+ extravagant salute, Metro-Goldwyn-Mayer producer Hunt Stromberg assigned William Powell and Myrna Loy, who had already co-starred successfully in MANHATTAN MELODRAMA (1934), THE THIN MAN (1934) and EVELYN PRENTICE (1934). Billie Burke had been scheduled to play herself when Universal was packaging the project, but when MGM took over she was given a term contract not to be in the picture and to serve, instead, as technical advisor. Viennese actress Luise Rainer, who had made her screen debut in MGM's ESCAPADE (1935), replacing Myrna Loy, was cast as the renowned stage attraction, Anna Held. Several celebrities closely associated with the great producer were cast as themselves in the epic: Ray Bolger (singing "She's a Follies Girl"), Fanny Brice (performing "Yiddle on the Fiddle" and "My Man"), Leon Errol, Gilda Gray and Harriet Hoctor (dancing in the "A Circus Must Be Different in a Ziegfeld Show" number). Initially, Ziegfeld's stage favorite, Marilyn Miller, was to appear in THE GREAT ZIEGFELD. However, her financial demands were so high that her real life cameo appearance was cancelled and Rosina Lawrence was used to impersonate the famed stage star of *Sally* and *Sunny* in a brief bit. In the film, Buddy Doyle impersonated Eddie Cantor (who wanted too much money for a guest cameo), performing "If You Knew Susie," and A. A. Trimble appeared as the late Will Rogers.

Harold Adamson and Walter Donaldson composed several songs for THE GREAT ZIEGFELD, but its best remembered production number was built around Irving Berlin's "A Pretty Girl Is Like A Melody," sung by Dennis Morgan (whose voice was dubbed by Allan Jones). The lavish number contained an unforgettably mammoth revolving pillar with 175 steps. The cylinder was decorated with 192 girls, with lovely Virginia Bruce lounging atop the column's pinnacle. Filmed in a circus tent set up on the backlot, the number cost $240,000.

When this movie opened in New York at a $2.20 ticket high, it was the studio's most costly production since BEN-HUR (1925). THE GREAT ZIEGFELD, along with GRAND HOTEL (1932), proved to be one of the studio's most memorable offerings of the decade. Because the final release ran three hours, a number of interesting sequences were sadly cut, such as Gilda Gray performing her famous "Shimmy" dance.

"You will never see another musical film that exceeds it in opulence, in visual inventiveness, in Babylonian splendor," was the verdict of the *New York Evening Post.* The *New York American* cheered, "THE GREAT ZIEGFELD is pretty nearly everything such an extravaganza should be. There are romance and reality, song and dance, gaiety and beauty, pathos and bathos, which is the restless heart of Broadway." Otis Ferguson wrote in *The New Republic,* "We have had romanticized biographies of show people before, but this is apart from them in scale if nothing else: three solid hours of tunes, girls, specialty numbers, and all the bustle of people and events in the lean and fat years of a national figure. The movie is fantastic, yet curiously appropriate, its atmosphere matching the topsy-turvey reality of all this blare and tinsel. Too glib for real life, it is persuasive for all that—possibly just because of that."

Named the Best Picture of 1936 by the Academy of Motion Picture Arts and Sciences, this opus also garnered an Oscar for Luise Rainer as Best Actress, who was exceedingly touching in the very theatrical but memorably pathetic telephone scene where she bids Ziegfeld great happiness in his forthcoming marriage to Billie Burke. Rainer also got to perform "Won't You Come and Play with Me?" and "It's Delightful to Be Married." While William Powell also claimed the Best Actor Oscar that year, it was for Universal's screwball comedy MY MAN GODFREY and *not* THE GREAT ZIEGFELD, in which he gave one of his most indelible performances. Nowhere matching Powell and Rainer's work in the lavish proceedings was Myrna Loy's rather bland portrayal of the always amusing, bubbling Billie Burke.

Glowing in the profits of THE GREAT ZIEGFELD, MGM produced ZIEGFELD GIRL (1941), *q.v.,* which concentrated on the lives of three Ziegfeld showgirls (Judy Garland, Hedy Lamarr and Lana Turner), and in 1946 offered ZIEGFELD FOLLIES, *q.v.,* a potpourri review which had a deceased Ziegfeld (William Powell again) looking down from heaven at the state and art of show business. On May 21, 1978 NBC-TV presented a three-hour, $3 million telefilm, ZIEGFELD: THE MAN AND HIS WOMEN. It starred Paul Shenar (Florenz Ziegfeld), Barbara Parkins (Anna Held), Samantha Eggar (Billie Burke), Valerie Perrine (Lilian Lorraine), Pamela Peadon (Marilyn Miller) and Inga Swenson (Nora Bayes). The *Hollywood Reporter* noted of this movie, ". . . [It] has all the glimmering ingredients essential to recreating the life of showman Florenz Ziegfeld. . . . However, this [the expensive production] comes to naught because the film's center—the man himself—is curiously cool."

GUYS AND DOLLS (Metro-Goldwyn-Mayer, 1955) Color 158 minutes.

Producer, Samuel Goldwyn; director, Joseph L. Mankiewicz; based on the musical play by Abe Burrows, Jo Swerling, Frank Loesser, and based on "The Idylls of Sarah Brown" by Damon Runyon; screenplay, Mankiewicz; production designer, Oliver Smith; art director, Joseph Wright; set decorator, Howard Bristol; costumes, Irene Sharaff; makeup, Ben Lane; orchestrators, Skip Martin, Nelson Riddle, Alexander Courage, Al Sendrey; choreographer, Michael Kidd; camera, Harry Stradling, Sr.; editor, Daniel Mandell.

Songs: "Fugue for Tin Horn," "Follow the Fold," "The Oldest Established," "I'll Know," "Adelaide's Lament," "A Woman in Love," "If I Were a Bell," "Take Back Your Mink," "Sue Me," "Luck Be a Lady," "Adelaide," "Sit Down, You're Rockin' the Boat," "Guys and Dolls," "Pet Me Poppa" (Frank Loesser).

Marlon Brando (Sky Masterson); Jean Simmons (Sarah Brown); Frank Sinatra (Nathan Detroit); Vivian Blaine (Miss Adelaide); Robert Keith (Lieutenant Brannigan); Stubby Kaye (Nicely-Nicely Johnson); B. S. Pully (Big Jule); Sheldon Leonard (Harry the Horse); Regis Toomey (Arvide Abernathy); Johnny Silver (Benny Southstreet); Dan Dayton (Rusty Charlie); George E. Stone (Society Max); Kathryn Givney (General Cartwright); Veda Ann Borg (Laverne); Mary Allan Hokanson (Agatha); Joe McTurk (Angie the Ox); Kay Kuter (Calvin); Stapleton Kent (Mission Member); Renee Renor (Cuban Singer); John Indrisao (Liverlips Louis); Earle Hodgins (Pitchman); Barry Tyler (Waiter); Matt Murphy (The Champ); Julian Rivero (Havana Waiter); Larri Thomas, Jann Darly, June Kirby, Madelyn Darrow, Barbara Brent (Goldwyn Girls); and: Franklyn Farnum, Major Sam Harris, Earle Hodgins, Frank Richards, Harry Tyler, Harry Wilson.

The American public has long been fascinated with the flavorful characters spawned by Damon Runyon (1880–1946) in his wonderful stories of colorful underworld types. Runyon's writings reflected a special never-never world more comical than real and always filled with oversized sentiments. Using Runyon's "The Idylls of Sarah Brown" as a basis, Jo Swerling and Abe Burrows created the book and Frank Loesser the songs for *Guys and Dolls.* The musical opened on Broadway on November 24, 1950 for a 1,200-performance run, starring Vivian Blaine, Robert Alda, Sam Levene, Isabel Bigley, Stubby Kaye and Pat Rooney, Sr. It included such popular songs as "A Bushel and a Peck," "I've Never Been in Love Before," "Luck Be a Lady" and "If I Were a Bell." Samuel Goldwyn paid $1,000,000 for the screen rights and surprised a great many by hiring Marlon Brando as Sky Masterson (a part originally planned for Gene Kelly, who was then under a confining MGM contract) and Frank Sinatra as Nathan Detroit. (More ideal casting would have been to have Brando and Sinatra switch roles.) Jean Simmons, more noted for her dramatic and light comedy appearances, was an offbeat (but very effective) selection as the sweet missionary heroine, Sarah Brown. Betty Grable was the first choice to play lovelorn showgirl Adelaide. However, she and Goldwyn (her former boss in the early 1930s) had a falling out and the role went to Vivian Blaine. Others repeating their Broadway assignments were Stubby Kaye (Nicely Nicely Johnson), B. S. Pully (Big Jule) and Johnny Silver (Benny Southstreet). It was a strange decision to give Joseph L. Mankiewicz, who had never directed a musical before, the directorial post on this project.

Amiable New York City gambler Nathan Detroit (Frank Sinatra) needs a fast $1,000 to get into a big floating crap game. He hopes to wangle the money from Sky Masterson (Marlon Brando), who has just returned to Manhattan. In order for Nathan to pry the funds from his pal, he must take up Masterson's bet that he can seduce any woman Nathan selects. Nathan stacks the odds in his own favor by selecting prim Salvation Army worker Sarah Brown (Jean Simmons) as the victim. Meanwhile, Nathan is in trouble with his fiancée, club performer Adelaide (Vivian Blaine), to whom he has been engaged for fourteen years. Sky romances Sarah and takes her with him to Havana. The two end up falling in love. When they marry it is a double-ring ceremony, with Nathan also marrying Adelaide.

In translating GUYS AND DOLLS to the screen, "My Time of Day" was dropped, as were "A Bushel and a Peck" and "I've Never Been in Love Before," the latter two replaced by the serviceable "Pet Me, Poppa" and "A Woman in Love." Another new addition to the film score was Loesser's "Adelaide," sung by Frank Sinatra. Thankfully, Marlon Brando was not disastrous in his characterization; he was rather charming and sang okay (his songs were pieced together from various takes). Blaine and the other Broadway veterans were appropriately delightful in their gusty performances and Jean Simmons did just fine. On the other hand, Sinatra proved far too laid-back for his own good. The real zest in the celluloid proceedings came from Michael Kidd's choreography of the show's Broadway street scene opening number and the "Luck Be a Lady" crap game sequence.

One of the prime complaints about GUYS AND DOLLS on-screen were the stylized settings. "For all the movement, artificial sets suggest theatrical enclosure," observed the *New York Times.* Stephen Sondheim, later to be a great Broadway composing talent, explained this point further in *Films in Review* (December 1955): "The two major flaws of GUYS AND DOLLS are Oliver Smith's sets and Frank Sinatra's performance. Samuel Goldwyn, Joseph Mankiewicz, and Mr. Smith apparently couldn't make up their minds whether the scenery should be realistic or stylized. As a result, they have the disadvantages of both, and these disadvantages work against the very special nature of Runyonesque story-telling. . . . GUYS AND DOLLS has much more success as a screen transference of a stage musical than OKLAHOMA!, BRIGADOON and KISS ME, KATE, but is not so successful as COVER GIRL, SEVEN BRIDES FOR SEVEN BROTHERS and SINGIN' IN THE RAIN, all of which were written for the screen."

Costing $5,500,000, the widescreen, color GUYS AND DOLLS grossed $7 million in domestic box-office receipts. GUYS AND DOLLS received four Oscar nominations: Scoring, Costume Design—Color, Cinematography—Color, and Art Direction-Set Direction—Color.

GYPSY (Warner Bros., 1962) Color 149 minutes.

Producer/director, Mervyn LeRoy; based on the musical play by Arthur Laurents, Jule Styne, Stephen Sondheim, and the book *Gypsy, a Memoir* by Gypsy Rose Lee [Rose Louise Hovick]; screenplay, Leonard Spigelgass; art director, John Beckman; set decorator, Ralph S. Hurst; costumes, Orry-Kelly, Howard Shoup, Bill Gaskin; makeup, Gordon Bau; music conductor/supervisor, Frank Perkins; orchestrators, Perkins, Carl Brandt; choreographer, Robert Tucker; assistant directors, Gil Kissel, Greg Peters, Mecca Graham; camera, Harry Stradling, Sr.; editor, Philip W. Anderson.

Songs: "Small World," "Baby June and Her Newsboys," "Mr. Goldstone, I Love You," "Little Lamb," "All I Need Is The Girl," "Together, Wherever We Go," "Broadway, Broadway," "Let Me Entertain You," "Dainty June and Her Farmboys," "If Mama Were Married," "Cow Song," "Everything's Coming Up Roses," "You'll Never Get Away from Me," "You Gotta Have a Gimmick," "Some People," "Rose's Turn" (Jule Styne, Stephen Sondheim).

Rosalind Russell (Rose); Natalie Wood (Gypsy [Louise]); Karl Malden (Herbie Sommers); Paul Wallace (Tulsa #2); Betty Bruce (Tessie Tura); Parley Baer (Mr. Kringelein); Harry Shannon (Grandpa); Suzanne Cupito ("Baby" June); Ann Jilliann [Jillian]

("Dainty" June); Diane Pace ("Baby" Louise); Faith Dane (Mazeppa); Roxanne Arlen (Electra); Jean Willes (Betty Cratchitt); George Petrie (George); Bewnn Lessy (Mervyn Goldstone); Guy Raymond (Patsy); Louis Quinn (Cigar); Jack Benny (Himself); Bert Michaels, Dick Foster, Jim Hubbard, Jeff Parker, Mike Cody, Bob Wagner (Farmboys); Terry Hope, Shirley Chandler, Francie Karath, Paula Martin, Dee Ann Johnston, Renee Aubry (Hollywood Blondes); Trudi Ames (Hawaiian Girl); Harvey Korman (Phil); James Millhollin (Mr. Beckman); William Fawcett (Mr. Willis); Danny Lockin (Yonker); Ian Tucker (Angie); Lois Roberts (Agnes); Dina Claire (Dolores); Lisa Kirk (Singing Voice for some of Rose's singing); Marni Nixon (High notes singing for Gypsy).

Louise Hovick (1914–1979), better known as Gypsy Rose Lee, was perhaps the best known stripper of her generation. She was also an accomplished actress, author and sparking personality, and the older sister of actress, director and author June Havoc. Hovick's 1957 autobiography, *Gypsy, a Memoir,* served as the basis for Arthur Laurent's book and Jule Styne-Stephen Sondheim's score for *Gypsy.* The trend-setting show, starring Ethel Merman, Jack Klugman and Sandra Church, opened on May 21, 1959 and ran for 702 performances. Despite the acclaim that brassy Ethel Merman won as pushy Mama Rose, Warner Bros. opted for safer casting by choosing brash Rosalind Russell for the lead assignment. (Most of her vocals were dubbed by Lisa Kirk.) Natalie Wood, who had scored in WEST SIDE STORY (1961), *q.v.,* was selected to play the reluctant stripper caught in a battle of wills with her dominating stage mama. (Wood's high notes were dubbed by Marni Nixon.) Bulbous-nosed Karl Malden proved surprisingly effective as the henpecked but loving Herbie Sommers. Paul Wallace, who had an effective solo dance-song ("All I Need Is the Girl"), recreated his stage role for the movie. Like the Broadway original, the movie version offered such popular numbers as "Let Me Entertain You," "Small World" and "Everything's Coming Up Roses."

During the Roaring Twenties hyperactive stage mother Rose (Rosalind Russell) insists on making stars of her two young daughters, June (Suzanne Cupito) and Louise (Diane Pace). With mama's tremendous prodding, June proves to be a success in vaudeville but Louise is too shy for the stage and remains firmly in the background. Meanwhile, Rose meets and falls in love with gentle Herbie Sommers (Karl Malden), a former candy salesman who tags along with the act. Eventually, June (Ann Jilliann [Jillian]) outgrows her child's act as vaudeville becomes passé, and she departs. A resourceful Rose is left to promote Louise (Natalie

Wood), who ends up in cheap burlesque but quickly becomes a star in the medium. As Gypsy Rose Lee the young woman emerges as a big moneymaker. Along the way she tries to rid herself of her mother's unwanted and suffocating influence. The two argue and decide to split. However, after Louise overhears her mother plaintively crying out her frustrations on an empty stage, the two reconcile.

The resultant GYPSY was a mixed bag, more successful in its recreation of vaudeville and burlesque than in fine-tuning the musical entertainment. "That tornado of a stage mother (and perfectly abominable woman) played and sung on Broadway by Ethel Merman is little more than a big wind now in the brassy, fiercely energetic and often amusing person of Rosalind Russell . . . there are too many dull intervals when the band snoozes and Miss Russell, an unappetizing Karl Malden and young Natalie Wood, who is charming throughout, simply talk. The real fire and lubricant here is the excellent Jule Styne score, most of it intact" (*New York Times*). One of the musical highlights of the film was the show-stopping "You've Got to Have a Gimmick," in which three strippers (Roxanne Arlen, Betty Bruce and Faith Dane) instruct the bewildered Gypsy on the need for a diverting gambit to succeed in their evocative but highly competitive art form. Both Wood and Russell were far better in their dramatic moments than in the musical sections. When all was said and done, however, anyone who had ever marveled at Ethel Merman's bravura stage performance sorely missed her presence in this screen translation about the world's most overpowering backstage mama.

GYPSY earned $6,000,000 in distributors' domestic film rentals. Its soundtrack album appeared on *Billboard* magazine's hits chart for thirteen weeks, rising to position #10. The movie received three Oscar nominations: Best Scoring of a Musical—Adaptation or a Treatment, Costume Design—Color, and Cinematography—Color.

The original musical play received a major Broadway revival in 1974, starring Angela Lansbury, and another in 1990, headlining Tyne Daly. Following the acclaimed latest staging of GYPSY, Barbra Streisand announced that she wanted to direct and star (as Mama Rose)—with Madonna as Gypsy—in a film remake of the property. However, its creators vetoed the startling idea, at least for the time being. "Not for all the money in the world will we let them make another film version of GYPSY," argued playwright Arthur Laurents. Co-collaborator Jule Styne noted that because of the 1962 movie: ". . . The show was dead in stock. It took almost 30 years to offset that lousy picture."

HAIR (United Artists, 1979) Color 121 minutes.

Producers, Lester Persky, Michael Butler; associate producer, Robert Greenhut; director, Milos Forman; based on the musical play by Galt MacDermot, Gerome Ragni, James Rado; screenplay, Michael Weller; production designer, Stuart Wurtzel; art director, Harold Michelson; set decorator/designer, Stuart Wurtzel; costumes, Ann Roth; makeup, Max Henriquez, Robert Mills; assistant director, Michael Hausman; choreographers, Twyla Tharp, Kenneth Rinker; sound, Chris Newman; sound re-recording, Bill Varney, Steve Maslow, Bob Minkler; supervising sound editor, Milton C. Burrow; special effects, Al Griswold; puppet creations, Larry Reehling; special camera, Miroslav Ondricek, Richard Kratina, Jean Talvin; second unit camera, Gerald Cotts; additional camera, Richard Perce; supervising editor, Lynzee Klingman; editors, Stanley Warnow, Alan Heim.

Songs: "Aquarius," "Colored Spade," "Ain't Got No," "Black Boys/White Boys," "Electric Blues," "Old Fashioned Melody," "Flesh Departures," "3-5-0-0," "Somebody to Hold," "Sodomy," "Donna," "Hashish," "Manchester," "Abie Baby," "Fourscore," "I'm Black," "Air," "Party Music," "My Conviction," "I Got Life," "Frank Mills," "Hair," "LBJ," "Hare Krishna," "Where Do I Go?" "Walking in Space," "Easy to Be Hard," "Good Morning Starshine," "What a Piece of Work Is Man," "Somebody to Love," "Don't Put It Down," "Let the Sunshine In" (Galt MacDermot, Gerome Ragni, James Rado).

John Savage (Claude Hooper Bukowski); Treat Williams (Berger); Beverly D'Angelo (Sheila); Annie Golden (Jeannie); Dorsey Wright (Hud); Don Dacus (Woof); Cheryl Barnes (Hud's Fiancée); Richard Bright (Fenton); Nicholas Ray (General); Charlotte Rae (Lady in Pink); Miles Chapin (Steve); Fern Tailer (Sheila's Mother); Charles Denny (Sheila's Father); Herman Meckler (Sheila's Uncle); Agness Breen (Sheila's Aunt); Antonia Rey (Berger's Mother); George Manos (Berger's Father); Linda Surh (Vietnamese Girl); Jane Booke (1st Debutante); Suki Love (2nd Debutante); Joe Acord (Claude's Father); Michael Jeter (Sheldon); Janet York (Prison Psychiatrist); Rahsaan Curry (Lafayette, Jr.); Harry Gittleson (Judge); Donald Alsdurf (M.P.); Steve Massicotte, Mario Nelson (Barracks Officers); Ken Woods, Tony Watkins, Carl Hall, Howard Porter, Nell Carter, Kurt Yahjan, Leata Galloway, Cyrena Lomba, Ron Young, Laurie Beechman, Debi Dye, Ellen Foley, John Maestro, Fred Ferrara, Jim Rosica, Charlaine Woodard, Trudy Perkins, Chuck Patterson, H. Douglas Berring, Russell Costen, Kenny Brawner, Lee Wells, Melba Moore, Ronnie Dyson, Rose Marie Wright, Tom Rawe, Jennifer Way, Shelley Washington,

Don Dacus, Annie Golden, Dorsey Wright and Treat Williams in HAIR (1979).

Christine Uchida, Raymond Kurshals, Richard Colton, Antony Ferro, Sara Rudner, Pat Benoye, Cameron Burke, Richard Caceres, Tony Constantine, Ron Dunham, Leonard Feiner, Ken Gildin, Kate Glasner, Christian Holder, Chris Komar, Nancy Lefkowith, Joseph Lennon, Robert Levithan, France Mayotte, Hector Mercado, Sharon Mirpolsky, Marta Renzi, Donna Ritchie, Ellen Saltonstall, Radha Sukhu, Byron Utley, Earlise Vails, Ronald Weeks, Kimmary Williams, Deborah Zalkind.

Hair caused a major sensation when it opened on Broadway in the spring of 1968, after having been first staged in 1967 Off-Broadway. This counter-culture play had a run of 1,742 performances with a cast that included Steve Curry, Paul Jabara, Diane Keaton, Melba Moore, James Rado and Gerome Ragni. Much of its notoriety derived from its staunch anti-Vietnam stand and on-stage nudity. A decade later the cultural atmosphere had so changed that a 1977 revival of the musical flopped. Thus it is surprising that it was even brought to the screen in 1979, although the movie version was somewhat changed from the stage production. Still, in the deepening inflation of the time, this movie musical only grossed a limp $6,237,965 in distributors' domestic film rentals.

Oklahoma youth Claude Hooper Bukowski (John Savage) goes to New York City for his induction into the army in the late 1960s, sure that he will end up serving in Vietnam. In Gotham he encounters a group of free-living hippies in Central Park, including Berger (Treat Williams), Jeannie (Annie Golden), Hud (Dorsey Wright) and Woof (Don Dacus). They preach the message of free love, free dope and freedom from wars and social conventions. The rather backward Claude is adopted by the group and they urge him on in his quest to seduce debutante Sheila (Beverly D'Angelo). Once Claude goes into the service, the hippies follow him to his basic training camp in Nevada. By error Berger is shipped off to Vietnam instead of Claude. A year later the group gathers at Berger's graveside in a huge cemetery.

For the movie, which was shot largely on location, the songwriters composed the new songs, "Party Music" and "Somebody to Love." As in the stage version, the most satisfying musical number in HAIR proved to be "Aquarius," which is creatively choreographed by Twyla Tharp (whose dance group is featured in the film). Other songs retained from the original production include "Black Boys/White Boys," which is about racial equality, "Good Morning Starshine," "Easy to Be Hard," and the anti-war "3-5-0-0." The picture was supervised by Czechoslovakian director Milos Forman who had directed such earlier anti-establishment motion pictures as TAKING OFF (1971) and ONE FLEW OVER THE CUCKOO'S NEST (1976). *Variety* pinpointed some of the film's problems, "There are moments in HAIR that are vibrant and innovative, in ways that no musical has succeeded in the late 1970s. . . . The spirit and elan that captivated the Vietnam protest era are long gone, and what [director Milos] Forman tries to make up with splash and verve fails to evoke potent nostalgia." Geoff Brown (British *Monthly Film Bulletin*) determined, " . . . Forman's earnestly enthusiastic approach to his subject makes the going doubly difficult: the whirling camerawork, kinetic editing and whimsical bits of business (like the cops' horses stepping in rhythm at the Central Park 'be-in') only make the musical numbers look more than ever like dinosaurs."

HALLELUJAH! (Metro-Goldwyn-Mayer, 1929) 109 minutes. (Also silent version: 6,579′).

Director/story, King Vidor; treatment, Richard Schayer; screenplay, Wanda Tuchock; dialogue, Ransom Rideout; titles, Marian Ainslee; art director, Cedric Gibbons; wardrobe, Henrietta Frazer; music supervisor, Eva Jessye; assistant directors, Robert A. Golden, William Allen Garrison; sound, Douglas Shearer; camera,

Gordon Avil; editors: (sound version) Hugh Wynn, (silent version) Anson Stevenson.

Songs: "Waiting at the End of the Road," "Swanee Shuffle" (Irving Berlin); "Goin' Home" (traditional); "Swing Low, Sweet Chariot" (traditional).

Daniel L. Haynes (Zeke); Nina Mae McKinney (Chick); William E. Fountaine (Hot Shot); Harry Gray (Parson); Fannie Belle De Night (Mammy); Everett McGarrity (Spunk); Victoria Spivey (Missy Rose); Milton Dickerson, Robert Couch, Walter Tait (Johnson Kids); Evelyn Pope Burwell, Eddie Connors (Singers); Slickem [William Allen Garrison] (The Heavy); and Dixie Jubilee Singers.

Although it is considered to be a serious social statement today, at the time of its release HALLELUJAH! was not a popular film in that it dealt with blacks. In the South it was hardly distributed at all and its exhibition in the North was not much more successful. Thus, despite the praise of critics, this $320,000 production lost $120,000 in its release, which substantiated the theory of many MGM executives; i.e., that the iconoclastic film should not have been produced. Director-scripter King Vidor made the picture without salary because of his extreme faith in it. *Photoplay* magazine judged it a "striking epic of the Negro, sensitively directed and spontaneously acted." For the leading roles Vidor cast popular black entertainers Daniel L. Haynes and Nina Mae McKinney, along with well-known blues singer and recording artist Victoria Spivey. The latter's career continued into the 1970s and, as a record producer the decade before, she was the first person to record Bob Dylan.

Black tenant farmer Zeke (Daniel L. Haynes) sells his family's cotton crop and when he receives $100 for it he becomes the target of the dancehall entertainer Chick (Nina Mae McKinney). She maneuvers him into a crap game with her boyfriend, Hot Shot (William E. Fountaine), who uses loaded dice to cheat Zeke out of his cotton earnings. When Zeke realizes he has been taken, a fight ensues. Getting hold of Hot Shot's gun, Zeke fires into the crowd, killing his own brother (Everett McGarrity). As a result, the shamed Zeke dedicates his life to religion and becomes a preacher. When he again meets Chick she converts to the church and leaves Hot Shot. Zeke is again attracted to Chick and now leaves his loving sweetheart, Missy Rose (Victoria Spivey). Meanwhile, Hot Shot returns and Chick runs off with him. Zeke pursues them and in a chase Chick dies when Hot Shot's buggy is wrecked. In the ensuing fight, Zeke kills Hot Shot. For his crime Zeke serves several years on a chain gang. However, when he returns home the faithful Missy Rose is waiting for him.

MGM's ad copy for HALLELUJAH! instructed, "Clap yo' hands! Slap yo' thigh! HALLELUJAH is here! HALLELUJAH the great! HALLELUJAH, the first truly epic picture portraying the soul of the colored race. . . . Every phase of their picturesque lives—their fierce loves, their joyous, carefree pursuit of happiness, their hates and passions—finds dramatic expression against vivid backgrounds of cabarets, cotton fields, gaming houses, and humble shacks called home. . . . [The cast] sing the songs of the negro as they have never been sung before. Don't miss this tremendous event in the history of the screen!"

Employing black spiritual songs and two songs composed by Irving Berlin, HALLELUJAH! was certainly a maverick production for elitist MGM. Lee Edward Stern wrote in *The Movie Musical* (1974), "From today's point of view, HALLELUJAH has many faults. The pace is often slow and overly deliberate . . . the characters are essentially stereotypes. . . . But HALLELUJAH retains, in addition, a strange kind of dignity, the inbred honesty Vidor was striving for. And a number of its successes are brilliant . . . most of all, a chase sequence unsurpassed in its masterful building of suspense and its dramatic use of sound." With location shooting in Memphis, Tennessee, John Kobal in *Gotta Sing, Gotta Dance* (1971) called it "a magnificent film and a remarkable achievement. . . ." In his book *Toms, Coons, Mulattoes, Mammies, and Bucks* (1973), Donald Bogle weighed, "In due time, HALLELUJAH! became not only an American classic, but the precursor of all-Negro musicals, setting the tone for the treatment of Negro casts and themes. . . . HALLELUJAH! remains the first of Hollywood's attempts to deal with the black family, and is directly related to subsequent black family dramas such as THE LEARNING TREE (1969) and SOUNDER (1972)."

HARMONY PARADE *see* PIGSKIN PARADE.

THE HARVEY GIRLS (Metro-Goldwyn-Mayer, 1946) Color 104 minutes.

Producer, Arthur Freed; associate producer, Roger Edens; director, George Sidney; based on the book by Samuel Hopkins Adams and the story by Eleanore Griffin, William Rankin; screenplay, Edmund Beloin, Nathaniel Curtis, Harry Crane, James O'Hanlon, Samson Raphaelson; additional dialogue by Kay Van Riper, (uncredited): Guy Bolton, Hagar Wilde; art directors,

Cedric Gibbons, William Ferrari; set decorators, Edwin B. Willis, Mildred Griffiths; costume supervisor, Irene; women's costumes, Helen Rose; men's costumes, Valles; makeup, Jack Dawn; music director, Lennie Hayton; orchestrator, Conrad Salinger; vocal arranger, Kay Thompson; choreographer, Robert Alton; color consultants, Natalie Kalmus, Henri Jaffa; assistant director, George Rheim; sound supervisor, Douglas Shearer; special effects, Warren Newcombe; camera, George Folsey; editor, Albert Akst.

Songs: "In the Valley (Where the Evening Sun Goes Down)," "Wait and See," "On the Atchison, Topeka and the Santa Fe," "Oh You Kid," "It's a Great Big World," "Swing Your Partner Round and Round," "The Wild Wild West" (Harry Warren, Johnny Mercer); "Training Sequence" (Roger Edens); "Judy's Rage" (Conrad Salinger); "Honky Tonk" (Duncan).

Judy Garland (Susan Bradley); John Hodiak (Ned Trent); Ray Bolger (Chris Maule); Preston Foster (Judge Sam Purvis); Virginia O'Brien (Alma); Angela Lansbury (Em); Marjorie Main (Sonora Cassidy); Chill Wills (H. H. Hartsey); Kenny Baker (Terry O'Halloran); Selena Royle (Miss Bliss); Cyd Charisse (Deborah); Ruth Brady (Ethel); Catherine McLeod (Louise); Jack Lambert (Marty Peters); Edward Earle (Jed Adams); Virginia Hunter (Jane); William "Bill" Phillips, Norman Levitt (Cowboys); Morris Ankrum (Reverend Claggett); Ben Carter (John Henry); Mitchell Lewis (Sandy); Stephen McNally (Goldust McClean); Bill Hall (Big Joe); Ray Teal, Robert Emmett O'Connor (Conductors); Vernon Dent (Engineer); Jim Toney (Mule Skinner); Ruth Brady, Dorothy Gilmore, Lucille Casey, Mary Jo Ellis, Mary Jean French, Joan Thorson, Jacqueline White, Daphne Moore, Dorothy Tuttle, Gloria Hope (Harvey Girls); Vera Lee, Dorothy Van Nuys, Eve Whitney, Jane Hall, Bunny Waters, Hazel Brooks, Erin O'Kelly, Peggy Maley, Kay English, Dallas Worth (Dance Hall Girls); Marion Doenges (Singing Voice of Deborah); Virginia Reese (Singing Voice of Em); and Byron Harvey, Jr.

One of the offshoots of the innovative Broadway musical *Oklahoma!* (1943) was its impact on Hollywood filmmakers. When Roger Edens, of the Arthur Freed musical film unit at MGM, saw the show, it led him to convince his superiors to produce a musical movie set in the West. Coincidentally, studio producer Bernard Hyman had died in September 1942, which caused the cancellation of THE HARVEY GIRLS, which was to star Lana Turner and was to be based on the book (1942) by Samuel Hopkins Adams and the unpublished story by Eleanore Griffin and William Rankin. MGM attempted to sell off the property rights to the project, but Fred Harvey's family insisted that only MGM—and no other studio—

Judy Garland in THE HARVEY GIRLS (1946).

could produce a film dealing with the founding of the Harvey restaurants. With the project back on go, it was assigned to Arthur Freed and Roger Edens, who wanted Judy Garland to star in this story of the old West. However, she was more interested in joining with Fred Astaire in the musical fantasy, YOLANDA AND THE THIEF (1945). Freed convinced Garland to accept THE HARVEY GIRLS and Freed's new protégée, Lucille Bremer, was substituted in YOLANDA AND THE THIEF. Despite production problems,* the film was completed on June 4, 1945. This was a few days after Judy Garland's divorce from composer David Rose and six days before her twenty-third birthday. On June 15, 1945 Garland married MGM film director Vincente Minnelli.

In 1890 young Susan Bradley (Judy Garland) arrives in the frontier community of Sandrock, New Mexico, supposedly to be the mail order bride of one H. H. Hartsey (Chill Wills), the town drunk. The whole matter, however, turns out to be a joke thought up by saloon owner-gambler Ned Trent (John Hodiak). Needing work, Susan accepts a job as one of the new waitresses in the Fred Harvey chain of restaurants. She and fellow new recruit Alma (Virginia O'Brien) are supervised by stern but loving Sonora Cassidy (Marjorie Main). In Sandrock, Susan comes to realize that the town is controlled by crooked Judge Sam Purvis (Preston Foster) and that one of the major seats of power is Trent's Alhambra Saloon, where brassy Em (Angela Lansbury) is in charge of the saloon girls. Idealistic but spunky Susan sets out to clean up Sandrock, while she and the jealous Em vie for Trent's affections. Soon Trent falls in love with Susan and admires her noble goals. He decides to move his operation to Flagstaff, which will end his emotional tussles with her. When the Harvey Girls organize a social dance the event is disrupted by Em and her girls, and Judge Purvis has the Harvey restaurant set on fire. Trent and Purvis have a showdown fight. The restaurant is relocated to the saloon. Thereafter Trent, Em and the saloon troupe board the train for Flagstaff, but at the last minute Trent decides to remain in Sandrock to be with Susan. She does not know this and has boarded the train, prepared even to be a saloon girl if it means remaining close to Trent. Em tells Susan of Trent's change of heart. She stops the train and Susan gets off. Trent arrives on horseback and together they

*Among the obstacles confronting the filmmakers on the making of THE HARVEY GIRLS were: cast member Ray Bolger being scalded by steam from a locomotive, John Hodiak being injured in a fight scene, Virginia O'Brien being pregnant (thus causing the restaging of her solo number "It's a Great Big World"), and problems with the Breen (censorship) Production Code Office over the handling of such items as the costumes for the saloon girls during the can-can number.

return to Sandrock to be married, with the Harvey Girls serving as bridesmaids.

For a screen musical, THE HARVEY GIRLS has an especially strong cast, ranging from spunky Judy Garland (in one of her most popular characterizations) to the romantic heel-turned-hero of John Hodiak. Moreover, there is Marjorie Main as the raucous cook, the pleasing supporting work of hoofer Ray Bolger, deadpan comedienne Virginia O'Brien, and the vocalizing of Kenny Baker. Certainly one of the highlights of the movie is Angela Lansbury's saloon hostess, an amoral personality who proves to have the proverbial heart-of-gold. It is a wonderfully gaudy characterization and buoys the entire film.

Of the Johnny Mercer-Harry Warren songs composed for the film, "On the Atchison, Topeka, and Santa Fe" was the most memorable, not only emerging as a big production sequence in the movie but winning an Academy Award as the Best Song of the year. (The tune would be a favorite of contemporary vocalists, with both Bing Crosby and Kate Smith having popular recordings of the hit melody.) Not to be overlooked was the hauntingly beautiful "In the Valley (Where the Evening Sun Goes Down)," sung by Judy Garland at the start of the film, as she heads westward for a new life. Cut from the release print of THE HARVEY GIRLS were "March of the Doagies" (Judy Garland and chorus), "Hayride" (Garland and Ray Bolger) and "My Intuition" (Garland and John Hodiak).

When THE HARVEY GIRLS opened in January 1946, the *New York Herald Tribune* congratulated, "THE HARVEY GIRLS is a perfect demonstration of what Hollywood can do with its vast resources when it wants to be really showy. A skeleton of a horse opera has been clothed sumptuously with pretty girls, period sets and costumes, brawls, and conflagrations. . . . It has about as much to do with the Fred Harvey chain of restaurants which followed the Atchison, Topeka, and Santa Fe across the country as a commercial calendar, but it is bustling and beautiful." Filmed at a cost of $2,524,315, THE HARVEY GIRLS grossed $5,175,000 in its initial release. THE HARVEY GIRLS received an Oscar nomination for Best Scoring but lost to Columbia Pictures' THE JOLSON STORY, *q.v.*

HEARTBREAK HOUSE *see* ELVIS (essay).

THE HELEN MORGAN STORY (Warner Bros., 1957) 118 minutes.

Producer, Martin Rackin; director, Michael Curtiz; screenplay, Oscar Saul, Dean Reisner, Stephen Longstreet, Nelson Gidding;

art director, John Beckman; costumes, Howard Shoup; music director, Larry Prinz; choreographer, LeRoy Prinz; assistant director, Paul Helmick; camera, Ted McCord; editor, Frank Bracht.

Songs: "Bill" (Jerome Kern, P. G. Wodehouse); "Can't Help Lovin' Dat Man," "Don't Ever Leave Me," "Why Was I Born?" (Kern, Oscar Hammerstein II); "If You Were the Only Girl in the World" (Clifford Grey, Nat D. Ayer); "I Can't Give You Anything But Love" (Dorothy Fields, Jimmy McHugh); "Avalon" (Vincent Rose, Al Jolson); "Breezin' Along with the Breeze" (Haven Gillespie, Seymour Simons, Richard Whiting); "Someone to Watch Over Me," "I've Got a Crush on You," "Do, Do, Do" (George Gershwin, Ira Gershwin); "Body and Soul" (Edward Heyman, Robert Sour, Frank Eyton, John Green); "I'll Get By" (Roy Turk, Fred Ahlert); "The Love Nest" (Otto Harbach, Louis A. Hirsch); "My Time Is Your Time" (Eric Little, Leo Dance).

Ann Blyth (Helen Morgan); Paul Newman (Larry); Richard Carlson (Wade); Gene Evans (Whitey Krause); Alan King (Ben); Cara Williams (Dolly); Virginia Vincent (Sue); Walter Woolf King (Florenz Ziegfeld); Dorothy Green (Mrs. Wade); Ed Platt (Haggerty); Warren Douglas (Hellinger); Sammy White (Sammy); Peggy De Castro, Cheri De Castro, Babette De Castro (Singers); Jimmy McHugh, Rudy Vallee, Walter Winchell (Themselves); Gogi Grant (Singing Voice of Helen Morgan).

Polly Bergen effectively portrayed torch singer Helen Morgan (1900–1941) on CBS-TV's "Playhouse 90" in the spring of 1957. Later that year Warner Bros. released a black-and-white feature film in CinemaScope about the life and times of Miss Morgan, with Ann Blyth in the title role. Ironically, the studio dubbed her singing voice with that of Gogi Grant, a full voiced singer, while Miss Blyth's own voice was far more suited to the soprano stylings of Helen Morgan.

Leaving her hometown of Danville, Illinois, singer Helen Morgan (Ann Blyth) comes to Chicago. She finds a job singing and dancing at an amusement park where she meets Larry (Paul Newman), who runs a concession there. After a night of passion, the two separate. Later, when she is auditioning for a singer's job at a speakeasy, she encounters Larry and his hoodlum pal Ben (Alan King), who help her gain the job. Her career progresses as does her romance with Larry. Later he convinces his underworld associate Whitey Krause (Gene Evans) to open a cafe for her. It is frequently raided by the law, and one night after law enforcers tear up her club, she departs for Europe where she continues her career. She later returns to New York and loses her savings in the stock market crash of 1929. Larry, meanwhile, has been injured trying to rob a liquor warehouse and is recuperating in a prison hospital. Trying to get Larry out of her life, she becomes drawn to an attorney, Wade (Richard Carlson), but learns he is married. By now Helen has become a top star of Broadway, but she drowns her personal sorrows in alcohol. This eventually causes the downfall of her career and she ends in the drug rehabilitation ward at Bellevue Hospital. When she is released, Larry is waiting for her. He takes her to the club, where her friends rally around her.

"Some indestructible old tunes and a fairly honest approach to the sleaziness of the speakeasy era are the mild compensations of this soap opera-biography supposedly dramatizing the rise and decline (rum and heartbreak, what else?) of the famed torch singer. Ann Blyth, sweet, fragile, timorous and trying desperately, is anything but a ruined woman in the central role. . . . [The film] is about as moving as a sail and as heart-warming as an electric pad" (*New York Times*).

The strong point of this picture is its revival of such Helen Morgan favorites as "Bill," "Can't Help Lovin' Dat Man" and "Why Was I Born?" Also of interest is Rudy Vallee's appearance (as himself), performing his theme song, "My Time Is Your Time." The soundtrack album to THE HELEN MORGAN STORY appeared on *Billboard* magazine's hits chart for one week, in position #25.

British release title: BOTH ENDS OF THE CANDLE.

HELLO, DOLLY! (20th Century-Fox, 1969) Color 148 minutes.

Producer, Ernest Lehman; associate producer, Roger Edens; director, Gene Kelly; based on the musical play by Jerry Herman, Michael Stewart and the play *The Matchmaker* by Thornton Wilder; screenplay, Lehman; production designer, John De Cuir; art directors, Jack Martin Smith, Herman Blumenthal; set decorators, Walter M. Scott, George James Hopkins, Raphael Bretton; costumes, Irene Sharaff; makeup, Dan Striepeke; music/music conductors, Lennie Hayton, Lionel Newman; orchestrators, Philip J. Lang, Hayton, Herbert Spencer, Alexander Courage, Don Costa, Warren Barker, Frank Comstock, Joseph Lipman; choral arranger, Jack Latimer; dance arranger, Marvin Laird; choreographer, Michael Kidd; assistant choreographer, Shelah Hackett; music editors, Robert Mayer, Kenneth Wannberg; assistant director, Paul Helmick; sound supervisor, James Corcoran; sound, Murray Spivack, Vinton Vernon, Jack Solomon, Douglas O. Williams; special camera effects, L. B. Abbott, Art Cruickshank, Emil Kosa, Jr.; camera, Harry Stradling; editor, William Reynolds.

Songs: "Just Leave Everything to Me," "Put On Your Sunday

Clothes," "So Long Dearie," "It Takes a Woman," "Ribbons Down My Back," "Before the Parade Passes By," "Love Is Only Love," "It Only Takes a Moment," "Dancing," "Waiter's Gavotte," "Hello, Dolly!" (Jerry Herman).

Barbra Streisand (Dolly Levi); Walter Matthau (Horace Vandergelder); Michael Crawford (Cornelius Hackl); Louis Armstrong (Orchestra Leader); Marianne McAndrew (Irene Molloy); E. J. Peaker (Minnie Fay); Danny Lockin (Barnaby Tucker); Joyce Ames (Ermengarde); Tommy Tune (Ambrose Kemper); Judy Kaniz (Gussie Granger); David Hurst (Rudolph Reisenweber); Fritz Feld (Fritz, the German Waiter); Richard Collier (Vandergelder's Barber); J. Pat O'Malley (Policeman in Park).

Jerry Herman and Michael Stewart based their hugely successful 1964 Broadway musical, *Hello, Dolly!,* starring Carol Channing, on Thornton Wilder's 1954 comedy, *The Matchmaker,* which itself was lensed in 1958 by Paramount Pictures with Shirley Booth in the title role. The mammoth hit (2,944 performances) was still running

Walter Matthau and Barbra Streisand in HELLY, DOLLY! (1969).

on Broadway when 20th Century-Fox finally filmed the property. On stage the pivotal role had been played by mature performers (from Channing to Ginger Rogers, Martha Raye, Pearl Bailey and Ethel Merman on Broadway), but to protect their hefty investment, the studio chose Barbra Streisand for the title part of Dolly Levi. Granted Oscar-winning Streisand was a bona fide movie star as the result of FUNNY GIRL (1968), *q.v.,* but she was far too young at twenty-seven to be effective in the characterization. Despite this *and* Gene Kelly's very old-fashioned direction, the screen musical captured some of the flavor of the stage vehicle. The much-needed exuberance emerged for the rendering of the title song and the rousing "Before the Parade Passes By" production number whose set cost $2,000,000 to construct. The movie grossed $15,200,000 in distributors' domestic film rentals, which, considering the high cost ($24,000,000) of the movie, was not a happy figure.

In the summer of 1890, New York widow Dolly Levi (Barbra Streisand) has set her sights on landing rich Yonkers grain merchant Horace Vandergelder (Walter Matthau). However, when she is summoned to his home she learns that the tight-fisted man wants her to escort his niece Ermengarde (Joyce Ames) to the city to protect her from struggling artist Ambrose Kemper (Tommy Tune). He also discloses that he plans to wed Irene Molloy (Marianne McAndrew), a milliner to whom Dolly had introduced him. Wanting Horace for herself, Dolly devises a complex plan which she inaugurates by telling the two young lovers to go to New York City and to enter a dance contest at the Harmonia Gardens restaurant. She then tells Horace's clerks, Cornelius Hackl (Michael Crawford) and Barnaby Tucker (Danny Lockin), to go to Irene's place of business and pretend to be wealthy clients. They do so and meet Irene and her co-worker, Minnie Fay (E. J. Peaker). When Dolly arrives with Horace, he breaks off his engagement to Irene. Dolly then instructs the young men to take Irene and Minnie to the Harmonia Gardens, where she also arranges a meeting between Horace and Ernestina Simple, a supposed heiress who is really Dolly's friend Gussie Granger (Judy Kaniz). At the restaurant, Dolly makes a grand entrance and romances Horace to the point where he is about to propose to her. However, he spots his niece and her beau on the dance floor and goes after them. In doing so, he also notices Cornelius and Barnaby who leave without paying their check. He fires them, and Dolly drops Horace. The next day, however, Horace admits the error of his ways and permits the marriage of Ermengarde and Ambrose. He promotes his two clerks and then proposes to Dolly.

Several numbers from the Broadway original were deleted,

including: "Call on Dolly," "I Put My Hand In," "Elegance" and "So Long Dearie." Reinstated for the film version were "Just Leave Everything to Me" and "Love Is Only Love," numbers cut during the pre-Broadway tryout of the play. During the protracted filming, there was much adverse publicity about the constant feuding of Walter Matthau and Barbra Streisand and the fact that director Kelly was having difficulty coping with "the" star and the enormous demands of the epic production. What emerged on screen was often unfelicitous, especially Streisand's uneven performance. At one point in the proceedings she, for some reason, decided to emulate the personae of Mae West to season her characterization. The results confirmed that there was only one Mae West and that in this motion picture Streisand was well out of her element. One of the few joyous creative decisions of this project was having Louis Armstrong join Streisand in the movie's big set piece, the title song number set in the Harmonia Gardens. Ebullient Armstrong briefly enlivened the wooden movie, which suffered from too many colorless supporting players and a disgruntled (dyspeptic) Matthau as leading man. Michael Kidd's striking choreography helped to divert attention from the by-now all too familiar storyline.

Elaine Rothschild argued in *Films in Review* magazine (January 1970), "HELLO, DOLLY! is a one-song show, and even that one song has an indifferent rendition in this expensive film version of the stage musical. . . . Barbra Streisand has the title role, and, except when she is imitating the movements and intonations of Mae West, is uninteresting and even downright incompetent. Gene Kelly . . . evidently lacked William Wyler's ability to extract a performance from Streisand. . . . This film comes to life only once: in the first shots of the parade."

HELLO, DOLLY! won Academy Awards for Music Score, Art Direction and Sound. Although nominated, it failed to win as Best Picture, losing to MIDNIGHT COWBOY. Undaunted by her adverse experience, Streisand next made another Broadway-to-Hollywood movie musical, ON A CLEAR DAY YOU CAN SEE FOREVER (1970), *q.v.*

HELLO, FRISCO, HELLO (20th Century-Fox, 1943) Color 98 minutes.

Producer, Milton Sperling; director, H. Bruce Humberstone; screenplay, Robert Ellis, Helen Logan, Richard Macauley; art directors, James Basevi, Boris Leven; set decorators, Thomas Little, Paul S. Fox; costumes, Helen Rose; music directors, Charles Henderson, Emil Newman; choreographers, Val Raset, Hermes Pan; assistant director, Charles Hall; color consultants, Natalie Kalmus,

Henri Jaffa; sound, Roger Heman; special effects, Fred Sersen; camera, Charles Clarke, Allen Davey; editor, Barbara McLean.

Songs: "You'll Never Know" (Mack Gordon, Harry Warren); "Ragtime Cowboy Joe" (Grant Clarke, Maurice Abrahams, Lewis F. Muir); "San Francisco" (Bronislau Kaper, Walter Jurmann, Gus Kahn); "Has Anybody Here Seen Kelly?" (Will Letters, C. W. Murphy, William J. McKenna); "Sweet Cider Time" (Percy Wenrich, Joseph McCarthy); "Hello, Frisco, Hello" (Louis A. Hirsch, Gene Buck); "Why Do They Always Pick On Me?" (Harry von Tilzer, Stanley Murphy); "Bedelia" (Jean Schwartz, William Jerome); "Doin' the Grizzly Bear" (George Botsford, Irving Berlin); "By the Light of the Silvery Moon" (Gus Edwards, Edward Madden); "Gee, But It's Great to Meet a Friend from Your Own Home Town" (James McGavisk, William G. Tracey); "It's Tulip Time in Holland" (Richard A. Whiting, Dave Radford); "I've Got a Girl in Every Port" (unknown); "When You Wore a Tulip" (Jack Mahoney, Wenrich); "Strike Up the Band, Here Comes a Sailor" (Andrew B. Sterling, Charles B. Ward); "King Chanticleer (Texas Tommy)" (Nat D. Ayer).

Alice Faye (Trudy Evans); John Payne (Johnnie Cornell); Jack Oakie (Dan Daley); Lynn Bari (Bernice Croft); Laird Cregar (Sam Weaver); June Havoc (Beulah Clancy); Ward Bond (Sharkey); Aubrey Mather (Charles Cochran); John Archer (Proprietor); Eddie Dunn (Foreman); Charles Cane (O'Riley); Frank Thomas (Auctioneer); Esther Dale (Aunt Harriett); Frank Darien (Missionary); Harry Hayden (Burkham); Mary Field (Cockney Maid); Fortunio Bonanova, Gino Corrado, Adia Kuznetzoff (Opera Singers); James Sills, Marie Brown (Roller Skating Specialty); Jackie Averill, Jimmie Clemens, Jr. (Child Dancers); Ed Mundy (Preacher); John Sinclair, Jack Stoney (Drunks); James Flavin, Ken Christy (Headwaiters); Edwin Earle (Stage Manager); Kirby Grant (Specialty Singer); Lorraine Elliott, Ruth Gillette (Singers).

Twentieth Century-Fox had a particular penchant for nostalgic screen musicals and, in the 1930s and 1940s, frequently starred Alice Faye in such wistful song-and-dance entries. HELLO, FRISCO, HELLO was one of Faye's most popular wartime Technicolor musicals and in it she introduced her most famous number, the Academy Award-winning song, "You'll Never Know." She also performed effectively several other tunes, including the title song, "Silver Moon" and "Why Do They Always Pick On Me?" (June Havoc's song, "I Gotta Have You," was cut before the film's release.)

During the heyday of San Francisco's Barbary Coast, entertainers Trudy Evans (Alice Faye), Johnnie Cornell (John Payne), Dan Daley (Jack Oakie) and Beulah (June Havoc) lose their jobs in a saloon when it is found that their songs draw customers away from the bar. Meanwhile, Johnnie grubstakes fast talking Sam Weaver (Laird Cregar) and then comes up with an idea to get money from saloon owners for *not* staging a show in front of their establishments. With these new funds, Johnnie opens his own place, called The Grizzly Bear, and makes Trudy his singing star. Both Trudy and the saloon are immediate successes, attracting even the Nob Hill crowd. Among the upper class visiting The Grizzly Bear are socialite Bernice Croft (Lynn Bari), with whom Cornell is taken romantically. Soon he opens three more saloons, while English theatrical producer Charles Cochran (Aubrey Mather) wants to feature Trudy in his new London show. At first she refuses, but when Johnnie suddenly elopes with Bernice the brokenhearted girl agrees to the proposal. Using his money to sponsor his wife's operatic ambition, Johnnie sees his fortunes decline. Meanwhile, Trudy becomes the toast of the London stage. Eventually she returns home to find that Johnnie and Bernice have separated after he was forced to sell all of his saloons to meet his expenses. Dan and Beulah have continued as entertainers and Johnnie now is a midway barker. Trudy secretly finances Johnnie through Dan, and Johnnie reopens the Grizzly Bear. On opening night he and Trudy are reunited.

Alice Faye had been off the screen for over a year—since WEEKEND IN HAVANA, 1941, *q.v.*—and her return was greeted enthusiastically. "The return of Alice Faye to motion pictures after a charmingly domestic recess is being celebrated with due and touching sentiment by Twentieth Century-Fox in a film which has all the standard qualities of a plush souvenir. It should afford a most pleasant reunion between Miss Faye and her loyal fans." (New York Times). *Photoplay* magazine noted, "There is something wistfully plaintive in la Faye's voice that tugs away at the love strings of a body's heart. In her belaced, beplumed, and befurbelowed gowns of the Gay Nineties, Alice is a picture of loveliness." *Variety* observed, "Her singing is quieter, more composed, very effective. The Technicolor cameras deal handsomely with her. . . ."

On November 15, 1943, Alice Faye repeated her role of Trudy Evans, opposite Robert Young, when "Lux Radio Theatre" broadcast "Hello, Frisco, Hello" on the CBS network.

HIGH SOCIETY (Metro-Goldwyn-Mayer, 1956) Color 107 minutes.

Producer, Sol C. Siegel; director, Charles Walters; based on the play *The Philadelphia Story* by Philip Barry; screenplay, John

Frank Sinatra and Bing Crosby in HIGH SOCIETY (1956).

Patrick; art directors, Cedric Gibbons, Hans Peters; set decorators, Edwin B. Willis, Richard Pefferle; costumes, Helen Rose; makeup, William Tuttle; music supervisors/adaptors, Johnny Green; Saul Chaplin; orchestrators, Conrad Salinger, Nelson Riddle; choreographer, Walters; special effects, A. Arnold Gillespie; camera, Paul C. Vogel; editor, Ralph E. Winters.

Songs: "High Society Calypso," "Little One," "Now You Have Jazz," "True Love," "You're Sensational," "I Love You, Samantha," "Well, Did You Evah," "Mind If I Make Love to You?" (Cole Porter); "Who Wants to Be a Millionaire?"

Bing Crosby (C. K. Dexter-Haven); Grace Kelly (Tracy Lord); Frank Sinatra (Mike Connor); Celeste Holm (Liz Imbrie); John Lund (George Kittredge); Louis Calhern (Uncle Willie); Sidney Blackmer (Seth Lord); Louis Armstrong (Himself); Margalo Gillmore (Mrs.

Seth Lord); Lydia Reed (Caroline Lord); Gordon Richards (Dexter-Haven's Butler); Richard Garrick (Lord's Butler); Richard Keen (Mac); Ruth Lee, Helen Spring (Matrons); Paul Keast (Editor); Reginald Simpson (Uncle Willie's Butler); Hugh Boswell (Parson).

HIGH SOCIETY was a musical remake of the classic THE PHILADELPHIA STORY (1940), which, in turn, was based on the witty Broadway comedy of 1939. The new film proved to be a potent box-office attraction starring Bing Crosby, Grace Kelly (in her singing debut) and Frank Sinatra. It also featured Louis Armstrong, who had first appeared with Bing two decades before in PENNIES FROM HEAVEN (1939), *q.v.* Grossing $5,878,365 in distributors' domestic film rentals, the class production nevertheless paled dramatically in comparison to the 1940 comedy, as noted by the *New York Times,* "Miss Kelly is downright pallid at times and good old Bing wanders in and out mellowly, Sinatra making a little more imprint. But the real lubricant, a fine Cole Porter score [drawn from both old and new compositions], keeps it gliding rather smoothly, as does Charles Walters' direction."

Socialite Tracy Lord (Grace Kelly) is about to marry dull George Kittredge (John Lund) when her ex-husband, songwriter-promoter C. K. Dexter-Haven (Bing Crosby), appears on the scene unexpectedly and tells her she will be miserable if she goes through with the wedding. Arriving to cover the wedding, which is to be the big social event of Newport, Rhode Island, are *Spy* magazine reporters Mike Connor (Frank Sinatra) and Liz Imbrie (Celeste Holm), who also plan to cover the city's annual jazz festival which this year features Louis Armstrong (himself) and His Band. By now the icy Tracy is having doubts about George and has a brief fling with Mike. Finally she realizes that she wants her former husband back and the two reunite.

While the plot of HIGH SOCIETY verged on staleness, the songs enlivened the glossy production greatly, especially the jazz-oriented numbers. Bing crooned "Little One" and "I Love You, Samantha" and dueted with buoyant Louis Armstrong on "Now You Have Jazz" and with Frank Sinatra on the jaunty "Well Did You Evah?" Sinatra crooned "Mind If I Make Love to You" and "You're Sensational" and joined Celeste Holm (very bouncy and cynical in her delightful characterization) in the cynical "Who Wants to Be a Millionaire?" Louis Armstrong and His Band performed "High Society Calypso" while the film's most popular song (which became a sentimental standard thereafter at weddings), "True Love," was harmonized by Crosby and Kelly (she in a wavering voice). The soundtrack album to HIGH SOCIETY was on *Billboard* magazine's hits chart for twenty-eight weeks, rising to position #5.

HIGH SOCIETY was also Oscar-nominated for Best Scoring. After Grace Kelly's next MGM film, THE SWAN (1956), she retired from the screen to wed Prince Rainier of Monaco. Cole Porter would prepare one more (mostly) original score for an MGM musical, LES GIRLS (1957), *q.v.* Charles Walters would direct seven more MGM features including the musicals, BILLY ROSE'S JUMBO (1962) and THE UNSINKABLE MOLLY BROWN (1964), *qq.v.*

HIGH, WIDE AND HANDSOME (Paramount, 1937) 110 minutes.

Producer, Arthur Hornblow, Jr.; director, Rouben Mamoulian; screenplay, Oscar Hammerstein, II, George O'Neill; art directors, Hans Dreier, John Goodman; set decorator, A. E. Freudeman; costumes, Travis Banton; music director, Boris Morros; orchestrator, Robert Russell Bennett; choreographer, LeRoy Prinz; special effects, Gordon Jennings; camera, Victor Milner, Theodor Sparkuhl; editor, Archie Marshek.

Songs: "Can I Forget You?" "The Things I Want," "Allegheny Al," "Folks Who Live on the Hill," "High Wide and Handsome," "Will You Marry Me Tomorrow, Maria?" (Oscar Hammerstein, II, Jerome Kern).

Irene Dunne (Sally Watterson); Randolph Scott (Peter Cortlandt); Dorothy Lamour (Molly Fuller); Elizabeth Patterson (Grandma Cortlandt); Raymond Walburn (Doc Watterson); Charles Bickford (Red Scanlon); Akim Tamiroff (Joe Varese); Ben Blue (Zeke); William Frawley (Mac); Alan Hale (Walt Brennan); Irving Pichel (Mr. Stark); Stanley Andrews (Lem Moulton); James Burke (Stackpole); Roger Imhof (Pop Bowers); Lucien Littlefield (Mr. Lippincott); Jack Clifford (Wash Miller); Russell Hopton (John Thompson, the Civil Engineer); Ivan Miller (Marble); Raymond Brown (P.T. Barnum); Constance Bergen (Singer); Tommy Bupp (Boy); Billy Bletcher (Shorty); Paul Kruger (Man); Claire McDowell (Seamstress); Fred Warren (Piano Player); Rolfe Sedan (Photographer); Marjorie Cameron (Blonde Singer); John T. Murray (Mr. Green); Edward Keane (Jones); Pat West (Razorback); John Maurice Sullivan (Old Gentleman); Ernest Wood (Hotel Clerk); Lew Kelly (Carpenter); Del Henderson (Bank President); John Marshall (Teller); Philip Morris (Teamster); Harry Semels (Bartender); Frank Sully (Gabby Johnson).

Hoping to duplicate the success of Universal's 1936 release, SHOW BOAT, *q.v.,* Paramount hired the star of that musical, Irene Dunne, and teamed her with director Rouben Mamoulian in a sprawling story by SHOW BOAT's creators, composers Jerome

Kern and Oscar Hammerstein, II. The resulting motion picture, the picturesque period musical HIGH, WIDE AND HANDSOME, cost nearly $2 million and was filmed partially on location in Chino, California. However, its melodramatics and aping of its predecessor failed to generate sufficient audience interest. It resulted in a box-office bust.

In 1859 young diva Sally Watterson (Irene Dunne) is stranded in a small western Pennsylvania community with her medicine show father (Raymond Walburn) who is promoting Indian Wizard Oil. There she meets and falls in love with a handsome farmer, Peter Cortlandt (Randolph Scott), and the two soon marry. Cortlandt organizes his neighbors in forming the Tidewater Oil Company but they are opposed by a corrupt railroad syndicate boss (Alan Hale) and his henchman (Charles Bickford) who are in league with a saloon owner (Akim Tamiroff) and his mistress (Dorothy Lamour), the latter having a yen for Cortlandt. When Sally realizes that her husband is more focused on laying the oil pipelines than on their marriage, the bride leaves home. She joins a traveling circus and becomes the star singing attraction. When she learns that her husband and his neighbors are having to fight the syndicate thugs she returns home, along with her helpful circus friends, and helps him in his efforts to complete the pipeline.

In HIGH, WIDE AND HANDSOME Irene Dunne, who was a bit too mature to play the ingenue properly, sings effectively "Can I Forget You" and "The Folks Who Live on the Hill." She and Dorothy Lamour do the bouncy "Allegheny Al" on a table top in a saloon sequence, while Lamour (looking far too exotic for the film's locale) solos with "The Things I Want." Not appearing in the final release print were "He Wore a Star" and "Grandma's Song."

Variety rated this sweeping musical Western ". . . A cross-section of Americana tinged with too much Hollywood hokum." The trade paper added, ". . . It flounders as it progresses, and winds up in a melodramatic shambles of fisticuffs, villainy and skullduggery which smacks of the serial film school." In retrospect, Tom Milne (*Mamoulian,* 1969) perceived that the film, ". . . Breaks all records for attack by having Irene Dunne, in close-up, belt into the title number from the first foot of the first shot. Significantly, perhaps, Mamoulian's camera seems here to have found a new, majestic freedom in the epic sweep of the action scenes, the breathtaking overhead set-ups for the circus rescue, the superb crane shot down from the banked candles in the circus big-top to a close shot of Irene Dunne as she starts to sing 'Can I Forget You?' "

In retrospect, HIGH, WIDE AND HANDSOME is a visually impressive motion picture that has been unduly neglected. This is all the more true since its director had helmed such path-finding screen musicals as APPLAUSE (1929) and LOVE ME TONIGHT (1932), *qq.v.*

British release title: BLACK GOLD.

HIT THE DECK (RKO, 1930) Color Sequences 93 minutes.

Director, Luther Reed; based on the musical play by Herbert Fields, Vincent Youmans, Leo Robin, Clifford Grey; and the play *Shore Leave* by Hubert Osborne; screenplay, Reed; set designer/costumes, Max Ree; music director, Victor Baravalle; choreographer, Pearl Eaton; assistant director, Frederick Fleck; sound, Hugh McDowell; camera, Robert Kurrle.

Songs: "Sometimes I'm Happy," "Hallelujah," "Why, Oh Why?" (Vincent Youmans, Clifford Grey, Leo Robin); "Keepin' Myself for You" (Youmans, Sidney Clare); "More Than You Know" (Youmans, Edward Eliscu, Billy Rose); "I Know That You Know" (Youmans, Anne Caldwell).

Jack Oakie (Bilge Smith); Polly Walker (Looloo); Roger Gray (Mat); Franker Woods (Bat); Harry Sweet (Bunny); Marguerita Padula (Lavinia); June Clyde (Toddy); Wallace MacDonald (Lieutenant Allen); George Ovey (Clarence); Ethel Clayton (Mrs. Payne); Nate Slott (Dan); Andy Clark (Dinty); Del Henderson (Admiral); Charles Sullivan (Lieutenant Jim Smith).

See: HIT THE DECK (1955) (essay).

HIT THE DECK (Metro-Goldwyn-Mayer, 1955) Color 112 minutes.

Producer, Joe Pasternak; director, Roy Rowland; based on the musical play by Herbert Fields, Vincent Youmans, Leo Robin, Clifford Grey; and the play *Shore Leave* by Hubert Osborne; screenplay, Sonya Levien, William Ludwig; art directors, Cedric Gibbons, Paul Groesse; costumes, Helen Rose; music director, George Stoll; orchestrators, Robert Van Eps, Will Beitel; choreographer, Hermes Pan; assistant director, George Rhein; camera, George Folsey; editor, John McSweeney, Jr.

Songs: "Keepin' Myself for You" (Vincent Youmans, Sidney Clare); "A Kiss or Two," "The Lady from the Bayou" (Youmans, Leo Robin); "Lucky Bird," "Loo-Loo," "Join the Navy," "Why, Oh Why?" "Hallelujah" (Youmans, Clifford Grey, Robin); "Sometimes I'm Happy" (Youmans, Grey, Irving Caesar); "I Know That You Know" (Youmans, Anne Caldwell); "More Than You Know" (Youmans, Edward Eliscu, Billy Rose); "Ciribiribee" (A. Pestalozza).

Jane Powell (Susan Smith); Tony Martin (Chief Boatswain's

Jane Powell, Vic Damone, Ann Miller, Tony Martin, Debbie Reynolds and Russ Tamblyn in HIT THE DECK (1955).

Mate William "Bilge" F. Clark); Debbie Reynolds (Carol Pace); Walter Pidgeon (Rear Admiral Daniel Xavier Smith); Vic Damone (Rico Ferrari); Gene Raymond (Wendell Craig); Ann Miller (Ginger); Russ Tamblyn (Danny Xavier Smith); J. Carrol Naish (Mr. Peroni); Kay Armen (Mrs. Ottavio Ferrari); Richard Anderson (Lieutenant Jackson); Jane Darwell (Jenny); Alan King, Henry Slate (Shore Patrol); Jubalaires (Themselves); Frank Reynolds (Dancer).

Hubert Osborne's 1922 comedy *Shore Leave* was adapted into a musical comedy by Herbert Fields in 1927 with a score by Vincent Youmans and staged as *Hit the Deck.* It became one of the composer's most memorable works. *Hit the Deck* debuted on Broadway in the spring of 1927 and had a 327-performance run with Louise Groody, Charles King, Stella Mayhew and Brian Donlevy in the cast. Later in the year it was staged in London with equal success, starring Ivy Tresmand and Stanley Holloway. With the coming of sound, RKO decided to film the Broadway musical, the original *Shore Leave* having already been filmed as a silent by First National in 1925, starring Richard Barthelmess and Dorothy Mackaill.

Several American sailors arrive in port with their ship and head to a favorite coffee shop, one owned by vivacious Looloo (Polly Walker). There they encounter rich Mrs. Payne (Ethel Clayton), who is there with her husband Admiral Payne (Del Henderson) and Lieutenant Allen (Wallace MacDonald). Mrs. Payne wants to buy Looloo's heirloom necklace. One of the sailors, Bilge Smith (Jack Oakie), falls for Looloo, while his pal Clarence (George Ovey) has been romancing her friend Lavinia (Marguerita Padula). Bilge tells Looloo his dream of becoming a ship's captain. To get money for Bilge to acquire his own ship, the lovestruck Looloo sells her prize necklace to Mrs. Payne. When the fleet later returns, Bilge proposes to Looloo, but is offended by her offer of money (to help make his nautical wish come true). He departs. Subsequently he is thrown out of the Navy. After Looloo tells Bilge she has lost all her money, the two agree to wed.

RKO heralded this production with: "A lavish Radio Pictures' musical extravaganza, in which flashes of sheer humor mingle with stirring drama. Glamorous scenes of Chinese revolution. Swinging choruses of gorgeous girls and gallant gobs. The rattle of distant gun-fire blends with lilting melodies." What emerged on screen did not live up to the hoopla. In *The RKO Story* (1982), Richard B. Jewell and Vernon Harbin reported, "In addition to the obvious drawbacks of a photographed stage play, the picture was little more than an awkward excuse to maintain as many musical numbers (Pearl Eaton staged the dances) as possible in a short period of time." The *New York Times* complained, "The fun is labored and the romance is more painful than sympathetic," while *Photoplay* magazine felt the film contained "some very routine performances." Fortunately the movie did retain such fine Vincent Youmans songs as "Sometimes I'm Happy" and the rousing "Hallelujah." "Keepin' Myself for You" was composed specifically for the film version by Youmans and Sidney Clare. Not to be overlooked in the movie was the lively presence of double-take specialist Jack Oakie, a joyful and recurring song-dance-comedy performer in Hollywood musicals of the 1930s and 1940s.

In 1936 RKO remade the property HIT THE DECK as FOLLOW THE FLEET (*q.v.*). However, it was reworked to the point that Youmans' score was deleted and mostly the plot of *Shore Leave* was left. Songs by Irving Berlin were employed for this new Fred Astaire-Ginger Rogers musical teaming.

MGM, which had a habit of purchasing remake rights to musicals from other studios,* did so again with HIT THE DECK, which it planned to use as a showcase for its young(er) talent in 1955. The new adaptation strayed from the plot of the original. Now it was the tale of three gobs—Bilge Clark (Tony Martin), Rico Ferrari (Vic Damone) and Danny Smith (Russ Tamblyn)—who have been stationed in Alaska. They are joyous to be finally experiencing their much-anticipated shore leave in San Francisco. For six years Bilge has been promising to marry nightclub performer Ginger (Ann Miller) and she intends to make it happen. Meanwhile, the admiral's (Walter Pidgeon) daughter Susan (Jane Powell) is rescued from licentious actor Wendell Craig (Gene Raymond) by her brother Danny. In the course of all this, Danny is attracted to young show business performer Carol Pace (Debbie Reynolds) and Rico is drawn to Susan. Finally, after several escapades in which they elude the pursuing shore patrol (Alan King, Henry Slate), the sailors clear themselves with the patrol. Rico's mother (Kay Armen), who has been providing a safe harbor for her son and his friends, resumes her romance with a local flower shop owner (J. Carrol Naish).

Again Vincent Youmans' melodious score was the cornerstone of the film. Musical highlights of the widescreen, color production include: Tony Martin's renditions of "More Than You Know" (added from Youmans' 1929 musical *Great Day!*) and "Keeping Myself for You"; Jane Powell singing "Sometimes I'm Happy" and dueting with Vic Damone on "I Know That You Know" (added from Youmans' 1926 stage play *Oh Please*); Debbie Reynolds doing "A Kiss or Two" as well as "Join the Navy" and "Loo Loo"; Ann Miller's ardent "Lady from the Bayou" and her "Keeping Myself for You" with Martin (from the 1930 film); and Kay Armen's energetic rendition of "Hallelujah," which was also performed by Martin, Damone and Tamblyn. The three male leads harmonized on "Why, Oh, Why?" in an alleyway setting and then the melody is later reprised by the three female stars, who ponder their romantic fates. The one non-Youmans song used in the film was "Ciribiribee," sung full-voiced by Armen.

Despite the enthusiasm of the cast, the richness of the score and the choreography of Hermes Pan (especially in the amusement park funhouse sequence), there was a synthetic quality to the new HIT THE DECK that all its bright trappings could not disguise.

---

*MGM had previously bought the rights to SHOW BOAT (1936), *q.v.*, from Universal for its 1951 musical remake; it purchased the rights to ROBERTA (1935), *q.v.*, from RKO to use for LOVELY TO LOOK AT (1952).

The *New York Times* analyzed that the production was: ". . . A goodly round-up of young talent, in a nearly plotless enterprise. . . . A good Vincent Youmans score still sounds fine. . . . But it remains a rather creaky property . . . and no more original now than way back then."

HOLIDAY INN (Paramount, 1942) 100 minutes.

Producer/director, Mark Sandrich; screen idea, Irving Berlin; screenplay, Claude Binyon, Elmer Rice; art directors, Hans Dreier, Roland Anderson; costumes, Edith Head; music director, Robert Emmett Dolan; choreographers, Fred Astaire, Danny Dare; camera, David Abel; editor, Ellsworth Hoagland.

Songs: "I'll Capture Your Heart Singing," "Lazy," "You're Easy to Dance With," "Happy Holiday," "Holiday Inn," "Let's Start the New Year Right," "Abraham," "Be Careful, It's My Heart," "I Can't Tell a Lie," "Easter Parade," "Let's Say It with Firecrackers," "Song of Freedom," "(I've Got) Plenty to Be Thankful For," "White Christmas" (Irving Berlin).

Bing Crosby (Jim Hardy); Fred Astaire (Ted Hanover); Marjorie Reynolds (Linda Mason); Virginia Dale (Lila Dixon); Walter Abel (Danny Reed); Louise Beavers (Mamie); Irving Bacon (Gus); Marek Windheim (Francois); James Bell (Dunbar); John Gallaudet (Parker); Shelby Bacon (Vanderbilt); Joan Arnold (Daphne); June Ealey (Dancer); David Tihmar (Specialty Dancer); Bob Crosby's Bobcats (Themselves); Leon Belasco (Proprietor in Flower Shop); Harry Barris, Ronnie Rondell (Orchestra Leaders); Jacques Vanaire (Assistant Headwaiter); Keith Richards, Reed Porter (Assistant Directors); Oscar G. Hendrian, Robert Homans (Doormen); Katharine Booth (Hatcheck Girl); Judith Gibson (Cigarette Girl); Lynda Grey (Dancing Girl); Kitty Kelly (Woman); Edward Arnold, Jr., Mel Ruick (Men); Bud Jamison (Santa Claus); Martha Mears (Singing Voice of Linda Mason).

"Loaded with a wealth of songs, it's meaty, not too kaleidoscopic and yet closely knit for a compact 100 minutes of tiptop filmusical entertainment. The titular 'Holiday Inn' idea is a natural, and [composer Irving] Berlin has fashioned some peachy songs to fit the highlight holidays. . . . The production is ultra, and the musical interpretations, with Bob Crosby's Bobcats backing up brother Bing, make the song idioms ultra-modern" (*Variety*).

Singer Jim Hardy (Bing Crosby) tires of the routine of being in show business and informs his pal, dancer Ted Hanover (Fred Astaire), that he plans to retire to his New England farm in Nibbsville, Connecticut. Once there he finds farm work even more exhausting than singing. After a rest he comes up with the idea of turning the farmhouse into a roadhouse nightclub that is only open on fifteen holidays during the year (which is a rather unenterprising concept). After considerable work he opens the club, called Holiday Inn, on New Year's Eve and draws a big crowd. Among the patrons are Linda Mason (Marjorie Reynolds), with whom he has already fallen in love, and tipsy Ted, who is upset because his fiancée, Lila Dixon (Virginia Dale), has jilted him to wed a Texas millionaire. During the evening Ted meets Linda and they cause a sensation when they dance together. Much to Hardy's chagrin, Ted begins romancing Linda and the two are offered the starring role in a film to be made about Holiday Inn. Jim does not like the idea but does not want to stand in the way of Ted and Linda's chances for professional success. Later, he becomes depressed when he reads that the two are Hollywood's hottest romantic team, both on and off screen. Going to maid Mamie (Louise Beavers) for advice, Jim is told to pour his heart out to Linda. He heads for Hollywood and learns that she is miserable and longs to return to the Holiday Inn with him. Hanover also finds happiness when Lila returns from Texas and they get back together.

Irving Berlin and Moss Hart had originally conceived of HOLIDAY INN as a stage musical, but when that did not come to be, Berlin discussed the concept with Paramount producer-director Mark Sandrich, who had directed five of the Fred Astaire-Ginger Rogers musicals at RKO, for some of which Berlin had composed the music. Casting purist dancer-singer Astaire with relaxed and mellow crooner Bing Crosby was a stroke of casting genius, for it provided a very pleasing set of leading men rivals whose performing styles meshed together nicely on screen. For a change of pace, in HOLIDAY INN, Astaire does not win the girl and there are times when "hero" Crosby is dour and conniving. The movie's major leading lady is Marjorie Reynolds, who had performed as a child actress under the name Marjorie Moore. While her dancing was not of the calibre of Ginger Rogers' or Rita Hayworth's* and her singing was dubbed (here by Martha Mears), she possessed a refreshing warmth that was displayed in several 1940s Paramount films.**

A perennial Christmas holiday favorite, first in theatres and later on TV and home video, HOLIDAY INN is most famous for

---

*Fred Astaire made HOLIDAY INN between two Columbia musicals with Rita Hayworth: YOU'LL NEVER GET RICH (1941) and YOU WERE NEVER LOVELIER (1942), *q.v.*

**Marjorie Reynolds would gain most fame playing Peg Riley on "The Life of Riley" teleseries (1953–58).

Bing Crosby's introduction of Irving Berlin's "White Christmas," which became the singer's most successful record, with over ten million copies sold. Fred Astaire choreographed an engrossing (and wild) firecracker dance for himself, while he and Reynolds also contributed a fine dance number to "Be Careful, It's My Heart." Crosby and Astaire duet on "I'll Capture Your Heart Singing." Of the score, only "Lazy" and "Easter Parade" were from Berlin's song trunk; the rest were composed for this motion picture. An unused number for the project was "It's a Great Country."

HOLIDAY INN won an Academy Award for Best Song ("White Christmas"). Irving Berlin was Oscar-nominated for Best Original Story and Robert Emmett Dolan for Best Scoring of a Musical Picture. Astaire and Crosby would reteam for BLUE SKIES (1946), *q.v.,* while Crosby and Reynolds would appear together in DIXIE (1943), as well as two Paramount all-star revue pictures, STAR-SPANGLED RHYTHM (1942) and DUFFY'S TAVERN (1945).

On January 11, 1943 Bing Crosby and Dinah Shore performed "Holiday Inn" on CBS radio's "Screen Guild Players."

HOLLYWOOD CANTEEN (Warner Bros., 1944) 124 minutes.

Producer, Alex Gottlieb; director/screenplay, Delmer Daves; art director, Leo Kuter; set decorator, Casey Roberts; costumes, Milo Anderson; makeup, Perc Westmore; music adaptor, Ray Heindorf; music director, Leo F. Forbstein; choreographer, LeRoy Prinz; assistant director, Art Lueker; sound, Oliver S. Garretson, Charles David Forrest; camera, Bert Glennon; editor, Christian Nyby.

Songs: "Don't Fence Me In" (Cole Porter); "You Can Always Tell a Yank" (E. Y. Harburg, Burton Lane); "What Are You Doing the Rest of Your Life?" (Ted Koehler, Burton Lane); "We're Having a Baby (My Baby and Me)" (Harold Adamson, Vernon Duke); "Sweet Dreams, Sweetheart," "Hollywood Canteen" (Ted Koehler, M. K. Jerome, Ray Heindorf); "I'm Gettin' Corns for My Country" (Jean Barry, Dick Charles); "Once to Every Heart" (Dorothy Donnelly, Sigmund Romberg); "Tumbling Tumbleweeds" (Bob Nolan); "King Porter Stomp" (Jelly Roll Morton); "The General Jumped at Dawn" (Larry Neal, Jimmy Mundy); "Ballet in Jive" (Heindorf); "The Bee" (Franz Schubert); "Slavonic Dance" (Antonin Dvorak); "Voodoo Moon" (Marion Sunshine, Julio Blanco, Obdulio Morales).

Joan Leslie (Herself); Robert Hutton (Slim); Dane Clark (Sergeant); Janis Paige (Angela); Jonathan Hale (Mr. Brodel); Barbara Brown (Mrs. Brodel); Steve Richards [Mark Stevens], Dick Erdman (Soldiers on Deck); James Flavin (Marine Sergeant);

Eddie Marr (Dance Director); Theodore von Eltz (Director); Ray Teal (Captain); Rudolph Friml, Jr. (Orchestra Leader); Betty Bryson, Willard Van Simons, William Alcorn, Jack Mattis, Jack Coffey (Dance Specialty); George Turner (Tough Marine); Jack Benny, Joe E. Brown, Eddie Cantor, Kitty Carlisle, Jack Carson, Joan Crawford, Helmut Dantine, Bette Davis, Faye Emerson, Victor Francen, John Garfield, Sydney Greenstreet, Alan Hale, Paul Henreid, Andrea King, Peter Lorre, Ida Lupino, Irene Manning, Nora Martin, Joan McCracken, Dolores Moran, Dennis Morgan, Eleanor Parker, William Prince, Joyce Reynolds, John Ridgely, Roy Rogers and Trigger, S. Z. Sakall, Alexis Smith, Zachary Scott, Barbara Stanwyck, Craig Stevens, Joseph Szigeti, Donald Woods, Jane Wyman, Jimmy Dorsey and His Band, Carmen Cavallaro and His Orchestra, Golden Gate Quartet, Rosario and Antonio, Sons of the Pioneers, Virginia Patton, Lynne Shayne, Johnny Mitchell, John Sheridan, Coleen Townsend, Angela Green, Paul Brooke, Marianne O'Brien, Dorothy Malone, Bill Kennedy, Mary Gordon, Chef Joseph Milani, Betty Brodel (Themselves).

Following its successful all-star effort, THANK YOUR LUCKY STARS, *q.v.,* the year before, Warner Bros. returned to the use of its name players doing musical numbers, the blackout routines being surrounded by a slim plot about the Hollywood Canteen and how movie stars did their bit to entertain servicemen while in the film capital. The *New York Herald Tribune* opined, "All in all HOLLYWOOD CANTEEN is a gaudy package of variety sketches which comes closer to a photograph of the canteen's activities than to a cohesive photoplay. . . . Call the whole thing a great big scrambled vaudeville show with enough talent to have made a dozen fine movies."

While on leave in Hollywood during World War II, soldiers Slim (Robert Hutton) and Sergeant (Dane Clark) visit the famous canteen there. Being the one millionth G.I. to enter the place, Slim wins a date with movie star Joan Leslie (herself), while Sergeant has the opportunity to dance with Joan Crawford (herself). While they are at the entertainment club, the two soldiers enjoy a variety of musical acts put on by assorted stars. Additionally, Bette Davis (herself), the president of the Canteen, and its vice-president, John Garfield (himself), relate the history behind the founding of the morale-boosting center. After spending three enjoyable nights at the Canteen, Slim and Sergeant return to active duty in New Guinea. Joan Leslie promises to wait for Slim.

Running more than two hours, HOLLYWOOD CANTEEN is most engaging when its variety of major stars are performing.

Among the musical highlights are Jack Benny joining classical violinist Joseph Szigeti for a rendition of "The Bee"—Szigeti also performs "Slavonic Dance"; Kitty Carlisle singing "Once to Every Heart" and "Sweet Dreams, Sweetheart"; Roy Rogers introducing Cole Porter's "Don't Fence Me In"; The Sons of the Pioneers performing "Tumbling Tumbleweeds"; Eddie Cantor and Nora Martin dueting on the comic patriotic song, "We're Having a Baby"; "Voodoo Moon" by Carmen Cavallaro; Joan McCracken's "Ballet in Jive"; the Andrews Sisters' rousing "Gettin' Corns for My Country," and Jimmy Dorsey and His Orchestra doing the swinging "King Porter Stomp."

HOLLYWOOD CANTEEN grossed $4,000,000 in distributors' domestic film rentals, a portion of which was donated to charity. HOLLYWOOD CANTEEN was nominated for three Oscars: Best Song ("Sweet Dreams, Sweetheart"), Best Scoring of a Musical Picture and Best Sound. Co-star Joan Leslie's sister (Betty Brodel) appears briefly in the picture.

THE HOLLYWOOD REVUE OF 1929 (Metro-Goldwyn-Mayer, 1929) Color Sequences 113 minutes.

Producer, Harry Rapf; director, Charles Reisner; dialogue, Al Boasberg, Robert E. Hopkins; skit, Joe Farnham; settings, Cedric Gibbons, Richard Day; costumes, David Cox, Henrietta Fraze, Joe Rapf; orchestrator, Arthur Lange; choreographer, Sammy Lee; assistant choreographer, George Cunningham; assistant directors, Jack Cummings, Sandy Roth, Al Shenberg; sound, Douglas Shearer; camera, John Arnold, Irving G. Ries, Maximilian Fabian; editor, William Gray.

Songs: "Singin' in the Rain," "Tommy Atkins on Parade," "You Were Meant for Me" (Arthur Freed, Nacio Herb Brown); "Low-Down Rhythm" (Raymond Klages, Jesse Greer); "For I'm the Queen" (Andy Rice, Martin Broones); "Gotta Feelin' For You" (Jo Trent, Louis Altger); "Bones and Tambourines," "Strike Up the Band," "Tableaux of Jewels" (Fred Fisher); "Lon Chaney Will Get You If You Don't Watch Out," "Strolling Through the Park One Day," "Your Mother and Mine," "Orange Blossom Time," "Minstrel Days," "Nobody But You," "I Never Knew I Could Do a Thing Like That" (Joe Goodwin, Gus Edwards).

Conrad Nagel, Jack Benny (Masters of Ceremony); John Gilbert, Norma Shearer, Joan Crawford, Bessie Love, Lionel Barrymore, Cliff Edwards, Stan Laurel, Oliver Hardy, Anita Page, Nils Asther, The Brox Sisters, Natacha Natova and Company, Marion Davies, William Haines, Buster Keaton, Marie Dressler, Charles King, Polly Moran, Gus Edwards, Karl Dane, George K.

Arthur, Gwen Lee, Albertina Rasch Ballet, The Rounders, The Biltmore Quartet (Specialties); Ann Dvorak (Chorus Girl); Charles King (Singing Voice of Conrad Nagel).

"Surpassing the dreams of the most optimistic, attaining a goal that was deemed impossible only a few months ago, Metro-Goldwyn-Mayer has created in its gigantic HOLLYWOOD REVUE an entertainment that will stand as a landmark in the annals of the talking screen. . . . It is star-studded with names, its choruses are picked beauties, its voices represent the choice of experts, its songs are from the genius of the country's most famed, its dialogue was conceived by the leaders of their craft, its settings and costumes, its recordings, each element of this mighty entertainment is the product of the top-notchers!" (Advertisement for THE HOLLYWOOD REVUE OF 1929).

Metro-Goldwyn-Mayer beat the rest of the studios to the finish line with the first of the early talkie all-star musical revues

Conrad Nagel and Anita Page in THE HOLLYWOOD REVUE OF 1929 (1929).

with this elaborate production. Hosted by Conrad Nagel and Jack Benny, it presented some two dozen studio stars doing blackout turns with moderate success. Sporting some Technicolor sequences, this motion picture was indeed a grab-bag of entertainment. It remains one of the most pleasing of these early sound extravaganzas. *Photoplay* magazine labeled it "A great big merry girl and music show," while John Kobal (in retrospect) stated in *Gotta Sing Gotta Dance* (1971), "The film's pleasure is that of seeing stars doing the unexpected, such as Bessie Love's furiously acrobatic dance with a male chorus, in which she is swung by her legs like a human pendulum." He also noted, "Seeing one such film is entertaining, but the pleasure would obviously pall rapidly if the type were a permanent staple of one's viewing."

The movie begins with a minstrel show and a dance number, with Conrad Nagel and Jack Benny introduced as the hosts. Joan Crawford appears and sings "Gotta Feelin' for You" and then dances with the Biltmore Quartet. (Some of this sequence and others from the film appear in THAT'S ENTERTAINMENT!, 1974, *q.v.*) Charles King then vocalizes "Your Mother and Mine," followed by Conrad Nagel (dubbed by Charles King) crooning "You Were Meant for Me" to Anita Page. Cliff "Ukulele Ike" Edwards does "Nobody But You" and then Jack Benny and William Haines engage in a (mild) battle of words before a miniature Bessie Love emerges from Benny's jacket pocket to perform "I Never Knew I Could Do a Thing Like That." Marie Dressler and Polly Moran team to do the comedy number "For I'm the Queen," followed by a comedy magician act by Stan Laurel and Oliver Hardy. "Tommy Atkins on Parade" is sung by Marion Davies and then by the Brox Sisters, while "The Tableau of the Jewels" offers a number of comedy blackout skits, including Marie Dressler as the queen of the ocean. Buster Keaton next appears in "The Dance of the Sea" and then Gus Edwards does "Lon Chaney Will Get You If You Don't Watch Out" while a masked performer appears claiming to be Chaney (he was not!). Natacha Natova and Company execute an adagio dance and in a Technicolor sequence John Gilbert and Norma Shearer perform the balcony scene from *Romeo and Juliet,* which turns out to be a film scene being directed by Lionel Barrymore. Cliff Edwards then does "Singin' in the Rain" in a well-staged production number. After additional comedy blackouts, the movie concludes in a color sequence with Charles King singing "Orange Blossom Time." The finale finds the entire cast doing "Singin' in the Rain."

Variety decided, "With a cast that reads like a benefit how can this one miss for coin? Besides which it's the top novelty film to be turned out to date." THE HOLLYWOOD REVUE OF 1929 was Oscar-nominated for Best Production (but lost to MGM's BROADWAY MELODY, *q.v.*) and for Best Interior Decorations (but lost to MGM's THE BRIDGE OF SAN LUIS REY).

Unlike some early talkie musicals THE HOLLYWOOD REVUE OF 1929 is not a chore to watch today. In fact, several sequences are still highly entertaining. The movie introduced to filmgoers "Singin' in the Rain" (which had been used in a stage revue the previous year and would be a perennial melody for MGM musicals). Cliff Edwards' rendering of it is quite pleasant, as are Marie Dressler's broad comedy, Charles King's crooning, and Laurel and Hardy's comedy magic act (despite the unfluidity of the camera).

L'HOMME DES FOLIES BERGERE *see* FOLIES BERGERE.

HONEY (Paramount, 1930) 73 minutes.

Director, Wesley Ruggles; based on the musical play *Come Out of the Kitchen* by Alice Duer Miller, A. E. Thomas, and the novel by Miller; adaptor/titles, Herman J. Mankiewicz; choreographer, David Bennett; sound, Harry M. Indgren; camera, Henry Gerrard.

Songs: "In My Little Hope Chest," "Sing You Sinners," "I Don't Need Atmosphere (to Fall in Love with You)," "Let's Be Domestic," "What Is This Power I Have?" (W. Frank Harling, Sam Coslow).

Nancy Carroll (Olivia Dangerfield); Stanley Smith (Burton Crane); Skeets Gallagher (Charles Dangerfield); Lillian Roth (Cora Falkner); Harry Green (J. William Burnstein); Mitzi Green (Doris); ZaSu Pitts (Mayme); Jobyna Howland (Mrs. Falkner); Charles Sellon (Randolph Weeks).

Following their successful teaming in SWEETIE (*q.v.*) in 1929, Nancy Carroll and Stanley Smith were reunited for another Paramount musical comedy, HONEY. The main attraction of the picture, however, is co-star Lillian Roth's powerful rendition of the Sam Coslow-W. Frank Harling song, "Sing You Sinners." *Photoplay* magazine announced the feature was "Light comedy, pleasing songs," while *Harrison's Reports* said, "A very good program picture. There is romance, fairly deep human interest, good singing (even though the singing seems to be out of place) and considerable comedy. . . ." The movie was taken from the 1921 play *Come Out of the Kitchen* by Alice Duer Miller and A. E. Thomas.

"At last a musical comedy has been written expressly for the screen instead of being adapted from a Broadway success. Following faithfully musical comedy tradition, the plot is the least of anybody's worries, including the audience's . . ." (*Motion Picture* magazine).

Southern aristocrats Olivia Dangerfield (Nancy Carroll) and her brother Charles (Skeets Gallagher) are in such a financial bind that they rent their home for six weeks to rich Mrs. Falkner (Jobyna Howland), whose daughter Cora (Lillian Roth) is engaged to marry equally rich Burton Crane (Stanley Smith). When all the servants except maid Mayme (ZaSu Pitts) quit, Olivia takes over as cook and Charles becomes the butler. When Burton comes to visit Cora, he meets Olivia and the two fall in love, while the same feeling is shared by Cora and Charles. Talkative little Doris (Mitzi Green), part of the household, tells Mrs. Falkner of the new love situation and she is scandalized, vowing to see that her daughter weds Crane. She fires Olivia but then orders her to cook a final dinner for Cora and Burton's engagement party. When Doris tells Mrs. Falkner who Cora and Charles really are, she agrees to let the new romances continue.

The storyline for HONEY had been filmed in 1919 as a silent vehicle for Marguerite Clark, COME OUT OF THE KITCHEN, based on the 1916 novel by Alice Duer Miller.

HONEYSUCKLE ROSE (Warner Bros., 1980) Color 119 minutes.

Executive producer, Sydney Pollack; producer, Gene Taft; director, Jerry Schatzberg; based on the story "Intermezzo" by Gosta Steven, Gustav Holander; screenplay, Carol Sobieski, William D. Wittliff, John Binder; production designer, Joel Schiller; set decorator, Jeff Haley; costumes, Jo Ynocencio; makeup, Lee Harman, Leo Lotito, Jr.; music supervisor, Richard Baskin; music consultant; Bradley Hartman; assistant directors, David McGiffert, Nick Marck; sound, Arthur Rochester; color consultant, Otto Paolini; concert lighting designer, Tim Phelps; additional sound, Portomatic Sound Effects; sound re-recording, Tom Fleischmann; concert recordings, The Enactron Truck; supervising sound editors, Stan Bochner, Lou Cerborino; camera, Robby Muller; editors, Aram Avakian, Norman Gay, Marc Laub, Evan Lottman.

Songs: "On the Road Again," "Crazy," "My Own Peculiar Way," "Yesterday's Wine," "Angels Flying Too Close to the Ground," "There's Two Sides to Every Story," "Uncloudy Day" (Willie Nelson); "Whiskey River" (John Bush Shinn); "So You Think You're a Cowboy" (Nelson, Hank Cochran); "Eighth of January," "Jumpin' Cotton Eyed Joe" (arranger, Johnny Gimble); "Singing the Yodelling Blues," "Coming Back to Texas" (Kenneth

Threadgill, Chuck Joyce, Julie Paul); "Loving Her Was Easier (Than Anything I'll Ever Do Again)," "You Show Me Yours (And I'll Show You Mine)" (Kris Kristofferson); "Under the 'X' in Texas" (Gimble); "Till I Gain Control Again," "Angel Eyes" (Rodney Crowell); "If You Could Touch Her at All" (Lee Clayton); "Make the World Go Away" (Cochran); "A Song for You" (Leon Russell); "I Didn't Write the Music" (Mickey Rooney, Jr.); "Amazing Grace," "Under the Double Eagle" (traditional).

Willie Nelson (Buck Bonham); Dyan Cannon (Viv Bonham); Amy Irving (Lily Ramsey); Slim Pickens (Garland Ramsey); Joey Floyd (Jamie Bonham); Charles Levin (Sid); Priscilla Pointer (Rosella Ramsey); Mickey Rooney, Jr. (Cotton Roberts); Pepe Serna (Rooster); Lane Smith (Brag); Diana Scarwid (Jeanne); Emmylou Harris (Herself); Rex Ludwick (Tex); Mickey Raphael (Kelly); Bee Spears (Bo); Chris Ethridge (Easter); Paul English (Paul); Bobby Nelson (Bonnie); Jody Payne (Jonas); Randy "Poodie" Locke (Poodie); T. Snake (Snake); Johnny Gimble (Fiddler); Kenneth Threadgill (Yodeller); Grady Martin (Grady); Hank Cochran (Hank); Jeannie Seely (Jeannie); Gene Rader (Owen); Frank Stewart (Dorsey Lee); Lu Belle Camp (Grandma Bonham); A. L. Camp (Grandpa Bonham); Bernadette Whitehead (Jessie); Jackie Ezzell (Country Girl); Harvey Christiansen (Mr. Eubanks); Hackberry Johnson (Hackberry); Kenneth Eric Hamilton (1st Boy); Nelson Fowler (2nd Boy); Guy Houston Garrett (3rd Boy); Centa Boyd, Cara Kanak (Women at Party); Augie Myers (Stage Manager); Robert Gotschall (Store Clerk); Emilio Gonzales (Cab Driver); Mary Jane Valle (Airline Clerk); Randy Arlyn Fletcher (Police Officer); Ray Liberto (Jim); Sam Allred (Contractor); Bob Baty, John Meadows (Carpenters); Cody Hubach (Cody); Dick Gimble, Maurice Anderson, Ray D. Hollingsworth, Bill Mounce, Kenny Frazier (The Reunion Swing Band).

Thanks to his success on the record charts and his critically acclaimed performance in THE ELECTRIC HORSEMAN (1979), veteran country music singer-composer Willie Nelson won his first movie starring role in HONEYSUCKLE ROSE. Many claim this film is semi-autobiographical, although its plotline actually derives from INTERMEZZO as transferred to the Texas plains. Loaded with familiar Willie Nelson music plus some new material, as well as solid performances and a fairly engrossing storyline, HONEYSUCKLE ROSE proved to be a box-office success with distributors' domestic film rentals of $10.4 million.

Texas country music performer Buck Bonham (Willie Nelson) and his band have traveled all over the southwest for fifteen years, entertaining and trying to capture that elusive stardom. Finally

Buck, who has a happy home life with his loyal wife-manager Viv (Dyan Cannon) and son Jamie (Joey Floyd), finds he and his music are on the threshold of national acceptance. As he is about to embark on the tour which should bring him stardom, Buck learns that his long-time lead guitar player, Garland Ramsey (Slim Pickens), intends to retire. Needing a replacement, he hires Garland's pretty college student daughter Lily (Amy Irving) for the summer tour, not realizing that the girl has been in love with him for several years. Leaving Viv and Jamie at home, Buck and the band start the tour. Once on the road, Buck and Lily begin an affair. Viv becomes suspicious and attends one of the concerts. Seeing Buck and Lily perform, she realizes something is going on and confronts Buck. When he admits his infidelity she leaves him. Caught between his need for both his wife and Lily and his impending stardom, Buck turns to drink. Garland returns and attempts to help him. Finally Buck realizes he has made a mistake with Lily and returns to Viv.

Philip Strick evaluated in *Films and Filming* magazine (October 1981), "The new ingredient in HONEYSUCKLE ROSE, surprisingly enough in this era of cinematic anonymity, is the battered, greying figure who stepped casually from his supporting role in ELECTRIC HORSEMAN into the status of potential superstar. Fron now on, there will be Willie Nelson movies."

Musically, HONEYSUCKLE ROSE (the title refers to the name on Viv's mail box) is a treasure trove for Willie Nelson fans, including many of his standards such as "Whiskey River" along with his renditions of new songs such as the title tune (which was a best-selling single for him on Columbia Records), "Angel Flying Too Close to the Ground" and "A Song for You." In addition, the movie had Nelson dueting with Dyan Cannon on "Loving You Was Easier" and "Uncloudy Day," and with Amy Irving on "You Show Me Yours." Country western favorite Emmylou Harris made a guest appearance in the feature, performing "So You Think You're a Cowboy" and dueting with Willie on "Angel Eyes." Several well-known country music names (Jeannie Seely, Hank Cochran, Johnny Gimble, Kenneth Threadgill, Jody Payne, Grady Martin) also appear in the feature. Mickey Rooney, Jr. has a delightful cameo as a self-centered flash-in-the-pan singer called Cotton Roberts.

HONEYSUCKLE ROSE was Oscar-nominated for Best Song, "On the Road Again," but lost to "Fame" from FAME, *q.v.* The soundtrack album remained on *Billboard* magazine's hits chart for thirteen weeks and rose to position #10.

TV title: ON THE ROAD AGAIN.

HONKY TONK (Warner Bros., 1929) 68 minutes. (Also silent version: 6,412′).

Director, Lloyd Bacon; story, Leslie S. Barrows; adaptor, C. Graham Baker; titles, De Leon Anthony; V. C. Graham Baker, Jack Yellen; choreographer, Larry Ceballos; assistant director, Frank Shaw; camera, Ben Reynolds.

Songs: "I'm the Last of the Red-Hot Mammas," "I'm Doin' What I'm Doin' for Love," "He's a Good Man to Have Around," "I'm Feathering a Nest (for a Little Bluebird)," "I Don't Want to Get Thin" (Jack Yellen, Milton Ager); "Some of These Days" (Shelton Brooks).

Sophie Tucker (Sophie Leonard); Lila Lee (Beth, Sophie's Daughter); Audrey Ferris (Jean Gilmore); George Duryea [Tom Keene/Richard Powers] (Freddie Gilmore); Mahlon Hamilton (Jim); John T. Murray (Cafe Manager); and: Wilbur Mack.

Already in her mid-forties, Broadway and club favorite Sophie Tucker (the last of the Red Hot Mamma songsters) made her film debut in HONKY TONK at a time when it was habit for Hollywood to trade on stage/vaudeville names for box-office insurance. The stocky, mature performer was signed for the part by Harry Warner against the advice of his two studio chief siblings. The resulting picture was hardly a dramatic feat but the personable Sophie Tucker and her songs helped to put it over and it made money. It remains the star's only solo starring feature film.* As noted by *Variety,* HONKY TONK was Tucker's show all the way: "You become so absorbed in Soph when she's singing that you forget everything. . . . Soph is beyond expectation all of the way."

Sophie Leonard (Sophie Tucker) is the headline attraction at a Gotham night spot where she is the hostess. She plans to retire when her daughter Beth (Lila Lee) returns home from Europe, where she has been expensively educated. Not knowing Sophie's (undignified) line of work, the snobbish girl is shocked at her mother's modest home. Later, Sophie is upset when her aristocratic daughter will not stay for dinner. The two have a fight about Beth going to wild parties with Freddie Gilmore (George Duryea [Tom Keene/Richard Powers]), her boyfriend. Despite hating her seamy way of life, Sophie continues to sing at the club, where at least she is appreciated. Freddie, to get even with Sophie, takes Beth there

---

*Sophie Tucker would portray herself in the British film, GAY LOVE (1934), play roles in BROADWAY MELODY OF 1938 (1937), *q.v.* and THOROUGHBREDS DON'T CRY (1937), perform specialities in FOLLOW THE BOYS (1944) and SENSATIONS OF 1945 and have a guest bit as herself in THE JOKER IS WILD (1957).

and seeing her mother perform, an embarrassed Beth leaves home and moves to a hotel. Sophie's friend Jim (Mahlon Hamilton) goes to Freddie and explains to him how Sophie has worked hard to support her daughter through the years. Freddie becomes understanding of the situation and asks Sophie's permission to marry Beth. Sophie agrees and is reconciled with her daughter. Later she becomes a happy grandmother.

The highlight of HONKY TONK is Sophie Tucker performing such numbers as "I'm the Last of the Red-Hot Mammas" (her trademark number), "He's a Good Man to Have Around" and "I'm Doin' What I'm Doin' for Love." While a print of HONKY TONK apparently no longer exists, the Vitaphone sound discs for it and its separate trailer, with footage of Sophie discussing the picture, have survived. Thus one can still hear "The Last of the Red Hot Mammas" belt out her songs in her famous style. There is a basic story parallel between HONKY TONK and APPLAUSE, *q.v.*, Paramount's far superior entry starring Helen Morgan. Director Lloyd Bacon had already helmed Al Jolson's THE SINGING FOOL (1928), *q.v.*, and would go on to direct such musicals as 42ND STREET (1933), *q.v.*, FOOTLIGHT PARADE (1933), GOLD DIGGERS OF 1937 (1936), *q.v.*, I WONDER WHO'S KISSING HER NOW (1947), CALL ME MISTER (1951) and his last musical, Jane Russell's THE FRENCH LINE (1954).

HOW TO SUCCEED IN BUSINESS WITHOUT REALLY TRYING (United Artists, 1967) Color 119 minutes.

Producer, David Swift; associate producer, Irving Temaner; director, Swift; based on the musical play by Abe Burrows, Willie Gilbert, Jack Weinstock, Frank Loesser, and the novel *How to Succeed in Business Without Really Trying: The Dastard's Guide to Fame and Fortune* by Shepherd Mead; screenplay, Swift; visual gags, Virgil Partch; art director, Robert Boyle; set decorator, Edward G. Boyle; costumes, Micheline; makeup, Robert Schiffer; music, Frank Loesser; music supervisor/conductor, Nelson Riddle; choreographer, Dale Moreda; assistant directors, John Bloss, Michael J. Dmytryk; sound, Robert Martin, James A. Richard; camera, Burnett Guffey; editors, Ralph E. Winters, Allan Jacobs.

Songs: "How To Succeed in Business Without Really Trying," "The Company Way," "A Secretary Is Not a Toy," "It's Been a Long Day," "I Believe in You," "Grand Old Ivy," "Rosemary," "Gotta Stop That Man," "Brotherhood of Man" (Frank Loesser).

Robert Morse (J. Pierpont Finch); Michele Lee (Rosemary Pilkington); Rudy Vallee (J. B. Biggley); Anthony Teague (Bud Frump); Maureen Arthur (Hedy LaRue); Murray Matheson (Benjamin Ovington); Kay Reynolds (Smitty); Sammy Smith (Mr. Twinble/Wally Womper); John Myhers (Bratt); Jeff DeBenning (Gatch); Ruth Kobart (Miss Jones); George Fenneman (TV Announcer); Anne Seymour (Mrs. Biggley); Erin O'Brien-Moore (Mrs. Frump); Joey Faye (Taxi Cab Driver); Helen Verbit (Finch's Landlady); Virginia Sale (Cleaning Woman); Al Nessor (Newspaper Seller); Carol Worthington (Miss Krumholtz); Janice Carroll (Brenda); Lory Patrick (Receptionist); Pat O'Moore, Wally Strauss (Media Men); Ivan Volkman (President of the U.S.); David Swift (Elevator Operator); Carl Princi (Voice of the Book); Paul Hartman (Toynbee); Dan Tobin (Johnson); Robert Q. Lewis (Tackaberry); John Holland (Matthews); Justin Smith (Jenkins); Hy Averback (2nd Executive); Bob Sweeney (3rd Executive); Paul Bradley (TV Board Member); Tucker Smith (Junior Executive); Don Koll (Passerby); and Sheila Rogers.

Prolific composer Frank Loesser had been a frequent contributor to Hollywood musicals, especially at Paramount, of the late 1930s (COLLEGE SWING, 1938, SOME LIKE IT HOT, 1939) and the 1940s (KISS THE BOYS GOODBYE, 1941, HAPPY GO LUCKY, 1943, THE PERILS OF PAULINE and RED, HOT AND BLUE, 1949). He also wrote the songs for hit Broadway musicals such as *Where's Charley?* (1948) and *Guys and Dolls* (1950), both of which were filmed. *How To Succeed in Business Without Really Trying,* starring Robert Morse and Rudy Vallee, opened on Broadway in the fall of 1961. It not only won the Pulitzer Prize, but also seven Tony Awards, including Best Musical, along with the New York Drama Critics Circle Award and the Theatre Club Award. The play ran for 1,417 performances and when United Artists brought it to the screen in 1967, the film version proved to be an overly faithful adaptation.

Ambitious J. Pierpont Finch (Robert Morse) works as a window cleaner at a New York high-rise office building. He latches onto an instant success book and putting the theories to work, quickly lands a job in the mail room of the World Wide Wickets Company run by pompous J. B. Biggley (Rudy Vallee), who is having an affair with his secretary Hedy (Maureen Arthur), unbeknownst to Biggley's wife (Anne Seymour). Finch meets pretty secretary Rosemary Pilkington (Michele Lee) and they fall in love. To rise up the corporate ladder, grasping Finch convinces Biggley that they attended the same college, that both love knitting, and that he shares the boss's dislike of his annoying nephew, Bud Frump (Anthony Teague). Biggley soon promotes Finch to vice president of advertising and he devises a TV treasure hunt stunt starring the statuesque Hedy. Everyone ends up in hot water when the program flops, but Finch wiggles out of the

Michelle Lee and Robert Morse in HOW TO SUCCEED IN BUSINESS WITHOUT REALLY TRYING (1967).

scrape when the Chairman of the Board, Wally Womper (Sammy Smith), learns that both started as window cleaners. Finch, in fact, takes over his job when Womper retires and marries Hedy. Now able to marry Rosemary, Finch sets his ambitions on an even higher job: that of U.S. president.

Robert Morse and Rudy Vallee both deftly recreated their stage roles and most of the humor in this very broad musical satire derives from their performances. Frank Loesser's score, while it failed to create any memorable tunes, fits well within the plot structure. Particularly well staged are "The Company Way," Morse's solo of "I Believe in You" and his duet with Vallee of "Grand Old Ivy." Missed from the stage version, however, was Vallee's romantic ballad, "Love From a Heart of Gold," which Biggley sang to Hedy.

The *New York Times* judged, "Nothing has happened in five

years to diminish the suitability or the sting of HOW TO SUCCEED IN BUSINESS WITHOUT REALLY TRYING as it was originally done on the Broadway stage. And certainly David Swift has done nothing to diminish the wit, the sparkle and the zing of the musical show in transferring it into the movie. . . . He has got the whole howling mockery of big business and the way it operates. . . ."

I DREAM TOO MUCH (RKO, 1935) 95 minutes.

Producer, Pandro S. Berman; director, John Cromwell; story, Elsie Finn, David G. Wittels; screenplay, James Gow, Edmund North; art director, Van Nest Polglase; costumes, Bernard Newman; music directors, Max Steiner, Andre Kostelanetz; choreographer, Hermes Pan; camera, David Abel; editor, William Morgan.

Songs: "Caro Nome" from the opera *Rigoletto* (Giuseppe Verdi); "Bell Song" from the opera *Lakmé* (Leo Delibes); "Jockey on the Carousel" (Jerome Kern, Dorothy Fields, Jimmy McHugh); "I Got Love," "I Dream Too Much," "I'm the Echo, You're the Song" (Kern, Fields).

Lily Pons (Annette Monard Street); Henry Fonda (Jonathan Street); Eric Blore (Roger Briggs); Osgood Perkins (Paul Darcy); Lucien Littlefield (Hubert Dilley); Esther Dale (Mrs. Dilley); Lucille Ball (Gwendolyn Dilley); Mischa Auer (Pianist); Paul Porcasi (Tito); Scotty Beckett (Boy on Merry-Go-Round); Clarence Wilson (Detective); Oscar Apfel (Cafe Owner); Ferdinand Munier (Carousel Owner); Billy Gilbert (Cook); Esther Dale (Tourist); Richard Carle, Ferdinand Gottschalk (Snobs); Russ Powell (Merry-Go-Round Operator); Al Haskel (Wagon Driver); Kirby Grant (Violinist/Quartet Singer); Elise Cavanna (Darcy's Secretary); June Storey (Girl in "I Dream Too Much" Number).

Grace Moore had scored a surprise hit in 1934 in Columbia's ONE NIGHT OF LOVE (*q.v.*), thus reviving interest in operatic films in Hollywood. RKO latched onto the services of Metropolitan opera star Lily Pons, who was also very popular on radio, and showcased her in the vehicle I DREAM TOO MUCH. Unfortunately she did not duplicate the success of Moore at Columbia; in fact, one unkind critic dubbed the movie, "I Scream Too Much." As the co-star, Henry Fonda, in his third feature film, was borrowed from producer Walter Wanger. However, I DREAM TOO MUCH was a box-office failure and did nothing to enhance his screen career.

Lovely French singer Annette Monard (Lily Pons) falls in love with American composer Jonathan Street (Henry Fonda) and they marry, each pursuing their own career. While Annette soon becomes a famous opera singer, Jonathan finds his works rejected.

This leads to marital trouble and their separation. Wanting to win her husband back, Annette sees to it that his opera is changed into a musical comedy. It is a big success, and the two are reconciled.

Lily Pons sang from assorted operas, most notably "Caro Nome" from *Rigoletto,* and Jerome Kern and Dorothy Fields also composed several songs for her to perform, including the title song. Kern, Fields and Jimmy McHugh wrote "Jockey on the Carousel." None of the tunes was especially memorable. Richard B. Jewell and Vernon Harbin assessed in *The RKO Story* (1982), "A clumsy melange of high brow artistry . . . and low-jinks comedy. . . . It was further weakened by soggy dialogue. Though hand-tailored to showcase the heroine's unquestionable vocal gifts, the film, not surprisingly, flopped."

Undaunted, RKO assigned Lily Pons to THAT GIRL FROM PARIS (1937), which did fare well. However, they sank her movie career with the disaster, HITTING A NEW HIGH, released the same year.

I MARRIED AN ANGEL (Metro-Goldwyn-Mayer, 1942) 84 minutes.

Producer, Hunt Stromberg; director, Major W. S. Van Dyke, II; based on the musical play by Richard Rodgers, Lorenz Hart, and the play by Vaszary Janos; screenplay, Anita Loos; art directors, Cedric Gibbons, John S. Detlie; set decorator, Edwin B. Willis; costumes, Motley; makeup, Jack Dawn; special effects, Arnold Gillespie, Warren Newcombe; camera, Ray June; editor, Conrad A. Nervig.

Songs: "I Married an Angel," "I'll Tell the Man in the Street," "Spring Is Here" (Richard Rodgers, Lorenz Hart); "Tira Lira La" (Rodgers, Bob Wright, Chet Forrest); "At the Roxy Music Hall" (with new lyrics); "A Twinkle In Your Eyes" (Rodgers, Hart; with additional lyrics by Wright, Forrest); "Caprice Viennoise" (Fritz Kreisler); "Chanson Bohème" from the opera *Carmen* (Georges Bizet; English lyrics, Wright, Forrest); "Anges Purs" from the opera *Faust* (Charles Gounod); "Aloha Oe" (Princess Lilivokalani of Hawaii); "Hey Butcher," "There Comes a Time," "To Count Palaffi," "May I Present the Girl," "Now You've Met the Angel," "But What of Truth" (Herbert Stothart, Wright Forrest).

Jeanette MacDonald (Anna Zador/Brigitta); Nelson Eddy (Count Willie Palaffi); Binnie Barnes (Peggy); Edward Everett Horton (Peter); Reginald Owen (Herman "Whiskers" Rothbart); Mona Maris (Marika); Janice [Janis] Carter (Sufi); Inez Cooper (Irene); Douglass Dumbrille (Baron Szigetti); Leonid Kinskey (Zinski); Marion Rosamond (Dolly); Anne Jeffreys (Polly); Marek

Windheim (Marcel); Georges Renavent (Pierre); Max Willenz (Assistant Manager); Francine Bordeaux (1st Maid); Mildred Shay (2nd Maid); Odette Myrtil (Modiste); Tyler Brooke (Lucien); Jacques Vanaire (Max); Luis Alberni (Jean Frederique); Micheline Cheirel (Annette); Rafaela Ottiano (Madelon); Margaret Moffat (Mother Zador); Vaughan Glaser (Father Andreas); Gino Corrado (Valet); Sid D'Albrook (Porter); Sig Arno (Waiter); Mitchell Lewis (Porter); Jacqueline Dalya (Olga); George Humbert (Taxi Driver); Ben Hall (Delivery Boy); Ferdinand Munier (Rich Man); George Davis (Pushcart Vendor); Jack Vlaskin (Milk Wagon Driver); Veda Ann Borg, Carol Hughes (Willie's Morning Ladies); Ludwig Stossel (Janitor); Robert Frieg (Major-Domo); Maxine Leslie, Lillian Eggers (Willie's Evening Ladies); Frederick Vogeding, Charles Judels (Customs Officer); Anthony Blair, Joel Friedkin, Major McNamara, Earle S. Dewey, Bert Roach (Board Members); Maude Eburne (Juli); Suzanne Kaaren (Simone); Lisl Valetti (Other Maid); Leonard Carey, Guy Bellis (Servants); Esther Dale (Mrs. Gherkin); Grace Hayle (Mrs. Gabby); Gertrude W. Hoffman (Lady Gimcrack); Maude Allen, Eva Dennison (Women); Florence Auer (Mrs. Roquefort); Walter Soderling (Mr. Kipper); Dick Elliott (Mr. Scallion); Oliver B. Prickett [Blake] (Mr. Gherkin); Almira Sessions (Mrs. Scallion); Lon Poff (Mr. Dodder); Charles Brabin (Mr. Fairmind); Otto Hoffman (Mr. Flitt); Beryl Wallace (Fifi); Anita Bolster (Mrs. Kipper); Frank Reicher (Driver); Rafael Storm (Berti); Cecil Cunningham (Mrs. Fairmind); Jack "Tiny" Lipson (Mr. Roquefort); Harry Worth, James B. Carson (Waiters); Alphonse Martell (Headwaiter); Arthur Dulac, Harry Horwitz (French News Vendors); Sam Savitsky (Doorman); Evelyn Atchinson (Marie Antoinette); Charles Bancroft (Chimney Sweep); Muriel Barr (Mermaid); Edwinia Coolidge (Queen Elizabeth); Ruth Adler (Night #1); Leda Nicova (Night #2); Vivian DuBois (Night #3); Betty Hayward (Night #4); George Ford (Neptune); Guy Gabriel, Dorothy Hans, Aileen Haley (Infantas); Joe Hartman (Marc Anthony); John Marlowe (Louis XIV); Paul Power (Scottish Highlander); Robert Spencer (Peacock).

I MARRIED AN ANGEL was the eighth and last MGM musical to star Jeanette MacDonald and Nelson Eddy. The *New York Times* chided, "A more painful and clumsy desecration of a lovely fiction has not been perpetrated in years." Originally Richard Rodgers and Lorenz Hart wrote the project as an MGM movie for MacDonald in 1934, but due to censorship problems it was shelved. Four years later it became a play by Vaszary Janos starring Dennis King, Vivienne Segal, Walter Slezak and Vera Zorina, which ran for 338 performances on Broadway.

Secretary Anna Zador (Jeanette MacDonald) works for Viennese playboy banker Count Willie Palaffi (Nelson Eddy). While she adores him, he pays her no attention, preferring to date many beautiful women and to leave the bank's mundane affairs in the hands of staid Herman "Whiskers" Rothbart (Reginald Owen). Willie's senior secretary, Marika (Mona Maris), and Whiskers stage an elaborate birthday gala for Willie, an affair to which Anna comes dressed as an angel. Later, in his dreams, Willie meets a real angel, Brigitta (Jeanette MacDonald), who predicts she will become his wife. Brigitta then materializes as a human and the two plan to wed. But at a party to introduce her to society, Brigitta upsets rich investor Baron Szigetti (Douglass Dumbrille), although Willie's ex-girlfriend, Peggy (Binnie Barnes), befriends her. Upset by Brigitta's actions, Willie leaves her and resumes his philandering ways, while Brigitta takes up with the Baron. After chasing Brigitta in his dreams, Willie awakens. He realizes it is Anna he truly loves and he quickly proposes to her.

Unlike most of Jeanette MacDonald and Nelson Eddy's operettas, I MARRIED AN ANGEL, even with its relatively brief running time, becomes tiresome after the first few reels. As edited for final release, the movie is especially convoluted at its finale, in which Eddy dreams he chases Jeanette through a variety of exotic locales, including a Spanish cafe and the beach at Waikiki. While MacDonald never looked more radiant and Eddy was in fine voice, the film failed to sufficiently entertain. Both sang the title song and Eddy recorded it for Columbia Records. Otherwise, the film was lax musically (in quality if not in quantity), although Jeanette had a brief occasion to do "Aloha Oe" in the Hawaiian dream scene. Interestingly, Nelson Eddy also waxed "Little Work-A-Day World" from the film, but this sequence was deleted from the release print; the record is most enjoyable, making one want to see the excised scene in which it was featured.

Through the years Jeanette MacDonald and Nelson Eddy continued to be reunited on radio, television and recordings. However, they never again worked together in films, although they continued to receive offers to re-team well into the 1960s. MacDonald died on January 14, 1965 of a heart attack and Nelson Eddy died of a stroke on March 6, 1967.

I'LL CRY TOMORROW (Metro-Goldwyn-Mayer, 1955) Color 117 minutes.

Producer, Lawrence Weingarten; director, Daniel Mann; based on the biography by Lillian Roth, Mike Connolly, Gerold Frank; screenplay, Helen Deutsch, Jay Richard Kennedy; art directors, Cedric Gibbons, Malcolm Brown; set decorators, Edwin B. Willis, Hugh Hunt; costumes, Helen Rose; background music, Alex North; music director, Charles Henderson; assistant director, Al Jennings; special effects, Warren Newcombe; camera, Arthur E. Arling; editor, Harold F. Kress.

Songs: "Sing You Sinners" (Sam Coslow, W. Frank Harling); "When the Red Red Robin Comes Bob Bob Bobbin' Along," "Happiness Is Just a Thing Called Joe" (E. Y. Harburg, Harold Arlen).

Susan Hayward (Lillian Roth); Richard Conte (Tony Bardeman); Eddie Albert (Burt McGuire); Jo Van Fleet (Katie Roth); Don Taylor (Wallie); Ray Danton (David Tredman); Margo (Selma); Virginia Gregg (Ellen); Don Barry (Jerry); David Kasday (David as a Child); Carole Ann Campbell (Lillian as a Child); Peter Leeds (Richard); Tol Avery (Fat Man); Jack Daley (Cab Driver); Ralph Edwards (Himself); Tim Carey (Derelict); Charles Tannen, Harlan Warde (Stage Managers); Ken Patterson, Stanley Farrar (Directors); Voltaire Perkins (Mr. Byrd); George Lloyd (Messenger); Nora Marlowe (Nurse); Peter Brocco (Doctor); Bob Dix (Henry); Anthony Jochim (Paul, the Butler); Kay English (Dress Designer); Eve McVeagh (Ethel); Veda Ann Borg (Waitress); Jack Gargan (Drug Clerk); Robert R. Stephenson, Joe DuVal (Bartenders); Vernon Rich (Club Manager); Cheerio Meredith (Elderly Lady); Gail Ganley (Lillian at Age Fifteen); Ruth Storey (Marge Belney); James Ogg (Usher); George Pembroke, Mary Bear (Couple); Bernadette Withers, Kathy Garner (Girls); Henry Kulky, Marc Krah, Guy Wilkerson (Men); Robert B. Williams (Stagehand); Bob Hopkins (Master of Ceremonies); Herbert C. Lytton (Conductor); George Selk (Switchman).

Once an extremely popular musical comedy star, Lillian Roth (1910–1980) sank into the depths of alcoholism before making an inspiring (highly publicized) return to normality and resuming her career. She detailed her see-saw life in the best-selling 1954 autobiography, *I'll Cry Tomorrow.* MGM purchased the screen rights to the book. Susan Hayward did an outstanding job as Lillian Roth, who was deprived of singing on the soundtrack since Hayward did her own vocals.

Starting out as a child performer (Carole Ann Campbell) in vaudeville, Lillian Roth grows into a teenager (Gail Ganley) on the stage; all the time her act is supervised by her domineering mother, Katie (Jo Van Fleet). Maturing into an attractive young woman, Lillian (Susan Hayward) becomes a star of Broadway and movies. However, she has an unsuccessful marriage to David Tredman (Ray Danton), followed by another unhappy marriage to sadistic Tony

Susan Hayward in I'LL CRY TOMORROW (1955).

Bardeman (Richard Conte), all of which propels her into drinking. Her addiction leads to the ruin of her life and career. Letting herself go, Lillian almost dies on Skid Row before she goes to Alcoholics Anonymous. There she meets Burt McGuire (Eddie Albert), her third husband, who helps her find faith in herself and resume her career. Her turnaround culminates with an appearance on Ralph Edwards' (himself) TV program, "This Is Your Life."

"Except for Susan Hayward's early, healthy appearance and seeming self-sufficiency as a vaudeville singer that sturdily nullify a need to take to the bottle, this drama of an alcoholic—her fall and regeneration—rings absolutely true, shattering and sad. So realistic is its development, once Miss Hayward gets into her cups, and so superb is she in portraying the singer-actress, Lillian Roth, that this autobiographical drama commands respects and admiration" (*New York Times*).

Susan Hayward, who had starred as another ill-fated songstress (Jane Frohman) in WITH A SONG IN MY HEART (1952), *q.v.*, was Oscar-nominated as Best Actress, but lost to Anna Magnani (THE ROSE TATTOO). The film was also nominated for Academy Awards for Best Cinematography—Black-and-White, Best Art Direction-Set Decoration—Black-and-White, and Best Costume Design—Black-and-White. I'LL CRY TOMORROW grossed $6,004,000 in distributors' domestic film rentals. One sequence deleted from I'LL CRY TOMORROW was the "Vagabond King Waltz" segment, showing Roth performing in THE VAGABOND KING (1930, *q.v.*), an early Paramount operetta.

MGM produced three screen biographies of musical performers in 1955. Besides I'LL CRY TOMORROW, there was Doris Day as cabaret/film torch singer Ruth Etting in LOVE ME OR LEAVE ME, *q.v.*, and Eleanor Parker (with Eileen Farrell dubbing the singing) as opera star Marjorie Lawrence in INTERRUPTED MELODY.

I'LL GET BY *see* TIN PAN ALLEY (essay).

I'LL SEE YOU IN MY DREAMS (Warner Bros., 1951) 110 minutes.

Producer, Louis F. Edelman; director, Michael Curtiz; story, Grace LeBoy Kahn, Edelman; screenplay, Melville Shavelson, Jack Rose; art director, Douglas Bacon; set decorator, George James Hopkins; costumes, Leah Rhodes, Marjorie Best; makeup, Gordon Bau; music director, Ray Heindorf; choreographer, LeRoy Prinz; assistant director, Chuck Hansen; second unit director, David C. Gardner; sound, Oliver S. Garretson, David Forrest; camera, Ted McCord; editor, Owen Marks.

Songs: "Ain't We Got Fun," "Ukulele Lady" (Richard A. Whiting, Gus Kahn); "The One I Love Belongs to Somebody Else," "I'll See You in My Dreams," "It Had to Be You," "Swingin' Down the Lane" (Isham Jones, Gus Kahn); "My Buddy," "Makin' Whoopee!" "Yes Sir, That's My Baby," "Carolina in the Morning," "Love Me or Leave Me" (Walter Donaldson, Gus Kahn); "I Wish I Had a Girl" (Grace LeBoy Kahn, Gus Kahn); "Nobody's Sweetheart" (Billy Meyers, Elmer Schoebel, Ernie Erdman, Gus Kahn); "Pretty Baby" (Egbert Van Alstyne, Tony Jackson, Gus Kahn); "Memories" (Van Alstyne, Gus Kahn); "I Never Knew" (Ted Fio Rito, Gus Kahn); "Toot Toot Tootsie Goodbye" (Al Jolson, Ernie Erdman, Gus Kahn); "No No Nora" (Fio Rito, Erdman, Gus Kahn); "I'm Through with Love" (Fud Livingston, Matt Malneck, Gus Kahn); "The Carioca" (Edward Eliscu, Vincent Youmans, Gus Kahn); "Your Eyes Have Told Me So" (Van Alstyne, Walter Blaufuss, Gus Kahn); "Liza" (George Gershwin, Ira Gershwin, Gus Kahn); "Shine on Harvest Moon" (Jack Norworth, Nora Bayes).

Doris Day (Grace LeBoy Kahn); Danny Thomas (Gus Kahn); Frank Lovejoy (Walter Donaldson); Patrice Wymore (Gloria Knight); James Gleason (Fred); Mary Wickes (Anna); Jim Backus (Sam Harris); Julie Oshins (Johnny); Minna Gombell (Mrs. LeBoy); Harry Antrim (Mr. LeBoy); William Forrest (Florenz Ziegfeld); Bunny Lewebel (Irene at Age Six); Robert Lyden (Donald at Age Eight); Mimi Gibson (Irene at Age Three); Christy Olson (Donald at Age Four); Dick Simmons (Bert); Else Neft (Mrs. Kahn); Jack Williams, Clarence Landry (Black Dancers); Ray Kellogg (John McCormack); George Neise (Isham Jones); Vince Barnett (Comic); Dan Barton (Hollywood Producer).

Gus Kahn (1886–1941), one of Tin Pan Alley's most famous lyricists, collaborated on scores of hit songs during the first four decades of the twentieth century. Kahn's life and music were brought to the screen in this rather simplistic, sentimental biopic which featured Danny Thomas as Kahn, but spotlighted Warner Bros. star Doris Day as his patient wife. Filmed in economical black and white, the conventional picture was at its best in its presentation of its subject's songs. Overall the movie lacked dramatic depth or realism and at times verged on the lachrymose. The choreography by LeRoy Prinz for the production numbers was better than his usual. This was Doris Day's fourth Warner Bros. film directed by Michael Curtiz; the others were: ROMANCE ON THE HIGH SEAS (1948), MY DREAM IS YOURS (1949), *q.v.*, and YOUNG MAN WITH A HORN (1950), *q.v.*

In the early part of the century, goods hauler Gus Kahn (Danny Thomas) has a facility for making up rhymes and this leads him to work on the words of songs. In 1908 in Chicago he meets music publisher's secretary Grace LeBoy (Doris Day) and together they collaborate on the tune, "I Wish I Had a Girl," and are a big success. The two wed and soon have a baby. After entertaining troops overseas during World War I, the Kahns move to New York City where Kahn becomes a well known songwriter, working with collaborators like Walter Donaldson (Frank Lovejoy) and for Broadway producers such as Florenz Ziegfeld (William Forrest). Trouble arises with Grace when Gus has an affair with stage star Gloria Knight (Patrice Wymore) and then he loses his savings in the 1929 Stock Market crash. For a time, Gus feels he has lost his ability to write songs and he toils in Hollywood. However, after recovering from a nervous breakdown he and Grace are reconciled and, with the help of old friend Walter Donaldson, he again finds show business success.

The *New York Times* judged of this standard biopic, "For all the wry humor that occasionally pops into the script, the verve of the other performers and the nostalgic lushness of the cavalcade of tunes, it is the warmth of Danny Thomas in the role of the lyricist, Gus Kahn, that keeps the entertainment from being just another sentimental over-the-years career story. By sheer virtuosity and charm, the actor makes it a cheerful and touching affair. . . . Doris Day does a good, solid job as the wife, likewise by several tunes." *Variety* reported, "Miss Day sells the Kahn tunes given her with a wallop and lends likable competence to the portrayal of Grace LeBoy Kahn."

IN OLD CHICAGO (20th Century-Fox, 1938) 110 minutes.

Producer, Darryl F. Zanuck; directors, Henry King, Robert Webb; based on the story "We the O'Learys" by Niven Busch; screenplay, Lamar Trotti, Sonya Levien; art directors, William Darling, Rudolph Sternad; set decorator, Thomas Little; costumes, Royer; music director, Louis Silvers; assistant director, Robert Webb; special effects, Fred Sersen, Ralph Hammeras, Louis J. White; camera, Peverell Marley; editor, Barbara McLean.

Songs: "In Old Chicago" (Mack Gordon, Harry Revel); "I'll Never Let You Cry," "I've Taken a Fancy to You," "Take a Dip in the Sea" (Sidney Mitchell, Lew Pollack); "Carry Me Back to Old Virginny" (James A. Bland); "Sweet Genevieve" (George Cooper, Henry Tucker); "How Many Miles to Dublin Town" (traditional); "The Irish Washerwoman" (traditional).

Tyrone Power (Dion O'Leary); Alice Faye (Belle Fawcett); Don Ameche (Jack O'Leary); Alice Brady (Molly O'Leary); Andy Devine (Pickle Bixby); Brian Donlevy (Gil Warren); Phyllis Brooks

(Ann Colby); Tom Brown (Bob O'Leary); Sidney Blackmer (General Phil Sheridan); Berton Churchill (Senator Colby); June Storey (Gretchen O'Leary); Paul Hurst (Mitch); Tyler Brooke (Specialty Singer); J. Anthony Hughes (Patrick O'Leary); Gene Reynolds (Dion as a Boy); Bobs Watson (Bob as a Boy); Billy Watson (Jack as a Boy); Mme. Sul-Te-Wan (Mattie); Spencer Charters (Beavers); Rondo Hatton (Rondo, the Bodyguard); Thelma Manning (Carrie Donahue); Ruth Gillette (Miss Lou); Eddie Collins (Drunk); Harry Stubbs (Fire Commissioner); Francis Ford (Driver); Gustav Von Seyffertitz, Russell Hicks (Men in Jack's Office); Charles Hummel Wilson (Lawyer); Frank Dee (Judge); Joe King (Ship's Captain); Robert Murphy, Wade Boteler (Police Officer); Rice and Cady (Specialty); Harry Hayden (Johnson, the Secretary); Vera Lewis (Witness); Ed Brady (Wagon Driver); Minerva Urecal (Frantic Mother); Scotty Mattraw (Beef Baron); Charles Lane (Booking Agent).

If MGM could produce the spectacular SAN FRANCISCO (1936) with Jeanette MacDonald and Clark Gable, and Samuel Goldwyn could turn out the elaborate THE HURRICANE (1937), then 20th Century-Fox mogul Darryl F. Zanuck could release his own disaster film, IN OLD CHICAGO, dealing with the great fire of 1871. Made at a cost of $1,800,000, IN OLD CHICAGO was lensed in 1937 but required several months thereafter to properly loop and edit the climactic twenty-minute fire sequence. Originally MGM's Jean Harlow was sought for the female lead, but after her death (June 7, 1937), director Henry King settled on Alice Faye for his leading lady.

Feisty widow Molly O'Leary (Alice Brady), a laundress living in poor quarters in the Chicago district known as The Patch, has three sons: lawyer Jack (Don Ameche), gambler-politician Dion (Tyrone Power), and laundry wagon driver Bob (Tom Brown). Dion is attracted to comely singer Belle Fawcett (Alice Faye), who works for saloon owner Gil Warren (Brian Donlevy). Dion promises her he will build a saloon better than Warren's where she will be the star attraction. He keeps his promise and opens a place called The Senate. Rather than compete with him, Warren announces he will run for the office of mayor of Chicago, and asks Dion's support. At first Belle is upset with Dion for taking money from Warren, but she does not know he has persuaded his brother Jack, now a successful attorney, to run for the office. To make sure Jack wins, Dion arranges a fight with Warren's supporters at a rally. When Gil's ballot-stuffers are carted off to jail, Jack is elected mayor. After taking office, Jack attempts to clean up the city's corruption and also tries to close Dion's Senate. After Belle promises to testify against Dion, he gets her to marry him, thus thwarting Jack's case. This causes a fight between the two brothers and Belle plans to leave Chicago. When Mrs. O'Leary hears about the dispute, she rushes to them, forgetting to put a bar between her cow's legs. The cow turns over a lantern which starts a conflagration that nearly destroys the entire city. General Sheridan (Sidney Blackmer) is called in with the Army and dynamite is used to blow up buildings. Jack and family friend Pickle (Andy Devine) are killed in the explosion and Warren dies when caught in the path of stampeding cattle from the stock yard. Dion and Tom struggle to find Belle, their mother and Gretchen (June Storey), Tom's wife. Eventually the family is reunited as Chicago burns.

It was a gamble having Alice Faye go dramatic in a film, when her public expected her merely to sing and dance. To hedge the bets in this spectacular film, the script provided for Faye to sing several songs in Tyrone Power's beer hall. Her most effective numbers were the rousing "In Old Chicago" and the traditional "Carry Me Back to Old Virginny" (in which she wore her famous bejeweled stockings). When originally released, IN OLD CHICAGO had an intermission after the first eighty minutes.

Variety noted how this film adroitly set the stage for the "cleansing" fire: "Scores of elaborate scenes establish the primitive types of architecture of the frame-built, rambling town. . . . Most of the action is laid in gaudy saloons and beer halls. . . . Chicago is pictured as a dirty and corrupt city, a Sodom on the brink, ready for the torch of annihilation." The trade paper also judged, "Picture is big and it is showy, but it is historically cockeyed in the placement of its main characters. . . . But as a film entertainment it is socko." The *New York Times* noted of the overwhelming climactic fire, "At the first cry of 'Fire' the screen suddenly flowers into beauty, violence and beauty. The ineffectual bucket brigades, the tangle of confused apparatus, the headlong plunging of fire horses around congested corners, the confusions of a fleeing populace. . . ."

Although released in 1938, IN OLD CHICAGO participated in the 1937 Academy Award balloting. The spectacle received Academy Awards for Best Supporting Actress (Alice Brady) and Best Assistant Director (Robert Webb). It was nominated for Oscars for Best Picture, Score, Original Story and Sound.

Because of the focus on beautifying Alice Faye's screen image in IN OLD CHICAGO, much attention was paid to her costuming and to exploiting her shapely figure (especially her legs). Her revealing costumes garnered her a great deal of publicity and set the tone for her future pictures. This was the first of three musicals in which Alice Faye co-starred with Tyrone Power; the others were

ALEXANDER'S RAGTIME BAND (1938) and ROSE OF WASHINGTON SQUARE (1939), *qq.v.* Don Ameche, a singing-acting leading man at 20th Century-Fox, teamed with Alice Faye four other times, in YOU CAN'T HAVE EVERYTHING (1937), ALEXANDER'S RAGTIME BAND (1938), LILLIAN RUSSELL (1940) and THAT NIGHT IN RIO (1941), *qq.v.*

20th Century-Fox utilized the spectacular fire sequences from IN OLD CHICAGO for "City in Flames" (CBS-TV, 3/6/57), an episode of "The Twentieth Century-Fox Hour" which was a weak remake of the original epic. Cast in leading roles were Anne Jeffreys, Kevin McCarthy, Jeff Morrow, Roland Winters and Lurene Tuttle.

For the record, it was always an unproved popular theory, which became legend, that Mrs. O'Leary's cow was responsible for the great Chicago fire.

INDIAN LOVE CALL *see* ROSE MARIE (1936).

INNOCENTS OF PARIS (Paramount, 1929) 78 minutes. (Also silent version: 7,816′).

Producer, Jesse Lasky; director, Richard Wallace; based on the story "Flea Market" by Charles E. Andrews; screenplay, Ethel Doherty, Ernest Vajda; art director, Hans Dreier; music director, Nathaniel W. Finston; choreographer, Fanchon and Marco, LeRoy Prinz; camera, Charles Lang; editor, George Arthur.

Songs: "Louise," "It's a Habit of Mine," "On Top of the World Alone," "Wait Till You See My Cherie" (Leo Robin, Richard A. Whiting).

Maurice Chevalier (Maurice Marny); Sylvia Beecher (Louise Leval); Russell Simpson (Emile Leval); George Fawcett (Monsieur Marny); Mrs. George Fawcett (Madame Marny); John Miljan (Monsieur Renard); Margaret Livingston (Madame Renard); David Durand (Jo-Jo); Johnnie Morris (Musician); Jack Luden (Jules).

Although forty years old, French entertainer Maurice Chevalier made his American (and sound) feature film debut in Paramount's INNOCENTS OF PARIS (1929), which was that studio's initial musical. John Douglas Eames observed in *The Paramount Story* (1985) that Chevalier, with ". . . His bubbling charm, polished technique and well-developed showmanship had an immediate impact on the moviegoing masses which propelled him into another 40 years of international renown." The picture, however, had difficulty even being made, as Eames further reported: "As the Hollywood studio's first musical, it was the production most disrupted when a fire destroyed the new sound stages, and shooting had to be completed in makeshift style on sets heavily draped against outside noises." No matter, the movie itself scored a big success. *Photoplay* magazine reviewed it as an "Inconsequential plot made delightful by the charming personality of Maurice Chevalier."

Paris junk dealer Maurice Marny (Maurice Chevalier) saves a little boy, Jo-Jo (David Durand), after his mother drowns herself. He takes the little fellow to his grandfather, Emile Leval (Russell Simpson). Maurice thereafter falls in love with Louise (Sylvia Beecher), the lad's aunt, but young Emile is opposed to the romance. While singing at a flea market, Maurice comes to the attention of theatrical producer Renard (John Miljan) and his wife (Margaret Livingston). They star him in their revue, although Louise is against the venture. When Emile tries to shoot Maurice, Louise has him arrested. Maurice scores a success as a singing junkman, but then gives up the stage to wed Louise.

INNOCENTS OF PARIS provided Maurice Chevalier with two of his most famous songs, "Louise" and "Wait Till You See My Cherie," both of which became best-sellers for him when he recorded them for Victor Records. The movie also started the French entertainer on a lengthy Hollywood stay. His next Paramount production, THE LOVE PARADE (1929), *q.v.,* began his successful screen teaming with Jeanette MacDonald.

IT HAPPENED IN BROOKLYN (Metro-Goldwyn-Mayer, 1947) 104 minutes.

Producer, Jack Cummings; director, Richard Whorf; story, John McGowan; screenplay, Isobel Lennart; art directors, Cedric Gibbons, Leonard Vasian; set decorators, Edwin B. Willis, Alfred E. Spencer; music director, Johnny Green; orchestrator, Ted Duncan; choreographer, Jack Donahue; assistant director, Earle McEvoy; sound supervisor, Douglas Shearer; camera, Robert Planck; editor, Blanche Sewell.

Songs: "La Ci Darem La Mano" from the opera *Don Giovanni* (Wolfgang Amadeus Mozart); "The Bell Song" from the opera *Lakmé* (Leo Delibes); "Time After Time," "The Song's Gotta Come from the Heart," "It's the Same Old Dream," "I Believe," "Whose Baby Are You?" (Jule Styne, Sammy Cahn); "Otchichornya" (traditional).

Frank Sinatra (Danny Webson Miller); Kathryn Grayson (Anne Fielding); Peter Lawford (Jamie Shellgrove); Jimmy Durante (Nick Lombardi); Gloria Grahame (Nurse); Marcy McGuire (Rae Jakobi); Aubrey Mather (Digby John); Tamara Shayne (Mrs. Kardos); Billy Roy (Leo Kardos); Bobby Long (Johnny O'Brien); William Haade (Police Sergeant); Lumsden Hare (Canon Green);

Wilson Wood (Fodderwing); Raymond Largay (Mr. Dobson); William Tannen (Captain); Al Hill (Driver); Dick Wessel (Cop); Lennie Bremen (Corporal); Bruce Cowling (Soldier); Mitchell Lewis (Printer); Andre Previn (Off-screen Pianist).

While Arthur Freed produced most of MGM's most famous musicals in the 1940s-1950s, Jack Cummings (the nephew of studio boss Louis B. Mayer) produced a wide variety of song-and-dance entries for the company. Eleanor Powell starred in five of his productions (including BORN TO DANCE, 1936, and BROADWAY MELODY OF 1940, *qq.v.*); Esther Williams in four (including BATHING BEAUTY, 1944, and NEPTUNE'S DAUGHTER, 1949) and Howard Keel in four (including KISS ME KATE, 1953, and SEVEN BRIDES FOR SEVEN BROTHERS, 1954, *qq.v.*). IT HAPPENED IN BROOKLYN was an economical venture (shot in black and white), featuring a congenial cast, a lighthearted script and several appealing musical numbers (in contrasting styles of classic, pop and razz-ma-tazz). The film offered Frank Sinatra at his most relaxed and unpretentious and was a definite audience pleaser.

G.I. Danny Miller (Frank Sinatra) is stationed in London, but is homesick for his Brooklyn home. He befriends titled Britisher Jamie Shellgrove (Peter Lawford) who is a well-meaning bore, and Danny attempts to bring some zip into his new pal's life. Returning home to Brooklyn, Danny goes to his old high school, where the draft board is located. There he meets pretty music teacher Anne Fielding (Kathryn Grayson) and is immediately attracted to her. He also encounters colorful school janitor Nick Lombardi (Jimmy Durante) and moves in with him when he cannot find an apartment due to the post-war housing shortage. As Danny continues to romance Anne, Jamie arrives on the scene, having been sent to Flatbush by his family, who hope the change in environment will humanize him. Jamie is soon enchanted by Anne. When Anne needs funds for a scholarship for her students, she joins Danny, Jamie and Nick in putting on a show which brings in the money. By now Anne realizes that she loves Jamie. Danny renews acquaintance with an Army nurse (Gloria Grahame) whom he met while in the service.

Sammy Cahn and Jule Styne wrote a number of listenable songs for the film, the most notable being "Time After Time," sung by Frank Sinatra who also crooned "It's the Same Old Dream." He and Kathryn Grayson did a comedy version of "La Ci Darem La Mano" and Grayson performed a straight solo of the classical "The Bell Song" from the opera *Lakmé.* Sinatra and Jimmy Durante cut loose on the comedy tune, "The Song's Gotta Come from the Heart." IT HAPPENED IN BROOKLYN was the second teaming of Sinatra and Grayson; they had been together in the classic ANCHORS AWEIGH (1945), *q.v.* Raucous clown Jimmy "Schnozzola" Durante had been a star at MGM in the early 1930s. The gravel-voiced comedian returned to MGM in the mid-1940s for a series of wonderful appearances in several MGM musicals: TWO GIRLS AND A SAILOR (1944), MUSIC FOR MILLIONS (1944), TWO SISTERS FROM BOSTON (1945), THIS TIME FOR KEEPS (1947), ON AN ISLAND WITH YOU (1948), and finally for BILLY ROSE'S JUMBO (1962), *q.v.* Clean-cut, elitist Britisher Peter Lawford, who never claimed to be a song-and-dance man, found himself in several MGM musicals, from GIRL CRAZY (1943), *q.v.,* to ROYAL WEDDING (1951), *q.v.,* and including GOOD NEWS (1947, which was his best effort), *q.v.,* and EASTER PARADE (1948), *q.v.*

Summing up IT HAPPENED IN BROOKLYN, James Agee wrote in *The Nation* magazine, "Aside from Sinatra and Durante the show amounts to practically nothing, but there is a general kindliness about it which I enjoyed."

IT HAPPENED ONE SUMMER *see* STATE FAIR (1945).

IT'S ALWAYS FAIR WEATHER (Metro-Goldwyn-Mayer, 1955) Color 102 minutes.

Producer, Arthur Freed; directors, Stanley Donen, Gene Kelly; story/screenplay, Betty Comden, Adolph Green; art directors, Cedric Gibbons, Arthur Lonergan; set decorators, Edwin B. Willis, Hugh Hunt; costumes, Helen Rose; makeup, Willam Tuttle; assistant director, Al Jennings; music arranger/conductor, Andre Previn; vocal supervisors, Robert Tucker, Jeff Alexander; choreographers, Kelly, Donen; color consultant, Alvord Eiseman; sound supervisor, Wesley C. Miller; special effects, Warren Newcombe, Irving G. Ries; camera, Robert Bronner; editor, Adrienne Fazan.

Songs: "March, March," "The Time for Parting," "Why Are We Here (Blue Danube)?" "Stillman's Gym," "Baby, You Knock Me Out," "Situation-Wise," "Once Upon a Time," "I Like Myself," "Thanks a Lot, But No Thanks" (Andre Previn, Betty Comden, Adolph Green); "Music Is Better than Words" (Previn, Roger Edens, Comden, Green); "Sleeper Phones" (Previn).

Gene Kelly (Ted Riley); Dan Dailey (Doug Hallerton); Cyd Charisse (Jackie Leighton); Dolores Gray (Madeleine Bradville); Michael Kidd (Angie Valentine); David Burns (Tim); Jay C. Flippen (Charles Z. Culloran); Steve Mitchell (Kid Mariacchi); Hal March (Rocky Lazar); Paul Maxey (Mr. Fielding); Peter Leeds (Mr. Trasker); Alex Gerrry (Mr. Stamper); Madge Blake (Mrs. Stamper); Wilson Wood (Roy, the TV Director); Richard Simmons (Mr. Grigman); Amira Sessions (Lady); Eugene Borden (Chef).

Conceived by Gene Kelly and Stanley Donen as a sequel to ON THE TOWN (1949), *q.v.,* IT'S ALWAYS FAIR WEATHER failed to line up Frank Sinatra and Jules Munshin from that production. They were replaced by Dan Dailey and Michael Kidd. With its satirical digs at television and some satisfying dance numbers (choreographed by Kelly and Donen), this musical was fairly entertaining and cleverly exploited the widescreen (CinemaScope) process. However, the score by Betty Comden, Adolph Green and Andre Previn was mediocre and the movie proved to be no box-office blockbuster. Although the feature focuses on three men, the two distaff players (Cyd Charisse, Dolores Gray) come off best. Charisse offers one of her best performances as the intellectual advertising worker, while Gray was zesty and grand as the sugar-coated but hard-as-nails TV hostess.

Three Army buddies, Ted Riley (Gene Kelly), Doug Hallerton (Dan Dailey) and Angie Valentine (Michael Kidd) celebrate the end of World War II at a bar run by Tim (David Burns) in New York City. The trio agree to meet there a decade later for a reunion celebration. When that time arrives, the three reunite. Ted is now a gambler, Doug an overworked advertising executive, and Angie the owner of a hamburger stand. All three are uncomfortable because each believes he is a failure. When they go to a restaurant for dinner, they meet Doug's co-worker, Jackie Leighton (Cyd Charisse), and Ted is attracted to her. Later, she comes to Stillman's Gymnasium where Ted works at fixing fights, and he quickly realizes he loves the woman. It leads him to want to abandon his crooked occupation. However, he faces retaliation from his rival, gangster Charles Z. Culloran (Jay C. Flippen). Knowing the story of the three Army buddies, Jackie maneuvers them onto Madeleine Bradville's (Dolores Gray) TV show, which features unknowns. When Culloran shows up to get even with Ted, the gangster is tricked into revealing his activities on live TV. Ted, Doug and Angie proceed to beat up the hoodlum and his thugs, and then go to Tim's bar to celebrate. Jackie arrives to pursue a romance with Ted.

In *The Films of Gene Kelly* (1974), Tony Thomas commented, "The dancing in this film remains its greatest asset. . . . The pleasing Dailey is brilliant in his 'Situation-Wise'. . . . As soon as he [Kidd] begins to dance it is obvious he is no meek, retiring nonentity. The street dance with the garbage can lids belongs in the select collection of great film choreography, and Kelly's routine on roller skates is amazing in its dexterity, especially in the ease of the tap-dancing."

Deleted before release of IT'S ALWAYS FAIR WEATHER was Michael Kidd's dance solo ("Jack and the Space Giants"), and not used were two Comden-Green-Previn numbers, "I Thought They'd Never Leave" and "Love Is Nothing But a Racket." Made at a cost of $2,062,256, IT'S ALWAYS FAIR WEATHER grossed $2,485,000 in its release. The movie was Oscar-nominated for its Story-Screenplay and Scoring of a Musical Picture.

Regarding the commercial failure of this picture, Gene Kelly would comment later, "We wanted to make an experiment by creating a serious subject within the context of a musical comedy. It was a good story for which we needed a little bit of realism, but we missed our goal, because we didn't succeed in giving it a feeling of nostalgia." Stanley Donen would add, "I didn't really want to co-direct another picture with Kelly at that point. . . . It was the only picture during which the atmosphere was really horrendous. We had to struggle from beginning to end. I can only say it was an absolute one hundred per cent nightmare."

JAILHOUSE ROCK (Metro-Goldwyn-Mayer, 1957) 96 minutes.

Producer, Pandro S. Berman; director, Richard Thorpe; story, Ned Young; screenplay, Guy Trosper; art directors, William A. Horning, Randell Duell; makeup, William Tuttle; music director, Jeff Alexander; assistant director, Robert Relyea; special effects, A. Arnold Gillespie; camera, Robert Bronner; editor, Ralph E. Winters.

Songs: "Treat Me Nice," "Jailhouse Rock," "Young and Beautiful," "I Want To Be Free," "Don't Leave Me Now," "You're So Square—Baby I Don't Care" (Jerry Lieber, Mike Stoller).

Elvis Presley (Vince Everett); Judy Tyler (Peggy Van Alden); Mickey Shaughnessy (Hunk Houghton); Jennifer Holden (Sherry Wilson); Dean Jones (Teddy Talbot); Anne Neyland (Laury Jackson); Hugh Sanders (Warden); Vaughn Taylor (Mr. Shores); Mike Stoller (Pianist); Grandon Rhodes (Professor August Van Alden); Katherine Warren (Mrs. Van Alden); Don Burnett (Mickey Alba); George Cisar (Jake, the Bartender); Glenn Strange (Simpson, the Convict); John Indrisano (Convict); Robert Bice (Barderman, the TV Studio Manager); Percy Helton (Sam Brewster); Peter Adams (Jack Lease); William Forrest (Studio Head); Dan White (Paymaster); Robin Raymond (Dotty); John Day (Ken); S. John Lauder (Judge); Dick Rich (Guard); Elizabeth Silfer (Cleaning Woman); Gloria Pall (Stripteaser); Fred Coby (Bartender); Walter Johnson (Shorty); Frank Kreig (Drunk); William Tannen (Record Distributor); Wilson Wood (Record Engineer); Tom McKee (TV Director); Donald Kerr (Photographer); Carl

Elvis Presley, Jennifer Holden and Mickey Shaughnessy in JAILHOUSE ROCK (1957).

Milletaire (Drummond); Francis DeSales (Surgeon); Harry Hines (Hotel Clerk); Dorothy Abbott (Woman in Cafe); The Jordanaires (Musicians).

Elvis Presley was impressive in his movie debut in the Western, LOVE ME TENDER (1956), in which he sang the title song and acted generally with conviction. His first solo starring role was in JAILHOUSE ROCK—shot in economical black-and-white—which further solidified his screen popularity. Additionally, the movie provided Presley with a number-one hit: "Jailhouse Rock" remained on the record charts for over five months. He also had a minor seller with another song from the picture, "Treat Me Nice." In the sequence in which he sang the title song, Elvis also executed a gyrating dance number with the other prisoners, the star having choreographed the impressive scene himself.

Following a barroom brawl in which a man is killed, Vince Everett (Elvis Presley) is sent to prison and is there indoctrinated in the ways of survival by cellmate Hunk Houghton (Mickey

Shaughnessy). Hunk also teaches him to sing and Vince proves to be a good vocalist. After he is released from jail, the embittered young man strives for a show business career. He is aided by agent Peggy Van Alden (Judy Tyler), who falls in love with him. The singer, who promptly rises to popularity, treats everyone ruthlessly, however, including Peggy and Hunk, the latter having become his flunky. Finally, Hunk gets fed up with the arrogant Vince. They have a fight which sends Vince to the hospital for a throat operation. When Vince realizes he will sing again, he comes to his senses and admits he loves Peggy.

Variety reported, "Film is packed with the type of sure-fire ingredients producers know Presley's followers go for, and it's likely a considerable portion of the populace, particularly the cats, will find this Metro release in their alley." The more staid *New York Times* termed the movie "A lumpy showcase for Elvis Presley. . . . This time some of the lyrics are actually audible. For the record the title tune is a convict jamboree, with Elvis breaking loose with his St. Vitus speciality."

Many filmgoers noted the plot similarities between JAILHOUSE ROCK and Warner Bros.' A FACE IN THE CROWD (1957) which starred Andy Griffith as a hobo turned into a TV star. Presley's co-star, Judy Tyler, was most noted for playing Princess Summer-Fall-Winter-Spring on television's "Howdy Doody Show" (1952–57). She died in an auto crash on July 4, 1957 at age twenty-four.

THE JAZZ SINGER (Warner Bros., 1927) 88 minutes. (Also silent version).

Director, Alan Crosland; based on the play by Samson Raphaelson; adaptor, Alfred A. Cohn; titles, Jack Jarmuth; music director, Louis Silvers; assistant director, Gordon Hollingshead; camera, Hal Mohr; editor, Harold McCord.

Songs: "Mammy" (Sam Lewis, Joe Young, Walter Davidson); "Toot Toot Tootsie Goodbye" (Gus Kahn, Ernie Erdman, Dan Russo); "Dirty Hands, Dirty Face" (Edgar Leslie, Grant Clarke, Al Jolson, Jimmy Monaco); "Blue Skies" (Irving Berlin); "Kol Nidre" (traditional); "Mother, I Still Have You" (Jolson, Louis Silvers); "Waiting for the Robert E. Lee" (L. Wolfe Gilbert, Lewis E. Muir); "My Gal Sal" (Paul Dresser).

Al Jolson (Jack Robins [Jakie Rabinowitz]); May McAvoy (Mary Dale); Warner Oland (Cantor Rabinowitz); Eugenie Besserer (Sara Rabinowitz); Bobby Gordon (Jakie at Age Thirteen); Otto Lederer (Moisha Yudelson); Cantor Josef Rosenblatt (Himself); Richard Tucker (Harry Lee); Nat Carr (Levi); William

Demarest (Buster Billings); Anders Randolf (Dillings); Will Walling (Doctor); Roscoe Karns (The Agent); Myrna Loy, Audrey Ferris (Chorus Girls); Jane Arden, Violet Bird, Ernest Clauson, Marie Stapleton, Edna Gregory, Margaret Oliver (Extras in Coffee Dan's Sequence).

See: THE JAZZ SINGER (1980) (essay).

THE JAZZ SINGER (Warner Bros., 1953) Color 107 minutes.

Producer, Louis F. Edelman; director, Michael Curtiz; based on the play by Samson Raphaelson; screenplay, Frank Davis, Leonard Stern, Lewis Meltzer; costumes, Howard Shoup; choreographer, LeRoy Prinz; camera, Carl Guthrie; editor, Alan Crosland, Jr.

Songs: "Lover" (Richard Rodgers, Lorenz Hart); "Just One of Those Things" (Cole Porter); "This Is a Very Special Day" (Peggy Lee); "Clover" (Mort Dixon, Harry Woods); "Birth of the Blues" (Buddy G. DeSylva, Lew Brown, Ray Henderson); "Living the Life I Love," "I Hear the Music Now," "What Are New Yorkers Made Of," "Hush-A-Bye," "Oh Moon" (Sammy Fain, Jerry Seelen); "I'll String Along with You" (Al Dubin, Harry Warren); "Breezin' Along with the Breeze" (Richard A. Whiting, Seymour Simons, Haven Gillespie); "If I Could Be with You" (Henry Creamer, Jimmy Johnson); "Kol Nidre" (traditional).

Danny Thomas (Jerry Golding); Peggy Lee (Judy Lane); Mildred Dunnock (Mrs. Golding); Eduard Franz (Cantor Golding); Tom Tully (McGurney); Alex Gerry (Uncle Louie); Allyn Joslyn (George Miller); Harold Gordon (Rabbi Roth); Hal Rose (Joseph); Justin Smith (Phil Stevens); Anitra Stevens (Yvonne).

See: THE JAZZ SINGER (1980) (essay).

THE JAZZ SINGER (Associated Film, 1980) Color 116 minutes.

Producer, Jerry Leider; associate producer, Joel Morwood; director, Richard Fleischer; based on the play by Samson Raphaelson; adaptor, Stephen H. Foreman; production designer, Harry Horner; art director, Spencer Deverill; set designers, Christopher Horner, Mark Poll; set decorators, Ruby Levitt, Robert de Vestel; graphic designer, Arthur Gelb; costumes, Albert Wolsky, Bill Whitten; makeup, Dan Striepeke, Leonard Engleman; incidental music, Leonard Rosenman; music editor, William Saracino; orchestral arrangers/conductors, Alan Lindgren, Tom Hensley; assistant directors, James Turley, Robert M. Webb, John Eyler, Jack Clinton, Alice Blanchard; stunt coordinator, Chris Howell; concert performance supervisor, Patrick Stansfield; technical advisor, Cantor Uri Frenkel; sound, T. G. Overton, Ron Hitchcock, Andy

Block; sound re-recording, Bill Varney, Steve Maslow, Gregg Landaker; sound designers, Ron Hitchcock, Andy Block; sound consultant, Bob Gaudio; supervising sound editor, William L. Stevenson; special effects, Lambert Powell; camera, Isidore Mankofsky; supervising editor, Frank J. Urioste; editor, Maury Winetrobe.

Songs: "You Baby," "Jerusalem," "America," "My Name Is Yussel" (Neil Diamond); "Love on the Rocks," "On the Robert E. Lee," "Summer Love," "Hey Louise," "Songs of Life" (Diamond, Gilbert Becaud); "Hello Again" (Diamond, Alan Lindgren); "Amazed and Confused" (Diamond, Richard Bennett); "Acapulco" (Diamond, Doug Rhone); "Hine Mah Tove," "Havah Nagilah" (traditional; adapted by Diamond); "Adon Olom," "Kol Nidre" (traditional; adapted by Uri Frenkel); "Heysur Bulgar" (traditional, arranged by Klezmorim Band).

Neil Diamond (Jess Robin [Yussel Rabinovitch]); Laurence Olivier (Cantor Rabinovitch); Lucie Arnaz (Molly Bell); Catlin Adams (Rivka Rabinovitch); Franklyn Ajaye (Bubba); Paul Nicholas (Keith Lennox); Sully Boyar (Eddie Gibbs); Mike Kellin (Leo); James Booth (Paul Rossini); Luther Waters (Teddy); Oren Waters (Mel); Rod Gist (Timmy); Walter Janowitz (Rabbi Birnbaum); Janet Brandt (Aunt Tillie); John Witherspoon (Master of Ceremonies at Cinderella Club); Dale Robinette (Tommy); David Coburn (Bar Mitzvah Boy); Judy Gibson (Peg); Hank Garrett (Police Sergeant); Ernie Hudson (Heckler); James Karen (Barney Callahan); Tim Herbert (1st Technician); Ed Jahnke (Guard); Hugh Gillin (Texas Bartender); Jill Jaress (Cowgirl); Victor Paul (Irate Driver); Cantor Uri Frenkel (Cantor); Rex Cutter (Semi Driver); Mike Pasternak (Zany Gray); Sandy Helberg (Sound Engineer); Brion James (Man in Bar); Douglas Nigh (2nd Technician); *The Neil Diamond Band:* Dennis St. Johns (Drums); Richard Bennett (Guitar); Alan Lindgren (Keyboards); Reinie Press (Bass); Doug Rhone (Guitar); Tom Hensley (Keyboards); King Errisson (Percussion); Linda Press (Vocals); Vince Charles (Percussion/Steel Drums).

The importance of the 1927 version of THE JAZZ SINGER cannot be overestimated. Singlehandedly this part-talkie struck the death knell for silent films. It not only brought motion pictures into the sound film era, but it also catapulted Warner Bros. into the hierarchy of movie-producing studios. The Samson Raphaelson play, on which the three films called THE JAZZ SINGER were based, debuted on Broadway in the fall of 1925 with George Jessel in the leading role and had a run of 315 performances. Warner Bros. acquired the screen rights to the work for $50,000 and, after Jessel demanded too much money to recreate his role on the screen, Al Jolson was hired for $75,000 to star in the movie, which made cinema history. Shot in Hollywood in August 1927, THE JAZZ SINGER debuted on October 6th of that year in New York City. The novelty of sound in a feature film caused a sensation, although earlier in the year the star had appeared in the Vitaphone one-reeler talkie, AL JOLSON IN A PLANTATION ACT SINGS APRIL SHOWERS.

Teenager Jakie Rabinowitz (Bobby Gordon), the son of Cantor Rabinowitz (Warner Oland), loves jazz music. He defers to his devout Jewish father's wishes and sings the "Kol Nidre" at high holiday services. Later he is punished when his stern father catches him singing jazz songs in a beer garden. Despite being close to his mother Sara (Eugenie Besserer), Jackie runs away from home to follow a career in show business. After ten years on the road he is known as singer Jack Robins (Al Jolson) and he comes to the attention of attractive dancer Mary Dale (May McAvoy), who helps him with his career. Now a star, he comes back to New York City and is reunited with his mother, but again has a falling out with his Cantor father over his singing jazz songs. Cantor Rabinowitz becomes ill and cannot sing the "Kol Nidre" on the eve of Yom Kippur. Sara implores Jack to cancel his Broadway debut and substitute for his father at the synagogue. He does so, and is reconciled with his father, who gives his blessing to Jack's career. Jack and Mary plan to wed.

THE JAZZ SINGER was essentially a silent production with added talkie sequences, including the song numbers and Jolson offering a little (hyperactive) dialogue like "Wait a minute, wait a minute. You ain't heard nothin' yet!" He sang such familiar favorites as "Toot Toot, Tootsie," "Dirty Hands, Dirty Face," "Blue Skies" and the heart-rending "My Mammy," as well as the traditional Jewish number, "Kol Nidre." Despite the novelty of sound, this photoplay was stilted and old-fashioned. But it lodged a mighty $3.5 million in box-office receipts and Al Jolson followed it with the even more successful THE SINGING FOOL (*q.v.*) the next year. *Photoplay* magazine noted wryly, "Neither a Broadway reputation nor 'Mammy' songs on the Vitaphone nor a good story can conceal the painful fact that Al Jolson is no movie actor." Still the film made showman Jolson a major star of motion pictures. He would repeat "The Jazz Singer" on "Lux Radio Theatre" on CBS radio on February 16, 1948. Four years later the production came to the small screen when WOR-TV in New York City presented "The Jazz Singer" on its "Broadway Television Theatre" program with Lionel Adams in the title part.

The 1927 THE JAZZ SINGER was Oscar-nominated for Best

Adaptation and Best Engineering Effects. Warner Bros. received a Special Academy Award Award for ". . . Producing THE JAZZ SINGER, the outstanding pioneer talking picture which has revolutionized the industry."

In 1952, Warner Bros., searching for a new vehicle for Danny Thomas, who had starred with Doris Day in I'LL SEE YOU IN MY DREAMS (1951), *q.v.,* remade the tear-jerking THE JAZZ SINGER (1953) in Technicolor. Large-nosed singer-comedian Thomas had already played a cantor on screen in MGM's BIG CITY (1948). At one time in the mid-1940s he had done a medley of Al Jolson numbers in his club act and had been briefly considered for the lead in THE JOLSON STORY (1946), *q.v.,* before Columbia Pictures contractee Larry Parks was handed the role. Big band vocalist-recording artist Peggy Lee was cast as the songstress who aids his career and falls in love with him. Eduard Franz appeared as his cantor father and Mildred Dunnock as his loving mother. In the updated, but still schmaltzy version, the "Kol Nidre" was retained but a new score by Sammy Fain and Jerry Seelen included "I Hear Music Now," "Living the Life I Love" and "This Is a Very Special Day." The *New York Times* decided, "If Danny Thomas and a basically-unaltered reprise of the old Al Jolson drama . . . don't improve the original, they do it intelligent justice, along with a color treatment that naturally includes a steady flow of tunes, sectarian and hit-parade. . . . Corn, highly sentimental corn, it remains, under Michael Curtiz' capable direction, but it is well-served, with hearts well to the fore." Eduard Franz repeated the role of Cantor Rabinowitz in "Ford Star Time's" presentation of "The Jazz Singer" on October 13, 1959. This one-hour NBC-TV drama miscast Jerry Lewis in the title role although the supporting cast of Franz, Molly Picon (as Sara) and Anna Marie Alberghetti (as the love interest) helped save the old chestnut from being a total debacle.

In 1980 Associated Films packaged a third version of THE JAZZ SINGER as a vehicle for Neil Diamond, with Laurence Olivier (in a badly over-exaggerated performance) as the cantor. There were many production problems, including the departure of Sidney J. Furie in the midst of production, with Richard Fleischer replacing him. Lucie Arnaz was also a replacement talent in this troubled production. This time around, the evergreen plot was not only updated but altered, minimizing the focus on the ethnic conflict since a great deal of the Jewish-assimilation-in-America issue had become a fait accompli.

Yussel Rabinovitch (Neil Diamond) is a fifth-generation cantor in a Lower East Side New York City synagogue. He is torn between his predestined life and his desire to be a songwriter and performer. (At nights, he sings in blackface with a Harlem soul group headed by his pal Bubba [Franklyn Ajaye].) When Yussel chooses the latter career and becomes known as Jess Robin, he is alienated from his traditionalist elderly father (Olivier) and breaks up his marriage with his parochial wife (Catlin Adams). During his rise to stardom, Jess is bolstered by record company executive/ manager (Lucie Arnaz). The two fall in love and later have a baby son. Later, back in New York City, the singer and his father are reconciled, after Jess substitutes for his ailing father at the synogogue's high holiday services.

In judging this rehash, Martyn Auty (British *Monthly Film Bulletin*) weighed, "There is even less to recommend this lackluster remake which, apart from the obvious desire to test Neil Diamond commercially as a movie star, merely trades on the dubious fame of the 1927 original. . . . The film occasionally catches in concert footage something of the raunchy, high-heeled strut and orchestral overkill of the Diamond style. But its more ludicrous sequences, notably the time-spanning montages backed by the oft-repeated hit

Lucie Arnaz and Neil Diamond in THE JAZZ SINGER (1980).

single 'Love on the Rocks' are slackly scripted and sepia-flooded hokum. . . ." *Variety* pointed out, "A vanity production from the word go. . . . Curiously, femme-slanted music biz tales, such as A STAR IS BORN [1976, *q.v.*], THE ROSE [1979, *q.v.*] and COAL MINER'S DAUGHTER [1980, *q.v.*] have performed well commercially, while male starrers have generally belly-flopped of late. . . . Old title has nothing to do with music on display here and would seem meaningless to modern audiences."

Made at a cost of $5,000,000, THE JAZZ SINGER (1980) grossed $13,000,000 in distributors' domestic film rentals. Perhaps the "highlight" of this dismal remake is Diamond's music score (only "Kol Nidre" is retained from the original version) which resulted in his best-selling singles, "America," "Hello Again" and "Love on the Rocks." The film's soundtrack album on Capitol Records sold over three million copies and was on *Billboard* magazine's hits chart for thirty-two weeks, rising briefly to position #3. Understandably, Neil Diamond has made no subsequent feature films to date.

JESUS CHRIST, SUPERSTAR (Universal, 1973) Color 107 minutes.

Producers, Norman Jewison, Robert Stigwood; associate producer, Patrick Palmer; director, Jewison; based on the rock opera by Andrew Lloyd Webber, Tim Rice; screenplay, Melvyn Bragg, Jewison; production designer, Richard MacDonald; art director, John Clark; costumes, Yvonne Blake; music director, Andre Previn; orchestrator, Webber; choreographer, Robert Iscove; assistant directors, Jack N. Reddish, Dusty Symonds; sound re-recording, Gordon K. McCallum, Keith Grant; sound editor, Les Wiggins; camera, Douglas Slocombe; editor, Antony Gibbs.

Songs: "Superstar," "Heaven on Their Minds," "What's the Buzz?" "Strange Things Mystifying," "Then We Are Decided," "Everything's Alright," "This Jesus Must Die," "Hosanna," "Simon Zealotes," "Poor Jerusalem," "Pilate's Dream," "Temple," "I Don't Know How to Love Him," "Damned for All Time/Blood Money," "The Last Supper," "Gethsemane," "The Arrest," "Peter's Denial," "Pilate and Christ," "King Herod's Song," "Could We Start Again Please?" "Judas' Death," "Trial Before Pilate," "The Crucifixion," "John Nineteen Forty-One" (Andrew Lloyd Webber, Tim Rice).

Ted Neeley (Jesus Christ); Carl Anderson (Judas Iscariot); Yvonne Elliman (Mary Magdalene); Barry Dennen (Pontius Pilate); Bob Bingham (Caiaphas); Larry T. Marshall (Simon Zealotes); Joshua Mostel (King Herod); Kurt Yaghijian (Annas); Philip Toubus (Peter); Pi Douglass, Robert LuPone, Jonathan Wynne, Thommie Walsh,

Richard Molinaire, David Devir, Jeffrey Hyslop, Richard Orbach, Shooki Wagner (Apostles); Darcel Wynne, Marcia McBroom, Sally Neal, Leeyan Granger, Vera Biloshinsky, Kathryn Wright, Wendy Maltby, Denise Pence, Baayork Lee, Wyetta Turner, Susan Allanson, Tamar Zafria, Ellen Hoffman, Riki Oren, Judith Daby, Lea Kestin, Adaya Pilo (Women); Zvulun Cohen, Amity Razi, Meir Israel, Avi Ben-Haim, Itzhak Sidranski, Haim Bashi, David Rejwan, David Duack (Priests); Steve Boockvor, Cliff Michaelevski, Peter Luria, Tom Guest, David Barkan, Stephen Denenberg, Danny Basevitch, Didi Liekov (Roman Soldiers); Doron Gaash, Zvi Lehat, Noam Cohen, Moshe Uziel (Temple Guards).

First composed as a church work and then translated into a successful 1968 record album, Andrew Lloyd Webber and Tim Rice's *Jesus Christ Superstar* became a hit musical play on Broadway (1971, with 711 performances) and in London (1972, with 3,358 performances). It emerged as a motion picture in 1973, the same year as GOSPEL, another film musical about Jesus Christ. JESUS CHRIST SUPERSTAR grossed $13,103,056 in distributors' domestic film rentals and is credited with bringing a generation of lost youth to the teachings of Christ with its rock music look at the Savior and his humanitarian message. Partially financed by the government of Israel, the movie was filmed on location there by director Norman Jewison in Technicolor and Todd-AO 35.

A varied group of young people arrive in the Holy Lands by bus to stage a version of *The Passion Play.* The troupe builds sets and dress in the manner of the people of Palestine in Christ's era, with the actor playing Jesus Christ (Ted Neeley) dressed in white. The actor portraying Judas Iscariot (Carl Anderson) leaves the group and goes into the hills, vowing to betray his master. The scene then switches to Bethany where Christ and his followers are in a cave with everyone celebrating until Christ and Judas have a falling out over Mary Magdalene (Yvonne Elliman). The local leader, Caiaphas (Bob Bingham), meanwhile, plots with ally Annas (Kurt Yaghigian) to get rid of Christ, whose popularity is fast rising with the people. Christ continues to minister in the land and when he arrives in Jerusalem he finds it full of prostitutes and dope pushers. Jesus retreats to the mountains to meditate while Judas betrays him to Caiaphas. The next day Christ meets with his disciples at the Last Supper and then is taken out of the Garden of Gethsemane and put before the Roman ruler Pilate (Barry Dennen). The latter sends him to King Herod (Joshua Mostel), who calls him a fraud and returns him to Pilate. The Roman ruler does not want to execute Christ but bows to the pressure of the excited crowd which demands his death. He is led to Golgotha where he is crucified. The play ends and the cast and crew pack up and leave, but the actor who has played the Christ is missing. In the distance, on one of three crosses, is the figure of a man.

The score fits well within the confines of the plot, but most of the songs cannot stand alone. However, Yvonne Elliman's (as Mary Magdalene) rendition of "I Don't Know How to Love Him" did prove to be a hit recording for her. Among the other memorable melodies are "Hosanna," performed by Ted Neeley, and Philip Toubus (as Peter) and Yvonne Elliman dueting on "Could We Start Again Please?" "Then We Are Decided," by Webber and Rice, was added for the film version. The soundtrack album to JESUS CHRIST SUPERSTAR remained on *Billboard* magazine's hits chart for eight weeks, rising to position #21.

Naturally, a rock opera about the life of Jesus Christ did not suit everyone's taste and the film was picketed in various cities by fundamentalist groups, mainly because Christ was depicted as a virile man with a hinted-at carnal interest in Mary Magdalene. Writing in *Films in Review* magazine (August-September, 1973), Alvin H. Marill noted, "This Christ, however, remains an acquired taste. Its followers are not likely to be among H. B. Warner's disciples, nor even Pasolini's."* In historical perspective, Clive Hirschhorn (*The Universal Story,* 1983) assessed, "The addition of a show-within-a-show format to the plot wasn't particularly helpful, but Douglas Slocombe's expert photography . . . Andre Previn's full-blooded musical direction, and some imaginative choreography from Robert Iscove, were. . . . In sum, an erratic movie whose mistakes were offset by some arresting sequences."

Joshua Mostel, in a hammy performance as King Herod (who sing's "Herod's Song"), is the son of stage-screen performer Zero Mostel.

JOLSON SINGS AGAIN (Columbia, 1949) Color 96 minutes.

Producer, Sidney Buchman; director, Henry Levin; screenplay, Buchman; art director, Walter Holscher; set decorator, William Kiernan; costumes, Jean Louis; makeup, Clay Campbell; incidental music, George Duning; music director, Morris Stoloff; music advisor, Saul Chaplin; orchestrator, Larry Russell; assistant director, Milton Feldman; sound, George Cooper, Philip Faulkner; camera, William Snyder; editor, William Lyon.

---

*On the other hand, the furor created by JESUS CHRIST, SUPERSTAR would pale in comparison to the tornado of protests engendered by Martin Scorsese's THE LAST TEMPTATION OF CHRIST (1988), also distributed by Universal Pictures.

Songs: "After You've Gone" (Harry Creamer, Turner Layton); "Chinatown, My Chinatown" (Joe Young, Sam Lewis, Jean Schwartz); "Give My Regards to Broadway" (George M. Cohan); "I Only Have Eyes for You," "About a Quarter to Nine" (Al Dubin, Harry Warren); "I'm Just Wild about Harry" (Noble Sissle, Eubie Blake); "You Made Me Love You" (Joseph McCarthy, James V. Monaco); "I'm Looking over a Four-Leaf Clover" (Mort Dixon, Harry M. Woods); "Is It True What They Say about Dixie?" (Sammy Lerner, Irving Caesar, Gerald Marks); "Ma Blushin' Rosie" (Robert B. Smith, John Stromberg); "Let Me Sing and I'm Happy" (Irving Berlin); "Baby Face" (Benny Davis, Harry Akst); "Sonny Boy" (Buddy G. DeSylva, Lew Brown, Ray Henderson); "Anniversary Song" (Al Jolson, Saul Chaplin, J. Ivanovici); "For Me and My Gal" (Edgar Leslie, E. Ray Goetz); "California, Here I Come" (DeSylva, Jolson, Joseph Meyer); "Rockabye Your Baby" (Sam Lewis, Joe Young, Jean Schwartz); "Carolina in the Morning" (Gus Kahn, Walter Donaldson); "Toot Toot Tootsie Goodbye" (Kahn, Ernie Erdman, Dan Russo); "April Showers" (DeSylva, Louis Silvers); "Swanee" (George Gershwin, Caesar); "My Mammy" (Sam Lewis, Joe Young, Walter Donaldson); "I'll Take Romance" (Oscar Hammerstein, II, Ben Oakland); "It's a Blue World" (Bob Wright, Chet Forrest); "Learn to Croon" (Sam Coslow, Arthur Johnston); "Back in Your Own Backyard" (Jolson, Billy Rose, Dave Dreyer); "When the Red Red Robin Comes Bob, Bob, Bobbin' Along" (Harry Woods).

Larry Parks (Al Jolson/Himself); Barbara Hale (Ellen Clark); William Demarest (Steve Martin); Ludwig Donath (Cantor Yoelson); Bill Goodwin (Tom Baron); Myron McCormick (Ralph Bryant); Tamara Shayne (Mama Yoelson); Eric Wilton (Henry); Robert Emmett Keane (Charlie); Frank McLure, Jock Mahoney (Men); Betty Hill (Woman); Margie Stapp (Nurse); Nelson Leigh (Theatre Manager); Virginia Mullen (Mrs. Bryant); Philip Faulkner Jr. (Sound Mixer); Morris Stoloff (Orchestra Leader); Helen Mowery (Script Girl); Michael Cisney, Ben Erway (Writers); Martin Garralaga (Mr. Estrada); Dick Cogan (Soldier); Peter Brocco (Captain of Waiters); Charles Regan, Charles Perry, Richard Gordon, David Newell, Joe Gilbert, David Horsley, Wanda Perry, Luise Illington, Gertrude Astor, Steve Benton, Eleanor Marvak (Bits); Al Jolson (Singing Voice for on-screen Al Jolson).

See: THE JOLSON STORY (essay).

THE JOLSON STORY (Columbia, 1946) Color 128 minutes.

Producers, Sidney Skolsky, (uncredited) Sidney Buchman; associate producer, Gordon S. Griffith; directors, Alfred E. Green, (uncredited) H. Bruce Humberstone; screenplay, Stephen Longstreet; adaptors, Harry Chandlee, Andrew Solt; art directors, Stephen Goosson, Walter Holscher; set decorators, Willam Kiernan, Louis Diage; gowns, Jean Louis; makeup, Clay Campbell; music director, Morris Stoloff; vocal arranger, Saul Chaplin; orchestrator, Martin Fried; music recording, Edwin Wetzel; music re-recording, Richard Olson; production numbers directed by Joseph H. Lewis; choreographer, Jack Cole; assistant director, Wilbur McGaugh; color consultants, Natalie Kalmus, Morgan Padelford; sound, John Livadary; montage, Lawrence W. Butler; camera, Joseph Walker; editor, William Lyon.

Songs: "Swanee" (Irving Caesar, George Gershwin); "You Made Me Love You" (Joseph McCarthy, James V. Monaco); "By the Light of the Silvery Moon" (Edward Madden, Gus Edwards); "I'm Sitting on Top of the World" (Sam Lewis, Joe Young, Ray Henderson); "There's a Rainbow Round My Shoulder" (Jolson, Billy Rose, Dave Dreyer); "My Mammy" (Lewis, Young, Walter Donaldson); "Rock-A-Bye Your Baby with a Dixie Melody" (Lewis, Young, Jean Schwartz); "Liza" (Gus Kahn, George Gershwin, Ira Gershwin); "Waiting for the Robert E. Lee" (L. Wolfe Gilbert, Lewis F. Muir); "April Showers" (Buddy G. DeSylva, Louis Silvers); "About a Quarter to Nine," "Lullaby of Broadway," "42nd Street," "She's a Latin from Manhattan," "We're in the Money" (Al Dubin, Harry Warren); "I Want a Girl Just Like the Girl That Married Dear Old Dad" (Will Dillon, Harry von Tilzer); "The Anniversary Song" (Jolson, Saul Chaplin, J. Ivanovici); "The Spaniard Who Blighted My Life" (Billy Merson); "Let Me Sing and I'm Happy" (Irving Berlin); "When You Were Sweet Sixteen" (James Thornton); "Toot Toot Tootsie Goodbye" (Gus Kahn, Ernie Erdman, Dan Russo); "Eli Eli" (Traditional); "On the Banks of the Wabash" (Paul Dresser) "Ma Blushin' Rosie" (Robert B. Smith, John Stromberg); "Ave Maria" (Franz Schubert); "After the Ball (Charles K. Harris); "Blue Bell" (Edward Madden, Theodore F. Morse); "Every Little Movement Has a Meaning of Its Own" (Otto Harbach, Karl Hoschna); "Avalon" (Jolson, Vincent Rose).

Larry Parks (Al Jolson); Evelyn Keyes (Julie Benson); William Demarest (Steve Martin); Bill Goodwin (Tom Baron); Ludwig Donath (Cantor Yoelson); Tamara Shayne (Mrs. Yoelson); John Alexander (Lew Dockstader); Jo-Carroll Dennison (Anny Murray); Ernest Cossart (Father McGee); Scotty Beckett (Young Al Jolson); William Forrest (Dick Glenn); Ann Todd (Young Ann); Edwin Maxwell (Oscar Hammerstein); Emmett Vogan (Jonsey); Eric Wilton (Henry); Coulter Irwin (Young Priest); Jimmy Lloyd (Roy Anderson); Adele Roberts (Ingenue); Bob Stevens [Robert Kellard] (Henry); Dan Stowell (Ticket Seller); Charles Marsh (Man at Theatre); Harry Shannon (Riley, the Policeman); John Tyrrell (Man in Line); Joseph Palma (Brakeman); Ted Stanhope (Electrician); P. J. Kelley (Doorman); Bud Gorman (Call Boy); Charles Jordan (Assistant Stage Manager); Edward Kane (Florenz Ziegfeld); Pierre Watkin (Architect); Fred Howard (Man); Lilian Bond (Woman); Eugene Borden (Headwaiter); Eddie Rio (Master of Ceremonies); Will Wright (Movie Crank); Arthur Loft (Stage Manager); Edward Keane (Director); Eddie Featherstone (Assistant Stage Manager); Bill Brandt (Orchestra Leader); Pat Lane (Cameraman); Ralph Linn (Recorder); Mike Lally (Lab Manager); George Magrill (Stage Gaffer); Helen O'Hara (Dancer-Actress); Jessie Arnold (Wardrobe Woman); Donna Dax (Publicist); Clay Campbell (Makeup Man); Louis Traeger ("Sonny Boy"); Fred Sears (Cutter); Elinor Vandiveer (Maid); Franklyn Farnum, Bess Flowers (Extras in Audience); Major Sam Harris (Man in Nightclub); George Martin, Ethel Martin, Rod Alexander, Virginia Hunter (Chorus); Al Jolson (Singing Voice for on-screen Al Jolson; double for Larry Parks as Al Jolson in Winter Garden Rampway Sequence).

Long known as "The World's Greatest Entertainer," Al Jolson (1886–1950) was experiencing a severe career eclipse in the 1940s. However, columnist Sidney Skolsky, who conceived the idea of filming Jolson's life story, finally convinced Harry Cohn—the crude but shrewd Columbia Pictures' studio chief who had long been a Jolson fan—to approve shooting the biopic. What resulted was THE JOLSON STORY, with Larry Parks* playing the title role and Jolson (then sixty-one years old) himself dubbing his voice in the many musical interludes. The result was a narrative which closely resembled the storyline of THE JAZZ SINGER (1927, *q.v.*), itself a loose rendering of Jolson's life and career. THE JOLSON STORY was a tremendous success, grossing $7.6 million in distributors' domestic film rentals. It quickly revitalized Jolson's sagging career. He went on to host NBC radio's "The Kraft Music Hall," and had many best-selling records on the Decca label.

At the turn of the century, little Al (Scotty Beckett), the son of Cantor (Ludwig Donath) and Mrs. Yoelson (Tamara Shayne), is attracted to popular music as a youngster in Washington, D.C.

*According to Doug McClelland in *Blackface to Blacklist: Al Jolson, Larry Parks, and "The Jolson Story"* (Scarecrow Press, 1987), among the contenders for the role of Al Jolson were Dane Clark, Gene Kelly, Ross Hunter, Jose Ferrer, Danny Thomas and Richard Conte. Also per McClelland's tome, H. Bruce Humberstone was the first director on THE JOLSON STORY, but left in a dispute with the film's unofficial producer, Sidney Buchman (who went on to produce JOLSON SINGS AGAIN). Humberstone was replaced by Alfred E. Green.

Larry Parks in THE JOLSON STORY (1946).

Growing up as Al Jolson (Larry Parks), he joins Lew Dockstader's (John Alexander) minstrel company and begins working in blackface as a singer of "mammy"-style songs. This leads to work in New Orleans and then to Broadway, where he is a singing sensation at the Winter Garden Theatre and later in several productions for Florenz Ziegfeld (Eddie Kane). He meets and falls in love with Julie Benson (Evelyn Keyes), a Ziegfeld girl. He stars in Hollywood's first talking picture, THE JAZZ SINGER in 1927, and becomes a major film star. Eventually Julie feels she is second to audiences in Al's life and she leaves him, but they are reconciled eventually.

THE JOLSON STORY certainly took dramatic licenses with facts, whitewashing Jolson's life. He was renowned as an exceedingly egotistical man and a selfish performer in any ensemble. The film distorted his actual marital relationships a great deal. (He was married a total of four times.) Because actress Ruby Keeler, his third wife (from 1928 to 1940), refused permission to be represented in the picture, a fictitious Julie Benson (Evelyn Keyes) was created for the storyline. Nevertheless, THE JOLSON STORY is still an amazingly effective entertainment package. Larry Parks performs a captivating feat in his striking, energetic impersonation of the great "Jolie." He is quite effective in his miming of the great entertainer who sang the soundtrack for such standards as "My Mammy," "You Made Me Love You," "Swanee" and "Rock-A-Bye Your Baby with a Dixie Melody." Jolson made one brief appearance before the cameras in THE JOLSON STORY when he stood in for Larry Parks in a long shot in a Winter Garden Theatre rampway sequence.

According to Howard Barnes (*New York Herald Tribune*), "The film is essentially a testament to the excitement of show business. As such, it is a captivating screen musical. . . . The blackface Mammy singer holds the center of the screen as he is dashingly portrayed by Larry Parks. . . . The songs are nostalgic and delightful." Bosley Crowther (*New York Times*) decided, "In this gaudy fictionalization of Al Jolson's hurly-burly life, it is not the story of the trouper which attracts the indifferently disposed, not the extreme and mawkish drooling over a popular star of stage and screen, but rather the generous sound-tracking of a sack full of familiar old songs which imparts to the film an appealing nostalgic quality. . . . There is little or no dramatic point—and certainly no quality of character—conveyed in this fat and fatuous tale."

THE JOLSON STORY won Oscars for Best Scoring of a Musical Picture (Morris Stoloff) and Best Sound (John Livadary). It received Academy Award nominations for Best Actor (Larry Parks), Best Supporting Actor (William Demarest), Cinematography—Color, and Editing.

Due to the phenomenal success of THE JOLSON STORY, Columbia could not resist filming a sequel in 1949 called JOLSON SINGS AGAIN. This time unused footage and songs from the original, plus flashback scenes from the first film, were employed to pad out the running time and the diminished budget. The sequel proved quite successful and grossed $5,000,000 in distributors' domestic film rentals. Again Larry Parks was Jolson, with Jolie doing the vocals, which included such perennial Jolson numbers as "Baby Face," "Sonny Boy," and "Carolina in the Morning" plus a new ballad Jolson co-wrote called "The Anniversary Song," which became a best-seller for him on Decca Records. One of the gimmicks in JOLSON SINGS AGAIN was having Larry Parks as himself playing Jolson coming face to face with Larry Parks as Jolson. One of the highlights of the new picture was the performance of Barbara Hale as his nurse-wife, Ellen Clark. She added a resiliency and warmth that balances the overpowering focus on Jolson. In actuality, the name of Jolson's fourth wife was Erle

Galbraith, then still married to Jolson and with whom he had adopted a son in 1945.

JOLSON SINGS AGAIN takes up where THE JOLSON STORY leaves off. Al (Larry Parks) is separated from Julie Benson and his career is in eclipse. During World War II he donates his time to entertaining soldiers and during the hostilities meets and falls in love with nurse Ellen Clark (Barbara Hale) and they are married. After the war, Jolson is idle again, but the production of the movie THE JOLSON STORY brings renewed career interest in him. Jolie finds that he is again a big singing star.

Regarding JOLSON SINGS AGAIN, Kate Cameron (in her 3½-star *New York Daily News* review) decided, "The second film is not as sentimental, nor as heart-warming in its domestic scenes, as its predecessor. It is however, well made and more interesting from a technical standpoint than the first, as it takes the audience into the Columbia studio in Hollywood to show just how THE JOLSON STORY was created." Thomas M. Pryor (*New York Times*) voiced, "Sidney Buchman . . . has so shrewdly bridged the gap between this Technicolored picture and its predecessor that a knowledge of the 1946 production is not necessary for complete understanding and enjoyment. There is heart, humor, tragedy and a warm sprinkling of sentiment in Mr. Buchman's story. Larry Parks comes close to perfection, though his speaking voice still lacks the resonance of Jolson's singing."

JOLSON SINGS AGAIN won Oscar nominations for Best Scoring of a Musical Picture, Best Story-Screenplay and Best Cinematography—Color.

When THE JOLSON STORY was heard on CBS radio's "Lux Radio Theatre" on February 16, 1945, Al Jolson portrayed himself in the musical drama and repeated the chore on May 22, 1950 on the program's presentation of JOLSON SINGS AGAIN, with Barbara Hale repeating her screen role as his wife. Jolson died of a heart attack in San Francisco on October 23, 1950. For Larry Parks, these two musicals proved the zenith of his movie career, which was wrecked by his contractual feuding with Harry Cohn and the Senator Joseph McCarthy anti-Communist hearings of the early 1950s, which branded Parks a Communist sympathizer. Parks died of a heart attack on April 13, 1975 in Studio City, California.

JUMBO *see* BILLY ROSE'S JUMBO.

JUNIOR PROM (Monogram, 1946) 69 minutes.

Producer, Sam Katzman; associate producer, Maurice Duke; director, Arthur Dreifuss; screenplay, Erna Lazarus, Hal Collins; art director, Ed Jewell; set decorator, Tommy Thompson; music director, Abe Lyman; orchestrators, Herschel Gilbert, Joe Sanns; choreographer, Dean Collins; assistant director, Mel DeLay; sound, Frank McWhorter; camera, Ira Morgan; editor, William Austin.

Songs: "Keep the Beat," "Teen Canteen" (Sid Robin); "Trimball for President" (Stanley Cowan); "(All of a Sudden) My Heart Sings" (Herpin; English lyrics, Harold Rome; French lyrics, Jamblan); "Loch Lomond" (traditional); "It's Me, Oh Lawd" (spiritual).

Freddie Stewart (Freddie); June Preisser (Dodie); Judy Clark (Addie); Noel Neill (Betty); Jackie Moran (Jimmy Forest); Frankie Darro (Roy); Warren Mills (Lee); Murray Davis (Tiny); Mira McKinney (Mrs. Rogers); Belle Mitchell (Miss Hinklefik); Milton Kibbee (Professor Townley); Sam Flint (Mr. Forest); Charles Evans (Uncle Daniel); Hank Henry (Tony); Abe Lyman and His Orchestra, Eddie Heywood and His Orchestra, Harry "The Hipster" Gibson, The Airliners (Themselves).

Not often did minor film studios attempt a musical. Even the medium league Republic Pictures eschewed the format most of the

Advertisement for JUNIOR PROM (1946).

time, and hardly any of the poverty row outfits tried them, simply because song material and production numbers were beyond their meager budgets. Monogram, however, did make musicals occasionally and in 1946–48 the studio turned out seven features in its "Teenagers" series starring Freddie Stewart and June Preisser. These episodes featured not only many songs but also some of the more popular bands of the day. Maurice Duke served as associate producer on all seven features. The first four were produced by Sam Katzman and directed by Arthur Dreifuss, while Will Jason took over as producer-director for the final three.

The principal (Milton Kibbee) of a local high school is informed by a rich contributor (Sam Flint) that unless his son Jimmy (Jackie Moran) is elected class president, he will forego his annual donation to the institution. Another student (Warren Mills) overhears the conversation and alerts the other candidate, Freddie (Freddie Stewart), who withdraws from the race, but re-enters when Jimmy tries to date his girl, Dodie (June Preisser). Meanwhile, Jimmy's campaign manager (Frankie Darro) romances Dodie's sister Betty (Noel Neill) so that the school paper will endorse his candidate—she is the editorial writer. The newspaper does back Jimmy, but Freddie's friends come to his rescue with a musical campaign and he wins the contest. At a dance to announce the election results, Jimmy learns that his father tried to buy the election for him. He pressures his dad into making the contribution anyway. He and Freddie and Dodie again become friends.

Variety favored this modest film, "Young talent and smooth, well-balanced production. . . . Melange of songs, dances and groovy music by featured orchs assure the juve appeal, but is also pleasant enough to get by with the oldsters." Musical highlights of the feature were Eddie Heywood and His Orchestra performing "Keep the Beat" and "Loch Lomond." June Preisser offered her usual display of acrobatic dancing.

THE KING AND I (20th Century-Fox, 1956) Color 133 minutes.

Producer Charles Brackett; director, Walter Lang; based on the musical play by Oscar Hammerstein, II and Richard Rodgers, the book *Anna and The King of Siam* by Margaret Landon, and the diaries of *The English Governess at the Siamese Court* by Anna Leonowens; screenplay, Ernest Lehman; art directors, Lyle R. Wheeler, John de Cuir; set decorators, Walter M. Scott, Paul S. Fox; costumes, Irene Sharaff; music director, Alfred Newman; orchestrators, Edward B. Powell, Gus Levene, Bernard Mayers, Robert Russell Bennett; choreographer, Jerome Robbins; assistant director, Eli Dunn; sound director, Carl Faulkner; camera, Leon Shamroy; editor, Robert Simpson.

Songs: "I Whistle a Happy Tune," "Hello Young Lovers," "March of the Siamese Children," "A Puzzlement," "Getting to Know You," "We Kiss in the Shadows," "I Have Dreamed," "The Small House of Uncle Thomas Ballet," "Something Wonderful," "Song of the King," "Shall We Dance?" (Richard Rodgers, Oscar Hammerstein, II).

Deborah Kerr (Anna Leonowens); Yul Brynner (The King); Rita Moreno (Tuptim); Martin Benson (Kralahome); Terry Saunders (Lady Thiung); Rex Thompson (Louis Leonowens); Carlos Rivas (Lun Tha); Patrick Adiarte (Prince Chulalongkorn); Alan Mowbray (British Ambassador); Geoffrey Toone (Ramsay); Yuriko (Eliza); Marion Jim (Simon Legree); Robert Banas (Keeper of the Dogs); Dusty Worrall (Uncle Thomas); Gemze deLappe (Specialty Dancer); Thomas Bonilla, Dennis Bonilla (Twins); Michiko Iseri (Angel in Ballet); Charles Irwin (Ship's Captain); Leonard Strong (Interpreter); Irene James (Siamese Girl); Jadin Wong, Jean Wong (Amazons); Fuji, Weaver Levy (Whipping Guards); William Yip (High Priest); Eddie Luke (Messenger); Josephine Smith (Guest at Palace); Jocelyn New (Princess Ying Yoowalak); Marni Nixon (Singing Voice of Anna Leonowens); Reuben Fuentes (Singing Voice of Lun Tha).

THE KING AND I had its origins in a nineteenth-century diary of an English schoolteacher which in turn inspired Margaret Landon's biography, *Anna and the King of Siam* (1944). The latter was filmed in 1946 in black and white by 20th Century-Fox, with favorable results, with Irene Dunne, Rex Harrison and Linda Darnell starred. In 1951 Richard Rodgers and Oscar Hammerstein, II adapted the work to the musical stage as *The King and I,* starring Gertrude Lawrence and Yul Brynner, and the show ran for 1,246 performances. (Gertrude Lawrence died of cancer during the run and was replaced by Constance Carpenter.) In 1956, 20th Century-Fox also did THE KING AND I on screen. The resplendent production won an Oscar for Yul Brynner as Best Actor, Deborah Kerr was nominated for Best Actress, and the movie was nominated for Best Picture. The musical received Academy Awards for Scoring, Art Direction-Set Decoration, Costumes and Sound. THE KING AND I grossed $8.5 million in distributors' domestic film rentals. The lavish THE KING AND I was lensed in the widescreen process, CinemaScope 55. Its soundtrack album remained on the *Billboard* magazine charts for thirty weeks, rising to #1 position.

In 1862 Britisher Anna Leonowens (Deborah Kerr), a widow, is hired to tutor the more than five dozen offspring of the King of Siam (Yul Brynner), to whom everyone is required to grovel by the country's supreme law. Anna arrives at the royal court with her young son Louis (Rex Thompson). The refined Anna is upset by the conditions in the country which she considers barbaric because of the King's many wives and concubines and his dictatorial rule over his subjects. While Anna eventually comes to respect the well-meaning King's desire for knowledge of Western customs, she is horrified by the way he treats his favorite wife Tuptim (Rita Moreno) after she has an affair with a handsome younger subject (Carlos Rivas). (The King has the two burned to death.) After a time Anna and the King become good friends, which helps when Louis dies in a riding accident. Later, the King also passes away and she aids his heir, Prince Chulalongkorn (Patrick Adiarte) to assume his monarchal duties. His first act is to abolish the law of groveling to the ruler. Anna leaves Siam feeling she has helped to modernize the country.

While much of Deborah Kerr's singing in THE KING AND I was dubbed by Marni Nixon, and that of Lun Tha by Reuben Fuentes, the rest of the cast performed the many memorable songs. The showpieces of the production were "The March of the Siamese Children" (a processional of the king's offspring), the costumed ballet, "The Small House of Uncle Thomas," and the climactic expression of friendship between Anna and the King, the show-stopping polka "Shall We Dance?" Of the original songs, "My Lord and Master" (Tuptim's sarcastic ode of obedience) and "Shall I Tell You What I Think of You?" (Anna's soliloquy) were cut from the release print of the film, as was "Western People Funny" (the King's wives/concubines). The ballad "I Have Dreamed" appeared in the film only as background music. Besides the exotic and vital Brynner's repeat of his Broadway assignment, other such carryover talent included dancers Michiko Iseri, Gemze deLappe, Dusty Worrall and Yuriko, as well as choreographer Jerome Robbins and costumer Irene Sharaff. The soundtrack album to THE KING AND I remained on *Billboard* magazine's hits chart for thirty weeks and was in position #1 for one week.

The *New York Times* called THE KING AND I "A splendid and splendiferous reprise of the Rodgers-and-Hammerstein stage musical . . . done with taste in color, decoration—and characterization, from Broadway, that is rare in a screen-transplanted musical. Deborah Kerr does a fine, alert job—and also in her ghost-sung numbers—as the heroine, and Yul Brynner is even more impressive as the monarch than on stage. . . . Ernest Lehman's scenario, more or less repeating the stage story, and Walter Lang's direction, plus some stunning choreography in the 'Uncle Thomas' ballet add to a movie that is all it should be."

The part of the King of Siam made Yul Brynner a star when he performed it in 1951 and he would continue to be associated with *The King and I* on stage for the balance of his career. (His shaved head for the part remained a trademark of the actor throughout the remainder of his life.) In addition to his lengthy Broadway sojourn in the role and his Academy Award-winning movie version, he did the part in 1954 at the War Memorial Opera House in San Francisco and successfully revived the character in 1977 on Broadway for a 695-performance run before going to London with *The King and I* at the Palladium Theatre in the summer of 1979. Also, from September to the end of December 1972 he played the part in the half-hour CBS-TV series, "Anna and the King," with Samantha Eggar as Anna Owens. Brynner continued to tour with the musical play until shortly before his death from lung cancer in 1985. Yul Brynner and Deborah Kerr would re-team on-screen for MGM's Iron Curtain melodrama, THE JOURNEY (1959).

KING CREOLE (Paramount, 1958) 116 minutes.

Producer, Hal B. Wallis; director, Michael Curtiz; based on the novel *A Stone for Danny Fisher* by Harold Robbins; screenplay, Herbert Baker, Michael Vincente Gazzo; art directors, Hal Pereira, Joseph MacMillan Johnson; costumes, Edith Head; makeup, Wally Westmore; music, Walter Scharf; choreographer, Charles O'Curran; assistant director, Michael Moore; special effects, John P. Fulton; camera, Russell Harlan; editor, Warren Low.

Songs: "King Creole," "Trouble," "Steadfast, Loyal and True" (Jerry Lieber, Mike Stoller); "Hard-Headed Woman" (Claude De Metrius); "As Long As I Have You," "Crawfish," "Don't Ask My Why" (Fred Wise, Ben Weisman); "New Orleans" (Sid Tepper, Roy C. Bennett); "Lover Doll" (Sid Wayne, Abner Silver); "Dixieland Rock" (De Metrius, Wise); "Young Dreams" (Schroeder, Martin Kalmanoff); "Turtles, Berries and Gumbo."

Elvis Presley (Danny Fisher); Carolyn Jones (Ronnie); Dolores Hart (Nellie); Dean Jagger (Mr. Fisher); Lilliane Montevecchi ("Forty" Nina); Walter Matthau (Maxie Fields); Jan Shepard (Mimi Fisher); Paul Stewart (Charlie LeGrand); Vic Morrow (Shark); Brian Hutton (Sal); Jack Grinnage (Dummy); Dick Winslow (Eddie Burton); Raymond Bailey (Mr. Evans); and: Minta Durfee Arbuckle, Hazel "Sonny" Boyne, Franklyn Farnum, Ziva Rodann.

In New Orleans high school boy Danny Fisher (Elvis Presley)

needs money to help his father (Dean Jagger) and he gets involved in petty theft. He vows to go straight but, as a result of his misdeed, he is denied a chance to graduate from school. Danny, who is in love with high school sweetheart Nellie (Dolores Hart), is a good singer and Charlie LeGrand (Paul Stewart) gives him the opportunity to sing at his Bourbon Street club, the Vieux Carée, where he becomes popular. Rival club owner-gangster Maxie Fields (Walter Matthau) wants Danny to sing for him. He blackmails the youth because of his past and, at the same time, the hoodlum's bitter moll Ronnie (Carolyn Jones) makes a play for the young talent. When competing gangsters engage in a shootout, Maxie and Ronnie are killed. Danny returns to his singing as well as to his romance with Nellie.

For his fourth feature film (and his third solo starring effort), Elvis Presley was more than convincing as the young man caught between right and wrong and the love of two women. (The movie was a considerably cleaned up version of Harold Robbins' classic piece of titillating drama.) The black and white feature provided Elvis with a baker's dozen songs, the most successful being his RCA chart numbers: "Hard-Headed Woman" and the extended play 45 rpm of "King Creole." In the supporting cast, Carolyn Jones was particularly impressive as the love-starved tart.

The *New York Times* said, "A surprisingly colorful and lively drama, with Elvis Presley doing some surprisingly credible acting flanked by a dandy supporting cast, although the picture finally lapses into standard gangster shenanigans. . . . [It] is generally a pleasure." *Variety* reported, "Hal Wallis has attempted to take the curse off Elvis Presley for those still resistant to his charms, by giving him an extraordinary backing in KING CREOLE, a solid melodrama with plenty of action and color. The Paramount presentation shows the young singer this time as a better-than-fair actor."

The soundtrack album to KING CREOLE appeared on *Billboard* magazine's hits chart for fifteen weeks and was in position #2 for one week.

KING OF JAZZ (Universal, 1930) Color 98 minutes.

Presenter, Carl Laemmle, Sr., producer, Carl Laemmle, Jr.; director/story deviser, John Murray Anderson; screenplay, Edward T. Lowe, Jr.; comedy sketches, Harry Ruskin; dialogue, Charles MacArthur; art directors, Herman Rosse, Thomas F. O'Neill; costumes, Rosse; orchestrator, Ferde Grofe; assistant director, Robert Ross; sound supervisor, C. Roy Hunter; camera, Hal Mohr, Jerome Ash, Ray Rennahan; supervising film editor, Maurice Pivar; film editor, Robert Carlisle.

Songs: "A Bench in the Park," "Happy Feet," "My Bridal Veil," "The Song of the Dawn," "I Like To Do Things for You," "Music Hath Charms," "My Lover" (Jack Yellen, Milton Ager); "It Happened in Monterey" (Billy Rose, Mabel Wayne); "Ragamuffin Romeo" (Wayne, Harry De Costa); "So the Bluebirds and the Blackbirds Got Together" (Billy Moll, Harry Barris); "Rhapsody in Blue" (George Gershwin); "Mississippi Mud" (Barris, James Cavanaugh); "When Day Is Done" (Buddy G. DeSylva, Robert Katscher); "Caprice Viennoise" (Fritz Kreisler); "Nola" (Felix Arndt, James Burns); "Linger Awhile" (Harry Owens, Vincent Rose); "Aba Daba Honeymoon" (Arthur Fields, Walter Donovan); "A-Hunting We Will Go" (traditional); "Ballet Egyptien" (Alexandre Luigini); "Rule Britannia" (traditional); "D'Ye Ken John Peel" (traditional), "Santa Lucia" (traditional); "Funiculi-Funicula" (traditional); "Comin' Through the Rye" (traditional), "Wiener Blut" (traditional); "Fair Killarney" (traditional); "The Irish Washerwoman" (traditional), "Ay-yi Ay-yi-yi" (traditional); "Song of the Volga Boatmen" (traditional); "Otchichornia" (traditional); "Has Anybody Seen Our Nelly?" (parody); "Oh, How I'd Like to Own a Fishstore" (parody).

Paul Whiteman and His Orchestra, John Boles, Laura La Plante, Glenn Tryon, Jeanette Loff, Merna Kennedy, Stanley Smith, Slim Summerville, Otis Harlan, William Kent, The Rhythm Boys [Harry Barris, Bing Crosby, Al Rimmer], The Sisters G, The Brox Sisters, George Chiles, Jacques Cartier, Frank Leslie, George Gerswhin, Charles Irwin, Al Norman, Grace Hayes, Paul Howard, Marion Stattler, Don Rose, Russell Markert Girls, Tommy Atkins Sextette, Nell O'Day, Wilbur Hall, John Fulton, Kathryn Crawford, Jeanie Lang, Beth Laemmle, Jack White, Walter Brennan, Churchill Ross, Johnson Arledge, Charlie Murray, George Sidney (Specialties).

Paul Whiteman was the most popular bandleader of the Roaring Twenties and his Victor records were best sellers. His renditions of "Whispering" and "Japanese Sandman" went over the one million mark in sales. At the beginning of the sound era, Whiteman, who was called "The King of Jazz," made a lush Technicolor musical revue feature for Universal, that studio's entry in the all-talking, all-dancing, all-singing sweepstakes. The result was a garish, overlong, mixed bag of music; but it was an entertaining item which holds up rather well today. At the time of its release, however, *Photoplay* magazine dubbed it "Pretentious" but added, "Unusual color and lighting effects, splendid choruses." In retrospect, John Springer decided in *All Talking! All Singing! All Dancing!* (1966) that director "John Murray Anderson made it all look fairly spectacular." The film cost the studio $2,000,000, a goodly portion of the cost due to having hired Whiteman and his group before a storyline was set, then trying to fabricate a love story about rotund Whiteman (which was later abandoned), and to hiring Broadway revue director John Murray Anderson, who had never directed a movie before.

KING OF JAZZ opens with Bing Crosby crooning "Music Has Charms" over the credits and then commences with an amusing animated cartoon about Paul Whiteman's scrapbook and how he became famed as The King of Jazz. In person Whiteman (himself) introduces his orchestra members and a dance number by chorus girls follows. The Rhythm Boys (themselves) sing "So the Bluebirds and the Blackbirds Got Together" and then a young bride dreams of wedding costumes through various ages. The Whiteman group performs "A Bench in the Park" and several comedy sequences with Slim Summerville, Glenn Tryon, Charlie Murray and George Sidney follow. In perhaps the most enjoyable sequence in KING OF JAZZ, John Boles romances Jeanette Loff in a Spanish setting as he sings "It Happened in Monterey" followed by "Song of the Dawn." The melodies "Happy Feet" and "Ragamuffin Romeo" are followed by George Gershwin (on piano) joining the Whiteman aggregation to perform his famous composition, "Rhapsody in Blue."* A comedy about the "Bogie Man" is next and the feature winds up with Whiteman's famous "The Melting Pot" number, about how all types of music came together to form jazz.

Despite its length and creaky production values, KING OF JAZZ remains a delightful vintage musical, especially for John Boles' crooning and the inclusion of the historically important Gershwin interlude. As a member of The Rhythm Boys, Bing Crosby made his film debut in the production. He was assigned the "Song of the Dawn" number but a drunk driving charge landed him in jail and the song went to John Boles, who was quickly becoming one of the sound era's first singing stars. Boles recorded both "It Happened in Monterey" and "Song of the Dawn" for Victor and had a best-selling record with the two numbers.

It should be noted that Universal issued a number of foreign-language versions of KING OF JAZZ, using a different

---

*Roy Hemming (*The Melody Lingers On,* 1986) judged of KING OF JAZZ that it ". . . boasts some incredibly extravagant sets and moving stages that have, even to this day, rarely been equaled. . . . The 'Rhapsody in Blue' number has one of the most eye-boggling sets of all. . . . It's a visually mesmerizing number in a bold, glittery, surreal style that few movies have ever attempted on such a scale."

host to introduce the film in each particular language version. For the Hungarian version, Bela Lugosi served as the host.

KISMET (Metro-Goldwyn-Mayer, 1955) Color 113 minutes.

Producer, Arthur Freed; directors, Vincente Minnelli, (uncredited) Stanley Donen; based on the musical play by Robert Wright, Chet Forrest as adapted from musical themes of Alexander Borodin; and the play by Edward Knoblock; screenplay, Charles Lederer, Luther Davis; art directors, Cedric Gibbons, Preston Ames; set decorators, Edwin B. Willis, Keogh Gleason; costumes, Tony Duquette; makeup, William Tuttle; music supervisors/conductors, Andre Previn, Jeff Alexander; orchestrators, Conrad Salinger, Alexander Courage, Arthur Morton; choreographer, Jack Cole; assistant director, William Shanks; color consultant, Charles K. Hagedon; sound supervisor, Dr. Wesley C. Miller; camera, Joseph Ruttenberg; editor, Adrienne Fazan.

Songs: "Fate," "Gesticulate," "The Olive Tree," "The Sands of Time," "Not Since Ninevah," "Bored," "Baubles, Bangles and Beads," "Stranger in Paradise," "Night of My Nights," "And This Is My Beloved," "Rahadlakum," "Rhymes Have I," "Dance of the Three Princesses of Ababu" (Bob Wright, Chet Forrest, based on melodies of Alexander Borodin).

Howard Keel (Hajj the Poet); Ann Blyth (Marsinah); Dolores Gray (Lalume); Vic Damone (Caliph); Monty Woolley (Omar); Sebastian Cabot (Grand Wazir); Jay C. Flippen (Jawan); Mike Mazurki (Chief Policeman); Jack Elam (Hassan-Ben); Ted De Corsia (Police Subaltern); Patricia Dunn, Reiko Sato, Wonci Lui (Princesses of A Ba Bu); Julie Robinson (Zubbediya); Ray Aghayan (Brave Shopkeeper); Aaron Spelling (Beggar).

Oscar Asche and Otis Skinner both had long associations with *Kismet,* Asche having first played the role of Haji the Poet on the London stage in the spring of 1911, with Otis Skinner doing the part on Broadway later that year. Asche also did the first screen version of KISMET as a silent in 1914 in English, while Otis starred in a 1920 production for Robertson-Cole and, when sound films came into being, repeated the role for First National in 1930, with Loretta Young as his daughter. A German version of that property was also produced in 1930, with Gustav Froehlich starring and William Dieterle directing. All of these productions were based on the Edward Knoblock play of 1911. It was not until the 1944 MGM version, starring Ronald Colman (the Beggar Poet), Marlene Dietrich (Jamilla), James Craig (Caliph) and Edward Arnold (Grand Vizier), that music was added, with two songs by Harold Arlen and E. Y. Harburg: "Willow in the Wind" and "Tell Me, Tell Me,

Evening Star." Costing $3 million, MGM's KISMET was an opulent production, the highlight being Dietrich's dance with her body painted in gold. *Cue* magazine noted, "The picture is escapist, amusing, merry and bubbling with good humor, sparkling with gay good spirits." Today it is shown on TV as ORIENTAL DREAM.

In 1953, Bob Wright and Chet Forrest, who had had great success utilizing the music of Edvard Grieg for the Broadway musical hit (*Song of Norway,* 1944), adapted the music of Russian composer Alexander Borodin for the stage musical, *Kismet.* Alfred Drake, Doretta Morrow and Joan Diener starred in the Tony-Award winning musical which ran for 583 performances in New York. Arthur Freed's musical film unit at MGM purchased the screen rights to *Kismet* and brought it to the screen with Howard Keel, Ann Blyth, Vic Damone and Dolores Gray.

In old Persia, street beggar-magician Hajj (Keel) has tricked a brigand (Jay C. Flippen) out of one hundred gold pieces and goes on a spending spree with his lovely daughter Marsinah (Blyth). Thereafter, he is arrested by the corrupt Wazir (Sebastian Cabot), who knows that Hajj is a thief, and Hajj is sentenced to lose his hands. The trickster poet, however, convinces the Wazir and his sultry wife Lalume (Dolores Gray) that he has magical powers. He is commissioned by the conniving Wazir to prevent a marriage between the Caliph (Vic Damone) and a new romantic interest. Hajj agrees, not knowing that the sweetheart is really Marsinah, who in turn thinks her beloved is really a gardener. Later, after a series of mix-ups, the poet kills the evil Vizier but is arrested by the Caliph's men. The Caliph, however, pardons him when he finds out he is Marsinah's father and that he has rid the land of the terrible Vizier. The poet is made a real prince on condition that he leave Bagdad. The Caliph plans to wed Marsinah, and Hajj takes Lalume with him when he leaves the city.

Of the original score, "He's in Love" and "Was I Wazir?" were deleted and the composers wrote "Bored" especially for the movie. The latter number was sung heartily by the much underrated Dolores Gray, who added the primary sparkle to this movie. She also enlivened a duet ("Rahadlakum") with Keel and soloed the very jaunty "Not Since Ninevah." Keel excelled as the roguish street beggar-poet and handled such numbers as "Fate," "Gesticulate" (in which he wittily pleads to save his hands from being chopped off), and the sonorous "Sands of Time." Blyth solos on "Baubles, Bangles and Beads," while Damone handles "Night of My Night" and Keel, Blyth and Damone perform "And This Is My Beloved" together.

Despite the material at hand and the bolstering performances of Keel and Gray, the movie was a great disappointment. Blyth and Damone were blah at best. *Harrison's Reports* noted that the picture was, ". . . Handicapped by excessive dialogue that, though humorous in spots, is not always interesting and slows down the action considerably." The *New York Times* confirmed, "But for all the opulence and some fitful humor in the Charles Lederer-Luther Davis revamping of their stage hit, the going gets ponderous."

What went wrong with the seemingly foolproof material? Director Vincente Minnelli had not wanted to do this screen musical, feeling it alien to his taste. He conceded to pressure because he hoped to make LUST FOR LIFE (1956) and this was the price for being given that screen biography of Vincent Van Gogh. Minnelli later admitted, "The cast tried hard. The whole enterprise sank. The experience taught me never again to accept an assignment when I lacked enthusiasm for it." Stanley Donen was brought in for some uncredited scene direction to help salvage the movie after Minnelli rushed off to France to begin location shooting on LUST FOR LIFE. The CinemaScope, color production cost $2,692,960 and grossed only $2,920,000 in distributors' domestic film rentals.

Kismet would emerge as an ABC-TV special (October 24, 1967) starring Jose Ferrer, Anna Marie Alberghetti, George Chakiris and Barbara Eden. It would be reworked into a black motif and presented on Broadway as the musical *Timbuktu!* (1978), starring Eartha Kitt, William Marshall, Melba Moore and Gilbert Price.

KISS ME KATE (Metro-Goldwyn-Mayer, 1953) Color 109 minutes.

Producer, Jack Cummings; director, George Sidney; based on the musical play by Cole Porter, Samuel Spewack, Bella Spewack, as adapted from the play *The Taming of the Shrew* by William Shakespeare; screenplay, Dorothy Kingsley; art directors, Cedric Gibbons, Urie McCleary; set decorators, Edwin B. Willis, Richard Pefferle; costumes, Walter Plunkett; music directors, Andre Previn, Saul Chaplin; choreographer, Hermes Pan; camera, Charles Rosher; editor, Ralph E. Winters.

Songs: "So In Love," "I Hate Men," "Wunderbar," "Were Thine That Special Face," "Tom, Dick and Harry," "From This Moment On," "Too Darn Hot," "I've Come to Wive It Wealthily in Padua," "Where Is the Life that Late I Led?" "We Open in Venice," "Always True to You Darling in My Fashion," "Brush Up Your Shakespeare," "Kiss Me Kate," "Why Can't You Behave?" (Cole Porter).

Kathryn Grayson (Lilli Vanessi/Katherine); Howard Keel (Fred Graham/Petruchio); Ann Miller (Lois Lane/Bianca); Tommy

Rall (Bill Calhoun/Lucentio); Bobby Van (Gremio); Keenan Wynn (Lippy); James Whitmore (Slug); Kurt Kasznar (Baptista); Bob Fosse (Hortensio); Ron Randell (Cole Porter); Willard Parker (Tex Callaway); Dave O'Brien (Ralph); Claud Allister (Paul); Ann Codee (Suzanne); Carol Haney, Jeanne Coyne (Specialty Dancers); Hermes Pan (Specialty, Sailor Dance); Ted Ecklelberry (Nathaniel); Mitchell Lewis (Stage Doorman).

One of the most spirited screen musicals of the 1950s or any decade is KISS ME KATE. Cole Porter's stage musical, based on William Shakespeare's *The Taming of the Shrew,* opened on Broadway late in 1948 and ran for 1,070 performances, starring Alfred Drake, Patricia Morison and Lisa Kirk. It won the Tony Award for the year's best musical and in 1953 MGM brought the production to the screen as the only musical ever to be filmed in 3-D (although most engagements projected it in a standard, flat version).

Fred Graham (Howard Keel), the director-star of a musical version of *The Taming of the Shrew,* tricks his tempestuous ex-wife Lilli Vanessi (Kathryn Grayson) into starring in the production by telling her that glamorous Lois Lane (Ann Miller) is slated for the key part. Both women end up in the show, with manipulative Graham keeping them competing with each other. Through a chain of mistakes, Lilli thinks Fred is in love with her again (which he is), but then she becomes jealous of his attention to Lois. In actuality, Lois is in love with cast member-dancer Bill Calhoun (Tommy Rall), who owes gangster Lippy (Keenan Wynn) a large sum of money. The upset Lilli plans to walk out of the show to marry a rich Texan (Willard Parker), but she is stopped by hoodlums Lippy and Slug (James Whitmore), who have appeared to collect Bill's debt. Meanwhile, the show goes on as the principals find their own lives interspersed with those in Shakespeare's comedy. When Lippy is accidentally bumped off, Bill's debt is cancelled. Bill vows to reform and marry Lois. Fred and Lilli realize they are still in love.

Initially MGM producer Jack Cummings had hoped to star Laurence Olivier in the lead role and to dub his voice for the singing sequences. Instead he re-teamed Howard Keel and Kathryn Grayson, who had already co-starred in the studio's SHOW BOAT (1951), *q.v.,* and LOVELY TO LOOK AT (1952).* While such

*KISS ME KATE was Kathryn Grayson's fifteenth and final musical at MGM, where she had been since 1941. In the early 1950s she had left the studio under a four-picture deal at Warner Bros. However, she departed that lot after two assignments—THE DESERT SONG (1953), and SO THIS IS LOVE (1953), *qq.v.*—and returned to MGM for her swan song there.

numbers as "I Sing of Love," "Bianca" and "I Am Ashamed That Women Are So Simple" were cut from the movie score, "From This Moment On" was added—a deleted song from Cole Porter's 1950 stage musical, *Out of This World.* For many, the highlight of KISS ME KATE was Ann Miller's terrific "Too Darn Hot" dance/song. However, there are other sparkling musical moments: Keel and Grayson dueting "So in Love" and "Wunderbar," Grayson's mocking "I Hate Men!" and Keel's swaggering rendition of "Where Is the Life That Late I Led?" Not to be overlooked is the comic number, "Brush Up Your Shakespeare," done by the cast's two Damon Runyonesque performers (Wynn, Whitmore). Equally impressive is the fine choreography of Hermes Pan (who appears in one dance scene) and its vivid interpretation by Miller, Tommy Rall, Bobby Van and Bob Fosse. In the dancing chorus were Carol Haney—who later starred on Broadway in *The Pajama Game* (1954)—and Jeanne Coyne who later married Gene Kelly.

The *New York Times* alerted, "Forget two things—an extremely messy, lumbering start and the constant jump of on-stage to backstage continuity of the plot—and you'll find a movie version that does Cole Porter's grand Broadway musical full justice. . . . The prankish spirit of the original is here, so are most of the dazzling Porter tunes . . . along with a splendid color production." In retrospect, Richard Oliver would state in the liner notes for a reissue of the MGM soundtrack album, "KISS ME KATE is a magnificent example of what movies can do with a Broadway show. It remains fresh and alive with enthusiasm and retains the flavor of the original while adding its own luster. The movie will not likely be forgotten." He also pointed out, "With KISS ME KATE, it was evident that Ann Miller had come a long way in films. Always providing zing, pzazz, and fun in her roles, she was usually cast as a not particularly bright character who had a healthy yearning for the opposite sex, especially if they were rich. In KISS ME KATE, her role had more dimension but still gave her ample opportunity to flash. . . ."

KISS ME KATE was Oscar-nominated for Best Scoring but lost to CALL ME MADAM (Alfred Newman), *q.v.*

LA BAMBA (Columbia, 1987) Color 108 minutes.

Executive producer, Stuart Benjamin; producers, Taylor Hackford, Bill Borden; associate producer, Daniel Valdez; director/screenplay, Luis Valdez; production designer, Vince Cresciman; set decorator, Rosemary Brandenburg; costumes, Sylvia

Joe Pantoliano and Lou Diamond Phillips in LA BAMBA (1987).

Vega-Vasquez; makeup, Richard Arrington; music, Carlos Santana, Miles Goodman; executive music producer, Joel Sill; supervising music editor, Curt Sobel; choreographer, Miguel Delgado; assistant directors, Stephen J. Fisher, Michael Katleman, Richard Graves; sound, Susumu Tokunow; sound re-recording, Donald O. Mitchell, Rick Kline, Kevin O'Connell; supervising sound editors, Fred Judkins, Tom C. McCarthy; special effects, Filmtrix, Inc. miniatures, Sessums & Slagle; camera, Adam Greenberg; second unit camera, Chuck Colwell; editors, Sheldon Kahn, Don Brochu.

Songs: "Rip It Up" (John Marascalco, Robert A. Blackwell); "Charlena" (Herman B. Chaney, Manuel G. Chavez); "Goodnight My Love" (George Motola, Marascalco); "Oh Boy" (Sunny West, Bill Tilghman, Norman Petty); "Framed" (Jerry Leiber, Mike Stoller); "We Belong Together" (S. Weiss, R. Carr, J. Mitchell); "Ooh! My Head," "The Paddi Wack Song," "Come On, Let's Go," "Donna" (Ritchie Valens); "La Bamba" (arranged/adapted by Valens); "Pajaro Loco," "Abuelitos Cortos," "Bakersfield Shuffle" (Los Lobos); "Cancion Mixteca" (Joseph Lopez Alvarez); "Who Do You Love?" (E. McDaniel); "Summertime Blues" (Eddie Cochran, Jerry Capehart); "Lonely Teardrops" (Berry Gordy, Tyran Carlo, Gwen Gordy); "Crying, Waiting, Hoping" (Buddy Holly); "Sleepwalk" (Santo Farina, Johnny Farina, Ann Farina); "I Got a Gal

Named Sue (That's My Little Suzie)" (Valens, Robert Kuhn, Arthur Brooks, Richard Brooks); "Ready Teddy" (Marascalco, Robert A. Blackwell); "Don't You Just Know It" (Huey P. Smith); "This I Swear" (Joseph Rock, Lennie Martin, James Beaumont, Janet Vogel, Joseph Verscharen, Walter Lester, John Taylor); "Blue Tango" (Leroy Anderson); "Chantilly Lace" (J. P. Richardson); "Betty Jean" (E. Anderson); "Tweedlee Dee" (Winfield Scott); "Smoke Gets in Your Eyes" (Jerome Kern, Otto Harbach); "Over the Mountain, Across the Sea" (Rex Garvin); "Armida," "Corrido del Compadre" (Daniel Valdez).

Lou Diamond Phillips (Ritchie Valens [Ricardo Valenzuela]); Esai Morales (Bob Morales); Rosana DeSoto (Connie Valenzuela); Elizabeth Pena (Rosie); Danielle von Zerneck (Donna Ludwig); Joe Pantoliano (Bob Keene); Rick Dees (Ted Quillin); Marshall Crenshaw (Buddy Holly); Howard Huntsberry (Jackie Wilson); Brian Setzer (Eddie Cochran); Daniel Valdez (Lelo); Felipe Cantu (Curandero); Eddie Frias (Chinbo); Mike Moroff (Mexican Ed); Geoffrey Rivas (Rudy Castro); Sam Anderson (Mr. Ludwig); Maggie Gwinn (Mrs. Ludwig); Jeffrey Alan Chandler (Alan Freed); Stephen Lee (Big Bopper); John Quade (Bartender); Lettie Ibarra (Vera); Diane Rodriquez (Ernestine); Kati Valdez (Connie, Jr.); Gloria Balcorta (Irma); Ernesto Hernandez (Garbage Man); Noble Willingham (Howard); Thom Pintello (Sound Engineer); Stephen Schmidt (Tommy Allsup); Rosanna Locke (Sharon Sheeley); Kim Sebastian (Donna's Girlfriend); Dyana Ortelli (Rosalinda); Andy Griggs (Mr. House); Art Koustik (Trucker); Tony Genaro (Mr. Caballero); Allison Robinson (Girl at Party); Hunter Payne (Baseball Announcer); Joe Miller. Maryann Tanedo, Barb Jittner, Brian Russell (Students); Los Lobos (Singing Voice of Ritchie Valens).

Ritchie Valens (1942–59) was only seventeen when he was killed in a plane crash on February 3, 1959 along with Buddy Holly and "The Big Bopper" (Jape Richardson), with whom he was touring. In his less than two years as a musical star Valens had hit records for the Del-Fi label with his self-penned "Donna," "Come On, Let's Go" and "La Bamba," along with an appearance in the movie GO, JOHNNY GO (1959). Over the years a coterie of avid followers kept Valens' memory alive and in 1987 his unpretentious biopic, LA BAMBA, was produced on a $6.5 million budget. It became one of the year's top grossers with distributors' domestic film rentals of $54.2 million, and revitalized interest in Valens' music, which was performed in the film by Los Lobos and his band.

Young Ricardo Valenzuela (Lou Diamond Phillips) works with his fruit-harvesting family in Northern California and exists with them in a tent in the run-down barrio. He then relocates with his mother (Rosana DeSoto), his sisters and ex-convict half-brother Bob Morales (Esai Morales) to Pacoima, in the San Fernando Valley outside of Los Angeles. Bob soon starts a romance with Ricardo's platonic friend Rosie (Elizabeth Pena). Ricardo attends high school and begins performing with his guitar. He falls in love with wealthy white girl Donna Ludwig (Danielle von Zerneck) but her bigoted family forbids the mixed ethnic romance. As a result the lovelorn Ricardo composes the song "Donna." In-person and television appearances bring recognition to the young Hispanic singer, who has now changed his name to Ritchie Valens. However, his half-brother Bob Morales (Esai Morales), a drug dealing, motorcycle gang member and ex-convict, arrives on the scene and seduces Donna. He makes a shambles of Ritchie's first major concert. With the aid of manager Bob Keene (Joe Pantoliano), the young man appears on Dick Clark's "American Bandstand" TV show and lands a place with Alan Freed's touring rock 'n' roll show. This leads to national stardom, his most popular number being his rendition of the traditional Mexican song, "La Bamba." From there he travels with Buddy Holly (Marshall Crenshaw), until the fatal air crash that claims his life on February 3, 1959 as they head from Iowa to North Dakota. Ironically he had always had a phobia about flying. Valens is buried in the San Fernando Mission Cemetery. On May 11, 1990 Ritchie Valens received a star on the Hollywood Boulevard Walk of Fame.

"As an exercise in traditional bio-pic embalming, this story of a teenage idol who was famous for just eight months has only one potentially unique angle; the fact that Valens was a Mexican who escaped from the fruit-picking ghetto of the barrio to succeed in the white-dominated world of rock 'n' roll. . . . The fresh-faced Lou Diamond Phillips mimes to Los Lobos' remarkably authentic-sounding cover versions of Valens' original recordings, and manages to play the singer as innocent rather than insipid . . ." (Nigel Floyd, British *Monthly Film Bulletin*). Roger Ebert (*Movie Home Companion,* 1989) assessed, "This is a good small movie, sweet and sentimental. . . . The best things in it are the most unexpected things: the portraits of everyday life, of a loving mother, of a brother who loves and resents him, of a kid growing up and tasting fame and leaving everyone standing around at this funeral shocked that his life ended just as it seemed to be beginning."

LA BAMBA was released in a trio of versions: English, Spanish, and one subtitled in Spanish.

LADY AND THE TRAMP (Buena Vista, 1955) Color 75 minutes.

Producer, Walt Disney; directors, Hamilton Luske, Clyde Geronimi, Wilfred Jackson; based on the novel by Ward Greene;

screenplay, Erdman Penner, Joe Rinaldi, Ralph Wright, Donald DeGradi; music, Oliver Wallace; animation directors, Milt Kahl, Franklin Thomas, Oliver Johnston, Jr., John Lounsbery, Wolfgang Reitherman, Eric Larson, Hal King, Les Clark; animators: George Nicholas, Hal Ambro, Ken O'Brien, Jerry Hathcock, Erik Cleworth, Marvin Woodward, Ed Aardal, John Sibley, Harvey Toombs, Cliff Nordberg, Don Lusk, George Kreisl, Hugh Fraser, John Freeman, Jack Campbell, Bob Carson; backgrounds: Claude Coats, Dick Anthony, Ralph Hulett, Albert Dempster, Thelma Witmer, Eyvind Earle, Jimi Trout, Ray Huffine, Brice Mack; layouts: Ken Anderson, Tom Codrick, Al Zinnen, A. Kendall O'Connor, Hugh Hennesy, Lance Nolley, Jacques Rupp, McLaren Stewart, Don Griffith, Thor Putnam, Collin Campbell, Victor Haboush, Bill Boesche; effects animation, George Rowley, Dan McManus; editor, Don Halliday.

Songs: "He's a Tramp," "La La Lu," "Siamese Cat Song," "Peace on Earth," "Bella Notte" (Sonny Burke, Peggy Lee).

Voices of: Peggy Lee (Darling/Peg/Si/Am); Barbara Luddy (Lady); Larry Roberts (Tramp); Bill Thompson (Jock/Bull/Dachsie); Bill Baucon (Trusty); Stan Freberg (Beaver); Verna Felton (Aunt Sarah); Alan Reed (Boris); George Givot (Tony); Dallas McKennon (Toughy/Professor); Lee Millar (Jim Dear); and: The Mello Men.

An endearing Walt Disney animated classic, the meticulously produced LADY AND THE TRAMP cost $4 million to make and has since grossed $40,249,000 in distributors' domestic film rentals. It remains a favorite via theatrical reissues and videocassette packaging. With songs by Peggy Lee (who also provides a quartet of voices for the feature) and Sonny Burke, the movie contains such memorable tunes as "He's a Tramp," "The Siamese Cat Song" and the very popular "Bella Notte." Leonard Maltin said of the feature in *The Disney Films* (1973), ". . . [It] is a well-thought-out, enjoyable cartoon feature, not as compelling as many earlier works, but certainly more handsome than some, due in large part to Disney's decision to make the film in Cinema-Scope. Thus, an added emphasis was given to the layout and design departments to create a succession of picturesque backgrounds against which the story could be played."

On Christmas Day in 1910 Jim Dear (voice of Lee Millar) gives his wife Darling (voice of Peggy Lee) a prim cocker spaniel puppy named Lady (voice of Barbara Luddy) as a pet. The three are very happy until Darling has a baby and Lady feels neglected. However, she is comforted by stray mutt Tramp (voice of Larry Roberts) whom Lady, along with neighborhood dog pals Jock (voice of Bill

Thompson) and Trusty (voice of Bill Baucon), had snubbed. Soon, though, the family shows Lady that she is not forgotten and all is peaceful again. Then trouble erupts when Jim and Darling leave for a trip and Aunt Sarah (voice of Verna Felton) arrives with her two Siamese cats, all of whom take a dislike to Lady. When Aunt Sarah muzzles her, Lady breaks loose and runs away. Again she is befriended by Tramp, who treats her to a spaghetti dinner behind Tony's (voice of George Givot) restaurant. The next day the two dogs end up in the pound. Aunt Sarah arrives, takes Lady home and chains her in the backyard. Tramp arrives and sees a large rat enter the house. He and Lady stop it from bothering the baby, but Tramp is accused of attacking the child. Jim and Darling arrive back home just as the dogcatcher takes Tramp away. They rescue him and he and Lady raise a family.

LADY BE GOOD (Metro-Goldwyn-Mayer, 1941) 110 minutes.

Producer, Arthur Freed; director, Norman Z. McLeod; story, Jack McGowan; screenplay, McGowan, Kay Van Riper, John McClain, (uncredited): Ralph Spence, Arnold Auerback, Herman Wouk, Robert McGunigle, Vincente Minnelli; art directors, Cedric Gibbons, John S. Detlie; set decorators, Edwin B. Willis, Merrill Pye; gowns, Adrian; music continuity (for Eleanor Powell numbers), Walter Ruick; vocal/orchestrators, Conrad Salinger, Leo Arnaud, George Bassman; musical numbers staged by Busby Berkeley; sound supervisor, Douglas Shearer; camera, Oliver T. Marsh, George Folsey; editor, Frederick Y. Smith.

Songs: "So Am I," "Oh, Lady Be Good," "Fascinating Rhythm," "Hang on to Me" (George Gershwin, Ira Gershwin); "You'll Never Know," "Saudades" (Roger Edens); "Your Words and My Music" (Arthur Freed, Edens); "The Last Time I Saw Paris" (Oscar Hammerstein, II, Jerome Kern); "Alone" (Nacio Herb Brown, Freed).

Eleanor Powell (Marilyn Marsh); Ann Sothern (Dixie Donegan); Robert Young (Eddie Crane); Lionel Barrymore (Judge Murdock); John Carroll (Buddy Crawford); Red Skelton (Joe "Red" Willet); Virginia O'Brien (Lull); Tom Conway (Mr. Blanton); Dan Dailey, Jr. (Bill Pattison); Reginald Owen (Max Milton); Rose Hobart (Mrs. Carter Wardley); Phil Silvers (Master of Ceremonies); The Berry Brothers (Themselves); Connie Russell (Singer); Edward Gargan (Policeman); Doris Day (Debutante).

George and Ira Gershwin's *Lady, Be Good!* was one of the most popular of Jazz Age musicals, opening on Broadway late in 1924 for a 330-performance run. The show launched the careers of Fred and Adele Astaire and Cliff Edwards as well as introducing such popular standards as the title song, "Fascinatin' Rhythm," "Hang on to Me" and "The Man I Love." (The last-named number was dropped from the show before it debuted, only to become a hit later in the decade.) First National Pictures filmed Guy Bolton's plot for LADY BE GOOD as a silent in 1928 with Jack Mulhall and Dorothy Mackaill. As a musical, the property did not reach the screen until the summer of 1941. By then, the plotline and most of the songs were gone. (MGM had paid Warner Bros. $61,500 just for the use of the title!)

Former waitress Dixie Donegan (Ann Sothern) meets unsuccessful composer Eddie Crane (Robert Young) and the two fall in love and marry. After Eddie and Dixie collaborate on songs and become a success in Tin Pan Alley, Eddie turns loafish and takes up with the society set. He and Dixie argue and divorce. The two are then reunited and retie the marital knot, only to have a falling out again and file for divorce. This time their domestic bliss is restored by the perceptive judge (Lionel Barrymore) who handled their first divorce hearing. Also involved are Dixie's dancer pal Marilyn Marsh (Eleanor Powell), goofy song plugger Joe "Red" Willet (Red Skelton) and handsome singer Buddy Crawford (John Carroll).

Although MGM dancing star Eleanor Powell was top-featured in the cast, her role was not integral to the storyline. She was on hand to perform three of her slick tap routines. The most rewarding was the intricate "Fascinatin' Rhythm" as staged by Busby Berkeley, who had originally been scheduled to direct the movie (until Eleanor Powell and Ann Sothern vetoed that). The "Fascinatin' Rhythm" number involved over eighty male dancers in white ties and tails, several grand pianos, as well as singer Connie Russell and the dancing Berry Brothers. Berkeley would recall years later, "She started the dance in front of a huge silver-beaded curtain, which circled to the left in a zig-zag course disclosing, on five-foot-high platforms, one grand piano after another. Eleanor followed and as the curtain circled each piano, a high lift would move in, pick up the platform with the piano on it, and pull it back out of the way of the camera boom which was following Eleanor as she danced. All of this was filmed in one continuous shot until the last piano disappeared and the moving curtain revealed Eleanor in a huge circular set surrounded by the hundred boys, with a full orchestra in the background. Toward the end of this number, the boys would throw Eleanor like a pendulum down through the tunnel they formed, ending with a big close-up of her at the end of the shot."

Made at a cost of $863,460, LADY BE GOOD grossed $1,692,000 in its initial release. "The Last Time I Saw Paris," one of the new songs for the movie (by Oscar Hammerstein, II and Jerome Kern) won an Academy Award as Best Song in a Musical Picture. The touching (and patriotic—it was World War II and Paris had fallen to the Germans) melody was performed effectively by Ann Sothern. Sothern, too infrequently allowed to step away from bread-and-butter entries (especially her "Maisie" comedy series), would next appear in the Arthur Freed-produced MGM musical, PANAMA HATTIE (1942), *q.v.* Eleanor Powell and rising screen comedian Red Skelton would be re-teamed by the studio for SHIP AHOY (1942) and I DOOD IT (1943).

THE LADY DANCES *see* THE MERRY WIDOW (1934).

LADY IN THE DARK (Paramount, 1944) Color 100 minutes.

Executive producer, Buddy G. DeSylva; associate producer, Richard Blumenthal; director, Mitchell Leisen; based on the musical play by Moss Hart, Kurt Weill, Ira Gershwin; screenplay, Frances Goodrich, Albert Hackett, (uncredited) Leisen; art directors, Hans Dreier, Raoul Pene du Bois; set decorator, Ray Moyer; costumes, du Bois, Edith Head, Leisen, Babs Wilmoez; makeup, Wally Westmore; music/music director, Robert Emmett Dolan; music associate, Arthur Franklin; vocal arranger, Joseph J. Lilley; choreographers, Billy Daniels, Don Loper; orchestrator, Robert Russell Bennett; color consultant, Natalie Kalmus; assistant directors, Chico Alonso, Richard McWhorter; sound, Earl Hayman, Walter Oberst; technical effects, Paul Lerpae; special effects, Gordon Jennings; process camera, Farciot Edouart; camera, Ray Rennahan; editor, Alma Macrorie.

Songs: "Girl of the Moment," "One Life to Live," "It Looks Like Liza," "This Is New," "The Saga of Jenny" (Ira Gershwin, Kurt Weill); "Suddenly It's Spring" (Johnny Burke, Jimmy Van Heusen); "Artist's Waltz" (Robert Emmett Dolan); "Dream Lover" (Clifford Grey, Victor Schertzinger).

Ginger Rogers (Liza Elliott); Ray Milland (Charley Johnson); Jon Hall (Randy Curtis); Warner Baxter (Kendall Nesbitt); Barry Sullivan (Dr. Brooks); Mischa Auer (Russell Paxton); Mary Philips (Maggie Grant); Phyllis Brooks (Allison DuBois); Edward Fielding (Dr. Carlton); Don Loper (Adams); Mary Parker (Miss Parker); Catherine Craig (Miss Foster); Marietta Canty (Matha); Virginia Farmer (Miss Edwards); Fay Helm (Miss Bowers); Gail Russell (Barbara at Age Seventeen); Kay Linaker (Liza's Mother); Harvey Stephens (Liza's Father); Rand Brooks (Ben); Pepito Perez (Clown); Charles Smith (Barbara's Boyfriend); Audrey Young, Eleanor DeVan, Jeanne Straser, Lynda Grey, Christopher King,

Maxine Ardell, Alice Kirby, Arlyne Varden, Angela Wilson, Dorothy O'Kelly, Betty Hall, Fran Shore, Louise LaPlanche (Office Girls); Paul Pierce, George Mayon, James Notaro, Jacques Karre, Byron Poindexter, Kit Carson (Specialty Dancers); Bunny Waters, Susan Paley, Dorothy Ford, Mary MacLaren (Models); Paul McVey (Librarian); Marten Lamont, Tristram Alper (Taxi Drivers); Dorothy Granger (Autograph Hunter); Emmett Vogan, Lester Dorr, Grandon Rhodes (Reporters): Johnnie Johnson, John O'Connor, Buster Brodie (Clowns); Herbert Corthell (Senator); Herb Holcomb (Aquatic Clown); Charles Bates (David); Theodore Marc (Daniel Boone Clown); Armand Tanny (Strong Man Clown); Stuart Barlow (Accordion Clown); Leonora Johnson (Bird's Nest Clown); Harry Bayfield (Snow Clown); Larry Rio (Farmer Clown); Buzz Buckley (Freckle-Faced Boy); Priscilla Lyon (Little Girl at Circus); Marjean Neville (Liza at Age Five and Seven); Billy Dawson (Boy at Circus); Billy Daniels (Office Boy); Phyllis M. Brooks (Barbara at Age Seven); Georgia Backus (Miss Sullivan); George Calliga (Captain of Waiters); Frances Robinson (Girl with Randy); Hillary Brooke (Miss Barr); Charles Coleman (Butler); Miriam Franklin (Dancer); Lester Sharpe (Pianist); Bobby Beers (Charley as a Boy); Jan Buckingham (Miss Shawn).

Gertrude Lawrence and Danny Kaye scored a sensation in 1941 in Broadway's *Lady in the Dark,* with book by Moss Hart, music by Kurt Weill and lyrics by Ira Gershwin. The innovative show lasted 467 performances, buoyed by its then avant-garde focus on psychoanalysis and its structural integration of book and songs. Originally the screen rights to the offbeat property were purchased by Alexander Korda, but they were then sold to Paramount Pictures (for nearly $300,000) as a vehicle in a multi-picture pact with Ginger Rogers, who had recently left RKO.* It required nearly two years of struggling to adapt the daring theme to the screen and to render its format conventional enough for consumption by the masses. During the transformation, director Mitchell Leisen abandoned the script devised by Albert Hackett and Frances Goodrich and rewrote it himself, going back to Moss Hart's original. Filming began in December 1942 and was completed in March 1943. During production Ginger Rogers disappeared for a time to marry husband #3. The Technicolor movie, which had become the bane of the Paramount lot, was not released until February 1944.

---

*In RKO's CAREFREE (1938), *q.v.*, with Fred Astaire, Ginger Rogers had kidded the subject of psychiatry, a contrast to LADY IN THE DARK, which was on a far more serious note.

Allure magazine editor Liza Elliott (Ginger Rogers), an efficient but uptight executive, suffers from headaches and continuous daydreams, to the point where she can no longer make decisions on her own. Feeling threatened by her insolent advertising manager Charley Johnson (Ray Milland) and being romanced by old friend Kendall Nesbitt (Warner Baxter) and a younger man, Randy Curtis (Jon Hall), she goes to psychiatrist Dr. Brooks (Barry Sullivan). Dr. Brooks helps Liza to understand that she is suffering from psychosomatic problems. She has three dreams: dream one in blue, another in gold and the third in a circus. After the dreams, she realizes that Charley is not really a threat to her and does not want to take her away from her work. They fall in love.

On its own, with its submerged theme of an Electra complex, its highly symbolized dream sequences and its unique Kurt Weill melodies, LADY IN THE DARK was incapable of appealing to the average moviegoer of the day. However, relying on the presence of Oscar-winner Ginger Rogers,* three popular leading men, bright Technicolor and gorgeous costumes, LADY IN THE DARK disguised its true self to a degree. Thus the *Los Angeles Times* could judge, "Put LADY IN THE DARK down as unique in the annals of the movies. It is one of the few attepts successfully to analyze mental processes, and the result is gaudy, glamorous and glittery."

In actuality, LADY IN THE DARK is a gaudy abortion, a mongrel adaptation of a Broadway classic that beneath the surface was unsatisfactory film fare. The focal Weill-Gershwin song "My Ship," from the Broadway score, was excised from the movie because Paramount executive producer Buddy G. DeSylva, himself a songwriter, did not like Weill's style and was upset that the movie (and this song) referred to the leading lady's mental aberrations. Added to the film were "Suddenly It's Spring," a new song by Johnny Burke and Jimmy Van Heusen; the musical interlude, "Artist's Waltz," by Robert Emmett Dolan; and the old chestnut, "Dream Lover," by Victor Schertzinger and Clifford Grey. The most elaborate and lively production is the climactic circus sequence in which Rogers sings "The Saga of Jenny," while in the process of unleashing some of her inhibitions. One of the great assets of the stage version had been Danny Kaye's hyperactive

---

*In *Hollywood Director* (1973), David Chierichetti interviewed Ray Milland about the creatively abortive LADY IN THE DARK: "Can you imagine anything more inappropriate than Ginger Rogers playing a Moss Hart script? . . . This was way beyond her. . . . All the time we were filming, I tried to be very philosophical. I kept saying to myself, 'Make the best of it. This too shall pass.' I did my own singing of the Circus dream, and of course I couldn't sing, although I'd been a good singer when I was a child. I kept thinking 'This too shall pass,' and I plunged in and did it."

performance as the chauffeur-photographer Russell Paxton, who had the show-stopping, tongue-twisting song, "Tchaikowsky." Mischa Auer played the role on screen in a far tamer variation and with the word-spewing song deleted.

In retrospect, Ted Sennett (*Hollywood Musicals,* 1981) judged of LADY IN THE DARK, "With Ginger Rogers solemn and grim-visaged . . . this film confined its musical sections to garish visualizations of Rogers's dreams. Her rendition of 'The Saga of Jenny,' the unfortunate lady who '*would* make up her mind,' was merely adequate. Mitchell Leisen directed with a heavy hand."

LADY IN THE DARK was Oscar-nominated for Best Interior Decoration—Color and Best Scoring of a Musical Picture.

This musical, whose once topical theme has become increasingly dated, has been revived many times over the decades. One of the more entertaining versions was done as a ninety-minute color special on NBC-TV (September 24, 1954) starring Ann Sothern and James Daly.

LADY SINGS THE BLUES (Paramount, 1972) Color 144 minutes.

Executive producer, Berry Gordy; producers, Jay Weston, James S. White; director, Sidney J. Furie; based on the book by Billie Holiday, William Duffy; screenplay, Terence McCloy, Chris Clark, Suzanne De Passe; production designer, Carl Anderson; set decorator, Reg Allen; costumes, Bob Mackie, Ray Aghayan, Norma Koch; makeup, Don Schoenfeld; music, Michel Legrand; assistant director, Charles Washburn; camera, John A. Alonzo; editor, Argyle Nelson.

Songs: "Lady Sings the Blues" (Billie Holiday, H. Nichols); "T'Ain't Nobody's Bizness If I Do" (Porter Grainger, Graham Prince, Clarence Williams); "All of Me" (Seymour Simons, Gerald Marks); "The Man I Love," "Our Love Is Here to Stay" (George Gershwin, Ira Gershwin); "Them There Eyes" (Maceo Pinkard, William Tracy, Doris Tauber); "I Cried for You" (Abe Lyman, Gus Arnheim, Arthur Freed); "Mean to Me" (Roy Turk, Fred Ahlert); "What a Little Moonlight Can Do" (Harry Woods); "Lover Man (Oh Where Can You Be?)" (Jimmy Davis, Jimmy Sherman, Roger "Ram" Ramirez); "You've Changed" (Bill Carey, Carl Fischer); "Gimme a Pigfoot and a Boot of Beer" ("Kid" Wesley, "Sox" Wilson); "Good Morning Heartache" (Irene Higginbotham, Ervin Drake, Dan Fisher); "My Man" (Maurice Yvain; English lyrics, Channing Pollock); "Strange Fruit" (Lewis Allan); "God Bless the Child," "Don't Explain" (Holiday, Arthur Herzog, Jr.).

Diana Ross (Billie Holiday); Billy Dee Williams (Louis

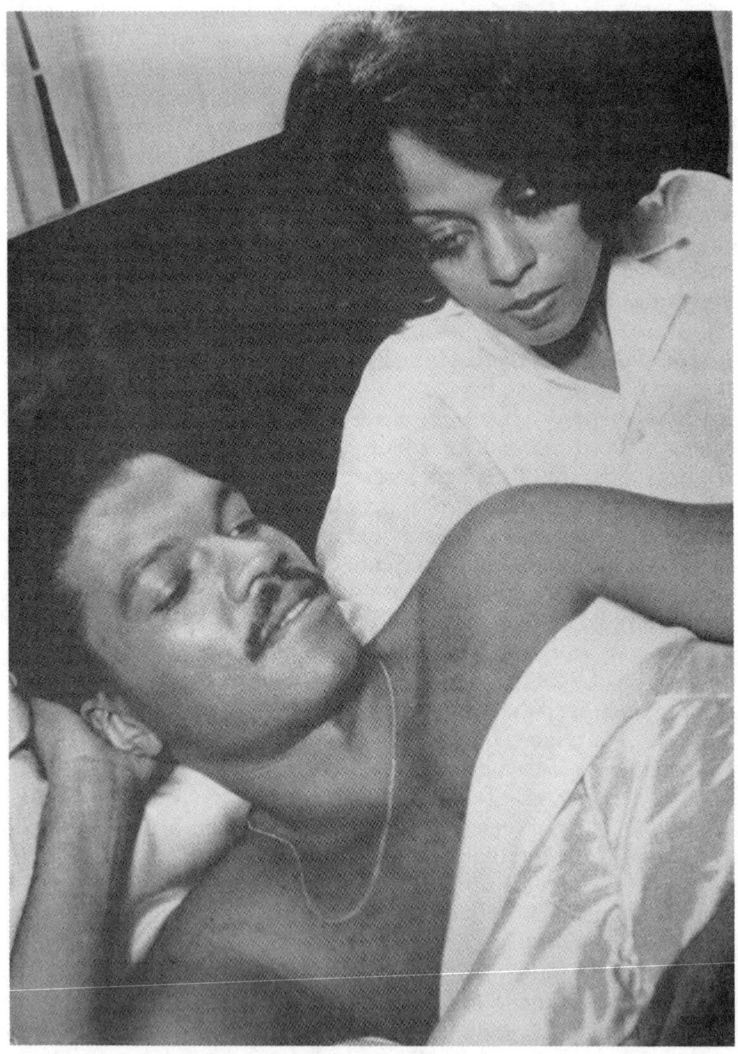

Billy Dee Williams and Diana Ross in LADY SINGS THE BLUES (1972).

McKay); Richard Pryor (Piano Man); James Callahan (Reg Hanley); Paul Hampton (Harry); Sid Melton (Jerry); Virginia Capers (Mama Holiday); Yvonne Fair (Yvonne); Scatman Crothers (Big Ben); Robert L. Gordy (Hawk); Harry Caesar (The Rapist); Milton Selzer (The Doctor); Ned Glass (The Agent); Paulene Myers (Mrs. Edson); Isabel Sanford (First Madame); Tracee Lyles (Whore); Norman Bartold (Detective); and: Michelle Aller, Denise Denise, Larry Duran, Jester Hairston, Lynn Hamilton, Byron Kane, Bert Kramer, Helen Lewis, Kay Lewis, Don McGovern, Shirley Melline, Paul Micale, Barbara Minkus, Victor Morosco, Dick Poston, Toby Russ, Ernie Robinson, Clay Tanner, Charles Woolf, George Wyner.

The cool on-the-surface, yet burning-within Billie Holiday (1915–1959) was a highly respected jazz vocalist known as "Lady Day." Her tragic life story, *Lady Sings the Blues* (1956), written with William Duffy, recounted not only her tremendous ups and down in show business and an essentially unhappy personal life, but also detailed her many bouts with drug addiction. The flamboyant Diana Ross, after breaking away from The Supremes and becoming a highly successful solo artist, made her solo film debut in the title role of the biopic, LADY SINGS THE BLUES. Her multi-dimensional performance earned her an Academy Award nomination as Best Actress. The musical film, which greatly distorted the facts of Holiday's seamy, sorrowful life, grossed $9,666,000 in distributors' domestic film rentals. It had a very well received soundtrack album (twenty-four weeks on *Billboard* magazine's hits chart) and successfully revived interest in the legendary Billie Holiday.*

In the 1930s, young Billie Holiday (Diana Ross) is growing up a poor child in the black ghetto of Baltimore. After she is raped by a drunk (Harry Caesar), her mother (Virginia Capers) sends her north to Harlem to live with a friend (Isabel Sanford) who, unbeknownst to her friend, runs a brothel. Billie soon works as a maid there, and later becomes one of the establishment's girls. Attracted to singing from an early age, Billie gains some recognition by performing for club owner Jerry (Sid Melton) in Gotham and then touring with bandleader Reg Hanley (James Callahan). Bandsman Harry (Paul Hampton) gets her hooked on drugs. With the aid of her agent (Ned Glass), Billie becomes a noted singer and is accompanied by her jivey musician pal, Piano Man (Richard Pryor), who also procures dope for her. Billie meets, falls in love with and marries freewheeling, free-loving Louis McKay (Billy Dee

*The soundtrack album to LADY SINGS THE BLUES remained on *Billboard* magazine's charts for twenty-four weeks, rising to #1 position for two weeks.

Williams). However, the pressures of her career and her drug addiction doom the union. Eventually, Billie is arrested for possession of drugs and Piano Man is murdered by thugs who demand that he pay for the dope he acquired for his employer. After years of hardships, Billie becomes the first black to perform at New York's Carnegie Hall. Afterwards, she fails in her latest attempt to obtain a Gotham work permit (because of her time in jail on a drug charge) and she dies in obscurity.

Variety reported that LADY SINGS THE BLUES contained: ". . . Excellent casting, handsome '30s physical values, and a script which is far better in dialog than structure." Regarding the movie's music, the reviewer noted, "A dozen or so of Miss Holiday's most remembered songs are included, all introduced logically (if anachronistically) and very neatly interpreted by Miss Ross with adroit overtones of Miss Holiday. What is lacking, however, is quality and calibre in the period music." John Douglas Eames (*The Paramount Story,* 1985) decided, "Sidney J. Furie's direction and . . . the production . . . combined to cast a glamorous, romantic aura over a story . . . requiring gritty realism. The result ranked among biofilms of addicted stars somewhere between the high of I'LL CRY TOMORROW [1955, *q.v.*] and the low of THE HELEN MORGAN STORY [1957, *q.v.*], but even the former was surpassed as a box-office success." The editors of *Consumer Guide* and Philip J. Kaplan wrote in *The Best, The Worst and The Most Unusual: Hollywood Musicals* (1983), "Though Ross is an excellent actress, the true mark of her success in the film is her singing. She evokes Holiday's style without imitating her, and captures the screen with every song." Donald Bogle in *Blacks in American Films and Television* judged, "The film simplifies the complex, irons out the complications to give a straightforward, conventional narrative and characters everyone can easily understand. . . . [Yet] LADY SINGS THE BLUES succeeded on another level, one that might well have pleased Lady Day herself: as lush, romantic reverie. There had never been (still has not been) a black movie like it."

In addition to Ross's Oscar bid (she lost to Liza Minnelli of CABARET, *q.v.*), LADY SINGS THE BLUES won Academy Award nominations for its Scoring, Screenplay, Art Direction-Set Decoration, and Costume Design. Despite such a promising beginning, Diana Ross made few motion pictures after LADY SINGS THE BLUES. After playing the lead in THE WIZ (1978), *q.v.,* she abandoned filmmaking altogether.

LADY SINGS THE BLUES was packaged as a film project by Berry Gordy's Motown Records, for which Diana Ross then recorded.

LES GIRLS (Metro-Goldwyn-Mayer, 1957) Color 114 minutes.

Producer, Sol C. Siegel; associate producer, Saul Chaplin; director, George Cukor; story, Vera Caspary; screenplay, John Patrick; art directors, William A. Horning, Gene Allen; set decorator, Edwin B. Willis; costumes, Orry-Kelly; music director, Adolph Deutsch; music adaptor/conductor, Adolph Deutsch; orchestrators, Alexander Courage, Skip Martin; choreographer, Jack Cole; camera, Robert Surtees; editor, Ferris Webster.

Songs: "Les Girls," "You're Just Too, Too," "Ca C'est L'Amour," "Ladies in Waiting," "Why Am I So Gone about That Gal?" (Cole Porter).

Gene Kelly (Barry Nichols); Mitzi Gaynor (Joy Henderson); Kay Kendall (Lady Wren); Taina Elg (Angèle Ducros); Jacques Bergerac (Pierre Ducros); Leslie Phillips (Sir Gerald Wren); Henry Daniell (Judge); Patrick MacNee (Sir Percy); Stephen Vercoe (Mr. Outward); Philip Tonge (Associate Judge); Owen McGiveney (Court Usher); Francis Ravel (French Stage Manager); Adrienne d'Ambricourt (Wardrobe Woman); Maurice Marsac (French House Manager); Cyril Delevanti (Fanatic); George Navarro (Waiter); Nestor Paiva (Spanish Peasant Man); Maya Van Horn (Stout French Woman); Louisa Triana (Flamenco Dancer); Genevieve Pasques (Shopkeeper); Lilyan Chauvin (Dancer); Dick Alexander (Stagehand).

LES GIRLS was Cole Porter's final Hollywood film scoring, and also Gene Kelly's last MGM musical. (Kelly also assisted with the choreography when choreographer Jack Cole became ill during production.) It was well-mounted in every department but it belonged more to the 1930s and 1940s than to the 1950s. Financially unsuccessful, the elegantly structured feature was amusing, but its comedy outshone its music. While the feature included "Ca, C'Est L'Amour," sung by Taina Elg, its other songs were more novelty tunes than satisfactory stand-alone numbers.

In a British court, a Judge (Henry Daniell) is hearing a case in which one-time dancer Angèle Ducros (Taina Elg), who is married to wealthy French businessman Pierre Ducros (Jacques Bergerac), is suing her former dancing partner, Sybil (Kay Kendall), because of the contents of her spicy memoirs. Sybil is now known as Lady Wren because of her marriage to Sir Gerald Wren (Leslie Phillips). As revealed in court, the two women, along with American Joy Henderson (Mitzi Gaynor), once danced on the Continent as part of the nightclub act of star Barry Nichols (Gene Kelly). On the witness stand, both Angèle and Sybil claim that the other tried to kill herself when Barry spurned her. Finally Barry is testified and he recounts how, after falling in love with and marrying Joy, he found both Sybil and Angèle near death from a faulty heating system in their apartment. The two women realize they were both wrong and again become friends.

Using a RASHOMON-like structure in which truth lies squarely in the eyes of the beholder, LES GIRLS borrows its charming heel-hoofer-hero from the World War II drama, IDIOT'S DELIGHT (1939), starring Clark Gable. In LES GIRLS, Gene Kelly should be the focal point, but he seemed less than his usual bouncy self and viewer attention gravitates all too frequently to the three female leads. All of them score well in LES GIRLS. Especially appealing are Mitzi Gaynor, who won the lead in SOUTH PACIFIC (1958), *q.v.,* as a result of her work in this picture, and British comedienne Kay Kendall, who stole the show from her co-stars with her witty performance and fine hoofing. Kelly and Elg have a good duet in "The Rope Dance," but more engaging is the spoof of Marlon Brando's THE WILD ONE (1953), with Kelly as a motorcycle riding hipster in black leather and leggy Gaynor as the juke box doll drawn to him.

LES GIRLS was Oscar-nominated for its Art Direction-Set Decoration, Costume Design, and Sound. Director George Cukor, far more comfortable with women's pictures, would later direct the stylish musical, MY FAIR LADY (1964), *q.v.* A "spinoff" from LES GIRLS and the earlier IDIOT'S DELIGHT was the short-lived sitcom series, "Harry's Girls" (NBC-TV, 1963–64), starring Larry Blyden as a vaudeville entertainer with a troupe of three girl dancers.

The financial failure of LES GIRLS was just another indicator that musicals, especially those with original scripts and scores, were fast declining or disappearing in the new Hollywood. They would be replaced in the 1960s by the likes of Elvis Presley's rock 'n' roll entries and the beach party musicals of Frankie Avalon-Annette Funciello.

LET'S DANCE (Paramount, 1950) Color 112 minutes.

Producer, Robert Fellows; director, Norman Z. McLeod; based on the story "Little Boy Blue" by Maurice Zolotow; screenplay, Allan Scott, Dane Lussier; art directors, Hans Dreier, Roland Anderson; set decorators, Sam Comer, Ross Dowd; costumes, Edith Head; makeup, Wally Westmore, Bill Woods, Frank Thayer; music director, Robert Emmett Dolan; music associate, Troy Sanders; orchestrator, Van Cleave; vocal arranger, Joseph J. Lilley; choreographer, Hermes Pan; assistant director, Eddie Silven; sound, Hugo Grenzbach, John Cope; camera, George Barnes; editor, Ellsworth Hoagland.

Songs: "Piano Dance," "Jack and the Beanstalk," "Why Fight the Feeling?" "The Hyacinth," "Tunnel of Love," "Can't Stop Talking," "Oh Them Dudes" (Frank Loesser).

Betty Hutton (Kitty McNeil); Fred Astaire (Donald Elwood); Roland Young (Mr. Edmund Pohlwhistle); Ruth Warrick (Carola Everett); Lucile Watson (Serena Everett); Gregory Moffett (Richard Everett); Barton MacLane (Larry Channock); Shepperd Strudwick (Timothy Bryant); Melville Cooper (Charles Wagstaffe); Harold Huber (Marcel); George Zucco (Judge); Peggy Badley (Bubbles Malone); Virginia Toland (Elsie); Sayre Dearing (Process Server); Ida Moore (Mrs. McGuire); Nana Bryant (Mrs. Bryant); Boyd Davis (Butler); Bobby Barber (Bartender); Herbert Vigran (Chili Parlor Owner); Rolfe Sedan (Jewelry Clerk); Ralph Peters (Cab Driver); Paul A. Pierce (Square Dance Caller); Eric Alden (Captain); Milton Delugg (Himself); Harry Woods (Police Lieutenant); Chester Conklin (Watchman); Major Sam Harris, Bess Flowers, Marion Gray (Guests); Peggy O'Neill (Woman).

Following her triumph in MGM's ANNIE GET YOUR GUN (1950), *q.v.,* blonde bombshell Betty Hutton returned to her home lot where she was joined by MGM's Fred Astaire in LET'S DANCE. Sad to say, the two contrasting performers hardly complemented one another (she was a hoydenish belter, he was a debonair hoofer).

During World War II entertainers Kitty McNeil (Betty Hutton) and Donald Elwood (Fred Astaire) have a successful show business act. However, when her flyer husband dies on a military mission, Kitty breaks up the partnership. She returns to Boston to raise her baby. After the war Donald becomes a successful financier and, by chance, the two meet five years later just as Kitty is planning a show business comeback for nightclub owner Larry Channock (Barton MacLane). To aid her effort, Donald is persuaded to rejoin the act and, after a time, the two fall in love. Trouble arises when Kitty's stern mother-in-law, wealthy Serena Everett (Lucile Watson), using lawyers Edmund Pohlwhistle (Roland Young) and Charles Wagstaffe (Melville Cooper), attempts to prove that Kitty is an unfit mother so that she can gain custody of her grandchild. Eventually the problems are worked out and Kitty keeps her child. She and Donald decide to wed.

The *New York Times* discerned, "Not the most effective Fred Astaire vehicle, likewise Betty Hutton as a partner, who occasionally shouts him and the picture down. This color musical, which has some fine musical highlights nevertheless, is a curious mixture of comedy, farce and sentimentality stretched much too long. . . . The best parts are an Astaire-Hutton cut-up as two western dudes and his tuneful gymnastics in a nightclub solo." In the film, bombastic Betty Hutton sang "Can't Stop Talking" (which she recorded for RCA Victor), "Why Fight the Feeling?" and "Tunnel of Love." She and Astaire dueted on "Oh Them Dudes," while Astaire had a fine (and far more typical) interlude in his dance solo to "Jack and the Beanstalk." Songwriter Frank Loesser had written the songs for Hutton's THE PERILS OF PAULINE (1947) and RED, HOT AND BLUE (1949).

LILI (Metro-Goldwyn-Mayer, 1953) Color 81 minutes.

Producer, Edwin H. Knopf; director, Charles Walters; based on the story by Paul Gallico; screenplay, Helen Deutsch; art directors, Cedric Gibbons, Paul Groesse; set decorators, Edwin B. Willis, Arthur Krams; costumes, Mary Anne Nyberg; makeup, William Tuttle; music, Bronislau Kaper; choreographers, Walters, Dorothy Jarnac; camera, Robert Planck; editor Ferris Webster.

Songs: "Hi-Lili, Hi-Lo" (Bronislau Kaper, Helen Deutsch); "Adoration," "Lili and the Puppets Ballet" (Kaper).

Leslie Caron (Lili Daurier); Mel Ferrer (Paul Berthalet); Jean-Pierre Aumont (Marc); Zsa Zsa Gabor (Rosalie); Kurt Kasznar (Jacquot); Amanda Blake (Peach Lips); Alex Gierry (Proprietor); Ralph Dumke (Monsieur Corvier); Wilton Graff (Monsieur Tonit); George Baxter (Monsieur Erique); Eda Reiss Merin (Fruit Peddler); George Davis (Workman); Reginald Simpson (Second Workman); Mitchell Lewis (Concessionaire); Fred Walton (Whistler); Richard Grayson (Flirting Vendor); Dorothy Jarnac (Specialty Dancer); Arthur Mendez, Dick Lerner, Frank Radcliffe, Lars Hensen (Specialty Dancers).

"You'll laugh, you'll cry, you'll love LILI!" insisted the MGM advertising copy for this infectious motion picture. Since making her film debut in MGM's AN AMERICAN IN PARIS (1951), *q.v.*, French-born Leslie Caron had not fared well in her studio assignments. She appeared in lesser melodramas like THE MAN WITH A CLOAK (1951) and the anthology romance drama, THE STORY OF THREE LOVES (1953). Fortunately, LILI re-established her in the limelight and provided a career transition that would lead her to GIGI (1958), *q.v.*

Sixteen-year-old French orphan Lili Daurier (Leslie Caron) becomes infatuated with suave circus magician Marc (Jean-Pierre Aumont). When he fails to seduce her, he gets her a job as a waitress with his show. However, she is fired the first night because she paid too much attention to Marc and his act. With nowhere to turn, Lili is brought out of her depression by puppeteer Paul Berthalet (Mel Ferrer), who does an impromptu act to cheer her up.

The routine proves so successful that Paul retains it in the performance he gives with Jacquot (Kurt Kasznar) and their quartet of puppets. Although he is distant with Lili, Paul actually loves her and in a fit of jealousy over her affection for Marc, he slaps her. (He also has been harboring a long-brewing frustration because a leg injury ended his dancing career years ago, forcing him to lose a Folies Bergère offer.) When Lili learns that Marc is married to his assistant (Zsa Zsa Gabor), she runs away from the circus. She soon realizes that she adores Paul and returns to the carnival and to him.

Initially Vincente Minnelli was asked to direct LILI but he felt it was too much like AN AMERICAN IN PARIS; instead, he chose to direct THE BAD AND THE BEAUTIFUL (1952). MGM utilitarian director and choreographer Charles Walters was substituted. LILI's three leading men provided a contrasting range of styles: sensitive Mel Ferrer, charming Jean-Pierre Aumont and proletarian Kurt Kasznar. The supporting cast included Zsa Zsa Gabor in her fourth film role, as well as Amanda Blake (who would gain fame as Miss Kitty of TV's "Gunsmoke" series).

In its low-keyed format, the sentimental LILI is atypical of the

Leslie Caron, Kurt Kasznar, Amanda Blake and Jean-Pierre Aumont in LILI (1953).

usual Hollywood musical. There are *no* brash intrusion of songs, *no* exploding production numbers; *no* hackneyed comedy relief. Instead, there are only three musical interludes: the instrumental "Adoration," a tender ballet entitled "Lili and the Puppets," and the captivating song, "Hi-Lili, Hi-Lo" (which became very popular). The fantasy magic of LILI is incorporated within the puppets' characterizations, including the little boy Carrot-Top and Bernardo, the lady-chasing fox.

"Sentiment, done with an air of charm, is the principal entertainment ingredient in LILI," judged *Variety*. "Leslie Caron does the title role with an ingratiating approach that wins sympathy and warm chuckles . . . although apparently considerable effort has been taken to set up two production dance numbers, there is no [real] dancing, not even by Miss Caron, an excellent terper." The *New York Times* enthused, "A lovely and beguiling little film, touched with the magic of romance, the shimmer of masquerade. . . . The production itself, in color photography and decor and the very musical arrangements, is tasteful and handsome."

LILI placed sixth in *Film Daily's* Ten Best Picture Poll of 1953. It won an Oscar for Best Scoring of a dramatic or comedy film (Bronislau Kaper). Leslie Caron was nominated for Best Actress but lost to Audrey Hepburn (then married to Mel Ferrer) for ROMAN HOLIDAY. Other Award nominees from the picture were: Best Director, Cinematography, and Art Direction-Set Direction—Color.

The charming LILI became a recurrent re-issue attraction from MGM. It served as the basis for the Broadway musical *Carnival,* which opened on April 13, 1961. With a book by Michael Stewart and lyrics and music by Bob Merrill, the show starred Anna Maria Alberghetti (Lili), Jerry Orbach (Paul) and James Mitchell (the Magician). It ran for 720 performances, but never was translated to the screen as MGM once intended. Instead, the studio chose a more economical option: to re-release LILI.

LILLIAN RUSSELL (20th Century-Fox, 1940) 127 minutes.

Producer, Darryl F. Zanuck; associate producer, Gene Markey; director, Irving Cummings; screenplay, William Anthony McGuire; art directors, Richard Day, Joseph C. Wright; set decorator, Thomas Little; costumes, Travis Banton; music director, Alfred Newman; choreographer, Seymour Felix; camera, Leon Shamroy; editor, Walter Thompson.

Songs: "Blue Lovebird" (Gus Kahn, Bronislau Kaper); "Adored One" (Mack Gordon, Alfred Newman); "Waltz Is King"

(Gordon, Charles Henderson); "Back in the Old Days of Broadway" (Henderson, Newman); "Come Down, Ma Evenin' Star," "Ma Blushin' Rosie" (John Stromberg, Robert B. Smith); "After the Ball" (Charles K. Harris); "The Band Played On" (John E. Palmer, Charles B. Ward).

Alice Faye (Lillian Russell); Don Ameche (Edward Solomon); Henry Fonda (Alexander Moore); Edward Arnold (Diamond Jim Brady); Warren William (Jesse Lewisohn); Leo Carrillo (Tony Pastor); Helen Westley (Grandma Leonard); Dorothy Peterson (Cynthia Leonard); Ernest Truex (Charles Leonard); Lynn Bari (Edna McCauley); Nigel Bruce (William Gilbert); Claud Allister (Arthur Sullivan); Joe Weber, Lew Fields (Themselves); Una O'Connor (Marie); Eddie Foy, Jr. (Eddie Foy, Sr.); Joseph Cawthorn (Leopold Damrosch); William B. Davidson (President Cleveland); Hal K. Dawson (Chauffeur); Robert Emmett Keane (Jeweler); Frank Darien (Coachman); Irving Bacon, William Haade, Paul Burns (Soldiers); Milburn Stone, Charles Tannen (Reporters): Leyland Hodgson (Hotel Clerk); Philip Winter (Tenor); Thaddeus Jones (Mose); Alex Pollard (Waiter); Tom London (Frank); Stella Shirpsor (Baby); Robert Shaw (Man); A. S. "Pop" Byron (Policeman); Floyd Shackelford (Valet); Diane Fisher (Dorothy); Charles Halton (Dr. Dobbins); Ferike Boros (Mrs. Rose); Frank Thomas (Official); Cecil Cunningham (Mrs. Hobbs); Elyse Knox, Joan Valerie, Alice Armand (Lillian Russell's Sisters); Paul McVey (Stage Manager); Dennis Kaye (New Born Baby); Harry Hayden (Mr. Sloane, the Newspaper Editor); Frank Sully (Hank); Bob Ryan (Owen); Dave Morris (Drunk); and: Richard Carle, Robert Homans, Ottola Newsmith.

The captivating Lillian Russell (1868–1922) was a lustrous entertainer in the pre-World War I era, renowned for her hourglass figure, her feathery hats and her assortment of offstage amours. In 1940, 20th Century-Fox's Darryl F. Zanuck, who had a strong penchant for period musical fare, brought this polished and entertaining biopic to the screen. The fact that it was historically inaccurate was apparently beside the point to the filmmakers and audiences alike. In the lead role Zanuck cast his (then) favorite leading lady, Alice Faye, who seemed born to appear in period costumes and to warble (with that fascinating quivering upper lip) nostalgic tunes. Co-starred with her were Don Ameche (for the fifth time), Henry Fonda and Edward Arnold as the men in Lillian's exciting life. Arnold was cast as rotund millionaire Diamond Jim Brady, a part he also played to the hilt in the 1935 Universal feature, DIAMOND JIM.

In Clinton, Iowa the youngest daughter of Charlie (Ernest Truex) and Cynthia Leonard (Dorothy Peterson), Helen Leonard (Alice Faye) grows up wanting to be an opera singer. She is encouraged by her grandmother (Helen Westley). Helen takes voice lessons from Leopold Damrosch (Joseph Cawthorn) who tells her she has a fine voice, but one not suited to opera. One day Helen and her grandmother are rescued by a mysterious young man, Alexander Moore (Henry Fonda), when their horses run away. Later, Helen is heard by theatre producer Tony Pastor (Leo Carrillo), who hires her to sing for him. He changes her name to Lillian Russell and bills her as "The greatest English Ballad Singer." Quickly the beguiling Lillian becomes the most famous star on the American stage and is courted by wealthy Diamond Jim Brady (Edward Arnold), but she marries musician Edward Solomon (Don Ameche). In London she again meets Moore, now a newspaperman, and he does a series of articles on her. When her husband dies suddenly Lillian returns home and continues her stage work. Several years later, she and Moore, who is now a newspaper publisher, meet for the third time and begin a romance.

Beautifully coiffed and gowned, Alice Faye sang such famous Lillian Russell songs as "Ma Blushin' Rosie" and "After the Ball," as well as such newer compositions as "Adored One," "Blue Love Bird" and "Back in the Days of Old Broadway." The "Last Rose of Summer" number was cut from the film's lengthy (127 minutes!) running time before release. Of historical interest, vaudeville greats Joe Weber and Lew Fields appeared as themselves in the feature while Eddie Foy, Jr. enacted the role of his famous father.

Despite the favorable reception from moviegoers, the critics were unimpressed by LILLIAN RUSSELL. The *New York Times* chided, "Miss Russell is said to have been a rather poor actress, and Miss Faye—even granting the thinness of her material—does not violate that reputation. Throughout she seems little more than a pampered and alarmingly virtuous family girl." *Variety* complained, "A story which is scarcely more than a broad burlesque of a career that was rich in sentiment and background. . . . Her cinematic biography is disappointing."

LILLIAN RUSSELL received an Oscar nomination for Best Interior Decoration—Black-and-White.

On screen Lillian Russell has been portrayed by Ruth Gillette in THE GREAT ZIEGFELD (1936), *q.v.,* and in THE GENTLEMAN FROM LOUISIANA (1936); by Louise Albritton in BOWERY TO BROADWAY (1944); and by Andrea King in MY WILD IRISH ROSE (1947).

LITTLE JOHNNY JONES (First National, 1929) 73 minutes. (Also silent version: 5,020′).

Director, Mervyn LeRoy; based on the play by George M. Cohan; screenplay, Adelaide Heilbron, Edward Buzzell; camera, Faxon Dean; editor, Frank Ware.

Songs: "Give My Regards to Broadway" (George M. Cohan); "Straight, Place, and Show" (Herman Ruby, M. K. Jerome); "Go Find Somebody to Love" (Herb Magidson, Michael Cleary); "My Paradise" (Herb Magidson, James Cavanaugh); "Painting the Clouds with Sunshine" (Al Dubin, Joe Burke).

Eddie Buzzell (Johnny Jones); Alice Day (Mary Baker); Edna Murphy (Vivian Dale); Robert Edeson (Ed Baker); Wheeler Oakman (George Wyman); Raymond Turner (Carbon); Donald Reed (Ramon Lopez).

George M. Cohan (1878–1942) first wrote and starred in *Little Johnny Jones* on Broadway in 1904, and in it he introduced two of his most enduring songs: "The Yankee Doodle Boy" and "Give My Regards to Broadway." In 1923 Warner Bros. filmed the stage play with Johnny Hines in the title role. However, as a silent picture it could not take advantage of Cohan's score, which had been the highlight of the stage production. This was remedied in 1929 when the studio remade the Cohan property at the beginning of the sound era. Star Eddie Buzzell sang the Cohan numbers along with other tunes including "Painting the Clouds with Sunshine," one of 1929's most popular melodies, introduced earlier in the year by Nick Lucas in Warner Bros.' THE GOLD DIGGERS OF BROADWAY (*q.v.*).

After successfully riding Ed Baker's (Robert Edeson) racehorse Yankee to victory in the Meadowbrook, New Jersey race, jockey Johnny Jones (Eddie Buzzell) is hired by a stable owner to ride for him in New York. Johnny leaves his girlfriend Mary Baker (Alice Day). In Gotham he comes under the spell of actress Vivian Dale (Edna Murphy). Under her influence, he is soon working in small clubs. He is so good at performing that he is offered a job in a major revue but he rejects the bid to remain in the racing game. When Mary and her father come to the city to enter Yankee in the same race that Johnny is riding in, she learns of his affair with Vivian, who has been trying to persuade him to throw the event. When his horse does lose, Johnny, due to an incriminating telegram from Vivian, is accused of throwing the race. In disgrace, he sails for England and ends up working in a Limehouse dive. Ed and Mary travel to London where Ed offers Johnny a chance to ride Yankee in an Epsom Downs race which he wins. He and Mary are reunited.

Photoplay magazine judged, "Eddie Buzzell, musical comedy star, and George M. Cohan music redeem this. Otherwise just another racetrack yarn." *Variety* termed it "a good light-weight diversion." Scenes from *Little Johnny Jones* would be incorporated into the George M. Cohan biopic, YANKEE DOODLE DANDY (1942), *q.v.*, starring Jimmy Cagney. Actor Edward Buzzell would become a director, handling such musicals as HONOLULU (1939), SHIP AHOY (1942), BEST FOOT FORWARD (1943), NEPTUNE'S DAUGHTER (1949) and AIN'T MISBEHAVIN' (1955).

LITTLE SHOP OF HORRORS (Warner Bros., 1986) Color 94 minutes.

Producer, David Geffen; associate producers, David Orton, Denis Holt; director, Frank Oz; based on the musical play by Howard Ashman, Alan Menken, and the screenplay by Charles Griffith; screenplay, Ashman; production designer, Roy Walker; art directors, Stephen Spence, John Fenner; set decorator, Tessa Davis; Audrey II designer/creator, Lyle Conway; costumes, Marit Allen; makeup, Paul Engelen, Lynda Armstrong; music, Miles Goodman; music arrangers/adaptors, Robby Merkin, Bob Gaudio; vocal arranger, Robert Billig; orchestrator/music supervisor, Robby Merkin; music producer, Gaudio; music editors, Nancy Fogart, Christopher Kennedy; music coordinator, Jim Henrikson; assistant directors, Dusty Symonds, Gareth Tandy, Nick Heckstall-Smith, Tim Reed; production coordinator, Vicki Manning; animatronics coordinator, Barbara Griffiths; sound, Peter Sutton, Joel Moss, Thomas Pasatieri; sound consultant, David Gray; sound re-recording, Robert W. Glass, Jr., Steve Maslow, Kevin O'Connell, Robert Ash; sound effects supervisor, Ron Davis; assistant sound editor, Colin Wilson; ADR editor, Bob Risk; special visual effects, Bran Ferren, James N. Shelly, Susan Coursey, Susan LeBer, David McDonough, Robert C. Francis, Chester T. Hartwell, John C. Huntington, III, Phillip Cullum, Kinnereth Ellentuck, Robert Kohut, Lars Pederson, Paul Pratt, Alan D. Webb; special optical effects, Robert Rowohlt, John Alagna, Bob Buckles, Sanford Duke, Mitch Wilson; special effects, Christine Overs, Tim Willis; camera, Robert Paynter; second unit camera, Ronnie Maasaz, James Devis; animatronics camera, Paul Wilson; editor, John Jympson.

Songs: "Little Shop of Horrors," "Skid Row (Downtown)," "Grow for Me," "Somewhere That's Green," "Dentist!" "Feed Me," "Suddenly Seymour," "Suppertime," "Mean Green Mother from Outer Space," "The Meek Shall Inherit" (Howard Ashman, Alan Menken).

Rick Moranis (Seymour Krelborn); Ellen Greene (Audrey);

Vincent Gardenia (Mushnik); Steve Martin (Orin Scrivello, DDS); Tichina Arnold (Crystal); Tisha Campbell (Chiffon); Michelle Weeks (Ronette); James Belushi (Patrick Martin); John Candy (Wink Wilkinson); Christopher Guest (1st Customer); Bill Murray (Arthur Denton); Stanley Jones (Narrator); Bertice Reading ("Downtown" Old Woman); Ed Wiley, Alan Tilvern, John Scott Martin ("Downtown" Bums); Vincent Wong (Chinese Florist); Mak Wilson, Danny Cunningham, Danny John-Jules, Gary Palmer, Paul Swaby (Doo Wop Street Singers); Mildred Shay, Melissa Wilsie, Kevin Scott, Barbara Rosenblat (Customers); Adeen Fogle (Radio Station Assistant); Kelly Huntley, Paul Reynolds (Audrey and Seymour's Children); Miriam Margolyes (Dental Nurse); Abbie Dabner (Boy Patient); Frank Dux (2nd Patient); Peter Whitman (Patient on Ceiling); Heather Henson (Girl Patient); Judith Morse (Girl's Mother); Bob Sherman (Agent); Doreen Hermitage (*Life* Magazine Lady); Kerry Shale (Her Assistant); Robert Arden, Stephen Hoye, Bob Sessions (Network Executives); Michael J. Shannon (TV Reporter); Levi Stubbs (Voice of Audrey II); Anthony Asbury, Mak Wilson, Sue Dacre, Marcus Clarke, David Greenaway, Michael Bayliss, Don Austen, William Todd Jones, Ian Tregonning, Michael Quinn, Brian Henson, Robert Tygner, David Barclay, Paul Springer, Toby Philpott, Michael Barclay, Chris Leith, Terry Lee, John Alexander, James Barton, Graham Fletcher (Principal Plant Performers); Madeline Adams, Tony Anthony, Ailsa Berk, Martin Bridle, Simon Brown, Georgia Clarke, Debbie Cummings, Mary Edwards, Mike Halford, Penny Hetherington, Ronnie Le Drew, Sally McCormack, Russell Nash, Graham Newton, Nigel Plaskitt, Peter Robbins, Anna Savva, John Styles, Ian Thom, Patti Webb, Francis Wright, Martin Antony, Joan Barton, Richard Brain, Fiona Benyon Brown, David Bulbeck, Richard Coombs, Phil Easton, Geoff Felix, Leslie Haynes, Helen Joannides, Patricia Martinelli, Stephen Mottram, Alsion Neil, Angie Passmore, Judy Preece, Gilly Robic, David Showler, Nicholas Temple, David Trainer, Simon Williamson, Saskia Wright (Additional Performers).

Roger Corman's 1961 cult movie classic, THE LITTLE SHOP OF HORRORS, was a broad parody of horror movies, shot in two days and two nights on standing sets. After its initial release it was quickly sold to TV, where it became a favorite. In the 1980s the black comedy storyline was adapted to the stage by Howard Ashman with music by Alan Menken and lyrics by Ashman, and became a surprise hit. In 1986 Ashman adapted the offbeat musical to film under the direction of Frank Oz (of TV "Muppets" fame), with Ellen Greene reprising her stage role of the flighty floral

Rick Moranis, Steve Martin and Ellen Greene in LITTLE SHOP OF HORRORS (1986).

arranger Audrey. The resulting movie grossed $38.7 million in distributors' domestic film rentals, making it one of the top twenty-five moneymaking films of the next year, as it was issued late in 1986. It was rated PG-13 for its strong language.

It is set in a Gotham slum. Loser Seymour Krelborn (Rick Moranis) is in love with pretty Audrey (Ellen Greene), both of them being employed in the skid row flower shop owned by Mushnik (Vincent Gardenia). Seymour grows a huge plant he calls Audrey II (voice of Levi Stubbs), named in honor of his lady love who is the victim of a sad romance with sadistic dentist Dr. Orin Scrivello (Steve Martin), who apes the mannerisms of Elvis Presley. Surprisingly the plant is intelligent and can talk. It demands to be fed with blood. The first feeding is slated to be provided by the unsuspecting Dr. Scrivello, who has been working on his masochistic patient, Arthur Denton (Bill Murray). Before Seymour can act, the dentist accidentally gasses himself to death. Now with a corpse at hand, Seymour feeds it to Audrey II. Next, Seymour proposes to Audrey. She accepts as they perform "Suddenly Seymour," about their hoped-for ideal life together in the suburbs. After a number of misadventures, the newlyweds get their dream house, only to find a flowerbed full of Audrey II's offspring growing there.

In *Magill's Cinema Annual 1987,* James M. Welsh determined, "The film is remarkably inventive in its handling of the musical spectacle," and added, "LITTLE SHOP OF HORRORS is a wonderfully entertaining adaptation of a stage musical to the screen and deserves to be considered one of the best pictures of 1986, even if it was too strange to warrant attention by the Academy of Motion Picture Arts and Sciences as one of the year's best. It delights both the eye and the ear, besides being satirically pleasing and offering an all-star comic cast." More critical was Tom Milne (British *Monthly Film Bulletin*). "The numbers are bright and catchy, and performed *con brio*. The Skid Row settings, solidly built and pitched to exactly the right note of formalised realism, are admirable. Audrey II . . . is superbly animated. But in stringing these elements together, alas, any sense of style in movement—so crucial to the musical—is signally lacking. . . . A mess, therefore, but not unenjoyable in its Muppety way."

Several songs from the Broadway production were deleted, including: "Don't It Go to Show Ya Never Know," "Closed for Renovations," "Mushnik and Son" and "Now," while "Mean Green Mother from Outer Space" was added for the movie version.

LOOK FOR THE SILVER LINING (Warner Bros., 1949) Color 106 minutes.

Producer, William Jacobs; director, David Butler; based on the story "Life of Marilyn Miller" by Bert Kalmar, Harry Ruby; screenplay, Phoebe Ephron, Henry Ephron, Marian Spitzer; art director, John Hughes; set decorator, Fred MacLean; costumes, Travilla; music/music director, Ray Heindorf; choreographer, LeRoy Prinz; assistant director, Phil Quinn; color consultants, Natalie Kalmus, Mitchell Kovaleski; sound, Francis J. Scheid, David Forrest; camera, Peverell Marley; editor, Irene Morra.

Songs: "Sunny," "Who" (Jerome Kern, Otto Harbach, Oscar Hammerstein, II); "Look for the Silver Lining," "Whip-Poor-Will," "A Kiss in the Dark" (Buddy G. DeSylva, Victor Herbert); "Pirouette" (Herman Finck); "Just a Memory" (DeSylva, Lew Brown, Ray Henderson); "Time on My Hands" (Mack Gordon, Harold Adamson, Vincent Youmans); "Wild Rose" (Clifford Grey, Kern); "Shine on Harvest Moon" (Nora Bayes, Jack Norworth); "Back, Back, Back to Baltimore" (Harry Williams, Egbert Van Alstyne); "Jingle Bells" (J. S. Pierpont); "Can't You Hear Me Callin', Caroline?" (William H. Gardner, Caro Roma); "Carolina in the Morning" (Gus Kahn, Walter Donaldson); "Yama Yama Man" (George Collin Davis, Karl Hoschna); "Dengozo" (Ernesto Nazareth); "Oh Gee! Oh Joy!" (P. G. Wodehouse, George Gershwin, Ira Gershwin).

June Haver (Marilyn Miller); Ray Bolger (Jack Donahue); Gordon MacRae (Frank Carter); Charlie Ruggles (Pop Miller); Rosemary DeCamp (Mom Miller); Lee Wilde (Claire Miller); Lyn Wilde ((Ruth Miller); Dick Simmons (Henry Doran); S. Z. Sakall (Shendorf); Walter Catlett (Himself); George Zoritch, Oleg Tupine (Ballet Specialty); Lillian Yarbo (Violet); Paul E. Burns (Mr. Beeman); Douglas Kennedy (Doctor); Ted Mapes (Driver); Monte Blue (St. Clair); Will Rogers, Jr. (Will Rogers); Esther Howard (Mrs. Moffitt); Jack Gargan (Stage Manager).

Although it bore little resemblance to the actual life of the great entertainer Marilyn ·Miller (1898–1936), the prefabricated LOOK FOR THE SILVER LINING was "one of the year's best musicals" according to a generous-feeling *Variety,* which also noted that it was "highly entertaining. . . . Picture captures the flavor of the era and is dressed in a fetching color garb. . . ." June Haver, on loan from 20th Century-Fox, had her best part in the title role and was more than ably assisted by Ray Bolger and Gordon MacRae as the men in her life.

Marilyn Miller (June Haver) is about to revive her famous stage musical *Sally* in Boston in 1936. She looks back on her career which began after the turn of the century when she joined her parents (Charles Ruggles, Rosemary DeCamp) and her two sisters (Lee Wilde, Lyn Wilde) in their vaudeville act, billed as The Five Columbians. When her family is stricken with the mumps, Marilyn is asked by dancer Jack Donahue (Ray Bolger) to join his act. By the age of fifteen she is a recognized performer and soon is starred in her first Broadway production. She falls in love with her co-star, singer Frank Carter (Gordon MacRae). Years pass and as her fame increases, so does her temperament and egotism. She is brought back to reality when Frank enlists in World War I. After the Armistice, Marilyn and Frank marry and she becomes a more famous name as a star of producer Florenz Ziegfeld's shows. On the opening night of *Sally,* Frank is killed in a car accident. Thereafter, having no personal life, she becomes obsessed with her stage and film career. Her health suffers. Although warned by her physicians not to tax her strength further, she accepts the lead in a revival of *Sally*.

Judging the picture pretty but with paper-thin results, *Harrison's Reports* has complaints about this account of the life and times of Marilyn Miller: ". . . Those familiar with her career will find that it has been by-passed for a moss-covered backstage story which, as presented, is dramatically and comically ineffective." On the other hand, the same trade journal admitted, "Mr. Bolger's solo dance routines are a delight to watch. Gordon MacRae, a popular 'crooner,' sings several of the old-time songs pleasantly." Bolger's tap dance to "Who" is a highlight of this film. For those not already favorably inclined toward comely June Haver as a screen presence, LOOK FOR THE SILVER LINING did not enhance her reputation.

LOST HORIZON (Columbia, 1973) Color 151 minutes.

Producer, Ross Hunter; associate producer, Jacques Mapes; director, Charles Jarrott; based on the novel by James Hilton; screenplay, Larry Kramer; art director, Preston Ames; set decorator, Jerry Wunderlich; costumes, Jean Louis; music/music director, Burt Bacharach; orchestrators, Leo Shuken, Jack Hayes; choreographer, Hermes Pan; second unit director, Russ Saunders; assistant directors, Sheldon Schrager, Jerry Ziesmer, Mike Frankovich, Jr., Mack Harding; climbing sequence supervisor, Lute Jerstad Adventures; aerial sequences, Frank Tallman; sound, Jack Solomon, Arthur Piantadosi, Richard Tyler, Dan Wallin; special camera effects, Butler-Glounder; camera, Robert Surtees; second unit camera, Harold Wellman, Bruce Surtees; editor, Maury Winetrobe.

Songs: "Lost Horizon," "Share the Joy," "The World Is a Circle," "Living Together, Growing Together," "I Might Frighten Her Away," "The Things I Will Not Miss," "If I Could Go Back," "Where Knowledge Ends (Faith Begins)," "Question Me an Answer," "I Come to You," "Reflections" (Burt Bacharach, Hal David).

Peter Finch (Richard Conway); Liv Ullmann (Catherine); Sally Kellerman (Sally Hughes); George Kennedy (Sam Cornelius [Simon Cosfield]); Michael York (George Conway); Olivia Hussey (Maria); Bobby Van (Harry Lovett); James Shigeta (Brother To-Linn); Charles Boyer (High Lama); John Gielgud (Chang); Larry Duran (Oriental Pilot); Kent Smith (Bill Ferguson); John Van Dreelen (Dr. Virdon); Miiko Taka (Nurse); Tybee Brascia (Dancer); Medley Mattingly (Airfield Official); Jerry Whitman (Singing Voice of Richard Conway); Diane Lee (Singing Voice of Catherine); Andra Willis (Singing Voice of Maria); Siam Phillips (Solo Voice for "Lost Horizon" number); and: Neil Jon, Virginia Ann Lee, Paul De Lucca.

A musical remake of the classic 1937 Frank Capra fantasy-drama based on James Hilton's 1933 novel, LOST HORIZON cost more than $6 million. It recouped less than half that amount when shown in theatres. Not only had the plot of the Hilton fantasy dated badly, but the music score contributed by Burt Bacharach and Hal David was one of their worst and Hermes Pan's choreography (which included a dancing bear!) is almost unbearable, including the steps given to wisecracking hoofer Bobby Van. Several of the stars were dubbed for their "singing" moments. The acting, script and sets were sub-par.

To escape a revolution in a small South Asian town, five people—British diplomat Richard Conway (Peter Finch), his hot-headed brother George (Michael York), *Newsweek* magazine photographer Sally Hughes (Sally Kellerman), businessman Sam Cornelius (George Kennedy) and nightclub comic Harry Lovett (Bobby Van)—escape in a small plane. The craft, which has been commandeered by a replacement pilot and is traveling in a non-charted direction, later crashes in the Himalayas, killing the pilot. The group is rescued by Chang (John Gielgud), an English-educated Oriental, who escorts them to the sheltered Valley of the Blue Moon, which the inhabitants call Shangri-La. In this paradise where there is no cold or darkness, the inhabitants lead a contented life. Among the locals are French teacher Catherine (Liv Ullmann) and ballerina Maria (Olivia Hussey), with whom George falls in love. After a time, George convinces Maria to return with him to America. Richard tries to stop him and seeks the help of the two-hundred-year-old High Lama (Charles Boyer), who warns that Maria will die if she leaves Shangri-La because the climate there keeps her eternally youthful. Maria convinces Richard the Lama is lying and he agrees to help the young lovers escape. The three abandon the city. As they climb down the snowy mountains Maria ages into an old hag. An avalanche kills both her and George. Richard goes on alone and is rescued eventually. Because he loves Catherine, he returns to Shangri-La.

The critics tore apart the ludicrously philosophical LOST HORIZON. Charles Champlin (*Los Angeles Times*) termed it "Cumbersome, unlyrical and tedious," while *Time* magazine branded it "Fatuous and tasteless." When it opened in England in the spring of 1973, the running time had been cut by seven minutes, including the Finch-Ullmann duet, "I Come to You." Jan Dawson (British *Monthly Film Bulletin*) reported, "Burt Bacharach's songs—catering simultaneously to the vogue for significant lyrics and the vocal shortcomings of the principal performers—are in fact among the film's keener disappointments. They are performed with much good will by the shamefully miscast Liv Ullmann and a hint of embarrassment by the more restrained Peter Finch, while Sally Kellerman—having shed her neuroses in the third reel—hops leggily about as if auditioning for the Ziegfeld Follies."

George Kennedy, Bobby Van, Sally Kellerman, Liv Ullmann and Peter Finch in LOST HORIZON (1973).

Former actor turned glossy film producer Ross Hunter had packaged an earlier musical, THE FLOWER DRUM SONG (1961), *q.v.,* to far better if not satisfactory results. Peter Finch and Liv Ullmann would re-team for the unsuccessful THE ABDICATION (1974), a continuation of the story of Queen Christina featured in the Greta Garbo movie of 1933.

LOVE IN LAS VEGAS *see* VIVA LAS VEGAS.

LOVE ME FOREVER (Columbia, 1935) 91 minutes.

Associate producer, Max Winslow; director/story, Victor Schertzinger; screenplay, Jo Swerling, Sidney Buchman; music, Louis Silvers; music directors, Silvers, Gaetano Muolo; camera, Joseph Walker; editors, Gene Milford, Viola Lawrence.

Songs: "Love Me Forever," "Whoa" (Victor Schertzinger, Gus Kahn); arias from the operas *La Bohème* (Giacomo Puccini); "The Quartet" from *Rigoletto* (Giuseppe Verdi); "Il Bacio" (Luigi Arditi); "Funiculi-Funicula" (Luigi Denza).

Grace Moore (Margaret Howard); Leo Carrillo (Steve Corelli); Michael Bartlett (Himself); Robert Allen (Philip Cameron); Spring

Byington (Fields); Thurston Hall (Maurizzio); Douglass Dumbrille (Miller); Luis Alberni (Luigi); and: Harry Barris, Gavin Gordon, Arthur Kaye.

Following their great success in ONE NIGHT OF LOVE (*q.v.*) the previous year, Columbia teamed opera diva Grace Moore and director Victor Schertzinger again for its follow-up. LOVE ME FOREVER proved to be a popular box-office item. For the production, versatile director Schertzinger and Gus Kahn composed the title theme and "Whoa!" for Grace Moore to sing. In addition, she also performed a wide variety of music, ranging from a duet with Michael Bartlett on "Tiny Hands" (from the opera *La Bohème*) and "Funiculi-Funicula" to such operatic work as "Il Bacio" and the quartet from *Rigoletto.*

Having begun his career as a stockman, earthy Steve Corelli (Leo Carrillo) has attained great riches and is now a gambler and a nightclub owner. He uses his money to further his greatest love: music. Steve meets impoverished society girl Margaret Howard (Grace Moore) at an auction to sell her home and possessions. When he later hears the soprano sing, he falls in love with both her and her voice. He soon hires her to sing at his club, but her highbrow music does not mix well with his lowbrow customers. He promises to make her a great opera star, refusing to accept that she cares for him *not* as a lover but as a friend. He has a swank club built in Margaret's honor, names it the La Margerita and makes her the star attraction. Meanwhile, Steve provides funds for Margaret to further her operatic training and arranges for her to have a singing audition at the Metropolitan Opera, which hires her. By now she has fallen in love with Boston aristocrat Philip Cameron (Robert Allen). When Steve learns this he turns to heavy drinking and reckless gambling. Margaret learns that he has a $15,000 gambling debt and she hastens to his aid, despite it being the night of her Metropolitan debut. She obtains a loan from the Opera and, after paying her benefactor's debt, breaks with Cameron. She returns to Steve who has done so much for her career.*

Variety cited one of the strategic problems involved in attempting to make LOVE ME FOREVER a lucrative follow-up to ONE NIGHT OF LOVE: "Choice of operatic arias is not so outstanding here simply because a majority of the surefires were crammed into the previous effort. But the *Bohème* climax is dynamite and will compensate for any differences the audiences may have with the picture up to that time." The trade paper

*In the original scenario for LOVE ME FOREVER, Leo Carrillo's character dies, leaving Grace Moore free to continue her romance with Robert Allen.

acknowledged, "Miss Moore once again looks well, is in glorious voice and gives a smart performance. . . . There's plenty of comedy, although some of it is forced. . . ." The *New York Times* was even more impressed: "Although the tale weeps too copiously for comfort after a splendidly comic beginning . . . [it] represents the musical cinema at its best and it deserves to rank as the most distinguished musical photoplay of the season."

Following LOVE ME FOREVER, Grace Moore made three more operatic musicals for Columbia: THE KING STEPS OUT (1936), I'LL TAKE ROMANCE (1937) and WHEN YOU'RE IN LOVE (1937). But by this time Moore, always demanding and battling weight, was wearing out her screen welcome. Moreover, by then MGM's Jeanette MacDonald had cemented her position as the screen's foremost operetta star and was the standard by whom all other competition was judged. Moore would return to the opera stage as well as starring in the French film production of LOUISE (1940). She died tragically in a plane crash early in 1947 at age forty-six.

British release title: ON WINGS OF SONG.

LOVE ME OR LEAVE ME (Metro-Goldwyn-Mayer, 1955) Color 122 minutes.

Producer, Joe Pasternak; director, Charles Vidor; story, Daniel Fuchs; screenplay, Fuchs, Isobel Lennart; art directors, Cedric Gibbons, Urie McCleary; set decorator, Edwin B. Willis; costumes, Helen Rose; Miss Day's music, Percy Faith; music director, George Stoll; choreographer, Alex Romero; sound, Wesley C. Miller; special effects, Warren Newcombe; camera, Arthur E. Arling; editor, Ralph E. Winters.

Songs: "Shaking the Blues Away" (Irving Berlin); "Mean to Me" (Roy Turk, Fred Ahlert); "Love Me or Leave Me" (Walter Donaldson, Gus Kahn); "Sam, the Old Accordion Man," "At Sundown" (Donaldson); "Everybody Loves My Baby" (Jack Palmer, Spencer Williams); "Stay on the Right Side, Sister" (Ted Koehler, Rube Bloom); "It All Depends on You" (Buddy G. DeSylva, Lew Brown, Ray Henderson); "Ten Cents a Dance" (Richard Rodgers, Lorenz Hart); "My Blue Heaven" (Donaldson, George Whiting); "You Made Me Love You" (Joseph McCarthy, James V. Monaco); "I'm Sitting on Top of the World," "Five Foot Two" (Sam M. Lewis, Joe Young, Henderson); "I'll Never Stop Loving You" (Nicholas Brodzky, Sammy Cahn); "Never Look Back" (Chilton Price).

Doris Day (Ruth Etting); James Cagney (Martin "The Gimp" Snyder); Cameron Mitchell (Johnny Alderman); Robert Keith

(Bernard V. Loomis); Tom Tully (Frobisher); Harry Bellaver (Georgie); Richard Gaines (Paul Hunter); Peter Leeds (Fred Taylor); Claude Stroud (Eddie Fulton); Audrey Young (Jingle Girl); John Harding (Greg Trent); Dorothy Abbott (Dancer); Phil Schumacher, Otto Reichow, Henry Kulky (Bouncers); Jay Adler (Orry); Mauritz Hugo (Irate Customer); Veda Ann Borg (Hostess); Claire Carleton (Claire); Benny Burt (Stage Manager); Robert B. Carson (Mr. Brelston, the Radio Station Manager); James Drury (Assistant Director); Richard Simmons (Dance Director); Michael Kostrick (Assistant Director); Roy Engel (1st Reporter); John Damler (2nd Reporter); Genevieve Aumont (Woman); Roy Engel (Propman); Dale Van Sickel, Johnny Day (Stagehands); Larri Thomas, Patti Nestor, Winona Smith, Shirley Wilson (Chorus Girls); Robert Malcolm (Doorman); Robert Stephenson (Waiter); Paul McGuire (Drapery Man); Barry Regan (Guard); Jimmy Cross, Henry Randolph (Photographers); Chet Brandenberg (Chauffeur).

Hollywood had a penchant for biographies of show business personalities (Lillian Roth, Helen Morgan, Grace Moore, Diana Barrymore, et al), especially when the subject had a tragic life to add dramatic bite to the presentation. In 1955 MGM produced the posh LOVE ME OR LEAVE ME, about Roaring Twenties' singing star Ruth Etting (1896–1978) and her tempestuous relationship with gangster Martin "The Gimp" Snyder. It was the first of several such genre studies to present a (somewhat) unvarnished look at the seamier side of the subject's life. While this musical took many liberties with actual events in the lives of the characters involved, it did recapture the era through its music and pictorial recreation of the Jazz Age.* The movie earned a half-dozen Oscar nominations, including James Cagney as Best Actor.** Daniel Fuchs won an Academy Award for Best Original Story. The film grossed $4,153,000 in distributors' domestic film rentals.

Following World War I, Ruth Etting (Doris Day), a Nebraska

---

*In *Ginger, Loretta and Irene Who?* (1976), in his career study of Ruth Etting, George Eels details some of the discrepancies between reality and the "facts" as presented in LOVE ME OR LEAVE ME. "Snyder's characteristics were heightened for theatrical effect. . . . The time span was compressed radically; instead of meeting Myrl [Alderman] in 1935, when her career was almost finished, he was her accompanist-tutor-suitor in the 1920s. Yet the portrayals by James Cagney, Doris Day, and Cameron Mitchell of Snyder, Ruth, and Alderman were so vivid and the gritty subject matter so much more pertinent than the perennial will-they-or-won't-they get the show on or be reunited that accuracy—or lack of it—bothered only those personally involved."

**LOVE ME OR LEAVE ME won other Oscar nominations for Best Song ("Love Me Or Leave Me"), Scoring, Screenplay and Sound.

farm girl, hopes to find singing stardom in Chicago. While struggling to become a success she meets Martin "The Gimp" Snyder (James Cagney), a gangster who makes a living by monopolizing the laundry business in the territory. Despite his many underworld ties and unsavory disposition, Ruth is attracted to the older man. He takes over the management of her career and soon makes her a top singing attraction in clubs on Broadway and recordings, with a weekly salary of $2,500. Snyder pressures Ruth into marrying him. Because of his abusive treatment of her and his recurring fits of jealousy, she begins drinking heavily. After a number of years Ruth falls in love with her accompanist, Johnny Alderman (Cameron Mitchell), and begs Snyder for a divorce. In a jealous rage the gangster shoots Johnny, but only wounds him. As a result, Snyder is imprisoned and Ruth divorces him. She is free now to wed the man she loves.

Originally, LOVE ME OR LEAVE ME was to be an MGM production starring Lana Turner or Ava Gardner and was to be directed by George Cukor. However, it was Doris Day, in her first film away from Warner Bros., who snared the choice role. Although the script and direction allowed little room for Day to reveal the mixture of fragility, pathetic courage and recurrent optimism that was all part of Ruth Etting, Day's performance was still a revelation for those used to her cotton candy assignments at Warner Bros. Obviously, interacting with a star of James Cagney's calibre brought forth a real performance from the actress.* A highlight of the feature was Doris Day's singing (in her style; not Etting's) of famous songs like "Shaking the Blues Away," "Mean to Me," "Ten Cents a Dance" and "Love Me or Leave Me." Surprisingly, however, the movie did not use one of Ruth Etting's most remembered numbers, her radio theme, "Shine On, Harvest Moon." The soundtrack album to LOVE ME OR LEAVE ME remained on *Billboard* magazine's hits chart for twenty-eight weeks and was in #1 position for seventeen of those weeks.

The *New York Herald Tribune* wrote, "It has plenty of songs of the jazz age to gratify the nostalgically-inclined; it has a story to grip those who don't care a Coolidge dollar about the music of yesteryear, and it has a performance by James Cagney that will be remembered for a long time. . . . Doris Day graduates out of her world of peppy collegiate revels with this picture, and the change is all to the good. She gives a mature performance." *Time* magazine

---

*Doris Day and James Cagney had previously been matched at Warner Bros. in WEST POINT STORY (1950), a lightweight musical excursion which taxed neither performer's skills.

opined, "LOVE ME OR LEAVE ME is a Hollywood paradox: a CinemaScope musical that has the bite of authenticity."

With LOVE ME OR LEAVE ME such a hit, a rash of further Hollywood musical biographies were turned out, including THE JOKER IS WILD (1957, with Frank Sinatra as Joe E. Lewis) and THE HELEN MORGAN STORY (1957 with Ann Blyth as the songstress; the singing voice of Gogi Grant), *q.v.*

In 1989, Michael Cristofer's adaptation of LOVE ME OR LEAVE ME tried out on the summer stock circuit. It featured Melissa Manchester as Ruth Etting, with Mark Margolis as Martin "The Gimp" Snyder.

LOVE ME TONIGHT (Paramount, 1932) 104 minutes.

Producer/director, Rouben Mamoulian; based on the play *Tailor in the Chateau* by Leopold Marchand, Paul Armont; screenplay, Samuel Hoffenstein, Waldemar Young, George Marion, Jr.; art director, Hans Dreier; set decorator, A. E. Freudeman; costumes, Edith Head, Travis Banton; music director, Nathaniel Finston; camera, Victor Milner; editor, Billy Shea.

Songs: "Isn't It Romantic?" "Mimi," "Lover," "A Woman Needs Something Like That," "The Poor Apache," "Love Me Tonight," "Song of Paree," "How Are You?" "The Son of a Gun Is Nothing But a Tailor" (Richard Rodgers, Lorenz Hart); "A Hot Time in the Old Town Tonight" (Theodore Matz).

Maurice Chevalier (Maurice Courtelin); Jeanette MacDonald (Princess Jeanette); Charlie Ruggles (Vicomte Gilbert de Vareze); Charles Butterworth (Count de Savignac); Myrna Loy (Countess Valentine); Sir C. Aubrey Smith (The Duke); Elizabeth Patterson, Ethel Griffies, Blanche Frederici (Aunts); Joseph Cawthorn (Dr. Armand de Fontinac); Major Sam Harris (Bridge Player); Robert Greig (Major Domo Flamond); Ethel Wales (Madame Dutoit the Dressmaker); Marion "Peanuts" Byron (Bakery Girl); Bert Roach (Emile); Tyler Brooke (Composer); Clarence Wilson (Shirtmaker); William H. Turner (Bootmaker); Tony Merlo (Hatmaker); Rolfe Sedan (Taxi Driver); Gordon Westcott (Collector); George [Gabby] Hayes (Grocer); Mary Doran (Madame Dupont); George Davis (Pierre Dupont); Edgar Norton (Valet); Cecil Cunningham (Laundress); Herbert Mundin (Groom); Rita Owin (Chambermaid); George Humbert (Chef); Tom Ricketts (Bit).

Gene Ringgold and DeWitt Bodeen wrote enthusiastically in *The Films of Maurice Chevalier* (1973), "Like vintage champagne, LOVE ME TONIGHT, 1932's most perfect film, improves with age and its screening at film retrospectives is always the event most anticipated and acclaimed. And no discerning film student or scholar disputes the word-of-mouth acclaim which so justly decrees it the all-time best screen musical."

Joyful French tailor Maurice Courtelin (Maurice Chevalier) is owed money from gambling debts by the Vicomte de Vareze (Charles Ruggles). However, when he attempts to collect the money, the tailor finds that the woman-chasing nobleman has left Paris because a jealous husband is pursuing him. Maurice learns that the Vicomte is hiding at his country chateau. Badly needing the money, Maurice follows de Vareze to his country home. En route, he meets the very attractive but snobbish widow, Princess Jeanette (Jeanette MacDonald), who is also staying at the chateau. When Maurice arrives, the Vicomte, fearing that his gruff uncle, the Duke d'Artelines (C. Aubrey Smith) will uncover the truth about his gambling and romantic activities, passes the tailor off as a baron. Maurice proceeds to charm everyone at the chateau including the man-hungry Countess Valentine (Myrna Loy) and three maiden aunts (Elizabeth Patterson, Ethel Griffies, Blanche Frederici), who are chaperones to the Princess. When the masquerade is revealed, an upset Maurice takes the train back to Paris. But, by now, the princess realizes she adores him. She pursues her loved one on horseback. The Princess stops the train and the two lovers return happily to the chateau.

The *Los Angeles Times* reported, "Really a stylized fairy tale, LOVE ME TONIGHT is a stunning example of co-ordination in the making of a musical movie. Excellently cast, kinetically photographed, flawlessly mounted, it rejoices additionally in a synchronic score which punctuates the flow of the gay comedy and lends a final fillip to each camera sentence."

Ken Hanke pinpointed the special musical joys of LOVE ME TONIGHT in an article on director Rouben Mamoulian for *Films in Review* magazine (August/September 1988): "Eight major musical numbers . . . and no two are approached in the same fashion. . . . Admittedly, the score itself is a great benefit, offering some of Rodgers' and Hart's best songs, three of which have become standards. . . . The unalloyed delight of LOVE ME TONIGHT rests on what Mamoulian does with those songs."* Among the melodious highlights of LOVE ME TONIGHT are Chevalier and Jeanette MacDonald singing "Love Me Tonight" and "Isn't It Romantic?"

*According to Lorenz Hart, to perfect their rhythmic conversation song concept for LOVE ME TONIGHT, Richard Rodgers and Lorenz Hart studied ". . . [Motion] pictures, not on the sound set but in the cutting room. Then, with [Maurice] Chevalier and [Rouben] Mamoulian, we developed for the first time dialogue with a sort of phony little half-rhyme, with a little music under it, cut to the situation."

(which became a perennial favorite at Paramount over the years), while Maurice performs "Mimi" and MacDonald solos on "Lover" (sung to her horse!). Regarding Mamoulian's innovative use of song to span time and space, Tom Milne in *Mamoulian* (1969) noted that the director's most striking example of this "gimmick" is in the song, "The Son of a Gun Is Nothing But a Tailor." Milne explains how this number ". . . Disposes of the entire plot crisis with maximum effect and minimum fuss in a single song." He also noted: ". . . All the songs are used with the same playful unpredictability; and this is undoubtedly why Mamoulian is able to adhere faithfully to the conventions of the time—at the same time sending them up—without ever becoming bogged down by them."

Stanley Green (*Encyclopaedia of Musical Films,* 1987) summarized, "Though owing some of its satirical touches to such directors as Rene Clair and Ernst Lubitsch, LOVE ME TONIGHT remains one of the screen's most innovative and imaginative musicals. By its close integration of story, dialogue, song, scoring, and locale, and its sweeping use of the camera and skillful editing, it set the standards in the creation of a purely cinematic form of musical comedy."

Maurice Chevalier and Jeanette MacDonald would be reunited next for MGM's THE MERRY WIDOW (1934), *q.v.,* their final screen musical together. Producer-director Rouben Mamoulian would go to direct such musicals as HIGH, WIDE AND HANDSOME (1937), *q.v.,* SUMMER HOLIDAY (1948) and SILK STOCKINGS (1957), *q.v.*

THE LOVE PARADE (Paramount, 1929) 107 minutes. (Also silent version: 7.094′).

Producer, Ernst Lubitsch; directors, Lubitsch, Perry Ivins; based on the play *The Prince Consort* by Leon Xanrof, Jules Chancel; screenplay, Ernst Vajda, Guy Bolton; art director/set decorator, Hans Dreier; sound, Franklin Hansen; camera, Victor Milner; editor, Merrill White.

Songs: "Paris," "Stay the Same," "Dream Lover," "Anything to Please the Queen," "Wedding March," "Let's Be Common," "March of the Grenadiers," "Champagne," "My Love Parade," "Sylvania's Queen," "The Queen Is Always Right" (Victor Schertzinger, Clifford Grey); "Valse Tatjana" (O. Potoker).

Maurice Chevalier (Count Alfred Renard); Jeanette MacDonald (Queen Louise of Sylvania); Lupino Lane (Jacques); Lillian Roth (Lulu); Edgar Norton (Major Domo); Lionel Belmore (Prime Minister); Albert Roccardi (Foreign Minister); Carl Stockdale (Admiral); Eugene Pallette (Minister of War); E. H. Calvert (Sylvanian Ambassador); Russell Powell (Afghan Ambassador);

Margaret Fealy (First Lady in Waiting); Virginia Bruce, Josephine Hall, Rosaline Charles, Helen Friend (Ladies in Waiting); Yola D'Avril (Paulette); Andre Cheron (Paulette's Husband); Winter Hall (Priest); Ben Turpin (Cross-Eyed Lackey); Anton Vaverka, Albert De Winton, William Von Hardenburg (Cabinet Ministers); Jean Harlow (Extra in Theatre); and: Jiggs the Dog.

Following his sound feature film debut in INNOCENTS OF PARIS *(q.v.)* in 1929, extremely personable Maurice Chevalier solidified his screen popularity the same year with the sophisticated THE LOVE PARADE, an operetta set principally in the boudoir. This motion picture also served to introduce Broadway's Jeanette MacDonald to the screen, thus creating what was to be a very popular movie musical love team. "Sparkling as Burgundy," *Photoplay* said of the feature, adding, "Director [Ernst] Lubitsch conquers light opera, and Maurice Chevalier conquers all. Jeanette MacDonald is a treat to the eyes and ears." In *The Paramount Story* (1985), John Douglas Eames wrote, "It was something new to musicals. No backstage show-must-go-on clichés here, no chorus cuties or wise-cracking comics, but a subtly sexy romance, light as a zephyr and floating on airs composed by Victor Schertzinger. . . . It was astonishing how smoothly Lubitsch, in his first sound film, blended the songs with the action instead of staging them as interruptive 'numbers'."

In the kingdom of Sylvania, the cabinet ministers worry because beautiful Queen Louise (Jeanette MacDonald) is unwed and there are no heirs to the throne. The queen, however, is attracted to Count Alfred Renard (Maurice Chevalier) who has just returned in disgrace from Paris where he romanced too many young women while on a diplomatic assignment. The two are attracted to one another and quickly fall in love, all of which pleases the cabinet members. Meanwhile, Jacques (Lupino Lane), Alfred's butler, and Lulu (Lillian Roth), the maid to the queen, are carrying on their own love affair. After Louise and Alfred wed, the Count finds he does not enjoy taking orders from his royal wife. When she instructs him to attend an opera, he refuses. Instead, he plans to head to Paris and file for divorce. However, after the Queen promises to make her husband the country's King and thus her equal, they are reconciled.

THE LOVE PARADE contained ten songs and provided best-selling records for both its stars, with Chevalier having "My Love Parade" and MacDonald waxing "Dream Lover," both recording for Victor. The acting duo also headlined a French-language version of the feature, called PARADE D'AMOUR.

The team of Chevalier, MacDonald and director Lubitsch

would be reunited for Paramount's ONE HOUR WITH YOU (1932) and MGM's THE MERRY WIDOW (1934), *qq.v.*

LUCKY ME (Warner Bros., 1954) Color 99 minutes.

Producer, Henry Blanke; director, Jack Donohue; story, James O'Hanlon; screenplay, O'Hanlon, Robert O'Brien, Irving Elinson; art director, John Beckman; set decorator, William Wallace; music director, Ray Heindorf; sound, Oliver Garretson; camera, Wilfrid M. Cline; editor, Owen Marks.

Songs: "Lucky Me," "Superstition Song," "I Speak to the Stars," "Take a Memo to the Moon," "Love You Dearly," "Bluebells of Broadway," "Parisian Pretties," "Wanna Sing Like an Angel," "High Hopes," "Men" (Sammy Fain, Paul Francis Webster).

Doris Day (Candy Williams); Robert Cummings (Dick Carson); Phil Silvers (Hap Snyder); Eddie Foy, Jr. (Duke McGee); Nancy Walker (Flo Neely); Martha Hyer (Lorraine Thayer); Bill Goodwin (Otis Thayer); Marcel Dalio (Anton); Hayden Rorke (Tommy Arthur); James Burke (Mahoney); Herb Vigran (Theatre Manager); George Sherwood (Smith); Percy Helton (Brown); James Hayward (Jones); Jack Shea (Cop); William Bakewell (Motorist); Cliff Ferne (Orchestra Leader); Charles Cane (Ser-

Hayden Rorke, Bob Cummings and Bill Goodwin in LUCKY ME (1954).

geant); Jean DeBriac (Captain); Ann Tyrrell (Fortune Teller); Ray Teal, Tom Powers (Cronies); Angie Dickinson, Lucy Marlow, Dolores Dorn, Emmaline Henry (Party Guests); Gladys Hurlbut (Dowager); Jac George (Waiter Captain).

Shot in wide screen (the first 1050s musical feature to do so) and WarnerColor, LUCKY ME came along when overly sweet movie musicals were losing out to television for audience attention. LUCKY ME was too weak to bring in the kind of receipts necessary to keep this type of genre affair alive. The *New York Herald Tribune* termed it ". . one of those factory-made shows produced when the machine wasn't running quite right."

Candy Williams (Doris Day), Hap Snyder (Phil Silvers), Duke McGee (Eddie Foy, Jr.) and Flo Neely (Nancy Walker) are members of the touring act "Parisian Pretties," which is reduced to playing in movie theatres between features. When the group is stranded in Miami, the quartet take jobs working a posh hotel. There Candy meets and falls in love with songwriter Dick Carson (Robert Cummings), who has been romancing Lorraine Thayer (Martha Hyer) in the hopes that her Texas millionaire oilman father (Bill Goodwin) will back his next show. Candy and Lorraine vie for Dick's attention. Eventually he decides he prefers Candy's love to Lorraine's bank account. All ends happily when his show, starring Candy and her song-and-dance pals, is staged.

While only snippets are heard of the title song in LUCKY ME, Doris Day had several solo numbers, including "I Speak to the Stars," "Love You Dearly," "I Wanna Sing Like an Angel" and the bouncy novelty item, "The Superstition Song." Phil Silvers performed the comic "Men," while he and Day along with Foy and Walker did "Blue Bells of Broadway" and the show's best melody, "High Hopes."

"The screenplay . . . is a tissue of tired, often tiresome, gags and situations without redeeming imagination or originality. This pat musical format doesn't inspire Jack Donohue's direction to any heights and his handling of the Henry Blanke production is poor. Picture is so full of high and low places that the 99 minutes of footage seems overly long," *Variety* complained. On the credit side of LUCKY ME, the use of CinemaScope did enhance the scenery, Doris Day was peppy, and the presence of three such wonderful second-banana entertainers as Silvers, Walker and Foy could not be overlooked. Leading man Robert Cummings had played in several musicals over the decades, ranging from COLLEGE SWING (1938) to Deanna Durbin's SPRING PARADE (1940). In 1941 he had co-starred with Betty Grable in another Florida-set musical, MOON OVER MIAMI, *q.v.,* in which he sang briefly.

MAD ABOUT MUSIC (Universal, 1938) 98 minutes.

Producer, Joe Pasternak; director, Norman Taurog; story, Marcella Burke, Frederick Kohner; screenplay, Bruce Manning, Felix Jackson; camera, Joseph Valentine; editor, Philip Cahn.

Songs: "I Love to Whistle," "Chapel Bells," "Serenade to the Stars," "There Isn't a Day Goes By" (Harold Adamson, Jimmy McHugh); "Ave Maria" (Charles Gounod).

Deanna Durbin (Gloria Harkinson); Herbert Marshall (Richard Todd); Arthur Treacher (Tripps); Gail Patrick (Gwen Taylor); William Frawley (Dusty Rhodes); Jackie Moran (Tommy); Helen Parrish (Felice); Marcia Mae Jones (Olga); Christian Rub (Pierre); Charles Peck (Henry); Elizabeth Risdon (Louise Fusenot); Nana Bryant (Annette Fusenot); Joan Tree (Patricia); Sid Grauman (Himself); Franklin Pangborn (Hotel Manager); Charles Judels, Bert Roach (Conductors); Martha O'Driscoll (Pretty Girl); and: Cappy Barra's Harmonica Band, The Vienna Boys Choir.

After her successful feature film debut in THREE SMART GIRLS (1937), *q.v.,* which was followed by the even more popular ONE HUNDRED MEN AND A GIRL (*q.v.*) the same year, young Deanna Durbin teamed with producer Joe Pasternak for the third time. MAD ABOUT MUSIC allowed her to have a puppy love boyfriend on screen for the first time. Under the direction of Norman Taurog (Henry Koster had helmed the first two Durbin vehicles), the picture continued the winning ways of the Deanna Durbin screen persona. It brought in a mint at the box-office, providing moviegoers with all the ingredients they had come to expect of a Deanna Durbin picture.

Because her movie star mother Gwen Taylor (Gail Patrick) does not want the world to know she has a fourteen-year-old daughter, Gloria Harkinson (Deanna Durbin) has been placed in a fashionable Swiss girls' boarding school run by the Fusenot sisters (Elizabeth Risdon, Nana Bryant). There she is friends with roommate Olga (Marcia Mae Jones), at odds with fellow student Felice (Helen Parrish), and carries on an innocent romance with Tommy (Jackie Moran), a boy her own age. Although Gloria worships her mother from afar, when the other students brag about their parents, she fabricates stories about an imaginary big game hunter father. When cornered by Felice into revealing his whereabouts Gloria enlists the aid of visiting British composer Richard Todd (Herbert Marshall), who pretends to be her parent. Problems arise when her mother arrives on the scene. It all works out when the movie star and the composer actually fall in love.

Variety weighed that MAD ABOUT MUSIC: ". . . Has a genuine and enthralling, if somewhat obvious story. It has been thoughtfully and tastefully produced and skillfully directed. It has a generous melodious score. And it is played with beguiling spirit by an exceptional cast. It's a natural."

Musically Deanna Durbin performed "Serenade to the Stars," "Chapel Bells," "There Isn't a Day Goes By," "I Love to Whistle" and Gounod's "Ave Maria," the latter number backed by the Vienna Boys Choir. With the presence of debonair Herbert Marshall, glamorous Gail Patrick and Arthur Treacher (as the stuffy butler), MAD ABOUT MUSIC was an upper-case production.

Universal would remake MAD ABOUT MUSIC as the non-musical comedy, TOY TIGER (1956), starring Jeff Chandler, Larraine Day and the child actor Tim Hovey.

MAME (Warner Bros., 1974) Color 132 minutes.

Producer, Robert Fryer, James Cresson; director, Gene Saks; based on the musical play by Jerome Lawrence, Jerry Herman, Robert E. Lee; the play by Lawrence and Lee and the novel *Auntie Mame* by Patrick Dennis; production designer, Robert F. Boyle; art director, Harold Michelson; set decorator, Marvin March; costumes, Theadora van Runkle; music directors, Ralph Burns, Billy Byers; orchestrators, Ralph Burns, Billy Byers; music supervisor, Fred Werner; choreographers, Onna White, Martin Allen; sound, Al Overton, Jr.; sound re-recording, Arthur Piantadosi; special camera effects, Albert Whitlock; camera, Phil Lathrop; editor, Maury Winetrobe.

Songs: "St. Bridget," "It's Today," "Open a New Window," "The Man in the Moon Is a Lady," "My Best Girl," "We Need a Little Christmas Now," "Mame," "Loving You," "The Letter," "Bosom Buddies," "Gooch's Song," "If He Walked into My Life" (Jerry Herman).

Lucille Ball (Mame); Beatrice Arthur (Vera Charles); Robert Preston (Beauregard Burnside); Bruce Davison (Patrick Dennis); Kirby Furlong (Patrick Dennis as a Boy); Jane Connell (Agnes Gooch); George Chiang (Ito); Joyce Van Patten (Sally Cato); Doria Cook (Gloria Upson); Don Porter (Mr. Upson); Audrey Christie (Mrs. Upson); John McGiver (Mr. Babcock); Bobbi Jordan (Pegeen); Patrick Laborteaux (Peter); Lucile Benson (Mother Burnside); Ruth McDevitt (Cousin Fan); Burt Mustin (Uncle Jeff); James Bodhead (Floorwalker); Leonard Stone (Stage Manager); Roger Price (Ralph Divine); John Wheeler (Judge Bregoff); Ned Wertimer (Fred Kates); Alice Nunn (Fat Lady); Jerry Ayres (Bunny); Michele Nichols (Midge); Eric Gordon (Boyd); Barbara Bosson (Emily).

With such a wonderful literary heritage, the movie MAME

should have been a winner. Instead it was a sore disappointment, showcasing a badly miscast Lucille Ball in what proved to be her final theatrical feature film.

Patrick Dennis' 1955 novel *Auntie Mame* was a comic delight. It was transformed into a stage comedy in 1956 (with book by Jerome Lawrence and Robert E. Lee) starring Rosalind Russell and ran for 639 performances.* It was brought to the screen roaringly by Warner Bros. in 1959 with Rosalind Russell recreating the title role. In 1966 the property was translated into the musical *Mame,* using the Lawrence-Lee book and with music-lyrics by Jerry Herman. Starring Angela Lansbury, Beatrice Arthur and Jane Connell, the show ran for 1,508 performances.** The song "Mame" was a best-selling record for Herb Alpert and the Tijuana Brass and a minor success for both Louis Armstrong and Bobby Darin. When Warner Bros. filmed the musical version in 1974—in the era of only filmed pre-sold Broadway musical hits—many of the Broadway cast and production crew were kept intact. However, Lucille Ball (who at the time had just retired from over two decades as the queen of television) was assigned the title role. When she broke her ankle skiing, filming was postponed. However, it was finally shot, with Ball in the pivotal title assignment. The combination of her weak ankle (which mitigated against her doing much hoofing), her age (causing her scenes to be shot under a heavy filter), and especially her non-affinity for the role spoiled what should have been a joyous motion picture.

In 1928 when he is ten years old, Patrick Dennis (Kirby Furlong) is orphaned. He is brought to New York City by his loyal governess Agnes Gooch (Jane Connell), to be cared for by his only living relative, the wealthy and eccentric Auntie Mame (Lucille Ball). The vivacious Mame determines to educate Patrick by her own unorthodox standards. The boy is briefly sent to a progressive school, much to the chagrin of stern Mr. Babcock (John McGiver), the trustee of the Dennis estate. When the 1929 Wall Street stock market crash wipes out her funds, Mame attempts to break into show business, accepting a small role in an operetta starring her friend Vera Charles (Bea Arthur). When that turns out to be a disaster, Mame goes to work selling shoes at Macy's Department Store. There she encounters wealthy Beauregard Burnside (Robert

---

*Among the others who played *Auntie Mame* on Broadway were Greer Garson and Beatrice Lillie; Sylvia Sidney and Constance Bennett were among the actresses who performed the star turn on tour.

**Among the others who starred in *Mame* on Broadway were Celeste Holm, Janis Paige and Ann Miller.

Preston), a handsome Southerner. Mame visits him at his family estate where she outfoxes her rival, Sally Cato (Joyce Van Patten), in the course of a hunt. She and Beauregard marry, but he is killed in an avalanche while skiing abroad. Back in America Mame again takes charge of Patrick. The latter is now an adult (Bruce Davison) and is planning to wed snobbish Gloria Upson (Doria Cook) of Connecticut. In a scheme to get rid of the superficial Gloria, Mame invites Mr. and Mrs. Upson (Don Porter, Audrey Christie) and Gloria to her Manhattan apartment. As planned, the visitors are aghast at Mame's bizarre array of friends, including bohemian Vera and a very pregnant (and unwed) Agnes Gooch. While Patrick loses Gloria he falls in love with Pegeen (Bobbi Jordan) who has replaced Agnes in the household. In 1948, the still bubbly Mame takes Patrick and Pegeen's small son on a summer adventure to Moscow. For Mame, life is still a banquet!

"That's How Young I Feel" was deleted from the Broadway score (for good reason) and "Loving You" was added for Robert Preston to sing. (He provides one of the strongest characterizations in the spiritless movie.) The set piece of the movie should have been the production number surrounding the title song, but as directed and choreographed it was an anti-climax. Fortunately, Bea Arthur ("The Man in the Moon Is a Lady") and Jane Connell ("Gooch's Song") were on hand to repeat their comic vocal turns. It was Arthur who carried the duet "Bosom Buddies," sung with a frog-voiced Lucille Ball.

Since comedy was Lucille Ball's forte, much was done to bring slapstick, instead of quick-witted comedy, into the proceedings. As such, on this lesser level, Ball strained to do her best with the fox hunt and get-rid-of-the-Upsons sequence, as well as her moments of bringing disaster to the stage operetta and chaos to Macy's department store.

Among the critics who minced no words when reviewing MAME was Pauline Kael (*New Yorker* magazine): "Too terrible to be boring; you can get fixated staring at it and wondering what exactly Lucille Ball thinks she's doing. When that sound comes out—it's somewhere between a bark, a croak, and a quaver—does she think she's singing? When she throws up her arms . . . and cries out 'Listen, everybody!' does she really think she's a fun person?"

When the film opened in England, fourteen minutes were deleted from the movie, including the "Bosom Buddies" number. Geoff Brown (British *Monthly Film Bulletin*) warned, "Put the blame on MAME, boys! For it makes one realise afresh the parlous state of the Hollywood musical, fighting to survive against misplaced superstars and elephantine budgets matched with minuscule imagination. . . . 'She'll coax the blues right out of your heart' boast the posters; on the whole, MAME coaxes more into it."

MAME grossed a disappointing $6,500,000 in distributors' domestic film rentals.

THE MAN FROM THE FOLIES BERGERE *see* FOLIES BERGERE.

MAN OF LA MANCHA (United Artists, 1972) Color 135 minutes.

Executive producer, Alberto Grimaldi; producer, Arthur Hiller; associate producer, Saul Chapin; director, Hiller; based on the musical play by Dale Wasserman, Mitch Leigh, Joe Darion, and suggested by *Don Quixote* by Miguel de Cervantes; screenplay, Wasserman; art director, Luciano Damiani; set decorator, Arrigo Breschi; costumes, Damiani; makeup, Charles Parker, Euclide Santoli, Guisse Giuseppe Annunziata; music director, Laurence Rosenthal; choreographer, Gillian Lynne; special effects, Adriano Pischiutta; camera, Giuseppe Rotunno; editors, Robert C. Jones, Folmar Blangsted.

Songs: "It's All the Same," "The Impossible Dream," "Barber's Song," "Man of La Mancha," "Dulcinea," "I'm Only Thinking of Him," "I Really Like Him," "Little Bird, Little Bird," "The Dubbing," "Life As It Really Is," "Aldonza," "A Little Gossip," "The Psalm," "Golden Helmet of Mambrino" (Mitch Leigh, Joe Darion).

Peter O'Toole (Miguel de Cervantes/Don Quixote/Alonso Quijana); Sophia Loren (Dulcinea/Aldonza); James Coco (Manservant/Sancho Panza); Harry Andrews (Governor/Innkeeper); John Castle (Duke/Dr. Carrasco/Black Knight/Knight of the Mirrors); Brian Blessed (Pedro); Ian Richardson (Padre); Julie Gregg (Antonio/Lady in White); Rosalee Crutchley (Housekeeper); Gino Conforti (Barber); Marne Maitland (Captain of the Guards); Dorothy Sinclair (Maria/Innkeeper's Wife); Miriam Acevedo (Fermina) Dominic Barto, Poldo Bendandi, Peppi Borza, Mario Donen, Fred Evans, Francesco Ferrini, Paolo Gozlino, Teddy Green, Peter Johnston, Roy Jones, Connel Miles, Steffen Zacharias, Lou Zamprogna, Calogero Caruana, Rolando De Santis (Muleteers); Simon Gilbert (Singing Voice of Miguel de Cervantes).

Dale Wasserman adapted his 1965 Tony and Drama Critics award-winning play, *Man of La Mancha,* to the screen, but the results were sadly disappointing. While Arthur Hiller did a decent job producing and directing this expansive effort, the musical screen version of MAN OF LA MANCHA was too often a lifeless affair. It was harmed by Peter O'Toole's performance as a loony Don Quixote, although one can find no fault with Sophia Loren as Dulcinea or James Coco as the rotund Sancho Panza. The screen musical proved to be a box-office dud (grossing less than $4,000,000 in distributors' domestic film rentals) and did disservice to the long-running stage version.*

In Seville, Spain, aging Miguel de Cervantes (Peter O'Toole) is thrown into a dungeon, awaiting trial by the Inquisition for an alleged offence against the Church. He soon finds himself the victim of a kangaroo court by his fellow prisoners. They snatch away all of his possessions including his manuscript to *Don Quixote.* To placate the mob, he tells them the story of Don Quixote (Peter O'Toole) and his associate, Sancho Panza (James Coco), and how they once set out to revive the age of chivalry. It was their goal to fight evil, defend the honor of women and right all wrongs. The addled Quixote does battle with a dragon which turns out to be a windmill and, later, he and Sancho encounter a servant girl, Aldonza (Sophia Loren) who is actually a whore. To Quixote she is the ideal female and he calls her Dulcinea (Sophia Loren). Thanks to his faith in her, the girl is transformed into a beautiful woman, while the Innkeeper (Harry Andrews) dubs Quixote "The Knight of the Woeful Countenance" after he defends Dulcinea's honor. Later, the girl is raped by a gang of muleteers and the Innkeeper denounces Quixote. When the old man realizes his own madness and gives up on life, Aldonza feels a sense of loss. As Quixote lies dying, she asks him to return to his quest. After he passes away, she informs Panza that her name is now Dulcinea. The story done, Cervantes finds he has had a powerful effect on the other prisoners in the dungeon. So deeply affected are they by Cervantes' tale that they return his manuscript to him. Cervantes now goes forth to face the Inquisition.

Besides the performances of Sophia Loren and James Coco, the best ingredient of MAN OF LA MANCHA was its score, with the former two actors doing their own vocals. On the other hand, Peter O'Toole's numbers, including the notable "The Impossible Dream," were dubbed by Simon Gilbert. Gilbert also did well by "Dulcinea," while Loren sang "It's All the Same" and dueted with Gilbert on "Aldonza." James Coco did the amusing "I Really Like

---

**Man of La Mancha*, starring Richard Kiley, Ray Middleton and Joan Diener opened in New York City on November 22, 1965 and ran for 2,329 performances. The musical was based on Miguel de Cervantes' *Don Quixote* and had music by Mitch Leigh and lyrics by Joe Darion. It became a stock theatrical staple with Allan Jones in the title role.

Him." Although Harry Andrews was adequate as the Innkeeper, his rendition of "The Dubbing" lacked the comic zest given it by Ray Middleton on Broadway. The original cast album of *Man of La Mancha* stayed on the record charts for over two years, while the film soundtrack lasted only some four months.

MARCH OF THE TOYS *see* BABES IN TOYLAND (1934).

MARCH OF THE WOODEN SOLDIERS *see* BABES IN TOYLAND (1934).

MARY POPPINS (Buena Vista, 1964) Color 140 minutes.

Producer, Walt Disney; co-producer, Bill Walsh; director, Robert Stevenson; based on the books by P. L. Travers; screenplay, Walsh, Don DaGradi; art directors, Carroll Clark, William H. Tuntke; set decorators, Emile Kuri, Hal Gausman; costumes, Tony Walton; makeup, Pat McNalley; animation art director, McLaren Stewart; nursery sequence designers, Bill Justice, Xavier Atencio; music supervisor/arranger/conductor, Irwin Kostal; music editor, Evelyn Kennedy; choreographers, Marc Breaux, Dee Dee Wood; assistant directors, Joseph L. McEveety, Paul Feiner; second unit director (live action), Arthur J. Vitarelli; special effects, Peter Ellenshaw, Hamilton Luske, Eustace Lycett, Robert A. Mattey; camera, Edward Colman; sound supervisor, Robert O. Cook; editor, Cotton Warburton.

Songs: "The Perfect Nanny," "Sister Suffragette," "The Life I Lead," "A Spoonful of Sugar," "Pavement Artist," "Chim Chim Cheree," "Jolly Holiday," "Super-Cali-Fragil-Istic-Expi-Ali-Docious," "Stay Awake," "I Love to Laugh," "Feed the Birds," "Fidelity Fiduciary Bank," "Step in Time," "A Man Has Dreams," "Let's Go Fly a Kite" (Richard M. Sherman, Robert B. Sherman).

Julie Andrews (Mary Poppins); Dick Van Dyke (Bert/Mr. Dawes, Sr.); David Tomlinson (Mr. Banks); Glynis Johns (Mrs. Banks); Hermione Baddeley (Ellen); Reta Shaw (Mrs. Brill); Karen Dotrice (Jane Banks); Matthew Garber (Michael Banks); Elsa Lanchester (Katie Nanna); Arthur Treacher (Constable Jones); Reginald Owen (Admiral Boom); Ed Wynn (Uncle Albert); Jane Darwell (The Bird Woman); Arthur Malet (Mr. Dawes, Jr.); Cyril Delevanti (Mr. Grubbs); Lester Matthews (Mr. Tornes); Clive L. Halliday (Mr. Mousely); Donald Barclay (Mr. Binnacle); Marjorie Bennett (Miss Lark); Alma Lawton (Mrs. Corry); Marjorie Eaton (Miss Persimmon); Doris Lloyd (Depositor); Major Sam Harris (Citizen); and: James Logan.

MARY POPPINS was one of the Disney Studio's most successful family films, with a gross of $45 million in distributors' domestic film rentals. It was the last really outstanding feature that Walt Disney personally supervised. Julie Andrews was named Best Actress by the Academy of Motion Picture Arts and Sciences for her work in this musical fantasy which was also nominated as Best Picture but lost to Warner Bros.' MY FAIR LADY (*q.v.*). Richard M. Sherman and Robert B. Sherman also won Oscars for Original Music Score and the song "Chim Chim Cher-ee." Peter Ellenshaw, Hamilton Luske, Eustace Lycett, and Robert A. Mattey won an Oscar for Special Visual Effects. The soundtrack album remained on *Billboard* magazine's charts for seventy-eight weeks, and in #1 position for fourteen weeks.

In London after the turn-of-the-century, street entertainer Bert (Dick Van Dyke) is told by Admiral Boom (Reginald Owen) that trouble exists in the household of banker George Banks (David Tomlinson) and his suffragette wife (Glynis Johns) because they cannot keep household help or a nanny for their children, Jane (Karen Dotrice) and Michael (Matthew Garber). When the latest nanny (Elsa Lanchester) resigns, Mr. Banks writes an ad for a new governess. However, his children, who have been escorted home

Dick Van Dyke and Julie Andrews in MARY POPPINS (1964).

by Constable Jones (Arthur Treacher), intercede and he throws the ad into the fire. It turns to smoky ashes and rises up the chimney, only to be intercepted by Mary Poppins (Julie Andrews). She is a magical young woman who arrives the next day at the Banks home at 17 Cherry Tree Lane and is given the job. With her charges in hand, Mary later meets Bert in the park. The quartet go to the country and the next day they visit Uncle Albert (Ed Wynn) who is dying of laughter. While Mr. Banks upbraids Mary for taking his offspring to the races (Mary wins a race riding a merry-go-round horse) and to tea parties, he has no effect on the unorthodox Miss. The next day she tells the youngsters about the old Bird Woman (Jane Darwell) at St. Paul's Cathedral. The children quarrel with their father at the bank and flee. They run into Bert, who is now a chimney sweep. The children embark on a tour of the London rooftops with Bert and Mary. Later, Bert helps Mr. Banks realize his shortcomings as a father. When Banks returns to the office thereafter, he is fired by the president, Mr. Dawes (Dick Van Dyke). But he takes the news happily, causing Uncle Albert to laugh himself to death. Mary can now leave the household, as the Banks family is a happy one, with the father planning to take over Uncle Albert's business position at the bank. As she floats upward, Mary Poppins is seen only by Bert.

In *The Disney Films* (1973), Leonard Maltin wrote, "Many regard MARY POPPINS as Walt Disney's crowning achievement, and that it may well be. Certainly it was the biggest hit in the history of the studio, both critically and financially; it is the kind of movie that will continue to play forever. And in most regards, it *does* have the feeling of a masterwork; that is to say, the film is really the culmination of thirty-five years' work, for no amount of enthusiasm or capability could take the place of the experience of the Disney staff, under the guidance of Walt himself, that worked together to make this film." In *Saturday Review* magazine, Hollis Alpert termed MARY POPPINS "One of the most magnificent pieces of entertainment ever to come from Hollywood."

In addition to their Oscar-winning "Chim Chim Cher-ee (sung by Julie Andrews, Dick Van Dyke and the Children) the Shermans composed a masterful music score for this delightful fantasy, including the unforgettable tongue-twister, "Super-Cali-Fragil-Istic-Expi-Ali-Docious," sung by Andrews and Van Dyke. Also memorable are Glynis Johns' "Sister Suffragette" and Ed Wynn's delightful "I Love to Laugh."

MARY POPPINS was the screen debut of Julie Andrews who ironically had lost out on recreating her role in Warner Bros.' MY FAIR LADY (starring Audrey Hepburn). It was the first of several screen musicals for Andrews, including THE SOUND OF MUSIC (1965), q.v., THOROUGHLY MODERN MILLIE (1967) and the disastrous STAR! (1968). Dick Van Dyke, who played dual roles in MARY POPPINS, would star in CHITTY CHITTY BANG BANG (1968), *q.v.,* United Artists' misfire attempt to duplicate the success of the whimsical MARY POPPINS. The Disney organization would turn out BEDKNOBS AND BROOMSTICKS (1971), another fantasy musical set in London and featuring a heroine (Angela Lansbury) who flies.

For several years, there have been recurring rumors of a sequel to MARY POPPINS starring Julie Andrews or Angela Lansbury, both of whom are now far closer to the age of the nanny from P. L. Travers' books.

MAYTIME (Metro-Goldwyn-Mayer, 1937) 132 minutes.

Producer, Hunt Stromberg; directors, Robert Z. Leonard, William Von Wymetal; based on the operetta by Rida Johnson Young, Sigmund Romberg; screenplay, Noel Langley; art directors, Cedric Gibbons, Frederic Hope; set decorator, Edwin B. Willis; costumes, Adrian; music director, Herbert Stothart; choreographer, Val Raset; camera, Oliver T. Marsh; editor, Conrad A. Nervig.

Songs: "Maytime" (Sigmund Romberg, Rida Johnson Young); "Summer Is a Cumin In" (traditional); "Love's Old Sweet Song" (J. L. Molloy, G. Clifton Bingham); "Vive L'Opera (folk song; lyrics, Bob Wright, Chet Forrest); "Student Drinking Song," (Herbert Stothart); "Le Regiment de Sambre et Meuse" (Robert Planquette); "Reverie" (based on Romberg airs); "Plantons La Vigne" (traditional); "Carry Me Back to Old Virginny" (James Bland); "Santa Lucia" (Teodoro Cottrau); "Jump Jim Crow," "Road to Paradise," "Dancing Will Keep You Young" (Young, Cyrus Wood, Romberg); "The Page's Aria (Nobles Seigneurs, Salut!)" from the opera *Les Huguenots* (Giacomo Meyerbeer); "Les Filles de Cadiz" by Leo Delibes; "Street Singer" (Wright, Forrest, Stothart); "Now Is the Month of Maying" (traditional; lyrics, Thomas Morley); "Chi Me Frena" from the opera *Lucia di Lammermoor* (Gaetano Donizetti); "William Tell Overture" from the opera *William Tell* (Giacchino Rossini); "Soldiers' Chorus" from the opera *Faust* (Charles Gounod); "Anvil Chorus," "Miserere" from the opera *Il Trovatore* (Giuseppe Verdi); "Largo Al Factotum" from the opera *The Barber of Seville* (Rossini); "Caro Nome," "La Donna E Mobile" from the opera *Rigoletto* (Verdi); "O, Du Mein Holder Abendstem" from the opera *Tannhauser* (Richard Wagner); "Liebestod" from the opera *Tristan und Isolde* (Wagner); "Sempre Libera" from the opera *La Traviata* (Verdi); "Mazurka" (traditional), "Napoleonic Waltz," "The Last Rose of Summer," "I Dreamt I Dwelt in Marble Halls," (Alfred Bunn, Michael Balfe); "Une Dame Noble Et Sage," "The Sidewalks of New York" (James Blake, Charles B. Lawlor); "Columbia, the Gem of the Ocean" (authorship disputed); arias from the "opera" *Czaritza* (music from the "Symphony No. 5 in E, Opus 64" by Peter Ilyich Tchaikovsky; French lyrics, Giles Guilbert).

Jeanette MacDonald (Marcia Morney [Miss Morrison]); Nelson Eddy (Paul Allison); John Barrymore (Nicholai Nazaroff); Herman Bing (August Archipenko); Tom Brown (Kip Stuart); Lynne Carver (Barbara Roberts); Rafaela Ottiano (Ellen); Charles Judels (Cabby); Paul Porcasi (Composer Trentini); Sig Rumann (Fanchon); Walter Kingsford (Rudyard); Edgar Norton (Secretary); Guy Bates Post (Emperor Louis Napoleon); Iphigenie Castiglioni (Empress Eugenie); Adia Kuznetzoff (Dubrovsky, Czaritza's Minister/Student in Cafe); John Le Sueur (Maypole Dancer); Russell Hicks (Monsieur Bulliet, the Voice Teacher); Harry Davenport, Harry Hayden, Howard Hickman, Robert C. Fischer (Opera Directors); Harlan Briggs (Bearded Director); Frank Sheridan (O'Brien, a Director); Billy Gilbert (Cafe Drunk); Ivan Lebedeff (Empress' Dinner Companion); Leonid Kinskey (Student in Bar); Clarence Wilson (Waiter); Maurice Cass (Opera House Manager); Douglas Wood (Massilon, the Hotel Manager); Barnard Suss (Assistant Manager); Henry Roquemore (Publicity Man); Alexander Schonberg (French Proprietor); Mariska Aldrich (Opera Contralto); Paul Weigel (Prompter); Ben Welden, Jose Rubio, Jack Murphy, Blair Davies, Agostino Borgato, Alberto Morin (Students); Delmar Watson, Buster Slavens, Grace Hayle, Luke Cosgrave, Diana Dean, Allen Cavan, Sarah Edwards (Bits); Christian Frank (Gendarme); George Davis (Usher); Pat Somerset (Gossiper); Ian Wolfe (Court Official); Gus Leonard (Concierge); Brandon Hurst (Master of Ceremonies); Eric Lonsdale, Guy D'Ennery (Aides); Claude King (Noble); Forbes Murray (Aide); Fred Graham, Frank O'Connor (Servants); Barlowe Borland (Stage Doorman); Charles Requa (Stage Manager); Arthur Stuart Hull, Harold Entwhistle (Roués); Frank Elliott (Aide): Jacques Lory (Drunk); Belle Mitchell (Maid); Hans Joby (Doctor); Christian Rub (Sleeper Outside Cafe); Genaro Spagnoli (Chef); Paul Cremonesi (Opera Critic); Oscar Rudolph, Herta Lind (Peasants); Jolly Lee Harvey (Fat Woman); Armand "Curley" Wright (Bow and Arrow Stand Man); Sidney Jarvis, Albert Pollet (Cabbies); Francisco Maran (Gendarme); Ed Goddard (Juggling Clown); Bob Watson, Helen Parris ("Merry Month of May" Singers); Joan Breslaw (Queen of the May); Nan Merriman, George London (*Les Hugenots*

Chorus); The Don Cossack Chorus (Chorus for "Le Regiment de Sambre et Meuse").

The third screen teaming of Jeanette MacDonald and Nelson Eddy, MAYTIME, was begun in Technicolor in 1936. However, it was scrapped when MGM executive-producer Irving Thalberg suddenly died in the fall of that year.* Production was resumed sometime later in black-and-white, with Hunt Stromberg supervising the lavish project which cost $1.5 million. Robert Z. Leonard replaced Edmund Goulding as director and some of the supporting cast was changed. It was based on the Sigmund Romberg operetta of 1917 which starred Peggy Wood and which had been filmed as a silent movie by Preferred Pictures in 1923. MAYTIME proved to be one of Jeanette MacDonald and Nelson Eddy's most popular vehicles.** It won an Academy Award nomination for Best Music Score for Herbert Stothart.

On May Day in 1906 in a small American town elderly Miss Morrison (Jeanette MacDonald) overhears a quarrel between Kip (Tom Brown) and Barbara (Lynne Carver), who wants to become a famous opera singer in New York City. When the two young lovers decide to break up, Miss Morrison tries to console Barbara. She tells her how she was once a famous diva named Marcia Morney. As she tells her story the film reverts to 1865 and to the court of Louis Napoleon (Guy Bates Post). There she is introduced to the nobility by her mentor-teacher, the much older Nicholai Nazaroff (John Barrymore). Following her success at court, the indebted Marcia agrees to marry Nicholai, but later at a cafe she meets handsome American baritone Paul Allison (Nelson Eddy). They tour the sights

---

*Among the $500,000 of footage scrapped from the first version of MAYTIME were a segment of Nelson Eddy and Jeanette MacDonald performing selections from the opera *Tosca* as well as "Farewell to Dream." In the revamped production, Frank Morgan was replaced by Herman Bing and John Barrymore substituted for Paul Lukas. At studio head Louis B. Mayer's dictate, the script was altered so that the lovers do *not* marry, but instead endure the more romantic fate of being unfulfilled lovers who, in the finale, are reunited and remain young eternally. In the first MAYTIME a good deal of the storyline occurred in America.

**In *Gotta Sing Gotta Dance* (1970) John Kobal observed, "All the resources of the world's most powerful film studio were lavished on . . . [MAYTIME]. The Empress Eugenie dresses designed by Adrian almost move themselves; Cedric Gibbons' reconstruction of the last days of the third Empire, requiring ball rooms, period apartments, Parisian bohemian quarters, and then the early American small town at the turn of the century, are uniformly superlative. Sydney Guilaroff designed the magnificent hairstyles, William Daniels' photography glows, and the story, based on the Sigmund Romberg operetta, gave MacDonald a part with greater range and depth than most she played at MGM. . . . [She] exhibits a self-mocking fundamental honesty and integrity that is part of her artless charm."

of Paris together and fall in love. Eventually the two break up, since Marcia feels she must keep her promise to the now insanely jealous maestro. The years pass and Marcia becomes a famous diva. On an American tour she is reunited on stage at the Metropolitan Opera with Paul and the two realize they are still in love. That night Marcia begs Nicholai for her freedom. He agrees reluctantly, but later, overtaken by jealousy he hastens to Paul's rooms and kills him. Returning to the present, Barbara promises Miss Morrison to make up with Kip. When she leaves, Miss Morrison dies. Marcia and Paul are reunited in spirit, appearing as they were when they were first in love.

The production provided MacDonald and Eddy with one of their most memorable duets, "Maytime (Will You Remember?)" It is first performed in a wondrously picturesque St. Cloud's May Day country fair setting and is then reprised frequently throughout the motion picture. Many of the film's most impressive opera sequences relied on a "shadow" opera, *Czaritza* (derived from themes of Tchaikovsky's Symphony No. 5), which was custom-composed for this movie. Additionally there is a montage sequence featuring MacDonald in a series of selections from actual operas. In these classical offerings a great deal of care is taken to interweave the operatic selections imaginatively into the storyline—for the benefit of the lowbrow among filmgoers and to present the stars at their optimum. In MAYTIME Nelson Eddy revealed a lighter side to his persona when he sings the "Students' Drinking Song" (harmonizing with the tavern group), and in the delightfully carefree breakfast scene—where he cooks ham and eggs—he and MacDonald duet on "Carry Me Back to Ole Virginny."

The *New York Daily Mirror* decided, "Abandoning the mood of light frivolity which pervaded their previous hits, MAYTIME is a perfect romance, a little sad, greatly charming and tender." The *New York Times* said "The screen can do no wrong while these two are singing: when, in addition it places a splendid production behind them, the result approaches perfection."

The two stars recreated their roles from MAYTIME on "Lux Radio Theatre" on CBS on September 4, 1944. This period operetta has become a favorite on television, frequently televised as a special May Day event.

MEET ME IN ST. LOUIS (Metro-Goldwyn-Mayer, 1944) Color 113 minutes.

Producer, Arthur Freed; director, Vincente Minnelli; based on the book by Sally Benson; screenplay, Irving Brecher, Fred F. Finklehoffe, (uncredited): Benson, Doris Gilbert, Sarah Y. Mason, Victor Heerman, William Ludwig; art directors, Cedric Gibbons,

Lemuel Ayers, Jack Martin Smith; set decorators, Edwin B. Willis, Paul Huldschinsky; costume supervisor, Irene; costumes designer, Irene Sharaff; makeup, Jack Dawn; music director, George Stoll, (uncredited) Lennie Hayton; music adaptor, Roger Edens; orchestrator, Conrad Salinger; choreographer, Charles Walters; color consultants, Natalie Kalmus, Henri Jaffa; sound supervisor, Douglas Shearer; camera, George Folsey; editor, Albert Akst.

Songs: "The Boy Next Door," "The Trolley Song," "Have Yourself a Merry Little Christmas" (Hugh Martin, Ralph Blane); "Under the Bamboo Tree" (Bob Cole, J. Rosamond Johnson); "Meet Me in St. Louis" (Andrew B. Sterling, Kerry Mills); "Skip to My Lou" (traditional; revised by Martin, Blane); "You and I" (Arthur Freed, Nacio Herb Brown); "I Was Drunk Last Night" (traditional); "Over the Bannister" (traditional; arranger, Conrad Salinger); "Brighten the Corner (Charles H. Gabriel, Jr.); "Summer in St. Louis," "The Invitation" (Roger Edens); "All Hallow's Eve," "The Horrible One," "Ah, Love!" (Salinger); "Good-Bye My Lady Love" (Joe Howard); "Under the Anheuser Bush" (Albert von Tilzer); "Little Brown Jug" (Eastburn; arranger, Lennie Hayton); "The Fair" (Hayton).

Judy Garland (Esther Smith); Margaret O'Brien ("Tootie" Smith); Mary Astor (Mrs. Anne Smith); Lucille Bremer (Rose Smith); June Lockhart (Lucille Ballard); Tom Drake (John Truett); Marjorie Main (Katie); Harry Davenport (Grandpa); Leon Ames (Alonzo Smith); Henry Daniels (Lon Smith, Jr.); Joan Carroll (Agnes Smith); Hugh Marlowe (Colonel Darly); Robert Sully (Warren Sheffield); Chill Wills (Mr. Neely); Donald Curtis (Dr. Terry); Mary Jo Ellis (Ida Boothby); Ken Wilson (Quentin); Robert Emmett O'Connor (Motorman); Darryl Hickman (Johnny Tevis); Leonard Walker (Conductor); Victor Kilian (Baggage Man); John Phipps (Mailman); Major Sam Harris (Mr. March); Mayo Newhall (Mr. Braukoff); Belle Mitchell (Mrs. Braukoff); Sidney Barnes (Hugo Borvis); Myron Tobias (George); Victor Cox (Driver); Kenneth Donner, Buddy Gorman, Joe Cobbs (Clinton Badgers); Helen Gilbert (Girl on Trolley); Arthur Freed (Singing Voice of Alonzo Smith); D. Markas (Singing Voice of Anne Smith).

In late 1944 John T. McManus wrote in *PM* newspaper, "If the archive keepers of film know their business, MEET ME IN ST. LOUIS should be in for a spell of immortality . . . as a technically excellent, warmly presented and charmingly produced item of musical Americana." His judgment has become prophetically true. This movie has become one of the most endearingly popular of all (MGM) musicals and is perhaps the film by which Judy Garland is best remembered today.

Margaret O'Brien, Judy Garland and Henry Daniels, Jr. in MEET ME IN ST. LOUIS (1944).

In 1941–42, the *New Yorker* magazine had published eight of Sally Benson's "The Kensington Stories," which affectionately dealt with life on 5135 Kensington Avenue in St. Louis at the turn of the century. The nostalgic material came to the attention of MGM producer Arthur Freed and, with the approval of studio chief Louis B. Mayer, he began the process of adapting the reminiscences to the screen. As the project expanded, it shifted from a near non-musical concept to one in which song, dance and music would help to convey the storyline. Judy Garland was fixed upon as the star, with George Cukor to direct. When the latter became involved in World War II military service, Vincente Minnelli replaced him. Van Johnson was a first choice to play John Truett (the "Boy Next Door") but later casting changed the assignment to contract performer Tom Drake. While the rest of the performers were being assembled, including Lucille Bremer (in her film debut) as sister

Rose, plans for the physical production kept expanding. The project was to have been shot originally on the "Andy Hardy" series Carvel Street set, but Freed wanted a very special and authentic look. Lemuel Ayers, the designer of the recent Broadway hit *Oklahoma!,* joined the creative force to prepare the elaborate St. Louis street set (which cost a then staggering $208,000).

Meanwhile, songwriters Hugh Martin and Ralph Blane, who had written the score for the Arthur Freed production of BEST FOOT FORWARD (1943) at MGM, prepared the songs for this major offering. Three of the solo numbers for Garland are classics which became an indelible part of her repertoire: the wistful ballad, "The Boy Next Door"; the bittersweet Yuletime tune, "Have Yourself a Merry Little Christmas"; and the expansive production number, "The Trolley Song." Garland was given a new arrangement of "Under the Bamboo Tree" to sing, a number which finds younger sister Tootie (Margaret O'Brien) joining her in a brief duet and for a cakewalk dance. Garland alone handled "Skip to My Lou," sung in the Smith family's parlor. Producer Arthur Freed was not only a co-writer of the old song, "You and I," but when it was decided to dub the voices of Mr. Smith (Leon Ames) and Mrs. Smith (Mary Astor), he provided the former's singing while D. Markas substituted for Astor on the vocals. It was a given that "Meet Me in St. Louis" (by Andrew B. Sterling and Kerry Mills) would be used; the genius was in having the song sung in snatches by members of the Smith household—including Katie the maid (Marjorie Main) and Grandpa (Harry Davenport)—helping to establish characterization and mood. One number which was deleted was "Boys and Girls Like You and Me," which had been written by Richard Rodgers and Oscar Hammerstein, II for *Oklahoma!* but had been cut from the stage show. In MEET ME IN ST. LOUIS the song was sung as Tom Drake carried Judy Garland across a mud puddle at the World's Fair site. It was decided that the number slowed down the pacing and it was excised from the release print.

In the summer of 1903, all of St. Louis is anticipating next year's World's Fair. So are the Smiths at 5135 Kensington Avenue. The household is comprised of attorney Alonzo Smith (Leon Ames) and his wife (Mary Astor) and their five offspring: Alonzo ("Lon") Jr. (Henry Daniels, Jr.), Rose (Lucille Bremer), Esther (Judy Garland), Agnes (Joan Carroll), and the youngest, "Tootie" (Margaret O'Brien). Not to be overlooked are Grandpa (Harry Davenport) and the efficient maid, Katie (Marjorie Main). Romance is a focal item at the Smiths. Rose has a beau away at college and another one locally, Lon has a St. Louis girlfriend, while Esther develops a strong crush on the new next-door neighbor, John Truett (Tom Drake). The little one, Tootie, happily engrossed in her world of childhood fantasy and fun, has her own passions. She spends a great deal of time riding about town with Mr. Neely (Chill Wills), the iceman. Tootie displays great bravery in meeting the challenge of scary Halloween, but, on occasion, tells a fib which leads to confusion among her elders. Mr. Smith announces that the family is going to relocate to New York City where he has a new business opportunity. The family is depressed by the news, and none more so than Tootie who smashes her beloved snowman in the backyard. Eventually Mr. Smith decides that his loved ones' peace of mind is more important than his career advancement. It is agreed they will remain in St. Louis. Later, the joyful Smith family sets out to explore the wonders of the St. Louis World's Fair.

Variety printed, "MEET ME IN ST. LOUIS is the answer to any exhibitor's prayer. Perhaps accented in these days as ideal 'escapist' fare, it would be surefire in any period. It holds everything for the film fan." The *New York Post* enthused, "At last MGM has gotten around to doing a musical memory book at once rich, tasteful, and a delight to experience. . . . The nicest part about it is that you feel the characters, not as quaint, costumed figures out of a past being commercialized for the easy laugh, but rather as people actually existing in those days." From the perspective of time, Tony Thomas (*The Films of the Forties,* 1975) assessed: "The art of the movie musical took a giant step forward in MEET ME IN ST. LOUIS, thanks largely to the direction of Vincente Minnelli. . . . This is an idealized and sentimental piece of Americana, but nothing about it is fake or mawkish. . . . The MGM art department excelled in this film. Their work graces the eye with pleasing sets exquisitely color photographed by George Folsey. But the master hand belongs to Minnelli."

MEET ME IN ST. LOUIS emerged seventh on the National Board of Review's Ten Best Pictures list for the year. Made at a cost of $1,707,561, the movie grossed over $7.56 million in its initial release. As a result of her work in this musical, Margaret O'Brien won a Special Academy Award as Outstanding Child Actress of 1944. The movie was Oscar-nominated for Best Song ("The Trolley Song"), Scoring, Cinematography—Color, and Screenplay.

On April 26, 1959 CBS-TV telecast a version of "Meet Me in St. Louis," using the movie's musical score. The cast included Jane Powell, Jeanne Crain, Tab Hunter, Myrna Loy, Walter Pidgeon, Patty Duke and Ed Wynn. In June 1960 a stage adaptation of the film, with additional songs composed by Hugh Martin and Ralph Blane, premiered at the St. Louis Municipal Opera. On November

2, 1989 a Broadway musical of *Meet Me in St. Louis* bowed, starring George Hearn (papa), Milo O'Shea (grandpa), Donna Kane (Esther), Jason Workman (John Truitt), Charlotte Moore (mama), Juliet Lambert (Rose), Rachel Graham (Rose), Courtney Peldon (Tootie), and Betty Garrett (Katie the maid). The $6 million stage version used ten new songs by Hugh Martin and Ralph Blane to bolster the few landmark songs taken from the original production. The show met with mixed reviews. Michael Kuchwara (Associated Press) reported, "It's reminiscent of those undemanding, undistinguished shows of yore, the kind that had big, expensive sets, pretty costumes, athletic dancing, maybe a star or two and a couple of hummable tunes. But what may have been, let's say, the best musical of 1953, has a tougher time on Broadway 1989." Howard Kissell (*New York Daily News*) offered, "There are dull stretches, songs that don't really pay off, but if the show doesn't charm you, your heart must be even harder than a theater critic's."

THE MERRY WIDOW (Metro-Goldwyn-Mayer, 1934) 99 minutes.

Producer, Irving Thalberg; director, Ernst Lubitsch; based on the operetta *Die Lustige Witwe* by Franz Lehar, Victor Leon, Leo Stein; screenplay, Samson Raphaelson, Ernest Vajda; art directors, Cedric Gibbons, Frederic Hope; set decorators, Edwin B. Willis, Gabriel Scognamillo; costumes, Ali Hubert; music, Lehar; music director, Herbert Stothart; choreographer, Albertina Rasch; sound supervisor, Douglas Shearer; camera, Oliver T. Marsh; editor, Frances March.

Songs: "Girls, Girls, Girls!" "I'm Going to Maxim's," "Vilia," "Tonight Will Teach Me to Forget," "Melody of Laughter," "Maxim's," "The Girls at Maxim's (Can-Can)," "The Merry Widow Waltz," "If Widows Are Rich," "Russian Dance" (Franz Lehar; new lyrics, Lorenz Hart, Gus Kahn, [uncredited] Richard Rodgers).

Maurice Chevalier (Prince Danilo); Jeanette MacDonald (Sonia); Edward Everett Horton (Ambassador Popoff); Una Merkel (Queen Dolores); George Barbier (King Achmed); Minna Gombell (Marcelle); Ruth Channing (Lulu); Sterling Holloway (Mischka); Henry Armetta (Turk); Barbara Leonard (Maid); Donald Meek (Valet); Akim Tamiroff (Maxim's Manager); Herman Bing (Zizipoff); Lucien Prival (Adamovitch); Luana Walters, Sheila Mannors [Sheila Bromley], Caryl Lincoln, Edna Waldron, Lona Andre (Sonia's Maids); Patricia Farley, Shirley Chambers, Maria Troubetskoy, Eleanor Hunt, Jean Hart, Dorothy Wilson, Barbara Barondess, Dorothy Granger, Jill Bennett, Mary Jane Halsey, Peggy Watts, Dorothy Dehn, Connie Lamont (Maxim Girls);

Charles Requa, George Lewis, Tyler Brooke, John Merkyl, Cosmo Kryle Bellew (Escorts); Roger Gray, Christian J. Frank, Otto Fries, George Magrill, John Roach (Policemen); Gino Corrado, Perry Ivins (Waiters); Katherine Burke [Virginia Field] (Prisoner); George Baxter (Ambassador); Paul Ellis (Dancer); Leonid Kinskey (Shepherd); Evelyn Selbie (Newspaper Woman); Wedgewood Nowell (Lackey); Richard Carle (Defense Attorney); Morgan Wallace (Prosecuting Attorney); Frank Sheridan (Judge); Arthur "Pop" Byron (Doorman); Claudia Coleman (Wardrobe Mistress); Lee Tin (Excited Chinese Man); Nora Cecil (Animal Woman); Tom Frances (Orthodox Priest); Winter Hall (Priest); Matty Roubert (Newsboy); Ferdinand Munier (Jailer); Dewey Robinson, Russell Powell, Billy Gilbert (Fat Lackeys); Arthur Housman, Johnny "Skins" Miller (Drunks); Hector Sarno (Gypsy Leader); Bella Loblov (Gypsy Violinist); Jan Rubini (Violinist); Jason Robards, Sr. (Arresting Officer); Albert Pollet (Head Waiter); Rolfe Sedan (Gabrielovitsch); Jacques Lory (Goatman); Lane Chandler (Soldier).

A.k.a.: THE LADY DANCES. French version: LA VEUVE JOYEUSE.

See: THE MERRY WIDOW (1952) (essay).

THE MERRY WIDOW (Metro-Goldwyn-Mayer, 1952) Color 105 minutes.

Producer, Joe Pasternak; director, Curtis Bernhardt; based on the operetta *Die Lustige Witwe* by Franz Lehar, Victor Leon, Leo Stein; screenplay, Sonya Levien, William Ludwig; art directors, Cedric Gibbons, Paul Groesse; set decorators, Edwin B. Willis, Arthur Krams; costumes, Helen Rose, Gile Steele; makeup, William Tuttle; music, Lehar; music director, Jay Blackton; choreographer, Jack Cole; color consultants, Henri Jaffa, Alvord Eiseman; special effects, A. Arnold Gillespie, Warren Newcombe; camera, Robert Surtees; editor, Conrad A. Nervig.

Songs: "Girls, Girls, Girls!", "I'm Going to Maxim's," "Can-Can," "Night," "Vilia," "The Merry Widow Waltz" (Franz Lehar; new lyrics, Paul Francis Webster).

Lana Turner (Crystal Radek); Fernando Lamas (Count Danilo); Una Merkel (Kitty Riley); Richard Haydn (Baron Popoff); Thomas Gomez (King of Marshovia); John Abbott (Marshovian Ambassador); Marcel Dalio (Police Sergeant); King Donovan (Nitki); Robert Coote (Marquis De Crillon); Sujata (Gypsy Girl); Lisa Ferraday (Marcella); Shepard Menken (Kunjany); Ludwig Stossel (Major Domo); Dave Willock (Attache); Wanda McKay (1st Girl); Anne Kimbell (2nd Girl); Edward Earle (Chestnut Vendor); Gwen

Verdon (Specialty Dancer); Gregg Sherwood, Joi Lansing (Maxim Girls); Trudy Erwin (Singing Voice of Crystal Radek).

Franz Lehar's bubbly operetta, *The Merry Widow* (1905 in Vienna; 1907 on Broadway), was first brought to the screen as a two-reeler in 1912, starring Alma Rubens and Wallace Reid. It emerged again as a mammoth MGM feature in 1925, directed in excess by Erich von Stroheim. But it was a popular silent vehicle for John Gilbert as Prince Danilo Petrovitch and Mae Murray as American dancer Sally O'Hara. (It was Murray who popularized "The Merry Widow Waltz" in this edition.) MGM executive Irving Thalberg, who had coped with the wildly extravagant, temperamental von Stroheim in 1925, had long wanted to remake the vehicle. He wanted to excise von Stroheim's intruding Freudian overtones and, of course, to make the story in sound, so that the operetta's famed songs and music could be a part of the actual film. Thus the new screenplay of Ernest Vajda and Samson Raphaelson somewhat restructured the flavor and slant of the original operetta.

Thalberg at once decided upon Maurice Chevalier to play the dashing Prince Danilo. The French star was then ending his Paramount Pictures contract and was planning to return to France. When the project was announced, MGM star Joan Crawford coveted the role of Sonia but she was rejected for the part. The studio briefly considered using opera singer Lily Pons or Broadway musical comedy star Vivienne Segal for the role. However, Chevalier wanted Metropolitan Opera singer Grace Moore for his leading lady. This idea was vetoed because Metro-Goldwyn-Mayer had had a bad working experience with Grace Moore in 1930 when she starred in their A LADY'S MORALS and NEW MOON (*q.v.*). She had proven temperamental and her soaring weight had caused consternation among the executives.* Meanwhile, Chevalier's former Paramount co-star, Jeanette MacDonald, had bowed at MGM in THE CAT AND THE FIDDLE (1934). She was the hierarchy's choice—along with recently hired director Ernst Lubitsch, who had directed Chevalier and MacDonald at Paramount—for the part of Sonia. Thus Chevalier and MacDonald were reunited on screen for the fourth time; their earlier pairings having been in THE LOVE PARADE (1929), *q.v.,* ONE HOUR WITH YOU (1932) and LOVE ME TONIGHT (1932), *q.v.*

In the kingdom of Marshovia the ruler (George Barbier) and his queen (Una Merkel) become alarmed when beautiful widow

*Ironically, after being rejected by MGM for THE MERRY WIDOW, Grace Moore would contract with Columbia Pictures to make ONE NIGHT OF LOVE (1934), *q.v.,* which restored her to screen stardom.

Sonia (Jeanette MacDonald) leaves the country to go to Paris because she controls the majority of the wealth in the land. When the king discovers roguish Prince Danilo (Maurice Chevalier) in his wife's boudoir, he orders the cad to Paris to romance Sonia. His instructions are to bring Sonia home or he will be court-martialed. In Paris, Danilo meets Sonia at Maxim's where she is in the guise of a cabaret girl. The two dance and fall in love, but they are forced to part without knowing each other's true identity. Back in Marshovia, Danilo and Sonia again meet at an embassy ball, where the young widow uncovers the truth about her lover. Although she threatens to leave Marshovia for good, Sonia testifies at Danilo's trial that he had done his best to romance her. Nevertheless, he is still found guilty. When she visits Danilo in his cell for the last time, the king arrives. He locks her in with the Prince and tells them they will stay there until they are married.

In THE MERRY WIDOW, Maurice Chevalier and Jeanette MacDonald dueted on the lilting "The Merry Widow Waltz," which was the grand set piece of the costume musical. It memorably featured a ballroom full of swirling dancers working their way down a mirrored corridor, providing a spectacular image. The jaunty Chevalier sang "Girls, Girls, Girls" and "I'm Going to Maxim's." MacDonald had the film's best melody, "Vilia," and also performed "Tonight Will Teach Me to Forget."

The *Los Angeles Times* assessed of the opulent product, "The Lubitsch picture is done lightly throughout. It is a pleasant revival. It lacks the ironic tinge Erich von Stroheim's silent version possessed when it was new. There is charm and effervescence instead permeating, and entertainment. One possibly should not ask for more." John Baxter (*Hollywood in the Thirties,* 1968) would champion, "Of all Lubitsch's operetta adaptations, THE MERRY WIDOW (1934) is the best. The film was made for Metro, but has all the Paramount polish, despite the problems Lubitsch had in getting Cedric Gibbons to fall in with his extravagant demands in the matter of sets. People criticized Metro for allowing Lubitsch to change a frothy romance into a satire on the ludicrousness of sex, but the combination of disenchanted dialogue and the lush Lehar music (with lyrics, by Rodgers, Hart and Kahn) gives this film a formal tension lacking in his earlier efforts. Chevalier plays the rake Danilo with style and charm, while MacDonald as the widow is at the height of her opulent pre-Raphaelite beauty. Her songs, especially 'Vilia' . . . are imaginatively directed, and her appearance in the film is, on balance, probably the peak of her career."

Despite its virtues, THE MERRY WIDOW was too sophisti-

Marcel Dalio and Lana Turner in THE MERRY WIDOW (1952).

cated for the hinterlands. Made at a cost of $1,605,000, the production lost $113,000 in its initial release. It did win an Academy Award for Best Interior Decoration. Director Ernst Lubitsch and stars Maurice Chevalier and Jeanette MacDonald also lensed a French-language version of THE MERRY WIDOW called LA VEUVE JOYEUSE. THE MERRY WIDOW would end Chevalier's tenure at MGM and the next year, after making FOLIES BERGERE (*q.v.*) at United Artists, he would return to France. Two decades later he would come back to MGM for the glorious GIGI (1958), *q.v.* As for Jeanette MacDonald, in 1935 she would co-star with Nelson Eddy in NAUGHTY MARIETTA, *q.v.*, which began a new wave of screen fame for her.

In 1952 MGM, needing to offer moviegoers grandiose visual productions to compete with the rival small screen medium of TV, decided to remake THE MERRY WIDOW.. It became a vehicle for glamorous studio star Lana Turner, with Fernando Lamas (replacing Ricardo Montalban) as Danilo and Una Merkel, who had played the queen in the 1934 version, now cast as Kitty Riley. The color production, which modernized and revamped the storyline, utilized

Paul Francis Webster's new lyrics, added to six of Lehar's original melodies, and boasted sets by Cedric Gibbons.* In the new version, Danilo had most of the song solos. According to *Newsweek* magazine, "The assets of the new production, directed by Curtis Bernhardt, are legion. This is a first class MERRY WIDOW and a fine tribute to the last grand master of the Viennese Waltz." The *New York Times* enthused, "Two things stand out here, one being probably the richest, most radiantly colorful dressing the old Lehar operetta ever received anywhere. The other solid surprise is a handsome Hollywood newcomer from the Argentine named Fernando Lamas, who is as dashing and fine-voiced a Count Danilo as could be imagined. Then there's Lana Turner, gowned and frilled to the teeth, who does well enough pictorially as the widow in a scenario carefully redraped around her." It should be noted that Lana Turner's vocals were dubbed by Trudy Erwin. THE MERRY WIDOW (1952) received Oscar nominations for Best Costumes—Color and Best Art Direction-Set Decoration—Color.

Following the newest MGM version of THE MERRY WIDOW there were two good TV productions: a 1954 outing with Patrice Munsel and Theodore Uppman on "Omnibus" on CBS-TV and, the next year, NBC-TV telecast a special of the Lehar operetta with Anne Jeffreys, Brian Sullivan and Edward Everett Horton starred. Still another film version of the operetta was done in Austria in 1962 as DIE LUSTIGE WITWE (The Merry Widow) with Karin Hubner in the title role and Peter Alexander as Danilo. In the 1970s it was announced repeatedly that Swedish director Ingmar Bergman would direct Barbra Streisand in a new version of THE MERRY WIDOW, but it never came to be.

---

*In the 1952 THE MERRY WIDOW Crystal Radek (Lana Turner), is a wealthy American widow, whose late husband came from the impecunious Balkan kingdom of Marshovia. That country's ministers persuade her to visit Marshovia on the pretext of viewing a monument to be erected in memory of her deceased spouse. In actuality, the King (Thomas Gomez) hopes to gain control of her money to prevent the country from going bankrupt. The King's playboy nephew, Count Danilo (Fernando Lamas), is designated to lead the reception committee. In a rash of mix-ups, Kitty Riley (Una Merkel)—Crystal's traveling companion—is mistaken for Crystal. When Crystal learns that Danilo had been ordered to romance her, she and Kitty flee to Paris. Once there, Crystal is determined to have a lark and persuades Kitty to continue being the "widow." When Danilo arrives in Paris and visits Maxim's, Crystal pretends to be Fifi, one of Maxim's good-time girls. Before long she and Danilo are in love. After further misunderstandings, Crystal saves Danilo's life by providing the King with a large check to help Marshovia balance its budget. Now believing Crystal is impoverished, the proud Danilo proposes to her. She accepts.

MISSISSIPPI (Paramount, 1935) 73 minutes.

Producer, Arthur Hornblow, Jr.; director, A. Edward Sutherland; based on the play *Magnolia* by Booth Tarkington; screenplay, Francis Martin, Jack Cunningham, Claude Binyon, Herbert Fields; art directors, Hans Dreier, Bernard Herzbrun; camera, Charles Lang; editor, Chandler House.

Songs: "Down by the River," "Soon," "It's So Easy to Remember (But So Hard to Forget)" (Richard Rodgers, Lorenz Hart); "Swanee River" (Stephen Foster).

Bing Crosby (Tom Grayson/Colonel Steele); W. C. Fields (Commmodore Orlando Jackson); Joan Bennett (Lucy Rumford); Queenie Smith (Alabam); Gail Patrick (Elvira Rumford); Claude Gillingwater, Sr. (General Rumford); John Miljan (Major Patterson); Edward Pawley (Joe Patterson); Fred Kohler, Sr. (Captain Blackie); John Larkin (Rumbo); Libby Taylor (Lavinia Washington); Harry Myers (Joe, the Stage Manager); Paul Hurst (Hefty); Theresa Maxwell Conover (Miss Markham); Al Richmond, Francis McDonald, Stanley Andrews, Eddie Sturgis, George Lloyd (Gamblers); Bruce Covington (Colonel); Jules Cowles (Bartender); Harry Cody (Abner, the Bartender); Lew Kelly, Matthew Betz (Men at Bar); Jack Mulhall (Duelist); Victor Potel (Guest); Bill Howard (Man in Auditorium); Jack Carlyle (Referee); Richard Scott (Second); Jan Duggan (Boat Passenger); James Burke (Passenger in Pilot House); Helene Chadwick, Jerome Storm (Extras at Opening); The Cabin Kids, Molasses, January (Themselves); King Baggot (1st Gambler); Mahlon Hamilton (2nd Gambler); Charles L. King (Desk Clerk); Jean Rouverol (Lucy's Friend); Mildred Stone, Mary Ellen Brown, Mabel Van Buren, Bill Harwood (Party Guests); J. P. McGowan (Dealer); Clarence Geldert (Hotel Proprietor); Fred "Snowflake" Toones (Valet); Forrest Taylor (Man at Bar who Orders Sarsaparilla); Warner Richmond (Man at Bar Who Draws a Gun); Oscar Smith (Valet); Robert McKenzie (Show Patron); Ann Sheridan (Extra at Engagement Party and Girls' School); Roy Bailey, Jean Clarendon, Dan Crimmins, Bud Flanagan [Dennis O'Keefe], William Howard Gould, Bert Lindley, Arthur Millet, Warren Rogers, Clarence L. Sherwood.

Booth Tarkington's 1923 novel *Magnolia* was first filmed by Paramount in 1924 as THE FIGHTING COWARD, with Ernest Torrance, Mary Astor, Noah Beery and Cullen Landis. In 1929 the studio redid the property as a talkie entitled RIVER OF ROMANCE, starring Charles "Buddy" Rogers, Mary Brian, June Collyer and Wallace Beery. The third studio version combined the talents of three diverse studio contractees: bulbous-nosed comedian W. C. Fields, crooner Bing Crosby (replacing the initially cast Lanny Ross), and beautiful leading lady Joan Bennett. The affable film, with its remarkable creation of the Mississippi riverboat era, provided Crosby with two of his most popular tunes: Richard Rodgers and Lorenz Hart's "Soon" and "It's So Easy to Remember (But So Hard to Forget)." Crosby also sang Rodgers and Hart's "Down by the River." The fourth number, Stephen Foster's "Swanee River" was sung by the Cabin Kids (a quintet of black youngsters) with Crosby joining in one of the chorus refrains.

In the Old South, Tom Grayson (Bing Crosby) disgraces himself in the eyes of his family and fiancée (Gail Patrick) by refusing to take part in a duel. Leaving home, he joins a riverboat performing troupe led by Commodore Jackson (W. C. Fields). Tom is soon featured as the company's lead singer. Roughneck Captain Blackie (Fred Kohler) breaks up one of Tom's performances and a brawl ensues in which Blackie is accidentally shot by his own gun. The crowd misconstrues the situation and Tom is acclaimed a hero. Conniving Jackson takes advantage of the situation and bills Tom as "Colonel Steele, the Singing Killer." Going back home, Tom sees Lucy Rumford (Joan Bennett), his ex-fiancée's younger sister. She now dislikes him because of his reputation as a killer. Eventually he confesses the truth to her and the two honeymoon on Jackson's boat.

While MISSISSIPPI provided relaxed Bing Crosby with a solid acting role (he was even allowed to use his fists in the saloon brawl with Fred Kohler), it also gave W. C. Fields a topnotch comedy assignment as the eccentric and none-too-honest riverboat skipper. His best comedy scene occurs when he is engaged in a poker game with several thugs and deals himself a poker hand containing five aces!

At the time of release, *Variety* was uncharmed by the production: "Paramount obviously couldn't make up its mind what it wanted to do with the film; it's rambling and hokey. For a few moments it's sheer farce, for a few moments it's romance. And it never jells." The trade paper also noted, "Some bits and sequences are not even followed through, but left in thin air."

MONTE CARLO (Paramount, 1930) 90 minutes. (Also silent version).

Producer, Adolph Zukor; director, Ernst Lubitsch; based on the play *The Blue Coast* by Hans Muller and the novel *Monsieur Beaucaire* by Booth Tarkington, Evelyn Sutherland; screenplay, Ernest Vajda; additional dialogue, Vincent Lawrence; set decorator,

Hans Dreier; costumes, Travis Banton; sound, Harry D. Mills; camera, Victor Milner; editor, Merrill White.

Songs: "Always in All Ways," "Give Me a Moment Please," "Beyond the Blue Horizon," "Day of Days," "Whatever It is, It's Grand," "Trimmin' the Women," "She'll Love Me and Like It," "I'm a Simple-Hearted Man," (Richard A. Whiting, W. Frank Harling, Leo Robin).

Jack Buchanan (Count Rudolph Falliere); Jeanette MacDonald (Countess Vera von Conti); ZaSu Pitts (Maria, Vera's Maid); Claude Allister (Prince Otto von Liebenheim); Lionel Belmore (Duke Gustave von Liebenheim); Tyler Brooke (Armand); John Roche (Paul, the "Real" Hairdresser); Albert Conti (Prince Otto's Companion/Master of Ceremonies); Helen Garden (Lady Mary in Stage Opera); Donald Novis (Monsieur Beaucaire in Stage Opera); David Percy (Herald); Erik Bey (Lord Winterset); Billy Bevan (Train Conductor); Sidney Bracey (Hunchback at Casino); Frances Dee (Receptionist); Rolfe Sedan (Hairdresser); John Carroll (Wedding Guest Officer); Geraldine Dvorak (Extra in Casino); and: Edgar Norton.

In Monte Carlo, Count Rudolph Falliere (Jack Buchanan) falls instantly in love with the beautiful Countess Vera von Conti (Jeanette MacDonald) who has been losing badly at the roulette wheel. Failing to meet the Countess, Rudolph takes on the guise of her new hairdresser, but finds out he is about to be fired because the Countess is too broke to pay his fee. In order to stay in her employ, Rudolph persuades the Countess to let him gamble with her last thousand pound note. Unbeknownst to her, he does not bet the money but instead supplements it with his own and returns to her with over one hundred thousand pounds. When he gives her the money the joyful Countess kisses him. However, the next day she reverts to her cold employer vs. employee attitude. Upset with her erratic behavior, Rudolph leaves the Countess's employ, although she begs him to return. When he does not, she agrees to marry elderly Prince Liebenheim (Claude Allister) because she needs his funding. In order to win the Countess back, Rudolph makes sure she sees a performance of *Monsieur Beaucaire.* Realizing the parallels between the play and her situation with Rudolph, the Countess breaks off her engagement to the Prince and agrees to marry the man she loves.

MONTE CARLO neatly reworked the premise of Booth Tarkington's novel *Monsieur Beaucaire* into a contemporary mode. A trademark of this and others of director Ernst Lubitsch's screen musicals was a sophisticated atmosphere filled with satirical japes at the hypocritical rituals of the affluent on the Continent. Jeanette

MacDonald, who frequently starred in Lubitsch's frou-frou, was at her coquettish best here (including a boudoir scene in scant attire). Britisher Jack Buchanan was her dapper leading man, a departure from her frequent co-star, Frenchman Maurice Chevalier. With its sly undertones, its adult relationships and its jovial mocking of how money affects romance among the wealthy set, MONTE CARLO is a sterling musical treat.

"Witty, piquant operetta in the best Lubitsch manner. Jeanette MacDonald sings gloriously," decided *Photoplay* magazine of this superior musical comedy with its fine score by Leo Robin, Richard Whiting and W. Frank Harling. From it came one of Jeanette MacDonald's most memorable songs, "Beyond the Blue Horizon." Discussing the production in retrospect, John Douglas Eames wrote in *The Paramount Story* (1985), "Jeanette MacDonald trilling 'Beyond the Blue Horizon' while leaning out of a train, accompanied by the wheels going clickety-clack and a chorus of railroad wavers, remains one of the screen's immortal sequences. As an example of blissful integration of sight and sound it was unique in those early days of the talkie. . . . The undeservedly disappointing grosses, except in Britain, were blamed on [Jack] Buchanan, whose name meant little elsewhere." (Jack Buchanan would return to Hollywood musicals in MGM's THE BAND WAGON [1953] *q.v.*)

MOON OVER MIAMI (20th Century-Fox, 1941) 91 minutes.

Producer, Harry Joe Brown; director, Walter Lang; based on the play *Three Blind Mice* by Stephen Powys; screenplay, Vincent Lawrence, Brown Holmes, George Seaton, Lynn Starling; art directors, Richard Day, Wiard B. Inhen; music director, Alfred Newman; choreographer. Hermes Pan; camera, Peverett Marley, Leon Shamroy, Allen M. Davey; editor, Walter Thompson.

Songs: "Moon Over Miami" (Edgar Leslie, Joe Burke); "What Can I Do for You?" "You Started Something," "Kindergarten Conga," "Oh Me Oh Mi-A-Mi," "Is That Good?" "Solitary Seminole," "Loveliness and Love," "I've Got You All to Myself" (Ralph Rainger, Leo Robin).

Don Ameche (Phil O'Neil); Betty Grable (Kay Latimer); Robert Cummings (Jeff Bolton); Charlotte Greenwood (Aunt Susie Latimer); Jack Haley (Jack O'Hara); Carole Landis (Barbara Latimer); Cobina Wright, Jr. (Connie Fentress); George Lessey (William Bolton); Robert Conway (Lester); Condos Brothers (Themselves); Robert Greig (Brearley); Minor Watson (Reynolds); Fortuno Bonanova (Mr. Pretto); George Humbert (Drive-In Boss); Spencer Charters (Postman); Lynn Roberts (Jennie May); Larry

McGrath (Bartender); Jack Cole and Company (Specialties); Mel Ruick (Band Leader); Leyland Hodgson (Victor the Waiter).

Under her new 20th Century-Fox pact, Betty Grable had already made DOWN ARGENTINE WAY (1940) and TIN PAN ALLEY (1940), *qq.v.* The next year the vivacious blonde musical comedy star was featured in a film noir detective yarn, I WAKE UP SCREAMING (a.k.a. HOT SPOT) and returned to form in the handsome Technicolor formula piece, MOON OVER MIAMI. It was a reworking of a studio property that had been filmed as THREE BLIND MICE with Loretta Young, Joel McCrea and David Niven.

After coming into a small inheritance of $4,500, beautiful sisters Kay Latimer (Betty Grable) and Barbara (Carole Landis), along with their Aunt Susie (Charlotte Greenwood)—who work in a roadside hamburger joint—head to Miami so the girls can find rich husbands among the city's society set. The three take rooms at a posh hotel, with Kay pretending to be a wealthy heiress (complete with a new, flashy wardrobe), Barbara posing as her secretary and Aunt Susie as her personal maid. The playboys, once rich Phil O'Neil (Don Ameche) and still rich Jeff Bolton (Robert Cummings), begin romancing Kay. She chooses Jeff and then realizes

Charlotte Greenwood, Betty Grable and Carole Landis in MOON OVER MIAMI (1941).

that she really loves Phil. The latter rejects her when he finds out her scheme. Jeff, however, is in love with Barbara, and Kay eventually wins Phil by admitting the truth to him. Meanwhile, spunky Aunt Susie has found romance with good-natured Jack O'Hara (Jack Haley).

Shot in the gaudy, captivating old Technicolor, MOON OVER MIAMI was fast-paced musical comedy froth which highlighted Betty Grable's dancing, especially in a number with the tap dancing Condos Brothers. Leo Robin and Ralph Rainger wrote eight songs for the picture, none of which became standards. Nevertheless, all the tunes fitted neatly into the surroundings of this slick production. Among the more notable are "Loveliness and Love," "You Started Something" and "I've Got You All to Myself." "Moon Over Miami" (written by Edgar Leslie and Joe Burke) is heard only as an orchestral salute over the film's opening titles. Of the three leading men Robert Cummings was the least experienced as a screen vocalist and was adequate at best in "You Started Something," which teamed him musically with Grable and Ameche. High-kicking Greenwood had a comedy duet with Haley on "Is That Good?" Hermes Pan staged the choreography which focused on the fancy footwork of Grable, the Condos Brothers and Jack Cole and Company.

Variety commended MOON OVER MIAMI for its "light, gay and tuneful spirit." One of this feature's nicer aspects is its on-location background shooting in Miami, showing the city as it once existed. Tony Thomas noted in *The Films of the Forties* (1975), "The film affords some fleeting shots of a 1941 Miami, almost quaint in comparison to the large, garish city of today, and interesting location sequences of aquatic and underwater activities in Cypress Gardens and Silver Springs."

MOON OVER MIAMI would be remade by 20th Century-Fox as the musical, THREE LITTLE GIRLS IN BLUE (1946), *q.v.*, with June Haver, Vivian Blaine, Celeste Holm and Vera-Ellen. It would provide the basis for the studio's comedy, HOW TO MARRY A MILLIONAIRE (1953), with Betty Grable, Marilyn Monroe and Lauren Bacall.

MOTHER WORE TIGHTS (20th Century-Fox, 1947) Color 107 minutes.

Producer, Lamar Trotti; director, Walter Lang; based on the novel by Miriam Young; screenplay, Trotti; art directors, Richard Day, Joseph C. Wright; set decorator, Thomas Little; costumes, Orry-Kelly; music directors, Alfred Newman, Charles Henderson; vocal arranger, Henderson; orchestrator, Gene Rose; choreographers, Seymour Felix, Kenny Williams; color consultants, Natalie Kalmus, Leonard Doss; assistant director, Gaston Glass; sound, Eugene Grossman, Roger Heman; camera, Harry Jackson; editor, J. Watson Webb, Jr.

Songs: "Ta-ra-ra-boom-de-ay" (Henry J. Sayers); "M-O-T-H-E-R" (Howard Johnson, Theodore F. Morse); "Put Your Arms Around Me, Honey" (Albert von Tilzer, Junie McCree); "Daddy, You've Been a Mother to Me" (Fred Fisher); "Burlington Bertie from Bow" (William Hargreaves); "Kokomo Indiana," "There's Nothing Like a Song," "Rolling Down to Bowling Green," "This Is My Favorite City," "Fare Thee Well, Dear Alma Mater," "You Do" (Mack Gordon, Joseph Myrow); "Tra-la-la-la-la" (Gordon, Harry Warren); "Swingin' Down the Lane" (Gus Kahn, Isham Jones); "Stumbling" (Zef Confrey); "Lily of the Valley" (L. Wolfe Gilbert, Anatole Friedland); "Choo'n Gum" (Mann Curtis, Vic Mizzy); "Silent Night" (Franz Gruber, Joseph Mohr).

Betty Grable (Myrtle McKinley Burt); Dan Dailey (Frank Burt); Mona Freeman (Iris Burt); Connie Marshall (Mikie Burt); Vanessa Brown (Bessie); Robert Arthur (Bob Clarkman); Sara Allgood (Grandmother McKinley); William Frawley (Mr. Schneider); Ruth Nelson (Miss Ridgeway); Anabel Shaw (Alice Flemmerhammer); Michael [Stephen] Dunne (Roy Bivens); George Cleveland (Grandfather McKinley); Veda Ann Borg (Rosemary Olcott); Sig Rumann (Papa): Lee Patrick (Lil); Señor Wences with Johnny (Specialty); Maude Eburne (Mrs. Muggins); William Forrest (Mr. Clarkman); Kathleen Lockhart (Mrs. Clarkman); Chick Chandler (Ed); Will Wright (Withers); Frank Orth (Stage Doorman); Harry Cheshire (Minister); Billy Greene (1st Policeman); David Thursby (2nd Policeman); Tom Stevenson (Hotel Clerk); Ann Gowland (Mikie at Age Three); Joan Gerians (Baby, One Month Old); Anne Baxter (Narrator); Kenny Williams (Dance Director); Eula Morgan (Opera Singer); Tom Moore, Harry Seymour (Men); Lee MacGregor (Boy); Stephen Kirchner (Myrtle's Dancing Partner); Alvin Hammer (Clarence); Brad Slaven, Ted Jordan (Sailors); George Davis (Waiter); Karolyn Grimes (Iris at Age Six); Lottie Stein (Mama); Antonioi Flauri (Papa Capucci).

MOTHER WORE TIGHTS was one of Betty Grable's most popular screen vehicles (with a gross of $4.1 million in distributors' domestic film rentals). This well-mounted, colorful piece of nostalgia marked the apex in the leggy, blonde star's screen popularity. The movie paired Betty Grable for the first time with Dan Dailey, who had just returned from military service. MOTHER WORE TIGHTS was yet another in 20th Century-Fox's Technicolor musicals which had been so popular with World War II

Betty Grable and Dan Dailey in MOTHER WORE TIGHTS (1947).

audiences. (However, as the post-war period progressed, such screen fare began to pale as audiences faced the Cold War.) *Variety* termed the musical "familiarly styled," adding: "Leisurely paced and loosely constructed as a series of undramatic vignettes, picture will appeal to patrons who prefer their nostalgia trowelled on thickly and sweetly."

Told in flashback by Mikie Burt (Connie Marshall), the story reverts to earlier in the century when Myrtle McKinley (Betty Grable) graduates from high school and is named the class's best dancer. Going against her grandparents' (Sara Allgood, George Cleveland) wishes, she becomes a professional hoofer. Along the way she falls in love with brash vaudeville comedian-dancer Frank Burt (Dan Dailey). The two marry and soon have two children, Iris (Mona Freeman) and Mikie. Burt persuades his wife to come out of retirement and to rejoin the act. Myrtle reluctantly leaves the girls with her grandparents. Over the years, the family reunites for summer vacations at various resorts. When the maturing Iris develops a crush on socialite Bob Clarkman (Robert Arthur), a disturbed Myrtle sends the girls to finishing school, hoping it might end the romance. Meanwhile, Iris has become a snob and is upset when her parents' act plays the theatre in the town where she is being educated. Afraid that her friends will make fun of her because of her parents' profession, Iris is surprised when the entire school turns up (at Myrtle's instigation) to see Myrtle and Frank perform. The troupers are given a rousing welcome by the students. On her graduation day, Iris, a music student major, sings the theme song from her parents' act, touchingly demonstrating her change of heart.

As was a given in any 20th Century-Fox nostalgia-laced musical, the proceedings were a cornucopia of old and new tunes, offered in breakneck succession. The novelty number "Burlington Bertie from Bow" was given renditions by Dailey and later, in a satirical parody, by Grable. The most impressive new tunes were Mack Gordon and Joseph Myrow's love ballad "You Do" and the sentimental "Kokomo, Indiana." A diversionary interlude was provided by the appearance of ventriloquist Señor Wences.

MOTHER WORE TIGHTS, which was in production for 76 days, was Academy Award-nominated for Best Song ("You Do") but lost to "Zip-A-Dee-Doo-Dah" from Walt Disney's SONG OF THE SOUTH. It also received Oscar bids for Scoring and Cinematography—Color. Betty Grable and Dan Dailey would re-team for YOU WERE MEANT FOR ME (1948), MY BLUE HEAVEN (1950) and CALL ME MISTER (1951).

MOVIETONE FOLLIES *see* FOX MOVIETONE FOLLIES.

MOVIETONE FOLLIES OF 1930 *see* FOX MOVIETONE FOLLIES (essay).

THE MUPPET MOVIE (Associated Film Distributors, 1979) Color 97 minutes.

Executive producer, Martin Starger; producer, Jim Henson; co-producer, David Lazer; director, James Frawley; screenplay, Jerry Juhl, Jack Burns; production designer, Joel Schiller; art director, Lee Gobruegge; set designers, Julia Harmount, Julius King; set decorator, Richard Goddard; Muppet designers: Caroly Wilcox, Mari Kaestle, Dave Goelz, Kathryn Mullen, Ed Christe, Larry Jameson, Faz Fazakas, Kermit Love, Sherry Amott, Wendy Midener, Janet Lerman-Graff, Bonnie Erickson, Don Sahlin, Amy Van Gilder; Muppet design consultant, Michael Firth; Muppet costumes, Calista Hendrickson; costumes, Gwen Capetanos; makeup, Ben Nye II; music, Paul Williams, Kenny Ascher; orchestrator/music director, Ian F. Smith; creative consultant, Frank Oz; assistant directors, Ron Wright, Penny Flowers; sound, Charles Lewis; sound re-recording, David Dockendorf; sound effects editor, Bill Wistrom; special effects, Robbie Knott; camera, Isidore Mankofsky; editor, Chris Greenbury.

Songs: "The Rainbow Connection," "Frogs' Legs So Fine," "Movin' Right Along," "Can You Picture That?" "Never Before," "Something Better," "This Looks Familiar," "I'm Going to Go Back There Some Day," "The Magic Store" (Paul Williams, Kenny Ascher).

Muppet Performers/Voices: Jim Henson (Kermit the Frog/Rowlf the Dog/Dr. Teeth/Waldorf); Frank Oz (Miss Piggy/Fozzie the Bear/Animal/Sam the Eagle); Jerry Nelson (Floyd Pepper/Crazy Harry/Robin the Frog/Lew Zealand); Richard Hunt (Scooter/Statler/Hanice/Sweetums/Beaker); Dave Goelz (The Great Gonzo/Zoot/Dr. Bunsen Honeydew); Carroll Spinney (Big Bird); Steve Whitmire, Kathryn Mullen, Bob Payne, Eren Ozker, Caroly Wilcox, Olga Felgemacher, Bruce Schwartz, Michael Davis, Buz Suraci, Tony Basilciato, Adam Hunt (Other Muppets); Charles Durning (Doc Hopper); Austin Pendleton (Max); Scott Walker ("Snake" Walker, the Frog Killer); Lawrence Gabriel Jr. (Sailor); Ira F. Grubman (Bartender); H. B. Haggerty (Lumberjack); Bruce Kirby (Gate Guard); Tommy Madden (One-Eyed Midget); James Frawley (Waiter); Arnold Roberts (Cowboy); Edgar Bergen (Himself); Milton Berle ("Mad Man" Mooney); Mel Brooks (Professor Max Krassman); James Coburn (Owner of El Sleezo Cafe); Dom DeLuise (Bernie, the Hollywood Agent;) Elliott Gould (Beauty Contest Compere); Bob Hope (Ice Cream Vendor); Madeline Kahn (El Sleezo Patron); Carol Kane (Myth); Cloris Leachman (Lord's Secretary); Steve Martin (Insolent Waiter); Richard Pryor (Balloon Vendor); Telly Savalas (El Sleezo Tough); Orson Welles (Lew Lord); Paul Williams (El Sleezo Pianist).

Jim Henson's Muppet puppets gained tremendous popularity on television in the PBS-TV series, "Sesame Street" and then on their own syndicated program, "The Muppet Show." The animal characters' chief asset seemed to be integrating successfully with live performers in a believable cohesion, with their comedy often going past lunacy. Thanks to their TV success, the Muppets came to the big screen in 1979 in THE MUPPET MOVIE, which had a gross of $32 million in distributors' domestic film rentals.

On his lilypad in the Georgia swamp, Kermit the Frog (voice of Jim Henson) meets a spaced-out Hollywood agent (Dom DeLuise) who, after hearing Kermit sing, urges him to give Hollywood a try. The Frog decides to take his advice and, with El Sleezo Cafe comedian Fozzie the Bear (voice of Frank Oz), he heads West. Along the way he meets other Muppets and they join up with him. En route the group also encounters a variety of wacky humans, including corrupt Doc Hopper (Charles Durning), who mightily wants to hire Kermit to be the spokesman for his fast food restaurant chain, which features deep-fried frog legs. Unable to gain Kermit's cooperation, Doc directs a mad scientist (Mel Brooks) to mold Kermit's mind to his will. But the two are thwarted bodily by Miss Piggy (voice of Frank Oz), who met Kermit at a county fair and now loves him dearly.

Paul Williams and Kenny Ascher composed the score for THE MUPPET MOVIE, which included Kermit singing "Rainbow Connection," his duet with Fozzie on "Movin' Right Along," Miss Piggy performing "Never Before, Never Again," Gonzo (voice of Dave Goelz) singing "I'm Going to Go Back There Someday," and the finale with all the Muppets harmonizing on "The Magic Store." Additionally, Kermit solos on the traditional "America."

Vincent Canby (*New York Times*) judged that THE MUPPET MOVIE "demonstrates once again that there's always room in movies for unbridled amiability when it's governed by intelligence and wit." On the other hand, John Pym (British *Monthly Film Bulletin*) warned, "The film, sadly, neglects to reproduce all the circumstances which made them 'famous.' " Pym explained, "Only Mel Brooks, that master of improvisation, emerges with any honour: he seizes his cameo and milks it with possessed energy. For the rest, the stars stand back and indulge the Muppets: a fatal ploy, as demonstrated by several unsuccessful episodes of the TV series. . . ."

THE MUPPET MOVIE received Oscar nominations for Best Song ("The Rainbow Connection") and Best Original Song Score. The soundtrack album was on *Billboard* magazine's charts for five weeks and rose to #32 position.

In 1981 Jim Henson brought the Muppets back to the big screen in THE GREAT MUPPET CAPER and in 1984 for THE MUPPETS TAKE MANHATTAN, the latter directed by Frank Oz.

MUSIC IN MY HEART (Columbia, 1940) 69 minutes.

Producer, Irving Starr; director, Joseph Santley; based on the story "Passport to Happiness" by James Edward Grant; screenplay, Grant; art director, Lionel Banks; costumes, Kalloch; music director, Morris W. Stoloff; dialogue director, William Castle; camera, John Stumar; editor, Otto Meyer.

Songs: "No Other Love," "Punchinello," "Oh What a Lovely Dream," "Prelude to Love," "I've Got Music in My Heart," "It's a Blue World" (Bob Wright, Chet Forrest).

Tony Martin (Robert Gregory); Rita Hayworth (Patricia O'Malley); Edith Fellows (Mary O'Malley); Alan Mowbray (Charles Gardner); Eric Blore (Griggs, the Butler); George Tobias (Sascha); Joseph Crehan (Mark C. Gilman); George Humbert (Luigi); Joey

Ray (Miller); Don Brodie (Taxi Driver); Julieta Novis (Leading Lady); Eddie Kane (Blake); Phil Tead (Marshall); Marten Lamont (Barrett) and: Andre Kostelanetz and His Orchestra.

While they were teamed for the CBS radio series "Tune-Up Time" during the 1939–40 season, Tony Martin and orchestra leader Andre Kostelanetz appeared in the Columbia musical MUSIC IN MY HEART, which surprisingly promoted their radio series. The movie was also the first Columbia musical to star Rita Hayworth and the pleasing picture did her no harm. Among the movie's tunes were "Music in My Heart," "Punchinello" and "It's a Blue World." The latter was nominated for an Oscar (but lost to PINOCCHIO'S "When You Wish Upon a Star") and was a best-selling disc for Tony Martin on Decca Records.

About to be deported, alien singer Robert Gregory (Tony Martin) is involved in a taxi accident. As a result, he meets pretty Patricia O'Malley (Rita Hayworth) and becomes infatuated with her. However, he learns she is engaged to marry wealthy, snobbish Charles Gardner (Alan Mowbray). Meanwhile, Robert wins a spot on Andre Kostelanetz's (himself) radio program and is a sensation on the airwaves. He continues to romance Patricia and is encouraged in his courtship by her younger sister, Mary (Edith Fellows); both young women live in an Avenue A tenement. Gardner finally learns that his fiancée has a boyfriend. He benignly forgives the two and, in order for Robert to remain in the United States, the millionaire adopts him. The singer is now free to wed Patricia.

Variety complained, "Plot is trite, threadworn affair which neither the direction nor the performance of the two leads and Andre Kostelanetz's superb music can overcome." The *New York Times* concurred, ". . . The only thing which keeps us from remarking that MUSIC IN MY HEART fills a long-felt need is the bare possibility that no one in particular has ever felt any particular need for such a union of musical comedy and conventional, low-budgeted cinema as Columbia's current exhibit presupposes." Still audiences liked the movie, especially comely Rita Hayworth and fine-voiced Tony Martin.

MUSIC MAN (Monogram, 1948) 66 minutes.

Producer, Will Jason; associate producer, Maurice Duke; director, Jason; story-screenplay, Sam Mintz; art director, Dave Milton; set decortor, Raymond Boltz, Jr.; music director, Edward Kay; assistant director, Melville Shyer; sound, L. J. Myers; camera, Jackson Rose; editor, William Austin.

Songs: "Little Man, You've Had a Busy Day," (Madel Wayel, Maurice Sigler, Al Hoffman), "I Could Swear It Was You" (Larry

Stock, Allan Flynn, Phil Brito); "Shy Ann" (Arnold Ross, Freddie Stewart); "Comm' e Bell 'a Stagione" (O. Pisano, R. Falvo); "Bella, Bella Marie" (Erhard Wimmler, Don Pelosi, Leo Towers).

Freddie Stewart (Freddie Russo); Phil Brito (Phil Russo); Jimmy Dorsey and His Orchestra (Themselves); Alan Hale, Jr. (Joe the Milkman); June Preisser (June Larkin); Noel Neill (Kitty); Grazia Narciso (Mrs. Russo); Chick Chandler (Sanders, the Music Publisher); Gertrude Astor (Mrs. Larkin); William Norton Bailey (Mr. Larkin); Roy Aversa (Luigi); Paul Bradley (Tony); Herman Cantor (Pianist); Norman Leavitt (Sam); Helen Woodford (Secretary).

After producing and directing the last three entries in Monogram's "Teenagers" series, Will Jason was reunited with the star of those pictures, Freddie Stewart, for MUSIC MAN. It co-starred popular Italian singer Phil Brito, presented Jimmy Dorsey and His Orchestra, and showcased two distaff holdovers from the "Teenagers" outings, June Preisser and Noel Neill. Among the tunes used in this compact, low-budget feature, one of Monogram's last attempts at a screen musical, were "Bella Bella Marie," "Little Man, You've Had a Busy Day," "I Could Swear It Was You" (co-written by Phil Brito), and "Shy Ann" (co-written by Freddie Stewart).

Songwriters and brothers Phil (Phil Brito) and Freddie Russo (Freddie Stewart) are constantly arguing over the quality of each other's compositions. Kitty (Noel Neill), a secretary, is in love with Phil but he does not realize it and romances June Larkin (June Preisser), who invites the brothers to sing at a benefit given by her parents (Gertrude Astor, William Norton Bailey). The boys' mother (Grazia Narciso) plans to throw a party to reconcile her sons, but Phil becomes upset when June gives Freddie a ride in her auto. The two brothers argue and go their separate ways. A music publisher (Chick Chandler) then refuses to handle Freddie's music and Freddie opens his own company. It fails because he will not take aid from his pal Jimmy Dorsey (himself). Kitty persuades milkman Joe (Alan Hale, Jr.) to secretly pose as a songwriter for a new show who is seeking a collaborator. In turn, he convinces each brother to help and a show is put together. When the brothers learn of the hoax, they threaten to sue one another., Eventually—after learning that their mother has invested her life's savings in the production—they allow the show to go on and it is a success. Phil plans to wed Kitty while Freddie and June agree to marry.

Harrison's Reports judged, "The presence in the cast of Jimmy Dorsey and his orchestra, and the singing of a few tuneful songs . . . may save the picture, but the story is trite. . . . [The] feud between the brothers seems artificial, and one's interest lags to the point of boresomeness."

THE MUSIC MAN (Warner Bros., 1962) Color 151 minutes.

Producer/director, Morton DaCosta; based on the musical play by Meredith Willson, Franklin Lacey; screenplay, Marion Hargrove; art director, Paul Groesse; set decorator, George James Hopkins; costumes Dorothy Jeakins; makeup, Gordon Bau; music supervisor/conductor, Ray Heindorf; vocal arranger, Charles Henderson; orchestrators, Heindorf, Frank Comstack, Gus Levene; choreographers, Oona White, Tom Panko; assistant director, Russsell Llewellyn; sound, M. A. Merrick, Dolph Thomas; camera, Robert Burks; editor, William Ziegler.

Songs: "Rock Island," "Iowa Stubborn," "Trouble," "Piano Lesson," "Goodnight, My Someone," "Seventy-Six Trombones," "Sincere," "The Sadder-But-Wiser Girl," "Pick-a-Little," "Goodnight Ladies," "Marian the Librarian," "Being in Love," "The Wells Fargo Wagon," "It's You," "Shipoopi," "Lida Rose," "Will I Ever Tell You," "Gary, Indiana," "Till There Was You," "If You Don't Mind" (Meredith Willson).

Robert Preston (Professor Harold Hill); Shirley Jones (Marian Paroo); Buddy Hackett (Marcellus Washburn); Hermione Gingold (Eulalie MacKechnie Shinn); Paul Ford (Mayor Shinn); Ewart Dunlop, Oliver Hix, Jacey Squires, Olin Britt (The Buffalo Bills); Pert Kelton (Mrs. Paroo); Timmy Everett (Tommy Djilas); Susan Luckey (Zaneeta Shinn); Ronny [Ron] Howard (Winthrop Paroo); Harry Hickox (Charlie Cowell); Charles Lane (Constable Locke); Mary Wickes (Mrs. Squires); Monique Vermont (Amaryllis); Ronnie Dapo (Norbert Smith); Jesslyn Fax (Avis Grubb); Patty Lee Hilka (Gracie Shinn); Garry Potter (Dewey); J. Delos Jewkes (Harley MacCauley); Ray Kellogg (Harry Joseph); William Fawcett (Lester Lonnergan); Rance Howard (Oscar Jackson); Roy Dean (Gilbert Hawthorne); David Swain (Chet Glanville); Arthur Mills (Herbert Malthouse); Rand Barker (Duncan Shyball); Jeannine Burnier (Jessie Shyball); Shirley Claire (Amy Dakin); Natalie Core (Truthful Smith); Therese Lyon (Dolly Higgins); Penelope Martin (Lila O'Brink); Barbara Pepper (Feril Hawkes); Anne Loos (Stella Jackson); Peggy Wynne (Ada Nutting); Hank Worden (Undertaker); Milton Parsons (Farmer); Natalie Masters (Farmer's Wife); Peggy Mondo, Sarah Seegar, Adnia Rice (Townswomen); Casey Adams, Charles Percheskly (Salesmen); Percy Helton (Conductor).

Meredith Willson and Franklin Lacey's musical comedy *The Music Man* opened on Broadway late in 1957 with Robert Preston and Barbara Cook in the leads, and enjoyed a tremendous run of

Robert Preston in THE MUSIC MAN (1962).

1,375 performances. Forrest Tucker and Van Johnson later headed successful touring companies of the musical. Warner Bros., which had a habit of purchasing the screen rights to Broadway musicals, bought this stage hit as well.* When THE MUSIC MAN was being readied for the screen, studio head Jack L. Warner wanted a younger actor to play Harold Hill, feeling Robert Preston was too old and not enough of a movie name. Eventually, Warner signed Preston to recreate the part. It was an excellent decision.

In the summer of 1912 fast-talking con artist Professor Harold Hill (Robert Preston) arrives in the sleepy rural town of River City, Iowa. He has a plan to fleece the citizens. His scheme involves organizing a boys' band and selling musical instruments and uniforms, and he fully intends to run off with the townspeople's money. Since Mayor Shinn (Paul Ford) is the owner of the local pool hall, he is opposed to Hill's plan because it will divert interest away from his money-making institution. Teaming up with stableboy Marcellus (Buddy Hackett), who has previously aided Hill in other towns, the Professor begins selling musical instruments. Meanwhile, he romances pretty but prim librarian Marian (Shirley Jones), who later finds out that Hill is a fraud. When Marian plans to reveal what she knows about Hill, he convinces her that he *can* create a band with his "think system" of learning to play musical instruments. In the process he brings harmony to the town. He sets up a barbershop quartet composed of the bothersome school board and appoints local gossips as head of the dance committee. He charms the mayor's wife (Hermione Gingold) into providing entertainment for the upcoming social event. By now, Marian has fallen deeply in love with Professor Hill and he returns her affections. He refuses to leave town, even after the instruments and band uniforms arrive. When a traveling salesman (Harry Hickox) appears in River City and informs the locals all about Hill, they quickly decide to tar and feather the imposter. But at the town hall the boys' band, led by Hill, does perform, resulting in a parade through the town's main street. For the amazed locals, the band seems to look and sound wonderful. With everyone content, Harold and Marian plan to marry.

Because director Morton DaCosta and choreographer Oona White repeated their tasks, the storyline, score and presentation point of view remained remarkably intact. For the motion picture, the

*Among the stage musicals hits Warner Bros. would convert to the screen in the late 1950s and 1960s were: THE PAJAMA GAME (1957), DAMN YANKEES (1958), *q.v.*, GYPSY (1962), *q.v.*, MY FAIR LADY (1964), *q.v.*, CAMELOT (1967), *q.v.*, and FINIAN'S RAINBOW (1968).

song "My White Knight" was restructured with additional lyrics and became "Being in Love." Robert Preston carried across his high-voltage stage performance to the screen and was extremely effective with his exuberant opening number ("Trouble"), his courtship melody ("Marian the Librarian") and his dynamic handling of the finale set piece ("Seventy-Six Trombones"). He and Shirley Jones dueted on "Goodnight My Someone" and "Till There Was You," he and young Ronny Howard handled "Gary, Indiana," and he and comedian Buddy Hackett sang "The Sadder But Wiser Girl." Jones joined with Pert Kelton for "If You Don't Mind," and sang "Will I Ever Tell You." For contrast, The Buffalo Bills provided barbershop harmony with "Sincere," "Lida Rose" and "Goodnight Ladies."

Not to be overlooked in this timeless foray into bucolic America is its engaging but bizarre conglomeration of characters. Only artistic license and a sense of joy could uncover one small American town that had such diverse personalities as the bumbling, greedy mayor (Paul Ford); his outré, unexplainably British wife (Hermione Gingold!); a goofy, pudgy stooge (Buddy Hackett); a sardonic mother (Pert Kelton); a tongue-tied little boy (Ronny Howard); and a bunch of busybodies, ranging from hawk-nosed Mary Wickes (delightful in the "Pick-a-Little" ensemble number) to the pompous school board members (The Buffalo Bills).

The *New York Times* reported, "Sophisticates may arch an eyebrow again at the Hollywood version of this breezy, broad-beamed and copiously sentimental show lifted more or less intact from Broadway, with everything expanded and elaborated. . . . The characters are the same (right out of vaudeville), the sentiments as tall as field-grown corn, the jokes as dependable . . . [and the songs] as thumping and precisely tailored as before." Wilfred Mifflin acknowledged in *Films in Review* magazine (August-September 1962), "The result may not be cinematic but it's certainly entertaining. [Robert] Preston's face, figure, bounce, and even age, are just right for the part of Harold Hill. . . . The film is really Preston's. It fits him like a glove."

THE MUSIC MAN grossed $8,100,000 in distributors' domestic film rentals. It won an Academy Award for Best Scoring of Music—Adaptation or Treatment, and received Oscar nominations for Art Direction-Set Decoration—Color, Costume Design—Color, and Sound. The soundtrack album was on *Billboard* magazine's chart for thirty-five weeks and rose to #2 position.

MY DREAM IS YOURS (Warner Bros., 1949) Color 101 minutes.

Producer, Michael Curtiz; associate producer, George Amy; director, Curtiz; based on the story "Hot Air" by Jerry Wald, Paul

Moss; screenplay, Harry Kurnitz, Dane Lussier, Allen Rivkin, Laura Kerr; art director, Robert Haas; set decorator, Howard Winterbottom; costumes, Milo Anderson; music, Harry Warren; music director, Ray Heindorf; choreographer, LeRoy Prinz; cartoon sequence director, I. Freeling; second unit director, David Curtiz; assistant director, Robert Vreeland; color consultants, Natalie Kalmus, Richard Mueller; sound, C. A. Riggs, David Forrest; special effects, Edwin DuPar; montage, Curtiz; camera, Ernest Haller, Wilfred M. Cline; editor, Folmar Blangsted.

Songs: "My Dream Is Yours," "Someone Like You," "Tic, Tic, Tic," "Love Finds a Way" (Ralph Freed, Harry Warren); "I'll String Along with You," "With Plenty of Money and You" (Al Dubin, Warren); "Canadian Capers" (Guy Chandler, Bert White, Henry Cohen, Earle Burnett); "Freddie Get Ready" (to the tune of the "Second Hungarian Rhapsody" by Franz Liszt); "You Must Have Been a Beautiful Baby," "Jeeper Creepers" (Johnny Mercer, Warren); "Nagasaki" (Mort Dixon, Warren).

Jack Carson (Doug Blake); Doris Day (Martha Gibson); Lee Bowman (Gary Mitchell); Adolphe Menjou (Thomas Hutchins); Eve Arden (Vivian Martin); S. Z. Sakall (Felix Hofer); Selena Royle (Freda Hofer); Edgar Kennedy (Uncle Charlie); Sheldon Leonard (Grimes); Franklin Pangborn (Sourpuss Manager); John Berkes (Character Actor); Ada Leonard (Herself); Frankie Carle (Himself); Ross Wesson (Hillard); Sandra Gould (Mildred); Iris Adrian (Peggy); Jan Kayne (Polly); Bob Carson (Jeff); Lennie Bremen (Louis); Marion Martin (Blonde); Frank Scannell (Car Salesman); Chili Williams (Fan Club President); Art Gilmore (Radio Announcer); Kenneth Britton (Richards, the Butler); James Flavin (Waiter); Rudolf Friml, Jr. (Orchestra Leader); Duncan Richardson (Freddie Manners); Jack Kenny (Cab Driver); Paul Maxey (Bald Man); Belle Daube (Elderly Actress); Louise Sarayder (Actress); Patricia Northrup (Gary Mitchell Fan); Don Brodie (Engineer); Tristram Coffin (Head Waiter); Edward Colmans (Radio Voice); Chester Clute, George Neise, Joan Vohns, Maynard Holmes, Eve Whitney (Party Guests).

"Unquestionably Miss Day has what is called 'talent' in Los Angeles. Her native good looks are gilded by long, blonde tresses; she has a certain swagger that gives illusion of vivacity in certain scenes, and her sense of rhythm does much for a husky voice in the film's many swing numbers" (*New York Herald Tribune*).

Following her impressive feature film debut in ROMANCE ON THE HIGH SEAS (1948), Warner Bros. again teamed their new girl-next-door star (Doris Day) with that film's leading man (Jack Carson) and director (Michael Curtiz) for MY DREAM IS

YOURS. It was a Technicolor remake of the studio's TWENTY MILLION SWEETHEARTS (1934) which starred Dick Powell, Ginger Rogers and Pat O'Brien. It reused the Harry Warren-Al Dubin song "I'll String Along with You," so fondly remembered from TWENTY MILLION SWEETHEARTS.

Talent scout Doug Blake (Jack Carson) is dropped by radio singer Gary Mitchell (Lee Bowman) when the latter turns into a snob with his growing success as a crooner. Looking for a client to replace Mitchell as his star celebrity, Doug finds pretty Martha Gibson (Doris Day), a young widow who has a baby boy. Hyperactive Blake has Martha audition for sponsor Felix Hofer (S. Z. Sakall), but Hofer is not impressed by her singing style. Meanwhile, Martha has become enamored of girl-chasing Mitchell, while Blake finds himself babysitting for Martha's child. Later, Gary Mitchell is fired from his radio show because of a drinking binge. On the other hand, Martha, who finally has found a suitable singing style, becomes a show business success. Others involved in her busy life are advertising agency executive Thomas Hutchins (Adolphe Menjou), his tart-mouthed assistant Vivian Martin (Eve Arden), and the radio show's sponsor, Hofer. Now backed by an all-girl orchestra, Martha quickly passes Gary in popularity. She persuades Doug to help Gary make a comeback. However, in the process, she realizes what a heel he is. Freed of her infatuation, she and Doug Blake pursue a romance together.

There are many pleasing ingredients in MY DREAM IS YOURS. Day brings her own special singing style—developed over years as a big band vocalist—to her interpretations of "My Dream Is Yours" (also sung by Lee Bowman's character), "I'll String Along with You" and "Canadian Capers" (a popular instrumental which was now given lyrics for the first time). Taking a cue from MGM's ANCHORS AWEIGH (1945), *q.v.,* which had Gene Kelly dancing with cartoon characters Tom and Jerry, MY DREAM IS YOURS had a Freudian dream sequence called "Freddie Get Ready" in which Warner Bros. cartoon figures Bugs Bunny and Tweedy Bird cavort with Day and Carson.

Not to be overlooked in this above-par formula film is the diverting presence of Jack Carson as the husky, hustling agent who beneath the tough surface is a loving soul. (He and Day would also co-star in the same year's IT'S A GREAT FEELING.) Then there is the joyful presence of several studio contract players: Eve Arden as the acidic agency person who is also an understanding and helpful confidant; and fluttery, tubby S. Z. "Cuddles" Sakall, who had more wiggles to his jowls than a bowl of jello. There were some down sides to the casting of this film. By this point, suave Adolphe

Menjou had played the high-powered movie executive and/or agency executive (e.g. THE HUCKSTERS, 1946) so often that his presence in such parts had become overly predictable and tiresome. And blah Lee Bowman, as the bad guy, was more a crushing bore than a fascinating heel.

The *Hollywood Reporter* cited as a deficiency in MY DREAM IS YOURS ". . . The overemphasis on the warbling of . . . Doris Day. Great performer though she is, it is too much to expect her to carry so many of the musical numbers, especially when they lack production values and consist essentially of solo singing spots. Naturally the girl gives everything she has—which is plenty. . . ." *Variety* tagged the movie "Average light entertainment." However, the public responded to Day, even in this vehicle, and the picture was a success. (Compared to the average new movie today, MY DREAM IS YOURS is solid entertainment.)

As a result of MY DREAM IS YOURS, Doris Day starred in a third screen version of *No, No, Nanette* called TEA FOR TWO (*q.v.*) the next year. In 1951 she and director Michael Curtiz (who had discovered her for the movies) again worked together in the musical I'LL SEE YOU IN MY DREAMS (*q.v.*).

MY FAIR LADY (Warner Bros., 1964) Color 170 minutes.

Producer, Jack L. Warner; director, George Cukor; based on the musical play by Alan Jay Lerner, Frederick Loewe and the play *Pygmalion* by George Bernard Shaw; screenplay, Lerner; production designer, Cecil Beaton; art director, Gene Allen; set decorator, George James Hopkins; costumes, Beaton; makeup, Gordon Bau; music supervisor/conductor, Andre Previn; orchestrators, Alexander Courage, Robert Franklyn, Al Woodbury; vocal arranger, Robert Tucker; choreographer, Hermes Pan; assistant director, David Hall; sound, Francis J. Scheid, Murray Spivak; camera, Harry Stradling; editor, William Ziegler.

Songs: "Why Can't the English?" "Wouldn't It Be Loverly?" "I'm an Ordinary Man," "With a Little Bit of Luck," "Just You Wait," "The Servant's Chorus," "The Rain in Spain," "I Could Have Danced All Night," "Ascot Gavotte," "On the Street Where You Live," "The Embassy Waltz," "You Did It," "Show Me," "The Flower Market," "Get Me to the Church on Time," "A Hymn to Him," "Without You," "I've Grown Accustomed to Her Face" (Alan Jay Lerner, Frederick Loewe).

Audrey Hepburn (Eliza Doolittle); Rex Harrison (Professor Henry Higgins); Stanley Holloway (Alfred P. Doolittle); Wilfred Hyde-White (Colonel Hugh Pickering); Gladys Cooper (Mrs. Higgins); Jeremy Brett (Freddy Eynsford-Hill); Theodore Bikel

(Zoltan Karpathy); Isobel Elsom (Mrs. Eynsford-Hill); Mona Washbourne (Mrs. Pearce); John Alderson (Jamie); John McLiam (Harry); Marni Nixon (Singing Voice of Eliza Doolittle); Bill Shirley (Singing Voice of Freddy Eynsford-Hill); Eric Heath, James O'Hara (Costermongers); Kendrick Huxham, Frank Baker (Elegant Bystanders); Walter Burke (Main Bystander); Queenie Leonard (Cockney Bystander); Laurie Main (Hoxton Man); Maurice Dallmore (Selsey Man); Owen Mcgiveney (Man at Coffee Stand); Jack Raine (Male Member); Marjorie Bennett (Cockney with Pipe); Britannia Beatey (Daughter of Elegant Bystander); Beatrice Greenough (Grand Lady); Hilda Plowright (Bystander); Dinah Anne Rogers, Lois Battle (Maids); Jacqueline Squire (Parlor Maid); Gwen Watts (Cook); Eugene Hoffman, Kai Farrelli (Jugglers); Raymond Foster, Joe Evans, Marie Busch, Mary Alexander, William Linkie, Henry Sweetman, Andrew Brown, Samuel Holmes, Thomas Dick, William Taylor, James Wood, Goldie Kleban, Elizabeth Aimers, Joy Tierney, Lenore Miller Donna Day, Corinne Ross, Phyllis Kennedy, Davie Robel (Cockneys); Iris Briston, Alma Lawton (Flower Girls); Gigi Michel, Sandy Steffens, Sandy Edmundson, Marlene Marrow, Carol Merrill, Sue Bronson, Lea Genovese (Toffs); Jack Greening (George); Ron Whelan (Algernon/Bartender); John Holland (Butler); Roy Dean (Footman); Charles Fredericks (King); Lily Kemble-Cooper (Lady Ambassador); Barbara Pepper (Doolittle's Dance Partner); Ayliene Gibbons (Fat Woman at Pub); Baroness Rothschild (Queen of Transylvania); Ben Wright (Footman at Ball); Oscar Beregi (Greek Ambassador); Buddy Bryan (Prince); Grady Sutton, Orville Sherman, Harvey Dunn, Barbara Morrison, Natalie Core, Helen Albrecht, Diana Bourbon (Ascot Types); Moyna MacGill (Lady Boxington); Colin Campbell (Ascot Gavotte); Marjory Hawtrey, Paulle Clark, Allison Daniell (Ad Libs at Ascot); Betty Blythe (Ad Lib at Ball); Nick Navarro (Dancer); Tom Cound, William Beckley (Footmen); Alan Napier (Ambassador); Geoffrey Steele (Taxi Driver); Jennifer Crier (Mrs. Higgins' Maid); Henry Daniell (Prince Gregor of Transylvania); Pat O'Moore (Man); Victor Rogers (Policeman); Michael St. Clair (Bartender); Brendon Dillon (Leaning Man); Olive Reeves-Smith (Mrs. Hopkins); Miriam Schiller (Landlady); Elzada Wilson, Jeanne Carson, Buddy Shea, Jack Goldie, Sid Marin, Stanley Fraser, George Pelling, Colin Kenny, Phyllis Kennedy, LaWana Backer, Monika Henreid, Anne Dore, Pauline Drake, Shirley Melline, Wendy Russell, Meg Brown, Clyde Howdy, Nicholas Wolcuff, Martin Eric, John Mitchum (Ad Libs at Church); Major Sam Harris (Guest at Ball).

If any show is the definitive twentieth-century Broadway

musical, it is *My Fair Lady*. In 1988, Stephen Holden assessed in the *New York Times*, "*My Fair Lady* transcended the Viennese tradition and incorporated powerful echoes of the English music hall. The songs seemed to spring directly from the personalities of the characters with a freshness and immediacy that seemed unprecedented." Dieter C. Deutsch concurred in his program notes for the 1988 CD album version of *My Fair Lady:* "There are Broadway musicals, and then there is *My Fair Lady*! . . . It has often been referred to as the most perfect expression of the Broadway musical as an art form, a sublime integration of the book, music and lyrics into a seamless whole."

Pygmalion, George Bernard Shaw's ironic study of English customs and habits, had debuted on the London stage in 1914. The story was transferred into a movie three times: in Germany (1935) with Gustaf Grundgens and Jenny Jugo, in the Netherlands in (1937) with John de Meester and Lily Bouwmeester; and in 1938 it became an acclaimed British movie starring Leslie Howard and Wendy Hiller, produced by Hungarian filmmaker Gabriel Pascal. For years thereafter, Pascal kept suggesting to Shaw that *Pygmalion* would make the basis for a wonderful musical comedy. On one occasion when the playwright was asked yet again about allowing his prize property to be converted into a musical, persnickety Shaw retorted, "I absolutely forbid such outrage. If *Pygmalion* is not good enough for your friends with its own verbal music, their talent must be altogether extraordinary." After Shaw's death in 1950, persistent Pascal proceeded to make his dream a reality. His concept was rejected by several composers (including E. Y. Harburg, Noel Coward, Cole Porter, Richard Rodgers-Oscar Hammerstein, II). Finally he settled on songwriters Alan Jay Lerner and Frederick Loewe, who had authored the hit musical, *Paint Your Wagon* (1951). The developing musical was originally known as *My Fair Liza* and at one juncture Mary Martin was considered for the leading role (she finally rejected it). Finally, on March 15, 1956, *My Fair Lady* opened on Broadway, starring Rex Harrison, Julie Andrews and Stanley Holloway. The show, which altered the original premise by adding a romantic finale, would run for 2,717 performances on Broadway, with 2,281 performances in London. The production garnered the New York Drama Critics Circle Award as the Best Musical of 1956; it also netted a half-dozen Tony Awards, including those of Lerner and Loewe and Rex Harrison for his extraordinary work as Professor Henry Higgins.

Warner Bros. purchased the screen rights to *My Fair Lady* for $5.5 million and spent another $12 million making the picture. Cary Grant was originally offered the screen lead but refused, adding that if Rex Harrison was not given the part he (Grant) would not go to see the movie. Harrison was signed for the role. As for the leading lady, studio head Jack L. Warner decreed that Broadway's Julie Andrews did not possess the potential to be a big box-office draw. Thus Audrey Hepburn, who had co-starred with Fred Astaire in the musical FUNNY FACE (1956), *q.v.,* was hired, with Marni Nixon assigned to dub her singing. Both Stanley Holloway (Alfred P. Doolittle) and costume designer Cecil Beaton were retained from the New York production. Elegant George Cukor, most noted as a tasteful director of women's pictures, was put in charge of the expensively-mounted screen musical. (He had previously directed the musical, LES GIRLS, 1957, *q.v.*)

In London, prior to World War I, phonetics teacher Henry Higgins (Rex Harrison) is fascinated by flowergirl Eliza Doolittle (Audrey Hepburn). He is shocked yet beguiled by her Cockney accent and, while he is taking notes on this creature, a row results. Higgins' colleague, Colonel Pickering (Wilfred Hyde-White), stops the fracas and Higgins brags to him that in three months' time he could have this Cockney lass speaking perfect English. In fact, Higgins boasts, he could pass her off as royalty! The two make a wager on the matter. The next day Eliza begins elocution lessons at Higgins' home, she agreeing because she wants to better herself and become a shop worker. While Henry's aristocratic mother (Gladys Cooper) is doubtful, the two men manage to transform the street urchin into a well-spoken young woman. However, her appearance at a high-toned horserace at Ascot is less than a success. With additional training, Eliza is coached for the social event of the season. At the grand ball she is smashing. Higgins and Pickering are so over-inflated by their achievement that they ignore Eliza. The angry young woman leaves Higgins' home and goes to see her father, Alfred Doolittle (Stanley Holloway), but finds he is finally planning to wed. Thus she goes to Henry's mother for advice. Later, Freddy Eynsford-Hill (Jeremy Brett) romances Eliza, and when Henry comes to visit her, they argue. Returning home, Higgins appreciates that he loves Eliza. Soon thereafter, she comes back to him with the same romantic realization.

The outstanding Lerner and Loewe music was retained for the screen version. Musical highlights included Stanley Holloway's rousing rendition of "Get Me to the Church on Time," Rex Harrison's talk-singing of "Why Can't the English?" "I've Grown Accustomed to Her Face" and "I'm an Ordinary Man." Harrison, Hepburn and Wilfred Hyde-White executed the enthusiastic "The Rain in Spain." Marni Nixon (dubbing Hepburn) sang "Wouldn't It Be Loverly?" "I Could Have Danced All Night" and "Without

You." Bill Shirley (dubbing for Jeremy Brett) did "On the Street Where You Live."

Regarding the transformation of the hit musical play into a successful musical film, Bosley Crowther (*New York Times*) judged, "They've made a superlative film from the musical stage show . . . a film that enchantingly conveys the rich endowments of the famous stage production in a fresh and flowing cinematic form." Less enchanted was Pauline Kael (*New Yorker* magazine): "The film seems to go on for about 45 minutes after the story is finished. Audrey Hepburn is an affecting Eliza, though she is totally unconvincing as a guttersnipe, and is made to sing with that dreadfully impersonal Marni Nixon voice that has issued from so many other screen stars. Rex Harrison had already played Higgins more than a bit too often."

Granted there are casting flaws to MY FAIR LADY and there is an almost slavish adherence to the Broadway musical original. On the other hand, MY FAIR LADY is pictorially splendiferous, especially in the stylish Ascot racetrack number where period costumes, sets and the music are elegantly combined for a stunning effect. MY FAIR LADY grossed $12 million in distributors' domestic film rentals and netted eight Academy Awards: Best Picture, Best Actor (Rex Harrison), Best Director, Best Scoring, Best Cinematography—Color, Best Art Direction-Set Decoration—Color, Best Sound, and Best Costumes—Color. It received Oscar nominations for Best Supporting Actor (Stanley Holloway), Best Supporting Actress (Gladys Cooper), and Best Screenplay—Adaptation. Ironically Audrey Hepburn was not even nominated for an Oscar, while Julie Andrews did win the Academy Award as Best Actress for her screen debut in Walt Disney's MARY POPPINS (*q.v.*). The soundtrack album to MY FAIR LADY remained on *Billboard* magazine's charts for seventy-seven weeks and rose to #4 position.

MY MAN (Warner Bros., 1928) 99 minutes. (Also silent version: 6,136′).

Director, Archie Mayo; story, Mark Canfield [Darryl F. Zanuck]; screenplay, Robert Lord; dialogue, Joe Jackson; titles, Jackson, James A. Starr; camera, Frank Kesson; editor, Owen Marks.

Songs: "My Man" (Maurice Yvain; English lyrics, Channing Pollock); "If You Want a Rainbow (You Must Have the Rain)" (Billy Rose, Mort Dixon, Oscar Levant); "I'm an Indian" (Blanche Merrill, Leo Edwards); "I Was a Floradora Baby" (Ballard MacDonald, Harry Carroll); "I'd Rather Be Blue with You (Than Happy with Somebody Else)" (Rose, Fred Fisher); "Second Hand Rose" (Grant Clarke, James Hanley).

Fanny Brice (Fannie Brand); Guinn "Big Boy" Williams (Joe Halsey); Edna Murphy (Edna Brand); Andre de Segurola (Landau, the Producer); Richard Tucker (Waldo); Billy Seay (Sammy); Arthur Hoyt (Thorne); Ann Brody (Mrs. Schultz); Clarissa Selwynne (Forelady).

Fanny Brice was nearly forty when she starred in this early part-talkie after having become one of the country's favorite revue stars, thanks to appearing in nine editions of Florenz Ziegfeld's *Follies,* dating back to 1910. She was no beauty in the traditional show business sense, but she had an inner radiance and sparkle. She was already famous for many songs, including her trademark "My Man," which was employed as the title and theme of this, her screen debut. *Photoplay* magazine reported that the film was "A chance to hear Fannie Brice sing all her best songs. Not much on story, but a good Vitaphone novelty." Much of the picture's dramatic action, as

Fanny Brice in MY MAN (1928).

with the earlier THE JAZZ SINGER (*q.v.*) in 1927, was silent with subtitles. However, MY MAN came to life with several tunes belted out by Brice, including "Second Hand Rose" and "I'd Rather Be Blue with You (than Happy with Somebody Else)."

Hard-working Fannie Brand (Fanny Brice) supports her brother Sammy (Billy Seay) and sister Edna (Edna Murphy) by her work as a seamstress in a theatrical costume shop. She meets rough-edged Joe Halsey (Guinn Williams), who demonstrates an elastic exerciser in a store window. The two soon fall in love and decide to marry. Edna, who is jealous of Fannie, makes a play for Joe. When Fannie finds out, she breaks off the engagement. Meanwhile, a theatrical producer (Andre De Segurola) hears Fannie sing and asks her to audition for his new show. She is cast in a Broadway revue and becomes a big success. As a result she and Joe are brought back together.

Following MY MAN, Fanny Brice made a second bid for screen stardom in United Artists' BE YOURSELF! (1930), in which she sang "Cooking Breakfast for the One I Love" and "When a Man Loves a Woman." However, she was to find more success on the stage and later on radio as the comic character "Baby Snooks." For later generations, it would be Barbra Streisand on Broadway and in the film version of Funny Girl (1968), *q.v.,* who "was" Fanny Brice.

NAUGHTY MARIETTA (Metro-Goldwyn-Mayer, 1935) 106 minutes.

Producer, Hunt Stromberg; director, W. S. Van Dyke, II; based on the operetta by Victor Herbert, Rida Johnson Young; screenplay, John Lee Mahin, Frances Goodrich, Albert Hackett; art director, Cedric Gibbons; costumes, Adrian; music adaptor, Herbert Stothart; assistant director, Eddie Woehler; sound, Douglas Shearer; camera, William Daniels; editor, Blanche Sewell.

Songs: "Chansonette," "Antoinette and Anatola," "Prayer," "Tramp, Tramp, Tramp," "The Owl and the Bob Cat," "'Neath the Southern Moon" (Victor Herbert, Gus Kahn); "Italian Street Song," "I'm Falling in Love with Someone," "Ah Sweet Mystery of Life" (Herbert, Rida Johnson Young); "Mon Ami Pierrot" (traditional).

Jeanette MacDonald (Marietta Franini [Princess Marie de Namours de la Bonfain]); Nelson Eddy (Captain Richard Warrington); Frank Morgan (Governor Gaspard d'Annard); Elsa Lanchester (Madame d'Annard); Douglass Dumbrille (Prince de Namours de la Bonfain); Joseph Cawthorn (Herr Schuman); Cecilia Parker (Julie); Walter Kingsford (Don Carlos de Braganza); Greta Meyer (Frau Schuman); Akim Tamiroff (Rudolpho, the Puppet Master);

Harold Huber (Abe [Abraham]); Edward Brophy (Zeke [Ezekiel Cramer]); Mary Doran, Jane Mercer, Marjorie Main, Jean Chatburn, Pat Farley, Jane Barnes, Kay English, Linda Parker (Casquette Girls); Arthur Belasco, Tex Driscoll, Edward Hearn, Edmund Cobb, Charles Dunbar, Ed Brady (Mercenary Scouts); Dr. Edouard Lippe (Landlord); Marietta (Cocker Spaniel); Olive Carey (Madame Renavent); William Desmond (Havre Gendarme Chief); Cora Sue Collins (Felice); Helen Shipman (Marietta Franini); William Burress (Bouget, the Pet Shop Keeper); Catherine Griffith (Prunella, Marie's Maid); Billy Dooley (Drunk, Marietta's "Brother"); Guy Usher (Ship's Captain); Walter Long (Pirate Captain); Harry Cording, Frank Hagney, Constantine Romanoff (Pirates); Henry Roquemore (Herald); Mary Foy (Duenna); James C. Morton (Barber); Louis Mercier (Duelist); Robert McKenzie (Town Crier); Delos Jewkes (Priest on Dock); Zarubi Elmassian (Voice of Suzette); William Moore (Jacques, the Suitor); Harry Tenbrook (Prospective Groom); Ben Hall (Mama's Boy); Ed Keane (Major Cornell); Roger Gray (Sergeant); Ralph Brooks, Edward Norris (Marie's Suitors); Richard Powell (Herald); Wilfred Lucas (Herald at Ball); Jack Mower (Nobleman).

By the mid-1930s movie operettas were considered passé. They had run their course in 1929–30 when the screen had first learned to talk. In 1933, film musicals had a rebirth with Warner Bros.' 42ND STREET, *q.v.*, and thereafter the Busby Berkeley-type celluloid extravaganza was the order of the day. MGM had copied the Berkeley formula in DANCING LADY (1933), *q.v.*, and later began a new series of screen musicals starring tap dancer Eleanor Powell. Meanwhile, MGM had hired ex-Paramount star Jeanette MacDonald, long a favorite of Metro studio chief Louis B. Mayer. In signing the titian-hair soprano, he offered her a choice of any vehicle, in his efforts to please this beautiful singing star. After much indecision, she chose to grace the operetta THE CAT AND THE FIDDLE (1934), with Ramon Novarro, and the same year she joined with her former Paramount teammate Maurice Chevalier for the big-budgeted THE MERRY WIDOW, *q.v.* For her next showcase, it was decided she was to star in NAUGHTY MARIETTA, based on the old Victor Herbert operetta.* It was one of Mayer's favorite works and he did not care that his co-executives thought the property too outdated and overly corny. Her co-lead was to be Allan Jones, whom MGM intended signing to a long-term studio pact. However, Jones was forced to complete obligations

*Victor Herbert's operetta *Naughty Marietta* debuted on Broadway in 1910, starring Emma Trentini and Orville Harold. It ran for 136 performances.

Jeanette MacDonald, Greta Meyer and Joseph Cawthorn in NAUGHTY MARIETTA (1935).

under his Shubert Brothers' stage contract. As a last-minute substitute, MGM cast Nelson Eddy opposite MacDonald. He had joined the studio in 1933, his most notable appearance being the vocalist in a production number of Joan Crawford's DANCING LADY.

In France, Princess Marie de la Bonfain, a red-haired beauty, is about to be married off to a Spanish grandee, Don Carlos de Braganza (Walter Kingsford). It is all part of a devious plan by her grasping uncle (Douglass Dumbrille) to get closer to the throne of King Louis XV of France. Realizing her fate, Marie exchanges places with servant girl Marietta (Helen Shipman) and sails for America as a Casquette Girl, one of those who will be sold as a wife to a settler in Louisiana. Aboard the ship bound for the New World, she befriends Julie (Cecilia Parker). As the vessel nears port, it is attacked by vicious pirates who kill the crew, kidnap the women and take them to their camp. The women are rescued by Captain Richard Warrington (Nelson Eddy) and his Yankee Scouts. Later, Warrington and his men escort the women to New Orleans. En route, he is attracted by Marie, but she remains standoffish.

Moreover, he is soon distracted by his military duties. When it comes time for Marie to wed one of the settlers, she seizes upon a ploy: she lies and announces that she is no longer a virgin. The flustered Governor (Frank Morgan) casts her adrift, to survive on her own. She joins a marionette show, run by the jovial Rudolpho (Akim Tamiroff). When Warrington encounters Marie again, the couple quickly discover that they love one another. At this juncture Marie is arrested by the Governor's men. Her true identity has been revealed by her uncle and Don Carlos, who have arrived in New Orleans. Her uncle informs her that unless she weds Don Carlos he will see to it that Warrington dies. Marie gives in to her fate. On the night of the Governor's big ball in New Orleans, the dashing Warrington sneaks in among the other guests. He persuades her to elope with him. They decide to escape into the wilderness, hoping that the French authorities will not pursue. Marie accepts the daring plan and the couple depart for a new life together, surrounded by Warrington's trusted troops.

There are many ingredients which insured NAUGHTY MARIETTA's popular reception. The production values were MGM-lavish; the supporting cast was adept at keeping the story moving entertainingly (especially Frank Morgan as the befuddled governor and Elsa Lanchester as his astute wife). The pacing was swift, handled by director W. S. Van Dyke, renowned for doing "one take" and moving on to the next scene. More importantly, Jeanette MacDonald and Nelson Eddy had a wonderful on-camera rapport, a mixture of posed sincerity, tongue-in-cheek playfulness, and superior voices which blended well in duets. Additionally, there was the wonderful music score, a mixture of songs from the original operetta with new numbers composed for this feature. Eddy fared best with "Tramp, Tramp, Tramp" and "I'm Falling in Love with Someone," while Jeanette sang "Ah, Sweet Mystery of Life" (which she and Nelson also dueted), "Chansonette," "Italian Street Song" and "Prayer." Finally, with America still in the midst of the Depression, NAUGHTY MARIETTA was ideal fantasy escapism. Its very romantic premise, boasting a lovely fairytale princess and her handsome soldier lover, hit just the right note with reality-fatigued filmgoers.

The critics were appreciative of this high-calibre production, which caught them off guard with its plush entertainment values. The *New York Herald Tribune* decided, "With all proper respect for Miss MacDonald, however, the triumph of the Van Dyke version is registered by Nelson Eddy. . . . Mr. Eddy has a brilliant baritone voice, he seems thoroughly masculine, he is engaging and good looking, and he gives the appearance of being unaffected." As to the leading lady, the *Los Angeles Times* reported that MacDonald ". . . Quite surpasses herself . . . invests her portrayal with charm and humanness."

NAUGHTY MARIETTA was named *Photoplay* magazine's Film of the Year, while *Film Daily* ranked it number four of the year's Ten Best pictures. It was Academy Award-nominated for Best Picture of the Year, but lost to MGM's MUTINY ON THE BOUNTY. It was also Oscar-nominated for Best Sound.

As a result of the huge success of NAUGHTY MARIETTA, Jeanette MacDonald and Nelson Eddy would team together for several follow-ups: ROSE MARIE (1936), MAYTIME (1937), THE GIRL OF THE GOLDEN WEST (1938), SWEETHEARTS (1938), NEW MOON (1940), BITTER SWEET (1940) and I MARRIED AN ANGEL (1942), *qq.v.* On June 12, 1944, MacDonald and Eddy reprised their roles of Princess Marie and Captain Warrington for "Lux Radio Theatre" on CBS. MacDonald co-starred with Gordon MacRae in "The Railroad Hour" version of the Victor Herbert operetta on January 17, 1949 on NBC. Both Jeanette MacDonald and Nelson Eddy successfully recorded their songs from NAUGHTY MARIETTA for RCA Victor when the film was issued in 1935. In the early 1950s Eddy re-recorded the score with Nadine Conner for Columbia Records.

NEW FACES (20th Century-Fox, 1954) Color 98 minutes.

Producers, Edward L. Alperson, Berman Schwartz; director, Harry Horner; based on the musical revue *New Faces of 1952* as produced by Leonard Stillman; screenplay, Ronny Graham, Melvin [Mel] Brooks, Paul Lynde, Luther Davis; camera, Lucien Ballard.

Songs: "Bal, Petit Bal" (F. Lemarque); "Monotonous," "Penny Candy" (Arthur Siegel, June Carroll); "Uska Dara" (adapted from a folk song); "C'est Si Bon" (Jerry Seelen, Henri Betti); "Santa Baby" (Joan Javits, Phil Springer, Tony Springer); "Guess Who I Saw Today?" (Murray Grand, Elisse Boyd); "I'm in Love with Miss Logan," "Lucky Pierre," "Waltzing in Venice," "Raining Memories," "He Takes Me Off His Income Tax" (Ronny Graham); "Boston Beguine" (Sheldon Harnick); "Take off the Mask" (Alice Ghostley, Graham); "We've Never Seen You Before" (Graham, Peter DeVries).

With: Ronny Graham, Eartha Kitt, Robert Clary, Virginia DeLuce, Alice Ghostley, June Carroll, Paul Lynde, Bill Mullikin, Rosemary O'Reilly, Allen Conroy, Jimmy Russell, George Smiley, Polly Ward, Carol Lawrence, Johnny Laverty, Elizabeth Logue, Faith Burwell, Clark Ranger.

Leonard Stillman's Broadway revue *New Faces* opened in May

1952 for a 365-performance run. After a follow-up tour, 20th Century-Fox transferred it to the screen as a CinemaScope widescreen production. It brought to public notice such stage/cafe performers as Eartha Kitt (who in the interim between the Broadway opening and the movie had had several best-selling RCA records), Robert Clary, Alice Ghostley and Paul Lynde. "Forgetting what takes place off stage, FACES is genuine entertainment, featuring a group of attractive and talented newcomers (to the screen)," wrote *Variety*.

Filmed as a stage revue, NEW FACES was highlighted by a number of entertaining blackout acts performed by the cast, with much of the material written and performed by creative comic Ronny Graham. The whole affair, like many movie musicals of the 1930s, was strung together by a very thin storyline about a theatrical group trying to stay together until a Texas backer provides the funds needed to sustain the show. Also the usual romantic subplot was included, here involving Robert Clary and Virginia DeLuce. Needless to say, all ends happily, but it is the music which entertains, not the story.

Among the musical highlights of NEW FACES are Eartha Kitt's rendition of "Monotonous" and her duet with Robert Clary on "Bal Petit Bal," plus the inclusion of her RCA hits, "Uska Dara," "C'est Si Bon" and "Santa Baby." Clary does a fine vocal on "I'm in Love with Miss Logan" and Alice Ghostley does the comedy piece, "Boston Beguine." She and Paul Lynde did "Death of a Salesman" and zany Lynde also does a funny monolog as an African travel lecturer. June Carroll nicely performs the song "Penny Candy" (which featured Carol Lawrence dancing).

Not everyone, however, liked the film and John Springer in *All Talking! All Singing! All Dancing!* (1966) termed the revue ". . . A straight transcription from the stage with the lack of movie production values spoiling even such a standout as Alice Ghostley's 'Boston Beguine.' " While there were additional chapters of Leonard Stillman's *New Faces* on stage, there were no further film episodes.

NEW MOON (Metro-Goldwyn-Mayer, 1930) 78 minutes.

Director Jack Conway; based on the operetta *The New Moon* by Oscar Hammerstein, II, Sigmund Romberg, Frank Mandel, Laurence Schwab; screenplay, Sylvia Thalberg, Frank Butler; dialogue, Cyril Hume; camera, Oliver T. Marsh; editor, Margaret Booth.

Songs: "Lover Come Back to Me," "One Kiss," "Stout-Hearted Men," "Wanting You," "Marianne," "Funny Little Sailor Men" (Sigmund Romberg-Oscar Hammerstein, II).

Lawrence Tibbett (Lieutenant Michael Petroff); Grace Moore (Princess Tanya Strogoff); Adolphe Menjou (Governor Boris Brusiloff); Roland Young (Count Strogoff); Gus Shy (Potkin); Emily Fitzroy (Countess Anastia Strogoff).

TV title: PARISIAN BELLE.

See: NEW MOON (1940) (essay).

NEW MOON (Metro-Goldwyn-Mayer, 1940) 105 minutes.

Producer/director, Robert Z. Leonard; based on the operetta *The New Moon* by Oscar Hammerstein, II, Sigmund Romberg, Frank Mandel, Laurence Schwab; screenplay, Jacques Deval, Robert Arthur; art directors, Cedric Gibbons, Eddie Imazu; set decorator, Edwin B. Willis; costumes, Adrian, Gile Steele; makeup, Jack Dawn; music, Romberg; music director, Herbert Stothart; choreographer, Val Raset; camera, William Daniels; editor, Harold F. Kress.

Songs: "Dance Your Cares Away," "Stranger in Paris," "The Way They Do It in Paris," "Shoes" (Romberg; new lyrics); "Lover Come Back," "Softly as in a Morning Sunrise," "One Kiss," "Wanting You," "Stout-Hearted Men," "Marianne" (Romberg, Oscar Hammerstein, II); "Troubles of the World," (traditional); "No More Weepin'" (traditional); "Wailing" (traditional); "Ombre Ma Fui," "Largo" from the opera *Serse* (George Frederic Handel); "The Marseillaise" (Claude Rouget de Lisle); "Bayou Trouble Tree" (Herbert Stothart, D. Jones).

Jeanette MacDonald (Marianne de Beaumanoir); Nelson Eddy (Charles Mission, Duc de Villiers); Mary Boland (Valerie de Rossac); George Zucco (Vicomte de Ribaud); H. B. Warner (Father Michell); Richard [Dick] Purcell (Alexander); Stanley Fields (Tambour); Bunty Cutler (Julie, the Maid); Grant Mitchell (Governor of New Orleans); Raymond Walker (Coco); John Miljan (Pierre Brugnon, the Overseer); Ivan Simpson (Guizot); George Irving (Ship Captain); Edwin Maxwell (Captain de Jean); Paul E. Burns (Guard on Ship); Trevor Bardette (Foulette); LeRoy Mason (Grant); William Tannen (Pierre); Cecil Cunningham (Governor's Wife); Claude King (Monsieur Dubois); Rafael Storm (de Piron); Winifred Harris (Lady); Robert Warwick (Commissar); Sarah Edwards (Marquise della Rosa); George Lloyd (Quartermaster); Gayne Whitman (Mate); Jean Fenwick (Woman); George Magrill (Guard); Christian J. Frank, Arthur Belasco, Edward Hearn, Nick Copeland, Gino Corrado, Fred Graham, Ralph Dunn, Harry Strang, Ray Teal, Ted Oliver (Bondsmen); Frank Remsden (Man); Ed O'Neill (Lookout); Warren Rock (Mate); Jewell Jordan (Woman); Joe Yule (Maurice); Max Marx (Officer); Alden

[Stephen] Chase (Citizen); Jack Perrin (Officer); Claire Rochelle (Drunken Girl); Frank Elliott, Kenneth Gibson, Victor Kendall, Gerald Fielding, Bea Nigro, Hillary Brooke (Guests); Dorothy Granger (Fat Bridesmaid); June Gittelson (Madeline); David Alison (Troubadour); Joe Dominguez (Wounded Bondsman); Florence Shirley (Guest); Forbes Murray (Commandant); Buster Keaton (Prisoner Aboard the *Lulu*).

Oscar Hammerstein, II and Sigmund Romberg's operetta *The New Moon* debuted on Broadway in September 1928 and had a run of over 500 performances with Evelyn Herbert, Robert Halliday, Olga Albani and Esther Howard in the cast. The production introduced such enduringly popular songs as "Lover, Come Back to Me," "Softly, As in a Morning Sunrise," "Stout-Hearted Men" and "Wanting You." Although there have been numerous mountings of the operetta on stage, there have been only two screen adaptations to date.

With great fanfare, MGM produced NEW MOON in 1930 and issued it for the Christmas holiday season that year. Opera stars Lawrence Tibbett, fresh from his Oscar-nominated role in MGM's THE ROGUE SONG (*q.v.*), and Grace Moore, who had made her screen debut as Jenny Lind in MGM's poorly received A LADY'S MORALS (1930), co-starred in this operetta which the studio revamped in storyline and concept. The ad copy boasted, "Every producer in motion pictures tried to get this prize stage sensation. M-G-M brings it to you with all the thrills that made it Broadway's wonder show for more than a year. Great stars—dramatic story—superb action—soul stirring love scenes—glorious voices. Don't miss it!" Then, hoping to widen its audience appeal, the studio utilized such titillating promotional copy as "She drew him quietly into her boudoir. Tonight she was his, but tomorrow she was to be the wife of another!"

In pre-Revolutionary Russia, on the ship *New Moon* the passengers include Lieutenant Michael Petroff (Lawrence Tibbett), who sings a gypsy song and charms the beautiful but arrogant Princess Tanya Strogoff (Grace Moore). She is engaged to marry Boris Brusiloff (Adolphe Menjou), the governor of an outlying province. The Lieutenant and the Princess make love, but later, when Brusiloff gives a ball to honor his fiancée, Michael arrives uninvited and dances with the princess, much to the dismay of her father (Roland Young) and her betrothed. To get revenge on Petroff, the governor orders him to the remote Fort Davaz, hoping that the unruly recruits there will kill him. As he leaves, Petroff denounces Tanya. At the fort he has to shoot the leaders of the rebellious troops and finally gets the outpost under control. Angry with Petroff and wanting revenge, Tanya follows him to Fort Davaz. However, by the time she arrives, she decides she loves him and the two marry. Petroff is soon called to lead his men into battle with the Tourkamens. Later it is reported (falsely) that he has been killed in action. He returns eventually to the fort and to Tanya.

The critical response was generally enthusiastic. The *New York Evening Journal* proclaimed it, ". . . An exceptional film adaptation . . . the best of the screen operettas yet filmed . . . in all respects the film is thoroughly entertaining." The *New York Tribune* opined, "Mr. Tibbett possesses the most effective singing voice in the motion pictures . . . much to be said for a film that offers two such superior voices as are possessed by Mr. Tibbett and Miss Moore." The *New York Times* printed, "This picture is an excellent combination of fine singing, romance and adventure." It added, "It was no wonder that the audience applauded his [Tibbett] songs, for if a singer ever deserved the enthusiasm, he did."

Well received as it was, both Lawrence Tibbett (after two more MGM pictures) and Grace Moore soon returned to the opera stage and concert platform. Each made a film comeback; she successfully in Columbia's ONE NIGHT OF LOVE (1934), *q.v.,* he to negligible results in UNDER YOUR SPELL (1936), *q.v.*

A decade after the initial release, MGM remade NEW MOON (the 1930 version then became known for some strange reason as PARISIAN BELLE) as a vehicle for Jeanette MacDonald and Nelson Eddy. The setting and plot were changed to more closely resemble the play; many felt it had become a close carbon copy of the singing team's earlier hit movie, NAUGHTY MARIETTA (1935), *q.v.*

In 1788 the beautiful Marianne de Beaumanoir (Jeanette MacDonald) sails to New Orleans from Paris to inspect a plantation left to her by an uncle. Aboard the *Joie-des-Anges* are a group of disgraced bondsmen being taken to the New World to be sold into slavery. Among them is Charles Mission, Duc de Villiers (Nelson Eddy), a political foe of the King who has escaped a death sentence by disguising himself as a bondsman. Encountering Charles in the captain's suite, she mistakes him for a ship's officer. Later, in New Orleans, Marianne is surprised to learn that he has been purchased by her plantation manager as the new domestic. Still carrying on his deception, Charles insists that he learned his good breeding from his employer, the Duc de Villiers. Meanwhile, she finds herself falling in love with Charles. When a pursuing French policeman (George Zucco) arrives in New Orleans, Marianne learns the truth about Charles. Knowing the danger facing him, Charles and his bondsmen followers plot their escape, taking over a ship in the harbor and sailing away. A discouraged Marianne voyages back to France, accompanied by her aunt (Mary Boland) and a group of brides-to-be who are destined for colonists in Martinique. En route, the *New Moon* is attacked by pirates. When they board, Marianne finds that Charles is their leader. A storm arises and the shipload of passengers heads for shore. On the island Charles establishes a new republic. Several of the girls choose husbands from among Charles's crew. The prideful Marianne remains aloof, but later agrees to marry Charles. When a French ship appears on the horizon, Charles decides to give himself up to save the others. By now Marianne realizes that she loves him. Representatives from the ship land on the island and Charles learns that because of the recent French Revolution, he is now a free man. A joyful Marianne and Charles begin their new life together.

As had become typical with MGM's adaptations of evergreen operettas, there was a mixture of songs from the original production with a blending of new lyrics to old melodies, a few opera arias added as showcases, and occasional traditional songs tossed into the mix. Jeanette MacDonald, adorned in attractive wigs and voluminous period gowns, passes through NEW MOON as a high-toned lady with a glorious voice. She sings "I Was a Stranger in Paris" (which Eddy mocks in his own rendition) and once in the New World, she performs the rondelet, "One Kiss." During a yard scene in which he is polishing shoes, the ever jocular (but now more stout) Eddy sings "Softly as in a Morning Sunrise." With the bondsmen he handles "Stout Hearted Men" (one of the film's few visually moving numbers) and, with the heroine, two love songs, "Wanting You" and "Lover Come Back to Me" (MacDonald first solos on this song). For musical variety, a group of black slaves are heard singing "No More Weepin'."

Unfortunately, by the time of NEW MOON, movie operettas were going through another decline. The comparisons of this picture with the earlier NAUGHTY MARIETTA were not favorable. Not only was the budget lessened for NEW MOON, but the two stars were fast maturing (too old to be the young hero and heroine) and their performing styles had frozen into a stylized rut. Regarding this, the sixth of MacDonald and Eddy's eight screen-teamings, *Variety* complained, "NEW MOON is another example of the inability of film writers and directors to transpose logical story qualities into picture form from operetta material. Despite the elaborate production mounting, and the general excellence of the songs, the synthetic story premise of the operetta still remains, with all the artificial trimmings of a stage piece."

In the mid-1950s Nelson Eddy recorded the score to *New*

Moon with Eleanor Steber on Columbia Records. One of the more recent outings for *New Moon* was the 1988 New York City Opera's production at Virginia's Wolf Trap Farm Park, with Leigh Munro and Richard White in the leading roles. The taped presentation was telecast on PBS-TV's "Great Performances" on April 7, 1989.

NIGHT AND DAY (Warner Bros., 1946) Color 128 minutes.

Producer, Arthur Schwartz; director, Michael Curtiz; based on the career of Cole Porter; adapter, Jack Moffitt; screenplay, Charles Hoffman, Leo Townsend, William Bowers; art director, John Hughes; set decorator, Armor Marlowe; costumes, Milo Anderson, Travilla; makeup, Perc Westmore; additional music, Max Steiner; music director, Leo F. Forbstein; orchestrator/conductor, Ray Heindorf; vocal arranger, Dudley Chambers; choreographer, LeRoy Prinz; assistant director, Frank Heath; dialogue director, Herschel Dougherty; color consultants, Natalie Kalmus, Leonard Doss; sound, Everett A. Brown, David Forrest; montages, James Leicester; special effects, Robert Burks; camera, Peverell Marley, William V. Skall; editor, David Weisbart.

Songs: "I'm in Love Again," "Bulldog," "In the Still of the Night," "An Old-Fashioned Garden," "You've Got That Thing," "Let's Do It," "You Do Something to Me," "Night and Day," "I'm Unlucky at Gambling," "Miss Otis Regrets," "What Is This Thing Called Love?" "I've Got You Under My Skin," "Rosalie," "Just One of Those Things," "Anything Goes," "You're the Top," "I Get a Kick Out of You," "Easy to Love," "My Heart Belongs to Daddy," "Do I Love You?" "Love for Sale," "Don't Fence Me In," "Begin the Beguine" (Cole Porter); "I Wonder What's Become of Sally" (Jack Yellen, Milton Ager).

Cary Grant (Cole Porter); Alexis Smith (Linda Lee Porter); Monty Woolley (Himself); Ginny Simms (Carle Hill); Jane Wyman (Gracie Harris); Eve Arden (Gabrielle); Victor Francen (Anatole Giron); Alan Hale (Leon Dowling); Dorothy Malone (Nancy); Tom D'Andrea (Bernie); Selena Royle (Kate Porter); Donald Woods (Ward Blackburn); Henry Stephenson (Omar Porter); Paul Cavanagh (Bart McClelland); Sig Rumann (Willowsky); Carlos Ramirez, Milada Mladova, Estelle Sloan, George Zoritch (Specialty Dancers); Adam and Jayne DiGalano (Specialty Team); Mary Martin (Herself); James Dobbs, John Compton, John Miles, Art Kassel, Paul Garkie, Laddie Rucker (Students); Frank Dae, Boyd Irwin, Sam Flint, Charles Miller (Professors); John Alvin (Petey); Harlan Briggs (Doorman); Harry Seymour (Clarence, the Piano Player); Clarence Muse (Caleb); JoAnn Marlowe (Tina); Regina Wallace, Frank Ferguson (Tina's Parents); George Meader (Minister);

Virginia Sale (Minister's Wife); Bertha Woolford, Armba Dandridge (Servants); Gregory Muradian (Small Caroler); Lisa Golm, Ernest Golm (Foreign Couple); John Goldsworthy (Yale Gentleman); Gary Owen (Bartender); Crane Whitley (Commercial Artist); Lynne Baggett (Sexboat); Rebel Randall, Arlyne Roberts (Chorus Girls); Paula Drew, Patricia Clark, Jane Harker (Specialty Trio); Creighton Hale, Paul Gustine (Men in Theatre); Bob McKenzie (Hansom Cab Driver); Alan Shute, Bill Hind, Eric Wilton (English Officers); Edgar Caldwell, George Volk, Allen Marston (American Officers); Leon Lenoir, Michael Panaieff, Pierre Duval (French Officers); James Dodd (Red); Emile Hilb (Orchestra Leader); Bernard Deroux (Assistant to Giron); George Suzanne, Henry DeSoto (Waiters); Marie Melesch (Scrub Woman); Adrian Doeshou, Rene Mimieux (Men at Bar); Fred Dash, Maurice Brierre, Albert Petit (French Waiters); Frank Marlowe (Army Driver); Rune Hultman (American Lieutenant); Peter Camlin (French Lieutenant); George Riley (O'Halloran); Fern Emmett (Secretary); Ruth Matthews, Betty Blair, Valerie Ardis, Edna Harris, Ellen Lowe, Joan Winfield (Nurses); Dick Erdman, Robert Arthur, Caren Harsh, Patsy Harmon, Dorothy Reisner (Young Customers); Claire Meade, Charles Williams (Customers); Mayo Newhall (Bearded Man); George Nokes (Wayne Blackburn); Gordon Richards (Coachman); Laura Treadwell (Woman in Theatre); Frank Miliott (Man in Theatre); Howard Freeman (Producer); Bobby Watson (Director); Philip Van Zandt (Librettist); Harry Crocker (Newspaperman); John "Red" Pierson, Herman Bing ("Peaches"); Chester Clute (Music Publisher); Joyce Compton, Helen O'Hara, Suzanne Rosser (Chorines); Dick Bartell (Photographer); Eddie Kane (Headwaiter); Louis Quince, Marion Gray, Willis Claire, Leota Lorraine (Couples); Rudolph Friml, Jr. (Orchestra Leader); John Vosper (Man); Helen Pender (Pretty Nurse); Eddie Kelly (Call Boy); Bill Hardsway, Jack Richardson, Tom McGuire, Ed Biby (Surgeons); Laurie Shermain (Intern); Hobart Cavanaugh, Almira Sessions (Couple in Hospital Corridor); Gene Garrick (Soldier); Jacquelinie Milo (French Girl); George Kirby (Cab Driver); Wally Scott (Chauffeur); Colin Kenny (Doorman); Herbert Evans (Bobby); Gladden James, Mike Lally, Dick Earle, J. W. Johnstone (Doctors); Buddy Gorman (English Page Boy); Harold DeBecker (English Workman); Jack Mower (Livery Chauffeur); Elizabeth Valentine (Matron in Hospital); Cyril Ring, Vivien Oakland (Married Couple); Pat Gleason (Dance Director); Don Roy (Band Leader); Hans Herbert (Headwaiter); Ruth Costello, Dorothy Costello (Twins, Dance Team); George Boyce (Stage Manager); Fred Deming (Guest); Bert Moorehouse,

Marshall Ruth, Fred Stanley (Yale Alumni, Class of 1916); Joe Kirkwood, Jr., Gene Stanley (Classmates of Cole Porter); Henry Hasting (Black Bartender); Nicodemus "Nick" Stewart (Black Waiter); Mel Torme (Drummer in Sideline Band during "You're the Top" number).

Cole Porter's beautiful songs are the highlights of this travesty of a biopic which pictured the composer (1891–1964) as a debonair romantic whose work was often inspired by his wife Linda; in reality Porter had no romantic or sexual interest in women. Taken in the context of fiction, and despite its 128-minute running time, NIGHT AND DAY does entertain. In its expensively mounted showcase of Porter tunes it presents an array of high-calibre musical talent in a host of star turns. As for the miscast Grant, he was gracious, charming and handsome, even if he gave no hint of the creative talent that was Cole Porter. Cole Porter was paid $300,000 for the screen rights to his life. The original concept included having Fred Astaire, Jimmy Durante, Danny Kaye, Bert Lahr, Mary Martin and Ethel Merman recreate numbers they had introduced in Porter musicals, but eventually only Martin agreed to the special guest appearance fee provided by the studio. To perform the rest of

Cary Grant, Jane Wyman, Pat Gleason and Monty Woolley in NIGHT AND DAY (1946).

the numbers, fictional composite figures were created.* NIGHT AND DAY grossed $4,990,000 in distributors' domestic film rentals.

In 1914 Cole Porter (Cary Grant) is a pre-law student at Yale University and his roommate is pre-medical student Ward Blackburn (Donald Woods). Cole is befriended by a fun-loving, egotistical professor, Monty Woolley (himself), who is at odds with the campus dean for too frequently joining in student activities. It is while at Yale that Porter begins composing songs for school productions and decides on a career as a songwriter. Meanwhile, during the Christmas holidays, Cole returns home to Indiana where he meets Kentucky socialite Linda Lee (Alexis Smith), who is a house guest of Porter's cousin (Dorothy Malone). Before the vacation is over, Cole and Woolley agree not to return to the campus; instead they intend to break into show business. Porter's grandfather (Henry Stephenson) is especially disappointed by his grandson's decision. Porter's first show is *See America First,* for which he writes the music, Woolley serves as director and Gracie Harris (Jane Wyman), a showgirl friend of Cole's from his Ivy League days, is the star. The musical, unfortunately, opens the night that the *Lusitania* is sunk. The show closes that same evening. During War I Porter joins the French Army and, on the front lines, a leg wound almost ends his life. During his recuperation he reencounters Linda, now a Red Cross nurse. She helps him regain his enthusiasm for composing music. Once back in the United States he writes the songs for such Broadway hits as *Fifty Million Frenchmen* and *The New Yorkers.* Later he goes to England to provide the tunes for the London stage show, *Wake Up and Dream.* While in England Porter and Linda meet yet again and are married. Returning to the States, Cole composes a succession of Broadway hits. As his career soars, his marriage falters, and chic Linda is pushed into the background. She eventually fades from his life. Years later, Cole returns to Indiana to attend his dying grandfather. While horseback riding in the countryside he is thrown by his horse and his leg is injured once more. He undergoes several operations

---

*In *The Melody Lingers On,* 1986, Roy Hemming judged, "The musical numbers . . . [the players] perform in NIGHT AND DAY are, with few exceptions, disappointing in staging and vocal execution. Morever, the script cavalierly introduces some of Porter's songs with little regard for actual compositional sequence, mixing them up in completely wrong periods of Porter's life. The script goes even further in whitewashing or fictionalizing Porter's private life, particularly a sequence in which he's depicted as a World War I hero. The silliest moment . . . comes when Grant is shown having difficulties composing 'Night and Day' and gets help from his adoring Linda (as a wartime nurse). . . ."

to save the limb; his only distraction is his songwriting. Meanwhile, Linda, who has been in Europe, learns of Cole's health problems and returns to America. At a Yale reunion, the couple is reunited and they decide to face the future together.

Within NIGHT AND DAY, vivacious Jane Wyman performs several numbers ("I'm in Love Again," "Let's Do It," "You Do Something to Me) in her usual sprightly manner. In an offbeat piece of casting, Eve Arden is seen as the French Gabrielle, who does "I'm Unlucky at Gambling." Later there is Ginny Simms (vocalizing several numbers, many of which were written originally for Ethel Merman): "I Wonder What's Become of Sally," "What Is This Thing Called Love?" "I've Got You Under My Skin," "Just One of Those Things" and "I Get a Kick Out of You." (The song "I Wonder What's Become of Sally" is a non-Porter number.) With Cary Grant, Simms duets "You're the Top." Game Grant provides snatches of "An Old-Fashioned Garden" and joins in "In the Still of the Night." The bewhiskered Monty Woolley, a delightful ham, has his own solo with "Miss Otis Regrets." Not to be overlooked is Mary Martin recreating her show-stopping Broadway number, "My Heart Belongs to Daddy" (from *Leave It to Me*). The production numbers are under-choreographed, but that was typical of LeRoy Prinz.

"In NIGHT AND DAY the music of Cole Porter comes through beautifully . . . but these good songs pop up like pegs in a story without drama. No doubt the writers thought in basing their script on Porter's 'career' instead of his life, they could avoid issues that might be precarious in portraying real people who are still alive," wrote *The Commonweal* magazine. Summing it all up in retrospect, Clive Hirschhorn (*The Hollywood Musical,* 1981) insisted, "Cole Porter deserved a better tribute to his life and work than NIGHT AND DAY . . . a shoddy Technicolored biopic in the worst Hollywood tradition that even contained the cliché 'Wait a minute, I think I've got it!' uttered by Porter as his muse finally descends to help him complete his most famous song, 'Night And Day.' "

NIGHT AND DAY was directed by Michael Curtiz, who had done a much finer job with the biopic of another Broadway composer-showman, that of George M. Cohan (James Cagney) in YANKEE DOODLE DANDY (1942), *q.v.* NIGHT AND DAY appeared in the same year as Warner Bros.' over-inflated RHAPSODY IN BLUE, *q.v.,* a 139-minute fabrication of the life and times of the great composer, George Gershwin, with Robert Alda failing in the title assignment.

A NIGHT AT THE OPERA (Metro-Goldwyn-Mayer, 1935) 90 minutes.

Producer, Irving Thalberg; director, Sam Wood; story, James Kevin McGuinness; screenplay, George S. Kaufman, Morrie Ryskind, Al Boasberg, Bert Kalmar, Harry Ruby; art directors, Cedric Gibbons, Ben Carre; set decorator, Edwin B. Willis; costumes, Dolly Tree; music, Herbert Stothart; choreographer, Chester Hale; camera, Merritt B. Gerstad; editor, William Levanway.

Songs: "All I Do Is Dream of You" (Nacio Herb Brown); "Alone" (Brown, Arthur Freed); "Cosi Cosa" (Ned Washington, Bronislau Kaper, Walter Jurmann); "Take Me Out to the Ballgame" (Jack Norworth); arias from the operas *Il Trovatore* (Giuseppe Verdi) and *I Pagliacci* (Ruggiero Leoncavallo).

Groucho Marx (Otis B. Driftwood); Chico Marx (Fiorello); Harpo Marx (Tomasso); Kitty Carlisle (Rosa Castaldi); Allan Jones (Riccardo Baroni); Walter Woolf King (Rodolfo Lassparri); Sig Rumann (Herman Gottlieb); Margaret Dumont (Mrs. Claypool); Edward Keane (Captain); Robert Emmett O'Connor (Detective Henderson); Gino Corrado (Steward); Purnell Pratt (Mayor); Frank Yaconelli (Engineer); Billy Gilbert (Engineer's Assistant/Peasant); Sam Marx (Extra on Ship and at Dock); Claude Peyton (Police Captain); Rita and Rubin (Dancers); Luther Hoobyar (Ruiz); Rodolfo Hoyos (Count di Luna); Olga Dane (Azucena); James J. Wolf (Ferrando); Inez Palange (Maid); Jonathan Hale (Stage Manager); Otto Fries (Elevator Man); William Gould (Captain of Police); Leo White, Jay Eaton, Rolfe Sedan (Aviators); Wilbur Mack, George Irving (Committee); George Guhl (Policeman); Harry Tyler (Sign Painter); Phillips Smalley, Selmer Jackson (Committee); Alan Bridge (Immigration Inspector); Harry Allen (Doorman); Lorraine Bridges (Louisa); Jack Lipson (Engineer's Assistant).

With their popularity slipping at the box-office, The Marx Brothers were dropped by Paramount in 1934 after DUCK SOUP. However, MGM, at the instigation of studio executive Irving Thalberg, picked up their option and cast them in A NIGHT AT THE OPERA. To insure the proper reception for the vehicle, Thalberg urged the brothers (now three on camera) to put together a vaudeville act based on scenes from the upcoming movie. They toured in it and polished the script, based on live audience reactions. The result was a movie which not only renewed their screen popularity but also helped to launch singer Allan Jones, who scored well with "Alone" and "Cosi Cosa," which he recorded successfully for Victor Records.

In Italy, slippery businessman Otis B. Driftwood (Groucho Marx) convinces social climbing millionairess Mrs. Claypool (Margaret Dumont) to sink $200,000 into an opera company. The group's director (Sig Rumann) signs famous Rodolfo Lassparri (Walter Woolf King) and Rosa Castaldi (Kitty Carlisle) to star in the production. Meanwhile, Driftwood has placed unknown chorus singer Riccardo Baroni (Allan Jones) under contract for the leading role, not knowing that he is Rosa's boyfriend. The opera company leaves Milan for New York City and Riccardo stows away on the ship, along with his pal Fiorello (Chico Marx) and Lassparri's dismissed valet, Tomasso (Harpo Marx). After much confusion on the high seas, they reach the United States and the opera is staged. However, Driftwood (who has been fired by Mrs. Claypool), Tomasso and Fiorello spoil the egotistical Lassparri's performance and kidnap him. Riccardo takes over and sings with Rosa (who had been dismissed from the troupe for not succumbing to Lassparri's lechery). Thus the company's rendition of *Il Trovatore* is a success and Mrs. Claypool recoups her investment.

Although it is centered around music, with the operatic sequences nicely handled by Allan Jones, Kitty Carlisle and Walter Woolf King, the highlights of A NIGHT AT THE OPERA are the comic antics of the Marx Brothers. Particularly memorable is the scene of the ship's cabin jammed with tangled bodies. Another sequence of inspired mayhem occurs at the opera house where Fiorello and Tomasso have caused havoc with the orchestra's sheet music. The classic overture suddenly becomes "Take Me Out to the Ball Game," with Driftwood lunging up and down the aisles hawking peanuts (in true ballpark style!). Before long the stage scenery is flying and Tomasso is swinging across the stage like Tarzan.

When this comedy with music premiered, the *New York Evening Post* heralded, "None of their previous films is as consistently and exhaustingly funny, or as rich in comic invention and satire, as A NIGHT AT THE OPERA." The *New York Daily Mirro*r insisted, "There is so much joy and inspired lunacy in A NIGHT AT THE OPERA it shouldn't be missed." A NIGHT AT THE OPERA earned $3 million in profits. The studio quicky re-teamed the three Marx Brothers with Allan Jones in A DAY AT THE RACES (1937), also directed by Sam Wood. It did not fare as well.

NO, NO, NANETTE (First National, 1930) Color Sequences 98 minutes. (Also silent version).

Producer, Ned Marin; director, Clarence Badger; based on the musical play by Otto Harbach, Emil Nyltray, Vincent Youmans,

Frank Mandel, Irving Caesar; adaptor, Howard Emmett Rogers; dialogue, Beatrice Van; choreographer, Larry Ceballos; camera, Sol Polito; editor, Mandel.

Songs: "King of the Air," "No, No, Nanette," "Dancing to Heaven" (Al Bryan, Ed Ward); "As Long as I'm with You" (Grant Clarke, Harry Akst); "Dance of the Wooden Shoes" (Ned Washington, Herb Magidson, Michael Cleary).

Bernice Claire (Nanette); Alexander Gray (Tom Trainor); Lucien Littlefield (Jim Smith) Louise Fazenda (Sue Smith); Lilyan Tashman (Lucille); Bert Roach (Bill Early); ZaSu Pitts (Pauline the Servant); Mildred Harris (Betty); Henry Stockbridge (Brody); Jocelyn Lee (Flora).

See: NO, NO, NANETTE (1940) (essay).

NO, NO, NANETTE (RKO, 1940) 96 minutes.

Producer-director, Herbert Wilcox; based on the musical play by Otto Harbach, Emil Nyltray, Vincent Youmans, Frank Mandel, Irving Caesar; screenplay, Ken Englund; costumes, Edward Stevenson; music director, Anthony Colins; camera, Russell Metty; editor, Elmo Williams.

Songs: "Tea for Two," "I Want to Be Happy," "Where Has My Hubby Gone?" "Take a Little One Step," "No, No, Nanette" (Irving Caesar, Otto Harbach, Vincent Youmans).

Anna Neagle (Nanette); Richard Carlson (Tom); Victor Mature (William); Roland Young (Mr. Smith); Helen Broderick (Mrs. Smith); ZaSu Pitts (Pauline); Eve Arden (Winnie); Tamara (Sonya); Billy Gilbert (Styles); Stuart Robertson (Stillwater, Jr./ Stillwater, Sr.); Dorothea Kent (Betty); Aubrey Mather (Remington); Mary Gordon (Gertrude); Russell Hicks (Hutch); Benny Rubin (Max); Margaret Armstrong (Dowager); George Nelson (Messenger Boy); Lester Dorr (Travel Agent); John Dilson, Cyril Ring, Joey Ray (Desk Clerks); Sally Payne (Maid); Torben Meyer (Furtlemertle); Victor Wong (Houseboy); Bud Geary (Taxi Driver); Chris Franke (Hansom Driver); Keye Luke, Ronnie Rondell (Men); Muriel Barr, Georgianna Young, Marion Graham (Show Girls); Minerva Urecal (Woman in Airport); Julius Tannen (Ship Passenger); Rosella Towne (Stewardess); Frank Puglia, Maurice Cass, Paul Irving (Art Critics); Mary Currier, Jean Fenwick, Joan Blair, Dora Clement (Women at Smith Home).

The popular musical comedy *No, No, Nanette* was based on Emil Nyltray and Frank Mandel's play *My Lady Friends,* which in turn came from the humorous novel *His Lady Friends* (1919) by May Eddington. MY LADY FRIENDS was filmed in 1921 starring Mr. and Mrs. Carter De Haven. In 1924 Frank Mandel and Otto

Harbach made the play into a musical comedy with music and lyrics by Vincent Youmans, Irving Caesar and Harbach. As *No, No, Nanette,* the production opened on Broadway in the fall of 1925 and ran for 321 performances with a cast including Louise Groody, Mary Lawlor, Charles Winninger and Frank Parker. Two of its songs, "Tea for Two" and "I Want to Be Happy," became popular song standards.

In the early days of sound films First National Pictures brought NO, NO, NANETTE to the screen in January 1930, but surprisingly it omitted the show's more popular tunes and added new material, the best being the song "As Long As I'm with You."

Tom Trainor (Alexander Gray) is writing a musical show for his girl, Nanette (Bernice Claire), but he cannot get backing for it. Finally he convinces Bible publisher Jimmy Smith (Lucien Littlefield), a friend of his father's, to finance the production. But Smith does not tell his staid wife Sue (Louise Fazenda). When Jimmy pays the bills for two chorus girls, their manager (Bert Roach) keeps the money for himself, and his wife (Lilyan Tashman) tells Mrs. Smith about the goings-on. She, in turn, hires detectives to trail her husband. When Jimmy later goes to Atlantic City for the show's opening the manager and both wives follow, but the women meet and like Nanette. Jimmy gets in trouble when the chorines arrive, but the show is well received and everyone is happy.

To ballyhoo its new musical, First National Picture advertised, "Here it comes!—The hit that made 'Tea for Two' a national anthem. . . . The smash that shattered all musical romance records in its one-year run on Broadway. . . . Brought to you on the screen in all its glory—and more!—More girls—more song hits—more stars—more stupendous settings than the stage production!" When it was released, *Photoplay* magazine said of the film, "A good girl-and-music picture with fine Technicolor trimmings, but notable chiefly for its rapid-fire succession of laughs." The *New York Times* concluded it was "Funny enough to tickle the risibles of almost anybody." Later in the year, First National teamed Alexander Gray and Bernice Claire again in the operetta, SONG OF THE FLAME, *q.v.,* with unremarkable results.

British producer Herbert Wilcox remade NO, NO, NANETTE in 1940 for RKO RADIO, starring his wife Anna Neagle in the title role. (Earlier in the year the studio, Wilcox and Neagle had converted another old stage warhorse into a film, IRENE.) This time the hit songs "Tea for Two" and "I Want to Be Happy" were retained, but the rest of the score was reduced to background music, except for the title tune (which had also been used in the 1930 version). Here, philandering Jimmy Smith (Roland Young), the uncle of Nanette (Anna Neagle), has been blackmailed by gold diggers. In order to help him, Nanette enlists the aid of artist Tom Trainor (Richard Carlson) and theatrical producer William (Victor Mature), both of whom romance Nanette.

"Though the romantic and golddigger troubles were sorted out in reasonably satisfactory fashion, Wilcox's stodgy direction weighed down the story's grace and gaiety," judged Richard B. Jewell and Vernon Harbin in *The RKO Story* (1982). Many thought Anna Neagle too coy in her characterization, although Victor Mature was approved for his virile presentation.

In 1950 Warner Bros. updated and redid the creaking property as the Doris Day musical, TEA FOR TWO (*q.v*). The next year, Jackie Gleason and Ann Crowley did a version of "No, No Nanette" on NBC-TV's "Musical Comedy Time." Early in 1971 the play was successful revived on Broadway with Busby Berkeley as its production supervisor. It starred Ruby Keeler, Jack Gilford, Helen Gallagher, Susan Watson, Bobby Van and Patsy Kelly (as the maid Pauline). Benny Baker later replaced Gilford as Jimmy Smith while Evelyn Keyes, Don Ameche and Ruth Donnelly starred in a road company of the show in 1972–73. Keeler and Cyril Ritchard did another 1973 road tour and a third company, on the road from 1973 to 1974, featured Keyes, Benny Baker and Betty Kean. Dame Anna Neagle, who had portrayed Nanette in the 1940 film version, portrayed Sue Smith in a 1973 London production of *No, No Nanette,* with Jenny Wren in the title role.

OKLAHOMA! (Magna, 1955) Color 145 minutes.

Executive producers, Richard Rodgers, Oscar Hammerstein, II; producer, Arthur Hornblow, Jr.; director, Fred Zinnemann; based on the musical play by Rodgers, Hammerstein, II, and the play *Green Grow the Lilacs* by Lynn Riggs; screenplay, Sonya Levien, William Ludwig; production designer, Oliver Smith; art director, Joseph Wright; costumes, Orry-Kelly, Motley; music director, Jay Blackton; orchestrator, Robert Russell Bennett; music adaptor, Adolph Deutsch; choreographer, Agnes DeMille; assistant director, Arthur Black, Jr.; sound director, Fred Hynes; camera, Robert Surtees; editor, Gene Ruggiero.

Songs: "Oh, What a Beautiful Morning," "Surrey with the Fringe on Top," "I Cain't Say No," "Many a New Day," "People Will Say We're in Love," "Pore Jud Is Daid," "All 'Er Nuthin'," "Everything's Up to Date in Kansas City," "The Farmer and the Cowman," "Out of My Dreams," "Oklahoma" (Richard Rodgers, Oscar Hammerstein, II).

Gordon MacRae (Curly); Gloria Grahame (Ado Annie); Gene

Nelson (Will Parker); Charlotte Greenwood (Aunt Eller); Shirley Jones (Laurey); Eddie Albert (Ali Hakim); James Whitmore (Carnes); Rod Steiger (Jud Fry); Barbara Lawrence (Gertie); J. C. Flippen (Skidmore); Roy Barcroft (Marshal); James Mitchell (Dream Curly); Bambi Linn (Dream Laurey); Jennie Workman, Kelly Brown, Marc Platt, Lizanne Truex, Virgina Bosler, Evelyn Taylor, Jane Fischer (Dancers); Ben Johnson (Cowboy at Train Depot).

When *Oklahoma!* leaped onto Broadway (March 31, 1943) it was credited with revolutionizing the American musical comedy form. This breakthrough show, bursting with folksy Americana, illustrated aptly how song, dance and plot could be melded together into a unified whole. It was based on the 1931 Broadway production of Lynn Riggs' *Green Grow the Lilacs,* a non-musical starring Franchot Tone, June Walker, Helen Westley, Richard Hale, Lee Strasberg and Woodward [Tex] Ritter. A dozen years later Richard Rodgers and Oscar Hammerstein, II adapted the play into *Oklahoma!* starring Alfred Drake, Joan Roberts, Celeste Holm, Betty Garde, Joan McCracken, Lee Dixon, Bambi Lynn and Howard DaSilva. This classic show ran for 2,212 performances, holding the record as the longest-running musical comedy on Broadway until *My Fair Lady* (1956), *q.v.* With *Oklahoma!* a hit, filmmakers were eager to translate this property to the screen, but Rodgers and Hammerstein held out, fearful that a competing (movie) version would harm the show's box-office. Finally, in 1953, the songwriters agreed to a movie edition and contracted with Todd-AO (a company producing films in a special widescreen process) to bring *Oklahoma!* to the cinema. Many of the exteriors for OKLAHOMA! were filmed near Nogales, New Mexico, not in Oklahoma, because the latter state had become too modernized to depict the early 1900s.

In rural Oklahoma at the turn of the century, cowboy Curly (Gordon MacRae) has fallen in love with beautiful Laurey (Shirley Jones), who lives with her feisty Aunt Eller (Charlotte Greenwood). Also lusting for Laurey is unrefined farmhand Jud Fry (Rod Steiger), while Curly's pal, Will Parker (Gene Nelson), wants to wed Ado Annie (Gloria Grahame), who flirts with peddler Ali Hakim (Eddie Albert). Needing money to marry Annie, Will enters a steer roping contest and wins, but loses his winnings to Ali (he later recovers them again). Curly also needs money and sells his horse and gun to acquire enough cash to outbid Jud on the lunch basket Laurey will bring to the annual picnic, since the man who wins a young lady's picnic basket then has an unspoken claim on her. Eventually Curly proposes marriage to Laurey and she accepts.

Shirley Jones and Gordon MacRae in OKLAHOMA! (1955)

However, Jud is out for revenge and, at a shivaree for the couple, he starts a fight with Curly. In the melee he falls on his own knife and is killed. Aunt Eller calls a quick trial in which Curly is exonerated of any crime. He and Laurey can proceed with their wedding/honeymoon.

While it seemed that much of America had already seen *Oklahoma!* in the twelve years between the stage debut and the film version, the movie managed (in many moments) to breathe some freshness into the production with its broad vistas of cornfields, its stereophonic sound, and by providing the cast more realistic settings and props to tell their love story. Gordon MacRae is first seen riding horseback through the fields singing "Oh, What a Beautiful Morning," and later, in an action sequence, performs "The Surrey with the Fringe on Top." He and Shirley Jones duet on "People Will Say We're in Love." Gloria Grahame, as the man-hungry Ado Annie, announces "I Cain't Say No" and Ron Steiger intones (along with MacRae) "Pore Jud is Daid." On the more exuberant side, wide-eyed, agile-legged Gene Nelson reports, "(Everything's Up to Date in) Kansas City." Lanky, high-kicking Charlotte Greenwood joined in on that number, as well as with the cast on "The Farmer and the Cowman" and the show's vigorous anthem, "Oklahoma." This movie carried over the concept from the stage production that a singer/actor was not necessarily able to be the best dancer. Thus the film also used the gimmick of having a Dream Curly (James Mitchell) and a Dream Laurey (Bambi Lynn) to handle the terpsichorean tasks during the Dream Dance sequence. Not used for the movie were two songs from the Broadway original: "It's a Scandal! It's a Outrage!" and "Lonely Room." Refreshingly, everyone in the movie edition of OKLAHOMA! sang their own songs.

When the movie of OKLAHOMA! had first been announced, a host of young name performers had been considered for the leads, including James Dean or Paul Newman as Curly, Joanne Woodward as Laurey and Eli Wallach as Jud. The actual cast chosen for the picture was exceptional in many ways. OKLAHOMA! marked the movie debut of beautiful and wholesome Shirley Jones, who had been performing on Broadway and in road companies of Rodgers and Hammerstein musicals. For handsome baritone Gordon MacRae, who had been a musical comedy star at Warner Bros., OKLAHOMA! brought new life to his film career. For Charlotte Greenwood, a long time veteran of the stage and movies (including many musicals at 20th Century-Fox in the 1940s), OKLAHOMA! provided her a chance to perform the role of Aunt Eller, one she had had to reject in 1943 because of movie commitments. For pouty-mouth, sultry Gloria Grahame and intense method actor Rod Steiger, their musical roles herein were remarkable changes of paces, as was Eddie Albert's role as the ethnic peddler. Both Bambi Lynn and Marc Platt had been in the Broadway cast of the musical, but not in the roles given them on screen. Director Fred Zinnemann, who had won an Academy Award for directing FROM HERE TO ETERNITY (1953), was a newcomer to the musical comedy format and OKLAHOMA! would be his only excursion into the genre.

The *New York Times* enthused of the released film, "It's a perfectly beautiful, fresh and melodiously flowing thing, with a superb cast . . . director Fred Zinnemann has superbly blended the action and musical sequences with a fittingly striking color canvas of the cornfield country—the open plains, red barns, yellow farmhouses and blue skyfulls of fleecy clouds. And wisely Agnes De Mille has been retained to recreate her dances, making of them eloquent movements that flow beneath the sky." On the other hand, John McCarten (*New Yorker* magazine) complained about the use of Todd-AO (widescreen) and the loudness of the movie's soundtrack, adding, "Although the method of presentation has been heavily altered, the picture does have the virtue of sticking close to the original script, and there are times when the songs and dances blend together with a kind of noisy charm."

OKLAHOMA! grossed $7.1 million in distributors' domestic film rentals. After its initial release in Todd-AO, it was re-released in CinemaScope by 20th Century-Fox. OKLAHOMA! won Academy Awards for Best Scoring of a Musical Picture and Sound. It was Oscar-nominated for Best Cinematography—Color and for Editing. The soundtrack album to OKLAHOMA! remained on the *Billboard* magazine hit charts for sixty-two weeks and was in #1 position for four weeks.

The next year, Gordon MacRae and Shirley Jones were reunited for the movie version of Rodgers and Hammerstein, II's CAROUSEL, *q.v.*

OLIVER! (Columbia, 1968) Color 153 minutes.

Producer, John Woolf; director, Carol Reed; based on the musical play by Lionel Bart, from the novel *Oliver Twist* by Charles Dickens; screenplay, Vernon Harris; production designer, John Box; art director, Terence Marsh; assistant art directors, Roy Walker, Bob Cartwright; set decorators, Vernon Dixon, Ken Mugglestone; costumes, Phyllis Dalton; wardrobe supervisor, John Wilson-Apperson; makeup, George Frost; music supervisor/orchestrator/choral arranger/music conductor, John Green; associate music supervisor/additional orchestrator, Eric Rogers; music coordinator, Dusty Buck; music editor, Kenneth Runyon; choreographer, Onna White; associate choreographer, Tom Panko; assistant directors, Colin Brewer, Ray Corbett; sound, Buster Ambler, Bob Jones; sound supervisor, John Cox; sound editor, Jim Groom; special effects, Allan Bryce; camera, Oswald Morris; second unit camera, Brian West; editor, Ralph Kemplen.

Songs: "Food, Glorious Food," "Oliver!", "Boy for Sale," "Where Is Love?" "Consider Yourself," "Pick a Pocket Or Two," "I'd Do Anything," "Be Back Soon," "As Long as He Needs Me," "Who Will Buy?" "It's a Fine Life," "Reviewing the Situation," "Oom-Pah-Pah" (Lionel Bart).

Ron Moody (Fagin); Shani Wallis (Nancy); Oliver Reed (Bill Sikes); Harry Secombe (Mr. Bumble); Mark Lester (Oliver Twist); Jack Wild (The Artful Dodger); Hugh Griffith (The Magistrate); Joseph O'Connor (Mr. Brownlow); Peggy Mount (Widow Corney); Leonard Rossiter (Mr. Sowerberry); Hylda Baker (Mrs. Sowerberry); Kenneth Cranham (Noah Claypole); Megs Jenkins (Mrs. Bedwin); Sheila White (Bet); Wensley Pithey (Dr. Grimwig); James Hayter (Mr. Jessop); Elizabeth Knight (Charlotte); Fred Emney (Chairman of Workhouse Governors); Edwin Finn, Foy Evans (Workhouse Paupers); Norman Mitchell (Arresting Policeman); Robert Bartlett, Graham Buttrose, Jeffrey Chandler, Kirk Clugeston, Dempsey Cook, Christopher Duff, Nigel Grace, Ronnie Johnson, Nigel Kingsley, Robert Langley, Brian Lloyd, Peter Lock, Ian Ramsey, Peter Renn, Bill Smith, Kim Smith, Freddie Stead, Raymond Ward, John Watters (Fagin's Boys); Clive Moss (Charlie Bates); Veronica Page (Oliver's Mother); Henry Kay (Doctor); Jane Peach (Rose, the Maid); Keith Roberts (Policeman in Magistrate's Court); Peter Hoar (Court Clerk); John Baskcombe, Norman Pitt, Arnold Locke, Frank Crawshaw (Workhouse Governors).

A musical version of Charles Dickens' beloved 1838 novel, *Oliver Twist,* OLIVER! opened in London in June 1960 and ran for 2,618 performances. The production, with music, lyrics and book by Lionel Bart, was staged on Broadway in January 1963 and lasted for 774 performances. As translated to the screen, OLIVER! won the Academy Award as Best Picture of 1968.* It also garnered Oscars for Art Direction, Scoring and Sound, while Onna White was given a Special Award for her Outstanding Choreography Achievement in the picture. Addtionally, Ron Moody (who played the role on the London stage) was nominated as Best Actor for his performance as the sinister Fagin, and Jack Wild as Best Supporting Actor for his lively appearance as the unremorseful The Artful Dodger. (Other nominations for the picture were: Best Screenplay, Cinematography, Editing and Costumes). The movie brought in $16,800,000 in distributors' domestic film rentals. The soundtrack album appeared on *Billboard* magazine's hit charts for eight weeks, rising to position #8.

In nineteenth-century England, young Oliver Twist (Mark Lester) is brought to an orphanage and, losing in a draw of straws, he requests a second helping of gruel. Because of this audacious behavior the proprietor (Harry Secombe) sells him to tightfisted undertaker Sowerberry (Leonard Rossiter) as an apprentice. When the undertaker's assistant (Kenneth Cranham) makes nasty remarks about Oliver's late mother, the boy runs away to London. There he meets a young scalawag called The Artful Dodger (Jack Wild), a

*Over the years there have been many dramatic screen interpretations of Charles Dickens' melodramatic novel, *Oliver Twist.* Among the several celluloid productions are: OLIVER TWIST (Crystal Studios, 1912), with Vinnie Burns (Oliver Twist) and Nat C. Goodwin (Fagin); OLIVER TWIST (Paramount Pictures, 1916), with Marie Doro (Oliver Twist) and Tully Marshall (Fagin); OLIVER TWIST (First National Pictures, 1922), with Jackie Coogan (Oliver Twist) and Lon Chaney (Fagin); OLIVER TWIST (Monogram Pictures, 1933), with Dickie Moore (Oliver Twist) and Irving Pichel (Fagin); and OLIVER TWIST (General Film Distributors, 1948), with John Howard Davies (Oliver Twist) and Alec Guinness (Fagin).

knowing soul who takes the naive Oliver under his wing. The Dodger works as a pickpocket for the miserly Fagin (Ron Moody), who trains young boys to steal. Fagin instructs Oliver in the methods of lifting money from strangers on the street. Oliver is later caught stealing and is put on trial. However, the victim, Mr. Brownlow (Joseph O'Connnor), whose wallet was stolen, takes mercy on the child and brings him to live in his home. Later he discovers that Oliver is really the son of his deceased niece. Meanwhile, Fagin fears Oliver will give evidence against him and orders his drunken associate, Bill Sikes (Oliver Reed), to find the boy. Bill forces his common-law wife Nancy (Shani Wallis) to set a trap for the youth. When Nancy finds out that Bill intends to kill Oliver, she alerts Brownlow. For her troubles, the loutish Sikes beats her to death and abducts the boy. Following Oliver's pet dog, a growing crowd makes it way to Fagin's hideout. The escaping Sikes is shot dead as he tries to leap across a rooftop. Oliver is reunited with Brownlow. As for Fagin, who has lost all his hoarded savings in the melee, he and The Artful Dodger set out to find new victims to fleece.

Deleted from the film production were such songs from the stage original as "I Shall Scream," "That's Your Funeral" and "My Name." Probably the best remembered songs from the score were "As Long as He Needs Me" (sung by Shani Wallis), which became a popular standard, and "Where Is Love?" (a wistful number performed by Mark Lester). Page Cook wrote in *Films in Review* magazine (January 1969), "When song and dance are inserted in the telling of a valid story all the usual dramaturgical rules are altered. Musical sequences should make characterization more believable and plot-turns more felicitous. In OLIVER!, I'm sorry to say, song and dance so prettifies Dickens' exposé of nineteenth century poverty and crime that the result, for the audience, is emotional confusion." Regarding the movie's music, Cook opined, "Lionel Bart's original score, with its bawdy English music-hall ditties and several lovely ballads, was pleasant enough. But Johnny Green's arrangement and orchestration of Bart's score for this film, and his conducting of the result, reek with ineptitudes and destroy Bart's best efforts." On the other hand, Ted Sennett (*Hollywood Musicals,* 1981) commended the song-and dance numbers, explaining that they ". . . have the requisite sweep and color. The largest, to the tune of 'Consider Yourself at Home,' is Oliver's introduction to London, bringing out scores of residents for a rousing welcome. On the glorious set of Mr. Brownlow's block, street vendors, followed by schoolgirls in yellow skirts, blue-coated schoolboys, and marching soldiers, greet a sparkling morning by singing 'Who Will Buy?' "

Sir Carol Reed was an offbeat but surprisingly effective choice for directing a musical. He had been noted for such dark brooding studies as ODD MAN OUT (1946), THE FALLEN IDOL (1948) and THE THIRD MAN (1949).

ON A CLEAR DAY YOU CAN SEE FOREVER (Paramount, 1970) Color 129 minutes.

Producer, Howard W. Koch; director, Vincente Minnelli; screenplay, based on the musical play by Burton Lane, Alan Jay Lerner; production designer, John De Cuir; set decorators, George James Hopkins, Raphael Bretton; Miss Streisand's contemporary clothes designer, Arnold Scassi; period costumes, Cecil Beaton; makeup, Harry Ray; music supervisor/arranger/conductor, Nelson Riddle; choral arranger, Joseph J. Lilley; vocal/dance arranger, Betty Walberg; choreographer, Howard Jeffrey; assistant directors, William McGarry, William R. Poole, Gene Anderson, Jr.; dialogue coach, Walter Kelley; sound, Ben Winkler, Elden Ruberg; camera, Harry Stradling; aerial camera, Tyler Camera Systems; time lapse camera, John Ott; editor, David Bretherton; assistant editor, Flo Williamson.

Songs: "On a Clear Day, You Can See Forever," "Come Back to Me," "What Did I Have That I Don't Have?" "He Isn't You," "Hurry, It's Lovely Up Here," "Go to Sleep," "Love with All the Trimmings," "Melinda" (Burton Lane, Alan Jay Lerner).

Barbra Streisand (Daisy Gamble); Yves Montand (Dr. Marc Chabot); Bob Newhart (Dr. Mason Hume); Larry Blyden (Warren Pratt); Simon Oakland (Dr. Conrad Fuller); Jack Nicholson (Tad Pringle); John Richardson (Robert Tentrees); Pamela Brown (Mrs. Fitzherbert); Irene Handl (Winnie Wainwhistle); Roy Kinnear (Prince Regent); Peter Crowcroft (Divorce Attorney); Byron Webster (Prosecuting Attorney); Mabel Albertson (Mrs. Hatch); Laurie Main (Lord Percy); Kermit Murdock (Hoyt III); Elaine Giftos (Muriel); John Le Mesurier (Pelham); Angela Pringle (Diana Smallwood); Leon Ames (Clews); Paul Carmen (Millard); George Neise (Wytelipt); Tony Colti (Preston).

Having tackled FUNNY GIRL (1968), *q.v.,* and HELLO DOLLY! (1969), *q.v.,* musical comedy megastar Barbra Streisand turned her attention to yet another Broadway musical then being transferred to the screen. The property, *On a Clear Day You Can See Forever,* with lyrics and book by Alan Jay Lerner and music by Burton Lane, had opened on Broadway in October 1965 for a 280-performance run. It had starred Barbara Harris and John Cullum (who replaced Louis Jourdan during the try-out tour).

In New York City, happy, unconventional Daisy Gamble

(Barbra Streisand) is romanced by conservative young executive Warren Pratt (Larry Blyden) as well as by her hippie "ex-stepbrother," Tad Pringle (Jack Nicholson). However, one evening she happens by a psychiatry class taught by Dr. Marc Chabot (Yves Montand) and falls into a trance while he is hypnotizing another student. As a result she decides to seek his aid to help her quit her incessant cigarette smoking. He quickly realizes that she has extraordinary mental powers. Under hypnosis, Daisy regresses back in time to the early nineteenth century when she was a poor girl named Melinda who advances herself by marrying a nobleman (Laurie Main) and then falling in love with handsome Robert Tentrees (John Richardson). Daisy has more sessions with Dr. Chabot and soon abandons her smoking habit. In the process, she reveals a remembrance of other past lives, and a common thread through all her reincarnations, that of transferring her affections from man to man. Meanwhile, the doctor finds himself greatly attracted to the personality of Melinda, while Daisy is becoming very infatuated with Chabot. The psychiatrist announces that he has found an extraordinary patient with ESP power, and officials at the university where he is employed are upset by the publicity. They demand that he deny the existence of ESP or resign. Meanwhile, Daisy hears the tapes Marc has made of their sessions. For the first time she consciously learns about Melinda and her past. She feels betrayed by the doctor and refuses to see him. In desperation, Marc uses telepathy to pursue Daisy. Eventually he not only convinces her she is a very sane young woman, but wins her love.

By the time ON A CLEAR DAY YOU CAN SEE FOREVER went into production, Oscar-winning Barbra Streisand was no longer playing characterizations in movies, she was playing Barbra Streisand. So great was her box-office power that she controlled the production more than the director. For sensitive director Vincente Minnelli, whose career had been faltering since the early 1960s, this movie was a nightmare of power control.* What emerged was a mishmash of confused style, abrupt editing and disjointed themes. On the plus side was a charming performance by the overshadowed Yves Montand and period costumes and coiffures which served to beautify the unique Miss Streisand.

Several songs from the Broadway edition were deleted, including "Ring Out the Bells," "Tosy and Cosh," "Don't Tamper

---

*Vincente Minnelli (1910–86), who directed several outstanding MGM musicals in the 1940s and 1950s, had won an Oscar for GIGI (1958), *q.v.* After the debacle of ON A CLEAR DAY YOU CAN SEE FOREVER, he directed one more picture, the non-musical A MATTER OF TIME (1976).

Barbra Streisand in ON A CLEAR DAY YOU CAN SEE FOREVER (1970).

with My Sister," "She Wasn't You" and "When I'm Being Born Again." Three new numbers were composed for the film; only one ("Love with All the Trimmings") survived the final cuts. Chopped from the release print were guitar-strumming Jack Nicholson's "Who Is There Among Us Who Knows?" and the duet number ("Wait Till You're Sixty-Five") between Streisand and Larry Blyden. Of the tunes left on screen, the best were the vigorous "Come Back to Me" (Yves Montand) and "On a Clear Day" (Montand; reprised by Streisand). For novelty there was Streisand's talking to her apartment plants in "Hurry! It's Lovely Up Here."

Page Cook rightly complained in *Films in Review* magazine (August-September 1970), "Miss Streisand's conception of Daisy Gamble . . . is that of an unimaginative boor, and her trumpeting through [Burton] Lane's score is an esthetic crime [director Vincente] Minnelli should not have permitted. . . . But I assume he was ordered to give Streisand her head, and she rewarded him by ruining some of his best scenes."

ON A CLEAR DAY YOU CAN SEE FOREVER grossed only $5,350,000 in distributors' domestic film rentals, making it a financial disaster. The soundtrack album did not reach the top forty charts. Streisand would not return to the musical format until FUNNY LADY (1975), *q.v.*

ON MOONLIGHT BAY (Warner Bros., 1951) Color 95 minutes.

Producer, William Jacobs; director, Roy Del Ruth; based on the "Penrod" stories by Booth Tarkington; screenplay, Jack Rose, Melville Shavelson; art director, Douglas Bacon; set decorator, William Wallace; costumes, Milo Anderson, Marjorie Best; makeup, Gordon Bau; music adaptor, Max Steiner; music director, Ray Heindorf; choreographer, LeRoy Prinz; sound, Francis J. Scheid, David Forrest; camera, Ernest Haller; editor, Thomas Reilly.

Songs: "Moonlight Bay" (Percy Wenrich, Edward Madden); "Till We Meet Again" (Ray Egan, Richard A. Whiting); "Pack Up Your Troubles in Your Old Kit Bag" (Felix Powell, George Asaf); "Christmas Story" (Pauline Walsh); "I'm Forever Blowing Bubbles" (Jean Kenbrovin, John W. Kellette); "Love Ya" (Charles Tobias, Peter DeRose); "Tell Me Why Nights Are Lonely" (Max Kortlander, W. J. Callahan); "Cuddle Up a Little Closer," "Every Little Movement Has a Meaning All Its Own" (Otto Harbach, Karl Hochna).

Doris Day (Marjorie Winfield); Gordon MacRae (William Sherman); Jack Smith (Hubert Wakeley); Leon Ames (George Winfield); Rosemary DeCamp (Mrs. Winfield); Mary Wickes (Stella); Ellen Corby (Miss Stevens); Billy Gray (Wesley Winfield); Jeffrey Stevens (Jim Sherman); Esther Dale (Aunt Martha): Suzanne Whitney (Cora); Eddie Marr (Barker); Sig Arno (Dancing Instructor); Jimmy Dobson (Soldier); Rolland Morris (Sleeping Soldier); *Silent Movie Cast:* Lois Austin (Mother); Creighton Hale (Father); Ann Kimball (Daughter); Ray Spiker (Bartender); Hank Mann, Jack Mower, Ralph Montgomery (Salesmen); and: Henry East.

"Although it strives to develop a genuine nostalgia mood, all that ON MOONLIGHT BAY seems to create, sadly enough, is the feeling that this film format is old hat" (*New York Times*). Trite though its conception and execution may have been, ON MOONLIGHT BAY was part of Warner Bros.' marketing plan to present its apple pie musical comedy star Doris Day in a series of lighthearted musicals; some period, some contemporary. No matter what the setting, these colorful Warner Bros. productions were merely structural threads to present a beamingly wholesome Day in a romantic tale that barely taxed her growing acting ability. The focus of these pictures was on her distinctive song styling and occasionally allowed her to display a few semi-graceful dance steps.

Thus in ON MOONLIGHT BAY, the spotlight was diverted from the Penrod character (here played by Billy Gray) and transferred to his hoydenish sister (Day).

In a small Indiana town in 1917, tomboy Marjorie Winfield (Doris Day) finds herself falling in love with Hoosier college student William "Bill" Sherman (Gordon MacRae) who lives across the street. In order to attract Bill, blonde Marjorie gives up her beloved baseball and her other unfeminine activities. She concentrates on being an attractive young lady (including taking dance lessons), but her efforts to win Bill's heart are complicated by interference from her pesky younger brother, Wesley (Billy Gray), the objections of her stern banker father (Leon Ames) and concerned mother (Rosemary DeCamp), the meddlesome but loving housekeeper Stella (Mary Wickes), and the fact that carefree Bill does not want to get married yet. Adding to the confusion is the fact that pretty Marjorie is also being courted by Hubert Wakely (Jack Smith). After many romantic hassles, Bill, who has finally abandoned his unconventional ideas about capitalists and matrimony, joins the Army. Mr. Winfield now agrees to Marjorie marrying Bill.

With its pre-World War I nostalgic setting, ON MOONLIGHT BAY was packed with vintage numbers like the title tune, "I'm Forever Blowing Bubbles" and "Cuddle Up a Little Closer." There were newer melodies as well: "Tell Me Why Nights Are Lonely" and "Every Little Moment Has a Meaning All Its Own." As *Variety* discerned, ". . . MOONLIGHT BAY makes no pretense at being anything other than good, soundly-valued entertainment with popular appeal."

ON MOONLIGHT BAY proved to be sufficiently successful to persuade Warner Bros. to reunite the cast (Day, MacRae, Ames, DeCamp, Wickes, Gray) for BY THE LIGHT OF THE SILVERY MOON (1953). This entry had newlyweds Day and MacRae trying to adjust to marriage after his wartime military service.*

ON THE AVENUE (20th Century-Fox, 1937) Color 90 minutes.

Producer, Darryl F. Zanuck; director, Roy Del Ruth; screenplay, Gene Markey, William Conselman; art directors, William Darling, Mark-Lee Kirk; set decorator, Thomas Little; costumes, Gwen Wakeling; music director, Arthur Lange; choreographer, Seymour Felix; camera, Lucien Andriot; editor, Allen McNeil.

*Doris Day and Gordon MacRae had first been teamed by Warner Bros. in TEA FOR TWO (1950), *q.v.*, and later that year played in THE WEST POINT STORY, *q.v.* Both Day and MacRae had guest appearances in the all-star revue, STARLIGHT (1951).

Songs: "He Ain't Got Rhythm," "You're Laughing at Me," "This Year's Kisses," "Slummin' on Park Avenue," "The Girl on the Police Gazette," "I've Got My Love to Keep Me Warm," "O Chi Chornia" (Irving Berlin).

Dick Powell (Gary Blake); Madeleine Carroll (Mimi Caraway); Alice Faye (Mona Merrick); The Ritz Brothers (Themselves); George Barbier (Commodore Caraway); Alan Mowbray (Frederick Sims); Cora Witherspoon (Aunt Fritz Peters); Walter Catlett (Jake Dribble); Douglas Fowley (Eddie Eads); Joan Davis (Miss Katz); Stepin Fetchit (Herman); Sig Rumann (Herr Hanfstangel); Billy Gilbert (Joe Papaloupas); E. E. Clive (Binns, the Cabby); Douglas Wood (Mr. Trivet); John Sheehan (Stage Manager); Paul Irving (Harry Morris); Harry Stubbs (Kelly); Ricardo Mandia (Luigi); Marjorie Weaver, Geneva Sawyer (Chorus Girls); Lynn Bari (Girl at Nightclub); Hank Mann (Footman in Sketch); Edward Cooper (Potts); Paul Gerrits (Joe Cherry); and: Frank Darien.

Producer Darryl F. Zanuck borrowed Dick Powell from Warner Bros. to headline this Irving Berlin musical which co-starred Britisher Madeleine Carroll. It surprisingly featured Alice Faye in a semi-villainous role as the other woman in the piece. Nevertheless, the combination of her good looks and her song delivery enabled Faye easily to steal the film from the two

Jimmy, Harry and Al Ritz in ON THE AVENUE (1937).

top-billed stars. Not only did Faye score well with "Slummin' on Park Avenue," "This Year's Kisses" and a brief duet with Dick Powell on "I've Got My Love to Keep Me Warm"; she also successfully recorded the trio of songs for Brunswick Records.* The British *Picturegoer* magazine noted, "Alice Faye has a role of a jealous actress which suits her admirably. She brings real character to it, and puts over her song numbers most efficiently." Never again would Alice Faye have less than star billing at 20th Century-Fox (except for her guest star appearance in FOUR JILLS IN A JEEP in 1944 and in her comeback picture for Fox, 1962's STATE FAIR, *q.v.*).

Broadway luminary Gary Blake (Dick Powell) has a success with his new show *On the Avenue.* In one scene co-star Mona Merrick (Alice Faye) performs a song called "The Richest Girl in the World." Heiress Mimi Caraway (Madeleine Carroll) believes the song is a snide dig at her family. The socialite goes backstage and protests to Gary, and he agrees to tone down the lampooning number. Meanwhile, he finds himself attracted to the well-bred Mimi, much to the chagrin of the envious Mona, who now schemes to get her competition (Mimi) out of the picture. Mona makes sure that Mimi, her father (George Barbier) and Aunt Fritz (Cora Witherspoon) are in the audience one night when she again does the contested satirical number. This time she makes it even more obvious that it is a send-up of the Caraway clan. The incensed Caraways sue Gary. Mimi then purchases the show from its producer (Walter Catlett) and alters Gary's role to make him look foolish. She also pays the audience to walk out on the revue. Gary refuses to continue with the show. Mimi is scheduled to marry Sims (Alan Mowbray), an Arctic explorer, but Aunt Fritz realizes that Gary and Mimi are really in love. She sees to it that the couple wed in city hall, while Mona begins romancing Mimi's affluent father.

Not to be overlooked in ON THE AVENUE, beyond the elaborate sets and breezy choreography (by Seymour Felix), is the diverting presence of the zany Ritz Brothers (who sing, clown and perform in drag) and knockabout comedienne Joan Davis.

ON THE ROAD AGAIN *see*: HONEYSUCKLE ROSE.

ON THE TOWN (Metro-Goldwyn-Mayer, 1949) Color 98 minutes.

Producer, Arthur Freed; associate producer, Roger Edens; directors, Gene Kelly, Stanley Donen; based on the musical play by

---

*Three numbers deleted from the release print of ON THE AVENUE were: "On the Avenue," "On the Steps of Grant's Tomb" and "Swing Sister."

Adolph Green, Betty Comden, Leonard Bernstein; from the ballet "Fancy Free" by Jerome Robbins, Bernstein; screenplay, Comden, Green; art directors, Cedric Gibbons, Jack Martin Smith; set decorators, Edwin B. Willis, Jack D. Moore; costumes, Helen Rose; makeup, Jack Dawn; music director, Lennie Hayton; orchestrator, Conrad Salinger; vocal arranger, Saul Chaplin; assistant director, Jack Gertsman; color consultants, Henri Jaffa, James Gooch; sound supervisor, Douglas Shearer; special effects, Warren Newcombe; camera, Harold Rosson; editor, Ralph E. Winters.

Songs: "New York, New York," "I Feel Like I'm Not Out of Bed Yet," "Come Up to My Place" (Leonard Bernstein, Betty Comden, Adolph Green); "Miss Turnstiles Ballet" (Bernstein); "Walking Down Main Street with You," "A Day in New York Ballet," "You're Awful (Awful Nice to Be With)," "On the Town," "You Can Count on Me," "Pearl of the Persian Sea," "Pre-Historic Man," "That's All There Is, Folks" (Roger Edens, Comden, Green); "Anniversary Fanfare" (Miklos Rozsa).

Gene Kelly (Gabey); Frank Sinatra (Chip); Betty Garrett (Brunhilde Esterhazy); Ann Miller (Claire Huddesen); Jules Munshin (Ozzie); Vera-Ellen (Ivy Smith); Florence Bates (Madame Dilyovska); Alice Pearce (Lucy Shmeeler); George Meader (Professor); Bern Hoffman (Worker); Lester Dorr (Subway Passenger); Bea Benaderet (Working Girl); Walter Baldwin (Sign Poster); Don Brodie (Photo Layout Man); Sid Melton (Spud); Robert B. Williams (Officer); Tom Dugan (Officer Tracy); Murray Alper (Cab Company Owner); Hans Conried (Francois); Claire Carleton (Redhead); Dick Wessel (Sailor Simpkins); William "Bill" Phillips (Sailor); Frank Hagney (Cop); Carol Haney (Dancer in Green); Eugene Borden (Waiter); Judy Holliday (Voice of a Sailor's Date); Gene Scott, Marie Grosscup (Dancers).

While ON THE TOWN may seem badly dated to today's viewers, it was a great trendsetter in its day. It was the first major Hollywood musical to go on location for much of its production. It was (and still is) an exuberant genre piece, full of rich vitality in both its songs and dance numbers. Because it was shot at such a breakneck speed (studio head Louis B. Mayer allowed the company only five days of costly location work!), there is a marvelous breathless quality to the movie, creating a pervasive and infectious joie de vivre.

ON THE TOWN had its origins in the modernistic ballet, *Fancy Free,* created by Leonard Bernstein and Jerome Robbins in 1949. Later that year Betty Comden and Adolph Green turned it into a Broadway musical called *On the Town,* which enjoyed a 463-performance run, starring Nancy Walker, Sono Osato and

Comden and Green. MGM purchased the screen rights for $250,000 in one of the industry's first cases of a pre-production deal. The chosen three male screen leads (Gene Kelly, Frank Sinatra and Jules Munshin) had just starred in the studio's TAKE ME OUT TO THE BALLGAME, *q.v.*, and the script was reshaped to fit their particular talents. A more major accommodation was coping with producer Arthur Freed's dislike of much of the show's score. As a result, only four of the Bernstein-Comden-Green numbers survived: "I Feel Like I'm Not Out of Bed Yet" (Bern Hoffman), "New York, New York" (Sinatra, Kelly, Munshin), "Miss Turnstiles Ballet" (Vera-Ellen) and "Come Up to My Place" (Betty Garrett, Sinatra). Comden and Green (at a fee of $85,000 for book rewrites, $25,000 for new lyrics, as well as sixty percent of the original $250,000 purchase price) wrote several new numbers: "Prehistoric Man" (Ann Miller, Kelly, Munshin, Garrett, Sinatra), "You're Awful (Awful Nice to Be With)" (Garrett, Sinatra), "When You Walk Down Main Street with Me" (Kelly, Vera-Ellen, song/dance), "You Can Count on Me" (Miller, Garrett), and the joking "That's All There Is, Folks."

On a brief shore leave, three sailors, Gabey (Gene Kelly), Chip (Frank Sinatra) and Ozzie (Jules Munshin), take a tour of New York City. Gabey falls in love with the subway poster image of a girl named Ivy Smith (Vera-Ellen), who has been named "Miss Turnstiles." The trio have frisky taxi driver Brunhilde Esterhazy (Betty Garrett) drive them to the Museum of Natural History and, because she is smitten with Chip, she quickly decides to join the boys on their whirlwind tour of the museum. There they encounter lovely Claire Huddesen (Ann Miller), a tap dancing anthropologist who is working on her thesis, *Modern Man, What Is It?* She is attracted to Ozzie. While Chip is being mothered by Brunhilde and Ozzie courts Claire, Gabey continues his search for Miss Turnstiles. He locates her at Carnegie Hall, where she is taking a ballet lesson from Madame Dilyovska (Florence Bates). He persuades her to accept a date. She does not tell him that she actually makes her living dancing in a Coney Island dive. That night the group go out on a joint date. Because Ivy must work, Brunhilde's homely, bronchial roommate (Alice Pearce) substitutes. Gabey eventually makes his way to the club where Ivy is working as a hootchy-kootchy dancer and tells her he does not mind her real occupation. The three sailors and their girls then head back to the boys' ship, since their leave is now over. Their new loves promise to wait for them.

There are several musical gems in ON THE TOWN, livened especially by the verve of the three male leads as they prance about

New York City from the Bronx to the Battery. There is the comic sequence in which Kelly, Sinatra and Munshin masquerade as harem girls and sing "Pearl of the Persian Seas" as the police raid Ivy's club. The very talented Betty Garrett is boisterously on key with her courtship plea, "Come Up to My Place," and leggy Ann Miller is snazzily proficient in her tap number/song, "Prehistoric Man" (which at its energetic finale finds the bones of a large dinosaur collapsing). Kelly and Vera-Ellen team for three dance sequences, providing the most stylized aspect of the movie. Regarding the dream sequence, Kelly would say in 1979, "There was nothing the censors could put their fingers on. The red color, the girl in black, and the sailor in white were very sensuous. The moves were sensuous. Yet I never laid a glove on her. There was nothing the censors could say. If they did, I could have said, 'What? do you have a dirty mind?' But, yes, it was very sensual and the colors did it."

The ads for ON THE TOWN read, "Skirts, skyscrapers and scamperings are the theme as these three skittering scamps take highways and byways of the big city!" *Time* magazine judged ON THE TOWN ". . . A film so exuberant that it threatens at moments to bounce right off the screen . . . leaves a happy impression that MGM has hit upon a bright new idiom for cinemusicals and a bright new directing team that knows how to use it." *Variety* championed, "Picture is crammed with songs and dance numbers, the book is sufficient to carry it along, the Technicolor hues are top flight, and the cast hard working." Made at a cost of $2,111,250, ON THE TOWN grossed $4.4 million in its initial release. ON THE TOWN won an Oscar for Best Scoring of a Musical Picture.

Writing in *The Films of Gene Kelly* (1974), Tony Thomas assessed ON THE TOWN as ". . . The most inventive and effervescent movie musical Hollywood had thus far produced and an important one in that it opened up the form and led to more development of modern dancing on the screen and a greater use of locations. More than any other, it took the musical out of the studio and into life."

There were two off-Broadway revivals of *On The Town* in 1959, a London revival in 1963 (with Elliot Gould and Don McKay) and a Broadway replay (of 73 performances) in November 1971, featuring Phyllis Newman, Bernadette Peters, Ron Husmann, Donna McKecknie and Marilyn Cooper. Plans to make IT'S ALWAYS FAIR WEATHER (1955), *q.v.*, a true sequel to ON THE TOWN, were diverted when neither Frank Sinatra nor Jules Munshin was available for the project.

ON WINGS OF SONGS *see* LOVE ME FOREVER.

ON WITH THE SHOW (Warner Bros., 1929) Color 120 minutes.

Director, Alan Crosland; based on the play *Shoestring* by Humphrey Pearson; screenplay, Robert Lord; choreographer, Larry Ceballos; camera, Tony Gaudio; editor, Jack Killifer.

Songs: "On with the Show," "Birmingham Bertha," "Let Me Have My Dreams," "Am I Blue?" "Welcome Home," "In the Land of Let's Pretend," "Don't It Mean a Thing to You?" "Lift the Juleps to Your Two Lips" (Harry Akst, Grant Clarke).

Betty Compson (Nita); Louise Fazenda (Sarah); Sally O'Neil (Kitty); Joe E. Brown (Ike); Purnell B. Pratt (Sam Bloom); William Bakewell (Jimmy); Fairbanks Twins (Twins); Wheeler Oakman (Durant); Sam Hardy (Jerry); Thomas Jefferson (Dad); Lee Moran (Pete); Harry Gribbon (Joe); Arthur Lake (Harold); Josephine Houston (Harold's Fiancée); Henry Fink (Father); Otto Hoffman (Bert); Ethel Waters, Harmony Four Quartette, Four Covans, Angelus Babe (Themselves); Josephine Houston (Singing Voice of Kitty).

"Now Warner Bros. pioneer again with another radical development in motion picture production.—COLOR! Full Colors—natural colors—real colors, reproduced direct from life! . . . For at ON WITH THE SHOW you can sit 'out front' and revel in all the color and rhythm of the spectacular singing and dancing numbers of a Broadway revue—then step behind the curtain to listen in on the strange drama and romance that wings and dressing-rooms hold secret . . . see heartbreak hiding behind hilarity because—'the show must go on!' " (Advertisement for ON WITH THE SHOW).

A Broadway musical is trying out in New Jersey and its manager, Jerry (Sam Hardy), is up against rising production costs and the cast's unpaid salaries. Especially troublesome is that star Nita (Betty Compson) is demanding the $400 in back salary owed to her . . . or else. The only money Jerry can muster to carry on the production is from old Dad (Thomas Jefferson), the stage doorman, since the main backer, Willie Durant (Wheeler Oakman), has ceased to be responsible for the play's debts. When the owner of the scenery, Sam Bloom (Purnell B. Pratt), threatens to remove it just as the curtain is about to go up, he is conveniently distracted by Sarah (Louise Fazenda), the comedienne of the production. While the show is in progress, the cast learns that the box-office has been robbed. However, Kitty (Sally O'Neil), the ingenue, is able to sweet talk Durant into again supporting the project. This leads to a breakup with her jealous sweetheart, leading man Jimmy (William Bakewell). Because she has not been paid, Nita refuses to perform and Kitty takes over her part at the last moment. She is a big success. Meanwhile, it is discovered that Dad took the receipts to protect his investment. Since the show is now a hit, Jimmy and Kitty are reconciled.

"Good on spectacle but weak on comedy," is how *Photoplay* magazine rated this early talkie which was highlighted by a fine Harry Akst-Grant Clarke score. One of the main virtues of the movie was Ethel Waters' singing of "Am I Blue?" and "Birmingham Bertha," two of her better known songs. (Because Waters was a star *and* black, pre-integration Hollywood solved the touchy situation of whether or not to have her interact with the white stars, by making her a specialty performer, seemingly disengaged from the rest of the storyline.) ON WITH THE SHOW was the forerunner of the classic 42ND STREET (1933), *q.v.*, but it does not compare favorably, as noted by Ted Sennett in *Warner Brothers Presents* (1971), "Filmed with the usual rigid camera, it dealt with the tribulations of a theatre troupe putting on a musical show called *Phantom Sweetheart.* There were several thin strands of plot involving a hatcheck girl with dreams of becoming a Broadway star (Sally O'Neil, in a performance that makes Ruby Keeler look like Bette Davis). . . . [it] is only a shade more than unbearable [as filmfare]."

In *The Hollywood Musical* (1981), Clive Hirschhorn observed, "What distinguished this offering was a story structure in which the musical numbers . . . were part of the show-within-a-show, whose plot the audience was able to follow simultaneously with the backstage intrigues. That aside, it was a catastrophe of misjudgements. . . . The movie was disadvantageously photographed through the claustrophobic camera booths of the time . . . [which] reduced the dancers to little specks." Hirschhorn also acknowledged, ". . . Simultaneous sound-recording was achieved by concealing 38 microphones—also at quite some distance from the performers [as were the cameras] which led to the music being drowned by the noise of dancing feet."

To be noted are the appearances of comedians Louise Fazenda (who turned to character roles in the 1930s), wide-mouthed Joe E. Brown, making his debut at Warner Bros., and, in a non-slapstick role, Arthur Lake, who gained later fame as the movies and TV's Dagwood Bumstead in the "Blondie" series.

ONE HUNDRED MEN AND A GIRL (Universal, 1937) 85 minutes.

Producer, Charles R. Rogers; associate producer, Joseph Pasternak; director, Henry Koster; story, Hans Kraly; screenplay,

Bruce Manning, Charles Kenyon, James Mulhauser, Kraly; music director, Charles Previn; camera, Joseph Valentine; editor, Bernard W. Burton.

Songs: "It's Raining Sunbeams" (Sam Coslow, Frederick Hollander); "A Heart That's Free" (Alfred G. Robyn, Thomas T. Bailey); "The Drinking Song" from the opera *La Traviata* (Giuseppe Verdi); "Hungarian Rhapsody No. 2" (Franz Liszt); excerpts from the opera *Lohengrin* (Richard Wagner); excerpts from "Symphony No. 5" (Peter Ilyich Tchaikovsky); "Alleluja" from the "Exultate, Jubilate, K165" (Wolfgang Amadeus Mozart).

Deanna Durbin (Patricia Cardwell); Leopold Stokowski (Himself); Adolphe Menjou (John Cardwell); Alice Brady (Mrs. Frost); Eugene Pallette (John R. Frost); Mischa Auer (Michael Borodoff); Billy Gilbert (Garage Owner); Alma Kruger (Mrs. Tyler); Jack [J. Scott] Smart (Marshall, the Doorman); Jed Prouty (Tommy Bitters); Jameson Thomas (Russell); Howard Hickman (Johnson); Frank Jenks (Taxi Driver); Christian Rub (Gustave Brandstetter); Gerald Oliver Smith (Stevens, the Butler); Jack Mulhall (Rudolph, a Bearded Musician/Boarder); James Bush (Music Lover); John Hamilton (Manager); Eric Wilton (Butler); Mary Forbes (Theatre Patron); Rolfe Sedan, Charles Coleman, Hooper Atchley (Guests); Leonid Kinskey (Pianist); Edwin Maxwell (Ira Westing, the Music Editor); Rosemary La Planche (Girl); Bess Flowers (Party Guest).

Universal Pictures struck a gold mine in 1937 when immigrants producer Joe Pasternak and director Henry Koster were teamed with teenager Deanna Durbin in her feature film debut, the comedy, THREE SMART GIRLS (*q.v.*). The picture, which emphasized Deanna's comedy and vocal accomplishments, was a surprise hit. For their second outing together, the trio did ONE HUNDRED MEN AND A GIRL, which not only solidified Durbin's screen popularity but also helped to revive the general public's interest in classical music.

The story of ONE HUNDRED MEN AND A GIRL is a simple affair. It told disarmingly of spunky teenager Patricia Cardwell (Deanna Durbin) who devises a scheme to gain work for her unemployed trombonist father (Adolphe Menjou). The Little Miss Fixit organizes a symphony orchestra composed of one hundred men, including her dad, and then persuades famed conductor Leopold Stokowski to lead the aggregation. The plan works and at the big concert, Patricia sings with Stokowski and the orchestra.

In his career study of Deanna Durbin in *Films in Review* magazine (November 1976), William K. Everson pointed out, ". . . Paul Fejos' old BROADWAY camera crane was brought in to play with some dizzying glides and descents to keep the classical stuff 'mobile,' and there was plenty of fun in Deanna's sometimes embarrassing attempts to crash society to get work for her father. [Adolphe] Menjou's performance as the harassed and desperate parent was first class, at times almost too poignant for the light-weight intent of the film. In any event, it was a huge critical and popular success."

Frederick Hollander and Sam Coslow composed the upbeat "It's Raining Sunbeams" for Deanna to sing, and she also performed "A Heart That's Free" by Alfred G. Robyn and Thomas T. Bailey. On the classical side she sang to Stokowski's accompaniment, Mozart's "Alleluja" and "The Drinking Song" aria from *La Traviata.* Stokowski conducted Liszt's "Hungarian Rhapsody No. 2," a portion of Tchaikovsky's "Fifth Symphony" and the prelude to the Third Act of the opera *Lohengrin.* As with most such films which exploited the "novelty" of presenting classical numbers in popularized format, the purity of vocal performance by the movie star lead was not as crucial as a delivery which would capture the attention of moviegoers.

ONE NIGHT OF LOVE (Columbia, 1934) 84 minutes.

Producer, Harry Cohn; director, Victor Schertzinger; story, Dorothy Speare, Charles Beahan; screenplay, S. K. Lauren, James Gow, Edmund North; art director, Stephen Gooson; costumes, Robert Kalloch; music, Louis Silvers; music director, Dr. Pietro Cimini; assistant director, Arthur Balch; sound, Paul Neal; special effects, John Hoffman; camera, Joseph Walker; editor, Gene Milford.

Songs: "One Night of Love" (Victor Schertzinger, Gus Kahn); "Ciri-Biri-Bin" (A. Pestaloza, Rudolf Thaler); arias from the operas: *Lucia de Lammermoor* (Gaetano Donizetti), *Madama Butterfly* (Giacomo Puccini) and *Carmen* (Georges Bizet).

Grace Moore (Mary Barrett); Tullio Carminati (Giulio Monteverdi); Lyle Talbot (Bill Houston); Mona Barrie (Lally); Jessie Ralph (Angelina, the Housekeeper); Luis Alberni (Giovanni, Monteverdi's Assistant); Andres De Segurola (Galuppi); Rosemary Glosz (Frappazini); Nydia Westman (Muriel); Jane Darwell (Mary's Mother); William Burress (Mary's Father); Frederick Burton (Impresario); Henry Armetta (Cafe Proprietor); Sam Hayes (Radio Announcer); Reginald Barlow (Stage Manager); Frederick Vogeding (1st Doctor); Arno Johnson (2nd Doctor); Olaf Hytten (Viennese Valet); Leo White (Florist); Herman Bing (Vegetable Man); Edward Keane (Stage Director); Reginald Le Borg (Opera Director); Paul Ellis (Pinkerton); Joseph Mack (Captain of Italian

Yacht); Marion Lessing (German Girl); Hans Joby (Taxi Driver); Victoria Stuart (Cora Florida); John Ardizoni (Radio Judge); Kurt Furberg (Stage Manager); Spec O'Donnell (Call Boy); Michael Mark (Flower Store Man); Richard La Marr (Steward); Wadsworth Harris (Judge); Arthur Stuart Hull (Sugar Daddy); and: Edmund Burns, Wilfred Lucas, Rafael Storm.

In America, pretty and talented Mary Barrett (Grace Moore) enters a singing contest on radio, the prize being a trip to Italy to study voice. She loses, but using her own money she sails for Italy anyway. Once there she sings in a cabaret and attracts the attention of the great vocal coach, Giulio Monteverdi (Tullio Carminati), and becomes his pupil. Giulio puts Mary through a strict regimen of exercise, diet and vocal training, and soon develops her into a potential star. In Vienna she is supposed to sing the role of "Carmen" but becomes incensed when she finds out that Giulio's former pupil and lover, Lally (Mona Barrie), is also in the city. To make Giulio jealous, Mary announces that she intends to wed her

Grace Moore, Jessie Ralph, Tullio Carminati and Mona Barrie in ONE NIGHT OF LOVE (1934).

ex-beau, rich Bill Houston (Lyle Talbot), who has followed her to Vienna. Finally Giulio realizes he loves Mary and the two are reconciled. But soon afterwards they have yet another misunderstanding and she departs for America to make her debut at the Metropolitan Opera. Previously, Giulio had told Mary she was not prepared for the Met. On opening night she has stage fright and fears he was correct. Yet when she looks up and sees him seated in the balcony, she had renewed confidence. Mary gives a perfect performance. She and Giulio plan to wed.

ONE NIGHT OF LOVE brought opera great Grace Moore back to the screen after she failed to register an impression earlier in MGM's A LADY'S MORALS (1930) as Jenny Lind, and in NEW MOON (1930), *q.v.* The feature, which she partially financed (as well as taking a reduced salary), turned out to be one of the biggest box-office successes of 1934. It was nominated for several Oscars: Best Picture, Best Actress (Grace Moore), Best Director (Victor Schertzinger, who also composed the title song with Gus Kahn) and Best Editing. It received Oscars for Paul Neal's Sound Recording and Louis Silvers' Score.

Variety printed, "Without hesitation this film can be given top rating from an artistic and general cinematographic standpoint." Regarding Grace Moore's rendition of "Sempre Libera" from the opera *La Traviata,* the same reviewer commented, "It's as musical a thrill as has been reached in sound pictures."

Assessing the film and its star, Ethan Mordden (*The Hollywood Musical,* 1981) wrote, ". . . ONE NIGHT OF LOVE is a small piece in modern dress. All it has is Grace Moore singing opera: all it needed. Moore was an exciting soprano who communicated not through acting but through musical intensity. . . . Moore is slim and confident; her phrasing caresses and her high notes blaze. The opera selections are not in English, the *Traviata* excerpt is horribly scrappy and a rehearsal of the sextet from *Lucia di Lammermoor* is covered by dialogue. But Moore makes all the points, especially in 'Ciribiribin,' an Italian pop song sung in a tavern to a rapt gathering who join in for the last chorus while Moore flies high on an extravagant obbligato."

With the raves and revenues harvested from ONE NIGHT OF LOVE Columbia and Grace Moore teamed for several more musical excursions; the next being LOVE ME FOREVER (1935), *q.v.* None of the follow-ups matched ONE NIGHT OF LOVE in audience or critical response.

ORIENTAL DREAM *see*: KISMET (essay).

PAGAN LOVE SONG (Metro-Goldwyn-Mayer, 1950) Color 76 minutes.

Producer, Arthur Freed; associate producers, Ben Feiner, Jr., (uncredited): Roger Edens, Lela Simone; director, Robert Alton; based on the novel *Tahiti Landfall* by William S. Stone; screenplay, Robert Nathan, Jerry Davis, (uncredited) Ivan Tors; art directors, Cedric Gibbons, Randall Duell; set decorators, Edwin B. Willis, Jack D. Moore; costumes, Helen Rose; makeup, William Tuttle; music director, Adolph Deutsch; orchestrator, Conrad Salinger; vocal arranger, Robert Tucker; technical advisor, Stone; assistant director, Al Jennings; color consultants, Henri Jaffa, James Gooch; sound supervisor, Douglas Shearer; special effects, A. Arnold Gillespie, Warren Newcombe; camera, Charles Rosher; editor, Adrienne Fazan.

Songs: "The House of Singing Bamboo," "Singing in the Sun," "Etiquette," "Why Is Love So Crazy?" "Tahiti," "Sea of the Moon" (Harry Warren, Arthur Freed); "Pagan Love Song" (Nacio Herb Brown, Freed); "Cocoanut Milk (Roger Edens).

Esther Williams (Mimi Bennett); Howard Keel (Hazard Endicott); Minna Gombell (Kate Bennett); Charles Muau (Tavae); Rita Moreno (Terru); Philip Costa (Manu); Dione Leilani (Tani); Charles Freund (Papera); Marcella Corday (Countess Mariani); Sam Maikai (Tua); Helen Rapoza (Angele); Birdie Debolt (Mama Ruau); Bill Kaliloa (Mato); Carlo Cook (Monsieur Bouchet).

Ramon Novarro introduced the Nacio Herb Brown-Arthur Freed number, "Pagan Love Song," in the 1929 part-talkie, THE PAGAN at MGM, and waxed the song for HMV Records in London in 1935. More than two decades later, prolific producer-songwriter Arthur Freed used the tune as the title for his latest Esther Williams aqua opus, which was filmed in Technicolor on location in the lushly tropical Hawaii. In addition, the movie interpolated a number of newer songs like Freed and Harry Warren's "House of Singing Bamboo," "Singing in the Sun," and "Sea of the Moon," the last of which Tony Martin recorded on RCA Victor Records.

Ohio school teacher Hazard Endicott (Howard Keel) arrives in Tahiti to take over a tattered coconut plantation left to him by a late uncle. There he meets Kate Bennett (Minna Gombell) and her beautiful niece Mimi (Esther Williams). He thinks Mimi is a full-bloom native girl. Actually she is a "haole" (half-white, half native) who had been college-bred on the mainland, but now enjoys an idyllic existence living a native's life on the isle. Hazard and Mimi promptly fall in love and decide to wed. Then everything goes amiss. During a storm, Endicott's workers leave the plantation to attend his wedding celebration, which Hazard insists is not proper behavior. When Mimi supports the natives' action, the couple fume and fuss. With the help of the interfering natives, the couple are reconciled and marry.

To showcase Williams' admirable physical charms and her swimming skills, PAGAN LOVE SONG featured several swimming sequences for its star, both above and beneath the waters (with an underwater garden scene incorporated into the storyline). There was also a dream scene in which she appears to be performing a water ballet in the sky! With his booming baritone, Howard Keel, who had made his MGM debut in ANNIE GET YOUR GUN (1950), *q.v.*, sang most of the numbers, but he and Williams dueted on "Singing in the Sun." (One number deleted from the release print was Keel's "Music of the Water.") When it was released in December 1950, MGM promoted the film with the tag lines, "Silvered with star, spangled with song, and wrapped up in romance. . . . MGM says 'Happy New Years' with the tops in Technicolor musicals!"

Despite all of its solid production values, PAGAN LOVE SONG did not gel as satisfying entertainment.* It seemed far longer than its seventy-six-minute running time would indicate. *Variety* evaluated the film as among ". . . other weaker entries in Arthur Freed's long string of Metro musicals. . . . With the exception of the boxoffice pull to be derived from the names of Esther Williams and Howard Keel, that's about all the picture has to offer." Made at a cost of nearly $2,000,000 (some $400,000 over budget), PAGAN LOVE SONG grossed over $3.2 million in its initial release, mostly on the basis of Esther Williams' marquee lure.

The next year Williams and Keel would be rematched in TEXAS CARNIVAL (which also featured Red Skelton) and in 1955 they would appear together for JUPITER'S DARLING, a

---

*The problems encountered in filming PAGAN LOVE SONG would have made a better movie than the script used. Esther Williams had just signed a new ten-year, $1,300,000 pact with the studio. Using her star power she refused to have Stanley Donen (who had co-directed her TAKE ME OUT TO THE BALL GAME, 1949, *q.v.*) direct the vehicle. Producer Arthur Freed replaced Donen with choreographer Robert Alton, who had only directed one film to that date, MERTON OF THE MOVIES (1946). Because filming on Tahiti was prohibitive (due to tourists), the company based itself on Kauai where, due to its inaccessibility and the primitive facilities available, the shooting proved extremely taxing. In the midst of production, the married Williams, who displayed no great on-camera affinity for her co-star Keel, was discovered to be pregnant and much effort was consumed in disguising her figure on screen. Adding to the problems were the fact that director Alton was having beginner's jitters and the Tahitian youths hired for the water ballet numbers were scampish, over-amorous, and not visually appealing.

limpid musical fantasy that neither spectacle nor CinemaScope could salvage.

To be spotted in PAGAN LOVE SONG as a native girl is Rita Moreno, who would win a Best Supporting Actress Oscar for WEST SIDE STORY (1961), *q.v.*

PAINT YOUR WAGON (Paramount, 1969) Color 166 minutes.

Producer, Alan Jay Lerner; associate producer, Tom Shaw; director, Joshua Logan; based on the musical play by Lerner, Frederick Loewe; screenplay, Lerner, Paddy Chayefsky; production designer, John Truscott; art director, Carl Braunger; set decorator, James I. Berkey; costumes, Truscott; makeup, Frank McCoy; music, Loewe; music director, Nelson Riddle; choral music director, Roger Wagner; choreographer, Jack Baker; second unit director, Shaw; assistant directors, Jack Roe, Al Murphy; sound, William Randall, Jr.; re-recording supervisor, Fred Hynes; special effects, Maurice Ayers, Larry Hampton; camera, William A. Fraker; second unit camera, Loyal Griggs; aerial camera, Nelson Tyler; editor, Robert C. Jones.

Songs: "I'm on My Way," "I Still See Elisa," "The First Thing You Know," "Hand Me Down That Can o' Beans," "They Call the Wind Maria," "A Million Miles Away Behind the Door," "I Talk to the Trees," "There's a Coach Comin' In," "Whoop-Ti-Ay!", "The Gospel of No Name City," "The Best Things in Life Are Dirty," "Wand'rin Star," "Gold Fever," "I'm on My Way" (Alan Jay Lerner, Frederick Loewe).

Lee Marvin (Ben Rumson); Clint Eastwood (Pardner); Jean Seberg (Elizabeth); Harve Presnell (Rotten Luck Willie); Ray Walston (Mad Jack Duncan); Tom Ligon (Horton Fenty); Alan Dexter (Parson); William O'Connor (Horace Tabor); Ben [Benny] Baker (Haywood Holbrook); Alan Baxter (Mr. Fenty); Paula Trueman (Mrs. Fenty); Robert Easton (Atwell); Geoffrey Norman (Foster); H. B. Haggerty (Steve Bull); Terry Jenkins (Joe Mooney); Karl Bruck (Schermerhorn); John Mitchum (Jacob Woodling); Sue Casey (Sarah Woodling); Eddie Little Sky (Indian); Harvey Parry (Higgins); H. W. Gim (Wong); William Mims (Frock-Coated Man); Roy Jenson (Hennessey); Pat Hawley (Clendennon); Anita Gordon (Singing Voice of Elizabeth); and: The Nitty Gritty Dirt Band.

Between 1951 (when *Paint Your Wagon* premiered on Broadway) and 1969 (when the movie version was released), the tastes and interests of entertainment seekers had changed vastly. What had seemed fresh and exuberant on stage now appeared old-fashioned, bloated and contrived on screen. The public and critical reactions to the movie of PAINT YOUR WAGON were further

Jean Seberg in PAINT YOUR WAGON (1969).

indicators that: (1) the public was turning off (almost altogether) Broadway-to-Hollywood musicals, and (2) spending a great deal of money (nearly $20,000,000) on a production did not guarantee distribution profits.

Alan Jay Lerner and Frederick Loewe's musical *Paint Your Wagon* arrived on Broadway on November 12, 1951 and ran for 289 performances, with James Barton, Olga San Juan, James Mitchell, Kay Medford and Tony Bavaar leading the cast. By the time Paramount had gotten around to filming the story, they opted for major box-office names to pull the weight rather than the vehicle itself. In their bid to lure in ticket buyers, they cast gruff Lee Marvin, who had won an Oscar for CAT BALLOU (1965), and Clint Eastwood, most noted for his several spaghetti Westerns for Sergio Leone. Neither popular performer was noted for his vocalizing talents; as was the case with attractive leading lady Jean Seberg (whose singing would be dubbed by Anita Gordon). Adding to the problems was the hiring of stage director Joshua Logan, who had previously not done well with such stage-to-film musicals as SOUTH PACIFIC (1958) and CAMELOT (1967), *qq.v.*

During the California gold rush, heavy drinking Ben Rumson

(Lee Marvin) and his quiet associate Pardner (Clint Eastwood) are working a gold claim in the raw mining town of No Name City, which has no women. When Mormon Jacob Woodling (John Mitchum) passes through with his wagon full of wives, Ben and Pardner buy one of the man's mates, Elizabeth (Jean Seberg). The two men vie with one another to see who will marry Elizabeth, but being a Mormon the young woman demands both of them as husbands. The two men are married to Elizabeth by local judge Haywood Holbrook (Benny Baker). To divert the town folk from being overly interested in Elizabeth, Rumson causes a group of French prostitutes to set up headquarters at No Name. Later a New England couple, Mr. and Fenty (Alan Baxter, Paula Trueman), arrive with their inhibited son Horton (Tom Ligon). Rumson and Pardner take the inhibited boy in tow, even introducing him to the wonders of the whorehouse. Meanwhile, the two prospectors have caused the town's streets to be laced with shallow mines to gather in any loose gold dust. Nevertheless, the gold vein is played out. A touring gospelman predicts the soulless town will be destroyed. His forecast comes true when a rampaging bull tears through No Name's streets and tunnels, collapsing the supports of the mines. Rumson leaves No Name seeking new excitement. Pardner and Elizabeth decide to farm the land.

Several songs did not survive the transition to the screen, including: "Rumson Town," "Lonely Men," "Movin'," "All for Him" and "Take the Wheels Off the Wagon." Newly written for the screen version by Lerner and Loewe were: "The First Thing You Know," "A Million Miles Away Behind the Door," "The Gospel of No Name City," "The Best Things in Life Are Dirty" and "Gold Fever." Surprisingly, raspy, deep-voiced Lee Marvin did a credible job with his rendition of "Wand'rin Star" and lanky Clint Eastwood was humble and gentle in his whispery performance of "I Talk to the Trees" (one of the hit songs of the stage show). It was no surprise that richly-voiced Harve Presnell (of THE UNSINKABLE MOLLY BROWN, 1964, *q.v.*) should do very well by "They Call the Wind Maria." As for the production ensembles ("Gold Fever," "The Best Things in Life Are Dirty"), they were heavy-handed and obvious.

In *The Film Encyclopedia: The Western* (1983) Phil Hardy wrote, "A disastrous film adaptation. . . . Virtually a succession of sterile set-pieces, the slow pace of the movie and its static plot . . . make for an overlong film. . . . The only real point of interest in the film lies in watching its two stars attempt to extend their screen images in such a bizarre fashion."

PAINT YOUR WAGON only grossed $14.5 million in distributors' domestic film rentals. It received an Oscar nomination for Best Score of a Musical Picture. The soundtrack album lasted a brief four weeks on *Billboard* magazine's hit charts, rising to position #28.

Location work for PAINT YOUR WAGON was done in Oregon. For some of the roadshow (reserve seat) engagements, the film was blown up to be shown in 70mm. widescreen. For later general release, the film was cut to 137 minutes. PAINT YOUR WAGON was rated "M" for its mature theme regarding matrimony and morality.

PAINTING THE CLOUDS WITH SUNSHINE *see:* GOLD DIGGERS OF BROADWAY (essay).

PAJAMA GAME *see*: DAMN YANKEES (essay).

PAJAMA PARTY (American International 1964) Color 82 minutes.

Producers, James. H. Nicholson, Samuel Z. Arkoff; co-producer, Anthony Carras; director, Don Weiss; screenplay, Louis M. Heyward; art director, Daniel Haller; set decorator, Harry Reif; costumes, Marjorie Corso; makeup, Bob Dawn; music, Les Baxter; music supervisor, Al Simms; choreographer, David Winters; music editor, Milton Lustig; motorcycle coordinator, George Dockstader; sound, Phil Mitchell, Robert J. Rubin; sound editor, James Nelson; special effects, Roger George, Joe Zomar; camera special effects, Butler-Glouner, Inc.; camera, Floyd Crosby; editors, Fred Feitshans, Eve Newman.

Songs: "It's That Kind of Day," "There Has to Be a Reason," "Where Did I Go Wrong?" "Pajama Party," "Beach Ball," "Among the Young," "Stuffed Animal" (Gus Hemric, Jerry Styner).

Tommy Kirk (Go-Go); Annette Funicello (Connie); Elsa Lanchester (Aunt Wendy); Harvey Lembeck (Eric Von Zipper); Jesse White (J. Sinister Hulk); Jody McCrea (Big Lunk); Ben Lessy (Fleegle); Donna Loren (Vikki); Susan Hart (Jilda); Bobbi Shaw (Helga); Cheryl Sweeten (Francine); Luree Holmes (Perfume Girl); Candy Johnson (Candy); Buster Keaton (Chief Rotten Eagle); Dorothy Lamour (Head Saleslady); Andy Romano, Linda Rogers, Alan Fife, Alberta Nelson, Jerry Brutsche, Bob Harvey (The Rat Pack); Renie Riano (Maid); Joi Holmes (Topless Bathing Suit Model); Kerry Kollmar (Little Boy); Joan Neel, Patricia O'Reilly, Marion Kildany, Linda Opie, Mary Hughes, Patti Chandler, Laura

Susan Hart, Donna Loren, Cheryl Sweeten and Annette Funicello in PAJAMA PARTY (1964).

Nicholson, Linda Benson, Casey Foster, Stacey Maxwell, Teri Hope, Margo Mehling, Diane Bond, Keva Page, Toni Basil, Kay Sutton, Connie Ducharme, Joyce Nizzari, Leslie Wenner (The Pajama Girls); Ray Atkinson, Frank Alesia, Ned Wynn, Ronnie Rondell, Howard Curtis, John Fain, Mike Nader, Rick Newton, Guy Hemric, Ed Garner, Frank Mortiforte, Ronnie David, Gus Trikonis, Bob Pane, Roger Bacon, Ronnie Dayton (The Pajama Boys); Nooney Rickett Four (Themselves); Don Rickles, Frankie Avalon (Cameo Appearances).

In an attempt to imitate its own successful "Beach Party" films, AIP made PAJAMA PARTY, a combination teenage musical comedy and science fiction feature. "Another American International musical aimed at youth market," sighed *Variety* about this silly affair, which was originally called THE MAID AND THE MARTIAN. Among its highlights are Annette Funicello singing "Where Did I Go Wrong?" Elsa Lanchester's spaced-out Aunt Wendy, Buster Keaton as Chief Rotten Eagle, and Harvey Lembeck's Eric Von Zipper, the inept biker gang leader (a satirical characterization which he had established in the other AIP beach movies).

Go-Go (Tommy Kirk) is dispatched from Mars to prepare the way for an invasion of the earth. He lands in the garden of Aunty Wendy (Elsa Lanchester) where he meets her nephew, Big Lunk (Jody McCrea), and his girl friend, Connie (Annette Funicello). Since Aunty Wendy is supposed to have a large amount of money hidden in her home, crook J. Sinister Hulk (Jesse White) and his cohort Fleegle (Ben Lessy) plan to rob her. Meanwhile, the house is about to be attacked by Eric Von Zipper (Harvey Lembeck) and his cycle gang, because Eric is seethingly jealous of Connie's affection for Big Lunk. Go-Go is unsuccessful in convincing Aunty Wendy, Big Lunk and Connie that he is a Martian and that there *will* be an invasion. At the same time, Chief Rotten Eagle (Buster Keaton) and Helga (Bobbi Shaw) ingratiate themselves with Aunty Wendy and aid their boss, Hulk, along with Fleegle, to crash her pajama party for the local teenagers. When the lawbreakers attempt to execute their caper, Go-Go sends the crooks to Mars. He also sidetracks Von Zipper and his bikers. As a result, the Martians cancel their invasion and Go-Go remains on Earth because he has fallen in love with Connie. Meanwhile, Big Lunk romances Helga.

Two years after the release of this inane comedy, AIP reworked the plot for a TV movie directed by Larry Buchanan called MARS NEEDS WOMEN. Star Tommy Kirk, whose career had fallen on very hard times, again played the invading Martian in this wretched affair.

PAL JOEY (Columbia, 1957) Color 111 minutes.

Producer, Fred Kohlmar; director, George Sidney; based on the musical play by John O'Hara, Richard Rodgers, Lorenz Hart from the stories by O'Hara; screenplay, Dorothy Kingsley; art director, Walter Holscher; set decorators, William Kiernan, Louis Diage; costumes, Jean Louis; makeup, Ben Lane; music adaptors, George Duning, Nelson Riddle; music supervisor/conductor, Morris Stoloff; orchestrator, Arthur Morton; choreographer, Hermes Pan; assistant director, Art Black; camera, Harold Lipstein; editors, Viola Lawrence, Jerome Thoms.

Songs: "That Terrific Rainbow," "I Didn't Know What Time It Was," "Do It the Hard Way," "Great Big Town," "There's a Small Hotel," "Zip," "I Could Write a Book," "Bewitched, Bothered and Bewildered," "The Lady Is a Tramp," "Plant You Now, Dig You Later," "My Funny Valentine," "You Mustn't Kick It Around," "What Do I Care for a Dame?" (Richard Rodgers, Lorenz Hart).

Rita Hayworth (Vera Simpson); Frank Sinatra (Joey Evans); Kim Novak (Linda English); Barbara Nichols (Gladys); Bobby Sherwood (Ned Galvin); Hank Henry (Mike Miggins); Elizabeth Patterson (Mrs. Casey); Robin Morse (Bartender); Frank Wilcox (Colonel Langley); Pierre Watkin (Mr. Forsythe); Barry Bernard (Anderson); Ellie Kent (Carol); Mara McAfee (Sabrina); Betty Utey (Patsy); Bek Nelson (Lola); Henry McCann (Shorty); John Hubbard (Stanley); James Seay (Livingston); Hermes Pan (Choreographer); Ernesto Molinari (Chef Tony); Jean Corbett (Specialty Dance Double); Robert Rietz (Boy Friend); Jules Davies (Red-Faced Man); Judy Dan (Hat Check Girl); Gail Bonney (Heavy Set Woman); Cheryl Kubert (Girl Friend); Tol Avery (Detective); Robert Anderson (Policeman); Genie Stone (Girl); Raymond McWalters (Army Captain); Bob Glenn (Sailor); Sue Boomer (Secretary); Helen Eliot (Traveler's Aid); Hermie Rose (Bald Club Owner); Jack Railey (Hot Dog Vendor); Frank Wilmarth (Sidewalk Artist); Roberto Piperio (Waiter); Ilsa Ostroffsky, Rita Barrett (Strippers); Howard Sigrist (Sidewalk Photographer); Paul Cesari, Everett Glass (Pet Store Owners); Maurice Argent, Michael Ferris (Tailors); Eddie Bartell, Albert Nalbandian, Joseph Miksak, Sydney Chatoo, Frank Sully (Barkers); Andrew Wong (Chinese Club Owner); George Chan (Chinese Pianist); Allen Gin (Chinese Drummer); Barbara Yung, Pat Lynn, Jean Nakaba, Elizabeth Fenton, Lessie Lynne Wong, Nellie Gee Ching (Chinese Dancers); George DeNormand, Oliver Cross, Bess Flowers, Franklyn Farnum (Bits); Giselle D'Arc (Vera's Maid); Leon Alton (Printer Salesman); Jane Chung (Flower Lady); George Ford, Steve Benton (Electricians); Ramon Martinez, George Nardelli (Headwaiters); Jo

Ann Greer (Singing Voice of Vera Simpson); Trudy Erwin (Singing Voice of Linda English).

PAL JOEY had a fascinating history: it was based on John O'Hara's 1930s *New Yorker* magazine stories which he turned into a musical which premiered late in 1940 on Broadway starring Vivienne Segal, Gene Kelly, June Havoc and Leila Ernst, with Van Johnson in the chorus. It ran for 374 performances. Despite its risque storyline and sleazy hero (which shocked theatregoers and critics of the day), Columbia Pictures purchased the screen rights, intending at one point to co-star Gene Kelly and Rita Hayworth (the COVER GIRL [1944], *q.v.*, team) in the musical. After a number of false starts, the studio lost interest in the project until a successful New York City revival in 1952 with Vivienne Segal and Harold Lang reactivated Columbia's enthusiasm. It was announced that Marlon Brando would have the title role, while Mae West (as did Marlene Dietrich) declined the feminine lead of the older woman. Finally, when it did come to the screen in 1957, the part of the prize heel Joey Evans went to Frank Sinatra, whose Essex Productions helped to finance the project. One-time studio queen Rita Hayworth was top-billed as the mature Vera Simpson, and her successor on the lot, Kim Novak, played the ingenue, Linda English. Helmed by George Sidney, the resilient color release earned $4.7 million in distributors' domestic film rentals.

Entertainer-heel Joey Evans (Frank Sinatra), whose luck is running out, arrives in San Francisco, broke and jobless. Through the help of orchestra leader Ned Galvin (Bobby Sherwood), the glib singer talks his way into a job at a small nightclub, initially as the master of ceremonies. There he meets chorus girl Linda English (Kim Novak), who is not drawn to his fast-living ways. Nevertheless, Joey pursues her, even renting a room adjacent to hers in a boarding house. One night Galvin and his group are booked to perform at the Nob Hill home of socialite-widow Vera Simpson (Rita Hayworth). He recognizes her as a former burlesque star named Vanessa, whom he had dated years before. He embarrasses her to perform one of her old numbers, which she does in pantomime. Furious with but also attracted to Joey, Vera intends to get even. Instead, she finds herself falling in love with the ne'er-do-well. Now that he is her lover, she promises to finance him in a new nightclub operation. He moves from the rooming house to Vera's yacht. When Vera observes Joey's continuing interest in Linda, she demands that he fire her, or else. Joey abandons the club project and gives up Vera. He intends to leave San Francisco alone. However, Linda convinces him that they should join forces to share the future together.

There were many changes from the stage *Pal Joey* to the movie. The locale was altered from Chicago to San Francisco. Because the leading man was more a singer than a dancer, Joey Evans on screen became a small-time club vocalist, and in the finale he is redeemed (which is a turnaround from the John O'Hara story original). Vera was softened from an adulterous married woman to a world-weary widow. Additionally, several numbers from the Broadway edition were dropped, including: "Chicago," "Happy Hunting Horn," "Now, Dig," "Den of Iniquity," and "Take Him," or became merely background music. To bolster the vocal catalog for Sinatra to sing, several numbers from other Rodgers and Hart shows were added: "I Didn't Know What Time It Was" (from *Too Many Girls,* 1939), "There's a Small Hotel" (from *On Your Toes,* 1936) and "The Lady Is a Tramp" (from *Babes in Arms,* 1937). Additionally, Rodgers and Hart's "My Funny Valentine" (from *Babes in Arms,* 1937) was included for Kim Novak's character to perform. Sinatra's rendition of the score was casual, but still mightily effective (and the soundtrack album remains a joy to hear).* While both the mature Hayworth and the young Novak were visually impressive, their "singing" was dubbed by Jo Ann Greer and Trudy Erwin respectively.

The *Los Angeles Mirror* reported, "Enough spice and ribald realism remains in this account of a night club lady-killer and the rich widow he mesmerizes to make PAL JOEY one of Hollywood's raciest movies of the season. Also I suspect, one of its most popular." The *Los Angeles Times* noted, "The innuendoes are broader than ever and the repartee—some of it obviously ad-libbed on the spot by Sinatra—is so racy that it had even blasé reviewers doing double-takes...." The *New York Times* termed it, "... Rather surprisingly, a gusty, swiftly-moving, cheerful and adult movie musical. . . . Although the superb Rodgers-and-Hart score is splintered and mixed in with a batter of R-and-H oldies, the musical result is pleasing."

The supremely entertaining PAL JOEY was nominated for a

---

*In *The Melody Lingers On,* 1986, Roy Hemming judged, "Best of all is the interplay as Sinatra sings 'The Lady Is a Tramp' to a first stunned and then amused Hayworth. It's the only one of the interpolated songs that really works in the PAL JOEY context. . . . As for Novak's version of 'My Funny Valentine' . . . it's as lifeless as the rest of her performance." Hemming also noted, "Of the original show's songs, 'Bewitched, Bothered and Bewildered' has had its lyrics laundered considerably, though Hayworth manages to imply a lot more than she's actually mouthing. . . . For the mock striptease of 'Zip' Hayworth lets loose with some provacative, bawdy strutting, obviously designed to recall her similar and classic 'Put the Blame on Mame' in GILDA (1946)—though it's not matched on the soundtrack by Greer's much-too-polite vocal."

quartet of Oscars (Art Direction-Set Direction, Costumes, Editing, Sound), but failed to win an award. The soundtrack album to PAL JOEY remained on *Bilboard* magazine's hit charts for twenty-seven weeks and rose to #2 position.

PALMY DAYS (United Artists, 1931) 80 minutes.

Producer, Samuel Goldwyn; director, A. Edward Sutherland; story, Morrie Ryskin, David Freeman, Eddie Cantor; screenplay, Ryskin, Keene Thompson, Freeman, Cantor; art director, Richard Day; set decorator, Willy Pogany; costumes, Chanel; music director, Alfred Newman; choreographer, Busby Berkeley; camera, Gregg Toland; editor, Sherman Todd.

Songs: "Bend Down, Sister," "Goose Pimples," "Dunk, Dunk Dunk" (Ballard MacDonald, Con Conrad); "My Baby Said Yes, Yes" (Cliff Friend); "There's Nothing Too Good for My Baby" (Eddie Cantor, Benny Davis, Harry Akst).

Eddie Cantor (Eddie Simpson); Charlotte Greenwood (Helen Martin); Spencer Charters (A. B. Clark); Barbara Weeks (Joan Clark); George Raft (Joe the Frog); Paul Page (Steve Clayton); Harry Woods (Plug Moynihan); Charles B. Middleton (Yolando); Loretta Andrews, Edna Callahan, Nadine Dore, Ruth Edding, Betty Grable, Amo Ingraham, Jean Lenivick, Betty Lorraine, Fay Pierre, Hylah Slocum, Betty Stockton, Nita Pike, Nancy Nash, Neva Lynn, Hazel Witter (The Goldwyn Girls); and: Walter Catlett.

In vaudeville, in Broadway musicals, in motion pictures and later on radio and television, Eddie Cantor (1892–1964) was a consummate entertainer. His typical persona—the well-meaning schnook with the high-pitched voice—which was so beloved in its day, seems at odds with today's standards. Then too, there was Cantor's need to turn every scene into a one-man marathon show as he bounded about the sets with jumping feet, fluttering hands and waving eyebrows. Because of his wide-eyed look, Cantor was affectionately known as "Banjo Eyes." Like Al Jolson and many performers of the early twentieth century, Eddie Cantor had a penchant for performing in blackface (which usually caused a disconcerting character change in his films' production numbers).

Having made silent films, Eddie Cantor returned to the screen in 1930 to star in the musical WHOOPEE (1930), a movie version of his great stage hit for producer Florenz Ziegfeld. Cantor's reception with moviegoers was so positive that producer Samuel Goldwyn contracted Cantor to star in many more movies for him and for United Artists release. All of these vehicles showcased Cantor as the poor jerk who succeeded in spite of himself. Each film surrounded him with a bevy of curvacious chorus girls (the

Goldwyn Girls) and these early 1930s' Goldwyn-Cantor musicals all boasted the services of innovative choreographer Busby Berkeley.

Eddie Simpson (Eddie Cantor) is unwittingly employed by gangster Yolando (Charles Middleton) as a part of the hoodlum's bogus medium operation. Eddie is in love with Joan Clark (Barbara Weeks), the daughter of bakery owner A. B. Clark (Spencer Charters). Yolando plans to take over Clark's business, but Eddie, to be near Joan, becomes the man's new efficiency expert. One day in the donut factory gymnasium, he attracts the attention of the Amazonian Miss Martin (Charlotte Greenwood), who begins an active romantic pursuit of Eddie. Meanwhile, Yolando and his cohorts—Joe the Frog (George Raft) and Plug Moynihan (Harry Woods)—steal Clark's holiday payroll and put the blame on Eddie. He, however, retrieves the money and hides it in a loaf of bread. With the aid of the athletic Miss Martin, Eddie subdues the gangsters in a fight and proves his innocence. When it is all over, Eddie realizes he loves Miss Martin and not Joan.

Cantor, who cavorts in drag and blackface in this picture, had a good solo number, "My Baby Says Yes, Yes," which became a part of his permanent repertoire. To display the pulchritude of the Goldwyn Girls (which included a very young Betty Grable) there was the prismatic, precision production number, "Bend Down Sister," which found gangly-legged Charlotte Greenwood instructing thirty-three factory workers in the art of exercise (with the camera focusing on their physique as the girls bent, turned and twisted). To be noted is Cantor's co-authorship of the song number "There's Nothing Too Good for My Baby."

The *New York Times* endorsed "It is quite a good entertainment. . . . The wit may not be as nimble as Mr. Cantor's image, but it is good enough to make one laugh heartily several times. . . . Mr. Cantor is up to his usual mark."

Eddie Cantor would continue to make an average of a film a year for the next several years for Samuel Goldwyn. While THE KID FROM SPAIN (1932) and ROMAN SCANDALS (1933) were popular enough, KID MILLIONS (1934) and STRIKE ME PINK (1936) were on the poor side. As a result, Cantor and Goldwyn came to a parting of the ways once their contract expired.

PANAMA HATTIE (Metro-Goldwyn-Mayer, 1942) 79 minutes.

Producer, Arthur Freed; directors, Norman Z. McLeod, (uncredited) Roy Del Ruth; based on the musical play by Herbert Fields, Buddy G. DeSylva, Cole Porter; screenplay, Jack McGowan, Wilkie Mahoney, (uncredited): Lillie Messinger, Mary

McCall, Joseph Schrank, Fred Finklehoff, Vincente Minnelli; art directors, Cedric Gibbons, John S. Detile; set decorators, Edwin B. Willis; musical presentation designer, Merrill Pye; gowns, Kalloch; music director, George Stoll; music adaptor, Roger Edens; vocal arrangers/orchestrators, Conrad Salinger, George Bassman, Leo Arnaud; musical numbers staged by Minnelli; choreographer, Danny Dare; technical advisor, Sergio R. Orta; sound supervisor, Douglas Shearer; camera, George Folsey; editor, Blanche Sewell.

Songs: "I've Still Got My Health," "Just One of Those Things," "Make It Another Old-Fashioned, Please," "Fresh as a Daisy," "Let's Be Buddies," "My Mother Would Like You," "They Ain't Done Right by Our Nell" (Cole Porter); "Hattie from Panama," "Good Neighbors," "I'll Do Anything for You" (Roger Edens); "The Son of a Gun Who Picks on Uncle Sam" (Burton Lane, E. Y. Harburg); "Did I Get Stinkin' at the Club Savoy?" (Walter Donaldson); "The Sping" (Phil Moore, J. Legon); "Berry Me Not" (Phil Moore); "La Bumba Rhumba" (Alex Hyde); "Hail, Hail, The Gangs's All Here" (based on the melody of "Come Friends Who Plough the Sea" [Sir Arthur Sullivan]; lyrics, Theodore F. Morse).

Ann Sothern (Hattie Maloney); Dan Dailey, Jr. (Dick Bulliet); Red Skelton (Red); Marsha Hunt (Leila Tree); Virginia O'Brien (Flo Foster); Rags Ragland (Rags); Alan Mowbray (Jay Perkins); Ben Blue (Howdy); Jackie Horner (Geraldine Bulliet); Carl Esmond (Lucas Kefler); Pierre Watkin (Admiral Tree); Stanley Andrews (Colonel John Briggs); Lena Horne (Specialty); George Watts (Mac, the Bartender); Lucien Prival (Hans); Joe Yule (Waiter); Duke York (Bruno); Fred Graham (Naval Policeman); Roger Moore (Spy); Max Wagner (Guard); Grant Withers (Shore Patrol); The Berry Brothers (Themselves); and: Carmen Amaya Dancers.

Cole Porter's musical *Panama Hattie,* with a book by Herbert Fields and Buddy G. DeSylva, opened on Broadway on October 30, 1940. Thanks to an adequate story, great songs, and the work of a dynamic cast—which included Ethel Merman, James Dunn, Virginia Field, Arthur Treacher, Rags Ragland, Betty Hutton, June Allyson and Vera-Ellen—the show had a 501-performance run. By the time MGM (who paid $130,000 for the screen rights) brought the property to the screen, the attack on Pearl Harbor had brought America into World War II, which caused the plotline to be altered. On stage the focus had been largely on the electrifying Ethel Merman; on screen the focus was changed to the comic antics of three high-jinks clowns: Red Skelton, Rags Ragland and Ben Blue.

Hattie Maloney (Ann Sothern) is a nightclub performer in Panama. She is romanced by Army Sergeant Dick Bulliet (Dan

Dailey, Jr.), a wealthy blueblood. Hattie's pals are three goofy gobs—Red (Red Skelton), Rags Ragland (Rags) and Ben Blue (Howdy)—who have a preoccupation with ferreting out real and imaginary spies. The loving but not-so-refined Hattie is initially at odds with Dick's seven-year-old daughter (Jackie Horner) who has just come to Central America from Philadelphia with the family butler (Alan Mowbray). Dick soon persuades his daughter that beneath Hattie's (vulgar) exterior, she is actually a swell person. Also arriving on the scene is snobbish socialite Leila Tree (Marsha Hunt), Dick's former girlfriend. Bumbling Red tries to help decoy the conniving Leila, but instead becomes involved in a Nazi spy plot. This leads the sailors to track down an Axis stronghold of explosive chemicals, but they do not capture any spies. Later, when Lucas Kefler (Carl Esmond), the actual head of the spy ring, insults Hattie, the three sailors defend her honor. Soon a melee develops. The military police appear on the scene to arrest the combatants. It is found that some of the prisoners are actual spies. The sailors are immediate heroes, and Hattie and Bulliet marry.

As was traditional with stage-to-film musicals, several numbers were cut. Among them were: "Visit Panama," "Join It Right Away," "I'm Throwing a Ball Tonight," "We Detest a Fiesta," "You Said It" and "God Bless the Women." Added for the movie was Cole Porter's "Just One of Those Things" (from Porter's *Jubilee,* 1934), as well as songs by other composers: "At the Savoy," "Hattie from Panama," "I'll Do Anything for You," "The Son of a Gun Who Picks on Uncle Sam," and "The Sping." Of the retained Porter numbers, Ann Sothern sings "I've Still Got My Health," "Make It Another Old-Fashioned, Please" and, with Jackie Horner, "Let's Be Buddies." Deadpan comedienne Virginia O'Brien performs "Fresh as a Daisy" and the three sailors handle "Let's Be Buddies." Sothern also handles "Hattie from Panama" and leads the cast in "Son of a Gun Who Picks on Uncle Sam," while O'Brien sings "(Did I Get Stinkin') At the Savoy" (a number Sothern refused to do in the movie). Skelton, Ragland and Blue execute "Good Neighbors." As an afterthought, when the unsuccessfully previewed PANAMA HATTIE was going through rewrites and additional shooting (under the direction of Roy Del Ruth and Vincente Minnelli), Lena Horne (who had just joined the studio's roster) was added to the proceedings. In the final release print Horne sings "Just One of Those Things" and the novelty rhumba number, "The Sping" (which also featured the dancing Berry Brothers). Horne proved to be a surprise hit with her musical offerings.

With so many fond memories of the stage *Panama Hattie* and Ethel Merman's vibrant performance, it was hard for the movie to compare favorably with critics. *Variety* termed the restructured musical, ". . . A jerky and spotty piece of entertainment that must be carried by Skelton's antics and some sparkling song and dance specialties." Because of the film's focus, Ann Sothern (who was very unhappy with the restructuring of the picture) is not seen to her best advantage and what had been a buoyant musical on Broadway became a slapstick comedy on screen.* Nevertheless, PANAMA HATTIE, which cost $1,097,907 to make, earned $4,326,000 in its initial release.

On November 10, 1954, on CBS-TV's "The Best of Broadway," Ethel Merman starred in a condensed version of "Panama Hattie." Her co-stars were Ray Middleton, Art Carney, Jack E. Leonard and Neil Hamilton.

PARAMOUNT ON PARADE (Paramount, 1930) Color Sequences 102 minutes.

Supervisor, Elsie Janis; directors, Dorothy Arzner, Otto Brower Edmund Goulding, Victor Heerman, Edwin H. Knopf, Rowland V. Lee, Ernst Lubitsch, Lothar Mendes, Victor Schertzinger, Edward Sutherland, Frank Tuttle; set designer, John Wenger; choreographer, David Bennett; camera, Harry Fischbeck, Victor Milner.

Songs: "Paramount on Parade," "Any Time's the Time to Fall in Love," "What Did Cleopatra Say?" "I'm True to the Navy Now" (Elsie Janis, Jack King); "We're the Masters of Ceremony" (Ballard MacDonald, Dave Dreyer); "Torna a Sorrento" (Leo Robin, Ernesto De Curtis); "I'm in Training for You," "Dancing to Save Your Sole," "Let Us Drink to the Girl of My Dreams" (L. Wolfe Gilbert, Abel Baer); "My Marine" (Richard A. Whiting, Raymond B. Eagan); "All I Want Is Just One Girl" (Richard A. Whiting, Leo Robin); "I'm Isadore, the Toreador" (David Franklin); "Sweepin' the Clouds Away" (Sam Coslow).

Richard Arlen, Jean Arthur, William Austin, George Bancroft, Clara Bow, Evelyn Brent, Mary Brian, Virginia Bruce, Nancy Carroll, Ruth Chatterton, Maurice Chevalier, Gary Cooper, Leon Errol, Stuart Erwin, Kay Francis, Skeets Gallagher, Harry Green, Mitzi Green, James Hall, Phillips Holmes, Helen Kane, Dennis King, Abe Lyman and His Band, Fredric March, Nino Martini, Mitzi Mayfair, Marion Morgan Dancers, David Newell, Jack Oakie,

*It was during the patch-and-repair of PANAMA HATTIE that the song-and-dance number, "I've Still Got My Health," was added back into the film, with Ann Sothern as the focal point. In the revamping, the song "The Son of a Gun who Picks on Uncle Sam" was utilized as a finale number for the full cast.

Zelma O'Neal, Joan Peers, Charles "Buddy" Rogers, Lillian Roth, Stanley Smith, Fay Wray (Specialties); Clive Brook (Sherlock Holmes); H. Reeves-Smith (Dr. Watson); Warner Oland (Dr. Fu Manchu); Eugene Pallette (Sergeant Heath); William Powell (Philo Vance); Iris Adrian (Chorus Girl in Chevalier Number); Rolfe Sedan (Bench Sitter); Henry Fink (Guest); Jack Pennick (Soldier); Robert Greig (Egyptian); Mischa Auer (Guest); Cecil Cunningham (Hostess); Edmund Goulding (Himself).

Although it was a bit of a late-comer in the major studio sweepstakes of all-star, all-talking, all-musical extravaganzas, PARAMOUNT ON PARADE was one of the best of the lot, with a number of Technicolor sequences among its thirteen reels of entertainment. Like its peers, the musical was basically plotless; a showcase for the talents (or non-talents) of its salaried stars, players and directors. "Take the family," opined *Photoplay* magazine of this opulent production.

The revue opens with a Technicolor rendition of "Showgirls on Parade" by a group of chorus girls and ushers, followed by the main titles which lead to studio scenes and to Mitzi Mayfair toe dancing. Jack Oakie, Skeets Gallagher and Leon Errol perform "We're The Masters of Ceremony" as the film's introduction. Next Charles "Buddy" Rogers and Lillian Roth duet on "Any Time's the Time to Fall in Love." This is followed by "Murder Will Out," a blackout sequence kidding movie detection with Clive Brook as Sherlock Holmes, H. Reeves-Smith as Dr. Watson, William Powell as Philo Vance, Eugene Pallette as Inspector Ernest Heath, Warner Oland as Dr. Fu Manchu and Jack Oakie as the murder victim. Next comes an Ernst Lubitsch-directed segment, with Maurice Chevalier and Evelyn Brent doing a bedroom apache dance. The Technicolor rendering of "Torna a Sorrento" is crooned by Nino Martini. A hospital comedy sketch features David Newell, Helen Kane and Leon Errol. In a girl's gym Jack Oakie and Zelma O'Neal sing "I'm in Training for You." Next comes "I'm Isadore, the Toreador," a satire on bullfighting, with Harry Green as the toreador and Kay Francis as Carmen, assisted by the Marion Morgan Dancers. In a Parisian setting, Ruth Chatterton offers "My Marine" as she romances Fredric March, Stuart Erwin and Stanley Smith, while in another Paris sequence Maurice Chevalier sings "All I Want Is Just One Girl." Child performer Mitzi Green imitates the singing style of Chevalier and Charlie Mack (of Moran and Mack) and this is followed by a comedy routine in a school with teacher Helen (the "Boop-Boop-a-Doop" Girl) Kane singing "What Did Cleopatra Say?" A Technicolor sequence has doomed man Dennis King singing "Nichavo" for Skeets Gallagher. Next, Nancy Carroll, backed by Abe Lyman and His Orchestra, sings and dances to "Dancing to Save Your Sole." "Let Us Drink to the Girl of My Dreams" is another Technicolor outing, headlined by Richard Arlen, Gary Cooper and James Hall to Jean Arthur, Mary Brian and Fay Wray. Clara Bow, assisted by Jack Oakie and Skeets Gallagher, and a forty-two-member chorus of sailors harmonizes on "I'm True to the Navy Now." A dull satire on society manners follows with George Bancroft, Kay Francis and William Austin. The revue concludes with Maurice Chevalier as a chimney sweep, backed by a girls' chorus, singing "Sweeping the Clouds Away."

Harrison's Reports said PARAMOUNT ON PARADE was "Better than the Warner SHOW OF SHOWS but nothing to brag about. . . . Picture as a whole is only fairly entertaining." The more easily pleased Mordaunt Hall (*New York Times*) called it a ". . . Bright and imaginative audible film . . . [and a] thoroughly enjoyable work."

The studio issued several foreign-language editions of PARAMOUNT ON PARADE for international distribution, cutting inappropriate segments and substituting masters of ceremonies who could speak the particular language (such as Jeanette MacDonald for the Spanish-language edition). Unlike some early talkie musicals, PARAMOUNT ON PARADE still exists and is sometimes screened, but most often in a truncated 75-minute version which deletes most of the color sequences, changing others to black and white (like the Maurice Chevalier finale). Still, even in this abridged format, this revue film retains much of its innate and innocent charm.

PARISIAN BELLE *see* NEW MOON (1930).

PENNIES FROM HEAVEN (Columbia, 1936) 90 minutes.

Producer, Emmanuel Cohen; director, Norman Z. McLeod; based on the story "The Peacock's Feather" by Katherine Leslie Moore; art director, Stephen Goosson; music, Arthur Johnston; music director, George Stoll; camera, Robert Pittack; editor, John Rawlins.

Songs: "Pennies from Heaven," "Skeleton in the Closet," "One, Two, Button Your Shoe," "So Do I," "Let's Call a Heart a Heart," "Now I've Got Some Dreaming to Do," "'What This Country Needs" (Arthur Johnston, Johnny Burke).

Bing Crosby (Larry); Madge Evans (Susan); Edith Fellows (Patsy); Donald Meek (Gramps); John Gallaudet (Hart); Louis Armstrong (Henry); Tom Dugan (Crowbar); Nana Bryant (Miss Howard); Charles Wilson (Warden); Harry Tyler (Concessionaire);

William Stack (Carmichael); Tom Ricketts (Briggs); and: Louis Armstrong and His Band; Lionel Hampton, Nydia Westman.

On loanout to Columbia from Paramount Pictures, Bing Crosby headlined this syrupy, low-budgeted musical which co-starred him with lovely Madge Evans, moppet performer Edith Fellows and, for the first time, Louis Armstrong, although Bing and Satchmo had little to do together in the tepid proceedings.*

Singer Larry (Bing Crosby) is sent to prison when he is falsely accused of being a smuggler. While inside he gets a note from a murderer who is about to go to the electric chair. The man gives him the name of a New Jersey family, the only relatives of the victim of the man's crime. He wants Larry to locate them when he gets out and give them his family estate. After Larry is released, he keeps his promise and finds the impoverished family, which is composed of Gramps (Donald Meek) and cute little Patsy (Edith Fellows). They agree to take over the convict's estate, but when they relocate there they discover it is a spooky old mansion. Larry convinces them to transform it into a restaurant, with him as the star singing attraction. Social worker Susan (Madge Evans) arrives to make sure that Patsy is taken care of properly. Soon Susan announces that the court intends to take the little girl away from Larry and Gramps. However, the restaurant and Larry are a success. He and Susan plan to wed and to adopt Patsy.

Arthur Johnston and Johnny Burke provided seven tunes for this weak comedy-drama-musical, the best being the title song, which Bing Crosby successfully recorded for Decca Records. The rest of the melodies are only adequate, although Louis Armstrong delivers strongly with "One, Two, Button My Shoe."

While star Bing Crosby tried hard, he had a difficult time saving this maudlin effort, as Robert Bookbinder noted in *The Films of Bing Crosby* (1977). ". . . Bing's first-rate performance is sadly wasted on a totally ineffectual motion picture."

PENNIES FROM HEAVEN (Metro-Goldwyn-Mayer/United Artists, 1981) Color 108 minutes.

Executive producer, Richard McCallum; producers, Herbert Ross, Nora Kaye; associate producer, Ken Adam; director, Ross; based on the television series by Dennis Potter; screenplay, Potter; art directors, Fred Tuch, Bernie Cutler; set decorator, Garrett Lewis; costumes, Bob Mackie; makeup supervisor, Frank Griffin; music,

*Besides PENNIES FROM HEAVEN, Bing Crosby and Louis Armstrong would appear together on-screen in DOCTOR RHYTHM (1938), HERE COMES THE GROOM (1951) and HIGH SOCIETY (1956), *q.v.*

Marvin Hamlisch, Billy May; music supervisor, Harry V. Lojewski; music coordinator, Louise Jaffe; music associate, Harper MacKay; music consultant, Kenith Trodd; music editors, George Korngold, Ken Wannberg; music research, Greg Gormick, Jim Bedoian, Joe Monte, Discontinued Records; choreographer, Danny Daniels; second unit director, Thomas J. Wright; assistant directors, L. Andrew Stone, Emmitt-Leon O'Neil, Hal Bell; sound, Al Overton; sound re-recording, Michael J. Kohut, Jay M. Harding, Richard Tuyler, Ted Keep; sound effects editor, John Dunn; special effects, Glen Robinson; camera, Gordon Willis; editor, Richard Marks.

"Pennies from Heaven" (Johnny Burke, Arthur Johnston); "The Clouds Will Soon Roll By" (Harry Woods, Nacio Herb Brown); "Yes, Yes!" (Con Conrad, Cliff Friend); "I'll Never Have to Dream Again" (Isham Jones, Charles Newman); "Roll Along Prairie Moon" (Ted Fio Rito, Harry MacPherson, Albert von Tilzer); "Did You Ever See a Dream Walking?" (Harry Revel, Mack Gordon); "It's the Girl" (Abel Baer, Dave Opppenheim); "Love Is Good for Anything that Ails You" (Matt Malneck, Cliff Friend); "Let's Put out the Lights and Go to Sleep" (Herman Hupfeld); "It's a Sin to Tell a Lie" (William Mayhew); "I Want to Be Bad" (Buddy G. DeSylva, Lew Brown, Ray Henderson); "Life is Just a Bowl of Cherries" (Henderson, Brown); "Let's Misbehave" (Cole Porter); "Serenade in the Night" (C. A. Bixio, B. Cherubini, Jimmy Kennedy); "Fancy Our Meeting" (Philip, Charig, Meyer, Douglas Furber); "Let's Face the Music and Dance" (Irving Berlin); "The Glory of Love" (William Hill).

Steve Martin (Arthur); Bernadette Peters (Eileen); Christopher Walken (Tom); Jessica Harper (Joan); Vernel Bagneris (Accordion Man); John McMartin (Mr. Warner); John Karlen (Detective); Jay Garner (Banker); Robert Fitch (Al); Tommy Rall (Ed); Eliska Krupka (Blind Girl); Frank McCarthy (Bartender); Raleigh Bond (Mr. Barrett); Gloria LeRoy (Prostitute); Nancy Parson (Old Whore); Tom Kaye, Shirley Kirkes (Tarts); Jack Fletcher (Elevator Operator); Hunter Watkins (Boy); Arell Blanton, George Wilbur (Motorcycle Police); M.C. Grainey (Young Policeman); Mark Campbell (Newsboy); Mark Martinez (Schoolboy); Duke Stroud, Joe Medalis (Countermen); Will Hare (Father Everson); Joshua Cadman (Jumbo); Paul Valentine, Bill Richards, John Craig, Alton Ruff (Bar Patrons); Karla Bush, Robin Hoff, Linda Montana, Dorothy Cronin (Bank Secretaries); Twink Caplan, Lillian D'Honau, Barbara Nordella, Dean Taliaferro (Bank Customers); Wayne Storm (Bank Guard); Gene Ross, Edward Heim, Dave Adams, Greg Finley, Paul Michael, Joe Ross (Bank Tellers); Conrad Palmisano, Dick Butler, Ronald Oliney (Stunts).

One of the more unique British Broadcasting Corporation's television offerings in the 1970s was the multi-part "Pennies from Heaven," a bittersweet musical drama based on a script by Dennis Potter and starring Bob Hoskins. Its structural gimmick was enunciated by the "hero" who sighs, "I want to live in a world where the songs come true." And they do, to a small degree, as the characters lip synch their way through song numbers which counterpoint the contrast between their mundane daily lives and the oversized optimism and romanticism of the songs' lyrics. In its offbeat satirical way, "Pennies from Heaven" was a captivating piece of entertainment. The telecasts caught the imagination of American choreographer-film director Herbert Ross, who along with his one-time dancer wife, Nora Kaye, produced this unusual feature.

In 1934 Chicago, during the height of the Depression, Arthur Parker (Steve Martin) is a sheet-music salesman who longs to have his own record store. His wife Joan (Jessica Harper) refuses to lend him the money from her inheritance so he can start his own business. She also rejects him sexually. After failing to obtain a bank loan, Arthur meets a hitchhiker-hobo, The Accordion Man (Vernel Bagneris). The two team up, with the musician singing the songs that Arthur is pitching. In a small town Arthur encounters school teacher Eileen Everson (Bernadette Peters). After he tells her he is a recent widower, the two become lovers. Returning home, Arthur is offered the money he needs by Joan and opens his shop. However, she soon suspects that he no longer loves her. She tries to stab him with her scissors. Some months pass and Eileen is fired from her teaching job by her principal (John McMartin), because she is pregnant. Meanwhile, Arthur opens his store. Going to see Eileen, Arthur meets a blind girl (Eliska Krupka) and offers her a ride, but she refuses. Later she is killed by the Accordion Man. Eileen comes to Chicago where pimp Tom (Christopher Walken) turns her into a hooker. Later she and Arthur are reunited accidentally, but he is arrested (due to leads provided to the police by a vindictive Joan) and convicted of the murder of the blind girl, and is sentenced to be executed. After he is hung, he and Eileen are (spiritually) reunited.

During the course of PENNIES FROM HEAVEN a number of vintage recordings are used on the soundtrack, including the title song (sung by Arthur Tracy), "Let's Put Out the Lights and Go to Sleep" (crooned by Rudy Vallee), "Did You Ever See a Dream Walking? (vocal by Bing Crosby) and "Let's Face the Music and Dance" (from the Fred Astaire-Ginger Rogers movie FOLLOW THE FLEET, *q.v.;* clips also shown). The movie version starred sarcastic, knock-about comedian Steve Martin, who proved surprisingly proficient in this change-of-pace casting. His co-star was his frequent on and off-screen teammate Bernadette Peters, a respected stage musical comedy player.

Michael Scragow (*Rolling Stone* magazine) decided of this offbeat production, "What I love is the audacity and brilliance of its craftsmen and performers. What I hate is its single-minded, monotonous rendering of the Great Depression and of depression generally." Scragow pinpointed, "What epitomizes the self-destruction of the entire film is the failure of the most daring number, in which Martin and Peters echo Astaire and Rogers . . . [who are dancing and singing on-screen to "Let's Face the Music and Dance" from FOLLOW THE FLEET, 1935, *q.v.,* with Martin and Peters soon dancing on the stage in front of the movie screen and then completing the dance themselves]. But the dance is clipped short; before we can catch our breath and appreciate the boldness and artistry, the number ends with the male chorus line's canes rising like prison bars." In *Magill's Cinema Annual 1982* (1982), Don K. Thompson analyzed, ". . . though PENNIES FROM HEAVEN pays tribute to the musicals of the 1930s, it is through the employment of these [lip-synching to old records] techniques, also creating an anti-nostalgic structure that provides a bitter reminder of what audiences of those old films experienced in their daily lives once they left the darkness of the movie palaces. Thus, the screenplay served a dual purpose, both re-creating the fantasies of the 1930s and exploring the nightmarish underside of those dreams. . . . PENNIES FROM HEAVEN is a wonderful film that has gone unrecognized by the audiences of 1981. Its appeal is timeless, however, and someday it will find the audience that it deserves."

Too offbeat for popular consumption, the expansive PENNIES FROM HEAVEN, with its heavily-mounted production dance numbers, was a box-office failure. It did receive an Oscar nomination for Best Costumes, but lost to CHARIOTS OF FIRE.

PETE KELLY'S BLUES (Warner Bros., 1955) Color 95 minutes.

Producer/director, Jack Webb; screenplay, Richard L. Breen; production designer, Harper Goff; art director, Feild Gray; set decorator, John Sturtevant; costumes, Howard Shoup; makeup, Gordon Bau; music, Ray Heindorf, Sammy Cahn, Arthur Hamilton; Kelly's Big 7 arrangements, Matty Matlock; assistant director, Harry D'Arcy; camera, Hal Rosson; editor, Robert M. Leeds.

Songs: "Pete Kelly's Blues" (Sammy Cahn, Ray Heindorf); "Sing a Rainbow," "He Needs Me" (Arthur Hamilton); "Somebody

Loves Me," "Sugar" (Maceo Pinkard, Sidney Mitchell, Edna Alexander); "I Never Knew" (Gus Kahn, Ted Fio Rito); "Hard-Hearted Hannah" (Jack Yellen, Milton Ager, Bob Bigelow, Charles Bates); "Bye, Bye Blackbird" (Mort Dixon, Ray Henderson); "What Can I Say After I Say I'm Sorry" (Walter Donaldson, Abe Lyman); "Oh, Didn't He Ramble" (Will Handy [Bob Cole, J. Rosamond Johnson]).

Jack Webb (Pete Kelly/Narrator); Janet Leigh (Ivy Conrad); Edmond O'Brien (Frank McCarg); Peggy Lee (Rose Hopkins); Andy Devine (George Tenell); Lee Marvin (Al Gannaway); Ella Fitzgerald (Maggie Jackson); Martin Milner (Joey Firestone); Jayne Mansfield (Cigarette Girl); Than Wyenn (Rudy); Herb Ellis (Bedido); John Dennis (Guy Bettenhouser); Mort Marshall (Cootie Jacobs); Nesdon Booth (Squat Henchman); William Lazerus (Dako); Dick Cathcart (Trumpet Work for Pete Kelly); Matty Matlock (Clarinetist); Moe Schneider (Trombonist); Eddie Miller (Saxophonist); George Van Eps (Guitarist); Nick Fatool (Drummer); Ray Sherman (Pianist); Jud de Naut (Bass Player); Snub Pollard (Waiter in Rudy's); Joe Venuti, Harper Goff, Perry Bodkin (Featured Members of the Tuxedo Band); and: The Israelite Spiritual Church Choir of New Orleans.

Jack Webb first appeared in the role of trumpet player Pete Kelly in the NBC network radio series, "Pete Kelly's Blues," which had a six-month run in 1951. The actual trumpet work was accomplished by Dick Cathcart, who did the same chore when Webb brought the character to the wide screen in 1955.

In Kansas City during Prohibition times, trumpet player Pete Kelly (Jack Webb) loves show girl Ivy Conrad (Janet Leigh). Meanwhile the local bootlegging empire is controlled by gangster Frank McCarg (Edmond O'Brien), whose moll is singer Rose Hopkins (Peggy Lee). McCarg decides to make even more money by taking over the band business and controlling all the musicians. Kelly stands up to him and eventually defeats the hoodlum in a shootout, while Rose goes insane.

Low-keyed, staccato-voiced Jack Webb, who would gain his greatest fame with radio/TV/motion picture episodes of "Dragnet," not only starred in the title role, but also produced and directed this feature film. Thanks to his supervision, the movie offers a fine recreation of the Roaring Twenties and its musical backgrounds. Besides a number of well-executed instrumentals, the picture also benefitted from the presence of co-star Peggy Lee, who was nominated for an Academy Award for her supporting actress performance. She sang "Somebody Loves Me" and "Sugar," while Ella Fitzgerald performed the title song and "Hard-Hearted

Hannah." The film grossed $5,000,000 in distributors' domestic film rentals. The album, SONGS FROM PETE KELLY'S BLUES, was on *Billboard* magazine's hit charts for ten weeks, rising to position #7.

The *New York Times* reported, "Although the plot of this standard, trashy gangster melodrama does look at backstage jazz and some show business intricacies that ring true, it is primarily an excuse for Jack Webb . . . to exchange his 'Dragnet' badge for a cornet [*sic*] and triumphantly battle some prohibition-era Kansas City mobsters."

In addition to the movie, Jack Webb narrated an RCA Victor record album called PETE KELLY'S BLUES which included a jazz combo comprised of Matty Matlock, Dick Cathcart, Nick Fatool,

Janet Leigh and Jack Webb in PETE KELLY'S BLUES (1955).

Elmer "Moe" Schneider, George Van Eps, Ray Sherman and Jud De Naut. He also produced the NBC-TV series, "Pete Kelly's Blues," starring William Reynolds (as Kelly) and Connee Boswell, which ran for six months in 1959 with Dick Cathcart again doing the trumpet solos.

PIGSKIN PARADE (20th Century-Fox, 1936) 95 minutes.

Associate producer, Bogart Rogers; director, David Butler; story, Arthur Sheekman, Nat Perrin, Mark Lelly; screenplay, Harry Turgend, Jack Yellen, Wiliam Conselman; costumes, Gwen Wakeling; music director, David Buttolph; camera, Arthur Miller; editor, Irene Morra.

Songs: "Balboa," "The Texas Tornado," "It's Love I'm After," "You Do the Darndest Things," "Baby," "T.S.U. Alma Mater," "Hold That Bulldog," "You're Slightly Terrific" (Sidney Mitchell, Lew Pollack); "Woo Woo," "We'd Rather Be in College" (The Yacht Club Boys).

Stuart Erwin (Amos Dodd); Patsy Kelly (Bessie Winters); Jack Haley ("Slug" [Winston Winters]); Johnny Downs (Chip Carson); Betty Grable (Laura Watson); Arline Judge (Sally Saxon); Dixie Dunbar (Ginger Jones); Judy Garland (Sairy Dodd); Anthony [Tony] Martin (Tommy Barker); Fred Kohler, Jr. (Biff Bentley); Elisha Cook, Jr. (Herbert Terwilliger Van Dyck); Eddie Nugent (Sparks); Grady Sutton (Mortimer Higgins); Julius Tannen (Dr. Burke); Sam Hayes (Himself as Radio Announcer); Robert McClung (Country Boy); George Herbert (Professor); Jack Murphy (Usher); Pat Flaherty (Referee); Dave Sharpe (Messenger Boy); Si Jenks (Baggage Master); John Dilson (Doctor); Jack Stoney (Policeman); George Y. Harvey (Brakeman); Ben Hall (Boy in Stadium); Lynn Bari (Girl in Stadium); Charles Wilson (Yale Coach); George Offerman, Jr. (Freddy, the Yale Reporter); Maurice Cass (Professor Tutweiler); Jack Best (Professor McCormick); Douglas Wood (Professor Dutton); Charles Crocker King (Professor Pillsbury); Alan Ladd (Student); Edward Le Saint (Judge); Jed Prouty (Mr. Van Dyke); Emma Dunn (Mrs. Van Dyke); and: The Yacht Club Boys.

PIGSKIN PARADE is today remembered chiefly because Judy Garland, on loan to 20th Century-Fox from MGM, made her feature film debut in this low-keyed musical. In its day, however, this movie was considered a popular programmer, not only for Garland's presence (in the days before she dieted, had her eyebrows plucked, etc.) but for the appearances of Betty Grable, Jack Haley and bumpkin comedian Stuart Erwin (who was Oscar-nominated for Best Supporting Actor). *Newsweek* magazine labeled

Betty Grable and Johnny Downs in PIGSKIN PARADE (1936).

the congenial movie, "A gleeful hybrid of the seasonable football picture and the ubiquitous campus musical comedy," while the *New York Times* cheered that it ". . . Moves down the entertainment field with gusto and eclat, engaging as a genuinely funny burlesque of football and its musical comedy concomitants."

Yale University needs an easy but reputable opponent for its annual pre-Harvard football match off. It chooses the University of Texas, but by accident the opponent ends up being the small, unknown Texas State University. At that school, newly arrived coach Slug Winters (Jack Haley) and his wife Bessie (Patsy Kelly) must put together a team to go up against Yale and save the pride of the institution which is currently the laughingstock of the football world. When they witness the throwing abilities of melon picker Amos Dodd (Stuart Erwin), the two enlist him as their lead player and get him into school on fake credentials. At the big game, where his young sister Sairy (Judy Garland) is on hand, Amos leads his team to victory over Yale on a snow-covered gridiron.

Sidney Mitchell and Lew Pollack composed a number of good tunes for PIGSKIN PARADE. Judy Garland sang "You're Slightly Terrific," "The Texas Tornado," and the rousing "Balboa." She performed "It's Love I'm After" in tandem with 20th Century-Fox contract player Tony Martin, who was then being billed as Anthony Martin. The Yacht Club Boys contributed both the composition and execution of "Woo Woo" and "We'd Rather Be in College," while Dixie Dunbar, as pert co-ed Ginger Jones, did a tap dance routine. Betty Grable, as fetching co-ed Laura Watson, was subordinated in the proceedings, performing in the "Balboa" segment with Garland, Johnny Downs and the chorus. It would be four years before Grable would return to 20th Century-Fox for DOWN ARGENTINE WAY. *q.v.,* which started her on the path to superstardom. Look for Alan Ladd in an early walk-on role as a student (who in one scene shows up twice, both on stage and in the audience).

British release title: HARMONY PARADE.

PINOCCHIO (RKO, 1940) Color 88 minutes.

Producer, Walt Disney; directors, Ben Sharpsteen, Hamilton Luske; sequence directors, Bill Roberts, Norman Ferguson, Jack Kinney, Wilfred Jackson, T. Hee [Disney]; animation directors, Fred Moore, Milton Kahl, Ward Kimball, Eric Larson, Franklin Thomas, Vladimir Tyta, Arthur Babbitt, Woolie Reatherman; based on the story by Collodi [Carlo Lorenzini]; screenplay, Ted Sears, Otto Englander, Webb Smith, William Cottrell, Joseph Sabo, Erdman Penner, Aurelius Battaglia; art directors, Charles Philippi, Hugh Hennesy, Dick Kelsey, Terrell Stapp, John Hubley, Kenneth Anderson, Kendall O'Connor, Thor Putnam, McLaren Stewart, Al Zinnen; character designers, Joe Grant, Albert Hurter, Campbell Grant, John P. Miller, Martin Provenson, John Walbridge; backgrounds, Claude Coats, Ed Starr, Merle Cox, Ray Huffine; animation, Jack Campbell, Berny Wolf, Don Lusk, Norman Tate, Lynn Karp, Oliver M. Johnston, Don Towsley, John Lunsberry, John Bradbury, Charles Nichols, Art Palmer, Don Tobin, George Rowley, Don Patterson, Lewis Clark, Hugh Fraser, Joshua Meador, Robert Martsch, John McManus, Preston Blair, Marvin Woodward, John Elliotte; music, Paul J. Smith.

Songs: "When You Wish Upon a Star," "Little Woodenhead," "Hi-Diddle-Dee-Dee (An Actor's Life for Me)," "I've Got No Strings," "Give a Little Whistle," "As I Was Say'n' to the Duchess," "Pinocchio," "Three Cheers for Anything," "Turn on the Old Box," "Jiminy Cricket" (Leigh Harline, Ned Washington).

Voices of: Dickie Jones (Pinocchio); Christian Rub (Geppetto);

Cliff Edwards (Jiminy Cricket); Evelyn Venable (The Blue Fairy); Walter Catlett (J. Worthington Foulfellow); Frankie Darro (Lampwick); Charles Judels (Stromboli the Coachman); Don Brodie (Barker).

Following the critical and financial success of SNOW WHITE AND THE SEVEN DWARFS (*q.v.*) in 1937, Walt Disney turned out his second animated feature film, PINOCCHIO, in 1940, at a cost of over $2.5 million. Like its predecessor, this motion picture was a huge success, grossing to date $32,957,000 in distributors' domestic film rentals. This magically escapist entertainment, whose richly emotional tale appeals to both children and adults, earned Academy Awards for its Original Music Score by Leigh Harline, Paul J. Smith and Ned Washington. Washington and Harline's "When You Wish Upon a Star" won the Oscar as Best Song. Other memorable tunes in the film were "Hi Diddle-Dee-Dee (An Actor's Life for Me)," "I've Got No Strings" and "Give a Little Whistle," all of which gave extra charm to this enchanting movie.

Lonely wood carver Geppetto (voice of Christian Rub) creates a wooden marionette of a young boy he calls Pinocchio (voice of Dickie Jones). One night The Blue Fairy (voice of Evelyn Venable) breathes life into the doll. Geppetto and his cat Figaro and goldfish Cleo are delighted to have Pinocchio alive. However, when the wooden boy goes to school the next day, he meets fox J. Worthington Foulfellow (voice of Walter Catlett) and his cat pal Gideon. Not listening to his conscience, Jiminy Cricket (voice of Cliff Edwards), Pinocchio agrees to work in a marionette show. Later he is imprisoned in a cage but the Blue Fairy comes to his rescue. Next the scheming Foulfellow talks Pinocchio into going to Pleasure Island with Lampwick (voice of Frankie Darro) and some other boys for a good time. He does so, again against Jiminy's wishes. After much celebration Pinocchio witnesses the other boys being turned into donkeys. He and Jiminy escape from the island and swim to Geppetto's workshop, only to find out that the old man has gone to sea and has been swallowed by the monster whale, Monstro. They set out to rescue Geppetto and eventually do so, but Monstro gives chase and they have to take refuge in a grotto. As a result Jiminy is killed. However, because he has proven himself worthy of being human, the Blue Fairy reappears and turns him into a real-life boy.

In *The Disney Films* (1973), Leonard Maltin wrote, "In PINOCCHIO, Disney reached not only the height of his powers, but the apex of what many of his (later) critics considered to be the realm of the animated cartoon. The wonder, the brilliance of PINOCCHIO, is in the depicting the wondrous fantasy of the story—a boy turned into a donkey, a man living on a boat inside the stomach of a whale—things that could not be shown with equal effectiveness by a live-action movie. It was when Disney tried to make his films more and more lifelike that the criticism mounted."

"Pinocchio" was performed as a segment of CBS radio's "Lux Radio Theatre" on December 25, 1939, prior to its theatrical release early the next year. The program was hosted by Cecil B. DeMille.

Perhaps as endearing as the title character in PINOCCHIO is the character of Jiminy Cricket, who sings the Oscar-winning title song, "When You Wish Upon a Star," the tune most associated with the Disney organization. Cliff "Ukulele Ike" Edwards continued to do the voice of Jiminy Cricket in Disney movies (FUN AND FANCY FREE, 1947), TV programs and records well into the 1960s. The title character reappeared in PINOCCHIO IN OUTER SPACE (1964) and PINOCCHIO AND THE EMPEROR OF THE NIGHT (1987), both animated theatrical features. It also turned up in the tepid X-rated feature, THE EROTIC ADVENTURES OF PINOCCHIO (1976), as well as in PINOCCHIO'S STORYBOOK ADVENTURES (1979), written and directed by Ron Merk.

THE PIRATE (Metro-Goldwyn-Mayer, 1948) Color 102 minutes.

Producer, Arthur Freed; director, Vincente Minnelli; based on the play by S. N. Behrman; screenplay, Albert Hackett, Frances Goodrich, (uncredited): Joseph L. Mankiewicz, Joseph Than, Lillian Braun, Anita Loos, Wilkie Mahoney; art directors, Cedric Gibbons. Jack Martin Smith; set decorators, Edwin B. Willis, Arthur Krams; costume supervisor, Irene; costumes, Tom Keogh; makeup, Jack Dawn; paintings, Doris Lee; music director, Lennie Hayton; instrumental arranger, Conrad Salinger; vocal arrangers, Kay Thompson, Robert Tucker, Roger Edens; choreographers, Robert Alton, Gene Kelly; assistant director, Wallace Worlsey; color consultants, Natalie Kalmus, Henri Jaffa; sound supervisor, Douglas Shearer; camera, Harry Stradling; editor, Blanche Sewell.

Songs: "Nina," "Love of My Life," "Mack the Black," "You Can Do No Wrong," "Be a Clown," "The Pirate Ballet" (Cole Porter); "Sweet Ices, Papayas, Berry Man," "Sea Wall," "Serafin" (Roger Edens); "The Ring," "Judy Awakens," "The Tight Rope," "Not Again" (Lennie Hayton); "Gene Meets Mack the Black," "The Mast" (Conrad Salinger).

Judy Garland (Manuela); Gene Kelly (Serafin); Walter Slezak (Don Pedro Vargas); Gladys Cooper (Aunt Inez); Reginald Owen (The Advocate); George Zucco (The Viceroy); The Nicholas

Brothers (Specialty Dancers); Lester Allen (Uncle Capucho); Lola Deem (Isabella); Ellen Ross (Mercedes); Mary Jo Eliis (Lizarda); Jean Dean (Casildo); Marion Murray (Eloise); Ben Lessy (Gumbo); Jerry Bergen (Bolo); Val Setz (Juggler); The Gaudsmith Brothers (Themselves); Cully Richards (Trillo).

In the 1820s West Indies, impressionable young Manuela (Judy Garland), a daughter of a rich Spanish family, falls in love with the image of the dashing pirate, Black Macoco. However, her more practical aunt (Gladys Cooper) informs her she is to be wed to the mayor of San Sebastian. The girl greets the news with horror for she detests the rotund Don Pedro Vargas (Walter Slezak). While in the town square, Manuela observes the strolling player Serafin (Gene Kelly) and his group of entertainers. He is entranced with her, but she does not reciprocate the feeling, convinced that he is a dabbler in romance. That evening Manuela attends the entertainers' show and Serafin uses her as a subject for his mesmerism act. Under hypnosis she reveals she has a dream lover pirate. Later, Serafin follows Manuela back to her house and comes into her bedroom. Hearing of this, Don Pedro arrives. Serafin recognizes him as the pirate Macoco and promises to keep his secret. Serafin then proclaims he is the famous pirate and takes over Don Pedro's house. He demands Manuela as a sacrifice, or he will burn down the town. When Serafin reveals the truth, Manuela hits him with a picture and knocks him out as Don Pedro arrives with his soldiers. Serafin is arrested on a fake robbery charge and is sentenced to be hung. The Viceroy (George Zucco) grants Serafin one final request. The prisoner's request is to die singing a happy song. Meanwhile, Manuela discovers that Don Pedro is the real thief and, on stage, tells the audience that Don Pedro is a coward. He responds by saying he is really Macoco, the now retired pirate. He tries to shoot Serafin but the entertainers prevent him. With all matters settled, Serafin announces that Manuela will be the new star of their show.

Based on Ludwig Fulda's 1911 play, *Der Seerauber,* which S. N. Behrman adapted as a comedy in 1942 for Alfred Lunt and Lynn Fontanne, THE PIRATE was an expensive fantasy-musical which proved troublesome from the time of conception to release. In 1943, MGM acquired the rights to the play (which had run for 177 performances) for $225,026. It was designated by the studio to be a Joseph Pasternak production with Henry Koster directing and Joseph L. Mankiewicz as scenarist. Then the project was shelved, only to have costume-set designer Lemuel Ayers suggest to producer Arthur Freed in 1944 that THE PIRATE would make a good musical and Cole Porter should write the score. Freed soon assigned various scriptwriters to the project, but when they diverted widely from the original storyline, he brought in the husband-wife writing team of Frances Goodrich and Albert Hackett to steer the scenario closer back to its origin. Cole Porter was hired at $100,000 to write the score. When his initial efforts were submitted, a displeased Freed demanded that he submit a new selection of tunes. By now the project had been designated as a reteaming of Judy Garland and Gene Kelly, who had scored so nicely in FOR ME AND MY GAL (1942), *q.v.* Garland began her prerecording of her numbers in late December 1946 and, by then, it was evident that the emotionally troubled actress was going through an especially difficult period. Undergoing severe stress and bouts of paranoia, Garland was absent from the set as frequently as she was there; when present, she was high-strung, temperamental and often unable to work. Meanwhile, her husband Vincente Minnelli, who was directing the project, was expanding Gene Kelly's role, believing this to be the only salvation of the jinxed project.* As Garland saw her importance in the film being diminished, she grew even more uncooperative. For a time, at the studio's demand, she was hospitalized in a sanatorium. Meanwhile, Kelly continued to exercise an increasing artistic participation in the project, in particular working closely with Cole Porter to tailor the songs to the changing concept. Garland's reaction to this growing rapport between Porter and Kelly was to become extremely antagonistic to the great songwriter. During the on-again, off-again filming of THE PIRATE, Kelly made another MGM movie, LIVING IN A BIG WAY (1947).

Despite all the production problems, there is much to recommend in this ultra-sophisticated screen musical. From the sets to the costumes, there is a wonderful sense of style and color, all captured admirably by cinematographer Harry Stradling. Garland—despite all her production travails—does marvelously with her solos: "Love of My Life," "Mack the Black" and "You Can Do No Wrong." Kelly is at his athletic best in his singing and dancing

*In 1979 Gene Kelly would admit, regarding THE PIRATE, "What really hurt the picture was that Vincente Minnelli and I really outsmarted ourselves. THE PIRATE had been the only flop the Lunts had. We'd both seen it on Broadway, and we knew something had to be changed. S. N. Behrman's dialogue was brilliant, but we wanted to get in a lot of action and a lot of dash. So we said, 'Let's make it obvious that the pirate is being played like Douglas Fairbanks, Sr. and the actor is being played like John Barrymore. Not too obvious, just enough to let everybody in on it.' Gee, we were being so clever. Then all the reviews hit us. 'This cheap actor tries to imitate the great. . . .' and so forth. The reviews were all of that ilk. Minnelli and I had to skulk behind bushes."

to "Nina" and "The Pirate Ballet," the latter an extravagant expression of creative eroticism. The finale number, "Be a Clown," proved to be a rousing highlight of the movie as Garland and Kelly sing enthusiastically about the joys of the life of an entertainer. Because the segment also featured the black specialty dancers, the Nicholas Brothers, when the film was distributed in the South much of their routine was cut. (Deleted from the film altogether was Garland's singing of "Voodoo" and Porter's song "Manuela," which was to have been a Kelly number.) One of the many retakes on THE PIRATE had been of Garland-Kelly's dance; studio head Louis B. Mayer thought it too "hair-curling" and that its torrid implications would destroy the wholesome image of the Garland-Kelly screen team. Reportedly, Mayer screamed, "Burn the negative! If that exhibition got on any screen, we'd be raided by the police." Kelly was brought to task for his on-screen abandon and the sequence was reshot.

Despite audience (and MGM executive) apathy, THE PIRATE garnered sterling reviews. *Newsweek* magazine endorsed it as ". . . One of the most delightful musicals to hit the screen in a month of Sundays. . . . THE PIRATE is a rare and happy combination of expert dancing, catchy tunes, and utterly unbelievable plot which manages to achieve pure escapism without becoming either sentimental or corny." The *New York Times* noted that it was "a dazzling, spectacular extravaganza," but conceded, "It takes this mammoth show some time to generate a full head of steam, but when it gets rolling it's thoroughly delightful. However, the momentum is far from steady and the result is a lopsided entertainment that is wonderfully flamboyant in its high spots and bordering on tedium elsewhere." *Time* magazine noted, ". . . As an all-out try at artful movie making, this is among the most interesting pictures of the year. Unluckily, much of the considerable artistry that has gone into this production collides head-on with artiness or is spoiled by simpler kinds of miscalculation. . . . The total effect of the picture is 'entertainment' troubled by delusions of 'art' and vice-versa."

THE PIRATE, made at a cost of $3,768,496, earned only $2,956,000 in its initial release. THE PIRATE received an Oscar nomination for Best Scoring of a Musical Picture but lost to the studio's EASTER PARADE, *q.v.,* which also starred Judy Garland. In analyzing the film's lack of audience appeal, producer Arthur Freed would say, years later, "I think today THE PIRATE would be a hit. It was twenty years ahead of its time. . . . I think one of the reasons [it was a flop] was, the public didn't want to see Judy as a sophisticate."

In the mid-1950s, when MGM was yielding to the rival medium of television by producing its own thirty-minute weekly ABC-TV show, "The MGM Parade," it chopped THE PIRATE into three parts and aired it for home consumption. It was a novelty in the era before the major studios sold their celluloid product to television.

PORGY AND BESS (Columbia, 1959) Color 138 minutes.

Producer, Samuel Goldwyn; directors, Otto Preminger, (uncredited pre-production), Rouben Mamoulian; based on the operetta by George Gershwin, Ira Gershwin, DuBose Heyward; from the play by DuBose and Dorothy Heyward, and the novel by Heyward; screenplay, N. Richard Nash; production designer, Oliver Smith; art directors, Serge Krizman, Joseph Wright; set decorator, Howard Bristol; costumes, Irene Sharaff; makeup, Frank McCoy, Layne Britton; music directors, Andre Previn, (uncredited) Ken Darby; choreography, Hermes Pan; camera, Leon Shamroy; editor, Daniel Mandell.

Songs: "Summertime," "Crap Game," "A Woman Is a Sometime Thing," "Honey Man's Call," "They Pass By Singing," "Yo' Mammy's Gone," "Gone, Gone, Gone," "Porgy's Prayer," "My Man's Gone Now," "The Train Is at the Station," "I Got Plenty O' Nuttin'," "Bess, You Is My Woman," "Oh, I Can't Sit Down," "I Ain't Got No Shame," "It Ain't Necessarily So," "What You Wan' Wid Bess," "It Takes a Long Pull to Get There," "De Police Put Me In," "Time and Time Again," "Strawberry Woman's Call," "Crab Man's Call," "A Red-Headed Woman," "Dere's a Boat Dat's Leavin' Soon for New York," "Good Mornin' Sistuh," "Bess, Oh Where's My Bess," "I'm on My Way" (George Gershwin, Ira Gershwin).

Sidney Poitier (Porgy); Dorothy Dandridge (Bess); Sammy Davis, Jr. (Sportin' Life); Pearl Bailey (Maria); Brock Peters (Crown); Leslie Scott (Jake); Diahann Carroll (Clara); Ruth Attaway (Serena); Clarence Muse (Peter); Everdinne Wilson (Annie); Joel Fluellen (Robbins); Earl Jackson (Mingo); Moses LaMarr (Nelson); Margaret Hairston (Lily); Ivan Dixon (Jim;); Antoine Durousseau (Scipio); Helen Thigpen (Strawberry Woman); Vince Townsend, Jr. (Elderly Man); William Walker (Undertaker); Roy Glenn (Frazier); Maurice Manson (Coroner); Claude Akins (Detective); Robert McFerrin (Singing Voice of Porgy); Adele Addison (Singing Voice of Bess); Loulie Jean Norman (Singing Voice of Clara); Inez Matthews (Singing Voice of Serena).

Director Otto Preminger brought the all-black musical CARMEN JONES (*q.v.*) to the screen in 1954 in a most heavy-handed manner. Five years later, a huge soundstage fire caused the disruption of filming PORGY AND BESS. Producer Samuel Goldwyn and director Rouben Mamoulian (who had directed the stage version) came to a stalemate as how to proceed creatively; Preminger was summoned to replace Mamoulian. It was a case of a bludgeoning, authoritarian helmsman replacing a creative, sensitive soul. The film was based on George Gershwin's 1935 Broadway folk opera, from DuBose Heyward's book (originally published as a novel in 1925 and as a dramatic play by Heyward and his wife Dorothy in 1927), with lyrics by Ira Gershwin and Heyward. Todd Duncan, Anne Brown and Buck & Bubbles headlined the New York production, which had a run of 124 performances. Even when memory of the Broadway staging faded, its rich score remained haunting and the property continued to have major revivals. Film producers had long wanted to transfer it to the screen, but feared its all-black theme would limit box-office revenue. It did.

PORGY AND BESS is set in the black ghetto of Charleston, South Carolina called Catfish Row. The brutish Crown (Brock Peters) kills Robbins (Joel Fluellen) over a hotly contested game of craps. Crown lusts after the sensuous, amoral Bess (Dorothy Dandridge) who, in turn, loves the well-meaning, crippled beggar Porgy (Sidney Poitier). Also involved in the conflict are flashy drug pusher Sportin' Life (Sammy Davis, Jr.) and the self-reliant cook Maria (Pearl Bailey), as well as Clara (Diahann Carroll), a young wife whose husband is hanged by a lynch mob. While Porgy and Bess attempt to find love and contentment, the perpetual evil and dangers within Catfish Row eventually thwart them.

PORGY AND BESS dutifully retained the fine Gershwin songs, but as in CARMEN JONES, most of the leading players were dubbed during their singing chores: Robert McFerrin sang for Sidney Poitier (in the role rejected by singer Harry Belafonte), Adele Addison dubbed Dorothy Dandridge, Inez Matthews substituted vocally for Ruth Attaway and Loulie Jean Norman sang "Summertime" instead of Diahann Carroll. Sammy Davis, Jr. and Pearl Bailey, however, did their own singing in the picture, which is perhaps one of the reasons their characters seem so much more realistic and full-bodied. Davis and Bailey dueted on "Oh, I Can't Sit Down," and Davis sang "It Ain't Necessarily So" and "A Boat Dat's Leavin' Soon for New York."

Many critics of the day were dutifully deferential toward the film. The *New York Times* reported that PORGY AND BESS was "a fine film version of the famous folk opera." The *New York Herald Tribune* decided: "Deserves respect as one of the most ambitious and, frankly, one of the finest cinematic versions of an opera, and even its flaws ought to be seen in the light of the serious magnitude of the task its makers set themselves." Nevertheless, PORGY AND BESS is actually so overstated in self-importance, so distorted by prettification of the sets and its characters, and so diminished by the hollowness of ghost singers that much of the majesty of the original property is lost. In retrospect, Donald Bogle (*Blacks in American Films and Television,* 1988) observed, "Far too stagey, the movie never opens up, breathes, or looks like anything other than something shot on a Hollywood soundstage. The exception is the picnic sequence which was filmed—thankfully—out of doors. . . . The picnic sequence reveals [Otto] Preminger, the director, best in this film, although at the moment when Brock Peters as the villainous Crown shows up, attacking Dandridge, the sequence slips into a sleaziness that's energetic but tacky. . . . As Sportin' Life, Sammy Davis, Jr. is a bit too slick but playing to his own rhythm. . . . As Maria, Pearl Bailey is unabashed, cantankerous energy, a high-rolling charismatic performer who's not encumbered by the script."

Made at a cost of $6,500,000, PORGY AND BESS did not even gross $4,000,000 in distributors' domestic film rentals. (Part of the audience apathy was due to white prejudice against a black story and, conversely, by black civil rights groups who contended that the story stereotyped the black race.) PORGY AND BESS won an Academy Award for Best Scoring of a Musical Picture. It received Oscar nominations for Cinematography—Color, Sound, and Costumes—Color. The soundtrack album remained on *Billboard* magazine's charts for fifty-eight weeks, rising to #8 position.

PORGY AND BESS was the final motion picture release of veteran producer Samuel Goldwyn. The Gershwin estate later bought back the music rights to PORGY AND BESS, which to date has prevented the film from being reissued theatrically or for home videocassette/disc.

PUTTIN' ON THE RITZ (United Artists, 1930) Color Sequences 88 minutes.

Presenter, Joseph M. Schenck; producer, John W. Considine, Jr.; director, Edward H. Sloman; story/screenplay, Considine; dialogue, William K. Wells; art directors, William Cameron Menzies, Park French; costumes, Alice O'Neill; orchestrator, Hugo Riesenfeld; choreographer, Maurice L. Kusell; assistant director, Jack Mintz; sound, Oscar Lagerstrom; camera, Ray June; editor, Hal Kern.

Songs: "With You," "Alice in Wonderland," "Puttin' on the Ritz" (Irving Berlin); "There's Danger in Your Eyes, Cherie" (Harry Richman, Jack Meskill, Peter Wendling).

Harry Richman (Harry Raymond); Joan Bennett (Dolores Fenton); James Gleason (James Tierney); Aileen Pringle (Mrs. Teddy Van Rensler); Lilyan Tashman (Goldie DeVere); Purnell Pratt (George Barnes); Richard Tucker (Fenway Brooks); Eddie Kane (Bob Wagner); George Irving (Dr. Blair); Sidney Franklin (Schmidt); James Bradbury, Jr. (Subway Guard); Oscar Apfel (House Manager); Budd Fine (Heckler); Lee Phelps (Listener in Audience).

Harry Richman (1895–1972) was one of the most colorful entertainers of the 1920s and 1930s, a dapper, woman-chasing showman who sold a song by combining a strong personality with a fair singing voice. He was a top vaudeville and club attraction and also performed in Broadway revues, in addition to running the Gotham speakeasy, Club Richman. PUTTIN' ON THE RITZ was his film debut. Like many other stage luminaries, he was not overly successful in talkies, although later in the 1930s he did do a trio of features: THE MUSIC GOES 'ROUND (1936), STARS OVER ARIZONA (1937) and the British-made KICKIN' THE MOON AROUND (1938). An enthusiastic aviator, in 1936 Richman teamed with Dick Merrill to make history's first trans-ocean round-trip flight.

Once famous vaudeville star Harry Raymond (Harry Richman) becomes a song plugger. However, he loses his job when pretty showgirl Dolores Fenton's (Joan Bennett) song is better than his. Dolores has an act with Goldie (Lilyan Tashman) and Harry's pal, Jim Tierney (James Gleason). Later, Harry causes an audience fight which leads to the trio splitting apart. The scheming Harry is soon teamed with Dolores and together they become a success singing "With You." The two fall in love and plan to marry. But sudden riches again cause Harry to philander, this time with wealthy Mrs. Van Rensler (Aileen Pringle). After a particularly wild party, bad booze causes Harry to temporarily lose his sight. Meanwhile, when Dolores opens in a new show, Jim takes Harry to her premiere. The audience demands to hear her sing "With You" with Harry. They do so and are a hit all over again. Dolores and Harry are reconciled.

Photoplay magazine noted, "Harry Richman warbles well in his first talkie. . . . Good Irving Berlin music." *Variety* hit right to the point—how did the star (who had recently gained tremendous publicity for his off-camera romance with screen sex symbol Clara Bow) register on camera? "Richman looks pretty good throughout. He's no beaut facially, although nifty in dress and of imposing carriage. His voice registers excellently. Most camera angles avoid close-ups, but in general the night club kid stands lens scrutiny well." While PUTTIN' ON THE RITZ may have had a schmaltzy plot, primitive technical support and lumbering song-and-dance routines, it did contain several substantial tunes, including the enduring "Puttin' on the Ritz." To be noted is that frequent song collaborator Richman had earlier co-written "There's Danger in Your Eyes, Cherie," which was sung in this production.

QUEEN OF THE NIGHTCLUBS (Warner Bros., 1929) 60 minutes. (Also silent version: 5,236′).

Director, Bryan Foy; screenplay, Murray Roth, Addison Burkhart; assistant director, Freddie Foy; camera, Ed Du Par.

Song: "It's Tough to Be a Hostess on Broadway."

Texas Guinan (Tex Malone); John Davidson (Don Holland); Lila Lee (Bee Walters): Arthur Housman (Andy Quinland); Eddie Foy, Jr. (Eddie Parr); Jack Norworth (Phil Parr); George Raft (Gigolo); Jimmie Phillips (Nick); William Davidson (Assistant District Attorney); John Miljan (Lawyer Grant); Lee Shumway (Crandall); Joe Depew (Roy); Agnes Franey (Flapper); Charlotte Merriam (Girl); James T. Mack (Judge).

During the Roaring Twenties boisterous and often crude Texas Guinan (188?-1934) was a well-known show business personality who sang in speakeasies and was noted for her trademark greeting, "Hello Sucker!" Actually she had a solid show business background, having been a "Gibson Girl" model in 1908, and later a revue star, before making motion pictures. (She ground out several "B" Westerns in which she was one of the screen's few cowgirl stars.) Even by the 1920s, this jaded blonde entertainer still had a a large following as a result of her well-publicized raucous act. Early in 1929 she came to Hollywood to star in Warner Bros.'s QUEEN OF THE NIGHTCLUBS, in which she belted out a number of ditties including "It's Tough to be a Hostess on Broadway."

Tex Malone (Texas Guinan) quits as a club hostess for Nick (Jimmie Phillips) and Andy (Arthur Housman). Instead, she opens her own joint and hires dancer Bee Walters (Lila Lee) as her star attraction. This breaks up Bee's act with boyfriend Eddie Parr (Eddie Foy, Jr.). To get even with Tex for becoming his rival, Andy murders her friend Holland (John Davidson) and puts the blame on Eddie. Eddie's father (Jack Norworth) tells Tex that Eddie is really her son, whom she gave up years before. During his trial, Tex persuades a member of the jury that Eddie may be innocent. She asks the court to let the jury come to her club, where she brings forth evidence of Eddie's innocence and Andy's guilt. With Eddie freed he is reunited with Bee, while Tex and Phil renew their marriage vows.

The cumbersome QUEEN OF THE NIGHTCLUBS did little to establish Texas Guinan as a talkie personality (although she did follow it with GLORIFYING THE AMERICAN GIRL the same year). *Photoplay* magazine reviewed, "Texas Guinan in a phoney story of silly revels. . . . Naturally it's a noise film." The movie did have a few interesting casting assignments, with George Raft making his screen debut doing a brief but fast Charleston dance. Texas Guinan's love interest was played by Jack Norworth, the composer of "Shine on Harvest Moon" and many other tunes.

REVENGE IS SWEET *see* BABES IN TOYLAND (1934).

RHAPSODY IN BLUE (Warner Bros., 1945) 139 minutes.

Producer, Jesse L. Lasky; director, Irving Rapper; story, Sonya Levien; screenplay, Howard Koch, Elliott Paul; art directors, John Hughes, Anton Grot; set decorators, Fred M. MacLean; music director, Leo F. Forbstein; music adaptor, Max Steiner; orchestrators, Ray Heindorf, Ferde Grofe; music conductor ("Rhapsody in Blue" number), Paul Whiteman; vocal arranger, Dudley Chambers; choreographer, Leroy Prinz; assistant director, Robert Vreeland; sound, David Forrest, Stanley Jones; special effects, Ray Davidson, Willard Van Enger; montage, James Leicester; camera, Sol Polito; editor, Folmer Blangsted.

Songs: "Rhapsody in Blue," "Concerto in F," "Variations on 'I Got Rhythm,' " "An American in Paris" (George Gershwin); "The Cuban Overture," "Fascinating Rhythm," "The Man I Love," "Mine," "Oh Lady Be Good," "Clap Yo' Hands," "Bidin' My Time," "Love Walked In," "Someone to Watch Over Me," "S' Wonderful," "I Got Rhythm," "My One and Only," "Delishious," "Embraceable You," "It Ain't Necessarily So" (George Gershwin, Ira Gershwin); "Yankee Doodle Blues" (George Gershwin, Buddy G. DeSylva, Irving Caesar); "Somebody Loves Me" (George Gershwin, DeSylva, Ballard MacDonald); "Swanee" (George Gershwin, Caesar); "Summertime," "I Got Plenty O' Nuttin' " (George Gershwin, Ira Gershwin, DuBose Heyward); "Liza" (George Gershwin, Ira Gershwin, Gus Kahn); "Do It Again," "Blue Monday Blues" (George Gershwin, DeSylva); "I'll Build a Stairway to Paradise" (George Gershwin, DeSylva, Arthur Frances [Ira Gershwin]).

Robert Alda (George Gershwin); Joan Leslie (Julie Adams); Alexis Smith (Christine Gilbert); Charles Coburn (Max Dreyfus); Julie Bishop (Lee Gershwin); Albert Basserman (Professor Frank); Morris Carnovsky (Papa Gershwin); Rosemary De Camp (Mama Gershwin); Anne Brown (Bess); Herbert Rudley (Ira Gershwin);

John B. Hughes (Commentator); Mickey Roth (George Gershwin as a Boy); Darryl Hickman (Ira Gershwin as a Boy); Charles Halton (Mr. Kast); Andrew Tombes (Mr. Milton); Gregory Gouluhoff (Mr. Katzman); Walter Soderling (Mr. Muscatel); Eddie Marr (Buddy G. DeSylva); Theodore Von Eltz (Foley); Bill Kennedy (Herbert Stone); Robert Shayne (Christine's Escort); Oscar Loraine (Ravel); Johnny Downs (Dancer); Ernest Golm (Otto Kahn); Martin Noble (Jascha Heifetz); Hugh Kirchhoffer (Walter Damrosch); Will Wright (Rachmaninoff); Ivan Lebedeff (Guest in Nightclub); George Riley (Comic); Virginia Sale (Cashier); Yola d'Avril (Prima Donna); Claire DuBrey (Receptionist); Christian Rub (Swedish Janitor); Odette Myrtil (Madame De Breteuil); Jay Novello (Orchestra Leader); Robert Johnson (Sport); William Gillespie (Porgy); Mark Stevens (Singer); Al Jolson, Paul Whiteman and His Orchestra, Oscar Levant, George White, Hazel Scott, Tom Patricola (Themselves); Louanna Hogan (Singing Voice for Julie Adams).

Warner Bros., which would popularize (and savage) the life of Cole Porter in NIGHT AND DAY (1946), *q.v.,* turned out another lavish biopic of a famous composer in RHAPSODY IN BLUE, supposedly the life of George Gershwin (1898–1937). As with most such inflated productions, the highlight of the picture was its use of the composer's well-known music. RHAPSODY IN BLUE runs more than two hours in its leisurely recreation of some of the best of Gershwin music. In addition, a number of major personalities (Paul Whiteman, Al Jolson, Oscar Levant, Hazel Scott, Anne Brown) who originally introduced Gershwin's music repeat their historic work in this presentation. On the other hand, the movie is plagued with the same creative troubles which bother many musical biogs: a lame plot and mediocre acting.

In 1910s New York City, tenement-bred George Gershwin (Robert Alda), brought up lovingly by his Old World Jewish parents (Morris Carnovsky, Rosemary DeCamp) begins working as a song plugger. He has ambitions of being a composer and is spurred on by his music teacher Professor Frank (Albert Basserman). After Al Jolson (himself) introduces Gershwin's song "Swanee," Gershwin starts to find success as a songwriter, often in tandem with his lyricist brother Ira (Herbert Rudley). George receives critical acclaim when Paul Whiteman (himself) introduces his lengthy "Rhapsody in Blue" concert piece. Thereafter, he begins composing a flow of hit Broadway shows. During these years he has many of his songs introduced by singer Julie Adams (Joan Leslie), with whom he falls in love, and he is also romanced by wealthy Christine Gilbert (Alexis Smith), an expatriate living in

Paris who eventually rejects him. Despite his success on Broadway and in films and his social life in New York and Beverly Hills, George Gershwin is not a happy man. He dies following a long illness.

Variety reported, "Those who knew Gershwin and the Gershwin saga may wax slightly vociferous at this or that miscue, but as cinematurgy, designed for escapism and entertainment, no matter the season, RHAPSODY IN BLUE can't miss." More accurate was Ted Sennett in *Warner Brothers Presents* (1971), "RHAPSODY IN BLUE . . . is a surprisingly mediocre effort. Burdened with a flat, conventional, and utterly fanciful plot line . . . it is a compendium of musical biography clichés . . . the acting is another liability, ranging from totally inadequate (Robert Alda as Gershwin) to wooden (Alexis Smith) to standard (Joan Leslie, Charles Coburn, and virtually everyone else)." When it was released the *New York Times* judged the film ". . . A hobbled and vague affair . . . disappointing to say the least." Roy Hemming (*The Melody Lingers On,* 1986) observed, "As with so many '40s musicals, there is also no resemblance whatsoever in that scene [the finale in which Levant is playing 'Concerto in F' as news of Gershwin's death is learned], nor in the two 'Rhapsody in Blue' sequences, to normal symphony stage-seating arrangements. Not only is the conductor half a block away from his players, but the orchestral groupings that Hollywood's designers apparently thought 'looked' better would probably also create some bizarre sounds and imbalances in most concert halls. . . . Moreover, the overly arty camera angles and boring visual presentation of the final 'Rhapsody in Blue' sequence (supposedly taking place at New York's Lewisohn Stadium) makes one realize how far the camerawork for today's concert telecasts has come since 1945."

Despite its several flaws, RHAPSODY IN BLUE has much to recommend it. Al Jolson is a delight as he reprises "Swanee" in blackface at a Winter Garden setting, while rotund band leader Paul Whiteman conducts "Rhapsody in Blue" with Oscar Levant at the piano, and wisecracking Levant also excels on a portion of "Concerto in F." Anne Brown recreates her role from Gershwin's *Porgy and Bess* and does superbly with "Summertime," while Hazel Scott performs "I Got Rhythm, "The Man I Love," "Fascinatin' Rhythm" and "Clap Yo' Hands." Tom Patricola offers "Somebody Loves Me," which he introduced in *George White's Scandals of 1924.* To be noted, Louanna Hogan dubbed Joan Leslie's singing as Julie Adams.

RHAPSODY IN BLUE received Oscar nominations for Best Scoring of a Musical Picture and Best Sound Recordings. Frequently, when shown on television, the film is condensed by omitting the opening childhood segment of the biography.

RHYTHM ON THE RANGE (Paramount, 1936) 85 minutes.

Producer, Benjamin Glazer; director, Norman Taurog; story, Mervin J. Houser; screenplay, John C. Moffett, Sidney Salkow, Walter DeLeon, Francis Martin; art directors, Hans Dreier, Robert Usher; set decorator, A. E. Fruedeman; costumes, Edith Head; music director, Boris Morros; camera, Karl Struss; editor, Ellsworth Hoagland.

Songs: "Empty Saddles" (based on a poem by J. Keirn Brennan; Billy Hill); "I'm an Old Cowhand" (Johnny Mercer); "Mr. Paganini" (Sam Coslow); "I Can't Escape from You" (Leo Robin, Richard A. Whiting); "The House Jack Built for Jill" (Robin, Frederick Hollander); "Drink It Down" (Ralph Rainger, Robin); "Hang Up My Saddle," "Rhythm on the Range" (Walter Bullock, Whiting); "Memories" (Whiting, Hollander); "Roundup Lullaby" (Bager Clark, Gertrude Rose).

Bing Crosby (Jeff Larrabee); Frances Farmer (Doris Halliday); Bob Burns (Buck Burns); Martha Raye (Emma); Samuel S. Hinds (Robert Halliday); Lucille Webster Gleason (Penelope Ryland); Warren Hymer (Big Brain); George E. Stone (Shorty); James Burke (Wabash); Martha Sleeper (Constance); Clem Bevans (Gila Bend); Leonid Kinskey (Mischa); Charles Williams (Gopher); Beau Baldwin (Cuddles); Emmett Vogan (Clerk); Bud Flanigan [Dennis O'Keefe] (Heckler); Duke York (Officer); James Blaine (Conductor); Herbert Ashley (Brakeman); James "Slim" Thompson (Porter); Jim Toney (Oil Station Proprietor); Syd Saylor (Gus); Sam McDaniel (Porter); Harry C. Bradley (Minister); Charles E. Arnt (Steward); Oscar Smith (Waiter); Bob McKenzie (Farmer); Heinie Conklin (Driver); Frank Dawson (Butler); Otto Yamaoka (Chinese Houseboy); Irving Bacon (Announcer); Eddy Waller (Field Judge); and: Louis Prima, Sons of the Pioneers [Bob Nolan, Tim Spencer, Carl Farr, Hugh Farr, Roy Rogers].

In her (auto)biography, *Will There Really Be a Morning?* (1972), troubled actress Frances Farmer claimed her happiest movie experience was making RHYTHM ON THE RANGE while she was under contract to Paramount Pictures. This "pleasant entertainment" (*Variety*) is best remembered today for introducing the song "I'm an Old Cowhand" as well as for being comedienne-songstress Martha Raye's first feature motion picture. She and fellow comedian Bob Burns would clown together in several subsequent Paramount comedies of the 1930s.

At a sophisticated dude ranch, Jeff Larrabee (Bing Crosby)

works as a cowhand for wealthy Penelope Ryland (Lucille Webster Gleason). The ranch is kept lively by the antics of dizzy Emma Mazda (Martha Raye), who has her romantic eye set on Jeff's pal, Buck Burns (Bob Burns). Things become even more involved when Penelope's pretty niece, the footloose heiress Doris Halliday (Frances Farmer), arrives from the east, on the lam from an unwanted marriage to a polo player. Doris and Jeff begin a romance but local bad guys, led by Big Brain (Warren Hymer), decide to kidnap Doris and hold her for ransom. Although they commit the crime, the hoodlums are eventually brought to justice by Jeff and Buck. Jeff and Doris resume their courtship.

In addition to "I'm an Old Cowhand," which relaxed Crosby croons in the film, bouncy Martha Raye does a rowdy version of "Mr. Paganini" (which began one of her standard concert numbers thereafter) and she and Crosby duet on "Mr. Paganini (If You Can't Sing It, You'll Have to Swing It)." The Sons of the Pioneers (including a very young Roy Rogers) perform "Empty Saddles." Cut from some release prints of RHYTHM ON THE RANGE is "The House That Jack Built for Jill," featuring Crosby and Frances Farmer.

In *The Films of Bing Crosby* (1977), Robert Bookbinder noted the film was ". . . A well-done musical panorama of life and love on a Western dude ranch, but it offered Crosby no real acting challenge." While RHYTHM ON THE RANGE was commercially successful, it was Crosby's only Western until he made the non-musical remake of STAGECOACH (1966). RHYTHM ON THE RANGE would be remade as PARDNERS (1956), a comedy vehicle for the team of Dean Martin and Jerry Lewis.

Martha Raye and Bing Crosby would re-team for Paramount's WAIKIKI WEDDING (1937) and DOUBLE OR NOTHING (1937).

RIO RITA (RKO, 1929) Color Sequences 135 minutes.

Producer, William LeBaron; director, Luther Reed; based on the musical play by Guy Bolton, Fred Thompson, Harry Tierney, Joseph McCarthy; screenplay, Reed, Russell Mack; art director/costumes Max Ree; music, Tierney; music director, Victor Baravalle; choreographer, Pearl Eaton; chorus master, Pietro Cimini; sound, Hugh McDowell; camera, Robert Kurrle, Lloyd Knechtel; editor, William Hamilton.

Songs: "You're Always in My Arms (But Only in My Dreams)," "Sweetheart, We Need Each Other," "Following the Sun Around," "Rio Rita," "If You're in Love You'll Waltz," "The Kinkajou," "The Ranger's Song" (Harry Tierney, Joseph McCarthy); "Long Before You Came Along" (E. Y. Harburg, Harold Arlen).

Bert Wheeler (Chick Bean); Robert Woolsey (Ed Lovett); Bebe Daniels (Rita Ferguson); John Boles (Captain Jim Stewart); Dorothy Lee (Dolly); Don Alvarado (Roberto Ferguson); Georges Renavent (General Ravenoff/"El Kinkajou"); Eva Rosita (Carmen); Sam Nelson (McGinn); Fred Burns (Wilkins); Sam Blum (Cafe Owner); Nick De Ruiz (Padrone); Tiny Sandford (Davalos); Helen Kaiser (Mrs. Bean); Benny Corbett, Fred Scott (Rangers).

See: RIO RITA (1942) (essay).

RIO RITA (Metro-Goldwyn-Mayer, 1942) 91 minutes.

Producer, Pandro S. Berman; director, S. Sylvan Simon; based on the musical play by Guy Bolton, Fred Thompson, Harry Tierney, Joseph McCarthy; screenplay, Richard Connell, Gladys Lehman, John Grant; costumes, Robert Kalloch, Gile Steele; music director, Herbert Stothart; special effects, Warren Newcombe; camera, George Folsey; editor, Ben Lewis.

Songs: "The Ranger's Song," "Rio Rita" (Harry Tierney, Joseph McCarthy); "Long Before You Came Along" (E. Y. Harburg, Harold Arlen); "Brazilian Dance" (Nilo Barnet); "Ora O Canga" (Lacerdo).

Bud Abbott (Doc); Lou Costello (Wishy); Kathryn Grayson (Rita Winslow); John Carroll (Ricardo Montera); Patricia Dane (Lucille Brunswick); Tom Conway (Maurice Craindall); Peter Whitney (Jake); Arthur Space (Trask); Joan Valerie (Dotty); Dick Rich (Gus); Barry Nelson (Harry Gantley); Eva Puig (Marianna); Mitchell Lewis (Julio); Eros Volusia (Dancer); Julian Rivero (Mexican Gent); Douglas Newland (Control Man); Lee Murray (Little Mexican); Inez Cooper (Pulque); Frank Perry (Chef).

Florenz Ziegfeld's production of *Rio Rita* first opened on Broadway in February 1927 and had a lengthy run of 494 performances, starring Ethelind Terry, J. Harold Murray, Walter Catlett and the comedy team of Bert Wheeler and Robert Woolsey, with a popular score by Joseph McCarthy and Harry Tierney. Two years later, RKO lavishly adapted the musical to the screen and included Technicolor sequences in its lengthy fifteen reels. Despite its slavish following of the conventions of its stage original and the obstacles of its primitive sound, the movie RIO RITA was considered trendsetting in its day.* *Photoplay* magazine enthused, "The finest of screen musicals to date. Comedy, singing, dancing and romance de luxe. Bebe Daniels wows 'em and John Boles sets

*In retrospect, Ethan Mordden (*The Hollywood Musical,* 1981) assessed, "One of the best of the Broadway adaptations, oddly, was the most faithful to the original, RKO'S RIO RITA (1929): full score . . . static camera, mixed cast of screen and stage veterans, the last third in color. It's horribly primitive—sound troubles on the set

hearts to fluttering anew." Grossing an amazing $2.4 million at the box-office, the film retained the stage vehicle's many lovely songs such as "If You're in Love You'll Waltz," "The Ranger's Song" and the title tune. "You're Always in My Arms (But Only in My Dreams)" was especially written for the film by the original composers, while the Harold Arlen-E. Y. Harburg tune "Long Before You Came Along" was added to the musical roster.

A notorious masked bandit called El Kinkajou is wanted by Mexican authorities. In a small border town a man named Jim (John Boles) arrives and romances pretty Rita Ferguson (Bebe Daniels) but makes an enemy of General Ravenoff (Georges Renavent). Ravenoff, who also desires Rita, tells her that Jim is really a Texas Ranger sent to arrest her brother Roberto (Don Alvarado), whom many believe is Kinkajou. When this is proved to be true, Rita turns her back on Jim. However, when Ravenoff sets a trap for the Ranger, Rita risks her life to save Jim's. On the Mexican side of the Rio Grande River, Ravenoff has built a barge which he uses as a gambling boat and he gives a party for Rita. Jim arrives in disguise and wins Rita's heart. With her keeping Ravenoff preoccupied, Jim cuts loose the barge and it floats to the Texas side of the border. There Jim arrests Ravenoff who is really El Kinkajou. In the midst of all this pell-mell activity, Chick Bean (Bert Wheeler) is attempting to arrange a divorce using a shady attorney called Ed Lovett (Robert Woolsey).

The comedy team of Bert Wheeler and Robert Woolsey repeated their stage roles as the comedy relief in RIO RITA and they were so successful that they became the top comedy duo at RKO, where they remained until Woolsey was forced off the screen in 1937 because of ill health; he died the next year. The dark-haired Bebe Daniels, once a leading star at Paramount who specialized in comedy roles, had been let go by that studio after sound came in. With RIO RITA she re-established her marquee power and starred in such musicals as DIXIANA (1930, also with Wheeler and Woolsey), 42ND STREET (1933), *q.v.,* and in England in such pictures as THE SONG YOU GAVE ME (1933) and MUSIC IS MAGIC (1935). For Broadway operetta star John Boles, who had

---

were almost insuperable. . . . As RIO RITA is a modern western, outdoor shots of mounted rangers were unavoidable, though this meant filming silent and then adding the sound. . . . The whole thing was shot in twenty-four days, and Bebe Daniels for one found it impossible to post-dub her part and had to get it down during filming or not at all; the choral singing clearly doesn't match the lip movements and must have been recorded separately. . . . Underscoring obscures the dialogue, balance in duets is a problem (especially in regard to Daniels' and Boles' relatively high voices) and at each new sound series the track cuts in with a little explosion. The camera, locked into its soundproof booth, also adds to the rough quality of the film. . . ."

acted in several silent features, RIO RITA was a continuation of his new screen vogue in screen operettas. The baritone (borrowed from Universal Pictures) had starred in THE DESERT SONG (1929), *q.v.*, and would appear in such other musicals as SONG OF THE WEST (1930), KING OF JAZZ (1930), *q.v.*, STAND UP AND CHEER (1934), *q.v.*, and ROSE OF THE RANCHO (1936), *q.v.*

Long before MGM decided to remake RIO RITA in 1942 as a vehicle for moneymakers Abbott and Costello (borrowed from Universal), the 1929 film and its Broadway original had become antique curiosity pieces. Because it was World War II, the plot was updated to include timely wartime espionage and most of the original score was deleted, except the title tune and "The Ranger's Song" from the play and "Long Before You Came Along" from the 1929 version.

Entertainers Doc (Bud Abbott) and Wishy (Lou Costello) are stranded on the West Coast and work in a pet store. They grab an opportunity to return to New York City by hiding in the trunk of a car they think will take them eastward. Actually, the driver, radio crooner Ricardo Montera (John Carroll), is heading to the Hotel Vista del Rio to see his girlfriend Rita Winslow (Kathryn Grayson). Doc and Wishy eventually become house detectives at the resort ranch. There they uncover a nest of Nazi spies led by hotel manager Maurice Craindall (Tom Conway). The latter intends to use an upcoming fiesta as a blind to send coded messages to the Fatherland. Doc and Wishy uncover the plot and stop the Nazi spying. Ricardo and Rita plan to wed.

Variety acknowledged: "Director S. Sylvan Simon has spaced the A & C nonsensities with a good sense of timing to properly break up the hoke, the libretto keeping it hanging together." The trade paper added, "John Carroll . . . is vocally impressive. . . . Ditto Kathryn Grayson, who evidences a fine coloratura soprano." Carroll handled the "The Ranger's Song" and "Rio Rita," while Grayson reprised "The Ranger's Song" and dueted with Carroll on "Long Before You Came Along," as well as singing operatic snatches. Brazilian Eros Volusia provided a sensuous South American dance during the fiesta, joined by a native troupe.

For the record, the heroine Rita is only called "Rio Rita" in the title song.

ROAD TO NASHVILLE (Crown International, 1966) Color 109 minutes.

Producer, Robert Patrick; associate producer, Marty Robbins; director/screenplay, Will Zens; makeup, Dorothy Kirkpatrick; camera, Leif Rise, William Zsigmond; editor, Michael David.

Songs: "Devil Woman," "Beggin' to You," "El Paso" (Marty

Robbins); "Working My Way Through a Heartache" (Buddy Mize); "Count Me Out" (Jerry Reed); "Love's Somethin' I Can't Understand" (Webb Pierce); "You Ain't No Better than Me" (Wayne Walker); "Anita, You're Dreaming" (Waylon Jennings); "Annie Lou" (H. Whittaker); "Put It Off Until Tomorrow" (Dolly Parton, Bill Owens); "I Miss You Already" (Faron Young); "I Love You Drops," "Nobody But a Fool Would Love You" (Bill Anderson); "Po' Folks" (Monda Dick); "Would You Hold It Against Me," "Here Comes My Baby" (Dottie West); "Just a Faded Petal from a Beautiful Bouquet" (Hank Snow); "Up This Hill and Down" (R. Staedtler); "Howdy Neighbor, Howdy" (J. Morris); "I Wouldn't Buy a Used Car from Him" (Harlan Howard); "I Walk the Line" (Johnny Cash); "Were You There (When They Crucified My Lord)" (traditional; arranger, Cash); "The One on the Right Is on the Left" (Jack Clement); "I Hope You'll Learn," "A Woman Half My Age," "No Dreams Like My Dreams," "A Thousand Ways," "I'll Never Get Over Lovin' You," "It Seemed that You'd Never Been Gone," "Write Me a Letter," "Goin', Goin', Gone," "My Baby's Coming Home" (William Leavitt, John Grady, Sherm Feller); "I've Been Everywhere" (Geoffrey Mack); "Skid Row Joe."

Marty Robbins (Himself); Doodles Weaver (Colonel Fiedelbaum); Connie Smith (Herself); Richard Arlen (J. B. Grover); Ralph Emery (Himself); The Stonemans, Webb Pierce, The Carter Family, Waylon Jennings, Margie Singleton, The Osborne Brothers, Porter Wagoner, Norma Jean, Johnny Cash, Hank Snow, Dottie West, Faron Young, Kitty Wells, Bill Anderson, Lefty Frizzell, Bill Phillips, Johnny Wright, Rudy Wright, Don Winters, Bobby Sykes, Quinine Gumstump and Buck (Guest Stars).

When his production company in Hollywood is about to shoot a country music jamboree in Nashville, executive J. B. Grover (Richard Arlen) sends a bumbling production assistant, Colonel Fiedelbaum (Doodles Weaver), to Music City to line up the acts for the production, In Nashville, the Colonel is befriended by Marty Robbins (himself) and Connie Smith (herself) and they help him to audition many famous country acts (Hank Snow, Johnny Cash, Kitty Wells, Webb Pierce, Lefty Frizzell, Waylon Jennings, Faron Young, Dottie West, among others) for his film. However, in his enthusiasm, the naive Colonel neglects to sign any of the talent to a contract. Fiedelbaum keeps assuring his boss that all is proceeding according to plan, but when J.B. and his crew are on their way to Nashville, the befuddled Colonel suddenly realizes his mistake. He again asks Marty and Connie for help. Thus he is able to sign some fifteen acts for the movie. When J. B. and the others arrive in Nashville, they are able to shoot the movie.

ROAD TO NASHVILLE is an interesting example of the phenomenon called "the country music movie," which began with COUNTRY MUSIC JUBILEE in 1960 and closed with 1972's THE NASHVILLE SOUND. In between were such features as COUNTRY MUSIC CARAVAN (1964), COUNTRY MUSIC ON BROADWAY (1964), MUSIC CITY U.S.A. (1966), SECOND FIDDLE TO A STEEL GUITAR (1966), COUNTRY WESTERN HOEDOWN (1967), FROM NASHVILLE WITH MUSIC (1968), and TRAVELIN' LIGHT (1971). They were all little more than a series of country music acts strung together with a wisp of a plot. In fact, ROAD TO NASHVILLE's storyline was a bit more detailed than in most such movies. Nevertheless, it did not get in the way of dozens of country performers doing some thirty-eight songs. Among the highlights were star Marty Robbins singing "El Paso" and "Devil Woman," Hank Snow's "I've Been Everywhere," Porter Wagoner's "Skid Row Joe," and "A Woman Half My Age" by Kitty Wells. The movie also provided Dolly Parton with her first screen credit. Although she does not appear in this motion picture, one of her songs, "Put It Off Until Tomorrow," is sung by Bill Phillips.

ROAD TO SINGAPORE (Paramount, 1940) 80 minutes.

Producer, Harlan Thompson; director, Victor Schertzinger; story, Harry Hervey; screenplay, Don Hartman, Frank Butler; art directors, Hans Dreier, Robert Odell; music director, Victor Young; choreographer, LeRoy Prinz; special effects, Farciot Edouart; camera, William C. Mellor; editor, Paul Weatherwax.

Songs: "Sweet Potato Piper," "Too Romantic," "Kaigoon" (Johnny Burke, James V. Monaco); "Captain Custard," "The Moon and the Willow Tree" (Burke, Victor Schertzinger).

Bing Crosby (Josh Mallon); Dorothy Lamour (Mima); Bob Hope (Ace Lannigan); Charles Coburn (Joshua Mallon, IV); Judith Barrett (Gloria Wycott); Anthony Quinn (Caesar); Jerry Colonna (Achilles Bombanassa); Johnny Arthur (Timothy Willow); Pierre Watkin (Morgan Wycott); Gaylord [Steve] Pendleton (Gordon Wycott); Miles Mander (Sir Malcolm Drake); Pedro Regas (Zato); Greta Grandstedt (Babe); Edward Gargan (Bill); Don Brodie (Fred); John Kelly (Sailor); Kitty Kelly (Sailor's Wife); Roger Gray (Father); Harry C. Bradley (Secretary); Richard Keene (Cameraman); Gloria Franklin (Ninky Poo); Carmen D'Antonio (Dancing Girl); Monte Blue (High Priest); Cyril Ring (Ship's Officer); Helen Lynd (Society Girl); Paula DeCardo (Native Dancing Girl); Benny Inocencio (Native Bouy); Jack Pepper (Columnist); Arthur Q. Bryan (Bartender); Robert Emmett O'Connor (Immigration Officer); Belle Mitchell (Shopkeeper); Fred Malatesta, Bob St. Angel (Native Policemen); Marguerita Padula (Proprietress); Bobby Barber (Dumb Looking Little Man); Claire James (Girl at Party); Grace Hayle (Chaperone); Richard Tucker (Ship's Officer); Elvia Allman (Homely Girl).

Often in the motion picture industry, the most inspired casting occurs accidentally. Such was the case with ROAD TO SINGAPORE (1940), the first in a series of seven comedies with music to star the triumvirate of Bing Crosby, Bob Hope and Dorothy Lamour.* Originally the property (a tropical drama) had been dusted off the shelf and converted into a comedy scheduled to star Fred MacMurray and Jack Oakie or MacMurray and George Burns. When they refused it, three of Paramount's stars who had never worked together on camera were matched for this property. The above-average ROAD TO SINGAPORE is perhaps the most neglected of the group, although without its success as a springboard, it is most likely that the series would have been stillborn.

Vagabondish Josh Mallon (Bing Crosby) and his pal Ace Lannigan (Bob Hope) lead a carefree existence, although Josh's rich father (Charles Coburn) and Josh's fiancée, Gloria Wycott (Judith Barrett), want him to succeed his dad as president of the family's profitable shipping business. To escape the family pressure, Josh and Ace head for exotic Singapore. There they rent a bungalow near the port city of Kaigoon, where they happen upon a beautiful native girl, Mima (Dorothy Lamour), who works in a sleazy vaudeville act as the assistant of whip-cracking Caesar (Anthony Quinn). Fearing Mima will get hurt in the act, the boys abduct her and take her back to their bungalow, and she agrees to become their housemaid. Quickly both men become enamored of her, but she refuses to admit which one of them she loves until she is sure of his commitment to her. Finally Josh tells Mima that he has to return to America because of his father and his fiancée. Mima insists that she really loves Ace. Actually her confession is a falsehood because she does not want to break up Josh's impending marriage. Josh departs, but when he discovers the truth he promptly returns to Mima.

ROAD TO SINGAPORE quickly established the formula for all "Road" pictures to come: a relaxed Bing Crosby and a hyperactive, wisecracking Bob Hope trade quips, engage in slapstick and constantly best one another in gaining the attention of

*The other "Road" pictures were: ROAD TO ZANZIBAR (1941), ROAD TO MOROCCO (1942), ROAD TO UTOPIA (1945), ROAD TO RIO (1947), ROAD TO BALI (1952) and THE ROAD TO HONG KONG (1962, in which Joan Collins had the feminine lead; Lamour had a cameo).

Gloria Franklin, Dorothy Lamour, Bing Crosby and Bob Hope in ROAD TO SINGAPORE (1940).

languorous, sarong-clad Dorothy Lamour. It became a maxim that the "Road" treks to exotic locale would all be filmed on the studio's backlot, that the dialogue would be peppered with topical ad libs and that the entire cast would play the comedy with tongue firmly in cheek. While songs were not the main focus of these amusing romps, they definitely played a role in balancing out the proceedings. Most of the songs in this entry were focused on Crosby, with director Victor Schertzinger and Johnny Burke composing the comic "Captain Custard" (handled by Crosby and Hope) and "The Moon and the Willow Tree" (warbled by Lamour).

Despite the fact that ROAD TO SINGAPORE did extremely well at the box-office, the critics were not enamored with the initial series' entry. ". . . ROAD TO SINGAPORE is cobbled with good intentions, is blessed intermittently with smooth-running strips of amiable nonsense, but is altogether too uneven, for regular use" (*New York Times*). In retrospect, Robert Bookbinder would judge in *The Films of Bing Crosby* (1977), "The film could stand as a prime example of how even a third-rate comedy script can be transformed into something successful when entrusted to performers like Hope and Crosby."

ROBERTA (RKO, 1935) 105 minutes.

Producer, Pandro S. Berman; director, William A. Seiter; based on the musical play by Jerome Kern, Otto Harbach; from the novel *Gowns by Roberta* by Alice Duer Miller; screenplay, Jane Murfin, Sam Mintz, Allan Scott, Glenn Tryon; art directors, Van Nest Polglase, Carroll Clark; set decorator, Thomas K. Little; costumes, Bernard Newman; music, Kern; music director, Max Steiner; choreographers, Fred Astaire, Hermes Pan; camera, Edward Cronjager; editor, William Hamilton.

Songs: "Let's Begin," "Smoke Gets in Your Eyes," "Yesterday," "I'll Be Hard to Handle" (Jerome Kern; new lyrics, Bernard Dougall); "You're Devastating," "The Touch of Your Hand," "Don't Ask Me Not to Sing" (Kern); "Lovely to Look At," "I Won't Dance" (Kern, Dorothy Fields); "Indiana" (Ballard MacDonald, James Hanley); "Russian Song" (traditional).

Irene Dunne (Stephanie); Fred Astaire (Huck Haines); Ginger Rogers (Countess Tanka Schwarwenka [Lizzie Gatz]); Randolph Scott (John Kent); Helen Westley (Roberta [Aunt Minnie]); Victor Varconi (Ladislaw); Claire Dodd (Sophie); Luis Alberni (Voyda); Ferdinand Munier (Lord Delves); Torben Meyer (Albert); Adrian Rosley (Professor); Bodil Rosing (Fernando); Lucille Ball, Jane Hamilton, Margaret McChrystal, Kay Sutton, Maxine Jennings, Virginia Reid, Lorna Low, Lorraine DeSart, Wanda Perry, Diane Cook, Virginia Carroll, Betty Dumbries, Donna Roberts (Mannequins); Mike Tellegen, Sam Savitsky (Cossacks); Zena Savine (Woman); Johnny "Candy" Candido, Muzzy Marcellino, Gene Sheldon, Howard Lily, William Carey, Paul McLarind, Hal Brown, Charles Shapre, Ivan Dow, Phil Cuthbert, Delmon Davis, William Dunn (Orchestra); Mary Forbes (Mrs. Teal); William B. Davidson (Purser); Grace Hayle (Reporter); Dale Van Sickel (Dance Extra); Judith Vosselli, Rita Gould (Bits).

The Otto Harbach-Jerome Kern musical *Roberta* caused a sensation on Broadway when it opened in the fall of 1933, due mainly to its enchanting song, "Smoke Gets in Your Eyes." The show starred Tamara, Lyda Roberti, George Murphy, Ray Middleton, Sydney Greenstreet, Bob Hope, Fred MacMurray and the California Collegians Orchestra. It enjoyed a 295-performance run. In 1935 RKO brought it to the screen starring Irene Dunne, Randolph Scott and the dancing team of Fred Astaire and Ginger Rogers. "If there is a flaw in the photoplay, it is the unfortunate

Irene Dunne in ROBERTA (1935).

circumstance that Mr. Astaire and his excellent partner, Miss Rogers, cannot be dancing during every minute of it," insisted the *New York Times*.

Coming to Paris for a cafe engagement, ex-football player John Kent (Randolph Scott) and his pal Huck Haines (Fred Astaire) find themselves stranded along with the members of Huck's band. While there, they visit John's Aunt Minnie (Helen Westley), who is known as the chic international dress designer, Roberta. Working for her as a couturier is Stephanie (Irene Dunne), a Russian princess in exile. Aunt Minnie asks one of her customers, club entertainer Countess Tanka Schwarwenka (Ginger Rogers), to use her contacts to find an engagement for John's band. Actually the phoney Polish Countess is really Lizzie Gatz, an old girlfriend of Huck's. She willingly persuades the cafe owners to hire the band. John begins a romance with the aristocratic Stephanie while Hick and Lizzie renew their affair. After Aunt Minnie suddenly dies, the quartet rush to get her new fashions to the public in a musical fashion program. After John explains away his former fiancée (Claire Dodd), who has arrived on the scene, he and the prideful Stephanie continue their romance, while Huck and Lizzie decide to wed as well.

When ROBERTA was produced, musical comedy-drama star Irene Dunne was queen of the RKO lot and thus the focal attention in the film is given to her. She sang the hauntingly beautiful "Smoke Gets in Your Eyes," "Yesterdays" and "Lovely to Look At" (at the fashion show). Astaire and Rogers danced to "Lovely to Look At" and "I Won't Dance," while Astaire crooned "Let's Begin"; he and Ginger sang and danced to the high-spirited "I'll Be Hard to Handle." Only four of the ten songs from the original Broadway score were retained, some with changed lyrics, while two new numbers were added for the film by Jerome Kern and lyricist Dorothy Fields: "I Won't Dance" and "Lovely to Look At."

If there are weak points in ROBERTA they are the blandness of Randolph Scott as the co-lead, the almost too faithful adherence to the stage plot, and the finale fashion show (in which Lucille Ball can be spotted as one of the models), which lasts too long. Otherwise, the expensively-mounted production is a well-balanced example of a screen musical at its stylish finest.

ROBERTA was Oscar-nominated for Best Song ("Lovely to Look At").

In 1952 MGM remade ROBERTA as LOVELY TO LOOK AT, starring Kathryn Grayson, Howard Keel, Red Skelton, Ann Miller and Marge and Gower Champion. The color remake added two new songs to Jerome Kern melodies: "Lafayette" (lyrics by

Dorothy Fields) and "The Most Exciting Night" (lyrics by Fields and Otto Harbach), but the revamped production did little to erase the memory of the superior 1935 version.

THE ROGUE SONG (Metro-Goldwyn-Mayer, 1930) Color 115 minutes.

Producer, Lionel Barrymore; directors, Barrymore, Hal Roach (Laurel and Hardy sequences); based on the operetta *Gypsy Love* by Franz Lehar, A. M. Willner, Robert Bodansky; screenplay, Frances Marion, John Colton; art director, Cedric Gibbons; costumes, Adrian; ballet music, Dimitri Tiomkin; ballet director, Madame Albertina Rasch; assistant director, Charles Dorian; sound, Paul Neal, Douglas Shearer; camera, Percy Hilburn, C. Edgar Schoenbaum; editor, Margaret Booth.

Songs: "The Rogue Song," "Once in the Georgian Hills," "When I'm Looking at You," "Song of the Shirt" (Herbert Stothart, Clifford Grey); "Love Comes Like a Bird on the Wing," "The White Dove" (Franz Lehar, Grey).

Lawrence Tibbett (Yegor); Catharine Dale Owen (Princess Vera); Judith Vosselli (Countess Tatiana); Nance O'Neil (Princess Alexandra); Stan Laurel (Ali-Bek); Oliver Hardy (Murza-Bek); Florence Lake (Nadja); Lionel Belmore (Ossman); Ullrich Haupt (Prince Sergei); Kate Price (Petrovna); Wallace McDonald (Hassan); Burr McIntosh (Count Peter); James Bradbury, Jr. (Azamat); H. A. Morgan (Frolov); Elsa Alsen (Yegor's Mother); Harry Bernard (Guard); The Albertina Rasch Ballet (Dancers).

In Czarist Russia, in a mountain area to the south, Yegor (Lawrence Tibbett) is the dashing and carefree leader of bandits who rob from the rich and give to the poor. At a remote inn belonging to Ossman the Turk (Lionel Belmore), Yegor is captivated with the splendid Princess Vera (Catherine Dale Owen), while spurning the advances of her companion, Countess Tatiana (Judith Vosselli). The latter tries to gain revenge by turning Yegor over to the Cossacks, who are led by Vera's evil brother, Prince Sergei (Ullrich Haupt). With Vera's aid, Yegor escapes, but not until he is forced to kill Ossman, who has been bribed by Tatiana. Yegor returns with his men to their mountain stronghold. However, upon arrival he finds that his sister Nadja (Florence Lake) has committed suicide after being kidnapped and violated by Sergei. Vowing revenge, Yegor disguises himself as a singer and goes to the Countess's palace where Prince Sergei is a guest. After performing for the royal guests, he kills Sergei and kidnaps Vera. Knowing the Cossacks will follow him and his band, Yegor orders his people to leave their stronghold. He leads them to a remote Caucasus region.

En route, Vera romances follower Hassan (Wallace McDonald), hoping to persuade him to betray Yegor. At the city of Kars, Hassan does betray Yegor to the Cossacks. However, by now Vera is in love with the rebel leader and regrets her actions. Nevertheless, Yegor is captured. When Vera rejects Hassan, he kills himself. As Yegor is flogged, he sings to Vera, further capturing her heart. She visits him in his jail cell and spends the night with him. She arranges for his escape, knowing she cannot accompany him. Yegor returns to the Caucasus, remembering his forbidden moments of love with the lovely princess.

Based on Franz Lehar's operetta *Gypsy Love* (1910), THE ROGUE SONG was a beautifully mounted Technicolor showcase for the film debut of Metropolitan opera star Lawrence Tibbett, who was nominated for an Academy Award for his virile, melodic performance in this film.* *Photoplay* magazine enthused, "Lawrence Tibbett, grand opera star, flashes across the photoplay horizon, an inimitable and dashing personality . . . this operetta is roistering, brilliant and dramatic—a feast for the eye and the ear." Not only did Tibbett score well as the roguish, moustached bandit; he also handled beautifully the movie's topnotch score, which included the title song, "When I'm Looking at You" and the lilting "The White Dove." Tibbett had a best-selling record for Victor with "The Rogue Song" and "The White Dove." Also of historical interest is the fact that Stan Laurel and Oliver Hardy made appearances in the feature as Tibbett's comical sidekicks. Regarding their work in the production, John McCabe wrote in *Laurel & Hardy* (1975), "To guarantee the success of the film in foreign markets, Laurel and Hardy were borrowed briefly from Hal Roach to add a few touches of comedy. . . . They are the archetypal comedy sidekicks with precious few opportunities for sidekicking. . . . Stan and Ollie do not appear in the film until 40 minutes [after the movie begins]. . . ."

Sadly, THE ROGUE SONG today is a lost film classic, with apparently only a few feet of Technicolor test film remaining from this once popular box-office success. On the other hand, thanks to the sound-on-disc process of the time, the movie's soundtrack is still intact and Tibbett's wonderful singing plus some dialogue and

*MGM boastfully announced in its advertising for THE ROGUE SONG, "Again Metro-Goldwyn-Mayer proves its leadership by being the first to present an operatic genius of such outstanding reputation as Lawrence Tibbett in a full-length motion picture production. Now you can hear in your favorite theatre the same glorious baritone that has thrilled thousands at the Metropolitan Opera House—that has carried his fame around the world!"

comedy by Laurel and Hardy are on a soundtrack album issued by Pelican Records in 1980.

MGM would next team Lawrence Tibbett in the far less successful NEW MOON (1930), *q.v.,* opposite Metropolitan opera diva Grace Moore.

ROLLER BOOGIE (United Artists, 1979) Color 103 minutes.

Executive producer, Irwin Yablans; producer, Bruce Cohn Curtis; associate producer, Joseph Wolf; director, Mark L. Lester; story, Yablans; screenplay, Barry Schneider; art director, Keith Michl; music, Bob Esty; choreographer, David Winters; assistant directors, Dan Allinham, Richard C. Wallace; camera, Dean Cundey; editor, Howard Kunin.

Songs: "Hell on Wheels," "All for One, One for All," "Takin' Life in My Own Hands," "Elektronix (Roller Dancin')," "Evil Man," "The Roller Boogie," "Love Fire" (Michele Aller, Bob Esty); "Good Girls" (John W. Brazas); "Boogie Wonderland" (Allee Willis, Jon Lind); "We've Got the Power," "Summer Love," "Rollin' Up a Storm (The Eye of the Hurricane)" (Esty, Michael Brooks); "Top Jammer" (Aller, Esty, S. A. Prudden); "Cunga" (Esty); "Lord Is It Mine" (R. Davies, R. Hodgson).

Linda Blair (Terry Barkley); Jim Bray (Bobby James); Beverly Garland (Lillian Barkley); Roger Perry (Roger Barkley); Jimmy Van Patten (Hoppy); Kimberly Beck (Lana); Rick Sciacca (Complete Control Conway); Sean McClory (Jammer); Mark Goddard (Thatcher); Albert Insinnia (Gordo); Stoney Jackson (Phones); M. G. Kelly (J. D.); Chris Nelson (Franklin); Patrick Wright (Sergeant Danner); Dorothy Meyer (Ada); Shelley Golden (Mrs. Potter); Bill Ross (Nick); Carey Fox (Sonny); Nina Axelrod (Bobby's Friend).

Fads in music have often resulted in motion pictures made on the cheap for fast playoff in the exploitation market, the practice being particularly common during the 1940s through the 1960s. Today, however, this marketing gambit is still in use and ROLLER BOOGIE is a perfect example of this type of cinema fare—in this case a film made to cash in on the very brief popularity of roller disco music. As a result, ROLLER BOOGIE is memorable neither as a drama, a musical or as a social commentary on its subject matter. ROLLER BOOGIE grossed $4,929,537 in distributors' domestic film rentals.

Unhappy Beverly Hills teenager Terry Barkley (Linda Blair) deserts her uncaring father Roger (Roger Perry) and pill-addicted mother Lillian (Beverly Garland) to take up with the beach skating crowd at Venice. There she is befriended by Bobby James (Jim Bray), who becomes her skating partner, Hoppy (Jimmy Van Patten), Lana (Kimberly Beck) and several other teenagers. All goes smoothly until gangsters led by Thatcher (Mark Goddard) attempt to take over the disco rink where the kids skate. The young adults unite to run off the hoodlums and stage a big roller boogie contest.

The musical numbers staged by David Winters are rather limp, but no more exciting are the skating sequences, and the finale contest lacks verve. Co-star Jim Bray, however, does impress with his skating gymnastics.

Variety reported, "After a slick opening which takes a great degree of interest in the mechanics and garb of roller disco, ROLLER BOOGIE grinds on as one of the more mindless, irrelevant concoctions churned out of late."

ROMAN SCANDALS (United Artists, 1933) 85 minutes.

Producer, Samuel Goldwyn; director, Frank Tuttle; story, George S. Kaufman, Robert E. Sherwood; adaptor, William Anthony McGuire, additional dialogue, George Oppenheimer, Arthur Sheekman, Nat Perrin; art director, Richard Day; costumes, John Harkrider; choreographer, Busby Berkeley; music director, Alfred Newman; chariot sequence director, Ralph Cedar; sound, Vinton Vernon; camera, Gregg Toland; editor, Stuart Heisler.

Songs: "No More Love," "Build a Little Home," "Keep Young and Beautiful," "Rome Wasn't Built in a Day" (Harry Warren, Al Dubin); "Put a Tax on Love" (Warren, L. Wolfe Gilbert).

Eddie Cantor (Eddie/Oedipus); Ruth Etting (Olga); Gloria Stuart (Princess Sylvia); David Manners (Josephus); Verree Teasdale (Empress Agrippa); Edward Arnold (Emperor Valerius); Alan Mowbray (Major Domo); Jack Rutherford (Manius); Grace Poggi (Slave Dancer); Willard Robertson (Warren F. Cooper); Harry Holman (Mayor of West Rome); Lee Kohlmar (Storekeeper); Stanley Fields (Slave Auctioneer); Charles C. Wilson (Police Chief Pratt); Clarence Wilson (Buggs, the Museum Keeper); Stanley Andrews (Official); Stanley Blystone (Cop/ Roman Jailer); Harry Cording, Lane Chandler, Duke York (Soldiers); William Wagner (Slave Buyer); Louise Carver (Lady Slave Bidder); Francis Ford (Citizen); Charles Arnt (Catus, the Food Tester); Leo Willis (Torturer); Frank Hagney (Lucius, the Aide); Michael Mark (Assistant Cook); Dick Alexander (Guard); Paul Porcasi (Chef); John Ince (Senator); Jane Darwell (Beauty Salon Manager); Billy Barty (Little Eddie); Iris Shunn [Meredith] (Girl); Aileen Riggin (Slave Dancer); Katharine Mauk, Rosalie Fromson, Mary Lange, Vivian Keefer, Barbara Pepper, Theo Plane, Lucille Ball (Slave Girls); and: The Abottiers [Florence Wilson, Rose

Kirsner, Genevieve Irwin, Dolly Bell, Jane Hamilton, Gigi Parrish, Bonnie Bannon, Dolores Casey].

For a performer with a very defined range of talents, the ebullient Eddie Cantor had a long (more than a half-century) and varied career, which encompassed vaudeville, Broadway, radio, movies, recordings and television. Much more of a personality than an actor, Cantor proved popular in early sound films. ROMAN SCANDALS, an interesting and elaborately mounted fantasy musical for producer Samuel Goldwyn, has proven to be one of his more enduring screen vehicles. It emerged as a result of Goldwyn wanting to feature his star in an adaptation of George Bernard Shaw's *Androcles and the Lion;* when this did not materialize he contracted Robert E. Sherwood and George S. Kaufman to write a comparable vehicle. Broadway's Kaufman and Sherwood had stipulated that Cantor was not to alter their script; when he did, they sued (and won and returned to New York). Goldwyn brought in a scad of additional writers to polish up the script, which bore more than passing parallels to Mark Twain's *A Connecticut Yankee in King Arthur's Court.* Nevertheless, ROMAN SCANDALS was the most spectacular of the Cantor-Goldwyn collaborations, filled with curvacious—and in one sequence nearly nude—chorines. It even managed to allow the rambunctious Cantor to perform his standard blackface number in the midst of a Roman bath house!

Wistful yet optimistic young Eddie (Eddie Cantor) resides in West Rome, Oklahoma. Because he has the simple-minded audacity to oppose the town's most influential and dishonest man, banker Warren F. Cooper (Willard Robertson), who wants to dispossess poor tenants from their homes to build a huge jail, he is ordered to leave town. Eddie daydreams that he is living in ancient times and is "transported" back to Rome, where as Oedipus he soon encounters the rapacious Emperor Valerius (Edward Arnold) who is so pleased to have been made to laugh (Eddie uses "magical" gas fumes) that he insists on bringing the newcomer back to the palace as the new official food taster. This places Eddie in a very precarious situation, for Empress Agrippa (Verree Teasdale) is attempting to poison her husband's food, so she can become ruler. Also at the royal domain—besides a bevy of gorgeous female slaves—is Princess Sylvia (Gloria Stuart), captured from another country. While the Emperor desires her, she loves Josephus (David Manners), an idealistic young nobleman who champions the poor. With Eddie's assistance, the couple escape from the imperial soldiers in a wild chariot race. In the midst of the chase Eddie falls from a cliff, at which point he awakens. He is back in West Rome, Oklahoma, where he discovers a check written by the banker. With this evidence he has the crook indicted and is soon restored to his position as grocery store clerk.

While the plot amounted to little more than a thread on which to hang amusing (and often anachronistic) gags and lush production numbers, ROMAN SCANDALS benefitted greatly from songs by Harry Warren and Al Dubin. As was customary in Eddie Cantor musicals, he had an upbeat, optimistic song, here called "Build a Little Home." In the ancient Roman setting, he dons blackface to exhort the bevy of girls at the sumptuous deco bath house to "Keep Young and Beautiful." Surrounded by rotating mirrored doors which magnified the intricate cast movements, the set piece was a lavish high point in the screen career of choreographer-stager Busby Berkeley. For a slave market scene, Berkeley convinced several of the chorines (here as Roman slave girls) to appear naked (with their long blonde wig tresses decorously covering their nudity). This was used as a backup to torch singer Ruth Etting—as the character Olga—singing "No More Love."

When it premiered on Christmas Eve Day in 1933, the *New York Times* noted, "Busby Berkeley is responsible for the costly numbers with the dancing girls, and he makes the most of the sequence in which Mr. Cantor sings 'Keep Young and Beautiful.' Some of the fun is effective without being especially keen wit. . . . Mr. Cantor does as well as possible in his role and he is exceptionally good in the episodes in which he sings."

ROMAN SCANDALS was Busby Berkeley's final film for Samuel Goldwyn at United Artists. He then returned to Warner Bros. to make the musical WONDER BAR (1934) with Al Jolson, Kay Francis, Dolores Del Rio and Dick Powell.

ROSALIE (Metro-Goldwyn-Mayer, 1937) 123 minutes.

Producer, William Anthony McGuire; director, W. S. Van Dyke II; based on the musical play by McGuire, Guy Bolton, Sigmund Romberg, George Gershwin; screenplay, McGuire; art director, Cedric Gibbons; set decorator, Edwin B. Willis; costumes, Dolly Tree; music director, Herbert Stothart; choreographer, Albertina Rasch; camera, Oliver T. Marsh; editor, Blanche Sewell.

Songs: "I've Got a Strange New Rhythm in My Heart," "Why Should I Care?" "Spring Love Is in the Air," "Rosalie," "It's All Over But the Shouting," "Who Knows?" "In the Still of the Night," "To Love or Not to Love," "Close" (Cole Porter); "The Caissons Go Rolling Along" (Edmund L. Gruber); "On, Brave Old Army Team" (Philip Enger); "Anchors Aweigh" (Alfred Miles, Royal Lovell, Charles A. Zimmerman); "M'Appari" from the opera *Martha* (Friedrich von Flotow); "Polovetsian Dances" from the opera *Prince Igor* (Alexander Borodin); excerpts from the ballet "Swan Lake," Act II (Peter Ilyich Tchaikovsky); "Goodbye Forever (Addio)" (Paolo Tosti); "Washington Post March," "Stars and Stripes Forever," "Semper Fidelis," "El Capitan" (John Philip Sousa); "Parade" (Herbert Stothart); "Wedding March" from the incidental music to a performance of William Shakespeare's *A Midsummer Night's Dream* (Felix Mendelssohn); "Gaudeamus Igitur" (traditional); "Oh Promise Me" (Reginald DeKoven, Scott Clement).

Nelson Eddy (Dick Thorpe); Eleanor Powell (Rosalie Romanikoff); Ray Bolger (Bill Delroy); Frank Morgan (King Frederic Romanikoff); Ilona Massey (Brenda); Edna May Oliver (Queen); Billy Gilbert (1st Officer Oloff); Reginald Owen (Chancellor); George Zucco (General Maroff); Virginia Grey (Mary Callahan); Tom Rutherford (Prince Paul); Janet Beecher (Miss Baker); Clay Clement (Captain Banner); Oscar O'Shea (Mr. Callahan); William Demarest (Army's Coach); Rush Hughes (Announcer); Wallis Clark (Major Prentice); Richard Tucker (Colonel Brandon); Jerry Colonna (2nd Officer Joseph); Wilson Benge (Steward); Pierre Watkin (Superintendent of the Academy); Tommy Bond (Mickey); Purnell Pratt (Ship Captain); Ricca Allen (School Teacher); Al Shean (Herman Schmidt); Frank Du Frane (Superintendent's Aide); Ocean Claypool, Katharine [Kay] Aldridge (Ladies in Waiting); Edward Earle (Navy Officer); George Magrill (Assistant Army Coach); Lane Chandler (Army Coach); Phillip Terry, William Tannen (Cadets); George Humbert (Carlo); Max Davidson (Chamberlain); Harry Semels, Roy Barcroft, John Picorri, Sidney Bracy (Conspirators); and: The Albertina Rasch Dancers.

For his first starring film role without Jeanette MacDonald, Nelson Eddy was assigned the lead in ROSALIE, a top-heavy effort which surprisingly did not sink his career. In fact, so popular was Nelson Eddy at the time that ROSALIE was one of MGM's top-grossing pictures for the 1937–38 season. Although it borrowed its title and some plotline from the 1928 Broadway show which had starred Marilyn Miller, the movie discarded the score by Sigmund Romberg and George Gershwin. Cole Porter was hired to provide Nelson Eddy with the title tune and "In the Still of the Night." Tap dancing co-star Eleanor Powell did well by "I've a Strange New Rhythm in My Heart." Overall, though, the *New York World Telegram* summed it up by dubbing ROSALIE "a long-winded and artificial operetta." ROSALIE utilized bits of footage from ROSALIE, MGM's 1930 Marion Davies musical that had never been released.

Dick Thorpe (Nelson Eddy) is the football hero of West Point.

In the big game with Navy he attempts to defer playing so that his pal Delroy (Ray Bolger) will look good for his girl Mary (Virginia Grey). However, Delroy nearly loses the match before Dick finally steps in to save the day. Watching the game are Vassar student Rosalie (Eleanor Powell) and her friend Brenda (Ilona Massey). Dick is attracted to Rosalie and tries to romance her with a song. Actually Rosalie is the Princess of the country of Romanza. Its General Maroff (George Zucco) soon comes to take her home to marry its Chancellor (Reginald Owen), a union arranged by her mother (Edna May Oliver) to save their kingdom. Rosalie consents reluctantly. With Delroy in tow, Dick follows her to Romanza in his plane, but he has trouble finding the country, thanks to two dizzy airport radio operators (Billy Gilbert, Jerry Colonna). The King (Frank Morgan), Rosalie's benign father, greets Dick upon his arrival and the visitor is soon reunited with Rosalie. Later, when a revolution threatens the homeland, all the principals depart for West Point, where Rosalie masquerades as a cadet before she and Dick are finally allowed to wed.

Whatever one may say about the cumbersome scenario or the fact that at age thirty-six Nelson Eddy was too mature to be a collegiate gridiron champ, ROSALIE provided Eddy with several excellent vocal opportunities. Additionally, it was a wonderful showcase for the precision tap dancing of athletic Eleanor Powell, especially in the awesome title number (with its scads of extras filling a cavernous set) and in her more intimate "I've a Strange New Rhythm in My Heart," which she performs at the Vassar dorm, gliding from room to room.

Variety assessed, "It is in the festival scenes that ROSALIE really shows its cinematic girth. Setting for the peasant's folk dances seems as big as Soldiers' Field, Chicago. . . . In the midst of this ensemble Miss Powell does an acrobatic tap atop some massive drums which must have been very difficult. . . ." Of the wedding scene finale, the trade paper gasped, "There are 10 massive organ keyboards for music, scores of lovely bridesmaids in candled 40-foot Valentines for decorations, and a regiment for the military escort. The newlywed couple probable [*sic*] have 15 bridal suites."

THE ROSE (20th Century-Fox, 1979) Color 134 minutes.

Executive producer, Tony Ray; producers, Marvin Worth, Aaron Russo; director, Mark Rydell; story, Bill Kerby; screenplay, Kerby, Bo Goldman; production designer, Richard MacDonald; art director, Jim Schoppe; set decorator, Bruce Weintraub; costume designer, Theoni V. Aldredge; costume supervisor, April Ferry; makeup, Jeff Angell; music arranger/music supervisor, Paul A.

Rothchild; choreographer, Toni Basil; concert supervisor, Ron DeBlasio; second unit director, Barry Primus; assistant directors, Larry Franco, Chris Doldo; sound, Jim Webb, Chris McLaughlin; sound re-recording, Theodore Soderberg, Douglas O. Williams, Paul Wells; supervising sound editor, Kay Rose; camera, Vilmos Zsigmond; additional concert camera, Bob Byrne, Conrad Hall, Jan Kiesser, Laszlo Kovacs, Steve Lydecker, Michael Margolies, David Meyers, Owen Roizman, Haskell Wexler; editor, Robert L. Wolfe; co-editor, Timothy O'Meara.

Songs: "The Rose" (Amanda McBroom); "Stay with Me" (Jerry Ragavoy, George Weiss); "Camellia" (Stephen Hunter); "The Night We Said Goodbye" (Bill Elliott); "Evil Lies" (Greg Prestopino, Carol Locatell); "Sold My Soul to Rock 'n' Roll" (Gene Pistilli); "Keep on Rockin' " (Sammy Hagar, John Carter); "Fire Down Below" (Bob Segar); "I've Written a Letter to Daddy" (Larry Vincent, Henry Tobias, Mo Jaffe); "When a Man Loves a Woman" (C. Lewis, A. Wright); "Midnight in Memphis" (Tony Johnson); "Whose Side Are You On?" (Kenny Hopkins, Charley Williams); "Let Me Call You Sweetheart" (Leo Friedman, Beth Slater Whitson).

Bette Midler (Rose [Mary Rose Foster]); Alan Bates (Rudge); Frederic Forrest (Houston Dyer); Harry Dean Stanton (Billy Ray); Barry Primus (Dennis); David Keith (Mal); Sandra McCabe (Sarah Willingham); Will Hare (Mr. Leonard); Rudy Bond (Monty); Don Calfa (Don Frank); James Keane (Dealer); Doris Roberts (Rose's Mother); Sandy Ward (Rose's Father); Michael Greer (Master of Ceremonies); Claude Sacha, Michael St. Laurent, Sylvester, Pearl Heart (Female Impersonators); Butch Ellis (Waiter); Richard Dioguardi, Luke Andreas, Seamon Glass (Truckers): John Dennis Johnston (Milledge); Jonathan Banks (Television Promoter); Jack O'Leary (Short Order Cook); Harry Northup (Skinny Guy); Cherie Latimer (Secretary); Pat Corley (Police Chief); Dennis Erdman (Billy Ray's Kid); Hugh Gillin (Guard); Joyce Roth (Waitress in Airport); Frank Speiser (Reporter at Rose's House); Constance Cawlfield, Dimo Condos, Lorrie Davis, David Garfield, Kathryn Grody, Jack Hollander, Sandra Seacat, Chip Zien, Ted Harris (Reporters); Annie McGuire (Don Frank's Wife); Hildy Brooks (Waitress in Diner); Jack Starrett (Dee); Victor Argo (Lockerman); Kelly Boyd (Blonde Girl in Leonard's); Cyndi Gottfried (Redhaired Girl in Leonard's); L. D. Frazier (Doorman at Nightclub); Lawrence Guardino (Cop at Police Station); Tom Hubiak (Cab Driver); Phil Rubenstein (Pot Belly); Charlie McCarthy (Cop in Luxor Baths); Danny Weiss, Steve Hunter, Robbie Louis Buchanan, Jerome Noel Jumonville, Norton Buffalo, Mark Leonard, Mark Underwood, Pentti "Whitey" Glan (The Rose Band); Rodney Dillard, Douglas Dillard, Byron Berline

Bette Midler in THE ROSE (1979).

(Billy Ray Band); Mark Jordan, Fred Beckmeier, David Kalish, Gary Ferguson (Club 77 Band); Greg Prestopino, Bill Elliot, Jon Sholle, Scott Chambers, Harry Stinson (Monty's Band).

THE ROSE, a tour-de-force for entertainer Bette Midler, was a sordid account of a Janis Joplin-like rock singer, who climbed to the heights of success only to end up killing herself by living in the fast lane too long. Grossing $22.6 million in distributors' domestic film rentals, THE ROSE obtained an Oscar nomination for its star, who lost as Best Actress to Sally Field (of NORMA RAE). Bette Midler did win a Grammy Award for Best Contemporary/Pop Female Solo vocal for the title song from the film. She also had a chart hit with "The Rose" and another song from the movie, "When a Man Loves a Woman." The soundtrack album to THE ROSE was also a best-seller, being on *Billboard* magazine's charts for twenty-three weeks and rising to #12 position. In THE ROSE, Bette Midler performed a variety of vocally difficult numbers which amply displayed her versatile singing style and poignant phrasing.

In the late 1960s, Rose, alias Mary Rose Foster (Bette Midler) is one of the biggest names in rock music. However, her personal life is a shambles of drink and drugs and is cluttered with the parasites who have surrounded her since she became famous. She has a love-hate relationship with her grasping, cold-hearted British manager Rudge (Alan Bates), who gives her drugs when she threatens to quit the business. On a series of one-night stands in the South she finds sexual satisfaction with her new employee, chauffeur Houston Dyer (Frederic Forrest), an Army sergeant who has gone AWOL. Also involved with the Rose are her road manager, Dennis (Barry Primus), and bodyguard Mal (David Keith). While on the tour her life becomes more complicated when a woman named Sarah Willingham (Sandra McCabe) competes with Dyer for Rose's physical favors and Dyer leaves her (although he later returns). Eventually Rose's hedonistic life style takes over her existence. Too much booze and dope cause her death while she is performing in a home town concert in Florida.

Variety intoned, "Director Mark Rydell has delivered a lengthy and impassioned exposé of the dark side of the music biz, but it's questionable to what degree contemporary audiences wish to identify with the subject matter. . . . It's a tribute to the talent of Midler herself that she makes the basically unsympathetic and unlikeable character attractive at all." The editors of *Consumer Guide* and Philip J. Kaplan wrote in *The Best, The Worst and the Most Unusual: Hollywood Musicals* (1983), "THE ROSE would not work without Bette Midler. She has a complex personality: vulnerable (crying when an old-time country and western singer says he doesn't like the way she recorded his songs), impulsive (starting a fight in a restaurant where they 'don't serve hippies'), and self-mocking (joining a nightclub's female impersonator in his version of 'The Rose'). The concert footage is dynamic because Midler brings this mix of emotion to every song." Richard Combs (British *Monthly Film Bulletin*) enthused, ". . . The film has a surprising freshness—its plot does not seem to have been dimly fabricated, as in most pop-music sagas, to get from one number to the next, and it avoids the concomitant danger of being left with no structure at all through the strength of its performances. . . . THE ROSE is certainly not as original a readjustment of the film musical as, say, NEW YORK, NEW YORK [1977], but it does allow an original performer to make the transition from one medium to another with more integrity (for both) than is usual."

Other Oscar nominations for THE ROSE were Best Supporting Actor (Frederic Forrest), Sound and Editing.

The next year Bette Midler would be seen on-screen in

DIVINE MADNESS (1980), *q.v.,* a recreation of a concert appearance. But thereafter her career moved away from screen musicals. After the disastrous comedy, JINXED (1982) she turned to comedies such as DOWN AND OUT IN BEVERLY HILLS (1986) and to dramas such as STELLA (1990). The soapy melodrama, BEACHES (1988), allowed her to sing several songs, including her extremely popular rendition of "Wind Beneath My Wings." The soundtrack album to BEACHES became a best-seller.

ROSE MARIE (Metro-Goldwyn-Mayer, 1936) 110 minutes.

Producer, Hunt Stromberg; director, W. S. Van Dyke, II; based on the operetta by Otto A. Harbach, Oscar Hammerstein, II, Rudolf Friml, Herbert Stothart; screenplay, Frances Goodrich, Albert Hackett, Alice Duer Miller; art directors, Cedric Gibbons, Joseph Wright, Edwin B. Willis; costumes, Adrian; music director, Stothart; Totem pole dance staged by Chester Hale; operatic sequences staged by William von Wymetal; Sheldon Brooks; sound supervisor, Douglas Shearer; camera, William Daniels; editor, Blanche Sewell.

Songs: "Indian Love Call," "Rose Marie" (Rudolf Friml, Otto Harbach, Oscar Hammerstein, II); "Pardon Me, Madame," "Finaletto" (Herbert Stothart, Gus Kahn); "The Mounties," "Totem Tom Tom" (Friml, Stothart, Harbach, Hammerstein, II); "Just For You" (Friml; adaptor, Stothart; new lyrics, Kahn); "Tes Yeux" (Rene Alphonse Rabey); "St. Louis Blues" (W. C. Handy); "Dinah" (Harry Akst, Sam Lewis, Joe Young); "Three Blind Mice" (traditional); "Some of These Days" (Shelton Brooks); arias from the opera *Romeo et Juliette* (Charles Gounod) and the opera *Tosca* (Giacomo Puccini).

Jeanette MacDonald (Marie de Flor); Nelson Eddy (Sergeant Bruce); James Stewart (John Flower); Reginald Owen (Myerson); George Regas (Boniface); Robert Greig (Cafe Manager); Una O'Connor (Anna); James Conlin (Joe, the Piano Player); Lucien Littlefield (Storekeeper); Dorothy Gray (Edith); Alan Mowbray (Premier); Mary Anita Loos (Corn Queen); Aileen Carlyle (Susan); Halliwell Hobbes (Mr. Gordon); Paul Porcasi (Emil, the Chef); David Niven (Teddy); Herman Bing (Mr. Danielle); Gilda Gray (Belle); Allan Jones (Romeo/Mario Cavaradossi); Bert Lindley (Pop); Edgar Dearing (Mounted Policeman); Pat West (Traveling Salesman); Milton Owen (Stage Manager); David Clyde (Doorman); Russel Hicks (Commandant); Rolfe Sedan, Louis Mercier (Admirers in Hall); Jack Pennick (Brawler); Leonard Carey (Louis); David Robel, Rinaldo Alacorn (Dancer); Matty Roubert (Newsboy); Major Sam Harris (Guest); Ernie Alexander (Elevator

Operator); James Mason (Trapper); John George, Lee Phelps (Barflies); Fred Graham (Corporal); Agostino Borgato, Adrian Rosley (Opera Fans); Delos Jewkes (Butcher at Hotel).

TV title: INDIAN LOVE CALL.

See: ROSE MARIE (1954) (essay).

ROSE MARIE (Metro-Goldwyn-Mayer, 1954) Color 115 minutes.

Producer/director, Mervyn LeRoy; based on the operetta by Otto A. Harbach, Oscar Hammerstein, II, Rudolf Friml, Herbert Stothart; screenplay, George Froeschel; art directors, Cedric Gibbons, Merrill Pye; costumes, Helen Rose; music director, George Stoll; choreographer, Busby Berkeley; camera, Paul Vogel; editor, Harold F. Kress.

Songs: "Rose Marie," "The Indian Love Call," "The Mounties," "Totem Tom Tom" (Rudolf Friml, Otto Harbach, Oscar Hammerstein, II); "The Right Place for a Girl," "Free to Be Free," "I Have Love," "Love and Kisses" (Friml, Paul Francis Webster); "The Mountie Who Never Got His Man" (George Stoll, Herbert Baker).

Ann Blyth (Rose Marie Lemaitre); Howard Keel (Mike Malone); Fernando Lamas (James Severn Duval); Bert Lahr (Barney McCorkle); Marjorie Main (Lady Jane Dunstock); Joan Taylor (Wanda); Ray Collins (Inspector Appleby); Chief Yowlachie (Black Eagle); James Logan (Clerk); Thurl Ravenscroft (Indian Medicine Man); Abel Fernandez (Indian Warrior); Billy Dix (Mess Waiter); Al Ferguson, Frank Hagney (Woodsmen); Marshall Reed (Mountie); Sheb Wooley (Corporal); Dabbs Greer (Committeeman); John Pickard, John Damler (Orderlies); Sally Yarnell (Hostess); Gordon Richards (Attorney); Lumsden Hare (Judge); Mickey Simpson (Trapper); Pepi Lanzi (Johnny Lang).

One of Rudolf Friml's most popular operettas, composed with Otto A. Harbach, Oscar Hammerstein, II and Herbert Stothart, was *Rose Marie.* It debuted on Broadway in the fall of 1924 starring Dennis King and Mary Ellis and had a run of 557 performances. The production included some of Friml's loveliest melodies, including "Indian Love Call," "Song of the Mounties," "Totem Tom Tom" and, of course, the title song. In 1928, MGM made the first of its three screen versions of the property, but this ROSE MARIE was a silent effort starring Joan Crawford, James Murray, House Peters, Creighton Hale and Gibson Gowland.

The definitive screen adaptation of ROSE MARIE came in 1936 when MGM re-teamed Jeanette MacDonald and Nelson Eddy—who had scored a sensation in NAUGHTY MARIETTA (*q.v.*) the year before—in a high-budget production which sported beautiful Lake Tahoe locations which focused on the majestic Sierra Nevadas.*

In Canada, glamorous opera star Marie de Flor (Jeanette MacDonald) is enjoying a tremendously successful concert tour. But she has personal problems. Her brother John Flower (James Stewart) has been jailed for his participation in a holdup. Marie intends to ask the premier of Canada, an admirer of her singing talents, to pardon her brother. Before she can put her plan into operation, she learns from a half-breed Indian guide named Boniface (George Regas) that John has escaped from jail, is wounded and has murdered a Mountie in the process. Abandoning her tour, and with Boniface as her guide, Marie sets out for the north woods wilderness to find her brother. Robbed and deserted by her shifty guide, Marie is left stranded in a trading post town. To earn extra money, she sings in a dance hall, much to the chagrin of local entertainer Belle (Gilda Gray), but she attracts the attention of handsome Mountie Sergeant Bruce (Nelson Eddy), who recognizes her as the diva. She, not knowing he is on her brother's trail, falls in love with him. He serves as her guide until Boniface happens to return. The latter returns her money and agrees to take her to John, but later again disappears. Sergeant Bruce follows her and later captures John. Seeing how her loved one has betrayed her, she leaves him in disgust and returns to the city. While performing the opera *Tosca* she collapses and has a complete breakdown. Her distraught manager (Reginald Owen) sends for Sergeant Bruce. With the Mountie's help, she regains her will to live and they plan their future together.

The richly appointed escapism of ROSE MARIE proved to be an ideal vehicle for Jeanette MacDonald and Nelson Eddy, and it was one of the most successful of their screen pairings. In it they sang "Indian Love Call," the song most associated with them (and one which sold over one million copies when they recorded it for RCA). Eddy also does well with "Rose Marie" and his stalwart version of "The Mounties," while the spectacular production dance number, "Totem Tom Tom," is well staged by Chester Hale.** In the film's early sequences MacDonald is given an opportunity to perform an excerpt from the opera *Romeo and Juliet* opposite Allan

*Originally Jeanette MacDonald and Nelson Eddy were to have teamed in a musical entitled CHAMPAGNE AND ORCHIDS, for which Jerome Kern and Oscar Hammerstein, II were commissioned to do the score. That project was dropped.

**The spectacular "Totem Tom-Tom" segment of the 1936 ROSE MARIE was shot at Emerald Bay on Lake Tahoe. It employed several hundred Indians as extras in its elaborate setting featuring enormous, grotesque totems.

Jones, and later she sings selections from *Tosca.* To show the down-to-earth side of the star, MacDonald is paired with Gilda Gray (famous for her "Shimmy" dance) in a cabaret sequence in which they give a rousing rendition of "Some of These Days."

Advertised with the slogan, "A pampered pet of the opera meets a rugged Canadian mountie," the film opened on January 31, 1936. The *New York Times* cheered, "As blithely melodious and rich in scenic beauty as any picture that has come from Hollywood . . . ," and added, of the two stars, "In splendid voice, whether singing solo or in duet, they prove to be fully as delightful a combination here as they were in the film of Victor Herbert's NAUGHTY MARIETTA [1935, *q.v.*]. . . ."

By acting standards of later generations, ROSE MARIE leaves much to be desired, for MacDonald is extremely coy and overly coquettish, and Eddy is often quite wooden. However, considered within its structural confines and the demands of movie operetta of the day, ROSE MARIE and its two stars are wonderfully effective. It was due to a concerned Nelson Eddy (whose marquee allure gave him great clout at the studio) that Allan Jones, a rival MGM

Nelson Eddy and Jeanette MacDonald in ROSE MARIE (1936).

contractee, had his role as MacDonald's opera partner diminished greatly in the final print of ROSE MARIE.

Due to the 1954 MGM remake, the 1936 edition of ROSE MARIE was retitled INDIAN LOVE CALL for TV showings.

The early 1950s saw Hollywood panicking over the inroads being made by competing television. They answered the onslaught with gimmicky 3-D and widescreen processes which gave filmmakers an excuse to remake a rash of old properties, now with the "bonus" of spectacular vistas and costly settings—anything to overshadow small-screen television. MGM found itself remaking operettas like THE MERRY WIDOW (1952), *q.v.,* and THE STUDENT PRINCE (1954), ignoring the fact that such old-fashioned operettas were alien to newer generations. ROSE MARIE, 1954-style, boasted CinemaScope, Eastman color, location work in the Canadian Northwest, and several plot changes from the 1936 adaptation.

Canadian Mounted policeman Sergeant Mike Malone (Howard Keel) attempts to tame tomboy Rose Marie (Ann Blyth), by carrying out a promise he made to her late father. He takes her to Fort McLeod to be civilized. Rose Marie soon grows accustomed to life at the post, but Malone's superior officer (Ray Collins) orders that she go to Maple Rock to live with raucous Lady Jane Dunstock (Marjorie Main), an innkeeper. Under Dunstock's big-hearted tutelage, Rose Marie blossoms into a lady and Mike falls in love with her. While she cares for the Sergeant, her romantic attentions are diverted by French Canadian trapper James Severn Duval (Fernando Lamas), a Robin Hood-like bandit. His interest in Rose Marie arouses the jealousy of Wanda (Joan Taylor), an Indian maiden who had been Duval's lover. Later, when Wanda is whipped by the chief (Chief Yowlachie) of her tribe for her indiscretions, she stabs him to death with a knife Duval once gave her. Duval is arrested for the crime and is sentenced to death. However, at the last minute, Malone proves the man's innocence. A grateful Rose Marie offers to marry the Mountie, but he accepts that she truly loves Duval. He leaves the scene, making way for Rose Marie and Duval to wed.

Musically the 1954 film (despite stereophonic sound) was far less exciting than the 1936 outing, although baritone Howard Keel does very well by the title song and "The Mounties." He does *not* duet with Ann Blyth on "Indian Love Call," that number going to her and Fernando Lamas. On a comedy note (which plays a far greater role in this version), Bert Lahr as Marjorie Main's cockeyed love interest, Barney McCorkle, clowned with "I'm a Mountie Who Never Got His Man." For the new production, Rudolf Friml

(1879–1972) wrote (with Paul Francis Webster) several new numbers, including "The Right Place for A Girl" (sung by Keel), "Free to Be Free" (performed by Blyth) and "Love and Kisses" (scratched out by the impish Lahr and the barrel-voiced Main).

Comparing the two talkie versions of ROSE MARIE, the *New York Times* decided, "The MacDonald-Eddy operetta . . . was golden compared to this generally flat-tasting Mulligan stew." The paper added, "Mainly, and interminably, a dull, wooden drama dominates. . . ."

In 1959 there appeared off-Broadway *Little Mary Sunshine,* with music, lyrics and book by Rick Besoyan. The satirical operetta was a send-up of *Rose Marie* and operettas of that ilk. It starred Eileen Brennan, William Graham, Elmarie Wendel and John McMartin. It lasted a rousing 1,143 performances.

ROSE OF THE RANCHO (Paramount, 1936) 85 minutes.

Producer, William LeBaron; director, Marion Gering; based on the play by Richard Walton Tully, David Belasco; screenplay, Frank Partos, Charles Brackett, Arthur Sheekman, Nat Perrin, Harlan Thompson, Brian Hoker; costumes, Travis Banton; camera, Leo Tover; editor, Hugh Bennett.

Songs: "If I Should Lose You," "Thunder Over Paradise," "Little Rose of the Rancho," "Got a Girl in Cal-i-for-ni-ay," "There's Gold in Monterey," "Where Is My Love?" "The Padre and the Bride" (Ralph Rainger, Leo Robin).

John Boles (Jim Kearney); Gladys Swarthout (Don Carlos [Rosita Castro]); Charles Bickford (Joe Kincaid); Willie Howard (Pancho Spiegelgass); Herb Williams (Phineas P. Jones); Grace Bradley (Flossie); H. B. Warner (Don Pasqual Castro); Charlotte Granville (Dona Petrona); Don Alvarado (Don Luis); Minor Watson (Jonathon Hill); Louise Carter (Guadalupe); Pedro de Cordoba (Gomez); Paul Harvey (Boss Martin); Arthur Aylesworth (Sheriff James); Russell Hopton (Frisco); and: Benny Baker, Harry Woods.

The popularity of screen opera and operetta in the mid-1930s persuaded Paramount to sign Metropolitan Opera star Gladys Swarthout to a contact. She made her screen debut in a version of the Richard Walton Tully-David Belasco play, *Rose of the Rancho* (1906). Ralph Rainger and Leo Robin composed a half-dozen tunes for the feature. John Boles, who had gained success in screen operettas in the early sound era, did well by songs like "If I Should Lose You," "Little Rose of the Rancho," and "Where Is My Love?" while Willie Howard (as a Jewish cowboy from the south!) did the comedy number, "A Girl in Cal-i-for-ni-ay."

In the 1850s Old California, just after it became a U.S. possession, the Spanish citizens are having their lands illegally confiscated by crooked Joe Kincaid (Charles Bickford) and his minions. They are opposed by the masked Don Carlos, the daring leader of the Spanish vigilantes. Government agent Jim Kearney (John Boles), along with bumbling assistant Pancho Spiegelgass (Willie Howard), are dispatched to stop Don Carlos. Upon his arrival Kincaid meets beautiful Rosita (Gladys Swarthout), whose father Don Pasqual Castro (H. B. Warner) is about to lose his rancho to the usurpers. Jim falls in love with Rosita and then discovers she is the masked Don Carlos. The revelation helps him to realize the plight of the Spanish citizens and he helps her in bringing Kearney and his underlings to justice.

Variety termed the movie "pretty out-moded plot stuff." *Harrison's Reports* decided, "Paramount 'muffed' this picture. Although it has produced it on a lavish scale, it is nothing but a glorified Western, with many defects . . . Gladys Swarthout, the Metropolitan Opera singer, makes a good impression in her first screen appearance; but her singing, particularly in the high notes, is spoiled by poor recording. And it is doubtful if the songs, with the exception of one, will prove popular." The *New York Times* complained, ". . . The enterprise is an unhappy, screen debut for Miss Swarthout, who possesses the qualities for a first-rate musical personality in the cinema. Mr. Boles doesn't get very far away from that prettiness which made some of us regret President Lincoln's decision to save him from the firing squad in THE LITTLEST REBEL [1935]."

Paramount would re-team Boles and Swarthout for ROMANCE IN THE DARK (1938), but when that minor effort flopped, the studio abandoned hopes of making her a rival to Jeanette MacDonald or Grace Moore. They put the opera star into her fifth and final studio release, the non-musical AMBUSH (a "B" action movie). Thereafter, she returned to the stage, radio and recordings.

ROSE OF WASHINGTON SQUARE (20th Century-Fox, 1939) 86 minutes.

Producer, Darryl F. Zanuck; associate producer, Nunnally Johnson; director, Gregory Ratoff; story, John Lark, Jerry Horwin; screenplay, Johnson; art directors, Richard Day, Rudolph Sternad; set decorator, Thomas Little; costumes, Royer; music director, Louis Silvers; choreographer, Seymour Felix; sound, Eugene Grossman, Roger Heman; camera, Karl Freund; editor, Louis Loeffler.

Songs: "I Never Knew Heaven Could Speak" (Mack Gordon, Harry Revel); "Rose of Washington Square" (James Hanley, Ballard MacDonald, Joseph McCarthy); "The Curse of An Aching Heart" (Al Piantadosi, Henry Fink); "I'm Sorry I Made You Cry" (N. J. Clesi); "The Vamp" (Byron Gay); "Ja-Da" (Bob Carleton); "I'm Just Wild about Harry" (Noble Sissle, Eubie Blake); "My Man" (Maurice Yvain; English lyrics, Channing Pollock); "California, Here I Come" (Buddy G. DeSylva, Joseph Meyer, Al Jolson); "My Mammy" (Joe Young, Sam Lewis, Walter Donaldson); "Pretty Baby" (Gus Kahn, Tony Jackson, Egbert Van Alstyne); "Toot Toot Tootsie Goodbye" (Kahn, Ernie Erdman, Dan Russo); "Rock-A-Bye Your Baby with a Dixie Melody" (Jean Schwartz, Lewis, Young).

Tyrone Power (Bart Clinton); Alice Faye (Rose Sargent); Al Jolson (Ted Cotter); William Frawley (Harry Long); Joyce Compton (Peggy); Hobart Cavanaugh (Whitney Boone); Moroni Olsen (Buck Russell); E. E. Clive (Barouche Driver); Louis Prima (Himself); Charles Wilson (Mike Cavanaugh); Hal K. Dawson, Paul Burns (Chumps); Ben Welden (Toby); Horace MacMahon (Irving); Paul Stanton (District Attorney); Harry Hayden (Dexter, the Apartment Owner); Charles Lane (Kress, the Booking Agent); Igor and Tanya (Specialty Performers); Chick Chandler (Master of Ceremonies); Murray Alper (Candy Butcher); Ralph Dunn (Officer); Edgar Dearing (Lieutenant); Robert Shaw (Reporter); James Flavin (Guard); Leonard Kibrick (Newsboy); Irene Wilsen (Miss Lust); Bert Roach (Mr. Paunch); Adrian Morris (Jim); John Hamilton (Judge); Winifred Harris (Mrs. Russell); Maurice Cass (Mr. Mork, the Furniture Buyer).

The third and final screen teaming of pretty Alice Faye and handsome Tyrone Power, who had scored well with IN OLD CHICAGO (1938), *q.v.*, and ALEXANDER'S RAGTIME BAND (1938), *q.v.*, was a 1920s musical loaded with many Jazz Age tunes and a syrupy plot. The script bore more than a slight resemblance to the life of comedienne-singer Fanny Brice (1891–1951), even to having Alice Faye warble Brice's trademark song, "My Man." Brice sued 20th Century-Fox, but the matter was settled out of court. This period musical proved to be another box-office boon for the studio. It was Al Jolson's next-to-last major film role, followed by SWANEE RIVER (1939), *q.v.* The *New York Times* noted that his contribution to the film was "something for the memory book." The film was directed by actor-turned-director Gregory Ratoff and the choreography was by Seymour Felix (a prolific dance director whose musicals extended from SUNNY SIDE UP, *q.v.*, in 1929 to THE "I DON'T CARE" GIRL in 1953).

In the 1920s cabaret singer Rose Sargent (Alice Faye) is down on her luck. She meets con man Bart Clinton (Tyrone Power) at a Long Island resort and is immediately attracted to the handsome chiseler, but he leaves when accused of stealing an expensive necklace. Better luck befalls Rose's pal, former singing waiter Ted Cotter (Al Jolson), who winds up with a hit act after a drunk (Hobart Cavanaugh) interrupts his singing and the two (star and stooge) are signed for a Broadway revue. Rose gets a job in a speakeasy. One evening Bart arrives just in time to rescue her when a police raid takes place. Soon the two fall in love. At a party for Ted, Rose sings a song and agent Harry Long (William Frawley) hears her and wants to sign her. However, Bart insists that he owns her contract—which he does not—and sells it to Long for $2,500. When Ted confronts him about it, Bart gets back the money by selling the furniture in the swanky apartment he is leasing from a friend. Despite her awareness of his shady past, Rose and Bart eventually marry and honeymoon in Europe. She returns to New York to appear in the *Ziegfeld Follies* and scores a big hit. Meanwhile, Bart almost goes to jail over the bogus furniture sale. Needing quick money, he joins a crime ring and is captured by the law during a robbery. Ted posts his $50,000 bail, but reading the newspaper headlines, a chagrined Bart, who fears going to prison, disappears. Sometime later he returns to hear Rose sing. He turns himself in and is sentenced to five years in prison. A tearful Rose promises to wait for him.

Naturally, the highlight of ROSE OF WASHINGTON SQUARE is its many finely staged period songs and production numbers (although the costumes, inexplicably, were very contemporary). Alice Faye's tune, "I Never Knew Heaven Could Speak," was especially written for the film. Her most touching moment in ROSE OF WASHINGTON SQUARE was her rendition of "My Man," sung on stage with Power in the audience. The emotional plight of her life gave the lyrics additional dimension. Al Jolson dynamically performed a number of his old favorites in this film, including "Rock-A-Bye Your Baby with a Dixie Melody," "My Mammy" and several others. Unfortunately, his renditions of "Avalon" and "I'm Always Chasing Rainbows" ended up on the cutting room floor, as did Faye's singing of "I'll See You in My Dreams."

The *New York Times* recorded, "Obviously designed as a thematic sequel to ALEXANDER'S RAGTIME BAND, the picture makes much the same capital of its sentimentally evocative score, its nostalgic reminders of the speakeasy era, its delicate reminder that the Nineteen Twenties already have become a 'costume period' . . . . The picture was at its best when the Mammy specialist [Al Jolson] held the spotlight."

Some decades later, the life of the real Fanny Brice would serve as the basis for the stage and movie version of FUNNY GIRL (1968), *q.v.*, with Barbra Streisand winning an Oscar for playing the comedienne. Streisand also filmed a sequel, FUNNY LADY (1975), *q.v.*

ROYAL WEDDING (Metro-Goldwyn-Mayer, 1951) Color 93 minutes.

Producer, Arthur Freed; director, Stanley Donen; story/screenplay, Alan Jay Lerner; art directors, Cedric Gibbons, Jack Martin Smith; set decorators, Edwin B. Willis, Alfred E. Spencer; makeup, William J. Tuttle; music director, Johnny Green; orchestrators, Conrad Salinger, Skip Martin; choreographer, Nick Castle; assistant director, Marvin Stuart; color consultants, Henri Jaffa, James Gooch; sound supervisor, Douglas Shearer; special effects, Warren Newcombe; camera, Robert Planck; editor, Albert Akst.

Songs: "Ev'ry Night at Seven," "Sunday Jumps," "Open Your Eyes," "The Happiest Day of My Life," "How Could You Believe Me When I Said I Love You When You Know I've Been a Liar All My Life?" "Too Late Now," "You're All the World to Me," "I Left My Hat in Haiti," "What a Lovely Day for a Wedding" (Burton Lane, Alan Jay Lerner); "How About You" (Lane, Arthur Freed); "The Devonshire Regiment" (traditional; arranger, Paul Marquardt).

Fred Astaire (Tom Bowen); Jane Powell (Ellen Bowen); Peter Lawford (Lord John Brindale); Sarah Churchill (Anne Ashmond); Keenan Wynn (Irving Klinger/Edgar Klinger); Albert Sharpe (James Ashmond); Viola Roache (Sarah Ashmond); Henri Letondal (Purser); James Finlayson (Cabby); Alex Frazer (Chester); Jack Reilly (Pete Cumberly); William Cabanne (Dick); John Hedloe (Billy); Francis Bethancourt (Charles Gordon); Jack Daley (Pop); James Horne (Young Man); Jack Gargan (Bartender); Kerry O'Day (Linda); Pat Williams (Barbara); Jimmy Fairfax (Harry); Eric Wilton (Man); Andre Charisse (Steward); Bess Flowers, Oliver Cross (Guests); Mae Clarke, Helen Winston (Phone Operators); Margaret Bert (Ellen's Maid); Wilson Benge (Stage Door Man); Leonard Mudie (Man); Phyllis Morris (Woman); David Thursby (Bobby); Wilson Wood (Man in Bar); Dee Turnell, Judy Lenson, Doreen Hayward, Shirley Rickert, Marian Horosko, Carmes Clifford, Italia DeNubelo, Betty Hannon, Charlotte Hunter, Janet Lavis, Sheila Meyers, Pat Simms, Dorothea Ward, Joan Vohs, Marietta Elliott, Svetlana McLe, Doris Wolcott, Bee Allen, Joane Dale, Shirley

Fred Astaire in ROYAL WEDDING (1951).

Glickan, Jean Harrison, Lucille Lamarr, Virginia Lee, Jetsy Parker, Dorothy Tuttle ("Haiti" Number).

To take advantage of the worldwide popularity of the marriage of Princess Elizabeth and Prince Philip in London, the Arthur Freed unit at MGM came up with ROYAL WEDDING. It deftly interpolated newsreel footage of the festivities into its London-based plot by Alan Jay Lerner, who also provided the lyrics to Burton Lane's songs. Originally June Allyson was set to co-star with Fred Astaire. It would have been her first musical assignment since WORDS AND MUSIC (1948) and her first co-starring role with Fred Astaire. However, Allyson, then married to Dick Powell, discovered she was pregnant. The MGM hierarchy replaced her with Judy Garland, who had been teamed with Astaire for EASTER PARADE (1948), *q.v.,* and had been scheduled to star with the dancing Fred in THE BARKLEYS OF BROADWAY (1949), *q.v.,* before emotional instability caused her exit from that. Since then Garland had made SUMMER STOCK (1950), *q.v.,* with Gene Kelly. Garland reported to the set of ROYAL WEDDING for one day, but after that her recurring personal problems became so severe that she was dropped from the project and soon left the studio. (This prevented her from accepting the role of Julie in MGM's remake of SHOW BOAT [1951], *q.v.,* which went to Ava Gardner.) The third choice for the role was MGM's soprano sweetheart, the young Jane Powell. Her performance in ROYAL WEDDING turned her into a full-fledged star and got her away from the squeaky clean ingenue roles she had specialized in during the 1940s. With such pre-production turmoil, it is amazing that director Stanley Donen turned out such a relaxed, proficient piece of celluloid musical comedy.

While the song-and-dance team of Tom Bowen (Fred Astaire) and his young sister Ellen (Jane Powell) enjoy their individual romantic flings, they avoid marriage, fearful of breaking up the partnership. Their agent, Irving Klinger (Keenan Wynn), books them for an engagement abroad. En route, Ellen is courted by charming John Brindale (Peter Lawford). Soon after arrival, Tom becomes entranced with earnest dancer Anne Ashmond (Sarah Churchill), who has auditioned for a part in the revue. Meanwhile, neither Tom nor Ellen will admit to one another that they are contemplating marriage, each insisting their career comes first. Complicating Tom's romance is that Anne feels a loyalty to a former beau who has gone abroad. However, Edgar Klinger (Keenan Wynn), Irving's twin brother and the team's London agent, discovers that her old beau is now married. On the day of the Royal wedding, Tom and Ellen find themselves in the London streets and caught up in the crowd's enthusiasm. They both decide to overcome their inhibitions and to get married. Each rushes off to find his/her mate and head to a church for a double wedding.

Despite its thin plotline, ROYAL WEDDING is a slick and entertaining production. It smartly gained additional publicity by casting British Prime Minister Sir Winston Churchill's daughter Sarah in the second female lead. In this film—her American screen debut—she gave one of her better celluloid performances. She even danced confidently in a brief sequence with Fred Astaire. While ROYAL WEDDING is not one of Alan Jay Lerner's best musicals, its numbers fit well within the framework of the movie's story. Jane Powell is in fine voice for "Too Late Now" (which became something of a song hit) and "The Happiest Day of My Life." She also sang "Open Your Eyes," which glides into a ballroom dance between her and Astaire aboard ship and ends with the performers frantically coping with the ship's pitching. "I Left My Hat in Haiti" is performed as a big production number, with Astaire singing and both he and Powell dancing. Astaire and Powell (in a black wig as a gum-chewing moll!) duet on the amusing "How Could You Believe Me When I Said I Loved You When You Know I've Been a Liar All of My Life" (a song reminiscent of the English musical hall). Astaire has two dance solos in ROYAL WEDDING. The first, "Sunday Jumps" (an instrumental), occurs in the ship's gym, and the second is set in his London hotel room. There, inspired by a picture of Sarah Churchill on his dresser, he announces "You're All the World to Me" and begins to dance exuberantly—not only on the floor but also (thanks to trick photography) on the walls and ceiling. (It would become one of his most celebrated gimmick dance numbers.) Prepared for ROYAL WEDDING but not used in the picture were the vocal versions of "Sunday Jumps" and "I Got Me a Baby."

"Like most of the big-scale MGM musicals in Technicolor, this one offers the type of entertainment that has always proved popular with most picture-goers. It is a breezy mixture of songs, dances, comedy and romance which, despite a featherweight story, keeps one fully entertained. The surprise of the picture is the excellent dancing ability displayed by Jane Powell . . ." (*Harrison's Reports*).

Shot on a thirty-three-day shooting schedule at a cost of $1,590,920, ROYAL WEDDING grossed over $3,925,000 in its initial release. ROYAL WEDDING was Oscar-nominated for Best Song ("Too Late Now").

British release title: WEDDING BELLS.

RUMBA *see* BOLERO (essay).

SALLY (First National, 1929) Color 103 minutes. (Also silent version).

Director, John Francis Dillon; based on the musical play by Guy Bolton, Jerome Kern, Clifford Grey, P. G. Wodehouse; screenplay/dialogue, Waldemar Young; art director, Jack Stone; costumes, Edward Stevenson; music director, Leo F. Forbstein; choreographer, Larry Ceballos; camera, Dev Jennings, C. Edgar Schoenbaum; editor, Leroy Stone.

Songs: "Look for the Silver Lining" (Jerome Kern, Buddy G. DeSylva); "Sally" (Kern, Clifford Grey); "Walking Off Those Balkan Blues," "After Business Hours (That Certain Business Begins)," "All I Want to Do, Do, Do Is Dance," "If I'm Dreaming Don't Wake Me Up Too Soon," "What Will I Do Without You?" (Al Dubin, Joe Burke).

Marilyn Miller (Sally); Alexander Gray (Blair Farquar); Joe E. Brown (Connie); T. Roy Barnes (Otis Hooper); Pert Kelton (Rosie); Ford Sterling (Pops Shendorff); Maude Turner Gordon (Mrs. Ten Brook); E. J. Ratcliffe (Josh Farquar); Jack Duffy (The Old Roué); Nora Lane (Marcia Ten Brook); and: the Albertina Rasch Ballet.

Popular musical comedy star Marilyn Miller (1898–1936) made her motion picture debut in SALLY, repeating her 1920 stage role. The play had been filmed as a silent in 1925 by First National with Colleen Moore top-featured. For her initial screen outing, Miller was paid $1,000 per hour by First National and the resultant color feature was a moneymaker.*

Cafe hostess Sally (Marilyn Miller) wants to be a dancer. She is in love with rich Blair Farquar (Alexander Gray), but his family wants him to marry equally wealthy Marcia Ten Brook (Nora Lane). When Sally spills food on booking agent Otis Hooper (T. Roy Barnes), she is fired from her job and goes to work at the Balkan Tavern for Pops Shendorff (Ford Sterling) and becomes a sensation by performing a Russian dance with a waiter (and former aristocrat) named Connie (Joe E. Brown). When Sally and Connie entertain at Mrs. Ten Brook's (Maude Turner Gordon) garden party, she learns about Blair's engagement to Marcia and leaves. Later Hooper finds Sally living in a tenement and hires her to star in a musical revue

*First National Pictures, which had Marilyn Miller under a four-year contract, proclaimed, "Now the Screen has robbed the stage of its most prize possession! . . . . Broadway's brightest dancing beauty will make her first film appearance. . . ." Regarding the musical itself, the studio's publicity department announced, "Every feature that kept Sally on Broadway for one solid year—stunning show girls, gorgeous gowns, lavish settings, and the matchless beauty of its famous star—ALL IN COLOR."

where she is well received. Blair breaks off with Marcia and he and Sally plan to wed.

"The glorious, scintillating dancing of Marilyn Miller, lovely Ziegfeld star, saves this from being merely a dull transcript of an outmoded musical comedy," wrote *Photoplay* magazine. *Variety* was more blunt, "Trouble seems to be that the studio took the stage script not only seriously, but literally. . . . Result is that the opening half hour is so deadly that the film never fully recovers." While Joe E. Brown did his best with his comedy antics, he had to live up to comparisons with his stage counterpart, Leon Errol, and the comparisons were not favorable. The picture was loaded with songs. Only two numbers ("Sally" and "Look for the Silver Lining") were retained from the original Broadway show (which had a run of 570 performances). Al Dubin and Joe Burke wrote five new numbers for the movie, including "All I Want to Do, Do, Do Is Dance," all geared to showcase the talents of the high-priced Miller.

By the time Marilyn Miller turned to motion pictures, she had passed her physical peak and the musical film was already losing its appeal. She would make two more starring features, SUNNY (1930), *q.v.,* and HER MAJESTY LOVE (1931), the latter with W. C. Fields. Shortly before her death she was scheduled to make a guest appearance in THE GREAT ZIEGFELD (1936), *q.v.,* but when she demanded an exorbitant salary, her guest cameo was deleted and Rosina Lawrence filled in a brief scene as Marilyn Miller.

SALLY, IRENE AND MARY (20th Century-Fox, 1938) 86 minutes.

Producer, Darryl F. Zanuck; associate producer, Gene Markey; director, William S. Seiter; based on the play by Edward Dowling, Cyril Wood; adaptors, Karl Tunberg, Don Ettinger; screenplay, Harry Tugend, Jack Yellen; art directors, Bernard Herzbrun, Rudolph Sternad; set decorator, Thomas Little; costumes, Gwen Wakeling; music director, Arthur Lange; choreographers, Nick Castle, Geneva Sawyer; sound, Arthur Von Kirbach, Roger Heman; camera, Peverell Marley; editor, Walter Thompson.

Songs: "Got My Mind on Music," "Sweet as a Song" (Mack Gordon, Harry Revel); "Minuet in Jazz" (Raymond Scott); "Half Moon on the Hudson," "I Could Use a Dream," "This Is Where I Came In," "Who Stole the Jam?" "Help Wanted: Male" (Walter Bullock, Harold Spina); "Hot Potata" (Jimmy Durante).

Alice Faye (Sally Day); Tony Martin (Tommy Reynolds); Fred Allen (Gabriel "Gabby" Green); Jimmy Durante (Jefferson Twitchell); Gregory Ratoff (Baron Zorka); Joan Davis (Irene Keene);

Marjorie Weaver (Mary Stevens); Louise Hovick [Gypsy Rose Lee] (Joyce Taylor); J. Edward Bromberg (Pawnbroker); Barnett Parker (Oscar); Raymond Scott Quintette (Themselves); Eddie Collins (Captain); Andrew Tombes (Judge); Brian Sisters (Themselves); Mary Treen (Miss Barkow); Charles Wilson (Cafe Manager).

Produced as a silent feature in 1925 starring Constance Bennett, Sally O'Neil and Joan Crawford, SALLY, IRENE AND MARY was converted into a musical by 20th Century-Fox as a screen pairing for Alice Faye and Tony Martin (who were married at the time). However, it proved to be a minor screen event at best. *Film Weekly* noted, "Played more 'straight' and shorn of some of its more extravagant moments, it would have been a first-rate musical comedy-romance." The *New York Times* was more explicit about the movie, "It's a forthright exploitation of the voice, full lips and other things of Alice Faye and her tenor-husband, Tony Martin. . . . Speaking personally, we've had enough close-ups of the luscious Miss Faye, whose inability to speak or sing without throwing her mouth into trembles has begun to wear us down."

Sally Day (Alice Faye), Irene Keene (Joan Davis) and Mary Stevens (Marjorie Weaver) are manicurists working for barber Oscar (Barnett Parker), but they long to be stage performers. An audition for Baron Zorka (Gregory Ratoff) is ruined by their agent Gabby Green (Fred Allen), but he gets them non-singing jobs at a Greenwich Village club called the Covered Wagon, where they meet singer Tommy Reynolds (Tony Martin). Glib Gabby persuades rich widow Joyce Taylor (Louise Hovick [Gypsy Rose Lee]) to finance a show to star Tommy and his three clients. However, Joyce has her romantic cap set for Tommy and becomes jealous of his growing affection for Sally. She demands that Sally be fired. When this happens, both Sally and Tommy leave and nearly starve before Mary comes to the rescue with the news that she has inherited an old ferry boat, the *General Freemont.* Gabby has the bright idea to turn it into a showboat-restaurant. To acquire the needed money to redecorate the vessel, Tommy agrees to wed Joyce, while Sally accepts the Baron's marriage proposal. (Neither knows that the other is about to make such a sacrifice.) With his partner, Jefferson Twitchell (Jimmy Durante), Gabby turns the boat into a classy showplace and Tommy and Sally are set to headline its big show. However, on opening night Twitchell almost ruins everything by causing the old boat to break away from its moorings. All is set right, though, and the show goes on, to a huge audience response. Sally and Tommy decide to wed, while the Baron and Joyce, who will make a profit from the club venture, decide to join forces.

As the star of the proceedings, Alice Faye sang "This Is Where I Came In," "Half Moon on the Hudson" and "Got My Mind on Music." She joined with Marjorie Weaver, Joan Davis and the young Brian Sisters for the "Big Apple" number, "Who Stole the Jam?" The mustachioed Martin crooned "I Could Use a Dream" and "This Is Where I Came In." Gangling Joan Davis, who struggled to provide some zany relief in SALLY, IRENE AND MARY, did the comic "Help Wanted: Male," and Jimmy "Schnozzola" Durante performed his old standby composition, "Hot Potata." The Raymond Scott Quintette did "Minuet in Jazz." Faye's "Think Twice" number was cut from the film, while for condensed showings of the picture on television, "Half Moon on the Hudson" is often deleted, as are Faye's dance moments from "Minuet in Jazz."

This was rubber-faced Joan Davis' fourth feature with Alice Faye; they had already shared screen time in ON THE AVENUE (1937), WAKE UP AND LIVE (1937) and YOU CAN'T HAVE EVERYTHING (1937), *qq.v.* They would be together one final time, in the abortive adventure drama, TAILSPIN (1939). At the time, 20th Century-Fox was promoting Marjorie Weaver for major stardom, but she never really shone in any of her many screen appearances. This was the final movie teaming of Faye and Tony Martin. They divorced in 1940.

SALSA (Cannon, 1988) Color 99 minutes.

Producers, Menahem Golan, Yoram Globus; associate producer, Kenny Ortega; director/story, Boaz Davidson; screenplay, Davidson, Tomas Benitez, Jeffrey Stacey, Simon Barron, Eric Wall, John Isabeau; production designer, Mark Haskins; set decorator, Kate Sullivan; costumes, Carin Hooper; makeup, Lesa Nielsen, Annette Fabrizi; music supervisors, Jack Fishman, Michael Linn; choreographers, Ortega, Miranda Garrison; music instrument staging, Jan Parent, Johnny Caswell; music editors, John Strauss, Robert Randles; second unit director, Ortega; assistant directors, Elie Cohn, Michael Kennedy, Jeffrey Stacey, Simon Barron, Eric Wall, John Isabeau; stunt coordinator, Al Jones; sound, Peter Bentley, Kim Ornitz, T-Bone Pascuzzo, Tina Canny; sound re-recording, Corey Bailey, Pat Cyccone, Frank A. Montano, Jr., David Cunningham; supervising sound editor, Bruce Bell; ADR/foley recording, Jim Bryan, Ben Wong; ADR editors, Ken Zimmerman, Nino Centurion; camera, David Gurfinkel; second unit camera, Frank Holgate, Gideon Porath; editor, Alain Jakubowicz.

Songs: "The Magic of Your Love" (David Friedman, Armanda George); "Every Teardrop" (Joyce Carlsen, Donald Cromwell);

"Which Way?" (Gabor Presser, Larry Kahn); "Son Matamoros" (Tata Guerra); "Chicos y Chicas" (Michelle Aller, Bob Esty); "My Blood Is Hot" (Michael Bishop, John Bigham, Wayne Linsey); "Maybe Baby" (Jean-Claude Naimro, Georges Decimus, Alex Masters); "Spanish Harlem" (Jerry Leiber, Phil Spector); "Loco" (Marco Antonio Cossio, Arturo Cabrera); "Lime Juice (Canto Limon)" (Barbara George); "Cali Pachanguero" (Jaairo Vorela, Georges Sigara); "Good Lovin' " (Arthur Resnik, Rudy Clark); "Oye Como Va," "Mambo Guzon" (Tito Puente); "Blue Suede Shoes" (Carl Perkins); "Under My Skin" (Michael Sembello, Randy Boydstun); "Apple Salsa" (Pat Kelly Bill Boydstun); "Salsa Heat" (Sembello, Rick Bell); "Puerto Rico" (Sembello, Bobby Caldwell, Randy Waldman, Wilkins); "Mucho Money" (L. Dermar, J. Galdo, R. Vigil).

Robby Rosa (Rico); Rodney Harvey (Ken); Magali Alvarado (Rita); Miranda Garrison (Luna); Moon Orona (Lola); Angela Alvarado (Vicki); Loyda Ramos (Mother); Valente Rodriguez (Chuey); Daniel Rojo (Orlando); Humberto Ortiz (Beto); Roxan Flores (Nena); Robert Gould (Boss); Deborah Chesher (Sister); Debra Ortega, Renee Victor (Aunts); Joanne Garcia (Waitress); Leroy Anderson, Chain Reaction, Celia Cruz, The Edwin Hawkins Singers, Grupo Latino, Mongo Santamaria, Tito Puente, Bobby Caldwell, Willie Sembello, H. Wilkins (Themselves); Patrick Alan, Marty Alvarez, Robert Alvarez, Eryn Bartman, Marylynn Benitez, Tony Burrer, Joanne Caballero, Juan Cabral, Tina Cardinale, Joyce Carlsen, Greg Carrillo, Bernard Ceballos, Carlos Eduardo Correa, Baruch Kozlo Darling, Charlie De Cali, Marco De La Cruz, Jose De Leon, Gregory De Silva, Toledo Diamond, Melissa Fahn, Daisy Flood, Jesus Fuentes, Joanne Garcia, Rafael Garcia, Marcial Hinestrosa, Monica Hinestrosa, Veronique Hinestrosa, Dr. Memo Huang, Liz Imperio, Louise Kawabata, Daniel Klein, Constance Marie Lopez, Tiger Martina, Steve Messina, David Norwood, Lisa Nunziella, Debra Ortega, Michael Parker, D. A. Pawley, Marla Rebert, Kamar Reyes, Jaqueline Rios, Kirk Rivera, Robert Rossi, Ana Marie Sanchez, Paul Guzman Sanchez, Thomas Guzman Sanchez, Pallas Sluyter, Linda Talcott, Nancy Todescheni, Paula Venise Vasquez, Eddie Vega, Renee Victor, Allen Walls, Adria Wilson, Mari Winsor, James Woodbury (Featured Dancers).

Following his successful choreography of DIRTY DANCING (1987), *q.v.*, Kenny Ortega did the same for SALSA. However, the results were not as good, according to Leonard Klady (*Los Angeles Times*) who said: ". . . [Ortega] could easily claim self-defense in killing director Boaz Davidson. Certainly Davidson's penchant for cutting away from the dancers to close-ups of elbows murders whatever artistry Ortega had evolved." He also noted, "SALSA just might be the hottest dirtiest dancing of the season, but we'll never know. The ads promise some flashy footwork, but the camera framing stubbornly insists on cutting its subjects off at the knees. Instead of sweep and sass, we get wall-to-wall musical coverage of that infectious Latin beat played at ear-splitting levels." Despite its new trappings, SALSA proved a distinct ripoff of SATURDAY NIGHT FEVER (1977), *q.v.,* and obviously hoped to cash in on the appeal of the similarly Latino-oriented LA BAMBA (1987), *q.v.*

Twenty-one-year-old Los Angeles auto mechanic Rico (Robby Rosa), a devoted "salsero" (salsa dancer), wants to become the "King of Salsa" at the forthcoming festival de San Juan. The prize is a trip to Puerto Rico. To do so, he teams with his girlfriend Vicki (Angela Alvarado), but it does not take him long to realize that they are not a good dance team, since the girl is not overly talented. At the East Los Angeles club, La Luna, Rico attracts the attention of its owner, Luna (Miranda Garrison), a former Queen of Salsa who is attempting a comeback. He dumps Vicki as a dance partner and joins with Luna in the hopes of winning the coveted dance title. Another beautiful, sensual young woman (Moon Orona) works at seducing Rico, while he becomes involved in trying to break up a romance between his sixteen-year-old sister Rita (Magali Alvarado) and his best friend, Ken (Rodney Harvey). In the process, Rico loses sight of his goal to win the contest. After Rita is slightly hurt in a car accident, she and Ken persuade the morose Rico to show up for the big competition. He does so, but partners not with Luna but with Vicki.

Certainly movie musicals have changed greatly since the days of Fred Astaire and Ginger Rogers, as can be seen in this tale of Los Angeles Latinos and their hot-blooded dances. Still, the plot remains no more realistic than those of bygone times, especially when the mechanic hero sports $600 duds and dances at a crowded club that has available parking spaces! Tongue-in-cheek the *Los Angeles Weekly* summed it up: "*Nada* story, *nada* and laughable dialogue, and whatever salsa there may have been (in the *bailes,* in the *musica*) is wasted by a distant camera, as distant as a *turista's* gaze upon our exotic *raza.*"

The ad campaign for SALSA read, "The Sun Goes Down, The Lights Come Up, The World Turns On To. . . . SALSA. . . . IT'S HOT!"

SATISFACTION (20th Century-Fox, 1988) Color 92 minutes.

Executive producers, Rob Alden, Armyan Bernstein; producers, Aaron Spelling, Alan Greisman; associate producer, Ilene

Chaiken; director, Joan Freeman; screenplay, Charles Purpura; production designer, Lynda Paradise; set decorator, Ernie Bishop; costumes, Eugenie Bafaloukos; makeup, Arlette Greenfield, Cheri Minns; music, Michael Colombier; music director, Peter Afterman; assistant director, Jerry Ketcham; special effects, John Gray; sound, Willy Burton; camera, Thomas Del Ruth; editor, Joel Goodman.

Songs: "(I Can't Get No) Satisfaction" (Mick Jagger, Keith Richards); "Knock on Wood" (Steve Cropper, Eddie Floyd); "Iko, Iko" (Joan Johnson, Joe Jones, Marilyn Jones, Sharon Jones, Jes Thomas, Barbara Hawkins, Rosa Hawkins); "C'mon Everybody" (Eddie Cochran, Jerry Capeheart); "Talk to Me" (Cropper); "Mr. Big Stuff" (Joe Broussard, Carol Jerry Capeheart); "Lies (Are Breaking My Heart)" (Beau Charles, Buddy Randell); "Dedicated to the One I Love" (Ralph Bass, Lowman Pauling); "Loving You Is Like a Suicide Mission" (David Bethany); "Rock & Roll Rebel" (John Kay, Michael Wilk, Rocket Ritchotte); "I've Been Down Before" (Antonina Armato, Kerry Knight); "Maybe" (Richard Barret); "Just Jump into My Life" (Mona Lisa Young); "God Bless the Child" (Billie Holiday); "Prelude No. 7, No. 28" (Frederic Chopin).

Justine Bateman (Jennie Lee); Liam Neeson (Martin Falcon); Trini Alvarado (May "Mooch" Stark); Scott Coffey (Nickie Longo); Britta Phillips (Billy Swan); Julia Roberts (Daryle Shane); Debbie Harry (Tina); Chris Nash (Frankie Malloy); Michael De Lorenzo (Bunny Slotz); Tom O'Brien (Hubba Lee); Kevin Haley (Josh); Peter Craig (Mig Lee); Steve Cropper (Sal); Alan Greisman (Bob Elden); Sheryl Ann Martin (Sylvia); Lia Romaine (Lexie); Wyatt Pringle (Man in Wild Pants at Party); Greg Roszyk (Guy at Party); "The Killer Whales" (The Blow Fish).

The trend of putting teenage TV stars in teenage theatrical movies was continued in SATISFACTION, which headlined Justine Bateman from the small screen's "Family Ties" sitcom program. "Watching SATISFACTION," Michael Wilmington wrote in the *Los Angeles Times,* "sometimes feels like being dropped into a time-warping Vegematic. This is a movie—supposedly about an '80s rock band—where the songs date from the '60s, the language and sexual attitudes suggest the '70s and the plot is pure '50s." Ironically, the film was produced by Steve Cropper, the guitarist with the popular 1960s Stax Band. He also made a brief appearance in the feature as a bartender, and rock star Debbie Harry also had a fleeting role.

Jennie Lee (Justice Bateman) is the lead singer of a garage band which features 1960s rock music. Also in the musical group are drummer-street hoodlum Mooch (Trini Alvarado), guitarist Billy

(Britta Phillips), who is on drugs, and Daryle (Julia Roberts), the bass player with boyfriend troubles. When a young man in the neighborhood, Nickie Longo (Scott Coffey), a classical pianist, is hired to round out the group, they land a summer job at an Atlantic Ocean beach resort, working for Martin Falcon (Liam Neeson), a once famous 1960s songwriter. Jennie falls in love with Martin as the band carries out its assignment, and Nickie romances Mooch. At the season's end, Jennie realize she does not love Martin, but was attracted only to his image.

Regarding the film's lack of entertainment value, *Daily Variety* noted, "If not for a song every 10 minutes or so, even the most easily entertained viewer might start nodding off. . . . It just reinforces what most adults have known for a long time—being a teenager can sure be dull." As for the musical's "name" star, the trade paper weighed, "SATISFACTION doesn't live up to its title and Justine Bateman singing of the w.k. [well known] Rolling Stone song, or any song for that matter, can't save this adolescent tale from being a bore."

SATURDAY NIGHT FEVER (Paramount, 1977) Color 119 minutes.

Executive producer, Kevin McCormick; producer, Robert Stigwood; associate producer, Milt Felsen; director, John Badham; based on the article "Tribal Rites of the New Saturday Night" by Nik Cohn; screenplay, Norman Wexler; set designers, George Detitta, John Godfrey; costumes, Patrizia Von Breandenstein, Jennifer Nichols; makeup, Max Herriquez; music, David Shire, Barry, Robin, and Maurice Gibb; choreographer, Lester Wilson [Lorraine Fields]; dance consultant, Jo-Jo Smith; assistant directors, Allan Wertheim, Joseph Ray; technical advisor, James Gambina; stunt coordinator, Paul Nuckles; sound, Les Lazarowitz; sound re-recording, John K. Wilkinson, Robert W. Glass, Jr., John T. Reitz; sound editor, Michael Colgan; camera, Ralf D. Bode; editor, David Rawlins.

Songs: "How Deep Is Your Love," "Night Fever," "Staying Alive," "You Should Be Dancing," "If I Can't Have You," "More Than a Woman," (Barry Gibb, Robin Gibb, Maurice Gibb); "Night on Disco Mountain," (based on "A Night on Bald Mountain" [Modest Mussorgsky]; adaptor, David Shire); "K-Jee" (Charles Hearndon); "A Fifth of Beethoven," adapted from "The Fifth Symphony" (Ludwig van Beethoven); "Disco Inferno" (Leo Green, Ron Kersey); "Open Sesame" (R. Bell, Kool and the Gang); "Dr. Disco," "Disco Duck" (Rick Dees); "Boogie Shoes" (H. W. Casey, R. Finch).

John Travolta in SATURDAY NIGHT FEVER (1977).

John Travolta (Tony Manero); Karen Lynn Gorney (Stephanie); Barry Miller (Bobby C.); Joseph Call (Joey); Paul Pape (Double J); Donna Pescow (Annette); Bruce Ornstein (Gus); Julie Bovasso (Flo); Martin Shakar (Frank, Jr.); Sam J. Coppola (Fusco); Nina Hansen (Grandmother); Lisa Peluso (Linda); Denny Dillon (Doreen); Bert Michaels (Pete); Robert Costanza (Paint Store Customer); Robert Weil (Becker); Shelly Batt (Girl in Disco); Fran Drescher (Connie); Donald Gantry (Jay Langhart); Murray Moston (Haberdashery Salesman); William Andrews (Detective); Ann Travolta (Pizza Girl); Monti Rock, III (DeeJay); Val Bisoglio (Frank, Sr.); Ellen Marca (Bartender); Helen Travolta (Woman in Paint Store).

To John Travolta goes the honor of starring in the two biggest moneymaking musical films, GREASE (1978), *q.v.,* and SATURDAY NIGHT FEVER, which brought in $74,100,000 in distributors' domestic film rentals. (The next year GREASE would generate $96,300,000 in distributors' domestic film rentals.) Unfortunately, Travolta's career, which began on Broadway (*Grease, Over Here!*) and spread to a TV sitcom series ("Welcome Back, Kotter"), did not sustain its popularity. However, for a brief time in the late 1970s, John Travolta was the king of movie musicals.

Nineteen-year-old Tony Manero (John Travolta) is a lower-middle-class Brooklyn youth who works as a clerk in a local paint store. Tony is at odds continually with his gross, unemployed father (Val Bisoglio), and his older brother (Martin Shakar) (who is studying for the priesthood, but is undergoing a questioning of his faith) tries to help smooth the path for his sibling. Tony is an excellent dancer and he and his pals hang out at the 2001 Odyssey disco where Tony excels at the flashy new dance craze. While he is lusted after by the promiscuous Annette (Donna Pescow), Tony spends his time dancing with the uppity Stephanie (Karen Lynn Gorney), whom he met recently at a dance studio. She belittles his narrow ambitions (to be a disco king) and boasts of her new secretarial job in a public relations agency and that she will soon relocate from Brooklyn to Manhattan. When Tony helps Stephanie make the move, he temporarily loses his job. He also discovers that she has been dating other men, which upsets him greatly. Meanwhile, his friends, feeling put upon by their Puerto Rican peers, raid a Puerto Rican gang, the Barracudas, who turn out not to be the ones who beat up Gus (Bruce Ornstein). That night at the dance contest, in a sudden rush of perspective and brotherhood, Tony turns over the first prize he and Stephanie have won, to a Puerto Rican couple. Still later that evening, Annette is raped by Tony's friends, and Bobby C (Barry Miller), distraught about a girl he made pregnant and is being forced to marry, falls to his death from a bridge. Meanwhile, a drunken Tony has made advances to Stephanie, who rejects him. A sobered Tony comes to Stephanie's apartment where he announces that he plans to leave Brooklyn and make something of his own life.

SATURDAY NIGHT FEVER is a musical in which the stars do NOT sing, only dance to the music of The Bee Gees on the soundtrack. (The soundtrack album was on *Billboard* magazine's hits chart for fifty-four weeks and in the number one position for twenty-four weeks.) As a result the film, as seen today, appears very outmoded. As noted by the editors of *Consumer Guide* and Philip J.

Kaplan in *The Best, The Worst and The Most Unusual: Hollywood Musicals* (1983), "SATURDAY NIGHT FEVER captures that glittering instant when disco music and disco dancing were the rage of the nation. The moment was only a short time ago, yet it already seems like history. Nothing dates faster than a dead fad. SATURDAY NIGHT FEVER already functions as nostalgia. Like so many good films, SATURDAY NIGHT FEVER survives because of its originality. The film did not merely recreate the disco phenomenon, it was instrumental in the movement's success. SATURDAY NIGHT FEVER helped spread disco dancing to its greatest heights and provided many of the most popular dance moves." In *The Paramount Story* (1985), John Douglas Eames wrote, "The whole theatre fairly vibrated with excitement while the audience caught SATURDAY NIGHT FEVER. Starting with a rather shabby, slice-of-life look, it quickly developed into one of those rare pictures glowing with the aura of a smash hit." On the other hand, *Variety* estimated, "SATURDAY NIGHT FEVER is nothing more than an updated '70s version of the Sam Katzman rock music cheapies of the '50s. That is to say, Robert Stigwood's production is a more shrill, more vulgar, more trifling, more superficial and more pretentious exploitation film."

In 1983 John Travolta, going through a career slump, repeated the role of Tony Manero, now trying to become a Broadway dancer while romancing two women, in STAYING ALIVE. The musical was directed and co-scripted by Sylvester Stallone. The picture, however, failed to recapture the magic of the original and did relatively mild business ($33,650,000 in distributors' domestic film rentals).

SAY IT WITH SONGS (Warner Bros., 1929) 95 minutes. (Also silent version: 5,699′).

Director, Lloyd Bacon; story, Darryl F. Zanuck, Harvey Gates; adaptor, Joseph Jackson; titles, De Leon Anthony; sound, George R. Groves; camera, Lee Garmes; editor, Owen Marks.

Songs: "Why Can't You?" "Used to You," "I'm in Seventh Heaven," "One Sweet Kiss" (Buddy G. DeSylva, Lew Brown, Ray Henderson); "Back in Your Own Backyard," "I'm Ka-razy about You" (Dave Dryer, Al Jolson, Billy Rose).

Al Jolson (Joe Lane); Davey Lee (Little Pal); Marion Nixon (Katherine Lane); Fred Kohler (Joe's Cellmate); Holmes Herbert (Dr. Robert Merrill); John Bowers (Surgeon); Kenneth Thompson (Arthur Phillips).

Popular songwriter and rising radio singer Joe Lane (Al Jolson) finds out that his best friend and the manager of the radio station for which he works, Arthur Phillips (Kenneth Thompson), has tried to romance Joe's wife Katherine (Marion Nixon). He confronts the man about her accusations. A fight ensues and Phillips is accidentally killed. Joe is sent to prison on manslaughter charges. When he is paroled, he visits his small son, Little Pal (Davey Lee). The boy begs his father to run away with him. Later, while earning extra money by selling newspapers, Little Pal is hit by a truck. The accident leaves his legs paralyzed; he is also unable to speak. While Joe was in jail, Katherine had become a nurse and has married Dr. Robert Merrill (Holmes Herbert). Joe takes the boy to Merrill for help and the doctor agrees to operate *if* Joe will return Little Pal to his mother. The surgery is a success and later Little Pal's voice returns after hearing one of his dad's recordings. Now that the boy is well again, Joe goes his own way.

SAY IT WITH SONGS was Al Jolson's third sound feature, following his huge success in THE JAZZ SINGER (1927) and THE SINGING FOOL (1928), *qq.v.* This movie also re-teamed him with Davey Lee from THE SINGING FOOL, although the little tyke does not sing in this entry. The feature, for which Jolson was paid $500,000, was loaded with songs sung by Jolson, including "Back in Your Own Backyard," co-written by the star. The tune "Little Pal" was a contrived attempt to repeat the hit status of "Sonny Boy" from THE SINGING FOOL. The more discerning filmgoer wondered where the background music came from, as Al Jolson chirped "Why Can't You?" from his jail cell.

By 1929 the musical and maudlin tearjerkers were growing stale. After a few more features Al Jolson would no longer be a major Hollywood screen property.

SCHOOL DAZE (Columbia, 1988) Color 120 minutes.

Executive producer, Grace Blake; producer, Spike Lee; co-producers, Loretha C. Jones, Monty Ross; director/screenplay, Spike Lee; production designer, Wynn Thomas; art director, Allan Trumpler; set decorator, Lynn Wolverton; costumes, Ruthe Carter; makeup, Teddy Jenkins; music, Bill Lee; choreographer, Otis Sallid; music editor, Lou Cerborino; assistant directors, Randy Fletcher, David Taylor, Parnes Cartwright, Lisa Jones, Roderick Giles, Shirlene Alice Blake; sound designer, Maurice Schell; sound, Rolf Pardula; sound consultant, Michael V. DiCosimo; sound re-recording, Tom Fleischman; sound editors, Kevin Lee, Peter Odabashian, Balsmeyer & Everett, Inc.; foley editor, Bruce Kitzmeyer; camera, Ernest Dickerson; editor, Barry Alexander Brown.

Songs: "I'm Building Me a Home" (arranger, Uzewe Brown);

"Straight and Nappy," "Be One," "Wake Up Suite" (Bill Lee); "I Can Only Be Me" (Stevie Wonder); "Perfect Match" (Lenny White, Tina Harris); "Kick It Out Tigers" (Consuela Lee Morehead); "Da Butt" (Marcus Miller, Mark Stevens); "We've Already Said Goodbye Before We Said Hello)" (Raymond Jones).

Larry Fishburne (Vaughn "Dap" Dunlap); Giancarlo Esposito (Julian "Big Brother Almighty" Eaves); Tisha Campbell (Jane Toussaint); Kyme (Rachel Meadows); Joe Seneca (President McPherson); Ellen Holly (Odrie McPherson); Art Eans (Cedar Cloud); Ossie Davis (Coach Odom); Bill Nunn (Grady); James Bond, III (Monroe); Branford Marsalis (Jordan); Kadeem Hardison (Edge); Eric A. Payne (Booker T.); Spike Lee (Half-Pint); Anthony Thompkins (Doo-Doo Breath); Guy Killum (Double Rubber); Dominic Hoffman (Mustafa); Roger Smith (Yoda); Kirk Taylor (Sir Nose); Kevin Rock (Mussolini); Eric Dellums (Slim Daddy); Darryl M. Bell (Big Brother X-Ray Vision); Rusty Cundieff (Big Brother Chucky); Cylk Cozart (Big Brother Dr. Feelgood); Tim Hutchinson (Big Brother Lance); Leonard Thomas (Big Brother General George Patton); Joie Lee (Lizzie Life); Alva Rogers (Doris Witherspoon); Delphine T. Mantz (Delphine); Terri Tracey (Traci); Sharon Ferrol (Sharon); Laurnea Wilkerson (Laurnea); Stephanie Clark (Stephanie); Eartha Robinson (Eartha); Angela Ali (Velda); Jhoe Breedlove (Kim); Paula Brown (Miriam); Tyra Ferrell (Tasha); Jasmine Guy (Dina); Karen Owens (Deidre); Michelle Whitney Morrison (Vivian); Greta Martin (Greta); Sharon Owens (Sharon); Frances Morgan (Frances); Monique Mannen (Monique "Mo-Freak"); Gregg Burge (Virgil Cloyd); Cinque Lee (Buckwheat); Kasi Lemmons (Perry); Toni Ann Johnson (Muriel); Paula Birth (Carla); Tracy Robinson (Roz); A. J. Johnson (Cecilia); Cassandra Davis (Paula); Michelle Bailey (Tina); Samuel L. Jackson (Leeds); Edward G. Bridges (Moses); Dennis Abrams (Eric); Albert Cooper (Spoon); Tracey Lewis (Counter Girl); Kelly Woolfolk (Vicky); Florante P. Galvez (Student in Bathroom); Leslie Sykes (Miss Mission); Dawn Jackson (1st Attendant); Angela Lewis (2nd Attendant); Phyllis Hyman, Bill Lee, Consuela Lee Morehead, Harold Vick, Joe Chambers (Phyllis Hyman Quartet); Valentino "Tino" Jackson; "Go Go" Mike Taylor, Gregory "Sugar Bear" Elliott, Jenario "Foxy Brown" Foxx, Kent Wood, Edward "Junie" Henderson, William "Ju Ju" Houyse, Ivan Goff, Darryl "Tidy" Hayes (EU Band); Keith John (Singer at Coronation); Reginald Tabor, Robert L. Cole, Jr., Lester McCorn, William N. Ross, Keith Wright, Derrek W. Jones, Harold L. Boyd II, Rod Hodge (Alpha Phi Alphas).

During the 1930s and 1940s, when many city theatres were

segregated racially, black film producers turned out scores of low-budget musicals for black audiences. With the 1950s and the climate of growing integration, such fare vanished from theatres. But in the 1980s a new interest in black musicals emerged, as exemplified by Spike Lee's SCHOOL DAZE. *Daily Variety* termed the feature, "A loosely connected series of musical set-pieces exploring the experience of blackness at an all-black university, film is a hybrid of forms and styles that never comes together in a coherent whole." Duane Byrge (*Hollywood Reporter*) decided, ". . . SCHOOL DAZE darts all over the place without a sympathetic central character and, right up to its fatuously righteous ending, its contending characters become progressively odious. . . . Spike Lee has given us no one to root for in SCHOOL DAZE."

At the all-black Mission College, a Southern university, there is growing friction between the black nationalist faction led by Vaughn Dunlap (Larry Fishburne) and the vigilantes, a reactionary group headed by Julian Eaves (Giancarlo Esposito). Dunlap seeks to incite the students to action in a rally which is interrupted by the members of Gamma Phi Gamma, a fraternity of which Eaves is a prime figure. The conflict causes repercussions on campus: the football coach (Ossie Davis) frets over the effect on the team, the college president (Joe Seneca) might be forced by the board of trustees to expel Vaughn, and the nervous student president (Gregg Burge) is caught in the middle as a mediator. In the midst of all this, Vaughn's cousin, Half-Pint (Spike Lee), goes undercover at the Gamma Phi Gamma house, but soon becomes so enamored with frat life that he wants to pledge the group. Moreover, Vaughn's girlfriend, Rachel Meadows (Kyme), insists that Vaughn is using her as a political expediency (because she is dark-skinned) and, in an act of rebellion, decides to pledge the Delta sorority. Bowing to a lack of support, Vaughn overcomes his idealistic nature and makes peace with the faction. He and Rachel are reunited, but the transformed Half-Pint has become an obnoxious rah rah frat boy. Vaughn is aghast at the dramatic changes in his cousin and this arouses him to a new crusade. He begins haranguing his peers anew.

While SCHOOL DAZE tries to incorporate various social issues into the framework of the musical, the ambitious attempt is too broad and ultimately unsatisfying. Overlong, the film "bumps and grinds along from the funky to the preach but without enough emotion," *Daily Variety* weighed. The trade paper also noted, "Almost as if he were trying to create a new genre single-handedly, Lee throws traditional rules of narrative filmmaking out the window in exchange for a collection of awkwardly-staged production numbers, one remarkably like the other. Lacking are characters to care about with compelling everyday problems." On the other hand, Roger Ebert (*Movie Home Companion, 1990,* 1989) was far more appreciative of multi-talented Lee's ambitious project: ". . . With utter frankness it addresses two subjects that are taboo in most 'black movies'—complexion and hair. Lee divides the women on his campus into two groups. . . . In a brilliant and startling song-and-dance sequence called 'Straight and Nappy,' they express their feelings for each other. Lee's choice of a musical production number to consider these emotionally charged subjects is an inspiration; there is possibly no way the same feeling could be expressed in spoken dialogue without great awkwardness and pain."

SCHOOL DAZE grossed $6,105,250 in distributors' domestic film rentals.

SEVEN BRIDES FOR SEVEN BROTHERS (Metro-Goldwyn-Mayer, 1954) Color 102 minutes.

Producer, Jack Cummings; director, Stanley Donen; based on the story "The Sobbin' Women" by Stephen Vincent Benet; screenplay, Albert Hackett, Frances Goodrich, Dorothy Kingsley; art directors, Cedric Gibbons, Urie McCleary; set decorators, Edwin B. Willis, Hugh Hunt; costumes, Walter Plunkett; music directors, Adolph Deutsch, Saul Chaplin; choreographer, Michael Kidd; assistant director, Ridgeway Callow; sound supervisor, Douglas Shearer; camera, George Folsey; editor, Ralph E. Winters.

Songs: "Bless Your Beautiful Hide," "Wonderful, Wonderful Day," "Lament," "Goin' Co'tin'," "Sobbin' Women," "June Bride," "Spring, Spring, Spring," "When You're in Love" (Gene dePaul, Johnny Mercer); "Lonesome Polecat."

Jane Powell (Milly); Howard Keel (Adam Pontabee); Jeff Richards (Benjamin Pontabee); Russ Tamblyn (Gideon Pontabee); Tommy Rall (Frank Pontabee); Howard Petrie (Pete Perkins); Virginia Gibson (Liza); Ian Wolfe (Reverend Elcott); Marc Platt (Daniel Pontabee); Matt Mattox (Caleb Pontabee); Jacques d'Amboise (Ephraim Pontabee); Julie Newmeyer [Newmar] (Dorcas); Nancy Kilgas (Alice); Betty Carr (Sarah); Ruta Kilmonis [Lee] (Ruth); Norma Doggett (Martha); Earl Barton (Harry); Dante DiPalo (Matt); Kelly Brown (Carl); Matt Moore (Ruth's Uncle); Dick Rich (Dorcas' Father); Marjorie Wood (Mrs. Bixby); Russell Simpson (Mr. Bixby); Anna Q. Nilsson (Mrs. Elcott); Larry Blake (Drunk); Phil Rich (Prospector); Lois Hall (Girl); Russ Saunders, Terry Wilson, George Robotham (Swains); Walter Beaver (Lem); Jarma Lewis (Lem's Girl Friend); Sheila James (Dorcas' Sister); Stan [I. Stanford] Joley, Tom Graham (Fathers); Betty Allen (Singing

Howard Keel and Jane Powell in SEVEN BRIDES FOR SEVEN BROTHERS (1954).

Voice of Dorcas); Marie Greene (Singing Voice of Alice); Betty Noyes (Singing Voice of Ruth); Bobbie Canvin (Singing Voice of Martha); Norma Zimmer (Singing Voice of Sarah); Bill Lee (Singing Voice of Caleb Pontabee); A. Davies, C. Parlato, Bob Wacker, Gene Lanham, M. Spergel, H. Hudson (Dubbers for Benjamin, Gideon, Frank, Daniel and Ephraim Pontabee and Chorus).

One of the most original and successful movie musicals of the 1950s was MGM's SEVEN BRIDES FOR SEVEN BROTHERS, which grossed $6.3 million in domestic film rentals. Based on the Stephen Vincent Benet story, "The Sobbin' Women," which in turn had its origin in the ancient Roman fable about the Rape of the Sabine Women, the production was highlighted by George Folsey's photography in Ansco Color and the athletic staging of the musical numbers by Michael Kidd. In fact, it is Kidd's energetic handling of the dances which gave the film most of its glow and zest, overshadowing the fact that this outdoors film was shot on confining MGM soundstages.

In frontier Oregon of the 1850s, Adam Pontabee (Howard

Keel), the oldest of seven brothers, comes home with a beautiful new bride, Milly (Jane Powell), a waitress in the town's cafe. His siblings, Benjamin (Jeff Richards), Gideon (Russ Tamblyn), Frank (Tommy Rall), Daniel (Marc Platt), Caleb (Matt Mattox) and Ephraim (Jacques d'Amboise), are taken with their new sister-in-law, not only because she is so nice and attractive, but because she is such a fine cook. The boys decide to get wives for themselves. After Adam relates to them the story of the "Sobbin' Women" who were kidnapped as brides in ancient times, the young men set out to accomplish the same thing after they fail to impress any of the local girls. The brothers kidnap Dorcas (Julie Newmeyer [Newmar]), Alice (Nancy Kilgas), Sarah (Betty Carr), Liza (Virginia Gibson), Ruth (Ruta Kilmonis [Lee]) and Martha (Norma Doggett). They take them to their mountain cabin. When a winter storm sets in the girls cannot be rescued by their families. During the winter, the couples learn to love each other. When the spring thaw comes, the girls' outraged parents arrive with a preacher (Ian Wolfe) to perform a mass shotgun wedding. Meanwhile, Milly has given birth to a baby.

The Johnny Mercer-Gene de Paul songs for SEVEN BRIDES FOR SEVEN BROTHERS are not memorable on their own, but the tunes work well within the framework of the picture. Baritone Howard Keel belts out "Bless Your Beautiful Hide" and with the brothers harmonizes on "Sobbin' Women." He and soprano Jane Powell duet on "When You're in Love." Powell solos with "Wonderful, Wonderful Day" and with the brothers, performs "Goin' Co'tin." The brothers do "Lonesome Polecat," while Virginia Gibson and the other young women do "June Bride." The brothers and the women together perform "Spring, Spring, Spring." The "Barn-Raising Ballet" features both the young men and women dancing.

In *Cue* magazine, Jesse Zunser wrote, "It's a cinematic barrel of fun—a large-scale CinemaScope color ramp, busting out all over the big screen with high spirits and young romancin', with great good humor, whistleable songs, lively lyrics, and an eye-popping screenful of high-speed acrobatic dancing. Any way you care to look at or listen to it, this SEVEN BRIDES is a full package of entertainment." The *New York Times* enthused, "A rarity—a genuinely original Hollywood musical, a warm and comic yarn about the rustic romances of a family of Oregonian pioneers with strikingly imaginative choreography, a good, melodic score and a contagious and talented cast, headed by Jane Powell and Howard Keel. . . . The choreography of Michael Kidd is a real treat." John Springer in *All Talking! All Singing! All Dancing!* (1966) stated that this film "must be included with the very finest original movie musicals" and added that it was ". . . Notable especially for some earthy humor and for some particularly lusty and virile dance numbers."

SEVEN BRIDES FOR SEVEN BROTHERS received an Academy Award for Best Scoring. It received Oscar nominations for Best Picture, Best Screenplay, and Cinematography—Color and Editing.

SEVEN BRIDES, which helped to counter the demise of the Hollywood musical, was the inspiration for the ABC-TV series, "Here Come the Brides" (1968–70), starring Robert Brown and Joan Blondell. In mid-1978 Jane Powell and Howard Keel toured in a pre-Broadway stage version of SEVEN BRIDES FOR SEVEN BROTHERS, which was adapted for the stage by Al Kasha and David Landay, with added songs by Kasha and Joel Hirschhorn. The show closed in Miami Beach in February 1979 but reemerged as a short-lived (five performances) Broadway production in July 1982, starring Debbie Boone, David-James Carroll, Craig Peralta, and Nancy Fox.

Howard Keel and Jane Powell had teamed in MGM's ROSE MARIE, *q.v.,* earlier in the year. In the 1970s they would perform together in touring versions of Broadway hits. Stanley Donen directed two more MGM musicals: DEEP IN MY HEART (1954), *q.v.,* which he co-choreographed, and IT'S ALWAYS FAIR WEATHER (1955), *q.v.,* co-directed with Gene Kelly.

1776 (Columbia, 1972) Color 141 minutes.

Producer, Jack L. Warner; director, Peter H. Hunt; based on the musical play by Peter Stone, Sherman Edwards; screenplay, Stone; art director, George Jenkins; set decorator, George James Hopkins; costumes, Patricia Zipprodt; makeup, Allan Snyder; music director, Ray Heindorf; orchestrators, Eddie Sauter, Peter Howard; choreographer, Onna White; music, Edwards; assistant director, Sheldon Shrager; camera, Harry Stradling, Jr.; editors, William Ziegler, Florence Williamson.

Songs: "Sit Down, John," "Piddle, Twiddle and Resolve," "Till Then," "The Lees of Old Virginia," "But, Mr. Adams," "Yours, Yours, Yours," "He Plays the Violin," "Momma Look Sharp," "The Egg," "Molasses to Rum," "Is Anybody There?" (Sherman Edwards).

William Daniels (John Adams); David Ford (John Hancock); Howard Da Silva (Benjamin Franklin); Donald Madden (John Dickinson); Emory Bass (James Wilson); Ken Howard (Thomas Jefferson); Ronald Holgate (Richard Henry Lee); Rex Robbins

(Roger Sherman); Peter Furstar (Oliver Wolcott); Frederic Downs (Samuel Huntington); Howard Caine (Lewis Morris); John Myhers (Robert Livingston); Richard McMurray (Francis Lewis); John Cullum (Edward Rutledge); Gordon De Vol (Thomas Lynch, Jr.); William H. Bassett (Thomas Heyward, Jr.); Jonathan Moore (Lyman Hull); William Engle (Button Gwinnett); Barry O'Hara (George Walton); William Hansen (Caesar Rodney); Ray Middleton (Thomas McKenan); Leo Layden (George Read); Patrick Hines (Samuel Chase); Heber Jentzsch (Charles Carroll); Andy Albin (William Paca); Charles Rule (Joseph Hewes); Jack De Mave (John Penn); Jordan Rhode (William Hooper); Ropy Poole (Stephen Hopkins); James Noble (John Witherspoon); Richard O'Shea (Francis Hopkinson); Fred Slyter (Richard Stockton); Daniel Keyes

William Daniels, Blythe Danner and Howard DaSilva in *1776*(1972).

(Joseph Bartlett); John Holland (William Whipple); Ralston Hill (Secretary Charles Thomson); Stephen Nathan (Courier); William Duell (Custodian Andrew McNair); Mark Montgomery (Leather Apron); Blythe Danner (Martha Jefferson); Virginia Vestoff (Abigail Adams).

Former Warner Bros. chief Jack L. Warner produced this ambitious musical history lesson for Columbia Pictures. While it certainly was not structured to be a rousing song-and-dance entry, it was a too respectful tailoring of the property to the film medium. Peter Stone adapted his play *1776* (1969) to the screen after it had a 1,217-performance run on Broadway, where it won a trio of Tony Awards, including Best Musical. Director Peter Hunt, who also won a Tony for the stage version, helmed the movie. William Daniels, Howard Da Silva, Virginia Vestoff, Ron Holgate, Ray Middleton and several others recreated their stage roles on camera. Onna White, who had fared better with OLIVER! (1968), *q.v.*, supplied the film's downplayed choreography.

In 1776 Philadelphia, colonists Benjamin Franklin (Howard Da Silva) and John Adams (William Daniels) perceive the need for the American colonies to unite into a strong union and to cast off the yoke of British rule. The two enlist the aid of young Thomas Jefferson (Ken Howard), who writes the Declaration of Independence. Also involved are Adams' loyal wife Abigail (Virginia Vestoff), Jefferson's wife Martha (Blythe Danner), Virginian Richard Henry Lee (Ron Holgate), John Hancock (David Ford), Edward Rutledge (John Cullum) and many other historical figures, including John Dickinson (Donald Madden) who opposes separation due to his loyalty to England. Eventually the crucial document of separation is composed, but then Adams, Franklin, Jefferson and others loyal to their cause must rally the votes necessary for its passage by the special Congress. By one vote, the Declaration of Independence is passed and the colonies formalize their break from the British crown.

Sherman Edwards' score for *1776* is a strong one within the confines of the plot. Among the better songs are William Daniels and Virginia Vestoff's duets on "Till Then" and "Yours, Yours, Yours," and Blythe Danner's "He Plays the Violin." Only the number "Cool, Cool Considerate Men" failed to make the transition from Broadway to the screen.

Newsday labeled *1776* ". . . A rarity among movie musicals—literate, frequently hilarious, continually engrossing historical drama. . . ." In retrospect, Clive Hirschhorn (*The Hollywood Musical*) was more on the mark when he assessed, ". . . The Panavision screen [version] emphasized the piece's pretensions: its coy, self-congratulatory pomposity, its flaccid score and arch lyrics. . . . The mood shifted uneasily as great figures of history . . . were diminished and trivialized in the name of humour. . . ."

The very expensively-produced *1776* failed to gross even $4,000,000 in distributors' domestic film rentals. It received an Oscar nomination for Best Cinematography but lost to CABARET, *q.v.*

SHAKE, RATTLE AND ROCK! (American International, 1956) 77 minutes.

Producers, James H. Nicholson, (uncredited) Alex Gordon; director, Edward L. Cahn; screenplay, Lou Rusoff; art director, Don Ament; music, Alexander Courage; assistant director, Bart Carre; camera, Frederick F. West; editors, Robert S. Eisen, Charles Gross, Jr.

Songs: "Honey Chile," "I'm in Love Again," "Ain't That a Shame" (David Bartholomew, Antoine "Fats" Domino); "Feelin' Happy," "Lipstick, Powder and Paint," "The Choker," "Rock, Rock, Rock" (Joe Turner); "Sweet Love on My Mind" (Wayne Walker); "Rockin' on Saturday Night" (George Matola, Johnny Lehman).

Antoine "Fats" Domino, Joe Turner (Themselves); Lisa Gaye (June); Touch [Mike] Connors (Garry); Sterling Holloway (Axe); Raymond Hatton (Horace); Douglass Dumbrille (Eustace); Margaret Dumont (Georgianna); Tommy Charles (Himself); Annita Ray (Herself); Paul Dubov (Bugsy); Eddie Kafafian (Nick); Clarence Kolb (Judge); Percy Helton (Hiram); Choker Campbell (Himself); Charles Evans (Bentley); Frank Jenks (Director); Pierre Watkin (Armstrong); Joe Devlin (Police Captain); Jimmy Pickford (Eddie); Nancy Kilgas (Nancy, the Ballerina); Giovanna Fiorino (Helen); Leon Tyler (Aloysius); Patricia Gregory (Pat); Rosie and Carlos (Themselves).

By the mid-1950s rock 'n' roll was taking hold of the music scene. Fledgling American International Pictures jumped onto the bandwagon, producing SHAKE, RATTLE AND ROCK!, the first of a series of movies it would make featuring this popular style of teenage music. Uncredited Alex Gordon produced this dual biller (which was issued with Gordon's melodrama, RUNAWAY DAUGHTERS) for slightly under $80,000. It grossed many times that amount when released, mainly due to the drive-in theatre trade. The title of the picture comes from a song hit by Joe Turner, who sang it in the feature, which also had guest appearances by Fats Domino (in his screen debut), Choker Campbell and His Band, Tommy Charles and Annita Ray.

Promoter Garry (Touch [Michael] Connors) intends to build a

Annita Ray, Sterling Holloway and Touch [Michael] Connors in SHAKE, RATTLE AND ROCK! (1956).

place where teenagers can enjoy rock 'n' roll music. However, his plans go awry when he is opposed by the parents (Sterling Holloway, Margaret Dumont) of his girlfriend June (Lisa Gaye). When he continues with his goal, the parents, along with disgruntled souls in the community, take him to court. He uncovers a film of June's mother doing the Charleston when she was a teenager, and the judge (Clarence Kolb) rules in Garry's favor. The rock house is built and the local teenagers, and their parents, enjoy a big concert.

"Rock 'N' Roll Vs. the 'Squares'—The Rockin' Rollin' Boogiest Jam Session You've Ever seen!" insisted the ads for this quickie musical. Its highlights are the musical interludes by the assorted artists, with Antoine "Fats" Domino getting the lion's share of the footage as he performs his hits "Honey Chile," "Ain't That a Shame" and "I'm in Love Again."

Soon after AIP issued this low-budget rock feature, the studio released Roger Corman's ROCK ALL NIGHT (1956), which featured The Platters.

SHALL WE DANCE (RKO, 1937) 101 minutes.

Producer, Pandro S. Berman; director, Mark Sandrich; based on the story "Watch Your Step" by Lee Loeb, Harold Buchman; screenplay, Allan Scott, Ernest Pagano, P. J. Wolfson; art director,

Van Nest Polglase; set decorator, Darrell Silvera; costumes, Irene; makeup, Mel Burns; music director, Nathaniel Shilkret; orchestrator, Robert Russell Bennett; choreographers, Fred Astaire, Hermes Pan, Harry Losee; special effects, Vernon Walker; camera, David Abel; editor, William Hamilton.

Songs: "Slap That Bass," "(I've Got) Beginner's Luck," "Let's Call the Whole Thing Off," "Walking the Dog," "They All Laughed," "They Can't Take That Away from Me," "Shall We Dance?" (George Gershwin, Ira Gershwin).

Fred Astaire (Petrov [Peter P. "Pete" Peters]); Ginger Rogers (Linda Keene [Linda Thompson]); Edward Everett Horton (Jeffrey Baird); Eric Blore (Cecil Flintridge); Jerome Cowan (Arthur Miller); Ketti Gallian (Lady Tarrington); William Brisbane (Jim Montgomery); Harriet Hoctor (Herself); Ann Shoemaker (Mrs. Fitzgerald); Ben Alexander (Bandleader); Emma Young (Tai); Sherwood Bailey (Newsboy); Pete Theodore ((Dancing Partner); Marek Windheim, Rolfe Sedan (Ballet Masters); George Magrill (Room Steward); Charles Coleman (Cop in Park); Frank Moran (Charlie, the Big Man); and: Norman Ainsley, William Burress, Jean de Briac, Pauline Garon, Helena Grant, Sam Hayes, Charles Irwin, J. M. Kerrigan, Alphonse Martell, Torben Meyer, Mantan Moreland, Leonard Mudie, Vasey O'Davoren, Matty Roubert, Spencer Teakle, Sam Wren.

By the time SHALL WE DANCE, the seventh teaming at RKO of Fred Astaire and Ginger Rogers, was released, the duo's box-office draw was showing signs of wear. While the film turned a profit, it was not in the same league with their previous movies. This was the screen team's only film with a Gershwin brothers' score and it was the last of the studio's efforts to surround the stars in a lavishly improbable ambiance. The rather pretentious storyline concept of a ballet dancer with a penchant for modern tap steps traces back to a screen idea devised two years earlier by Richard Rodgers and Lorenz Hart as a potential Astaire project. When the dancer rejected the conception, the composers converted the script into Broadway's *On Your Toes* (1936) starring Ray Bolger. After that stage musical's success, RKO tried to buy the property for Astaire-Rogers, but when that failed, SHALL WE DANCE was fashioned. (ON YOUR TOES would be filmed by Warner Bros. in 1939 with Eddie Albert and Vera Zorina.)

In Paris, world renowned ballet star, the Russian Petrov (Fred Astaire) becomes aware of musical comedy star Linda Keene (Ginger Rogers), much to the chagrin of his protective impresario, Jeffrey Baird (Edward Everett Horton). Actually Petrov is Peter P. "Pete" Peters, an American from Pittsburgh, Pennsylvania with a

Ginger Rogers and Fred Astaire in SHALL WE DANCE (1937).

phoney accent, and she is really Linda Thompson, who intends to marry into society. He pursues her across the Atlantic in a luxury liner and soon is in love with her. As they settle into life in Manhattan, the two unite romantically and on stage. Because both prove to have flashy tempers and large egos, they bicker constantly and soon decide to break up their popular act. Not wanting to lose a good audience draw, their manager, Arthur Miller (Jerome Cowan), concocts a publicity gimmick (that they are married). As the furor mounts, the couple decide the only way to end the "scandal" is to really marry and then divorce. Despite the interference of their associates, the pair finally realize that they are truly in love and remain married.

Fred Astaire did an imaginative dance set in the ocean liner's steam room to "Slap That Bass," while several black crew members look on. He crooned "They Can't Take That Away From Me" and it was nominated for an Oscar. He and Ginger were delightful dancing to "They All Laughed" (which she also sang) and "Shall We Dance?" (The latter was the film's finale number set in the club theatre at the top of a majestic New York hotel where Astaire, in white tie and tails, dances with Rogers and a rash of chorus girls all wearing Ginger Rogers masks.) Especially sparkling was the stars' roller skating duet, in a Central Park rink, on "Let's Call the Whole Thing Off," with the mocking song lyrics adding spice to the proceedings.* The film also provided the stars an opportunity to change partners: Fred dancing with ballerina Harriet Hoctor, while Ginger performed with Pete Theodore. Prepared but unused in the picture were the two Gershwin numbers, "Hi-Ho!" and "Wake Up, Brother, and Dance."

"One of the best things the screen's premiere dance team has done, a zestful, prancing, sophisticated musical show. It has a grand score by George Gershwin (lyrics by brother Ira), a generous leavening of comedy, a plot or so, and forever, and ever, the nimble hoofing of a chap with quick-silver in his feet and a young woman who has leaped to follow him with assurance" (*New York Times*). Yet, despite everything, there was a certain spark missing from SHALL WE DANCE—call it deja vu or a childish script with

---

*Regarding the "Let's Call the Whole Thing Off" number, Roy Hemming (*The Melody Lingers On,* 1986) observed, ". . . Neither Astaire nor Rogers look at ease or completely comfortable as they glide and tap away on their skates. The song itself is another matter. It comes across as the catchiest and cleverest song in the movie, thanks especially to the fun that Ira's lyrics poke at any number of words in the English language that some people pronounce one way, others another. . . . 'Let's Call the Whole Thing Off' was the first Gershwin movie song to make radio's 'Your Hit Parade.' "

scatterbrain logic or the forced comedy antics of those perennially snobbish stooges (Edward Everett Horton, Eric Blore). As Ted Sennett (*Hollywood Musicals,* 1981) determined, ". . . Although the film has its share of musical numbers, too few of them take advantage of the intimate, romantic, and infinitely graceful style the team had perfected in their films together. Only one, 'They All Laughed,' has a full quota of the Astaire-Rogers artistry; others are either perfunctory or ill-considered."

After SHALL WE DANCE, Astaire made A DAMSEL IN DISTRESS (1937), *q.v.,* again with a Gershwin brothers' score and with Joan Fontaine now as his leading lady. But the next year it was back to Ginger Rogers. Although the team had passed their apex of creativity and popularity, they reunited for three additional features: CAREFREE (1938, at RKO), THE STORY OF VERNON AND IRENE CASTLE (1939, at RKO) and THE BARKLEYS OF BROADWAY (1949, at MGM), *qq.v.*

SHOW BOAT (Universal, 1929) 130 minutes. (Also silent version: 10,290′).

Producer, Carl Laemmle; director, Harry Pollard; additional director, Arch Heath; based on the novel by Edna Ferber and the musical play by Jerome Kern, Oscar Hammerstein, II; production by Florenz Ziegfeld; screenplay, Charles Kenyon; dialogue, Harry Pollard, Tom Reed; titles, Reed; music, Joseph Cherniavsky; sound, C. Roy Hunter; special camera effects, Frank H. Booth; camera, Gilbert Warrenton; editorial supervisor, Edward J. Montagne; editors, Maurice Pivar, Daniel Mandell.

Songs: "C'Mon, Folks," "Hey, Feller," "Ol' Man River," "Can't Help Lovin' Dat Man" (Joseph Cherniavsky, Jerome Kern, Oscar Hammerstein, II); "Bill" (P. G. Wodehouse, Jerome Kern, Oscar Hammerstein, II); "The Lonesome Road" (Gene Austin, Nathaniel Shilkret); "Here Comes That Show Boat" (Billy Rose, Maceo Pinkard); "Down South" (William H. Myddleton, Sigmund Spaeth); "Love Sings a Song in My Heart" (Cherniavsky, Clarence J. Mark); "Coon, Coon, Coon" (Leo Friedmann, Gene Jefferson); "Deep River" (traditional); "I've Got Shoes" (traditional).

Prologue: Tess Gardella, Otis Harlan, Helen Morgan, Jules Bledsoe, The Jubilee Singers, The Plantation Singers, Carl Laemmle, Florenz Ziegfeld; *The Story:* Laura La Plante (Magnolia Hawks); Joseph Schildkraut (Gaylord Ravenal); Otis Harlan (Captain Andy Hawks); Emily Fitzroy (Parthenia Ann Hawks); Alma Rubens (Julie); Elsie Bartlett (Elly); Jack McDonald (Windy); Jane La Verne (Magnolia as a Child/Kim); Neely Edwards (Schultzy); Theodore Lorch (Frank); Stepin Fetchit (Joe); Gertrude Howard

(Queenie); Ralph Yearsley (The Killer); George Chesebro (Steve); Harry Holden (Means); Max Asher (Utility Man); Jim Coleman (Stagehand); Carl Herlinger (Wheelsman); Eva Olivetti (Singing Voice of Magnolia Hawks); voices of: the Billbrew Chorus, Silverstone Quartet, The Four Emperors of Harmony, Claude Collins.

See: SHOW BOAT (1951) (essay).

SHOW BOAT (Universal, 1936) 110 minutes.

Producer, Carl Laemmle, Jr.; director, James Whale; based on the novel by Edna Ferber and the musical play by Jerome Kern, Oscar Hammerstein, II; screenplay, Hammerstein, II; art director, Charles D. Hall; costumes, Doris Zinkeison; music director, Victor Baravalle; choreographer, LeRoy Prinz; camera, John Mescall; editors, Ted Kent, Bernard W. Burton.

Songs: "Ol' Man River," "Ah Still Suits Me," "Bill," "Can't Help Lovin' Dat Man," "Only Make Believe," "I Have the Room Above," "You Are Love," "Gallivantin' Around," "Cotton Blossom," "Cap'n Andy's Ballyhoo," "Where's the Mate for Me?" "Mis'ry's Comin' Around," "Why Do I Love You?" (instrumental) (Jerome Kern, Oscar Hammerstein, II); "After the Ball" (Charles K. Harris); "Goodbye, My Lady Love" (Joe Howard); "At a Georgia Camp Meeting" (Kerry Mills); "Washington Post March" (John Phillip Sousa).

Irene Dunne (Magnolia Hawks); Allan Jones (Gaylord Ravenal); Charles Winninger (Captain Andy Hawks); Helen Westley (Parthenia Ann Hawks); Paul Robeson (Joe); Helen Morgan (Julie); Donald Cook (Steve); Sammy White (Frank Schultz); Queenie Smith (Ellie); J. Farrell MacDonald (Windy McClain); Arthur Hohl (Pete); Charles Middleton (Sheriff Vallon); Hattie McDaniel (Queenie, Joe's Wife); Francis X. Mahoney (Rubberface); Sunnie O'Dea (Elder Kim); Marilyn Knowlden (Younger Kim); Patricia Barry (Baby Kim); Dorothy Granger, Barbara Pepper, Renee Whitney (Chorus Girls); Harry Barris (Jake); Charles Wilson (Jim Green); Clarence Muse (Sam, the Janitor); Stanley Fields (Zebe); "Tiny" [Stanley J.] Sanford (Backwoodsman); May Beatty (Landlady); Bobby Watson (Lost Child); Jane Keckley (Mrs. Ewing); E. E. Clive (Englishman); Helen Jerome Eddy (Reporter); Donald Briggs (Press Agent); LeRoy Prinz (Dance Director); Eddie "Rochester" Anderson (Young Black Man); Patti Patterson (Banjo Player); Helen Hayward (Mrs. Brencenbridge); Flora Finch (Woman); Theodore Lorch (Simon Legree); Arthur Housman (Drunk); Elspeth Dudgeon (Mother Superior); Monte Montague (Old Man); Lois Verner (Small Girl); Grace Cunard (Mother); Marilyn Harris

(Little Girl); Jimmy Jackson (Young Man); Eddy Chandler, Lee Phelps, Frank Mayo, Ed Peil, Sr., Edmund Cobb, Al Ferguson (Gamblers); Maude Allen (Fat Woman); Artye Folz, Barbara Bletcher (Fat Girls); Forrest Stanley (Theatre Manager); Jack Latham (Juvenile) George H. Reed (Old Black Man); Georgia O'Dell (Schoolteacher); Selmer Jackson (Hotel Clerk); George Hackathorne (YMCA Worker); Ernest Hilliard, Jack Mulhall, Brooks Benedict (Race Fans).

See: SHOW BOAT (1951) (essay).

SHOW BOAT (Metro-Goldwyn-Mayer, 1951) Color 107 minutes.

Producer, Arthur Freed; associate producers, Ben Feiner, Jr., (uncredited) Roger Edens; director, George Sidney; based on the novel by Edna Ferber and the musical play by Jerome Kern, Oscar Hammerstein, II; screenplay, John Lee Mahn, (uncredited): George Wells, Jack McGowan; art directors, Cedric Gibbons, Jack Martin Smith; set decorators, Edwin B. Willis, Alfred Spencer; costumes, Walter Plunkett; makeup, William J. Tuttle; music director, Adolph Deutsch; orchestrator, Conrad Salinger; vocal arranger, Robert Tucker; choreographer, Robert Alton; color consultants, Henri Jaffa, James Gooch; assistant director, George Rheim; sound supervisor, Douglas Shearer; special montage director, Peter Ballbusch; special effects, Warren Newcombe; camera, Charles Rosher; editor, Albert Akst.

Songs: "Ol' Man River," "Where's the Mate for Me?" "You Are Love," "Make Believe," "Why Do I Love You?" "Can't Help Lovin' That Man," "Cotton Blossom," "Mis'ry Comin' Round," "I Might Fall Back on You," "Life Upon the Wicked Stage," "Buck and Wing Dance," "Cap'n Andy's Ballyhoo," "Hey Fella" (Jerome Kern, Oscar Hammerstein, II); "After the Ball" (Charles K. Harris); "Bill" (Kern, P. G. Wodehouse, Guy Bolton); "Auld Lang Syne" (adaptor, Adolph Deutsch).

Kathryn Grayson (Magnolia Hawks); Ava Gardner (Julie LaVerne); Howard Keel (Gaylord Ravenal); Joe E. Brown (Captain Andy Hawks); Marge Champion (Ellie May Shipley); Gower Champion (Frank Schultz); Robert Sterling (Stephen Baker); Agnes Moorehead (Parthenia Ann Hawks); Adele Jergens (Cameo McQueen); William Warfield (Joe); Leif Erickson (Pete); Owen McGiveney (Windy McClain); Frances Williams (Queenie); Regis Toomey (Sheriff Ike Vallon); Frank Wilcox (Mark Hallson); Chick Chandler (Herman); Emory Parnell (Jake Green); Sheila Clark (Kim Ravenal); Ian MacDonald (Drunken Sport); Fuzzy Knight (Troc Piano Player); Norman Leavitt (George, the Calliope Player); Anne Marie Dore, Christian Lind, Lyn Wilde, Marietta Elliott,

Joyce Jameson, Bette Arlen, Helen Kimbell, Tac Porchon, Mitzie Uehlein, Judy Landon, Nova Dale, Mary Jane French, Marilyn Kinsley, Alice Markham (Showboat Cast Girls); Michael Dugan, Robert Fortier, George Ford, Cass Jaeger, Boyd Ackerman, Roy Damron, Joseph Roach (Showboat Cast Boys); George Lynn (Dealer); Louis Mercier (Dabney); Lisa Ferraday (Renee); Anna Q. Nilsson (Seamstress); Ida Moore (Little Old Lady); Alphonse Martell (Headwaiter); Edward Keane (Hotel Manager); Tom Irish (Bellboy); Jim Pierce (Doorman); William Tannen (Man with Julie); Bert Roach (Drunk); Earle Hodgins (Bartender); Annette Warren (Singing for Julie LaVerne).

One of the perennially successful musicals of the American theatre, Edna Ferber's *Show Boat* (1926) was first adapted to the stage the year after it was published as a book. It debuted on Broadway on December 27, 1927 and the Florenz Ziegfeld production had a 572-performance run. With music by Jerome Kern and lyrics by Oscar Hammerstein, II, the musical starred Norma Terris, Helen Morgan, Charles Winninger, Edna May Oliver and Aunt Jemima (Tess Gardella). Its tale of marital strife and miscegenation became a classic, enhanced by a melodious score. Three motion pictures would be made from the stage play, the first two by Universal Pictures and the last by MGM.

Universal acquired the screen rights to the Broadway musical hit and began filming the story as a major silent production, not an uncommon practice in the 1920s. The very slick European Joseph Schildkraut was cast as the very American Gaylord Ravenal, with popular Laura La Plante as his leading lady, Magnolia Hawks. With the sound revolution already in vogue, the studio belatedly determined to add spoken dialogue and songs to the proceedings and reshot several scenes, as well as adding others. This presented new problems, for Schildkraut had a slight accent (which became noticeable in the sound sequences) and La Plante was not a proficient vocalist (her songs were dubbed by Eva Olivetti). To complicate matters more, it was decided to have several members of the original Broadway cast perform in a special all-talking, all-singing eighteen-minute overture, highlighting numbers from the acclaimed show. (This was shot in haste in New York City.) Thus there was Helen Morgan performing "Bill" and "Can't Help Lovin' Dat Man," Aunt Jemima (Tess Gardella) and the Jubilee Singers doing "C'Mon Folks" and "Hey Feller," and Jules Bledsoe singing "Ol' Man River," joined by the chorus from the original Broadway version. Universal's founder, Carl Laemmle, and Broadway's Florenz Ziegfeld introduced these numbers, which only served, by comparison, to make the remainder of the proceedings anticlimactic and inferior. The bowdlerizing of the storyline was yet another insult to the original.

Magnolia Hawks (Laura La Plante) is the star of her family's riverboat revue on the Mississippi. She marries gambler Gaylord Ravenal (Joseph Schildkraut), but after her father, Captain Andy (Otis Harlan), falls overboard during a storm, Magnolia and her husband cannot get along with her domineering mother (Emily Fitzroy). Magnolia sells her interest in *The Cotton Palace* and the couple move to Chicago. There Gaylord drifts into a life as a gambler who suffers a long losing streak. The interfering Mrs. Hawks tells him to leave Magnolia since she would be "happier" without him. Thinking she is correct, the weakling dandy disappears. To make a living for herself and her baby, Magnolia begins singing Negro spirituals on stage, where she becomes a success. When her mother dies later, Magnolia returns to take over the show boat. There she is reconciled with a repentant Gaylord, who has given up his gambling ways.

Between the elongated prologue and the film proper, much of the original score was utilized, with several additional numbers, including traditional spirituals, interpolated. Gene Austin and Nathaniel Shilkret wrote a new number, "The Lonesome Road," for the picture.

The highly ballyhooed SHOW BOAT was roadshown with an intermission breaking up the running time. Universal proclaimed, "THE GREATEST LOVE STORY EVER TOLD. . . . Pictured with all the movement, beauty, thrills and grandeur of the colorful floating theaters on the Mississippi River. That is Edna Ferber's romance of the ages transferred to the screen." Reacting to the promotional overkill, the critics were sorely disappointed with the actual results, particularly as to storyline development, direction and the acting. "Lavish production of a colorful novel that deserved less obvious direction," opined a polite *Photoplay* magazine. *Variety* was aghast at the sloppy editing and the length (130 minutes) of the movie. It also complained about ". . . The drama, and with drama an overdose of each and every scene. . . ." The same trade paper added, "Production on interiors so-so, not calling for anything else. Exteriors are so sweeping they become enough." The *New York Times*' Mordaunt Hall recorded, "It's a pity that . . . [director Harry Pollard] has such a passion for pathos, for he does not realize where misfortunes on the screen becomes tedious to the onlooker."

It was a strange decision by Carl Laemmle, Jr. to place Britisher James Whale, most noted for macabre horror films such as FRANKENSTEIN (1931) and THE INVISIBLE MAN (1933), in charge of the remake of SHOW BOAT (1936). However, he did a

Paul Robeson in SHOW BOAT (1936).

magnificent job with the stage masterpiece. The splendid new black-and-white version retained the plot (Oscar Hammerstein, II did the adaptation) and the music of the stage play, and was enhanced by dance numbers staged by LeRoy Prinz (who can be spotted briefly in the movie). Irene Dunne, who had played the role in road tours before coming to Hollywood, was cast as Magnolia, with Allan Jones as Gaylord and Helen Westley as Magnolia's shrewish mother. Charles Winninger repeated his Broadway role as the irrepressible Captain Andy. Also recreating her stage role of Julie, the tragic mulatto, was Helen Morgan, and a highlight of the new version was her touching rendering of her famous "My Bill." Also notable were Paul Robeson's deep-voiced rendition of "Ol' Man River" and Hattie McDaniel's light-hearted performance as his wife. For the 1936 screen version, Jerome Kern and Oscar Hammerstein, II added: "Gallivantin' Around" (done in blackface by a cavorting Irene Dunne!), "Ah Still Suits Me" (a duet by Paul Robeson and Hattie McDaniel) and "I Have the Room Above Her" (sung by Allan Jones). Written but not used by the songwriting team was "Got My Eye on You." Also interpolated into the film were: "Washington Post March" and "At a Georgia Camp Meeting." Cut from the original production were "Got My Eye on You" and "Why Do I Love You?" (done only as an instrumental in the 1936 picture). Intact and done in wonderful harmony and taste were the show's two big duets, "Make Believe" and "You are Love," performed to perfection by Dunne and Jones.

The *New York Times*' Frank S. Nugent enthused, "Here is one of the few musical shows which is not merely a screen concert. The picture has a rhythmic pace and a balanced continuity of movement which is as exceptional as it is welcome." Nugent judged Dunne "splendid" and Jones "equally well-cast."

The 1936 SHOW BOAT proved to be a huge financial success for the studio, the last for Universal's Carl Laemmles (father and son) before the studio was sold the same year. On June 24, 1940, Irene Dunne and Allan Jones repeated their roles in a radio adaptation of "Show Boat" on CBS' "Lux Radio Theatre."

MGM acquired the screen rights to *Show Boat* from a financially troubled Universal Pictures. It was planning its own expansive new version, at one point as a vehicle for Jeanette MacDonald and Nelson Eddy. That casting did not come to be, but at the instigation of producer Arthur Freed, MGM financed a Broadway revival (January 5, 1946) of the venerable property, hoping to stir up fresh interest in the show. In the studio's 1946 biopic of Jerome Kern, TILL THE CLOUDS ROLL BY, *q.v.*, MGM recreated a portion of *Show Boat*. It served to test the waters for its projected full remake of the show. Kathryn Grayson as Magnolia and Tony Martin as Gaylord did a duet on "Make Believe," while Caleb Peterson as Joe sang "Ol' Man River." Five years later, MGM produced the first color film version of SHOW BOAT, with Kathryn Grayson again cast as Magnolia, Howard Keel as Gaylord and Ava Gardner (replacing Judy Garland and a briefly considered Dinah Shore) as the mulatto Julie (with her singing dubbed by Annette Warren).

The newest screen rendition of SHOW BOAT benefitted greatly from Technicolor and the impressive MGM mounting. The plot was restructured to keep shy Magnolia and Gaylord's daughter, Kim, a child and not show her a grownup stage success, as had been done in the Broadway original and the 1936 movie. It was decided not to allow Julie to disappear from the storyline midway through the picture and not to have Magnolia and Gaylord conclude their romance as elderly people. To enhance its casting of Grayson, Keel and Gardner, William Warfield was signed as Joe and there were the comic scamperings of Joe E. Brown (Cap'n Andy) and Agnes

Howard Keel and Kathryn Grayson in SHOW BOAT (1951).

Moorehead as his authoritative wife, Parthenia. For musical comedy variation, Marge and Gower Champion—as Ellie and Frank—were given Robert Alton-choreographed dance numbers ("I Might Fall Back on You" and "Life Upon the Wicked Stage")—as well as a "Buck and Wing Dance." But the focal star of the production remained the glorious show boat itself, a marvelous piece of craftsmanship, built at a cost of $126,468.

The most favored numbers remained intact in the new SHOW BOAT: "Where's the Mate for Me?" (Keel), "Make Believe" (Grayson-Keel), "Why Do I Love You?" (Grayson-Keel) and "You Are Love" (Grayson-Keel). The 1951 edition deleted "Nobody Else but Me," "I Have the Room Above" and "Ah Still Suits Me."

The *New York Times* endorsed, "For visual splendor and rich, ripe musical tastefulness, this third version dims the other two. . . . This one has glitter and opulence, without losing heart and drama."

Made at a cost of $2,295,429, SHOW BOAT (1951) grossed over $8,650,000. It received Oscar nominations for Best Scoring and Best Cinematography—Color.

The legend of SHOW BOAT continued on. In 1977 Miles

Kreuger wrote the reference book *Show Boat: The Story of a Classic American Musical,* tracing the landmark show's history in great detail. In 1988 EMI produced a three-disc cast recording of the musical, including all the songs from the original 1927 production, even including numbers excised during the pre-Broadway tryouts. The comprehensive new recording, which rose to number one on the hit album charts, featured opera stars Frederica von Stade (Magnolia), Jerry Hadley (Gaylord), Bruce Hubbard (Joe), Teresa Stratas (Julie) and, in a special appearance, Lillian Gish as the Lady on the Levee. *Newsweek* magazine noted of the revived interest in the classic musical, "With its serious theme and an integrated cast, *Show Boat* was revolutionary. Unlike other musical-theater staples, it not only changed during its pre-Broadway try-out but went through radical permutations over the years, often to suit changing taste. An entire generation, brought up on telecasts of M-G-M's execrable 1951 extravaganza . . . has a misconception of *Show Boat* as a gooey operetta."

In October 1989 PBS-TV aired a three-hour version of "Show Boat," capturing a stage version performed at the Paper Mill Playhouse in Millburn, New Jersey. It starred Rebecca Baxter (Magnolia), Richard White (Gaylord), Shelly Burch (Julie), Eddie Bracken (Cap'n Andy), Marshall Bagwell (Parthenia) and P. L. Brown (Joe). *Daily Variety* reported, "For anyone unfamiliar with *Show Boat,* this version is a good intro. . . . This isn't the music Center, and it isn't Broadway, it's regional theater, and it's doing what show boats that rode the Mississippi used to do—it's bringing honest, well-played theater to local audiences. As such, it's a humdinger."

THE SHOW OF SHOWS (Warner Bros., 1929) Color 127 minutes.

Supervising director, Darryl F. Zanuck; director, John G. Adolfi; special material, Frank Fay, J. Keirn Brennan; choreographers, Larry Ceballos, Jack Haskell; sound, George R. Groves; camera, Bernard McGill.

Songs: "Military March," "What's Become of the Floradora Boys?" "Lady Luck" (Ray Perkins); "Motion Picture Pirates" (M. K. Jerome); "If I Could Learn to Love" (Herman Ruby, Jerome); "Pingo Pongo," "If Your Best Friend Won't Tell You" (Al Dubin, Joe Burke); "Dear Little Pup," "The Only Song I Know," "Meet My Sister" (J. Keirn Brennan, Ray Perkins); "Your Mother and Mine" (Joe Goodwin, Gus Edwards); "Singin' in the Bath-Tub" (Ned Washington, Herb Magidson, Michael Cleary); "Believe Me" (Eddie Ward); "Just an Hour of Love," "Li-Po-Li" (Al Bryan, Ward);

"Rockabye Your Baby with a Dixie Melody" (Jean Schwartz, Joe Young, Sam Lewis); "Jumping Jack" (Herman Ruby, Rube Bloom); "Your Love Is All That I Crave" (Dubin, Perry Bradford, Jimmy Johnson); "You Were Meant for Me" (Arthur Freed, Nacio Herb Brown).

Prologue: Frank Fay (Master of Ceremonies); William Courtenay (The Minister); H. B. Warner (The Victim); Hobart Bosworth (The Executioner); *Military Parade:* Monte Blue, Pasadena's American Legion Fife and Drum Corps, 300 dancing girls (Specialties); *Floradora:* Marian Nixon, Sally O'Neil, Myrna Loy, Patsy Ruth Miller, Lila Lee, Alice Day (Floradora Sextette); Ben Turpin (Waiter); Heinie Conklin (Ice Man); Lupino Lane (Street Cleaner); Lee Moran (Plumber); Bert Roach (Father); Lloyd Hamilton (Hansom Cabby); *Skull and Crossbones:* Frank Fay, Jack Mulhall, Chester Morris, Sojin, Ted Lewis and His Band, Ted Williams Adagio Dancer (Specialties); Noah Beery, Tully Marshall, Wheeler Oakman, Bull Montana, Kalla Pasha, Anders Randof, Philo McCullough, Otto Matiesen, Jack Curtis (Pirates); Johnny Arthur (The Hero); Carmel Myers, Ruth Clifford, Sally Eilers, Viola Dana, Shirley Mason, Ethlyne Claire, France Lee, Julianne Johnston (Ladies); Marcelle (Dancer); *Eiffel Tower:* Georges Carpentier, Patsy Ruth Miller, Alice White, chorus of 75 (Specialties); *Recitations:* Beatrice Lillie, Louise Fazenda, Lloyd Hamilton, Frank Fay; *Eight Sister Acts:* Richard Barthelmess (Introduction); Dolores and Helene Costello, Sally O'Neil and Molly O'Day, Alice and Marceline Day, Sally Blane and Loretta Young, Lola and Armida, Marion Byron and Harriet Lake [Ann Sothern], Ada Mae and Alberta Vaughan, Shirley Mason and Viola Dana (Sisters); *Singin' in the Bath-Tub:* Winnie Lightner, Bull Montana, male chorus of 50 (Specialties); *Irene Bordoni Act:* Irene Bordoni (Specialty); Eddie Ward, Lou Silvers, Ray Perkins, Harry Akst, Michael Cleary, Norman Specer, Dave Silverman, Joe Burke, M. K. Jerome, Lester Stevens (The Composers); *Chinese Fantasy:* Rin-Tin-Tin (Introduction); Nick Lucas, Myrna Loy, the Jack Haskell Girls (Specialties); *Bicycle Built for Two:* Frank Fay, Sid Silvers (Introduction); Douglas Fairbanks, Jr. (Ambrose); Chester Conklin (Cop); Grant Withers, William Collier, Jr., Jack Mulhall, Chester Morris, William Bakewell (Boys); Lois Wilson, Gertrude Olmsted, Pauline Garon, Sally Eilers, Edna Murphy, Jacqueline Logan (Girls); *Black and White:* Frank Fay, Sid Silvers, Louise Fazenda, 75 dancing girls (Specialties); *Your Love Is All That I Crave:* Frank Fay (Specialty); Harry Akst (Accompanist); *King Richard III:* John Barrymore (King Richard III); Anthony Bushell, E. J. Radcliffe, Reginald Sharland (Others); *Mexican Moonshine:* Frank Fay (The General); Monte

Blue (Condemned Man); Albert Gran, Noah Beery, Lloyd Hamilton, Tully Marshall, Kalla Pasha, Lee Moran (Soldiers); *Lady Luck:* Betty Compson, Alexander Gray, Chorus (Specialties).

Warner Bros.' entry in the all-star musical sweepstakes that swept the major Hollywood studios at the beginning of the sound era was THE SHOW OF SHOWS. Like the later PARAMOUNT ON PARADE (1930), *q.v.,* it was a filmed mammoth vaudeville show with a long parade of blackouts by a host of—in this case seventy-seven—studio stars. "You'll be too busy enjoying yourself to count all the celebs in this super-revue. . . . And besides there are stunning stage effects and dance routines, gorgeous Technicolor, and millions of laughs," decided *Photoplay* magazine. In the tradition of the vaudeville stage, the lengthy fifteen-reel production was held together by Master of Ceremonies Frank Fay, who (unfortunately) often participated in the various stars' acts.

THE SHOW OF SHOWS begins on a rather dour note in a French Revolution setting with a victim (H. B. Warner) about to lose his head to The Executioner (Hobart Bosworth). The show itself commences with a military dance featuring Monte Blue and a host of chorines. Next comes one of the film's highlights, comedienne Winnie Lightner performing "Singing in the Bathtub" with several burly men dressed as bathing girls; she then does a comedy routine with Bull Montana. Boxing champion Georges Carpentier is featured in "If I Could Learn to Love" with Alice White and Patsy Ruth Miller. This is followed by Irene Bordoni performing a number of tunes, and next come dancing and songs by the Floradora Girls and Boys. Frank Fay then attempts to serenade his dog but is interrupted by Nick Lucas who sings "Lady Luck" and "That's the Only Song I Know." Fay and Beatrice Lillie do a scene in which the latter sings "Your Mother and Mine," and Ted Lewis and Noah Beery as his henchman appear as pirates in a large production routine. Winnie Lightner offers the comedy number, "Pingo-Pongo," followed by "The Chinese Fantasy" in which a prince (Nick Lucas) serenades his lady love (Myrna Loy) with a song called "Li-Po-Li," about an amorous bandit. Frank Fay and Sid Silvers, the latter imitating Al Jolson, do some comedy. Richard Barthelmess is the host for "Meet My Sister," with the rhythmic dance/song performed by several real-life sister acts including Loretta Young and Sally Blane. Louise Fazenda and Lupino Lane provide a tramp ballet. In a dramatic scene John Barrymore is *Richard III,* with Anthony Bushell and E. J. Radcliffe in support. "Bicycle Built for Two" spotlights Douglas Fairbanks Jr. Next Monte Blue chases bandit Noah Beery into the badlands. Betty Compson and Alexander Gray lead the "Lucky Lady" interlude, and the film closes by showing the production's stars in head shots as they sing the song.

Fortunately THE SHOW OF SHOWS still exists (although only in a black and white print). Although issued in the fall of 1929, this extravagant revue did not get much general release until early 1930. By that time, such screen fare was beginning to pale with filmgoers.

SILK STOCKINGS (Metro-Goldwyn-Mayer, 1957) Color 117 minutes.

Producer, Arthur Freed; director, Rouben Mamoulian; based on the musical play by George S. Kaufman, Leueen McGrath, Abe Burrows, Cole Porter; suggested by the play *Ninotchka* by Melchior Lengyel and the screenplay to *Ninotchka* by Billy Wilder, Charles Brackett, Walter Reisch; art directors, Cedric Gibbons, Randall Duell; set decorators, Edwin B. Willis, Hugh Hunt; costumes, Helen Rose; makeup, William Tuttle; music supervisor/conductor, Andre Previn; orchestrator, Conrad Salinger; additional orchestrators, Skip Martin, Al Woodbury; music coordinator, Lela Simone; choreographers, Hermes Pan, Eugene Loring; assistant director, Al Jennings; color consultant, Charles K. Hagedon; sound supervisor, Dr. Wesley C. Miller; camera, Robert Bronner; editor, Harold F. Kress.

Songs: "Too Bad," "Paris Loves Lovers," "Fated to Be Mated," "The Ritz Rock and Roll," "Silk Stockings," "Red Blues," "Stereophonic Sound," "Josephine," "Satin and Silk," "Without Love," "It's a Chemical Reaction, That's All," "Siberia," "Red Blues," "I've Got You Under My Skin," "Easy to Love," "I Concentrate on You" (Cole Porter); "All of You."

Fred Astaire (Steve Canfield); Cyd Charisse (Nina "Ninotchka" Yoshenka); Janis Paige (Peggy Dainton); Peter Lorre (Brankov); Jules Munshin (Bibinski); Joseph Buloff (Ivanov); George Tobias (Commissar Vassili Markovich); Wim Sonneveld (Peter Ilyitch Boroff); Belita (Vera, the Dancer); Ivan Triesault (Russian Embassy Official); [Betty] Barrie Chase (Gabrielle, the Dancer); Da Utti, Tybee Afra (Dancers); Carole Richards (Singing Voice of Ninotchka).

In the MGM movie *Ninotchka* (1939), the inestimable Greta Garbo laughed in a sophisticated satirical comedy about a stiff Russian Communist (Garbo) who succumbs to Western ways while being kidded and courted by a debonair playboy (Melvyn Douglas) in Paris. The screen story, itself based on a play, served as the basis for Cole Porter's twenty-fifth Broadway musical. *Silk Stockings* opened early in 1955 and had a 478-performance run, starring Don

Ameche, Hildegarde Neff and Gretchen Wyler. Their performances were ranked better than the score, which only had the title song and "All of You" as its better numbers. While this was happening, Paramount Pictures released the rather unfunny comedy THE IRON PETTICOAT, an uncredited updating of the Ninotchka theme set in the Cold War. The only saving grace of that British-made comedy was the surprising chemistry between stars Bob Hope and Katharine Hepburn.

MGM, not to be left out of Cold War genre pieces, brought *Silk Stockings* to the screen in 1957. It was directed by the elegantly tasteful Rouben Mamoulian, who had last worked at MGM and for producer Arthur Freed on the ill-fated SUMMER HOLIDAY (1948), starring Mickey Rooney and Gloria DeHaven. In bringing the project to the screen, Mamoulian steered the focus of the musical away from song and more to dance. As he explained later, "I had two of the best dancers in the world, and what interested me was to give greater importance to the dancing than to the action proper. . . . The psychological and dramatic development existed only in the dances. It was by dancing that the characters became aware of something or other. . . ." Eugene Loring was hired to recreate his Broadway choreography for the project, while Hermes Pan was reunited with Fred Astaire once again to work with him on his dance numbers. It was the first teaming of Astaire and Cyd Charisse since they had worked together in THE BAND WAGON (1953), *q.v.*

Dapper American film director Steve Canfield (Fred Astaire) has come to Paris with his lady friend, glamorous movie swimming star Peggy Dainton (Janis Paige) to do a new spectacle based on the loves of Napoleon Bonaparte and Josephine. There he meets beautiful Ninotchka (Cyd Charisse), a stern Russian Communist who spouts the party line. She has been sent to the French capital to check on the activities of three errant envoys, Brankov (Peter Lorre), Bibinski (Jules Munshin) and Ivanov (Joseph Buloff), who are in the West to retrieve a straying music composer (Wim Sonneveld) who is to write music for Canfield's film. The hedonistic Canfield is immediately taken with the rigid Ninotchka and sets out to win her love. She comes under the spell of Paris and his charm, and he finally succeeds. As a result the young woman abandons her Soviet propaganda for the decadent joys of love and capitalism.

On-camera, the lyrics of Fred Astaire's vocal on "All of You" were censored somewhat, but the melody provided inspiration for him and Charisse to dance elegantly. He and Cyd Charisse (dubbed by Carole Richards) dueted/danced to "Fated to Be Mated," written by Porter for the film. The other newly composed Porter effort was

Fred Astaire and Janis Paige in SILK STOCKINGS (1957).

"The Ritz Rock and Roll," which allowed Astaire a tour de force dance solo—with supporting chorus—in which to contrast and blend his more traditional dance style with the new rock craze. Astaire and Charisse also joined together for "It's a Chemical Reaction, That's All" and "Paris Loves Lovers." What had been a song ("Silk Stockings") for the leading man on stage became a dance for Charisse on screen. Comedy relief was provided by the Red bureaucratic trio of Lorre, Buloff and Munshin, who worry about being exiled to "Siberia" but later enjoy the fruits of capitalism and sing and dance to the song spoof, "Too Bad" (joined by Charisse). The too-often overlooked Janis Paige lent a special zip to "Stereophonic Sound," which she performed with Astaire, and soloed on the deliberately vulgar "Josephine" and the brassy "Satin and Silk." Not used from the stage original was "Hail Bibinski" and "As on Through the Seasons We Sail."

The chic SILK STOCKINGS received guarded praise from the critics, who expected something a little more contemporary in the ever-changing late 1950s. "The follow-up movie flows and sparkles musically. . . . But for some reason, director [Rouben] Mamoulian camps it under a glass-bell, with some arid dialogue patches and only the vaguest suggestions of the city of Paris, the point of it all. . . . Otherwise, the picture is highly enjoyable" (*New York Times*).

Made at a cost of $1,953,463, SILK STOCKINGS grossed $4,417,753. By the time of its release, MGM had gone through more corporate changes and it was the last of fifty-eight-year-old Fred Astaire's musicals for the studio. He would make one more genre piece, FINIAN'S RAINBOW (1968). The golden age of MGM song-and-dance films had ended.

SING, BABY, SING (20th Century-Fox, 1936) 90 minutes.

Producer, Darryl F. Zanuck; associate producer, Buddy G. DeSylva; director, Sidney Lanfield; story, Milton Sperling, Jack Yellen; screenplay, Sperling, Yellen, Harry Tugend; art director, Mark-Lee Kirk; set decorator, Thomas Little; costumes, Royer; music director, Louis Silvers; sound, Arthur Von Kirbach, Roger Heman; camera, Peverell Marley; editor, Barbara McLean.

Songs: "When Did You Leave Heaven?" (Walter Bullock, Richard A. Whiting); "You Turned the Tables on Me" (Sidney D. Mitchell, Louis Alter); "Love Will Tell," "Sing, Baby, Sing" (Lew Pollack, Yellen); "The Music Goes 'Round and 'Round" (Mike Riley, Red Hodgson, Ed Farley); "Singing a Vagabond Song" (Harry Richman, Sam Messenheimer, Val Burton); "When My Baby Smiles at Me" (Andrew B. Sterling, Bill Munro, Ted Lewis).

Alice Faye (Joan Warren); Adolphe Menjou (Bruce Farraday); Gregory Ratoff (Nicky); Ted Healy (Al Craven); Patsy Kelly (Fitz); Michael Whalen (Ted Blake); The Ritz Brothers (Themselves); Montagu Love (Robert Wilson); Dixie Dunbar (Telephone Operator); Douglas Fowley (Mac); Paul Stanton (Brewster); Tony Martin (Tony Renaldo); Virginia Field (Farraday's Nurse); Paul McVey (Doctor); Carol Tevis (Tessie); Cully Richards (Joe); and: Lynn Bari.

Singer Joan Warren (Alice Faye) loses her job at Club 41 because she is not a blue blood. Her hard working agent, Nicky (Gregory Ratoff), maneuvers her a radio audition, but that too fails because of her lack of a pedigree. At her last club performance she meets drunken Hollywood star Bruce Farraday (Adolphe Menjou), who thinks beautiful Joan is Juliet to his lovelorn Romeo. Soon thereafter, the inebriated Farraday is taken to a hospital to recover. The next day newspapers carry the headlines about Farraday's whirlwind romance with Joan. Buoyed by such fodder, Nicky parlays a radio offer for Joan. However, the sponsor-to-be demands that Farraday appear with her on the air. Meanwhile, the movie star's cousin, Robert Wilson (Montagu Love), arrives and packs his relative off to Hollywood, convinced that Joan is only after Bruce's money. Farraday and Wilson board a train bound for the west, while Joan and Nicky pursue the two men via plane. In Kansas City, where the two sets of passengers are to cross paths, Joan and Nicky present the test radio broadcast using local talent, including husky-voiced singer Tony Renaldo (Tony Martin), as support players. Wilson does his best to keep Farraday off the program, but Nicky coerces the movie star into making a guest appearance on the show. Joan then wins the coveted radio contract.

Although it carried an on-screen disclaimer, SING, BABY, SING was based on an actual incident, the romance between John Barrymore and the much-younger Elaine Barrie. The picture, however, is a delightful comedy and gives both Alice Faye and Adolphe Menjou strong roles. Faye has several good songs to present, including "Sing, Baby, Sing," "Love Will Tell" and "You Turned the Tables on Me." Tony Martin (who would soon become Alice's off-camera husband) made a very good impression warbling "When Did You Leave Heaven?" which he recorded for Decca Records. The latter song was nominated for an Academy Award but lost to "The Way You Look Tonight" from SWING TIME, *q.v.* Tyrone Power was set originally for the role of the gossip columnist, but at the last minute he was replaced by Michael Whalen. The daffy, talented Ritz Brothers made their 20th Century-Fox debut in this movie. They provided comedy relief by clowning, singing ("The Music Goes 'Round and 'Round") and doing their zany impersonations of show business icons.

Variety applauded the film as "a melody for the box office," deciding that the "cast gets along swell" and approving the "original yarn of unique character."

SING YOU SINNERS (Paramount, 1938) 88 minutes.

Producer/director, Wesley Ruggles; screenplay, Claude Binyon; art directors, Hans Dreier, Ernst Fegte; set decorator, A. E. Freudeman; music director, Boris Morros; camera, Karl Struss; editor, Alma Macrorie.

Songs: "Small Fry" (Hoagy Carmichael, Frank Loesser); "Don't Let that Moon Get Away," "I've Got a Pocketful of Dreams," "Laugh and Call It Love," "Where Is Central Park?" (James V. Monaco, Johnny Burke).

Bing Crosby (Joe Beebe); Fred MacMurray (David Beebe); Donald O'Connor (Mike Beebe); Elizabeth Patterson (Mrs.

Beebe); Ellen Drew (Martha); John Gallaudet (Harry Ringmer); William Haade (Pete); Paul White (Filter); Irving Bacon (Lecturer); Tom Dugan (Race Fan); Herbert Corthell (Nightclub Manager); Earl Roach (Drummer).

Mrs. Beebe (Elizabeth Patterson) has three sons: somewhat shiftless Joe (Bing Crosby), hard working mechanic David (Fred MacMurray) and young Mike (Donald O'Connor). Joe and David are not always in agreement because of Joe's inability to settle down. However, all three brothers are devoted to music and earn extra money working as a performing trio. When Joe becomes restless with life, he moves to Los Angeles where he has success in the second-hand trade. When his mother hears this, she sells her home and she and Mike move West to be with Joe. However, when they arrive, they discover that he has sold his business and has used the money to purchase a race horse. The next week David and his fiancée Martha (Ellen Drew) come to the West Coast to see Joe. The family and David have a falling out with Joe over the race horse. However, when Joe's horse wins the big race, David is happily proven wrong.

Johnny Burke and James V. Monaco provided Bing Crosby with several good songs in SING YOU SINNERS, including "I've Got a Pocketful of Dreams" and "Don't Let the Moon Get Away." By far the movie's biggest hit melody was Frank Loesser and Hoagy Carmichael's "Small Fry," which Crosby sang with Donald O'Connor.

"The happily accidental conjunction of Bing Crosby and horse racing . . . has turned out to be the funniest comedy on Broadway. . . . You've got to know the character of Bing to appreciate the family comedy of SING YOU SINNERS. Bing is the type that's lovable, but that lies around reading in hammocks, or goes out and drinks too much and comes home pie-eyed, and that propagates a new scheme for getting rich quick every week-end or so" (*New York Times*). SING YOU SINNERS gave Bing Crosby his first really in-depth screen part. In *The Films of Bing Crosby* (1977), Robert Bookbinder noted, "It is a skillful characterization, revealing for the first time the more serious side of Bing's talent."

Bing Crosby repeated the part of Joe Beebe when "Sing You Sinners" was broadcast on January 15, 1940 on CBS' "Lux Radio Theatre."

SINGIN' IN THE RAIN (Metro-Goldwyn-Mayer, 1952) Color 103 minutes.

Producer, Arthur Freed; associate producer, Roger Edens; directors, Gene Kelly, Stanley Donen; suggested by the song

"Singin' in the Rain" by Nacio Herb Brown, Freed; story/screenplay, Adolph Green, Betty Comden; art directors, Cedric Gibbons, Randall Duell; set decorators, Edwin B. Willis, Jacques Mapes; costumes, Walter Plunkett; makeup, William Tuttle; music director, Lennie Hayton; orchestrators, Conrad Salinger, Wally Heglin, Skip Alexander; vocal arrangers, Jeff Alexander, (uncredited) Edens; choreographers, Kelly, Donen; color consultants, Henri Jaffa, James Gooch; sound supervisor, Douglas Shearer; special effects, Warren Newcombe, Irving G. Ries; camera, Harold Rosson, (uncredited) John Alton; editor, Adrienne Fazan.

Songs: "Singin' in the Rain," "Temptation," "All I Do Is Dream of You," "Make 'Em Laugh," "I've Got a Feelin' You're Foolin'," "Wedding of the Painted Doll," "Should I," "Beautiful Girl," "You Were Meant for Me," "Good Morning," "Broadway Melody," "Broadway Rhythm," "You Are My Lucky Star" (Nacio Herb Brown, Arthur Freed); "Fit As a Fiddle and Ready for Love" (Al Hoffman, Al Goodhart, Freed); "Moses" (Roger Edens, Betty Comden, Adolph Green).

Gene Kelly (Don Lockwood); Donald O'Connor (Cosmo Brown); Debbie Reynolds (Kathy Selden); Jean Hagen (Lina Lamont); Millard Mitchell (R. F. Simpson); Rita Moreno (Zelda Zanders); Douglas Fowley (Roscoe Dexter); Cyd Charisse (Dancer); Madge Blake (Dora Bailey); King Donovan (Rod); Kathleen Freeman (Phoebe Dinsmore); Bobby Watson (Diction Coach); Jimmie Thompson (Male Lead in "Beautiful Girls" Number); Dan Foster (Assistant Director); Margaret Bert (Wardrobe Woman); Mae Clarke (Hairdresser); Judy Landon (Olga Mara); John Dodsworth (Baron de la May de la Toulon); Stuart Holmes (J. C. Spendrill, III); Dennis Ross (Don as a Boy); Bill Lewin (Bert, the Villain in the Western); Richard Emory (Phil, the Cowboy Hero); Julius Tannen (Man on Screen); Dawn Addams, Elaine Stewart (Ladies in Waiting); Carl Milletaire (Villain in "Dueling Cavalier" and "Broadway Rhythm" Numbers); Jack George (Orchestra Leader); Wilson Wood (Rudy Vallee Impersonator); Dorothy Patrick, William Lester, Charles Evans, Joi Lansing (Audience); Dave Sharpe, Russ Saunders (Fencers); Patricia Denise, Jeanne Coyne (Girl Dancers); Bill Catham, Ernest Flatt, Don Hulbert, Robert Dayo (Male Dancing Quartet); David Kasday (Kid); Betty Royce (Singing Voice of Kathy Selden).

"I've made a lot of films that were bigger hits and made a lot more money, but now they look dated. But this one, out of all my pictures, has a chance to last." (Gene Kelly, 1977.)

Gene Kelly was, of course, referring to SINGIN' IN THE

Carl Milletaire (center), Cyd Charisse and Gene Kelly in SINGIN' IN THE RAIN (1952).

RAIN, which many regard as the classic movie satire on Hollywood (during the transition from silents to sound) and the apex of American musical movies made in the 1950s. Originally, the concept for this motion picture—even more appreciated in later years than at the time of release—sprang from a thought at the Arthur Freed production unit at MGM about doing a musical version of Jean Harlow's old studio picture, BOMBSHELL (1933), and/or doing a satire (starring Howard Keel) of an actor who rises to fame as a singing cowboy star in the 1930s. The creative process moved on to paralleling the downfall of MGM's own John Gilbert, whose career was ruined by self-indulgence, studio politics and his highly romantic image which did not adapt well to the sound medium. As the concept developed still further, the focal point switched from an actor to an actress, and thus was born the character of Lina Lamont. Originally, Oscar Levant was thought of to play Cosmo Brown, but the creative team on SINGIN' IN THE RAIN insisted on Donald O'Connor for the role. Young Debbie Reynolds, who had appeared in the studio's THREE LITTLE

WORDS (1950), *q.v.,* and MR. IMPERIUM (1951), was a surprising choice (even to her) for the female lead. Ironically, given the film's storyline, her vocals in the movie would be dubbed by Betty Royce.* Years afterward Reynolds would recount the horrors of the martinet-like training she underwent to prepare for the picture.

In 1920s Hollywood, at the premiere of their new movie, screen lovers Don Lockwood (Gene Kelly) and Lina Lamont (Jean Hagen) tell a gushy Louella Parsons-like columnist (Madge Blake) a fabrication of how they became movie stars and such good friends both on and off the set. In reality, ex-vaudevillian and former movie stunt man Don thinks blonde Lina is an idiot and she, in turn, is too egomaniacal to acknowledge his existence. Later, in order to avoid his screaming female fans, Don escapes by leaping from the top of a bus into an open-topped jalopy driven by Kathy Selden (Debbie Reynolds). She wants to become a big singing star, but snobbishly insists she wants nothing to do with movies. When Don later attends a big party he finds that Kathy is part of the hired entertainment. Her job is to jump out of a huge cake and do a frantic Charleston dance. So much for her artistic pretensions! Don and Kathy begin to fall in love as he starts a new movie with Lina called THE DUELING CAVALIER. The production is scheduled to have dialogue sequences, sound having just come to the film industry. The rushes prove that the costume picture is hopelessly dated and that Lina's scratchy voice is too high-pitched and unsuitable for sound. To salvage the production, Don's friend Cosmo Brown (Donald O'Connor), a vaudeville pal turned studio musician, has the studio re-do the feature as a musical comedy and Kathy is hired to dub Lina's voice. This works and the resulting film is a success at its premiere. Lina, in attendance, is asked to sing for her adoring fans. Quickly Kathy is placed behind a curtain and she sings as Lina mouths the words. Don and Cosmo, however, raise the curtain and reveal the truth about Lina's ghostly talents. Lina's career is finished while Kathy is on the verge of becoming a star, with plans for her and Don to become the new singing love team of Monumental Pictures.

Cliff Edwards first introduced the song "Singin' in the Rain" in MGM's HOLLYWOOD REVUE OF 1929 (*q.v.*) and the studio

---

*Because it was decided that Debbie Reynolds' own voice (at this point in her career) was not cultivated enough for the task, in the scenes of SINGIN' IN THE RAIN in which Reynolds is seen dubbing her voice for that of Jean Hagen's, the studio actually used Hagen's own refined voice to dub that of Reynolds dubbing her.

employed it on several occasions in ensuing years.* (A montage of such uses is featured in THAT'S ENTERTAINMENT! [1974], *q.v.*) However, the tune is best remembered for its effective presentation in this 1952 musical, thanks to Gene Kelly's strenuous dance routine to the number.** The next best remembered song from the movie is Donald O'Connor's solo of "Make 'Em Laugh," which he sings and dances to in a highly athletic, acrobatic sequence. ("Make 'Em Laugh" was written as a deliberate parallel/ satire on Cole Porter's "Be a Clown," which had appeared in THE PIRATE [1948], *q.v.*) O'Connor and Kelly duet on the fast-paced "Moses," while the latter and Debbie Reynolds join together for "Good Mornin'." Among the many older numbers enhancing the period flavor of this musical are "Broadway Rhythm" and "Broadway Melody." Gene Kelly and Cyd Charisse have an impressively mammoth dance sequence in the fifteen-minute narrative, "Broadway Ballet," which was lensed at a cost of $600,000 *after* the rest of the picture had been completed. Reynolds' "singing" of "You Are My Lucky Star" was deleted from the release print.

Using much the same technical talent, as well as the star, of ON THE TOWN (1949), *q.v.*, SINGIN' IN THE RAIN emerged as a breezy genre entry, full of youthful exuberance and brimming with talent. The *New York Times'* Bosley Crowther reported, "This song-and-dance contrivance is an impudent, offhand comedy about the outlandish making of movies back in the sheik-and-flapper days when they were bridging the perilous chasm from silent to talking films. . . . At times it reaches the level of first-class satiric burlesque."

Made at a cost of $2,540,800, SINGIN' IN THE RAIN grossed $7,665,000 in its initial release. SINGIN' IN THE RAIN received Oscar nominations for Best Supporting Actress (Jean Hagen) and for Best Scoring.

Debbie Reynolds and Donald O'Connor would re-team the next year for MGM's I LOVE MELVIN.

On July 2, 1985 a Broadway musical version of SINGIN' IN THE RAIN, starring Don Correia (Don Lockwood), Mary D'Arcy (Kathy Selden), Peter Slutsker (Cosmo Brown) and Faye Grant (Lina Lamont) debuted. Making use of Nacio Herb Brown and Arthur Freed's songs, the screenplay by Betty Comden and Adolph

*Prolific song writer Arthur Freed made a practice of using his own vast catalog of compositions for a variety of his own productions at MGM. One of the guiding goals in making SINGIN' IN THE RAIN was to use a basketful of Freed tunes, both a self-serving and an economical rationale.

**In PUNCHLINE (1988), Tom Hanks would execute a wonderful mime parody of Gene Kelly's famous dance while "Singin' in the Rain."

Green and some of the original choreography by Gene Kelly and Stanley Donen (with new choreography by director Twyla Tharp), the derivative stage show lasted for 367 performances.

THE SINGING FOOL (Warner Bros., 1928) 105 minutes. (Also silent version: 7,444′).

Director, Lloyd Bacon; based on the story by Leslie S. Barrows; screenplay, C. Graham Baker; dialogue/titles, Joseph Jackson; music arranger, Louis Silvers; assistant director, Frank Shaw; sound, George R. Groves; camera, Byron Haskin; editors, Ralph Dawson, Harold McCord.

Songs: "Sonny Boy," "It All Depends on You," "I'm Sittin' on Top of the World" (Buddy G. DeSylva, Lew Brown, Ray Henderson); "There's a Rainbow Round My Shoulder," "Keep Smiling at Trouble," "Golden Gate," "The Spaniard Who Blighted My Life" (Billy Rose, Al Jolson, Dave Dreyer).

Al Jolson (Al Stone); Betty Bronson (Grace); Josephine Dunn (Molly Winton); Arthur Housman (Blackie Joe); Reed Howes (John Perry); Davey Lee (Sonny Boy); Edward Martindel (Louis Marcus); Robert Emmett O'Connor (Cafe Manager); and: Helen Lynch.

Al Jolson followed his phenomenal success with THE JAZZ SINGER (1927), *q.v.*, with another part-talkie the following year, for which he was paid $150,000. THE SINGING FOOL had more talk and music than silence, the reversal of his prior feature. Over-long at eleven reels, but filled with many famous Jolson songs, THE SINGING FOOL had a corny plot (even for 1928) and Jolie hopelessly overacted to milk every drop of sentiment from the naive tale. (*Photoplay* magazine admitted it was a "Saga of a mammy shouter. . . . Sobs and Vitaphone Songs.") Despite all, THE SINGING FOOL grossed $5.5 million at the box-office, a record not broken for eleven years until GONE WITH THE WIND (1939).

While working as a singing waiter at Blackie Joe's (Arthur Housman) cafe, Al Stone (Al Jolson) writes a best-selling song for grasping club performer Molly Winton (Josephine Dunn), whom he loves. She is too engrossed in furthering her own career to care about Al's infatuation with her. However, when his song is suddenly proclaimed a success, she becomes interested in him. They marry and have a child called Sonny Boy (Davey Lee). Meanwhile, Al has become a star on Broadway. Eventually Molly deserts Al for gangster John Perry (Reed Howes) and takes Sonny Boy with her. As a result of losing his family, a morose Al gives up his career and becomes a vagabond. Eventually he goes back to

Al Jolson in THE SINGING FOOL (1928).

Blackie Joe's place, where he receives loyalty and understanding from winsome cigarette girl Grace (Betty Bronson), who has loved Al from the start. She convinces him to start singing again. When Sonny Boy becomes very sick, Al goes to him in the hospital and sings to his son the child's favorite song. Nevertheless, the boy dies. Al resumes his career and he and Grace marry and go to live and work in California.

While saccharine is the best word to describe the primitive proceedings, THE SINGING FOOL comes alive when Jolie belts out his many grand songs, including "I'm Sitting on Top of the World," "Keep Smiling at Trouble" and a tune from early in his stage career, "The Spaniard Who Blighted My Life." The film's biggest hit was the contrived tearjerker, "Sonny Boy" (allegedly written as a joke), which sold over three million records when Al recorded it for Brunswick.

Al Jolson and Davey Lee would be reunited for the lugubrious SAY IT WITH SONGS (1929), *q.v.*

SMALL TOWN GIRL (Metro-Goldwyn-Mayer, 1953) Color 93 minutes.

Producer, Joe Pasternak; director, Leslie Kardos; story, Dorothy Cooper; screenplay, Cooper, Dorothy Kingsley; art directors, Cedric Gibbons, Hans Peters; makeup, William Tuttle; music director, Andre Previn; choreographer, Busby Berkeley; camera, Joseph Ruttenberg; editor, Albert Akst.

Songs: "My Flaming Heart," "Fine, Fine, Fine," "The Fellow I'd Follow," "Lullaby of the Lord," "Small Towns Are Smile Towns," "My Gaucho," "Take Me to Broadway," "I've Got to Hear that Beat" (Nicholas Brodzky, Leo Robin).

Jane Powell (Cindy Kimbell); Farley Granger (Rick Belrow Livingston); Ann Miller (Lisa Bellmount); S. Z. Sakall (Eric Schlemmer); Robert Keith (Judge Gordon Kimbell); Bobby Van (Ludwig Schlemmer); Billie Burke (Mrs. Livingston); Fay Wray (Mrs. Gordon Kimbell); Chill Wills (Happy, the Jailer); Nat "King" Cole (Himself); Dean Miller (Mac); William Campbell (Ted); Philip Tonge (Hemmingway); Jonathan Cott (Jim, the Cop); Bobby Hyatt (Dennis); Rudy Lee (Jimmy); Beverly Wills (Deirdre); Gloria Noble (Patsy); Jane Liddell (Betty); Nancy Valentine (Mary); Janet Stewart (Sandra); Pegi McIntire (Susie); Virginia Hall (Girl Friend); and: Marie Blake.

When MGM produced SMALL TOWN GIRL in 1936 it had been a congenial girl-meets/loses/wins-boy comedy featuring Janet Gaynor, Robert Taylor and Lew Ayres. The *New York Times* had labeled it "another pleasant, if incurably romantic, bit of Metro-

Goldwyn-Mayer." Nearly two decades later the studio, already fallen on harder times, chose to remake the slight property, this time as a musical starring Jane Powell and Farley Granger. For a conservatively budgeted entry with a stale story, the lightweight remake had several impressive ingredients: splashy hoofers Ann Miller and Bobby Van, a guest appearance by silky-voiced Nat "King" Cole, and the still fertile creativity of veteran choreographer Busby Berkeley. And, being a Joe Pasternak production, it was geared to be glossy, appealing to a wide range of taste, and to be very colorful.

Self-centered young millionaire Rick Belrow Livingston (Farley Granger) is arrested for speeding through the small town of Duck Creek. The local judge, Gordon Kimbell (Robert Keith), sentences him to thirty days in jail, thus postponing his elopement with gold-digging Broadway musical comedy star Lisa Bellmount (Ann Miller). While in jail Rick meets the judge's wholesome daughter, Cindy (Jane Powell), and the two display an attraction for one another. By feigning a hunger strike, Rick talks his jailer (Chill Wills) into permitting him one night of freedom so he can go to New York City, allegedly to spend the evening with his mother (Billie Burke), celebrating her birthday. Actually he plans to meet his fiancée. Lisa. His scheme is disrupted when Cindy decides to go along as his "guardian." Rick manages to sneak away from Cindy when they are at his mother's home, but later must retrieve the troublesome girl when she gets locked in his mother's walk-in fur storage locker. Later that evening Rick and Cindy go on a tour of Manhattan nightclubs. By the time they return to Duck Creek, they are in love. All of this is embarrassing to Cindy's father and mother (Fay Wray) as well as to her boyfriend, Ludwig Schlemmer (Bobby Van). The latter has show business ambitions, while his own father, Eric (S. Z. Sakall), a local merchant, wants his offspring to marry Cindy and settle down. Rick and Cindy announce they are in love. After solving other complications, and learning that Lisa has found a new and rich beau, the young couple plan their future together.

Co-stars Ann Miller and Bobby Van received the lion's share of the notices for their energetic work in SMALL TOWN GIRL. Miller was especially impressive in her two Busby Berkeley-conceived dance numbers, "I've Gotta Hear that Beat" and "My Gaucho." In the former, the inventive Berkeley created a setting in which eighty-six sets of hands protruded up from the stage to play assorted instruments while Miller ferociously tap danced about the stage. Van literally stole the show with his "Street Dance," and especially his exhausting plea for a show business career in "Take Me to Broadway." He also sang with Jane Powell on "Fine, Fine,

Fine," while Jane soloed on "The Lullaby of the Lord," "Small Towns Are Smile Towns" and "The Fellow I'd Follow." Another musical highlight was a special guest appearance by Nat "King" Cole who sang the ballad "My Flaming Heart." (Interestingly, Farley Granger, who did not sing in this movie, had an opportunity to do so in the stage musical *First Impressions,* 1959, in which he co-starred with Polly Bergen.)

The *New York Times* called this musical remake, "Another of those wholesome, pastel musicals that comes to life when the band hits it, and this one has some fine singing and a few dancing sequences that are plain wonderful." *Variety* noted of the movie, ". . . Packages an engaging round of light musical comedy offering fun for most all ages and audience groups. Familiar names for the marquee, Technicolor, spritely songs and dances, and a plot with just enough substance to hold attention without wearing. . . ."

SMALL TOWN GIRL won an Academy Award nomination for Best Song ("My Flaming Heart") but lost to "Secret Love" from CALAMITY JANE, *q.v.*

SNOW WHITE AND THE SEVEN DWARFS (RKO, 1937) Color 82 minutes.

Producer, Walt Disney; supervising director, David Hand; sequence directors, Perce Pearce, Larry Morey, William Cottrell, Wilfred Jackson, Ben Sharpsteen; based on the fairy tale "Sneewittchen" by Jacob Grimm, Wilhelm Grimm; screenplay, Ted Sears, Otto Englander, Earl Hurd, Dorothy Ann Blank, Richard Creedo, Dick Richard, Merril De Maris, Webb Smith; art directors, Charles Phillippi, Hugh Hennessy, Terrell Stapp, McLaren Stewart, Harold Miles, Tom Codrick, Gustaf Tenggren, Kenneth Anderson, Kendall O'Connor, Hazel Sewell; character designers, Albert Hunter, Joe Grant; supervising animators, Hamilton Kuske, Vladimir Tytla, Fred Moore, Norman Ferguson; animators, Frank Thomas, Dick Lundy, Arthur Babbitt, Eric Larson, Milton Kahl, Robert Stokes, James Algar, Al Eugster, Cy Young, Joshua Meador, Ugo D'Orsi, George Rowley, Lee Clark, Fred Spencer, Bill Roberts, Bernard Garbutt, Grim Natwick, Jack Campbell, Marvin Woodward, James Culhane, Stan Quackenbush, Ward Kimball, Wolfgang Reitherman, Robert Martsch; backgrounds, Samuel Armstrong, Mique Nelson, Merle Cox, Claude Coats, Phil Dike, Ray Lockrem, Maurice Noble; music, Leigh Harline, Paul J. Smith.

Songs: "Heigh Ho," "Just Whistle While You Work," "Some Day My Prince Will Come," "I'm Wishing," "One Song," "With a

Smile and a Song" "The Washing Song," "Is This a Silly Song?" "Bluddle-Uddle-Um-Dum," "The Dwarfs' Yodel Song" (Larry Morey, Frank Churchill).

Voices: Adriana Caselotti (Snow White); Harry Stockwell (Prince Charming); Lucille LaVerne (The Queen); Moroni Olsen (Magic Mirror); Billy Gilbert (Sneezy); Pinto Colvig (Sleepy/Grumpy); Otis Harlan (Happy); Scotty Mattraw (Bashful); Roy Atwell (Doc); Stuart Buchanan (Humbert, the Queen's Huntsman); Marion Darlington (Bird Sounds/Warbling); The Fraunfelder Family, Jim MacDonald (Yodeling).

After a decade of making Hollywood cartoons, Walt Disney entered the feature-length animated field with SNOW WHITE AND THE SEVEN DWARFS, adapting the famous Grimms' fairy tale to the screen. (It required nearly three years of production to complete, and effective use of the multiplane camera, which gave the setting added realism.) Interpolated into the embellished plot were a number of colorful songs with music by Frank Churchill and lyrics by Larry Morey. Leigh Harline and Paul J. Smith wrote the background score. Costing $1.75 million (its original budget had been set at $250,000), SNOW WHITE AND THE SEVEN DWARFS has grossed $27 million in distributors' domestic film rentals, having been issued on several occasions and now, in videocassette format.

Pretty young Snow White (voice of Adriana Caselotti) lives at the castle of the Wicked Queen (voice of Lucille LaVerne) who prides herself as being the most beautiful woman in the land. Snow White longs for a handsome prince to rescue her, but when she sees the courtly prince (voice of Harry Stockwell) she runs away from him out of shyness. Because the Wicked Queen's magic mirror tells her that Snow White is *now* the fairest in the land, she orders a huntsman to kill the girl. However, the kind-hearted soul cannot carry out his deadly assignment. He permits Snow White to escape into the forest where she comes upon the cottage of the Seven Dwarfs. The little men adopt the bewildered young girl. Snow White is happy with the Dwarfs. Through her magic mirror, the Wicked Queen learns that Snow White still lives. Taking on the guise of an old crone, she goes to the Dwarfs' cottage and gives the girl a poisoned apple which puts her into a deep sleep. In a rainstorm, the Dwarfs give chase to the evil Queen, who falls from a ravine and is killed. The Prince comes to see the sleeping Snow White and kisses the girl. She awakens and now can live happily ever after with the handsome man of her dreams.

SNOW WHITE AND THE SEVEN DWARFS contains two pleasant love ballads, "Someday My Prince Will Come" and "I'm

Wishing." However, it is the numbers assigned to the irrepressible Dwarfs that really stand out in retrospect; they range from "Heigh Ho" to "Just Whistle While You Work." Cut from the film's final release print were the songs, "Music in Your Soup" and "You're Never Too Old to Be Young."

Writing in the *New York Herald Tribune,* Howard Barnes said that the film "belongs with the few great masterpieces of the screen." He added, "It is one of those rare works of inspired artistry that weaves an irresistible spell around the beholder. Walt Disney has created worlds of sheer enchantment before with his animated cartoons, but never has he taken us so completely within their magic bounds. SNOW WHITE AND THE SEVEN DWARFS is more than completely satisfying entertainment, more than a perfect moving picture, in the full sense of that term. It offers one a memorable and deeply enriching experience."

SNOW WHITE AND THE SEVEN DWARFS received an Oscar nomination for Best Score, but lost to 100 MEN AND A GIRL, *q.v.* For the record it was Marjorie Belcher—later known as Marge Champion—who served as the model for Snow White.

A stage version of SNOW WHITE AND THE SEVEN DWARFS opened at New York City's Radio City Music Hall on October 18, 1979 for a thirty-three-performance run before going on tour. It starred Mary Jo Salerno, Richard Bowne, Ann Francine, Thomas Ruisinger and Charles Hall. It utilized some of the Frank Churchill-Larry Morey score from the Walt Disney production, but added new songs by Joe Blackton and Joe Cook (who also wrote the new book).

SO THIS IS LOVE (Warner Bros., 1953) Color 101 minutes.

Producer, Henry Blanke; director, Gordon Douglas; based on the book *You're Only Human Once* by Grace Moore; screenplay, John Monk, Jr.; art director, Edward Carrere; costumes, Leah Rhodes; music, Max Steiner; music director, Ray Heindorf; choreographer, LeRoy Prinz; camera, Robert Burks; editor, Folmar Blangsted.

Songs: "The Kiss Waltz," "Time On My Hands" (Harold Adamson, Mack Gordon, Vincent Youmans); "Remember" (Irving Berlin); "I Wish I Could Shimmy Like My Sister Kate" (Armand J. Prion, Peter Bocage); "Ciribiribin" (Harry James, Jack Lawrence, A. Pestalozza); excerpts from the operas *The Marriage of Figaro* (Wolfgang Amadeus Mozart); *Faust* (Charles Gounod); *La Bohème* (Giacomo Puccini).

Kathryn Grayson (Grace Moore); Merv Griffin (Buddy Nash); Joan Weldon (Ruth Obre); Walter Abel (Colonel Moore); Rosemary DeCamp (Aunt Laura Stokley); Jeff Donnell (Henrietta Van Dyke); Douglas Dick (Byron Curtis); Ann Doran (Mrs. Moore); Margaret Field (Edna Wallace); Mabel Albertson (Mary Garden); Fortunio Bonanova (Dr. Marafioti); Marie Windsor (Marilyn Montgomery); Noreen Corcoran (Grace Moore at Age Eight); The Szonys (Dance Specialty); Lillian Bronson (Mrs. Wilson Green); Ray Kellogg (John McCormack); Roy Gordon (Otto Kahn); Moroni Olsen (Arnold Reuben); Mario Siletti (Gatti Casazza); Charles Meredith (Arthur Bodansky); William Boyett (George Gershwin).

Grace Moore (1901–1947) was a popular opera diva who had her first success in popular music before becoming a major star of the Metropolitan Opera in 1928. In the early days of sound films she appeared in two MGM musicals, A LADY'S MORALS (1930) and NEW MOON (1930), *q.v.* However, her greatest celluloid success came in 1934 for Columbia Pictures in ONE NIGHT OF LOVE (q.v.). She did other feature films after that. Through her movies, personal appearances and recordings she was one of the most popular singers of opera until her tragic death in a plane crash in 1947 in Denmark. In 1953, Warner Bros. who had made a deal to utilize the screen services of MGM's Kathryn Grayson, produced SO THIS IS LOVE, a rather mundane movie biography focusing on the early life of the opera star. It is also one of the few feature film appearances of Merv Griffin, who gained later fame and fortune as a TV game and talk show host.

As a child, rural Tennessee-born Grace Moore (Noreen Corcoran), a self-willed young lady with ambitions for show business, upsets her staid father, Colonel Moore (Walter Abel), by riding an elephant when they visit the circus. As a young woman (Kathryn Grayson) she leaves her Washington, D.C. music school to go to New York to find a job on the stage. She sings in a Manhattan nightclub and falls in love with song-and-dance man, Buddy Nash (Merv Griffin). However, because she neglects him for her career, he later marries one of her friends. Grace wins a role in a musical, but a bad case of laryngitis intervenes. After a rest cure ordered by her coach Dr. Marafioti (Fortunio Bonanova), she earns another singing role. When the star of the show is taken ill, she successfully steps on in her place. Soon she is a rising young luminary on the Broadway stage. Meanwhile, she meets well-bred Byron Curtis (Douglas Dick), who proposes to her. Still driven to become an opera singer, she auditions for the Metropolitan Opera but is advised that her voice is not yet ready. Turning her back on the Broadway stage and Byron's love, she goes abroad (for eighteen months) to study opera with the great Mary Garden (Mabel

Kathryn Grayson and Merv Griffin in SO THIS IS LOVE (1953).

Albertson). Upon her return to the United States, Grace makes a triumphant appearance at the Metropolitan Opera, debuting as Mimi in *La Bohème.* Despite stardom she finds she is all alone.

SO THIS IS LOVE was very loosely based on Grace Moore's autobiography, *You're Only Human Once* (1944), and in the film Kathryn Grayson was showcased in a variety of songs which ranged from popular numbers ("Time on My Hands," "Ciribiribin") to novelty tunes ("I Wish I Could Shimmy Like My Sister Kate") to classical offerings ("Voi Che Sapete," "Mi Chiamano Mimi"). As usual, she was musically proficient but emotionally distant.

The *New York Times* decided: ". . . [The film is] more effective musically than in its depiction of a colorful success story . . . the tale is a succession of entertaining but rarely exciting incidents." More to the point was *Harrison's Reports,* "Unfortunately, the picture offers little to set it apart from numerous other musical films; it is equipped with the same dramatic situations, none of which are too convincing, and except for the lush production values and the fine color photography, it impresses one as being just another assembly job."

If Warner Bros. was hoping to duplicate the success of MGM's THE GREAT CARUSO (1951), *q.v.*, they were sorely disappointed.

British release title: THE GRACE MOORE STORY.

SOMETHING FOR THE BOYS (20th Century-Fox, 1944) Color 87 minutes.

Producer, Irving Starr; director, Lewis Seiler; based on the musical play by Herbert Fields, Dorothy Fields, Cole Porter; screenplay, Robert Ellis, Helen Logan, Frank Gabrielson; art directors, Lyle Wheeler, Albert Hogsett; set decorators, Thomas Little, Walter M. Scott; musical settings, Joseph C. Wright; music director, Emil Newman; choreographer, Nick Castle; assistant director, Arthur Jacobson; color consultant, Natalie Kalmus; sound, W. D. Flick; special camera effects, Fred Sersen; camera, Ernest Palmer; editor, Robert Simpson.

Songs: "Something for the Boys" (Cole Porter); "Wouldn't It Be Nice?" "I Wish We Didn't Have to Say Goodnight," "80 Miles Outside of Atlanta," "I'm in the Middle of Nowhere," "Boom Brachee," "Samba Boogie" (Harold Adamson, Frank Loesser, Jimmy McHugh).

Carmen Miranda (Chiquita Hart); Michael O'Shea (Staff Sergeant Rocky Fulton); Vivian Blaine (Blossom Hart); Phil Silvers (Harry Hart); Sheila Ryan (Melanie Walker); Perry Como (Sergeant Laddie Green); Glenn Langan (Lieutenant Ashley Crothers); Roger Clark (Lieutenant); Cara Williams (Secretary); Thurston Hall (Colonel Jefferson L. Calhoun); Clarence Kolb (Colonel Grubbs); Paul Hurst (Supervisor); Andrew Tombes (Southern Colonel); Judy Holliday (1st Girl at Defense Plant); Murray Alper (Sergeant); Eddie Acuff (Operator).

In the mid-1940s, 20th Century-Fox churned out a trio of musicals directed by Lewis Seiler, with Carmen Miranda, Vivian Blaine and Perry Como starred. SOMETHING FOR THE BOYS was the initial outing, followed by two 1946 songfests: DOLL FACE and IF I'M LUCKY. The first film was based on the 1942 Broadway play of the same title starring Ethel Merman, with a score by Cole Porter and book by Herbert and Dorothy Fields; on stage the musical ran for a healthy 422 performances. In the loosely-conceived Hollywood rendition, it was converted into another splashy vehicle for the exotic Brazilian export, Carmen Miranda, then earning over $200,000 annually in tinseltown. This was the film debut for radio and recording crooner Perry Como. To be noted in a tiny bit in the film as a defense plant worker was future stage/film star Judy Holliday.

Chiquita Hart (Carmen Miranda) works in a defense plant polishing carborundum. Her cousin, Blossom Hart (Vivian Blaine), is a club singer. Both of them have another cousin, Harry Hart (Phil Silvers), who is a sidewalk salesman. They finally meet when they discover they have inherited a debt-drenched Thomasville, Georgia mansion. After visiting the rundown place they are persuaded by Staff Sergeant Rocky Fulton (Michael O'Shea), from a nearby military camp, to convert the manse into a boarding home for soldiers' wives. To finance the operation, they put on several shows. Once the transformation is accomplished, Blossom finds herself being romanced by Fulton, much to the chagrin of his socialite fiancée, Melanie Walker (Sheila Ryan), who arrives on the scene. Meanwhile, volatile Chiquita has all kinds of problems when her mouth turns into a radio receiver due to a carborundum cap on her teeth. During a Red-Blue Army war game, the manse becomes a strategic operations point and thanks to radio information transmitted over Chiquita's teeth, Rocky's team wins the maneuvers.

SOMETHING FOR THE BOYS retained only one (!) of the Cole Porter stage songs ("Something for the Boys"), while adding several new tunes by the team of Harold Adamson, Frank Loesser and Jimmy McHugh. Carmen Miranda performed the splashy "Samba Boogie," and "Boom Brachee," while Perry Como crooned "I Wish We Didn't Have to Say Goodnight" and "I'm in the Middle of Nowhere." Michael O'Shea dueted with Vivian Blaine on "Wouldn't It Be Nice?" while Blaine—ever a proficient trouper—performed effectively on "80 Miles Outside of Atlanta" (a production number). Nick Castle provided his usual, flashy choreography to enliven the proceedings.

Variety judged, ". . . Taken as a whole, the story does not have particular punch in dialog or otherwise. . . . The comedy values are somewhat spotty. . . . Phil Silvers works hard on the comic end and, in one clowning number, provides several minutes of surefire nature."

While SOMETHING FOR THE BOYS was lensed in Technicolor, its two "follow-ups" with Blaine, Miranda and Como were done in economical black and white. None of the three musicals was successful in converting Como into a solid screen personality.

SONG OF NORWAY (Cinerama, 1970) Color 138 minutes.

Producers, Andrew L. Stone, Virginia Stone; director, Andrew L. Stone; based on the musical play by Milton Lazarus, Robert Wright, George Forrest from the play by Homer Curran; art director, William Albert Havemeyer; costumes, David Walker, Fiorella Mariani; music supervisor/orchestrator/conductor, Roland

Shaw; choreographer, Lee Theodore; second unit director, Yakima Canutt; assistant director, Leif Jul; animation director, Jack Kinney; sound, John Purchese; sound editor, Virginia Stone; camera, David Boulton; second unit camera, Terry Gould; editor, Virginia Stone.

Songs: "Opening Piano Concert—The Life of a Wife of a Sailor," "Freddie and His Fiddle," "Strange Music," "The Song of Norway," "A Rhyme and a Reason," "The Little House," "Hill of Dreams," "I Love You," "Hymn of Betrothal," "Be a Boy Again," "Midsummer's Eve, Hand in Hand," "Three There Were," "The Solitary Wanderer," "A Welcome Toast," "Wrong to Dream," "Solvejg's Song—Norwegian National Anthem," "Grieg's Piano Concerto," "At Christmas Time," "John Heggerstrom," "When We Wed," "Ribbons and Wrappings" (Bob Wright, Chet Forrest; based on the compositions of Edvard Grieg).

Toralv Maurstad (Edvard Grieg); Florence Henderson (Nina Hagerup Grieg); Christina Schollin (Therese Berg); Frank Porretta (Rikard Nordraak); Harry Secombe (Bjornsterne Bjornson); Robert Morley (Berg); Edward G. Robinson (Krogstad); Elizabeth Larner (Mrs. Bjornson); Oscar Homolka (Engstrand); Frederick Jaeger (Henrik Ibsen); Henry Gilbert (Franz Liszt); Richard

Florence Henderson in SONG OF NORWAY (1970).

Wordsworth (Hans Christian Andersen); Bernard Archard (George Nordraak); Susan Richards Chitty (Aunt Aline); John Barrie (Hagerup); Wenke Foss (Mrs. Hagerup); Ronald Adam (Gade); Carl Rigg (Captain Hansen); Aline Towne (Mrs. Thoresen); Nan Munro (Irate Woman); James Hayter (Berg's Butler); Avind Harum (Freddie); Rolf Berntzen (Doctor); Tordis Maurstad (Mrs. Schmidt); Erik Chitty (Helsted); Charles Lloyd Pack (Chevalier); Robert Rietty (Winding); Rosalind Speight, Ros Drinkwater (Liszt's Friends); Tracey Crisp (Receptionist); Cyril Renison (Rome Butler); Manoug Parikian (Violinist); Richard Vernon (1st Councilman); Eli Lindstner (Bjornson's Secretary); Ilke Tromm (Girl's Mother); Ernest Clark (2nd Councilman); Jeffrey Taylor, Peter Salmon, Roy Jones, Gordon Coster, Paddy McIntyre, Barrie Wilkinson, Rupert Lupone, Stephen Reinhardt, Jane Darling, Barbara von der Heyde, Hermione Fathingale, Jennie Walton, Michele Hardy, Susan Claire, Denise O'Brien, Jane Kells (Dancers).

Bob Wright and Chet Forrest's musical, *Song of Norway,* opened on Broadway late in the summer of 1944 and had a then tremendous run of 860 performances. It starred Lawrence Brooks, Irra Petina, Helena Bliss and Sig Arno, and the music in the production was adapted from the melodies of Edvard Grieg (1843–1907) and resulted in the hit song, "Strange Music." In 1958 Guy Lombardo produced a successful revival of the musical at Jones Beach (New York) with Brenda Lewis, John Reardon, Helena Scott and Sig Arno, the latter reprising his Broadway role. A dozen years later Andrew and Virginia Stone brought the Wright-Forrest work to the screen. However, the multi-million dollar production, which included forty-five musical numbers and more than two dozen songs, turned out be a box-office fiasco, recouping only $4.55 million in distributors' domestic film rentals. Filmgoers wanted more diversion than this clichéd and archaic production had to offer. Not even the international cast (including a non-singing Edward G. Robinson) nor a few interpolated animated sequences could give the project any verisimilitude.

Wealthy Theresa Berg (Christina Schollin), a classmate of Norwegian composer-pianist Edvard Grieg (Toralv Maurstad), strikes a bargain with her stern-willed father (Robert Morley). If he will finance a recital for Grieg and persuade Stockholm's respected critics to attend, she promises not ever to see again the man (Grieg) she loves. The concert is a success, but Grieg is upset by Theresa's disappearance from his life. Grieg next goes to Copenhagen where he is influenced by the compositions of Rikard Nordraak (Frank Porretta), who becomes his good friend. Edvard marries his cousin, Nina Hagerup (Florence Henderson), and on the day of his wedding again hears from Theresa, who announces that she wants to see him again. Grieg and Nina go to Kristiania, where he hopes to become the conductor of the national theatre. However, he loses the appointment due to political infighting. He embarks on another concert tour, again secretly financed by Theresa, which is a failure. Sailing to Rome, Grieg meets Franz Liszt (Henry Gilbert) and works with Henrik Ibsen (Frederick Jaeger) on *Peer Gynt.* Theresa arrives in Rome and becomes his patroness. Later, from the piano dealer Krogstad (Edward G. Robinson), he learns that Nina, who he had thought had gone home to live with her mother, is struggling on alone. Understanding his selfishness, Grieg returns home to Nina and begins composing Norway's national music.

With its bloated musical offerings, stuffy plotline and lugubrious pacing, it was little wonder that Richard Schickel (*Life* magazine) dubbed the feature "Godawful." He added, "The musical numbers, when not downright ugly, are ludicrous . . . truly an amazing work of unintentional humor." Vincent Canby (*New York Times*) "SONG OF NORWAY is no ordinary movie kitsch, but a display to turn Guy Lombardo livid with envy. . . ." He pointed out that the reason the cast ". . . Appear to be a little more foolish than they need be is not only because of the scenario, but also because of [Andrew] Stone's pursuit of realism, in this case, of scenery, which is so overwhelming that the people are reduced to being scenic obstructions." In *The Films of the Seventies* (1984), Marc Sigoloff wrote, "Silly musical biography . . . [it] is filled with dismal and phoney sweetness, and the film does not even do justice to Grieg's music."

SONG OF THE FLAME (First National, 1930) Color 72 minutes.

Director, Alan Crosland; based on the operetta by Oscar Hammerstein, II, Otto Harbach, George Gershwin, Herbert Stothart; screenplay/dialogue, Gordon Rigby; set designer, Anton Grot; costumes, Edward Stevenson; music director, Leo F. Forbstein; chorus director, Ernest Grooney; choreographer, Jack Haskell; assistant director, Ben Silvey; sound, George R. Groves; camera, Lee Garmes; editor, Al Hall.

Songs: "The Cossack Love Song," "Song of the Flame" (Oscar Hammerstein, II, Herbert Stothart); "Petrograd," "Liberty Song," "The Goose Hangs High," "Passing Fancy," "One Little Drink" (Grant Clarke, Harry Akst, Ed Ward); "When Love Calls" (Ward).

Alexander Gray (Prince Volodya); Bernice Claire (Anuita the Flame); Noah Beery (Konstantin); Alice Gentle (Natasha); Bert Roach (Count Boris); Inez Courtney (Grusha); Shep Camp (Officer); Iva Linow (Konstantin's Pal); Janina Smolinska (Dancer).

Based on the 1925 Broadway operetta with music by Herbert Stothart and George Gershwin and book/lyrics by Otto Harbach and Oscar Hammerstein, II, *Song of the Flame* had a 219-performance run on Broadway. It was filled with all the extravaganzas of emotion, setting and songs that the musical format required. As such it was a natural property to be acquired during Hollywood's craze with turning out musical movies in the late 1920s. First National Pictures, which had a proclivity for such movie operettas, heralded their newest entry with: "Gigantic scenes in gorgeous color vivify its sweeping drama. Thundering choruses set your senses tingling. A sumptuous revel with scores of sinuous dancing girls exposes the pleasures of nobility on the brink of doom!" As an added gimmick for the feature, during the course of the movie, the screen expanded for a wide-lens sequence. Only a few songs from the original stage version remained in the movie edition; Harry Akst and Grant Clarke composed several new numbers for the film.

On the eve of the Russian Revolution, beautiful Anuita (Bernice Claire), "The Flame," sings to her people as she incites them to revolt against Czar Nicholas. Prince Volodya (Alexander Gray) uses his Cossack forces to capture the young woman, but she is protected by fellow revolutionary Konstantin (Noah Beery). The latter lusts for her, even though he is betrothed to Natasha (Alice Gentle), who is very jealous of the alluring Anuita. When the revolution comes, the Czar is overthrown but Konstantin and his conspirators become more brutal and oppressive than the Czarists ever were. Sickened by what has happened, the disillusioned Anuita returns to her small Polish village for the Festival of the Harvest. There she meets Prince Volodya and the two fall in love. Konstantin and his men arrive and place the Prince under arrest. To save him from execution, Anuita tells Konstantin she will become his mistress. Instead, she is jailed. The Prince manages to escape his bonds and, in disguise, rescues Anuita as Natasha murders Konstantin. Anuita and the Prince escape to the West and to freedom.

Alexander Gray and Bernice Claire had just starred in NO, NO NANETTE (1930), *q.v.,* for First National when the studio paired them in this Technicolor operetta. (Gray would follow it with yet another color operetta for Warner Bros., VIENNESE NIGHTS, *q.v.,* the same year.) Sadly none of these well-mounted musicals was successful, as noted by John Springer in *All Talking! All Singing! All Dancing!* (1966): "If the moment had been right, it might have been Bernice Claire and Alexander Gray as the King and Queen of movie operetta instead of MacDonald and Eddy. However, by the time they made their appearance in NO, NO

NANETTE and SONG OF THE FLAME, fickle movie fans were staying away from anything with song. . . ." This is sad because SONG OF THE FLAME was an entertaining production which provided Noah Beery with one of his few screen chances to show off his fine deep bass voice.

Because movie operetta was fast becoming anathema at the box-office, THE SONG OF THE FLAME was trimmed to a relatively brief 72 minutes, deleting some of the musical sequences.

A SONG TO REMEMBER (Columbia, 1945) Color 113 minutes.

Producer, Louis F. Edelman; director, Charles Vidor; story, Ernst Marischka; screenplay, Sidney Buchman; art directors, Lionel Banks, Van Nest Polglase; set decorator, Frank Tuttle; costumes, Walter Plunkett, Travis Banton; makeup, Clay Campbell; music director, Morris W. Stoloff; music adaptor, Miklos Rozsa; music supervisor, Mario Silva; music recordings, William Randall; color consultant, Natalie Kalmus; assistant director, Abby Berlin; sound, Lodge Cunningham; camera, Tony Gaudio, Allen M. Davey; editor, Charles Nelson.

Musical numbers: "Valse in D Flat (Minute Waltz)," "Mazurka in B Flat, Opus 7, No. 1," "Fantasie Impromptu, Opus 66," "Etude in A Flat, Opus 25, No. 1," "Polonaise in A Flat, Opus 53," "Scherzo in B Flat Minor," "Etude in C Minor, Opus 10, No. 12," "Nocturne in C Minor, Opus 48, No. 1," "Nocturne in E Flat, Opus 9, No. 2," "Valse in A Flat, Opus 34, No. 1," "Ballade in A Flat, Opus 47," "Waltz in C Sharp Minor, Opus 64, No. 2," "Berceuse in D Flat, Opus 57," "Etude in E, Opus 10, No. 3" (Frederic Chopin).

Paul Muni (Professor Joseph Elsner); Merle Oberon (George Sand [Amandine Dupin]); Cornel Wilde (Frederic Chopin); Stephen Bekassy (Franz Liszt); Nina Foch (Constantia); George Coulouris (Louis Pleyel); Sig Arno (Henri Dupont); Howard Freeman (Kalkbrenner); George Macready (Alfred DeMusset); Claire Dubrey (Madame Mercier); Frank Puglia (Monsieur Jollet); Fern Emmett (Madame Lambert); Sybil Merritt (Isabelle Chopin); Ivan Triesault (Monsieur Chopin); Fay Helm (Madame Chopin); Dawn Bender (Isabelle Chopin at Age Nine); Maurice Tauzin (Frederic Chopin at Age Ten); Roxy Roth (Niccolo Paganini); Peter Cusannelli (Honoré de Balzac); William Challee (Titus); William Richardson (Jan); Alfred Piax (Headwaiter); Charles Wagenheim, Paul Zaeremba (Waiters); Charles Latorre (Postman); Earl Easton (Albert); Gregory Gaye (Young Russian); Walter Bonn (Major Domo); Henry Sharp (Russian Count); Zoia Karabanova (Countess); Michael Visaroff (Russian Governor); John George (Servant); Ian Wolfe (Pleyel's Clerk); Lucy Von Boden (Window Washer);

Norman Drury (Duchess of Orleans); Alfred Allegro, Cosmo Sardo (Lackeys); Al Luttringer (De La Croux); Darren McGavin (Printer); Eugene Borden (Duc of Orleans); Jose Iturbi (Piano Playing for Frederic Chopin).

In the mid-1940s Hollywood had a penchant for biopics of popular contemporary composers. However, it was Columbia's successful A SONG TO REMEMBER, a fabrication about Polish composer Frederic Chopin (1810–1849), which paved the way for more such screen studies on classical composers, such as THE SONG OF LOVE (1947) about Robert Schumann and Johannes Brahms, SONG OF SCHEHERAZADE (1947) with Jean-Pierre Aumont as Nikolai Rimsky-Korsakoff, and, later, MAGIC FIRE (1956), with Carlos Thompson as Franz Liszt. The lavishly-mounted A SONG TO REMEMBER not only presented virile Cornel Wilde as Chopin, but it also starred glamorous Merle Oberon, cast against type as nineteenth-century feminist George Sand. Filmed in color, A SONG TO REMEMBER managed to make a potentially stuffy biographic set piece an engrossing period romantic drama.

As a young boy (Maurice Tauzin) Frederic Chopin displays great promise as a virtuoso and composer in his native Poland, which is constantly under attack from Czarist Russia. He is guided by his good-natured but forceful teacher, Professor Joseph Elsner (Paul Muni), who trains the boy for an eventual career in Europe's music center, Paris. When he is twenty-two Chopin (Cornel Wilde) leaves Warsaw for Paris. After some difficult times, he is aided by fellow composer Franz Liszt (Stephen Bekassy). He meets the beautiful writer Amandine Dupin, who calls herself George Sand (Merle Oberon) and who affects wearing mannish clothes. The two fall in love, with Frederic forgetting loyal Constantia (Nina Foch), who remained in Poland. While Sand urges him to abandon his classical works and compose waltzes, he disregards her advice and becomes successful under his own terms. In the process, he forgets his roots and the urgings of Elsner to use his position to inspire freedom for his people. Finally Chopin breaks with Sand and embarks on a concert tour to raise money for Poland and the liberation of its soldiers held captive in Russia. He dies of consumption, rejected by Sand, with whom he wants to reconcile.

The highlight of A SONG TO REMEMBER, which stunningly recaptured the flavor of nineteenth-century Paris, was unbilled Jose Iturbi's off-screen playing of Chopin's piano compositions. In 1945 Iturbi had a million-selling record of Chopin's "Polonaise in A-Flat" for RCA Victor. Both Cornel Wilde as Chopin and Paul Muni as his overbearing mentor handled their roles intelligently. However, pretty Merle Oberon as a mannish, cigar-smoking George Sand was hard to accept. Particularly good were supporting performances by Nina Foch as Chopin's devoted friend, Howard Freeman as Chopin's music critic enemy, Kalkbrenner, George Coulouris as impresario Louis Pleyel, and Stephen Bekassy as Franz Liszt.

The *Hollywood Reporter* termed A SONG TO REMEMBER ". . . A major event in film history. It is one of the finest and most beautiful screen productions yet given to the world, and in the field of music films of its kind it stands alone. . . . The actual presentation of the music itself is a thrilling triumph, particularly as the major medium of musical expression employed is the piano, admittedly the most difficult of all instruments to record. But here the recording is so perfect that there is no sense that it is recorded." The *New York Times* acknowledged, "Since movie producers usually approach classical music in an obvious state of trepidation, Columbia Pictures deserves to be heartily congratulated for the generous assortment of Chopin's popular piano compositions rendered in the new music-drama. . . . If you accept the picture for what it represents, a stunningly beautiful and melodious entertainment, it should provide you with a memorable screen experience." On the other hand, the no-nonsense James Agee (*The Nation* magazine) said, ". . . A SONG TO REMEMBER contains a good deal of nicely played Chopin, and is as infuriating and funny a misrepresentation of an artist's life and work as I have ever seen . . ."

A SONG TO REMEMBER received five Oscar nominations: Best Actor (Cornel Wilde), Scoring of a Dramatic or Comedy Picture, Original Story, Cinematography—Color, and Editing.

THE SOUND OF MUSIC (20th Century-Fox, 1965) Color 174 minutes.

Producer, Robert Wise; associate producer, Saul Chaplin; director, Wise; based on the musical play by Richard Rodgers, Oscar Hammerstein, II, Howard Lindsay, Russel Crouse; screenplay, Ernest Lehman; production designer, Boris Leven; art director, Harry Kemm; set decorator, Walter M. Scott, Ruby Levitt; costumes, Dorothy Jeakins; makeup, Ben Nye, Willard Buell; music supervisor/arranger/conductor, Irwin Kostal; vocal supervisor, Robert Tucker; choreographers, Marc Breaux, Dee Dee Wood; second unit supervisor, Maurice Zuberano; puppeteers, Bill Baird, Cora Baird; sound, Murray Spivack, Bernard Freerick; special camera effects, L. B. Abbott, Emil Kosa, Jr.; camera, Ted McCord; additional camera, Paul Beeson; editor, William Reynolds; assistant editor, Larry Allen.

Songs: "The Sound of Music," "Preludium (Dixit Dominus),"

"Morning Hymn," "Alleluia," "Maria," "I Have Confidence!" "Sixteen Going on Seventeen," "My Favorite Things," "Climb Every Mountain," "The Lonely Goatherd," "Do-Re-Mi," "Something Good," "Maria," "Edelweiss," "So Long, Farewell" (Richard Rodgers, Oscar Hammerstein, II).

Julie Andrews (Maria); Christopher Plummer (Captain Von Trapp); Eleanor Parker (The Baroness); Richard Haydn (Max Detweiler); Peggy Wood (Mother Abbess); Charmian Carr (Liesl); Heather Menzies (Louisa); Nicholas Hammond (Friedrich); Duane Chase (Kurt); Angela Cartwright (Brigitta); Debbie Turner (Marta); Kym Karath (Gretl); Anna Lee (Sister Margaretta); Portia Nelson (Sister Berthe); Ben Wright (Herr Zeller); Daniel Truhitte (Rolfe); Norma Varden (Frau Schmidt); Gil Stuart (Franz); Marni Nixon (Sister Sophia); Evadne Baker (Sister Bernice); Doris Lloyd (Baroness Ebberfield); Bill Lee (Singing Voice of Captain Von Trapp); Margery McKay (Singing Voice of Mother Abbess).

The final collaboration of Richard Rodgers and Oscar Hammerstein, II (who died nine months after it premiered), *The Sound of Music* debuted on Broadway in 1959 starring Mary Martin, Theodore Bikel and Kurt Kasznar. During its five-year stay it went for 1,442 performances, with Martin scoring a personal triumph in the role of Maria von Trapp. When 20th Century-Fox purchased the screen rights to the property for $1,250,000, Mary Martin was deemed too old for the lead (as she had been for SOUTH PACIFIC [*q.v.*] seven years earlier) and Julie Andrews starred, following up her Oscar-winning success in MARY POPPINS (1964), q.v.* Grossing $80 million in distributors' domestic film rentals, THE SOUND OF MUSIC won the Oscar for Best Picture of 1965, with Robert Wise being named Best Director. Other Academy Awards won by the film were William Reynolds for Film Editor, Irwin Kostal for Music Score Adaptation and for Sound. Julie Andrews was nominated for Best Actress but lost to Julie Christie of DARLING.**

The exuberant Maria (Julie Andrews) is a postulant at an

*As part of the financial package involved in gaining the screen rights to A SOUND OF MUSIC and catering to the Von Trapp family (then living in Vermont), 20th Century-Fox acquired the distribution rights to the German-made THE TRAPP FAMILY (1961) which blended together portions of DIE TRAPP FAMILIE (on which THE SOUND OF MUSIC had been partially based) and its sequel, DIE TRAPP FAMILIE IN AMERIKA. The dramatized documentary was dubbed for its American release.

**Other Oscar nominations for THE SOUND OF MUSIC were Best Supporting Actress (Peggy Wood), Cinematography—Color, Art Direction-Set Decoration—Color, and Costume Design—Color.

Abbey in Saltzburg in the Austrian Alps in the 1930s. She is frequently absent and derelict in her duties and has become a great source of concern for the veteran head of the Abbey, Mother Abbess (Peggy Wood). The nuns finally conclude that Maria must resolve her feeling about life and Mother Abbess sends her to the family of Captain von Trapp (Christopher Plummer), a widower, to be the governess of his seven children. Maria finds that von Trapp, a retired naval officer, rules his motherless family with an iron hand and that the children are hostile to her. Meanwhile, the oldest daughter, Liesl (Charmian Carr), is romancing the local delivery boy (Dan Truhitte). When a thunderstorm erupts, Maria wins the children over to her by calming their fears and she protects Liesl when her father demands to know where she has been that evening. The captain leaves for Vienna to visit with the beautiful Baroness Schraeder (Eleanor Parker). When he returns with her and their friend Max Detweiler (Richard Haydn) he fires Maria for not keeping the children on their strict regimen. He later relents and asks her to stay. After Maria leads the children in singing and giving a puppet show, Max suggests that they participate in the forthcoming Saltzburg Festival. At first the conservative von Trapp refuses to allow them to do so, until Max urges him to join the act as well. By now the Nazi movement is taking hold in the area. Meanwhile, Maria realizes she is in love with her employer. When von Trapp continues with his plan to marry the wealthy Baroness, Maria is hurt and returns to the Abbey. The wise Mother Abbess dispatches Maria back to von Trapp and they are reunited. They soon marry. When they return from their honeymoon, the Captain and Maria find Max has entered the children in the Saltzburg Festival. The Nazis have invaded Austria and the Captain is ordered to return to service for Hitler's regime. When the family attempts to flee Austria, they are caught, but Max tells the authorities they are on the way to the festival to perform. The von Trapps and Maria take advantage of the staging of their number to disappear. As they leave the country, they win first prize in their absence. The von Trapps, however, have left Austria for a new life.

A few numbers ("How Can Love Survive?" "No Way to Stop It") from the Broadway original did not survive the transition to film. Rodgers and Hammerstein wrote two new songs for the picture: "I Have Confidence!" (sung by Julie Andrews) and "Something Good" (sung by Andrews and Bill Lee, the latter dubbing for Christopher Plummer). The bulk of the songs were sung by Andrews, including the title tune, "My Favorite Things," and "Do-Re-Mi" with the children. The kids perform a reprise of "The Sound of Music" and "So Long, Farewell" and join with

Julie Andrews in THE SOUND OF MUSIC (1965).

Andrews et al in "Edelweiss." It is the courting young adults (Charmian Carr and Dan Truhitte) who perform "Sixteen Going on Seventeen." The nuns' chorus offers several religious hymns. The film's most stirring number, "Climb Ev'ry Mountain," is sung by Margery McKay, dubbing for Peggy Wood (who had sung musical roles on Broadway decades before). It is interesting to note that the first choice for the role of Mother Abbess was Kate Smith, but she declined the screen assignment. Christopher Plummer, who proved very wooden in his performance herein (and who later referred to the project as "The Sound of Mucus"), was dubbed by Bill Lee for his singing sequences. Marni Nixon, who had dubbed many stars for their on-screen singing, was cast in THE SOUND OF MUSIC as a nun.

Originally William Wyler was to have directed THE SOUND OF MUSIC, but the assignment eventually went to Robert Wise, who had won an Academy Award for WEST SIDE STORY (1961), *q.v.* If any one ingredient bolstered THE SOUND OF MUSIC to its staggering success, it was its lush cinematography, which breathtakingly captured the landmarks and splendid natural scenery of Saltzburg. The aerial shots of Julie Andrews scampering on a grassy plateau of the Alps with arms outstretched as she sings the title tune in her crystal clear tones remains a visual classic of cinema (and was later much satirized).

While the very mainstream, cozily safe THE SOUND OF MUSIC received much praise for Julie Andrews' effervescent performance, its luscious backdrops and its technical expertise in presenting the well known score, there was some critical backlash to the syrupy approach of the filmmakers. Pauline Kael (*New Yorker* magazine) enunciated, ". . . This is a tribute to freshness that is so mechanically engineered and so shrewdly calculated that the background music rises, the already soft focus blurs and melts, and, upon the instant, you can hear all those noses blowing in the theatre. Whom could this operetta offend? Only those of us who . . . loathe being manipulated in this way and are aware of how cheap and ready-made are the responses we are made to feel."

In retrospect, Clive Hirshhorn (*The Hollywood Musical,* 1981) assessed, ". . . The mawkish sentimentality it oozed from every frame of its 174-minute running time made it difficult to enjoy without the uneasy feeling that one's emotions were being mercilessly manipulated. Yet, as a piece of old-fashioned popular entertainment with both eyes firmly on the box-office cash registers of the world, it was a shrewdly professional piece of work, stunningly presented, and crafted with awesome expertise."

Julie Andrews went on to one more Hollywood musical triumph, THOROUGHLY MODERN MILLIE (1967), before her superstardom backfired with such flops as STAR! (1968), also produced and directed by Robert Wise.

SOUTH PACIFIC (20th Century-Fox, 1958) Color 171 minutes.

Producer, Buddy Adler; director, Joshua Logan; based on the musical play by Richard Rodgers, Oscar Hammerstein, II, from the book *Tales of the South Pacific* by James A. Michener; screenplay, Paul Osborn; art directors, Lyle Wheeler, John De Cuir, Walter M. Scott, Paul S. Fox; costumes, Dorothy Jeakins; music directors,

Alfred Newman, Ken Darby; orchestrators, Edward B. Powell, Pete King, Bernard Mayers, Robert Russell Bennett; choreographer, LeRoy Prinz; sound director, Fred Hynes; special effects, L. B. Abbott; camera, Leon Shamroy; editor, Robert Simpson.

Songs: "My Girl Back Home," "Dites-Moi," "Bali Ha'i," "Happy Talk," "A Cockeyed Optimist," "Soliloquies," "Some Enchanted Evening," "Bloody Mary," "I'm Gonna Wash that Man Right Outa My Hair," "There Is Nothing Like a Dame," "Younger than Springtime," "Honey Bun," "You've Got to Be Carefully Taught," "I'm in Love with a Wonderful Guy," "This Nearly Was Mine" (Richard Rodgers, Oscar Hammerstein, II)

Rossano Brazzi (Emile De Becque); Mitzi Gaynor (Nellie Forbush); John Kerr (Lieutenant Joseph Cable); Ray Walston (Luther Billis); Juanita Hall (Bloody Mary); France Nuyen (Liat); Russ Brown (Captain Brackett); Jack Mullaney (Professor); Ken Clark (Stewpot); Floyd Simmons (Harbison); Candace Lee (Ngana, Emile's Daughter); Warren Hsieh (Jerome, Emile's Son); Tom Laughlin (Buzz Adams); Beverly Aadland (Dancer); Galvan De Leon (Sub Chief); Ron Ely (Co-Pilot); Archie Savage (Native Chief); Robert Jacobs (Communications Man); Richard Cutting (Admiral Kester); John Gabriel (Radio Man); Darleen Engle, Evelyn Ford (Nurses); Doug McClure, Stephen Ferry (Pilots); Joe Bailey (U.S. Commander); Joan Fontaine (Bit); Giorgio Tozzi (Singing Voice of Emile De Becque); Bill Lee (Singing Voice of Lieutenant Joseph Cable); Muriel Smith (Singing Voice of Bloody Mary); Thurl Ravenscroft (Singing Voice of Stewpot); Marie Greene (Singing Voice of Ngana); Betty Wand (Singing Voice of Jerome).

South Pacific is one of the most famous of all American musicals, having debuted on Broadway in the spring of 1949 for a lengthy 1,925-performance run starring Mary Martin, Ezio Pinza, Juanita Hall, Myron McCormick and William Tabbert. This Tony Award-winning show was based on James Michener's Pulitzer Prize-winning book, *Tales of the South Pacific* (1947), in particular on two stories, "Our Heroine" and "Fo' Dolla." After a decade of stage success, SOUTH PACIFIC finally was turned into a film in 1958. Its belated screen production caused one of the greatest star searches since GONE WITH THE WIND. Joshua Logan, who had directed the stage version, wanted Elizabeth Taylor for the lead part of Nellie Forbush, while composer Richard Rodgers favored Doris Day. Others in the running were Jean Simmons (who had acquitted herself well in GUYS AND DOLLS [1955], *q.v.*), Ginger Rogers (a candidate on her own ticket), and Shirley Jones, a protégée of Rodgers and Hammerstein's who had already starred on screen for them in OKLAHOMA! (1955) and CAROUSEL (1956), *qq.v.* A decidedly dark horse candidate was ex-20th Century-Fox star Mitzi Gaynor, who displayed so much spunk and vitality at the several auditions that she became the compromise choice for the coveted assignment. Several other roles in the screen adaptation went to performers who had already played the part on Broadway (Juanita Hall), in London (Ray Walston) or in touring companies (Russ Brown). Italian actor Rossano Brazzi, then at his box-office peak, was hired as Gaynor's vis-à-vis. To portray the two idealistic lovers, John Kerr, who specialized in sensitive young adult roles, and France Nuyen, a former model and then a 20th Century-Fox contractee, were hired.

During World War II in the South Seas, midwesterner Nellie Forbush (Mitzi Gaynor), a nurse for the United States Navy, meets and falls in love with French plantation owner Emile de Becque (Rossano Brazzi). However, when she finds out he is the father of two children by a native woman (now deceased), she vows to get him out of her life. Meanwhile, the American Lieutenant Joseph Cable (John Kerr) has fallen in love with native girl Liat (France Nuyen), although he cannot bring himself to marry her due to their cultural and ethnic differences. Also involved in the activities are conniving sailor Luther Billis (Ray Walston) and wise native woman Bloody Mary (Juanita Hall), the latter Liat's mother. Eventually Nellie and de Becque decide their love is more important than their differences and her motherly instincts for his children come to the fore. As for Liat and Cable, their love ends in tragedy when he is killed in action on a mission against the Japanese.

More so than most major musicals, SOUTH PACIFIC is filled with ghost dubbers. In the cases of Rossano Brazzi and John Kerr, on hand for their box-office and/or visual presence, this was understandable; as it was with the singing of Brazzi's two on-screen children. However, it was a case of perfectionism that led the filmmakers to replace the singing of Juanita Hall (who had handled the role on Broadway) with that of Muriel Smith (who had performed the part in London). Many of the musical numbers in SOUTH PACIFIC have a distinctly vicarious appeal to them. "Dites-Moi" is sung by de Becque's two youngsters; Cable sings of "My Girl Back Home" and later admits that he feels "Younger than Springtime" and abhors his inbred racial prejudice in "Carefully Taught." De Becque essays "Some Enchanted Evening," the wistful "This Nearly Was Mine" and duets with Nellie Forbush on "Twin Soliloquies." It is the rotund Bloody Mary who instructs the younger generation on the virtues of "Happy Talk" and remarks on the geographic/romantic splendors of "Bali Ha'i." The chorus of

Naval Seabees recites the virtues of "Bloody Mary" and "There Is Nothin' Like A Dame." In the pivotal assignment, Nellie Forbush admits she is "A Cockeyed Optimist." She displays a duality of emotion when she insists "I'm Gonna Wash That Man Right Outa My Hair," while she confesses, "(I'm in Love with) A Wonderful Guy." She can also be rambunctious, as in the camp show with her rendition of "Honey Bun." ("My Girl Back Home" had been cut from the stage version, but was added back in for the motion picture.)

Much of the location work for SOUTH PACIFIC was accomplished on the Hawaiian island of Kauai, with backgrounds lensed in the Fiji Islands. It was shot in the widescreen Todd AO process in color with stereophonic sound. With such meticulous, expansive production work, SOUTH PACIFIC *should* have been a grand experience. But there were several problems. The film had to compete with the highly regarded stage edition and the stellar performance of Mary Martin. The movie faced the recurrent problems of filmed Broadway musicals: How to combine the fantasy of a genre plot with the realism demanded by a big screen production? How to bridge the crescendos of song and plot that on stage rely so heavily on audience interaction? Director Joshua Logan thought he had the answer to one of the problems. He used a much publicized series of color light filters (and colored gases) to give the settings an almost surrealistic look, hoping to distort the realities of location filming into a magical half-fantasy ambiance. Not only did the concept not work, it caused tremendous distraction to filmgoers and received much criticism. At the heart of the problem was the fact that Mitzi Gaynor, no matter how pert, curvacious and talented she was, lacked that essential natural warmth so needed to make the role succeed. She did her best, but she was more a wind-up Kewpie doll than a fully dimensional heroine.

Bosley Crowther (*New York Times*), while overly enthusiastic about this major release from a major studio and advertiser, did note obliquely, ". . . What it lacks in the more subtle values the show had upon the stage is balanced by frank spectacular features that will probably fascinate folks who go to films." *Variety* observed that the "expansion" of the ". . . libretto may give cause to ponder the values where the visualization eclipses the imaginative." The trade paper added, "The pseudo-religious tribal custom terps [choreographed by LeRoy Prinz] borders somewhat on the Fanchon & Marco out of the yesteryear brand of Warner Bros. filmusicals."

For its roadshown editions (with an intermission after the first 105 minutes) SOUTH PACIFIC was shown in the Todd AO process; for later general distribution it was distributed in a CinemaScope version.

SOUTH PACIFIC grossed $17,500,000 in distributors' domestic film rentals. It won an Academy Award for Best Sound, and received Oscar nominations for Best Cinematography—Color and for Best Scoring of a Musical Picture. The soundtrack album to SOUTH PACIFIC was on the charts for sixty-five weeks and in number one position for thirty-one weeks.

To be noted in small roles in SOUTH PACIFIC are: Ron Ely (who later became television's "Tarzan"), Tom Laughlin (of the motion picture series, BILLY JACK), Doug McClure (of TV's "The Virginian") and Joan Fontaine. The latter, an Oscar-winning star, was a personal friend of director Joshua Logan and was then under contract to 20th Century-Fox. She did the walk-on (in native garb) as a lark.

SPRINGTIME IN THE ROCKIES (20th Century-Fox, 1942) Color 91 minutes.

Producer, William LeBaron; director, Irving Cummings; story, Philip Wylie; screenplay, Walter Bullock, Ken Englund, Jacques Thery; art directors, Richard Day, Joseph C. Wright; music director, Alfred Newman; choreographer, Hermes Pan; camera, Ernest Palmer; editor, Robert Simpson.

Songs: "I Had the Craziest Dream," "Run, Little Raindrop, Run," "A Poem Set to Music," "I Like to Be Loved by You," "Chattanooga Choo Choo," "Pan American Jubilee" (Mack Gordon, Harry Warren); "Tic-Tac Do Meu Coracao" (Alcyr Peres Vermelho, Walfrido Silva).

Betty Grable (Vicky); John Payne (Dan); Carmen Miranda (Rosita); Cesar Romero (Victor); Charlotte Greenwood (Phoebe Gray); Edward Everett Horton (McTavish, the Valet); Frank Orth (Bickle); Harry Hayden (Brown); Jackie Gleason (Dan's Agent); Chick Chandler (Stage Manager); Iron Eyes Cody (Indian); Trudy Marshall (Marilyn); Bess Flowers (Mrs. Jeepers); Banda da Lua (Themselves); Billy Wayne (Assistant Stage Manager); Harry James and His Music Makers (Themselves); Helen Forrest (Band Vocalist).

Vicky (Betty Grable) and Dan (John Payne) are the successful singing stars of a Broadway musical, but their romantic life is not ideal due to his constant philandering. By the end of the show's run, Vicky is disgusted with Dan's roving eye for pretty girls. She goes on a tour of the Western states with her former dance partner, Victor (Cesar Romero). While the two are appearing with Harry James (himself) and His Music Makers at Lake Louise, Dan arrives. He tries to persuade Vicky to reunite with him, both romantically and in an upcoming Broadway show. A number of complications arise, including Dan's new valet McTavish (Edward Everett Horton) and his fiery secretary, Rosita (Carmen Miranda). Eventually Vicky and Dan are brought back together.

With its Technicolor cinematography by Ernest Palmer and some on-location footage of Lake Louise, SPRINGTIME IN THE ROCKIES is a strikingly gorgeous musical which moves briskly when the plot does not get in the way of the abundance of music. It benefits from the fiery presence of Carmen Miranda (still a novelty on screen), the high-kicking zest of Charlotte Greenwood (a 20th Century-Fox musical staple of the 1940), the suavity of expert dancer Cesar Romero, and the buffoonery (an acquired taste) of bumbling Edward Everett Horton. Added into the very commercial mix was the highly popular trumpeter Harry James and his swing musicians, as well as the starring team of Grable and John Payne. It was little wonder that SPRINGTIME IN THE ROCKIES was such a box-office success.

Within this musical, Betty Grable and John Payne share a fine production number, "Run, Little Raindrop, Run" and later she and Cesar Romero dance together gracefully in expansive sequences backed by Harry James and His Music Makers. The latter scored well with a number of songs, especially his Columbia record hit, "I Had the Craziest Dream," with the vocal by Helen Forrest. (It was staged extremely well in the film, in an outdoor setting with Forrest intermingling with the rapt audience.) Carmen Miranda danced energetically to "Chattanooga Choo Choo" (whose distinctively North American lyrics she manipulated with her very South American accent). She later sang "Tic-Tac Do Meu Coracao," backed by her own Banda Da Lua. The film's stars closed out the proceedings with the nicely staged "Pan American Jubilee," which begins as a Miranda number and later encompasses all the stars.

Variety termed the film "solid entertainment," adding, "Script is studded with laugh lines which are well distributed among the cast. Picture sags considerably toward the end, when the story has to devote extended amount of footage to the romantic interludes without interruption of any song or dance specialities. But this is minor in the overall content of entertainment provided."

Betty Grable and Harry James, who met on the set of SPRINGTIME IN THE ROCKIES, were married on July 11, 1943 in Las Vegas. In later years they would use "I Had the Craziest Dream" as a pivotal number in their personal appearance tours. SPRINGTIME IN THE ROCKIES was Grable's third of four screen teamings with John Payne, the others being: TIN PAN ALLEY (1940), *q.v.,* FOOTLIGHT SERENADE (1942) and THE

DOLLY SISTERS (1945), *q.v.* By 1942 the fast-rising Betty Grable would be number 8 of the top ten moneymaking stars (as ranked by *Motion Picture Herald*). By the next year she would be number one and remained on the list through 1951.

STAND UP AND CHEER (Fox, 1934) 80 minutes.

Producer, Winfield Sheehan; director, Hamilton MacFadden; screen idea, Will Rogers, Philip Klein; screenplay, Ralph Spence, Lew Brown; art directors, Gordon Wiles, Russell Patterson; music, Brown, Jay Gorney; music director, Arthur Lange; choreographer, Sammy Lee; camera, Ernest Palmer, L. W. O'Connell; editor, Margaret Clancy.

Songs: "I'm Laughing," "We're Out of the Red," "Broadway's Gone Hillbilly," "Baby Take a Bow," "This Is Our Last Night Together," (Jay Gorney, Lew Brown); "She's Way Up Thar" (Brown); "Stand Up and Cheer" (Brown, Harry Akst).

Warner Baxter (Lawrence Cromwell); Madge Evans (Mary Adams); Nigel Bruce (Eustace Dinwiddie); Stepin Fetchit (George Bernard Shaw); Frank Melton (Fosdick); Lila Lee (Zelda); Ralph Morgan (President's Secretary); Frank Mitchell (Senator Danforth); Jack Durant (Senator Short); Arthur Byron (Harley); James Dunn (Dugan); Skins Miller (Hillbilly); Tess Gardella (Aunt Jemima); Nick [Dick] Foran, Shirley Temple, John Boles, Sylvia Froos, Jimmy Dallas (Specialty Numbers); Frances Morris, Lurene Tuttle, Dorothy Gulliver, Bess Flowers, Lillian West (Stenographers); Selmer Jackson, Clyde Dilson (Correspondents); Edward Earle (Secret Service Man); Gayne Whitman (Voice for President); Frank Sheridan, Paul Stanton, Wallis Clark, Arthur Stuart Hull (Senators); Si Jenks (Rube Farmer); Aggie Herring (Irish Washerwoman); Phil Tead (Vaudevillian); Randall Sisters (Trio); George K. Arthur (Dance Director); Baby Alice Raetz (Child Bit); Ruth Beckett (Child's Mother); Bobby Caldwell (General Lee); Wilbur Mack (Beamish); Elspeth Dudgeon, Jessie Perry, Harry Northrup (Reformers); John Davidson (Sour Radio Announcer); Harry Dunkinson, Gilbert Clayton, Herbert Prior, Carlton Stockdale (Quartette); Lucien Littlefield (Professor Hi-De-Ho); Arthur Loft, Jack Richardson, Dagmar Oakland, Vivian Winston (Bits); Joe Smith Marba (Elephant Trainer); Carleton E. Griffin, Paul McVey, Rolin Ray, Reginald Simpson (Male Secretaries); Arthur Vinton (Turner); Sam Hayes (Radio Announcer); Tina Marshall (Boy's Mother); Dora Clement, Peggy Watt, Dorothy Dehn, Ruth Clifford (Female Secretaries); Glen Walters (Hillbilly's Wife); Lew Brown, Patricia Lee, Guy Usher, Lynn Bari, Morris Ankrum, Scotty Beckett (Bits).

Based on a story idea by Will Rogers and screen writer Philip Klein, STAND UP AND CHEER is remembered chiefly today as the feature film which brought Shirley Temple to the attention of the movie-going public and launched the astronomically successful career of the moppet star. On its own merits, the movie is a decent vaudeville-type song-and-dance entry. However, at the time of its release, *Variety* complained, "This musical is a hodge-podge principally handicapped by a national depression premise. Americans now like to think of themselves in the light of being on the upturn and having rounded that long-awaited corner, so CHEER'S plot motivation is basically questionable."

In order to help the country get over the blues of its economic depression, the President orders his secretary (Ralph Morgan) to find a Secretary of Amusements, whose responsibility it will be to bring entertainment to the American public. The position goes to Broadway producer Lawrence Cromwell (Warner Baxter) and, with the aid of pretty Mary Adams (Madge Evans) and the unwanted "help" of silly senators Danforth (Frank Mitchell) and Short (Jack Durant), he is finally able to produce the big show which fulfills his obligations.

Of course, the highlight of STAND UP AND CHEER is the climactic colossal showcase. Its best remembered number is one with Shirley Temple winning the nation's heart singing "Baby Take a Bow," with James Dunn and Patricia Lee. (Later that year Temple and Dunn would co-star in a Fox movie entitled BABY TAKE A BOW.) Stepin Fetchit provided comedy relief, while the musical numbers included such fare (all co-written by Lew Brown) as John Boles and Sylvia Froos' duet of "This Is Our Last Night Together," Froos's solo on "Broadway's Gone Hillbilly," a duet by Nick (later Dick) Foran and Aunt Jemima (Tess Gardella) on "I'm Laughin'," backed by Earl Dancer's chorus, and Aunt Jemimia and Boles singing "Out of the Red."

Shirley Temple would receive a special Academy Award in recognition of her contributions to screen entertainment during the year 1934. In the late 1980s, a computer colorized version of STAND UP AND CHEER was released for television/videocassette showings.

A STAR IS BORN (Warner Bros., 1954) Color 176 minutes.

Producer, Sidney Luft; director, George Cukor; based on the screenplay by Dorothy Parker, Alan Campbell, Robert Carson, from the screen story by William A. Wellman, Carson, inspired by the film WHAT PRICE HOLLYWOOD; screenplay, Moss Hart; production designer, Gene Allen; art director, Malcolm Bert; set decorator, George James Hopkins; costumes, Jean Louis, Mary Ann Nyberg, Irene Sharaff; music director, Ray Heindorf; choreographer, Richard Barstow; assistant directors, Earl Bellamy, Edward Graham, Russell Llewellyn; special effects, H. F. Koenekamp; camera, Sam Leavitt; editor, Folmar Blangsted.

Songs: "Gotta Have Me Go with You," "It's a New World," "Here's What I'm Here For," "The Man that Got Away," "Someone at Last," "Lose that Long Face" (Harold Arlen, Ira Gershwin); "Born in a Trunk" (Leonard Gershe); "I'll Get By" (Roy Turk, Fred Ahlert); "You Took Advantage of Me" (Richard Rodgers, Lorenz Hart); "Black Bottom" (Buddy G. DeSylva, Lew Brown, Ray Henderson); "Peanut Vendor" (L. Wolfe Gilbert, Marion Sunshine, Moises Simon); "My Melancholy Baby" (George A. Norton, Ernie Burnett); "Swanee" (Irving Caesar, Gershwin).

Judy Garland (Vicki Lester [Esther Blodgett]); James Mason (Norman Maine); Jack Carson (Matt Libby); Charles Bickford (Oliver Niles); Tommy Noonan (Danny McGuire); Lucy Marlow (Lola Lavery); Amanda Blake (Susan Ettinger); Irving Bacon (Graves); Hazel Shermet (Libby's Secretary); James Brown (Glenn Williams); Lotus Robb (Miss Markham); Joan Shawlee (Announcer); Dub Taylor (Driver); Louis Jean Heydt, Leonard Penn, Tristram Coffin (Directors); Olin Howland (Charley); Willis Bouchey (Director McBride); Kathryn Card (Landlady); Rex Evans (Master of Ceremonies); Emerson Treacy (Justice of the Peace); Bob Jellison (Eddie); Chick Chandler (Man in Car); Blythe Daly (Miss Fusselow); Mae Marsh (Party Guest); Frank Ferguson (Judge); Nadene Ashdown (Esther at Age Six); Heidi Meadows (Esther at Age Three); Henry Kulky (Cuddles); Jack Harmon (1st Dancer); Don McCabe (2nd Dancer); Eric Wilton (Valet); Grady Sutton (Carver); Henry Russell (Orchestra Leader); Robert Dumas (Drummer); Laurindo Almeida (Guitarist); Bobby Sailes (Dancer); Percy Helton (Drunk); Charles Watts (Harrison); Pat O'Malley, Samuel Barrymore Colt (Men at Race Track); Charles Halton, Joseph Mell (Studio Employees); Stuart Holmes (Spectator); Grandon Rhodes (Producer); Frank Puglia (Bruno); Wilton Graff (Master of Ceremonies, Final Scene); and: Phil Arnold, Rudolph Anders, Bess Flowers, Allen Kramer.

See: A STAR IS BORN (1976) (essay).

A STAR IS BORN (Warner Bros., 1976) Color 140 minutes.

Executive producer, Barbra Streisand; producer, Jon Peters; director, Frank Pierson; based on the screen story by William A. Wellman, Robert Carson; screenplay, John Gregory Dunne, Joan Didion, Frank Pierson; production designer, Polly Platt; art director, William Hiney; set decorator, Ruby Levitt; costumes, Shirlee Strahm, Seth Banks; makeup, Allan Snyder, Marvin C. Thompson; music supervisor, Paul Williams; music coordinator, Kenny Ascher; music concepts, Barbra Streisand; music underscore, Roger Kellaway; choreographer, David Winters; assistant directors, Stu Fleming, Michele Ader, Ed Ledding; sound, Tom Overton; sound re-recording, Dan Wallin, Robert Knudson, Bob Glass; sound effects editors, Joe Von Stroheim, Marvin I. Kosberg; special effects, Chuck Gasper; camera, Robert Surtees; editor, Peter Zinner.

Songs: "Watch Closely Now," "Spanish Lies," "Hellacious Acres," "Woman in the Moon," "With One More Look at You" (Paul Williams, Kenny Ascher); "Queen Bee" (Rupert Holmes); "Everything" (Holmes, Williams); "Lost Inside of You" (Leon Russell, Barbra Streisand); "Evergreen" (Streisand, Williams); "I

Advertisement for A STAR IS BORN (1954).

Believe in Love" (Kenny Loggins, Alan Bergman, Marilyn Bergman); "Crippled Crow" (Donna Weiss).

Barbra Streisand (Esther Hoffman); Kris Kristofferson (John Norman Howard); Paul Mazursky (Brian); Gary Busey (Bobby Ritchie); Oliver Clark (Gary Danziger); Venette Fields, Clydie King (The Oreos); Marta Heflin (Quentin); M. G. Kelly (Bebe Jesus); Sally Kirkland (Photographer); Joanne Linville (Freddie); Uncle Rudy (Mo); Stephen Bruton, Sam Creson, Cleve Dupin, Donna Fritts, Dean Hagen, Booker T. Jones, Jerry McGee, Art Munson, Charles Owens, Terry Paul, Jack Redmond, Bobby Shew, Mike Utley (The Speedway); Tony Orlando (Himself); Robert Englund (Patron).

The old story of a great Hollywood star who goes downhill while his lady love takes her place in the limelight was first filmed as WHAT PRICE HOLLYWOOD by RKO in 1932, with Constance Bennett and Lowell Sherman. It was allegedly suggested by the real life events involved in the lives of silent screen players Marguerite de la Motte and John Bowers. It was redone as A STAR IS BORN by David O. Selznick for United Artists in 1937. Both films were straight dramas and the Selznick version (filmed in color) was especially popular thanks to its stars, Janet Gaynor and Fredric March. In the early 1950s, Judy Garland, who had played the lead in "A Star Is Born" when it was broadcast on NBC's "Lux Radio Theatre" in 1942, and her husband-promoter Sid Luft, decided to make a musical version of the story as a comeback vehicle for Garland. George Cukor, who had helmed WHAT PRICE HOLLYWOOD, was signed to direct the project for Warner Bros. Originally Cary Grant, Laurence Olivier, Humphrey Bogart or Ray Milland (or others) were sought for the leading male role, but it was Britisher James Mason who was finally cast in the role. (He would later say he took the role "because I was not getting anywhere very fast.") Initially the picture was to have been shot in a more conventional screen ratio, but belatedly studio head Jack L. Warner agreed to use the voguish widescreen CinemaScope process (controlled by 20th Century-Fox). It required several scenes already shot to be refilmed.

Alcoholic film star Norman Maine (James Mason) and his publicist Matt Libby (Jack Carson) attend a charity benefit. There the drunken Maine is saved from making a fool of himself onstage by band vocalist Esther Blodgett (Judy Garland). Later, when he has sobered, Norman seeks out his benefactor and locates her at a musicians' joint where he is enchanted by her singing. Enthused by her freshness and her great potential, he convinces her to quit the band. He promises to arrange a screen test for her. However, he soon goes off on location for a new movie and the two do not meet for several weeks until he tracks her down at a drab rooming house. Keeping his word, he brings Esther to the attention of cynical studio chief Oliver Niles (Charles Bickford). Soon she is cast in a major role in a new musical. She is given a new name, Vicki Lester, and a brand new look. The picture makes her a star and she and Maine wed. Later Maine, whose career is slipping due to his addiction, is dropped by the studio. With no film roles forthcoming, he remains at home drinking and sulking. On the evening that Vicki wins an Academy Award, the washed up celebrity appears at the ceremonies and lurches onto the stage in a drunken stupor. In a moment of wild gesturing he slaps her across the face. Thereafter, he is hospitalized for a cure and emerges a "new" man. However, the sardonic Matt Libby, who never forgave Norman for treating him so badly in the past, accuses Maine of being kept by his superstar wife. Maine returns to heavy drinking and is jailed for drunken driving. Vicki rescues him and decides to abandon her career to nurse him back to health. He, however, understands that he has become a tremendous burden to her. He commits suicide by drowning himself in the ocean. The distraught Vicki goes into seclusion, but later is convinced to return to her movie career. Appearing in public, she announces her presence with, "This is Mrs. Norman Maine."

As a dramatic structure, there is much to recommend in the solidly constructed A STAR IS BORN, a corrosive study of the film industry. As a musical it is a stunning tour-de-force for Judy Garland, who handles all the numbers (mostly written by Harold Arlen and Ira Gershwin) in her distinctive, captivating manner. She is bluesy with the torch ballad, "The Man That Got Away" (which became one of her trademark numbers), reassuring in "Here's What I'm Here For" (cut from some release prints), bouncy in "Lose That Long Face" (cut from some release prints), and touching in "It's a New World." She displays her too frequently overlooked talent for mimicry and satire in "Someone at Last" (a send-up of Hollywood musical production numbers). Her major production number, "Born in a Trunk," is almost a mini-movie in itself, with Leonard Gershe creating a set piece that mirror-images the public vision of Garland's own show business career beginnings. Within the elaborate (and for some, too long) eighteen-minute number, she has the opportunity to essay a characterization of a fledgling chorine looking for that big industry break, and vocalizes a variety of songs ranging from "Black Bottom" to "My Melancholy Baby" and including the vibrant "Swanee." This afterthought segment was shot after George Cukor had gone on to other projects. Unused in the film were three song numbers, "Dancing Partner," "Green Light Ahead" and "I'm Off the Downbeat."

If there had been many creative and financial production problems before *and* during production (with the emotionally fragile Garland having to be coaxed into appearing at the studio, let alone doing her scenes), they were nothing compared to what happened just before *and* after the motion picture debuted in October 1954. Jack L. Warner decided the picture played too long and on his own authority decided to cut particular scenes. After it opened, he cut more scenes (Garland would claim he had "gummed the picture to death"), including her newsboy song number, "Lose that Long Face." In total, twenty-seven minutes were cut from the picture. Director George Cukor would bemoan years later, ". . . I could have sweated out twenty-five minutes here and there, and nobody would have missed them. Instead, they took an axe to the movie."

Regarding the film—as it first played in release—Bosley Crowther (*New York Times*) cheered the filmmakers: ". . . [They] have really and truly gone to town in giving this hackneyed Hollywood story an abundance of fullness and form. . . . They have fattened it up with musical numbers that are among the finest things in the show. . . . Through it all, [there is] a gentle tracing of clever satire of Hollywood, not as sharp as it was in the original, but sharp enough to be stimulating fun." *Variety* judged, "The reel and the real-life values sometimes play back and forth, in pendulum fashion, and the unspooling is never wanting for heart-wallop and gusty entertainment values. . . . Just as it threatens to become a vocalisthenic tour-de-force . . . the meaty plot strands pick up again, and the whole cloth reaffirms its basic dramatic pattern."

Many insisted all the tampering harmed the film in box-office returns (costing nearly $5 million, A STAR IS BORN grossed just over $6 million in distributors' domestic film rentals). However, all the tampering with the picture, which diminished Garland's impact, also cost her an Oscar for Best Actress. (The Award was won by Grace Kelly for THE COUNTRY GIRL.) James Mason was nominated as Best Actor, but lost to Marlon Brando of ON THE WATERFRONT. Other Oscar nominations for A STAR IS BORN were: Best Song ("The Man That Got Away"), Scoring, Art Direction-Set Decoration—Color, and Costume Design—Color.

In 1983, Ronald Haver, head of the film department at the Los Angeles County Museum of Art, supervised the reconstruction of A STAR IS BORN, replacing as many of the deleted scenes as possible, in some situations using production still shots on screen while recording tracks are heard on the soundtrack.* The restored film had a highly promoted new premiere at Radio City Music Hall and later was issued for the home videocassette market. George Cukor died the night before he was to view a rough cut of the restored print. Viewing the restored version, Roger Ebert (*Home Movie Companion,* 1989) reported, "The missing scenes are good to have back again. But the movie's central scenes are even better to see again. . . . A STAR IS BORN is one of the rare films that successfully integrate music with drama; it's not exactly a musical, but it has more music than most musicals."

Meanwhile, in 1974 Barbra Streisand, looking for a musical movie follow-up to FUNNY LADY (1975), *q.v.*—her sequel to the more popular FUNNY GIRL (1968), *q.v.*—fastened on A STAR IS BORN as an appropriate vehicle. It was considered great "chutzpah" for anyone to want to remake the Judy Garland classic, but such was Streisand's ego that she brooked every obstacle to get the project underway. Elvis Presley was initially thought of to play the restructured male lead role in this revamped tale set in the contemporary rock concert scene. When he turned down the assignment, Kris Kristofferson (who off-screen had his own drug problems) accepted the role of the drink and drug-addicted John Norman Howard. Filming began late in 1974 under the direction of Jerry Schatzberg, then when he left the project Streisand's then hairdresser-romantic partner, Jon Peters, temporarily took over control of the project. Assorted screenwriters were brought in to do rewrites and one of them, Frank Pierson, later took over as the credited director. Through all the expensive travails, the multi-talented Streisand remained in full control of the project, as executive producer, star, co-composer of two songs, as well as providing her own wardrobe and offering "musical concepts" for the picture.

Rock star John Norman Howard (Kris Kristofferson) is on a career downslide, unable to maintain a hold on his public. Returning from an unfulfilling concert tour, he visits a club where he disrupts the performance of Esther Hoffman (Barbra Streisand) and the Oreos. A fight breaks out, and Esther helps Howard make his getaway. Howard is impressed by her song-writing talent and, in a moment of whim he invites her to fly (by helicopter) with him to his next concert gig. It is a flop and the overlooked Esther must find her own way home. The two later encounter one another at a recording studio where she is taping backgrounds for commercials. They start a relationship both as songwriting collaborators and

*An excellent and very detailed account of the travails of producing editing and restoring A STAR IS BORN is presented by Ronald Haver in *A Star Is Born* (1988).

Kris Kristofferson in A STAR IS BORN (1976).

romantically. Because John Howard has lost his self-confidence, he is a disaster at a benefit concert and pulls Esther from the wings to sing in his place. She becomes an overnight star and the happy couple marry soon thereafter. Her career escalates, his descends as his drinking hampers his career. When she is accepting her Grammy Award at the televised ceremonies he drunkenly disrupts her speech. After further disillusionment (she finds him in bed with one of his groupie followers), the couple reunite. They plan a joint tour, but while out driving, John Norman is killed in a car crash. At the memorial concert, an anguished Esther sings a song dedicated to her late husband.

Running well over two hours, the glossy R-rated production was self-indulgent and vapid and filled with several anti-climaxes in the last portions of the remake. Streisand and Paul Williams did win an Oscar for their title song composition "Evergreen." Besides performing that popular song in the film, the star also did "Queen Bee," "Everything," "The Woman in the Moon," "I Believe in Love," "With One More Look at You" and "Watch Closely Now." Kristofferson soloed on "Crippled Crow," "Watch Closely Now," and "Hellacious Acres." The two dueted on "Lost Inside of You."

With so many preceding film versions of the time-worn story, A STAR IS BORN received a scathing critical reception from most of the fourth estate. Geoff Brown (British *Monthly Film Bulletin*) pointed out, "Updating and transposing the story-line from Hollywood to the rock world has proved a grave mistake; the plot's hackneyed pattern of intertwined careers . . . simply does not suit the unglamorous world of monster open-air concerts, thunderous decibels, drugs and groupies. . . . The present script is distinguished only by large amounts of foul language and even larger amounts of addled sentimentality." The film's virtues lie in its documentary-like display of rock concerts and the urgency attendant on performers in gaining rapport with their highly responsive audiences.

A STAR IS BORN (1976) grossed $36,100,000. In addition to its Oscar for Best Song, A STAR IS BORN won Academy Award nominations for Best Original Song Score, Cinematography and Sound. The soundtrack album to the new remake was on the charts for twenty-eight weeks, being in first place for six weeks.

STATE FAIR (20th Century-Fox, 1945) Color 100 minutes.

Producer, William Perlberg; director, Walter Lang; based on the novel by Phil Stong; adaptors, Sonya Levien, Paul Eliot Green; screenplay, Oscar Hammerstein, II; art directors, Lyle Wheeler, Lewis Creber; set decorator, Thomas Little, Al Orenbach; music directors, Alfred Newman, Charles Henderson; orchestrator, Edward Powell; color consultants, Natalie Kalmus, Richard Mueller; assistant director, Gaston Glass; sound, Bernard Freericks, Roger Heman; special effects, Fred Sersen; camera, Leon Shamroy; editor, J. Watson Webb.

Songs: "It Might as Well Be Spring," "It's a Grand Night for Singing," "That's for Me," "Isn't It Kinda Fun?" "All I Owe Iowa," "Our State Fair" (Richard Rodgers, Oscar Hammerstein, II).

Jeanne Crain (Margy Frake); Dana Andrews (Pat Gilbert); Dick Haymes (Wayne Frake); Vivian Blaine (Emily Edwards); Charles Winninger (Abel Frake); Fay Bainter (Melissa Frake); Donald Meek (Hippenstahl); Frank McHugh (McGee); Percy Kilbride (Miller); Henry [Harry] Morgan (Barker); Jane Nigh (Eleanor); William Marshall (Marty); Phil Brown (Harry Ware); Paul E. Burns (Hank); Tom Fadden (Eph); William Frambes (Pappy); Steve Olson (Barker); Josephine Whittell (Mrs. Metcalfe); Paul Harvey (Simpson); John Dehner (Announcer); Harlan Briggs, Will Wright, Alice Fleming (Judges); Walter Baldwin (Farmer); Ralph Sanford (Police Chief); Frank Mayo (Man); Minerva Urecal (Woman); Almira Sessions, Virginia Brissac (Farmers' Wives); Earl

S. Dewey, Wheaton Chambers (Assistant Judges); Harry Depp (Secretary to Judge); Francis Ford (Mr. Martin, Whirlwind's Owner); Margo Wood, Jo-Carrol Dennison, Coleen Gray (Girls); Neal Hart (Farmer); Emory Parnell (Senator); Louanne Hogan (Singing Voice of Margy Frake); Charles Boyer, Bing Crosby (Voices in Margy's Dream Sequence).

TV title: IT HAPPENED ONE SUMMER.

See: STATE FAIR (1962) (essay).

STATE FAIR (20th Century-Fox, 1962) Color 118 minutes.

Producer, Charles Brackett; director, Jose Ferrer; based on the novel by Philip Stong; adaptors, Oscar Hammerstein, II, Sonya Levien, Paul Eliot Green; screenplay, Richard Breen; art directors, Jack Martin Smith, Walter M. Simonds; set decorators, Walter M. Scott, Lou Hafley; costumes, Marjorie Best; makeup, Ben Nye; music supervisor/conductor, Alfred Newman; associate music supervisor, Ken Darby; orchestrators, George Bassman, Henry Beau, Benny Carter, Pete King, Gus Levene, Bernard Mayers; choreographer, Nick Castle; assistant director, Ad Schaumer; sound, Alfred Bruzlin, Warren B. Delaplain; special camera effects, L. B. Abbott, Emil Kosa, Jr.; camera, William C. Mellor; editor, David Bretherton.

Songs: "It Might as Well Be Spring," "Our State Fair," "It's a Grand Night for Singing," "That's for Me," "Isn't It Kinda Fun?" (Richard Rodgers, Oscar Hammerstein, II); "It's the Little Things in Texas," "More than Just a Friend," "Willing and Eager," "This Isn't Heaven," "Never Say No to a Man" (Rodgers).

Pat Boone (Wayne Frake); Bobby Darin (Jerry Dundee); Pamela Tiffin (Margie Frake); Ann-Margret (Emily Porter); Tom Ewell (Abel Frake); Alice Faye (Melissa Frake); Wally Cox (Hipplewaite); David Brandon (Harry); Clem Harvey (Doc Cramer); Robert Foulk (Squat Judge); Linda Henrich (Betty Jean); Edward "Tap" Canutt (Red Hoerter); Margaret Deramee (Lilya); Albert Harris (Jim); Bebe Allan (Usherette); George Russell (George Hoffer); Edwin McClure (Announcer); Walter Beilbey (Swine Judge); Tom Loughney (Dick Burdick); Claude Hall (Sime); Tony Zoppi (The Masher); Mary Durant (Woman Judge); Sheila Mathews (Hipplewaite's Girl); Anita Gordon (Singing Voice of Margie Frake); and: Tommy Allen, Jack Carr, Mamie Harris, Ken Hudgins, Bob Larkin, Freeman Morse, Carl Princi, Paul Rhone, Louis Roussel, Milton Stolz, Kay Sutton, Dan Terrell.

Will Rogers first starred in STATE FAIR for Fox in 1933, co-starred with Janet Gaynor and Norman Foster as his children and Louise Dresser as his wife. Lew Ayres and Sally Eilers provided

Dick Haymes, Fay Bainter, Jeanne Crain and Charles Winninger in STATE FAIR (1945).

the romantic interest for Gaynor and Foster respectively. This homey bit of Americana was based on Phil Stong's novel (1932) of the same title and proved a very popular release. A dozen years later, 20th Century-Fox, wanting to reap profits from war-weary filmgoers' renewed interest in family-oriented, grassroot stories, decided to refilm the vehicle as a musical in Technicolor. To write the score, it hired Richard Rodgers and Oscar Hammerstein, II, who had enjoyed great success on Broadway with their *Oklahoma!* (1943). The songwriting team provided their only original film score, with Hammerstein also contributing the screenplay. "The script and the songs lift this simple little story to a level of great warmth and appeal. As they had in the legitimate theater, Rodgers and Hammerstein deepened the concept of the movie musical by making the songs a part of the plot," wrote Tony Thomas (*The Films of the Forties,* 1975).

In rural Iowa, the Frake family is getting ready for the state's annual fair week. Father Abel Frake (Charles Winninger) is hoping to win the top prize for his 880-pound boar hog ("Blue Boy"), while his wife Melissa (Fay Bainter) is after the blue ribbon for her mincemeat pie. Also looking forward to the event are the family's young adults, Margy (Jeanne Crain) and Wayne (Dick Haymes), both of whom are eager for the excitement of new romance. At the fair, Wayne is attracted to vivacious redheaded Emily Edwards (Vivian Blaine), who sings with a dance band. Margy meets and falls in love with cynical newspaper reporter Pat Gilbert (Dana Andrews). Even the pet boar finds an attachment with a sow. On the final day of the fair, Wayne discovers that Emily is unable to marry him because she has a husband (from whom she is only separated) and Margy has her romance halted abruptly when Gilbert's newspaper editor dispatches him to Chicago to cover a story. The family returns home, the adults happy about their valued prizes, while their offspring bemoan their romantic problems. Back on the farm, Margy has no patience with her well-meaning but unimaginative farmer suitor (Phil Brown). Later, she is happily surprised when the elusive Pat arrives at the farm asking her hand in marriage. As for Wayne he overcomes his attachment for Emily by reestablishing his romance with a neighboring farm girl (Jane Nigh).

Of the half-dozen tunes Rodgers and Hammerstein composed for the feature, the best are "It Might As Well Be Spring," which is sung by Jeanne Crain (dubbed by Louanne Hogan), and Dick Haymes' rendition of "It's a Grand Night for Singing," which is reprised by Vivian Blaine, William Marshall and the chorus, and again at the finale by Haymes and the cast. Blaine, a much overlooked star of 1940s musicals, nicely handles "That's for Me" and joins with Charles Winninger, Fay Bainter, Donald Meek et al in "All I Owe Iowa." Using the same gimmick as MEET ME IN ST. LOUIS (1944), *q.v.,* "Our State Fair" provides character delineation as sung by Winninger, Bainter and Percy Kilbride. For the record, Dana Andrews' participation in the "It's a Grand Night for Singing" fairway production number was dubbed. Andrews admitted later, of his few choruses of singing, "I let them hire another singer to dub me. They paid him $150 for it. I could have saved the studio some money and sung the tune a lot better. But I kept my mouth shut. I [still] don't like what happens to singers in Hollywood."

Interestingly, the critics of the day were not overwhelmed by STATE FAIR. Bosley Crowther (*New York Times*) insisted that the production was ". . . No more than an average screen musical, with a nice bucolic flavor here and there." The critic added that Rodgers and Hammerstein ". . . Let Hollywood get them—the Hollywood stencil, that is—and their film is much closer to Vine Street than it is to Iowa. . . . They have let the film be concerned with the routine romantic adventures of a couple of boys and girls. And these boys and girls are the usual Hollywood musical types, cut more to the patterns of the night clubs and the fashion salons than to the last of a State fair." James Agee (*The Nation* magazine) admitted there were "nice performances" and "pretty tunes, graceful lyrics." However, he insisted the film was "Otherwise lacking any real delicateness, vitality, or imagination, and painfully air-conditioned-looking, for a bucolic film. . . ."

Despite the unspectacular critical reception, audiences responded very favorably and STATE FAIR grossed over $4,000,000 in distributors' domestic film rentals. STATE FAIR (1945) won an Academy Award for Best Song ("It Might as Well Be Spring"), and received an Oscar nomination for Best Scoring of a Musical Picture, but lost to ANCHORS AWEIGH (*q.v.*).

And then came the 1962 remake of STATE FAIR, which is as pale as the 1945 version is bright. For this version Richard Rodgers (whose partner, Oscar Hammerstein, II, had died) composed five new songs. None of them are distinguished, the best being Alice Faye's rendition of "Never Say No to a Man." Faye, whom 20th Century-Fox wanted to play Emily in the 1945 version, returned to the screen after a sixteen-year absence to play the mother; Don Ameche had been suggested as her husband, but the part went to Tom Ewell. The new version also changed the plot somewhat, the setting now being Texas. The Dana Andrews role of a newspaper reporter became fast-talking announcer Jerry Dundee, played by Bobby Darin. Ann-Margret played Emily, now a song and dance performer with "a" past. As in the 1945 edition, Pat Boone's Wayne Frake has a girl back home, Betty Jean (Linda Henrich), to whom he returns after his infatuation with Emily.

The best part of the remake—directed in lackluster fashion by Jose Ferrer (a very bizarre choice!), in CinemaScope and color—is the original Rodgers and Hammerstein melodies: Anita Gordon (dubbing Pamela Tiffin as sister Margie) singing "It Might as Well Be Spring"; the opening number of "Our State Fair" performed by Pat Boone, Faye and Tom Ewell, and the finale with Boone, Bobby Darin and Anita Gordon doing "It's a Grand Night for Singing." The nadir of the film came in the song number, "More than Just a Friend," with Ewell crooning the melody to the pet boar, "Blue Boy"! Perhaps the fault of the remake of STATE FAIR was its overly synthetic look and direction, as noted by the *San Francisco Chronicle,* "In spite of color, of music, and of comely personalities, what STATE FAIR lacks most of all is a good, healthy vigorous aroma of a country fair, with which one senses director Jose Ferrer is totally unfamiliar."

Location filming for the 1962 edition was accomplished at the Dallas State Fair.

STEP LIVELY (RKO, 1944) 88 minutes.

Producer, Robert Fellows; director, Tim Whelan; based on the play *Room Service* by John Murray, Allen Boretz; screenplay, Warren Duff, Peter Milne; art directors, Albert S. D'Agostino, Carroll Clark; set decorators, Darrell Silvera, Claude Carpenter; costumes, Edward Stevenson; music director, Constantin Bakaleinikoff; orchestrator, Gene Rose; vocal arranger for Frank Sinatra, Alex Stordahl; vocal arranger, Ken Darby; choreographer, Ernest Matray; assistant director, Clem Beauchamp; sound, Jean L. Speak; camera, Robert DeGrasse; editor, Gene Milford.

Songs: "Some Other Time," "As Long as There's Music," "Where Does Love Begin?" "Come Out, Come Out, Wherever You Are," "Why Must There Be an Opening Song?" "And Then You Kissed Me," "Ask the Madame" (Sammy Cahn, Jule Styne).

Frank Sinatra (Glen); George Murphy (Miller); Adolphe Menjou (Wagner); Gloria DeHaven (Christine); Walter Slezak (Gribble); Eugene Pallette (Jenkins); Wally Brown (Binion); Alan Carney (Harry); Grant Mitchell (Dr. Glass); Anne Jeffreys (Miss Abbott); Frances King (Mother); Harry Noble (Father); George Chandler (Country Yokel); Rosemary LaPlanche (Louella); Shirley O'Hara (Louise); Elaine Riley (Lois); Dorothy Malone (Telephone Operator); Frank Mayo (Doorman).

Fast-talking Broadway producer Miller (George Murphy) swindles naive Glen (Frank Sinatra) out of $1,500, telling him he will produce his very amateurish play. Meanwhile Miller is really packaging a new musical comedy. He is also in debt to his brother-in-law, hotel manager Gribble (Walter Slezak), for $1,500 for the rent on a hotel penthouse and rooms for his cast. At this juncture, Gribble's seething employer, Wagner (Adolphe Menjou), arrives, demanding to know why the hotel is in debt. Meanwhile, blonde Miss Abbott (Anne Jeffreys) appears on the scene, accompanied by her manager, Jenkins (Eugene Pallette). She announces she can provide a check for $50,000 (from a mysterious sugar daddy) to finance Miller's production, *if* she is given the lead in the pending musical. While the potential backer is not impressed by the book of the show nor by its leading lady Christine (Gloria DeHaven)—Miller has been forced to stage a phoney rehearsal of Glen's script—Miss Abbott is entranced by Glen's singing. She excitedly tells her attorney/manager to close the deal immediately. Miller now must make Glen realize the truth about his play and he asks Christine to tell Glen the bad news, and to persuade him to sing in the upcoming musical comedy now in rehearsal. Thereafter, the $50,000 check bounces and the disillusioned Glen, wanting to help his new friends, pretends to take poison so that the hotel will not throw the troupe out. The musical finally debuts and is a big success. The backers have a hit on their hands and Glen, having forgiven Christine for lying to him, pursues a romance with her.

This was a remake by RKO of its 1938 Marx Brothers' comedy, ROOM SERVICE, which in turn was based on the 1937 stage hit which ran for 500 performances and for which RKO had paid $225,000 for the screen rights. It was the screen acting debut of Frank Sinatra, who had already appeared as a guest band vocalist in prior feature films. He also received his first movie kisses, here from Anne Jeffreys and Gloria DeHaven. STEP LIVELY presented a group of songs by Sammy Cahn and Jule Styne. Frank Sinatra had his best vocal opportunities with "Where Does Love Begin?" (first sung by Gloria DeHaven, George Murphy and the chorus and then reprised by Sinatra and Anne Jeffreys) and "As Long As There's Music."

Variety reported the film had ". . . Song trimming palpably designed to fit Frank Sinatra. As a tailormade vehicle it's somewhat loosely fitted but in the main it will please. . . . Musically there is some final choral and orchestral work evident in all the arrange-

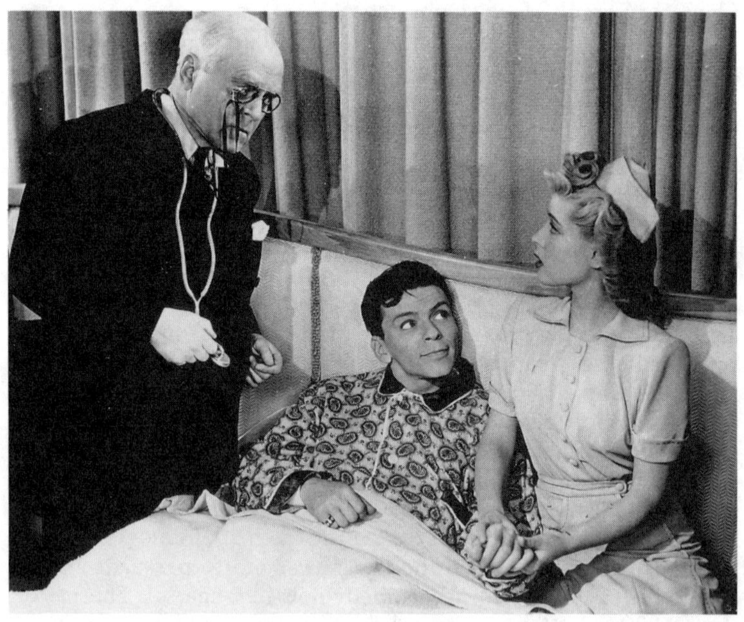

Grant Mitchell, Frank Sinatra and Gloria DeHaven in STEP LIVELY (1944).

ments." Richard B. Jewell and Vernon Harbin wrote in *The RKO Story* (1982), "Though the musical numbers tended to break the comic momentum on occasion, Tim Whelan's pacey direction brought the events back to high gear in a remarkably short time."

STORMY WEATHER (20th Century-Fox, 1943) 77 minutes.

Producer, William Le Baron; director, Andrew Stone; story, Jerry Horwin, Seymour B. Robinson; screenplay, Frederick Jackson, Ted Koehler, H. S. Kraft; art directors, James Basevi, Joseph C. Wright; set decorators, Thomas Little, Fred J. Rode; costumes, Helen Rose; music director, Emil Newman; choreographer, Clarence Robinson; musical numbers supervisor, Fanchon; production advisor, Irving Mills; assistant director, Abe Steinberg; sound, Alfred Bruzlin, Roger Heman; special effects, Fred Sersen; camera, Leon Shamroy; editor, James B. Clark.

Songs: "There's No Two Ways about Love" (Ted Koehler, Irving Mills, James P. Johnson); "Stormy Weather" (Harold Arlen, Koehler); "Ain't Misbehavin" (Fats Waller, Andy Razaf, Harry Brooks); "Rhythm Cocktail" (Cab Calloway); "Rang Tang Tang," "Dat, Dot, Dah" (Cyril Mockridge); "That Ain't Right" (Irving Mills, Nat "King" Cole); "I Can't Give You Anything But Love, Baby," "Digga Digga Doo" (Dorothy Fields, Jimmy McHugh); "I Lost My Sugar in Salt Lake City" (Leon Rene, Johnny Lange); "Geechy Joe" (Andy Gibson, Jack Palmer); "Jumpin' Jive" (Palmer, Calloway, Frank Froebe); "My, My Ain't that Somethin'?" (Harry Tobias, Pinkly Tomlin); "De Camptown Races" (Stephen Foster); "At a Georgia Camp Meeting" (Kerry Mills); "Linda Brown" (Al Cowans); "Nobody's Sweetheart" (Billy Meyers, Elmer Schoebel, Ernie Erdman, Gus Kahn); "Beale Street Blues" (traditional); "Basin Street Blues" (traditional).

Lena Horne (Selina Rogers); Bill Robinson (Corky); Cab Calloway and His Band (Themselves); Katherine Dunham and Her Troupe (Themselves); Fats Waller (Fats); Nicholas Bros. (Themselves); Ada Brown (Ada); Dooley Wilson (Gabe); The Tramp Band (Themselves); Net Stanfield, Johnny Horace (The Shadracks); Babe Wallace (Chick Bailey); Ernest Whitman (Jim Europe); Zuttie Singleton (Zuttie); Mae E. Johnson (Mae); Flournoy E. Miller (Miller); Johnny Lee (Lyles); Robert Felder (Cab Calloway, Jr.); Nicodemus Stewart (Chauffeur).

The same year MGM brought the all-black cast musical CABIN IN THE SKY (*q.v.*) to the big screen, 20th Century-Fox released STORMY WEATHER, which starred Lena Horne and Bill Robinson. The former was featured in both movie musicals. STORMY WEATHER was a loosely fabricated account of the life and times of the legendary Bill "Bojangles" Robinson (1878–1949), who had co-starred with Shirley Temple in several Fox musicals of the 1930s.* While STORMY WEATHER was delightful for its music soundtrack, it had a tacky look about it and appeared more like a film produced by companies catering to the black film theatre circuit rather than the product of a major Hollywood studio. Despite its frivolous story and mediocre look, STORMY WEATHER remains well worth viewing for the talent showcase it presents.

Corky (Bill Robinson) and his pal Gabe (Dooley Wilson) return home after service in First World War. They attend a welcome home party at a Harlem nightclub and meet singer Selina Rogers (Lena Horne). She is the sister of one of Corky's dead army pals. Selina, knowing Corky's proficiency as a dancer, soon urges him to remain in New York to try for a show business career there. However, the insecure man insists on going to Memphis, Tennessee where he has an offered job on a riverboat. As a result of an impromptu dance he performs on the boat, Corky is given a job in a Memphis honkytonk. Some months later, Selina, accompanied by her manager, Chick Bailey (Babe Wallace), happens onto the Beale Street cafe and sees Corky perform. At Selina's insistence Babe offers Corky a job in her upcoming show, but because Bailey is jealous of Corky he makes the role a very minor one. The angered Corky does an unscheduled specialty number during the show and is a hit. Nevertheless, Bailey fires him. Time passes and Corky becomes a major star. He asks Selina to marry him but she refuses to give up her career. Later, Corky goes to Hollywood, where he performs in several motion pictures. One evening, Cab Calloway (himself) asks Corky to visit a club to entertain World War II soldiers. There he encounters Selina for the first time in many years. He gives the performance of his career, and he and Selina renew their romance.

While the plotline of STORMY WEATHER offers little that is novel or perceptive, both agile Bill Robinson and sultry Lena Horne handle their roles well, although he was far too old to play her romantic interest convincingly. More importantly, the picture bubbles with fine musical talent, often not given a chance to shine by the white-dominated Hollywood of the 1940s. Robinson dances at intervals throughout the picture. Horne is finely showcased as

*Bill Robinson and young Shirley Temple had played together in THE LITTLE COLONEL (1935), THE LITTLEST REBEL (1935), REBECCA OF SUNNYBROOK FARM (1938) and JUST AROUND THE CORNER (1938). He had provided choreography for Temple's DIMPLES (1936).

she sings the title song, "I Can't Give You Anything But Love" and "Digga Digga Doo." (Horne, backed by Cab Calloway and His Orchestra, would record several of these numbers for V-Discs during World War II.) In addition to the two focal stars, STORMY WEATHER also featured a number of top black acts, including Fats Waller performing his famous composition, "Ain't Misbehavin'," Calloway and his group doing "Geechy Joe," and an energetic tap dance number provided by the dexterous Nicholas Brothers as part of the finale.*

When it debuted in New York in July 1943, 20th Century-Fox gave STORMY WEATHER a dual premiere: at the Roxy Theatre in midtown Manhattan and at the Alhambra Theatre in Harlem. The *New York Times* reported, "STORMY WEATHER is a first-rate show, just the kind of spirited divertissement that will make you forget all about your own momentary weather troubles. . . . Musically . . . it is a joy to the ear, especially when Miss Horne digs deep into the depths of romantic despair to put across the classic blues number, after which the picture is titled, in a manner that is distinctive and refreshing even at this late day." *Variety* added, "As a backstage colored musical, it is in itself a novelty. There is convincing flavor to the stars and featured talent who play themselves."

In *The Best, Worst and Most Unusual: Hollywood Musicals* (1983), the editors of *Consumer Guide* and Philip J. Kaplan judged of the film, "Sometimes condescending, it nonetheless contains some of the most amazing individual performances ever recorded on film, and therefore deserves serious consideration. . . . [It] is a frustrating film because it is so extreme. It is both excellent and horrible."

To be noted was that Irving Mills, head of Mills Music, served as production advisor for this movie project. As *Variety* detailed, "Mills, vet manager of colored talent, and whose Mills Music firm has published most of the notable Harlem songsmiths, unquestionably figured importantly in the assembling of this galaxy of music, talent and other values."

THE STORY OF VERNON AND IRENE CASTLE (RKO, 1939) 90 minutes.

Producers, George Haight, Pandro S. Berman; director, H. C. Potter; based on the books *My Husband* and *My Memories of Vernon*

*Regarding the spectacular dance by the Nicholas Brothers, Donald Bogle enthused in *Blacks in American Films and Television* (1988), "Dressed elegantly in tuxedos, their faces lighted up with enthusiasm for their work, the two—Harold and Fayard—perform a staircase/split number that is, in intricate technical terms, a marvel. . . . Their work frames the movie, bringing it to an almost intolerably pleasurable peak."

Castle by Irene Castle; adaptors, Oscar Hammerstein II, Dorothy Yost; screenplay, Richard Sherman; art directors, Van Nest Polglase, Perry Ferguson; set decorator, Darrell Silvera; costumes, Walter Plunkett, Edward Stevenson, Castle; makeup, Mel Burns; music director, Victor Baravalle; choreographer, Hermes Pan; technical advisor, Castle; assistant director, Argyle Nelson; special effects, Vernon L. Walker; camera, Robert DeGrasse; editor, William Hamilton.

Songs: "Only When You're in My Arms" (Con Conrad, Harry Ruby, Bert Kalmar); "Missouri Waltz" (John Eppell, Frederick Logan, J. R. Shannon); "Oh, You Beautiful Doll" (Nat Ayer, A. Seymour Brown); "Nights of Gladness" (Charles Ancliffe); "By the Beautiful Sea" (Harry Carroll, Harold Atteridge); "Glow, Little Glow Worm" (Paul Lincke, Lillian Cayley Robinson); "Destiny Waltz" (Sidney Baynes); "Row, Row, Row" (James V. Monaco, William Jerome); "The Yama Yama Man" (Karl Hoschna, Collin Davis); "Hello, Hello, Who's Your Lady Friend?" (Bert Lee, Harry Fragson, Worton David); "Take Me Back to New York Town" (Harry von Tilzer, Andrew B. Sterling); "It's a Long Way to Tipperary" (Harry Williams, Jack Judge); "Come, Josephine in My Flying Machine" (Fred Fisher, Alfred Bryan); "By the Light of the Silvery Moon" (Gus Edwards, Ed Madden); "Cuddle Up a Little Closer" (Karl Hoschna, Otto Harbach); "Way Down Yonder in New Orleans" (Henry Creamer, Turner Layton); "King Chanticleer" ["Texas Tommy"] (Nat D. Ayer); "The Darktown Strutters' Ball" (Shelton Brooks; French lyric by Elsie Janis); "While They Were Dancing Around" (Monaco, Joseph McCarthy); "Rose Room" (Art Hickman, Harry Williams); "Hello, Frisco, Hello" (Louis Hirsch, Gene Buck); "Très Jolie Waltz" (Emil Waldteufel); "You're Here and I'm Here" (Jerome Kern, Harry B. Smith); "Syncopated Walk" (Irving Berlin); "Maxixe Dengozo" (Ernesto Nazareth); "Little Brown Jug" (Joseph E. Winters); "Too Much Mustard" (Cecil Macklin); "Waitin' for the Robert E. Lee" (Abel Baer, L. Wolfe Gilbert).

Fred Astaire (Vernon Castle); Ginger Rogers (Irene Foote Castle); Edna May Oliver (Maggie Sutton); Walter Brennan (Walter); Lew Fields (Himself); Etienne Girardot (Papa Aubel); Janet Beecher (Mrs. Foote); Rolfe Sedan (Emile Aubel); Leonid Kinskey (Artist); Robert Strange (Dr. Foote); Douglas Walton (Student Pilot); Clarence Derwent (Papa Louis); Sonny Lamont (Charlie); Frances Mercer (Claire Ford); Victor Varconi (Grand Duke); Donald MacBride (Hotel Manager); Dick Elliott (Conductor); David McDonald, John Meredith (Army Pilots); Tiny Jones (Lady in Revolving Door); Marjorie Belcher [Marge Champion]

(Irene's Girl Friend); and: Adrienne d'Ambricourt, Roy D'Arcy, "Buzz" Barton, Joe Bordeaux, Eugene Borden, Don Brodie, Neil Burns, Willis Clare, Armand Cortez, Max Darwyn, Hal K. Dawson, Elspeth Dudgeon, Bill Franey, Neal Hart, Ethyl Haworth, Russell Hicks, George Irving, Dorothy Lovett, Hugh McArthur, Bruce Mitchell, Leonard Mudie, Esther Muir, Frank O'Connor, Bill Patton, Jack Perrin, Kay Sutton, D. H. Turner, Allen Wood, Theodore Von Eltz.

A great deal had changed on the Hollywood musical scene since Fred Astaire and Ginger Rogers had first united on-camera for FLYING DOWN TO RIO (1933), *q.v.* They had co-starred in eight sleek musicals, reaching their zenith with THE GAY DIVORCEE (1934) and TOP HAT (1935), *qq.v.* It was only natural, after eight films together, that audiences should be tiring of the set formula and special production values that were associated with an Astaire-Rogers musical. Astaire had already gone solo in the not-so-well received DAMSEL IN DISTRESS (1937), *q.v.*, and he and Rogers were not so felicitously reunited in CAREFREE (1938), *q.v.* Astaire, in fact, would soon be labeled box-office poison by an industry magazine survey. However, RKO in financial peril, needed another hoped-for Astaire-Rogers success to bolster their profit and loss statements. So the stars were persuaded to join together "for one final time" (as the publicity copy boasted) in THE STORY OF VERNON AND IRENE CASTLE. With its heavily biographical plot and its period trappings, it was the most uncharacteristic of all the 1930s Astaire-Rogers movies.

In 1911 vaudeville slapstick comedian Vernon Castle (Fred Astaire) meets pretty young Irene Foote (Ginger Rogers) in New Rochelle, New York and the two quickly fall in love. She has ambitions to become a dancer and she persuades him to abandon his stale comedy act to perfect a dance team with her. After a long period of struggle, they go to Paris, ostensibly to appear in a musical comedy. However, they are disappointed to learn that the manager had thought he was hiring Vernon to perform his old comedy routines. They are downhearted. By pure luck, they encounter Maggie Sutton (Edna May Oliver), a manager-promoter who obtains an engagement for the couple at the chic Café de Paris. They become sensations overnight and money offers pour in. They return to America where they make well-received cross country tours. They become a craze, their fans copying their clothing and hair styles, and many items are merchandized with their names attached. They later decide to retire and settle down. However, Vernon, an Englishman by birth, enlists in the Aviation Corps at the start of World War I, much to Irene's consternation. They have a reunion in Paris just as America enters the war. Vernon becomes an aviator instructor, while she goes to Hollywood to make pictures. Some months later she is thrilled to learn that Vernon has been transferred to America and that he is on his way to Texas to instruct Army students in aviation. They agree upon a rendezvous. However, on the day they are to meet, Vernon is killed in an aerial accident. In a dream-like sequence, Irene and Vernon are reunited for a last waltz.

Although the film was based (*very* loosely) on two books by Irene Castle and she was an advisor on the film (causing many problems because of her interference on the set), THE STORY OF VERNON AND IRENE CASTLE is only a retelling of the Castles' life in spirit.* If Astaire seemed more dimensional with his more substantial than usual character, Rogers was more coy and arch in the opening young girl scenes and a bit too grand as the successful star. Because of the confines of the scenario, there was very little opportunity for the boy meets/chases/loses/wins girl structure that had been the foundation of the team's past pictures together. (In fact, with the film's tragic finale, it provided another first for an Astaire-Rogers movie—the death of one of the leads.) Although the period settings and costumes offered a welcome change of pace, it carried the stars away from the elegant art deco ambiance of their earlier successes. And, most of all, because the music was comprised almost entirely of authentic songs from past generations, it lacked the special tailor-made romantic quality of the contemporary numbers composed for the screen pair by the likes of Irving Berlin, Cole Porter and George and Ira Gershwin in their past movies.**

Despite all these departures from the established ingredients, and the sluggish direction of H. C. Potter, *Variety* kindly called the movie "one of the best Astaire-Rogers films," and added, "Miss Rogers and Astaire are excellent as the Castles. The illusion is always there; their deportment is more Vernon and Irene Castle than Astaire and Rogers. Their dance sequences [again choreographed by Hermes Pan] are less spectacular but more consistent with the normal plot progression." The *New York Journal* stated: ". . . A thoroughly entertaining piece in which the two most delightful

---

* Vernon and Irene Castle had appeared together on screen in THE WHIRL OF LIFE (1915).

** The one new number for THE STORY OF VERNON AND IRENE CASTLE was "Only When You're in My Arms" by Con Conrad and Harry Ruby, and Bert Kalmar. Fred Astaire would portray Kalmar in the MGM musical biography, THREE LITTLE WORDS (1950), *q.v.*

dancers of the present day impersonate the most glamorous dancing pair of another generation." Two of the highlights of the production were Ginger Rogers' performing "The Yama Yama Man" and the montage sequence which found Astaire and Rogers dancing across a huge map of the United States.

While THE STORY OF VERNON AND IRENE CASTLE did modestly well at the box-office, it was the finale of Astaire and Rogers as a RKO song-and-dance team. He went on to MGM and BROADWAY MELODY OF 1940 (*q.v.*), teamed with Eleanor Powell for the first time. Ginger Rogers, now under a non-exclusive contract with RKO, focused on dramas and comedies, winning an Oscar for KITTY FOYLE (1940). Her next musical was the overblown LADY IN THE DARK (1944), *q.v.*, at Paramount. She would be called in to replace an emotionally ailing Judy Garland for MGM's THE BARKLEYS OF BROADWAY (1949), *q.v.*, which reunited her with Fred Astaire for the tenth and final time on the big screen.

STRIKE UP THE BAND (Metro-Goldwyn-Mayer, 1940) 120 minutes.

Producer, Arthur Freed; director, Busby Berkeley; screenplay, John Monks, Jr., Fred Finklehoffe, (uncredited): Herbert Fields, Kay Van Riper; art directors, Cedric Gibbons, John S. Detlie; set decorator, Edwin B. Willis; costumes, Dolly Tree, Gile Steele; makeup, Jack Dawn; fruit models created by Henry Rox; music director, George Stoll; choral arrangers/orchestrators, Conrad Salinger, Leo Arnaud; musical presentation, Merrill Pye; sound supervisor, Douglas Shearer; camera, Ray June; editor, Ben Lewis.

Songs: "Strike Up the Band" (George Gershwin, Ira Gershwin); "Our Love Affair" (Roger Edens, Arthur Freed); "Do the La Conga," "Nobody," "Drummer Boy," "Nell of New Rochelle" (Edens); "Sidewalks of New York" (James Blake, Charles Lawlor); "Sing, Sing, Sing" (Louis Prima); "Walking Down Broadway" (arranger: Edens); "Light Cavalry Overture" (Franz von Suppe); "Over the Waves" (Juventino Rosas); "Heaven Protect the Working Girl" (A. Baldwin Sloane, Edgar Smith); "I Just Can't Make My Eyes Behave" (Gus Edwards, Will Cobb); "The Curse of an Aching Heart" (Al Piantadosi, Henry Fink); "Five Foot Two, Eyes of Blue" (Ray Henderson); "After the Ball" (Charles K. Harris).

Mickey Rooney (Jimmy Connors); Judy Garland (Mary Holden); Paul Whiteman and His Orchestra (Themselves); June Preisser (Barbara Frances Morgan); William Tracy (Phillip Turner); Ann Shoemaker (Mrs. Connors); Larry Nunn (Willie Brewster);

George Lessey (Mr. Morgan); Francis Pierlot (Mr. Judd); Harry McCrillis (Booper Barton); Margaret Early (Annie); Sarah Edwards (Miss Hodges); Elliot Carpenter (Henry); Virginia Brissac (Mrs. May Holden); Howard Hickman (The Doctor); Virginia Sale (Music Teacher); Milton Kibbee (Mr. Holden); Mickey Martin, Charles Smith (Boys); Sherrie Overton, Margaret Marquis, Maxine Cook (Girls); Phil Silvers (Pitch Man); Billy Wayne (Clown); Joe Devlin (Attendant); Don Castle (Charlie); Enid Bennett (Mrs. Morgan); Helen Jerome Eddy (Mrs. Brewster); Harlan Briggs (Doctor); Dick Allen (Policeman); Jimmie Lucas, Jack Albertson (Barkers); Earle Hodgins (Hammer Concessionaire); Harry Harvey (Shooting Gallery Concessionaire); Jack Baxley (Ice Cream Concessionaire); Harry Lahs, Jack Kenny (Hot Dog Concessionaires); Roland Got (House Boy); Lowden Adams (Butler); Margaret Seddon, Margaret McWade (Old Ladies); Louise LaPlanche, Lois James, Helen Seamon, Mary Jo Ellis, Naida Reynolds, Linda Johnson, Wallace Musselwhite, Myron Speth, Douglas Wilson, Sidney Miller, Vendell Darr (Students); Jack Mulhall, Henry Roquemore (Men); Leonard Sues (Trumpet Player).

Having succeeded so well with the formula in BABES IN ARMS (1939), *q.v.,* MGM rematched its young song-and-dance stars, Mickey Rooney and Judy Garland, in another festive study of teenage hi-jinks, also with a show business motif. Producer Arthur Freed and director Busby Berkeley outdid themselves in stuffing the production with musical offerings. The abundance led the *New York Times* to print, "As they say in Hollywood, this show has everything—music, laughter, tears. . . . As usual, everything is a little too much." As the basis for this movie, MGM acquired the screen rights to George and Ira Gershwin's musical *Strike Up the Band,* which had premiered on Broadway early in 1930. It had a 191-performance run, featuring the comedy team of Clark & McCullough, Blanche Ring and Red Nichols and His Orchestra. The show introduced the title song, "Soon" and "I've Got a Crush on You," while "The Man I Love" was dropped from the production. In typical movieland fashion, the studio completely revamped the project, retaining only the title song for its rousing climax. Since big band music was so popular at the time, adding famed bandleader Paul Whiteman to the proceedings not only made the production more topical, it gave added inducement to moviegoers to flock to STRIKE UP THE BAND.

The widowed Mrs. Connors (Ann Shoemaker) hopes that her son, Jimmy (Mickey Rooney), will become a physician, but his aspirations are to become a drummer in a swing band. However, once he explains just how much music really means to him, she relents. She realizes he should do whatever is best for himself. Meanwhile, Jimmy organizes a band, composed of his Riverwood High School classmates, with Mary Holden (Judy Garland) as group vocalist. He plans to have the band become so proficient that they can enter and win the competition being sponsored by renowned bandleader Paul Whiteman (himself). To earn the $200 necessary to provide transportation for Chicago, the band performs at a school dance and later at an Elks' affair. Shortly before the troupe is to leave for the audition, Jimmy discovers that one of the boys, Willie Brewster (Larry Nunn), is extremely ill and that his mother (Helen Jerome Eddy) needs the $200 to take her son to Chicago for immediate surgery. Jimmy and the band give Mrs. Brewster the money, but now the band is stranded. However, all is not lost. The wealthy father (George Lessey) of Barbara Frances Morgan (June Preisser)—who has a crush on Jimmy, much to the chagrin of part-time school librarian Mary—takes Jimmy and the band to Chicago on a special train. The group competes in the contest and wins it. Jimmy is given the honor of leading all the competing bands in one final grand number, which is broadcast to the nation.

More so than in BABES IN ARMS, STRIKE UP THE BAND is a tour-de-force for versatile Mickey Rooney. He frantically plays the drums and the xylophone, sings, dances, romances, cries, sacrifices himself for the betterment of one of his peers, all the while cavorting in the best/worst show business tradition. It led the *New York Herald Tribune* to judge, "Master Rooney, who amply deserves the screen title of America's Sweetheart without Curls, mugs and acts his way through two hours of film cut-ups without one moment of indecision." The *New York Times* added, "Call him cocky and brash, but he has the sort of exuberant talent that keeps your eyes on the screen, whether he's banging the trap-drums, prancing through a Conga, or hamming the old ham actors." In this phase of his lengthy career, Rooney could do no wrong at the studio or with the public. Soon this half pint of T.N.T. would be named number one at the box-office. Not only was Rooney a multi-talented quick study at an assortment of song-and-dance tricks, but he was very willing to rehearse, something absolutely necessary to carry out the complex routines devised by taskmaster Busby Berkeley.

On the other hand, eighteen-year-old Judy Garland, even in 1940, was an emotionally tender star. She relied on an abundance of talent and instincts to carry her through her screen assignments. Her spontaneous, undisciplined nature rebelled at practicing routines over and over again, leading to great on-set friction between her and Busby Berkeley. Thus, frequently, MGM filmmakers were forced to rely on Rooney to carry more than his share of the Rooney-Garland outings. That is not to say that Judy Garland was not effective in STRIKE UP THE BAND. It showcased her as a talented songstress, a good-hearted lass who worked after classes in the school library and who adored band leader Mickey Rooney so much that she would willingly sacrifice her happiness (and her chance to shine) to vixenish June Preisser if the latter would provide the funding to get the band to Chicago on time. *Variety* judged, "Miss Garland catches major attention for her all-around achievements. She's right there with Rooney in much of the story as his mentoring girlfriend, teams with him in the production numbers for both songs and dances, and rings the bell with several songs sold to the utmost." By now, Garland had slimmed down into an attractive, mature young woman.

There are many highlights in the (over)-long STRIKE UP THE BAND. Rooney solos on "Drummer Boy" while Garland—with that wonderful catch in her voice—vocalizes on "Our Love Affair." In an effective gimmicky moment, Rooney explains to Garland just how he intends to set up the band for the competition. The devout Garland listens with rapt attention as the pieces of fruit Rooney has been using for examples spring to life as small puppet musicians who begin playing their respective instruments. The intricate "Do the Conga" production number displays Rooney and Garland leading their tireless classmates in a sweeping gymnastic follow-the-leader. Also included (and which well could have been deleted) is the youths' overzealous performance of a dreadful old-fashioned melodrama, *Nell of New Rochelle,* which they romp through in period costumes and exaggerated gestures. Then there is the expansive climactic number, a patriotic salute.

Less fortuitous moments in STRIKE UP THE BAND include the lachrymose sentiments that engulf the discussions between Ann Shoemaker and her music-obsessed son, and the wallowing in self-pity of good sport Garland, who fears she will lose her beloved (albeit cocky) Rooney to pampered, pouty blonde, June Preisser. A low point of sentimentality occurs when the ailing Larry Nunn, lying in his sickbed, is more worried about the band's fate than his own condition. However, this is not the nadir of tugging at the audience's heart strings. There is the fatherly chat that bandleader Paul Whiteman has with overachiever Rooney. In this conversation the rotund legend explains metaphorically to Rooney that life has its special rhythm from start to finish, even to those final "last eight bars" in the sky. All this helps to convince Rooney that he must not accept the offer of a New York gig to drum with a big group.

Instead his responsibility is to remain with his school pals and to help launch the whole gang on the big road to success.

Made at a cost of $838,661, STRIKE UP THE BAND grossed $3,494,000 in its initial release. The picture received an Academy Award for Best Sound Recording. It earned Oscar nominations for Best Song, "Our Love Affair," and Best Score.

Mickey Rooney and Judy Garland would repeat their "Strike Up the Band" roles on CBS network's "Lux Radio Theatre" on October 28, 1940. They would next be teamed in BABES ON BROADWAY (1941) and GIRL CRAZY (1943), *q.v.,* and would both appear in the all-star salute, THOUSANDS CHEER (1943).

SUMMER STOCK (Metro-Goldwyn-Mayer, 1950), Color 109 minutes.

Producer, Joe Pasternak; director, Charles Walters; story, Sy Gomberg; screenplay, George Wells, Gomberg; art directors, Cedric Gibbons, Jack Martin Smith; set decorators, Edwin B. Willis, Alfred E. Spencer; costumes, Walter Plunkett, Helen Rose; makeup, William Tuttle, John Truwe; music directors, Johnny Green, Saul Chaplin; choreographers, Nick Castle, Gene Kelly, Walters; assistant director, Al Jennings; color consultants, Henri Jaffi, James Gooch; sound, Douglas Shearer, John Williams; camera, Robert Planck; editor, Albert Akst.

Songs: "Howdy Neighbor," "Friendly Star," "Mem'ry Island," "Dig-Dig-Dig for Your Dinner," "If You Feel Like Singing, Sing," "All for You," "Blue Jean Polka" (Harry Warren, Mack Gordon); "You, Wonderful You" (Warren, Jack Brooks, Saul Chaplin); "Get Happy" (Ted Koehler, Harold Arlen); "Heavenly Music" (Chaplin).

Judy Garland (Jane Falbury); Gene Kelly (Joe D. Ross); Eddie Bracken (Orville Wingait); Gloria DeHaven (Abigail Falbury); Marjorie Main (Esme); Phil Silvers (Herb Blake); Ray Collins (Jasper G. Wingait); Carleton Carpenter (Artie); Nita Bieber (Sarah Higgins); Hans Conried (Harrison I. Kerath); Paul E. Burns (Frank); Carol Haney, Dorothy Tuttle, Arthur Loew, Jr., Dick Humphreys, Jimmy Thompson, Bridget Carr, Joanne Tree, Jean Coyne, Jean Adcock, Rena Lenart, Joan Dale, Betty Hannon, Elynne Ray, Marilyn Reiss, Carol West, Eugene Freedley, Don Powell, Joe Roach, Albert Ruiz (Stock Company Members); Roy Butler, Henry Sylvester, George Bunny, Frank Pharr (Townsmen); Cameron Grant, Jack Daley, Reginald Simpson (Producers); Michael Chapin, Teddy Infuhr (Boys); Almira Sessions (Constance Fliggerton); Kathryn Sheldon (Amy Fliggerton); Jack Gargan

Judy Garland and Gene Kelly in SUMMER STOCK (1950).

(Clerk); Eddie Dunn (Sheriff); Erville Alderson (Zeb); Bette Arlen, Bunny Waters (Showgirls).

On the surface, SUMMER STOCK was just another pleasant MGM musical diversion. However, it has a larger role in cinema history. It was Judy Garland's final picture for her home lot, Metro-Goldwyn-Mayer. If the studio had dealt with her myriad emotional and physical problems in the past, the end began when she caused so many production problems during the filming of THE PIRATE (1948) and EASTER PARADE (1948), *qq.v.* The Arthur Freed unit at MGM had barely managed to cope with these severely trying situations. However, even by her standards, Garland became impossible on the set of THE BARKLEYS OF BROADWAY (1949), *q.v.,* and had to be replaced by Ginger Rogers. When that situation had cleared and she had allegedly stabilized from her emotional problems, she was cast in ANNIE GET YOUR GUN (1950), *q.v.,* and actually got through the pre-recordings of her song numbers and a few sequences before recurrent problems forced her to leave the project and Paramount's Betty Hutton was substituted. After a stay at a Boston hospital to help her withdraw from drug dependency, she returned (too soon?) to the studio for SUMMER STOCK, a Joe Pasternak production. It reunited her for the third and final time on-camera with Gene Kelly.*

Jane Falbury (Judy Garland) is an impoverished farm owner in Connecticut. She eagerly awaits the arrival of her younger sister Abigail (Gloria DeHaven) to help her gather in the crops. Unexpectedly, the headstrong Abigail arrives with a summer stock company headed by Joe D. Ross (Gene Kelly). The latter is Abigail's newest boyfriend and he and the troupe want to put on their new musical revue in the farm's barn. All this exasperates the hard-working Jane. Jane reluctantly agrees to allow them to use her farm when she learns that Joe and the others have invested all their savings in staging the show. The bargain is that if they help with the farmyard chores, they can stay. Not so happy about the situation are Jane's pragmatic boyfriend, Orville Wingait (Eddie Bracken), and his conservative father, general store owner Jasper G. Wingait (Ray Collins). As rehearsals proceed, Jane and Joe become attracted to one another, but Jane remains distant, not wanting to break up her sister's romance. A few days before the big opening, Abigail and Joe argue and she runs off to New York. Joe begs Jane to take over

*Judy Garland had already starred with Gene Kelly at MGM in FOR ME AND MY GAL (1942) and THE PIRATE (1948), *qq.v.* Later they were scheduled to perform together in EASTER PARADE (1948), *q.v.,* but an injury forced Kelly to drop out and Fred Astaire was lured out of semi-retirement to substitute.

the role. She agrees, over the objections of Orville, who rushes off to Manhattan to retrieve Abigail. On opening night Orville and Abigail return in time to see the show's warm reception. Abigail sees how much Jane and Joe care for one another. She willingly steps aside, for she finds Orville much more to her liking.

If SUMMER STOCK had been made a decade earlier, it surely would have starred Judy Garland and Mickey Rooney in another of their "gee, let's put on the big show" epics. As it was, SUMMER STOCK is a mature expression of such youthful capering. Considering all the production problems involved in catering to Garland, it is a wonder that the film was ever completed. For comedy relief there was raucous Marjorie Main,* boisterous Phil Silvers and bucolic Eddie Bracken.

Harry Warren and Mack Gordon wrote several of the numbers for SUMMER STOCK, all of them serviceable, none especially memorable. The opening sequence has a coverall-clad Garland riding on a tractor and singing "Howdy Neighbor." Later, she wistfully (her speciality) sings "Friendly Star." She is seen showering as she expounds "If You Feel Like Singing, Sing." Gene Kelly performs the production number ("All for You"), does a solo dance ("You Wonderful You") on an empty stage, and escorts Garland about the dance floor in the "Portland Fancy" routine. He and Phil Silvers perform the jocular "Dig, Dig for Your Dinner" and harmonize on "Heavenly Music" (as broken-toothed hillbillies sporting oversized fake feet). The upbeat show piece of the film, "Get Happy" (by Harold Arlen and Ted Koehler), was an afterthought. By the time it was shot choreographer Nick Castle had left the production and director Charles Walters (who began as a dancer-choreographer) took over. Garland, whose weight had fluctuated greatly throughout production, was in one of her slim periods and for this number she donned leotards, a man's tuxedo jacket and a black fedora pushed down over one eye. It offers Garland at her most vividly exciting. (Because there was such a vast physical difference between the Garland of this number and the rest of the picture, it was assumed by many filmgoers that the segment had been lifted from earlier shot footage.)

When SUMMER STOCK debuted in the late summer of 1950, *Time* magazine noted, "SUMMER STOCK, no great shakes as a cinemusical, serves nonetheless as a welcome reminder of Judy Garland's unerring way with a song. Ill, and in and out of trouble with her studio, actress Garland has been off the screen since last

---

*Marjorie Main appeared in three musicals with Judy Garland: MEET ME IN ST. LOUIS (1944), THE HARVEY GIRLS (1946) and SUMMER STOCK (1950), *qq.v.*

year's IN THE GOOD OLD SUMMERTIME. A rest cure left her chubbily overweight for her first return performance. But none of it seems to have affected her ability as one of Hollywood's few triple-threat girls. Thanks to actress Garland's singing, dancing, and acting (and some imaginative dancing by Gene Kelly) the picture seems considerably better than it is."

SUMMER STOCK was a moneyearner. Garland had left the studio for a vacation when she was summoned back to Culver City to replace a pregnant June Allyson opposite Fred Astaire in ROYAL WEDDING (1951), *q.v.* The reluctant star reported to the studio for rehearsals, but after a few weeks—by June 17, 1950—her ill-behavior led the studio to drop her from the company's payroll. After a nearly fifteen-year tenure, Judy Garland was through at MGM. She would not make another picture for four years, until she made a triumphant comeback in Warner Bros.' A STAR IS BORN (1954), *q.v.*

British release title: IF YOU FEEL LIKE SINGING.

SUN VALLEY SERENADE (20th Century-Fox, 1941) 86 minutes.

Producer, Milton Sperling; director, H. Bruce Humberstone; screen idea, Darryl F. Zanuck; story, Art Arthur, Robert Harari; screenplay, Robert Ellis, Helen Logan; art directors, Richard Day, Lewis Creber; choreographer, Hermes Pan; camera, Edward Cronjager; editor, James B. Clark.

Songs: "Chattanooga Choo Choo," "I Know Why (and So Do You)," "It Happened in Sun Valley," "At Last," "The Kiss Polka" (Harry Warren, Mack Gordon); "In the Mood" (Andy Razaf, Joe Garland); "Sun Valley Jump," "The Spirit Is Willing" (music, Jerry Grey); "Measure for Measure" (music, Arletta May).

Sonja Henie (Karen Benson); John Payne (Ted Scott); Glenn Miller (Phil Carey); Milton Berle (Nifty Allen); Lynn Bari (Vivian Dawn); Joan Davis (Miss Carstairs); Nicholas Brothers (Specialty); William Davidson (Murray); Dorothy Dandridge (Specialty); Alira Sessions (Nurse); Mel Ruick (Band Leader); Forbes Murray (Headwaiter); Ralph Dunn (Customs Officer); Chester Clute (Process Server); Edward Earle, Edward Kane (Men); Lynne Roberts (Receptionist); Ann Doran (Waitress); Walter "Spec" O'Donnell (Western Union Boy); Bruce Edwards (Ski Instructor); John "Skins" Miller (Sleigh Driver); Fred "Snowflakes" Toones (Porter); Ernie Alexander (Boy); Sheila Ryan (Telephone Operator); William Forrest (Husband); Dora Clement (Wife); Herbert Gunn, Kenneth Alexander (Ski Patrol Men); The Modernaires (Themselves); Tex Beneke, Jimmy Priddy, "Chommy" MacGregor, Ernie Caceres, Hal McIntyre, Willie Schwarz, Al Klink, Ray

Anthony, Johnny Best, Billy May, Maurice Purtill, Trigger Alpert, Paul Tanner, Frank D'Anolfo, Ralph Brewster, Mickey McMickle, Jack Lathrop (Glenn Miller Orchestra); Paula Kelly, Ray Eberle (Vocalists); Pat Friday (Singing Voice of Vivian Dawn).

Phil Carey (Glenn Miller) and His Orchestra find they have widely spaced bookings, but through the efforts of singer Vivian Dawn (Lynn Bari) they gain an audition at a Sun Valley resort and land the job. Some months before, the band's pianist, Ted Scott (John Payne), obtained publicity by becoming the guardian of a Norwegian war refugee named Karen Benson (Sonja Henie). Just as the band is about to depart for Sun Valley, she appears on the scene. Frantically Ted and the band's publicist, Nifty Allen (Milton Berle), conceal the girl on their train. By now, Karen has become infatuated with Ted. When the band arrives in Sun Valley, Karen proves to be their star attraction since she is a sensational skater (and skier), while Nifty finds himself romantically pursued by secretary Miss Carstairs (Joan Davis). The band and Karen are a big success at the resort. After they are stranded together in a mountain ski hut, Ted discovers he loves Karen.

Scandinavian skating wiz Sonja Henie had been a 20th Century-Fox (novelty) star since 1936's ONE IN A MILLION. On skates she was a sparkling, rhythmic wonder; on terra firma she left much to be desired as an actress. By the time of SUN VALLEY SERENADE, her seventh studio outing, the magic had worn off the relationship between the athletic Henie and dictatorial studio chief, Darryl F. Zanuck. He had grown tired of arguing with the shrewd businesswoman who made more money from ice skating than she did from her Hollywood contract. When Henie demanded that she be given a third ice skating routine for SUN VALLEY SERENADE, Zanuck balked. He said she could have it on condition that she pay for it. That ended the discussion.

Glenn Miller and His Orchestra were at the peak of their popularity and were drawn to Hollywood in the early 1940s as were nearly all of the big swing bands. SUN VALLEY SERENADE was the first (and more heavily budgeted) of two features the group would make for 20th Century-Fox, the second being ORCHESTRA WIVES (1942). The joy of SUN VALLEY SERENADE is having the opportunity to watch the famed Miller troupe perform several of their most popular numbers. If they seem a bit nervous in front of the camera, their musicianship overcomes this deficit. Pat Friday dubbed for the on-camera Lynn Bari performing "At Last" in duet with John Payne, as well as "I Know Why," which Friday did in harmony with Payne and Miller's group, The Modernaires. The Modernaires provide the backing, joined by a chorus, for the lilting "It Happened in Sun Valley," which has on-location background filming to bolster the sequence. During the Miller rendition of "Chattanooga Choo Choo," sung by Tex Beneke, Paula Kelly and the Modernaires, the amazing Nicholas Brothers perform one of their sensational dances and singer Dorothy Dandridge does a specialty.

Variety acknowledged of SUN VALLEY SERENADE that it was "an excellent compound of entertaining ingredients" and noted, "the winter resort activities of Sun Valley are displayed without intrusion on the main story unreeling. . . . Production is excellently mounted, with camera work by Edward Cronjager highly meritorious." Not to be overlooked was the presence of angular, deep-voiced Joan Davis (in her final film under her studio contract) and a youngish Milton Berle.

So popular was SUN VALLEY SERENADE that Darryl F. Zanuck was forced to renegotiate a new contract with Henie (who had left the studio and gone East). Their uneasy relationship continued for two more pictures. Her next, ICELAND (1942) also co-starred John Payne.

SUNNY (First National, 1930) 67 minutes.

Director, William A. Seiter; based on the musical play by Otto Harbach, Oscar Hammerstein, II, Jerome Kern; adaptors, Humphrey Pearson, Henry McCarty; dialogue, Pearson; music director, Erno Rapee; director of ballet sequences, Theodore Kosloff; camera, Ernest Haller; editor, LeRoy Stone.

Songs: "Sunny," "Who?" "D'Ya Love Me?" "Two Little Love Birds," "I Was Alone" (Otto Harbach, Oscar Hammerstein, II, Jerome Kern).

Marilyn Miller (Sunny); Lawrence Gray (Tom Warren); Joe Donahue (Jim Deming); Mackenzie Ward (Wendell-Wendell); O. P. Heggie (Peters); Inez Courtney ("Weenie"); Barbara Bedford (Marcia Manners); Judith Vosselli (Sue); Clyde Cook (Sam); Barry Allen (The Barker); William Davidson (1st Officer); Ben Hendrickson, Jr. (2nd Officer).

Sunny, with book and lyrics by Otto Harbach and Oscar Hammerstein, II and music by Jerome Kern, opened on Broadway in the fall of 1925 and ran for 517 performances, starring Marilyn Miller, Jack Donahue, Clifton Webb, Cliff Edwards and George Olsen and His Orchestra. It produced two popular standards, "Sunny" and "Who?" With the coming of sound films, Marilyn Miller (she invented the name Marilyn for herself by combining her given name of Mary Ellen into one) came to Hollywood and did a trio of features, SALLY (1930), *q.v.,* being her first, followed by SUNNY and by HER MAJESTY, LOVE (1931).

Beautiful Sunny (Marilyn Miller) is a circus bareback performer who goes against her father's (O.P. Heggie) wishes to marry English nobleman Wendell-Wendell (Mackenzie Ward). She stows away on an ocean liner bound for the U.S., with her dad also aboard. When the two are found, the old man is forced to pay his passage by scrubbing the decks, while Sunny must sing and dance for the passengers, who include the man she loves, American Tom Warren (Lawrence Gray). The latter is engaged to socialite Marcia Manners (Barbara Bedford). Unable to enter the U.S. without a passport, Sunny engineers a marriage of convenience with Jim Deming (Joe Donahue), Tom's pal, who owns a profitable gymnasium. Things become complicated when Jim's former fiancée, Weenie (Inez Courtney), and Wendell-Wendell arrive from England. When Marcia overhears Sunny tell Tom she knows he loves her, Marcia announces she and Tom will marry. However, before Sunny can leave the country, after having divorced Jim, Tom proposes and they agree to marry.

Because musicals were nearly passé, SUNNY, with its nonsensical storyline, was shorn of several of its musical numbers and was released in a relatively brief sixty-seven-minute format. The camerawork was not especially flattering to Miller and she did not shine as she had in the stage edition. Nevertheless, the magical name of Marilyn Miller still lured moviegoers. The critical response was respectful. *Photoplay* magazine challenged, "Who said singies were through? A gem of a picture like this makes us wonder. The radiant personality of Marilyn Miller smashes over this gay and tasteful version of the stage. . . . To rave about her dancing would be to gild the lily. . . . Swell!" The *New York Times* stated, "Miss Miller is captivating . . . an ably directed film, with pleasing light touches." For the culture-minded, there were ballet sequences choreographed by Theodore Kosloff.

Marilyn Miller died in 1936. Judy Garland would play Miller in a segment of TILL THE CLOUDS ROLL BY (1946), *q.v.* A fanciful account of Miller's life would be presented in LOOK FOR THE SILVER LINING (1949), *q.v.,* with June Haver cast as the legendary star. Pamela Peadon appeared as Marilyn Miller in ZIEGFELD: THE MAN AND HIS WOMEN, an NBC-TV 1978 telefeature.

SUNNY SIDE UP (Fox, 1929) Color Sequences 80 minutes.

Presenter, William Fox; director, David Butler; story/dialogue, Buddy G. DeSylva, Ray Henderson, Lew Brown; adaptor, Butler; art director, Harry Oliver; costumes, Sophie Wachner; music directors, Howard Jackson, Arthur Kay; choreographer, Seymour

Felix; assistant director, Ad Schaumer; sound, Joseph Aiken; camera, Ernest Palmer, John Schmitz; editor, Irene Morra.

Songs: "I'm a Dreamer, Aren't We All," "If I Had a Talking Picture of You," "Turn on the Heat," "Sunny Side Up," "You've Got Me Picking Petals Off o' Daisies," "Anytime You're Necht on a Broad Bricht Moonlicht Nicht," "You Find the Time and I'll Find the Place" (Buddy G. DeSylva, Lew Brown, Ray Henderson).

Janet Gaynor (Molly Carr); Charles Farrell (Jack Cromwell); El Brendel (Eric Swenson); Marjorie White (Bee Nichols); Frank Richardson (Eddie Rafferty); Sharon Lynn (Jane Worth); Mary Forbes (Mrs. Cromwell); Joe E. Brown (Joe Vitto); Alan Paull (Raoul); Peter Gawthorne (Lake); Jackie Cooper (Tenement Boy).

Janet Gaynor and Charles Farrell became the world's favorite screen love team after having made SEVENTH HEAVEN in 1927 for Fox Films. They followed it with STREET ANGEL in 1928 and then made their sound debut as a team in the part-talkie, LUCKY STAR (1929). Then came the musical comedy-drama, SUNNY SIDE UP. It was so successful that it grossed over $3 million at the box-office. In reviewing SUNNY SIDE UP, *Photoplay* magazine enthused, "The royal Gaynor-Farrell team go into their song and dance and prove their versatility. . . . This is real entertainment."

In New York City, department store worker Molly Carr (Janet Gaynor) lives in a lower east side tenement. In contrast, young society playboy Jack Cromwell (Charles Farrell) spends his summers at the chic Long Island resort of Southampton. When Jack and Molly meet one day, she is suddenly provided with the opportunity to sample the rarified life of the rich. The snooty Mrs. Cromwell (Mary Forbes) immediately disapproves of Molly, even though the young lady has done her best to disguise her impoverished background by having her pals Bee Nichols (Marjorie White), Eddie Rafferty (Frank Richardson) and Eric Swenson (El Brendel) serve as her maid, chauffeur and valet. For a spell it seems that Jack is so overwhelmed by his gold-digging upper-crust girl friend, the flapper Jane Worth (Sharon Lynn), that there is no hope for Molly. Eventually, however, after the Cromwells' big charity show, Jack comes to his senses and is reunited with the ever-forgiving Molly.

In retrospect, *neither* nasal-twanged Janet Gaynor nor high-pitched Charles Farrell were appropriate candidates for song-and-dance features. However, it was Hollywood, where anything was possible, they were stars, and in the early days of sound features, everyone had a go at musicals. It was what the public wanted and what (heaven help the audiences in many instances) they got. The Gaynor-Farrell love team was not helped by the hackneyed plotline devised by song composers Buddy G. DeSylva, Ray Henderson and

Lew Brown, nor by the intrusive ethnic humor of then voguish comedy star El Brendel, but they were bolstered by the songwriters' fine score, their first original one for movies.

It was Gaynor who "vocalized" on the plaintive "I'm a Dreamer, Aren't We All?" several times and who "sang" and "danced" to the buoyant anti-Depression number, "Sunny Side Up," performed on the sidewalk streets. For the Gaynor-Farrell duet, "If I Had a Talking Picture of You," the literal filmmakers could not resist superimposing a close-up of Gaynor over the sheet music as Farrell sighs about his new romance. Marjorie White and Frank Richardson, who provided comedy relief, handled "Pickin' Petals Off Daisies" and perky White did "Anytime You're Necht on a Broad Bricht Moonlicht Nicht." Vivacious Sharon Lynn was given "You Find the Time and I'll Find the Place" and led "Turn on the Heat." The latter is a rather audacious production number which switched from a line of chorines posing as Eskimos in igloos, to tropical hula girls with very little clothing who eventually escape the burning sun by jumping into the pool which separates the cast from the society audience. (This number, which seems high camp today, was filmed in color and is often deleted from TV prints.)

Mordaunt Hall judged in the *New York Times,* "Miss Gaynor's voice may not be especially clear, but the sincerity with which she renders at least two of her songs is most appealing. Her performance is as fine as anything she has done on the screen. So far as her singing is concerned, she is not supposed to be any prima donna. . . . Mr. Farrell's singing is possibly just what one might expect from the average young man taking a chance on singing a song at a private entertainment. His presence is, however, ingratiating and his acting and talking are natural. He may not strike one as an experienced stage actor, but his speeches and even his singing suits the part."

Gaynor and Farrell would guest star in the studio's HAPPY DAYS (1929), singing "We'll Build a Little World of Our Own." They starred in another musical, HIGH SOCIETY BLUES (1930), which was not particularly successful, and then returned to drama/comedy in THE MAN WHO CAME BACK (1931), MERELY MARY ANN (1931), DELICIOUS (1931), TESS OF THE STORM COUNTRY (1932), THE FIRST YEAR (1932), and their twelfth and final film together, CHANGE OF HEART (1934).

SWEET ADELINE (Warner Bros., 1935) 87 minutes.

Producer, Edward Chodorov; director, Mervyn LeRoy; based on the musical play by Jerome Kern, Oscar Hammerstein, II; screenplay, Erwin S. Gelsey; art director, Robert Haas; costumes,

Orry-Kelly; music director, Leo F. Forbstein; choreographer, Bobby Connolly; camera, Sol Polito; editor, Harold McLernon.

Songs: "Here Am I," "Don't Ever Leave Me," "Why Was I Born?" "Twas Not So Long Ago," "Out of the Blue," "We Were So Very Young," "Lonely Feet," "Pretty Little Jenny Lee" (Jerome Kern, Oscar Hammerstein, II); "Down Where the Wertzberger Flows" (Harry von Tilzer, Vincent Bryan); "I'd Leave My Happy Home for You" (von Tilzer).

Irene Dunne (Adeline Schmidt); Donald Woods (Sid Barnett); Ned Sparks (Dan Herzig); Hugh Herbert (Rupert Rockingham); Winifred Shaw (Elysie); Louis Calhern (Major Jim Day); Nydia Westman (Nellie Schmidt); Joseph Cawthorn (Oscar Schmidt); Dorothy Dare (Dot, the Band Leader); Phil Regan (Juvenile); Noah Beery, Sr. (Sultan); Don Alvarado (Renaldo); Martin Garralaga (Dark Young Man); Emmett Vogan (Captain); Howard Dickinson (Civilian); Eddie Shubert (Eddie); Nick Copeland (Prop Man); Ferdinand Munier (General Hawks); William V. Mong (Cobbler, a Spy); Johnny Eppelite (Young Jolson); Mary Tree (Girl); Milton Kibbee (Stagehand); Joseph Bernard (Waiter); Charles Hickman (Manx); Howard H. Mitchell (Bartender); Landers Stevens, William Arnold (Men); David Newell (Young Man); Evelyn Wynans (Woman); Harry Tyler (Louis); Jack Mulhall (Bob).

In the year that versatile Irene Dunne shone in Universal's drama MAGNIFICENT OBSESSION, and sparkled in RKO's ROBERTA, *q.v.,* it is little wonder that her period operetta trifle for Warner Bros., SWEET ADELINE, could go overlooked.

Jerome Kern and Oscar Hammerstein, II composed *Sweet Adeline* for Helen Morgan after she scored so well as Julie in their production of *Show Boat.* The new musical opened on Broadway on September 3, 1929 and ran for 234 performances. In it Helen Morgan sang two of her most famous tunes, "Why Was I Born?" and "Don't Ever Leave Me." When Warner Bros. obtained the screen rights to the vehicle in 1934, Irene Dunne was borrowed from RKO to do the Helen Morgan part. While she handled the assignment well, her performance lacked the vitality which Morgan brought to the stage version.

Adeline Schmidt (Irene Dunne) is the daughter of a German beer garden operator (Joseph Cawthorn), headquartered in Hoboken. He longs to marry her off, along with her flighty sister (Nydia Westman). In the process, Adeline ends up with two beaus, a dashing composer (Donald Woods) and a stuffy Spanish-American War Army major (Louis Calhern). The composer has penned an operetta which he takes to a producer (Ned Sparks), and he gains a backer (Hugh Herbert), who is also a secret service agent. Adeline is wanted for the lead role since the Major also plans to back the production, but she has a rival (Winifred Shaw). Eventually the operetta proves to be a hit on Broadway, with Adeline in the lead. She and the composer have a falling out and she returns to her father's beer garden to perform, but they are later reconciled.

To replace some of the deleted songs from the Broadway score, three new numbers ("Lonely Feet," "We Were So Very Young," "Pretty Little Jenny Lee") were written by Kern and Hammerstein for SWEET ADELINE, as well as "I'd Leave My Happy Home for You" (Harry von Tilzer) and "Down Where the Wertzberger Flows" (von Tilzer and Vincent Bryan). While Dunne was visually appealing in her bustle-skirted outfits and moved through the turn-of-the-century ambiance with ease, she was too regal and cosmopolitan to properly play the innocent young maid. Her coolly efficient, high soprano singing of "Don't Ever Leave Me" and "Why Was I Born?" and her duet on "We Were So Very Young" (with Irish tenor Phil Regan) were proficient but not engaging.

Director Mervyn LeRoy, who had helmed THE GOLD DIGGERS OF 1933 (*q.v.*) and HAPPINESS AHEAD (1934), made this his last Warner Bros. musical and it certainly lacked the zest of his initial outing in the field. *Variety* correctly graded the production, "Strictly on merit, it rates no better than fair." It should be noted that the part Winifred Shaw played in the film was written especially for the production, and her villainous character had to sing off key in order to lose the lead role to Irene Dunne.

SWEET CHARITY (Universal, 1969) Color 157 minutes.

Producer, Robert Arthur; director, Bob Fosse; based on the musical play by Neil Simon, Cy Coleman, Dorothy Fields; screenplay, Peter Stone; art directors, Alexander Golitzen, George C. Webb; set decorator, Jack D. Moore; costumes, Edith Head; makeup, Bud Westmore; music supervisor/conductor, Joseph Gershenson; orchestrator, Ralph Burns; music editor, Arnold Schwarzwald; choreographer, Fosse; assistant director, Douglas Green; sound, Waldon O. Watson, Wilson Russell, Ronald Pierce, Len Peterson; camera, Robert Surtees; editor, Stuart Gilmore.

Songs: "My Personal Property," "Hey, Big Spender," "Rich Man's Frug," "If My Friends Could See Me Now," "There's Gotta Be Something Better Than This," "The Hustle," "It's a Nice Face," "Rhythm of Life," "Sweet Charity," "I'm a Brass Band," "I Love to Cry at Weddings," "Where Am I Going?" (Cy Coleman, Dorothy Fields).

Shirley MacLaine (Charity Hope Valentine); Sammy Davis, Jr.

(Big Daddy); Ricardo Montalban (Vittorio Vitale); John McMartin (Oscar Lindquist); Chita Rivera (Nickie); Paula Kelly (Helene); Stubby Kaye (Herman); Barbara Bouchet (Ursula); Alan Hewitt (Nicholsby); Dante D'Paulo (Charlie); John Wheeler (Rhythm of Life Dancer); John Craig (Man in Fandango Ballroom); Dee Carroll (Woman on Tandem); Tom Hatten (Man on Tandem); Sharon Harvey (Young Woman on Bridge); Charles Brewer (Young Man on Bridge); Richard Angarola (Maitre d'); Henry Beckman, Jeff Burton (Policemen); Ceil Cabot (Married Woman); Alfred Dennis (Waiter at Chile Hacienda); David Gold (Panhandler); Nolan Leary (Manfred); Diki Lerner (Man with Dog on Bridge); Buddy Lewis (Appliance Salesman); Joseph Mell (Man on Bridge); Geraldine O'Brien (Lady on Bridge); Alma Platt (Lady with Hat on Bridge); Maudie Prickett (Nurse on Bridge); Chet Stratton (Waiter); Robert Terry (Doorman); Roger Til (Greeter at Pompeii Club); Buddy Hart, Bill Harrison (Baseball Players); Suzanne Charny (Lead Frug Dancer); Bick Goss (Drummer Boy); Chelsea Brown, Ray Chabeau, Bryan Da Silva, Lynn Fields, Roy Fitzell, Ellen Halpin, Dick Korthaze, April Nevins, Maris O'Neill, Lee Roy Reams, Sandy Roveta, Charleen Ryan, Juleste Salve, Patrick Spohn, Jerry Trent, Ben Vereen, Bud Vest, Lorene Yarnell (Frug Dancers); John Frayer, Dom Salinaro, Paul Shipton, Walter Stratton (Patrons at Dancehall); Larry Billman, Herman Boden, Dick Colacino, Lynn McMurrey, Ted Monson, Ed Robinson (Waiters/Dancers); Leon Bing, Sue Linden, Jackie Mitchell, Carroll Roebke (Models); Kathryn Doby, Al Lanti, Gloria Mills, Louise Quick, Victoria Scruton, Tiffin Twitchell, Renata Vaselle, Adele Yoshioka (Dancers in "Big Spender" Number); Chuck Harrod, Charles Lunard, Jerry Mann, Frank Radcliff (Singers); Marie Bahruth, Toni Basil, Carol Birner, Donald Bradburn, Lonnie Burr, Cheryl Christiansen, Marguerite De Lain, Jimmy Fields, Ben Gooding, Carlton Johnson, Kirk Kirksey, Lance Le Gault, Trish Mahoney, Walter Painter, Bob Thompson, Jr., Bonnie G. West, Kay York (Dancers in "Rhythm of Life" Number); Leon Alton, Norman Stevans (Conversions).

By the late 1960s Hollywood had almost abandoned the original screen musical and was relying on proven hits from the Broadway stage for its genre entries. One of the most overblown, distorted translations from stage to screen was SWEET CHARITY. Plagued with many production problems and an escalating budget, SWEET CHARITY was a mediocre exercise. It grossed only $4 million at the box-office, lost in the shuffle of more successful (but still unsatisfying tunefeasts) like the same year's HELLO, DOLLY! (*q.v.*).

SWEET CHARITY was based on Federico Fellini's 1957 film,

NOTTI DI CABIRIA (Nights of Cabiria). The Neil Simon-Cy Coleman-Dorothy Fields musical comedy, directed and choreographed by Bob Fosse, opened on Broadway on January 29, 1966, with Gwen Verdon, John McMartin and Helen Gallagher starred. It ran for 608 performances. It was purchased by Universal Pictures as a vehicle for Shirley MacLaine, an ex-Broadway hoofer (*Pajama Game*) who specialized in vulnerable gamin roles on camera. Her only real Hollywood musicals to that date had been CAN-CAN (1960), *q.v.,* opposite her Rat Pack pal Frank Sinatra, and the belabored WHAT A WAY TO GO (1964) with Gene Kelly. At age thirty-five she badly wanted a showcase to prove that she still had the talents and looks to handle a demanding musical-dance assignment.

Ever optimistic Charity Hope Valentine (Shirley MacLaine) is a "hostess" at the sleazy Fandango Ballroom, a third-rate Gotham dance hall and pick-up joint. Although life has not been kind to her, Charity has high hopes for the future, including her romance with hoodlum Charlie (Dante D'Paulo). However, he takes all her money and pushes her off a bridge in Central Park, making her regret having had his name tattooed on her arm. One evening Charity observes a fracas between Italian film star Vittorio Vitale (Ricardo Montalban) and his lover, Ursula (Barbara Bouchet). When the latter leaves, Vittorio notices Charity and takes her to a club and dinner. After they return to his apartment, Ursula suddenly reappears and Charity is forced to spend the night in a closet. Hoping to better herself, Charity goes to an employment agency, but they reject her for lack of skills. She next gets trapped in an elevator with insurance actuary Oscar Lindquist (John McMartin) and they begin dating, he thinking she is a bank employee. Ignoring the warning of her earthy Fandango cohorts, Helene (Paula Kelly) and Nickie (Chita Rivera), Charity tells Oscar the truth about herself. Surprisingly, he still proposes. At the marriage license bureau, however, he backs out after meeting Helen and Nickie and observing Charity's tattoo. Back on the same bridge where Charlie tried to kill her, Charity once again finds her hopes renewed when some hippies offer her a fresh daisy.

Bob Fosse (1927–1987) had been around Hollywood since the early 1950s when he danced at MGM in THE AFFAIRS OF DOBIE GILLIS (1953), GIVE A GIRL A BREAK and KISS ME, KATE (1953, also as assistant choreographer), *q.v.* SWEET CHARITY was his first excursion as a full-fledged movie director-choreographer. The challenge and the heady power led him to excesses which distorted the intimate, sensitive feel of the stage original. The actual highlights of SWEET CHARITY are two supporting players, Paula Kelly and Chita Rivera, who are wonderfully electric in the famous "Hey, Big Spender" number and who join with Shirley MacLaine in "There's Got to Be Something Better Than This." Fosse is at his inventive best choreographing "Rich Man's Frug" and "The Hustle." MacLaine was touching in the semi-show stopping "If They Could See Me Now" and really came alive with the "I'm a Brass Band." John McMartin, from the stage production, was adequate but colorless (on purpose?) in his rendition of the title song. Sammy Davis, Jr. almost diverted the picture into a new direction with his role of the cult religious evangelist who chants "The Rhythm of Life." For comedy relief, Stubby Kaye, as a dance hall crew member, sang "I Love to Cry at Weddings." Written especially for the movie were "My Personal Property" (sung by MacLaine), "It's a Nice Face" (sung by MacLaine) and "Sweet Charity" (a revamping of the stage show version, sung by McMartin).

After the poorly attended initial roadshow release, with an intermission after the first eighty-three minutes, SWEET CHARITY was trimmed for later general distribution. It received Oscar nominations for Best Score of a Musical Picture, Art Direction-Set Decoration, and Costumes.

In retrospect Pauline Kael (*5001 Nights at the Movies,* 1984) would say of SWEET CHARITY, "The tricky camera effects that Fosse later brought off in CABARET [1972, *q.v.*] and in the TV special 'Liza with a Z' are jangling here, and although Shirley MacLaine tries hard, it's obvious that her dancing isn't up to the demands of the role. It's a disaster, but zoom-happy Fosse's choreographic conceptions are intensely dramatic, and the movie has some of the best dancing in American musicals of the picture."

Bob Fosse would bounce back on-screen with the Oscar-winning CABARET (1972), *q.v.,* and his remarkable if flawed ALL THAT JAZZ (1979), *q.v.*

SWEET ROSIE O'GRADY *see:* THE DAUGHTER OF ROSIE O'GRADY (essay).

SWEETHEARTS (Metro-Goldwyn-Mayer, 1938) Color 120 minutes.

Producer, Hunt Stromberg; director, W. S. Van Dyke, II; based on the operetta by Harry B. Smith, Fred DeGresac, Robert B. Smith, Victor Herbert; screenplay, Dorothy Parker, Alan Campbell; art director, Cedric Gibbons; set decorator, Edwin B. Willis; costumes, Adrian; music adaptor, Herbert Stothart; choreographer, Albertina Rasch; sound supervisor, Douglas Shearer;

special effects, Slavko Vorkapich; camera, Oliver Marsh, Allen Davey; editor, Robert J. Kern.

Songs: "Wooden Shoes," "Every Lover Must Meet His Fate," "Happy Day," "Sweethearts," "Pretty as a Picture," "Game of Love," "Badinage," "On Parade," "Summer Serenade" (Victor Herbert, new lyrics by Bob Wright, Chet Forrest); "In the Convent Garden They Never Taught Me That," "Angelus" (Herbert, Robert B. Smith); "Auld Lang Syne" (traditional); "The Message of the Violet" and "Keep It Dark" from the opera *The Prince of Pilsen* by Gustav Luders, Frank Pixley; "Little Gray Home in the West" (Hermann Lohr, D. Eardley-Wilmot); "Give My Regards to Broadway" (George M. Cohan); "Sidewalks of New York" (Charles Lawlor, James Blake); "St. Louis Blues" (W. C. Handy); "Missouri Waltz" (Frederick Knight Logan, James Royce Shannon); "Home, Sweet Home" (Henry Bishop); "Tea for Two" (Irving Caesar, Vincent Youmans); "Night and Day" (Cole Porter).

Jeanette MacDonald (Gwen Marlowe); Nelson Eddy (Ernest Lane); Frank Morgan (Felix Lehman); Ray Bolger (Hans, the Dancer); Florence Rice (Kay Jordan); Mischa Auer (Leo Kronk); Fay Holden (Hannah, the Dresser); Terry Kilburn (Junior, Gwen's Brother); Betty Jaynes (Una Wilson); Douglas McPhail (Harvey Horton); Reginald Gardiner (Norman Trumpett); Herman Bing (Oscar Engel); Allyn Joslyn (Dink Rogers); Raymond Walburn (Orlando Lane); Lucile Watson (Mrs. Marlowe); George Barbier (Benjamin Silver); Kathleen Lockhart (Aunt Amelia Lane); Gene Lockhart (Augustus Marlowe); Berton Churchill (Sheridan Lane); Olin Howland (Appleby, the Box-Office Man); Gerald Hamer (Harry); Marvin Jones (Boy in Lobby); Dorothy Gray (His Girl Friend); Emory Parnell (Fire Inspector); Maude Turner Gordon (Dowager); Jack George (Violinist); Roger Converse (Usher); Reid Kilpatrick (Radio Announcer); Wilson Benge (2nd Valet to Ernest); George Ernest (1st Call Boy); Billy McCullough (2nd Call Boy); Lee Phelps (Doorman at St. Regis); Pat Gleason, Ralph Malone, David Kerman, Jack Gardner (Reporters); Ralph W. Berry, Rollin B. Berry, Chester L. Berolund, Leo Berolund (Lawyer Twins); Mira McKinney, Grace Hayle (Telephone Operators): Hal K. Dawson (Morty, the Stage Manager); Forrester Harvey (Tailor's Assistant); Gayne Whitman (Commentator); Margaret Irving (Madame); Irving Bacon (Assistant Director); Barbara Pepper, Marjorie "Babe" Kane (Telephone Operators); Jimmy Conlin (Property Man); Dick Rich (1st Stage Hand); Ralph Sanford (2nd Stage Hand); James Flavin (Theatre Doorman); Richard Tucker, Edwin Stanley, Edward Earle, Brent Sargent (Men in Lobby); Betty Ross Clarke, Dorothy Christy, Suzanne Kaaren, Lulu May Bohrman (Women in Lobby);

Hal Cooke, Jenifer Gray (Mr. Silver's Secretaries); Fred Santley (Music Vendor); Don Barclay (Taxi Driver from Bridgeport); Arthur "Pop" Byron (Policeman); James Farley (Carriage Starter); Bruce Mitchell (Stagehand); George Cooper, Frank Mills (Electricians); Mary Howard, Joan Barclay, Sharon Lewis, Vivian Reid, Lucille Brown, Valerie Day, Ethelreda Leopold (Chorus Girls); Lester Dorr (Dance Director); Anne Wigton (Saleswoman); Dalies Frantz (Pianist for "Badinage" Number); Paul Marquardt (Marine Band Conductor); Paul Kerby (Orchestra Conductor); Joe A. Devlin (New York Cabbie); Ralph Brooks, Brooks Benedict (Radio Audience Extras); Toby Wing (Telephone Operator); Cyril Ring (Waiter).

For their fifth screen teaming, Jeanette MacDonald and Nelson Eddy were paired in Victor Herbert's operetta, *Sweethearts,* which was first staged in 1913 with Christie MacDonald and Edwin Wilson in the leads. This plush 1938 MGM film version was lensed in three-color Technicolor and earned Oliver Marsh and Allen Davey a special Academy Award citation. The film also drew Oscar nominations for Best Score and Best Sound. *Photoplay* magazine gave it its Gold Medal Award as Best Picture of 1938. The movie was the first to present its stars in a modern setting and proved to be one of MGM's top grossers for 1939, the film having been issued late in 1938. The studio advertised the feature with "Your heart will pound with excitement at the wonders of this great Show of Shows."

Gwen Marlowe (Jeanette MacDonald) and her husband Ernest Lane (Nelson Eddy) have been starring on Broadway for six years in the musical *Sweethearts,* which shows no sign of fading. This makes the play's author, Leo Kronk (Mischa Auer), composer Oscar Engel (Herman Bing), producer Felix Lehman (Frank Morgan) and press agent Dink Rogers (Allyn Joslyn) very happy indeed. Then along comes suave Hollywood agent Norman Trumpett (Reginald Gardiner), who tries to lure the two stars to the film mecca. Following the anniversary performance, Gwen and Ernest plan to celebrate their wedding anniversary, but instead are talked into attending a cast party which turns out to be a nationwide radio broadcast. Finally at home, the two find themselves in the middle of a continuous squabble involving Gwen's secretary, Kay Jordan (Florence Rice), and their various relatives; they are also invaded by a theatrical troupe headed by their zany cousin (Raymond Walburn). To escape the craziness, they decide to try Hollywood. This panics the people involved with *Sweethearts,* who do their best to dissuade the stars from heading westward. Things become complicated when Gwen comes to believe that Ernest is in love with Kay and Gwen leaves him. They still continue to do the play and, with the Hollywood contract cancelled by their separation, the producers use Gwen and Ernest in two separate road companies of *Sweethearts.* On the road, the two stars realize how much they miss one another and they are eventually reconciled.

For this heavily-mounted screen adaptation, not only was the plot changed greatly but the play's original songs were given new lyrics by Bob Wright and Chet Forrest. Ray Bolger had appeared in MacDonald-Eddy's THE GIRL OF THE GOLDEN WEST (1938), *q.v.,* but his role had been excised from that feature. However, in SWEETHEARTS he is very much a focal point, In the play-within-the-play he performs the "Zuyder Zee" dance and joins with MacDonald in the "Wooden Shoes" number. Jeanette and Nelson Eddy duet on "Sweethearts" and "Every Lover Must Meet His Fate," as well as "Pretty as a Picture" and "Little Gray Home in the West." For her solos MacDonald performs "Angelus" and "Summer Serenade"—for which she is backed by Dalies Frantz at the piano and an eighty-piece orchestra. Eddy does "On Parade" supported by a Marine Band contingent. What makes the stars' musical offerings so unique in SWEETHEARTS is the effort the filmmakers made to present the songs in contrasting settings (a radio broadcast studio, the Broadway stage, at home, etc.). One of the lesser ingredients of the picture was the dull presence of chubby Douglas McPhail and Betty Jaynes (married off-camera), who appear as MacDonald and Eddy's lackluster partners when the couple split up for separate road companies of *Sweethearts.*

When SWEETHEARTS, which contained an Adrian-design fashion show as an added bonus, debuted in November 1938, the *New York Times* judged it "a dream of ribbons, tinsel, Technicolor, and sweet, theatrical sentiment." More demanding was Archer Winsten (*New York Post*) who complained, "somewhere in the course of modernizing SWEETHEARTS both the heart and the sweetness have been lost."

On December 15, 1947 Jeanette MacDonald and Nelson Eddy again performed "Sweethearts" on NBC radio's "Camel Screen Guild Theatre." They would not be reunited on-screen again until 1940's NEW MOON, *q.v.*

SWEETIE (Paramount, 1929) 95 minutes. (Also silent version: 6,303′).

Director, Frank Tuttle; story/screenplay/dialogue, George Marion, Jr., Lloyd Corrigan; titles, Marion, Jr.; choreographer, Earl Lindsay; sound, Eugene Merritt; camera, Alfred Gilks; editor, Verna Willis.

Advertisement for SWEETIE (1929).

Songs: "Sweeter than Sweet," "Alma Mammy," "The Prep Step," "I Think You'll Like It," "Bear Down Pelham" (Richard A. Whiting, George Marion, Jr.).

Nancy Carroll (Barbara Pell); Helen Kane (Helen Fry); Stanley Smith (Biff Bentley); Jack Oakie (Tap-Tap Thompson); William Austin (Professor Percy "Pussy" Willow); Stuart Erwin (Axel Bronstrup); Wallace MacDonald (Bill Barrington); Charles Sellon (Dr. Oglethorpe); Aileen Manning (Miss Twill).

Broadway hoofer Barbara Pell (Nancy Carroll) falls madly in love with college football player Biff Bentley (Stanley Smith), and they plan to marry. However, things turn sour when Biff tells Barbara they must postpone the nuptials until after the big football game between his school (Pelham College) and their arch rival (Oglethorpe). Barbara returns to Gotham with fellow performer Tap-Tap Thompson (Jack Oakie). She soon learns she has inherited Pelham College from a deceased relative, its founder. To get even with Biff, Barbara makes him take a tough English examination in order to remain eligible to play football. He fails. She also gives rival college dean Dr. Oglethorpe (Charles Sellon) an option to buy

Pelham, which he intends to tear down. After Biff's pal Axel Bronstrup (Stuart Erwin) begs Barbara to let Biff play and offers to give up his own position on the team so that Biff can, she relents. She has Biff take a make-up test which he passes. On the day of the big game, which will decide Pelham's fate, Biff does not play well. At half-time Barbara gives the team a pep talk which inspires the players to save the day. Biff even scores the big touchdown which wins the game. Biff and Barbara are then reunited and marry.

Certainly the definite stage/film campus tale of the big football game was GOOD NEWS (1927 on stage; 1930 on film), *q.v.* One of the earlier movie distillations of the theme was SWEETIE, which boasts perennial college student Jack Oakie (a boisterous, engaging and talented delight). It also offered exceedingly popular Paramount star Nancy Carroll in one of her several musical comedy assignments. In retrospect, the film is a badly dated early talkie. But at the time of release, *Photoplay* magazine dubbed it "pleasant, youthful and lively," while *Film Daily* said, "the story was well constructed. . . . Nicely balanced with love interest, football and show life."

SWING TIME (RKO, 1936) 105 minutes.

Producer, Pandro S. Berman; director, George Stevens; story, Erwin Gelsey; screenplay, Howard Lindsay, Allan Scott; art directors, Van Nest Polglase, Carroll Clark; set decorator, Darrell Silvera; special settings/costumes, John Harkrider; gowns, Bernard Newman; makeup, Mel Burns; music director, Nathaniel Shilkret; choreographer, Hermes Pan; sound, Hugh McDowell; special effects, Vernon L. Walker; camera, David Abel; editor, Henry Berman.

Songs: "It's Not in the Cards," "The Way You Look Tonight," "A Fine Romance," "The Waltz in Swing Time," "Never Gonna Dance," "Pick Yourself Up," "Bojangles of Harlem" (Jerome Kern, Dorothy Fields).

Fred Astaire (John "Lucky" Garrett); Ginger Rogers (Penelope "Penny" Carroll); Victor Moore (Pop [Dr. Ed Cardetti]); Helen Broderick (Mabel Anderson); Eric Blore (Mr. Gordon); Betty Furness (Margaret Watson); George Metaza (Ricardo Romero); Landers Stevens (Judge Watson); John Harrington (Dice Raymond); Pierre Watkin (Al Simpson); Abe Reynolds (Schmidt); Gerald Hamer (Eric Facannistrom); Edgar Dearing (Policeman); Harry Bowen, Harry Bernard (Stagehands); Donald Kerr, Jack Good, Ted O'Shea, Frank Edmunds, Bill Brand (Dancers): Frank Jenks (Red); Ralph Byrd (Hotel Clerk); Charles Hall (Taxi Driver);

Jean Perry (Roulette Dealer); Olin Francis (Muggsy); Floyd Schackleford (Romero's Butler); Joey Ray (Announcer); Jack Rice (Wedding Guest); Howard Hickman (1st Minister); Ferdinand Munier (2nd Minister); Fern Emmett (Maid); Frank Mills (Croupier); Dale Van Sickel (Diner); Dennis O'Keefe, Bess Flowers, Ralph Brooks (Dance Extras); Jack Good (Dancer); and: Baby Marie Osborne, Sailor Vincent, Blanca Vischer.

The sixth screen teaming of Fred Astaire and Ginger Rogers, SWING TIME was one of their more popular vehicles, due to a surprisingly good plot, top-notch songs by Jerome Kern and Dorothy Fields, and the usual eloquent dancing by the two stars. Still, some critics were beginning to tire of the RKO plots given to Astaire and Rogers. "It is high time that Fred Astaire and Ginger Rogers were relieved of the necessity of going through a lot of romantic nonsense in their screen musicals," the *New York Herald Tribune* opined, with the reviewer calling SWING TIME "uneven and definitely disappointing in its conclusion."

Having failed to show up on time for his wedding dancer John Garrett (Fred Astaire), who is also a gambler, is dismissed by the father (Landers Stevens) of the bride-to-be (Betty Furness), and ordered not to return until he can become reliable and is solvent. Thereafter, the jaunty Garrett spots lovely Penelope Carroll (Ginger Rogers) on the street and is immediately attracted to her. He follows her to her place of employment, a dance studio run by Gordon (Eric Blore). To get closer to the elusive Penelope, Garrett pretends he knows nothing about dancing and after a while the girl gives up and refuses to take his money. She is fired on the spot by Gordon. Garrett, however, saves Penelope's job by showing Gordon an intricate dance routine he claims he has just learned from the pretty teacher. Garrett then begins to romance Penelope. Trouble arrives in the person of his ex-hometown sweetheart, Margaret Watson (Betty Furness), but with the aid of his pal, Pop (Victor Moore), Garrett gets rid of Margaret and keeps Penelope. Meanwhile, he and Penelope team to win success performing their dance routines at the Club Raymond and the Silver Sandal nightclub.

The highlights of SWING TIME are Fred and Ginger dancing to "Never Gonna Dance" (their big romantic ballroom number of the film)* and Astaire's solo hoofing in blackface (his only time) to "Bojangles of Harlem," the choreography of which won Hermes

*In *The Melody Lingers On,* 1986, Roy Hemming decided, " 'Never Gonna Dance' may well be the best torch song ever written for a man to sing. It's a plaintive ballad expressing Astaire's despair at what he believes is the end of his affair with Rogers."

Pan an Oscar nomination. Astaire crooned Kern's "The Way You Look Tonight," which won an Academy Award as Best Song. In a snowy scene, Astaire courts Rogers with "A Fine Romance," termed by the composers a "sarcastic love song." He and Ginger perform "Pick Yourself Up" (which found him dancing delightfully awkwardly per the story's plot) and they also danced together in the glittering "Waltz in Swing Time."

It is interesting to note that while Astaire still got the better of the songs in their joint films, Ginger Rogers outdistanced him in acting, paving the way for her soon to turn to dramatic roles in movies. For comedy relief there was once again sharp-tongued Helen Broderick (as Rogers' pal), Eric Blore (as the snobbish, slippery dance school proprietor) and, making his debut in the series, bumbling Victor Moore (as a sort of man Friday to Astaire).

TAKE ME OUT TO THE BALL GAME (Metro-Goldwyn-Mayer, 1949) Color 93 minutes.

Producer, Arthur Freed; associate producer, Roger Edens; director, Busby Berkeley; story, Gene Kelly, Stanley Donen; screenplay, Harry Tugend, George Wells, (uncredited) Harry Crane; art directors, Cedric Gibbons, Daniel B. Cathcart; set decorators, Edwin B. Willis, Henry W. Grace; women's costumes, Helen Rose; men's costumes, Valles; makeup, Jack Dawn; music director, Adolph Deutsch; vocal arranger, Robert Tucker; choreographers, Kelly, Donen; assistant director, Dolf Zimmer; color consultants, Natalie Kalmus, James Gooch; sound supervisor, Douglas Shearer; special effects, Warren Newcombe; montage sequence, Peter Ballbusch; camera, George Folsey; editor, Blanche Sewell.

Songs: "Take Me Out to the Ball Game" (Albert von Tilzer, Jack Norworth); "The Hat My Father Wore on St. Patrick's Day" (William Jerome, Jean Schwartz); "O'Brien to Ryan to Goldberg," "The Right Girl for Me," "It's Fate, Baby, It's Fate," "Yes, Indeedy," "Strictly U.S.A." (Roger Edens, Betty Comden, Adolph Green)

Frank Sinatra (Dennis Ryan); Esther Williams (K. C. Higgins); Gene Kelly (Eddie O'Brien); Betty Garrett (Shirley Delwyn); Edward Arnold (Joe Lorgan); Jules Munshin (Nat Goldberg); Richard Lane (Michael Gilhuly); Tom Dugan (Slappy Burke); Murray Alper (Zalinka); Wilton Graff (Nick Donford); Mack Gray, Charles Regan (Henchmen); Saul Gorss (Steve); Douglas Fowley (Karl); Eddie Parkes (Dr. Winston); James Burke (Cop in Park); The Blackburn Twins (Specialty); Gordon Jones (Senator Catcher); Jack Bruce, John "Red" Burger, Aaron Phillips, Edward Cutler,

Ellsworth Blake, Harry Allen, Joseph Roach, Hubert Kerns, Pete Kooy, Robert Simpson, Richard Landry, Jack Boyle, Richard Beavers (Wolves' Team); Virginia Bates, Joi Lansing (Girls on Train); Mitchell Lewis (Fisherman); Esther Michaelson (Fisherman's Wife); Almira Sessions, Isabel O'Madigan, Gil Perkins, Robert Stephenson, Charles Sullivan, Edna Harris (Fans); Frank Scannell (Reporter); Henry Kulky (Burly Acrobat); Dorothy Abbott (Girl Dancer); Jackie Jackson (Kid); Si Jenks (Sam); Jack Rice (Room Clerk); Ed Cassidy (Teddy Roosevelt); Dick Wessel (Umpire); Sally Forrest (Dancer).

Busby Berkeley directed his final movie musical in this MGM entertainment, although he would work as the sequence director on eight additional film productions. Most of TAKE ME OUT TO THE BALL GAME's music sequences were directed by Gene Kelly and Stanley Donen, who had originally wanted to helm the film. In fact, their success here behind the camera led to the duo's first credited directorial assignment later in the year with ON THE TOWN (*q.v.*).

In 1910, baseball players Dennis Ryan (Frank Sinatra) and Eddie O'Brien (Gene Kelly), who moonlight each winter as vaudevillians, report to Florida for spring training on The Wolves, a professional baseball team. They are surprised when the team's new owner turns out to be comely K.C. Higgins (Esther Williams). Eddie persuades his friend to show a romantic interest in K.C., to divert attention from his own night life. Not to be outsmarted, K.C. demands that O'Brien adhere to the team's rules, or else. Their feud slowly turns into a romance. Meanwhile, Shirley Delwyn (Betty Garrett), an avid baseball fan, is increasingly intrigued with Dennis. Eddie becomes involved with crooked gambler Joe Lorgan (Edward Arnold), who intends to destroy the Wolves in order to win bets on their opponents. He dupes O'Brien into accepting a nightclub contract, knowing that the late hours will adversely affect his playing. When K.C. learns of Eddie's violations of the team's rules, she suspends him from the game. Finally, realizing he has been duped by Lorgan, Eddie manages to return to the team. With the aid of Dennis and teammate Nat Goldberg (Jules Munshin) they win the pennant. Lorgan and his cronies are corralled by the police. By now Eddie has won the heart of his employer, while Dennis and Shirley are also in love.

Originally, Judy Garland was to have starred in TAKE ME OUT TO THE BALL GAME, but she was replaced by aquatic star Esther Williams, who received second-billing to Frank Sinatra. So that Williams' devout fans would not be disappointed, she does have one swimming sequence, garbed in bloomer-type swim attire and with Sinatra crooning to her, "The Right Girl for Me." Sinatra and Betty Garrett join on "It's Fate, Baby, It's Fate," while Gene Kelly has the rousing "The Hat My Father Wore on St. Patrick's Day." (He danced to this number as well as to the title tune and "Yes, Indeedy.") The trio of Kelly, Sinatra and Jules Munshin handle the comic turns of "O'Brien to Ryan to Goldberg," a song devoted to the intricacies of making a double play on the diamond. The four leads provide the patriotic finale, "Strictly U.S.A." Cut from the film were: "Boys and Girls Like You and Me" (written by Richard Rodgers and Oscar Hammerstein, II and sung by Frank Sinatra), "Sand Man" (by Roger Edens, Betty Comden and Adolph Green); "Hayride" and "Baby Doll" (both by Harry Warren and Johnny Mercer).

This was Busby Berkeley's first film since 1946. He and Kelly had previously worked together in FOR ME AND MY GAL (1942), *q.v.* TAKE ME OUT TO THE BALL GAME was the second screen teaming for Kelly and Sinatra, who would rejoin with Jules Munshin and Betty Garrett later in the year for ON THE TOWN. The latter musical also had songs by Broadway's Comden

Esther Williams, Tom Dugan, Gene Kelly and Richard Lane in TAKE ME OUT TO THE BALL GAME (1949).

and Green. Esther Williams was so displeased at working with disciplinarian Berkeley that she refused to work under his direction in PAGAN LOVE SONG (1950), *q.v.*

Bosley Crowther (*New York Times*) agreed that TAKE ME OUT TO THE BALL GAME was a "rowdy-dow musical show" and "The only hits in this BALL GAME are those which are danced and sung." However, he conceded, ". . . The show lacks consistent style and pace, and the stars are forced to clown and grimace much more than becomes their speed. Actually, the plotted humor is conspicuously bush-league stuff."

Breaking the old axiom that movies about baseball have two strikes against them, TAKE ME OUT TO THE BALL GAME was very profitable. Made at a cost of $1,725,940, it grossed over $4,344,000 in its initial release.

British release title: EVERYBODY'S CHEERING.

TEA FOR TWO (Warner Bros., 1950) Color 98 minutes.

Producer, William Jacobs; director, David Butler; based on the musical play *No, No, Nanette* by Frank Mandel, Otto Harbach, Vincent Youmans, Emil Nyitray; screenplay, Harry Clork; art director, Douglas Bacon; set decorator, Lyle B. Reifsnider; costumes, Leah Rhodes; makeup, Al Greenway; music director/orchestrator, Ray Heindorf; choreographer, LeRoy Prinz; assistant director, Phil Quinn; sound, Dolph Thomas, David Forrest; camera, Wilfred M. Cline; editor, Irene Morra.

Songs: "I Know that You Know" (Anne Caldwell, Vincent Youmans); "Crazy Rhythm" (Irving Caesar, Roger Wolfe Kahn, Joseph Meyer); "Charleston" (Cecil Mack, Jimmie Johnson); "I Only Have Eyes for You" (Harry Warren, Al Dubin); "Tea for Two," "I Want to Be Happy" (Caesar, Vincent Youmans); "Oh Me, Oh My" (Arthur Francis [Ira Gershwin], Youmans); "The Call of the Sea" (Youmans, Caesar, Otto Harbach); "Do Do, Do" (George Gershwin, Ira Gershwin); "No, No, Nanette" (Youmans, Harbach).

Doris Day (Nanette Carter); Gordon MacRae (Jimmy Smith); Gene Nelson (Tommy Trainor); Patrice Wymore (Beatrice Darcy); Eve Arden (Pauline Hastings); Billy De Wolfe (Larry Blair); S. Z. Sakall (J. Maxwell Bloomhaus); Bill Goodwin (William Early); Virginia Gibson (Mabel Wiley); Crauford Kent (Stevens); Mary Eleanor Donahue (Lynne); Johnny McGovern (Richard); Harry Harvey (Crotchety Man); George Baxter (Backer); Herschel Dougherty (Theatre Manager); Abe Dinovitch (Taxi Driver); Elizabeth Flournoy (Secretary); Buddy Shaw (Piano Mover); John Hedloe (Chorus Boy); Jack Daley (Truck Driver); Art Gilmore (Radio Announcer).

Doris Day and Gordon MacRae in TEA FOR TWO (1950).

For a third screen rendition (the first two were done in 1930 and 1940, *qq.v.*) of *No, No, Nanette,* Warner Bros. altered the plot of the old chestnut. It added some new music and called it TEA FOR TWO, a vehicle for Doris Day and Gordon MacRae. Shot in Technicolor, the production continued the studio's successful string of Doris Day genre pieces.

The movie is told in flashback, with Uncle Max (S.Z. Sakall) telling the events to his great-nieces and nephews. The plot reverts back to 1929 with rich songstress Nanette (Doris Day) *not* being advised that she has lost most of her money in the recent stock market crash. The impetuous miss continues with her plans to finance a new musical which is being promoted by the fast-talking Larry Blair (Billy De Wolfe) and has music by struggling songwriter-singer Jimmy Smith (Gordon MacRae). Blair had actually promised the lead in the show to Beatrice Darcy (Patrice Wymore) but he tells Nanette the part is hers to insure her financial participation. Meanwhile, Uncle Max informs Nanette that he will provide additional funding if she learns to say no to every question asked her in a forty-eight-hour period. He hopes this will thwart her tendency to get mixed up in crazy schemes and unsuccessful romances. Sticking to her promise, Nanette continually says "no," which causes a great deal of consternation during show rehearsals and confusion between her and Jimmy—they are falling in love. Having won her bet, Nanette now explains her sudden binge of "no's" and turns to Uncle Max to pay up. At that juncture, Nanette's attorney William Early (Bill Goodwin) arrives to announce that his client has no money. However, sharp-tongued Pauline Hastings (Eve Arden), Nanette's practical secretary, is quick-witted enough to use her charms on Early, and he is convinced to back the show himself.

TEA FOR TWO marked Doris Day's first real dancing on-screen. Her partner was agile Gene Nelson, who in many respects stole the show. Together they hoofed to "I Know That You Know" and handled "No, No Nanette." Day and Gordon MacRae dueted on "Do, Do, Do" as well as on the title song, where they were joined by Nelson. Day and MacRae performed "I Want to Be Happy." Nelson did "I Only Have Eyes for You" with Patrice Wymore.

"Good music and snappy comedy do the trick here, in a surprisingly palatable once-over (once more) of the old musical play, *No, No Nanette,* that is as spritely and graceful as it can be . . . ," wrote the *New York Times.* "Miss Day and MacRae treat the songs with a zest that should zoom the numbers to new popularity on the Hit Parade, especially since they are brand new to this generation of youthful moviegoers" (*Film Bulletin*).

Doris Day, Gordon MacRae and Gene Nelson, who were so refreshingly bright in TEA FOR TWO, would be re-teamed in THE WEST POINT STORY (1950), *q.v.,* which co-starred James Cagney and Virginia Mayo.

THANK YOUR LUCKY STARS (Warner Bros., 1943) 127 minutes.

Producer, Mark Hellinger; director, David Butler; story, Everett Freeman, Arthur Schwartz; screenplay, Norman Panama, Melvin Frank, James V. Kern; art directors, Anton Grot, Leo K. Kuter; set decorator, Walter F. Tilford; costumes, Milo Anderson; makeup, Perc Westmore; music director, Leo F. Forbstein; music adaptor, Heinz Roemheld; orchestrator, Maurice de Packh; choreographer, Leroy Prinz; assistant director, Phil Quinn; sound, Francis J. Scheid, Charles David Forrest; special effects, H. F. Koenekamp; camera, Arthur Edeson; editor, Irene Morra.

Songs: "They're Either Too Young or Too Old," "The Dreamer," "Ridin' for a Fall," "We're Staying Home Tonight," "Goin' North," "Love Isn't Born, It's Made," "No You, No Me," "Ice-Cold Katie," "How Sweet You Are," "That's What You Jolly Well Get," "Good Night, Good Neighbor," "Thank Your Lucky Stars," "Finale" (Frank Loesser, Arthur Schwartz); "Blues in the Night" (Harold Arlen, Johnny Mercer); "Hotcha Cornia [Otchichornia]" (traditional; adapted).

Eddie Cantor (Joe Sampson/Himself); Joan Leslie (Pat Dixon); Dennis Morgan (Tommy Randolph); Dinah Shore (Herself); S. Z. Sakall (Dr. Schlenna); Edward Everett Horton (Farnsworth); Ruth Donnelly (Nurse Hamilton); Joyce Reynolds (Girl with Book); Richard Lane (Barney Jackson); Don Wilson (Himself); Henry Armetta (Angelo); Willie Best (Soldier); Humphrey Bogart, Jack Carson, Bette Davis, Olivia de Havilland, Errol Flynn, John Garfield, Alan Hale, Ida Lupino, Ann Sheridan, Alexis Smith, George Tobias, Spike Jones and His City Slickers (Specialties); Frank Faylen (Sailor); Creighton Hale, Jack Mower (Engineers); Noble Johnson (Charlie, the Indian); Ed Gargan (Doorman); Billy Benedict (Busboy); Hank Mann (Assistant Photographer); Don Barclay (Pete); Stanley Clements, James Copedge (Boys); Leah Baird, Joan Matthews, Phyllis Godfrey, Lillian West, Morgan Brown, George French (Bus Passengers); Joe De Rita (Milquetoast Type); Eleanor Counts (Sailor's Girl Friend); Charles Soldani, J. W. Cody (Indians); Harry Pilcer (Man in Broadcasting Station); Mike Mazurki (Olaf); Bennie Bartlett (Page Boy); Marjorie Hoshelle, Anne O'Neal (Maids); Jerry Mandy (Chef); Betty Farrington (Assistant Chef); William Haade (Butler); Lou Marcelle (Commentator); Mary Treen (Fan); Juanita Stark (Secretary); Paul Harvey (Dr. Kirby); Bert Gordon (Patient); David Butler, Mark Hellinger (Themselves); Billy Wayne (Chauffeur); Howard Mitchell, James Flavin (Policemen); Dick Rich (Fred); Ralph Dunn (Marty); James Burke (Bill, the Intern Guard); Frank Mayo (Dr. Wheaton); Angi O. Poulos (Waiter); Boyd Irwin (Man); Helen O'Hara (Show Girl); *Ice Cold Katie Number:* Hattie McDaniel (Gossip); Rita Christiani (Ice-Cold Katie); Jess Lee Brooks (Justice); Ford, Harris and Jones (Trio); Matthew Jones (Gambler); *Errol Flynn Number:* Monte Blue (Bartender); Art Foster, Fred Kelsey, Elmer Ballard, Buster Wiles, Howard Davies, Tudor Williams, Alan Cook, Fred McEvoy, Bobby Hale, Will Stanton, Charles Irwin, David Thursby, Henry Ibling, Earl Hunsaker, Hubert Hend, Dudley Kuzello, Ted Billings (Pub Characters); *Bette Davis Number:* Jack Norton (Drunk); Henri DeSoto (Maitre d'Hotel); Dick Elliott, Dick Earle (Customers); Harry Adams (Doorman); Sam Adams (Bartender); Conrad Weidell (Jitterbug); Charles Francis, Harry Bailey (Bald-Headed Men); Joan Winfield (Cigarette Girl); Nancy Worth, Sylvia Opert (Hatcheck Girls); *The Lucky Stars:* Harriette Haddon, Harriett Olsen, Joy Barlowe, Nancy Worth, Janet Barrett, Dorothy Schoemer, Dorothy Dayton, Lucille LaMarr, Mary Landa, Sylvia Opert (the Lucky Stars); *Humphrey Bogart Sequence:* Matt McHgh (Fireman); *Ann Sheridan Number:* Georgia Lee Settle, Virgina Patton (Girls); *Good Neighbor Number:* Igor DeNavrotsky (Dancer);

Brandon Hurst (Cab Driver); Angelita Mari (Duenna); Lynne Baggett (Miss Latin America); Mary Landa (Miss Spain).

For many filmgoers one Eddie Cantor performance in a picture is an overdose of a "good" thing. However, in THANK YOUR LUCKY STARS there are two (!) Cantors gyrating through his range of traditional shtick. Actually the highlights of this 127-minute extravaganza are the assorted song-and-dance turns by a variety of (Warner Bros.) stars better known for their dramatic and/or comedy talents, as well as interludes by such songsters as Dinah Shore and such bands as Spike Jones and His City Slickers. If audiences were agog at viewing some of their favorite celluloid personalities popping in for quick cameos, they were more astounded at witnessing swashbuckling Errol Flynn singing and lampooning his he-man image. By any count, the most remarkable segment of THANK YOUR LUCKY STARS is the appearance of Bette Davis, the Queen of Warner Bros. drama, headlining a jitterbug segment.

Trying to put on a Cavalcade of Stars benefit show, producers Farnsworth (Edward Everett Horton) and Dr. Schlenna (S.Z. Sakall) learn that they must feature Eddie Cantor (himself) if they want to get his singing star, Dinah Shore (herself), on the program. Cantor, however, takes over control of the show at its first rehearsal, while singer Tom Randolph (Dennis Morgan) finds he is

Dennis Morgan, Joan Leslie and Eddie Cantor in THANK YOUR LUCKY STARS (1943).

not on the bill due to a phony contract by an agent who has also fleeced composer Pat Dixon (Joan Leslie). Tom meets Joe Sampson (Eddie Cantor), a bus driver who cannot get a break because he looks like Eddie Cantor. They go to the show business hangout at Gower Gulch where they meet the distraught Pat. The three come up with a scheme to become part of the benefit show. They have Cantor kidnapped by a group of Gower Gulch "Indians" and Joe then pretends to be the banjo-eyed star and hosts the revue himself. The real Cantor escapes and returns to the theatre. However, Joe convinces everyone that the real Cantor is a fraud and he is tossed out. Meanwhile, Joe, Tom and Pat are the hits of the charity show.

Dinah Shore has the lion's share of songs in this war-time salute, performing "Thank Your Lucky Stars," "How Sweet You Are" and "The Dreamer." Cantor, in his own inimitable fashion, does "We're Staying Home Tonight" (to adhere to the rationing of critical items like fuel), while a very earnest John Garfield sweats through a parody of "Blues in the Night." In an English pub sequence Errol Flynn nicely kids his war hero image with "That's What You Jolly Well Get." Dennis Morgan and Joan Leslie duet on "Ridin' for a Fall" and "No You, No Me." Morgan also croons "Good Night, Good Neighbor," which is danced to by a svelte Alexis Smith. Two of Hollywood's best second bananas, Jack Carson and Alan Hale, team to sing and dance to "Goin' North," while Ann Sheridan (the "Ooomph Girl") has a rare chance to sing on-camera with "Love Isn't Born." Olivia de Havilland, Ida Lupino and George Tobias do their best (which is a mixed blessing) with a reprise of "The Dreamer," set to a contemporary beat. The most solidly musical and entertaining item of the whole movie is Hattie McDaniel's jiving rendition of "Ice Cold Katie," with Willie Best. Racial stereotypes to one side, it is a pure delight! The capper to this celebrity outing is Bette Davis's "They're Either Too Young or Too Old," in which she jitterbugs while decrying—in her own unique rhythm and pitch—the fate of women left on the home front while all the fit men of proper age have gone off to the battlefront.

James Agee (*The Nation* magazine) judged, "THANK YOUR LUCKY STARS is the loudest and most vulgar of the current musicals. It is also the most fun, if you are amused when show people kid their own idiom, and if you find a cruel-compassionate sort of interest in watching amateurs like Bette Davis do what they can with a song."

THANK YOUR LUCKY STARS received an Oscar nomination for Best Song ("They're Either Too Young Or Too Old") but lost to "You'll Never Know" of HELLO, FRISCO, HELLO, *q.v.* To be noted is that both the producer (Mark Hellinger) and the director (David Butler) of THANK YOUR LUCKY STARS make brief cameo appearances as themselves. The next year many of the same celebrities from this entertainment fest would appear in Warner Bros.' HOLLYWOOD CANTEEN, *q.v.*

THAT'S DANCING! (Metro-Goldwyn-Mayer/United Artists, 1985) Color 104 minutes.

Executive producer, Gene Kelly; producers, David Niven, Jr., Jack Haley, Jr.; associate producer, Bud Friedgen; director/screenplay, Haley, Jr.; costumes, Ron Talsky; music, Henry Mancini; music supervisor, Harry V. Lojewski; music coordinator, Bob Emmer; music editors, William Saracino, Scott Perry; assistant directors, Ira Halberstadt, Richard Hinds, Joel Tuber, Paul Hornstein, David Dreyfuss; sound re-recording, William McCaughey, Lyle Burbridge, Ray O'Reilly; sound editor, Paul Hochman; additional camera, Andrew Laszlo, Paul Lohmann; supervising editor, Bud Friedgen; editor, Michael J. Sheridan.

New songs: "That's Dancing!" (Henry Mancini, Larry Grossman, Ellen Fitzhugh); "Invitation to Dance" (Kim Carnes, Dave Ellingson, Martin Page, Brian Fairweather).

Gene Kelly, Sammy Davis, Jr., Mikhail Baryshnikov, Ray Bolger, Liza Minnelli (Narrators).

Extracts from: SO THIS IS PARIS ("Charleston" sequence); SHOW OF SHOWS ("Lady Luck" with The Vitaphone Dancing Girls); FLYING HIGH ("We'll Dance Until Dawn" with The Berkeley Dancers); 42nd STREET ("42nd Street" with Ruby Keeler, Dick Powell, The Berkeley Dancers); GOLD DIGGERS OF 1933 ("The Shadow Waltz" with Ruby Keeler, The Berkeley Girls); DAMES ("I Only Have Eyes for You" with Ruby Keeler, Dick Powell, The Berkeley Dancers); GOLD DIGGERS OF 1935 ("Lullaby of Broadway" with The Berkeley Dancers); RUFUS JONES FOR PRESIDENT ("Great Day Here" with Sammy Davis, Jr.); ROBERTA ("I Won't Dance" with Fred Astaire); THE GAY DIVORCEE ("Night and Day" with Fred Astaire, Ginger Rogers); SWING TIME ("Pick Yourself Up" with Fred Astaire, Ginger Rogers); THE LITTLEST REBEL ("Ad-lib Dance" with Shirley Temple, Bill "Bojangles' Robinson); KING FOR A DAY ("Swanee," "Smiles," "The Lindy Hop" with Bill "Bojangles Robinson); BROADWAY MELODY OF 1936 ("Broadway Rhythm" with Eleanor Powell); HONOLULU ("Honolulu" with Eleanor Powell); DOWN ARGENTINE WAY ("Down Argentine Way" with The Nicholas Brothers); THE HARVEY GIRLS ("The Atcheson, Topeka and the Santa Fe" with Ray Bolger); THE WIZARD OF OZ ("If I Only Had a Brain" with Ray Bolger, Judy

Garland); THE TURNING POINT ("Le Corsaire" with Mikhail Baryshnikov); silent footage from assorted sources (Loie Fuller, Annabella, Isadora Duncan); THE DUMB GIRL OF PORTICI (Anna Pavlova); THE HOLLYWOOD REVUE OF 1929 ("Orange Blossom Time" with The Albertina Rasch Ballet); ON YOUR TOES ("The Princess Zenobia Ballet" with Vera Zorina, Charles Laskey); THE RED SHOES ("The Red Shoes Ballet" with Moira Shearer, Robert Helpmann, Leonide Massine); TONIGHT WE SING ("The Adam Ballet" with Tamara Toumanova); CAROUSEL ("The Carousel Waltz" with Jacques D'Amboise); AN EVENING WITH THE ROYAL BALLET ("Le Corsaire" with Rudolf Nureyev, Dame Margot Fonteyn); GIVE A GIRL A BREAK ("Nothing Is Impossible" with Debbie Reynolds, Bob Fosse); ROYAL WEDDING ("I Left My Heart in Haiti" with Fred Astaire, Jane Powell); SINGIN' IN THE RAIN ("Moses" with Gene Kelly, Donald O'Connor); THREE LITTLE WORDS ("Thinking of You" with Fred Astaire, Vera-Ellen); INVITATION TO THE DANCE ("Scheherezade" with Gene Kelly, Carol Haney); THE BAND WAGON ("A Shine on Your Shoes" with Fred Astaire, Leroy Daniels); IT'S ALWAYS FAIR WEATHER ("We're Civilians Now" with Gene Kelly, Dan Dailey, Michael Kidd); YANKEE DOODLE DANDY ("Give My Regards to Broadway" with James Cagney); KISS ME KATE ("Tom, Dick or Harry" with Ann Miller, Tommy Rall, Bobby Van, Bob Fosse); OKLAHOMA! ("Out of My Dreams Ballet" with Bambi Lynn, James Mitchell); SWEET CHARITY ("There's Gotta Be Something Better than This" with Shirley MacLaine, Chita Rivera, Paula Kelly); SILK STOCKINGS ("The Red Blues" with Cyd Charisse); WEST SIDE STORY ("Cool" with The Jets and their Girls); SATURDAY NIGHT FEVER ("You Should Be Dancing" with John Travolta, The Bee Gees); FAME ("Fame" with The Fame Dancers, Irene Cara); FLASHDANCE ("Flashdance/What a Feeling" with Marine Jahan, Jennifer Beals, Irene Cara); BEAT IT ("Beat It!" with Michael Jackson).

Attempting to repeat the screen success of THAT'S ENTERTAINMENT! (1974) (*q.v.*), producer-director-scenarist Jack Haley, Jr. put together a compilation feature of Hollywood-lensed footage tracing the history of movie dancing from the beginning of the sound era to the present. Haley not only used the archives of his home studio, MGM, but also obtained footage from other lots, to give a hopefully well-rounded look at celluloid hoofing. As with his preceding film, and its less successful follow-up, THAT'S ENTERTAINMENT: PART II (1976), *q.v.*, Haley employed noted genre performers to introduce various segments. His hosts here were

Gene Kelly (executive producer of this venture), actress Liza Minnelli, ballet star Mikhail Baryshnikov and song-and-dance man Sammy Davis, Jr. Sadly, these framing sequences were not imaginatively structured and served only to burden a film already too long in running time.

Historically THAT'S DANCING! contains an interesting conglomeration of movie dance sequences, ranging from the Warner Bros.' Busby Berkeley spectacles with Ruby Keeler and Dick Powell to Fred Astaire and Ginger Rogers' classic ballroom routines at RKO Radio. These, along with the terpsichorean display from WEST SIDE STORY (1961), *q.v.,* are the highlights of this compilation feature. Unfortunately the movie is beefed up with too much filler, like the poorly staged dance routine with Judy Garland and Ray Bolger which was deleted from the release print of THE WIZARD OF OZ (1939), *q.v.,* Michael Jackson's music video "Beat It!" and John Travolta's body gyrations from SATURDAY NIGHT FEVER (1977), *q.v.*

The novelty of any compilation feature lies in its choice of material and, unfortunately, much of the prime footage had been used (for the first time) in THAT'S ENTERTAINMENT! So the producers were left with two barren choices: using far less spectacular footage *and/or* clips already too familiar with viewers. *Variety* observed, "As far as quality, what hurts DANCING is an understandable effort toward the end to add present-day appeal by including clips of recent teenthrobs. . . ." *TV Movies and Video Guide* (1989) concurred: "1980s selections that end the film seem lumbering and ludicrous compared to the marvels of movement that precede them."

THAT'S ENTERTAINMENT! (Metro-Goldwyn-Mayer/United Artists, 1974) Color 132 minutes.

Executive producer, Daniel Melnick; producer/director/script, Jack Haley, Jr.; music supervisor, Jesse Kaye; additional music adaptor, Henry Mancini; assistant directors, Richard Bremerkamp, David Silver, Claude Binyon, Jr.; film librarian, Mort Feinstein; sound re-recording, Hal Watkins, Aaron Rochin, Lyle Burbridge, Harry W. Tetrick, William L. McCaughey; opticals, Robert Hoag, Jim Liles; camera, Gene Polito, Ernest Laszlo, Russell Metty, Ennio Guarnieri, Allan Green; editors, Bud Friedgen, David E. Blewitt.

Fred Astaire, Bing Crosby, Gene Kelly, Peter Lawford, Liza Minnelli, Donald O'Connor, Debbie Reynolds, Mickey Rooney, Frank Sinatra, James Stewart, Elizabeth Taylor (Narrators/Hosts).

Extracts from: THE HOLLYWOOD REVUE OF 1929 ("Singin' in the Rain" with Cliff Edwards); SPEAK EASILY ("Singin' in the Rain" with Jimmy Durante); LITTLE NELLIE

KELLY ("Singin' in the Rain" with Judy Garland); SINGIN' IN THE RAIN ("Singin' in the Rain" with Gene Kelly, Donald O'Connor, Debbie Reynolds); BROADWAY MELODY ("Broadway Melody" with Charles King); ROSALIE ("Rosalie" with Eleanor Powell); ROSE MARIE ("Indian Love Call" with Jeanette MacDonald, Nelson Eddy); THE GREAT ZIEGFELD ("A Pretty Girl Is Like a Melody" with Dennis Morgan [dubbed by Allan Jones], Virginia Bruce); BROADWAY MELODY OF 1940 ("Begin the Beguine" with Fred Astaire, Eleanor Powell); "IT HAPPENED IN BROOKLYN ("The Song's Gotta Come from the Heart" with Frank Sinatra, Jimmy Durante); "CYNTHIA ("Melody of Spring" with Elizabeth Taylor); THOUSANDS CHEER ("Honeysuckle Rose" with Lena Horne); TAKE ME OUT TO THE BALL GAME ("Take Me Out to the Ball Game" with Frank Sinatra, Gene Kelly); WORDS AND MUSIC ("Thou Swell" with June Allyson); GOOD NEWS ("Varsity Drag" and "French Lesson" with June Allyson, Peter Lawford); TWO WEEKS WITH LOVE ("Aba Daba Honeymoon" with Debbie Reynolds, Carleton Carpenter); A DATE WITH JUDY ("It's a Most Unusual Day" with Elizabeth Taylor, Jane Powell, Wallace Beery, Selena Royle, Robert Stack, George Cleveland, Scotty Beckett, Jerry Hunter, Leon Ames); THE HARVEY GIRLS ("On the Atcheson, Topeka and Santa Fe" with Judy Garland, Ray Bolger); FREE AND EASY ("It Must Be You" with Robert Montgomery, Lottice Howell); THE HOLLYWOOD REVUE ("I've Got a Feelin' for You" with Joan Crawford); RECKLESS ("Reckless" with Jean Harlow [dubbed by Virginia Verrell]); SUZY ("Did I Remember?" with Jean Harlow [dubbed by Virginia Verrell], Cary Grant); BORN TO DANCE ("Easy to Love" with James Stewart, Eleanor Powell); IDIOT'S DELIGHT ("Puttin' on the Ritz" with Clark Gable); BROADWAY TO HOLLYWOOD (montage dance number with Mickey Rooney); BROADWAY MELODY OF 1938 ("You Made Me Love You" with Judy Garland); BABES IN ARMS ("Babes in Arms" with Douglas McPhail and chorus); BABES ON BROADWAY ("Hoedown" with Judy Garland, Mickey Rooney); BABES ON BROADWAY ("Waitin for the Robert E. Lee" and "Babes on Broadway" with Judy Garland, Mickey Rooney); STRIKE UP THE BAND ("Strike Up the Band" with Judy Garland, Mickey Rooney); ZIEGFELD FOLLIES ("The Babbitt and the Bromide" with Gene Kelly, Fred Astaire); THE BARKLEYS OF BROADWAY ("They Can't Take That Away from Me" with Fred Astaire, Ginger Rogers); DANCING LADY ("Rhythm of the Day" with Fred Astaire, Joan Crawford); THE BAND WAGON ("I Guess I'll Have to Change My Plans" with Fred Astaire, Jack Buchanan);

ROYAL WEDDING ("Sunday Jumps" with Fred Astaire); THE BARKLEYS OF BROADWAY ("Shoes with Wings On" with Fred Astaire); ROYAL WEDDING ("You're All the World to Me" with Fred Astaire); THE BAND WAGON ("Dancing in the Dark" with Fred Astaire, Cyd Charisse); PAGAN LOVE SONG ("Pagan Love Song" with Esther Williams); BATHING BEAUTY (production number with Esther Williams); MILLION DOLLAR MERMAID (production number with Esther Williams); THREE LITTLE WORDS ("I Wanna Be Loved by You" with Debbie Reynolds [dubbed by Helen Kane], Carleton Carpenter); SMALL TOWN GIRL ("I Gotta Hear That Beat" with Ann Miller); THE TOAST OF NEW ORLEANS ("Be My Love" with Mario Lanza, Kathryn Grayson); SINGIN' IN THE RAIN ("Make 'em Laugh" with Donald O'Connor); SHOW BOAT ("Cotton Blossom" with cast; "Make Believe" with Kathryn Grayson, Howard Keel; "Ol' Man River" with William Warfield); THE BAND WAGON ("By Myself" with Fred Astaire); THE PIRATE ("Mack the Black" with Gene Kelly); ON THE TOWN ("New York, New York" with Frank Sinatra, Gene Kelly, Jules Munshin); ANCHORS AWEIGH ("The Worry Song" with Gene Kelly, Jerry the Mouse); SINGIN' IN THE RAIN ("Singin' in the Rain" and "Broadway Melody" with Gene Kelly); IN THE GOOD OLD SUMMERTIME ("In the Good Old Summertime" with Judy Garland, Van Johnson, Liza Minnelli); LA FIESTA SANTA BARBARA ("La Cucaracha" with The Gumm Sisters with Judy Garland); EVERY SUNDAY ("Opera Versus Jazz" with Judy Garland, Deanna Durbin); BROADWAY MELODY OF 1938 (dance with Judy Garland, Buddy Ebsen); THE WIZARD OF OZ ("We're Off to See the Wizard" with Judy Garland; "If I Only Had a Brain" with Judy Garland, Ray Bolger, Jack Haley, Bert Lahr; "Over the Rainbow" with Judy Garland); MEET ME IN ST. LOUIS ("The Trolley Song" with Judy Garland; "Under the Bamboo Tree" with Judy Garland, Margaret O'Brien; "The Boy Next Door" with Judy Garland); SUMMER STOCK ("Get Happy" with Judy Garland); GOING HOLLYWOOD ("Going Hollywood" with Bing Crosby); HIGH SOCIETY ("Well, Did You Evah!" with Bing Crosby, Frank Sinatra); "True Love" with Bing Crosby, Grace Kelly); HIT THE DECK ("Hallelujah" with Kay Armen, Debbie Reynolds, Jane Powell, Ann Miller, Tony Martin, Russ Tamblyn, Vic Damone); SEVEN BRIDES FOR SEVEN BROTHERS ("Barnraising Ballet" with cast); GIGI ("Gigi" with Louis Jourdan; "Thank Heaven for Little Girls" with Maurice Chevalier); AN AMERICAN IN PARIS ("An American in Paris" with Gene Kelly, Leslie Caron).

See: THAT'S ENTERTAINMENT: PART II (essay).

THAT'S ENTERTAINMENT: PART II (Metro-Goldwyn-Mayer/United Artists, 1976) Color 133 minutes.

Producers, Saul Chaplin, Daniel Melnick; new sequences director, Gene Kelly; commentary, Leonard Gershe; production designer, John De Cuir; music director/music arranger, Nelson Riddle; music supervisor, Harry V. Lojewski; special lyrics, Howard Dietz, Saul Chaplin; assistant director, William R. Poole; animators, Hanna-Barbera Productions; sound, Bill Edmonson, sound re-recording, Hal Watkins, Aaron Rochin; camera, George Folsey; editors, Bud Friedgen, David Blewitt; contributing editors, David Bretherton, Peter C. Johnson.

Fred Astaire, Gene Kelly (Hosts).

Extracts from: THE BAND WAGON ("That's Entertainment" with Fred Astaire, Nanette Fabray, Oscar Levant, Jack Buchanan, Cyd Charisse; "Triplets" with Fred Astaire, Nanette Fabray, Jack Buchanan); FOR ME AND MY GAL ("For Me and My Gal" with Judy Garland, Gene Kelly); LADY BE GOOD ("Fascinatin' Rhythm" with Eleanor Powell); BROADWAY MELODY OF 1936 ("I've Got a Feeling You're Fooling" with Robert Taylor); TWO-FACED WOMAN ("La Chica Chaca" with Greta Garbo); THE BELLE OF NEW YORK ("I Wanna Be a Dancin' Man" with Fred Astaire); LILI ("Hi-Lili, Hi-Lo" with Leslie Caron); THE PIRATE ("Be a Clown" with Judy Garland, Gene Kelly); KISS ME KATE ("From This Moment On" with Ann Miller, Tommy Rall, Carol Haney, Bobby Van, Bob Fosse, Jeanne Coyne); SILK STOCKINGS ("All of You" with Fred Astaire, Cyd Charisse); SEVEN BRIDES FOR SEVEN BROTHERS ("Lonesome Polecat" with Howard Keel); LOVELY TO LOOK AT ("Smoke Gets in Your Eyes" with Kathryn Grayson, Marge Champion, Gower Champion); EASTER PARADE ("Easter Parade" with Fred Astaire, Judy Garland; "Steppin' Out with My Baby" with Fred Astaire; "A Couple of Swells" with Fred Astaire, Judy Garland); GOING HOLLYWOOD ("Temptation" with Bing Crosby, Fifi D'Orsay); LISTEN, DARLING ("Zing Went the Strings of My Heart" with Judy Garland); CABIN IN THE SKY ("Taking a Chance on Love" with Ethel Waters, Eddie "Rochester" Anderson); BORN TO DANCE ("Swingin' the Jinx Away" with Eleanor Powell); NEW MOON ("Stouthearted Men" with Nelson Eddy; "Lover Come Back to Me" with Nelson Eddy, Jeanette MacDonald); HOLLYWOOD PARTY ("Inka Dinka Doo" with Jimmy Durante); GIRL CRAZY ("I Got Rhythm" with Judy Garland, Mickey Rooney); SONGWRITERS REVUE ("Songwriters Revue of 1929" with Jack Benny); THE BROADWAY MELODY ("Wedding of the Painted Doll" with the original troupe); LADY BE GOOD ("Lady Be

Good" with Ann Sothern, Robert Young); BROADWAY SERENADE ("Broadway Serenade" with Lew Ayres, Al Shean; "For Every Lonely Heart" with Jeanette MacDonald); WORDS AND MUSIC ("The Lady Is a Tramp" with Lena Horne; "Manhattan" with Mickey Rooney, Tom Drake, Marshall Thompson); THREE LITTLE WORDS ("Three Little Words" with Fred Astaire, Red Skelton); THE GREAT WALTZ ("Tales from the Vienna Woods" with Fernand Gravet, Miliza Korjus); SINGIN' IN THE RAIN ("Good Morning" with Gene Kelly, Debbie Reynolds, Donald O'Connor; "Broadway Rhythm" with Gene Kelly, Cyd Charisse); AN AMERICAN IN PARIS ("Concerto in F" with Oscar Levant; "I Got Rhythm" with Gene Kelly; "Our Love Is Here to Stay" with Gene Kelly, Leslie Caron; "I'll Build a Stairway to Paradise" with Georges Guetary); MEET ME IN ST. LOUIS ("Have Yourself a Merry Little Christmas" with Judy Garland, Margaret O'Brien); LOVE ME OR LEAVE ME ("Ten Cents a Dance" with Doris Day, James Cagney); THE TENDER TRAP ("The Tender Trap" with Frank Sinatra); TILL THE CLOUDS ROLL BY ("Ol' Man River" with Frank Sinatra; "The Last Time I Saw Paris" with Dinah Shore); ANCHORS AWEIGH ("I Fall in Love Too Easily" with Frank Sinatra; "I Begged Her" with Frank Sinatra, Gene Kelly); IT HAPPENED IN BROOKLYN ("I Believe" with Frank Sinatra, Jimmy Durante, Billy Roy); HIGH SOCIETY ("You're Sensational" with Frank Sinatra, Grace Kelly; "Now You Has Jazz" with Bing Crosby, Louis Armstrong); THE MERRY WIDOW (1934) "Maxim's" and "Girls, Girls, Girls" with Maurice Chevalier; "The Merry Widow Waltz"); THE MERRY WIDOW (1952) ("Can-Can" with Gwen Verdon and dancers); INVITATION TO THE DANCE ("Sinbad" with Gene Kelly); SMALL TOWN GIRL ("Take Me to Broadway" with Bobby Van); ANNIE GET YOUR GUN ("There's No Business Like Show Business" with Betty Hutton, Howard Keel, Keenan Wynn, Louis Calhern); IT'S ALWAYS FAIR WEATHER ("I Like Myself" with Gene Kelly); GIGI ("I Remember It Well" with Maurice Chevalier, Hermione Gingold); THE BARKLEYS OF BROADWAY ("Bouncin' the Blues" with Fred Astaire, Ginger Rogers); EASY TO LOVE ("Water Ski Ballet" with Esther Williams); BUD ABBOTT AND LOU COSTELLO IN HOLLYWOOD (Bit); ADAM'S RIB (Spencer Tracy, Katharine Hepburn); A DAY AT THE RACES (The Three Marx Brothers); A TALE OF TWO CITIES (Bit); BOMBSHELL (Jean Harlow); BOOM TOWN (Spencer Tracy, Clark Gable); BOYS TOWN (Spencer Tracy, Mickey Rooney); CHINA SEAS (Robert Benchley); DANCING LADY (Bit); DAVID COPPERFIELD (W.C. Fields); DINNER AT EIGHT

Fred Astaire and Gene Kelly co-hosting THAT'S ENTERTAINMENT: PART II (1976).

(Jean Harlow); GONE WITH THE WIND (Vivien Leigh, Clark Gable); GOODBYE, MR. CHIPS (Bit); GRAND HOTEL (Greta Garbo, John Barrymore); BILLY ROSE'S JUMBO (Jimmy Durante); LASSIE COME HOME (Roddy McDowall); LAUREL AND HARDY'S LAUGHING TWENTIES (Bits); NINOTCHKA (Greta Garbo); PAT AND MIKE (Spencer Tracy, Katharine Hepburn); THE PHILADELPHIA STORY (Katharine Hepburn, Cary Grant); PRIVATE LIVES (Bit); SARATOGA (Jean Harlow, Clark Gable); STRANGE CARGO (Bit); TARZAN THE APE MAN (Johnny Weissmuller); THE THIN MAN (William Powell); TWO GIRLS AND A SAILOR (Bit); WHITE CARGO (Bit); WITHOUT LOVE (Bit); ZIEGFELD GIRL (Bit); and scenes from the travelogues: HONG KONG, HUB OF THE ORIENT; STOCKHOLM, PRIDE OF SWEDEN; BEAUTIFUL BANFF AND LAKE LOUISE; LAND OF THE TAJ MAHAL; COLORFUL GUATEMALA; JAPAN, IN CHERRY BLOSSOM TIME; IRELAND, THE EMERALD ISLE; SWITZERLAND, THE BEAUTIFUL; PICTURESQUE UDAIPUR; OLD NEW ORLEANS; A DAY ON TREASURE ISLAND; MADEIRA, ISLAND OF ROMANCE; COPENHAGEN, CITY OF TOWERS.

One of the most satisfying of all historical film compilations, THAT'S ENTERTAINMENT! traces the MGM sound musical from its beginnings in 1929 through its golden age of the 1930s and 1940s, and up to the late 1950s. Conceived, written, produced and directed by Jack Haley, Jr., this production meticulously used prime prints for its production, re-channeling the sound to contemporary standards and employing a wide screen where appropriate to dramatize the juxtaposition of employed clips. What really made this novelty entry so special was the choice of hosts to introduce each segment of the carefully structured documentary. Not only were the celebrities chosen for their marquee/nostalgia allure, but they were provided with props (old sets even) to bridge from the present back to the past when particular productions were being made. If Liza Minnelli (Jack Haley Jr.'s ex-wife) was gushy about her late mother (Judy Garland), Peter Lawford was humble about his role in the history of song-and-dance, and Elizabeth Taylor made such a breathtakingly beautiful entry that audiences could only gasp with approval.

Nothing is more of a crowd pleaser than to show current generations the foibles of their forebears and the early musicals of MGM demonstrate that perfectly: fat-thighed chorines thumping on the dance floor, inane dialogue being spouted in syrupy, amateurish fashion, and production numbers that would be laughed off MTV in a moment. Equally engaging was the montage of scenes from MGM movies that utilized "Singin' in the Rain." For those who had never seen Eleanor Powell's spectacular dancing her display of athletic precision tapping in ROSALIE (1937), *q.v.* was astounding. The sight of an aged, pudgy Mickey Rooney (one of the hosts) could not take away from the joy of witnessing a fresh and young Rooney teamed with an equally sparkling Judy Garland in moments from several of their infectious let's-put-on-the-show MGM musicals. There was Gene Kelly dancing and singing, Esther Williams diving in and out of water in aquatic ballet numbers, and June Allyson and Peter Lawford scampering to "The Varsity Drag" from GOOD NEWS (1947), *q.v.* For amusement's sake there were snippets of Clark Gable attempting to be a song-and-dance man in IDIOT'S DELIGHT (1939) and a dubbed Jean Harlow singing in RECKLESS (1933). James Stewart hosted a segment where he self-effacingly commented on the process of having nonmusical stars sing in movies, which led into clips of several MGM luminaries who "sang" on-camera. Most touching of all was having Fred Astaire walk through the run-down train station set from THE BAND WAGON (1953), *q.v.,* and then the film switch to the movie itself with Astaire performing "By Myself." If anything seemed extraneous in this cornucopia of entertainment it was "The American in Paris" ballet from that movie (1950). Seen in retrospect; it appears pretentious, overly-arty and not so marvelous.

MGM, which was going through difficult times in the mid-1970s and had become a nearly non-functioning studio, made a great ballyhoo about THAT'S ENTERTAINMENT! It rounded up over fifty surviving MGM alumni to attend the U.S. premieres of the film and sent many of the personalities on tour to promote the documentary. Among the still living studio greats who did *not* participate were Greta Garbo, Greer Garson, Walter Pidgeon, and, very surprisingly, Esther Williams.

In praising this effective compilation outing, the *Hollywood Reporter* noted, "Those lavish musical films are genuine American folk art, masterfully made and performed, and uncluttered by neurotic agony. Their purpose was to create pleasure, a form of entertainment the movies have, hopefully, only temporarily set aside." *Variety* praised, "Outstanding, stunning, sentimental, exciting, colorful, enjoyable, spirit-lifting, tuneful, youthful, invigorating, zesty, respectful, heartwarming, awesome, cheerful, dazzling, and richly satisfying."

THAT'S ENTERTAINMENT! grossed over $12,083,620, making it the ninth-greatest earner in the studio's history to that date. The theme song for the film had come from the Howard Dietz-Arthur Schwartz song penned for THE BAND WAGON (1953).

With such a bonanza from THAT'S ENTERTAINMENT! the studio could not resist doing a sequel. Because so much of the "best" footage had been included in the original, the producers decided to expand the concept by including comedy and drama sequences in the new offering. Nothing seemed to work as well the second time around. The novelty had worn off, the choice of material was not as spectacular, and the hosts (Fred Astaire and Gene Kelly) were too self-conscious and archly cute rather than straightforward and informative. Clips from seventy-two MGM films were used in the sequel. There were some musical scenes, including Jeanette MacDonald singing "Lover Come Back to Me" (done to appease fans incensed at the scant attention given her in the first compilation), Cyd Charisse's dance from SINGIN' IN THE RAIN (1952), *q.v.* and Judy Garland and Gene Kelly singing "Be a Clown" from THE PIRATE (1948), *q.v.* This go-round had a subordinate comedy film theme. Included was a montage tribute to the Marx Brothers, bits of Laurel and Hardy and Abbott and Costello, as well as smidgeons of Greta Garbo from NINOTCHKA (1939) and Spencer Tracy and Katharine Hepburn from PAT AND MIKE (1952). For obvious filler, several MGM travelogues were included, poking fun of the format which usually concluded with a pompous narrator insisting, "As we bid farewell to. . . ."

Overall, this too long entry (133 minutes) was not a happy experience. Cut from the release print were Sammy Cahn as a co-host and scenes from SEVEN BRIDES FOR SEVEN BROTHERS (1954), *q.v.* One unhappy participant in the films was Esther Williams. In September 1976 she sued MGM for $1 million for breach of contract and invasion of privacy, claiming the studio had no legal permission to use footage from her old movies in a new offering. The matter was settled out-of-court. Another unhappy participant was Elizabeth Taylor, who felt the studio was exploiting her appearance in the second film, when it only contained a few brief moments of her.

THAT'S ENTERTAINMENT: PART II premiered at New York's Ziegfeld Theatre on May 10, 1976, which was Fred Astaire's seventy-seventh birthday. The gala was a benefit for the Film Society of Lincoln Center. While MGM promoted this follow-up heavily, it did not even gross $4 million in distributors' domestic film rentals.

THERE'S NO BUSINESS LIKE SHOW BUSINESS (20th Century-Fox, 1954) Color 117 minutes.

Producer, Sol C. Siegel; director, Walter Lang; story, Lamar Trotti; screenplay, Phoebe Ephron, Henry Ephron; art directors, Lyle Wheeler, John De Cuir; music directors, Alfred Newman, Lionel Newman; choreographer, Robert Alton; camera, Leon Shamroy; editor, Robert Simpson.

Songs: "When the Midnight Choo Choo Leaves for Alabam'," "Let's Have Another Cup of Coffee," "Play a Simple Melody," "After You Get What You Want You Don't Want It," "Heat Wave," "You'd Be Surprised," "A Sailor's Not a Sailor," "A Pretty Girl Is Like a Melody," "Lazy," "If You Believe Me," "A Man Chases a Girl (Until She Catches Him)," "Marie," "There's No Business Like Show Business" (Irving Berlin); "Alexander's Ragtime Band."

Ethel Merman (Molly Donahue); Donald O'Connor (Tim Donahue); Marilyn Monroe (Vicky); Dan Dailey (Terrance Donahue); Johnnie Ray (Steve Donahue); Mitzi Gaynor (Katy Donahue); Richard Eastham (Lew Harris); Hugh O'Brian (Charles Gibbs); Frank McHugh (Eddie Duggan); Rhys Williams (Father Dineen); Lee Patrick (Marge); Chick Chandler (Harry); Eve Miller (Hatcheck Girl); Robin Raymond (Lillian Sawyer); Lyle Talbot (Stage Manager); George Melford (Stage Doorman); Alvy Moore (Katy's Boy Friend;) Henry Slate (Dance Director); Gavin Gordon (Geoffrey); Nolan Leary (Archbishop); Mimi Gibson (Katy at Age Four) Linda Lowel (Katy at Age Eight); John Potter (Steve at Age Two); Jimmy Baird (Steve at Age Six); Billy Chapin (Steve at Age Ten); Neal McCaskill (Tim at Age Two); Donald Gamble (Tim at Age Six); Charlotte Austin (Lorna); John Doucette (Stage Manager); Isabelle Dwan (Sophie Tucker); Donald Kerr (Bobby Clark).

By the mid-1950s, in an era of changing tastes and tightening film budgets, the traditional Hollywood musical was fading from the scene. However, THERE'S NO BUSINESS LIKE SHOW BUSINESS was a joyful throwback to the 1930s and the likes of ALEXANDER'S RAGTIME BAND (1938), *q.v.* It was directed with polish by veteran Walter Lang, who had handled such 20th Century-Fox musicals as TIN PAN ALLEY (1940), STATE FAIR (1945) and MOTHER WORE TIGHTS (1947), *qq.v.* He had also helmed CALL ME MADAM (1953), *q.v.* at the studio which starred Ethel Merman and Donald O'Connor. The splashy THERE'S NO BUSINESS LIKE SHOW BUSINESS used a grab bag of wonderful Irving Berlin tunes as a basis for what the *New York Times* termed "A lavish, spangly and gorgeously-colored wallow in style and sentiment."

In 1919 the Donahue family are all members of vaudeville.

There is mother Molly (Ethel Merman), father Terrance (Dan Dailey), and their three children. Although Molly wants her children to have formal schooling, they insist on being part of the act and continually reappear to perform with their parents. Finally she relents and lets them stay with the act. The youngsters grow to adulthood—Tim (Donald O'Connor), Katy (Mitzi Gaynor) and Steve (Johnnie Ray)—as the family continues to tour the country. When Steve drops out of the act to enter the priesthood, the family is billed as the Four Donahues. Tim meets ambitious singer Vicky (Marilyn Monroe) and the two fall in love. When Vicky has a lucky break and is picked to star in a Broadway show, she arranges for both Tim and Katy to have roles in the musical. Later, Tim, misunderstanding her relationship with the show's producer, gets drunk and is injured in a car accident. He is hospitalized and Molly goes on stage in his place. She is warmly received by the audience. Meanwhile, Terrance reprimands the recuperating Tim and the latter disappears. A remorseful Terrance goes off in search of Tim and he too vanishes. Frustrated at seeing her family torn apart, Molly takes out her concerns on the well-meaning Vicky. Eventually Katy convinces Molly that Vicky is not a villain. At an Actors Fund Benefit at the Hippodrome, the Five Donahues are reunited on stage. Steve has become an Army chaplain, Tim is in the Navy and Terrance is just glad to be back home.

In addition to his old standbys, Irving Berlin composed some new songs for THERE'S NO BUSINESS LIKE SHOW BUSINESS: "If You Believe Me" for Johnnie Ray; "A Man Chases a Girl (Until She Catches Him)," which gave Donald O'Connor a wild dance solo; and "A Sailor's Not a Sailor (Till a Sailor's Been Tattoed)," a novelty duet for Ethel Merman and Mitzi Gaynor (with Merman in a sailor suit and sporting a moustache!). Marilyn Monroe's best remembered number in the production is the sizzling "Heat Wave." Her "After You Get What You Want" is a close second, thanks to her form-fitting (partial) see-through white gown and her purring of the lyrics. In the vaudeville tradition, Merman and Dan Dailey perform "When the Midnight Choo-Choo Leaves for Alabam'," and Merman, joined by Dailey, Donald O'Connor, Gaynor, and Johnnie Ray, slams through "Alexander's Ragtime Band." Merman vibrates with her anthem, "There's No Business Like Show Business" (which came from her *Annie Get Your Gun*), which is reprised at the finale by the six leads.

Filmed in CinemaScope and color, THERE'S NO BUSINESS LIKE SHOW BUSINESS received generally positive reviews (except for the drubbing taken by non-actor Johnnie Ray). Jesse Zunser in *Cue* magazine commented, "What makes this story palatable, in addition to 'Alexander's Ragtime Band' reprised five times, is the presence of such veteran troupers as Ethel Merman as Ma, Dan Dailey as Pa, and Donald O'Connor and Mitzi Gaynor as two of the kids. . . . The singing—solo and ensemble—is good; there are plenty of lively lines, jokes, gags, skits and revues, and the film overflows with sentimentality and nostalgia."

THERE'S NO BUSINESS LIKE SHOW BUSINESS grossed $5,000,000 in distributors' domestic film rentals. It received Oscar nominations for Best Scoring, Motion Picture Story and Costumes—Color.

When Decca released the soundtrack album to THERE'S NO BUSINESS LIKE SHOW BUSINESS in 1954, Dolores Gray replaced Marilyn Monroe on her numbers: "Lazy" and "Heat Wave."

THIS IS THE ARMY (Warner Bros., 1943) Color 121 minutes.

Producers, Jack L. Warner, Hal B. Wallis; director, Michael Curtiz; based on the musical play by Irving Berlin; screenplay, Casey Robinson, Claude Binyon; art directors, John Keonig, John Hughes; costumes, Orry-Kelly; music directors, Leo F. Forbstein, Frank Heath; orchestrator, Ray Heindorf; choreographers, LeRoy Prinz, Robert Sidney; technical advisor, Lieutenant Colonel Frank McCabe; assistant director, Frank Heath; dialogue director, Edward Blatt; sound, C. A. Riggs; montages, James Leicester, Don Siegel; special effects, Jack Cosgrove; camera, Bert Glennon, Sol Polito; editor, George Amy.

Songs: "Your Country and My Country," "My Sweetie," "Poor Little Me, I'm on K.P.," "We're On Our Way to France," "God Bless America," "What Does He Look Like?" "This Is the Army, Mr. Jones," "I'm Gettin' Tired So I Can Sleep," "Mandy," "The Army Made a Man Out of Me," "Ladies of the Chorus," "That's What the Well-Dressed Man in Harlem Will Wear," "How About a Cheer for the Navy?" "I Left My Heart at the Stage Door Canteen," "With My Head in the Clouds," "American Eagles," "Oh, How I Hate to Get Up in the Morning," "This Time Is the Last Time" (Irving Berlin).

Irving Berlin (Himself); George Murphy (Jerry Jones); Joan Leslie (Eileen Dibble); George Tobias (Maxie Twardofsky); Alan Hale (Sergeant McGee); Charles Butterworth (Eddie Dibble); Rosemary DeCamp (Ethel); Dolores Costello (Mrs. Davidson); Una Merkel (Rose Dibble); Stanley Ridges (Major Davidson); Ruth Donnelly (Mrs. O'Brien); Dorothy Peterson (Mrs. Nelson); Kate Smith (Herself); Frances Langford (Cafe Singer); Gertrude Niesen (Singer); Ronald Reagan (Johnny Jones); Joe Louis (Himself); Julie

Oshins (Ollie Twardofsky) Alan Anderson, Ezra Stone, Tom D'Andrea, James Burrell, Ross Elliott, Alan Manson, John Prince Mendes, Earl Oxford, Robert Shanley, Philip Truex, James MacColl, Ralph Magelssen, Tileston Perry, Joe Cook, Jr., Larry Weeks, The Allon Trio [Louis Bednarcik, Angelo Buono, Gene Erbisto] (Soldiers); Robert Shenley (Ted Nelson); Herbert Anderson (Danny Davidson); Sergeant Fisher (Blake Nelson); Victor Moore, Ernest Truex (Fathers of Soldiers); Jackie Brown (Mike Nelson); Patsy Moran (Marie Twardofsky); James Conlin (Doorman); Ilka Gruning (Mrs. Twardofsky); Irving Bacon (Waiter); Murray Alper (Soldier); Pierre Watkin (Stranger); Frank Coghlan, Jr., Dick Crane, Arthur Space, Arthur Foster, Jimmy Butler, Ross Ford, Gayle de Camp, John Daheim, Alan Pomeroy, John Jones (Soldiers at Camp Cook); Henry Jones (Soldier/Singer); Doddles Weaver (Soldier on Cot); Leah Baird (Old Timer's Wife); Warner Anderson (Sports Announcer); Jack Young (Franklin D. Roosevelt); Sidney Robin, William Roerich, Dick Bernie, John Draper, Richard Irving, Fred Kelly, Henry J. P. Mandes, Gene Berg, Arthur Steiner, Belmonte Cristiani, Pinkie Mitchell.

On July 4, 1942 the flag waving *This Is the Army* debuted on Broadway. It had a book and music by Irving Berlin and the composer himself appeared in the show, which featured an all-soldier cast. After 113 performances this zealously patriotic musical went on tour (without Berlin). Warner Bros. obtained the rights to the stage musical and allocated $1.4 million to bringing it to the screen in Technicolor. Michael Curtiz, having recently directed YANKEE DOODLE DANDY (1942), *q.v.,* and CASABLANCA (1943, for which Curtiz won an Academy Award), was assigned to direct. The movie grossed $8.5 million in distributors' domestic film rentals, with the profits going to the war effort. Many of those involved in the making of this motion picture donated their salaries to the Army Relief Fund.

In 1917 New York, Ziegfeld Follies dancing star Jerry Jones (George Murphy) is drafted. While in basic training at Camp Upton, Jerry encounters musician Eddie Dibble (Charles Butterworth), East Side fruit peddler Maxie Twardofsky (George Tobias), and gruff but good-hearted top sergeant McGee (Alan Hale). Commanding officer Major Davidson (Stanley Ridges) permits a soldier show to be produced, with Jerry in charge. The production is called *Yip, Yip, Yaphank* and is a huge hit on Broadway. After its run the cast goes overseas, and Jerry receives a leg injury in the front lines. After the Armistice the men return to America and to civilian life. When the Second World War breaks out, Jerry is now a theatrical producer, with his son Johnny (Ronald Reagan) as his assistant. Maxie now owns a posh fruit emporium, with his son Ollie (Julie Oshins, repeating his Broadway role) as his helper. Eddie now operates a music store, assisted by his daughter Eileen (Joan Leslie). Johnny and Eileen are engaged to marry. Both Johnny and Ollie enlist and find themselves at Camp Upton with McGee as their sergeant. The alumni of *Yip, Yip, Yaphank* come to visit their offspring and convince the new commanding officer to allow the men to stage a show. The new production is called *This Is the Army.* With Jerry as his consultant, Johnny is placed in charge of the show. After a tremendous reception on Broadway a nationwide tour is organized. During the engagement in Washington, Johnny and Eileen are married in the theatre alley, with Jerry as their best man.

Running two hours, THIS IS THE ARMY—when not trapped by its plot of convenience—is a delightful musical romp which highlights music of both war eras. The highlight of this movie is the appearance of Kate Smith (in a radio broadcast studio setting) singing "God Bless America," the Berlin composition she introduced on radio in 1938 and which she turned into a second (unofficial) national anthem. Other musical treats include Irving Berlin* croaking "Oh, How I Hate to Get Up in the Morning," Alan Hale and company in drag, performing "Ladies of the Chorus," Gertrude Niesen singing "Your Country and My Country," Frances Langford's rendition of "What Does He Look Like?" (the only new number Berlin wrote for this movie), and the all-black production number, "That's What the Well-Dressed Man in Harlem Will Wear" (which included heavyweight boxing champion Joe Louis). Actually, the last portion of this film is a staging of the music from the stage production of THIS IS THE ARMY, done by an all-soldier cast, although the star of the Broadway production, Ezra Stone, had his scenes cut from the final release print.

Variety (over)enthused, "After the history of World War II is written, the Warner Bros. filmization will stand out like the Empire State Building amidst the many other highlights in the motion picture industry's contributions to the home front and war front. It's that kind of an all-embracing job."

THIS IS THE ARMY grossed $8,301,000 in distributors' domestic film rentals. The film received an Academy Award for

---

*Of his "singing" in THIS IS THE ARMY, composer Berlin enjoyed relating the story that when a member of the studio crew heard him recording the selection for the soundtrack, he turned to a colleague and said, "If the guy who wrote *this* song could hear the way this guy is singing it, he'd turn over in his grave!"

Best Scoring of a Musical Picture. It received Oscar nominations for Best Interior Decoration—Color and Best Sound.

Today THIS IS THE ARMY is one of the most widely seen of World War II-era musicals because it has become a public domain picture and has many TV screenings as well as various videocassette releases.

THREE LITTLE GIRLS IN BLUE (20th Century-Fox, 1946) Color 90 minutes.

Producer, Mack Gordon; director, H. Bruce Humberstone; based on the play *Three Blind Mice* by Stephen Powys; adaptors, Brown Holmes, Lynn Starling, Robert Ellis, Helen Logan; screenplay, Valentine Davis; art directors, Lyle Wheeler, Joseph C. Wright; set decorators, Thomas Little, Walter M. Scott; costumes, Bonnie Cashin; music director, Alfred Newman; vocal arranger, Charles Henderson; orchestrators, Maurice de Packh, Edward Powell; choreographers, Seymour Felix, Babe Pearce; color consultants, Natalie Kalmus, Richard Mueller; assistant director, Henry Weinberger; sound, E. Clayton Ward, Roger Heman; special camera effects, Fred Sersen; camera, Ernest Palmer; editor, Barbara McLean.

Songs: "Three Little Girls in Blue," "You Make Me Feel So Young," "On the Boardwalk in Atlantic City," "Somewhere in the Night," "I Feel Like Mike," "A Farmer's Life Is a Very Merry Life," "Oh, My Love," "Always a Lady" (Josef Myrow, Gordon); "If You Can't Get a Girl in the Summertime" (Bert Kalmar, Harry Tierney).

June Haver (Pam); George Montgomery (Van Damm Smith); Vivian Blaine (Liz); Celeste Holm (Miriam); Vera-Ellen (Myra); Frank Latimore (Steve); Charles Smith (Mike); Charles Halton (Hoskins); Ruby Dandridge (Mammy); Thurston Hall (Colonel); Clinton Rosemond (Ben); William Forrest, Jr. (Head Clerk); Theresa Harris (Maid); Eddie Acuff (Josh); Al Murphy (Bartender); Robert Neury (Headwaiter); Coleen Gray (Girl); Robert "Smoky" Whitfield (Sam); Jesse Graves (Headwaiter); Don Garner (Boy on Beach); Carol Stewart (Singing Voice of Myra); Ben Gage (Singing Voice of Van Damm Smith); Del Porter (Singing Voice of Mike).

Having been made as a comedy in 1938 called THREE BLIND MICE and as the 1941 musical MOON OVER MIAMI (*q.v.*), Stephen Powys' play *Three Blind Mice* (1938) was dusted off and lensed for a third time in Technicolor as THREE LITTLE GIRLS IN BLUE, with a music score by Mack Gordon (who also made his debut as a producer with this musical) and Josef Myrow. The film underwent a lengthy production schedule because of the miscasting

Vera-Ellen, June Haver and Vivian Blaine in THREE LITTLE GIRLS IN BLUE (1946).

of its leads and the inability of director H. Bruce Humberstone to gel the cast and plotline into a workable unit. Today the musical is best remembered as the film debut of sparkling Celeste Holm, who made such a hit on Broadway as Ado Annie in *Oklahoma!*

In 1905, three sisters, Pam (June Haver), Liz (Vivian Blaine) and Myra (Vera-Ellen) come into a small inheritance ($3,000) and leave their farm for the excitement of Atlantic City. They are intent on finding millionaire spouses. Pam pretends to be a wealthy woman, with her sisters serving as part of her entourage. Once they are settled in their expensive suite at a swank hotel, Pam is romanced by both Van Damm Smith (George Montgomery) and Steve (Frank Latimore), while Myra is courted by bellboy Mike (Charles Smith). Pam decides on Smith as her husband-to-be and confesses the truth about her pedigree to him. He, in turn, admits he is penniless and that he was hoping to marry a wealthy woman. Pam insists she still wants to wed him, but he now refuses. Later, Pam accepts Steve's marriage offer and they depart for a visit to his Maryland estate. There Steve's sister Miriam (Celeste Holm) realizes that Pam still loves Van Damm. She invites him to the house, hoping nature and her prodding help will solve matters. By now the aristocratic Steve has fallen in love with Myra and is pleased to see that Pam has found love with Van Damm. To everyone's surprise, Myra announces she has already married her bellboy beau, Mike.

Despite the presence of several dubbers to handle the vocals for the several non-singing cast members, THREE LITTLE GIRLS IN BLUE has its pleasing moments. June Haver, Vivian Blaine and Vera-Ellen sang "A Farmer's Life Is a Very Merry Life," "On the Boardwalk at Atlantic City" and the title tune. Blaine (20th Century-Fox's strawberry blonde star and, like June Haver, a backup for the studio's top musical comedy star Betty Grable) handled "Somewhere in the Night." Vera-Ellen did "I Feel Like Mike" and dueted with Charles Smith on "You Make Me Feel So Young" (a dream ballet which allowed Vera-Ellen to dance). Celeste Holm scored well kidding "Always a Lady."

Variety termed the period outing "Pleasant musical filmfare with extra value of color. . . . It's a good first try (for producer Mack Gordon), making excellent use of stock musical ingredients for general entertainment."

In 1953 20th Century-Fox filmed the property for the fourth time as the CinemaScope color comedy, HOW TO MARRY A MILLIONAIRE, starring Betty Grable, Marilyn Monroe and Lauren Bacall. The locale was now changed to New York City.

THREE LITTLE WORDS (Metro-Goldwyn-Mayer, 1950) Color 102 minutes.

Producer, Jack Cummings; director, Richard Thorpe; based on the lives and songs of Bert Kalmar, Harry Ruby; screenplay, George Wells; art directors, Cedric Gibbons, Urie McCleary; set decorators, Edwin B. Willis, Arthur Krams; costumes, Helen Rose; makeup, Jack Dawn, Eddie Polo; music director, Andre Previn; orchestrator, Leo Arnaud; choreographer, Hermes Pan; color consultants, Henri Jaffa, James Gooch; assistant director, Bert Glazer; technical advisor, Harry Ruby; sound, Douglas Shearer, Ralph Pender; camera, Harry Jackson; editor, Ben Lewis.

Songs: "I Wanna Be Loved By You," "Who's Sorry Now?" "Three Little Words," "I Love You So Much," "She's Mine, All Mine," "So Long, Oo-Long," "Hooray for Captain Spaulding," "Up in the Clouds," "All Alone Monday," "Thinking of You," "Mr. and Mrs. Hoofer at Home" (Bert Kalmar, Harry Ruby); "Where Did You Get That Girl?" (Kalmar, Harry Ruby, Harry Puck); "My Sunny Tennessee" (Kalmar, Harry Ruby, Herman Ruby); "Come on Papa" (Harry Ruby, Edgar Leslie); "You Are My Lucky Star" (Arthur Freed, Nacio Herb Brown).

Fred Astaire (Bert Kalmar); Red Skelton (Harry Ruby); Vera-Ellen (Jessie Brown Kalmar); Arlene Dahl (Eileen Percy); Keenan Wynn (Charlie Kope); Gale Robbins (Terry Lordel); Gloria DeHaven (Mrs. Carter DeHaven); Phil Regan (Himself); Harry Shannon (Clanahan); Debbie Reynolds (Helen Kane); Paul Harvey (Al Masters); Carleton Carpenter (Dan Healy); George Metkovich (Al Schact); Harry Mendoza (Mendoza the Great); Billy Gray (Boy); Pat Flaherty (Coach); Pierre Watkin (Philip Goodman); Syd Saylor (Barker); Elzie Emanuel (Black Boy); Sherry Hall (Pianist); Pat Williams (Assistant); Charles Wagenheim (Waiter); Tony Taylor (Kid); Phyllis Kennedy (Mother); Donald Kerr (Stage Manager); Beverly Michaels (Francesca Ladovan); Bert Davidson, William Tannen (Photographers); George Sherwood (Director); Harry Barris (Guest Piano Player); Alex Gerry (Marty Collister); Harry Ruby (Baseball Player); Helen Kane (Singing Voice of Helen Kane); Anita Ellis (Singing Voice of Jessie Brown Kalmar).

MGM continued its penchant for making glossy and superficial biopics of famous composers with THREE LITTLE WORDS, about Bert Kalmar (1884–1947) and Harry Ruby (1895–1974), who were prolific but not highly regarded tunesmiths. This film, however, went against all odds and proved to be a highly satisfying musical, both for its songs and for Fred Astaire and Vera-Ellen's dancing. In addition, Debbie Reynolds received her first taste of public adulation for her playing Helen "Boop-Boop-a-Doop" Kane, although the latter supplied her own vocal on her most famous Kalmar-Ruby melody, "I Wanna Be Loved By You."

Bert Kalmar (Fred Astaire) begins his career as a dancer partnered with Jessie Brown (Vera-Ellen). She is in love with him, but he is preoccupied with his career. Kalmar's passion is his love of magic and while he is performing his tricks on stage, his act is ruined by stagehand Harry Ruby (Red Skelton), the latter an amateur songwriter and a devout baseball fan and player. With his career as a magician aborted, Bert returns to dancing with Jessie. However, a knee injury soon forces him to temporarily retire. Instead of getting married (as Jessie hopes), Kalmar decides to team with Ruby in writing songs. Jessie goes off on a vaudeville tour on her own. Kalmar and Ruby become successful, but Bert misses Jessie. Ruby intervenes and brings the two together and they are married. Jessie retires from the stage and devotes herself to domestic life and to refereeing the feuds between Bert and Harry, who are so different in temperament and interests. She and Bert also work at protecting Harry from the assortment of predatory females he dates, including entertainer Terry Lordel (Gale Robbins). Along the way Harry and Bert, guided by their manager (Keenan Wynn), meet showgirl Helen Kane (Debbie Reynolds), who popularizes their tune "I Wanna Be Loved By You" by adding her own "boop-boop-a-doop" styling to the lyrics. Meanwhile, Harry meets young actress Eileen Percy (Arlene Dahl) and they soon wed. The songwriting team find great success on Broadway and in Hollywood, but they break apart over a minor matter. Eventually their wives manipulates their spouses into a reunion.

Richard Thorpe, best known for robust action pictures, deftly directed THREE LITTLE WORDS into what the *New York Times* termed "A grand musical, well-nigh flawless and for several reasons. First and last is Fred Astaire, superbly teamed on the hoof with the nimble, lovely Vera-Ellen and extraordinarily fine on his own, but splendidly convincing and warm in personifying the career of Bert Kalmar. . . . An excellent, uncluttered script by George Wells recounts it smoothly. . . ."

Fred Astaire and Vera-Ellen (whose singing voice was dubbed by Anita Ellis) had an outstanding pantomime dance number ("Mr and Mrs. Hoofer") about the home life of two married dancers. Among the Kalmar-Ruby songs recreated on film were Astaire singing "Three Little Words," Astaire and Red Skelton dueting on "My Sunny Tennessee," "So Long, Oo-Long," and "Nevertheless" with Anita Ellis. She also soloed on "Thinking of You," while she and Astaire dueted on "Where Did You Get That Girl?" Arlene Dahl sang "I Love You So Much," Gale Robbins sang "All Alone Monday," and Gloria DeHaven (playing her mother, Mrs. Carter DeHaven) sang "Who's Sorry Now?"

To be noted in the film is the presence of songwriter Harry Ruby, playing a baseball player. Irish tenor Phil Regan played himself. Red Skelton proved that when he was restrained he could be a very effective entertainer.

THREE LITTLE WORDS received an Oscar nomination for Best Scoring of a Musical Picture but lost to ANNIE GET YOUR GUN (*q.v.*).

Fred Astaire and Vera-Ellen would reunite for THE BELLE OF NEW YORK (1952). Debbie Reynolds, who shared her "I Wanna Be Loved By You" number with Carleton Carpenter in THREE LITTLE WORDS, was rematched with him for MGM's TWO WEEKS WITH LOVE (1950), in which they performed the near-classic novelty tune, "Aba Dabba Honeymoon."

THREE SMART GIRLS (Universal, 1937) 86 minutes.

Executive producer, Charles R. Rogers; producer, Joseph Pasternak; director, Henry Koster; story, Adele Comandini; screenplay, Comandini, Austin Parker; art director/costumes, John

Harkrider; music director, Charles Previn; camera, Joseph Valentine; editor, Ted J. Kent.

Songs: "My Heart Is Singing," "Someone to Care for Me" (Gus Kahn, Walter Jurmann, Bronislau Kaper); "Il Bacio" (Luigi Arditi).

Deanna Durbin (Penny Craig); Binnie Barnes (Donna Lyons); Alice Brady (Mrs. Lyons); Ray Milland (Lord Michael Stuart); Charles Winninger (Judson Craig); Mischa Auer (Count Arisztid); Nan Grey (Joan Craig); Barbara Read (Kay Craig); Ernest Cossart (Binns, the Butler); Hobart Cavanaugh (Wilbur Lamb); John King (Bill Evans); Lucile Watson (Trudel); Nella Walker (Dorothy Craig); Bud Flanagan [Dennis O'Keefe] (Club Extra); Gladden James (Waiter); Wade Boteler, John Hamilton (Sergeants); Lane Chandler (Cop); Charles Coleman (Butler); Franklin Pangborn (Jeweler); Albert Conti (Count's Friend); and Selmer Jackson.

See: THREE SMART GIRLS GROW UP (essay).

THREE SMART GIRLS GROW UP (Universal, 1939) 90 minutes.

Producer, Joe Pasternak; director, Henry Koster; screenplay, Bruce Manning, Felix Jackson; costumes, Vera West; music director, Charles Previn; camera, Joe Valentine, editor, Ted J. Kent.

Songs: "Because" (Edward Teschemacher, Guy D'Hardelot); "The Last Rose of Summer" (Thomas Moore, Richard Alfred Milliken); "La Capinera"; "Invitation to the Dance."

Deanna Durbin (Penny "Mouse" Craig); Charles Winninger (Judson Craig); Nan Grey (Joan Craig); Helen Parrish (Kay Craig); Robert Cummings (Harry Loren); William Lundigan (Richard Watkins); Ernest Cossart (Binns, the Butler); Nella Walker (Mrs. Dorothy Craig); Felix Bressart (Penny's Music Teacher).

Canadian-born Deanna Durbin became one of the most popular stars on the screen, at age sixteen, when starred in Universal's THREE SMART GIRLS, her feature movie debut. The picture is credited with saving Universal from financial disaster and it began a successful association involving producer Joe Pasternak, director Henry Koster and the teenage star, who is also credited with reviving the popularity of classical music among young people.

Three sisters, young Penny (Deanna Durbin), Joan (Nan Grey) and Kay (Barbara Read), are determined to see their estranged parents, Dorothy (Nella Walker) and Judson Craig (Charles Winninger) reconciled. Trouble arises, however, when congenial Judson is chased by gold digger Donna Lyons (Binnie Barnes) and her grasping mother (Alice Brady). The girls devise a plan to get rid of Donna and her mother. The scheme involves an English lord (Ray Milland) and an impoverished Hungarian count (Mischa

Auer). Thanks to the ingenuity of Penny, it all works out and Dorothy and Judson are reunited.

Regarding the screen's newest Miss Fix-It, the *New York Times* lauded this young soprano: ". . . [She] carols most sweetly in an immature, but surprisingly well trained voice. Her notes are rounded, velvety and bell-like; the manner of her rendition is agreeably artless; she has, besides, an ingratiating impudence which peppers her performance and makes it mischievously natural." In the production, Durbin sang "Il Bacio," "Someone to Care for Me" and "My Heart Is Singing," all of which she waxed for Decca Records. *Variety* opined that the modestly budgeted film ". . . has that rare quality of making an audience feel better for having seen it." It made Deanna Durbin an overnight star.

By 1939 Deanna Durbin was firmly established as a major star, her chief rival being MGM's Judy Garland. While the former specialized in classical songs, the latter concentrated on singing "hot," much as they had done in their one celluloid excursion together, the MGM short subject, EVERY SUNDAY (1936). In the year that Judy Garland starred in THE WIZARD OF OZ and BABES IN ARMS, *qq.v.,* at plush Metro-Goldwyn-Mayer, Durbin was headlined in a sequel to THREE SMART GIRLS entitled THREE SMART GIRLS GROW UP. In the interim the dulcet-toned actress had appeared in ONE HUNDRED MEN AND A GIRL (1937), *q.v.,* MAD ABOUT MUSIC (1938), *q.v.,* and THAT CERTAIN AGE (1938), all of which solidified her screen popularity.

In THREE SMART GIRLS GROW UP, youngest sister Penny (Deanna Durbin)—who is also called "Mouse"—wants to help her sisters Joan (Nan Grey) and Kay (Helen Parrish) find romance. She steps in when she discovers that Joan is entranced with Richard Watkins (William Lundigan), who really adores Kay. Mrs. Craig (Nella Walker) is too inured to Penny's non-stop outpourings to pay attention, and portly Mr. Craig (Charles Winninger) is too preoccupied with his brokerage business. Penny decides to take matters into her own hands. On the advice of the Craigs' butler (Ernest Cossart), she searches for a candidate to win Kay's heart. Her victim is young musician Harry Loren (Robert Cummings), whom Penny meets in the studio next to hers where she is taking singing lessons. Introduced into the Craig household, Loren is attracted to Joan and not Kay, as Penny had planned. When Miss Fix-It becomes upset, the family thinks it is because she loves Harry. After much rushing about, and the intervention of Mr. Craig, matters are righted. Joan and Harry marry, as do Richard and Kay.

Variety termed the well-mounted picture a "warm, thoroughly delightful family entertainment." In it Deanna Durbin sang "The Last Rose of Summer," "La Capiera," "Invitation to the Dance" and "Because." The latter song was to become her largest-selling Decca recording.

Still a third entry in the Penny Craig saga came from Universal in 1943 when Deanna Durbin played the part again in the drama HERS TO HOLD, with Charles Winninger and Nella Walker again playing her parents. Here adult Penny falls in love with a bomber pilot (Joseph Cotten). It contained footage, used in the plot as home movies, from the previous features, and here Deanna sang "Begin the Beguine," "Say a Prayer for the Boys Over There," "The Kashmiri Song," and "Seguidilla" from Georges Bizet's opera, *Carmen.*

TILL THE CLOUDS ROLL BY (Metro-Goldwyn-Mayer, 1946) Color 120 minutes.

Producer, Arthur Freed; directors, Richard Whorf, (uncredited): George Sidney, Vincente Minnelli; based on the life and music of Jerome Kern; story, Guy Bolton; adaptor, George Wells; screenplay, Myles Connolly, Jean Holloway, (uncredited) Fred F. Finklehoffe. John Lee Mahin, Lemuel Ayers, Hans Willheim; art directors, Cedric Gibbons, Daniel B. Cathcart; set decorators, Edwin B. Willis, Richard Pefferle; costume supervisor, Irene; women's costumes, Helen Rose; men's costumes, Valles; makeup, Jack Dawn; music director, Lennie Hayton; orchestrator, Conrad Salinger; vocal arranger, Kay Thompson; choreographer, Robert Alton; assistant director, Wally Worsley; color consultants, Natalie Kalmus, Henri Jaffa; sound supervisor, Douglas Shearer; montage, Peter Ballbusch; camera, Harry Stradling, George J. Folsey; editor, Albert Akst.

Songs: "Who Cares If My Boat Goes Upstream," "Life Upon the Wicked Stage," "Can't Help Lovin' Dat Man," "Ol' Man River," "Make Believe," "Who?" "Sunny," "One More Dance," "The Last Time I Saw Paris," "All the Things You Are," "Why Was I Born?" (Jerome Kern, Oscar Hammerstein, II); "Ka-lu-a" (Kern, Anne Caldwell); "How'd You Like to Spoon with Me?" (Kern, Ed Laska); "They Didn't Believe Me" (Kern, Herbert Reynolds); "Till the Clouds Roll By" (Kern, P. G. Wodehouse, Guy Bolton); "Leave It to Jane," "Cleopatterer," "Land Where the Good Songs Go" (Kern-Wodehouse); "Look for the Silver Lining" (Kern, Buddy G. DeSylva); "Try to Forget," "Yesterdays" (Kern, Otto Harbach); "Long Ago (and Far Away)" (Kern, George Gershwin); "A Fine Romance" (Kern, Dorothy Fields); "The Touch of Your Hand,"

"Siren's Song," "Why Do I Love You," "Twas Not So Long," "Mark Twain Suite," "Go Little Boat," "Sun Shines Brighter," "La Jeunne Fille," "Passionate Pilgrim," "You Never Knew about Me," "Pal Like You," "You Are Love," "Crickets Are Calling," "In the Egern of the Tegern Sea," "I Dream Too Much," entr'acte of *Cat and the Fiddle,* "Don't Ever Leave Me," "Smoke Gets in Your Eyes" (Kern and various composers); "I Won't Dance" (Harbach, Fields).

Robert Walker (Jerome Kern); Judy Garland (Marilyn Miller); Lucille Bremer (Sally); Joan Wells (Sally as a Girl); Van Heflin (James I. Hessler); Paul Langton (Oscar Hammerstein, II); Dorothy Patrick (Mrs. Jerome Kern); Mary Nash (Mrs. Muller); Harry Hayden (Charles Frohman); Paul Maxey (Victor Herbert); Rex Evans (Cecil Keller); William "Bill" Phillips (Hennessey); Dinah Shore (Julie Sanderson); Van Johnson (Band Leader); June Allyson, Angela Lansbury, Ray McDonald (Guest Performers); Maurice Kelly, Cyd Charisse, Gower Champion (Dance Specialties); Ray Teal (Orchestra Conductor); Wilde Twins (Specialty); *Showboat Number:* William Halligan (Captain Andy); Tony Martin (Gaylord Ravenal); Kathryn Grayson (Magnolia); Virginia O'Brien (Ellie); Lena Horne (Julie); Caleb Peterson (Joe); Bruce Cowling (Steve); Frank Sinatra, Johnny Johnston (Finale); Herschel Graham, Fred Hueston, Dick Earle, Larry Steers, Reed Howes, Hazard Newsberry, Ed Elby, Lee Smith, Larry Williams, James Plato, Leonard Mellen, James Darrell, Tony Merlo, Charles Madrin, Charles Griffin (Opening Night Critics); Byron Foulger (Charles Frohman's Secretary); Lee Phelps, Ralph Dunn (Moving Men); Lucille Casey, Mary Jane French, Beryl McCutcheon, Alice Wallace, Irene Vernon, Gloria Joy Arden, Mickey Malloy, Alma Carroll, Wesley Brent (Showgirls); George Peters, Harry Denny, Bob McLean, Frank McClure, George Murray, John Alban, Lee Bennett (Stage Door Johnnies); Jean Andren (Secretary); John Albright (Call Boy); Margaret Bert (Maid); Herbert Heywood (Stagehand); Thomas Louden (Rural Postman); Ann Codee (Miss Laroche); James Finlayson (Candy Vendor); Elspeth Dudgeon, Margaret Bert (Maids); Lilyan Irene (Barmaid); Tom Stevenson (Genius); Penny Parker (Punch and Judy Operator); Robert Emmett O'Connor (Clerk); Stanley Andrews (Doctor); Russell Hicks (Motion Picture Producer); William Forrest (Motion Picture Director); Arnaut Brothers (Bird Act); Jim Grey, Douglas Wright (Bull Clown); Louis Manley (Swivel Chair Lady); Don Wayson, Howard Mitchell (Detectives); Sally Forrest, Mary Hatcher (Chorus Girls); Esther Williams (Movie Star Signing Autographs at Los Angeles Train Station).

To disguise a bland plotline, producer Arthur Freed clogged

TILL THE CLOUDS ROLL BY, the biopic of composer Jerome Kern (1885–1945), with an almost endless series of musical interludes by MGM contract stars. Surprisingly, none of the numbers were done in period detail. Still these musical diversions were the highlight of the top-heavy feature because, as James Agee wrote in *The Nation,* "The story is enough of the life and not very hard times of the late Jerome Kern to make you want either not to hear any of it at all or to get the real story instead. . . ." The posh color feature, however, did gross $6,724,000 in its initial release (based on a production cost of $2,841,608, with the splashy finale alone costing $170,174). Any resemblances between the screen chronicle and the real life of Jerome Kern were mostly coincidental; the same can be said of casting lanky, tall, amiable Robert Walker to play the short, finicky, inhibited Kern.

TILL THE CLOUDS ROLL BY opens with the December 1927 Broadway bow of *Show Boat* by Jerome Kern (Robert Walker). It flashes back to several years earlier. Kern, a young songwriter, comes to veteran music arranger James Hessler (Van Heflin) for assistance. The two soon become good friends. Because Kern is convinced that Broadway producers are only interested in shows imported from England, he goes to London, where he manages to sell one of his compositions to a local producer. It becomes a hit and others follow. Before long Broadway producer Charles Frohman (Harry Hayden) hears about Kern across the ocean and commissions him to write the music for a new Broadway show. Meanwhile, Kern falls in love with a young English woman named Eva Leale (Dorothy Patrick). After a trip to New York about his music, Kern returns to England to wed Eva. Years pass. Hessler's daughter Sally (Lucille Bremer) is promised the opportunity to introduce one of Kern's songs in his next musical. However, the producer of the show insists that Marilyn Miller (Judy Garland) be given the number. The heartbroken Sally runs away, while the long-infirm Hessler dies. It now becomes an obsession with Kern to find Sally and he permits his songwriting career to falter. He finally locates Sally in a Memphis club where she explains that she intends to become a show business success on her own, and says that she has always appreciated his kindness. Now at ease over Sally's future, Kern returns to music writing and prepares the score for *Show Boat.*

The parade of tunes and their various performers are the highlights of the frequently mushy TILL THE CLOUDS ROLL BY. While Richard Whorf (replacing Busby Berkeley) directed the movie, Judy Garland (as Marilyn Miller) was directed in her scenes by her then husband Vincente Minnelli, and she does especially

June Allyson and Ray McDonald in TILL THE CLOUDS ROLL BY (1946).

well by "Look for the Silver Lining" (done in a kitchen setting with a besmudged, dishwashing Garland singing from behind a pile of dishes) and "Who?" (handled in a circus setting). Other attention-getters include Angela Lansbury singing the musical hall number, "How'd You Like to Spoon with Me?"; an effervescent and very cute June Allyson giving bubbly renditions of "Cleopatterer" and "Leave It to Jane"; and the stylish recreation of several *Show Boat* sequences. From that Kern classic comes Tony Martin singing "Who Cares If My Boat Goes Upstream" and Martin and Kathryn Grayson (who played Magnolia in MGM's 1951 production of SHOW BOAT [*q.v.*]) dueting on "Make Believe." Also well done (if too dreamy) from this capsule show are Lena Horne as the tragic Julie singing "Can't Help Lovin' Dat Man," Virginia O'Brien's humorous deadpan rendering of "Life Upon the Wicked Stage," and Caleb Peterson's touching "Ol' Man River." Far less appealing was Frank Sinatra, in a white tuxedo, doing "Ol' Man River" in a concert sequence (directed by George Sidney), and almost as embarrassing were Van Johnson and Lucille Bremer hoofing to "I Won't Dance."* Two young MGM contractees spotted in the movie were Gower Champion and Cyd Charisse, dancing to "Smoke Gets in Your Eyes." To be noted in one quick unbilled cameo is MGM swimming star Esther Williams, seen as a movie star at a Los Angeles train station signing autographs. Cut from the final release print were Lena Horne singing "Bill," Kathryn Grayson performing "I've Told Every Little Star," and Judy Garland doing "D'Ye Love Me?"

TILL THE CLOUDS ROLL BY was the first soundtrack album (on 78 rpm records) to be issued by MGM Records in 1946.

TIN PAN ALLEY (20th Century-Fox, 1940) 92 minutes.

Associate producer, Kenneth MacGowan; director, Walter Lang; story, Pamela Harris; screenplay, Robert Ellis, Helen Logan; art directors, Richard Day, Joseph C. Wright; set decorator, Thomas Little; costumes, Travis Banton; music director, Alfred Newman; choreographer, Seymour Felix; sound, Eugene Grossman, Roger Heman; camera, Leon Shamroy; editor, Walter Thompson.

Songs: "Sheik of Araby" (Harry B. Smith, Francis Wheeler, Ted Snyder); "You Say the Sweetest Things, Baby" (Mack Gordon, Harry Warren); "America, I Love You" (Edgar Leslie, Archie Gottler); "Goodbye Broadway, Hello France" (Francis Riesner, Benny Davis, Billy Baskette); "K-K-K-Katy" (Geoffrey O'Hara); "On Moonlight Bay" (Edward Madden, Percy Wenrich); "Honeysuckle Rose" (Andy Razaf, Thomas "Fats" Waller); "Moonlight and Roses" (Ben Black, Neil Moret, Edwin H. Lemare).

Alice Faye (Katie Blane); Betty Grable (Lily Blane); Jack Oakie (Harry Calhoun); John Payne (Skeets Harrigan); Allen Jenkins (Sergeant Casey); Esther Ralston (Nora Bayes); Harold Nicholas, Fayard Nicholas (Dance Specialty); Ben Carter (Boy); John Loder (Reggie Carstairs); Elisha Cook, Jr. (Joe Cadd); Fred Keating (Harvey Raymond); Billy Gilbert (Sheik); Lillian Porter (Telephone Operator); Brian Sisters (Specialty); Robert Brothers (Specialty); Princess Vanessa Ammon (Specialty); Tyler Brooke (Bert Melville); Hal K. Dawson (Hotel Clerk); William B.

*In *Hollywood Musicals*, 1981, Ted Sennett pointed out about the finale of TILL THE CLOUDS ROLL BY, "Chorus girls emerge, and following a portentous drum roll, the audience beholds Frank Sinatra . . . as he sings a perfectly enunciated version of 'Ol' Man River.' Nobody seems to notice the disparity between his elegant appearance and Oscar Hammerstein's despairing lyrics. . . . It is one of the truly insensitive musical numbers in film history, and it climaxes a movie that has only one true virtue: it leaves the music of Jerome Kern undiminished."

Davidson (Hotel Manager); Lionel Pape (Lord Stanley); Billy Bevan (Doorman); Dewey Robinson (Dumb Guy); Robert Emmett Keane (Manager); John Sheehan (Announcer); George Watts (Mike Buckner); Jack Roper (Nick Palerno); James Flavin (Sergeant); Franklyn Farnum (Man in Audience); Harry Strang (Doughboy).

The first of a quartet of features to co-star Alice Faye with John Payne, TIN PAN ALLEY was a beautiful musical recreation of the pre-World War I era, especially with its well-executed production numbers and overall period costuming. *Variety* reported, "TIN PAN ALLEY unfolds at a consistently fast clip throughout and is provided with top A production mounting. Photography by Leon Shamroy is of highest standard." TIN PAN ALLEY had originally been conceived of as a vehicle for Alice Faye, Tyrone Power and Don Ameche, the stars of ALEXANDER'S RAGTIME BAND (1938), *q.v.* The role for Betty Grable was introduced into the scenario after she proved such a sensation in DOWN ARGENTINE WAY (1940), *q.v.*

Songwriters Harry Calhoun (Jack Oakie) and Skeets Harrigan (John Payne) are down to their last dollar and about to be evicted from their lodgings. At the last moment they convince the singing sister act of Katie (Alice Faye) and Lily Blane (Betty Grable) to introduce their new song. The girls almost lose their jobs, but thankfully the song is a success and Katie helps the boys enter the song publishing business by purchasing a tune by Joe Cadd (Elisha Cook, Jr.) which also becomes a big hit. When Lily goes into a new show, Katie gives up the stage to work for Harry and Skeets, successfully plugging their new songs. For a time the trio prospers but Katie becomes upset with Skeets' absorption in the business and his willingness to use everyone to succeed. In a peak of despair, she goes to London to team up again with Lily after Harry gives a sensational new number to Nora Bayes (Esther Ralston) to introduce at a benefit performance. After that the tunesmiths' business goes downhill and they enlist in the Army when World War I breaks out. They are sent to London, where they see Katie and Lily perform on stage. A remorseful Skeets is upset to learn that Katie is engaged to a British lord (John Loder) and leaves the theatre without seeing her. When Katie learns of this, she and Lily, with the help of the understanding nobleman, head for the docks, where the sisters manage to say their goodbyes to the doughboys as they embark for France. When the war is over, Katie and Skeets resume their romance in New York City.

Highlights of TIN PAN ALLEY include the somewhat censored "The Sheik of Araby" production number, which featured a somewhat scantily clad Alice Faye and Betty Grable, with rotund Billy Gilbert as the sheik. Also memorable is the scene near the end of the picture where Jack Oakie falls into the London harbor, resulting in the composition of the song "K-K-K Katy" (part of a running gag about Oakie finding socko lyrics to go with a melody that has been haunting him). Other songs in the movie included "You Say the Sweetest Things" and "America, I Love You" (which Kate Smith popularized on radio and on Columbia Records), plus such standards as "On Moonlight Bay" and "Honeysuckle Rose." Cut from the film was the Faye-Grable-Oakie number, "Get Out and Get Under," performed while the trio are out riding in a car.

Harrison's Reports enthused, "The picture does not depend on music alone to put it over; it has deep human appeal, fine comedy and romance. All this is tied together by a lavish production. The old times and places are reproduced realistically."

TIN PAN ALLEY won an Academy Award for Best Scoring (Alfred Newman). It was remade in an updated version by 20th Century-Fox as I'LL GET BY (1951), starring June Haver, William Lundigan and Gloria DeHaven.

TOP HAT (RKO, 1935) 101 minutes.

Producer, Pandro S. Berman; director, Mark Sandrich; based on the play *The Gay Divorcee* by Dwight Taylor, Cole Porter; from the play *The Girl Who Dared* by Alexander Farago, Aladar Laszlo; screenplay, Taylor, Alan Scott; art directors, Van Nest Polglase, Carroll Clark; set decorator, Thomas Little; costumes, Bernard Newman; makeup, Mel Burns; music director, Max Steiner; orchestrator, Edward Powell; choreographers, Fred Astaire, Hermes Pan; special effects, Vernon L. Walker; camera, David Abel, Walker; editor, William Hamilton.

Songs: "No Strings (I'm Fancy Free)," "Isn't This a Lovely Day?" "St. Vitus' Dance," "Top Hat, White Tie and Tails," "Cheek to Cheek," "The Piccolino" (Irving Berlin).

Fred Astaire (Jerry Travers); Ginger Rogers (Dale Tremont); Edward Everett Horton (Horace Hardwick); Helen Broderick (Madge Hardwick); Erik Rhodes (Alberto Beddini); Eric Blore (Bates, the Butler); Lucille Ball (Flower Clerk); Leonard Mudie (Flower Salesman); Donald Meek (Curate); Florence Roberts (Curate's Wife); Edgar Norton (Hotel Manager in London); Gino Corrado (Hotel Manager in Venice); Peter Hobbes (Call Boy); Frank Mills (Lido Waiter); Tom Ricketts (Thackeray Club Waiter); Bud Flanagan [Dennis O'Keefe] (Elevator Passenger); and: Phyllis Coghlan, Tom Costello, Charles Hall, Ben Holmes, John Impolito, Rita Rozelle, Genaro Spagnoli, Nick Thompson.

Probably the most successful and the best remembered screen teaming of Fred Astaire and Ginger Rogers was TOP HAT, which grossed more than $3.2 million at the box-office, making it RKO's most successful musical feature of the 1930s. It also included a highly memorable score by Irving Berlin, including "Cheek to Cheek" and "Isn't This a Lovely Day?" For "The Piccolino" production number, Astaire and Rogers rehearsed for more than 125 hours to bring it to the screen. Few filmgoers seemed to mind that TOP HAT paralleled, very closely indeed, all the ingredients that had made THE GAY DIVORCEE (1934) so popular. Not only was the plot extremely similar, but the new picture had the same producer, director and co-author as the former, besides three of the same supporting cast (Edward Everett Horton, Erik Rhodes and Eric Blore).

American entertainer Jerry Travers (Fred Astaire) is working on the London stage and, while on the street one day, meets pretty American Dale Tremont (Ginger Rogers). He is immediately attracted to her. He follows her all over the city, attempting to win her affections. However, it is all in vain since she thinks he is married to her old friend, Madge Hardwick (Helen Broderick). This is not the case: stuffy Horace Hardwick (Edward Everett Horton) is actually her mate. Meanwhile, Dale is also pursued by hyperactive Italian dress designer Alberto Beddini (Erik Rhodes). Dale eventually succumbs to his courtship. A determined Jerry connives to separate Dale and Alberto on their wedding night in Venice. Later he learns from Horace's butler (Eric Blore) that he (Bates) had been trailing Dale on Horace's orders, and had performed the marriage ceremony pretending to be a minister. With the legalities now resolved, Jerry and Dale marry.

This, the fourth screen teaming of Astaire and Rogers, gave them their best all-around film score. Astaire successfully soloed on "No Strings (I'm Fancy Free)" and "Top Hat, White Tie and Tails" (a near definitive dance number).* He and Ginger danced together in "Cheek to Cheek" and "Isn't This a Lovely Day?" while Rogers sang in the grandiose production number, "The Piccolino," at the Venetian resort, with her and Astaire dancing through and around the hotel setting. Unused in the film were three Berlin numbers:

---

*Roy Hemming (*The Melody Lingers On,* 1986) argues, "One other song in TOP HAT has been virtually forgotten over the years—unfairly. . . . It's a delightful elegy to the single life, 'No Strings (I'm Fancy Free)'. . . . It's the song that really sets the plot in motion, when Astaire's dancing wakes up Rogers, sleeping in a room below. But even as a song on its own, it remains a marvelous and refreshing antidote to all those pop songs that equate romance with wedding bells."

"Get Thee Behind Me, Satan," "Wild About You" and "You're the Cause."

Stanley Green (*The Encyclopaedia of the Musical Film,* 1987) judged of TOP HAT, ". . . The movie was raised into Pantheon position in the world of Astaire and Rogers because of the remarkable interplay between the two stars, the imaginative, varied dance routines, the memorable Irving Berlin score, and the stylized, dazzling white art-deco decor, all of which established the tone and spirit of the subsequent movies the team did together."

TOP HAT earned Oscar nominations for Best Picture, Art Direction-Set Decoration, Dance Direction (Hermes Pan) and Best Song ("Cheek to Cheek").

TWENTY MILLION SWEETHEARTS *see* MY DREAM IS YOURS (essay).

UNDER YOUR SPELL (20th Century-Fox, 1936) 62 minutes.

Producer, John Stone; director, Otto Preminger; story, Bernice Mason, Sy Bartlett; screenplay, Frances Hyland, Saul Elkins; costumes, Herschel; music director, Arthur Lange; choreographer, Sammy Lee; camera, Sidney Wagner; editor, Fred Allen.

Songs: "Amigo," "My Little Mule Wagon," "Under Your Spell" (Arthur Schwartz, Howard Dietz); arias from the operas *The Marriage of Figaro* (Wolfgang Amadeus Mozart) and *Faust* (Charles Gounod).

Lawrence Tibbett (Anthony Allen); Wendy Barrie (Cynthia Drexel); Gregory Ratoff (Petroff, the Manager); Arthur Treacher (Botts, the Butler); Gregory Gaye (Count Raul Du Rienne); Berton Churchill (Judge); Jed Prouty (Mr. Twerp); Claudia Coleman (Mrs. Twerp); Charles Richman (Uncle Bob); Madge Bellamy (Miss Stafford); Nora Cecil (School Teacher); Bobby Samarzich (Pupil); Joyce Compton, June Gittelson (Secretaries); Clyde Dilson, Boyd Irwin, John Dilson, Lloyd Whitlock, Frank Sheridan, Edward Mortimer, Sam Blum, Jay Eaton, Scott Mattraw, Harry Stafford (Sponsors); Edward Gargan, Frank Fanning (Detectives); Cedric Stevens (Steward); Creighton Hale, Harry Harvey, Charles Sherlock (Photographers); Edward Cooper (Butler); Lee Phelps, Bruce Mitchell (Bailiffs); Clarence Kolb (Judge); Pierre Watkin (Allen's Lawyer); Theodore Von Eltz (Cynthia's Lawyer); Sherry Hall, Jack Mulhall (Court Clerks); Dink Trout (Small Man); Kate Murray, Mariska Aldrich (Tall Women); Frank Arthur Swales (Man with Glasses); Troy Brown (Porter); Florence Wix (Dowager); George Magrill (Angry Man); Josef Swickard (Amigo); Ann Gillis (Gwendolyn); Robert Dalton (Announcer); Muriel Evans (Governess); Alan Davis (Pilot).

Despite a fabulous singing voice, handsome features, a winning personality and good acting ability, Lawrence Tibbett never caught on as a Hollywood film star. At the beginning of the talking era he made a quartet of features for MGM, including his Oscar-nominated debut in THE ROGUE SONG (1930) and NEW MOON (1930), *qq.v.,* with Grace Moore. In the mid-1930s, after Grace Moore had a runaway hit with ONE NIGHT OF LOVE (1934), *q.v.,* musicals with opera stars were back in vogue. Tibbett signed a two-picture contract with 20th Century-Fox and starred in METROPOLITAN (1935). When that film proved unsuccessful, the studio negotiated to cancel the agreement. However, Tibbett insisted on finishing out his contract. To punish him and to avoid wasting any more money than need be, the studio put him in UNDER YOUR SPELL, a programmer which 20th Century-Fox tossed away on the lower half of a double bill.

Opera singer Anthony Allen (Lawrence Tibbett) is weary from overwork. He longs for a rest. With the aid of his butler Botts (Arthur Treacher), he attempts to hide away from his overbearing manager, Petroff (Gregory Ratoff). He meets society heiress Cynthia Drexel (Wendy Barrie), who soon wants him to perform at a charity show she is hostessing. Anthony abandons her and goes into retreat into the desert. However, she pursues him and the two end up telling their stories before a judge (Clarence Kolb). By now, they realize they are in love.

The *New York Times* observed, "On the most ridiculously romantic or trumped-up occasions, however, his [Tibbett] voice remains the richest, most dramatic, the most beautifully controlled vocal instrument on the contemporary screen. . . . The fact that the Tibbett voice could stand a more studiously thought-out setting will hardly be contested by anyone."

Outside of the title song, which Lawrence Tibbett performed beautifully, the Howard Dietz-Arthur Schwartz score, including "Amigo" and "My Little Mule Wagon," did little for the opera star's screen image.

THE UNSINKABLE MOLLY BROWN (Metro-Goldwyn-Mayer, 1964) Color 128 minutes.

Producer, Lawrence Weingarten; associate producer, Roger Edens; director, Charles Walters; based on the musical play by Meredith Willson, Richard Morris; screenplay, Helen Deutsch; art directors, George W. Davis, Preston Ames; set decorators, Henry

Grace, Hugh Hunt; costumes, Morton Haack; makeup, William Tuttle; music conductor/supervisor, Robert Armbruster; orchestrators, Calvin Jackson, Leo Arnaud, Jack Elliott, Alexander Courage; music arranger, Edens; choreographer, Peter Gennaro; assistant director, Hank Moonjean; sound supervisor, Franklin Milton; sound, Larry Jost; special visual effects, A. Arnold Gillespie, Robert R. Hoag, J. McMillan Johnson; camera, Daniel L. Fapp; editor, Fredric Steinkamp.

Songs: "I Ain't Down Yet," "Colorado Is My Home," "Belly Up to the Bar, Boys," "I'll Never Say No," "Leadville Johnny Brown," "He's My Friend," "I've Already Started," "Up Where the People Are," "Dolce Far Niente" (Meredith Willson).

Debbie Reynolds (Molly Brown); Harve Presnell (Johnny Brown); Ed Begley (Shamus Tobin); Jack Kruschen (Christmas Morgan); Hermione Baddeley (Mrs. Grogan); Vassili Lambrinos (Prince Louis de Laniere); Fred Essler (Baron Karl Ludwig von Ettenburg); Harvey Lembeck (Polak); Lauren Gilbert (Mr. Fitzgerald); Kathryn Card (Mrs. Wadlington); Hayden Rorke (Broderick); Harry Holcombe (Mr. Wadlington); Amy Douglass (Mrs. Fitzgerald); George Mitchell (Monsignor Ryan); Martita Hunt (Grand Duchess Elise Lupovinova); Vaughn Taylor (Mr. Cartwright); Anthony Eustrel (Roberts); Audrey Christie (Mrs. McGraw); Grover Dale (Jam); Brendan Dillon (Murphy); Maria Karnilova (Daphne); Gus Trikonis (Joe); Mary Ann Niles (Dancehall Girl); Anna Lee (Passenger); George Nicholson (Hotchkiss); C. Ramsay Hill (Lord Simon Primdale); Moyna Macgill (Lady Primdale); Pat Benedetto (Count Feranti); Mary Andre (Countess Feranti); Pat Moran (Vicar); Herb Vigran (Spieler); Eleanor Audley (Mrs. Cartwright).

Based on the exploits of Margaret "Molly" Tobin Brown of Denver, Colorado, Meredith Willson's musical *The Unsinkable Molly Brown* bowed on Broadway in the fall of 1960 and ran for 532 performances, with Tammy Grimes in the title role and Harve Presnell as Molly's husband. MGM purchased the rights to film the production, initially intended for Doris Day. However, with the poor reception accorded Day's BILLY ROSE'S JUMBO (1962), *q.v.,* Debbie Reynolds was substituted.

In the Old West, Molly Tobin (Debbie Reynolds) weds prospector Johnny Brown (Harve Presnell) and they strike it rich with the "Little Johnny" mine, worth over $20 million. Socially ambitious, Molly convinces Johnny to move to Denver, Colorado where they are snubbed by society because of their unpolished ways. The two then go to Europe, where the irrepressible Molly makes many friends among royalty. She brings some of them back with her to Denver to show off to the locals who had rebuffed her. Molly and Johnny give a big society ball for the visiting royalty but it turns into a brawl when Johnny's miner pals crash the festivities. Upset, Molly returns to Europe where she is pursued by a prince (Vassili Lambrinos). However, she misses Johnny and returns home on the Titanic. When it sinks, she becomes a hero by taking command of a lifeboat and rescuing passengers. Saved by another ship, Molly is later reunited with Johnny in Denver.

THE UNSINKABLE MOLLY BROWN was a tour-de-force for rambunctious Debbie Reynolds. It provided her with a rowdier, more mature characterization than had her notable role as the backwoods girl in TAMMY AND THE BACHELOR (1957), which had produced a major hit song ("Tammy") for her. The new musical offered her songs like "I Ain't Down Yet," "Belly Up to the Bar, Boys" and "I'll Never Say No," with the bulk of the remaining songs going to baritone Harve Presnell (including "He's My Friend," added for the movie version). One of the bolstering forces of the film was Peter Gennaro's spirited choreography.

The *New York Times* labeled the film, which grossed $8.5 million in distributors' domestic film rentals, "Cheerful, spirited, with the sweet corn-high score from Meredith Willson's Broadway musical, some down-to-earth tomboyish strutting from Debbie Reynolds and fine, manly singing by Harve Presnell. . . . The picture is bountiful and beaming."

THE UNSINKABLE MOLLY BROWN earned Debbie Reynolds an Academy Award nomination for Best Actress, but she lost to Julie Andrews of MARY POPPINS, *q.v.* The picture was also Oscar-nominated for Best Scoring, Cinematography—Color, Art Direction-Set Decoration—Color, Costumes—Color, and Sound.

In 1989 Debbie Reynolds and Harve Presnell reprised their roles from THE UNSINKABLE MOLLY BROWN when the musical was revived in a national stage tour.

THE VAGABOND KING (Paramount, 1930) Color 104 minutes.

Producer, Adolph Zukor; director, Ludwig Berger; based on the novel by R. H. Russell, the play *If I Were King* by Justin Huntly McCarthy and the operetta by William H. Post, Rudolf Friml, Brian Hooker; adaptor/dialogue, Herman J. Mankiewicz; art director, Hans Dreier; wardrobe, Travis Banton; color consultant, Natalie Kalmus; sound, Franklin Hansen; camera, Ray Rennahan; editor, Merrill White.

Songs: "Huguette's Waltz," "Love for Sale," "Love Me Tonight," "Only a Rose," "Some Day," "Song of the Vagabonds,"

"Nocturne" (Rudolph Friml, Brian Hooker); "If I Were King," "King Louie," "Mary Queen of Heaven," "What France Needs" (Leo Robin, Sam Coslow, Newell Chase); "Death March" (Robin, Chase).

Dennis King (François Villon); Jeanette MacDonald (Katherine de Vaucelles); O.P. Heggie (King Louis XI); Lillian Roth (Huguette); Warner Oland (Thibault); Arthur Stone (Oliver, the Barber); Thomas Ricketts (The Astrologer); Lawford Davidson (Tristan); Christian J. Frank (Executioner); Elda Voelkel (Girl); Dorothy Davis, Thora Waverly, Cecile Cameron (Brunettes); Jean Douglas, Eugenia Woodbury, Rae Murray, Blanche Saunders, Francis Waverly (Blondes); Gloria Faith, Theresa Allen, Sue Patterson (Pages).

See: THE VAGABOND KING (1956) (essay).

THE VAGABOND KING (Paramount, 1956) Color 88 minutes.

Producer, Pat Duggan; director, Michael Curtiz; based on the novel by R. H. Russell, the play *If I Were King* by Justin Huntly McCarthy and the operetta by William H. Post, Rudolf Friml, Brian Hooker; screenplay, Ken Englund, Noel Langley; art directors, Hal Pereira, Henry Bumstead; costumes, Mary Grant; music, Victor Young; choreographer, Hanya Holm; special effects, John P. Fulton; camera, Robert Burke; editor, Arthur Schmidt.

Songs: "Some Day," "Huguette's Waltz," "Song of the Vagabonds," "Love Me Tonight" (Rudolph Friml, Brian Hooker); "Vive Le You," "Watch Out for the Devil," "This Same Heart," "Bon Jour," "Comparisons" (Friml, Johnny Burke); "Lord, I'm Glad I Know Thee" (V. Giovane, K. C. Rogan [Friml, Burke]).

Kathryn Grayson (Catherine De Vaucelles); Oreste "Kirkop" (François Villon); Rita Moreno (Huguette); Sir Cedric Hardwicke (Tristan); Walter Hampden (King Louis XI); Leslie Nielsen (Thibault); William Prince (Rene); Jack Lord (Ferrebone); Billy Vine (Jacques); Harry McNaughton (Colin); Florence Sundstrom (Laughing Margot); Lucie Lancaster (Margaret); Raymond Bramley (The Scar); Gregory Morton (General Antoine De Chabannes); Richard Tone (Quicksilver); Ralph Sumpter (Bishop of Paris and Turin); G. Thomas Duggan (Burgundy); Gavin Gordon (Major Domo); Joel Ashley (Duke of Normandy); Ralph Clanton (Duke of Anjou); Gordon Mills (Duke of Bourbon); Vincent Price (Narrator); Sam Schwartz (One Eye); Phyllis Newman (Lulu); Slim Gaut (Jehan "the Wolf"); Albie Gaye (Jeannie); Laura Raynair, Frances Lansing, Jeanette Miller (Ladies in Waiting); Richard Shannon (Sergeant); Larry Pennell (1st Soldier); Nancy Bajer (Blanche); Rita Marie Tanno (Belle); Dolores Starr, David Nillo (Specialty Dancers).

Rudolf Friml's acclaimed operetta, *The Vagabond King,* first appeared on Broadway in the fall of 1925 and ran for 511 performances, with Dennis King starring as romantic poet François Villon. In 1930 Paramount brought the vehicle to the screen with Dennis King repeating his role. He was co-starred with Jeanette MacDonald and Lillian Roth, the latter gaining much deserved attention for her robust performance as tavern wench Huguette. Shot in Technicolor, the production retained several of the Friml melodies, including "Song of the Vagabonds," "Some Day," "Only a Rose" and "Love For Sale." Newell Chase, Leo Robin and Sam Coslow wrote several numbers especially for the picture, including "If I Were King."

In 1463 Paris, the city is under siege from the Burgundians who are revolting against the weak King Louis XI (O.P. Heggie) who will not defend the metropolis. Thibault (Warner Oland), the king's grand marshal, is really a spy for the Burgundians and plans to kill the monarch and his niece Katherine (Jeanette MacDonald). However, the beautiful young maiden is saved by swashbuckling poet François Villon (Dennis King), the leader of the city's vagabonds. Before long, Katherine and Villon have fallen in love. An astrologer (Thomas Ricketts) informs the king that a vagabond will save Paris. Later, the king, in disguise, goes to a tavern and hears Villon mock him in song. He orders the man's arrest, along with that of tavern girl Huguette (Lillian Roth), who loves Villon. The king offers to let Villon take his place for a week before being executed. The poet accepts. Meanwhile, Thibault leads the vagabonds in freeing their leader, hoping that the king will be killed. However, it is Huguette who dies in the fracas. Villon then leads a successful attack on the Burgundians and, with them out of the way, the king pardons him when Katherine offers her life for that of her lover. Thus Villon and Katherine are free to be together.

THE VAGABOND KING was Paramount's first Technicolor all-talking musical and it was Jeanette MacDonald's second screen appearance following her debut in THE LOVE PARADE (*q.v.*) the year before. Although he gave a solid (some insisted stolid) acting and vocal performance in the lead role, the film failed to establish Dennis King as a movie star. He was just too theatrical, which, combined with MacDonald's very mannered performance, did not go over with moviegoers. (At least Warner Oland was dastardly villainous in his characterization.) Much of the blame for the static production goes to German director Ludwig Berger, who was making his sound film debut.

THE VAGABOND KING garnered Hans Dreier an Academy Award nomination for Art Direction.

Paramount and the legend of François Villon continued onward. In 1938 Paramount produced a sweeping swashbuckling entry, IF I WERE KING, starring Ronald Colman, Frances Dee and Basil Rathbone. It was a wonderful, romantic and rousing dramatic entry. In 1956, Paramount, searching for ways to compete against television and to find their own answer to Hollywood's Mario Lanza, refilmed THE VAGABOND KING as a vehicle for European opera star Oreste who made his motion picture debut in the role of François Villon. The project was shot in color and widescreen VistaVision and co-starred Kathryn Grayson as Catherine De Vaucelles (which was her last feature film to date). Rita Moreno was cast as Huguette.

For this new production, Rudolf Friml, along with Johnny Burke, composed new songs including "Bon Jour" and "This Same Heart." Under the direction of Michael Curtiz, the film proved to be a solid adaptation of the Friml work. However, the plotline was far too dated for 1950s audiences. John Kobal noted in *Gotta Sing Gotta Dance* (1971), "Grayson sang enchantingly, but the time for this sort of film was long gone, and certainly the time for its revival could not have been less apt." John Douglas Eames concurred in *The Paramount Story* (1985), "Such an old-fashioned operetta was a dead duck to the fifties public, and VistaVision and all the other technical innovations of the modern cinema merely served to make it look embalmed."

To promote its very expensive remake of THE VAGABOND KING and to help make audiences familiar with Oreste, Paramount released the short film, BING PRESENTS ORESTE, in 1956, in which Bing Crosby introduced the European opera baritone to Americans. When RCA released a cast album of the 1956 THE VAGABOND KING it was Jean Fenn who appeared on the recordings opposite Oreste, not Grayson. As for Oreste, THE VAGABOND KING was the start and finish of his movie career.

THE VAGABOND LOVER (RKO, 1929) 65 minutes. (Also silent version).

Producers, James Ashmore Creelman, Louis Sarecky; director, Marshall Neilan; story/screenplay/dialogue, Creelman; art director, Max Ree; assistant director, Wallace Fox; camera, Leo Tover.

Songs: "If You Were the Only Girl in the World" (Clifford Grey, Nat D. Ayer); "A Little Kiss Each Morning," "Heigh Ho Everybody," (Harry M. Woods); "Piccolo Pete" (Phil Baxter); "I Love You" (Ruby Cowan, Philip Bartholomae, Phil Bouteljie); "I'll Be Reminded of You" (Ken Smith, Edward Heyman); "I'm Just a Vagabond Lover" (Leon Zimmerman, Rudy Vallee).

Rudy Vallee (Rudy Bronson); Sally Blane (Jean); Marie Dressler (Mrs. Whitehall); Charles Sellon (Officer Tuttle); Eddie Nugent (Sport); Nella Walker (Mrs. Todd Hunter); Malcolm Waite (Ted Grant); Alan Roscoe (Manager); and The Connecticut Yankees.

Rudy Vallee burst onto the entertainment scene in 1928, quickly becoming a popular club, radio, vaudeville and record attraction with his band, The Connecticut Yankees. By 1929 he was quickly developing into the nation's first singing idol. As a result he and his band were rushed to Hollywood that year to star in their first feature film, THE VAGABOND LOVER, for Radio Pictures. Simplistic at best, the movie was hampered by Rudy's wooden acting performance and by the fact that director Marshal Neilan went on a drunken spree in the midst of production, following the death of his mother. The movie had to be completed by assistant director Wallace Fox. *Photoplay* magazine announced, "Rudy goes through the whole gamut of emotions without moving a muscle. But when he sings—ah, that's another story. (A better one, too.) Vallee fans will be pleased."

Bandleader Rudy Bronson (Rudy Vallee) dreams of becoming a big star with his college band. He feels his big hope rests with his idol, impresario Ted Grant (Malcolm Waite), with whom he has been studying by correspondence. When the band finds out that Grant is to perform at a garden party hosted by dowager socialite Mrs. Whitehall (Marie Dressler), they head to her Long Island estate. Rudy is mistaken for Ted by the woman's pretty niece, Jean (Sally Blane). The band is hired to play for a charity event for homeless children and, while there, Rudy and Jean fall in love. When the real Ted Grant and his manager (Alan Roscoe) arrive on the scene, Rudy's hoax is exposed. He and the band make a hasty retreat, with Jean's help. However, on the night of the benefit, they return and Rudy and the band score a sensation. They end up with a radio contract, while Jean forgives Rudy and they are reunited.

While it was spare on plot and dramatics, THE VAGABOND LOVER does showcase Rudy Vallee at the height of his popularity, singing several of his best known songs, including "I'm Just a Vagabond Lover" and "A Little Kiss Each Morning." The film is also credited with bringing Marie Dressler back to the screen; she stole the show as the society dame who carries on a feud with rival Mrs. Todd Hunter, nicely played by Nella Walker. In later years, Rudy Vallee used THE VAGABOND LOVER as part of his club act, insisting that the picture was so bad that theatres which screened it had to be fumigated and that in recent years it was shown only to captive audiences in prisons and comfort stations.

LA VEUVE JOYEUSE *see*: THE MERRY WIDOW (1934).

VIENNESE NIGHTS (Warner Bros., 1930) Color 107 minutes.

Director, Alan Crosland; screenplay, Oscar Hammerstein, II; music, Sigmund Romberg; music conductor, Louis Silvers; choreographer, Jack Haskell; sound, George R. Groves; camera, James Van Trees; editor, Hal McLaren.

Songs: "I Bring a Love Song," "I'm Lonely," "Will You Remember Vienna?" "Here We Are," "Regimental March," "Yes, Yes, Yes," "Viennese Nights," "Goodbye My Love" (Oscar Hammerstein, II, Sigmund Romberg).

Alexander Gray (Otto); Vivienne Segal (Elsa); Bert Roach (Gus); Milton Douglas (Bill Jones); Jean Hersholt (Hochter); June Purcell (Mary); Walter Pidgeon (Franz); Louise Fazenda (Gretl); Lothar Mayring (Baron); Alice Day (Barbara); Bela Lugosi (Ambassador).

One of the very few early sound operettas to be written especially for the screen, VIENNESE NIGHTS was scripted by Oscar Hammerstein, II, who collaborated on the score with Sigmund Romberg. Warner Bros. gave the production a lush Technicolor mounting and it was one of the more successful genre pieces of the day. *Photoplay* magazine called it "The best operetta in recent months—with oh, what waltzes!" In addition to a sturdy plot, the film contained eight songs by Hammerstein-Romberg, including "I Bring a Love Song," "I'm Lonely" and "Viennese Nights." The cast included Alexander Gray, who had been in several screen musicals/operettas: THE SHOW OF SHOWS (1929), *q.v.,* SALLY (1929), *q.v.,* NO NO NANETTE (1930), *q.v.,* SONG OF THE FLAME (1930), *q.v.,* and SPRING IS HERE (1930), the latter three with Bernice Claire, with whom he also appeared in vaudeville. Vivienne Segal, a leading Broadway singing star, had been on-camera in SONG OF THE WEST (1930), BRIDE OF THE REGIMENT (1930) and GOLDEN DAW (1930). Walter Pidgeon, who would gain later fame for his screen teamings with Greer Garson, had appeared on-camera in such musicals as MELODY OF LOVE (1928) and BRIDE OF THE REGIMENT (1930). Today, however, this early screen musical is practically forgotten except for the fact that in it Bela Lugosi played one of his earliest sound roles, that of an (unbilled) ambassador.

In Austria, three men, Otto (Alexander Gray), Gus (Bert Roach) and Franz (Walter Pidgeon), are good friends until they all join the army to fight in the latest war. Franz becomes an officer while Otto and Gus are his subordinates. Otto meets beautiful Elsa (Vivienne Segal), the daughter of a cobbler, and the two fall in love.

However, when Franz spots Elsa, he wants her for himself and Otto is powerless to stop him. After the war, Otto and Gus come to America where Otto becomes a successful orchestra violinist. Meanwhile, he has married and has a child. One night at the theatre, Otto encounters Elsa, now a rich woman and the wife of nobleman Franz. He learns that she is unhappy and decides to see her again. The two fall in love once more, but Elsa breaks off with Otto when she learns of his wife and baby. Forty years pass, and Elsa hopes her granddaughter Barbara (Alice Day) will marry a rich man and bring money back to their family. However, the girl elopes with an American songwriter (Milton Douglas) who, she discovers, is really Otto's grandson. Happy that her granddaughter has found happiness with the grandson of the man she loved, Elsa dreams that Otto has come to serenade her.

When VIENNESE NIGHTS opened, Warner Bros. promoted it with: "THE greatest love story ever told! Old Vienna—gay, charming—capital of glorious romance; the inspiration of artists and the home of love and youth! . . . Old times, rich with remembrance . . . mirrored again in the new life of today. Beauty that never dies; love that lives on forever, each growing more beautiful as the long years pass."

VIVA LAS VEGAS (Metro-Goldwyn-Mayer, 1964) Color 85 minutes.

Producers, Jack Cummings, George Sidney; director, Sidney; screenplay, Sally Benson; art directors, George W. Davis, Edward Carfagno; set decorators, Henry Grace, George R. Nelson; costumes, Don Feld; makeup, William Tuttle; music director, George Stoll; choreographer, David Winters; assistant director, Milton Feldman; sound supervisor, Franklin Milton; camera, Joseph Biroc; editor, John McSweeney, Jr.

Songs: "Viva Las Vegas," "I Need Somebody to Lean On" (Doc Pomus); "The Lady Loves Me" (Sid Tepper, Roy C. Bennett); "Come On, Everybody" (Stanley Chianese); "Today, Tomorrow, and Forever" (Bill Grant, Bernie Baum, Florence Kaye); "If You Think I Don't Need You" (Bob "Red" West); "Appreciation," "My Rival" (Marvin More, Bernie Wayne); "The Climb," "The Yellow Rose of Texas" (Don George); "The Eyes of Texas Are Upon You."

Elvis Presley (Lucky Jackson); Ann-Margret (Rusty Martin); Cesare Danova (Count Elmo Mancini); William Demarest (Mr. Martin); Nicky Blair (Shorty Farnsworth); Jack Carter (Himself); Robert B. Williams (Swanson); Bob Nash (Big Gus Olson); Roy Engel (Baker); Barnaby Hale (Mechanic); Ford Dunhill (Driver); Eddie Quillan (Master of Ceremonies); George Cisar (Manager);

Ivan Triesault (Head Captain); Francis Raval (Francois); Mike Ragan [Holly Bane] (Man).

One of the last good-sized-budget movies to star Elvis Presley, VIVA LAS VEGAS was a tuneful affair combining music with race car driving, plus the added attraction of sex kitten Ann-Margret as the slinky feminine lead. With location filming in Las Vegas and at Boulder Dam Lake, the movie was a colorful entry. *Variety* reported, "Potent pairing of Presley and Ann-Margret insures bright b.o. [box office] future for its sleek but skimpy concoction of romance and songs." The *New York Times* wrote, "This fetching entertainment may not rate that withheld exclamation point, but is one of several Elvis Presley musical frolics that can hold its head high enough, with no apologies. Friendly, wholesome. . . . It's good, easy entertainment all the way. . . . The climax is a wing-ding of an auto race across the countryside."

Ann-Margret and Elvis Presley in VIVA LAS VEGAS (1964).

When racer Lucky Jackson (Elvis Presley) beats Italian champ Count Elmo Mancini (Cesare Danova) in a competition, continental Mancini asks Lucky to drive for him. Lucky declines; he intends to get a new engine for his own car so he can enter the Las Vegas Grand Prix. In the gambling capital, both Lucky and Mancini try to romance pretty swimming instructress Rusty Martin (Ann-Margret). When he is pushed into a resort pool, Lucky loses all his funds and is forced to work as a waiter. However, in the process, he wins Rusty's affections and she wants him to quit the dangerous sport of racing. To make Lucky jealous and hopefully win her point, Rusty flirts with Mancini. Later, both Rusty and Lucky enter a hotel talent contest, with the two ending up in a tie. Their prizes are a paid honeymoon for Lucky and a pool table for Rusty. So Lucky can participate in the big race, Rusty's father (William Demarest) loans him the needed funds. During the race Mancini's car is destroyed in a crash and Lucky wins the event. With the prize money he and Rusty decide to wed.

While VIVA LAS VEGAS had a good plot and plenty of action at the climax, it was weak in the music department. The song highlights were Elvis singing "Yellow Rose of Texas" and dueting with Ann-Margret on "The Lady Loves Me." The picture grossed over $5 million in distributors' domestic film rentals. Elvis would return to the car racing scene in SPINOUT (1966) and SPEEDWAY (1968), both directed by Norman Taurog. The screenplay for VIVA LAS VEGAS was by ex-film critic and novelist Sally Benson, whose magazine stories had provided the basis for MEET ME IN ST. LOUIS (1944), *q.v.,* and who had co-written such musicals as Betty Grable's THE FARMER TAKES A WIFE (1953) and Debbie Reynold's THE SINGING NUN (1966).

British release title: LOVE IN LAS VEGAS.

WAKE UP AND LIVE (20th Century-Fox, 1937) 91 minutes.

Producer, Darryl F. Zanuck; associate producer, Kenneth MacGowan; director, Sidney Lanfield; based on the story by Curtis Kenyon, the novel by Dorothea Brande; screenplay, Harry Tugend, Jack Yellen; art directors, Mark-Lee Kirk, Haldane Douglas; set decorator, Thomas Little; costumes, Gwen Wakeling; music director, Louis Silvers; choreographer, Jack Haskell; assistant director, A. F. Erickson; sound, W. D. Flick, Roger Heman; camera, Edward Cronjager; editor, Robert Simpson.

Songs: "There's a Lull in My Life," "I Love You Too Much, Muchacha," "Wake Up and Live," "Never in a Million Years," "It's Swell of You" "Red Seal Malt," "I'm Bubbling Over," "Oh, But I'm

Happy" (Mack Gordon, Harry Revel); "De Camptown Races" (Stephen Foster).

Walter Winchell (Himself); Ben Bernie and His Band (Themselves); Alice Faye (Alice Huntley); Patsy Kelly (Patsy Kane); Ned Sparks (Steve Clushey); Jack Haley (Eddie Kane); Grace Bradley (Jean Roberts); Walter Catlett (Gus Avery); Leah Ray (Cafe Singer); Joan Davis (Spanish Dancer); Douglas Fowley (Herman); Miles Mander (James Stratton); The Condos Brothers (Specialty); The Brewster Twins (Themselves); Etienne Girardot (Waldo Peebles); Paul Hurst (McCabe); George Givot (Manager); Barnett Parker (Foster); Charles Williams (Albers); Warren Hymer (1st Gunman); Ed Gargan (Murphy, the Doorman); William Demarest, John Sheehan (Attendants); Rosemary Glosz (Singer); Robert Lowery (Chauffeur); George Chandler (Janitor); Gary Breckner (Announcer); Elyse Knox (Nurse); Ellen Prescott (Girl); Harry Tyler (Buick Driver); Andre Beranger (Accompanist); Buddy Clark (Singing Voice of Eddie Kane).

One of radio's continuing comedy feuds was that between columnist Walter Winchell and bandleader Ben Bernie. This publicity gimmick was the crux of WAKE UP AND LIVE, which was a delightful satire on radio as well as an outstanding musical. Encompassed in the storyline were such top Mack Gordon-Harry Revel songs as the "Wake Up and Live," "It's Swell of You" and "Never in a Million Years," all of which star Alice Faye recorded successfully for Brunswick Records. Another outstanding song in the movie was "I Love You Much Too Much, Muchacha," sung by Leah Ray and comically danced to by comedienne Joan Davis. While Jack Haley was cast as a radio crooner in the movie, his vocals were dubbed by Buddy Clark, who would become one of radio's most popular singers in the 1940s.

Singers Eddie Kane (Jack Haley) and Jean Roberts (Grace Bradley) arrive in New York City to audition for Walter Winchell's (himself) radio show, thanks to arrangements made by Eddie's sister, Patsy (Patsy Kelly), who works for the famed columnist. Eddie, however, suffers from mike fright and faints. A disgusted Jean leaves him and takes a club job negotiated by booking agent Gus Avery (Walter Catlett). Landing a job as a uniformed guide at Radio Center, Eddie is befriended by Winchell's rival, bandleader Ben Bernie (himself) and radio songstress Alice Huntley (Alice Faye), who tries to help Eddie get over his fear of the microphone. One evening Eddie sings into what he believes is a turned-off microphone in a deserted control room. Actually Ben Bernie is on the air and Eddie's voice is carried out over the station. His voice causes such a sensation that the station is deluged with requests to hear him sing again. He soon becomes known as the "Phantom Troubadour" and when Bernie cannot find the Phantom and substitutes another singer, Winchell exposes him. Thereafter, both vie to locate the real crooner. Eventually Alice discovers that Eddie is the sought-after performer, but so do Jean and Avery, who kidnap him. However, after a long chase Alice gets Eddie to sing with Bernie's band at a nightclub and Winchell carries the big scoop over his own gossip show. Now Alice and Eddie are radio's new singing sweethearts as well as having a romance for real.

The *New York Times* cheered, "The compound forms a brisk and diverting musical show, fresher than most and considerably funnier. . . . Miss Faye still is a grand song-plugger." *Variety* concurred, "Both Miss Faye and Haley are capital as the love interest, former never looking better and now handling light emotional scenes with conviction. For Haley this picture has excited much sudden highly favorable comment in film circles." Bolstering the proceedings were wisecracking Patsy Kelly and dyspeptic Ned Sparks. Musically, the two specialty dances of the agile Condos Brothers added to the diversity of this song-and-dance entry.

Wide-eyed Jack Haley, who co-starred with Alice Faye in STOWAWAY (1936), would appear in ALEXANDER'S RAGTIME BAND (1938), *q.v.,* in which he supported Alice Faye, Tyrone Power and Don Ameche.

WEDDING BELLS *see* ROYAL WEDDING.

WEEKEND IN HAVANA (20th Century-Fox, 1941) Color 80 minutes.

Producer, William Le Baron; director, Walter Lang; screenplay, Karl Tunberg, Darrell Ware; art directors, Richard Day, Joseph C. Wright; set decorator, Thomas Little; costumes, Gwen Wakeling; makeup, Guy Pearce; music director, Alfred Newman; choreographer, Hermes Pan; sound, E. Clayton Ward, Roger Heman; camera, Ernest Palmer; editor, Allen McNeil.

Songs: "Romance and Rhumba" (Mack Gordon, James V. Monaco); "Tropical Magic," "The Man with the Lollipop Song," "The Nango," "When I Love, I Love," "A Weekend in Havana" (Gordon, Harry Warren); "Maria Inez" (L. Wolfe Gilbert, Eliseo Grenet); "Rebola a Bola" (Aloysio Oliviera, Nestor Almaro); "Mama Inez" (Eliseo Grenet, L. Wolfe Gilbert).

Alice Faye (Nan Spencer); Carmen Miranda (Rosita Rivas); John Payne (Jay Williams); Cesar Romero (Monte Blanca); Cobina Wright, Jr. (Terry McCracken); George Barbier (Walter

McCracken); Sheldon Leonard (Boris); Leonid Kinskey (Rafael); Billy Gilbert (Arbolado); Chris-Pin Martin (Driver); Hal K. Dawson (Mr. Marks); William B. Davidson (Captain Moss); Hugh Beaumont (Officer); Maurice Cass (Tailor); Leona Roberts, Harry Hayden (Passengers); Major Sam Harris (Gambler).

A cruise ship wrecks off the coast of Florida on its way to Havana. Passenger Nan Spencer (Alice Faye), a Macy's Department Store salesgirl from New York City, refuses to sign a waiver which would absolve the steamship company's liability in the accident. The head (George Barbier) of the company orders his soon-to-be son-in-law, Jay Williams (John Payne), to fly Nan to Havana, hoping he can persuade her to see the company's point of view. All this angers Jay's fiancée, Terry (Cobina Wright, Jr.), who must postpone their wedding. In Havana Nan asks Jay to take her to the Casino Madrilena to see headliner Rosita Rivas (Carmen Miranda). Upset at Jay's cold attitude toward her, she flirts with Monte Blanca (Cesar Romero), Rosita's boyfriend-manager. The latter is a compulsive gambler who thinks Nan is a rich tourist. Believing he can erase his gambling debts to club manager Boris (Sheldon Leonard), Monte gets him to credit Nan's gambling losses to his account. However, when the girl wins, he gets deeper in debt to the club. Since Monte is romancing Nan, Jay agrees to pay off his losses. Meanwhile, fiery Rosita becomes jealous when she accompanies Jay to a restaurant in the country and sees Monte there; he is with Nan. Nan leaves with Jay, who wrecks his car on a deserted road. While they are coping with the accident, they fall in love. The next day, Terry arrives in Havana and Nan, not wanting to break up her pending marriage to Jay, signs the waiver. She gives the check to Monte, who surprisingly wins at gaming tables. Meanwhile, Jay and Terry break off their relationship and he joyfully returns to Havana and to Nan.

Alice Faye, John Payne, Carmen Miranda and director Walter Lang were reunited in WEEKEND IN HAVANA following their success with TIN PAN ALLEY (*q.v.*) the previous year. This colorful outing offered Alice Faye two good songs, "Tropical Magic" and "Romance and Rhumba." Her third number, "The Man with the Lollipop Song," was recorded but cut from the film; it was only heard briefly in a scene at the country inn, with the owner (Billy Gilbert) singing a snatch of the tune. For tongue-twisting, fruit-laden Carmen Miranda, WEEKEND IN HAVANA was indeed a showcase. She sang the title song, did the South American number "Rebola a Bola" and the North American "When I Love I Love," backed by her own group, the Bando Da Lua. Hermes Pan choreographed her big production routine, "The Nango," and with her co-stars she reprised "Weekend in Havana" at the finale.

Bosley Crowther (*New York Times*), who approved of this splashy musical, inquired, "Where else can you see such grandeur and Technicolored swank as you can see in a Fox-filmed night club jammed with extras, dancing girls and Alice Faye? Where else can you find so much music compressed in such a short space of time? Where else can you meet Carmen Miranda, wriggling devilishly with harvest baskets on her head, except in whatever capital a Fox musical is set?" *Variety* found flaws with the class-A production: "The book is conventional in pattern, lightweight in texture, and slow getting anywhere. The laughs are also a bit spaced. . . . Walter Lang's direction is smooth, keeping the camera well on the move although that does not save the film from its dragginess."

This was the third 20th Century-Fox musical within a year to salute a South American capital, others being DOWN ARGENTINE WAY (1940), *q.v.*, and THAT NIGHT IN RIO (1941). At one point, Betty Grable had been mentioned for the lead in WEEKEND IN HAVANA.

THE WEST POINT STORY (Warner Bros., 1950) 107 minutes.

Producer, Louis F. Edelman; director, Roy Del Ruth; based on the story "Classmates" by Irving Wallace; screenplay, John Monks, Jr., Charles Hoffman, Wallace; art director, Charles H. Clarke; set decorator, Armor E. Marlowe; costumes, Milo Anderson, Marjorie Best; makeup, Otis Malcolm; music director, Ray Heindorf; orchestrator, Frank Perkins; choreographer, LeRoy Prinz; dance stagers, Eddie Prinz, Al White; Mr. Cagney's dances created by Johnny Boyle, Jr.; assistant director, Mel Deller; sound, Francis J. Scheid; special effects, Edwin DuPar; camera, Sid Hichox; editor, Owen Marks.

Songs: "Ten Thousand Sheep," "You Love Me," "By the Kissing Rock," "Long Before I Knew You," "Brooklyn," "It Could Only Happen in Brooklyn," "Military Polka," "The Corps" (Jule Styne, Sammy Cahn).

James Cagney (Elwin Bixby); Virginia Mayo (Eve Dillon); Doris Day (Jan Wilson); Gordon MacRae (Tom Fletcher); Gene Nelson (Hal Courtland); Alan Hale, Jr. (Bull Gilbert); Roland Winters (Harry Eberhart); Raymond Roe (Bixby's "Wife"); Wilton Graff (Lieutenant Colonel Martin); Jerome Cowan (Jocelyn); Frank Ferguson (Commandant); Russ Saunders (Acrobat); Jack Kelly (Officer-in-Charge); Glen Turnbull (Hoofer); Walter Ruick (Piano Player); Lute Crockett (Senator); Victor Desney (French Attaché); Wheaton Chambers (Secretary); James Dobson, Joel Marston, Bob

Hayden, DeWitt Bishop, John Hedloe, Don Shartel, James Young (Cadets).

Back in December 1934 the love team of Ruby Keeler and Dick Powell had strolled down FLIRTATION WALK, one of their several Busby Berkeley musicals at Warner Bros. The studio returned to the military training school for another song-and-dance foray in THE WEST POINT STORY. It was James Cagney's first screen musical since YANKEE DOODLE DANDY (*q.v.*), which earned him an Oscar eight years before. This film also produced an Academy Award nomination, for Ray Heindorf's music scoring. Otherwise it was a mundane offering which wasted its bright cast in a trivial story with mediocre songs. "THE WEST POINT STORY crossbreeds two thin Hollywood strains: the backstage musical and the plot that glories the U.S. Military Academy. The result is a little monster of a flag-waving, hip-wagging movie combining the misshapen features of both. In a fine burst of freakishness, the Warners have even stuffed over-age (46) James Cagney, into the uniform of a West Point plebe" (*Time* magazine).

Needing money, hot-tempered Broadway producer Elwin Bixby (James Cagney) accepts the job of producing the annual West Point show from producer Harry Eberhart (Roland Winters). The book and songs for the production have been written by cadet Tom Fletcher (Gordon MacRae) who happens to be Eberhart's nephew. Eberhart thinks the boy is so talented that he should quit the Academy and that the work should be launched on Broadway. Once on the grounds of West Point, Bixby, a former soldier, is always razzing the cadets. They finally make the temperamental man a freshman plebe to keep him under control. Bixby is in love with his assistant, Eve Dillon (Virginia Mayo), and he persuades her to perform in the production. He also enlists the services of Jan Wilson (Doris Day), a movie star, who wins the heart of Tom. Tom is nearly expelled for pursuing his romance with Jan, who has been summoned back to Hollywood. However, crafty Elwin rights matters at West Point and the show is staged with Tom performing the male lead. It is a big success.

Despite James Cagney's energetic performance in the lead and good work from Virginia Mayo (who along with Doris Day became Warner Bros.' queen of musicals in the early 1950s), Gordon MacRae and Doris Day in support, the film failed to garner a popular following. Gordon MacRae had the best song showcase with his rousing "The Corps," while James Cagney vocalized "It Could Only Happen in Brooklyn" and "Brooklyn," and appeared with MacRae, Day and Mayo in the "Military Polka" production number. Veteran hoofer Cagney was so unimpressed with veteran choreographer LeRoy Prinz that he insisted on having his own special stager (Johnny Boyle, Jr.) to handle his numbers.

Gordon MacRae and Doris Day had previously appeared in TEA FOR TWO (1950), *q.v.*, and would next appear in ON MOONLIGHT BAY (1952), *q.v.*

British release title: FINE AND DANDY.

WEST SIDE STORY (United Artists, 1961) Color 155 minutes.

Producer, Robert Wise; associate producer, Saul Chaplin; directors, Wise, Jerome Robbins; based on the musical play by Arthur Laurents, Leonard Bernstein, Stephen Sondheim; screenplay, Ernest Lehman; production designer, Boris Leven; set decorator, Victor Gangelin; costumes, Irene Sharaff; makeup, Emile La Vigne; music conductor, Johnny Green; orchestrators, Sid Ramin, Irwin Kostal; music editor, Richard Carruth; choreographer, Robbins; assistant directors, Robert E. Relyea, Jerome M. Siegel; sound, Murray Spivack, Fred Lau, Vinton Vernon; sound editor, Gilbert D. Marchant; camera effects, Linwood Dunn, Film Effects of Hollywood; camera, Daniel L. Fapp; editor, Thomas Stanford; assistant editor, Marshall M. Borden.

Songs: "Prologue," "Jet Song," "Something's Coming," "Dance at the Gym," "Maria," "America," "Tonight," "One Hand, One Heart," "Gee, Officer Krupke," "Quintet," "Rumble," "Cool," "I Feel Pretty," "A Boy Like That," "I Have a Heart" (Bernstein, Sondheim).

Natalie Wood (Maria); Richard Beymer (Tony); Russ Tamblyn (Riff); Rita Moreno (Anita); George Chakiris (Bernardo); *The Jets:* Tucker Smith (Ice); Tony Mordente (Action); Eliot Feld (Baby John); David Winters (A-Rab); Burt Michaels (Snowboy); Robert Banas (Joyboy); Scooter Teague (Big Deal); Tommy Abbott (Gee-Tar); Harvey Hohnecker (Mouthpiece); David Bean (Tiger); Sue Oakes (Anybodys); Gina Trikonis (Graziella); Carole D'Andrea (Velma); *The Sharks:* Jose De Vega (Chino); Jay Norman (Pepe); Gus Trikonis (Indio); Robert Thompson (Luis); Larry Roquemore (Rocco); Jaime Rogers (Loco); Eddie Verso (Juano); Andre Tayir (Chile); Nich Covvacevich (Toro); Rudy Del Campo (Del Campo); Suzie Kay (Rosalia); Yvonne Othon (Consuelo); Joanna Miya (Francisca); *The Adults:* Simon Oakland (Lieutenant Schrank); Bill Bramley (Officer Krupke); Ned Glass (Doc); John Astin (Glad Hand, the Social Worker); Penny Santon (Madame Lucia); Marni Nixon (Singing Voice of Maria); Jimmy Bryant (Singing Voice of Tony); Betty Wand and Marni Nixon (Singing Voice of Anita).

"From the opening helicopter shots of New York's soaring

skyline, gradually moving closer and closer to the threatening finger snapping of a juvenile street gang lounging against a fence, through the sometimes violent, sometimes bitter-sweet story of two New York gangs, told in terms of *Romeo and Juliet,* WEST SIDE STORY was a work of art" (Paul Michael, *The Academy Awards: A Pictorial History,* 1978). He added, "It is most unusual when a work of art also captures the popular imagination, but in the case of this drama-musical ballet, popularity and art danced arm in arm through the teeming city streets, the gymnasium, the tenements."

WEST SIDE STORY, with book by Arthur Laurents, music by Leonard Bernstein, lyrics by Stephen Sondheim and choreography by Jerome Robbins, opened on Broadway on September 26, 1957. It starred Carol Lawrence, Larry Kert, Chita Rivera, Art Smith and Mickey Callin. The innovative show amazed viewers with its musical richness and shocked theatregoers with its candid depictions of street gangs in the slums of the "Big Apple." It ran for 732 performances. (It would reopen April 27, 1960 for an additional 249 performances on Broadway.)

In the slums of New York City, two rival teenage gangs, the white Jets and the Puerto Rican Sharks, are frequently at war. Puerto Rican girl Maria (Natalie Wood) moves to the city where her brother Bernardo (George Chakiris) is the leader of the Sharks. At a dance Maria meets and falls in love with Tony (Richard Beymer), a member of the Jets, who has a job at Doc's (Ned Glass) candy store. They begin a romance, despite the protests of Bernardo's strong-willed, prejudiced girlfriend Anita (Rita Moreno). When the relationship becomes known, the two gangs plan a showdown, despite the protests of the cop on the beat, Officer Krupke (Bill Bramley). Maria attempts to persuade Tony to stop the troubles, but he fails as Bernardo murders the leader of the Jets, Riff (Russ Tamblyn). An enraged Tony then stabs Bernardo to death and later goes to Maria to ask her forgiveness. The two plan to leave the city. The Sharks, however, hunt down Tony, who, mistakenly believing that Maria has been murdered, has turned reckless. The Sharks corner him in a playground and he is shot to death by Chino (Jose De Vega). Maria finds his body as the members of both gangs converge on the area. She shouts at both factions, "You all killed him. And my brother and Riff too." Hurling the gun away, she holds the dead Tony in her arms, whispering, "Te adore, Anton." Tony's body is carried off by members of both the Sharks and the Jets. Temporarily, the two rival groups have formed a truce born of tragedy.

With five weeks on location in the slums of New York, WEST SIDE STORY contained a memorable score, highlighted by the

Natalie Wood in WEST SIDE STORY (1961).

energetic choreography of Jerome Robbins, who co-directed the feature. (Robbins restaged his dances to suit the film medium.) When Ernest Lehman was scripting the motion picture he became so caught up in the sociological significance of the thematic material that finally producer and co-director Robert Wise told him, "Look, Ernie, we're not doing the definitive study of Puerto Rican problems in New York. We're making a musical, and we've already got something awfully good to go on." To give the movie a stronger continuity, a few of the songs (the whole Broadway score was used) were juxtaposed; for example, Maria's "I Feel Pretty" was moved from the second act to earlier in the proceedings. "America," which on stage had played in front of a scrim, became a production number on the rooftop in the movie, utilizing revised lyrics.

In analyzing this topical musical, Pauline Kael wrote in *The New Yorker* magazine, ". . . The dance movements are so sudden and huge, so portentously 'alive' they're always near the explosion point. . . . The irony of this hyped-up, slam-bang production is that those involved apparently don't really believe that beauty and romance *can* be expressed in modern rhythms, because whenever their Romeo and Juliet enter the scene, the dialogue becomes painfully old-fashioned and mawkish, the dancing turns to simpering, sickly romantic ballet, and sugary old stars hover in the sky. When true loves enters the film, Bernstein abandons Gershwin and begins to echo Richard Rodgers, Rudolf Friml, and Victor Herbert. There's even a heavenly choir."

Despite or because of its catering to the use of visually appealing leads for the movie (with several dubbers utilized), WEST SIDE STORY is both commercially crass and muted in energy. The two leads (Natalie Wood and Richard Beymer) are romantically starry-eyed, but it is the vibrant performances of George Chakiris and Rita Moreno, especially in their dancing, that brings the film to life, helped by the snappy dancing of the gang choruses.

Grossing almost $20 million in distributors' domestic film rentals, WEST SIDE STORY was a major Academy Award victor with ten wins. It was honored for Best Picture, Best Director, Best Supporting Actor (George Chakiris), Best Supporting Actress (Rita Moreno), Scoring, Costumes—Color, Art Direction-Set Decoration—Color, Editing, Cinematography, Sound. It was also nominated for Best Screenplay—Adaptation. The soundtrack album was on the charts for forty-four weeks, reaching #1 position for several weeks.

Ironically, in later decades, the frightening realities of intensified urban gang warfare would make WEST SIDE STORY seem so tame and prettified that it lost much of its credibility for later generations. Nevertheless, in its melodious score and its vigorous choreography it is a triumph of collaborative creation.

George Chakiris had played Riff in the London company of *West Side Story*. Robert Wise would later direct such musicals as THE SOUND OF MUSIC (1965), *q.v.*, and STAR! (1968). In 1989 he returned to a Manhattan ghetto setting with ROOFTOPS, a failed musical which starred Jason Gedrick and Troy Beyer. In contrasting WEST SIDE STORY to ROOFTOPS, *Variety* observed, ". . . [The former] was compelling entertainment with its unique combination of stunning choreography, clever libretto and a cast of engaging characters equal to their Shakespearean roots. . . . ROOFTOPS is sadly lacking in these categories, with the weakest element being the story itself."

WHAT LOLA WANTS *see* DAMN YANKEES.

WHEN MY BABY SMILES AT ME *see* DANCE OF LIFE (essay).

WHEN THE BOYS MEET THE GIRLS *see* GIRL CRAZY (1943) (essay).

WHERE DO WE GO FROM HERE? (20th Century-Fox, 1945) Color 77 minutes.

Producer, William Perlberg; director, Gregory Ratoff; story, Morrie Ryskind, Sig Herzig; screenplay, Ryskind; art directors, Lyle Wheeler, Leland Fuller; set decorators, Thomas Little, Walter Scott; music directors, Emil Newman, Charles Henderson; orchestrator, Maurice de Packh; choreographer, Fanchon; color consultants, Natalie Kalmus, Richard Mueller; assistant director, Ad Schaumer; sound, Arthur von Kirbach, Harry M. Leonard; special effects, Fred Sersen; camera, Leon Shamroy; editor, J. Watson Webb.

Songs: "Morale," "If Love Remains," "All at Once," "Song of the Rhineland," "Christopher Columbus," "The Nina, the Pinta, and the Santa Maria" (Kurt Weill, Ira Gershwin).

Fred MacMurray (Bill); Joan Leslie (Molly); June Haver (Lucille); Gene Sheldon (Genie/Ali); Anthony Quinn (Indian Chief); Carlos Ramirez (Benito); Alan Mowbray (General George Washington); Fortunio Bonanova (Christopher Columbus); Herman Bing (Hessian Colonel); Otto Preminger (General Rahl); Howard Freeman (Kreiger); John Davidson (Benedict Arnold); Rosina Galli (Old Lady); Fred Essler (Dutch Councilman); Joseph Haworth, Scott Elliott, Robert Castaine, William Carter (Service Men); Arno Frey (German Lieutenant); Max Wagner (Sergeant); Larry Thompson (Soldier); Bob Stephenson, Will Kaufman, Walter Bonn (Dutchmen); Hans Von Morhart (Blacksmith); Bert Roach, Paul Weigel, Ferdinand Munier, Harry Holman, Harrison Greene (Dutch Councilmen); Joe Bernard (Burgher); Hope Landin (Elderly Wife); Dick Elliott (Father); Norman Field (Minister); Edward Clark (Organist); Cyril Ring (Army Doctor); Sam Bernard (Warden); Ralph Dunn, Ralph Sanford (Policemen).

Twentieth Century-Fox announced that WHERE DO WE GO FROM HERE? was "the funniest picture ever set to music." It is a fantasy tale of a 4-F man who is transported back in American history by a genie. While the color picture made money, star Fred MacMurray seemed distinctly uneasy in the lead role. The film's premise had been executed better in the non-musical comedy, THE REMARKABLE ANDREW, three years earlier by Paramount. Kurt Weill (always too offbeat and innovative for Hollywood) and Ira Gershwin composed a quintet of songs for WHERE DO WE GO FROM HERE?, but none was especially memorable. The bounciest number was "The Nina, the Pinta and the Santa Maria," sung by MacMurray, Fortunio Bonanova and Carlos Ramirez as Columbus and his crew bound across the Atlantic in 1492.

Although he wants to be a Marine, Bill (Fred MacMurray) is declared 4-F and assigned to guard a salvage depot. Wanting to help the war effort he washes dishes at a local armed forces canteen. There, not realizing he has already won the affections of Molly (Joan Leslie), he is attracted to Lucille (June Haver), who loves men in uniform. One day while performing his tasks, Bill uncovers an old Arabian lamp and it produces Ali (Gene Sheldon), a genie, who sends Bill on three adventures back through history. First he arrives at Valley Forge, where he warns General George Washington (Alan Mowbray) about the evil intent of treacherous Benedict Arnold (John Davidson). Next he is a sailor aboard one of Christopher Columbus' (Fortunio Bonanova) ships, and informs the explorer that he has discovered Cuba. Finally, Bill aids the Dutch in purchasing Manhattan Island from an Indian chief (Anthony Quinn). After his time travel, in which he constantly meets girls who look like Molly and Lucille, Bill is given his final wish. He becomes a soldier, with Ali a part of his regiment. Billy finally realizes he loves Molly.

Variety assessed, "Perhaps the idea, thrice-repeated, militates against a wholly satisfactory sum total. More like the shortcoming lies in the sameness of the comedy." It should be noted that while June Haver did not win Fred MacMurray in the film, the two were married in the next decade.

WHITE CHRISTMAS (Paramount, 1954) Color 120 minutes.

Producer, Robert Emmett Dolan; director, Michael Curtiz; screenplay, Norman Krasna, Norman Panama, Melvin Frank; art directors, Hal Pereira, Roland Anderson; set decorators, Sam Comer, Grace Gregory; costumes, Edith Head; music director, Joseph J. Lilley; choreographer, Robert Alton; sound, Hugo Grenzbach, John Cope; camera, Loyal Griggs; editor, Frank Bracht.

Songs: "The Best Things Happen While You're Dancing," "Love, You Didn't Do Right by Me," "Choreography," "Count

Your Blessings Instead of Sheep," "What Can You Do with a General?" "Mandy," "The Minstrel Show," "Sisters," "Heat Wave," "Blue Skies," "Let Me Sing," "Abraham," "Snow," "The Old Man," "Gee, I Wish I Were Back in the Army," "White Christmas" (Irving Berlin).

Bing Crosby (Bob Wallace); Danny Kaye (Phil Davis); Rosemary Clooney (Betty); Vera-Ellen (Judy); Dean Jagger (General Waverly); Mary Wickes (Emma); John Brascia (Joe); Anne Whitfield (Susan); Richard Shannon (Adjutant); Grady Sutton (General's Guest); Sig Rumann (Landlord); Robert Crosson (Albert); Herb Vigran (Novello); Dick Keene (Assistant Stage Manager); Johnny Grant (Ed Harrison); Gavin Gordon (General Carlton); Marcel De La Brosse (Maitre d'); James Parnell (Sheriff); Percy Helton (Conductor); Elizabeth Holmes (Fat Lady); Barrie Chase (Doris); I. Stanford Jolley (Station Master); George Chakiris (Specialty Dancer); Trudy Stevens (Singing Voice of Judy); and: Bea Allen, Joan Bayley, Glen Carlyle, Lester Clark, Lorraine Crawford, Mike P. Donovan, Ernest Flatt.

Bing Crosby was no stranger to the lyrics of "White Christ-

Rosemary Clooney and Bing Crosby in WHITE CHRISTMAS (1954).

mas," the Irving Berlin song which is ranked as the number one non-religious Yuletime song of all time. Crosby had first performed it in HOLIDAY INN (1942), *q.v.*, and then reprised the hit melody in BLUES SKIES (1946), *q.v.* Originally this musical was to have teamed Crosby with Donald O'Connor, but when the latter broke his leg, he was replaced by funny man Danny Kaye. To compensate for the use of a "non"-dancing co-lead, John Brascia was hired to perform several of the dance numbers with Vera-Ellen.

During World War II, entertainers Bob Wallace (Bing Crosby) and Phil Davis (Danny Kaye) put together an act to perform on U.S.O. tours. After they are discharged they quickly become a big success on the club circuit. The duo find themselves in Florida after the close of a pre-Broadway tryout of a new show. The two producer-directors are asked to audition the sister team of singer Betty (Rosemary Clooney) and dancer Judy (Vera-Ellen). After a series of events, Bob and Phil decide to join the girls at a Vermont ski lodge resort where the sisters are set to perform. Arriving there they discover that the inn is owned by their former service commander, General Waverly (Dean Jagger). Bob and Phil also learn that the general's posh lodge is doing poor business (there has been no snow in weeks) and he is about to lose it. The two ex-soldiers decide to bring the cast of their Broadway-bound show to the lodge to rehearse during Christmas week. Phil, anxious to get the work-obsessed Bob married off, decides that Betty would be the perfect spouse. However, Betty is controlled by her big sister syndrome and is afraid of leaving Judy on her own. To solve this, Phil and Judy pretend to be engaged. Meanwhile, the depressed General has requested a return to military duty, but he is refused because of his age. To perk up his spirits, the boys arrange for members of his old Division to come to the lodge for a surprise reunion. Bob and Phil arrange for their show to be telecast as part of the festivities. Betty misunderstands Bob's motives and storms off in a huff. However, she learns the truth and returns on Christmas eve to help participate in the show. The telecast is a big success. Bob and Betty admit their love, as do Phil and Judy. To make matters even better, the snow begins to fall, covering the ski slopes.

The *New York Times* wrote, "Fans of Bing Crosby and Danny Kaye, who have every right to expect more, for all this picture's dressy appointments will find only a routine accumulation of standard romance and sentiment, blessed by a few funny set-ups usually grabbed with most effect by Kaye. And, of course, the music of Irving Berlin, plentiful but a good bit of it less than inspired." *Harrison's Reports* decided, "There are . . . spots where it becomes quite slow and boresome, the slowness in the action being caused by the many rehearsals in preparation for the big show." Robert Bookbinder concurred in *The Films of Big Crosby* (1977), "Actually amounting to little more than an impressive succession of stunning visual images punctuated form time to time by an Irving Berlin song, WHITE CHRISTMAS resembles BLUE SKIES in appearance, just as it resembles HOLIDAY INN in plot, but it fails to project the charm and appeal of either of the Berlin-Crosby vehicles that preceded it."

In addition to the title song, the best Berlin numbers in the feature are "Love, You Didn't Do Right By Me" (sung by Rosemary Clooney) and "Count Your Blessings Instead of Sheep" sung by Crosby and Clooney. The most amusing segment is when Crosby-Kaye reprise in lip-synch and mime "Sisters," done earlier by Clooney and Vera-Ellen. The Crosby-Kaye number, "A Crooner, a Comic," was deleted before release.

WHITE CHRISTMAS was lensed in Paramount's own new widescreen process (VistaVision) and grossed an impressive $12 million in distributors' domestic film rentals at the box-office. WHITE CHRISTMAS received an Oscar nomination for Best Song ("Count Your Blessings Instead of Sheep") but lost to "Three Coins in the Fountain" from the picture of the same title.

To be noted as one of the dancers in WHITE CHRISTMAS was future WEST SIDE STORY (1961), *q.v.,* Oscar-winner, George Chakiris.

WITH A SONG IN MY HEART (20th Century-Fox, 1952) Color 116 minutes.

Producer, Lamar Trotti; director, Walter Lang; screenplay, Trotti; art directors, Lyle Wheeler, Joseph C. Wright, Earle Hagen; set decorators, Thomas Little, Walter M. Scott; costumes, Charles LeMaire; makeup, Ben Nye; music director, Alfred Newman; choreographer, Billy Daniel; technical adviser, Jan Froman; color consultant, Leonard Doss; special effects, Fred Sersen; sound, Arlan I. Kirlbrick; camera, Leon Shamroy; editor, J. Watson Webb.

Songs: "California, Here I Come" (Buddy G. DeSylva, Al Jolson, Joseph Meyer); "Alabamy Bound" (DeSylva, Jolson, Meyer, Bud Green); "Blue Moon," "With a Song in My Heart" (Richard Rodgers, Lorenz Hart); "Dixie" (Daniel D. Emmett); "Tea for Two" (Irving Caesar, Vincent Youmans); "That Old Feeling" (Sammy Fain, Lew Brown); "I've Got a Feelin' You're Foolin'" (Nacio Herb Brown, Arthur Freed); "It's a Good Day" (Dave Barbour, Peggy Lee); "I'll Walk Alone" (Sammy Cahn, Jule Styne); "They're Either Too Young or Too Old" (Frank Loesser, Arthur

Robert Wagner and Susan Hayward in WITH A SONG IN MY HEART (1952).

Schwartz); "Chicago" (Fred Fisher); "America the Beautiful" (Samuel Ward, Katherine Lee Bates); "I'm Through with Love" (Gus Kahn, Matty Malneck, Fud Livingston); "On the Gay White Way" (Ralph Rainger, Leo Robin); "Embraceable You" (George Gershwin, Ira Gershwin); "Jim's Toasted Peanuts," "The Right Kind of Love" (Charles Henderson, Don George); "Wonderful Home Sweet Home" (Ken Darby); "Get Happy (Ted Koehler, Harold Arlen); "Carry Me Back to Old Virginny" (James Bland); "Give My Regards to Broadway" (George M. Cohan); "Deep in the Heart of Texas" (Don Swander, June Hershey); "Maine Stein

Song" (Lincoln Colcord, E. A. Henderson, Don George); "Montparnasse" (Eliot Daniel, Newman); "Hoe that Corn" (Jack Woodford, Max Showalter); "Back Home Again in Indiana" (James F. Hanley, Ballard MacDonald).

Susan Hayward (Jane Froman); Rory Calhoun (John Burns); David Wayne (Don Ross); Thelma Ritter (Clancy); Robert Wagner (Paratrooper); Helen Westcott (Jennifer March); Una Merkel (Sister Marie); Richard Allan (Dancer); Max Showalter (Guild); Lyle Talbot (Radio Director); Leif Erickson (General); Stanley Logan (Diplomat); Jane Froman (Singing Voice of Jane Froman); Frank Sully (Texas); George Offerman (Muleface); Ernest Newton (Specialty); William Baldwin (Announcer); Carlos Molina, Nestor Paiva, Emmett Vogan (Doctors); Maude Wallace (Sister Margaret); Dick Ryan (Officer); Douglas Evans (Colonel); Beverly Thompson (USO Girl); Eddie Firestone (USO Man); The Skylarks, The Modernaires, The Melody Men, The King's Men, The Starlighters, The Four Girlfriends (Background Singers).

Jane Froman (1907–1980), a popular singing star of radio, Broadway, movies, records and clubs, was badly injured in a plane crash in 1943 while entertaining troops overseas. She gallantly carried on her career despite extensive injuries from which she never fully recovered. Her inspiring story was chronicled in the biopic, WITH A SONG IN MY HEART, in which Susan Hayward portrayed Jane Froman. However, it was the singer who did the vocals on the some two dozen songs used in the feature, including the title song, "Embraceable You" and "That Old Feeling."

In the mid-1930s singer Jane Froman (Susan Hayward) struggles to become a show business success. While auditioning to sing commercials at radio station WCKX in Cincinatti, Ohio, she meets unsuccessful vaudevillians Don Ross (David Wayne) and Guild (Max Showalter). Don offers her moral support and boosts her career as she rises to become a headline attraction in Chicago, appearing on radio, at clubs and in stage revues at big motion picture palaces. Eventually she marries Don and finds contentment for a time; he abandons his stage and songwriting activities to become her manager. Her career escalates and she becomes an increasingly popular personality on radio, recordings and in club engagements. However, her success causes an emotional break between Jane and Don, but they do not divorce. During World War II, Jane volunteers to sing for troops in Europe. On a flight over Lisbon in 1943 she is involved in a plane accident, which leaves her crippled. She is saved from the crash by Pan-American pilot John Burns (Rory Calhoun). The two begin a romance, and Froman is aided in her partial recovery by peppery nurse Clancy (Thelma

Ritter). Although never able to regain full use of her legs, Jane Froman valiantly resumes her career (on crutches) and completes her promised engagement (a 30,000-mile trek) to sing for grateful G.I.s. Meanwhile, Don steps aside so that Jane and John can marry.

Variety termed the feature, ". . . A drama with the kind of strong entertainment values that should sell well in any situation. It is tops on songs. . . . It is effectively performed with great heart, and glossed with a Technicolor coating and emphasizes the presentation." The *New York Times* dubbed it a ". . . . Splashily-colored, starry-eyed and sticky gob of tribute to the genuine gallantry of the singer. . . ."

WITH A SONG IN MY HEART received an Academy Award for Best Scoring (Alfred Newman). It earned Oscar nominations for Best Actress (Susan Hayward), Costumes—Color, and Sound.

Susan Hayward, who had played a songstress in SMASH-UP, THE STORY OF A WOMAN (1947), brought great verve and dimension to her characterization, an especially difficult task when all her vocal numbers were dubbed. (She would again play a show business figure—this time Lillian Roth—in I'LL CRY TOMORROW [1955], *q.v.*) As the shell-shocked paratrooper brought up on stage to join Froman's performance, Robert Wagner made such an impact with audiences that he soon became a star at his home studio, 20th Century-Fox.

THE WIZ (Universal, 1978) Color 134 minutes.

Executive producer, Ken Harper; producer, Rob Cohen; associate producer, Burtt Harris; director, Sidney Lumet; based on the book *The Wonderful Wizard of Oz* by L. Frank Baum, and the musical play by William F. Brown, Charlie Smalls; screenplay, Joel Schumacher; production designer, Tony Walton; art director, Philip Rosenberg; set decorators, Edward Stewart, Robert Drumheller; costumes, Walton; makeup, Stan Winston; music adaptor/supervisor, Quincy Jones; music director, Robert N. Tucker, Jr.; choir arranger/conductor, Tom Bahler; dance arrangers, Jones, Frank Owens; vocal arranger, Jones; orchestrators, Jones, Pete Meyers, Mendel Balitz, Bob Freedman, Ralph Ferraro, Greg MacRitchie, Bob Florence, Chris Boardman, Dick Hazard, Wayne Robinson; choreographer, Louis Johnson; assistant directors, Harris, Alan Hopkins; stunt coordinator, Everett Creach; sound, James T. Sabat; sound rerecording, Richard Nahmias, Richard Vorisek; supervising sound editor/music editor, Jack Fitzstephens; special sound consultant, Guy Costa; special effects, Albert Whitlock, Al Griswold; camera, Oswald Morris; second unit camera, Jack Priestly; matte camera, Bill Taylor, Dennis Glouner; editor, Dede Allen.

Songs: "The Feeling that We Have," "He's the Wizard," "Soon as I Get Home," "You Can't Win," "Ease on Down the Road," "What Would I Do If I Could Feel?" "Slide Some Oil to Me," "(I'm a) Mean Old Lion," "Be a Lion," "Don't Nobody Bring Me No Bad News," "Believe in Yourself," "Brand New Day," "So You Wanted to See the Wizard," "He's the Wizard" (Charles Smalls); "Can I Go On Not Knowing?" "Is This What Feeling Gets?" (Quincy Jones, Nick Ashford, Valerie Simpson); "Glinda's Theme," "Poppy Girls," "Liberation Agitato," "The Wiz," "March of the Munchkins," "Now Watch Me Dance," "End of the Yellow Brick Road," "A Sorry Phoney" (Jones); "Emerald City Ballet" (Jones, Smalls); "Everybody Rejoice" (Luther Vandross).

Diana Ross (Dorothy); Michael Jackson (Scarecrow); Nipsey Russell (Tinman); Ted Ross (Lion); Mabel King (Evillene); Theresa Merritt (Aunt Em); Thelma Carpenter (Miss One); Lena Horne (Glinda the Good); Richard Pryor (The Wiz); Stanley Greene (Uncle Henry); Clyde J. Barrett (Subway Peddler); Derrick Bell, Roderick Spencer Sibert, Kashka Banjoko, Ronald "Smokey" Stevens (Crows); Tony Brealond, Joe Lynn (Gold Footmen); Cointon Jackson, Charles Rodriguez (Green Footmen); Carlton Johnson (Head Winkie); Ted Williams (1st Munchkin) Mabel Robinson (2nd Munchkin); Damon Pearce (3rd Munchkin); Donna Patrice Ingram (4th Munchkin); Harry Madsen (Cheetah); Glory Van Scott (Rolls-Royce Lady); Vicki Baltimore (Green Lady); Carlos Cleveland, Mariann Aalda, Aaron Boddie, Gay Faulkner, Ted Butler, T. B. Skinner, Jamie Perry, Daphne McWilliams, Douglas Berring, James Shaw, Johnny Brown, Gyle Waddy, Dorothy Fox, Frances Salisbury, Beatrice Dunmore, Traci Core, Donald King, Claude Brooks, Billie Allen, Willie Carpenter, Denice Dejon, Kevin Stockton, Alvin Alexis (Guests at Aunt Em's Party); and Dancers from the Louis Johnson Dance Theatre.

In the 1970s, with black culture receiving its belated due in the American entertainment arts, several stage shows came forth with all-black casts performing stories which once had been the domain of white entertainers. One of the most successful translations to the black idiom was *The Wiz,* based on L. Frank Baum's *The Wonderful Wizard of Oz* (1900). With a book by William F. Brown and music and lyrics by Charles Smalls, *The Wiz* debuted on January 5, 1975 for a 1,672-performance run. It starred Stephanie Mills, Tiger Haynes, Ted Ross, Hinton Battle, Mabel King and Dee Dee Bridgewater. Its special vitality and hip point of view almost made one put aside memories of Judy Garland's 1939 MGM classic, THE WIZARD OF OZ, *q.v.* Costing $24 million to produce, THE WIZ on screen (which changed the setting to a hip excursion in the "Big

Apple") received a big ballyhoo from the press. However, after a good start at the box-office, it failed to appeal to a mass audience and resulted in a big flop for Universal. It generated only $13.6 million in distributors' domestic film rentals.

At a holiday gathering of her family, twenty-four-year-old Harlem school teacher Dorothy (Diana Ross) is prodded by her nagging Aunt Em (Theresa Merritt) to get on with life. Aunt Em insists she should switch jobs, go out into the world, or even marry. Later, when Dorothy is putting out the garbage from the holiday dinner, she chases her dog Toto who has run off into the snow. Soon they are whisked away by a tornado and they find themselves in Munchkinland; another part of New York City. She is congratulated for having accidentally killed Evermean, the Wicked Witch of the East. Miss One (Thelma Carpenter) provides Dorothy with the dead witch's magic slippers and tells her to follow the yellow brick road to find the Wiz (Richard Pryor), who hopefully will assist Dorothy in getting back home. En route, Dorothy teams with the Scarecrow (Michael Jackson), the Tinman (Nipsey Russell) and a Cowardly Lion (Ted Ross) as they truck on down the road to locate the elusive Wizard. After misadventures in the subway system and on drug-infested Poppy Street, the group reaches Emerald City. The Wiz informs the newcomers that if he is to help them, they must destroy Evillene (Mabel King), the Wicked Witch of the West, who runs a sweat shop. They succeed in their mission—dissolving Evillene in a spray of water—and demand their reward from the Wizard. However, he turns out to be a fraud, a failed politician. Discouraged but not defeated, Dorothy bolsters the spirits of her comrades. Meanwhile, the Good Witch returns to tell Dorothy that she always had the way to return home in her heart. If she believes enough she will return to her loved ones. Dorothy bids farewell to her new friends and returns to Harlem.

For the film, "You Can't Win," which had been cut from the Broadway show, was reinstated. Quincy Jones wrote/collaborated on new numbers and background music for the movie, including "Can I Go On Without Knowing?" and "Is This What Feeling Gets?" (sung by Diana Ross), and the revamped Emerald City ballet sequence. The peppiest song remained "Ease on Down the Road," performed by a hyperactive Michael Jackson and Ross (and later reprised by the duo with Ted Ross and Nipsey Russell). Radiant Lena Horne, the mother-in-law of this film's director, Sidney Lumet, was unfortunately short-shrifted, with only a duet ("Believe In Yourself"), a black pride tune sung with Diana Ross. Mabel King, from the Broadway cast, reprised her wonderful rendition of the evil witch who sings "Don't Bring Me No Bad News."

One of the major problems with THE WIZ was the casting of thirty-four-year-old Diana Ross as the lead. She was too mature, sophisticated, and stylized to play the young and optimistic Dorothy. Tom Milne (British *Monthly Film Bulletin*) cited several other creative problems with the production: "As so often nowadays, a rather nice little musical seems to be peeping out from behind the fulsome distractions of this expanded version of a Broadway success. . . . The film also has delusions of grandeur. . . . Quincy Jones seems to have expanded all the ensemble numbers to inordinate length. . . . THE WIZ is very much a thing of fits and starts." Donald Bogle (*Blacks in American Films and Television,* 1988) noted, "At first glance, Tony Walton's sets look sensational, dazzling the eye. . . . But the script can never turn these overscaled backdrops into intimate settings. The characters are always removed from their environment and seldom give an indication of being part of urban life. . . . At the same time, director [Sidney] Lumet doesn't connect to his characters." Bonnie Allen (*Essence* magazine) pondered, "Maybe the project was too big for a director working on his first musical." The editors of *Consumer Guide* and Philip J. Kaplan had a different slant when they reported in *The Best, The Worst and the Most Unusual: Hollywood Musicals* (1983), "While many of the scenes in the film are delightful, they never quite equal the stunning sets they're being played in front of. The dance numbers are sloppily choreographed and shot in a chaotic fashion with pointless, jarring editing. . . . It is important to note that the problems with THE WIZ have nothing to do with its concept, which is continually winning and innovative. For all its flaws, THE WIZ is one of the most imaginative musicals in recent years." Far more enthusiastic at the time of release was *Variety,* "Frank Baum would never recognize his simple little story in this fantastically blown-up version, but the heart of this tale—that a person must find what he's searching for within himself—is still there. . . . Director Sidney Lumet has created what amounts to a love letter to the city of New York, which he equates to Oz."

THE WIZ received Oscar nominations for Best Original Song Score—Adaptation, Costumes, Art Direction and Cinematography. Its soundtrack album was on the charts for one week, at position #40.

After the disappointment of THE WIZ, Diana Ross, who had shown such promise with LADY SINGS THE BLUES (1972), *q.v.,* returned to recordings, videos, and concert tours.

THE WIZARD OF OZ (Metro-Goldwyn-Mayer, 1939) Color Sequences 101 minutes.

Producer, Mervyn LeRoy; directors, Victor Fleming, (uncredited) King Vidor, Richard Thorpe; based on the novel by L. Frank Baum; screenplay, Noel Langley; art directors, Cedric Gibbons, William A. Horning; set decorator, Edwin B. Willis; costumes, Adrian; makeup, Jack Dawn; music director/adaptor, Herbert Stothart; associate conductor, George Stoll; orchestrators, George Bassman, Murray Cutter, Paul Marquardt; vocal arranger, Ken Darby; choreographer, Bobby Connolly; special effects, Arnold Gillespie; camera, Harold Rosson; editor, Blanche Sewell.

"Over the Rainbow," "Munchkinland," "Ding Dong the Witch Is Dead," "Follow the Yellow Brick Road," "If I Only Had a Brain/If I Only Had a Heart/If I Only Had the Nerve," "If I Were the King of the Forest," "The Merry Old Land of Oz," "Come Out, Come Out, Wherever You Are," "It Really Was No Miracle," "Lions and Tigers and Bears," "You're Out of the Woods" (Harold Arlen, E. Y. Harburg); "Threatening Witch," "Into the Forest of the Wild Beast," "The City Gates Are Open," "At the Gates of the Emerald City," "Magic Smoke Chords," "Toto's Chase," "On the Castle Wall," "Delirious Escape," "Poppies" (music, Herbert Stothart); "The Cornfields" (music, Stothart, George Stoll, George Bassman); "Optimistic Voices" (Arlen, Stothart, Harburg); "The Witch's Castle" (music, Stothart, Felix Mendelssohn); "March of The Winkies" (Stothart, Roger Edens); "Dorothy Rescue" (based on "Night on Bald Mountain" by Modest Petrovich Mussorgsky as arranged by Edens); "In the Shade of the Old Apple Tree" (Egbert Van Alstyne, Harry Williams);

Judy Garland (Dorothy Gale); Ray Bolger (Hunk/The Scarecrow); Bert Lahr (Zeke/The Cowardly Lion); Jack Haley (Hickory/The Tin Woodsman); Billie Burke (Glinda, the Good Witch); Margaret Hamilton (Miss Gulch/The Wicked Witch); Charles Grapewin (Uncle Henry); Clara Blandick (Auntie Em); Pat Walshy (Nikko); Frank Morgan (Professor Marvel/The Wizard/Guard/Doorman/Coachman); The Singer Midgets (Munchkins); Mitchell Lewis (Monkey Officer); Terry the Dog (Toto); Jerry Marenghi [Jerry Maren] (A Munchkin); Lorraine Bridges (Singing Voice of Glinda the Good Witch).

One of the most memorable of Hollywood musical fantasies, THE WIZARD OF OZ was made on a $3,700,000 budget and grossed only $3,017,000 in its initial release.* However, its true

*One of the problems facing THE WIZARD OF OZ in 1939 was the rich abundance of product available to filmgoers. In 1939 alone, MGM released such popular other entries as GONE WITH THE WIND, NINOTCHKA, IDIOT'S DELIGHT, BABES ON BROADWAY and GOODBYE MR. CHIPS.

fame and continued popularity derive from its more than two dozen annual runs on network television, which have kept it alive for successive generations.* As the years passed after its original release, critics and moviegoers began appreciating THE WIZARD OF OZ as a marvelous movie geared for all ages, and not just for children.** For its fiftieth anniversary, MGM caused a new print to be struck (with the addition of outtakes and historical/publicity material) for videocassette and laser disc release.

Of course, this classic fantasy musical is best remembered for making Judy Garland into a major star and for the song "Over the Rainbow" by E. Y Harburg and Harold Arlen. The number won the Oscar as Best Song for 1939 and Herbert Stothart won the Academy Award for Best Original Music Score. The film lost the Oscar to MGM's GONE WITH THE WIND as Best Picture. Judy Garland received a special award from the Academy of Motion Picture Arts and Sciences ". . . For her outstanding performance as a screen juvenile during the past year." The picture was also nominated for Oscars for Best Art Direction-Set Decoration—Color, Cinematography, and Special Effects.

The L. Frank Baum novel, *The Wonderful Wizard of Oz* (1900), and the other volumes in the series by him and other authors have had a long cinema history, dating back to 1908 when Baum himself produced a series of short silent films for Radio Plays called THE WIZARD OF OZ. In 1910 Selig did a one-reel version of the tale and the same year produced DOROTHY AND THE SCARECROW and THE LAND OF OZ. Four years later HIS MAJESTY THE SCARECROW OF OZ, THE MAGIC CLOAK OF OZ and THE PATCHWORK GIRL OF OZ appeared. In 1919, scenes from the last-named film were interpolated with new footage to make a new movie entitled THE RAGGED GIRL OF OZ, starring Mildred Harris, Juanita Hansen and Vivian Reed. Perhaps the best known silent version of THE WIZARD OF OZ was issued by Chadwick Pictures in 1924, with L. Frank Baum, Jr. co-authoring

*Trivia facts concerning the milestone THE WIZARD OF OZ (1939): the film shot for twenty-two weeks; there were three directors involved (Richard Thorpe, Victor Fleming, King Vidor); ten writers contributed to the screenplay, with three receiving screen credit. There were six hundred actors employed, including 124 midgets. Over 1,000 costumes were employed in the Technicolor production. Judy Garland's weekly salary was $400; while Ray Bolger received $3,000 weekly, Jack Haley $3,000 weekly and Bert Lahr $2,500 weekly. Terry, the female Cairn Terrier, one of two dogs who played Toto, earned $125 weekly.

**When THE WIZARD OF OZ was first released in England in January of 1940, the censors judged it for "adults only" because they felt Margaret Hamilton's Wicked Witch was too terrifying for little children to watch.

the screenplay with Leon Lee. The film was directed by popular comedy star Larry Semon, who played The Scarecrow, with Dorothy Dwan as Dorothy and Oliver Hardy as The Tin Man.

When MGM began preparation for filming THE WIZARD OF OZ, it was hoped to borrow moppet star Shirley Temple from 20th Century-Fox, but they refused to loan their valuable property. Seventeen-year-old Judy Garland, heavily corseted and made up, was substituted. For the key assignment of the Wizard, MGM's own gruff Wallace Beery coveted the role. However, studio chieftain Louis B. Mayer was so disturbed by the constantly crass and crude Beery that he refused to have him in this "A" production. Stage comedian Ed Wynn rejected the part of the Wizard as being too small, as did W. C. Fields, who wanted $100,000 for the job. (MGM only offered him $75,000.) The part finally went to MGM contractee Frank Morgan, who did yeoman's duty in the film, also playing Professor Marvel, The Doorman of Emerald City, the Carriage Driver and the Guard of Oz's palace. Early drafts of the project had roles set for Fanny Brice (a witch), singer Betty Jaynes (a princess), and Kenny Baker (a prince), but they were deleted as the project progressed. Initially Edna May Oliver was wanted for the role of The Wicked Witch of the West, but when she was unavailable, Academy Award-winning Best Supporting Actress Gale Sondergard was contracted. After costume tests, it was agreed that she was wrong for the concept and Margaret Hamilton was hired. Buddy Ebsen was first assigned to play The Scarecrow, a part lanky Ray Bolger coveted, instead of the role of The Tin Woodman that he was given. After much persuasion, producer Mervyn LeRoy agreed to allow Bolger and Ebsen to switch characters. Ironically, after Ebsen began working on the production (October 22, 1938) he developed a strong allergic reaction to the aluminum dust used for his outer makeup. While he was hospitalized, MGM replaced him with Jack Haley, borrowed from 20th Century-Fox. There was little question about Broadway veteran Bert Lahr being cast for the role of The Cowardly Lion. He was the first and only choice for the role. At first, the role of Glinda the Good Witch was given to starlet Helen Gilbert, but when she was unavailable it was reassigned to Billie Burke, whose few lines of singing "Come Out, Come Out, Wherever You Are" were dubbed by Lorraine Bridges. Clara Blandick was a final replacement for May Robson and then Janet Beecher in the role as Auntie Em. For the pivotal roles of the Munchkins, MGM turned to Leo Singer and his Singer's Midgets.

Young Dorothy Gale (Judy Garland) lives on a Kansas farm with her dog Toto (Terry the dog), Uncle Henry (Charley Grapewin) and Aunt Em (Clara Blandick). The shrewish local busybody, Miss Gulch (Margaret Hamilton), has threatened to have Dorothy's mischievous dog taken away. One day Dorothy and Toto encounter the charlatan Professor Marvel (Frank Morgan) and later are caught in a summer tornado. They are quickly lifted into the fantasy world of Oz. Her landing accidentally causes the death of the Wicked Witch of the East. In Oz, Dorothy soon meets The Scarecrow (Ray Bolger), The Tin Man (Jack Haley) and The Cowardly Lion (Bert Lahr), each of whom has unfulfilled dreams. Meanwhile, the dead witch's sister, The Wicked Witch of the West (Margaret Hamilton), vows revenge. However, Glinda The Good Witch (Billie Burke) comes to Dorothy's rescue and informs her and her pals that the only way Dorothy might get home is to find the Wizard of Oz (Frank Morgan). According to Glinda, he can help her. The group heads down the Yellow Brick Road to find the Wizard's headquarters in the mysterious Emerald City. Once they are there, the Wizard bargains with Dorothy that he will help her if she brings him the Witch's broom. She sets out to accomplish her task, but she and Toto are soon captured by the Witch. Dorothy's three friends come to her rescue and the Witch is killed when the girl tosses a bucket of water on her, which causes her to melt. Back at the Wizard's stronghold, Dorothy and her friends discover he is a fake. However, Glinda returns and gives Dorothy the secret of how to return home. Her benefactress explains that Dorothy could have returned to Kansas at any time by means of her magical ruby red slippers, but she had to discover for herself that "there's no place like home." She and Toto are happy to be reunited with her aunt and uncle and the friendly farmhands (Ray Bolger, Jack Haley, Bert Lahr). After relating her wondrous experiences and being reassured that Miss Gulch will not be able to harm Toto, the jubilant Dorothy exclaims, "I love you all, and . . . oh, Auntie Em . . . there's no place like home!"

Within the magic spell weaved by THE WIZARD OF OZ—through costumes, scenery and special effects (the Kansas "twister," the talking apple trees, the melting evil Witch) and the wondrous cast—music plays a very central role. Beyond the lilting "Over the Rainbow" each of Dorothy's prime friends has his own wish-fulfillment song, and there is the catchy "Follow the Yellow Brick Road" (Dorothy and Her Friends) and "Ding Dong, the Witch Is Dead" (The Munchkins). During previews of THE WIZARD OF OZ it was decided to cut "The Jitterbug" production number, which focused on Bert Lahr's Cowardly Lion and had Judy Garland "cutting the rug" with her trio of special friends. There was even great feeling among many studio executives, for a spell, that "Over the Rainbow" was too sophisticated, too sad and too literate a number to be kept in a children's picture. Fortunately, more rational thought prevailed.

When THE WIZARD OF OZ was released, *Variety* enthused, "Nothing comparable has come out of Hollywood in the past few years to approximate the lavish scale of this filmusical extravaganza, in the making of which the ingenuity and inventiveness of technical forces were employed without stint of effort or cost. Except for opening and closing stretches of prolog and epilog, which are visioned in a rich sepia, the greater portion of the film is in Technicolor. Some of the scenic passages are so beautiful in design and composition as to stir audiences by their sheer unfoldment."

On June 29, 1939 as part of the "Maxwell House Good News" show on NBC network radio, Judy Garland, Ray Bolger, Bert Lahr, Frank Morgan, and songwriters Harold Arlen and E. Y. Harburg appeared to promote the feature film. Judy Garland would repeat her role of Dorothy on "Lux Radio Theatre" on CBS-TV on December 2, 1950.

In its first twenty years of theatrical engagements, THE WIZARD OF OZ surprisingly earned only $4 million in domestic rentals. However, with the advent of CBS-TV showing the children's classic on TV annually (at $800,000 per telecast), THE WIZARD OF OZ gained in stature, spawning further merchandizing of all sorts and reminding new generations what a treat this colorful musical was. Since the 1939 version, the Baum story has been filmed as THE WONDERFUL LAND OF OZ in 1969 by producer-director Barry Mahon; JOURNEY BACK TO OZ (1974), an animated feature made in the mid-1960s, with Judy Garland's daughter, Liza Minnelli, supplying the voice of Dorothy and Margaret Hamilton recreating her role of the Wicked Witch of the West. In 1985 a vapid sequel to the 1939 landmark film appeared, called RETURN TO OZ, with Jean Marsh as Dorothy going back to Oz and finding it controlled by wicked rulers. On Broadway, a black ethnic-oriented musical based on THE WIZARD OF OZ, entitled *The Wiz* (1975), became a long-running hit and was turned into an unsuccessful motion picture (1978), *q.v.,* with Diana Ross and Michael Jackson. The MGM/United Artists movie, UNDER THE RAINBOW (1982), featuring Carrie Fisher, Chevy Chase and Eve Arden, dealt satirically and fictitiously with the turmoil engendered by the midget actors during the lensing of THE WIZARD OF OZ. In December 1988 a U.S./Canadian tour of *The Wizard of Oz,* a live musical arena show, began at Radio City Music Hall. It was produced-directed by Mike Grilikhes, who in 1956 had staged the live introduction portion to the first CBS-TV airing of the 1939 movie, with Liza Minnelli and Bert Lahr as live hosts. For an Easter 1990 telecast, NBC-TV filmed "The Dreamer of Oz," starring John Ritter as author L. Frank Baum.

The legend of Baum's stories and the 1939 classic movie continues to grow.*

For the record, there were at least six different pairs of ruby red slippers created for Judy Garland (as Dorothy) to use in THE WIZARD OF OZ. One set was auctioned in 1988 for $165,000.

WORDS AND MUSIC (Metro-Goldwyn-Mayer, 1948) Color 121 minutes.

Producer, Arthur Freed; associate producers, Ben Feiner, Jr., (uncredited) Roger Edens; director, Norman Taurog; based on the lives and music of Richard Rodgers, Lorenz Hart; story, Guy Bolton; adaptors, Feiner, Jr., (uncredited): Jean Holloway, Bolton, Isabel Lennart, Jack Mintz; art directors, Cedric Gibbons, Jack Martin Smith; set decorators, Edwin B. Willis, Richard A. Pefferle; women's costumes, Helen Rose; men's costumes, Valles; makeup, Jack Dawn; music director, Lennie Hayton; orchestrator, Conrad Salinger; vocal arranger, Robert Tucker; choreographer, Robert Alton; color consultants, Natalie Kalmus, James Gooch; sound supervisor, Douglas Shearer; camera, Charles Rosher, Harry Stradling; editors, Albert Akst, Ferris Webster.

Songs: "Lover," "Mountain Greenery," "Manhattan," "There's a Small Hotel," "Way Out West on West End Avenue," "A Tree in the Park," "Where's that Rainbow?" "On Your Toes," "You Took Advantage of Me," "Blue Room," "Someone Should Tell Them," "Thou Swell," "With a Song in My Heart," "Where or When," "Lady Is a Tramp," "I Didn't Know What Time It Was," "I Wish I Were in Love Again," "Johnny One Note," "I Married an Angel," "Blue Moon," "Spring Is Here," "My Romance," "Slaughter on Tenth Avenue," "We'll Be the Same," "Here In My Arms," "Yours Sincerely," "This Can't Be Love," "The Girl Friend," "Ship Without a Sail," "March of the Knights," "Nothing But You," "Hollywood Party," "Dancing on the Ceiling" (Richard Rodgers, Lorenz Hart).

Perry Como (Eddie Lorrison Anders); Mickey Rooney (Lorenz "Larry" Hart); Ann Sothern (Joyce Harmon); Tom Drake (Richard "Dick" Rodgers); Betty Garrett (Peggy Lorgan McNeil); Janet

*Among the several books minutely detailing the background, production and legacy of THE WIZARD OF OZ (1939) are Doug McClelland's *Down the Yellow Brick Road* (1976), Aljean Harmetz's *The Making of the Wizard of Oz* (1977) and John Fricke's *The Wizard of Oz: The Official 50th Anniversary Pictorial History* (1989). Stephen Cox wrote *Oz Remembered: Memoirs of the Munchkins* (1989), which followed the history thereafter of the little people performers who were cast in THE WIZARD OF OZ.

Leigh (Dorothy Feiner); Marshall Thompson (Herbert Fields); Jeanette Nolan (Mrs. Hart); Richard Quine (Ben Feiner, Jr.); Clinton Sundberg (Shoe Clerk); Harry Antrim (Dr. Rodgers); Ilka Gruning (Mrs. Rodgers); Emory Parnell (Mr. Feiner); Helen Spring (Mrs. Feiner); Edward Earle (James Fernby Kelly); Cyd Charisse (Margo Grant); Judy Garland, June Allyson, The Blackburn Twins, Gene Kelly, Vera-Ellen, Mel Torme (Guest Stars); and John Butler, Sid Frohlich, Allyn Ann McLerie, Dee Turnell.

Thanks to the box-office returns on TILL THE CLOUDS ROLL BY (1946), *q.v.,* the Jerome Kern story, MGM turned to the lives of musical collaborators Richard Rodgers (1902–1979) and Lorenz Hart (1895–1943). Plotwise, WORDS AND MUSIC was just as specious and contrived as the Kern feature. Musically it had a less lavish recreation of the Rodgers-Hart numbers, with fewer studio stars performing the composers' most noted songs. As a result, it was a dull biopic highlighted by only a few sparkling musical interludes. Also, the movie had to skirt around the same structural problem which befell Warner Bros.' NIGHT AND DAY (1946), *q.v.,* in that Lorenz Hart, like Cole Porter, had homosexual preferences, something that was taboo on screens at the time.

After an overture of music and introduction with Richard Rodgers (Tom Drake) speaking to the audience about Rodgers and Hart being "two lucky fellas who had success very young," WORDS AND MUSIC flashes back to its story. In 1920s New York, two young composers, freewheeling Lorenz Hart (Mickey Rooney) and business-like Richard Rodgers, begin a successful collaboration. The more sedate Rodgers finds happiness in his marriage to Dorothy Feiner (Janet Leigh) while Hart romances Peggy Lorgan McNeil (Betty Garrett). She finally discards Hart for another suitor. Although Rodgers and Hart continue their very lucrative work together, penning one hit song and show after another, Hart begins to lose his health while Rodgers and his wife happily raise a family. Their work together ends when Hart dies. In a finale, Gene Kelly (as himself) offers a tribute to the composers, with a montage of flashbacks providing curtain calls for the stars.

Like TILL THE CLOUDS ROLL BY, WORDS AND MUSIC is at its most effective when presenting the composers' works. Among the best outings are Gene Kelly's choreographed "Slaughter on Tenth Avenue" sequence, featuring himself and Vera-Ellen; a high-strung Judy Garland singing "Johnny One Note"; and June Allyson and the Blackburn Twins' rendition of "Thou Swell," which displayed the trio's abilities at song and tap and soft shoe dancing. Mickey Rooney and Garland do a fairly substantial duet on "I Wish I Were in Love Again," and Betty Garrett, a most underrated trouper, shines with "There's a Small Hotel." (Two of her other numbers, "Way Out West" and "It Never Entered My Mind," were cut from the film.) Lena Horne is chic and alluring with her gutsy "The Lady Is a Tramp," and also does "Where Or When." Relaxed Perry Como (as an actor who appears in several of the composers' shows) performs "Blue Room" and "With a Song in My Heart," while Mel Torme offers "Blue Moon" (to which Cyd Charisse dances). Ann Sothern (as an actress who spurns Richard Rodgers' crush on her) is given too little to do and only has the wistful "Where's That Rainbow" song-dance number to showcase her musical talents. Cyd Charisse and Dee Turnell perform a classical ballet duet with a jazz upbeat. While the quality of many of these individual musical turns was superior, too frequently they were inserted in the picture just to pad out the thin scenario. An effort was made to present all the musical numbers in natural settings rather than elaborate Hollywood versions of same.

In the *New York Times* Bosley Crowther lambasted WORDS AND MUSIC saying it was ". . . A patently juvenile specimen of musical biography . . . played with fantastic incompetence by Tom Drake and Mickey Rooney in the principal roles. . . . Around . . . [some] commendable numbers—and several others which are not so good (but loud)—there oozes and gums the heavy treacle of a sluggish, maudlin plot." Perhaps most embarrassing of all excesses in WORDS AND MUSIC was cigar-chomping, puffy Mickey Rooney's expiration in the picture. It has attained the status of high camp, with Rooney's character groping and gasping his way from his hospital sick bed to the theatre where his new show is being performed.

Made on a budget of $2,799,970, WORDS AND MUSIC, which boasted lavish sets, grossed over $4,552,000 in its initial release. This was Mickey Rooney's final film under his long-time MGM contract. Associate producer and co-scripter Ben Feiner, Jr. was Richard Rodgers' brother-in-law.

XANADU (Universal, 1980) Color 93 minutes.

Executive producer, Lee Kramer; producer, Lawrence Gordon; associate producer, Tery Nelson; director, Robert Greenwald; screenplay, Richard Christian Danus, Marc Reid Rubel, Michael Kane; production designer, John W. Corso; set decorator, Marc E. Meyer, Jr.; costumes, Bobbie Mannix; makeup, Rick Sharp, Harry Blake, Craig Smith; music, Barry DeVorzon; orchestrator for DeVorzon, Dick Hazard; big band/string arranger for John Farrar, Richard Hewson; choreographer, Kenny Ortega; dance effects supervisor, Alex Romero; animation design supervisor, Kenneth

Stytzer; animation designer, Randy Balsmeyer; animation, Don Bluth; assistant directors, Dan Kolsrud, Lisa Marmon, Venita Ozols; color consultant supervisor, Dick Ritchie; special visual effects supervisor, Richard Greenberg; camera, Victor J. Kemper; time-lapse camera, Lou Schwartzberg; model editor, Dennis Virker; associate editor, Tina Hirsch; special effects editor, Larry Plastrik; supervising visual effects editor, Ruth Smerek.

Songs: "I'm Alive," "The Fall," "Don't Walk Away," "All Over the World," "Xanadu" (Jeff Lynne); "Magic," "Suddenly," "Dancing," "Suspended in Time," "Whenever You're Away from Me" (John Farrar).

Olivia Newton-John (Kira); Gene Kelly (Danny McGuire); Michael Beck (Sonny Malone); James Sloyan (Simpson); Dimitra Arliss (Helen); Katie Hanley (Sandra); Fred McCarren (Richie); Ren Woods (Jo); Sandhal Bergman, Lynn Latham, Melinda Phelps, Cherise Bate, Juliette Marshall, Marilyn Tokuda, Yvette Van Voorhees, Teri Beckerman (Muses); Marty Davis (Male Guard); Bebe Drake-Massey (Female Guard); Mickey McMeel (Accountant); Aharon Ipale (Photographer); Lise Lang (Popcorn Girl); Melvin Jones (Big Al); Matt Lattanzi (Young Danny McGuire); Ira Newborn ('40s Band Leader); Jo Ann Harris, Cindy Leake, Patty Keene ('40s Singers); John "Fee" Waybill ('80s Rock Singer); Stephen Pearlman (Foreman); Church Ortiz (1st Worker); Randy T. Williams (2nd Worker); David Tress (Nick); Madison Arnold (Vargas); Wilfrid Hyde-White (Male Heavenly Voice); Coral Browne (Female Heavenly Voice); Maria V. Langston (Dizzy Heights); Clyde Barrett, Cheryl Baxter, Hilary Beane, Annie Behringer, Judith Bernett, Teda Bracci, Ellen Cadwallader, Stelio Calagias, Lonny Carabajal, Hillary Carlip, Lynda Chase, Russell Clark, Contessa Cohn, Derrick Cross, Gary Dio, Marisol Garcia, Miranda Garrison, Sandy Gray, Jei Guerrero, Cheryl Hangland, Yolanda Hernandez, Susan Inouye, Veda Jackson, Michael James, Deborah Jenssen, Leroy Jones, Fred Kirby, Lise Lang, Brenda Lee, Dale Leeche, Victoria Mansi, Michael Martinez, Yvette Matthews, Tykin Mikals, Glenn Nash, Christine Nazareth, Tim O'Brien, Jeff Osser, Shelley Pang, Sally Pansing, Arlette Patterson, Alan Peterson, Lena Pousette, Vic Prim, Melody Santangelo, Tony Selesnick, Kathy Singleton, Cindy Spooner, Michael Springer, Re Styles, Jim Thompson, Francisco Torres, Bobby Walker, Michael Watkins, Adria Wilson, Darcel Wynne, Noreen Xavier, Mark Ziebell, The Mumm Brothers, Chain Reaction Dancers, Tom Sachelle, Paul Sachelle, Kyle Hanford, Michael Donley, Robert Winters (Dancers); Rick Anderson, Michael Cotton, Prairie Prince, Bill Spooner, Roger Steen, Fee Waybill, Vince Welnick (The Tubes).

Musical fantasy had not worked well on-screen as a plot device in YOLANDA AND THE THIEF (1945), in DOWN TO EARTH (1947), or in ONE TOUCH OF VENUS (1948). However, such whimsy was again the unfortunate focal point of XANADU. It headlined Olivia Newton-John, who had starred in GREASE (1978), *q.v.*, the biggest moneymaking musical of all time. She was allowed to sing, dance and even figure roller-skate. To bring in older viewers, Gene Kelly was coaxed out of semi-retirement to be her co-star. Unfortunately, the hugely expensive project turned out to be a mess of gigantic proportions, which grossed only $10.2 million in distributors' domestic film rentals. In *The Best, The Worst and the Most Unusual: Hollywood Musicals* (1983), the editors of *Consumer Guide* and Philip J. Kaplan termed the film ". . . The ultimate disco movie—all flashy images, high tech effects, and nothing else. . . . The entertainment value is akin to watching war newsreel while someone shines a bright light in your eye."

Muse Kira (Olivia Newton-John) is dispatched to Earth to inspire Los Angeles commercial artist Sonny Malone (Michael Beck), who specializes in creating record album covers. Sonny becomes infatuated with the image of Kira and she keeps popping up on the record sleeves he is designing. He sets out to find her and along the way encounters ex-bandleader-clarinetist Danny McGuire (Gene Kelly), who abandoned music to become a successful New York businessman and now wants to open a new club like the one he had decades before. In fact, Danny still longs for a WAAF who sang with his band during World War II and then disappeared. (It was actually Kira in an earlier visit to Earth.) Sonny dreams of opening a rock palace and, with the help of McGuire, converts an old wrestling arena into the disco club Xanadu. When Kira realizes Sonny loves her, she returns to the wall mural from which she emerged, having told him that she is the daughter of Zeus and cannot have human emotions. A love-torn Sonny follows her, and in the heavens she receives the blessings from the gods to return to Earth for an "eternal" moment. She reappears at the opening night party at the disco, performing for a pleased crowd.

Long-time collaborator John Farrar wrote several tunes for English-born Olivia Newton-John to sing in the film. There was "Magic," a duet ("Suddenly") with her former mentor Cliff Richard, "Dancin'," a duet ("Suspended in Time") with The Tubes, a song/dance pairing ("Whenever You're Away from Me") with Gene Kelly, and the title song composed by Jeff Lynne. The poorly conceived dance numbers were staged by Kenny Ortega of SATURDAY NIGHT FEVER (1977), *q.v.*, fame. Newton-John had two hit singles from the soundtrack, "Magic," which reached #1 on the charts, and "Xanadu," which climbed to the eighth spot. The album itself was on the charts for fifteen weeks, reaching #4 position.

Most of the critics trounced the ill-conceived movie. "XANADU is a mushy and limp musical fantasy, so insubstantial it evaporates before our eyes. It's one of those rare movies in which every scene seemed to be the final scene . . ." Roger Ebert (*Movie Home Companion, 1988,* 1987). For Ebert, one of the film's saving graces was ". . . it's not as bad as CAN'T STOP THE MUSIC [1980, *q.v.*]."

Kelly was again playing the character of Danny McGuire which he had originated in 1944's COVER GIRL, *q.v.* All the exuberance, creativity and sparkle that had blessed that earlier movie were missing from XANADU. As Jill Forbes (British *Monthly Film Bulletin*) observed, "XANADU tries to offer something for everyone, but its eclecticism seems motivated less by nostalgia or generosity towards the past than by the absence of any new material. Pastiche can often be a compliment, but here it is simply cruel to Gene Kelly when the resemblance of two show-girls, across a generation, is used to remind us of the splendid COVER GIRL."

Evidently not having learned her lesson, Olivia Newton-John's next film, TWO OF A KIND (1983), was a nonmusical comedy in which she and John Travolta were involved with heavenly messengers. It was a box-office dud.

YANKEE DOODLE DANDY (Warner Bros., 1942) 126 minutes.

Producer, Hal B. Wallis; director, Michael Curtiz; story, Robert Buckner; screenplay, Buckner, Edmund Joseph, (uncredited) Julius Epstein, Philip Epstein; art director, Carl Jules Weyl; costumes, Milo Anderson; makeup, Perc Westmore; music director, Leo F. Forbstein; music adaptors, Ray Heindorf, Heinz Roemheld; choreographers, LeRoy Prinz, Seymour Felix, John Boyle; technical advisor, William Collier, Sr.; sound, Nathan Levinson; camera, James Wong Howe; editor, George Amy.

Songs: "I Was Born in Virginia," "Off the Record," "You're a Wonderful Girl," "Blue Skies, Grey Skies," "Oh You Wonderful Girl," "The Barbers' Ball," "The Warmest Baby in the Bunch," "Little Nellie Kelly," "In a Kingdom of Our Own," "The Man Who Owns Broadway," "Molly Malone," "Billie," "So Long Mary," "Mary's a Grand Old Name," "Forty-Five Minutes from Broadway," "Give My Regards to Broadway," "Yankee Doodle Boy," "You're a Grand Old Flag," "Over There" (George M. Cohan); "All Aboard for Old Broadway" (Jack Scholl, M. K. Jerome); "The Love Nest" (Louis A. Hirsch, Otto Harbach).

James Cagney (George Michael Cohan); Joan Leslie (Mary);

Walter Huston (Jerry Cohan); Richard Whorf (Sam Harris); George Tobias (Dietz); Irene Manning (Fay Templeton); Rosemary De Camp (Nellie Cohan); Jeanne Cagney (Josie Cohan); S. Z. Sakall (Schwab); George Barbier (Erlanger); Walter Catlett (Manager); Frances Langford (Nora Bayes); Minor Watson (Ed Albee); Eddie Foy, Jr. (Eddie Foy); Chester Clute (Harold Goff); Douglas Croft (George M. Cohan at Age Thirteen); Patsy Lee Parsons (Josie Cohan at Age Twelve); Captain Jack Young (Franklin D. Roosevelt); Audrey Long (Receptionist); Odette Myrtil (Madame Bartholdi); Clinton Rosemond (White House Butler); Spencer Charters (Stage Manager in Providence); Dorothy Kelly, Marijo James (Sister Act); Henry Blair (George M. Cohan at Age Seven); Jo Ann Marlow (Josie Cohan at Age Six); Thomas Jackson (Stage Manager); Phyllis Kennedy (Fanny); Pat Flaherty (White House Guard); Leon Belasco (Magician); Syd Saylor (Star Boarder); William B. Davidson (New York Stage Manager); Harry Hayden (Dr. Lewellyn); Francis Pierlot (Dr. Anderson); Charles Smith, Joyce Reynolds, Dick Chandlee, Joyce Horne (Teenagers); Frank Faylen (Sergeant); Wallis Clark (Theodore Roosevelt); Georgia Carroll (Betsy Ross); Joan Winfield (Sally); Dick Wessel, James Flavin (Union Army Veterans); Sailor Vincent (Schultz in *Peck's Bad Boy* Scene); Fred Kelsey (Irish Cop in *Peck's Bad Boy* Scene); Tom Dugan (Actor at Railway Station); Garry Owen (Army Clerk); Murray Alper (Wise Guy); Creighton Hale (Telegraph Operator); Ruth Robinson (Nurse); Eddie Acuff, Walter Brooke, Bill Edwards, William Hopper (Reporters); William Forrest, Ed Keane (Critics); Dolores Moran (Girl); Poppy Wilde, Leslie Brooks (Chorus Girls in "Little Johnny Jones" Number); Jerrie Lynn (Singer); Vivien Coe (Pianist).

The dynamic George M. Cohan (1878–1942), the composer of such songs as "Give My Regards to Broadway" and "Yankee Doodle Dandy," was a remarkable show businessman. He not only performed as a song-and-dance entertainer in vaudeville and on Broadway for decades, but was also a playwright, librettist, producer and director. He only starred in one motion picture, THE PHANTOM PRESIDENT (1932), and that, ironically, had songs by Richard Rodgers and Lorenz Hart. Only two of Cohan's stage musicals were brought to the screen, LITTLE JOHNNY JONES (1930), *q.v.*, and LITTLE NELLIE KELLY (1940), the latter starring Judy Garland and George Murphy.

Cohan had been negotiating for years to sell the movie rights to his flavorful life story. Warner Bros. bid the highest price, giving Cohan $100,000 *plus* screenplay and cast approval. Flag-waving Cohan liked Warners' concept, which would make the George M.

Cohan story a patriotic salute, very appropriate in those World War II times. Studio head Jack L. Warner later reflected, "When the time came to choose a star for YANKEE DOODLE DANDY . . . I knew that [James] Cagney, despite the law suits [against the studio] and his Irish stubbornness, was the only man for the part." Pugnacious Cagney would admit, "It was an exciting picture from an actor's point of view. I had knocked around in all kinds of shows and knew that every actor of Cohan's generation had been influenced by him. Cohan had unbounded energy and an interest in everything. He was bright as hell and had a drive second to none. Writing, dancing, and acting—he was a triple threat man. That's what made him interesting." Throughout production there were daily conflicts between Cagney, who insisted on rewriting scenes, and the studio, who feared that Cohan might veto the project at any stage.* One of the wedges the studio held against the rambunctious Cagney was that his actress sister Jeanne was cast in the movie (as his sister), and if the film were not released, it would harm the progress of her career. Finally, after a cost of $1,500,000, the lavish musical biography was completed by director Michael Curtiz and received Cohan's approval. The picture debuted on Broadway in May 1942 in a special charity gala which raised $5,750,000 in war bond sales. Cohan would die on October 5, 1942.

The Cohan family, vaudevillians, consist of Jerry (Walter Huston) and Nellie Cohan (Rosemary De Camp) and their offspring George (James Cagney) and Josie (Jeanne Cagney), who have been in the act since they were children in the 1880s. When an agent offers the family a major engagement, the brash George loses it for them with his boastfulness. While playing a bill in Buffalo, George meets and falls in love with stagestruck Mary (Joan Leslie). Later, George takes her with him when he tries to peddle his latest work, a stage musical. While he fails to sell it, he does meet producer Sam Harris (Richard Whorf) and the two become partners, with funding provided by Lawrence Schwab (S. Z. Sakall). Their show, *Yankee Doodle Dandy,* is a huge hit. *George Washington, Jr.* is composed especially to re-team the Four Cohans for a final smash entry. For the last time at curtain call, Cohan can say, "My father thanks you, my mother thanks you, my sister thanks you and I thank you." After this production, George's parents retire and Josie becomes engaged to wed. Later his parents die and, thereafter, Cohan and Harris produce their only flop, *Popularity.* When

*Although Cohan had been married twice and his ailing second spouse was still living, he refused to have the film depict these two women. Studio scripters devised "Mary," a harmless amalgam of both women.

World War I breaks out, Cohan tries to enlist but is told he is too old. As his part for the war effort George composes the song, "Over There," which Nora Bayes (Frances Langford) introduces at Camp Merritt. After the Armistice, Cohan and Harris dissolve their firm, while he and Mary, who have been married for years, take a long delayed honeymoon trip around the world. When they return, Harris convinces Cohan to star in a new Broadway show called *I'd Rather Be Right,* in which Cohan plays the President. Later, Cohan is summoned to the White House, where the President (Jack Young) gives him the Congressional Medal of Honor in recognition of his having written "Over There" and "It's a Grand Old Flag." It is while talking to the President that Cohan recites the facts of his life. When it is concluded, he walks out onto the streets of Washington, D.C., where his spirits are sparked by a patriotic parade in which everyone is singing "Over There."

YANKEE DOODLE DANDY was geared from the start to be a very sentimental film, relying more on safe conventions than fact or dramatic bite. It is at its best when energetic Cagney recreates the many famous George M. Cohan tunes, like "Mary Is a Grand Old Name," "You're a Grand Old Flag" and "Yankee Doodle Boy," plus a new song written for the film, "All Aboard for Old Broadway." One of the most riveting song-and-dance sequences from this movie (or any movie) occurs during the Broadway opening of *Little Johnny Jones* (1904) when Cagney (as Cohan) performs some of the star's famous hoofing, which included his trademark tapping, strutting and bouncing off the proscenium walls.

In its leisurely fashion, YANKEE DOODLE DANDY not only recreated the works of George M. Cohan, but its plot also focused on several of the greats of the American stage, including Irene Manning as Fay Templeton, Frances Langford as Nora Bayes, and Eddie Foy, Jr. as his famous father. In addition, there was Wallis Clark as Theodore Roosevelt and Captain Jack Young as President Franklin D. Roosevelt.

The *New York Times* termed the movie a "delightful film biography" and noted, ". . . Mr. Cagney's Mr. Cohan is not so much an image of George M. as it is an exhilarating portrait of a spirited trouper and a warmly emotional man." The *New York Post* noted, "The picture YANKEE DOODLE DANDY is a triumph not only for its superb timeliness but also for its portrait of a man and its vitality as a period piece. . . ." *Time* magazine stated, "YANKEE DOODLE DANDY is possibly the most genial screen biography ever made. Few films have bestowed such loving care on any hero as this one does on the beaming, buoyant, dry-mouthed George M. Cohan."

YANKEE DOODLE DANDY grossed $4,719,681 in distributors' domestic film rentals. For his stellar performance, James Cagney was awarded an Academy Award. YANKEE DOODLE DANDY also earned Oscars for Best Scoring and Sound. It was nominated for Best Supporting Actor (Walter Huston), Original Story, Director, and Editing.

For James Cagney, a Broadway hoofer who had danced only twice on screen previously (FOOTLIGHT PARADE, 1933, *q.v.*, and SOMETHING TO SING ABOUT, 1937), YANKEE DOODLE DANDY was not the end of the Cohan trail. In THE SEVEN LITTLE FOYS (1955), with Bob Hope as performer Eddie Foy, Cagney would do a guest cameo as George M. Cohan and join Hope for a wonderful sequence, trading quips and hoofing. Others who have played George M. Cohan included Mark Baker in the motion picture AFTER THE BALL (1957), Joel Grey on Broadway in the musical *George M!* (1968), and Mickey Rooney interpreted the great showman in "Mr. Broadway" (1957), an NBC-TV special.

YENTL (Metro-Goldwyn-Mayer/United Artists, 1983) Color 133 minutes.

Executive producer, Larry De Waay; producers, Barbra Streisand, Rusty Lemorande; director, Streisand; based on the story "Yentl, the Yeshiva Boy" by Isaac Bashevis Singer; screenplay, Jack Rosenthal, Streisand; production designer, Roy Walker; art director, Leslie Tomkins; set decorator, Tessa Davies; costumes, Judy Moorcroft; makeup, Wally Schneiderman, Beryl Lerman; music/music director/orchestrator, Michel Legrand; music editors, Robin Clarke, George Brand; choreographer, Gillian Lynne; assistant directors, Steve Lanning, Peter Waller, Steven Harding; technical consultants, Michael Bloom, Shimeon Brisman, Dr. Lucjan Dobroszycki, Rabbi Laura Geller, Dr. Louis Jacobs, Rabbi Daniel Lapin, Rabbi Dr. Harry Rabinowicz, Rabbi Chaim Seidler-Feller, Josh Waltzky, Yivo Institute for Jewish Research; special consultant, Rick Edelstein; sound, David Hildyard, Keith Grant; sound re-recording, Bill Rowe; special effects, Alan Whibley; camera, David Watkin; second unit camera, Gordon Hayman, Doug Milsome; editor, Terry Rawlings.

Songs: "A Piece of Sky," "No Matter What Happens," "This Is One of Those Moments," "Tomorrow Night," "Where Is It Written?" "No Wonder," "The Way He Makes Me Feel," "Papa, Can You Hear Me?" "Will Someone Ever Look at Me That Way?" (Alan Bergman, Marilyn Bergman, Michel Legrand).

Barbra Streisand (Yentl); Mandy Patinkin (Avigdor); Amy Irving (Hadass); Nehemiah Persoff (Papa); Steven Hill (Reb Alter

Vishkower); Allan Corduner (Shimmele); Ruth Goring (Esther Rachel); David DeKeyser (Rabbi Zalman); Bernard Spear (Tailor); Doreen Mantle (Mrs. Shaemen); Lynda Barron (Peshe); Jack Lynn (Bookseller); Anna Tzelniker (Mrs. Kovner); Miriam Margolyes (Sarah); Mary Henry (Mrs. Jacobs); Robbie Barnett (Tailor's Assistant); Ian Sears (David); Renata Buser (Mrs. Shaemen's Daughter); Frank Baker, Anthony Rubes (Village Students); Kerry Shale, Gary Brown, Peter Whitman, Danny Brainin, Jonathan Tafler, Teddy Kempner (Students).

The fifteen-year saga of Barbra Streisand's compulsion to turn Isaac Bashevis Singer's story, "Yentl, the Yeshiva Boy," into a motion picture would have made a wonderful TV movie of the week, full of determination, egotism, and the many conflicts between a powerful, multi-talented superstar and the film industry, with each refusing to bend to the other's will. When Streisand could not convince a studio to package the property, she eventually gambled and co-produced and co-scripted the project herself, in addition to playing the leading role and directing the venture. Although the resultant musical grossed $19,680,127 in distributors' domestic film rentals, it was such an expensive project ($14.5 million) to produce that it was not a significant money earner. While it earned Golden Globe Awards, it failed to earn any major Oscars; which says a lot not only for the qualities of the film but for Hollywood's way of handling rich mavericks. The fact that it did not garner a mass audience can be attributed both to its plot and to the fact that the star was far too old (forty-one) to play the lead assignment. Some of the feature was shot on location in Czechoslovakia.

One can look at the plot device of YENTL as a charming old world fable or as a disturbingly coy convention. Whichever interpretation the filmgoer takes, the picture is badly damaged by its too leisurely pace, its over-emphasis on Streisand, and the blandness of most of the numbers created by lyricists Alan and Marilyn Bergman with music by Michel Legrand. The fact that Streisand sang all the songs was not surprising; what was unfortunate was that personable co-star Mandy Patinkin (who handled his throwaway role charmingly) would later reveal, in other media a most admirable singing voice.

Just after the turn of the century in Poland, Yentl (Barbra Streisand) is insistent upon becoming a Yeshiva student, even though this traditional Jewish education is available only to men. To circumvent the situation, she crops her hair and dresses as a young man. She moves from her native village to a larger city where she gains admittance to religious studies. She meets handsome fellow student Avigdor (Mandy Patinkin) and falls in love with him, but cannot reveal her real identity. The two become friends and when Avigdor is unable to marry his radiant fiancée, Hadass (Amy Irving), because his brother had committed suicide—which shows an instability in the family—he convinces Yentl to marry the girl. This ploy will allow the love-struck Avigdor to still be near his beloved. Yentl reluctantly goes through with the ceremony but uses various excuses to keep Hadass from discovering the truth. On a trip to Lublin, Yentl reveals the facts to Avigdor. The couple is forced to part the next morning. Months later, Hadass and Avigdor are married, while Yentl takes passage for the United States.

Interestingly, like Barbra Streisand's devout legion of fans, the critics were more favorably impressed with YENTL than the average moviegoer. *Variety* diplomatically assessed that YENTL was "a large-scaled but intimate musical," adding, "Carefully and lovingly done in every respect, pic starts out well, but ultimately bogs down due to repetitious musical numbers and overly methodical telling of a rather predictable story." More favorable was *People* magazine, which insisted, "This is no A STAR IS BORN [1976, *q.v.*] vanity production; Streisand leans heavily on the members of her crew and her co-stars, and they deliver . . . her voice, flowing like eiderdown over the score . . . has never sounded lovelier. The thirteen songs, sung by Streisand as interior monologues, sometimes slow down the action. . . . These are minor faults. Streisand gives YENTL a heart that sings and a spirit that soars." Roger Ebert (*Chicago Sun-Times*) observed, "There was speculation from Hollywood that YENTL would be 'too Jewish' for middle-American audiences. I don't think it is. . . . At one time or another, almost everyone has wanted to do something and been told they couldn't, and almost everyone has loved the wrong person for the right reason. That's the emotional ground that YENTL covers, and it always has its heart in the right place."

YENTL won an Academy Award for Best Original Score. It was Oscar-nominated for Best Song ("Papa Can You Hear Me" and "The Way He Makes Me Feel") and for Best Art Direction-Set Decoration. The sole song from YENTL to make its mark in the pop music world was "The Way He Makes Me Feel," which was a minor record-seller for Streisand on the CBS label. The soundtrack album was on the charts for thirteen weeks, rising only as high as #9 on the charts.

YES, GIORGIO (Metro-Goldwyn-Mayer/United Artists, 1982) Color 110 minutes.

Producer, Peter Fetterman; director, Franklin J. Schaffner; suggested by the novel by Anne Piper; screenplay, Norman Steinberg; production designer, William J. Creber; set decorators,

William Durrell, Jr., Perry Gray; costumes, Rita Riggs; music, John Williams; camera, Fred J. Koenekamp; editor, Michael F. Anderson.

Songs: "If We Were in Love" (Alan Bergman, Marilyn Bergman, John Williams); "I Left My Heart in San Francisco" (George Cory, Douglas Cross); arias from the opera *Turandot* (Giacomo Puccini); "Santa Lucia" (traditional; arranger, Alexander Courage); "Comme Facette Mammeto" (Capaldo, Gambardella; arranger, Courage); "O Sole Mio" (Giovanni Capurro, Russo, Edoardo Di Capua; adapted); "Una Furtiva Lagrima" from the opera *L'Elisir d'Amore*" (Gaetano Donizetti); "La Donna e Mobile" from the opera *Rigoletto* (Giuseppe Verdi); "Ave Maria" (Franz Schubert); "This Heart of Mine" (instrumental) (music, Harry Warren); "Did I Remember?" (instrumental) (music, Walter Donaldson); "Cielo e Mar" from the opera *La Gioconda* (Amilcare Ponchielli); Ballet Music from the opera *Aida* (Verdi); "Donna non Vida Mai" from the opera *Manon Lescaut* (Puccini).

Luciano Pavarotti (Giorgio Fini); Kathryn Harrold (Pamela Taylor); Eddie Albert (Henry Pollack); Paola Borboni (Sister Teresa); James Hong (Kwan); Beulah Quo (Mei Ling); Norman Steinberg (Dr. Barmen); Rod Colbin (Ted Mullane); Kathryn Fuller

Luciano Pavarotti and Kathryn Harrold in YES, GEORGIO (1982).

(Faye Kennedy); Joseph Mascolo (Dominic Giordano); Karen Kondazian (Francesca Giordano); Leona Mitchell, Kurt Adler, Emerson Buckley (Themselves).

Take one 300-pound operatic tenor and star him in an $18 million romantic musical comedy in the early 1980s. One might undoubtedly expect a box-office flop, and that is exactly what happened with YES, GIORGIO, starring internationally famous opera singer Luciano Pavarotti. Long gone were the stellar days of Nelson Eddy, Allan Jones and Mario Lanza, when MGM/United Artists issued this operatic musical. Despite its failing at the box-office, YES, GIORGIO has commanded its own coterie of loyal admirers.

Opera star Giorgio Fini (Luciano Pavarotti) is the toast of the highbrow music world, both in Europe and in the United States, where he is a beloved personality. The married and self-centered Fini comes to Boston to give an outdoor concert, with his manager Henry Pollack (Eddie Albert). During a rehearsal he loses his voice. Throat specialist Dr. Pamela Taylor (Kathryn Harrold) is called in to treat Giorgio but due to his chauvinism he mistakes her for a nurse, causing tension between the two. Eventually the singer and the doctor are attracted to each other and begin a love affair. Conniving Pollack wants Giorgio to return to sing at the Metropolitan Opera and attempts to persuade Pamela to aid him in his quest. After several romantic upsets, she finally convinces Fini to return to the Met. The two decide to carry on their romance, although Pamela does not approve of the fact that Giorgio will remain married.

Musically this flashy and well made production makes good use of its star's glorious singing abilities. Pavarotti performs five arias, including the climactic "Nessun Dorma" (from the opera *Turandot*) in his Met return. Other songs range from "O Sole Mio" and "Santa Lucia" to "I Left My Heart in San Francisco" and "If We Were in Love," the latter composed especially for the picture.

Variety recorded, "Material is far afield from anything director Franklin J. Schaffner has attempted in the past, and he's done his job of mounting a lushly professional setting and not allowing his star to embarrass himself. It will be easy for hipsters, critics and opera purists to snicker at this one even before seeing it, but it's just as easy to ignore the filler and enjoy the musical treats on hand."

YOU CAN'T HAVE EVERYTHING (20th Century-Fox, 1937) 99 minutes.

Producer, Darryl F. Zanuck; associate producer, Laurence Schwab; director, Norman Taurog; story, Gregory Ratoff; screenplay, Harry Tugend, Jack Yellen, Karl Tunberg; art director, Duncan Cramer; set decorator, Thomas Little; costumes, Royer; music director, David Buttolph; choreographer, Harry Losee; sound, Arthur Von Kirbach, Roger Heman; camera, Lucien Andriot; editor, Hansen Fritch.

Songs: "Danger—Love at Work," "Please Pardon Us We're in Love," "The Loveliness of You," "You Can't Have Everything," "Afraid to Dream," "Long Underwear" (Mack Gordon, Harry Revel); "It's a Southern Holiday" (Louis Prima, Jack Loman, Dave Franklin); "Rhythm on the Radio" (Prima).

Alice Faye (Judith Poe Wells); Harry Ritz, Al Ritz, Jimmy Ritz [The Ritz Brothers] (Themselves); Don Ameche (George Macrae); Charles Winninger (Sam Gordon); Louise Hovick [Gypsy Rose Lee] (Lulu Riley); David Rubinoff (Himself); Tony Martin (Bobby Walker); Arthur Treacher (Bevins); Phyllis Brooks (Evelyn Moore); Louis Prima (Orchestra Leader); Tip, Tap and Toe [Samuel Green, Ted Fraser, Ray Winfield] (Specialty Dancers); George Humbert (Romano); Wally Vernon (Jerry); Jed Prouty (Mr. Whiteman); George Davis, Frank Puglia (Waiters); Paul Hurst (Truck Driver); Frank Yaconelli (Accordion Player); Nick Moro (Guitar Player); Dorothy Christy (Blonde); Gordon [Bill] Elliott (Lulu's Bathing Companion); Margaret Fielding (Miss Barkow); Robert Murphy (Alderman Barney Callahan); Inez Palange (Mrs. Romano); Joan Davis (Dance Bit); Si Jenks (Janitor); Jane Kerr, Mary Gordon, Bonita Weber (Scrubwomen); Clara Blandick (Townswoman); Robert Lowery (Co-Pilot); June Gale (Girl in YWCA); Hank Mann (Cab Driver); Jayne Regan (Stewardess); Lynne Berkeley (Joan); William Mathieson (Bagpiper); Thomas Pogue (Standee); Claudia Coleman (Matron in YWCA); Sam Ash (Publicity Agent); Howard Cantonwine (Tony).

Without funds and unable to sell her play, *North Winds,* Judith Poe Wells (Alice Faye), the granddaughter of Edgar Allan Poe, orders a big meal in a restaurant, knowing she cannot pay for the food. As a result, she is forced to carry a sign advertising the restaurant because she is too proud to permit another customer, somewhat intoxicated George Macrae (Don Ameche), to pay her tab. She does, however, tell George about her play which she sent to producer Sam Gordon (Charles Winninger), who has not yet replied to her. George goes home and finds his girlfriend Lulu Riley (Louise Hovick [Gypsy Rose Lee]) in a rage over his attentions to Judith. The next day he and Gordon read Judith's play and think it is terrible. However, they pay her some money for its rights. Meanwhile, George dispatches Lulu on a vacation. George produces a musical and asks Judith to appear in it, but Lulu returns on

Don Ameche and Alice Faye in a publicity pose for YOU CAN'T HAVE EVERYTHING (1937).

opening night. She emphatically warns Judith to stay away from her George. Judith leaves New York City and returns home to the small town where she finds employment as a music store song plugger. Since he cannot locate Judith, George turns her play into a musical. When she learns this, she angrily returns to Broadway, only to find the show a success. She and George renew their romance.

YOU CAN'T HAVE EVERYTHING, the first of a half-dozen screen pairings of Alice Faye and Don Ameche, contained a quintet of fine Mack Gordon-Harry Revel songs, with Alice doing outstanding work on "Please Pardon Us, We're in Love," "Danger—Love at Work" (which had her backed by trumpeter Louis Prima), a good duet ("Afraid to Dream") with Tony Martin (whom Alice would marry that year), and her rendition of the title song, backed by violinist David Rubinoff. The movie also marked the screen debut of Louise Hovick, who was better known as stripper Gypsy Rose Lee. It was also the third and last 20th Century-Fox film to pair beautiful Alice Faye with the zany Ritz brothers.

The *New York Times* was unimpressed by this breezy entertainment. "There is Miss Faye, who continues to be the screen's foremost songplugger. There is Mr. Ameche, still with that 'distinguished' pomade about the temples. There are the Ritz Brothers, whom we can resist effortlessly, even though audiences are not able to. There is the backstage plot, with a fillip here and there to give it a pretense of originality. It is a patented formula, relentless, inescapable, and always effective to a degree. Second degree here."

YOU LIGHT UP MY LIFE (Columbia, 1977) Color 91 minutes.

Producer, Joseph Brooks; associate producers, Nicholas Grippo, Edwin Morgan; director/screenplay, Brooks; special comedy material, Gerald Segal; art director, Tom Rasmussen; costumes, Nancy Chadwick, John Patton; makeup, Donna Turner; music director, Brooks; assistant director, Ed Morgan; sound, Art Names; sound re-recording, Richard Vorisek, Rick Dior; sound transfer, Bill Cooper; sound editors, Kate Hirson, Bernard Hajdenberg; camera, Eric Saarnen; editor, Lynzee Klingman.

Songs: "California Daydreams," "Do You Have a Piano?" "Rollin' the Chords," "You Light Up My Life," "The Morning of My Life" (Joseph Brooks).

Didi Conn (Laurie Robinson); Joe Silver (Si Robinson); Michael Zaslow (Cris Nolan); Stephen Nathan (Ken Rothenberg); Melanie Mayron (Annie Gerrard); Jerry Keller (Conductor); Lisa Reeves (Carla Wright); John Gowans (Charley Nelson); Simmy

Bow (Mr. Granek); Bernice Nicholson (Mrs. Granek); Ed Morgan (Account Executive); Joe Brooks (Creative Director); Amy Letterman (Laurie as a Child); Marty Zagon (Mr. Nussbaum); Martin Gish (Harold Nussbaum); Brian Byers (Singer); Tom Gerrard (Best Man); Arnold Weiss, Terry Brannen, Barry Godwin, John Miller, Stephen Tice (Ushers); Eileen Dietz, Lindsey Jones, Kasey Ciszk, Greta Ronnegan, Lisa Nicholson (Bridesmaids); Ruth Manning (Mrs. Rothenberg); Rosemary Lovell, Judy Novgrad (Receptionists); Jeffrey Kramer (Background Singer); Frank Conn (Stage Manager); Mary Kwan, Edward Steefe, Cynthia Szijeti (Cousins); Sparky Watts (Uncle Fritz); Robin O'Hara (Aunt Emma); Ken Olfson (1st Commercial Director); Richmond Shepard (2nd Commercial Director); Aurora Roland (Gail Gerrard); Thelma Pelish (Rachel); John Millerberg (Studio Musician); Nancy Chadwick (Producer); Matt Hyde, Jerry Barnes (Engineers); Bob Manahan (Assistant Engineers); Kasey Ciszk (Singing Voice of Laurie Robinson).

YOU LIGHT UP MY LIFE was one of the surprise movie sleepers of 1977, with distributors' domestic film rentals of $8.4 million. This gross was far more than it cost to make this independent effort by producer-director-writer Joe Brooks which was picked up for distribution by Columbia Pictures. Besides boasting good production values and performances, what made the film such a popular item was its title song, which won the Academy Award as Best Song. It became a record chart blockbuster for Debbie Boone who recorded it for Warner Bros. Records. The song remained on the *Cashbox* magazine charts for twenty-seven weeks. It was the number one song on that popular music singles listings for two consecutive months, almost an unheard-of feat for a song in the 1970s.

Laurie Robinson (Didi Conn) is a young woman who finds that her life has become meaningless in her attempt to become a show business success. She is the daughter of Catskills comedian Si Robinson (Joe Silver), who had forced his shy child to perform as a stand-up comedian. She is still doing the same old, tired routines on television's "The Kids Komedy Hour." To try and bring her life together she plans to marry Ken Rothenberg (Stephen Nathan), whom she finds rather dull. Laurie's friend, Annie Gerrard (Melanie Mayron), attempts to give her some guidance, but it is not until filmmaker Cris Nolan (Michael Zaslow) wants to record Laurie's own composition, "You Light Up My Life," that she begins to emerge from her shell. She soon finds herself in love with Nolan, who promises her a lead in his new film. However, as with his claim of a long-term love affair, this proves to be a lie. Unable to continue being a second-rate comedian any more, she confronts her father and he reluctantly accepts her need to be a singer. She leaves for New York to pursue fame.

While the title song dominates the movie, four other tunes are also used in the feature, and in the recording studio sequence Didi Conn (dubbed by Kasey Ciszk) is backed by members of the New York Philharmonic. The soundtrack LP to YOU LIGHT UP MY LIFE remained on *Billboard* magazine's album charts for five weeks, rising to #19 position.

Variety noted the feature ". . . Has all the virtues and all the liabilities of a low budget effort. There's an earnest sincerity in the story. . . . There's also a lot of cutesy, cornball, convenient and compacted plotting. . . ." Pauline Kael (*New Yorker* magazine) summed up the film with, "The whole thing is like a commercial for the insistent title song."

The gamin-like Didi Conn would co-star as Frenchie in GREASE (1978) and GREASE 2 (1982), *qq.v.*

YOU WERE NEVER LOVELIER (Columbia, 1942) 97 minutes.

Producer, Louis F. Edelman; director, William A. Seiter; based on the story/screenplay "The Gay Senorita" by Carlos Olvari, Sixto Pondal Rios; screenplay, Michael Fessier, Ernest Pagano, Delmer Daves; art directors, Lionel Banks, Rudolph Sternad; set decorator, Frank Tuttle; costumes, Irene; music director, Leigh Harline; choreographer, Val Raset; sound, John Livardy; camera, Ted Tetzlaff; editor, William Lyon.

Songs: "Dearly Beloved," "Audition Dance," "Wedding in the Spring," "I'm Old Fashioned," "You Were Never Lovelier," "The Shorty George," "These Orchids If You Please," "Ding Dong Bell," "On the Beam" (Jerome Kern, Johnny Mercer); "Chiu Chiu" (Alan Surgal, Nicanor Molinare).

Fred Astaire (Robert Davis); Rita Hayworth (Maria Acuna); Adolphe Menjou (Eduardo Acuna); Leslie Brooks (Cecy Acuna); Adele Mara (Lita Acuna); Isobel Elsom (Mrs. Maria Castro); Gus Schilling (Fernando); Barbara Brown (Mrs. Delfina Acuna); Douglas Leavitt (Juan Castro); Catherine Craig (Julia Acuna); Kathleen Howard (Grandmother Acuna); Mary Field (Louise); Larry Parks (Tony); Stanley Brown (Roddy); Xavier Cugat and His Orchestra (Themselves); Kirk Alyn (Groom); George Bunny (Flower Man); Ralph Peters (Chauffeur); Lina Romay (Singer); Nan Wynn (Singing Voice of Maria Acuna).

Fred Astaire and Rita Hayworth had gracefully teamed for

YOU'LL NEVER GET RICH (1941) with a Cole Porter score.* The next year Columbia Pictures reunited them for the romantic escapism, YOU WERE NEVER LOVELIER, which because of wartime restrictions and limited markets was shot on a restricted budget. It provided Astaire with two of his most successful movie songs, "Dearly Beloved" and "I'm Old Fashioned," both of which he recorded for Decca Records. The two stars, who complemented one another so well, had a very successful jitterbug dance duet, "The Shorty George," choreographed by Val Raset.

In Argentina, hotel magnate Eduardo Acuna (Adolphe Menjou) will not permit his younger daughters Cecy (Leslie Brooks) and Lita (Adele Mara) to marry until their beautiful older sister, Maria (Rita Hayworth), has wed. Because she is so fickle and particular, she has no current beau. To stimulate her romantic inclinations, Eduardo clandestinely sends Maria flowers accompanied by unsigned love notes, hoping she will take a liking to some eligible bachelor, thinking that man had sent her the flowers and messages. Much to Eduardo's chagrin, Maria soon thinks the attention is being paid to her by out-of-work American dancer Robert Davis (Fred Astaire). They begin a romance of sort. After several squabbles and various mix-ups, Eduardo sees his daughter married to Davis, paving the way for her other sisters to wed.

YOU WERE NEVER LOVELIER was nominated for three Academy Awards: Best Song ("You Were Never Lovelier"), Scoring and Sound. Rita Hayworth's vocals were dubbed by Nan Wynn. An unknown double provided some of the dance steps for Hayworth in "The Shorty George" routine. Outside the two stars, the film's music included, among others, Xavier Cugat and His Orchestra performing "Chiu Chiu" with the vocal by Lina Romay.**

Despite its pleasing settings and the well-calculated musical interludes, the *Hollywood Reporter* was not satisfied: "When two

*Some thirty years before YOU WERE NEVER LOVELIER, Fred Astaire and Rita Hayworth's father (Eduardo Cansino) had shared the same vaudeville bills. Forty-three-year-old Astaire was nearly twenty years Hayworth's senior; she was nearly his height and he was a known perfectionist. When asked how he liked working on screen with Hayworth, the always diplomatic Astaire commented, "She learned steps faster than anyone I've ever known. I'd show her a routine before lunch. She'd be back right after lunch and have it down to perfection. She apparently figured it out in her mind while she was eating."

**In *The Melody Lingers On,* 1986, Roy Hemming insists about the score of YOU WERE NEVER LOVELIER, "One other song deserves a mention, the wonderfully hummable 'These Orchids If You Please,' even though it's virtually thrown away in two brief, plot-related uses. The score's only clinker is 'Wedding in the Spring' sung by Cugat vocalist Lina Romay—a song that owes more to Middle European operetta than to anything Latin American."

such accomplished dancers as Astaire and Miss Hayworth are brought together, their public has a right to expect a brilliant display of terpsichorean skill. Instead, the accent is on featherweight romance, its prolonged outcome never for a moment in doubt. . . . The picture is more than half over before he (Astaire) and Miss Hayworth join in a dance that is followed by two more routines, all dazzlingly executed but not numerous enough to satisfy fans." In retrospect, Stanley Green (*Encyclopaedia of the Musical Film,* 1987) recorded, ". . . Despite the movie's attempt to do its wartime bit for the Good Neighbor Policy, just about the only Latin American touches in it were provided by Xavier Cugat's accent and orchestra. Included among choreographic pleasures were Astaire's playfully brash audition for Adolphe Menjou and the ecstatic manner in which he wafted Miss Hayworth all over her elegant garden."

YOUNG MAN WITH A HORN (Warner Bros., 1950) 112 minutes.

Producer, Jerry Wald; director, Michael Curtiz; based on the novel by Dorothy Baker; screenplay, Carl Foreman, Edmund H. North; art director, Edward Carrere; set decorator, William Wallace; costumes, Milo Anderson; makeup, Perc Westmore; music director, Ray Heindorf; musical advisor, Harry James; sound, Everett A. Brown; camera, Ted McCord; editor, Alan Crosland, Jr.

Songs: "The Very Thought of You" (Ray Noble); "I May Be Wrong" (Henry Sullivan, Harry Ruskin); "The Man I Love" (George Gershwin, Ira Gershwin); "Too Marvelous for Words" (Johnny Mercer, Richard A. Whiting); "With a Song in My Heart" (Richard Rodgers, Lorenz Hart); "Pretty Baby" (Egberg Van Alstyne, Tony Jackson); "I Only Have Eyes for You," "Lullaby of Broadway" (Harry Warren, Al Dubin); "Limehouse Blues" (Philip Braham, Douglas Furber); "Melancholy Rhapsody" (Sammy Cahn, Heindorf); "Get Happy" (Harold Arlen, Ted Koehler).

Kirk Douglas (Rick Martin); Lauren Bacall (Amy North); Doris Day (Jo Jordan); Hoagy Carmichael (Smoke Willoughby); Juano Hernandez (Art Hazzard); Jerome Cowan (Phil Morrison); Mary Beth Hughes (Margo Martin); Nestor Paiva (Louis Galba); Orley Lindgren (Rick Martin as a Boy); Walter Reed (Jack Chandler); Jack Kruschen (Cab Driver); Alex Gerry (Dr. Weaver); Jack Shea (Male Nurse); James Griffith (Walter); Dean Reisner (Joe); Everett Glass (Man Leading Song); Dave Dunbar (Alcoholic Bum); Robert O'Neill (Bum); Paul E. Burns (Pawnbroker); Julius Wechter (Boy Drummer); Ivor James (Boy Banjoist); Larry Rio

(Owner); Hugh Charles, Sid Kane (Men); Vivian Mallah, Lorna Jordan, Lewell Enge (Molls); Bridget Brown (Girl); Dan Seymour (Mike); Paul Dubov (Maxie); Keye Luke (Ramundo); Frank Cady (Hotel Clerk); Murray Leonard (Bartender); Hugh Murray (Doctor); Dick Cogan (Interne); Katharine Kurasch (Miss Carson); Burk Symon (Pawnbroker); Bill Walker (Black Minister); Helene Heigh (Tweedy Woman); Ted Eckleberry (Elevator Boy); Harry James (Trumpet Playing for Rick Martin); Jimmy Zito (Trumpet Playing for Art Hazzard); Buddy Cole (Some of the Piano Playing for Smoke Willoughby).

Rick Martin (Orley Lindgren) is orphaned at age ten and turns to music as the most important thing in his life. He is taught the trumpet by veteran jazzman Art Hazzard (Juano Hernandez). As he matures, Rick (Kirk Douglas) begins performing in low-class bars and clubs and eventually is given a boost by pianist Smoke Willoughby (Hoagy Carmichael). He begins working in bands, where he meets vocalist Jo Jordan (Doris Day). She promptly falls in love with the temperamental Rick. Meanwhile, he becomes entangled with neurotic, wealthy Amy North (Lauren Bacall). Rick and Amy marry but their union is an unhappy one and Rick turns to drink, despite the fact that his career is moving along well and he is now a top solo star. Eventually Rick and Amy break up and his life falls apart. He is saved from skid row and an alcoholic's death by Smoke's loyalty and Jo's love. Rick slowly reactivates his career. He finally reaches his dream of hitting that impossibly high note on the horn.

YOUNG MAN WITH A HORN is set in the late 1920s and early 1930s and narrated by Hoagy Carmichael's character. The film is a distortion (among other items, removing the miscegenation issue) of the well-regarded Dorothy Baker novel (1938) dealing with the life and hard times of jazz trumpeter Bix Beiderbecke (1903–1931). Kirk Douglas practiced for three months with Harry James (whose trumpeting was heard on the soundtrack) to get the proper fingering and breath control needed for his musical numbers.* It was Douglas's riveting, driven performance which gave the film its focus and saved it from becoming another tiresome musical biography. His co-star, Lauren Bacall, had been a friend of his from their New York theatre days and it was she who had helped to bring him to the attention of Hollywood producers. For

---

***Young Man with a Horn* had been bought by Warner Bros. in 1945 as a possible vehicle for John Garfield, but there had been great problems in dealing with the racial and drug addiction issues of the story.

Doris Day, who had begun her career as a big band vocalist, her role as wholesome Jo Jordan was *deja vu*.

Time magazine insisted, ". . . [The film], which starts out to adapt the best selling story of a jazz musician's integrity, winds up badly in need of some integrity of its own. . . . Actor Douglas gives plenty of vitality to the central role, but he is called on to repeat a good deal of what he did in CHAMPION [1949]; one scene, in which he bangs a trumpet to pieces and breaks into sobs, is almost a remake of the climax of his earlier film." The *New York Times* reported, "A fine jazz earful, an admirably tense performance by Kirk Douglas, as a sensitive genius who loves his trumpet, and the slick, pictorial smoothness of Michael Curtiz' direction more than compensate for the banalities of a script. . . ."

British release title: YOUNG MAN OF MUSIC.

YOUNG MAN OF MUSIC *see* YOUNG MAN WITH A HORN.

ZIEGFELD FOLLIES (Metro-Goldwyn-Mayer, 1946) Color 110 minutes.

Producer, Arthur Freed; directors, Vincente Minnelli, (uncredited): George Sidney, Norman Taurog, Charles Walters, Roy Del Ruth, Lemuel Ayres; screenplay, E. Y. Harburg, Jack McGowan, Guy Bolton, Frank Sullivan, John Murray Anderson, Ayres, Don Loper, Kay Thompson, Roger Edens, Hugh Martin, Ralph Blane, William Noble, Wilkie Mahoney, Cal Howard, Erick Charell, Max Liebman, Bill Schorr, Harry Crane, Lou Holtz, Eddie Cantor, Allan Boretz, Edgar Allan Woolf, Phil Rapp, Al Lewis, Joseph Schrank, Robert Alton, Eugene Loring, Robert Lewis, Walters, James O'Hanlon, David Freedman, Joseph Erons, Irving Brecher, Samson Raphaelson, Everett Freeman, Devery Freeman; art directors, Cedric Gibbons, Jack Martin Smith, Merrill Pye, Ayres; set decorators, Edwin B. Willis, Mac Alper; costume supervisor, Irene; costumes, Irene Sharaff, Helen Rose; puppets/puppet costumes, Florence Bunin; makeup, Jack Dawn; music director, Lennie Hayton; orchestrators, Conrad Salinger, Wally Heglin; vocal arranger, Thompson; choreographer, Robert Alton; color consultants, Natalie Kalmus, Henri Jaffa; sound supervisor, Douglas Shearer; camera, George Folsey, Charles Rosher, Ray June; puppet sequence camera, William Ferrari; editor, Albert Akst.

Songs: "Bring on Those Wonderful Girls" (Earl Brent, Roger Edens); "This Heart of Mine" (Harry Warren, Arthur Freed); "The Drinking Song" from the opera *La Traviata* (Giuseppe Verdi); "Love" (Ralph Blane, Hugh Martin); "Limehouse Blues" (Philip Graham, Douglas Furber); "The Babbit and the Bromide" (George

Gershwin, Ira Gershwin); "There's Beauty Everywhere" (Freed, Brent).

William Powell (The Great Ziegfeld); *Ziegfeld Days:* Fred Astaire, Bunin's Puppets; *Meet the Ladies:* Astaire, Lucille Ball, Cyd Charisse, Virginia O'Brien; *Love:* Lena Horne; *This Heart of Mine:* Astaire (The Imposter); Lucille Bremer (The Princess); Count Stenfenelli (The Duke); Naomi Childers (The Duchess); Helen Boice (The Countess); Robert Wayne (Retired Dyspeptic); Charles Coleman (The Major); Feodor Chaliapin (The Lieutenant); Sam Flint (The Flunky); Shirlee Howard, Natalie Draper, Noreen Roth, Dorothy Van Nuys, Katherine Booth, Lucille Casey, Eve Whitney, Elaine Shepard, Frances Donelan, Helen O'Hara, Aina Constant, Aileen Haley (Showgirls); *We Will Meet Again:* Esther Williams, James Melton; *A Great Lady Has an Interview:* Judy Garland (Herself); Rex Evans (The Butler); *When Televison Comes:* Red Skelton; *The Babbit and the Bromide:* Astaire, Gene Kelly; *Traviata:* James Melton, Marion Bell, Lena Horne, Avon Long; *The Sweepstakes Ticket:* Fannie Brice (Norma); Hume Cronyn (Monty); William Frawley (Martin); Arthur Walsh (Telegraph Boy); *Pay the Two Dollars:* Victor Moore, Edward Arnold (Themselves), Ray Teal (Special Officer); Joseph Crehan (Judge); William B. Davidson (Presiding Judge); Eddie Dunn, Garry Owens (Officers); Harry Hayden (Warden); *Limehouse Blues:* Astaire (Tai Long); Bremer (Moy Ling); Captain George Hill, Jack Deery (Men); Charles Lunard, Robert Ames, Jack Regas, Sid Gordon (Four Men with Masks); Charisse (Chicken); James King (Rooster); Eugene Loring (Costermonger); Harriet Lee (Singer in Dive), Dane Dipaolo, Robert Chetwood, Jack Purcell, Herb Luri, Walter Stane, Edward Brown, Milton Chisholm, Jack Regas, Bert May, Richard D'Arch, Alex Romero, Don Hulbert, Ricky Ricardi, Robert Trout, Bill Hawley, Rita Dunn, Charlotte Hunter, Patricia Lynn, Ruth Merman, Melba Snowden, Patricia Jackson, Marilyn Christine, Wanda Stevenson, Judi Blacque, Virginia Hunter, Seazn Francis, Dorothy Gilmore, Doreen Hayward (Ensemble); Ellen Ray, Billy Shead (Couple with Parasols); Eleanor Biley, Ronnie Stanton (Couple with Branches); Jean Ashton, Rod Alexander (Couple with Banners); Mary Jo Ellis, James Barron (Couple with Birds); *Number Please:* Keenan Wynn, Kay Williams (On Phone); Peter Lawford (Phone Voice); Audrey Totter (Voice of Telephone Operator); *Beauty:* Kathryn Grayson, the Ziegfeld Girls.

Every studio is entitled to its creative miscalculations. For MGM it was the nearly unmanageable ZIEGFELD FOLLIES, which struggled through three years of production and near hysterical reshaping. Meanwhile, many of its stars worked on other pictures which found release before this hodgepodge presentation was nationally distributed.

In his posh digs in Heaven, famed Broadway producer Florenz Ziegfeld (William Powell, who played the same role a decade before in THE GREAT ZIEGFELD, *q.v.*) plots a new musical revue. He prepares a list of possible stars. A puppet show (by the Bunin Puppets) boasting some of Ziegfeld's early luminaries follows and then Fred Astaire (himself) appears to pay tribute to the legendary producer, followed by a dozen blackout sequences. First Lucille Ball (never looking more glamorous) and Virginia O'Brien do the circus number, "Bring on the Beautiful Girls," followed by "A Water Ballet" featuring Esther Williams. From Verdi's opera *La Traviata,* operatic tenor James Melton and soprano Marion Bell perform "The Drinking Song," while Victor Moore and Edward Arnold recreate the old vaudeville/burlesque sketch, "Pay the Two Dollars." Astaire and Lucille Bremer dance in a ballroom sequence to "This Heart of Mine" and Keenan Wynn does the hoary comedy routine, "Number Please." Fanny Brice and Hume Cronyn play a married couple who have a domestic mix-up over the ownership of a winning "Sweepstakes Ticket." Next, Lena Horne sings a sultry "Love." Buffoon Red Skelton provides the sketch, "When Television Comes." Astaire and Bremer appear again for the elaborate Oriental ballet, "Limehouse Blues," and Judy Garland (a replacement for Greer Garson) impersonates a movie queen in "The Great Lady Has an Interview." Astaire and Gene Kelly—with very different dance styles—try to blend for "The Babbit and the Bromide." The revue closes with Kathryn Grayson singing "There's Beauty Everywhere."

ZIEGFELD FOLLIES was conceived originally by producer Arthur Freed as a salute to MGM's twentieth anniversary in 1944 and a follow-up to the studio's earlier THE GREAT ZIEGFELD and ZIEGFELD GIRL (1941), *qq.v.* Metro-Goldwyn-Mayer chief Louis B. Mayer allotted Freed a $3 million budget. (Reportedly, MGM acquired the film, radio and TV rights to the title *Ziegfeld Follies* from Ziegfeld's widow, actress Billie Burke, for $100,000.) From the start it was agreed that the movie musical would be a revue, with no (or little) storyline. Initially George Sidney was the project's director but, along the way, he was replaced by Vincente Minnelli with additional work by director Norman Taurog. Many numbers were discarded in the process: "If Swing Goes, I Go Too" (a Fred Astaire dance), "A Cowboy's Life" (a western number sung by James Melton), "Death and Taxes" (a comedy skit featuring Jimmy Durante, Edward Arnold and Stephen McNally), "Baby Snooks" (Fanny Brice doing her specialty characterization from her radio series), "Liza" (sung by Avon Long to Lena Horne and ten dancers), "Brindisi" (James Melton and Marion Bell dueting on this aria from *La Traviata*); "The Pied Piper" (a comedy skit with Jimmy Durante), and "Honolulu" (James Melton singing while Esther Williams swims underwater, although the aquatic ballet remained; his vocal contributions were cut). Many of the cuts, especially the comedy sequences, were trimmed because of disastrous early previews of the film, in which the supposedly funny routines fell flat. Fred Astaire voluntarily agreed to have "If Swing Goes, I Go Too" removed from the release print.* Added to the proceedings was the framing device of the celestial Florenz Ziegfeld looking down on earthly show business.

One of the highlights of this potpourri was Garland's satirical "A Great Lady Has an Interview." Equally enjoyable was the elaborately staged story-dance, "Limehouse Blues," a stunning production number shot on the revamped London street set from THE PICTURE OF DORIAN GRAY (1945). It took ten days of shooting and a cost of $228,225. For many the comedy antics of Red Skelton are an acquired taste. His shenanigans as the drink-guzzling soul in the "When Television Comes" routine is unimaginative and cloying. Equally unfelicitous is "The Babbit and the Bromide," which, until their co-hosting chores on THAT'S ENTERTAINMENT: PART II (1976), *q.v.,* was the only screen teaming of two great screen dancers, Fred Astaire and Gene Kelly. Even Kelly would admit later of his performance in this unesthetic number (which finds the two hoofers dancing together as young men, mature men and bearded angels), "I thought I looked like a klotz!" The "There's Beauty Everywhere" finale had its own share of problems. On screen Kathryn Grayson was buried behind a burst of colored bubbles and odd backgrounds. In actuality, the special effects spraying of the set with these bubbles emitted so noxious a gas that the studio fire brigade had to be called to stage 27 where it was being shot. As a result, the planned-for dance finale by

*Other numbers planned for ZIEGFELD FOLLIES but not used in the film were: "Fireside Chat" (Judy Garland, Ann Sothern and Lucille Ball), "Pass That Peace Pipe" (June Allyson, Gene Kelly, Nancy Walker and chorus), "Reading of the Play" (Garland and Frank Morgan), "As Long As I Have My Art" (Garland and Mickey Rooney), "Glorifying the American Girl" (Ball, Marilyn Maxwell, Lucille Bremer, Lena Horne and Elaine Shephard), "A Trip to Hollywood" (Jimmy Durante, Ball and Maxwell), "Fairy Tale Ballet" (Katharine Hepburn, Margaret O'Brien and Jackie "Butch" Jenkins), and "You're Dream Like" (based on the Howard Dietz-Arthur Schwartz song). Judy Garland and Mickey Rooney had already pre-recorded the song, "Will You Love Me in Technicolor as You Do in Black and White?" but it was not in the released film.

Astaire-Bremer to the vocal accompaniment of James Melton's singing was spoiled and it was largely deleted.

When the film was released in April 1946, the *New York World-Telegram* observed that ZIEGFELD FOLLIES contained ". . . All those stars and not one really star act." *PM* newspaper dismissed the film as ". . . Nothing more or less than a parade of celebrity short subjects."

Made at a cost of $3,240,816, ZIEGFELD FOLLIES nevertheless grossed over $5,344,000 in its initial release, thanks to its star lineup.

ZIEGFELD GIRL (Metro-Goldwyn-Mayer, 1941) Sepia 131 minutes.

Producer, Pandro S. Berman; director, Robert Z. Leonard; story, William Anthony McGuire; screenplay, Marguerite Roberts, Sonya Levien; art directors, Cedric Gibbons, Daniel B. Cathcart; set decorator, Edwin B. Willis; costumes, Adrian; makeup, Jack Dawn; music, Herbert Stothart; music director, George Stoll; vocal arrangers/orchestrators, Leo Arnaud, George Bassman, Conrad Salinger; music presenter, Merrill Pye; choreographer, Busby Berkeley; sound supervisor, Douglas Shearer; camera, Ray June; editor, Blanche Sewell.

Songs: "Minnie fron Trinidad," "Laugh? I Thought I'd Split My Sides" (Roger Edens); "I'm Always Chasing Rainbows" (Joseph McCarthy, Harry Carroll); "You Never Looked So Beautiful Before," "You Gotta Pull Strings" (Walter Donaldson, Harold Adamson); "Caribbean Love Song" (Ralph Freed, Edens); "Whispering" (John Schonberger, Richard Coburn, Vincent Rose); "Mr. Gallagher and Mr. Shean" (Edgar Gallagher, Al Shean); "You Stepped Out of a Dream" (Gus Kahn, Nacio Herb Brown).

James Stewart (Gilbert Young); Judy Garland (Susan Gallagher); Hedy Lamarr (Sandra Kolter); Lana Turner (Sheila Regan); Tony Martin (Frank Merton); Jackie Cooper (Jerry Regan); Ian Hunter (Geoffrey Collins); Charles Winninger (Pop Gallagher); Edward Everett Horton (Noble Sage); Philip Dorn (Franz Kolter); Paul Kelly (John Slayton); Eve Arden (Patsy Dixon); Dan Dailey, Jr. (Jimmy Walters); Al Shean (Himself); Fay Holden (Mrs. Regan); Felix Bressart (Mischa); Rose Hobart (Mrs. Merton); Bernard Nedell (Nick Capalini); Ed McNamara (Mr. Regan); Mae Busch (Jenny); Josephine Whittell (Perkins); Renie Riano (Annie); Six Hits and a Miss (Singers); Elliott Sullivan, James Flavin (Truckers); Joyce Compton (Miss Sawyer); Ruth Tobey (Beth Regan); Bess Flowers (Palm Beach Casino Patron); Jean Wallace, Myrna Dell, Georgia Carrol, Louise La Planche, Virginia Curzon, Alaine

Brandeis, Patricia Dana, Irma Wilson, Lorraine Gettman [Leslie Brooks], Madeleine Martin, Vivien Mason, Harriet Bennett, Nina Bissell, Frances Gladwin, Anya Taranda (Ziegfeld Girls); Antonio and Rosario (Specialty Dancers); Fred Santley (Floorwalker); Claire James (Hopeful); Sergio Orta (Native Dancer); Reed Hadley (Geoffrey's Friend); Armand Kaliz (Pierre); Joan Barclay (Actress in Slayton's Office); Donald Kirke (Playboy); Ray Teal (Pawnbroker); Al Hill (Truck Driver); Roscoe Ates (Theatre Worker); George Lloyd (Bartender); Ginger Pearson (Salesgirl).

Ever since the exceedingly popular THE GREAT ZIEGFELD (1936), *q.v.*, MGM had been hoping to deal with the great showman again on screen. Five years later, using a new story created by William Anthony McGuire (who had provided the original storyline for THE GREAT ZIEGFELD), the studio released ZIEGFELD GIRL. It was devised as a vehicle for three of MGM's very diverse leading ladies: Judy Garland, Hedy Lamarr and Lana Turner. Actually, Florenz Ziegfeld as a character does not appear in the storyline.

Elevator girl Sheila Regan (Lana Turner) is spotted on her job by a *Ziegfeld Follies* recruiter. Agent Noble Sage (Edward Everett Horton) tells her she has been chosen and she is so stunned that her boyfriend, truck driver Gilbert Young (James Stewart), has to work

Hedy Lamarr and Tony Martin in ZIEGFELD GIRL (1941).

out all the details for her. Another young woman signed for the *Follies* is Sandra Kolter (Hedy Lamarr), who is married to concert violinist Franz Kolter (Philip Dorn). A third girl brought into the show is Susan Gallagher (Judy Garland), the singing offspring of show business veteran Pop Gallagher (Charles Winninger). Being part of the famed *Follies* affects each of the young women differently. Success causes Sheila to lose her perspective and she drops Gilbert in favor of playboy Geoffrey Collins (Ian Hunter). Sandra's overshadowed husband leaves her. Susan uses her success to obtain her dad and his partner (Al Shean) a spot in the new production. Sandra eventually realizes that Franz is far more important than the glamour of show business and they are reconciled. However, the excessive life Susan has led weakens her heart and on opening night she suffers a fatal heart attack.

Lana Turner, had by far, the meatiest acting assignment of the three female leads of ZIEGFELD GIRL, while Hedy Lamarr was photographed most advantageously.* Judy Garland scored well singing "I'm Always Chasing Rainbows" and had a comic production number, "Minnie from Trinidad." Top-billed James Stewart had a "thankless role" (*Newsweek* magazine) as Turner's boyfriend. On the other hand, Tony Martin, as singer Frank Merton, was outstanding as he crooned "You Stepped Out of a Dream" to Lamarr, Turner and Garland in a Busby Berkeley-directed production ensemble. Other songs included in the black-and-white feature were "You Never Looked So Beautiful Before" and "You Gotta Pull Strings," both numbers from THE GREAT ZIEGFELD. Of historical note, the famous vaudevillian Al Shean recreated his famous 1922 patter song, "Mr. Gallagher and Mr. Shean," here teamed with Charles Winninger playing his partner, Ed Gallagher. For this movie Nacio Herb Brown and Gus Kahn especially composed the aforementioned "You Stepped Out of a Dream." The Judy Garland-Tony Martin number, "We Must Have Music," was cut from the release print.

The *New York Times* acknowledged, "The girls, especially Lana Turner, who must have been born on Olympus, are breathtaking . . . it is the perilously lovely Miss Turner who gets this department's bouquet for a surprisingly solid performance as the little girl from Brooklyn." *Variety* printed, "When Metro-Goldwyn-

*Lana Turner's role as the reddish blonde Sheila Regan was built up in the course of filming ZIEGFELD GIRL. According to Turner, "By the end of the picture, they added a drunk scene and a death scene. It was the first time anyone realized I could play something beside a co-ed." The movie contains the well-remembered sequence in which Turner slowly descends a staircase and collapses.

Mayer plans a super-filmusical, the studio goes 'all out' in every department. . . . Several elaborate production numbers out-dazzle the original Ziegfeld presentations through expanded opportunities afforded by the screen medium. . . . It's highly effective." On the other hand, the trade paper noted that the movie was too long, that three parallel stories requiring equal time were confusing to the continuity, and that "Interpolation of two extended displays of Ziegfeldian production sequences, with parades of the glorified girls, prevents smooth unfolding of the piece and results in several dull passages."

MGM would return next to the Florenz Ziegfeld story with ZIEGFELD FOLLIES (1946), *q.v.*

CHRONOLOGY

1927
The Jazz Singer

1928
My Man
The Singing Fool

1929
Applause
The Broadway Melody
Close Harmony
Dance of Life
The Desert Song
The Fox Movietone Follies
Gold Diggers of Broadway
Hallelujah!
The Hollywood Revue of 1929
Honky Tonk
Innocents of Paris
Little Johnny Jones
The Love Parade
On with the Show
Queen of the Nightclubs
Rio Rita
Sally
Say It with Songs
Show Boat
The Show of Shows
Sunny Side Up
Sweetie
The Vagabond Lover

1930
Good News
Hit the Deck
Honey
King of Jazz
Monte Carlo
New Moon
No, No, Nanette
Paramount on Parade
Puttin' on the Ritz
The Rogue Song
Song of the Flame
Sunny
The Vagabond King
Viennese Nights

1931
Palmy Days

1932
The Big Broadcast
Girl Crazy
Love Me Tonight

1933
College Humor
Dancing Lady
Flying Down to Rio
Footlight Parade
42nd Street
Going Hollywood
Gold Diggers of 1933
Roman Scandals

1934
Babes in Toyland
Bolero
Dames
The Gay Divorcee
George White's Scandals
The Merry Widow
One Night of Love
Stand Up and Cheer

1935
After the Dance
Big Broadcast of 1936
Broadway Melody of 1936
Curly Top
Every Night at Eight
Folies Bergere
George White's 1935 Scandals
Gold Diggers of 1935
I Dream Too Much
Love Me Forever
Mississippi
Naughty Marietta
A Night at the Opera
Roberta
Sweet Adeline
Top Hat

1936
Big Broadcast of 1937
Born to Dance
Collegiate
Follow the Fleet
Gold Diggers of 1937
The Great Ziegfeld
Pennies from Heaven
Pigskin Parade
Rhythm on the Range
Rose Marie
Rose of the Rancho
Show Boat
Sing, Baby, Sing
Swing Time
Under Your Spell

1937
Big Broadcast of 1938
Broadway Melody of 1938
A Damsel in Distress
The Firefly
High, Wide and Handsome
Maytime
On the Avenue
One Hundred Men and a Girl
Rosalie
Shall We Dance?
Snow White and the Seven Dwarfs
Three Smart Girls
Wake Up and Live
You Can't Have Everything

1938
Alexander's Ragtime Band
Carefree
The Girl of the Golden West
Gold Diggers in Paris
In Old Chicago
Mad About Music
Sally, Irene and Mary
Sing You Sinners
Sweethearts

1939
Babes in Arms
Balalaika
The Great Victor Herbert
Rose of Washington Square
The Story of Vernon and Irene Castle
Three Smart Girls Grow Up
The Wizard of Oz

1940
Bitter Sweet
The Boys from Syracuse
Broadway Melody of 1940
Down Argentine Way
Fantasia

Lillian Russell
Music in My Heart
New Moon
No, No, Nanette
Pinocchio
Road to Singapore
Strike Up the Band
Tin Pan Alley

1941
The Chocolate Soldier
Lady Be Good
Moon Over Miami
Sun Valley Serenade
Weekend in Havana
Ziegfeld Girl

1942
Cabin in the Sky
For Me and My Gal
Holiday Inn
I Married an Angel
Panama Hattie
Rio Rita
Springtime in the Rockies
Yankee Doodle Dandy
You Were Never Lovelier

1943
The Desert Song
The Gang's All Here
Girl Crazy
Hello, Frisco, Hello
Stormy Weather
Thank Your Lucky Stars
This Is the Army

1944
Cover Girl
Going My Way
Hollywood Canteen
Lady in the Dark
Meet Me in St. Louis
Something for the Boys
Step Lively

1945
Anchors Aweigh
The Dolly Sisters
George White's Scandals
Rhapsody in Blue
A Song to Remember
State Fair
Where Do We Go from Here?

1946
Blue Skies
Centennial Summer
The Harvey Girls
The Jolson Story
Junior Prom
Night and Day
Three Little Girls in Blue
Till the Clouds Roll By
Ziegfeld Follies

1947
Good News
It Happened in Brooklyn
Mother Wore Tights

1948
April Showers
A Date with Judy
Easter Parade
The Emperor Waltz
Music Man
The Pirate
Words and Music

1949
The Barkleys of Broadway
Jolson Sings Again
Look for the Silver Lining
My Dream Is Yours
On the Town
Take Me Out to the Ball Game

1950
Annie Get Your Gun
The Daughter of Rosie O'Grady
Let's Dance
Pagan Love Song
Summer Stock
Tea for Two
Three Little Words
The West Point Story
Young Man with a Horn

1951
An American in Paris
Disc Jockey
The Great Caruso
I'll See You in My Dreams
On Moonlight Bay
Royal Wedding
Show Boat

1952
The Merry Widow
Singin' in the Rain
With a Song in My Heart

1953
The Band Wagon
Calamity Jane
Call Me Madam
The Desert Song
Easy to Love
Gentlemen Prefer Blondes
The Jazz Singer
Kiss Me Kate
Lili
Small Town Girl
So This Is Love

1954
Brigadoon
Carmen Jones
Deep in My Heart
The Glenn Miller Story
Lucky Me
New Faces
Rose Marie
Seven Brides for Seven Brothers
A Star Is Born
There's No Business Like Show Business
White Christmas

1955
Daddy Long Legs
Gentlemen Marry Brunettes
Guys and Dolls
Hit the Deck
I'll Cry Tomorrow
It's Always Fair Weather
Kismet
Lady and the Tramp
Love Me or Leave Me
Oklahoma!
Pete Kelly's Blues

1956
Carousel
High Society
The King and I
Shake, Rattle and Rock!
The Vagabond King

1957
Carnival Rock
Funny Face
The Helen Morgan Story
Jailhouse Rock
Les Girls
Pal Joey
Silk Stockings

1958
Bells Are Ringing
Damn Yankees
Gigi
King Creole
South Pacific

1959
Porgy and Bess

1960
Can Can
G.I. Blues

1961
Babes in Toyland
Blue Hawaii
The Flower Drum Song
West Side Story

1962
Billy Rose's Jumbo
Gypsy
The Music Man
State Fair

1963
Beach Party
Bye Bye Birdie
Follow the Boys

1964
Mary Poppins
My Fair Lady
Pajama Party
The Unsinkable Molly Brown
Viva Las Vegas

1965
The Sound of Music

1966
A Funny Thing Happened on the Way to the Forum
Road to Nashville

1967
Camelot
How to Succeed in Business Without Really Trying

1968
Funny Girl
Oliver!

1969
Chitty Chitty Bang Bang
Hello Dolly!
Paint Your Wagon
Sweet Charity

1970
On a Clear Day You Can See Forever
Song of Norway

1971
Fiddler on the Roof

1972
Cabaret
Lady Sings the Blues
Man of La Mancha
1776

1973
Jesus Christ Superstar
Lost Horizon

1974
Mame
That's Entertainment!

1975
At Long Last Love
Funny Lady

1976
The First Nudie Musical
A Star Is Born
That's Entertainment: Part II

1977
Saturday Night Fever
You Light Up My Life

1978
The Buddy Holly Story
Grease
The Wiz

1979
All That Jazz
Elvis
Hair
The Muppet Movie
Roller Boogie
The Rose

1980
Can't Stop the Music
Coal Miner's Daughter
Divine Madness
Fame
Honeysuckle Rose
The Jazz Singer
Xanadu

1981
Pennies from Heaven

1982
Annie
The Best Little Whorehouse in Texas
Grease 2
Yentl
Yes, Georgio

1984
Body Rock

1985
That's Dancing!

1986
The Little Shop of Horrors

1987
Dirty Dancing
La Bamba

1988
Baja Oklahoma
Salsa
Satisfaction
School Daze

ABOUT THE AUTHORS

JAMES ROBERT PARISH, Studio City, California-based direct marketing consultant and free-lance writer, was born in Cambridge, Massachusetts. He attended the University of Pennsylvania and graduated Phi Beta Kappa with a degree in English. A graduate of the University of Pennsylvania Law School, he is a member of the New York Bar. As president of Entertainment Copyright Research Co., Inc. he headed a major researching facility for the film and television industries. Later he was a film reviewer-interviewer for *Motion Picture Daily* and *Variety* trade newspapers. He is the author of over 75 volumes, including: THE GREAT COP PICTURES, THE FOX GIRLS, GOOD DAMES, THE SLAPSTICK QUEENS, THE RKO GALS, THE TOUGH GUYS, THE JEANETTE MACDONALD STORY, THE ELVIS PRESLEY SCRAPBOOK, THE HOLLYWOOD BEAUTIES and THE GREAT COMBAT PICTURES. Among those he has co-written are: HOLLYWOOD BABY BOOMERS, THE MGM STOCK COMPANY, THE DEBONAIRS, LIZA!, HOLLYWOOD CHARACTER ACTORS, THE HOLLYWOOD RELIABLES, THE FUNSTERS, THE BEST OF MGM, BLACK ACTION PICTURES FROM HOLLYWOOD, and his ongoing series, COMPLETE ACTORS TELEVISION CREDITS with Vincent Terrace. With Michael R. Pitts, he has co-written such tomes as HOLLYWOOD ON HOLLYWOOD, THE GREAT WESTERN PICTURES (base and companion volumes), THE GREAT GANGSTER PICTURES (base and companion volumes), THE GREAT SPY PICTURES (base and companion volumes), THE GREAT SCIENCE FICTION PICTURES (base and companion volumes), THE GREAT DETECTIVE PICTURES, and HOLLYWOOD SONGSTERS. Mr. Parish is advisor for Greenwood Press's Bio-Bibliography in the Performing Arts series. Mr. Parish's entertainment research collection is archived at Kent State University Library in Kent, Ohio.

MICHAEL R. PITTS is a free-lance writer who has written or co-authored numerous books on entertainment, including KATE SMITH: A BIO-BIBLIOGRAPHY, WESTERN MOVIES, HOLLYWOOD AND AMERICAN HISTORY, HORROR FILM STARS, FAMOUS MOVIE DETECTIVES, HOLLYWOOD ON RECORD, THE BIBLE ON FILM, and two editions of RADIO SOUNDTRACKS. With Mr. Parish he has written THE HOLLYWOOD SONGSTERS and THE GREAT . . . PICTURES series and its companion volumes. In addition he has contributed to several other published books and his magazine articles have been published both here and abroad. With degrees in history and journalism, Mr. Pitts writes columns on record collecting for *The Big Reel* and *Classic Images* magazines. He has written record album liner notes and lectures on film history and entertainment. Mr. Pitts resides in Indiana with his wife, Carolyn, and daughter, Angela.